SVG
UNLEASHED

Andrew Watt
Chris Lilley
Daniel J. Ayers
Randy George
Christian Wenz
Tobias Hauser
Kevin Lindsey
Niklas Gustavsson

 201 West 103rd Street, Indianapolis, Indiana 46290

SVG Unleashed

International Standard Book Number: 0-67232-429-6

Library of Congress Catalog Card Number: 2002104076

Printed in the United States of America

First Printing: September 2002

05   04   03   02   4   3   2   1

Trademarks

All terms mentioned in this book that are known to be trademarks or service marks have been appropriately capitalized. Sams Publishing cannot attest to the accuracy of this information. Use of a term in this book should not be regarded as affecting the validity of any trademark or service mark.

Warning and Disclaimer

Every effort has been made to make this book as complete and as accurate as possible, but no warranty or fitness is implied. The information provided is on an "as is" basis. The authors and the publisher shall have neither liability nor responsibility to any person or entity with respect to any loss or damages arising from the information contained in this book or from the use of the programs accompanying it.

Acquisitions Editor
Jill Reed

Development Editor
Heather Goodell

Managing Editor
Charlotte Clapp

Project Editors
Elizabeth Finney
Katelyn Cozatt

Copy Editor
Chuck Hutchinson

Indexer
Rebecca Salerno

Proofreader
Jessica McCarty

Technical Editors
Kevin Lindsey
Niklas Gustavsson
Marcel Salathe
Max Dunn
Andrew Watt
Ronan Oger
Robert A. DiBlasi

Team Coordinator
Amy Patton

Multimedia Developer
Dan Scherf

Interior Designer
Gary Adair

Cover Designer
Alan Clements

Graphics
Tammy Graham
Oliver Jackson

Contents at a Glance

Table of Contents

Foreword

The release of the SVG 1.0 specification as a full W3C Recommendation was proof of the enabling effect of a strong, active, and vocal user and developer community. Less visibly to the public, it was also a demonstration of the W3C process that enables competing companies to come together in a vendor-neutral space and work on commonly agreed, open specifications for the benefit of the Web in general and to grow the market.

SVG was the first specification to not only have a test suite, but also to publish the results of testing on named implementations. During the Candidate Recommendation phase, implementers and content creators gave a large amount of valuable feedback that helped to improve the clarity and technical accuracy of the specification. As a result, compared to other specifications at an equivalent level of maturity, SVG was extremely well implemented by the time it became a W3C Recommendation on September 4, 2001.

That event was also, for me, a personal triumph and the culmination of a long journey. Graphics was the reason I first became involved with Web development, in 1993. When I attended the first-ever Web conference at CERN, Geneva, in May 1994, I was working for a computer graphics facility and was involved with the emerging PNG specification and the IETF HTML Working Group that produced HTML 2.0. In December 1995, I presented a paper on future development challenges for Web graphics at the fourth Web conference in Boston, was hired by W3C to head up the graphics area, and published (in 1996) a requirements document for scalable graphics.

At times, it seemed that the world was not ready for vector graphics on the Web; it took a lot of work raising awareness and gathering support before finally, in September 1998, the first SVG Working Group was formed. Then, suddenly, we were off and running. There was a flurry of ideas and discussions. Graphics experts from many leading companies were enjoying the experience of freely sharing ideas and wished to create a new format that did what, we all felt, graphics should have been doing all along! The first working draft was released in February 1999 and the second in April of that year. By May, there were already three implementations (from IBM, BlackDirt, and Adobe). And this pace continued throughout the development of SVG 1.0.

I have been asked how the world would be different if a vector graphics standard had been available early on. The answer is that certainly it would have been better to have something sooner, but that we would also have a legacy problem and have to reinvent something like SVG anyhow. Early in the development of the Web, XML did not exist. Vector graphics might have been an HTML extension, or a binary format, but would not have had the benefits that XML has brought. Style sheets were not available, so it would have been unstyled. The XML DOM was not available, so scripting and dynamic content generation would have been specific to the format and not shared tools and techniques with other content. The Web Accessibility Initiative had not started, the Unicode standard was not yet accepted by the industry, and the general state of software internationalization was immature; so an early graphics standard would not have been universally accessible. In a sense, it was possible to create SVG only after the shared infrastructure on which it is built had been developed.

So, SVG was developed when its time had come, and is now successful. There are many implementations of viewers and content creation tools. The ease of generating and modifying SVG, using visual tools or simple text editors, has been a boon for content developers and has clearly boosted adoption. The ready integration into existing XML-based workflows has meant that SVG rapidly found a place in information delivery—representing graphics, not text—but in terms of processing, just another XML component.

That one crucial difference from other XML languages—that it produces a rendered result—has made it a natural target for XML transformations using XSLT or generation with programming and scripting languages. Regardless of what the origin XML language is representing—weather data, geographical information, chemical molecules—transforming it to SVG allows this specialized, domain-specific markup to be given a visual form that can be understood and interacted with. You will meet many examples of this process in the course of the book. Unlike with some "write once" binary formats, it is common and expected that SVG graphics will be revised, rewritten, or include components that change over time.

Programmers have been generating graphics programmatically for some time, but while the resulting graphics were standard—one of a handful of raster formats widely used on the Web—the programming interface and underlying model varied widely and were specific to the particular graphics toolkit used. Programmers were unable to share skills or transfer experience from one project to the next. SVG changes all that. Not only is the output graphic standard, but the programming interface and underlying model are also standard. You can build experience over several projects, discuss experiences with colleagues, and apply lessons and techniques from one project to the next one. In the course of this book, you will see many approaches to creating graphics programmatically, but they are all variations on a theme. They all rely on the underlying model of SVG in terms of vector graphics objects and the Document Object Model. The SVG rendering model and syntax are presented in the first part of this book; you can read through it or refer to it as you study the programming examples in subsequent parts. Thus, your understanding builds as you work through the material. Be sure to read parts that use programming languages you are not familiar with, too.

Many graphics represent text, and here a key difference from other graphics formats emerges. In SVG, the graphic text to be displayed is stored in the SVG file as a Unicode text string. It doesn't matter if the text is in an unusual font, stretched, skewed, placed on a spiral, or filtered—it is still selectable text. It may be directly edited, generated on the fly by the server, or created in response to user interaction on the client. Unlike special "alternate text" added as an afterthought to provide some measure of accessibility, the text in SVG is real text. It will not become out of date or out of sync with the graphic presentation; it *is* the graphic presentation. This is an enormous benefit in terms of accessibility for the disabled community; screen readers and text-to-speech or Braille generators can access this structured text and allow the visually disabled to navigate through the graphic content.

As is often the case, an accessibility advantage gives benefits to the nondisabled community as well. By using live text, SVG can be searched and indexed, both by users and by search engines. When you're interacting with an SVG graphic, you can look for specific text strings, to copy and paste them into other applications. Text in SVG is also well internationalized. Text in any of the world's languages can be used and is still searchable and selectable. In today's multilingual society, this capability provides a significant advantage. It is no longer sufficient to assume that people in Europe or the Americas need simple, "single-byte" languages, that the Middle East needs only bidirectional languages, that the Far East is the only place that needs "double-byte" languages, and that we treat any other combination as an insignificant minority. Instead, the reality is that there is a single, cosmopolitan, global market. SVG reflects that realization.

Another change in the market is the rise of handheld devices—personal digital assistants, Pocket PCs, PalmOS devices, mobile phones—and other nontraditional devices such as game consoles, set-top boxes, and information kiosks. Bringing challenges due to lower CPU power and memory, these devices also have a refreshing lack of legacy problems and are often the first to adopt new W3C specifications such as XHTML, SMIL, and SVG. Their use is widespread and growing; not only are mobile devices easier to carry—in a pocket, not a backpack—but they are also more affordable to a larger segment of the population. Over time, the number of people accessing the Web using such devices is likely to greatly exceed the number using traditional desktop or laptop computers. It is vitally important, to avoid fragmentation of the information space, that the same specifications—URLs, HTTP, and content formats including SVG—are used in the mobile Web as well as the "desktop Web."

Recognizing this fact, work on SVG has not stopped at W3C. Indeed, SVG 1.1 and SVG Mobile moved to Candidate Recommendation on April 30, 2002, and work on SVG 1.2 has started. Rest assured, though, that SVG 1.1 has the same features and syntax as SVG 1.0; the specification of those features is expressed differently to allow subsetting. SVG Tiny and SVG Basic, collectively called SVG Mobile, are interoperable subsets of SVG 1.1 specifically designed for mobile devices. You can read more about the future of SVG in Chapter 27. For now, it is sufficient to know that by reading this book about SVG 1.0, you are making the best possible preparation for also doing work on SVG Mobile.

Welcome to the future.

Chris Lilley
W3C Graphics Activity Lead and SVG Working Group Chair
http://www.w3.org/Conferences/WWW4/Papers/53/gq-boston.html
http://www.w3.org/Graphics/ScalableReq.html
http://www.w3.org/Graphics/SVG

About the Authors

Andrew Watt is an independent consultant and author with an interest and expertise in XML technologies, including SVG. He created the world's first continuing all-SVG Web site at http://www.svgspider.com. He is author of *Designing SVG Web Graphics* (published by New Riders)—the world's first book in print on SVG—and *XPath Essentials* (published by Wiley). He is coauthor of *XML Schema Essentials* (published by Wiley) and *Sams Teach Yourself JavaScript in 21 Days* (published by Sams). He is a contributing author to *XHTML, XML & Java 2 Platinum Edition* and *XHTML By Example* (published by Que); *Professional XSL, Professional XML 2nd Edition,* and *Professional XML Meta Data* (published by Wrox); and *Special Edition Using XML, 2nd Edition* (in press at Que). Andrew contributed Chapters 1–12 and the Introduction.

Chris Lilley has been employed by the World Wide Web Consortium (W3C) since April 1996. There, he is the Graphics Activity Lead and a member of the Technical Architecture Group (TAG). He chairs the current SVG Working Group and was also chair and team contact for the previous SVG Working Group. He has also been a member of the HTML and XSL Working Groups and was for five years chair of the CSS Working Group. He has spoken at numerous Web, XML, Graphics, and Internationalization conferences and is a member of the conference committee for the Unicode, XML Europe, and SVG Open conferences.

Prior to working for the W3C, he was a staff member at the Computer Graphics Unit, University of Manchester, England, where he participated in the standardization of HTML 2.0 and the development of the PNG format. He holds a BSc with honors in Biochemistry from the University of Stirling, Scotland; an MSc in Computing from the University of York, England; and a postgraduate diploma in bioinformatics from the Global Network Academy. Chris contributed Chapter 27 and the Foreword.

Daniel J. Ayers is a freelance developer and author who specializes in leading-edge Internet technologies, primarily using server-side Java and XML. He lives in rural Italy with his wife Caroline and cat Sassi. He is a strong advocate of SVG, believing that it will play an important role in the next-generation Web. Danny contributed Chapters 13, 17, 19, 20, and Appendix A.

Randy George has had a long history with graphics programming going back to his college days in the early seventies. He is currently CTO of Geotechnologies, Inc., as well as the owner of Micro Map & CAD. He has developed a number of map translation programs for the CAD market and also authored more than a dozen articles for journals in the CAD and GIS industries. As CTO for Geotechnologies, he has developed a number of SVG prototypes for the GIS, AEC, and FMS industries as well as some medical and military applications. Over the last couple of years, he has become increasingly excited about the potential for SVG/XML coupled with server-side Java and native XML databases. When not experimenting with SVG and Java, he helps out around the house in Colorado, home-schooling some of his eight children. Randy contributed Chapters 24–26.

Christian Wenz is author of more than two dozen books. He specializes in Web programming and Web scripting (most notable publications are on JavaScript, ASP/ASP.NET, PHP, and WAP; some of them translated into other languages). He is also a regular speaker at both national and international conferences. He lives in Munich, Germany. Christian contributed Chapters 14–16, 18, 22, and 23 jointly with Tobias Hauser.

Tobias Hauser is author of more than 20 books on various topics of computing and the Internet. Apart from Web development, his second focus is on graphics. He has written books on ASP.NET, GIMP, Photoshop, Web Publishing, and PHP and WAP, among other topics. He lives and works in southern Germany. Tobias contributed Chapters 14–16, 18, 22, and 23 jointly with Christian Wenz.

Kevin Lindsey currently lives in the Dallas-Fort Worth area with his wife Liz. He has been involved in the publishing and medical industries for more than 10 years. Kevin has been an active member in the SVG community since 2000 and frequently posts to Yahoo!'s SVG Developers group. He is also the maintainer of and sole contributor to the KevLinDev.com Web site. Kevin contributed Chapter 21.

Niklas Gustavsson has taken up technical management, doing mostly Web application development while on sabbatical from his work as a molecular biologist studying regulatory mechanisms in E. coli. in Gothenburg, Sweden. In his spare time, he's involved in several open-source projects, keeps his blog and experiments at protocol7.com and is the housekeeper of the SVG-wiki (http://www.protocol7.com/svg-wiki). When away from computers, he is planning his upcoming wedding, rides his mountain bike, or spends time with friends. Niklas contributed Appendixes B, C, and D.

Dedications

I would like to dedicate my part in this book to the memory of my late father, George Alec Watt, a very special human being.
—Andrew Watt

Dedicated to my father, Don, who introduced me to black letter typefaces.
—Daniel J. Ayers

This book is dedicated to all nonideologic supporters of SVG.
—Christian Wenz

Acknowledgments

I would like to thank all the members of the svg-developers mailing list who have made learning about the exciting new graphics format, SVG, so much fun. The input on the list from Chris Lilley and Jon Ferraiolo has been particularly valuable. I would also like to thank Chris for taking time from his busy schedule to contribute his unique perspectives on SVG to this book. I would like to thank the technical editors, Kevin Lindsey and Niklas Gustavsson, for the quality of their comments on draft text. I would also like to thank all those at Sams Publishing who have helped get this project off the ground and through to completion: Jennifer Kost-Barker, Jill Reed, Heather Goodell, Elizabeth Finney, and Mark Taber. **—Andrew Watt**

I would like to acknowledge the members of the first and second W3C SVG Working Groups who put so much time and effort into the SVG specification and test suite; the programmers who created implementations of SVG to let us know what parts of the emerging specification worked and what needed fixing; and the members of the svg-developers mailing list who created content, fully exercised the specification, and gave valuable detailed feedback. All of this made the SVG specification much better than it would otherwise have been. It was, and continues to be, a privilege to work with such a great community. **—Chris Lilley**

I'd like to thank the "Golden Girls" at Sams Publishing (but they are much younger!), in alphabetical order: Elizabeth, Heather, and Jill. Without you, this book would not be in this excellent shape. Furthermore, many thanks to the excellent technical reviewers who found more than one embarrassing mistake on my side. Finally, shout-outs to Marsha and Vic. **—Christian Wenz**

Many thanks to Jill, Heather, Jennifer, and Elizabeth at Sams Publishing and the other authors and editors for their help, and making this a pleasure. Special thanks to Andrew for his support, contagious enthusiasm, and remarkable determination. Thanks to the Batik developers and Jim Ley, Dave Pawson, Sean B. Palmer, and William Loughborough for all their help and inspirational work; and of course the folks on the svg-developers, wai-ig, and rdf-interest lists for constant stimulation. Thanks as ever to Caroline for her tolerance and patience. —**Danny Ayers**

I would like to acknowledge the W3C and specifically the SVG Working Groups. Their efforts have given me the unique opportunity to be a part of a wonderful and ever-growing SVG community. SVG continues to fascinate me, and as I dig deeper into the specification, I gain renewed admiration for the efforts of the SVG Working Groups. I would also like to acknowledge Andrew Watt for talking me into participating in this book, Jill Reed for keeping the project focused and running smoothly, the svg-developers list for helping me to better understand SVG, and to all of you who have given me encouragement to continue exploring the possibilities of SVG. —**Kevin Lindsey**

We Want to Hear from You!

As the reader of this book, *you* are our most important critic and commentator. We value your opinion and want to know what we're doing right, what we could do better, what areas you'd like to see us publish in, and any other words of wisdom you're willing to pass our way.

You can e-mail or write me directly to let me know what you did or didn't like about this book—as well as what we can do to make our books stronger.

Please note that I cannot help you with technical problems related to the topic of this book, and that due to the high volume of mail I receive, I might not be able to reply to every message.

When you write, please be sure to include this book's title as well as your name and phone or e-mail address. I will carefully review your comments and share them with the authors and editors who worked on the book.

Email: webdev@samspublishing.com

Mail: Mark Taber
Associate Publisher
Sams Publishing
201 West 103rd Street
Indianapolis, IN 46290 USA

Reader Services

For more information about this book or others from Sams Publishing, visit our Web site at www.samspublishing.com. Type the ISBN (excluding hyphens) or the title of the book in the Search box to find the book you're looking for.

Introduction

Congratulations! You have just chosen a book that will provide you with information to unleash the power of Scalable Vector Graphics (SVG).

SVG is an immensely powerful graphics tool for use on the Web and elsewhere. In parallel with its immense power and potential, it is also based on a relatively complex specification. Reading *SVG Unleashed* will provide you with the perspective to understand how to use most of the SVG specification and also provide you with lots of working SVG code that you can use to get up to speed in this exciting new vector graphics world.

SVG Unleashed covers the SVG elements themselves, showing you essential syntax and techniques. In addition, you will see how to use SVG with JavaScript, Java, XSLT, and other languages. The XML and SVG Document Object Models are also described, with examples showing how you can manipulate the Document Object Model, the DOM, of an SVG document.

Creating SVG on the server is an important technique to master for dynamic creation of SVG, and in several chapters, you are introduced to techniques that enable you to create SVG on the server to meet diverse needs.

Who This Book's Intended Audience Is

This book is written for those with at least some experience with Web development using at least a scripting language, such as JavaScript, or who have significant programming experience with a full programming language such as Java, C++, or Perl. We also assume that you have at least some basic understanding of XML.

The main focus of this book is SVG, and we don't assume that you already know much SVG. However, we do assume that you have experience using the Web and that you are a quick learner, so that the maximum information about SVG can be contained in the available space.

Any knowledge you have of one of the programming languages in this book will help you get the most from the relevant chapters. We have, however, worked hard to try to help you gain an understanding of the techniques to be used with SVG, even if you aren't already familiar with each of the scripting and programming languages we use.

We assume that you want to use SVG in the real world and will want to get your hands dirty using SVG code. If you choose, you can do that by typing in code. Likely, you will want to make use of the code downloads available from the Sams Publishing Web site (`http://www.samspublishing.com`). Running the code and viewing the result in an SVG viewer are essential if you want fully to appreciate the animations and interactivity that are incorporated in many of the examples created in the book.

What You Will Learn from Reading This Book

This book covers a broad range of topics that give you the necessary knowledge to create static and animated SVG documents. Each of the SVG version 1.0 elements is described, with many examples showing how to use various attributes for an element. The interfaces of the XML DOM and version 1.0 of the SVG DOM are introduced and many examples shown.

Later chapters in the book cover the use of JavaScript with SVG and also show you how several programming languages can be used server-side to generate SVG. The case studies will help you appreciate where SVG creation fits into real-life development scenarios.

What Software You Will Need to Complete the Examples Provided with This Book

To create SVG by hand, you can use any simple text editor. Having an XML-aware text editor with code highlighting will ease the task of identifying syntax errors. An editor that can validate against the SVG 1.0 Document Type Definition (DTD) will provide another level of assistance.

To view SVG, you will need an SVG rendering engine, also known as an SVG viewer. Installation of these tools is described in Chapter 1, "SVG Overview."

To use the programming languages employed to script or generate SVG, you will need appropriate language tools. In many cases, free open-source tools are available.

How This Book Is Organized

This book is divided into the following parts.

Part I: SVG Fundamentals

The book begins with a personal insight into the creation of SVG from Chris Lilley, Chairman of the W3C's SVG Working Group.

Most of Part I of the book builds a foundation for your use of SVG by describing the SVG 1.0 elements and providing examples that show how to use them. The XML DOM and SVG DOM are also introduced, and examples of using the DOM with JavaScript are shown. Many SVG animations and transformations are demonstrated. The final chapter in this part describes how SVG can be used to aid accessibility.

Part II: Programming SVG Client-Side

SVG animations can be created using declarative syntax alone. However, adding scripting using a language such as JavaScript appends powerful options for control of interactivity with the user of the SVG that you create. Part II is intended to ensure that you understand how to use JavaScript with SVG.

Part III: Producing SVG Server-Side

In many scenarios, you will likely want to create SVG dynamically on a Web server. In this part of the book, you will be introduced to general issues of creating SVG on a Web server, including configuration of the server to allow SVG to be served.

In addition, we will discuss and demonstrate the creation of SVG using Java, with servlets or JavaServer Pages (JSP), the Extensible Stylesheet Language Transformations (XSLT), and Perl.

Part IV: Case Studies

This part of the book consists of several case studies that demonstrate how SVG can be used in the production of architectural and construction diagrams and creation of SVG maps.

Part V: Looking Ahead

The final part of the book is a look ahead to the future of SVG written by Chris Lilley. Chris is in a unique position to point to future developments in SVG, as it moves through the upcoming versions 1.1, 1.2, and 2.0. This part will provide you with a vista into SVG's future, showing you some of the exciting things you will be able to do to build further on the skills you have learned in *SVG Unleashed* using SVG 1.0.

What's on the Sams Web Site for This Book

The code files for this book, chapter by chapter, are available at `http://www.samspublishing.com/`. Enter the ISBN for this book without the hyphens in the Search box and click the Search button. When the book's title is displayed, click the title to go to a page where you can download all the code.

Conventions Used in This Book

This book uses certain conventions to help make the book more readable and helpful:

- Code listings, methods, elements, functions, and other code terms appear in a `monospace font`.

- Placeholders (words with substitutes for what you actually type) appear in a `monospace italic` font.

- Sometimes a code line that should appear on one line is unable to fit on a single line in this book. When this happens, the line is broken and continued on the next line, preceded by a ➥ character.

In addition, this book uses special sidebars that are set apart from the rest of the text, including Notes, Tips, and Cautions.

PART I

SVG Fundamentals

IN THIS PART

SVG Overview

Scalable Vector Graphics (SVG) is an XML-based graphics standard from the World Wide Web Consortium (W3C), which opens up new and powerful ways for programmers to generate graphics for display on a variety of devices. SVG is intended for the production of two-dimensional vector graphics and so is useful for display of many types of information, including quantitative statistics, graphs, maps, and technical diagrams. SVG is particularly suited to the creation of graphics that are created from data held as XML.

It is the combination of qualities that SVG possesses that makes it so powerful and flexible. As your knowledge of SVG increases, you will likely come to appreciate more the power, flexibility, and control that you have to determine the visual appearance of the SVG documents and images you create. Later in this chapter, we will examine some of the positive characteristics of SVG.

Before we dive into an appraisal of SVG's strengths and weaknesses, let's quickly look at a few scenarios in which SVG can provide you, your employers, or your customers with viable and efficient solutions to aid communication with customers or colleagues.

Imagine having a diagram of a piece of equipment or a circuit onscreen, and you need to see more detail in a particular part of the diagram. With SVG, you can simply zoom in to a greater magnification and see whatever level of detail the creator of the diagram has provided for you. With a bitmap graphic, a user would have to go back to the server for another version of the graphic, if such a magnified version exists at all. In SVG if you want to look at a different part of the diagram, you simply pan the image to the point you want to study. Imagine you are looking at a map onscreen, and you need to see greater detail about a particular part, perhaps your destination for an upcoming trip. Again, you simply zoom in to the SVG map and see the area of interest in detail. You want to follow a road or railway to see where it goes? Simply pan the SVG image in the desired direction.

Suppose you want to create a statistical graph from data you hold as XML for presentation, or update a graph of share prices by the hour, or even more often. SVG images can be created dynamically using Java (or other languages server-side) resulting in an up-to-date SVG graph being presented to users of your site. If your data is held as XML, or in a DBMS (Database Management System), which "speaks" XML, then SVG is talking your language. If the graph you create has detail that a user might want or need to see, there is no need for a new image to be fetched from the server. Again, an SVG viewer will allow zooming in to examine relevant parts of the graph. With appropriate scripting, the SVG image may be able to offer more than one presentation of the data.

In the preceding scenarios, I have given you a brief taste of some of the many advantages that SVG can provide, to help you present business data to colleagues, customers, or sales contacts or help you convey information in training or other settings. This book will cover SVG elements and their attributes, as well as ways to combine those elements to create static and animated graphic shapes. You will also be shown how to manipulate and create SVG by using its Document Object Model (DOM), using languages such as ECMAScript (JavaScript), Java, PHP, and Perl.

Understanding SVG

SVG is an application language of XML, the Extensible Markup (Meta) Language. All SVG documents follow the syntax rules of XML 1.0. If you are not already familiar with the syntax requirements of XML, they are summarized in Chapter 2, "Document Structure in SVG," where we examine the structure of an SVG document.

SVG is intended to display three types of visual entities:

- **Graphics shapes**—SVG has several predefined graphics shapes as well as `path` elements, which can describe any arbitrary two-dimensional shape.

- **Text**—SVG provides `text` and `tspan` elements for the layout of text.

- **Bitmap graphics**—SVG allows conventional bitmap graphics, such as PNGs, to be embedded in an SVG image or document.

> **NOTE**
>
> Full information on the SVG 1.0 Recommendation is located at
> http://www.w3.org/TR/2001/REC-SVG-20010904/.

An SVG image is unusual in that the source code for the SVG image is a succession of characters, which are always editable (as in any XML file). Contrast that with a bitmap graphic in which the data to describe the graphic is unintelligible to most human beings except when rendered by a graphics editor.

The SVG specification defines a Document Object Model (DOM) for SVG images, which is based on DOM Level 2 Core (`http://www.w3.org/TR/2000/REC-DOM-Level-2-Core-20001113`). The DOM provides an Application Programming Interface (API) to allow the creation, deletion, or alteration of parts of the object model and therefore of the corresponding SVG document to which the object model applies.

> **NOTE**
>
> If you plan to use the W3C DOM Level 2 documents, be sure to check the errata page located at http://www.w3.org/2000/11/DOM-Level-2-errata.

To be able to create SVG images dynamically, we need to understand how an SVG document is structured to produce the SVG image we see onscreen.

Let's look at a short SVG document that conveys a welcome to this book. A simple SVG document has many similarities to documents written in other markup languages such as HTML. Listing 1.1 shows a simple animated greeting created using SVG to welcome you to this book.

LISTING 1.1   Greeting.svg—A Welcome to SVG Unleashed

```
<?xml version="1.0" standalone="no"?>
<!DOCTYPE svg PUBLIC "-//W3C//DTD SVG 20010904//EN"
"http://www.w3.org/TR/2001/REC-SVG-20010904/DTD/svg10.dtd">
<svg width="468" height="60">
    <rect x="0" y="0" width="100%" height="100%" style="fill:#CCCCCC"/>
    <text x="500" y="40" style="fill:red; stroke:none; font-size:24;">
      Welcome to SVG Unleashed!
        <animate begin="0s" attributeName="x" from="500" to="-300"
         dur="11s" repeatCount="indefinite"/>
    </text>
</svg>
```

Figure 1.1 shows the appearance in a Web browser (in this case Internet Explorer 5.5) with the Adobe SVG Viewer installed partway through the ticker-tape animation that displays the welcome message.

> **SVG Viewers**
>
> To view SVG, you will need an SVG viewer. An SVG viewer can be a plug-in for conventional Web browsers—the Adobe SVG Viewer takes that approach—or a standalone SVG viewer such as Batik or X-Smiles. For instructions to help you download and install SVG viewers, see the "Tools to View SVG" section later in this chapter.

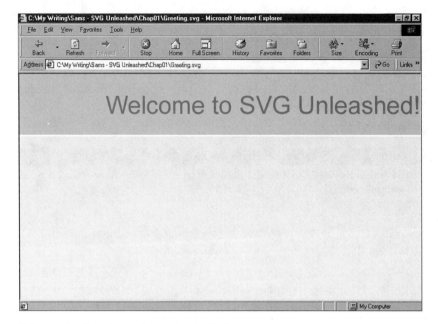

FIGURE 1.1   A simple animated greeting in SVG.

SVG is ideally suited to the display of mapping and similar data because most maps consist of many graphics shapes, some simple and some of arbitrary complexity.

A simple SVG document to display five lines, representing a simplified urban map, is shown in Listing 1.2.

LISTING 1.2   FiveLines.svg—A Highly Simplified SVG "Map"

```
<?xml version="1.0" standalone="no"?>
<!DOCTYPE svg PUBLIC "-//W3C//DTD SVG 20010904//EN"
"http://www.w3.org/TR/2001/REC-SVG-20010904/DTD/svg10.dtd">
<svg width="100%" height="100%">
    <!-- Horizontal line, black stroke representing road -->
    <line x1="0" y1="200" x2="800" y2="200"
     style="stroke:#000000; stroke-width:0.5"/>
    <!-- Horizontal line, black stroke representing road -->
    <line x1="0" y1="300" x2="800" y2="300"
     style="stroke:#000000; stroke-width:0.5"/>
    <!-- Vertical line, black stroke representing road -->
    <line x1="400" y1="0" x2="400" y2="600"
     style="stroke:#000000; stroke-width:0.5"/>
    <!-- Diagonal line, black intermittent stroke, representing rail line -->
```

LISTING 1.2   Continued

```
    <line x1="0" y1="50" x2="800" y2="250"
     style="stroke:#000000; stroke-width:0.5; stroke-dasharray:5,3,2"/>
    <!-- Horizontal line, blue stroke, representing canal -->
    <line x1="0" y1="250" x2="800" y2="250"
     style="stroke:#0000FF; stroke-width:0.5"/>
</svg>
```

An SVG document begins, optionally, with an XML declaration. The DOCTYPE declaration indicates that the document conforms to the SVG 1.0 Recommendation and gives the location of the Document Type Definition (DTD) for SVG 1.0 documents to support validation of documents you may create.

As you can see in Listing 1.2, we can use standard XML comments to document our code. SVG has a number of predefined graphics shapes represented in the source code by SVG elements. You can see five line elements, each of which has attributes that describe the location of each end of a straight line and provide information to the SVG rendering engine about how the line is to be displayed onscreen.

The onscreen appearance of Listing 1.2 is shown in Figure 1.2.

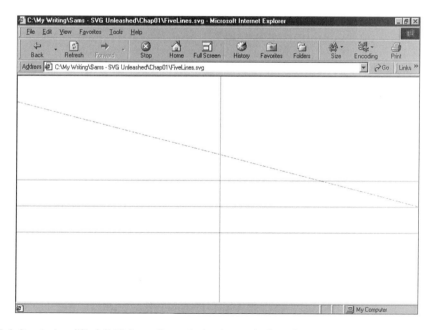

FIGURE 1.2   A simplified SVG "map" created using only line elements.

> **NOTE**
>
> The SVG graphics elements for basic shapes such as lines, rectangles, and circles are described in Chapter 3, "Basic SVG Elements and Shapes."

Advantages of SVG

SVG has many potential advantages over existing graphics standards. Many of the positive characteristics of SVG have been available individually in previous graphics formats. It is the combination of characteristics that makes SVG potentially so powerful and useful for programmatically orientated or created graphics. In this section, we will briefly consider a number of the positive aspects of SVG. Taken together, they place SVG in a league of its own.

File Size

The W3C, in the SVG requirements document, specifically intended SVG as a replacement for many uses of bitmap graphics on the Web. One of the aspirations was that SVG file sizes be smaller than those of bitmap graphics, such as GIFs and JPEGs. The size of SVG images, of course, depends on the complexity of the vector image that is to be rendered. In practice, it is possible to create logos, banner ads, and other SVG images that are significantly smaller than all but the smallest and simplest bitmap images. Equally, when a large, detailed, and complex SVG map or diagram is served, the file size may be substantial. However, that one image is likely to provide functionality at least equal to several bitmap images, and provide panning and zooming functionality that bitmap images are not capable of.

> **NOTE**
>
> SVG documents can be zipped to reduce file size. For unzipped SVG files, the file extension is .svg. For zipped SVG files, the file extension is .svgz.

Zooming Images

SVG images can be zoomed without the need to go back to the server to reload another version of the image. This capability is a big advantage in fields such as mapping and engineering. Listing 1.3, FiveLinesPlusRects.svg, adds some simple rectangles to the previous image to represent some buildings.

LISTING 1.3   FiveLinesPlusRects.svg—Further Development of the Map with Some "Buildings" Added

```
<?xml version="1.0" standalone="no"?>
<!DOCTYPE svg PUBLIC "-//W3C//DTD SVG 20010904//EN"
```

LISTING 1.3   Continued

```
"http://www.w3.org/TR/2001/REC-SVG-20010904/DTD/svg10.dtd">
<svg width="100%" height="100%">
    <!-- Horizontal line, black stroke representing road -->
    <line x1="0" y1="200" x2="800" y2="200"
     style="stroke:#000000; stroke-width:0.5"/>
    <!-- Horizontal line, black stroke representing road -->
    <line x1="0" y1="300" x2="800" y2="300"
     style="stroke:#000000; stroke-width:0.5"/>
    <!-- Vertical line, black stroke representing road -->
    <line x1="400" y1="0" x2="400" y2="600"
     style="stroke:#000000; stroke-width:0.5"/>
    <!-- Diagonal line, black intermittent stroke, representing rail line -->
    <line x1="0" y1="50" x2="800" y2="250"
     style="stroke:#000000; stroke-width:0.5; stroke-dasharray:5,3,2"/>
    <!-- Horizontal line, blue stroke, representing canal -->
    <line x1="0" y1="250" x2="800" y2="250"
     style="stroke:#0000FF; stroke-width:0.5"/>
    <!-- Add some rectangles to represent buildings -->
    <rect x="401" y="196" height="3" width="7" />
    <rect x="409" y="196" height="3" width="9" />
    <rect x="420" y="196" height="3" width="12" />
    <rect x="433" y="196" height="3" width="8" />
    <rect x="401" y="186" height="9" width="4"
     style="fill:#FF0000; stroke:none" />
    <rect x="401" y="180" height="5" width="3"
     style="fill:#FF0000; stroke:none" />
    <rect x="401" y="174" height="5" width="5"
     style="fill:#00FF00; stroke:none" />
</svg>
```

Onscreen, the image produced looks like that shown in Figure 1.3.

If, however, we use the zoom facility available in the Adobe SVG Viewer and other SVG viewers, we can magnify selected areas of the screen to allow a closer inspection of detail in an image. The Adobe viewer, for example, allows four magnification (zoom) steps of x2, x4, x8, and x16. Thus, if we zoom in to see a x16 magnification of our simple map, we can see considerably more detail than was apparent when the SVG image was viewed in its original form. Figure 1.4 shows the image zoomed x4.

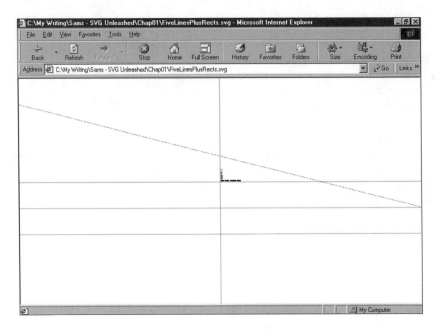

FIGURE 1.3   Adding buildings, using rect elements, to the map.

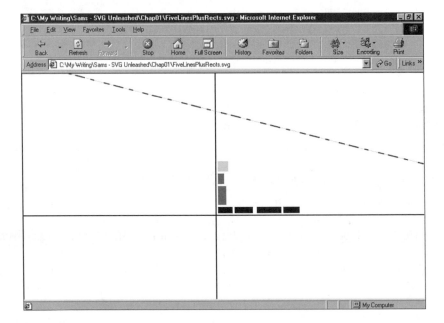

FIGURE 1.4   Zooming in to see more detail of the "buildings."

Just as we can zoom in to see detail, so we can zoom out (see Figure 1.5) from either a zoomed size or the original view so that we can see a broader perspective on where a particular part of a diagram or map fits into a larger whole. In the Adobe SVG Viewer, we can zoom out so that the image is as small as one-sixteenth of its original size.

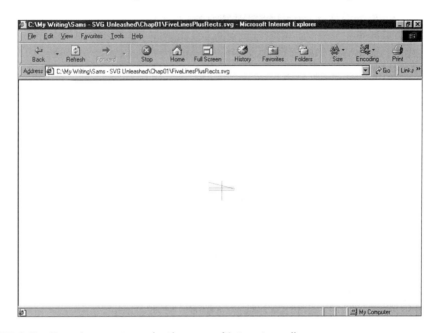

FIGURE 1.5   Zooming out to make the area of interest smaller.

As you can see in Figure 1.5, the graphic that filled the screen when shown at normal size is now a little bigger than the mouse cursor.

Clearly, how useful zooming is in a particular context depends on how much detail is encoded in the original SVG image. Adding detail to SVG images to maximize the benefits attainable from zooming in a particular context can be expected to have an adverse effect on file size and therefore on download time. However, in a mapping context, it can provide significant added value to a user.

NOTE

The key and mouse combinations to zoom vary between SVG viewers. The Adobe SVG Viewer requires the user to right-click and then choose Zoom In or Zoom Out or Original View from the offered menu. In Batik, to zoom, you hold down the Ctrl key and drag out an area to be zoomed.

Panning Images

When an image is zoomed, the user has some control of the zoomed area, but the area first displayed after the image is zoomed may not be exactly the area desired. SVG viewers provide panning of an image to allow us to either frame a zoomed image exactly as we want or to explore beyond the edges of the browser window.

In our simple example, let's suppose that the triangular area between the two intersecting roads and the railway had been purchased by a property developer. Panning the SVG image as shown in Figure 1.6 allows attention to be focused precisely on the area of interest. Notice that the cursor has changed to a hand shape, indicating that panning is available.

> **NOTE**
>
> Individual SVG viewers have different key/mouse combinations to enable panning. The Adobe SVG Viewer, for example, requires that you press both an Alt key and the left mouse button. In that circumstance, moving the mouse pans the onscreen SVG image in parallel with the direction and distance the mouse is moved. In Batik, to pan you hold down the Alt and Shift keys and the left mouse button and drag.

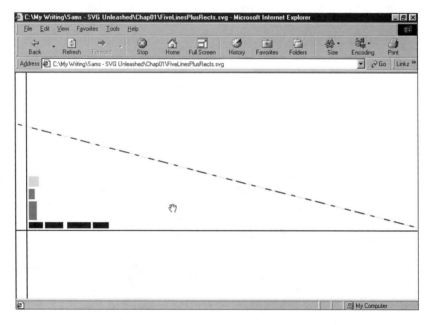

FIGURE 1.6   Panning to selectively view an area in a zoomed image.

Figure 1.6 shows the image panned to focus on the triangular area of interest.

Selective Display of Elements

In some situations, viewing images that focus in on selected types of data can be useful. SVG, when combined with a more conventional programming language such as ECMAScript (JavaScript), allows selective display of information interactively. When a user is, for example, displaying a complex map, with visual data for roads, rivers, buildings, and so on, it can be useful to suppress display of some aspects of the image to closely study the inter-relationship of particular features. An SVG image that includes suitable scripting code enables this type of control, which is customizable to user needs in a particular context. Listing 1.4 shows a simple way to hide and show the "canal" in our simple map.

LISTING 1.4   FiveLinesInteractive.svg—An Interactive Map That Allows Us to Selectively Hide or Show the "Canal"

```
<?xml version="1.0" standalone="no"?>
<!DOCTYPE svg PUBLIC "-//W3C//DTD SVG 20010904//EN"
"http://www.w3.org/TR/2001/REC-SVG-20010904/DTD/svg10.dtd">
<svg width="" height="">
    <script type="text/javascript">
        <![CDATA[
            function HideShowCanal(){
            SVGDoc = evt.getTarget().getOwnerDocument;
            myCanal = SVGDoc.getElementById("Canal");
            CurrentVisibility = myCanal.getAttribute("visibility");
            if (CurrentVisibility=="visible"){
            myCanal.setAttribute("visibility","hidden");
            } //end if
            else if (CurrentVisibility=="hidden"){
            myCanal.setAttribute("visibility", "visible");
            } // end else
            }
        ]]>
    </script>
    <!-- Horizontal line, black stroke representing road -->
    <line x1="0" y1="200" x2="800" y2="200"
     style="stroke:#000000;stroke-width:0.5"/>
    <!-- Horizontal line, black stroke representing road -->
    <line x1="0" y1="300" x2="800" y2="300"
     style="stroke:#000000; stroke-width:0.5"/>
    <!-- Vertical line, black stroke representing road -->
    <line x1="400" y1="0" x2="400" y2="600"
     style="stroke:#000000; stroke-width:0.5"/>
```

LISTING 1.4   Continued

```
    <!-- Diagonal line, black intermittent stroke, representing rail line -->
    <line x1="0" y1="50" x2="800" y2="250"
     style="stroke:#000000; stroke-width:0.5;
stroke-dasharray:5,3,2"/>
    <!-- Horizontal line, blue stroke, representing canal -->
    <line id="Canal" x1="0" y1="250" x2="800" y2="250"
     style="stroke:#0000FF;
stroke-width:2" visibility="visible" onclick="HideShowCanal(evt)"/>
    <text x="20" y="270" font-size="14pt"
     onclick="HideShowCanal(evt)">Canal Visibility</text>
</svg>
```

If you click on the text Canal Visibility, you can hide the canal if it is currently visible, or if the canal is hidden, you can make it visible again. Figure 1.7 shows the appearance after the text is first clicked. Figure 1.8 shows the visibility of the canal restored. On this occasion, the screenshots were taken in the Internet Explorer browser because scripting Mozilla later than version 0.9.1 can be problematic because Mozilla changed APIs that the Adobe SVG Viewer used.

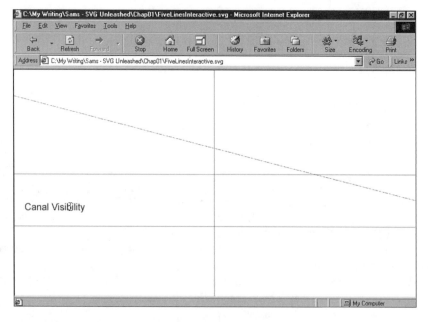

FIGURE 1.7   The canal is hidden by clicking the text.

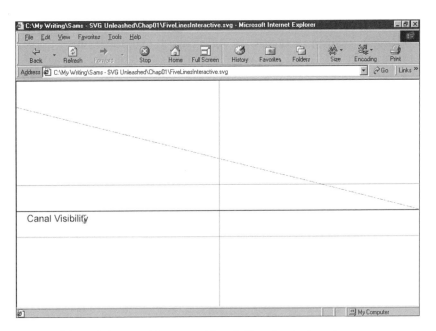

FIGURE 1.8   Visibility of the canal is restored by clicking the text again.

Real-world examples of such an interactive selective display on maps can be seen online at
`http://www.academy-computing.com/svg-oilgas/og04.htm` and elsewhere.

Open Source Code

The source code for an SVG image can be displayed by an SVG viewer. In the Adobe SVG
Viewer, right-clicking on an image brings up a menu that includes the option View Source
(see Figure 1.9). Choosing that option causes a browser window to open with the source
code for the image being displayed. That code may be inspected to assist understanding of
how the image was constructed, and the option to save the SVG code to disc is also available. The ready accessibility of SVG source code is likely to help spread SVG skills in a
manner similar to that which led to the explosion of use of HTML several years ago.

Internationalization of Content

Increasingly, Web sites are being designed to reach a multilingual, international audience.
SVG has support for internationalization of text content. In addition, it provides support
for conditional display of text in an appropriate language corresponding to the locale or
language settings of the consuming browser.

Listing 1.5, International.svg, is a simple example of text display conditional on language
settings in the consuming browser. The code will display white text on a red background
no matter what the language setting is. However, the content of the displayed text will

vary depending on the language settings of the user agent. In this example, we will use the Batik SVG Browser. If the language setting is English (en), the greeting displayed is "Good Evening!". If the language setting is French (fr), the greeting "Bonsoir!" is displayed. With a language setting of German (de), "Guten Abend!" is displayed. In the absence of any of the specified language settings, a default text is displayed; in this example, the default happens also to be in English.

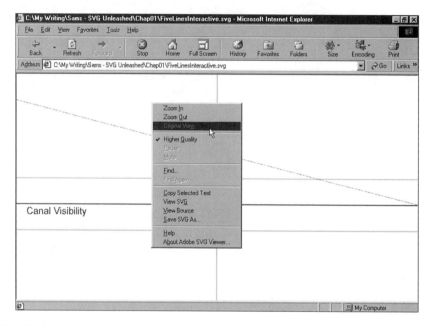

FIGURE 1.9   The menu available when you right-click in Adobe SVG Viewer.

LISTING 1.5   International.svg—The Language of the Greeting Depends on the User's Language Settings

```
<?xml version="1.0" standalone="no"?>
<!DOCTYPE svg PUBLIC "-//W3C//DTD SVG 20010904//EN"
"http://www.w3.org/TR/2001/REC-SVG-20010904/DTD/svg10.dtd">
<svg width="400" height="150">
    <rect x="40" y="40" rx="8" ry="8" width="200"
     height="40" style="fill:#FF0000; stroke:none"/>
    <switch>
        <text x="65" y="65" style="stroke:none; fill:#FFFFFF;
         font-family:Arial, sans-serif; font-size:18"
         systemLanguage="en">
            Good Evening!
        </text>
        <text x="65" y="65" style="stroke:none; fill:#FFFFFF;
```

LISTING 1.5 Continued

```
            font-family:Arial, sans-serif; font-size:18"
            systemLanguage="fr">
                Bonsoir!
        </text>
        <text x="65" y="65" style="stroke:none; fill:#FFFFFF;
         font-family:Arial, sans-serif; font-size:18"
         systemLanguage="de">
            Guten Abend!
        </text>
        <text x="65" y="65" style="stroke:none; fill:#FFFFFF;
         font-family:Arial, sans-serif; font-size:18">
            Good Evening!
        </text>
    </switch>
</svg>
```

Figure 1.10 was made with the language in Batik set to English (en). Thus, the child element of the <switch> element with a systemLanguage attribute with a value of en is to be displayed. As you can see in the source code, the text to be displayed for the English language setting is Good Evening!.

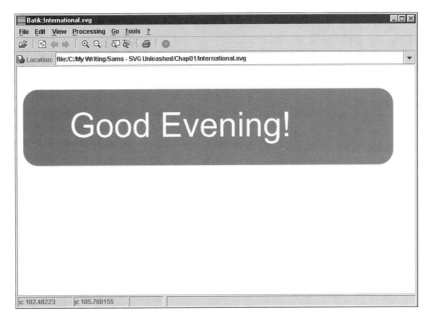

FIGURE 1.10 A greeting in English to correspond to Batik language settings.

Using the Batik SVG Browser, you can set system languages by choosing Edit, Preferences, and then adjusting the Language preferences. Thus, if the language preference were French (fr), the greeting "Bonsoir!" would be displayed, as you can see in Figure 1.11 (shot still using International.svg as the SVG document to be displayed).

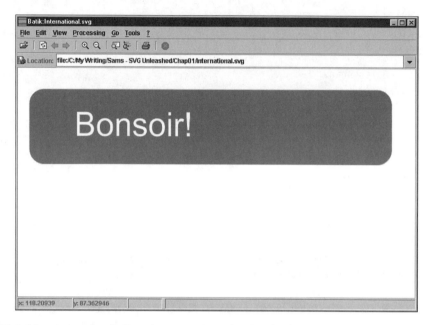

FIGURE 1.11   A greeting in French to correspond to Batik language settings.

The ability to create images that can be used on the Web for a multilingual audience provides significant potential efficiency savings over situations in which separate bitmap graphics must be created for each supported language. With SVG, it is possible, as you have seen, to serve a single graphic that displays text appropriate to the user's language settings and, presumably, language skills.

You can achieve conditional display of text using the Adobe SVG Viewer in, for example, Internet Explorer. However, adjusting language settings is a little less convenient. In Windows 98, for example, open the Control Panel, select Regional Settings, and choose a language of interest. When the language is set as German, the Adobe viewer causes the text in Figure 1.12 to be displayed. You may find that, to get the browser to display German text (assuming your original setting was English), you need to close all Internet Explorer windows and then open Internet Explorer after adjusting the language in Regional Settings before the desired text displays.

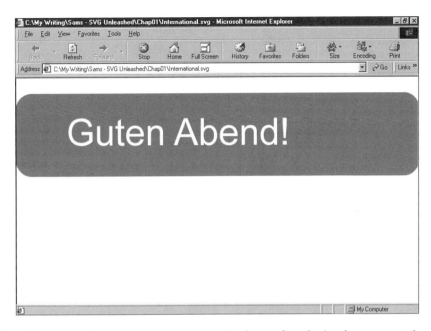

FIGURE 1.12   A greeting in German in Internet Explorer, after altering language settings.

Accessible to Search Engines

Text within SVG images remains as text because the displayed text is simply the character content of one of the SVG elements, `text` or `tspan`, which determine the display of text in SVG images. This text is searchable by XML-aware search engines. This contrasts favorably with bitmap graphics used in Web pages, where any text is converted to no more than a pattern of colored pixels. Although the pixel pattern is likely decipherable as text by the human eye viewing the page, the text is inaccessible to current or likely future search engines. Similarly, text content in Flash Web pages is contained within a proprietary binary format and is likely to be inaccessible to many search engines. SVG images, or Web pages (see Chapter 12, "SVG for Web Authoring"), will preserve or enhance the accessibility of text content.

Display of text in SVG is discussed fully in Chapter 8, "Laying Out Text in SVG."

Data-Driven Graphics

SVG files can be static or can be created dynamically at the time a Web page or an image on it is served to a client. The SVG document, when created dynamically, can make use of data held elsewhere, such as in XML or in an RDBMS to provide part of the information that is to be displayed in the graphic. The use of data-driven SVG graphics provides a multiplicity of possible applications. Imagine a Web page with local weather with temperatures graphed out, or attractive graphics appropriate to the temperature or weather, making the site more attractive for the general user.

In fact, a significant part of this book will consider how data-driven SVG graphics can be created using current technologies combined with SVG.

Resolution Independent

SVG images are rendered in a manner that is independent of the resolution of the device on which it is being rendered. Unlike bitmap images that consist essentially of a two-dimensional array of information related to individual pixels (compressed where possible), SVG images are drawn from instructions contained in the elements of the source code. Thus, the image is rendered in a manner appropriate to the display device and its resolution. Having different versions of a graphic for individual types of devices or screen resolution is not necessary.

Display on Mobile Devices

One of the aims in the original Requirements document for SVG was that it be available on a range of display devices, not only on the conventional desktop browser. Already some prototype implementations of SVG 1.0 are available on mobile devices. Imagine having a mobile device with an SVG map that you scroll as you make your journey, zooming in to the area of interest as you come closer to your destination.

SVG 1.1, currently in the Candidate Recommendation phase, will offer modularization of the SVG specification and, likely, a number of SVG profiles that will make appropriate parts of SVG usable on devices with resources too limited to implement the full SVG 1.0 specification.

Declarative Rollovers

A common use of bitmap graphics on Web pages is to provide rollover functionality—for example, a change in shape or color of a button or other object in response to mousing the object. When creating a rollover in HTML Web pages, you would typically have more than one bitmap image with the transition between images being controlled by JavaScript code. SVG introduces a capability to create rollovers declaratively, using SVG elements borrowed from SMIL Animation. The use of SMIL Animation elements in SVG animations is described more fully in Chapter 11, "SVG Animation Elements."

> **NOTE**
>
> SMIL is the Synchronized Multimedia Integration Language, another application language of XML. Full information on SMIL is located at http://www.w3.org/TR/2001/REC-smil20-20010807/ and http://www.w3.org/TR/2001/REC-smil-animation-20010904/.

An example rollover effect on the SVGSpider.com all-SVG Web site shown in Figure 1.13 is produced by declarative SVG code.

The text link to Page07 on the SVGSpider.com Web site (`http://www.SVGSpider.com/`) is created as follows:

```
<a xlink:href="Page07.svg" id="Page07">
    <text style="fill:black; stroke:black; font-size:12;"
     x="25" y="280" > Page 7 </text>
</a>
```

The `id` attribute of the SVG a element in the preceding code is referenced from an SVG animate element:

```
<animate begin="Page07.mouseover" dur="0.1s"
 attributeName="visibility" from="hidden" to="visible" fill="freeze"/>
```

You can examine the full SVG listing at `www.svgspider.com/default.svg`.

Rollovers are only one example of interactivity that SVG can provide by means of declarative code in response to user actions. Of course, because SVG images can be scripted by JavaScript, the declarative interactivity can be supplemented by customized JavaScript code.

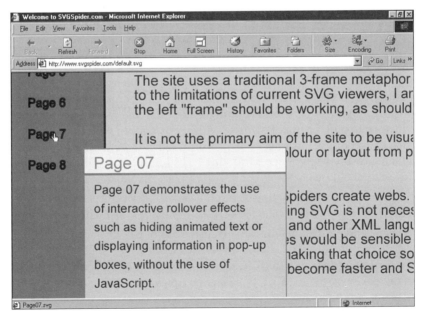

FIGURE 1.13 A rollover created using declarative SVG syntax.

Let's move on to consider some of the potential and actual limitations that currently apply to SVG 1.0.

Limitations of SVG

Inevitably with any new technology, it is necessary to balance a description of its strengths with an assessment of its limitations or weaknesses. In my view, the advantages of SVG far outweigh its shortcomings although, of course, in certain specific settings other technologies may offer advantages over SVG.

Size of Download for Viewer

A negative point put forward regarding the Adobe SVG Viewer is that it is a much larger download than the competitor vector graphics rendering engine for Macromedia Flash. Because Adobe is distributing its SVG viewer with other products, many Web users will have the Adobe plug-in available (and installed) with other products, such as the Adobe Acrobat Reader.

> **CAUTION**
>
> At least some distributions of Adobe software automatically install version 2 of the Adobe SVG Viewer when version 3 is already installed on the system. That can cause problems, particularly if you have copied Adobe SVG Viewer version 3 to browsers where automatic installation is not possible. See the "Tools to View SVG" section later in this chapter for further information.

Open Source Code

Some SVG creators may be concerned that source code for their graphics is made available to Web site users. This could create fears, for example, for companies that produce maps for online consumption—that some users might use them in breach of copyright. However, many mapping companies and organizations appear, with good reason, to consider that the technical advantages of SVG outweigh the potential for abuse of the SVG maps. Additionally, the Requirements Working Draft for SVG 2.0 indicates that encryption may be part of SVG 2.0 (see http://www.w3.org/TR/SVG2Reqs).

CPU Intensive

An SVG viewer (rendering engine) makes extensive use of the CPU during the multiple screen recalculations required by complex SVG animations. The load on the CPU speed is determined partly by the size of the SVG image—a larger image places a greater load on the CPU—and partly by the number, type, and complexity of animations, or other redrawing requirements, of the image.

You can view an example of an SVG image that can display jerkily with slower CPUs at `http://www.svgspider.com/BubblesLava01.svg`. That example will run at sustained 100% CPU usage on a 550MHz machine and 75% CPU usage on a 1.3GHz CPU. With animations that require similarly intensive recalculations on computers with very slow CPUs, the machine can seem to lock totally.

This limitation of SVG is likely to improve with time. The Adobe SVG Viewer and other SVG viewers are becoming more efficient at display of SVG. In addition, with the steady increase in CPU speed available on new computers, a greater proportion will be able to give good display speeds with SVG.

Limited Tools

The SVG Recommendation was completed in September 2001. Inevitably, it takes time after a technology is completed for a range of tools to be finalized and made generally available. Likely during the lifetime of this book, the number of SVG tools available will increase substantially. Tools available at the time of writing are described in the following section.

Basic Tools

To make use of SVG images, you need two types of tools: something with which to create the SVG and something with which to view the SVG.

Tools to Create SVG

SVG code can be generated by hand, if you understand SVG syntax sufficiently, or can be automatically generated by a number of drawing tools. Of course, SVG code can also be generated server-side, as will be described in later chapters of this book.

Text Editor

For the purposes of the early part of this book, we will assume that you have access to a text editor, ideally an XML-aware one, which you can use to create SVG. Later chapters of the book will introduce you to tools that allow SVG documents to be created dynamically server-side.

Many XML editors are available. One inexpensive editor that provides syntax color coding as well as checks for well-formedness and validity is XML Writer (`www.xmlwriter.net`). XML Writer was last released before the SVG specification was finalized, but the creation of an SVG document template is straightforward and can be added to those available as standard. An SVG template, SVGTemplate.svg, suitable for XML Writer or use in any other XML-aware text editor is shown in Listing 1.6.

LISTING 1.6   Template.svg—A Basic Template for an SVG 1.0 Document

```
<?xml version="1.0" standalone="no"?>
<!DOCTYPE svg PUBLIC "-//W3C//DTD SVG 20010904//EN"
"http://www.w3.org/TR/2001/REC-SVG-20010904/DTD/svg10.dtd">
<svg width="" height="">
</svg>
```

Additionally, you might want to have a template for SVG documents that include JavaScript, such as the template shown in Listing 1.7.

LISTING 1.7   JSTemplate.svg—A Template for an SVG Document to Include JavaScript Code

```
<?xml version="1.0" standalone="no"?>
<!DOCTYPE svg PUBLIC "-//W3C//DTD SVG 20010904//EN"
"http://www.w3.org/TR/2001/REC-SVG-20010904/DTD/svg10.dtd">
<svg width="" height="">
<script type="text/javascript">
<![CDATA[

]]>
</script>

</svg>
```

Many other XML editors are available, including XML Spy 4.4, which provides several views of an SVG document's structure. XML Spy is more expensive than XML Writer. An evaluation download of XML Spy is available from `http://www.xmlspy.com`.

SVG Drawing Tools

SVG functionality is being added to a number of existing drawing tools, such as Adobe Illustrator and CorelDRAW. In addition, the first dedicated SVG drawing and animation tool, Jasc WebDraw, is now in version 1.02.

Jasc WebDraw

A useful tool for creating SVG code, recently released as version 1, is Jasc's WebDraw. WebDraw (formerly called Trajectory Pro) is intended as a tool that allows designers to draw vector graphics and create animations in SVG. Its relevance to the process of under-standing SVG and the relationship that exists between SVG code and the visual rendering of the SVG image is that WebDraw has both Canvas and Source tabs. You can draw on the Canvas tab, as in a traditional vector drawing tool, and view the source code by clicking on the Source tab. You can then modify either the drawing on the Canvas tab or the source code on the Source tab. Any changes made are reflected on the other tab. This is a powerful learning tool. Occasionally, however, WebDraw has problems with opened files, as shown in Figure 1.14, where the horizontal lines are not rendered. Further improvements to WebDraw are anticipated. Check `www.jasc.com` for the latest version.

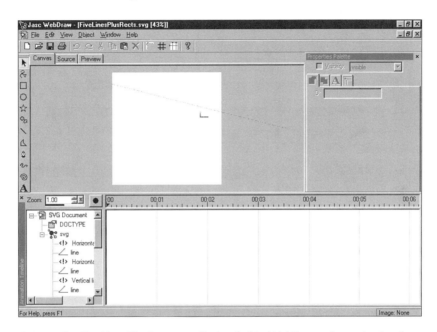

FIGURE 1.14   The FiveLinesPlusRects.svg file loaded in WebDraw, shown in the Canvas tab.

Figures 1.14 and 1.15 show, respectively, FiveLinesPlusRects.svg opened in WebDraw from a file on disc and the source code shown when the Source tab is clicked.

The WebDraw Source tab has syntax highlighting. If you, for example, add a stroke (outline) to a shape in the Source tab, the change is shown in the Canvas tab when you switch back to it. The use of a tool like WebDraw helps you to understand how different parts of the code impact the visual appearance of an SVG graphic. An alternative approach is an XML editor, such as XML Writer, with repeated Preview in Browser choices.

Like many other drawing tools, WebDraw can be fairly hungry for memory.

WebDraw tends to produce code that, at least to my eye, is significantly more readable than code produced from Adobe Illustrator. Listing 1.8 shows the code to produce a simple banner-ad-size SVG image. (Compare Listing 1.8 with Listing 2.2 in Chapter 2.)

LISTING 1.8   JascWebDraw.svg—A Simple Image Produced by Jasc WebDraw 1.0

```
<?xml version="1.0" standalone="no"?>
<!DOCTYPE svg PUBLIC "-//W3C//DTD SVG 1.0//EN"
 "http://www.w3.org/TR/2001/REC-SVG-20010904/DTD/svg10.dtd">
```

LISTING 1.8   Continued

```
<svg width="468" height="60">
    <polygon points="86.5,12 104.398,43 68.6021,43"
     transform="matrix(1.98348 0 0 1 -85.0708 0) translate(0 0)"
     style="fill:none;stroke:rgb(0,0,0);stroke-width:2"/>
    <rect x="154" y="12" width="256" height="34" rx="5" ry="5"
     style="fill:none;stroke:rgb(0,0,0);stroke-width:1"/>
</svg>
```

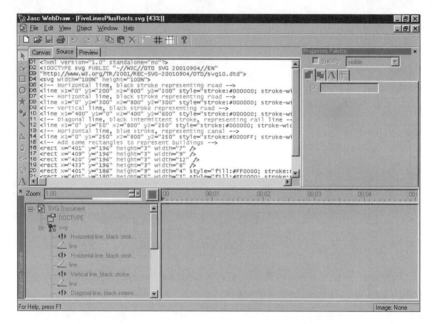

FIGURE 1.15   The source code in the Source tab corresponding to the drawing in Figure 1.14.

For the triangle and rectangle used in the image, notice that the SVG polygon and rect elements are used. Contrast that with the path elements and multiple entities in Listing 2.2 exported from Adobe Illustrator, which are significantly less readable.

Adobe Illustrator 10

Adobe Illustrator 10 is a well-regarded drawing tool among graphic designers. It has SVG export facilities. You may find that graphic designers with which you work use Adobe Illustrator to produce their work.

TIP

If you are using Illustrator to create SVG code to act as a template for dynamic generation of the same visual appearance, be sure to save two versions of the code, to ensure you can edit again in Illustrator. One version will have the information to allow further editing in Illustrator, if necessary, and the other will have the extraneous Illustrator-specific information removed to provide an optimally sized SVG file.

Adobe Illustrator is a powerful drawing tool. At the time of writing, it is at version 10—the first version to implement the SVG 1.0 Recommendation. Given its familiarity, you may find that you are required to handle the code it outputs with many path elements and ENTITY definitions and references.

CAUTION

Adobe Illustrator 9 produces SVG code for export that complies with a non-final version of the SVG 1.0 specification. CorelDRAW 9 also produces a non-final version of SVG. If you are using either of those tools, you will likely want to update the DOCTYPE declaration to that for SVG 1.0. The correct DOCTYPE is described in Chapter 2.

CAUTION

Adobe Illustrator 10 occasionally loses information from an SVG file in the process or exporting and re-importing, even if the check box to preserve editing information is checked. Be sure to check that the final SVG matches the intended visual appearance.

So which SVG drawing tool is best for you or your graphic designer? If your designer is already using Illustrator, he or she will likely prefer to continue with what he or she knows. If the choice is being made without a company commitment to either tool, there are several trade-offs. Jasc WebDraw produces cleaner SVG code. You can edit SVG code directly in Jasc WebDraw, using the Source tab. Adobe Illustrator is a more mature drawing tool but tends to produce long code that isn't too easily read. And Adobe Illustrator is more than twice the price of Jasc WebDraw. The choice is yours.

Other SVG drawing tools are available, but Jasc WebDraw and Adobe Illustrator are two of the best specified SVG drawing tools at the time of writing.

Tools to View SVG

Whatever technique you choose to create SVG, you will need an SVG viewer (also called an SVG rendering engine) to view SVG images onscreen. Three SVG viewers provide implementations that vary in completeness. In addition, three browsers, Mozilla, Konquerer, and Amaya, provide very limited SVG implementations.

In turn, we will look at the three principal SVG viewers available at the time of writing: the Adobe SVG Viewer, Batik, and X-Smiles.

NOTE

You may find it useful to check out the current conformance of viewers located at http://www.w3.org/Graphics/SVG/Test/ and follow the link to current conformance data.

Adobe SVG Viewer

The Adobe SVG Viewer is, at the time of writing, the SVG viewer that comes closest to having a complete implementation of the SVG 1.0 Recommendation. The Adobe viewer has an implementation of SVG animation that is far superior to that currently in any of the alternative browsers. In addition, it provides extensive, but not yet complete, support for scripting of SVG. Adobe SVG Viewer version 3.0 was released in November 2001.

The Adobe SVG Viewer is a plug-in for a conventional HTML browser such as Microsoft Internet Explorer or Netscape Navigator. Further information and free downloads are available at `http://www.adobe.com/svg/` and `http://www.adobe.com/svg/viewer/install/main.html`.

Batik

The Batik SVG Viewer is part of a Java-based SVG toolkit. The Batik SVG toolkit consists of an SVG viewer and modules to allow you to create SVG in Java.

At the time of writing, the most recent release version of Batik is version 1.1. Batik 1.1 supports most of static SVG but lacks support for animation and has only limited support for scripting.

A beta version of Batik 1.5 is also available for download. The beta version of 1.5 adds substantial support for scripting of SVG. Support of SVG animation has yet to be added and is expected in Batik 2.0, scheduled for release around the end of 2002. When these parts of SVG functionality have been added, Batik will have the potential to threaten the current dominance of the Adobe SVG Viewer.

A growing number of projects use Batik for implementing SVG support. Because Batik is written in Java, it is not surprising that Java-based projects dominate in that regard. For an up-to-date list of projects that use Batik, visit `http://xml.apache.org/batik/index.html`.

X-Smiles

The X-Smiles browser is a multinamespace XML browser that supports such XML application languages as XSL-FO, SMIL, XForms, and SVG.

The X-Smiles browser is available for download from `http://www.x-smiles.org`. X-Smiles, which is currently at version 0.6, uses the CSIRO SVG Viewer to support SVG.

Native Browser Support for SVG

The SVG viewers, just mentioned, provide good and improving functionality for viewing SVG. However, it would be better if Web browsers natively supported viewing of SVG without the need for a plug-in. At the time of writing, however, native browser support for SVG is poor.

Mozilla   Mozilla has an ongoing project to develop native SVG support. Mozilla version 1.0, the latest version at this writing, has no native SVG support. It is unlikely that native SVG support will be added to a regular release of Mozilla in the short term, in part due to some licensing issues. For up-to-date information on the implementation of SVG in Mozilla, visit `http://www.mozilla.org/projects/svg/`.

Konqueror   This Linux browser is described at `http://www.kde.org/svg`.

Amaya   Amaya is a combined Web browser and authoring tool produced by the W3C. It has limited SVG support at the time of writing. Further information on the Amaya project can be obtained at `http://www.w3.org/Amaya/`.

Internet Explorer   At the time of writing, Microsoft's Internet Explorer browser does not have native SVG support. The Adobe SVG Viewer version 3 works well with the Internet Explorer browser, and many screenshots in this book will demonstrate that synergy.

Despite the absence of any announcement by Microsoft of support for SVG, there are indications at the time of writing that Microsoft has some exploratory work on SVG underway. Whether that work will lead to a decision on the part of Microsoft to support SVG natively in Internet Explorer remains to be seen. Another possible application would be to implement SVG within the .NET family of servers.

SVG Painter's Model

It may seem odd in a book for programmers to discuss up front a topic called the **painter's model**. However, a basic or better understanding of the SVG painter's model is important to anyone writing SVG code.

The creation of both the **fills** of SVG shapes and the creation of their outline—referred to as the **stroke**—can be considered as painting for the purposes of this discussion.

The SVG painter's model works similarly to painting with oil or acrylic paints. Paint that is applied later is applied over paint that was applied earlier. If the second paint applied is fully opaque, anywhere that the paint covers the first paint, the first paint is concealed. SVG documents work similarly. Code that comes early in an SVG document causes an onscreen object to be rendered. The next piece of code that relates to that same screen area is rendered, with any area where it overlaps the first object causing the first object to be hidden.

Listing 1.9 shows how two rectangles overlap. The rectangle that comes later in the code paints over the first. Don't worry about the detail of the animation syntax. If you run the code, you will see the second rectangle painting over the first one.

LISTING 1.9   TwoRects.svg—Two Rectangles Illustrating the Painter's Model

```
<?xml version="1.0" standalone="no"?>
<!DOCTYPE svg PUBLIC "-//W3C//DTD SVG 20010904//EN"
"http://www.w3.org/TR/2001/REC-SVG-20010904/DTD/svg10.dtd">
<svg width="400" height="250">
    <rect x="25" y="25" width="350" height="175" style="fill:#CCCCCC"/>
    <rect x="50" y="50" width="0" height="175" style="fill:green">
        <animate begin="2s" attributeName="width"
          from="0" to="350" dur="5s" fill="freeze"/>
    </rect>
</svg>
```

Figure 1.16 shows the zoomed appearance after the second rectangle has reached its full width. Notice that where the second rectangle has overlapped the first rectangle, the first is completely concealed.

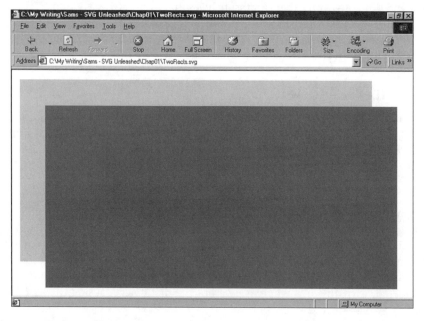

FIGURE 1.16   Effect of the SVG painter's model when two SVG objects overlap.

Paint in SVG needn't be fully opaque. The opacity of an SVG element can range from zero (fully transparent) to one (fully opaque).

Listing 1.10 shows the two rectangles but with the opacity of the second rectangle reduced to 0.3.

LISTING 1.10   TwoRectsOpacity.svg—Illustrating the Painter's Model with a Partially Transparent Object

```
<?xml version="1.0" standalone="no"?>
<!DOCTYPE svg PUBLIC "-//W3C//DTD SVG 20010904//EN"
"http://www.w3.org/TR/2001/REC-SVG-20010904/DTD/svg10.dtd">
<svg width="400" height="250">
    <rect x="25" y="25" width="350" height="175" style="fill:#CCCCCC"/>
    <rect x="50" y="50" width="0" height="175" style="fill:green; opacity:0.3">
        <animate begin="2s" attributeName="width"
        from="0" to="350" dur="5s" fill="freeze"/>
    </rect>
</svg>
```

The appearance of the rectangles after running Listing 1.10 is shown in Figure 1.17. Notice that, because the second rectangle is partially transparent, the paint of the first rectangle shows through the second. Of course, the color of the first is modified by the color of the second.

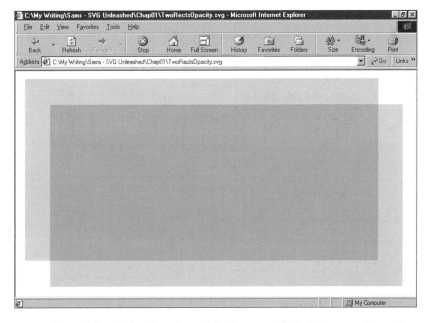

FIGURE 1.17   Effect of the SVG painter's model when two SVG objects overlap and one is semi-transparent.

Some SVG Examples

In this section, we will look at some short examples of SVG code and the visual appearances produced.

Documenting an Image

An SVG document is written in XML; therefore, simple XML comments can be added in all the locations where such comments are legal in a generic XML document. In addition, SVG provides a desc element, which is intended for use in storing a description of an SVG image (see Listing 1.11).

LISTING 1.11   FiveLineswithDesc.svg—Using a desc Element to Document an SVG Document

```
<?xml version="1.0" standalone="no"?>
<!DOCTYPE svg PUBLIC "-//W3C//DTD SVG 20010904//EN"
"http://www.w3.org/TR/2001/REC-SVG-20010904/DTD/svg10.dtd">
<svg width="100%" height="100%" xmlns="http://www.w3.org/2000/svg">
    <desc>This SVG image consists simply of five SVG &lt;line&gt;
          elements which provide simple representations of features on a map.
    </desc>

    <line x1="0" y1="200" x2="800" y2="200" style="stroke:#000000;
     stroke-width:0.5"/>
    <desc>The line above is a horizontal line which has a
     black stroke and in this simple map represents a road
    </desc>

    <line x1="0" y1="300" x2="800" y2="300" style="stroke:#000000;
     stroke-width:0.5"/>
    <desc>The line above is a horizontal line
     which has a black stroke and represents a road
    </desc>

    <line x1="400" y1="0" x2="400" y2="600" style="stroke:#000000;
     stroke-width:0.5"/>
    <desc>The line above is a vertical line which
     has a black stroke and represents a road
    </desc>

    <line x1="0" y1="50" x2="800" y2="250"
     style="stroke:#000000; stroke-width:0.5;
     stroke-dasharray:5,3,2"/>
    <desc>The line above is a diagonal line which has
```

LISTING 1.11   Continued

```
    a black intermittent stroke and represents a railway.
  </desc>

  <line x1="0" y1="250" x2="800" y2="250"
style="stroke:#0000FF;stroke-width:0.5"/>
    <desc>The line above is a horizontal line which
    has a blue stroke and represents a canal.
    </desc>
</svg>
```

Notice the several desc elements in Listing 1.11. The text in the first desc element provides a description of the whole SVG document. The content of the desc elements associated with line elements provides descriptions of the purpose and meaning of each line.

Simple Text Example

Graphs where data is plotted or technical diagrams of whatever type convey more meaning if they include clear and appropriate labels. Thus, to be able to use SVG to create expressive diagrams, maps, and other images, we need to understand how text is handled within an SVG document or image. Listing 1.12 demonstrates the lack of automatic text wrapping.

LISTING 1.12   SimpleText.svg—A Demonstration of the Lack of Automatic Text Wrapping

```
<?xml version="1.0" standalone="no"?>
<!DOCTYPE svg PUBLIC "-//W3C//DTD SVG 20010904//EN"
"http://www.w3.org/TR/2001/REC-SVG-20010904/DTD/svg10.dtd">
<svg width="400" height="200">
    <text x="10" y="25" style="fill:#000000; stroke:none;
    font-family:Arial, sans-serif; font-size:20">
    SVG differs from HTML in that text is not automatically
    wrapped to fit a browser window.
    </text>
</svg>
```

The absence of automatic wrapping of text in an SVG viewer places demands on a programmer to calculate line length when outputting text other than very short strings.

As you can see in Figure 1.18, the text in our example is curtailed at the edge of the size defined by the svg element (400 pixels wide).

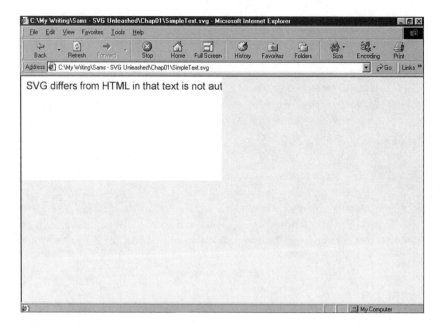

FIGURE 1.18   SVG text does not automatically wrap; separate elements are needed.

> **NOTE**
>
> It seems likely that at least some automatic text wrapping functionality will be added in SVG 1.2. For further information about the current status, visit http://www.w3.org/tr/svg12/. Additional automatic text flow functionality is likely in SVG 2.0. When the first SVG 2.0 Working Draft is released, it will likely be located at http://www.w3.org/TR/svg20.

When text in SVG 1.0 is laid out in multiple lines, two options exist for defining the layout. It is possible to lay text out using only `text` elements, and that is the approach we will look at first. The second approach, which we will look at in a moment, is to nest `tspan` elements within a `text` element.

Listing 1.13, SimpleText02.svg, shows text laid out using two `text` elements.

LISTING 1.13   SimpleText02.svg—Using Multiple text Elements to Break Text into Lines

```
<?xml version="1.0" standalone="no"?>
<!DOCTYPE svg PUBLIC "-//W3C//DTD SVG 20010904//EN"
"http://www.w3.org/TR/2001/REC-SVG-20010904/DTD/svg10.dtd">
<svg width="400" height="200">
    <text x="10" y="25" style="fill:#000000; stroke:none;
    font-family:Arial, sans-serif; font-size:20">
```

LISTING 1.13   Continued

```
    Welcome to SVG Unleashed
    </text>
    <text x="20" y="55" style="fill:#000000; stroke:none;
     font-family:Arial, sans-serif; font-size:16">
     A foundation in SVG for programmers.
    </text>
</svg>
```

A difficulty arises with using this approach if there is any likelihood that a user will want to copy all the text because, as you can see in Figure 1.19, it is possible to select the text in only one text element at a time.

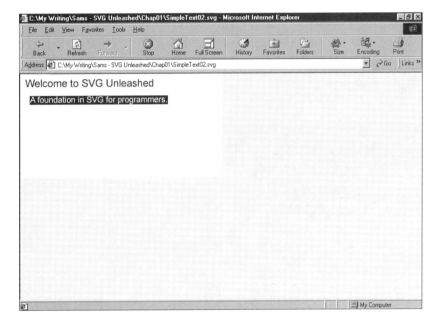

FIGURE 1.19   You can select the content of only one text element at a time.

The use of text elements in this way also causes difficulties in accessibility because logically connected information is treated as separate chunks. Thus, an aural browser would treat, for example, the beginning of a sentence in one text element as a separate thing from the completion of the sentence in a following text element, possibly causing significant comprehension problems for a visually impaired listener.

If we place the text within tspan elements, which are nested within text elements, as in Listing 1.14, Text03.svg, we can keep logically related text together. In this way, for example, all the content of a text element can be selected for copying together, as you can see in Figure 1.20.

LISTING 1.14   SimpleText03.svg—Using tspan Elements to Facilitate Selection of Text Content

```
<?xml version="1.0" standalone="no"?>
<!DOCTYPE svg PUBLIC "-//W3C//DTD SVG 20010904//EN"
"http://www.w3.org/TR/2001/REC-SVG-20010904/DTD/svg10.dtd">
<svg width="400" height="200">
    <text>
        <tspan x="10" y="25" style="fill:#000000; stroke:none;
         font-family:Arial, sans-serif; font-size:20">
        Welcome to SVG Unleashed
        </tspan>
        <tspan x="20" y="55" style="fill:#000000; stroke:none;
         font-family:Arial, sans-serif; font-size:16">
        A foundation in SVG for programmers.
        </tspan>
    </text>
</svg>
```

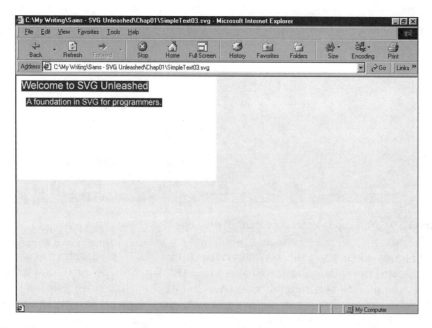

FIGURE 1.20   Using tspan elements allows all text within a text element to be selected.

Introducing the XML DOM

The examples you have seen so far in this chapter typically used SVG declarative syntax. In other words, they exclusively used markup, but no programming was involved. However, the interactivity and animation of SVG graphics can be enhanced by using programming languages such as ECMAScript to add control logic to define the effects possible in an SVG image, as you saw in the simple example in Listing 1.4.

SVG is an application language of XML. Therefore, it is not surprising that SVG makes use of the Document Object Model (DOM), which the W3C has defined as an Application Programming Interface (API) for the programmatic manipulation of XML documents.

The DOM at the W3C

The first version of the XML Document Object Model at W3C, called DOM Level 1, was a development of the so-called DOM Level 0, the JavaScript DOM for an HTML Web page. W3C DOM Level 1 was focused on the manipulation of either HTML or XML documents, as appropriate.

DOM Level 2 built on the functionality in DOM Level 1. You can find an overview of the DOM work at W3C at `http://www.w3.org/DOM/`.

XML DOM Basics

The XML Document Object Model models an XML document, and therefore an SVG document, as a hierarchy of node objects, or **nodes**. Some types of nodes may have other nodes as **child nodes**, whereas some nodes, called **leaf nodes**, are not permitted to have child nodes. Listing 1.15 shows a very simple XML document.

LISTING 1.15   SimpleXML.xml—A Simple XML Document

```
<?xml version='1.0'?>
<!-- This is a comment -->
<someElement>
 Some text.
</someElement>
```

The hierarchy of nodes for the document in Listing 1.15 would consist of a `Document` node. That `Document` node would have two child nodes. One child node is a `Comment` node, and the other child node is an `Element` node.

The `Comment` node has no child nodes. However, the `Element` node that represents the `someElement` element has a child node that is a `Text` node.

XML DOM Node Types

This section introduces each of the node types defined in the DOM Level 2 Core Recommendation (`http://www.w3.org/TR/2000/REC-DOM-Level-2-Core-20001113`).

Document Node

The `Document` node represents the **document entity** in XML 1.0 parlance—the invisible document itself.

A `Document` node may have several types of child nodes. There is always one `Element` node, corresponding to the document element of the XML document. Other permitted child node types are `ProcessingInstruction` nodes (corresponding to an XML processing instruction), `Comment` nodes (corresponding to an XML comment), and `DocumentType` nodes (corresponding to the document type, `DOCTYPE`, declaration of the XML document).

All nodes of other types present in an XML document have an `ownerDocument` attribute, which associates them with the document within which they exist.

> **CAUTION**
>
> Be careful not to confuse the DOM notion of an **attribute**, which relates to a property of a node, with the XML notion of an **attribute**, which is found in the start tag of an XML element.

DocumentType Node

Each `Document` node has a `DocumentType` attribute. If the corresponding XML document has no `DOCTYPE` declaration, the attribute is `null`. If the XML document has a `DOCTYPE` declaration, the `DocumentType` attribute of the `Document` node is an object reflecting that `DOCTYPE` declaration. The `DocumentType` interface provides access to information about entities associated with the document. A `DocumentType` node has no child nodes.

Element Node

An `Element` node corresponds to an element in the XML document. An `Element` node has an `attributes` attribute, which contains information about the attributes associated with the element. Additionally, an `Element` node has methods to retrieve an `Attr` object by name.

An `Element` node has a `tagName` attribute:

```
<myElement ...>
<!-- Some content could go here -->
</myElement>
```

For the preceding code, the value of the `tagName` attribute of the `Element` node would be the string `"myElement"`.

When two `Element` nodes share a parent node, they are said to be siblings:

```
<myElement ...>
    <anElement ... />
    <anotherElement ... />
</myElement>
```

The `Element` nodes with `tagName` attributes of `anElement` and `anotherElement` are sibling nodes.

The permitted child node types for an `Element` node are `Element`, `Text`, `ProcessingInstruction`, `Comment`, `CDATASection`, and `EntityReference`.

Attr Node

An `Attr` node represents an attribute in the corresponding XML document. The DOM does not consider `Attr` nodes part of the document tree, so the `parentNode`, `nextSibling`, and `previousSibling` attributes of an `Attr` node have a `null` value.

The value of an attribute in an XML document may be text or an entity reference, so an `Attr` node may have a child node that is either a `Text` node or an `EntityReference` node. If you are unfamiliar with entity references as the value of an attribute, see Listing 2.2 where the code output by Adobe Illustrator demonstrates that.

EntityReference Node

XML documents may use entities as a convenient means of storing information that is used repeatedly. You are likely familiar with the built-in entities such as `&lt;` and `&gt;` which are used to represent left- and right-angled brackets, respectively, in parsed text.

In XML the value of an attribute may be an entity reference. The permitted child node types for an `EntityReference` node are `Element`, `Text`, `ProcessingInstruction`, `Comment`, `CDATASection`, and `EntityReference`.

ProcessingInstruction Node

A `ProcessingInstruction` node in the DOM corresponds to a processing instruction in the corresponding XML document. A `ProcessingInstruction` node has no child nodes.

Comment Node

A `Comment` node in the DOM corresponds to a comment in the corresponding XML document. A `Comment` node has no child nodes.

Text Node

A `Text` node corresponds to text content of an element or an attribute in the XML document. A `Text` node has no child nodes.

CDATASection Node

A CDATASection node in the DOM corresponds to a CDATA section in the XML document. A CDATASection node has no child nodes.

Entity Node

An Entity node in the DOM corresponds to an XML entity. An Entity node may have the following types of child nodes: Element, ProcessingInstruction, Comment, Text, CDATASection, and EntityReference.

Requirements for SVG Rendering Engines

SVG rendering engines must support all the DOM Level 2 Core specification as well as parts of the Events, Traversal, and Range. If an SVG rendering engine supports Cascading Style Sheets (CSS), it must also support DOM Level 2 CSS. Support for DOM Level 2 Traversal and Range interfaces is optional.

Introducing the SVG DOM

The XML DOM introduced in the previous section provides generic ways to manipulate an XML document through a standard API. SVG has its own Document Object Model, which is built on the XML DOM and enables SVG-specific manipulation of the object model of an SVG document.

The Batik SVG Viewer allows you to view a representation of the SVG DOM. Figure 1.21 shows the DOM Viewer in the Batik SVG Browser with FiveLines.svg (Listing 1.2) loaded.

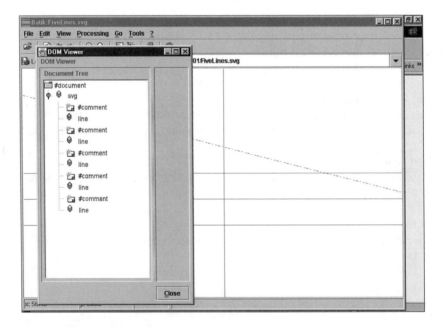

FIGURE 1.21   The SVG Document Object Model as represented in the Batik SVG Viewer.

Jasc WebDraw also provides a visual representation of the SVG DOM. Figure 1.22 shows how the DOM is displayed in WebDraw. The DOM is shown in the bottom left. One `line` element node is highlighted, and the attributes for that `line` element are shown in the Properties Palette at the top right.

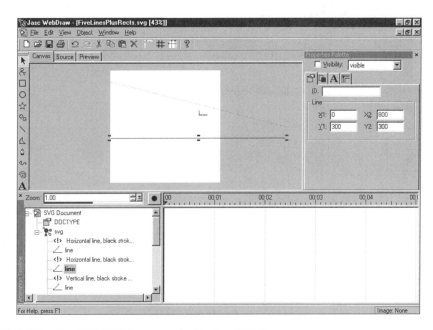

FIGURE 1.22   The SVG DOM represented in Jasc WebDraw.

It is helpful to use these visual presentations of the DOM, specifically the SVG DOM, to familiarize yourself with how the SVG DOM corresponds to the structure of an SVG document. The Jasc WebDraw visualization is particularly useful. You can click on a node in the SVG DOM and see its properties displayed in the Properties Palette and also see the visible object displayed in the Canvas tab, as Figure 1.22 shows.

Of course, the purpose of the SVG DOM is not primarily to allow you to visualize it; rather it is to give you the control to programmatically manipulate the structure and content of an SVG document.

For example, the SVG DOM can be used to add a new element to an SVG document. Listing 1.16 shows a simple example in which JavaScript is used to manipulate the DOM.

LISTING 1.16   AddCircle.svg—Adding a Circle to an SVG Document Using JavaScript and the SVG DOM

```
<?xml version="1.0" standalone="no"?>
<!DOCTYPE svg PUBLIC "-//W3C//DTD SVG 20010904//EN"
"http://www.w3.org/TR/2001/REC-SVG-20010904/DTD/svg10.dtd">
```

LISTING 1.16   Continued

```
<svg width="400px" height="250px" >
 <script type="text/javascript">
 <![CDATA[
    function createShape(evt) {
       var SVGDoc  = evt.getTarget().getOwnerDocument();
       var SVGRoot = SVGDoc.getDocumentElement();
       var myShape;

       myShape = SVGDoc.createElement("circle");
       myShape.setAttribute("cx", 125);
       myShape.setAttribute("cy", 125);
       myShape.setAttribute("r",  50);
       myShape.setAttribute("style", "fill: #FFCCCC; stroke:#FF0000");
       SVGRoot.appendChild(myShape);
       }
       ]]>
 </script>
<circle cx="60px" cy="100px" r="50px"
 style="fill:white; stroke:red; stroke-width:4"
 onclick="createShape(evt)"/>
</svg>
```

If you are not familiar with JavaScript, you may find the introduction to JavaScript in Part II helpful. However, even if you don't regularly use JavaScript, we hope the following description will give you an impression of how to use JavaScript to manipulate the SVG DOM.

```
<circle cx="60px" cy="100px" r="50px"
 style="fill:white; stroke:red; stroke-width:4"
 onclick="createShape(evt)"/>
```

The preceding code has an onclick attribute, which defines what happens when the circle is clicked. In this instance, a JavaScript function named createShape() is called.

Within the CDATA section, we see the first lines of code for the createShape()function:

```
function createShape(evt) {
  var SVGDoc  = evt.getTarget().getOwnerDocument();
  var SVGRoot = SVGDoc.getDocumentElement();
  var myShape;
```

> **NOTE**
>
> You can use an alternate syntax for the above function so that the first two of the preceding variable declarations would look like this:
>
> ```
> var SVGDoc = evt.target.ownerDocument;
> var SVGRoot = SVGDoc.documentElement;
> ```

The first variable declaration uses the getOwnerDocument() method to find information about the document that contains the circle to be clicked. The SVGDoc variable stores that information. The SVGRoot variable stores information about the document element, which in the case of an SVG document is always the outer svg element.

We then declare a myShape variable, which we will use to store information about the element we are about to create:

```
myShape = SVGDoc.createElement("circle");
myShape.setAttribute("cx", 125);
myShape.setAttribute("cy", 125);
myShape.setAttribute("r",  50);
myShape.setAttribute("style", "fill: #FFCCCC; stroke:#FF0000");
SVGRoot.appendChild(myShape);
```

Next, we use the createElement() method to create a node corresponding to a circle element. Then we use the setAttribute() method four times to set the values of the circle's attributes.

Up to this point, we have simply created a node that corresponds to a circle element, which isn't part of any particular document. We, of course, want the newly created circle element to be part of AddCircle.svg, so we use the appendChild() method to add the node corresponding to the node corresponding to the svg element of our document. It is only after that is done that the newly created circle element is part of the document. As you can see in Figure 1.23, the circle element is then displayed onscreen.

Figure 1.23 shows the appearance before the circle is clicked and the createShape() function is called. Figure 1.24 shows the appearance after the createShape() function has been called and a second circle element has been added to the document.

Of course, there is much more to the SVG DOM than you have seen here. In the following chapters of this book, we will discuss and demonstrate the SVG DOM further. Typically, when we introduce an SVG element, we will discuss the SVG DOM for that element and, for some DOM objects, use it in an example toward the end of the chapter.

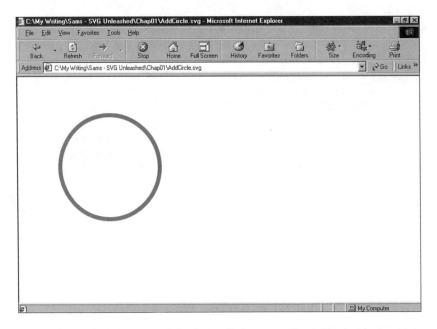

FIGURE 1.23   The circle before it is clicked to call the createShape() function.

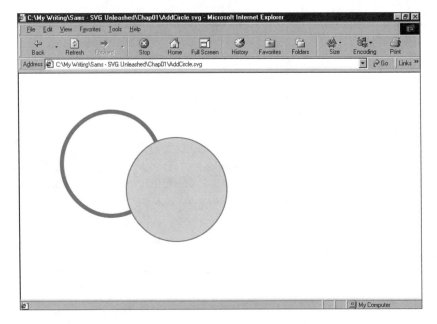

FIGURE 1.24   The circle after it has been clicked to call the createShape() function.

Summary

SVG is an XML-based declarative language for the description of two-dimensional vector graphics. As you can probably tell by now, SVG opens up new and powerful ways for programmers to generate graphics.

To view an SVG image, you need an SVG rendering engine, also known as an SVG viewer. To create SVG, you can use a text editor or a vector drawing program that can export SVG.

SVG has a Document Object Model (DOM) based on the DOM Level 2 for XML. The SVG DOM can be scripted. You'll see more about the DOM and scripting throughout the rest of this book.

CHAPTER 2

Document Structure in SVG

This chapter will introduce you to the permitted structure of SVG documents. It will also introduce you to several of the SVG elements. In later chapters, we will examine the other SVG elements; for example, in Chapter 3, "Basic SVG Elements and Shapes," we will look at the SVG elements that provide the basic SVG graphic shapes.

SVG is an application language of XML; therefore, all general XML syntax rules apply to SVG documents. Some basic rules of XML syntax as they apply to SVG will be reviewed in the first section of this chapter. Following that, we will discuss the necessary and permitted elements that, in various combinations, form the general structure of an SVG document.

The final part of this chapter will focus on the DOM interfaces that apply to the elements discussed in the chapter.

SVG Is XML

An SVG document is written in XML 1.0 syntax. Full details of the syntax requirements of XML 1.0 (2nd Edition) are located at `http://www.w3.org/TR/2000/REC-xml-20001006`. If you are already familiar with the basic rules of XML, then likely you can skip this section.

If most of your programming has been in an HTML environment, you will notice that SVG syntax has similarities to HTML, but if you want your SVG images to be displayed correctly, you need to follow some rules for XML and SVG that a Web browser and HTML won't demand that you follow.

Optional XML Declaration

An SVG document may begin with an optional XML declaration:

```
<?xml version="1.0"?>
```

If an XML declaration is present, it must be on the first line of the document, and no characters, not even a single space character, can precede it. A version attribute is compulsory. At the time of writing, the only permitted value of the version attribute is "1.0".

The XML declaration can also take a standalone attribute, with permitted values of "yes" and "no". Additionally, an encoding attribute can be used to specify character encoding for the document. All XML parsers must support UTF-8 and UTF-16, at a minimum.

Document Type Declaration

An XML document can include a Document Type Declaration, sometimes referred to as a DOCTYPE declaration, to indicate information about the structure of the document.

For an SVG 1.0 document, the DOCTYPE declaration typically takes the following form:

```
<!DOCTYPE svg PUBLIC "-//W3C//DTD SVG 20010904//EN"
"http://www.w3.org/TR/2001/REC-SVG-20010904/DTD/svg10.dtd">
```

The svg in the first line indicates the **element type name** of the **document element**, that is, the element within which all other elements in the document are nested. The string enclosed in quotation marks in the latter part of the first line, following the word PUBLIC, is the public identifier for the document type. The string on the second line, enclosed in quotation marks, is the URL at which the **Document Type Definition** (DTD) for an SVG 1.0 document is located. A DTD defines the permitted structure of an SVG document. In the case of an SVG 1.0 document, the document type definition is held external to the SVG document (and its DOCTYPE declaration) and its URL is referenced in the **external subset** of the DOCTYPE declaration.

CAUTION

Be careful not to confuse the **Document Type Declaration** (DOCTYPE declaration) with the **Document Type Definition** (DTD). The DOCTYPE declaration includes the **internal subset** of the document type definition (there is none for the SVG DTD) and a reference to the **external subset**, typically a separate DTD file.

If the XML jargon is confusing, simply copy the DOCTYPE declaration shown at the beginning of this section into the correct point in your SVG code listings, and you will be okay. In some settings, you may not need the DOCTYPE declaration at all—for example, if your browser recognizes an SVG file by the .svg file extension. But for general usage, it is wiser to include the DOCTYPE declaration.

2

> **NOTE**
>
> You may see DOCTYPE declarations that differ from the one shown earlier. They may refer to nonfinal versions of the SVG specification. Some vector drawing packages, for example, Adobe Illustrator 9 and CorelDRAW 10, produce SVG code that does not correspond exactly to the final SVG 1.0 Recommendation. Usually, the code will still run successfully in the Adobe SVG Viewer.

If you are interested in looking at the DTD for SVG 1.0, it is located at `http://www.w3.org/TR/2001/REC-SVG-20010904/DTD/svg10.dtd`. Attempting to display it in Internet Explorer 5.5 causes an error, but the DTD displays in Mozilla 0.9.9.

Element Names Are Case Sensitive

Element type names in all XML-based languages are case sensitive. Most, but not all, element type names in SVG use lowercase only. One exception is the `clipPath` element. In any case, it is essential that you use the case of all characters in an element type name exactly as defined in the SVG specification. Thus, for example, the following code is legal and will be recognized by an SVG processor:

```
<svg></svg>
```

However, the SVG language does *not* contain an `SVG` element. Using uppercase will cause an error. You must write `svg`, not `SVG`, when creating start and end tags for the `svg` element.

Similarly,

```
<clipPath ...>
<!-- Content can go here. -->
</clipPath>
```

will be recognized and processed by an SVG rendering engine, whereas

```
<ClipPath ...>
<!-- Do not use this element name -
the case of one letter is wrong!! -->
<!-- Content can go here. -->
</ClipPath>
```

will cause an error because the case of the first character is wrong.

Matching Start and End Tags

All elements that have content must have a start tag:

```
<svg>
```

They also must have a matching end tag:

```
</svg>
```

Omitting the end tag will cause an error. The content of an element, if it has any, must be placed between the start and end tags.

Empty elements can be written as a single tag with a forward slash before the final closing angled bracket:

```
<rect .... />
```

Quotation Marks with Attributes

When you add attributes to an SVG element, you must use quotation marks to delimit the value of an attribute. You can use either a pair of single quotation marks or a pair of double quotation marks. So to define the position of the top left of a rect element, you could write the following:

```
<rect x="0" y='0' .... />
```

Notice that the value for the x attribute is delimited by a pair of double quotation marks, and the value of the y attribute is delimited by a pair of single quotation marks.

CAUTION

Be careful not to use a combination of single and double quotation marks on the same attribute value. Both the following are wrong and will cause an error:

```
x="0'
y='0"
```

The quotation marks must be used in matching pairs, such as x="20" or y='10'.

Comments

You can add comments to SVG documents. The syntax is the same as that for HTML/XHTML comments:

```
<!-- This is a comment. -->
```

SVG additionally has desc elements, described later in this chapter, which you can use to provide descriptions of an SVG document, an individual element and its purpose, and so on.

Processing Instructions

XML 1.0 provides for processing instructions to be included in XML documents. In SVG, you can use a processing instruction to associate an external cascading style sheet (CSS) with the SVG document. For example, the following shows the code necessary to access an external CSS named XMML02.css:

```
<?xml-stylesheet type="text/css" href="XMML02.css" ?>
```

You can see an example of this process in action at http://www.XMML.com/, if you have an SVG viewer correctly installed.

A processing instruction begins with the characters <? followed by the name of the processing instruction (in this case, xml-stylesheet), followed by text, which in the case of the xml-stylesheet processing instruction typically consists of the type and href attributes with appropriate values, similar to those shown in the sample code.

Entities and Entity References

A number of SVG drawing tools, including Adobe Illustrator, will generate **entities** in the SVG code that they export. An entity is an XML 1.0 term that refers to a way to store information that may be used more than once. XML processors, and therefore SVG, have a few built-in entities:

- <—The left-angled bracket, <
- >—The right-angled bracket, >
- "—A double quotation mark, "
- '—A single quotation mark, or apostrophe, '
- &—The ampersand, &

If you wanted to display the following text in an SVG document

```
An SVG document has an <svg> element
```

you would need to use the < and > entities in your code, as shown in Listing 2.1.

LISTING 2.1   EntityExample.svg—An Example of Using Entities

```
<?xml version="1.0" standalone="no"?>
<!DOCTYPE svg PUBLIC "-//W3C//DTD SVG 20010904//EN"
"http://www.w3.org/TR/2001/REC-SVG-20010904/DTD/svg10.dtd">
<svg width="500px" height="300px">
<text x="50px" y="30px" style="fill:red; stroke:none; font-size:18">
Every SVG document has an &lt;svg&gt; element.
</text>
</svg>
```

If the third last line of code was literally

```
Every SVG document has an <svg> element
```

an error would occur because the SVG processor would recognize what seemed to be the start tag of an svg element and look for its corresponding end tag. When that tag could not be located, an error would occur.

Listing 2.2 shows a sample SVG document produced by Adobe Illustrator 10. Look for the parts of the code that contain the keyword ENTITY (there you will see the entity definitions) and strings that begin with the character & (which are the entity references).

LISTING 2.2   AdobeIllustrator.svg—An SVG Document Including Entities Automatically
Generated by Adobe Illustrator

```
<?xml version="1.0" encoding="utf-8"?>
<!-- Generator: Adobe Illustrator 10.0, SVG Export Plug-In . SVG Version: 3.0.0
Build 76)  -->
<!DOCTYPE svg PUBLIC "-//W3C//DTD SVG 1.0//EN"
"http://www.w3.org/TR/2001/REC-SVG-20010904/DTD/svg10.dtd" [
    <!ENTITY ns_flows "http://ns.adobe.com/Flows/1.0/">
    <!ENTITY ns_svg "http://www.w3.org/2000/svg">
    <!ENTITY ns_xlink "http://www.w3.org/1999/xlink">
    <!ENTITY st0 "fill:#FFFFFF;stroke:#000000;">
]>
<svg  xmlns="&ns_svg;" xmlns:xlink="&ns_xlink;"
xmlns:a="http://ns.adobe.com/AdobeSVGViewerExtensions/3.0/"
    width="227.071" height="39.261" viewBox="0 0 227.071 39.261"
style="overflow:visible;enable-background:new 0 0 227.071 39.261"
    xml:space="preserve">
    <g id="Layer_1">
        <path style="&st0;"
d="M36.817,20.288L24.911,25.441-2.504,12.731-8.58-9.73L0.946,29.991l6.603-
➥11.167L2.093,7.053l12.662,2.829
            19.508-8.827l1.222,12.916L36.817,20.288z"/>
        <path style="&st0;"
d="M226.574,18.531c0,6.627-5.373,12-12,12H72.72c-6.627,0-12-5.373-
➥12-12v-4.78c0-6.627,5.373-12,12-12
            h141.854c6.627,0,12,5.373,12,12V18.531z"/>
    </g>
</svg>
```

Listing 2.2 contains several entities. Notice the following line:

```
<path style="&st0;"
```

The value of the `style` attribute is `&st0;`. The string `&st0` is an entity reference to an entity definition contained in the following line:

```
<!ENTITY st0 "fill:#FFFFFF;stroke:#000000;">
```

Putting the two lines of code together is equivalent to having the following line of code:

```
<path style="fill:#FFFFFF;stroke:#000000;">
```

The entity reference in the value of the `style` attribute is replaced by the **replacement text**, which is defined in the `ENTITY` declaration.

> **NOTE**
>
> The entities st0, ns_svg, ns_xlink, and so on shown in Listing 2.2 are generated automatically by Adobe Illustrator. They must be matched by corresponding ENTITY declarations. These entities are not part of the SVG language as specified, but are part of the syntax of XML and so can be used with SVG.

If that same style is used multiple times in the same SVG document, having an entity declaration and entity references can be more efficient in terms of file size than specifying a long style description for each of possibly several occurrences. In practice, the use of entities does make it significantly more difficult to find your way around code, particularly when—as with Illustrator—the entities do not have names that are meaningful to human readers. Some of the entities in Listing 2.2 are used in namespace declarations, which we will discuss next.

Namespace Declarations

As the number of application languages of XML has increased, so the likelihood of collisions of **element type names** has become more real. How, for example, could you tell if

```
<title>
XMML.com - XML technologies consultancy services
</title>
```

contained in a Web page that included both XHTML and SVG was an SVG `title` element or an XHTML `title` element? Similarly, on the same page, you might have two `script` elements—one an XHTML `script` element and the other an SVG `script` element. In both cases, and in the general case, you need to distinguish which **namespace** the element belongs to. The namespace is an indication to a processor of the XML language that the element belongs to.

To distinguish similarly named elements from each other, XML documents use **namespace declarations**. A namespace declaration is a way to associate a **namespace prefix** with a **namespace URI** (also called a **namespace name**). A **URI** is a Uniform Resource Identifier.

A namespace prefix can contain any legal XML name that does not contain a colon character. This is referred to as an NCName, meaning a noncolon name. The namespace prefix, when present, is separated from the **local part** of the element type name by a colon character:

```
<myPrefix:myElementTypeName .../>
```

In the preceding line of code, the namespace prefix is myPrefix, and the local part of the element type name is myElementTypeName. Not all elements require a namespace prefix:

```
<myElementTypeName .../>
```

In the preceding line of code, there is no namespace prefix and therefore no colon character separator. The local part of the element type name is myElementTypeName.

A namespace declaration looks similar to an attribute and is placed in the start tag of an element:

```
<svg xmlns="http://www.w3.org/2000/svg" ...>
```

The preceding code using the reserved string xmlns declares that the default namespace is associated with the namespace URI http://www.w3.org/2000/svg. That means that you can write SVG elements like this:

```
<svg xmlns="http://www.w3.org/2000/svg"
width="800px" height="600px">
    <text x="200px" y="150px">
    Welcome to SVG Unleashed!
    </text>
</svg>
```

If that SVG code were to be used in some way with code from another XML namespace, we might want to make it clear which elements were SVG elements:

```
<svg:svg xmlns:svg="http://www.w3.org/2000/svg" ...>
```

The preceding namespace declaration associates the namespace prefix svg with the namespace URI http://www.w3.org/2000/svg. If we use that namespace declaration, each SVG element, when written within the scope of that namespace declaration, must include the namespace prefix svg on each start tag and end tag, as in the following code:

```
<svg:svg xmlns:svg="http://www.w3.org/2000/svg"
width="800px" height="600px">
    <svg:text x="200px" y="150px">
    Welcome to SVG Unleashed!
    </svg:text>
</svg:svg>
```

You can use any namespace prefix you prefer for SVG elements, but it must be associated with the namespace URI `http://www.w3.org/2000/svg`. Typically, for SVG documents the svg namespace prefix is used, and it is sometimes referred to as the **indicative namespace prefix**.

In these examples, we have simply provided the namespace URI literally. However, some SVG drawing tools, such as Adobe Illustrator, produce entities for namespace declarations. Let's consider entities and how they can be used in namespace declarations. Notice this line of code from Listing 2.2, shown earlier:

```
<svg  xmlns="&ns_svg;" xmlns:xlink="&ns_xlink;"
```

This line is part of the start tag of the svg document element. It contains two namespace declarations—the first for the SVG namespace, `http://www.w3.org/2000/svg`, and the second for the XLink (XML Linking Language) namespace, `http://www.w3.org/1999/xlink`. However, instead of declaring these namespace URIs, Illustrator uses entities. Notice the entity references &ns_svg; and &ns_xlink;. Those entities are defined elsewhere in Listing 2.2, as shown in the following two lines:

```
<!ENTITY ns_svg "http://www.w3.org/2000/svg">
<!ENTITY ns_xlink "http://www.w3.org/1999/xlink">
```

Notice that the entity ns_svg is defined as meaning `http://www.w3.org/2000/svg`, the namespace for SVG elements, and the entity ns_xlink is defined as meaning `http://www.w3.org/1999/xlink`.

CDATA Sections

When scripting code is added to an SVG document by simply placing the code nested within the tags of a script element, the SVG rendering engine would attempt to parse that code as XML. Typical script code, such as JavaScript, differs significantly from the syntax of a well-formed XML document, and so an error would inevitably result.

To prevent such errors, you place scripting code within a **CDATA section**. A CDATA section is placed between the start tag and end tag of the script element, as shown here:

```
<script type="text/javascript">
<![CDATA[
// Scripting code would go here
]]>
</script>
```

A CDATA section begins with the characters <![CDATA[and ends with the character sequence]]>. Characters between these two delimiters are not to be parsed as XML and therefore not as SVG. Processing of the content of a CDATA section that is itself nested within an SVG script element is passed to a JavaScript or other script interpreter for processing.

Having looked at some basic XML concepts, let's move on to examine the structure of an SVG document, including several SVG elements that will appear in many SVG documents.

The svg Element

An SVG **document fragment** consists of an svg element and all its content. When the SVG document fragment exists as a standalone file, it is termed an **SVG document**. An SVG document fragment can be embedded in an SVG document or can be embedded in a document from another XML application language—for example, an XSL-FO (Extensible Stylesheet Language Formatting Objects) document.

An SVG document fragment need not have any content (but, of course, in that situation there is nothing to render other than a blank SVG **viewport**) or can contain a complex, deeply nested hierarchy of elements, for example, describing static SVG graphics shapes, SVG animation elements, and scripting code.

The viewport is the area into which the SVG is to be rendered. The width and height attributes on the document element svg element are used to define its dimensions. A detailed consideration of viewports and coordinates system is to be found in Chapter 5, "Coordinate Systems in SVG."

All SVG documents have an svg element as the **document element**. An SVG element can take width and height attributes, which define the size of the **viewport**. Listing 2.3 shows a skeleton SVG document that you may want to use as a template for your code.

LISTING 2.3   Skeleton.svg—A Skeleton SVG Document Fragment

```
<?xml version="1.0" standalone="no"?>
<!DOCTYPE svg PUBLIC "-//W3C//DTD SVG 20010904//EN"
"http://www.w3.org/TR/2001/REC-SVG-20010904/DTD/svg10.dtd">
<svg width="300px" height="200px">
<!-- Other content can be added here. -->
</svg>
```

It is possible to have an even more minimalist SVG document fragment, as shown in Listing 2.4.

LISTING 2.4   BareSkeleton.svg—Just About the Smallest Possible SVG Document Fragment

```
<svg width="300px" height="200px">
<!-- Other content can be added here. -->
</svg>
```

When Listing 2.3 or 2.4 is rendered in a browser that has SVG display facility, likely because the Adobe SVG Viewer is supported, the appearance is similar to that shown in

Figure 2.1. Notice the cursor at the bottom right of the paler area, which is the SVG viewport.

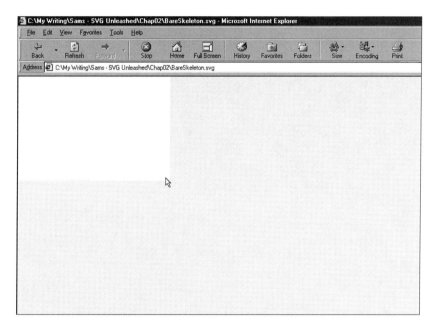

FIGURE 2.1   The SVG viewport shows as a paler area against the pale gray background within the browser window.

In SVG 1.0 there is no way directly to alter the default off-white color of the SVG viewport. To create the appearance of having altered the background color for the viewport, simply add a `rect` element (discussed in detail in Chapter 3) with the x, y, `width`, and `height` attributes and the desired color set as the value of a `style` attribute, as shown in Listing 2.5. This produces a pale green background to the SVG viewport.

LISTING 2.5   ColoredViewport.svg—Creating the Appearance of a Colored Background to the SVG Viewport

```
<?xml version="1.0" standalone="no"?>
<!DOCTYPE svg PUBLIC "-//W3C//DTD SVG 20010904//EN"
"http://www.w3.org/TR/2001/REC-SVG-20010904/DTD/svg10.dtd">
<svg width="300px" height="200px">
    <rect x="0" y="0" width="100%" height="100%" style="fill:#CCFFCC"/>
    <!-- Other content can be added here. -->
</svg>
```

Figure 2.2 shows the colored viewport background produced using Listing 2.5.

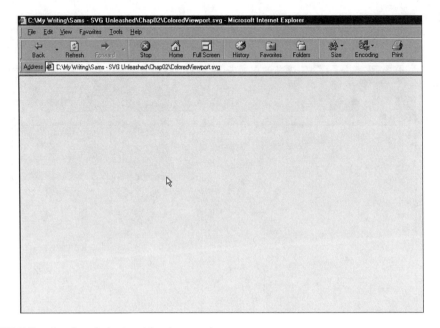

FIGURE 2.2   A colored viewport background.

If an svg element lacks any width and height attributes, a default width of 100% and a default height of 100% of the browser window, or similar user space, is applied.

You can specify the value of the x, y, width, or height attributes in any of the units permitted in SVG. They are shown in Table 2.1.

TABLE 2.1   Units Allowed in SVG

Units	Meaning
em	Same as font-size.
ex	The x-height of the current font-size.
px	Pixels.
pt	Points. There are 72 points to 1 inch.
cm	Centimeters.
mm	Millimeters.
pc	Picas. There are 6 picas to 1 inch.
%	A percentage of the relevant dimension of the browser window or similar space.
in	Inches.

You can specify dimensions without any units of measurement, in which case they are treated as being defined in **user units**. User units will be considered in more detail in Chapter 5.

The version Attribute

The svg element can take a version attribute. For SVG processors supporting SVG version 1.0, this attribute need not be expressed. If it is present, the value of the version attribute must be "1.0".

In future versions of SVG, including SVG 1.1, which is under early development at the World Wide Web Consortium (W3C), the version attribute will be required.

Nesting svg Elements

You can embed SVG document fragments inside each other by nesting one svg element within the svg element that is the document element. Such svg elements can be nested with arbitrary complexity. Nesting svg elements within the svg element that is the document element has several potential advantages.

For example, each nested svg element and its content can be treated as a visual component. If you adjust the value of the x or y attribute of the nested svg element, the whole component is moved around the screen accordingly. Alternatively, the content of the nested svg element can be imported from a free-standing SVG document using the image element.

Establishing a New Viewport

When an svg element is nested within another, the nested svg element opens a new viewport. This has a number of effects, depending on how the svg document element and the nested svg element are used.

Listing 2.6 shows a simple example in which all values of attributes are expressed as pixels.

LISTING 2.6   NestedSVGCoordinates.svg—An Example Showing the Alteration of Coordinates on Using a Nested svg Element

```
<?xml version="1.0" standalone="no"?>
<!DOCTYPE svg PUBLIC "-//W3C//DTD SVG 20010904//EN"
"http://www.w3.org/TR/2001/REC-SVG-20010904/DTD/svg10.dtd">
<svg width="400px" height="300px">
    <rect x="0" y="0" width="100%" height="100%"
     style="stroke:red; stroke-width:5; fill: white"/>
    <svg x="50px" y="50px" width="300px" height="200px">
        <rect x="0" y="0" width="100%" height="100%"
         style="stroke:blue; stroke-width:5;
         stroke-dasharray:5,5; fill: white"/>
    </svg> <!-- End tag of the nested svg element. -->
</svg>
```

Notice that Listing 2.6 contains two rect elements. One of the rect elements—the one with the solid red outline—is contained in the svg document element. The second rect element is contained within the nested svg element. Both rect elements have x and y attributes with a value of zero, indicating that the top-left corner of the rectangle is at the top left of the viewport, yet as you can see in Figure 2.3, the top-left corners of the two rectangles are not at the same position onscreen. They are not in the same place because there are two viewports. The viewport created by the svg document element is at the top left of the browser window. The nested svg element creates a second viewport whose top-left corner is defined by the value of the x and y attributes of the nested svg element—which is 50 pixels to the right and 50 pixels down from the top-left corner of the viewport created by the svg document element.

> **NOTE**
>
> Elements such as the rect element used in Listing 2.6 are described in detail in Chapter 3.

> **NOTE**
>
> In SVG the svg, symbol, image, and foreignObject elements create a new viewport.

The x and y Attributes

An svg element can have x and y attributes. On the outermost svg element—that is, the document element—in an SVG document, the x and y attributes have no meaning. On other svg elements—that is, nested svg elements—the x and y attributes specify the position of the upper-left corner of the viewport created by the nested svg element.

FIGURE 2.3   The limits of two SVG viewports illustrated by the outline of two rect elements.

The viewBox Attribute

The viewBox attribute helps to define what the onscreen size of objects will be. It does that by defining a new coordinate system. This process and how to control it will be described in detail in Chapter 5.

The viewBox attribute provides a way of scaling content within an svg element. A viewBox attribute contains four numeric values separated by whitespace. The difference between the first and third values corresponds to the width of the viewport. The difference between the second and fourth values corresponds to the height of the viewport.

Listing 2.7 shows an example of using the viewBox attribute.

LISTING 2.7   ViewBoxDemo.svg—Using the viewBox Attribute to Alter Visual Appearance

```
<?xml version="1.0" standalone="no"?>
<!DOCTYPE svg PUBLIC "-//W3C//DTD SVG 20010904//EN"
"http://www.w3.org/TR/2001/REC-SVG-20010904/DTD/svg10.dtd">
<svg width="800px" height="400px" viewBox="0 0 800 400">
    <rect x="20" y="20" width="200" height="100"
      style="stroke:black; stroke-width:5; fill:none;"/>
```

LISTING 2.7   Continued

```
<svg x="0px" y="200px" width="400px" height="200px" viewBox="0 0 800 400">
    <rect x="20" y="20" width="200" height="100"
     style="stroke:black; stroke-width:5; fill:none;"/>
</svg>

<svg x="400px" y="200px" width="400px" height="200px" viewBox="0 0 200 100">
    <rect x="20" y="20" width="200" height="100"
     style="stroke:black; stroke-width:5; fill:none;"/>
</svg>
</svg>
```

Each of the three rectangles, created using a `rect` element, has the same code describing it:

```
<rect x="20" y="20" width="200" height="100"
 style="stroke:black; stroke-width:5; fill:none;"/>
```

However, if you look at Figure 2.4, you can see that the three rectangles are of different sizes.

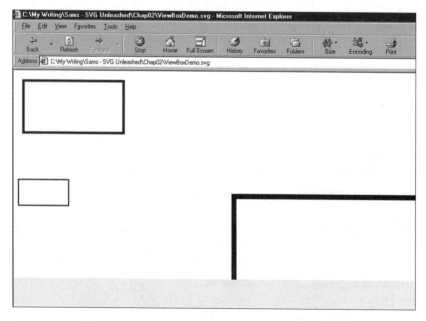

FIGURE 2.4   Three rectangles whose size is controlled by viewBox attributes.

For the top-left rectangle, its onscreen size is controlled by the `viewBox` attribute on the svg document element:

```
<svg width="800px" height="400px" viewBox="0 0 800 400">
```

The difference between the first and third values of the `viewBox` attribute is 800. That value of 800 user units corresponds to the value of the `width` attribute of the `svg` element, which is `800px`. Thus, the scale is 800 units to 800 pixels, or 1 unit to 1 pixel.

For the second `rect` element, the scale is defined by the `viewBox` attribute on the second svg element (the first nested `svg` element):

```
<svg x="0px" y="200px" width="400px" height="200px"
 viewBox="0 0 800 400">
```

In this case, the difference between the first and third values of the `viewBox` attribute is 800 units again, but on this occasion the `width` attribute of the `svg` element has a value of `400px`. Thus, the scale is 800 units to 400 pixels, or 2 units per pixel. Thus, the second rectangle is half the size of the first.

For the third `rect` element, the scale is defined by the `viewBox` attribute on the second nested `svg` element:

```
<svg x="0px" y="200px" width="400px" height="200px"
 viewBox="0 0 200 100">
```

In this case, the difference between the first and third values of the `viewBox` attribute is 200 units, and the `width` attribute of the `svg` element has a value of `400px`. Thus, the scale is 200 units to 400 pixels, or 1 unit equal to 2 pixels. Thus, the third rectangle is twice the size of the first.

> **CAUTION**
>
> Be sure to keep the scale for the horizontal and vertical axes the same; otherwise, you run into problems of preserving **aspect ratio**. Aspect ratio is discussed in more detail in Chapter 5.

The `viewBox` attribute will be considered in more detail in Chapter 5.

The g Element

The purpose of the g element is to group SVG elements. A g element can contain nested within it graphic elements such as those described in Chapter 3. Additionally, a g element can also contain `desc` and `title` elements, which provide information about the content of the g element, thus facilitating accessibility. Accessibility is discussed in more detail in Chapter 13, "Accessibility, Internationalization, and Metadata."

TIP

A g element and its associated nested SVG elements may be **transformed**. A transformation moves an object in some way on the screen, due to an alteration in the coordinate system (see Chapter 5). An svg element, whether the document element or a nested svg element, cannot be transformed. So, if you think it is likely that you will want to use SVG transformations, group elements using the g element rather than a nested svg element. Transformations are described in Chapter 7, "Transformations in SVG."

Grouping elements can make code shorter. For example, we could specify the style on several graphics shapes by specifying style for the containing g element. Listing 2.8 shows three rectangles with the style specified on each.

LISTING 2.8   ViewBoxDemo.svg—Styling of Three Rectangles Expressed on Each Rectangle

```
<?xml version="1.0" standalone="no"?>
<!DOCTYPE svg PUBLIC "-//W3C//DTD SVG 20010904//EN"
"http://www.w3.org/TR/2001/REC-SVG-20010904/DTD/svg10.dtd">
<svg width="400px" height="300px">
    <rect x="10px" y="20px" width="100px" height="50px"
    style="fill:none;stroke:red; stroke-width:4px"/>
    <rect x="10px" y="120px" width="100px" height="50px"
    style="fill:none;stroke:red; stroke-width:4px"/>
    <rect x="10px" y="220px" width="100px" height="50px"
    style="fill:none;stroke:red; stroke-width:4px"/>
</svg>
```

Listing 2.9 shows the style specified on the container g element.

LISTING 2.9   ThreeRectsGrouped.svg—Styling of Three Rectangles Expressed on a Container g Element

```
<?xml version="1.0" standalone="no"?>
<!DOCTYPE svg PUBLIC "-//W3C//DTD SVG 20010904//EN"
"http://www.w3.org/TR/2001/REC-SVG-20010904/DTD/svg10.dtd">
<svg width="400px" height="300px">
<g style="fill:none; stroke:red; stroke-width:4px" >
<rect x="10px" y="20px" width="100px" height="50px" />
<rect x="10px" y="120px" width="100px" height="50px" />
<rect x="10px" y="220px" width="100px" height="50px" />
</g>
</svg>
```

You can also use a g element to transform all the elements contained in the group. Listing 2.10 shows a **translate** transformation of 100 pixels across and 100 pixels down for the two rectangles contained within the g element. Transformations are described in more detail in Chapter 7.

LISTING 2.10   GroupedRects.svg—Applying a Transformation to All Elements Contained in a g Element

```
<?xml version="1.0" standalone="no"?>
<!DOCTYPE svg PUBLIC "-//W3C//DTD SVG 20010904//EN"
"http://www.w3.org/TR/2001/REC-SVG-20010904/DTD/svg10.dtd">
<svg width="500px" height="400px">
    <g transform="translate(100px,100px)">
        <rect x="0px" y="0px" width="50px" height="50px" style="fill:red"/>
        <rect x="0px" y="100px" width="50px" height="50px"
         style="fill:red; opacity:0.4;"/>
    </g>
</svg>
```

Similarly, grouping a number of elements in a g element allows you to apply a transformation animation (see Chapter 11, "SVG Animation Elements," for further details) to the group as a whole.

A g element can contain further g elements nested within it, to any desired depth.

The title and defs Elements

The title and defs elements typically occur early in an SVG document.

The title Element

The title element provides information about the SVG element within which it is nested. A title element can be nested within the svg document element, in which case an SVG viewer may render the text of the title in the title bar of the browser or SVG viewer.

Listing 2.11 shows a title for an SVG document supplied in a title element that is nested within the svg document element.

LISTING 2.11   SimpleTitle.svg—Supplying a Title for an SVG Document

```
<?xml version="1.0" standalone="no"?>
<!DOCTYPE svg PUBLIC "-//W3C//DTD SVG 20010904//EN"
"http://www.w3.org/TR/2001/REC-SVG-20010904/DTD/svg10.dtd">
<svg width="400px" height="200px">
    <title>A simple demo of the title element
```

LISTING 2.11   Continued

```
    </title>
    <text x="50px" y="40px" font-size="14pt">
    A simple demo of the &lt;title&gt; element.
    </text>
</svg>
```

> **TIP**
>
> Be sure to avoid any whitespace immediately following the start tag of the title element. In the
> Adobe SVG Viewer 3.0, adding whitespace or breaking a line in the code can result in a title that
> fails to display or only partially displays.

The defs Element

The defs element contains definitions. Such definitions will typically be referenced, and possibly reused many times, by elements that occur later in an SVG document. Elements nested within a defs element are not rendered but are available to be referenced by elements later in an SVG document.

A defs element may, for example, contain linearGradient or radialGradient elements (see Chapter 3) that define gradients which may be applied to graphics shapes. Similarly, a filter element may be present in the defs element. The filter element and the elements within it, which describe filter primitives, define visual effects that can be applied to graphics shapes. Filter elements and their effects are described in Chapter 10, "SVG Filters."

Graphics shapes can also be stored in a defs element. If, for example, you wanted to create a grid of lines, you might define a line element within the defs element and reference that line element by multiple use elements.

Listing 2.12, in the next section, shows an example of referencing line elements that are nested within a defs element. The use element is employed to cause the referenced element to be rendered.

The symbol Element

The symbol element defines graphics objects that can be used later in the SVG document by using the use element. A symbol element itself is not rendered onscreen. It is the instance of the symbol element, created using the use element that is rendered.

A symbol element can contain one or multiple graphics shapes.

A symbol element can have viewBox and preserveAspectRatio attributes, which may be used to allow it to scale to fit within a viewport defined by a use element. This topic will be discussed further in Chapter 5.

The use Element

It is common for a graphic to have many similar shapes within it. One example is a rectangular grid, which consists simply of multiple horizontal and vertical lines. In SVG each of those lines could be created by using multiple individual line elements. An alternative approach is to define line elements within a defs element and then reference those line elements by using use elements. Listing 2.12 shows an example.

LISTING 2.12   UseExample.svg—An Example of Reusing Graphic Shapes Using use Elements

```
<?xml version="1.0" standalone="no"?>
<!DOCTYPE svg PUBLIC "-//W3C//DTD SVG 20010904//EN"
"http://www.w3.org/TR/2001/REC-SVG-20010904/DTD/svg10.dtd">
<svg width="600px" height="400px">
    <title>Demonstrating the use element</title>
    <defs>
        <line id="horiz" x1="20px" y1="30px" x2="420px" y2="30px"
         style="stroke:red; stroke-width:5px; stroke-dasharray:3,3;
         fill:none;"/>
        <line id="vert" x1="20px" y1="30px" x2="20px" y2="330px"
         style="stroke:red; stroke-width:5px; stroke-dasharray:1,9,3;
         fill:none;"/>
    </defs>
<!-- Horizontal lines -->
    <use xlink:href="#horiz" />
    <g transform="translate(0,100)">
        <use xlink:href="#horiz" />
    </g>
    <g transform="translate(0,200)">
        <use xlink:href="#horiz"  />
    </g>
    <g transform="translate(0,300)">
        <use xlink:href="#horiz"  />
    </g>
<!-- Vertical lines -->
    <use xlink:href="#vert" />
    <g transform="translate(100,0)">
        <use xlink:href="#vert" />
    </g>
    <g transform="translate(200,0)">
        <use xlink:href="#vert" />
    </g>
    <g transform="translate(300,0)">
        <use xlink:href="#vert" />
```

LISTING 2.12   Continued

```
    </g>
    <g transform="translate(400,0)">
        <use xlink:href="#vert" />
    </g>
</svg>
```

NOTE

You can achieve a similar visual appearance by using x and y attributes on a use element. Thus,

```
<g transform="translate(300,0)">
<use xlink:href="#vert" />
</g>
```

could be written as

```
<use xlink:href="#vert" x="300" y="0" />
```

However, the x and y attributes are relative to any position of the element defined within the defs element.

Two line elements are defined within the defs element. Each line element has an id attribute, indicating, respectively, whether it is a horizontal or vertical line.

Within the main body of the SVG document are multiple use elements that reference the line element definitions by means of an xlink:href attribute. The value #horiz or #vert refers to the value of the id attribute of the line elements defined earlier in the document.

In this example, we reuse the line elements by translating them using a transform attribute on a containing g element for each use element. When the object being reused is as simple as a line element, it would be just as easy to code the line elements individually. When reusing more complex graphic objects, the use element can be a significant aid to code reuse.

The use element can reference only elements or objects within the same SVG document. In that respect, it contrasts with the image element, which can import an external graphic.

The use of the use element with symbol elements will be demonstrated in Chapter 5.

The script Element

All SVG scripting code is related to a script element. Typically, the script element will, when used, have no namespace prefix on the element type name to distinguish it from the HTML/XHTML script element. However, although the script elements have a similar function, they are from two different markup languages, and their syntax is not identical.

The SVG `script` element has a `type` attribute. Typical examples of the `type` attribute include `"text/javascript"` or `"text/ecmascript"`.

> **NOTE**
>
> Unlike the HTML script element, the SVG script element should not have a language attribute. The type attribute fulfills that function.

Scripting code, such as JavaScript, does not satisfy the syntax requirements of XML 1.0. To avoid errors when the SVG viewer attempts to interpret JavaScript, or other scripting code as XML, you must enclose the scripting code in a `CDATA` section. As mentioned previously, a `CDATA` section begins with `<![CDATA[` and ends with `]]>`. Listing 2.13 shows a template you might want to use for scripting code.

LISTING 2.13   ScriptingTemplate.svg—A Template for Scripting SVG

```
<?xml version="1.0" standalone="no"?>
<!DOCTYPE svg PUBLIC "-//W3C//DTD SVG 20010904//EN"
"http://www.w3.org/TR/2001/REC-SVG-20010904/DTD/svg10.dtd">
<svg width="" height="">
<script type="text/javascript">
<![CDATA[
// JavaScript code goes here
]]>
</script>
<!-- SVG code goes here -->
</svg>
```

Alternatively, JavaScript code can be held in an external JavaScript file that is referenced using the `xlink:href` attribute on a `script` element, as shown in Listing 2.14.

LISTING 2.14   ExternalJSTemplate.svg—A Scripting Template That References an External JavaScript File

```
<?xml version="1.0" standalone="no"?>
<!DOCTYPE svg PUBLIC "-//W3C//DTD SVG 20010904//EN"
"http://www.w3.org/TR/2001/REC-SVG-20010904/DTD/svg10.dtd">
<svg width="" height=""
xmlns:xlink="http://www.w3.org/1999/xlink">
<script type="text/javascript" xlink:href="SomeJSFile.js"/>
<script type="text/javascript" >
<![CDATA[
// More JavaScript code could go here
]]>
```

LISTING 2.14   Continued

```
</script>
<!-- SVG elements can be nested here. -->
</svg>
```

Many of the early chapters of this book include JavaScript examples that demonstrate aspects of how to manipulate the SVG DOM. A fuller description of JavaScript is found in Part II.

Zoom and Pan

SVG supports both zooming and panning. Zooming allows display of an SVG image at different magnifications. Panning allows the SVG image to be moved around the screen.

SVG provides the facility to turn off zooming and panning. To do so, you use the zoomAndPan attribute on the svg element that is the document element:

```
<svg zoomAndPan="disable" ....>
```

> **TIP**
>
> If you want to disable zoom and pan, you must place the zoomAndPan attribute with a value of "disable" on the outermost svg element. Adding a zoomAndPan attribute to a nested svg element has no effect on the document.

Zooming

Zooming is the ability to magnify a selected part of an image. In the Adobe SVG Viewer, if you want to zoom an image, simply right-click it, select the Zoom In option from those offered, and the image will be magnified to double its size.

Similarly, you zoom out by selecting the Zoom Out option. Zooming in or out can magnify to 16 times the original size or reduce to one-sixteenth of original size.

If you want to zoom in or out farther than the Adobe SVG Viewer allows, you can use scripting code similar to that shown in Listing 2.15.

LISTING 2.15   DynamicZoom03.svg—A Demonstration of Zooming In or Out by Scripting

```
<?xml version="1.0" standalone="no"?>
<!DOCTYPE svg PUBLIC "-//W3C//DTD SVG 20010904//EN"
"http://www.w3.org/TR/2001/REC-SVG-20010904/DTD/svg10.dtd">
<svg id="SVG" width="" height="" onload="Initialize(evt)">
<script type="text/javascript">
<![CDATA[
var SVGRoot;
```

LISTING 2.15   Continued

```
var MyRect;
var SVGDoc;
var ZoomFactor = 1.5;
var Growing = true;
window.status = ZoomFactor;

function Initialize(evt){
SVGDoc = evt.getTarget().getOwnerDocument();
SVGRoot = SVGDoc.getDocumentElement();
MyRect = SVGDoc.getElementById("MyRect");
SVGDoc.getElementById("SVG").addEventListener("click", ZoomOnClick, false);
}

function ZoomOnClick(evt){

if (SVGRoot.currentScale > 20)
{ Growing = false;
 } // end if
else if (SVGRoot.currentScale < 0.1 )
 {
 Growing = true;
 } // end else

if (Growing == true){
ZoomFactor = ZoomFactor * 1.5}
else
{ ZoomFactor = ZoomFactor * 0.5;
}

SVGRoot.setCurrentScale(ZoomFactor);
window.status = SVGRoot.currentScale;

} // End function ZoomOnClick()
]]>
</script>
<text x="20" y="20" style="font-family:Arial, sans-serif; fill:red;
stroke:none">
Click this text or the rectangle and watch our size change
</text>
<rect id="MyRect" x="75" y="75" width="300" height="150" style="fill:red;
opacity:0.4"/>
</svg>
```

The text and rectangle can be magnified to more than 20 times the starting size and
reduced to less than one-tenth of the starting size. You can easily modify the code to
provide any arbitrary limit on zooming out or zooming in.

Panning

Panning allows your viewpoint on the theoretically infinite SVG canvas to change.

Individual SVG viewers vary in the techniques used to pan. In the Adobe SVG Viewer on a
Windows platform, you hold down the Alt key, hold down the left mouse button too, and
then move the mouse. The cursor will change to a clenched fist. If you move the mouse,
you can pan around the image.

Unfortunately, the Adobe SVG Viewer failed to implement scrollbars.

In the Batik browser, if you want to pan the image, you hold down the Alt key and the
Shift key, while also holding down the left mouse button and moving the mouse.

Linking in SVG

Linking in SVG depends on the XML Linking Language, XLink. All internal and external
links in SVG images, including those that use fragment identifiers, make use of XLink
attributes.

XLink: The XML Linking Language

XLink is a W3C specification for the description of links among resources. Unusually
among W3C specifications expressed in XML syntax, XLink adds no new elements. All the
semantics of XLink links are expressed in **global attributes**, which are in the XLink namespace. XLink provides both **extended links** and **simple links**. SVG implements only simple
XLink links.

Explicitly declaring the XLink namespace is not essential because the declaration is
included in the SVG DTD (Document Type Definition), assuming that the SVG viewer has
access to the DTD. In production code where that may not always be true, it is wise to add
a namespace declaration for the XLink namespace to the document element svg element:

```
<svg
 xmlns="http://www.w3.org/2000/svg"
 xmlns:xlink="http://www.w3.org/1999/xlink"
>
```

> **NOTE**
>
> General information on XLink at W3C is located at http://www.w3.org/XML/Linking.

First, let's look at linking from SVG documents.

The SVG a Element

The SVG a element is similar in its functioning to the HTML/XHTML a element.

An SVG a element associates exactly two resources: a **local starting resource** and a **remote ending resource**. The more complex parts of XLink are hidden. The **arc** between the starting resource and ending resource is implicit. Only **outbound** XLink links are supported.

Listing 2.16 shows a simple link.

LISTING 2.16   FirstLink.svg—A Simple Link Using the SVG a Element

```
<?xml version="1.0" standalone="no"?>
<!DOCTYPE svg PUBLIC "-//W3C//DTD SVG 20010904//EN"
"http://www.w3.org/TR/2001/REC-SVG-20010904/DTD/svg10.dtd">
<svg width="400px" height="250px">
<a xlink:href="http://www.XMML.com">
<text x="30px" y="50px" style="stroke:blue;">
Click here to access XMML.com
</text>
</a>
</svg>
```

Notice that I have specified a blue color for the linking text. In SVG 1.0, there is no automatic alteration of color to indicate a link. Figure 2.5 shows the zoomed and panned appearance in a browser that uses the Adobe SVG Viewer. Notice the cursor change to a hand when over the link text.

The default behavior of a simple link in SVG is to replace the document within which the starting resource is located with the ending resource. Thus, if you click on the link produced by Listing 2.16, the XMML.com home page will open in the browser window.

XLink specifies a way to open the ending resource in a new window by means of the `xlink:show` attribute. The default value of `xlink:show` is `"replace"`. You ought to be able to open a new window by using `xlink:href="new"`, but in Adobe SVG Viewer 3.0, at least, that approach does not work. A workaround is to use a `target` attribute on the a element.

Listing 2.17 shows a similar listing but with the `target` attribute added with a value of `"new"`. When you run Listing 2.17, the ending resource is opened in a new browser window.

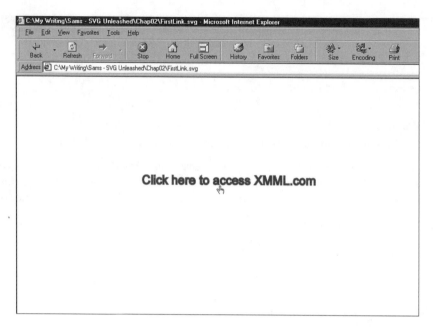

FIGURE 2.5   A simple XLink link in SVG.

LISTING 2.17   FirstLink02.svg—An XLink Link in SVG to Open a New Browser Window

```
<?xml version="1.0" standalone="no"?>
<!DOCTYPE svg PUBLIC "-//W3C//DTD SVG 20010904//EN"
"http://www.w3.org/TR/2001/REC-SVG-20010904/DTD/svg10.dtd">
<svg width="400px" height="250px">
<a xlink:href="http://www.XMML.com"
   target="new">
<text x="30px" y="50px" style="stroke:blue;">
Click here to access XMML.com in a new browser window.
<tspan x="30px" dy="1.5em">
This code uses the xlink:show attribute with value of "new"
</tspan>
</text>
</a>
</svg>
```

You do not need to specify a value for the `xlink:actuate` attribute. The SVG DTD fixes the value at `"onRequest"`. This, of course, prevents the use of SVG images or Web pages to open linked pop-up windows automatically when the SVG image or Web page loads.

You can use the `xlink:role` and `xlink:arcrole` attributes if you want to provide information to a user. These attributes are not necessary to the functioning of the link.

Linking Using XPointer

SVG provides a partial implementation of the XML Pointer Language, XPointer. XPointer is the fragment identifier language for generic XML documents and external parsed entities. A limited subset of XPointer is used in SVG to enable reuse of elements contained within the `defs` element part of an SVG document.

The XPointer specification was not complete at the time the SVG Recommendation was finalized. Up-to-date information on the XPointer specification is located at `http://www.w3.org/tr/xptr`.

SVG supports the **bare names** form of XPointer plus the use of the **xpointer scheme**. For either of these forms of XPointer to operate successfully, the document fragment to which you want to link must possess an `id` attribute.

Let's examine the use of both of these forms of XPointer using an SVG document where a `rect` element is defined in the `defs` section of the document and is used twice using the `use` element. Listing 2.18 shows an XPointer example.

LISTING 2.18   XPointerDemo.svg—Illustrating the Use of XPointers in SVG

```
<?xml version="1.0" standalone="no"?>
<!DOCTYPE svg PUBLIC "-//W3C//DTD SVG 20010904//EN"
"http://www.w3.org/TR/2001/REC-SVG-20010904/DTD/svg10.dtd">
<svg width="400px" height="300px">
<defs>
<rect id="simpleRect" width="100px" height="75px"/>
</defs>
<use xlink:href="#simpleRect" x="50" y="50" style="fill:red"/>
<use xlink:href="#xpointer(id('simpleRect'))" x="250"
 y="50" style="fill:yellow"/>
</svg>
```

Figure 2.6 shows the result when the two `use` elements successfully reference the `rect` element that is nested within the `defs` element.

Notice the `xlink:href` attribute on each `use` element.

Linking by Specifying an SVG View

In SVG there is an additional way to link into a particular fragment of a document—by specifying an SVG view within the URL that specifies the link. To understand how this works, we need to take a step aside to look at the SVG `view` element. The `view` element is also described in Chapter 5.

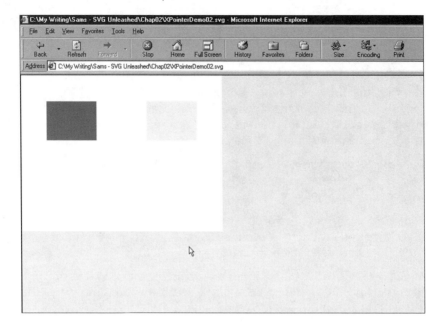

FIGURE 2.6   Using XPointer fragment identifiers.

The view Element

The view element allows you to change the appearance of the content of the svg element that contains it. Listing 2.19 shows a simple example.

CAUTION

Make sure that the vertical and horizontal ratios between the dimensions of the viewport and the third and fourth values in the viewBox attribute are the same; otherwise, issues of aspect ratio (discussed in Chapter 5) become important. If you do not understand aspect ratios, make sure to keep the two ratios (in the example, 500 pixels to 100 units both horizontally and vertically) the same.

LISTING 2.19   ViewElement.svg—Using the view Element to Scale an Image

```
<?xml version="1.0" standalone="no"?>
<!DOCTYPE svg PUBLIC "-//W3C//DTD SVG 20010904//EN"
"http://www.w3.org/TR/2001/REC-SVG-20010904/DTD/svg10.dtd">
<svg xmlns="http://www.w3.org/2000/svg"
     xmlns:xlink="http://www.w3.org/1999/xlink"
     width="500px"
     height="500px"
```

LISTING 2.19   Continued

```
     viewBox="0 0 100 100">
<view id="NormalView" viewBox="0 0 100 100"/>
<view id="DoubleSize" viewBox="0 0 50 50"/>
<view id="TripleSize" viewBox="0 0 33 33"/>
<a xlink:href="#NormalView">
<text x="0" y="10" font-size="5"> Normal Size</text>
</a>
<a xlink:href="#DoubleSize">
<text x="0" y="20" font-size="5"> Double Size</text>
</a>
<a xlink:href="#TripleSize">
<text x="0" y="30" font-size="5"> Triple Size</text>
</a>
</svg>
```

The wording of the content of each text element indicates the relative size obtained by clicking on each piece of linked text.

Let's examine how Listing 2.19 works by looking at what happens when you click the text "Double Size". The value of the xlink:href attribute indicates a fragment identifier corresponding to an id attribute elsewhere in the document with value "DoubleSize":

```
<a xlink:href="#DoubleSize">
<text x="0" y="20" font-size="5"> Double Size</text>
</a>
```

That id attribute is situated on a view element:

```
<view id="DoubleSize" viewBox="0 0 50 50"/>
```

The values in the viewBox attribute of the view element are applied to the viewBox attribute of its parent svg element. This means that clicking the text "Double Size" is broadly equivalent to rewriting the start tag of the svg document element as follows:

```
<svg xmlns="http://www.w3.org/2000/svg"
     xmlns:xlink="http://www.w3.org/1999/xlink"
     width="500px"
     height="500px"
     viewBox="0 0 50 50">
```

Thus, instead of a ratio of 100 units to 500 pixels in the viewport, the ratio becomes 50 units to 500 pixels. In other words, each unit becomes twice as large. Visually, that means that the text doubles in size when the text "Double Size" is clicked.

Clicking on the text "Normal Size" effectively changes the viewBox attribute of the svg document element to

```
viewBox="0 0 100 100"
```

Here, the visual appearance is restored to its original appearance because 100 units again corresponds to 500 pixels in the viewport.

> **NOTE**
>
> The Adobe SVG Viewer version 3.0, the latest at the time of writing, does not support the viewTarget attribute on the view element.

In the final section of the chapter, we will look at some SVG DOM interfaces that are relevant to material we covered earlier in the chapter. If you are not interested in manipulating the SVG DOM at this time, you can leave the following section for review at a later time.

SVG DOM Interfaces

The SVG DOM's primary purpose is to allow a programmer to have a standard Application Programming Interface (API) for access to and modification of the SVG document to which the Document Object Model relates. The SVG DOM builds on the basic functionality of the W3C Document Object Model specifications.

In a couple of early examples in this section, the meaning of the code will be explained in detail. In later chapters, less full explanation will be given. If you need further understanding of JavaScript used with SVG, look at Part II.

A Sample Document

Let's look at how a simple SVG document is viewed when represented in the concepts of the XML DOM and the SVG DOM. Listing 2.20 shows a simple document.

LISTING 2.20   SimpleExample.svg—A Simple SVG Document to Demonstrate the DOM

```
<?xml version="1.0" standalone="no"?>
<!DOCTYPE svg PUBLIC "-//W3C//DTD SVG 20010904//EN"
"http://www.w3.org/TR/2001/REC-SVG-20010904/DTD/svg10.dtd">
<svg width="400px" height="300px" onload="Initialize(evt)">

<script type="text/javascript">
<![CDATA[
var SVGDoc;
var SVGRoot;
```

LISTING 2.20   Continued

```
function Initialize (evt) {
SVGDoc = evt.getTarget().getOwnerDocument();
}

function reportDOM(evt){
SVGRoot = SVGDoc.getDocumentElement();
window.alert("The value of the width attribute of the <svg> element is
➥" + SVGRoot.getAttribute("width"));
}

]]>
</script>
<desc>A simple example SVG document to demonstrate the DOM</desc>
<rect x="20px" y="20px" width="360px" height="260px"
 style="fill:#DDDDDD; stroke:red; stroke-width:4;"
 onclick="reportDOM(evt)"/>
</svg>
```

The purpose of Listing 2.20 is simply to report the value contained in the width attribute of the svg element. The example will illustrate how we can access the values of attributes on SVG elements more generally.

First, we declare two variables, SVGDoc and SVGRoot:

```
var SVGDoc;
var SVGRoot;
```

They are declared within the script element but outside any functions so that they will be global variables, accessible from any function that we may create within the script element.

When the SVG image loads, the onload attribute on the svg element causes the Initialize() function to be called:

```
<svg width="400px" height="300px" onload="Initialize(evt)">
```

The Initialize() function simply assigns a value to the SVGDoc variable, specifically the identity of the SVG document within which the svg element is contained:

```
function Initialize (evt) {
SVGDoc = evt.getTarget().getOwnerDocument();
}
```

The SVGDoc variable corresponds to the Document node in terms of the XML DOM. You may recall from the description in Chapter 1, "SVG Overview," that the Document node is not represented in the code contained in the document but may be considered to represent the document as a container or, in terms of XML 1.0, to represent the **document entity**.

TIP

Choose a variable name for the Document node and stick to it in your coding. It is best to choose a meaningful name such as SVGDoc, svgdoc, or something like that.

If we click on the rect element contained in the SVG document, the onclick attribute captures the click event on the rectangle and calls the reportDOM()function:

```
<rect x="20px" y="20px" width="360px" height="260px"
 style="fill:#DDDDDD; stroke:red; stroke-width:4;"
onclick="reportDOM(evt)"/>
```

The reportDOM() function first assigns a value to the SVGRoot variable. The variable assignment makes use of the getDocumentElement() method of the Document node and assigns the value returned by that method to the SVGRoot variable. The SVGRoot variable represents the **document element** of the SVG document, which is the svg element:

```
function reportDOM(evt){
SVGRoot = SVGDoc.getDocumentElement();
window.alert("The value of the width attribute of the
 <svg> element is " + SVGRoot.getAttribute("width"));
}
```

Finally, the window.alert() function causes an alert window to open onscreen, similar to that shown in Figure 2.7.

The DOM Representation of the Document

NOTE

If you are unfamiliar with the XML and SVG Document Object Models, you may find it helpful to review the introduction to the DOM in Chapter 1, "SVG Overview."

The SVG document itself would, in the XML DOM, be represented by a Document node. In XML DOM terms, the Document node is the root of the hierarchy of the DOM.

NOTE

The DOM term root is very similar to the notion of a root node in the XML Path Language, XPath, and terminology. However, the object models of XML DOM and XPath differ significantly.

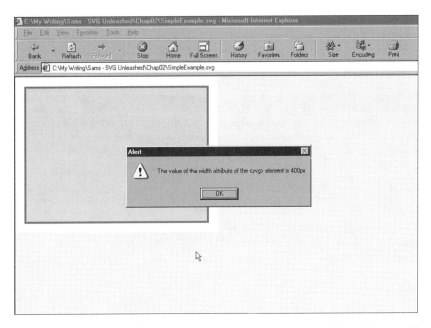

FIGURE 2.7 An alert window displays the value contained by the width attribute of the svg element.

All other nodes in the Document Object Model are viewed in relation to the DOM root node. The Document node has **child nodes,** and some types of child nodes may themselves have further child nodes, and so on.

The Document node in an SVG document has all the methods and properties described for a Document node in the DOM Level 2 Core specification and in the DOM Level 2 Events specification. In addition, it has the following SVG-specific properties.

The Document node has five SVG-specific properties:

- title—of type DOMString

- referrer—of type DOMString

- domain—of type DOMString

- URL—of type DOMString

- rootElement—an object of type SVGSVGElement

Listing 2.21 demonstrates all the SVG-specific properties. There are no SVG-specific methods, other than those that get the value of the SVG-specific properties. The get methods typically take the form *getPropertyName()*. So, for the title property, the get method is getTitle(). Notice that the property name—title, for example—begins with a lowercase letter. However, when that name is used as part of a get method, the first letter of the property name is in uppercase, as in the getTitle() method. Some methods used, such as getTitle(), are specific to the Adobe SVG Viewer, the only SVG viewer that, at the time of writing, allows scripting.

CAUTION

JavaScript is case sensitive. You cannot write gettitle() and expect to retrieve the desired title property. You must use the correct case for each letter, as in getTitle().

LISTING 2.21   DocumentDOM.svg—Demonstrating the Properties of the Document Node

```
<?xml version="1.0" standalone="no"?>
<!DOCTYPE svg PUBLIC "-//W3C//DTD SVG 20010904//EN"
"http://www.w3.org/TR/2001/REC-SVG-20010904/DTD/svg10.dtd">
<svg width="400px" height="300px" onload="Initialize(evt)">

<script type="text/javascript">
<![CDATA[
var SVGDoc;
var SVGRoot;
function Initialize (evt) {
SVGDoc = evt.getTarget().getOwnerDocument();
}

function reportDOMDocument(evt){
var documentProperties = "";
var titleVar = SVGDoc.getTitle();
titleVar = "The document's title property is: " + titleVar +"\n"
documentProperties += titleVar;

var referrerVar = SVGDoc.getReferrer();
referrerVar = "The document's referrer property is: " + referrerVar +"\n"
documentProperties += referrerVar;

var domainVar = SVGDoc.getDomain();
domainVar = "The document's domain property is: " + domainVar +"\n"
documentProperties += domainVar;

var URLVar = SVGDoc.getURL();
URLVar = "The document's URL property is: " + URLVar +"\n"
documentProperties += URLVar;
```

LISTING 2.21 Continued

```
var documentElementVar = SVGDoc.getRootElement();
documentElementVar = "The document's rootElement property is: " +
documentElementVar + "\n"
documentProperties += documentElementVar;

window.alert(documentProperties);
}


]]>
</script>
<desc>A simple example SVG document to demonstrate the DOM</desc>
<rect x="20px" y="20px" width="360px" height="260px"
 style="fill:#DDDDDD; stroke:red; stroke-width:4;"
onclick="reportDOMDocument(evt)"/>
</svg>
```

Let's look step by step at how the example works.

When the SVG document loads, the `Initialize()` function is called:

```
<svg width="400px" height="300px" onload="Initialize(evt)">
```

Two global variables are already defined:

```
var SVGDoc;
var SVGRoot;
```

These variables can be used in all functions present within a `script` element.

The `Initialize()` function assigns a value to the `SVGDoc` variable, using the `getOwnerDocument()` method:

```
function Initialize (evt) {
SVGDoc = evt.getTarget().getOwnerDocument();
}
```

The `rect` element has an `onclick` attribute. When the rectangle is clicked, the `reportDOMDocument()` function is called:

```
<rect x="20px" y="20px" width="360px" height="260px"
 style="fill:#DDDDDD; stroke:red; stroke-width:4;"
onclick="reportDOMDocument(evt)"/>
```

The `reportDOMDocument()` function consists mostly of several similar parts. We will look here at the code needed to access and display the `title` property of the `Document` node.

First, the local variable `documentProperties` is created and assigned the empty string as its value:

```
function reportDOMDocument(evt){
var documentProperties = "";
var titleVar = SVGDoc.getTitle();
titleVar = "The document's title property is: " + titleVar +"\n"
documentProperties += titleVar;
```

Then another variable, `titleVar`, is declared (to hold the value of the `title` property) and is assigned the value returned by the `getTitle()` method of the `Document` node, whose value is held in the `SVGDoc` variable:

```
var titleVar = SVGDoc.getTitle();
```

Then we modify the value contained in the `titleVar` variable so that when it is displayed, it is more informative than a bare value. The code \n indicates that a new line is to be displayed:

```
titleVar = "The document's title property is: " + titleVar +"\n"
```

Finally, we add the value of the `titleVar` variable to the value of the `documentProperties` variable:

```
documentProperties += titleVar;
```

We follow a similar process for each of the other four properties listed earlier. We use the relevant get method to assign a value to a new variable and then add suitable explanatory text (and a newline character). Then we add that newly created string to the values already stored in the `documentProperties` variable.

When DocumentDOM.svg is run locally, the output will be similar to that shown in Figure 2.8. The value of the `title` property is null. The value of the `referrer` property is the empty string. The `domain` property indicates /, the root directory of the host computer. The URL property holds the filename of the SVG document on the local computer. The value of the `rootElement` property indicates that it is an object and that the object is of type `SVGSVGElement`.

If, however, we run the code on a Web server—for example, from http://www.svgenius.com/SVGUnleashed/DocumentDOM.svg—we will see output similar to that shown in Figure 2.9. Notice that the value of the `domain` property is now www.svgenius.com, and the value of the URL property is now http://www.svgenius.com/SVGUnleashed/DocumentDOM.svg.

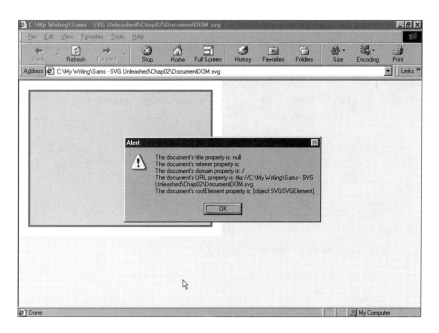

FIGURE 2.8   The SVG-specific properties of the Document node when run locally.

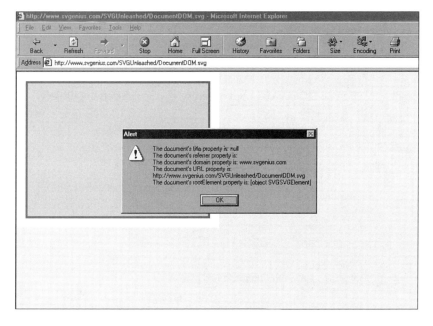

FIGURE 2.9   The SVG-specific properties of the Document node when run on a Web server.

The svg Element

Let's now look at how the svg element is viewed in the SVG DOM. The svg element is variously referred to as the **document element**, **root element**, or **element root**.

It may be most helpful to consider the SVG-specific properties of the svg element in two parts: the properties common to all SVG elements and those specific to svg elements. First, let's look at the SVGElement object, which has the properties common to all SVG elements.

The SVGElement Object

The SVGElement object has all the properties of an XML DOM Element object. In addition, it has the following properties:

- id—of type DOMString
- xmlbase—of type DOMString
- ownerSVGElement—of type SVGSVGElement
- viewportElement—of type SVGElement

The id property corresponds to an id attribute, if the SVG element possesses one. The xmlbase property corresponds to the base URI, as defined in XML Base, which applies to the element. The ownerSVGElement property corresponds to the document element svg element of the SVG document. The viewportElement property corresponds to the SVG element that defines the viewport for the element.

In the Adobe SVG Viewer version 3.0 (ASV3), only the id and viewportElement properties are accessible. Listing 2.22 provides code to access all the properties, with properties unsupported at the time of writing commented out.

LISTING 2.22   SVGElementDOM.svg—The Properties of the SVGElement Object

```
<?xml version="1.0" standalone="no"?>
<!DOCTYPE svg PUBLIC "-//W3C//DTD SVG 20010904//EN"
"http://www.w3.org/TR/2001/REC-SVG-20010904/DTD/svg10.dtd">
<svg width="400px" height="300px" onload="Initialize(evt)">

<script type="text/javascript">
<![CDATA[
var SVGDoc;
var SVGRoot;
function Initialize (evt) {
SVGDoc = evt.getTarget().getOwnerDocument();
}

function reportDOMSVGElement(evt){
SVGRoot = SVGDoc.getDocumentElement();
```

LISTING 2.22 Continued

```
MyElement = SVGRoot.getElementById("MyRect");
var elementProperties = "";
var idVar = MyElement.getId();
idVar = "The element's id property is: " + idVar +"\n"
elementProperties += idVar;

//var xmlbaseVar = MyElement.getXmlbase();
//xmlbaseVar = "The element's xmlbase property is: " + xmlbaseVar +"\n"
//elementProperties += xmlbaseVar;

//var ownerSVGElementVar = MyElement.getOwnerSVGElement();
//ownerSVGElementVar = "The element's ownerSVGElement property is: "
// + ownerSVGElementVar +"\n"
//elementProperties += ownerSVGElementVar;

var viewportElementVar = MyElement.getViewportElement();
viewportElementVar = "The element's viewportElement property is: "
 + viewportElementVar +"\n"
elementProperties += viewportElementVar;

window.alert(elementProperties);
}

]]>
</script>
<desc>A simple example SVG document to demonstrate the DOM</desc>
<rect id="MyRect" x="20px" y="20px" width="360px" height="260px"
 style="fill:#DDDDDD; stroke:red; stroke-width:4;"
onclick="reportDOMSVGElement(evt)"/>
</svg>
```

If you run the code, you will see the value of the id property, MyRect, and the value of the
viewportElement property, which indicates that the viewport element is an object of type
SVGSVGElement.

Figure 2.10 shows the output with the limitations of ASV3 at the time of writing.

Let's now move on to consider the properties that are specific to the SVGSVGElement
object.

The SVGSVGElement Object

The SVGSVGElement object is specific only to an svg element. The SVGSVGElement object
has a substantial number of both properties and methods specific to itself.

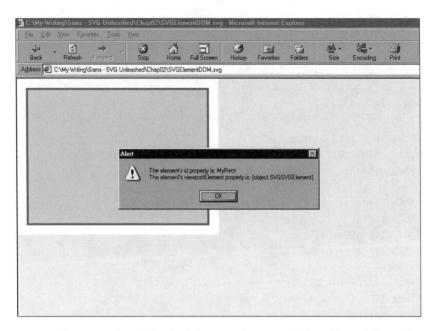

FIGURE 2.10   The properties of the SVGElement object available in the Adobe SVG Viewer.

The properties of the SVGSVGElement object are listed here:

- x—of type SVGAnimatedLength

- y—of type SVGAnimatedLength

- width—of type SVGAnimatedLength

- height—of type SVGAnimatedLength

- contentScriptType—of type DOMString

- contentStyleType—of type DOMString

- viewport—of type SVGRect

- pixelUnitToMillimeterX—of type float

- pixelUnitToMillimeterY—of type float

- screenPixelToMillimeterX—of type float

- screenPixelToMillimeterY—of type float

- useCurrentView—of type boolean

- currentView—of type SVGViewSpec

- currentScale—of type `float`
- currentTranslate—of type `SVGPoint`

The `x`, `y`, `width`, and `height` attributes of an `svg` element can be animated; therefore, we find that the corresponding properties of the `SVGSVGElement` object are of type `SVGAnimatedLength`. We will look at an example demonstrating some of the properties of the `SVGSVGElement` object a little later.

At the time of writing, the Adobe SVG Viewer 3.0 implements only the `currentScale` and `currentTranslate` properties, the latter as read-only. The use of the `currentScale` property was illustrated in Listing 2.15.

The `SVGSVGElement` object also has several methods, in addition to the `get` and `set` methods for the properties:

- suspendRedraw(*max_wait_milliseconds*)—The method returns a value of type `unsigned long`. The *max_wait_milliseconds* argument is of type `unsigned long`.

- unsuspendRedraw(*suspend_handle_id*)—The method returns a value of type `void`. The *suspend_handle_id* argument is of type `unsigned long`.

- unsuspendRedrawAll()—The method returns a value of type `void`. It takes no argument.

- forceRedraw()—The method returns a value of type `void`. It takes no argument.

- pauseAnimations()—The method returns a value of type `void`. It takes no argument.

- unpauseAnimations()—The method returns a value of type `void`. It takes no argument.

- animationsPaused()—The method returns a value of type `boolean`. It takes no argument.

- getCurrentTime()—The method returns a value of type `float`. It takes no argument.

- setCurrentTime(*seconds*)—The method returns a value of type `void`. The *seconds* argument is of type `float`.

- getIntersectionList(*rect*, *referenceElement*)—The method returns a DOM NodeList. The *rect* argument is of type `SVGRect`. The *referenceElement* argument is of type `SVGElement`.

- getEnclosureList(*rect*, *referenceElement*)—The method returns a DOM NodeList. The *rect* argument is of type `SVGRect`. The *referenceElement* argument is of type `SVGElement`.

- checkIntersection(*element*, *rect*)—The method returns a value of type `boolean`. The *element* argument is of type `SVGElement`. The *rect* argument is of type `SVGRect`.

- checkEnclosure(*element*, *rect*)—The method returns a value of type boolean. The *element* argument is of type SVGElement. The *rect* argument is of type SVGRect.

- deselectAll()—The method returns a value of type void. It takes no argument.

- createSVGNumber()—The method returns a value of type SVGNumber. It takes no argument.

- createSVGLength()—The method returns a value of type SVGLength. It takes no argument.

- createSVGAngle()—The method returns a value of type SVGAngle. It takes no argument.

- createSVGPoint()—The method returns a value of type SVGPoint. It takes no argument.

- createSVGMatrix()—The method returns a value of type SVGMatrix. It takes no argument.

- createSVGRect()—The method returns a value of type SVGRect. It takes no argument.

- createSVGTransform()—The method returns a value of type SVGTransform. It takes no argument.

- createSVGTransformFromMatrix(*matrix*)—The method returns a value of type SVGTransform. The *matrix* argument is of type SVGTransform.

- getElementById(*ElementId*)—The method returns a value that is a DOM Element. The *ElementId* argument is of type DOMString.

If you feel exhausted after simply reading about all these properties and methods, it isn't too threatening if you take them one at a time. Fortunately, most other SVG objects have substantially fewer properties and methods.

The Adobe SVG Viewer 3.0 implements the following methods of the SVGSVGElement object: pauseAnimations(), unpauseAnimations(), animationsPaused(), getCurrentTime(), setCurrentTime(), deselectAll(), createSVGPoint(), createSVGMatrix(), createSVGRect(), and getElementById(). The getElementById() method is one you are likely to use frequently.

We can view the properties of the SVGSVGElement object using techniques similar to those in previous examples. We simply use get methods to extract the value of the relevant properties of the SVGSVGElement object. Listing 2.23 allows examination of some of the properties and methods of the SVGSVGElement object.

LISTING 2.23   SVGSVGElementDOM.svg—Some SVGSVGElement Object Properties and Methods

```
<?xml version="1.0" standalone="no"?>
<!DOCTYPE svg PUBLIC "-//W3C//DTD SVG 20010904//EN"
"http://www.w3.org/TR/2001/REC-SVG-20010904/DTD/svg10.dtd">
<svg width="400px" height="300px" viewBox="0 0 1000 750" onload="Initialize(evt)">

<script type="text/javascript">
<![CDATA[
var SVGDoc;
var SVGRoot;
function Initialize (evt) {
SVGDoc = evt.getTarget().getOwnerDocument();
}

function reportDOMSVGSVGElement(evt){
SVGRoot = SVGDoc.getDocumentElement();
var elementProperties = "";
var xVar = SVGRoot.getAttribute("x");
xVar = "The <svg> element's x property is: " + xVar +"\n"
elementProperties += xVar;

var yVar = SVGRoot.getAttribute("y");
yVar = "The <svg> element's y property is: " + yVar +"\n"
elementProperties += yVar;

var currentScaleVar = SVGRoot.getCurrentScale();
currentScaleVar = "The <svg> element's currentScale property is: "
 + currentScaleVar +"\n"
elementProperties += currentScaleVar;

var currentTranslateVar = SVGRoot.getCurrentTranslate();
currentTranslateVar = "The <svg> element's currentTranslate property is: "
 + currentTranslateVar +"\n"
elementProperties += currentTranslateVar;

var currentTimeVar = SVGRoot.getCurrentTime();
currentTimeVar = "The <svg> element's getCurrentTime() method returns: "
 + currentTimeVar +"\n"
elementProperties += currentTimeVar;
window.alert(elementProperties);
}
```

LISTING 2.23   Continued

```
]]>
</script>
<desc>A simple example SVG document to demonstrate the DOM</desc>
<rect id="MyRect" x="20px" y="20px" width="360px" height="260px"
 style="fill:#DDDDDD; stroke:red; stroke-width:4;"
onclick="reportDOMSVGSVGElement(evt)"/>
</svg>
```

As you can see in Figure 2.11, the x and y properties return the empty string. For the
SVGSVGElementDOM.svg document, the currentScale property is 1. The value of the
currentTranslate property is an object of type SVGPoint. If you run the code, you may be
surprised at the value returned by the getCurrentTime() method. It does not, as you
might intuitively expect, return a date something like November 30th 2002, 20:22:38 but
returns a float value that may be less than 1. The time being returned by the
getCurrentTime() method is the time since the SVG document finished loading. This
value is used in the control of the begin and dur attributes of SVG animations.

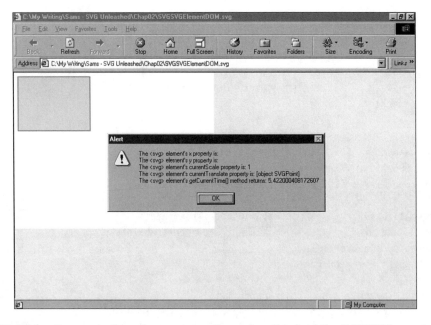

FIGURE 2.11   Demonstration of some properties and methods of the SVGSVGElement object.

The SVGLength Object

In the descriptions of the x, y, width, and height properties of the SVGSVGElement object, we indicated that these properties were of type SVGAnimatedLength. To fully understand the SVGAnimatedLength object, we must also look at the SVGLength object.

The SVGLength object has the following constants associated with it:

- SVGLength.SVG_LENGTHTYPE_UNKNOWN—This is of type short and has a value of 0.

- SVGLength.SVG_LENGTHTYPE_NUMBER—This is of type short and has a value of 1. This applies when we assign a numerical value without units to an attribute such as the x attribute, x="200".

- SVGLength.SVG_LENGTHTYPE_PERCENTAGE—This is of type short and has a value of 2. This applies when we assign a percentage value to an attribute such as the x attribute, x="100%".

- SVGLength.SVG_LENGTHTYPE_EMS—This is of type short and has a value of 3. This applies when we assign a numerical value with em units to an attribute such as the dy attribute, dy="2em".

- SVGLength.SVG_LENGTHTYPE_EXS—This is of type short and has a value of 4. This applies when we assign a numerical value with ex units to an attribute such as the dx attribute, dx="2ex".

- SVGLength.SVG_LENGTHTYPE_PX—This is of type short and has a value of 5. This applies when we assign a numerical value with px units, that is pixels, to an attribute such as the y attribute, y="200px".

- SVGLength.SVG_LENGTHTYPE_CM—This is of type short and has a value of 6. This applies when we assign a numerical value with cm units, that is centimeters, to an attribute such as the y attribute, y="2cm".

- SVGLength.SVG_LENGTHTYPE_MM—This is of type short and has a value of 7. This applies when we assign a numerical value with mm units, that is millimeters, to an attribute such as the y attribute, y="20mm".

- SVGLength.SVG_LENGTHTYPE_IN—This is of type short and has a value of 8. This applies when we assign a numerical value with in units, that is inches, to an attribute such as the y attribute, y="1in".

- SVGLength.SVG_LENGTHTYPE_PT—This is of type short and has a value of 9. This applies when we assign a numerical value with pt units, that is points, to an attribute such as the font-size attribute, font-size="18pt". There are 72 points in 1 inch.

- SVGLength.SVG_LENGTHTYPE_PC—This is of type short and has a value of 10. This applies when we assign a numerical value with pc units, that is picas, to an attribute such as the dy attribute, dy="2pc". There are 6 picas to 1 inch, or 12 points to 1 pica.

The SVGLength object also has the following properties:

- unitType—of type unsigned short

- value—of type float

- valueInSpecifiedUnits—of type float

- valueAsString—of type DOMString

The SVGLength object has two methods that are specific to it and are in addition to the get and set methods for its properties:

- newValueSpecifiedUnits(*unitType, valueInSpecifiedUnits*)—The method returns a value of type void. The *unitType* argument is of type unsigned short. The *valueInSpecifiedUnits* argument is of type float.

- convertToSpecifiedUnits(*unitType*)—The method returns a value of type void. The *unitType* argument is of type unsigned short.

Miscellaneous SVG DOM Objects

In this section, we will describe a number of miscellaneous SVG DOM objects.

The GetSVGDocument Object

The GetSVGDocument object is used to return an SVG document using scripting.

The GetSVGDocument object has no constants or properties specific to it. The GetSVGDocument object has the following method:

- getSVGDocument()—The method returns a value of type SVGDocument. The method takes no argument.

The SVGAElement Object

The SVGAElement object corresponds to an a element in the SVG code.

The SVGAElement object has the properties and methods of the SVGElement object, the SVGURIReference object, the SVGTests object, the SVGLangSpace object, the SVGExternalResourcesRequired object, the SVGStylable object, the SVGTransformable object, and the DOM Level 2 Events EventTarget element (events::EventTarget).

The SVGAElement object has the following property:

- target—of type SVGAnimatedString

The SVGAElement object has no methods specific to it.

The SVGAngle Object

The SVGAngle object is used to specify the type of units used to specify an angle.

The SVGAngle object has the following constants associated with it:

- SVGAngle.SVG_ANGLETYPE_UNKNOWN—This is of type short and has a value of 0.

- SVGAngle.SVG_ANGLETYPE_UNSPECIFIED—This is of type short and has a value of 1.

- SVGAngle.SVG_ANGLETYPE_DEG—This is of type short and has a value of 2.

- SVGAngle.SVG_ANGLETYPE_RAD—This is of type short and has a value of 3.

- SVGAngle.SVG_ANGLETYPE_GRAD—This is of type short and has a value of 4.

The SVGAngle object has the following properties:

- unitType—of type unsigned short

- value—of type float

- valueInSpecifiedUnits—of type float

- valueAsString—of type DOMString

The SVGAngle object has the following methods:

- newValueSpecifiedUnits(*unitType*, *valueInSpecifiedUnits*)—The method returns a value of type void. The *unitType* argument is of type unsigned short. The *valueInSpecifiedUnits* argument is of type float.

- convertToSpecifiedUnits(*unitType*)—The method returns a value of type void. The *unitType* argument is of type unsigned short.

The SVGCursorElement Object

The SVGCursorElement object has the properties and methods of the SVGElement object, the SVGURIReference object, the SVGTests object, and the SVGExternalResourcesRequired object.

In addition, the SVGCursorElement object has the following properties:

- x—of type SVGAnimatedLength

- y—of type SVGAnimatedLength

The SVGCursorElement object has no methods specific to it.

The SVGDefsElement Object

The SVGDefsElement corresponds in the SVG DOM to the defs element in an SVG document.

The SVGDefsElement object has all the properties and methods of the SVGElement object, the SVGTests object, the SVGLangSpace object, the SVGExternalResourcesRequired object, the SVGStylable object, the SVGTransformable object, and the DOM Level 2 Events EventTarget object (events::EventTarget).

The SVGDescElement Object

The SVGDescElement object is the SVG DOM object corresponding to the desc element in an SVG document.

The SVGDescElement object has all the properties and methods of the SVGElement object, the SVGLangSpace object, and the SVGStylable object.

The SVGDocument Object

The SVGDocument object corresponds to the document entity of an SVG document.

The SVGDocument object has the properties and methods of the DOM Level 2 Document object (dom::Document) and of the DOM Level 2 Events DocumentEvent object (events::DocumentEvent).

The SVGDocument object has the following properties specific to it:

- title—of type DOMString
- referrer—of type DOMString
- domain—of type DOMString
- URL—of type DOMString
- rootElement—an object of type SVGSVGElement

The SVGDocument object has no objects specific to it.

The SVGElementInstance Object

A use element has a corresponding SVGElementInstance object in the SVG DOM. Where there are multiple use elements, an SVGElementInstanceList object has several associated SVGElementInstance objects.

The SVGElementInstance object has the properties and methods of the DOM Level 2 Events EventTarget object (events::EventTarget).

In addition, the SVGElementInstance object has the following properties specific to it:

- correspondingElement—of type SVGElement
- correspondingUseElement—of type SVGUseElement
- parentNode—of type SVGElementInstance
- childNodes—of type SVGElementInstanceList
- firstChild—of type SVGElementInstance
- lastChild—of type SVGElementInstance
- previousSibling—of type SVGElementInstance
- nextSibling—of type SVGElementInstance

The SVGElementInstance object has no methods specific to it.

The SVGElementInstanceList Object

The instances of an element or object defined within a defs element have a corresponding SVGElementInstanceList object in the SVG DOM.

The SVGElementInstanceList object has the following property specific to it:

- length—of type unsigned long

The SVGElementInstanceList object has the following method specific to it:

- item(*index*)—The method returns a value of type SVGElementInstance. The *index* argument is of type unsigned long.

The SVGEvent Object

The SVGEvent object has the properties and methods of the DOM Level 2 Events Event object (events::Event).

The SVGEvent object has no properties or methods specific to it.

The SVGExternalResourcesRequired Object

The SVGExternalResourcesRequired object has the following property specific to it:

- externalResourcesRequired—of type SVGAnimatedBoolean

The SVGExternalResourcesRequired object has no methods specific to it.

The SVGGElement Object

The SVGGElement object in the SVG DOM corresponds to a g element in an SVG document.

The SVGGElement object has all the properties and methods of the SVGElement object, the SVGTests object, the SVGLangSpace object, the SVGExternalResourcesRequired object, the SVGStylable object, the SVGTransformable object, the DOM Level 2 Events EventTarget object (events::EventTarget).

The SVGLangSpace Object

The SVGLangSpace object stores information corresponding to the xml:lang and xml:space attributes.

The SVGLangSpace Object has the following properties specific to it:

- xmllang—of type DOMString

- xmlspace—of type DOMString

The SVGLangSpace object has no methods specific to it.

The SVGLengthList Object

The SVGLengthList object has the following property:

- numberOfItems—of type unsigned long

The SVGLengthList object has the following methods:

- clear()—The method returns a value of type void. The method takes no arguments.

- initialize(*newItem*)—The method returns a value of type SVGLength. The *newItem* argument is of type SVGLength.

- getItem(*index*)—The method returns a value of type SVGLength. The *index* argument is of type unsigned long.

- insertItemBefore(*newItem*, *index*)—The method returns a value of type SVGLength. The *newItem* argument is of type SVGLength. The *index* argument is of type unsigned long.

- replaceItem(*newItem*, *index*)—The method returns a value of type SVGLength. The *newItem* argument is of type SVGLength. The *index* argument is of type unsigned long.

- removeItem(*index*)—The method returns a value of type SVGLength. The *index* argument is of type unsigned long.

- appendItem(*newItem*)—The method returns a value of type SVGLength. The *newItem* argument is of type SVGLength.

The SVGLocatable Object

The SVGLocatable object has the following properties:

- nearestViewportElement—of type SVGElement
- farthestViewportElement—of type SVGElement

The SVGLocatable object has the following methods specific to it:

- getBBox()—The method returns a value of type SVGRect. It takes no argument.
- getCTM()—The method returns a value of type SVGMatrix. It takes no argument.
- getScreenCTM()—The method returns a value of type SVGMatrix. It takes no argument.
- getTransformToElement(*element*)—The method returns a value of type SVGMatrix. The *element* argument is of type SVGElement.

The SVGMetadataElement Object

The SVGMetadataElement object has the properties and methods of the SVGElement object.

The SVGNumber Object

The SVGNumber object has the following property:

- value—of type float

The SVGNumber object has no methods specific to it.

The SVGNumberList Object

The SVGNumberList object has the following property:

- numberOfItems—of type unsigned long

The SVGNumberList object has the following properties:

- clear()—The method returns a value of type void. The method takes no arguments.
- initialize(*newItem*)—The method returns a value of type SVGNumber. The *newItem* argument is of type SVGNumber.

- getItem(*index*)—The method returns a value of type SVGNumber. The *index* argument is of type unsigned long.

- insertItemBefore(*newItem*, *index*)—The method returns a value of type SVGNumber. The *newItem* argument is of type SVGNumber. The *index* argument is of type unsigned long.

- replaceItem(*newItem*, *index*)—The method returns a value of type SVGNumber. The *newItem* argument is of type SVGNumber. The *index* argument is of type unsigned long.

- removeItem(*index*)—The method returns a value of type SVGNumber. The *index* argument is of type unsigned long.

- appendItem(*newItem*)—The method returns a value of type SVGNumber. The *newItem* argument is of type SVGNumber.

The SVGRect Object

The SVGRect object has the following properties:

- x—of type float

- y—of type float

- width—of type float

- height—of type float

The SVGRect object has no methods specific to it.

The SVGScriptElement Object

The SVGScriptElement object is the SVG DOM representation of a script element in an SVG document.

The SVGScriptElement object has the properties and methods of the SVGElement object, the SVGURIReference object, and the SVGExternalResourcesRequired object.

In addition, the SVGScriptElement object has the following property:

- type—of type DOMString

The SVGScriptElement object has no methods specific to it.

The SVGStringList Object

The SVGStringList object has the following properties:

- numberOfItems—of type unsigned long

The `SVGStringList` object has the following methods:

- `clear()`—The method returns a value of type `void`. The method takes no arguments.

- `initialize(newItem)`—The method returns a value of type `DOMString`. The *newItem* argument is of type `DOMString`.

- `getItem(index)`—The method returns a value of type `DOMString`. The *index* argument is of type `unsigned long`.

- `insertItemBefore(newItem, index)`—The method returns a value of type `DOMString`. The *newItem* argument is of type `DOMString`. The *index* argument is of type `unsigned long`.

- `replaceItem(newItem, index)`—The method returns a value of type `DOMString`. The *newItem* argument is of type `DOMString`. The *index* argument is of type `unsigned long`.

- `removeItem(index)`—The method returns a value of type `DOMString`. The *index* argument is of type `unsigned long`.

- `appendItem(newItem)`—The method returns a value of type `DOMString`. The *newItem* argument is of type `DOMString`.

The SVGSymbolElement Object

The `SVGSymbolElement` object is the SVG DOM representation of a `symbol` element in an SVG document.

The `SVGSymbolElement` object has all the properties and methods of the `SVGElement` object, the `SVGLangSpace` object, the `SVGExternalResourcesRequired` object, the `SVGStylable` object, the `SVGFitToViewBox` object, and the DOM Level 2 Events `EventTarget` object (`events::EventTarget`).

The SVGTests Object

The `SVGTests` object has the following properties specific to it:

- `requiredFeatures`—of type `SVGStringList`

- `requiredExtensions`—of type `SVGStringList`

- `systemLanguage`—of type `SVGStringList`

The `SVGTests` object has the following method specific to it:

- `hasExtension(extension)`—The method returns a value of type `boolean`. The *extension* argument is of type `DOMString`.

The SVGTitleElement Object

The SVGTitleElement object is the SVG DOM representation of a title element.

The SVGTitleElement object has all the properties and methods of the SVGElement object, the SVGLangSpace object, and the SVGStylable object.

The SVGURIReference Object

The SVGURIReference object has the following property specific to it:

- href—of type SVGAnimatedString

The SVGURIReference object has no methods specific to it.

The SVGUseElement Object

The SVGUseElement object is the SVG DOM representation of a use element in an SVG document.

The SVGUseElement object has all the properties and methods of the SVGElement object, the SVGURIReference object, the SVGTests object, the SVGLangSpace object, the SVGExternalResourcesRequired object, the SVGStylable object, the SVGTransformable object, and the DOM Level 2 Events EventTarget object (events::EventTarget).

The SVGUseElement object has the following properties specific to it:

- x—of type SVGAnimatedLength
- y—of type SVGAnimatedLength
- width—of type SVGAnimatedLength
- height—of type SVGAnimatedLength
- instanceRoot—of type SVGElementInstance
- animatedInstanceRoot—of type SVGElementInstance

The SVGUseElement object has no methods specific to it.

The SVGViewElement Object

The SVGViewElement object is the SVG DOM representation of a view element in an SVG document.

The SVGViewElement object has the properties and methods of the SVGElement object, the SVGExternalResourcesRequired object, the SVGFitToViewBox object, and the SVGZoomAndPan object.

In addition, the `SVGViewElement` object has the following property:

- `viewTarget`—of type `SVGStringList`

The `SVGViewElement` object has no methods specific to it.

The SVGViewSpec Object

The `SVGViewSpec` object has the properties and methods of the `SVGZoomAndPan` object and the `SVGFitToViewBox` object.

The `SVGViewSpec` object has the following properties specific to it:

- `transform`—of type `SVGTransformList`
- `viewTarget`—of type `SVGElement`
- `viewBoxString`—of type `DOMString`
- `preserveAspectRatioString`—of type `DOMString`
- `transformString`—of type `DOMString`
- `viewTargetString`—of type `DOMString`

The `SVGViewSpec` object has no methods specific to it.

The SVGZoomAndPan Object

The `SVGZoomAndPan` object is the SVG DOM representation of the value of the `zoomAndPan` attribute on the `svg` document element in an SVG document.

The `SVGZoomAndPan` object has the following constants associated with it:

- `SVGZoomAndPan.SVG_ZOOMANDPAN_UNKNOWN`—This constant is of type `short` and has a value of 0.
- `SVGZoomAndPan.SVG_ZOOMANDPAN_DISABLE`—This constant is of type `short` and has a value of 1.
- `SVGZoomAndPan.SVG_ZOOMANDPAN_MAGNIFY`—This constant is of type `short` and has a value of 2.

The `SVGZoomAndPan` object has the following property specific to it:

- `zoomAndPan`—of type `unsigned short`

The `SVGZoomAndPan` object has no methods specific to it.

The SVGZoomEvent Object

The SVGZoomEvent object has the properties and methods of the DOM Level 2 Events UIEvent object (events::UIEvent).

In addition, the SVGZoomEvent object has the following properties:

- zoomRectScreen—of type SVGRect

- previousScale—of type float

- previousTranslate—of type SVGPoint

- newScale—of type float

- newTranslate—of type SVGPoint

The SVGZoomEvent object has no methods specific to it.

Summary

Understanding XML syntax is relevant to your use of SVG. If you make XML syntax errors, quite likely your SVG code will not run correctly and may not display at all.

You have been introduced to several SVG elements, such as the svg, g, defs, title, and use elements. Such elements provide the basic structure of many SVG documents.

The SVG Document Object Model provides a specific representation of an SVG document, to augment the generic properties and methods provided by the XML Document Object Model.

In later chapters, we will introduce and demonstrate further SVG elements and further parts of the SVG Document Object Model. Chapter 3 covers basic SVG graphic shapes.

Basic SVG Elements and Shapes

SVG provides several elements that describe commonly used graphic shapes.

In this chapter, we will examine six of the SVG elements that provide basic graphic shapes we can use, and reuse, as visual components. In particular, we will examine in detail the following elements and many of their attributes that SVG provides for a developer to modify the visual appearance produced by an SVG rendering engine:

- The line element, which describes a straight line
- The rect element, which describes a rectangle or square
- The circle element, which describes a circle
- The ellipse element, which describes an ellipse
- The polyline element, which describes a shape created by a number of straight lines
- The polygon element, which describes a closed multi-sided shape with straight edges

Each basic graphic shape will be described in this chapter. We will describe and demonstrate the ways in which each shape can be used and explore the techniques to use the permitted attributes to alter the visual appearance of each shape. In addition, we will also describe the interfaces in the Document Object Model that relate to each shape.

Not all SVG shapes can be described using the graphic shapes discussed in this chapter. The path element can express any arbitrary shape and is described in Chapter 6, "Paths in SVG." In this chapter, the focus is on static graphic shapes. The techniques to animate SVG graphic shapes are described in

Chapter 11, "SVG Animation Elements." In addition, each of the SVG basic graphic shapes may be used in clipping paths, which are described in Chapter 9, "Clipping, Masking, Compositing."

In addition to the basic graphic shapes, the syntax for use of gradients and patterns in SVG will be described. SVG DOM interfaces relevant to the SVG basic graphic shapes, gradients, and patterns will also be described.

The line Element

The line element describes a single straight line. To draw a straight line in a coordinate system, you need to know the coordinates of each end of the line. In SVG, the coordinates of one end of the line are defined by the x1 and y1 attributes. The coordinates of the other end of the line are defined by x2 and y2 attributes.

Listing 3.1 shows four straight lines, each being created using a line element.

LISTING 3.1   FourLines.svg—Creating Straight Lines Using the line Element

```
<?xml version="1.0" standalone="no"?>
<!DOCTYPE svg PUBLIC "-//W3C//DTD SVG 20010904//EN"
"http://www.w3.org/TR/2001/REC-SVG-20010904/DTD/svg10.dtd">
<svg width="400px" height="250px">
<line x1="50px" y1="100px" x2="350px" y2="100px" stroke="black"/>
<line x1="20px" y1="50px" x2="20px" y2="350px" stroke="black"/>
<line x1="0px" y1="0px" x2="400px" y2="250px" stroke="black"/>
<line x1="300px" y1="30px" x2="200px" y2="50px" stroke="black"/>
</svg>
```

Figure 3.1 shows the onscreen appearance of Listing 3.1. Recall that when the value of the x attribute and the value of the y attribute equal 0, the top-left corner of the viewport is being referred to. The viewport is the area (of the potentially infinite SVG canvas) which is rendered onscreen.

The onscreen appearance of these lines is dull. No style information is present on the line elements in Listing 3.1. Listing 3.2 shows some possible ways in which we can style line elements.

LISTING 3.2   FourLinesStyled.svg—Applying Style Information to line Elements

```
<?xml version="1.0" standalone="no"?>
<!DOCTYPE svg PUBLIC "-//W3C//DTD SVG 20010904//EN"
"http://www.w3.org/TR/2001/REC-SVG-20010904/DTD/svg10.dtd">
<svg width="400px" height="250px">
<line x1="50px" y1="100px" x2="350px" y2="100px"
```

LISTING 3.2   Continued

```
style="stroke:red; stroke-width:5" />
<line x1="20px" y1="50px" x2="20px" y2="350px"
 stroke="green" stroke-width="2" />
<line x1="0px" y1="0px" x2="400px" y2="250px"
 style="stroke:blue; fill:none; stroke-dasharray:9,9;"/>
<line x1="300px" y1="30px" x2="200px" y2="50px"
 style="stroke:blue; fill:none; stroke-dasharray:3,3;"/>
</svg>
```

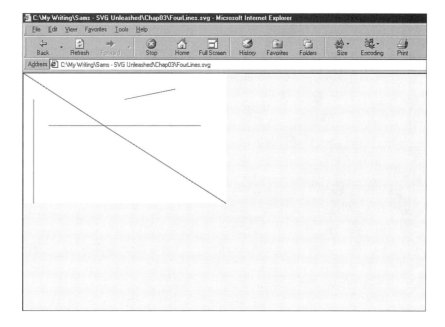

FIGURE 3.1   Four lines created using the SVG line element.

The appearance produced by Listing 3.2 is shown in Figure 3.2.

You may wonder why it is necessary to specify `fill:none;` for the third and fourth `line` elements in Listing 3.2. If you don't do so, as in Listing 3.3, a faint gray line will appear onscreen in Adobe SVG Viewer 3.

LISTING 3.3   TwoLinesStyled.svg—The Need for Specifying No Fill on Dashed line Elements

```
<?xml version="1.0" standalone="no"?>
<!DOCTYPE svg PUBLIC "-//W3C//DTD SVG 20010904//EN"
"http://www.w3.org/TR/2001/REC-SVG-20010904/DTD/svg10.dtd">
<svg width="400px" height="250px">
```

LISTING 3.3   Continued

```
<line x1="0px" y1="0px" x2="400px" y2="250px"
 style="stroke:blue; stroke-width:5; fill:none; stroke-dasharray:9,9;"/>
<line x1="0px" y1="20px" x2="400px" y2="270px"
 style="stroke:blue; stroke-width:5; stroke-dasharray:9,9;"/>
</svg>
```

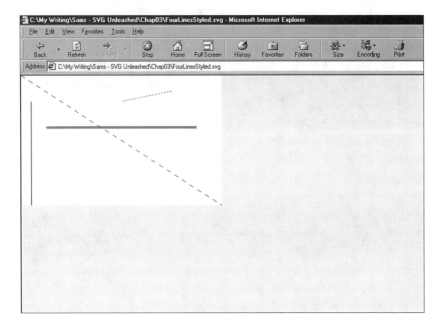

FIGURE 3.2   Styling applied to the four lines.

Figure 3.3 shows the two lines zoomed in the Adobe SVG Viewer.

We don't need to specify `fill:none` on a solid line—the color of the stroke will completely cover the faint gray default line produced in the Adobe Viewer.

You can specify `opacity` for the `line` element either by adding an `opacity` attribute or specifying an `opacity` property within a `style` attribute. The latter technique is used in Listing 3.4.

LISTING 3.4   ThreeSimpleLines.svg—Opacity of Three Lines

```
<?xml version="1.0" standalone="no"?>
<!DOCTYPE svg PUBLIC "-//W3C//DTD SVG 20010904//EN"
"http://www.w3.org/TR/2001/REC-SVG-20010904/DTD/svg10.dtd">
<svg width="300" height="300">
```

LISTING 3.4   Continued

```
<line x1="20" y1="20" x2="220" y2="20"
 style="stroke:#FF0000; stroke-width:4; opacity:0.1"/>
<line x1="20" y1="120" x2="220" y2="120"
 style="stroke:#FF0000; stroke-width:4; opacity:0.4"/>
<line x1="20" y1="220" x2="220" y2="220"
 style="stroke:#FF0000; stroke-width:4; opacity:1"/>
</svg>
```

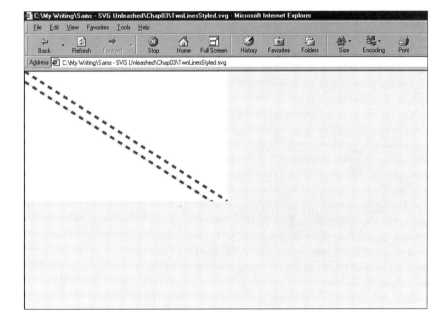

FIGURE 3.3   The effect of the presence and absence of fill:none on a dashed line element.

Figure 3.4 shows the visual effect, slightly zoomed, of three levels of opacity on otherwise identical lines.

In Figure 3.4, you will notice that the topmost of the three lines is fairly faint, due to its opacity being only 0.1. The bottom line is fully opaque, having an opacity of 1, and the middle line is semitransparent, having an opacity of 0.4.

We can use line elements to create the axes of a graph, as well as the scale marks for each axis. Listing 3.5 shows the use of line elements to create the skeleton of a graph. The comments within the code indicate the purpose of each line element.

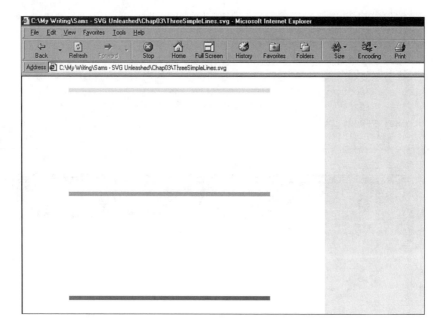

FIGURE 3.4   Three lines of different opacity values.

LISTING 3.5   GraphAxes.svg—A Skeleton for a Graph Created with line Elements

```
<?xml version="1.0" standalone="no"?>
<!DOCTYPE svg PUBLIC "-//W3C//DTD SVG 20010904//EN"
"http://www.w3.org/TR/2001/REC-SVG-20010904/DTD/svg10.dtd">
<svg width="600" height="400">
<!-- The vertical axis -->
<line x1="40" y1="360" x2="40" y2="40"
 style="stroke:#000000; stroke-width:0.5;"/>

<!-- The scale marks on the vertical axis -->
<line x1="40" y1="110" x2="48" y2="110"
 style="stroke:#000000; stroke-width:0.5;"/>
<line x1="40" y1="160" x2="48" y2="160"
 style="stroke:#000000; stroke-width:0.5;"/>
<line x1="40" y1="210" x2="48" y2="210"
 style="stroke:#000000; stroke-width:0.5;"/>
<line x1="40" y1="260" x2="48" y2="260"
 style="stroke:#000000; stroke-width:0.5;"/>
<line x1="40" y1="310" x2="48" y2="310"
 style="stroke:#000000; stroke-width:0.5;"/>
```

LISTING 3.5   Continued

```
<!-- The horizontal axis -->
<line x1="40" y1="360" x2="550" y2="360"
 style="stroke:#000000; stroke-width:0.5;"/>

<!-- The scale marks on the horizontal axis -->
<line x1="80" y1="360" x2="80" y2="352"
 style="stroke:#000000; stroke-width:0.5;"/>
<line x1="120" y1="360" x2="120" y2="352"
 style="stroke:#000000; stroke-width:0.5;"/>
<line x1="160" y1="360" x2="160" y2="352"
 style="stroke:#000000; stroke-width:0.5;"/>
<line x1="200" y1="360" x2="200" y2="352"
 style="stroke:#000000; stroke-width:0.5;"/>
<line x1="240" y1="360" x2="240" y2="352"
 style="stroke:#000000; stroke-width:0.5;"/>
<line x1="280" y1="360" x2="280" y2="352"
 style="stroke:#000000; stroke-width:0.5;"/>
<line x1="320" y1="360" x2="320" y2="352"
 style="stroke:#000000; stroke-width:0.5;"/>
<line x1="360" y1="360" x2="360" y2="352"
 style="stroke:#000000; stroke-width:0.5;"/>
<line x1="400" y1="360" x2="400" y2="352"
 style="stroke:#000000; stroke-width:0.5;"/>
<line x1="440" y1="360" x2="440" y2="352"
 style="stroke:#000000; stroke-width:0.5;"/>
<line x1="480" y1="360" x2="480" y2="352"
 style="stroke:#000000; stroke-width:0.5;"/>
<line x1="520" y1="360" x2="520" y2="352"
 style="stroke:#000000; stroke-width:0.5;"/>
</svg>
```

As you can see in Figure 3.5, using only the `line` element, we can create the basis of a graph in SVG. Clearly, to create a more respectable graph, we will need to learn how to control the display of text in SVG, which is described in Chapter 8, "Laying Out Text in SVG."

It is straightforward to add further `line` elements to produce a bar chart, which might indicate monthly sales for a particular product or division of a corporation. This procedure is shown in Listing 3.6.

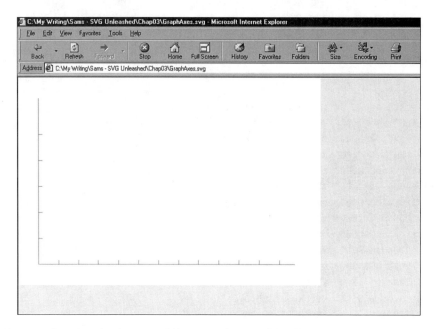

FIGURE 3.5   Creating the framework for a graph using line elements.

LISTING 3.6   GraphAxes02.svg—Adding Bars to the Graph

```
<?xml version="1.0" standalone="no"?>
<!DOCTYPE svg PUBLIC "-//W3C//DTD SVG 20010904//EN"
"http://www.w3.org/TR/2001/REC-SVG-20010904/DTD/svg10.dtd">
<svg width="600" height="400">
<!-- The vertical axis -->
<line x1="40" y1="360" x2="40" y2="40"
 style="stroke:#000000; stroke-width:0.5;"/>

<!-- The scale marks on the vertical axis -->
<line x1="40" y1="110" x2="48" y2="110"
 style="stroke:#000000; stroke-width:0.5;"/>
<line x1="40" y1="160" x2="48" y2="160"
 style="stroke:#000000; stroke-width:0.5;"/>
<line x1="40" y1="210" x2="48" y2="210"
 style="stroke:#000000; stroke-width:0.5;"/>
<line x1="40" y1="260" x2="48" y2="260"
 style="stroke:#000000; stroke-width:0.5;"/>
<line x1="40" y1="310" x2="48" y2="310"
 style="stroke:#000000; stroke-width:0.5;"/>
```

LISTING 3.6   Continued

```
<!-- The horizontal axis -->
<line x1="40" y1="360" x2="550" y2="360"
 style="stroke:#000000; stroke-width:0.5;"/>

<!-- The scale marks on the horizontal axis -->
<line x1="80" y1="360" x2="80" y2="352"
 style="stroke:#000000; stroke-width:0.5;"/>
<line x1="120" y1="360" x2="120" y2="352"
 style="stroke:#000000; stroke-width:0.5;"/>
<line x1="160" y1="360" x2="160" y2="352"
 style="stroke:#000000; stroke-width:0.5;"/>
<line x1="200" y1="360" x2="200" y2="352"
 style="stroke:#000000; stroke-width:0.5;"/>
<line x1="240" y1="360" x2="240" y2="352"
 style="stroke:#000000; stroke-width:0.5;"/>
<line x1="280" y1="360" x2="280" y2="352"
 style="stroke:#000000; stroke-width:0.5;"/>
<line x1="320" y1="360" x2="320" y2="352"
 style="stroke:#000000; stroke-width:0.5;"/>
<line x1="360" y1="360" x2="360" y2="352"
 style="stroke:#000000; stroke-width:0.5;"/>
<line x1="400" y1="360" x2="400" y2="352"
 style="stroke:#000000; stroke-width:0.5;"/>
<line x1="440" y1="360" x2="440" y2="352"
 style="stroke:#000000; stroke-width:0.5;"/>
<line x1="480" y1="360" x2="480" y2="352"
 style="stroke:#000000; stroke-width:0.5;"/>
<line x1="520" y1="360" x2="520" y2="352"
 style="stroke:#000000; stroke-width:0.5;"/>

<!-- The lines representing monthly sales -->
<line x1="83" y1="360" x2="83" y2="250"
 style="stroke:#FF0000; stroke-width:4;"/>
<line x1="123" y1="360" x2="123" y2="240"
 style="stroke:#FF0000; stroke-width:4;"/>
<line x1="163" y1="360" x2="163" y2="230"
 style="stroke:#FF0000; stroke-width:4;"/>
<line x1="203" y1="360" x2="203" y2="240"
 style="stroke:#FF0000; stroke-width:4;"/>
<line x1="243" y1="360" x2="243" y2="210"
 style="stroke:#FF0000; stroke-width:4;"/>
<line x1="283" y1="360" x2="283" y2="220"
 style="stroke:#FF0000; stroke-width:4;"/>
```

LISTING 3.6   Continued

```
<line x1="323" y1="360" x2="323" y2="230"
 style="stroke:#FF0000; stroke-width:4;"/>
<line x1="363" y1="360" x2="363" y2="220"
 style="stroke:#FF0000; stroke-width:4;"/>
<line x1="403" y1="360" x2="403" y2="240"
 style="stroke:#FF0000; stroke-width:4;"/>
<line x1="443" y1="360" x2="443" y2="190"
 style="stroke:#FF0000; stroke-width:4;"/>
<line x1="483" y1="360" x2="483" y2="210"
 style="stroke:#FF0000; stroke-width:4;"/>
<line x1="523" y1="360" x2="523" y2="200"
 style="stroke:#FF0000; stroke-width:4;"/>
</svg>
```

Figure 3.6 shows the bars added to the skeleton of the graph.

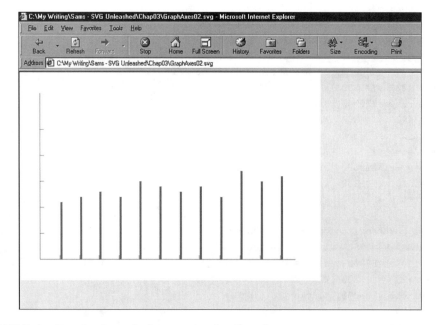

FIGURE 3.6   Creating bars of a bar graph using line elements.

The line element, in common with many other SVG elements, can be animated using declarative SVG animations. SVG declarative animations are discussed in Chapter 11.

The rect Element

The rect element defines a rectangular shape. The SVG rect element can be used to describe both a rectangle and a square. A square is simply a special case of a rectangle—one in which the width and height of the rectangle are equal.

To fully describe a rectangle in SVG, we need to define the coordinates of its top-left corner together with its width and height. Those key pieces of information are specified in the x, y, width, and height attributes, respectively, of the rect element.

In addition to defining the position and dimensions of the rectangle, we need to define its appearance using the style attribute (or one of the alternative techniques described in Chapter 4, "Using CSS with SVG"). If we omit any style information, the rectangle will be rendered as a solid black shape. Like the line element, the rect element has a stroke property that defines the color of the outline of the rectangle. A rect element also may have a fill color that is defined by the value of its fill property.

In Listing 3.7, SimpleRects.svg, we produce two rectangular shapes. The upper shape appears onscreen to be a solid red rectangle, whereas the lower shape is a pale gray rectangle with a red outline. In fact, for both shapes, the stroke property (which defines the color of the outline) is defined separately from the color of the fill. In the first rectangle, which appears to have no outline, the stroke is simply the same color as the fill.

LISTING 3.7   SimpleRects.svg—Two Rectangles Using the rect Element

```
<?xml version="1.0" standalone="no"?>
<!DOCTYPE svg PUBLIC "-//W3C//DTD SVG 20010904//EN"
"http://www.w3.org/TR/2001/REC-SVG-20010904/DTD/svg10.dtd">
<svg width="300" height="300">
<rect x="50" y="50" width="150" height="50"
 style="stroke:#FF0000; fill:#FF0000"/>
<rect x="50" y="200" width="150" height="50"
 style="stroke:#FF0000; fill:#CCCCCC"/>
</svg>
```

A common use of the rect element is in graphs, such as bar graphs. Listing 3.8, GraphAxes03.svg, shows how to use rect elements in a manner similar to that shown earlier to produce vertical bars in a bar chart.

LISTING 3.8   GraphAxes03.svg—Using the rect Element in a Bar Graph

```
<?xml version="1.0" standalone="no"?>
<!DOCTYPE svg PUBLIC "-//W3C//DTD SVG 20010904//EN"
"http://www.w3.org/TR/2001/REC-SVG-20010904/DTD/svg10.dtd">
<svg width="600" height="400">
```

LISTING 3.8   Continued

```
<!-- The vertical axis -->
<line x1="40" y1="360" x2="40" y2="40"
 style="stroke:#000000; stroke-width:0.5;"/>

<!-- The scale marks on the vertical axis -->
<line x1="40" y1="110" x2="48" y2="110"
 style="stroke:#000000; stroke-width:0.5;"/>
<line x1="40" y1="160" x2="48" y2="160"
 style="stroke:#000000; stroke-width:0.5;"/>
<line x1="40" y1="210" x2="48" y2="210"
 style="stroke:#000000; stroke-width:0.5;"/>
<line x1="40" y1="260" x2="48" y2="260"
 style="stroke:#000000; stroke-width:0.5;"/>
<line x1="40" y1="310" x2="48" y2="310"
 style="stroke:#000000; stroke-width:0.5;"/>

<!-- The horizontal axis -->
<line x1="40" y1="360" x2="550" y2="360"
 style="stroke:#000000; stroke-width:0.5;"/>

<!-- The scale marks on the horizontal axis -->
<line x1="80" y1="360" x2="80" y2="368"
 style="stroke:#000000; stroke-width:0.5;"/>
<line x1="120" y1="360" x2="120" y2="368"
 style="stroke:#000000; stroke-width:0.5;"/>
<line x1="160" y1="360" x2="160" y2="368"
 style="stroke:#000000; stroke-width:0.5;"/>
<line x1="200" y1="360" x2="200" y2="368"
 style="stroke:#000000; stroke-width:0.5;"/>
<line x1="240" y1="360" x2="240" y2="368"
 style="stroke:#000000; stroke-width:0.5;"/>
<line x1="280" y1="360" x2="280" y2="368"
 style="stroke:#000000; stroke-width:0.5;"/>
<line x1="320" y1="360" x2="320" y2="368"
 style="stroke:#000000; stroke-width:0.5;"/>
<line x1="360" y1="360" x2="360" y2="368"
 style="stroke:#000000; stroke-width:0.5;"/>
<line x1="400" y1="360" x2="400" y2="368"
 style="stroke:#000000; stroke-width:0.5;"/>
<line x1="440" y1="360" x2="440" y2="368"
 style="stroke:#000000; stroke-width:0.5;"/>
<line x1="480" y1="360" x2="480" y2="368"
```

LISTING 3.8   Continued

```
style="stroke:#000000; stroke-width:0.5;"/>
<line x1="520" y1="360" x2="520" y2="368"
 style="stroke:#000000; stroke-width:0.5;"/>

<!-- The rectangles representing monthly sales -->
<rect x="77" y="250" width="6" height="110"
 style="stroke:#FF0000; fill:#CCCCCC; stroke-width:1;"/>
<rect x="117" y="240" width="6" height="120"
 style="stroke:#FF0000; fill:#CCCCCC; stroke-width:1;"/>
<rect x="157" y="230" width="6" height="130"
 style="stroke:#FF0000; fill:#CCCCCC; stroke-width:1;"/>
<rect x="197" y="240" width="6" height="120"
 style="stroke:#FF0000; fill:#CCCCCC; stroke-width:1;"/>
<rect x="237" y="210" width="6" height="150"
 style="stroke:#FF0000; fill:#CCCCCC; stroke-width:1;"/>
<rect x="277" y="220" width="6" height="140"
 style="stroke:#FF0000; fill:#CCCCCC; stroke-width:1;"/>
<rect x="317" y="230" width="6" height="130"
 style="stroke:#FF0000; fill:#CCCCCC; stroke-width:1;"/>
<rect x="357" y="220" width="6" height="140"
 style="stroke:#FF0000; fill:#CCCCCC; stroke-width:1;"/>
<rect x="397" y="240" width="6" height="120"
 style="stroke:#FF0000; fill:#CCCCCC; stroke-width:1;"/>
<rect x="437" y="190" width="6" height="170"
 style="stroke:#FF0000; fill:#CCCCCC; stroke-width:1;"/>
<rect x="477" y="210" width="6" height="150"
 style="stroke:#FF0000; fill:#CCCCCC; stroke-width:1;"/>
<rect x="517" y="200" width="6" height="160"
 style="stroke:#FF0000; fill:#CCCCCC; stroke-width:1;"/>
</svg>
```

In Listing 3.8, the direction of the scale marks on the horizontal axis has been reversed—they now point down. The rect elements allow us to create bars that are two colors, having a red stroke and a pale gray fill, as you can see in Figure 3.7, or if you run the code onscreen.

An SVG rect element may be given rounded corners by means of the rx and ry attributes. Listing 3.9 shows how the rx and ry attributes can be used and also a limitation of the use of the use element—you can only use the shape exactly as defined and cannot, for example, add rx and ry attributes.

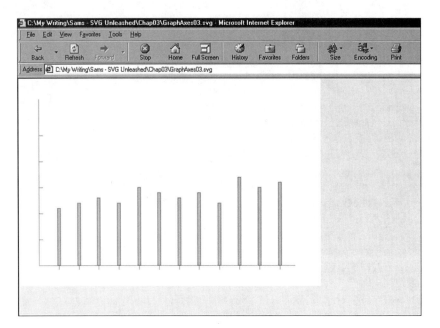

FIGURE 3.7   A bar graph using rect and line elements.

LISTING 3.9   RectRoundCorners.svg—Creating Rectangles with Rounded Corners

```
<?xml version="1.0" standalone="no"?>
<!DOCTYPE svg PUBLIC "-//W3C//DTD SVG 20010904//EN"
"http://www.w3.org/TR/2001/REC-SVG-20010904/DTD/svg10.dtd">
<svg width="800px" height="600px">
<defs>
<rect id="MyRect" x="0px" y="0px" width="100px" height="75px"
 style="fill:none; stroke:blue; stroke-width:3"/>
</defs>
<g transform="translate(25,25)">
<use xlink:href="#MyRect" rx="0px" ry="0px" />
</g>
<g transform="translate(225,25)">
<use xlink:href="#MyRect" rx="5px" ry="5px" />
</g>
<g transform="translate(425,25)">
<use xlink:href="#MyRect" rx="10px" ry="10px" />
</g>
<rect id="MyRect" x="225px" y="150px" width="100px" height="75px"
 style="fill:none; stroke:blue; stroke-width:3" rx="5px" ry="5px"/>
```

LISTING 3.9 Continued

```
<rect id="MyRect" x="425px" y="150px" width="100px" height="75px"
 style="fill:none; stroke:blue; stroke-width:3" rx="10px" ry="10px"/>
</svg>
```

The final two `rect` elements in Listing 3.9 produce the two rectangles in the lower row in Figure 3.8, each of which has rounded corners. Unfortunately, when you make use of the `use` element, you cannot modify the shape by, for example, adding `rx` and `ry` attributes.

> **TIP**
>
> If you want to apply unequal rx and ry values, you must be sure to specify a desired value, even zero, for both attributes. If you omit one of the two attributes, the SVG rendering engine will assign the same value to the other.

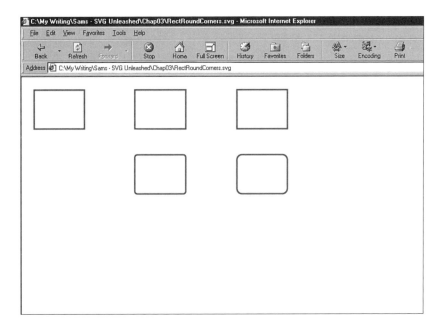

FIGURE 3.8 Adding rounded corners to rectangles in SVG.

A `rect` element may be animated by any of the SVG animation elements—`animate`, `set`, `animateColor`, `animateMotion`, or `animateTransform`—which are described in Chapter 11.

The circle Element

Circular objects may appear in many graphics, whether as functional parts of an object or as decorative additions. In maps, a circle may be used as a simple representation of a traffic circle, for example.

> **NOTE**
>
> Strictly speaking, the circle element is not needed in SVG because a circle can be described as an ellipse element (described in the next section), which has equal values for its rx and ry attributes.

The circle element, not surprisingly, is used to produce circles. If you studied basic geometry, you may remember that a circle is completely described if the position of its center and its radius are both known. In the SVG circle element, the x coordinate of the center of the circle is denoted by the cx attribute, the y coordinate of the center is denoted by the cy attribute, and the radius is denoted by the r attribute. As well as the essential geometric information, we can also add style information. Thus, to define a circle of radius 50, centered at coordinates 100,100, we can use the code in Listing 3.10.

LISTING 3.10   FirstCircle.svg—A Circle in SVG

```
<?xml version="1.0" standalone="no"?>
<!DOCTYPE svg PUBLIC "-//W3C//DTD SVG 20010904//EN"
"http://www.w3.org/TR/2001/REC-SVG-20010904/DTD/svg10.dtd">
<svg width="" height="">
<circle cx="100" cy="100" r="50"
 style="stroke:#FF0000; stroke-width:2; fill:#CCCCFF"/>
</svg>
```

As you can see in Figure 3.9, which is zoomed and panned, we produce a circle whose outline color differs from its fill color.

A circle element may be animated by any of the SVG animation elements—animate, set, animateColor, animateMotion, or animateTransform—which are described in Chapter 11.

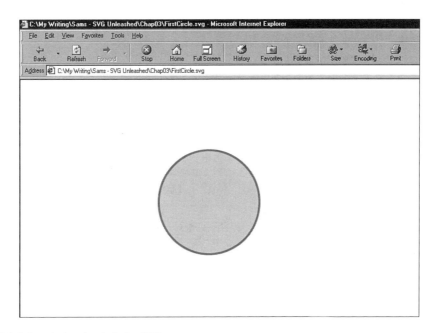

FIGURE 3.9   A simple circle in SVG.

The ellipse Element

The `circle` element is adequate to describe a circle but is inadequate to describe an ellipse because an ellipse has two radii, an x radius and a y radius. The SVG `ellipse` element is used to describe an ellipse. The center of the ellipse is described, as with the `circle` element, using a `cx` and a `cy` attribute. The x radius of an ellipse is described using an `rx` attribute, and the y radius is described using an `ry` attribute. Listing 3.11 shows how we can describe a simple ellipse using the `ellipse` element.

LISTING 3.11   SimpleEllipse.svg—A Simple SVG Ellipse

```
<?xml version="1.0" standalone="no"?>
<!DOCTYPE svg PUBLIC "-//W3C//DTD SVG 20010904//EN"
"http://www.w3.org/TR/2001/REC-SVG-20010904/DTD/svg10.dtd">
<svg width="400" height="300">
<ellipse cx="200" cy="100" rx="150" ry="50"
 style="stroke:#FF0000; stroke-width:2; fill:#FFFFFF"/>
</svg>
```

An ellipse element may be animated by any of the SVG animation elements—animate, set, animateColor, animateMotion, or animateTransform—which are described in Chapter 11.

The polyline Element

The polyline element allows us to create shapes that consist of a number of straight lines. Such polyline shapes may be filled or have no fill.

The position of the ends of each line that makes up the polyline shape are defined in the points attribute of the polyline element. Style information is applied, as previously described, by using the style attribute (or individual attributes corresponding to style properties).

Listing 3.12 shows two polyline shapes, one of which is filled; whereas the other is specified, within the style attribute, as having no fill.

LISTING 3.12   SimplePolyline.svg—Two Simple Polyline Shapes

```
<?xml version="1.0" standalone="no"?>
<!DOCTYPE svg PUBLIC "-//W3C//DTD SVG 20010904//EN"
"http://www.w3.org/TR/2001/REC-SVG-20010904/DTD/svg10.dtd">
<svg width="500" height="300">
<polyline style="stroke:#000000; stroke-width:2; fill:#CCCCCC;"
  points="30,200 30,50 130 50" />
<polyline style="stroke:#000000; stroke-width:2; fill:none;"
  points="230,200 230,50 330 50" />
</svg>
```

As you can see in Figure 3.10, which is zoomed and panned, the fill of the left polyline element is pale gray. If we did not specify a value for the fill property within the style attribute, the default black fill would be applied. For the polyline element on the right, we specify within the style attribute that there is no fill using the CSS declaration fill:none.

Typically, a polyline element is used to create an open shape. However, if you include a pair of coordinates within the points attribute that match the starting point, for example, you can create a closed shape, as shown in Listing 3.13, SimplePolyline02.svg.

LISTING 3.13   SimplePolyline02.svg—A Closed Polyline Shape

```
<?xml version="1.0" standalone="no"?>
<!DOCTYPE svg PUBLIC "-//W3C//DTD SVG 20010904//EN"
"http://www.w3.org/TR/2001/REC-SVG-20010904/DTD/svg10.dtd">
<svg width="500" height="300">
```

LISTING 3.13 Continued

```
<polyline style="stroke:#000000; stroke-width:2; fill:#CCCCCC;"
  points="30,200 30,50 130,50 30,200" />
<polyline style="stroke:#000000; stroke-width:2; fill:none;"
  points="230,200 230,50 330,50 230,200" />
</svg>
```

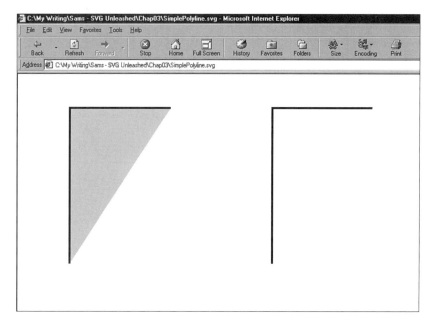

FIGURE 3.10 A filled and nonfilled polyline.

As you can see in Figure 3.11, which is zoomed and panned, Listing 3.13 creates two triangles, one filled and one that lacks a fill. You can create closed shapes with an arbitrary number of sides using the same technique, but the `polygon` element described in the next section is specifically designed to create such shapes. The advantage of the polygon is that the point at which the shape is closed has a neat line join, while the line join for the `polyline` elements is not sharp, as you can see if you zoom in on the bottom vertex of either of the triangles when you run Listing 3.13.

A polyline element may be animated by any of the SVG animation elements—`animate`, `set`, `animateColor`, `animateMotion`, or `animateTransform`—which are described in Chapter 11.

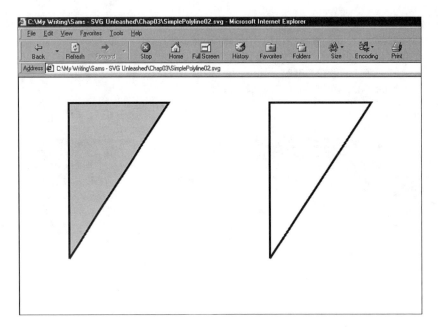

FIGURE 3.11   Two closed polyline shapes.

The polygon Element

The `polygon` element is designed to create closed shapes, the edges of which consist of multiple (that is, three or more) straight lines. The syntax of the `polygon` element is essentially identical to that of the `polyline` element. Listing 3.14, SimplePolygons.svg, was created by simply replacing `polyline` with `polygon` in the start tags of Listing 3.13.

LISTING 3.14   SimplePolygons.svg—Two Simple Polygon Shapes

```
<?xml version="1.0" standalone="no"?>
<!DOCTYPE svg PUBLIC "-//W3C//DTD SVG 20010904//EN"
"http://www.w3.org/TR/2001/REC-SVG-20010904/DTD/svg10.dtd">
<svg width="500" height="300">
<polygon style="stroke:#000000; stroke-width:2; fill:#CCCCCC;"
  points="30,200 30,50 130,50 30,200" />
<polygon style="stroke:#000000; stroke-width:2; fill:none;"
  points="230,200 230,50 330,50 230,200" />
</svg>
```

Not surprisingly, the visual appearance produced is identical to that shown in Figure 3.11 in the preceding section, except that zooming in on the bottom vertex of either triangle shows that the `polygon` element produces a sharp, neat line join.

A polygon element may be animated by any of the SVG animation elements—animate, set, animateColor, animateMotion, or animateTransform—which are described in Chapter 11.

Color in SVG

Hitherto, we have used only one of the three possible syntaxes to refer to the color of the stroke or fill of SVG elements. Let's take a closer look at the syntax options for defining color.

SVG provides two separate numeric syntaxes for defining the color of the stroke (outline) or fill of SVG graphic shapes. In addition, for certain commonly used colors, a third option exists—using a named color. I suggest you avoid named colors except for simple colors such as black, red, and white because the numeric syntax provides far more color options.

> **NOTE**
>
> The SVG 1.0 specification allows an ICC color profile to be specified.

For example, Listing 3.15, ColorSyntaxes.svg, shows three lines, each of which has an identical appearance onscreen. Each of the three lines is red. The first line element uses the syntax #FF0000 to describe the red color. The # character is essential. If you omit it, you will typically find that you have inadvertently produced a black outline or fill, rather than the color you intended. Following the # character are three couplets in hexadecimal notation. The first couplet, FF, indicates a red color value of 255 (hexadecimal FF); the second, 00, indicates a 0 value for the green color value; and the third, 00, indicates a 0 value for the blue color value.

> **TIP**
>
> If you use the red, green, and blue components of the color value as paired numbers—for example, #CCFFCC—you can write those values as #CFC, which will be interpreted as meaning the same as #CCFFCC by the SVG rendering engine.

The second line element expresses the same color, red, by using the syntax rgb(255,0,0). Notice that the full use of red is expressed as 255, not as 100, as may be the case in some other graphics settings. The third line element simply uses the name "red" to produce the same color onscreen. SVG provides a significant number of named colors.

> **NOTE**
>
> When using the rgb(...) syntax, you can use percentages. Thus, rgb(255,0,0) and rgb(100%, 0%, 0%) mean the same and produce a red color onscreen.

LISTING 3.15　ColorSyntaxes.svg—Using the Three Syntaxes to Specify Color

```
<?xml version="1.0" standalone="no"?>
<!DOCTYPE svg PUBLIC "-//W3C//DTD SVG 20010904//EN"
"http://www.w3.org/TR/2001/REC-SVG-20010904/DTD/svg10.dtd">
<svg width="300" height="300">
<line x1="20" y1="20" x2="220" y2="20"
 style="stroke:#FF0000; stroke-width:4"/>
<line x1="20" y1="40" x2="220" y2="40"
 style="stroke:rgb(255,0,0); stroke-width:4"/>
<line x1="20" y1="60" x2="220" y2="60"
 style="stroke:red; stroke-width:4"/>
</svg>
```

If you run the code and examine the output onscreen, you can see that the three lines are identical in appearance.

> **CAUTION**
>
> One of the few situations in which letters are not case sensitive occurs when you use the letters in a color value expressed as hexadecimal. This is true because the use of hexadecimal letters (as numbers) existed before XML was created. Be sure to use lowercase only for rgb(12,23,34) because those letters are case sensitive.

SVG is rendered on the client machine, which opens up the possibilities of removing restrictions imposed in Web-safe palettes. Instead of a color cube of 6 colors × 6 colors × 6 colors, the SVG designer or developer can use a color cube that is 255 colors × 255 colors × 255 colors, thus greatly increasing the creative possibilities available in graphics delivered across the Web.

Additionally, as shown earlier in the chapter, SVG colors can have a variable opacity applied to any color in a graphic. No longer is transparency limited to a single color that must be fully transparent. In SVG images, any color may be transparent, fully opaque, or any of a potentially infinite number of semitransparent variants. In addition, the opacity of any part of a graphic may be animated using SVG declarative animation.

The SVG DOM interfaces for the SVGColor object are described in Chapter 4.

Gradients in SVG

As well as allowing a greater choice of solid colors, SVG provides elements to allow us to create color gradients. A gradient is a change in color value along a line. For example, a rectangle could be blue at one side and gradually change to pale gray on the other side. In SVG terminology, that is a linear gradient.

In SVG, gradients may be applied to either the stroke or fill of an SVG shape, or both if you prefer. SVG provides two elements, the linearGradient element and the radialGradient element, that, respectively describe linear and radial gradients.

Linear Gradients

A gradient is typically defined using the relevant SVG gradient element nested within a defs element, where all definitions that are to be used elsewhere in an SVG document are located. The relevant element in the definition section is then referenced using a "bare names" form of XPointer as the value of the relevant property of the graphic shape. For example, to define and use a simple linear gradient for a line, we could use code like that shown in Listing 3.16.

LISTING 3.16   SimpleLinearGradient.svg—An SVG Linear Gradient

```
<?xml version="1.0" standalone="no"?>
<!DOCTYPE svg PUBLIC "-//W3C//DTD SVG 20010904//EN"
"http://www.w3.org/TR/2001/REC-SVG-20010904/DTD/svg10.dtd">
<svg width="" height="">
<defs>
<linearGradient id="FirstGradient" >
 <stop offset="0%" style="stop-color:#FF00FF"/>
 <stop offset="100%" style="stop-color:#FFFF00"/>
</linearGradient>
</defs>
<line x1="50" y1="70" x2="250" y2="70"
 style="stroke:url(#FirstGradient); stroke-width:6"/>
</svg>
```

The visual appearance produced is a line that is magenta in color at the left, gradually changing to yellow at the right end of the line. To see the gradient best, you need to run the code onscreen, but Figure 3.12 may give you some indication of the visual appearance.

Notice that the linear gradient is defined in a linearGradient element nested within the defs element of the SVG document:

```
<defs>
<linearGradient id="FirstGradient" >
 <stop offset="0%" style="stop-color:#FF00FF"/>
 <stop offset="100%" style="stop-color:#FFFF00"/>
</linearGradient>
</defs>
```

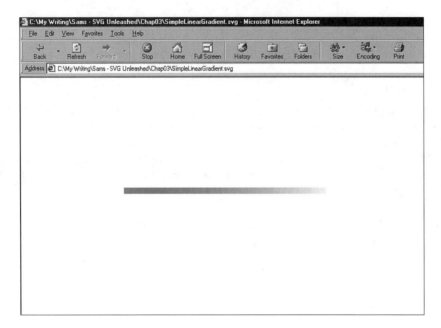

FIGURE 3.12   A horizontal SVG linear gradient.

This code snippet defines only a horizontal linear gradient from magenta on the left to yellow on the right. If it is not referenced elsewhere in the SVG document by an SVG element that is to be rendered, the presence of the gradient within the definitions of the document has no effect on the visual appearance produced by the SVG rendering engine. Thus, the code

```
<line x1="50" y1="70" x2="250" y2="70"
 style="stroke:url(#FirstGradient); stroke-width:6"/>
```

which references the gradient, is essential to produce a visual effect from the gradient onscreen.

Linear gradients in SVG may be horizontal, vertical, or may be applied diagonally. The default behavior is to produce a horizontal gradient. A linear gradient may have two stop colors, as shown in the earlier example, or may have several, thus producing a number of color transitions within a single graphic.

Let's look at a number of the options for using a linear gradient in SVG. First, let's look at how to apply simple horizontal gradients to the stroke and/or fill of SVG shapes.

Listing 3.17 illustrates the use of three gradients to control the appearance of a linear gradient in the stroke of three SVG line elements.

LISTING 3.17   StrokeGradients.svg—Linear Gradients in line Elements

```
<?xml version="1.0" standalone="no"?>
<!DOCTYPE svg PUBLIC "-//W3C//DTD SVG 20010904//EN"
"http://www.w3.org/TR/2001/REC-SVG-20010904/DTD/svg10.dtd">
<svg width="400" height="500">
<defs>
<linearGradient id="Gradient1" >
 <stop offset="0%" style="stop-color:#FF0000"/>
 <stop offset="100%" style="stop-color:#00FF00"/>
</linearGradient>
<linearGradient id="Gradient2" >
 <stop offset="0%" style="stop-color:#0000FF"/>
 <stop offset="100%" style="stop-color:#FFFFFF"/>
</linearGradient>
<linearGradient id="Gradient3" >
 <stop offset="0%" style="stop-color:#FFFF00"/>
 <stop offset="100%" style="stop-color:#0000FF"/>
</linearGradient>
</defs>
<line x1="20" y1="20" x2="220" y2="20"
 style="stroke:url(#Gradient1); stroke-width:4"/>
<line x1="20" y1="40" x2="220" y2="40"
 style="stroke:url(#Gradient2); stroke-width:4"/>
<line x1="20" y1="60" x2="220" y2="60"
 style="stroke:url(#Gradient3); stroke-width:4"/>
</svg>
```

As you can see in Figure 3.13, which is zoomed and panned, we again have three lines. If you download and run the code, you will see that each of the three lines has a simple linear gradient, but the color values for each gradient are distinct. The first line has a gradient from red at the left to green at the right. The second line has a gradient from blue at the left to white at the right, and the third line has a linear gradient from yellow at the left to blue at the right.

We can apply similar gradients to the fill of shapes. For example, we can create simple linear gradients in the fill of SVG rect elements, as well as in the fill of other graphic shapes. Listing 3.18 shows how simple linear gradients can be applied to rectangular shapes, such as those you might use in a bar chart.

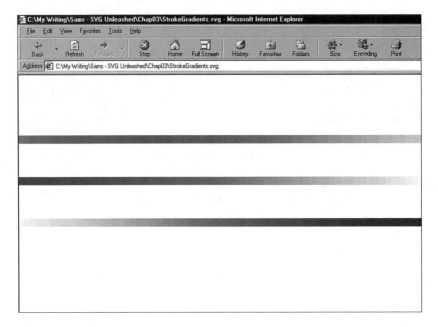

FIGURE 3.13   Three linear gradients on line elements.

LISTING 3.18   FillGradients.svg—Applying a Linear Gradient to the Fill of a Shape

```
<?xml version="1.0" standalone="no"?>
<!DOCTYPE svg PUBLIC "-//W3C//DTD SVG 20010904//EN"
"http://www.w3.org/TR/2001/REC-SVG-20010904/DTD/svg10.dtd">
<svg width="400" height="500">
<defs>
<linearGradient id="Gradient1" >
 <stop offset="0%" style="stop-color:#FF0000"/>
 <stop offset="100%" style="stop-color:#00FF00"/>
</linearGradient>
<linearGradient id="Gradient2" >
 <stop offset="0%" style="stop-color:#0000FF"/>
 <stop offset="100%" style="stop-color:#FFFFFF"/>
</linearGradient>
<linearGradient id="Gradient3" >
 <stop offset="0%" style="stop-color:#FFFF00"/>
 <stop offset="100%" style="stop-color:#0000FF"/>
</linearGradient>
</defs>
<rect x="40" y="25" width="300" height="75"
```

LISTING 3.18   Continued

```
 style="stroke:red; fill:url(#Gradient1)"/>
<rect x="40" y="175" width="300" height="75"
 style="stroke:red; fill:url(#Gradient2)"/>
<rect x="40" y="325" width="300" height="75"
 style="stroke:red; fill:url(#Gradient3)"/>
</svg>
```

Each rectangle has a red stroke. The fill of each rectangle is defined in the `linearGradient` elements, which are then referenced by the `fill` property of the `style` attribute of each `rect` element. For example, we apply the previously defined linear gradient to the fill of the top rectangle using the following code:

```
style="stroke:red; fill:url(#Gradient1)"
```

Up to this point, we have relied on the default behavior of the SVG rendering engine to produce a horizontal linear gradient. We can make that explicit by adding x1, y1, x2, and y2 attributes to the `linearGradient` element nested within the `defs` element. Listing 3.19 shows how this is done.

LISTING 3.19   ExplicitHorizGradients.svg—Creating Horizontal Gradients Explicitly

```
<?xml version="1.0" standalone="no"?>
<!DOCTYPE svg PUBLIC "-//W3C//DTD SVG 20010904//EN"
"http://www.w3.org/TR/2001/REC-SVG-20010904/DTD/svg10.dtd">
<svg width="400" height="500">
<defs>
<linearGradient x1="0%" y1="0%" x2="100%" y2="0%" id="Gradient1" >
 <stop offset="0%" style="stop-color:#FF0000"/>
 <stop offset="100%" style="stop-color:#00FF00"/>
</linearGradient>
<linearGradient x1="0%" y1="0%" x2="100%" y2="0%" id="Gradient2" >
 <stop offset="0%" style="stop-color:#0000FF"/>
 <stop offset="100%" style="stop-color:#FFFFFF"/>
</linearGradient>
<linearGradient x1="0%" y1="0%" x2="100%" y2="0%" id="Gradient3" >
 <stop offset="0%" style="stop-color:#FFFF00"/>
 <stop offset="100%" style="stop-color:#0000FF"/>
</linearGradient>
</defs>
<rect x="40" y="25" width="300" height="75"
 style="stroke:red; fill:url(#Gradient1)"/>
<rect x="40" y="175" width="300" height="75"
 style="stroke:red; fill:url(#Gradient2)"/>
```

LISTING 3.19   Continued

```
<rect x="40" y="325" width="300" height="75"
 style="stroke:red; fill:url(#Gradient3)"/>
</svg>
```

Notice that the values of the x1 and x2 attributes of each linearGradient element differ, indicating that the gradient changes on a horizontal axis, that is, as we move from the x1 to x2 positions. The visual appearance is as before.

We can produce a vertical gradient in each rectangle by making the values of the x1 and x2 attributes the same, indicating no change in the gradient along a horizontal axis, and by introducing a difference in the values of the y1 and y2 attributes, indicating that there is a change in the appearance of the gradient along the y axis; that is, it is a vertical gradient. Listing 3.20 shows how to do this.

LISTING 3.20   ExplicitVertGradients.svg—Creating Vertical Gradients in SVG

```
<?xml version="1.0" standalone="no"?>
<!DOCTYPE svg PUBLIC "-//W3C//DTD SVG 20010904//EN"
"http://www.w3.org/TR/2001/REC-SVG-20010904/DTD/svg10.dtd">
<svg width="400" height="500">
<defs>
<linearGradient x1="0%" y1="0%" x2="0%" y2="100%" id="Gradient1" >
 <stop offset="0%" style="stop-color:#FF0000"/>
 <stop offset="100%" style="stop-color:#00FF00"/>
</linearGradient>
<linearGradient x1="0%" y1="0%" x2="0%" y2="100%" id="Gradient2" >
 <stop offset="0%" style="stop-color:#0000FF"/>
 <stop offset="100%" style="stop-color:#FFFFFF"/>
</linearGradient>
<linearGradient x1="0%" y1="0%" x2="0%" y2="100%" id="Gradient3" >
 <stop offset="0%" style="stop-color:#FFFF00"/>
 <stop offset="100%" style="stop-color:#0000FF"/>
</linearGradient>
</defs>
<rect x="40" y="25" width="300" height="75"
 style="stroke:red; fill:url(#Gradient1)"/>
<rect x="40" y="175" width="300" height="75"
 style="stroke:red; fill:url(#Gradient2)"/>
<rect x="40" y="325" width="300" height="75"
 style="stroke:red; fill:url(#Gradient3)"/>
</svg>
```

You have seen how we can explicitly produce a horizontal gradient by specifying differing values for the x1 and x2 attributes of the linearGradient element and how we can produce a vertical gradient by using different values for the y1 and y2 attributes. To produce a diagonal gradient, we simply ensure that both attribute pairs—the x1 and x2 and y1 and y2 attributes—have different values. Listing 3.21 shows this in practice.

LISTING 3.21   SimpleDiagonalGradient.svg—A Diagonal Linear Gradient

```
<?xml version="1.0" standalone="no"?>
<!DOCTYPE svg PUBLIC "-//W3C//DTD SVG 20010904//EN"
"http://www.w3.org/TR/2001/REC-SVG-20010904/DTD/svg10.dtd">
<svg width="400" height="500">
<defs>
<linearGradient x1="0%" y1="0%" x2="100%" y2="100%" id="Gradient2" >
 <stop offset="0%" style="stop-color:#0000FF"/>
 <stop offset="100%" style="stop-color:#FF0000"/>
</linearGradient>
</defs>
<rect x="40" y="25" width="300" height="300"
 style="stroke:red; fill:url(#Gradient2)"/>
</svg>
```

Onscreen you will see a square that is blue in the top-left corner, shading through various shades of purple down and to the right, finishing with red in the bottom-right corner.

As well as specifying a stop-color property for each stop element, you may also specify a stop-opacity property, thus allowing partially transparent gradients to be created.

Radial Gradients

Producing a radial gradient rather than a linear gradient requires a syntax that is very similar to that for a linear gradient. The radialGradient element is nested within a defs element and has an id attribute that is then referenced as the fill or stroke property of an SVG graphic shape. The syntax of the radialGradient element differs slightly, as you can see in Listing 3.22.

LISTING 3.22   SimpleRadialGradient.svg—Creating a Simple Radial Gradient in SVG

```
<?xml version="1.0" standalone="no"?>
<!DOCTYPE svg PUBLIC "-//W3C//DTD SVG 20010904//EN"
"http://www.w3.org/TR/2001/REC-SVG-20010904/DTD/svg10.dtd">
<svg width="400" height="400">
<defs>
<radialGradient id="FirstRadialGradient" gradientUnits="userSpaceOnUse"
```

LISTING 3.22   Continued

```
  cx="200" cy="200" r="150" fx="200" fy="200">
  <stop offset="0%" style="stop-color:#FF00FF"/>
  <stop offset="25%" style="stop-color:#00FF00"/>
  <stop offset="50%" style="stop-color:#FFFF00"/>
  <stop offset="75%" style="stop-color:#0000FF"/>
  <stop offset="100%" style="stop-color:#FFFF00"/>
</radialGradient>
</defs>
<rect x="0" y="0" width="400" height="400"
 style="fill:url(#FirstRadialGradient);"/>
</svg>
```

The cx and cy attributes on the radialGradient element define the center position of the gradient. The r attribute defines the radius over which the radius applies. The fx and fy attributes define the focal point for the gradient.

The visual appearance produced onscreen is pretty strident but does give you some indication of the types of visual effects that can be produced using radial gradients. Figure 3.14 shows the onscreen appearance when Listing 3.22 is run.

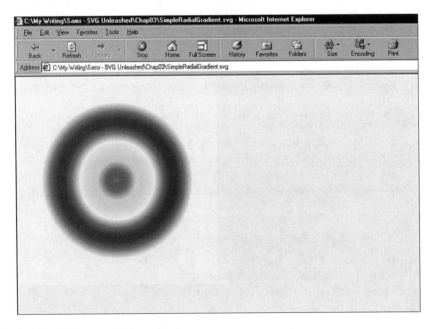

FIGURE 3.14   A vibrant radial gradient.

Radial gradients on a much smaller scale can, when combined with declarative animation elements, be used to create visually unmissable markers for important content. Be careful, however, not to overdo the effect, or you may simply irritate the users.

SVG Patterns

Many visual objects have some kind of periodicity or pattern in their appearance. Likely, you will want to mimic that effect onscreen. The SVG `pattern` element provides us with a technique to create repeating visual patterns.

An SVG pattern is defined within a `pattern` element, typically nested within a `defs` element. The `pattern` element must have an `id` attribute to allow the pattern to be referenced as the paint to be used in a `fill` or `stroke` property later in the document.

A `pattern` element, apart from a necessary `id` attribute, has `x`, `y`, `width`, and `height` attributes, which define part of how the pattern will be laid out onscreen. In addition, this element has a `viewBox` attribute, which can be used to adjust the scaling of the pattern. The element or elements nested within the `pattern` element define the shape or shapes that make up a pattern. In Listing 3.23, there is single `rect` element nested within the `pattern` element, creating a pattern that consists of rectangles, which are used to fill an ellipse shape.

Listing 3.23 illustrates the use of the `pattern` element.

LISTING 3.23   RectPattern.svg—A Straightforward SVG Pattern

```
<?xml version="1.0" standalone="no"?>
<!DOCTYPE svg PUBLIC "-//W3C//DTD SVG 20010904//EN"
"http://www.w3.org/TR/2001/REC-SVG-20010904/DTD/svg10.dtd">
<svg width="600px" height="500px" viewBox="0 0 600 500"
xmlns="http://www.w3.org/2000/svg">
<defs>
<pattern id="RectanglePattern" patternUnits="userSpaceOnUse"
x="0" y="0" width="100" height="100" viewBox="0 0 20 20" >
<rect x="0" y="0" width="10" height="5" fill="red"/>
</pattern>
</defs>
<rect fill="none" stroke="red" x="1" y="1" width="598" height="498"/>
<ellipse fill="url(#RectanglePattern)" stroke="black" stroke-width="5"
cx="300" cy="200" rx="250" ry="150" />
</svg>
```

Figure 3.15 shows the visual appearance produced by Listing 3.23.

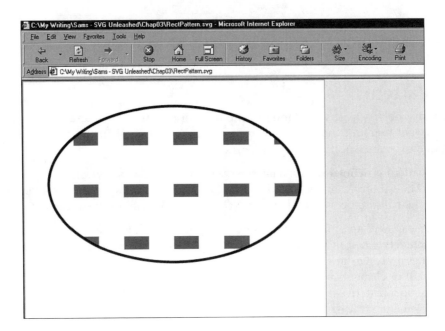

FIGURE 3.15   A pattern of rectangles contained in an ellipse.

By altering values in the viewBox attribute of the pattern element, we can adjust the periodicity of the pattern. In Listing 3.24, we alter the final value in the viewBox attribute from 20 to 10. Effectively, that means we double the repeat of the pattern in a vertical direction.

LISTING 3.24   RectPattern02.svg—Altering the Vertical Periodicity of the Pattern

```
<?xml version="1.0" standalone="no"?>
<!DOCTYPE svg PUBLIC "-//W3C//DTD SVG 20010904//EN"
"http://www.w3.org/TR/2001/REC-SVG-20010904/DTD/svg10.dtd">
<svg width="600px" height="500px" viewBox="0 0 600 500"
xmlns="http://www.w3.org/2000/svg">
<defs>
<pattern id="RectanglePattern" patternUnits="userSpaceOnUse"
x="0" y="0" width="100" height="50" viewBox="0 0 20 10" >
<rect x="0" y="0" width="10" height="5" fill="red"/>
</pattern>
</defs>
<rect fill="none" stroke="red"
```

LISTING 3.24   Continued

```
x="1" y="1" width="598" height="498"/>
<ellipse fill="url(#RectanglePattern)" stroke="black" stroke-width="5"
cx="300" cy="200" rx="250" ry="150" />
</svg>
```

Figure 3.16 shows the doubling of the vertical periodicity of the pattern.

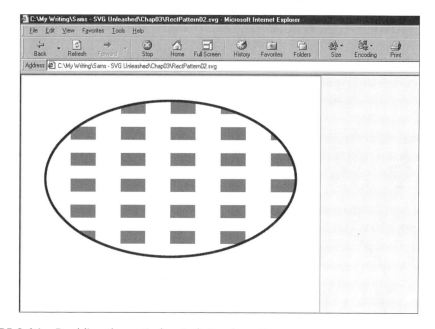

FIGURE 3.16   Doubling the vertical periodicity of a pattern.

The `patternTransform` attribute permits us to transform the individual components of the pattern. Listing 3.25 shows a skew transform applied to the rectangles that made up the pattern in Listing 3.23, RectPattern.svg. Transforms are described in Chapter 7, "Transformations in SVG."

LISTING 3.25   RectPattern03.svg—Using the patternTransform Attribute

```
<?xml version="1.0" standalone="no"?>
<!DOCTYPE svg PUBLIC "-//W3C//DTD SVG 20010904//EN"
"http://www.w3.org/TR/2001/REC-SVG-20010904/DTD/svg10.dtd">
<svg width="600px" height="500px" viewBox="0 0 600 500"
xmlns="http://www.w3.org/2000/svg">
<defs>
```

LISTING 3.25   Continued

```
<pattern id="RectanglePattern" patternUnits="userSpaceOnUse"
x="0" y="0" width="100" height="100" viewBox="0 0 20 20"
 patternTransform="skewX(15)">
<rect x="0" y="0" width="10" height="5" fill="red"/>
</pattern>
</defs>
<rect fill="none" stroke="red" x="1" y="1" width="598" height="498"/>
<ellipse fill="url(#RectanglePattern)" stroke="black" stroke-width="5"
cx="300" cy="200" rx="250" ry="150" />
</svg>
```

Figure 3.17 shows the skewed rectangles that create the modified pattern as defined by the `patternTransform` attribute.

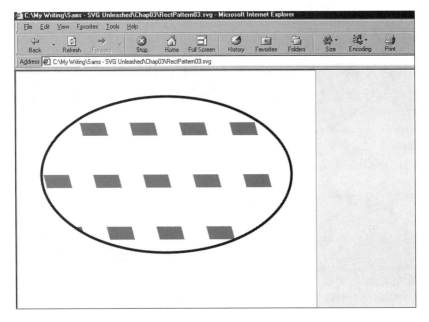

FIGURE 3.17   Using a skew transform in the patternTransform attribute.

Patterns can be used in many ways. Many different graphic shapes, including path elements, may be nested within a pattern element definition. Therefore, any arbitrary shape can be used in an SVG pattern. To achieve a particular effect, you need to choose appropriate element content for the pattern element and likely adjust one or several of the attributes. In Chapter 21, "SVG and Perl," an example is developed using SVG and Perl.

SVG DOM Interfaces for the SVG Basic Shapes

In this section, we will examine the SVG DOM interfaces that correspond to the SVG elements we looked at earlier in the chapter. The interfaces are described in an order similar to that in which elements were presented earlier in the chapter.

The SVGLineElement Object

The SVGLineElement object is the SVG DOM representation of a line element. The SVGLineElement object is accessed when you want to manipulate a line element in an SVG document. The properties of the SVGLineElement object correspond closely to the attributes of a line element.

The SVGLineElement object has the properties and methods of the SVGElement object (described in Chapter 2, "Document Structure in SVG"), the SVGTests object, the SVGLangSpace object, the SVGExternalResourcesRequired object, the SVGStylable object, the SVGTransformable object, and the EventTarget object of the DOM 2 Events specification.

The SVGLineElement object has the following properties:

- x1—of type SVGAnimatedLength
- y1—of type SVGAnimatedLength
- x2—of type SVGAnimatedLength
- y2—of type SVGAnimatedLength

The SVGLineElement object has no methods specific to it.

The SVGRectElement Object

The SVGRectElement object is the SVG DOM representation of a rect element. The SVGRectElement object allows the attributes of a rect element to be accessed and manipulated using a scripting language. The properties of the SVGRectElement object correspond closely to the attributes of a rect element.

The SVGRectElement object has the properties and methods of the SVGElement object (described in Chapter 2), the SVGTests object, the SVGLangSpace object, the SVGExternalResourcesRequired object, the SVGStylable object, the SVGTransformable object, and the EventTarget object of the DOM 2 Events specification.

In addition, the SVGRectElement object has the following properties:

- x—of type SVGAnimatedLength
- y—of type SVGAnimatedLength
- width—of type SVGAnimatedLength

- height—of type SVGAnimatedLength

- rx—of type SVGAnimatedLength

- ry—of type SVGAnimatedLength

The SVGRectElement object has no methods specific to it.

The SVGCircleElement Object

The SVGCircleElement object is the SVG DOM representation of a circle element. The SVGCircleElement object allows the attributes of a circle element to be accessed and manipulated programmatically. The properties of the SVGCircleElement object correspond closely to the attributes of a circle element.

The SVGCircleElement object has the properties and methods of the SVGElement object (described in Chapter 2), the SVGTests object, the SVGLangSpace object, the SVGExternalResourcesRequired object, the SVGStylable object, the SVGTransformable object, and the EventTarget object of the DOM 2 Events specification.

The SVGCircleElement object has the following properties:

- cx—of type SVGAnimatedLength

- cy—of type SVGAnimatedLength

- r—of type SVGAnimatedLength

The SVGCircleElement object has no methods specific to it.

The SVGEllipseElement Object

The SVGEllipseElement object is the SVG DOM representation of an ellipse element. The properties of the SVGEllipseElement object correspond closely to the attributes of an ellipse element.

The SVGEllipseElement object has the properties and methods of the SVGElement object (described in Chapter 2), the SVGTests object, the SVGLangSpace object, the SVGExternalResourcesRequired object, the SVGStylable object, the SVGTransformable object, and the EventTarget object of the DOM 2 Events specification.

The SVGEllipseElement object has the following properties:

- cx—of type SVGAnimatedLength

- cy—of type SVGAnimatedLength

- rx—of type SVGAnimatedLength

- ry—of type SVGAnimatedLength

The `SVGEllipseElement` object has no methods specific to it.

The SVGPolylineElement Object

The `SVGPolylineElement` object is the SVG DOM representation of a `polyline` element.

The `SVGPolylineElement` object has the properties and methods of the `SVGElement` object (described in Chapter 2), the `SVGTests` object, the `SVGLangSpace` object, the `SVGExternalResourcesRequired` object, the `SVGStylable` object, the `SVGTransformable` object, the `SVGAnimatedPoints` object, and the `EventTarget` object of the DOM 2 Events specification.

The `SVGPolylineElement` object has no specific properties or methods.

The SVGPolygonElement Object

The `SVGPolygonElement` object is the SVG DOM representation of a `polygon` element.

The `SVGPolygonElement` object has the properties and methods of the `SVGElement` object (described in Chapter 2), the `SVGTests` object, the `SVGLangSpace` object, the `SVGExternalResourcesRequired` object, the `SVGStylable` object, the `SVGTransformable` object, the `SVGAnimatedPoints` object, and the `EventTarget` object of the DOM 2 Events specification.

The `SVGPolygonElement` object has no specific properties or methods.

Other SVG DOM Interfaces

This section describes SVG DOM objects other than those that relate to the basic graphic shape elements and that relate to topics discussed earlier in this chapter.

The SVGGradientElement Object

Three SVG DOM objects are directly related to the `linearGradient` and `radialGradient` elements: the `SVGGradientElement` object, the `SVGLinearGradientElement` object, and the `SVGRadialGradientElement` object.

The `SVGGradientElement` object has the properties and methods of the `SVGElement` object (described in Chapter 2), the `SVGURIReference` object, the `SVGExternalResourcesRequired` object, the `SVGStylable` object, and the `SVGUnitTypes` object.

The `SVGGradientElement` object has the following constants associated with it:

- `SVGGradientElement.SVG_SPREADMETHOD_UNKNOWN`—This constant is of type `short` and has a value of `0`.

- `SVGGradientElement.SVG_SPREADMETHOD_PAD`—This constant is of type `short` and has a value of `1`.

- SVGGradientElement.SVG_SPREADMETHOD_REFLECT—This constant is of type short and has a value of 2.

- SVGGradientElement.SVG_SPREADMETHOD_REPEAT—This constant is of type short and has a value of 3.

The SVGGradientElement object has the following properties:

- gradientUnits—of type SVGAnimatedEnumeration

- gradientTransform—of type SVGAnimatedTransformList

- spreadMethod—of type SVGAnimatedEnumeration

The SVGGradientElement object has no specific methods.

The SVGLinearGradientElement Object

The SVGLinearGradientElement object is the DOM representation of the linearGradient element. The SVGLinearGradientElement object has the properties of the SVGGradientElement, plus the following properties:

- x1—of type SVGAnimatedLength

- y1—of type SVGAnimatedLength

- x2—of type SVGAnimatedLength

- y2—of type SVGAnimatedLength

The SVGLinearGradientElement object has no methods specific to it.

The SVGPaint Object

The SVGPaint object has the properties and methods of the SVGColor object (which is described in Chapter 4).

The SVGPaint object has the following constants associated with it:

- SVGPaint.SVG_PAINTTYPE_UNKNOWN—The constant is of type short and has a value of 0.

- SVGPaint.SVG_PAINTTYPE_RGBCOLOR—The constant is of type short and has a value of 1.

- SVGPaint.SVG_PAINTTYPE_RGBCOLOR_ICCCOLOR—The constant is of type short and has a value of 2.

- SVGPaint.SVG_PAINTTYPE_NONE—The constant is of type short and has a value of 101.

- SVGPaint.SVG_PAINTTYPE_CURRENTCOLOR—The constant is of type short and has a value of 102.

- SVGPaint.SVG_PAINTTYPE_URI_NONE—The constant is of type short and has a value of 103.

- SVGPaint.SVG_PAINTTYPE_URI_CURRENTCOLOR—The constant is of type short and has a value of 104.

- SVGPaint.SVG_PAINTTYPE_URI_RGBCOLOR—The constant is of type short and has a value of 105.

- SVGPaint.SVG_PAINTTYPE_URI_RGBCOLOR_ICCCOLOR—The constant is of type short and has a value of 106.

- SVGPaint.SVG_PAINTTYPE_URI—The constant is of type short and has a value of 107.

In addition, the SVGPaint object has the following properties:

- paintType—of type unsigned short

- uri—of type DOMString

The SVGPaint object has the following methods:

- setUri(*uri*)—The method returns a value of type void. The *uri* argument is of type DOMString.

- setPaint(*paintType*,*uri*,*rgbColor*,*iccColor*)—The method returns a value of type void. The *paintType* argument is of type unsigned short; the *uri*, *rgbColor*, and *iccColor* arguments are of type DOMString.

The SVGPatternElement Object

The SVGPatternElement object is the SVG DOM representation of the pattern element. The properties of the SVGPatternElement object correspond closely to the attributes of the pattern element.

The SVGPatternElement object has the properties and methods of the SVGElement object, the SVGURIReference object, the SVGTests object, the SVGLangSpace object, the SVGExternalResourcesRequired object, the SVGStylable obect, the SVGFitToViewBox object, and the SVGUnitTypes object.

In addition, the SVGPatternElement object has the following properties:

- patternUnits—of type SVGAnimatedEnumeration

- patternContentUnits—of type SVGAnimatedEnumeration

- patternTransform—of type SVGAnimatedTransformList

- x—of type SVGAnimatedLength

- y—of type SVGAnimatedLength

- width—of type SVGAnimatedLength

- height—of type SVGAnimatedLength

The SVGPatternElement object has no methods specific to it.

The SVGRadialGradientElement Object

The SVGRadialGradientElement object is the DOM representation of the radialGradient element. The SVGRadialGradientElement object has the properties of the SVGGradientElement, plus the following properties:

- cx—of type SVGAnimatedLength

- cy—of type SVGAnimatedLength

- r—of type SVGAnimatedLength

- fx—of type SVGAnimatedLength

- fy—of type SVGAnimatedLength

The SVGRadialGradientElement object has no methods specific to it.

The SVGStopElement Object

The SVGStopElement object has the properties and methods of the SVGElement object and the SVGStylable object.

In addition, the SVGStopElement object has the following property:

- offset—of type SVGAnimatedNumber

The SVGStopElement object has no methods specific to it.

The SVGSwitchElement Object

The SVGSwitchElement object has the properties and methods of the SVGElement object, the SVGTests object, the SVGLangSpace object, the SVGExternalResourcesRequired object, the SVGStylable object, the SVGTransformable object, and the DOM Level 2 Events EventTarget object (events::EventTarget).

To complete this section on the SVG DOM, let's look at an example of how to script an object representing an element described earlier in this chapter.

Creating a Line Using the SVG DOM

Listing 3.26 is an example of creating a line. The `line` element is created using the `createElement()` method of the `SVGDocument` object. The attributes needed to describe the position of the two ends of the `line` element and its `style` attribute are added using the `setAttribute()` method.

LISTING 3.26 MakeLine.svg—Creating a Line Using JavaScript and the SVG DOM

```
<?xml version="1.0" standalone="no"?>
<!DOCTYPE svg PUBLIC "-//W3C//DTD SVG 20010904//EN"
"http://www.w3.org/TR/2001/REC-SVG-20010904/DTD/svg10.dtd">
<svg width="400px" height="200px" onload="MakeLine()">
<script type="text/javascript">
<![CDATA[
function MakeLine(){
SVGDoc = evt.getTarget().getOwnerDocument();
SVGRoot = SVGDoc.getDocumentElement();
myLine = SVGDoc.createElement("line");
myLine.setAttribute("x1", 50);
myLine.setAttribute("y1", 100);
myLine.setAttribute("x2", 375);
myLine.setAttribute("y2", 100);
myLine.setAttribute("style", "stroke:red; stroke-width:4");
SVGRoot.appendChild(myLine);
}
]]>
</script>
<rect x="75" y="75" width="300" height="50" style="fill:red; opacity:0.4"/>
</svg>
```

Summary

This chapter introduced the basic SVG graphic shapes: the `line`, `rect`, `circle`, `ellipse`, `polyline`, and `polygon` elements. These elements allow commonly used regular shapes, such as lines, rectangles, and circles to be created. The attributes of these SVG elements are used to position them onscreen and to control their size and styling.

In addition, you saw how to use linear and radial gradients in SVG, as well as the syntax to create arbitrary patterns in your SVG images.

We also described the SVG DOM interfaces for the basic shapes, gradients, and patterns.

CHAPTER 4

Using CSS with SVG

The styling of any graphic is important in determining the visual impact it will have on the person viewing it and with respect to how much information it can convey. The use of styling to assist the conveying of information is crucial in modern Web graphics. Therefore, it is not surprising that SVG provides sophisticated and flexible means to style graphic shapes of all supported types as well as styling text.

In Chapters 1 to 3, you have already seen, in passing, styling being used in examples. This chapter will consider each of the five available techniques for applying styling in SVG in greater detail. The final part of the chapter will introduce the SVG DOM interfaces, which are particularly relevant to the styling of SVG documents.

What Is Styling in SVG?

SVG provides us with many techniques to alter the visual appearance of any arbitrary graphic shape. We can, for example, make a solid line or a dashed line, a thin line or a thick line, a black line or any other color of line, a fully opaque line or a semi-transparent line. We can specify that a shape has no fill or has a fill of a particular color. We can specify the size of a font to be used to display text; its color; whether it is normal, bold, or italic; and so on. All these presentation aspects of an SVG object can be defined using one or more of the techniques that SVG provides for the developer to have precise control of styling.

Styling in SVG is founded on the Cascading Style Sheets specifications, which are also produced by the W3C. Just as there are several ways to apply CSS styles to HTML elements, so SVG provides more than one way to apply styles to an SVG image. If you know how to use CSS with HTML or XHTML, parts of this chapter will seem familiar. The needs of the individual designer who wants to tweak the appearance of a single element are supported. Equally, at the other end of the spectrum, the needs to control site-wide corporate styles using external CSS style sheets are also supported in SVG.

This chapter will assume that you have some basic understanding of the Cascading Style Sheets Level 2 specifications. Many SVG styling properties are fully defined in the CSS2 documentation.

You can view the Cascading Style Sheets Level 2 specification at `http://www.w3.org/TR/1998/REC-CSS2-19980512`.

Why Do We Need Styles?

We need styles because graphics with styling information can be visually more attractive or more expressive of the information stored within the graphics. Listing 4.1 shows an unstyled simple SVG graphic, representing a highly simplified urban map.

LISTING 4.1   Unstyled.svg—Unstyled SVG Shapes

```
<?xml version="1.0" standalone="no"?>
<!DOCTYPE svg PUBLIC "-//W3C//DTD SVG 20010904//EN"
"http://www.w3.org/TR/2001/REC-SVG-20010904/DTD/svg10.dtd">
<svg width="" height="">
<line x1="0px" y1="0px" x2="1050px" y2="600px" />
<line x1="0px" y1="220px" x2="1050px" y2="220px" />
<line x1="0px" y1="290px" x2="1050px" y2="290px" />
<line x1="0px" y1="370px" x2="1050px" y2="370px" />
<line x1="400px" y1="0px" x2="400px" y2="1050px" />
</svg>
```

Figure 4.1 shows the appearance onscreen when Listing 4.1 is run. The information conveyed is limited because there is no way to distinguish the meaning of one line from another, apart from its coordinates. SVG images without styling information are dull.

Listing 4.2 shows the same graphic but with style information added.

LISTING 4.2   Styled.svg—Style Information Added to Listing 4.1

```
<?xml version="1.0" standalone="no"?>
<!DOCTYPE svg PUBLIC "-//W3C//DTD SVG 20010904//EN"
"http://www.w3.org/TR/2001/REC-SVG-20010904/DTD/svg10.dtd">
<svg width="" height="">
<line x1="0px" y1="0px" x2="100%" y2="1050px"
  style="stroke-dasharray:8,4; stroke:black; stroke-width:4"/>
<line x1="0px" y1="220px" x2="1050px" y2="220px"
  style="stroke:black; stroke-width:3"/>
```

LISTING 4.2   Continued

```
<line x1="0px" y1="290px" x2="1050px" y2="290px"
 style="stroke:blue; stroke-width:4"/>
<line x1="0px" y1="370px" x2="1050px" y2="370px"
 style="stroke:black; stroke-width:3"/>
<line x1="400px" y1="0px" x2="400px" y2="1050px"
 style="stroke:black; stroke-width:3"/>
</svg>
```

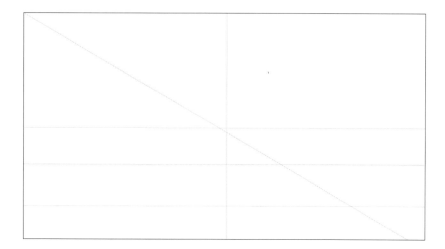

FIGURE 4.1   Unstyled line elements convey limited information.

Figure 4.2 shows the onscreen appearance when Listing 4.2 is run. The diagonal dashed line is instantly recognizable as different from the plain black lines. A familiarity with visual metaphor in some maps might, even in the absence of a legend, lead us to think the dashed line represents a railway. At a minimum, it strongly suggests a distinct meaning from the other uniform, solid black lines. Similarly, the fact that the middle horizontal line is blue (as you can see when you run the code) might lead us to conclude that it is a water feature such as a canal. If a legend that interprets the styling is provided, the diagram becomes much more information rich than its unstyled counterpart.

The power of styling is enormous. To exploit the power of SVG visually to compare information, we need to understand how to apply styling using SVG.

In addition to static styling information, SVG allows us to alter the appearance of SVG elements by means of declarative animation (described in Chapter 11, "SVG Animation Elements") or by means of scripting using languages such as JavaScript. For example, using SVG animation elements, we could cause objects of particular interest to flash, by changing the `stroke` or `fill` properties from one value to another. Or, using scripting, we could selectively show or hide selected elements by setting the `visibility` property to a value of `visible` or `hidden`. Such interactive styling allows customized highlighting of particular parts of a diagram or map that are of interest in a particular context or for particular users. Such interactive or dynamic uses of styling help us better to transmit information to the user.

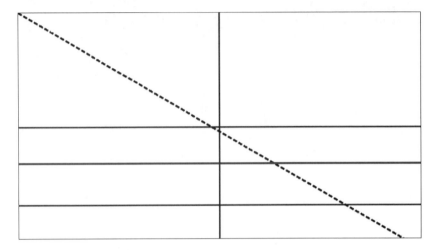

FIGURE 4.2   Styled line elements convey or hint at additional information.

How Is SVG Styling Information Expressed?

Style in SVG is expressed in terms of **styling properties**. Styling properties, broadly, can be divided into three types:

- Visual cues such as color, stroke width, and so on

- Text-specific properties such as font family and font size

- Techniques that affect how a graphic is rendered, such as clipping paths, masks, or filters

In this chapter, we will primarily consider the first two types of styling properties. Text-specific styling should be considered in the context of text layout, as described in Chapter 8, "Laying Out Text in SVG." Clipping paths and masking are described in Chapter 9, "Clipping, Masking, Compositing," and filters are described in Chapter 10, "SVG Filters."

Specifying a Style

SVG provides four CSS techniques to style a graphic shape:

- Individual CSS properties expressed as **presentation attributes**
- A `style` attribute containing a list of CSS declarations
- A `style` element that allows internal style sheets to be created
- External CSS style sheets

A fifth technique, the use of entities, is described in a following section.

These techniques are listed in decreasing order of priority. In other words, if a style is specified in an external style sheet, a style rule in an internal style sheet will override it. Similarly, a style rule in an internal style sheet will be overridden by either a `style` attribute or an individual style property such as `fill` or `stroke`.

For much of the remainder of this chapter, we will look at each of these four available styling techniques.

Individual Presentation Attributes

The first option for specifying styling properties on an SVG element is to use SVG attributes that individually correspond to single CSS properties. Such attributes are termed **presentation attributes**. We can consider each of the other techniques as convenient syntax to group these individual styling properties.

To specify the `stroke` and `stroke-width` properties of a `line` element, for example, we would write something like this:

```
<line x1="20px" y1="20px" x2="400px" y2="20px"
 stroke="red" stroke-width='4'/>
```

As you can see, the **attribute name** (which is also the name of the styling property) is followed by an equals sign and then the **attribute value** enclosed in a pair of double quotation marks or a pair of single quotation marks. This technique follows the syntax conventions for all XML and SVG attributes. In this simple example, the `stroke` and `stroke-width` properties are expressed as two separate presentation attributes.

> **CAUTION**
>
> When used in presentation attributes, the names of styling properties are case sensitive. In SVG, they are written as lowercase only. If you use styling property names within a style attribute or in style sheets, they are not case sensitive.

When to Use Individual Presentation Attributes

If you begin to hand-code lengthy SVG documents, you will soon find that the process of coding and maintaining individual presentation attributes is tedious. Imagine you have 10

SVG Web pages, each with 20 elements with individual presentation attributes, and restyling of the site is required. It would be tedious to change the individual values many times in many documents and very easy to overlook one or more presentation attributes.

The main use for individual presentation attributes in a production setting is locally to override a setting specified in, for example, an external CSS style sheet.

Properties Defined in CSS2

In this section, we will list and briefly describe the styling properties used in SVG that are defined by the CSS Level 2 specification. Examples using some of these properties will be demonstrated in following sections. Later in the chapter, we will go on to look at how to use these CSS properties in internal and external CSS style sheets.

The following font-related properties used in SVG are defined in CSS2:

- `font`—Provides a shorthand notation for setting `font-style`, `font-variant`, `font-weight`, `font-size`, `line-height`, and `font-family` properties

- `font-family`—Specifies which font family is to be used in rendering text, as a prioritized list of font family or generic family names

- `font-size`—Specifies the size of the font from baseline to baseline when in multiple consecutive lines of text

- `font-size-adjust`—Allows the x-height of a preferred font to be maintained in a substitute font

- `font-stretch`—Specifies the amount of stretch or compression of glyphs to be applied

- `font-style`—Specifies whether text is to be rendered as normal, italic, or oblique

- `font-variant`—Specifies whether normal lowercase glyphs or small caps are to be used

- `font-weight`—Defines the heaviness or lightness of the glyphs to be rendered, relative to members of the same font family

The following text properties are defined in CSS2:

- `direction`—Specifies whether text is written left-to-right or right-to-left

- `letter-spacing`—Specifies spacing between text characters, additional to any spacing specified in the `kerning` property

- `text-decoration`—Specifies text decoration, such as underline or line-through, which is to be applied to text

- `unicode-bidi`—Allows overriding of the Unicode bidirectionality algorithm

- `word-spacing`—Specifies spacing between words

> **NOTE**
>
> SVG uses the term *line-through* for what many people call **strikethrough**.

The following properties are also defined in CSS2:

- `clip`—Determines an initial clipping path

- `color`—Provides the `currentColor` for the `fill`, `stroke`, `stop-color`, `flood-color`, and `lighting-color` properties

- `cursor`—Specifies the appearance of the pointing device onscreen

- `display`—Indicates whether or how an SVG object is to be rendered

- `overflow`—Determines an initial clipping path

- `visibility`—Specifies whether the current graphics element is visible

Next, let's briefly look at the styling properties defined in SVG but not in CSS2.

Properties Not Defined in CSS2

The properties listed and briefly described in this section perform styling or quasi-styling functions but are not defined in the CSS Level 2 specification, but are part of the SVG specification.

The following SVG styling properties are related to clipping, masking, and compositing (see Chapter 9):

- `clip-path`—References a `clipPath` element to allow it to be rendered

- `clip-rule`—Specifies the clipping rule to be applied to elements contained within a `clipPath` element

- `mask`—References a `mask` element

- `opacity`—Specifies the opacity of an SVG object

The following SVG styling properties are related to the use of SVG filters (described in Chapter 10):

- `enable-background`—Specifies on **container elements** how the rendering engine manages the accumulating background image

- `filter`—Defines the filter to be applied to an element using a URI reference to the filter

- `flood-color`—Indicates the color to use to flood the current filter primitive sub-region

- `flood-opacity`—Indicates the opacity to use for the flood for the current filter primitive subregion

- `lighting-color`—Defines the lighting color to be used with filter primitives `feDiffuseLighting` and `feSpecularLighting`

The following styling properties are related to the use of gradients (described in Chapter 3, "Basic SVG Elements and Shapes"):

- `stop-color`—Specifies the stop color to be used in a gradient

- `stop-opacity`—Specifies the stop opacity to be used in a gradient

The following styling property relates to interactive events:

- `pointer-events`—Specifies whether an SVG object will respond to the onscreen pointer

The following styling properties relate to color and paint in SVG:

- `color-interpolation`—Controls the color space used for gradients and color animations

- `color-interpolation-filters`—Controls the color space used for filter effects

- `color-profile`—Specifies the color profile to be used (the default is `sRGB`)

- `color-rendering`—Indicates to the rendering engine whether speed or quality should be given priority

- `fill`—Defines the presence (or not) or color of the fill of an object

- `fill-opacity`—Specifies the opacity of the fill color of an SVG object

- `fill-rule`—Specifies the algorithm to be used to determine what parts of the SVG canvas are inside a shape

- `image-rendering`—Specifies to the rendering engine whether speed or quality should be prioritized when rendering an image

- `marker`—Specifies the marker symbol to be used at the vertices of a path or basic graphic shape

- `marker-end`—Defines the marker at the final vertex of a path or basic graphic shape

- `marker-mid`—Specifies the marker to be used when `marker-start` and `marker-end` do not apply

- `marker-start`—Defines the marker at the first vertex of a path or basic graphic shape

- `shape-rendering`—Specifies the trade-offs among speed, edge definition, and geometric precision when rendering an SVG object

- `stroke`—Defines the presence (or not) or color of the outline of a graphic object

- `stroke-dasharray`—Specifies the pattern for a dashed `stroke` of an SVG object

- `stroke-dashoffset`—Specifies the distance into a dash pattern at which the pattern should be started

- `stroke-linecap`—Specifies the shape to be used at the end of an open subpath when it is stroked

- `stroke-linejoin`—Specifies the shape to be used at corners of a path of basic graphic shape

- `stroke-miterlimit`—Specifies, when `stroke-linejoin` is `miter`, that stroke miter is limited to the value of `stroke-width`

- `stroke-opacity`—Allows the opacity of the stroke to be defined separately from the opacity of the fill (see `fill-opacity`)

- `stroke-width`—Specifies the width of the stroke (outline) of an SVG object.

The following text-related styling properties are defined in SVG but not in CSS:

- `alignment-baseline`—Specifies how an object is to be aligned relative to its parent

- `baseline-shift`—Allows the dominant baseline to be repositioned relative to the dominant baseline of its parent

- `dominant-baseline`—Determines or adjusts a scaled baseline table

- `glyph-orientation-horizontal`—Controls glyph orientation when inline progression direction is horizontal

- `glyph-orientation-vertical`—Controls glyph orientation when inline progression direction is vertical

- `kerning`—Specifies whether and how a rendering engine should adjust inter-glyph space based on kerning tables

- `text-anchor`—Specifies the alignment of text relative to a given point

- `text-rendering`—Specifies whether speed or precision should take precedence when rendering text

- `writing-mode`—Specifies whether the initial inline writing direction is left-to-right, right-to-left, or vertical

Having looked briefly at many styling properties, let's move on and look at some examples of how to use some commonly used styling properties.

The stroke and fill Properties

For many basic SVG graphic shapes, we will want to specify the color of the stroke (the outline) and the fill properties. Specifying these styling properties is straightforward using the hexadecimal or rgb color notations described in Chapter 3 or a named color when one is available. Listing 4.3 shows an example.

LISTING 4.3   FillAndStroke.svg—Using the stroke and fill Properties

```
<?xml version="1.0" standalone="no"?>
<!DOCTYPE svg PUBLIC "-//W3C//DTD SVG 20010904//EN"
"http://www.w3.org/TR/2001/REC-SVG-20010904/DTD/svg10.dtd">
<svg width="600px" height="500px">
<rect x="40px" y="40px" width="150px" height="100px"
 fill="#DDDDDD" stroke="blue" />
<rect x="240px" y="40px" width="150px" height="100px"
 fill="#FFFFCC" stroke="#FFCC00"/>
<rect x="440px" y="40px" width="150px" height="100px"
 fill="rgb(255,255,0)" stroke="#CC00CC"/>
</svg>
```

The stroke and fill properties in Listing 4.3 use all three of the color notations available in SVG 1.0.

The stroke-width and stroke-dasharray Properties

Examples of the stroke-width and stroke-dasharray properties were used in Chapter 3. The stroke-width property controls the width of a stroke (outline). The actual onscreen width of the stroke depends on the current user coordinate system. Coordinate systems are discussed in more detail in Chapter 5, "Coordinate Systems in SVG." Listing 4.4 shows how varying the stroke-width property depends on the user coordinate system. The coordinate system within nested svg elements is different for each of them, as specified by the value of the viewBox attribute.

LISTING 4.4   StrokeWidths.svg—Varying the stroke-width Property in Different User Coordinate Systems

```
<?xml version="1.0" standalone="no"?>
<!DOCTYPE svg PUBLIC "-//W3C//DTD SVG 20010904//EN"
"http://www.w3.org/TR/2001/REC-SVG-20010904/DTD/svg10.dtd">
<svg width="" height="">
<svg x="0px" y="0px" width="200px" height="600px"
 viewBox="0 0 100 300">
<line x1="0px" y1="20px" x2="200px" y2="20px"
 stroke-width="1" stroke="red"/>
```

LISTING 4.4 Continued

```
<line x1="0px" y1="40px" x2="200px" y2="40px"
 stroke-width="2" stroke="red"/>
<line x1="0px" y1="60px" x2="200px" y2="60px"
 stroke-width="4" stroke="red"/>
</svg> <!-- End of left coordinate system -->
<svg x="200px" y="0px" width="200px" height="600px"
 viewBox="0 0 200 600">
<line x1="0px" y1="40" x2="200px" y2="40"
 stroke-width="1" stroke="green"/>
<line x1="0px" y1="80" x2="200px" y2="80"
 stroke-width="2" stroke="green"/>
<line x1="0px" y1="120" x2="200px" y2="120"
 stroke-width="4" stroke="green"/>
</svg> <!-- End of middle coordinate system -->
<svg x="400px" y="0px" width="200px" height="600px"
 viewBox="0 0 50 150">
<line x1="0px" y1="10" x2="200px" y2="10"
 stroke-width="1" stroke="yellow"/>
<line x1="0px" y1="20" x2="200px" y2="20"
 stroke-width="2" stroke="yellow"/>
<line x1="0px" y1="30" x2="200px" y2="30"
 stroke-width="4" stroke="yellow"/>
</svg> <!-- End of right coordinate system -->
</svg>
```

In Figure 4.3 (slightly zoomed), you can see that the left (red) line is twice as wide as the middle (green) line and that the middle line is a quarter as wide as the right (yellow) line. But for each set of lines, the progression of values for stroke-width is 1, 2, 4. However, the viewBox attribute on each of the nested svg elements means that the scale in the viewports created by each of those svg elements is different. For the left, middle, and right nested svg elements, the scale is, respectively, 100 user units to 200 pixels, 200 user units to 200 pixels, and 50 user units to 200 pixels. Because, in the right nested svg coordinate system, a user unit equals 4 pixels, it is not surprising that a stroke-width of 4 (16 pixels) is wider onscreen than for the left, where a user unit equals 2 pixels (8 pixels total).

The visibility Property

The visibility property allows us to control whether a particular SVG graphics element is visible. Listing 4.5 shows a simple example.

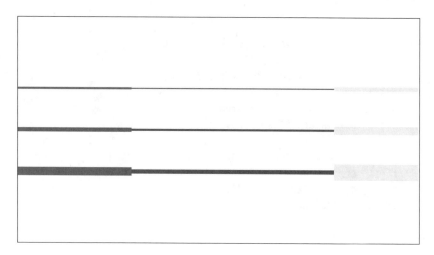

FIGURE 4.3   The effect of the stroke-width property depends on the user coordinate system.

LISTING 4.5   TextVisibility.svg—Setting the visibility Property on Text

```
<?xml version="1.0" standalone="no"?>
<!DOCTYPE svg PUBLIC "-//W3C//DTD SVG 20010904//EN"
"http://www.w3.org/TR/2001/REC-SVG-20010904/DTD/svg10.dtd">
<svg width="" height="">
<text x="30px" y="40px" font-family="Arial, sans-serif"
 font-size="28pt" visibility="visible">
This text should be visible
</text>
<text id="Clickable" x="30px" y="80px" font-family="Arial, sans-serif"
 font-size="28pt" visibility="visible" stroke="blue" fill="blue">
Click here
</text>
<text x="30px" y="140px" font-family="Arial, sans-serif"
 font-size="28pt" visibility="hidden">
<set attributeName="visibility" from="hidden" to="visible"
 begin="Clickable.click"/>
This text should now be visible, after you clicked
</text>
</svg>
```

The content of the third text element in Listing 4.5 is hidden when the SVG document loads, as you can see in Figure 4.4. Clicking on the content of the second text element alters the value of the visibility property of the third text element from hidden to `visible`. The content of the third `text` element is then visible onscreen, as you can see in Figure 4.5.

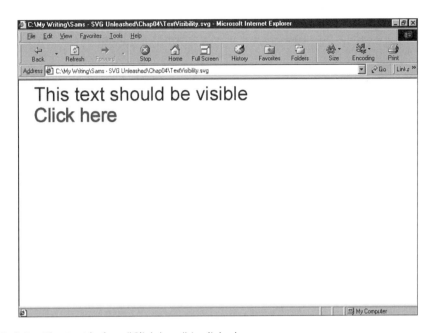

FIGURE 4.4   The text before "Click here" is clicked.

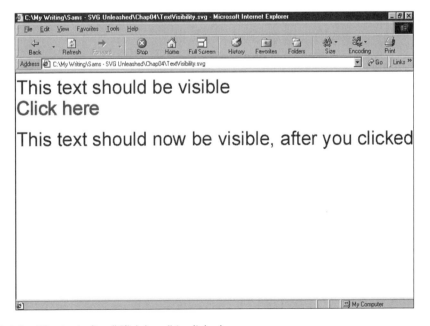

FIGURE 4.5   The text after "Click here" is clicked.

The way this type of declarative animation works is discussed in Chapter 11.

The pointer-events Property

The `pointer-events` property does not change the visual appearance of a graphic object. However, it does affect how that graphic object responds to pointer events, such as moving the mouse over the object.

Listing 4.6 shows an example of how setting `pointer-events` to none alters the behavior of the cursor.

LISTING 4.6   PointerEvents.svg—A pointer-events Property Example

```
<?xml version="1.0" standalone="no"?>
<!DOCTYPE svg PUBLIC "-//W3C//DTD SVG 20010904//EN"
"http://www.w3.org/TR/2001/REC-SVG-20010904/DTD/svg10.dtd">
<svg width="" height="">
<text x="30px" y="30px" fill="red" stroke="none"
 font-size="24">
This text changes the cursor to an I-bar
</text>
<text x="30px" y="80px" fill="red" stroke="none"
 font-size="24" pointer-events="none">
This text does not change the cursor
</text>
<a xlink:href="">
<text x="30px" y="130px" fill="red" stroke="none"
 font-size="24" >
This text shows a pointing finger when moused
</text>
</a>
<a xlink:href="">
<text x="30px" y="180px" fill="red" stroke="none"
 font-size="24" pointer-events="none">
This text shows the normal pointer when moused
</text>
</a>
</svg>
```

The first and third pieces of text behave normally. The first shows an I-bar (also called I-beam) cursor when the mouse is moved over it. The third, because it is nested within an a element, causes the pointer to change to a pointing finger. On the second and fourth `text` elements, the `pointer-events` attribute has a value of none; therefore, when they are moused, no change in the cursor appearance takes place (contrast with the first and third; see Figure 4.6).

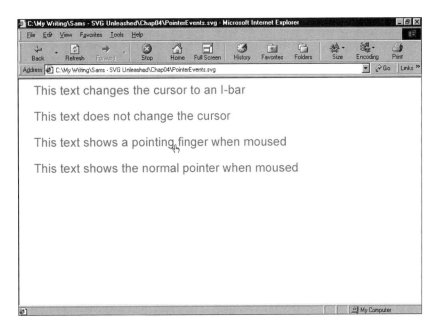

FIGURE 4.6 Altering the response to the mouse cursor using the pointer-events property.

Having looked at a number of styling properties used individually, as presentation attributes, let's move on to examine one of the techniques available to group these properties—the style attribute.

The SVG style Attribute

The SVG style attribute allows us to group several CSS styling properties within a single attribute.

The syntax when using the style attribute differs from that which we saw in the previous section where we used individual presentation attributes. There is now only one attribute, the style attribute, and the value of that attribute consists of CSS **declarations** separated by a semicolon and optional whitespace. Thus, we have code like the following:

```
style="stroke:red; fill:green; stroke-width:3;"
```

A single CSS declaration looks like this:

```
stroke:red;
```

The separator within a CSS declaration between the property name and its value is the colon character.

If you read the earlier chapters in this book, you saw many examples using the style attribute; therefore, further similar examples are not given here. Any appropriate combination of styling properties may be combined within a style attribute, separated by semicolons and optional whitespace.

The contentStyleType Attribute

The contentStyleType attribute of the svg element specifies a default content type to be applied to the values of style attributes within the SVG document fragment nested within the svg element. The default value of the contentStyleType attribute is "text/css". Therefore, if you plan to use only CSS styling, you don't need to specify the contentStyleType attribute on the svg document element.

CAUTION

It is not sufficient to set the contentStyleType attribute if you plan to use internal CSS style sheets. You must add a type attribute to the style element. The contentStyleType attribute affects the style attribute, not the style element. The style element is described in "Internal CSS Style Sheets," later in the chapter.

Opacity and Transparency

In SVG, a graphic shape may be fully opaque, partly transparent, or fully transparent. SVG also allows us to control, for example, the opacity of the fill of an SVG shape while leaving its stroke fully opaque.

Listing 4.7 illustrates a semi-transparent stroke, controlled by a stroke-opacity property combined with a fully opaque fill. The listing animates the rectangle from the left to the right of the screen, so you can see the changing background color through the semi-transparent stroke.

LISTING 4.7   Opacity01.svg—A Semi-Transparent Stroke Using the stroke-opacity Property

```
<?xml version="1.0" standalone="no"?>
<!DOCTYPE svg PUBLIC "-//W3C//DTD SVG 20010904//EN"
"http://www.w3.org/TR/2001/REC-SVG-20010904/DTD/svg10.dtd">
<svg width="" height="">
<rect x="400px" y="0px" width="500px" height="400px" />
<rect x="0px" y="50px" width="200px" height="125px"
 style="stroke-opacity:0.3; stroke-width:10; fill:red; stroke:#FFFF00;">
<animate attributeName="x" begin="3s"
 from="0px" to="800px" dur="20s" repeatCount="3"/>
</rect>
</svg>
```

The second `rect` element is animated from the left to the right of the screen. As it moves from a white background to black and back to white, you can see that the stroke color is semi-transparent. Figure 4.7 shows the animated rectangle part through its animation, zoomed to show the semi-transparent stroke.

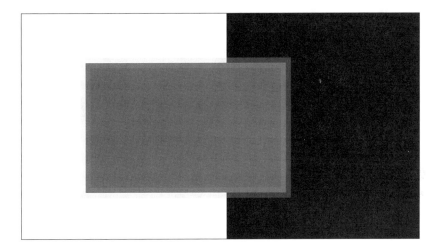

FIGURE 4.7   The semi-transparent stroke shown against contrasting backgrounds.

Equally, by using the `fill-opacity` property, we can make the fill semi-transparent while either leaving the stroke fully opaque or separately adjusting its opacity using the `stroke-opacity` property. If we want to adjust transparency equally for `stroke` and `fill`, we can use the `opacity` property, omitting both the `fill-opacity` and `stroke-opacity` properties.

Internal CSS Style Sheets

The third technique for applying style is to create an internal CSS style sheet nested within the `defs` element.

The basic structure of an internal style sheet is shown in Listing 4.8. Notice the `CDATA` section within the `style` element. CSS rules do not follow the syntax requirements of XML, and therefore the SVG rendering engine must be told that the CSS style rules are not to be treated as XML. The `CDATA` section marks its content as not being appropriate to parse as XML.

LISTING 4.8   CSSSkeleton.svg—A Skeleton for Creating an Internal CSS

```
<?xml version="1.0" standalone="no"?>
<!DOCTYPE svg PUBLIC "-//W3C//DTD SVG 20010904//EN"
"http://www.w3.org/TR/2001/REC-SVG-20010904/DTD/svg10.dtd">
<svg width="" height="">
```

LISTING 4.8   Continued

```
<style type="text/css">
<![CDATA[
// CSS Rules can go here.
]]>
</style>
<!-- SVG elements go here. -->
</svg>
```

CAUTION

The style element must have a type attribute with a value of "text/css" if the style rules contained in it are to be recognized as CSS rules.

CSS rules that correspond to the CSS2 specification can be placed within the style element. We can, for example, specify styles to be applied to particular element types. For example, we might want to create circles with no fill and a red outline together with rectangles with a blue, dotted stroke and a gray fill. Listing 4.9 shows the necessary code.

LISTING 4.9   StyleByElement.svg—Applying Style by Element Type

```
<?xml version="1.0" standalone="no"?>
<!DOCTYPE svg PUBLIC "-//W3C//DTD SVG 20010904//EN"
"http://www.w3.org/TR/2001/REC-SVG-20010904/DTD/svg10.dtd">
<svg width="" height="">
<style type="text/css">
<![CDATA[
circle{
fill:none;
stroke:red;
}
rect{
fill:#CCCCCC;
stroke:blue;
stroke-dasharray:4,4;
}
]]>
</style>
<circle cx="30px" cy="80px" r="20px"/>
<circle cx="70px" cy="80px" r="20px"/>
<circle cx="110px" cy="80px" r="20px"/>
<rect x="40px" y="120px" width="30px" height="30px" />
```

LISTING 4.9   Continued

```
<rect x="80px" y="120px" width="30px" height="30px" />
<rect x="120px" y="120px" width="30px" height="30px" />
</svg>
```

Figure 4.8 shows the appearance (zoomed) when you run Listing 4.9.

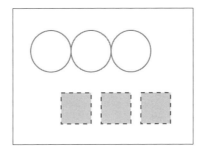

FIGURE 4.8   Applying style using CSS rules.

Element types can be grouped in CSS rules. The following would assign the same style to rect and circle elements in a document:

```
rect,circle{
stroke:red;
fill:#CC00CC;
stroke-width:6;
}
```

The grouped selector consists of the element type names separated by a comma.

You may not want to apply the same style to all elements of a particular element type. CSS classes and the class attribute provide the means to achieve that.

The class Attribute

To achieve, within an internal style sheet, different styles on individual elements of a particular type, we can use a class rule within the style sheet and add a class attribute to the SVG graphics element. Listing 4.10 shows how to apply two different styles to two different classes of rect elements.

LISTING 4.10   ClassRules.svg—Using CSS Class Rules

```
<?xml version="1.0" standalone="no"?>
<!DOCTYPE svg PUBLIC "-//W3C//DTD SVG 20010904//EN"
"http://www.w3.org/TR/2001/REC-SVG-20010904/DTD/svg10.dtd">
```

LISTING 4.10   Continued

```
<svg width="" height="">
<style type="text/css">
<![CDATA[
rect{
fill:#CCCCCC;
stroke:blue;
stroke-dasharray:4,4;
}
rect.Big{
fill:green;
stroke:red;
stroke-width:4;
}
]]>
</style>
<rect x="40px" y="120px" width="30px" height="30px" />
<rect x="80px" y="120px" width="30px" height="30px" />
<rect x="120px" y="120px" width="30px" height="30px" />
<rect class="Big" x="40px" y="20px" width="50px" height="50px" />
<rect class="Big" x="100px" y="20px" width="50px" height="50px" />
<rect class="Big" x="160px" y="20px" width="50px" height="50px" />
</svg>
```

Figure 4.9 shows the onscreen appearance when you run Listing 4.10. Notice that the default style to be applied to all rect elements is defined in the following rule:

```
rect{
fill:#CCCCCC;
stroke:blue;
stroke-dasharray:4,4;
}
```

Because there is a stroke-dasharray declaration in the default rule for the rect element, that stroke-dasharray rule also applies to any class rules defined for rect elements, as for the Big class in the following rule, unless it is explicitly overruled in a more specific style rule:

```
rect.Big{
fill:green;
stroke:red;
stroke-width:4;
}
```

The syntax for a class rule is a **selector**, followed by an opening curly bracket ({), followed by one or more CSS declarations, separated by semicolons and optional whitespace, followed by a closing curly bracket (}). A **class selector** consists of the element type name, followed by a period, followed by the class name. In the present example, `rect` is the element type name and `Big` is the class name. For that CSS rule to be applied to a particular element, the value of the `class` attribute on the element must match the class name in the CSS selector.

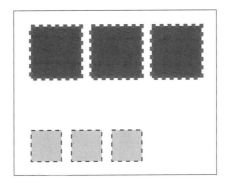

FIGURE 4.9   Using class rules to style rectangles.

When to Use Internal Style Sheets

Using internal CSS style sheets allows all styling information for an SVG document to be brought together in one location. This result can be convenient during the design phase when various styling options are being considered. Having an internal style sheet makes it much easier to try out different styles, compared to using individual presentation attributes or a `style` attribute on each element in the document.

Similar advantages occur during site maintenance. Thus, for example, if a site redesign meant that you wanted to change the `stroke` color for all `line` elements with a `class` attribute of value `Separator`, you need only look for the selector `line.Separator` and adjust the value of the `stroke` property in that one place. The style change will be reflected throughout the document.

If visitors to your site have slow Web connections, an internal, as opposed to an external, CSS style sheet may give better initial rendering of a graphic. When an external style sheet is used, an SVG rendering engine may render an SVG image or Web page in various shades of black and gray until the CSS style sheet is retrieved.

External CSS Style Sheets

The fourth CSS styling technique that SVG offers is the use of external CSS style sheets. This offers significant advantages when a style in SVG images or Web pages extends across many documents. During the design phase, we can apply a style option across the site and test it for its visual appeal by making changes in, likely, a single external CSS style sheet. Similar advantages are available during site maintenance or style upgrade.

External style sheets do slow correct rendering of SVG images if your users have slow Web connections. The image or SVG Web page can render initially with only blacks and grays until the styling information is retrieved and made available to the SVG rendering engine. On a slow connection, the delay can be noticeable. The Web page at `http://www.xmml.com/default.svg` uses an external style sheet, and this effect can be seen if you have a slow connection.

Associating a Style Sheet with an SVG Document

To associate an external CSS style sheet with an SVG document, you simply use the `xml-stylesheet` processing instruction.

The following code would associate a style sheet called myStylesheet.css with the SVG document containing the `xml-stylesheet` processing instruction:

```
<?xml-stylesheet href="myStylesheet.css" type="text/css"?>
```

> **NOTE**
>
> In the xml-stylesheet processing instruction, an href attribute is used, not an xlink:href attribute as is used widely in other parts of SVG.

Listings 4.11 and 4.12 show how we can apply the same styling information as we used in Listing 4.10 but this time using an external style sheet.

LISTING 4.11   ClassExternal.svg—Linking to an External CSS Style Sheet

```
<?xml version="1.0" standalone="no"?>
<?xml-stylesheet type="text/css" href="External.css" ?>
<!DOCTYPE svg PUBLIC "-//W3C//DTD SVG 20010904//EN"
"http://www.w3.org/TR/2001/REC-SVG-20010904/DTD/svg10.dtd">
<svg width="" height="">
<rect x="40px" y="120px" width="30px" height="30px" />
<rect x="80px" y="120px" width="30px" height="30px" />
<rect x="120px" y="120px" width="30px" height="30px" />
<rect class="Big" x="40px" y="20px" width="50px" height="50px" />
<rect class="Big" x="100px" y="20px" width="50px" height="50px" />
<rect class="Big" x="160px" y="20px" width="50px" height="50px" />
</svg>
```

The `xml-stylesheet` processing instruction references the CSS style sheet, External.css, which is shown in Listing 4.12. Notice that the `style` element and its nested `CDATA` section have been removed in Listing 4.11 (refer to Listing 4.10).

LISTING 4.12   External.css—An External CSS Style Sheet

```
rect{
fill:#CCCCCC;
stroke:blue;
stroke-dasharray:4,4;
}
rect.Big{
fill:green;
stroke:red;
stroke-width:4;
}
```

When Listing 4.11 is run, the onscreen appearance is the same as that shown in Figure 4.9.

Using Entities When Styling

It is tempting to refer to the use of entities to define styles as the fifth of the techniques for defining styles in SVG. In fact, entities can be applied with individual properties or when using the `style` attribute.

The use of entities is, strictly speaking, an XML technique rather than an SVG one. If you, or a designer colleague, use Adobe Illustrator to generate SVG graphics, you will almost certainly meet many entities in all but the simplest code (as you saw in Chapter 2, "Document Structure in SVG").

An entity is a way to reuse character strings. In SVG, the **external subset** of the Document Type Definition (DTD) is defined at a location on the W3C site. However, you can add entities to the **internal subset** of the Document Type Definition that is located within the Document Type Declaration (also called the `DOCTYPE` declaration) early in your SVG documents.

Listing 4.13 shows a brief example of declaring and using an entity in an SVG document.

LISTING 4.13   Entity01.svg—A Simple Example Using a User-Defined Entity

```
<?xml version="1.0" standalone="no"?>
<!DOCTYPE svg PUBLIC "-//W3C//DTD SVG 20010904//EN"
"http://www.w3.org/TR/2001/REC-SVG-20010904/DTD/svg10.dtd"
[
```

LISTING 4.13   Continued

```
<!ENTITY myEntity "stroke:red; stroke-width:8; fill:#CCFFCC">
]
>
<svg width="" height="">
<rect x="50" y="50" width="500" height="400" style="&myEntity;" />
</svg>
```

CAUTION

In many parts of SVG, you define things you want to reuse within a defs element. Declaring entities is an XML technique and is done within the DOCTYPE declaration before the start tag of the svg document element.

To add an **entity declaration** to your document, you add an **internal subset** of the DTD to the DOCTYPE declaration. Immediately before the closing angled bracket of the DOCTYPE declaration, you indicate the beginning of the internal subset by using a [character. Then you can add entity declarations (or, in principle, other additions to the DTD) using normal DTD syntax. The end of the internal subset is indicated by the] character. Then the closing angled bracket finishes the DOCTYPE declaration.

In Listing 4.13, we declare the ENTITY called myEntity. The value of the style attribute of the rect element is &myEntity; indicating that the text which defines the myEntity entity is substituted as the value of the style attribute. This is equivalent to simply writing the style attribute as follows:

```
style="stroke:red; stroke-width:8; fill:#CCFFCC"
```

Figure 4.10 shows the style defined in the ENTITY declaration applied to the rect element.

Aural Style Sheets

In Level 2 of the CSS specifications, style sheets need not be applied only to onscreen presentations. Aural style sheets provide a way of defining "style" for aural presentations of material.

At the time of writing, Aural style sheets have not yet been implemented in any generally available SVG rendering engine.

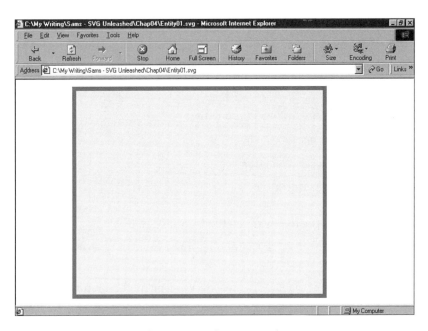

FIGURE 4.10   Using a user-defined entity to style a rectangle.

Style SVG DOM Interface

The objects from the SVG DOM that are particularly relevant to styling are presented in this section. Objects are listed in alphabetical order.

> **NOTE**
>
> The prefix css is used in this section to designate objects from the CSS Level 2 specifications. Thus, the CSSValue object from CSS2 will be presented as css::CSSValue.

The SVGColor Object

The SVGColor object has the properties and methods of the CSSValue object (css:CSSValue) of the Cascading Style Sheets Level 2 Recommendation.

In addition, the SVGColor object has the following constants associated with it:

- SVGColor.SVG_COLORTYPE_UNKNOWN—This constant is of type short and has a value of 0.

- SVGColor.SVG_COLORTYPE_RGBCOLOR—This constant is of type short and has a value of 1.

- `SVGColor.SVG_COLORTYPE_RGBCOLORICCCOLOR`—This constant is of type short and has a value of 2.

- `SVGColor.SVG_COLORTYPE_CURRENTCOLOR`—This constant is of type short and has a value of 3.

The SVGColor object has the following properties:

- `colorType`—of type unsigned short

- `rgbColor`—of type css::RGBColor

- `iccColor`—of type SVGICCColor

The SVGColor object has the following methods specific to it:

- `setRGBColor(rgbColor)`—The method returns a value of type void. The rgbColor argument is of type DOMString.

- `setRGBColorICCColor(rgbColor, iccColor)`—The method returns a value of type void. The rgbColor argument is of type DOMString. The iccColor argument is of type DOMString.

- `setColor(colorType, rgbColor, iccColor)`—The method returns a value of type void. The colorType argument is of type unsigned short. The rgbColor argument is of type DOMString. The iccColor argument is of type DOMString.

The SVGColorProfileElement Object

The SVGColorProfileElement object has the properties and methods of the SVGElement object, the SVGURIReference object, and the SVGRenderingIntent object.

In addition, the SVGColorProfileElement object has the following properties:

- `local`—of type DOMString

- `name`—of type DOMString

- `renderingIntent`—of type unsigned short

The SVGColorProfileElement object has no methods specific to it.

The SVGColorProfileRule Object

The SVGColorProfileRule object has the properties and methods of the SVGCSSRule object and the SVGRenderingIntent object.

In addition, the `SVGColorProfileRule` object has the following properties:

- `src`—of type `DOMString`
- `name`—of type `DOMString`
- `renderingIntent`—of type `unsigned short`

The `SVGColorProfileRule` object has no methods specific to it.

The SVGCSSRule Object

The `SVGCSSRule` object has the properties and methods of the CSS Level 2 `CSSRule` object (`css::CSSRule`).

In addition, the `SVGCSSRule` object has the following constant associated with it:

- `SVGCSSRule.COLOR_PROFILE_RULE`—This constant is of type `short` and has a value of 7.

The `SVGCSSRule` object has no properties or methods specific to it.

The SVGICCColor Object

The `SVGICCColor` object has the following properties:

- `colorProfile`—of type `DOMString`
- `colors`—of type `SVGNumberList`

The `SVGICCColor` object has no methods specific to it.

The SVGStylable Object

The `SVGStylable` object has the following properties:

- `className`—of type `SVGAnimatedString`
- `style`—of type `css::CSSStyleDeclaration`

The `SVGStylable` object has the following method specific to it:

- `getPresentationAttribute(name)`—The method returns a value of type `css:CSSValue`. The `name` argument is of type `DOMString`.

The SVGStyleElement Object

The SVGStyleElement object has the properties and methods of the SVGElement object.

In addition, the SVGStyleElement object has the following properties specific to it:

- xmlspace—of type DOMString

- type—of type DOMString

- media—of type DOMString

- title—of type DOMString

The SVGStyleElement object has no methods specific to it.

The DOM Level 2 Style Specification

When we come to the Document Object Model as it applies to style in an SVG document, we not only have available to us techniques from the XML DOM (DOM Level 2) and the specific objects, properties, and methods defined in the SVG DOM, but we also have objects, properties, and methods that are defined in the DOM Level 2 Style Recommendation.

The DOM Level 2 Style specification is fully described at http://www.w3.org/TR/2000/REC-DOM-Level-2-Style-20001113/.

Examples of Styling Using the DOMs

This section will show some ways in which you might choose to use the SVG DOM to control or alter styling on SVG objects. The techniques that you are likely to use frequently are straightforward, often involving the setting of a new value for a style property.

NOTE

The explanation of the JavaScript that follows is brief. If you are not familiar with JavaScript, you may find it helpful to read Part II before studying the code examples in detail.

Changing Fill Color Using the DOM

Listing 4.14 shows a simple interactive way to alter styling on an SVG shape—in this case, a rectangle. The three words displayed by the code describe a fixed choice of colors to alter the fill color of the rectangle.

LISTING 4.14   ChangeFill.svg—Altering the fill Property of a rect Element

```
<?xml version="1.0" standalone="no"?>
<!DOCTYPE svg PUBLIC "-//W3C//DTD SVG 20010904//EN"
"http://www.w3.org/TR/2001/REC-SVG-20010904/DTD/svg10.dtd">
<svg width="" height="" onload="Initialize(evt)">
<script type="text/javascript">
<![CDATA[
var SVGDoc;
var SVGRoot;
var myRect;
function Initialize(){
SVGDoc = evt.target.ownerDocument;
SVGRoot = SVGDoc.documentElement;
}

function ToGreen(){
myRect = SVGDoc.getElementById("theRect");
myRect.setAttribute("fill", "green");
}
function ToRed(){
myRect = SVGDoc.getElementById("theRect");
myRect.setAttribute("fill", "red");
}
function ToBlue(){
myRect = SVGDoc.getElementById("theRect");
myRect.setAttribute("fill", "blue");
}
]]>
</script>
<text x="50" y="50" font-size="20" >Click a word below to change
➥the fill of the rectangle
<tspan x="50" y="100" onclick="ToGreen(evt)"
 style="fill:green; stroke:none; font-size:20">green
</tspan>
<tspan dx="50" y="100" onclick="ToRed(evt)"
 style="fill:red; stroke:none; font-size:20">red
</tspan>
<tspan dx="50" y="100" onclick="ToBlue(evt)"
style="fill:blue; stroke:none; font-size:20">blue
</tspan>
</text>
<rect id="theRect" x="50" y="150" width="100" height="50" fill="#CCCCCC"/>
</svg>
```

The `rect` element whose style is being changed has an `id` attribute with value of `theRect`. Each of three `tspan` elements possesses an `onclick` attribute, with the function called being specific for each color.

The `svg` document element possesses an `onload` attribute, which calls the `Initialize()` function. That sets a couple of global variables, ready for use by any of the functions that may be called by user action.

When the text contained in one of the `tspan` elements is clicked, the function specified in the `onclick` attribute is called. For each function, we use the `getElementById()` method on the `SVGDocument` object to access the DOM object representing the desired `rect` element. The `setAttribute()` method is used to change the value of the `fill` property of the rectangle.

Figure 4.11 shows the onscreen appearance when Listing 4.14 is run.

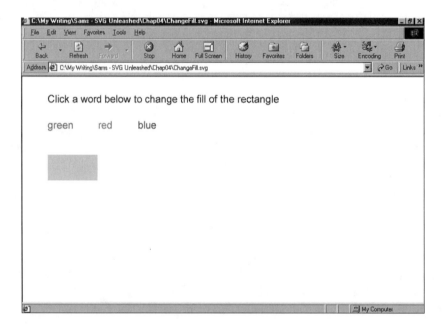

FIGURE 4.11   Clicking on the text description of a color changes the fill property of the rectangle.

Changing Opacity Using the DOM

Listing 4.15 allows us to define fixed values of opacity for a rectangle.

LISTING 4.15   ChangeOpacity.svg—Selecting Fixed Options for Opacity of a Rectangle

```
<?xml version="1.0" standalone="no"?>
<!DOCTYPE svg PUBLIC "-//W3C//DTD SVG 20010904//EN"
"http://www.w3.org/TR/2001/REC-SVG-20010904/DTD/svg10.dtd">
<svg width="" height="" >
<script type="text/javascript">
<![CDATA[
//var SVGDoc;
var SVGRoot;
var myRect;
//function Initialize(){
//SVGDoc = evt.target.ownerDocument;
//SVGRoot = SVGDoc.documentElement;
//}

function To75(){
myRect = document.getElementById("theRect");
myRect.setAttribute("opacity", "0.75");
}
function To50(){
myRect = document.getElementById("theRect");
myRect.setAttribute("opacity", "0.5");
}
function To25(){
myRect = document.getElementById("theRect");
myRect.setAttribute("opacity", "0.25");}
]]>
</script>
<text x="50" y="50" font-size="20" >Click a word below to change
➥the opacity of the rectangle
<tspan x="50" y="100" onclick="To75(evt)"
 style="fill:green; stroke:none; font-size:20">75%
</tspan>
<tspan dx="50" y="100" onclick="To50(evt)"
 style="fill:red; stroke:none; font-size:20">50%
</tspan>
<tspan dx="50" y="100" onclick="To25(evt)"
style="fill:blue; stroke:none; font-size:20">25%
</tspan>
</text>
<rect id="theRect" x="50" y="150" width="100" height="50" fill="#FF6600"/>
</svg>
```

Notice that inside the To75(), To50(), and To25() functions, we use a different syntax option document.getElementById("theRect") rather than the option used in Listing 4.14. This technique is a useful shortcut for standalone SVG images or Web pages, but if you embed the SVG in an XHTML document, the document object will select the XHTML within which the SVG is contained. In that case, use the commented out code in Listing 4.15.

Changing Inherited Styling Properties

The g element was introduced in Chapter 2. If a style attribute is placed on a g element, the corresponding style attributes on the nested elements can be changed. Listing 4.16 demonstrates how we can alter the value of an attribute on a g element—in this case, the hexadecimal color value of its stroke—and see the change in property inherited by the elements nested within the g element.

LISTING 4.16   InheritedStroke.svg—Inheritance of a Scripted Change

```
<?xml version="1.0" standalone="no"?>
<!DOCTYPE svg PUBLIC "-//W3C//DTD SVG 20010904//EN"
"http://www.w3.org/TR/2001/REC-SVG-20010904/DTD/svg10.dtd">
<svg width="200" height="200" onload="Initialize()">
  <script type="text/javascript">
  <![CDATA[

var crosshairs = null;
var crosshairsInterval = null;

function Initialize() {
    crosshairs = document.getElementById('crosshairs');
    crosshairsInterval = setInterval('fade()', 200);
}

function fade() {
    var stroke = crosshairs.style.getPropertyValue('stroke');
    var hexVal = stroke.substr(1, 1);
    var decVal = parseInt(hexVal, 16);
    decVal--;
    if (decVal < 0)
        decVal = 15;
    hexVal = decVal.toString(16);
    var cssColor = "#" + hexVal + hexVal + hexVal;
    crosshairs.style.setProperty('stroke', cssColor);
}
```

LISTING 4.16   Continued

```
/*
getPropertyValue and setProperty come from css::CSSStyleDeclaration
*/

  ]]>
  </script>
  <g id="crosshairs" style="stroke: #fff">
    <circle cx="100" cy="100" r="75" stroke="inherit" fill="none"/>
    <line x1="100" y1="25" x2="100" y2="75" stroke="inherit"/>
    <line x1="175" y1="100" x2="125" y2="100" stroke="inherit"/>
    <line x1="100" y1="175" x2="100" y2="125" stroke="inherit"/>
    <line x1="25" y1="100" x2="75" y2="100" stroke="inherit"/>
  </g>
</svg>
```

The getElementById() method is used to reference the g element whose id attribute has the value of crosshairs.

When the document is loaded, the value of the stroke property is #fff (which is a short form for #ffffff). In other words, the crosshairs are initially white.

The setInterval() method in the Initialize() function determines the speed of the fade. When the fade() function is called, we use the getPropertyValue() method (described in DOM Level 2 - Style, http://www.w3.org/TR/2000/REC-DOM-Level-2-Style-20001113/) to retrieve the value of the stroke property of the g element whose id attribute has the value of crosshairs.

The value #fff and its successor values are parsed and progressively decremented. Thus, initial values would be #fff, #eee, #ddd, #ccc, and so on. Eventually, the values reach #111, #000, and then when the value of each character is below zero, it is set back to 15, which is f in hexadecimal. So the color of the stroke property on the g element is progressively changed from white to black in an endless loop. The scripted changes on the stroke property of the g element are also reflected in the stroke properties of the elements nested within the g element. Figure 4.12 shows the onscreen appearance partway through the animation.

Changing a Style Property from HTML

In the example in this section, we change the fill property of text in an SVG image embedded in an HTML Web page. Listing 4.17 is the HTML page.

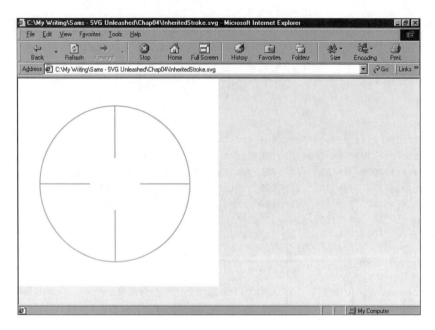

FIGURE 4.12   A time-based inherited scripted change in value of the stroke property.

LISTING 4.17   HTMLtoSVG.html—The HTML Document That Contains the SVG Image

```
<html >
<head>
<title>Accessing SVG Style Properties from HTML</title>
<script type="text/javascript" >

var htmlObj, SVGDoc, svgText, colorInterval;
var colors    = ['#f00', '#ff0', '#0f0', '#0ff', '#00f', '#f0f'];
var colorIndex = 0;

function Initialize() {
    htmlObj = document.getElementById('htmlObj');
    SVGDoc   = htmlObj.getSVGDocument();
    svgText  = SVGDoc.getElementById('svgText');
    colorInterval = setInterval('changeTextColor()', 2000)
}

function changeTextColor() {
    svgText.style.setProperty('fill', colors[colorIndex++]);
    if (colorIndex >5){
```

LISTING 4.17   Continued

```
        colorIndex = 0;


    }
}

</script>
</head>
<body onload="Initialize()">
<p>The script on this HTML page changes the color of the text in the SVG
document below. </p>
<embed id="htmlObj" src="HTMLtoSVG.svg" type="image/svg+xml"
width="200px" height="200px" />
</body>
</html>
```

Listing 4.18 is the SVG image.

LISTING 4.18   HTMLtoSVG.svg—An SVG Image for Embedding in an HTML Web Page

```
<?xml version="1.0" standalone="no"?>
<!DOCTYPE svg PUBLIC "-//W3C//DTD SVG 20010904//EN"
"http://www.w3.org/TR/2001/REC-SVG-20010904/DTD/svg10.dtd">
<svg width="200" height="200" >
<rect x="0" y="0" width="100%" height="100%"
 style="fill:#CCCCCC; stroke:black; stroke-width:3;" />
  <text id="svgText" x="20px" y="70px"
    style="fill: #000; font-size: 20pt">
Colored Text</text>
</svg>
```

When the body of the HTML page loads, the Initialize() function is called. We use the getElementById() method to reference the embed element whose id attribute has the value of htmlObj. The getSVGDocument() method is then used to select the relevant SVG document.

The setInterval() method is then used to call the changeTextColor() function every 2,000 milliseconds.

The svgText variable is assigned the result of calling the getElementById() method, thus referencing the relevant (only one in this example) text element in the SVG code. We then use the setProperty() method to change the value of the fill property of the text.

Onscreen the color of the text changes every 2,000 milliseconds, the colors displayed being determined by the elements of the `colors` array.

Summary

This chapter introduced the importance of styling in helping to convey information. You saw how to use styling in SVG by employing five techniques: using individual presentation attributes, using the `style` attribute, using internal or external CSS style sheets, and by using entities.

The SVG DOM interfaces that are relevant to styling in SVG were also described. Some examples of styling SVG objects by scripting the DOM have been demonstrated.

CHAPTER 5

Coordinate Systems in SVG

A good understanding of the use of coordinates in SVG is important for fully exploiting the power of SVG. If you don't understand SVG coordinates, in some circumstances you will be unable to achieve the visual appearance you want to produce onscreen.

Sometimes the use of coordinates in SVG can seem relatively intuitive. In some circumstances, coordinates in SVG have some pitfalls for the unwary. This chapter will cover several important topics relating to SVG coordinates, helping you to understand how an SVG rendering engine interprets and renders coordinates.

If SVG supported only a single, fixed coordinate system, things would be pretty simple. However, the flexibility in how to use coordinate systems—for example, to zoom and pan images—which SVG provides to developers who create SVG, creates potential pitfalls. To be able to confidently generate SVG images, you need a good understanding of how coordinate systems are handled in SVG.

The SVG Canvas

An SVG image is two dimensional. That image is drawn on the **SVG canvas**, which is a two-dimensional plane that is potentially infinite in size. SVG can, in a sense, be considered to be three dimensional in that certain parts of SVG—for example, some of the lighting filter primitives discussed in Chapter 10, "SVG Filters,"—make implicit use of a third dimension. However, an SVG image is rendered only in two dimensions.

You may find it helpful to imagine the SVG canvas as an infinitely large piece of paper (or canvas, if you prefer) onto which SVG "paint" is applied. At any one time, you can see only a finite rectangular part of the canvas. You can think of that rectangular shape—the viewport—as being similar to a rectangular porthole that you look through to see part of the canvas. It is up to you, as the creator of an SVG document, to decide whether your code should relate only to the rectangular **viewport** that a user will have onto the infinite SVG canvas or whether to code over a much larger area. In the latter case, you will likely expect the user to scroll or pan to a desired part of the image that your code defines.

So how do we define the size of the viewport?

The Initial Viewport

You can envisage the initial viewport as being created by a process of negotiation between an SVG document fragment and a container or parent document. If an SVG image is located within, say, an XHTML document, the latter is the parent document. If the SVG document fragment is standalone, the parent is notional.

> **NOTE**
>
> In SVG, the svg, symbol, image, and foreignObject elements create a new viewport.

The initial viewport differs depending on whether the SVG document is a standalone document or is embedded within another XML or HTML document. We will consider the two situations separately.

Initial Viewport for Standalone SVG

The initial viewport is created by the svg element that is the document element for an SVG document. The width and height attributes on the svg element, assuming they are present, give values in pixels for the width and height of the initial viewport. Ideally, the SVG rendering engine also has information that allows the size of a pixel to be mapped to real-world units such as millimeters or inches.

If a viewBox attribute is present on the document element svg element, the width and height in pixels (as described in the preceding paragraph) are mapped to the number of user units specified in the third and fourth values (assuming the first two values are zero) that make up the value of the viewBox attribute.

For example, the viewBox attribute

```
viewBox = "0 0 1000 500"
```

specifies a viewport that is 1,000 user units wide (third value minus first value) and 500 user units high (fourth value minus second value).

The larger the third and fourth values are, for any given pair of first and second values, the more user units there are in any given number of pixels and the smaller the onscreen size of any SVG object of a defined dimension measured in user units.

Listing 5.1 shows a simple SVG document with an svg document element that possesses a viewBox attribute.

LISTING 5.1   InitialViewport01.svg—A viewBox Attribute Example

```
<?xml version="1.0" standalone="no"?>
<!DOCTYPE svg PUBLIC "-//W3C//DTD SVG 20010904//EN"
"http://www.w3.org/TR/2001/REC-SVG-20010904/DTD/svg10.dtd">
<svg width="800px" height="400px" viewBox="0 0 800 400">
<rect x="0" y="0" width="200" height="200"
 style="fill:red"/>
<rect x="800" y="0" width="200" height="200"
 style="fill:red"/>
</svg>
```

The width attribute of the svg document element is 800 pixels. The width in user units is also 800—800 (third value of the viewBox attribute) minus 0 (first value of the viewBox attribute). Similarly, the height attribute defines a viewport height of 400 pixels, and this height contains 400 user units (fourth value minus second value in the viewBox attribute).

As you can see in Figure 5.1, a square is displayed onscreen. Notice that in Listing 5.1 there is a second rect element that you can't see onscreen when the document loads (it is positioned immediately to the right of the initial viewport and therefore cannot be seen). Its purpose will become clear as we develop this example.

The value of the viewBox attribute takes the following general form:

```
viewBox="originX, originY, width, height"
```

or

```
viewBox="originX originY width height"
```

In other words the value of the viewBox attribute consists of four values separated by whitespace and, optionally, a comma. The first value, originX, indicates the x coordinate at the top-left corner of the viewport. The second value, originY, indicates the y coordinate at the top-left corner of the viewport. The third and fourth values, width and height, indicate the value—in user units—of the viewport.

If we change either or both of the first two values, then, effectively, we pan the viewport to a different place on the SVG canvas. If we increase the third and fourth values, an object of any given size (in user units) is smaller onscreen. Conversely, if we decrease the third and fourth values, an object of any given size (in user units) is larger onscreen.

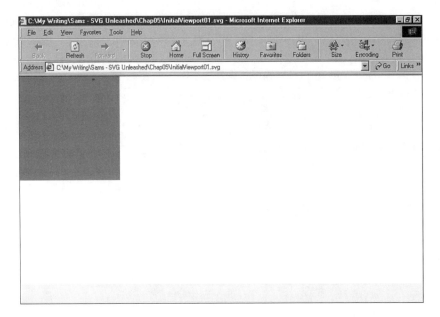

FIGURE 5.1   A rectangle displayed in the initial viewport.

Listing 5.2 shows the effect when the first two values of the value of the viewBox attribute are not zero.

LISTING 5.2   InitialViewport02.svg—Modifying the First Two Values of the viewBox Attribute

```
<?xml version="1.0" standalone="no"?>
<!DOCTYPE svg PUBLIC "-//W3C//DTD SVG 20010904//EN"
"http://www.w3.org/TR/2001/REC-SVG-20010904/DTD/svg10.dtd">
<svg width="800px" height="400px" viewBox="-100 -100 800 400">
<rect x="0" y="0" width="200" height="200"
 style="fill:red"/>
 <rect x="800" y="0" width="200" height="200"
 style="fill:red"/>
</svg>
```

As you can see, the square shown in Figure 5.2 is displaced down and to the right because the x coordinate of the top-left corner of the screen now represents the first value of the viewBox attribute— –100 user units. Similarly, the y coordinate of the top-left corner of the screen represents the second value of the viewBox attribute—again, –100 user units.

If we give the first two values of the viewBox attribute positive values, the top-left corner of the screen represents a value such as (100,50), so that the first rectangle moves off the screen partly, upward and to the left. The second rectangle becomes partly visible because its x coordinate is now only 700 user units from the left of the screen. Listing 5.3 shows the necessary code.

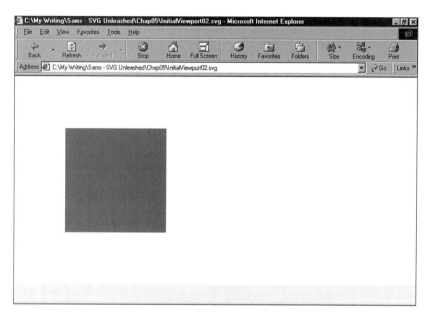

FIGURE 5.2   A rectangle displayed in an initial viewport with a displaced origin.

LISTING 5.3   InitialViewport03.svg—Using Positive Values in the viewBox Attribute

```
<?xml version="1.0" standalone="no"?>
<!DOCTYPE svg PUBLIC "-//W3C//DTD SVG 20010904//EN"
"http://www.w3.org/TR/2001/REC-SVG-20010904/DTD/svg10.dtd">
<svg width="800px" height="400px" viewBox="100 50 800 400">
<rect x="0" y="0" width="200" height="200"
 style="fill:red"/>
 <rect x="800" y="0" width="200" height="200"
 style="fill:red"/>
</svg>
```

Figure 5.3 shows the appearance onscreen.

If you have read the explanation and studied the code listings and figures, I hope that the effect of the `viewBox` attribute on what you see onscreen will now be clear. If not, I suggest you go back and review this material because the concepts are developed further throughout the chapter.

Initial Viewport for Embedded SVG

When an SVG document is embedded in an XML document from another namespace or an HTML document, the process used to determine the initial viewport is a little different. The parent document has a significant say in how much screen real estate the SVG image is allowed to use.

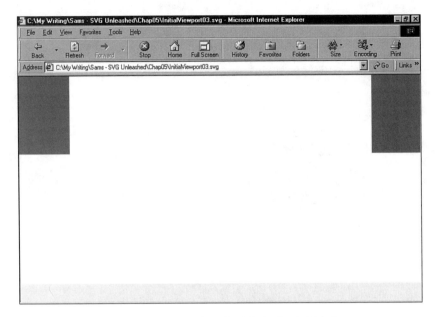

FIGURE 5.3   A rectangle displaced up and to the left in the initial viewport.

Suppose we want to embed a 200-pixel-square SVG document. Listing 5.4 shows a place-holder image whose outline is a rectangle to make clear whether or not all the image is shown.

LISTING 5.4   InitialViewport04.svg—A Placeholder SVG Document to Be Embedded

```
<?xml version="1.0" standalone="no"?>
<!DOCTYPE svg PUBLIC "-//W3C//DTD SVG 20010904//EN"
"http://www.w3.org/TR/2001/REC-SVG-20010904/DTD/svg10.dtd">
<svg width="200px" height="200px" viewBox="0 0 200 200">
<rect x="0" y="0" width="100%" height="100%"
 style="fill:none; stroke:red; stroke-width:6"/>
</svg>
```

Listing 5.5 shows a simple HTML document within which we can embed the SVG document.

LISTING 5.5   HTMLInitialViewport.html—Embedding SVG in HTML

```
<!DOCTYPE HTML PUBLIC "-//W3C//DTD HTML 4.0 Transitional//EN"
"http://www.w3.org/TR/REC-html40/loose.dtd">
<HTML>
<HEAD>
<TITLE>Untitled</TITLE>
```

LISTING 5.5   Continued

```
</HEAD>
<BODY>
<embed src="InitialViewport04.svg" width="50px"
 height="50px" type="image/svg+xml">
</BODY>
</HTML>
```

Figure 5.4 shows the onscreen appearance, without any zooming in or out. You may be surprised to see that all the square is shown, but it has been scaled to fit the permitted size of 50 pixels by 50 pixels. We will return to the topic of scaling to fit when we consider aspect ratios later in this chapter.

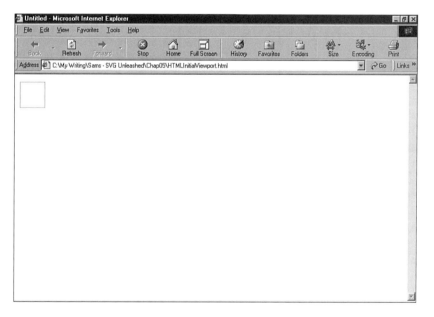

FIGURE 5.4   A scaled-to-fit SVG image in a small initial viewport.

If you alter the value of the width and height attributes of the embed element to 200px, the SVG image will be displayed full size. Later in the chapter, we will look at the preserveAspectRatio attribute, which is used to control how scale to fit works.

Adding a Nested svg Element

When you nest an svg element within an SVG document, a new viewport is created, with an associated new **viewport coordinate system** and a new **user coordinate system**. The boundaries of the new viewport are defined by the values of the x, y, width, and height attributes on the nested svg element. The new viewport coordinate system and the new user coordinate system have their origin at (x,y) in the parent coordinate system, where x and y are the values of the x and y attributes of the nested svg element.

Adding a viewBox attribute to the nested svg element helps determine the new user coordinate system. Listing 5.6 shows 3 squares that are each 100 user units square; however, they display differently onscreen because they are in different viewports opened by separate nested svg elements that have different values in their respective viewBox attributes.

LISTING 5.6   NewViewports.svg—Opening New Viewports Using Nested svg Elements

```
<?xml version="1.0" standalone="no"?>
<!DOCTYPE svg PUBLIC "-//W3C//DTD SVG 20010904//EN"
"http://www.w3.org/TR/2001/REC-SVG-20010904/DTD/svg10.dtd">
<svg width="" height="">
<svg x="40px" y="40px" width="200px" height="200px" viewBox="0 0 400 400">
<rect x="0" y="0" width="100%" height="100%"
 style="stroke:red; stroke-width:10; fill:none;"/>
<rect x="20" y="20" width="100" height="100"
 style="fill:red; stroke:#CCCCCC; stroke-width:4"/>
</svg>
<svg x="250px" y="40px" width="200px" height="200px" viewBox="0 0 200 200">
<rect x="0" y="0" width="100%" height="100%"
 style="stroke:red; stroke-width:10; fill:none;"/>
<rect x="20" y="20" width="100" height="100"
 style="fill:red; stroke:#CCCCCC; stroke-width:4"/>
</svg>
<svg x="460px" y="40px" width="200px" height="200px" viewBox="0 0 100 100">
<rect x="0" y="0" width="100%" height="100%"
 style="stroke:red; stroke-width:10; fill:none;"/>
<rect x="20" y="20" width="100" height="100"
 style="fill:red; stroke:#CCCCCC; stroke-width:4"/>
</svg>
</svg>
```

The three new viewports are each outlined in red, using a rect element with no fill. Notice that the values of the viewBox attributes on each nested svg element are different. Effectively, the user unit in the left viewport is half the size of a user unit in the middle viewport, which in turn is half the size of a user unit in the right viewport. Each new viewport is 200 pixels wide by 200 pixels high. However, the width and height in user units are, respectively from left to right, 400 user units, 200 user units, and 100 user units. Figure 5.5 shows the onscreen appearance when the code is run.

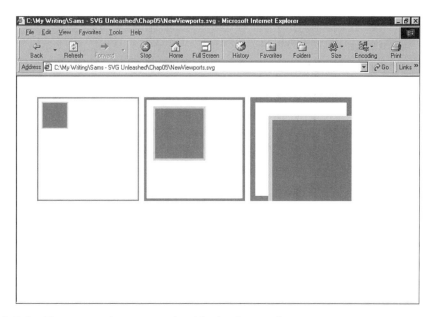

FIGURE 5.5   Three new viewports each with viewBox attributes.

Other SVG elements that can create a new viewport are the `symbol` element (when instanced by a `use` element), the `image` element, and the `foreignObject` element. They are discussed and demonstrated later in this chapter.

Preserving Aspect Ratio

Many beginner users of SVG find the topic of aspect ratios a difficult one. First, let's look at what preserving aspect ratio consists of and why it can hold traps for the unwary.

Listing 5.7 shows a description of a simple SVG square.

LISTING 5.7   Square01.svg—A Square in SVG

```
<?xml version="1.0" standalone="no"?>
<!DOCTYPE svg PUBLIC "-//W3C//DTD SVG 20010904//EN"
"http://www.w3.org/TR/2001/REC-SVG-20010904/DTD/svg10.dtd">
<svg width="800px" height="600px">
<rect x="0px" y="100px" width="200px" height="200px" style="fill:none;
stroke:red; stroke-width:5"/>
</svg>
```

If you run the code, you will see onscreen a square with a red outline and no fill positioned to the extreme left of the browser window, as shown in Figure 5.6.

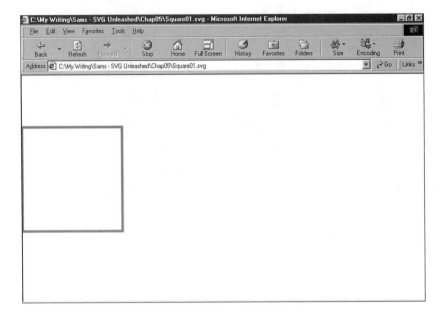

FIGURE 5.6   A square displayed onscreen using pixel measurements.

Suppose, however, you wanted to create a similar square onscreen using the code in Listing 5.8.

LISTING 5.8   Square02.svg—A Square Displayed in a Viewport with a viewBox Attribute

```
<?xml version="1.0" standalone="no"?>
<!DOCTYPE svg PUBLIC "-//W3C//DTD SVG 20010904//EN"
"http://www.w3.org/TR/2001/REC-SVG-20010904/DTD/svg10.dtd">
<svg width="800px" height="600px" viewBox="0 0 1000 1000">
<rect x="0" y="100" width="200" height="200"
 style="fill:none; stroke:red; stroke-width:5"/>
</svg>
```

The appearance onscreen may surprise you. Figure 5.7 shows the result of running Listing 5.8. You do see a square, but it is "incorrectly" positioned in that it is positioned significantly away from the left edge of the screen despite the fact that the x attribute of the rect element has a value of 0.

So what is happening? First, look at the viewBox attribute and notice that both the third and fourth values are 1000. However, the width of the viewport is 800px and the height is 600px. In other words, the horizontal and vertical scales are different. If the SVG rendering engine tried to strictly apply the scales, it would draw a "square" that was 200 user units (160 pixels) wide and 200 user units (120 pixels) high. But a shape 160 pixels wide and 120 pixels high is not a square! So we have given the SVG rendering engine values for scaling horizontally and vertically that cannot be literally implemented and still produce the desired shape—a square.

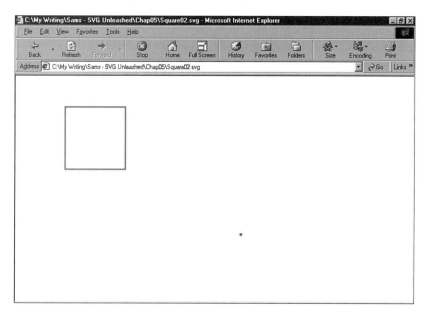

FIGURE 5.7   The appearance of the square when a viewBox attribute is present.

SVG provides a way of defining how an image should stretch to fit the provided viewport in "impossible" situations such as the one we have just looked at. The preserveAspectRatio attribute allows us this control.

Broadly, the preserveAspectRatio allows us to use an image so that it *meets* an edge of the viewport exactly (or is placed midway between two edges) or use the image so that we *slice* part of the image.

The value of the preserveAspectRatio attribute consists of two strings separated by white-space. The first string conveys alignment information, and the second string is meet or slice. Thus, the attribute may take a value such as the following:

preserveAspectRatio="*xMinYMin* meet"

First, let's look at situations in which the second part of the value of the preserveAspectRatio attribute is meet.

The preserveAspectRatio Attribute with meet

The most effective way to try to convey how the `preserveAspectRatio` attribute works is to demonstrate it in action. Listing 5.9 shows multiple viewports with different values for the `preserveAspectRatio` attribute.

For each value of the `preserveAspectRatio` attribute, we have the form

preserveAspectRatio = "*xPosYPos* meet"

where the *Pos* may be `Min`, `Mid`, or `Max`. So, for example, we could have a value of `xMidYMax meet`.

To demonstrate the results, we will create a graphic that is 50 units square and position it in viewports of 2 sizes—35 units wide by 100 units high and 100 units wide by 35 units high. The outline of each viewport is illustrated by a rectangle placed behind it.

LISTING 5.9   PARWithMeet.svg—The preserveAspectRatio Attribute with meet

```
<?xml version="1.0" standalone="no"?>
<!DOCTYPE svg PUBLIC "-//W3C//DTD SVG 20010904//EN"
"http://www.w3.org/TR/2001/REC-SVG-20010904/DTD/svg10.dtd"
>
<svg width="800px" height="600px" viewBox="0 0 800 600"
xmlns:xlink="http://www.w3.org/1999/xlink">
<defs>
<rect id="myRect"  x="0" y="0" width="50" height="50"
 style="fill:#DDDDDD;stroke:red; stroke-width:4"/>
</defs>
<!-- First row is 35 units wide by 100 high -->
<rect x="20" y="20" width="35" height="100" style="fill:none;stroke:blue"/>
<rect x="60" y="20" width="35" height="100" style="fill:none;stroke:blue"/>
<rect x="100" y="20" width="35" height="100" style="fill:none;stroke:blue"/>
<svg x="20" y="20" preserveAspectRatio="xMinYMin meet"
width="35" height="100" viewBox="0 0 50 50">
<use xlink:href="#myRect"/>
</svg>
<svg x="60" y="20" preserveAspectRatio="xMinYMid meet"
width="35" height="100" viewBox="0 0 50 50">
<use xlink:href="#myRect"/>
</svg>
<svg x="100" y="20" preserveAspectRatio="xMinYMax meet"
width="35" height="100" viewBox="0 0 50 50">
<use xlink:href="#myRect"/>
</svg>
<!-- Second row is 100 units wide by 35 high -->
```

LISTING 5.9   Continued

```
<rect x="20" y="140" width="100" height="35" style="fill:none;stroke:blue"/>
<rect x="130" y="140" width="100" height="35" style="fill:none;stroke:blue"/>
<rect x="240" y="140" width="100" height="35" style="fill:none;stroke:blue"/>
<svg x="20" y="140" preserveAspectRatio="xMinYMin meet"
width="100" height="35" viewBox="0 0 50 50">
<use xlink:href="#myRect"/>
</svg>
<svg x="130" y="140" preserveAspectRatio="xMidYMid meet"
width="100" height="35" viewBox="0 0 50 50">
<use xlink:href="#myRect"/>
</svg>
<svg x="240" y="140" preserveAspectRatio="xMaxYMax meet"
width="100" height="35" viewBox="0 0 50 50">
<use xlink:href="#myRect"/>
</svg>
</svg>
```

Figure 5.8 shows the appearance when you run Listing 5.9.

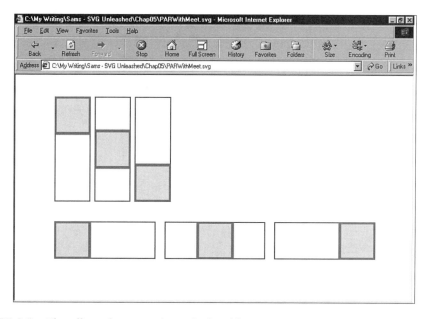

FIGURE 5.8   The effect of preserveAspectRatio with meet.

The first row in Figure 5.8 shows the effect of having xMinYMin meet, xMinYMid meet, and xMinYMax meet as the values of the preserveAspectRatio attribute.

YMin, YMid, and YMax indicate where vertically the object is placed within the viewport, as you can see in the first, second, and third viewports in the first row. In the left image, we have xMinYMin meet, and the value YMin means that the square is located at the top of the viewport because YMin means that we minimize the position in respect of Y; that is, we place the object against the top edge of the viewport. When we have xMinYMid meet, the value YMid means that the square is located at the midpoint vertically of the viewport. When we have xMinYMax meet, the value YMax means that the square is located at the bottom of the viewport.

The second row in Figure 5.8 shows the effect of having xMinYMin meet, xMidYMid meet, and xMaxYMax meet as the values of the preserveAspectRatio attribute. xMin, xMid, and xMax indicate where horizontally the object is placed within the viewport, as you can see in the first, second, and third viewports in the second row. The value xMin places the square at the left of the viewport (because the value of x is at a minimum at the left of the viewport), the value xMid places the square at the midpoint horizontally of the viewport, and the value xMax places the square at the right edge of the viewport.

You can see that the values of the preserveAspectRatio attribute with meet preserve the shape of an object at the cost of placing it in a specified position that may not correspond strictly with the position specified by, for example, x and y attributes.

Let's move on to examine what happens when the second value in the preserveAspectRatio attribute is slice.

The preserveAspectRatio Attribute with slice

In this situation, the value of the preserveAspectRatio attribute looks like

preserveAspectRatio = "*xPosYPos* slice"

where *Pos* can, as previously, be Min, Mid, or Max.

When the final part of the value of the preserveAspectRatio attribute is slice, instead of displaying the whole shape in the viewport only a *slice* of the shape (or object) is displayed. A slice that fills the viewport is created.

When *xPos* is xMin, we take a slice from the left side of the object to be displayed; when it is xMid, we take a slice from the middle of the object; and when it is xMax, we take a slice from the right side of the object. Similarly, when *YPos* is YMin, we take a slice from the top of the object; when it is YMid, we take a slice from the middle (vertically) of the object; and when it is YMax, we take a slice from the bottom of the object.

Listing 5.10 illustrates the use of the slice value.

LISTING 5.10   PARWithSlice.svg—Using the slice Value in preserveAspectRatio

```
<?xml version="1.0" standalone="no"?>
<!DOCTYPE svg PUBLIC "-//W3C//DTD SVG 20010904//EN"
"http://www.w3.org/TR/2001/REC-SVG-20010904/DTD/svg10.dtd"
>
<svg width="800px" height="600px" viewBox="0 0 800 600"
xmlns:xlink="http://www.w3.org/1999/xlink">
<defs>
<rect id="myRect"  x="0" y="0" width="50" height="50"
 style="fill:#DDDDDD;stroke:red; stroke-width:4"/>
</defs>
<!-- First row is 35 units wide by 100 high -->
<rect x="20" y="20" width="35" height="100" style="fill:none;stroke:blue"/>
<rect x="60" y="20" width="35" height="100" style="fill:none;stroke:blue"/>
<rect x="100" y="20" width="35" height="100" style="fill:none;stroke:blue"/>
<svg x="20" y="20" preserveAspectRatio="xMinYMin slice"
width="35" height="100" viewBox="0 0 50 50">
<use xlink:href="#myRect"/>
</svg>
<svg x="60" y="20" preserveAspectRatio="xMidYMid slice"
width="35" height="100" viewBox="0 0 50 50">
<use xlink:href="#myRect"/>
</svg>
<svg x="100" y="20" preserveAspectRatio="xMaxYMax slice"
width="35" height="100" viewBox="0 0 50 50">
<use xlink:href="#myRect"/>
</svg>
<!-- Second row is 100 units wide by 35 high -->
<rect x="20" y="140" width="100" height="35" style="fill:none;stroke:blue"/>
<rect x="130" y="140" width="100" height="35" style="fill:none;stroke:blue"/>
<rect x="240" y="140" width="100" height="35" style="fill:none;stroke:blue"/>
<svg x="20" y="140" preserveAspectRatio="xMinYMin slice"
width="100" height="35" viewBox="0 0 50 50">
<use xlink:href="#myRect"/>
</svg>
<svg x="130" y="140" preserveAspectRatio="xMidYMid slice"
width="100" height="35" viewBox="0 0 50 50">
<use xlink:href="#myRect"/>
</svg>
<svg x="240" y="140" preserveAspectRatio="xMaxYMax slice"
width="100" height="35" viewBox="0 0 50 50">
<use xlink:href="#myRect"/>
</svg>
</svg>
```

5

Figure 5.9 shows the appearances produced by running Listing 5.10.

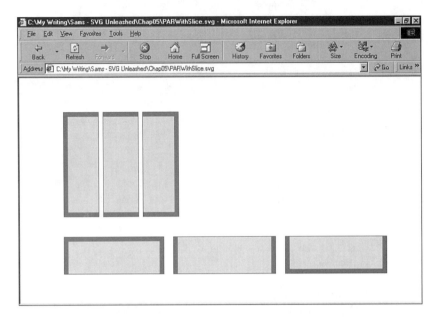

FIGURE 5.9   Effect of preserveAspectRatio with slice.

Let's look first at the visual appearance produced in the first row.

The left viewport is 50 units by 50 units. The value of `preserveAspectRatio` is `xMinYMin slice`. The square is expanded to fill the viewport vertically, and then the `xMin` value indicates that the left edge of the square is aligned with the left edge of the viewport and the square overflows the viewport to the right.

On the second viewport, the value of `preserveAspectRatio` is `xMidYMid slice`. Again, the square fills the viewport vertically but the `xMid` indicates that the square is centered horizontally in the viewport, so we see neither the left nor right edges of the square.

On the third viewport in the first row, the value of `preserveAspectRatio` is `xMaxYMax slice`. Again, the square fills the viewport vertically, but the `xMax` value indicates that the right edge of the square is aligned with the right edge of the viewport, so we see the right edge of the square aligned with the right edge of the viewport.

Let's now move on to look at the second row of viewports.

The left viewport is 50 units by 50 units. The value of `preserveAspectRatio` is `xMinYMin slice`. The square is expanded to fill the viewport horizontally, and then the `YMin` value indicates that the top edge of the square is aligned with the top edge of the viewport and the square overflows the viewport below.

On the second viewport, the value of preserveAspectRatio is xMidYMid slice. Again, the square fills the viewport horizontally, but the YMid value indicates that the square is centered vertically in the viewport, so we see neither the top nor bottom edges of the square.

On the third viewport in the second row, the value of preserveAspectRatio is xMaxYMax slice. Again, the square fills the viewport horizontally, but the YMax value indicates that the bottom edge of the square is aligned with the bottom edge of the viewport.

The x and y parts of the first value of the preserveAspectRatio attribute are not required to be identical.

The final option we need to look at occurs when the first value of the preserveAspectRatio attribute is none.

The preserveAspectRatio Attribute with the Value none

When the first part of the value of the preserveAspectRatio attribute is none, the second part of the value (whether meet or slice) is ignored. When the first part of the value of the preserveAspectRatio attribute is none, no attempt is made to preserve the aspect ratio, and the shape is simply adjusted to fill the viewport.

Listing 5.11 shows an example. The shape to be displayed is a square (a rect element with width equal to height), but the onscreen display is a rectangle that fills the available viewport. The "square" shape is scaled to fit, but in that process, we don't preserve the aspect ratio; that is, it is no longer a square.

LISTING 5.11   AspectRatio03.svg—The preserveAspectRatio attribute with the Value none

```
<?xml version="1.0" standalone="no"?>
<!DOCTYPE svg PUBLIC "-//W3C//DTD SVG 20010904//EN"
"http://www.w3.org/TR/2001/REC-SVG-20010904/DTD/svg10.dtd">
<svg width="800px" height="400px" viewBox="0 0 800 800"
 preserveAspectRatio="none">
<rect x="0" y="0" width="100%" height="100%"
 style="fill:none; stroke:red; stroke-width:5"/>
<rect x="300" y="100" width="200" height="200"
 style="fill:#999999; stroke:red; stroke-width:5"/>
</svg>
```

Figure 5.10 shows the appearance onscreen.

When preserveAspectRatio is none, we can make use of that setting to ensure that a graphic scales to fit its assigned viewport. Listing 5.12 shows an SVG document that we will embed in an HTML document.

LISTING 5.12   AspectRatioNone.svg—SVG Document with preserveAspectRatio Set to none

```
<?xml version="1.0" standalone="no"?>
<!DOCTYPE svg PUBLIC "-//W3C//DTD SVG 20010904//EN"
"http://www.w3.org/TR/2001/REC-SVG-20010904/DTD/svg10.dtd">
<svg width="200px" height="125px" viewBox="0 0 200 125"
 preserveAspectRatio="none meet">
<rect x="0" y="0" width="200" height="125"
 style="stroke:red; fill:#CCCCFF; stroke-width:5"/>
<text x="20" y="65" style="font-size:20">
SVG is elastic
</text>
</svg>
```

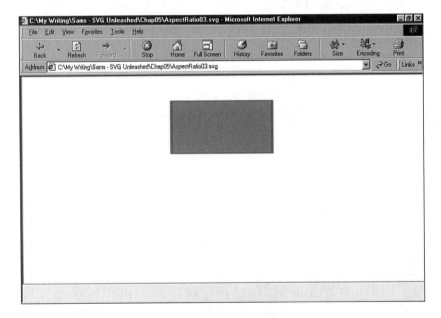

FIGURE 5.10   Effect of preserveAspectRatio with the value none.

Listing 5.13 is an HTML document that includes four embed elements of different sizes to illustrate how the SVG content will scale to fit.

LISTING 5.13   MultiAspectRatio.html—An HTML Document to Create Four Differently Sized Viewports

```
<!DOCTYPE HTML PUBLIC "-//W3C//DTD HTML 4.0 Transitional//EN"
"http://www.w3.org/TR/REC-html40/loose.dtd">
<HTML>
<HEAD>
```

LISTING 5.13   Continued

```
<TITLE>Multiple viewports with SVG stretching to fit</TITLE>
</HEAD>
<BODY>
<embed src="AspectRatioNone.svg" width="150px" height="200px"
type="image/svg+xml">
<embed src="AspectRatioNone.svg" width="100px" height="300px"
type="image/svg+xml">
<embed src="AspectRatioNone.svg" width="175px" height="90px"
type="image/svg+xml">
<embed src="AspectRatioNone.svg" width="400px" height="90px"
type="image/svg+xml">
</BODY>
</HTML>
```

Figure 5.11 shows the onscreen appearance when Listing 5.13 is run.

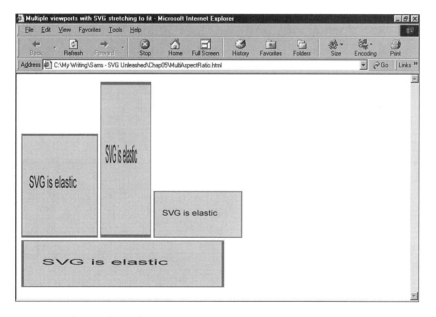

FIGURE 5.11   Scaling to fit with preserveAspectRatio having a value of none.

> **TIP**
>
> Remember to include both a viewBox attribute and a preserveAspectRatio with the first value of
> none on the document element svg element of the SVG document. If you omit them, likely the
> scale to fit won't work.

Transformations and Coordinates

In SVG terminology, a **transformation** appears to change the position or shape of an SVG shape or object. Transformations can be of the following types:

- translate—Moves a shape horizontally, vertically, or diagonally onscreen
- rotate—Rotates a shape about a defined point
- scale—Changes the size of a shape
- skewX—Distorts a shape in the horizontal direction and also moves it horizontally
- skewY—Distorts a shape in the vertical direction and also moves it vertically

When a transformation is applied, a new user coordinate system is created. The following sections will illustrate the alterations in the user coordinate system using the simple transformations available in SVG. The simple transformations are translate(), rotate(), scale(), skewX(), and skewY(). Each example in the following sections will illustrate the effect on the x- and y-axes when a particular simple transformation is applied.

translate() Transformations and the Coordinate System

First, let's look at how a translate() transformation affects the coordinate system. A translate() function takes two values, as shown here:

```
translate(20,30)
```

The preceding code indicates that the coordinate system is moved 20 user units to the right and 30 user units downward.

Listing 5.14 illustrates the alteration in the axes of the user coordinate system produced by a translate() transformation.

LISTING 5.14   Translate01.svg—Alteration in the Axes of the Coordinate System After Applying a translate() Transformation

```
<?xml version="1.0" standalone="no"?>
<!DOCTYPE svg PUBLIC "-//W3C//DTD SVG 20010904//EN"
"http://www.w3.org/TR/2001/REC-SVG-20010904/DTD/svg10.dtd">
<svg width="" height="">
<g transform="translate(0,0)">
<line x1="0" y1="0" x2="400" y2="0"
 style="stroke-width:6; stroke:black"/>
<line x1="0" y1="0" x2="0" y2="400"
 style="stroke-width:6; stroke:black"/>
</g>
<g transform="translate(50,50)">
```

LISTING 5.14   Continued

```
<line x1="0" y1="0" x2="400" y2="0"
 style="stroke-width:9; stroke:red; stroke-dasharray:4,4;"/>
<line x1="0" y1="0" x2="0" y2="400"
 style="stroke-width:9; stroke:red; stroke-dasharray:4,4;"/>
</g>
</svg>
```

The slightly panned result of running Listing 5.14 is shown in Figure 5.12.

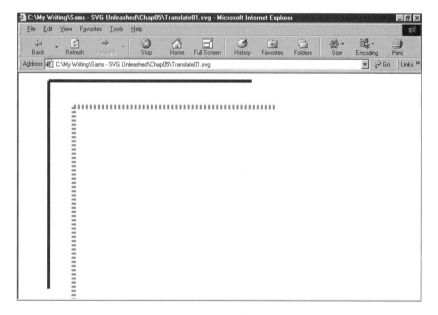

FIGURE 5.12   Applying a translate() transformation to the user coordinate system.

The user coordinate system following the transformation is shown as a dashed line. You can see that it is moved down and to the right relative to the original axes (shown in a solid line).

So, when a shape has a translate transformation applied, it is not just the shape that is moved, but the coordinate system in which it is displayed changes.

rotate() Transformations and the Coordinate System

A rotate() transformation involves rotating the coordinate system either around the origin of the coordinate system (the top left of the viewport),

```
rotate(90)
```

or around a specified point in the current coordinate system,

```
rotate(90, 100, 100)
```

In the preceding code, the first argument is an angle (measured in degrees). The second argument is the x coordinate of the point about which rotation is to take place. The third argument is the y coordinate of that point.

Listing 5.15 illustrates the effect of two `rotate()` transformations on the user coordinate system.

LISTING 5.15   Rotate01.svg—Applying rotate() Transformations to the User Coordinate System

```
<?xml version="1.0" standalone="no"?>
<!DOCTYPE svg PUBLIC "-//W3C//DTD SVG 20010904//EN"
"http://www.w3.org/TR/2001/REC-SVG-20010904/DTD/svg10.dtd">
<svg width="" height="">
<g transform="rotate(0)">
<line x1="0" y1="0" x2="400" y2="0"
 style="stroke-width:6; stroke:black"/>
<line x1="0" y1="0" x2="0" y2="250"
 style="stroke-width:6; stroke:black"/>
</g>
<g transform="rotate(30)">
<line x1="0" y1="0" x2="400" y2="0"
 style="stroke-width:9; stroke:red; stroke-dasharray:4,4;"/>
<line x1="0" y1="0" x2="0" y2="250"
 style="stroke-width:9; stroke:red; stroke-dasharray:4,4;"/>
</g>
<g transform="rotate(30, 200, 125)">
<line x1="0" y1="0" x2="400" y2="0"
 style="stroke-width:9; stroke:red; stroke-dasharray:8,8;"/>
<line x1="0" y1="0" x2="0" y2="250"
 style="stroke-width:9; stroke:red; stroke-dasharray:8,8;"/>
</g>
</svg>
```

The result of running Listing 5.15 is shown in Figure 5.13, with the image panned to best show the coordinate axes.

The solid line represents the initial coordinate system (the figure is panned). The point where the two lines join is (0,0) in the initial system. The dotted line with the smaller dots is rotated around (0,0) and is produced by the `rotate(30)` transformation because the default is to rotate around (0,0). The dotted line with the larger dots represents the `rotate(30, 200, 125)` transformation. The first value is the rotation (in degrees), the second value is the x coordinate of the point about which rotation takes place, and the third value is the y coordinate of the point about which rotation takes place.

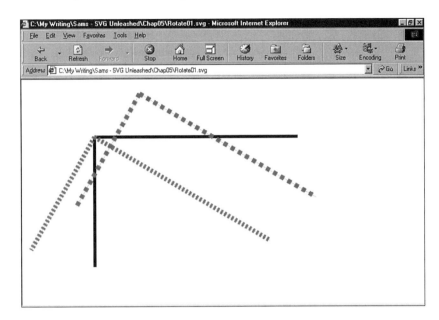

FIGURE 5.13   Applying rotate() transformations to the user coordinate system.

For the user coordinate systems we have typically looked at in this book, the origin is at the top left of the screen or viewport. However, that isn't always the case. Listing 5.16 shows a situation in which the origin of the user coordinate system is at the top right for two of the three shapes because the whole coordinate system is rotated through 90 degrees.

LISTING 5.16   Rotate02.svg—Altering the Position of the User Coordinate System's Origin

```
<?xml version="1.0" standalone="no"?>
<!DOCTYPE svg PUBLIC "-//W3C//DTD SVG 20010904//EN"
"http://www.w3.org/TR/2001/REC-SVG-20010904/DTD/svg10.dtd">
<svg width="" height="">
<g transform="rotate(0)">
<line x1="0" y1="0" x2="400" y2="0"
 style="stroke-width:6; stroke:black"/>
<line x1="0" y1="0" x2="0" y2="250"
 style="stroke-width:6; stroke:black"/>
</g>
<g transform="rotate(90)">
<line x1="0" y1="0" x2="400" y2="0"
```

LISTING 5.16   Continued

```
style="stroke-width:9; stroke:red; stroke-dasharray:4,4;"/>
<line x1="0" y1="0" x2="0" y2="250"
 style="stroke-width:9; stroke:red; stroke-dasharray:4,4;"/>
</g>
<g transform="rotate(90, 200, 125)">
<line x1="0" y1="0" x2="400" y2="0"
 style="stroke-width:9; stroke:red; stroke-dasharray:8,8;"/>
<line x1="0" y1="0" x2="0" y2="250"
 style="stroke-width:9; stroke:red; stroke-dasharray:8,8;"/>
</g>
</svg>
```

The origin of the user coordinate system of all three viewports is the place where the two lines meet at right angles. The screenshot in Figure 5.14, which shows the result of running Listing 5.16, has been panned a little so that the original (0,0) position is away from the top-left corner of the screen. The origin of the user coordinate system in the first `rotate()` transformation is still at the top left of the screen (before the image was panned) but is at the top right of the new viewport. The origin of the user coordinate system for the second `rotate()` transformation is moved to the right and upward. In addition, the origin of the user coordinate system is again at the top right of the new viewport.

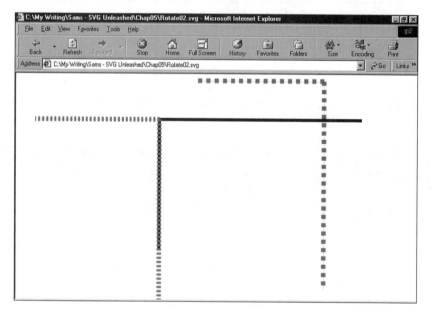

FIGURE 5.14   Moving the position of the user coordinate system's origin.

scale() Transformations and the Coordinate System

A scale() transformation alters the size of user units in the current user coordinate system. You can visualize the SVG canvas as being stretched uniformly.

Listing 5.17 illustrates the effect on the axes of the user coordinate system of applying a scale() transformation.

LISTING 5.17 Scale01.svg—Effect of Applying a scale() Transformation

```
<?xml version="1.0" standalone="no"?>
<!DOCTYPE svg PUBLIC "-//W3C//DTD SVG 20010904//EN"
"http://www.w3.org/TR/2001/REC-SVG-20010904/DTD/svg10.dtd">
<svg width="" height="">
<g transform="scale(1.0)">
<line x1="0" y1="0" x2="400" y2="0"
 style="stroke-width:6; stroke:black"/>
<line x1="0" y1="0" x2="0" y2="250"
 style="stroke-width:6; stroke:black"/>
</g>
<g transform="scale(2.0)">
<line x1="0" y1="0" x2="400" y2="0"
 style="stroke-width:9; stroke:red; stroke-dasharray:4,4;"/>
<line x1="0" y1="0" x2="0" y2="250"
 style="stroke-width:9; stroke:red; stroke-dasharray:4,4;"/>
</g>
</svg>
```

Figure 5.15 shows the result (panned and slightly zoomed out) of running Listing 5.17. The solid line represents the axes before scaling. The dotted line represents the axes after scaling. As you can see, the dotted line is twice as long as the corresponding solid line.

A scale transformation, by default, takes place around the points (0,0). For shapes that are placed away from the origin, their onscreen position changes, as well as their size. Scale transformations are discussed in more depth in Chapter 7, "Transformations in SVG."

skewX() Transformations and the Coordinate System

The skewX() transformation distorts the user coordinate system. It functions as if someone is stretching the SVG canvas by pulling horizontally on the top left and bottom right.

Listing 5.18 shows the effect of skewing the user coordinate system by 20 degrees, using transform="skewX(20)". Instead of being vertical onscreen, the "vertical" edges of a rectangle are skewed by 20 degrees. Because the x coordinates are distorted, the shape also moves onscreen.

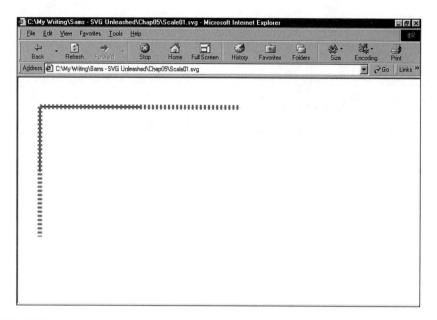

FIGURE 5.15   Applying a scale() transformation to the user coordinate system.

LISTING 5.18   SkewX01.svg—Showing the Effect on the Axes of Applying a skewX()
Transformation

```
<?xml version="1.0" standalone="no"?>
<!DOCTYPE svg PUBLIC "-//W3C//DTD SVG 20010904//EN"
"http://www.w3.org/TR/2001/REC-SVG-20010904/DTD/svg10.dtd">
<svg width="" height="">
<g transform="skewX(0)">
<line x1="0" y1="0" x2="400" y2="0"
 style="stroke-width:6; stroke:black"/>
<line x1="0" y1="0" x2="0" y2="400"
 style="stroke-width:6; stroke:black"/>
</g>
<g transform="skewX(20)">
<line x1="0" y1="0" x2="400" y2="0"
 style="stroke-width:9; stroke:red; stroke-dasharray:4,4;"/>
<line x1="0" y1="0" x2="0" y2="400"
 style="stroke-width:9; stroke:red; stroke-dasharray:4,4;"/>
</g>
</svg>
```

Figure 5.16 shows the result of running Listing 5.18.

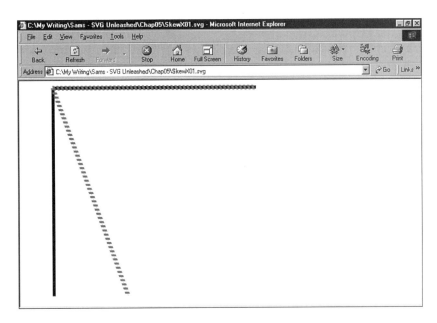

FIGURE 5.16   Applying a skewX() transformation to the user coordinate system.

skewY() Transformations and the Coordinate System

The skewY() transformation functions as if someone is stretching the SVG canvas by pulling vertically on the top left and bottom right.

Listing 5.19 illustrates the effect on the axes of the user coordinate system of applying a skewY transformation. When we apply transform="skewY(20)", the horizontal edges of a rectangle are pulled down by 20 degrees. When an object is positioned away from the origin of the coordinate system, the object's position also appears to change onscreen because the y component of the coordinate system has been skewed.

LISTING 5.19   SkewY01.svg—Altering the User Coordinate System Axes Using a skewY Transformation

```
<?xml version="1.0" standalone="no"?>
<!DOCTYPE svg PUBLIC "-//W3C//DTD SVG 20010904//EN"
"http://www.w3.org/TR/2001/REC-SVG-20010904/DTD/svg10.dtd">
<svg width="" height="">
<g transform="skewY(0)">
<line x1="0" y1="0" x2="400" y2="0"
 style="stroke-width:6; stroke:black"/>
<line x1="0" y1="0" x2="0" y2="400"
 style="stroke-width:6; stroke:black"/>
</g>
<g transform="skewY(20)">
```

LISTING 5.19   Continued

```
<line x1="0" y1="0" x2="400" y2="0"
 style="stroke-width:9; stroke:red; stroke-dasharray:4,4;"/>
<line x1="0" y1="0" x2="0" y2="400"
 style="stroke-width:9; stroke:red; stroke-dasharray:4,4;"/>
</g>
</svg>
```

Figure 5.17 shows the (slightly panned) result of running Listing 5.19.

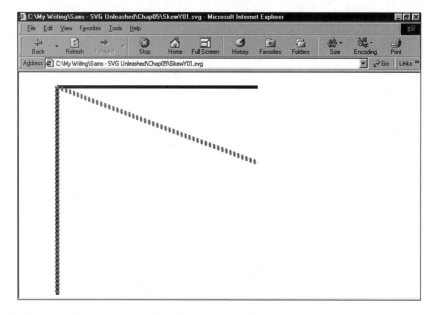

FIGURE 5.17   Applying a skewY() transformation to the user coordinate system.

Other Elements That Affect Coordinates

In this section, we will look at several SVG elements that affect the coordinate system.

The view Element

The view element was introduced in Chapter 2, "Document Structure in SVG." In this section, we will focus on the effects of the view element on coordinates in an SVG document. You may remember that the view element possesses a viewBox attribute. The viewBox attribute on the view element works similarly to the viewBox attribute on the svg element.

Essentially, the view element allows us to offer a choice to the user about what sort of scaling or translation we might want to use. Listing 5.20 shows an example to offer different scaling.

LISTING 5.20   ViewBox01.svg—Using the viewBox Attribute to Scale an Image

```
<?xml version="1.0" standalone="no"?>
<!DOCTYPE svg PUBLIC "-//W3C//DTD SVG 20010904//EN"
"http://www.w3.org/TR/2001/REC-SVG-20010904/DTD/svg10.dtd">
<svg width="700px" height="500px" viewBox="0 0 700 500">
<view id="NormalSize" viewBox="0 0 1320 800"/>
<view id="LargeSize" viewBox="0 0 700 500"/>
<view id="SmallSize" viewBox="0 0 2100 1500"/>
<rect x="100" y="100" width="500" height="300"
 style="fill:blue"/>
<a xlink:href="#SmallSize">
<text x="50" y="450">Small</text>
</a>
<a xlink:href="#NormalSize">
<text x="150" y="450">Normal</text>
</a>
<a xlink:href="#LargeSize">
<text x="250" y="450">Large</text>
</a>
</svg>
```

Clicking the text that says Small, Normal, or Large changes the viewBox attribute, contained on the matching view element, which is applied to the document element svg element. Figure 5.18 shows the (slightly panned) onscreen appearance after the document is loaded.

We can also use the view element to pan an image. Listing 5.21 shows an example.

LISTING 5.21   ViewBox02.svg—Using the view Element to Pan an Image

```
<?xml version="1.0" standalone="no"?>
<!DOCTYPE svg PUBLIC "-//W3C//DTD SVG 20010904//EN"
"http://www.w3.org/TR/2001/REC-SVG-20010904/DTD/svg10.dtd">
<svg width="700px" height="500px" viewBox="0 0 700 500">
<view id="LeftPosition" viewBox="100 0 700 500"/>
<view id="CenterPosition" viewBox="0 0 700 500"/>
<view id="RightPosition" viewBox="-100 0 700 500"/>
<rect x="100" y="100" width="500" height="300"
```

LISTING 5.21   Continued

```
 style="fill:blue"/>
<a xlink:href="#LeftPosition">
<text x="250" y="450">Go Left</text>
</a>
<a xlink:href="#CenterPosition">
<text x="350" y="450">Center</text>
</a>
<a xlink:href="#RightPosition">
<text x="450" y="450">Go Right</text>
</a>
</svg>
```

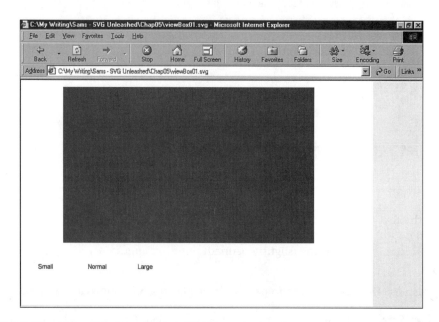

FIGURE 5.18   Using the view element to scale an image.

Figure 5.19 shows the result of running Listing 5.21. Clicking the text causes the rectangle to move to one of three fixed positions.

By combining the scaling and panning capabilities of a `view` element, you could pan and zoom to a fixed point at a fixed magnification to highlight a particular part of a map or diagram.

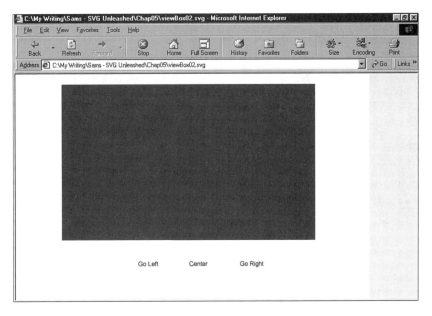

FIGURE 5.19   Using the view element to pan an image.

The image Element

The image element causes a new viewport to be created when it is used. The image element can be used to import external SVG files or bitmap graphics. All conforming SVG viewers must support the import of SVG, JPEG, and PNG files.

The preserveAspectRatio attribute of the image element determines how an image is (or is not) scaled, depending on the size of the image, the size of the viewport, and the values of the preserveAspectRatio and viewBox attributes on the image element.

> **NOTE**
>
> The preserveAspectRatio attribute is not supported on the image element in Adobe SVG Viewer version 3.0.

The foreignObject Element

The foreignObject element is intended to allow objects from non-SVG namespaces to be embedded in an SVG document. For example, you might want to embed some XHTML text within an SVG 1.0 Web page to achieve automatic text flow. Alternatively, you might want to embed SMIL (Synchronized Multimedia Integration Language) code to allow video to be shown with SVG.

Using the `foreignObject` element causes a new viewport to be created. It may take x, y, width, and height attributes as well as a `requiredExtensions` attribute, where appropriate.

NOTE

The foreignObject element is not supported in Adobe SVG Viewer version 3.0.

The symbol Element

The `symbol` element may take a `viewBox` attribute and `preserveAspectRatio` attribute, as illustrated for other elements earlier in this chapter.

Listing 5.22 shows an example of using the `symbol` element. A logo for XMML.com is created using a `symbol` element and `text` and `rect` elements.

LISTING 5.22   Symbol01.svg—Creating a Logo Using the symbol Element

```
<?xml version="1.0" standalone="no"?>
<!DOCTYPE svg PUBLIC "-//W3C//DTD SVG 20010904//EN"
"http://www.w3.org/TR/2001/REC-SVG-20010904/DTD/svg10.dtd">
<svg width="800px" height="500px" viewBox="0 0 800 500">
<defs>
<symbol id="XMMLLogo" viewBox="0 0 800 500">
<text x="5" y="15" >XMML.com</text>
<rect x="5" y="20" width="15" height="15"
 style="fill:red"/>
<rect x="25" y="20" width="15" height="15"
 style="fill:yellow"/>
 <rect x="45" y="20" width="15" height="15"
 style="fill:blue"/>
</symbol>
</defs>
<use xlink:href="#XMMLLogo" />
<use xlink:href="#XMMLLogo" transform="translate(700,0)"/>
</svg>
```

The symbol can be scaled or scaled to fit by adjusting the values contained in the `viewBox` attribute.

The two use elements in Listing 5.22 allow the symbol to be used twice. The second use element alters the user coordinate system by means of its `transform` attribute. The result is shown in Figure 5.20.

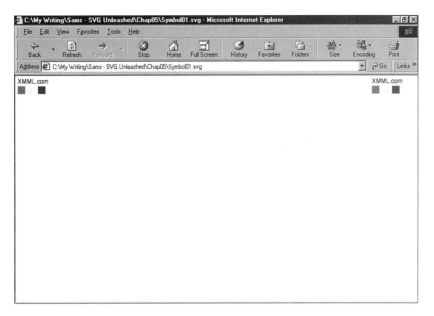

FIGURE 5.20   Using the symbol and use elements.

The use Element

When we use a use element to instance a symbol or other element, it may take a transform attribute. This allows the alterations in the coordinate system illustrated earlier in this chapter to be applied to the object instanced by the use element. This usage was shown in Listing 5.22 in the preceding section.

The pattern Element

You may recall from the discussion of the pattern element in Chapter 3, "Basic SVG Elements and Shapes," that it uses a viewBox attribute. This allows the scaling of objects within the pattern to be adjusted to a desired size. When the first two values of the viewBox attribute are altered, the positioning of the pattern may be adjusted precisely.

SVG DOM Interfaces

This section describes SVG DOM interfaces that are relevant to coordinate systems.

The SVGFitToViewBox Object

The SVGFitToViewBox object's properties and methods are used by the SVGViewSpec object (which is used in relation to the view element) and the SVGSVGElement object (which represents the svg element).

The `SVGFitToViewBox` object has the following properties specific to it:

- `viewBox`—of type `SVGAnimatedRect`
- `preserveAspectRatio`—of type `SVGAnimatedPreserveAspectRatio`

The `SVGFitToViewBox` object has no methods specific to it.

The SVGForeignObjectElement Object

The `SVGForeignObjectElement` object corresponds to the `foreignObject` element in an SVG document.

The `SVGForeignObjectElement` object has the properties and methods of the `SVGElement` object, the `SVGTests` object, the `SVGLangSpace` object, the `SVGExternalResourcesRequired` object, the `SVGStylable` object, the `SVGTransformable` object, and the DOM Level 2 Events EventTarget object (events::EventTarget).

In addition, the `SVGForeignObjectElement` object has the following properties:

- `x`—of type `SVGAnimatedLength`
- `y`—of type `SVGAnimatedLength`
- `width`—of type `SVGAnimatedLength`
- `height`—of type `SVGAnimatedLength`

The `SVGForeignObjectElement` object has no methods specific to it.

The SVGImageElement Object

The `SVGImageElement` object corresponds to an `image` element in an SVG document.

The `SVGImageElement` object has all the properties and methods of the `SVGElement` object, the `SVGURIReference` object, the `SVGTests` object, the `SVGLangSpace` object, the `SVGExternalResourcesRequired` object, the `SVGStylable` object, the `SVGTransformable` object, and the DOM Level 2 Events EventTarget object (events::EventTarget).

In addition, the `SVGImageElement` object has the following properties specific to it:

- `x`—of type `SVGAnimatedLength`
- `y`—of type `SVGAnimatedLength`
- `width`—of type `SVGAnimatedLength`
- `height`—of type `SVGAnimatedLength`
- `preserveAspectRatio`—of type `SVGAnimatedPreserveAspectRatio`

The `SVGImageElement` object has no methods specific to it.

The SVGMarkerElement Object

The `SVGMarkerElement` object has the properties and methods of the `SVGElement` object, the `SVGLangSpace` object, the `SVGExternalResourcesRequired` object, the `SVGStylable` object, and the `SVGFitToViewBox` object.

The `SVGMarkerElement` object has the following constants associated with it:

- `SVGMarkerElement.SVG_MARKERUNITS_UNKNOWN`—The constant is of type short and has a value of 0.

- `SVGMarkerElement.SVG_MARKERUNITS_USERSPACEONUSE`—The constant is of type short and has a value of 1.

- `SVGMarkerElement.SVG_MARKERUNITS_STROKEWIDTH`—The constant is of type short and has a value of 2.

- `SVGMarkerElement.SVG_MARKER_ORIENT_UNKNOWN`—The constant is of type short and has a value of 0.

- `SVGMarkerElement.SVG_MARKER_ORIENT_AUTO`—The constant is of type short and has a value of 1.

- `SVGMarkerElement.SVG_MARKER_ORIENT_ANGLE`—The constant is of type short and has a value of 2.

The `SVGMarkerElement` object has the following properties associated with it:

- `refX`—of type `SVGAnimatedLength`

- `refY`—of type `SVGAnimatedLength`

- `markerUnits`—of type `SVGAnimatedEnumeration`

- `markerWidth`—of type `SVGAnimatedLength`

- `markerHeight`—of type `SVGAnimatedLength`

- `orientType`—of type `SVGAnimatedEnumeration`

- `orientAngle`—of type `SVGAnimatedAngle`

The `SVGMarkerElement` object has the following methods:

- `setOrientToAuto()`—The method returns a value of type void. The method takes no argument.

- `setOrientToAngle(angle)`—The method returns a value of type void. The *angle* argument is of type `SVGAngle`.

The SVGPreserveAspectRatio Object

The SVGPreserveAspectRatio object has the following constants associated with it:

- SVGPreserveAspectRatio.SVG_PRESERVEASPECTRATIO_UNKNOWN—The constant is of type short and has a value of 0.

- SVGPreserveAspectRatio.SVG_PRESERVEASPECTRATIO_NONE—The constant is of type short and has a value of 1.

- SVGPreserveAspectRatio.SVG_PRESERVEASPECTRATIO_XMINYMIN—The constant is of type short and has a value of 2.

- SVGPreserveAspectRatio.SVG_PRESERVEASPECTRATIO_XMIDYMIN—The constant is of type short and has a value of 3.

- SVGPreserveAspectRatio.SVG_PRESERVEASPECTRATIO_XMAXYMIN—The constant is of type short and has a value of 4.

- SVGPreserveAspectRatio.SVG_PRESERVEASPECTRATIO_XMINYMID—The constant is of type short and has a value of 5.

- SVGPreserveAspectRatio.SVG_PRESERVEASPECTRATIO_XMIDYMID—The constant is of type short and has a value of 6.

- SVGPreserveAspectRatio.SVG_PRESERVEASPECTRATIO_XMAXYMID—The constant is of type short and has a value of 7.

- SVGPreserveAspectRatio.SVG_PRESERVEASPECTRATIO_XMINYMAX—The constant is of type short and has a value of 8.

- SVGPreserveAspectRatio.SVG_PRESERVEASPECTRATIO_XMIDYMAX—The constant is of type short and has a value of 9.

- SVGPreserveAspectRatio.SVG_PRESERVEASPECTRATIO_XMAXYMAX—The constant is of type short and has a value of 10.

- SVGPreserveAspectRatio.SVG_MEETORSLICE_UNKNOWN—The constant is of type short and has a value of 0.

- SVGPreserveAspectRatio.SVG_MEETORSLICE_MEET—The constant is of type short and has a value of 1.

- SVGPreserveAspectRatio.SVG_MEETORSLICE_SLICE—The constant is of type short and has a value of 2.

The SVGPreserveAspectRatio object has the following properties:

- align—of type unsigned short

- meetOrSlice—of type unsigned short

The SVGPreserveAspectRatio object has no methods specific to it.

Manipulating Coordinates Using the DOM

In this section, we will show a few examples to illustrate how you can manipulate coordinates or the SVG DOM objects mentioned earlier in this chapter.

Panning Under Scripting Control

Listing 5.23 shows how we can pan across the SVG canvas using scripting and the DOM.

LISTING 5.23   Panning.svg—Panning Across the SVG Canvas

```
<?xml version="1.0" standalone="no"?>
<!DOCTYPE svg PUBLIC "-//W3C//DTD SVG 20010904//EN"
"http://www.w3.org/TR/2001/REC-SVG-20010904/DTD/svg10.dtd">
<svg width="800px" height="600px" xmlns="http://www.w3.org/2000/svg"
xmlns:xlink="http://www.w3.org/1999/xlink" viewBox="0 0 800 600"
onload="Initialize()">
  <script type="text/javascript">
  <![CDATA[

var arrows;
var SVGRoot = document.documentElement;

function Initialize() {
    arrows = document.getElementsByTagName('use');
    for (var i=0; i<arrows.length; i++)
        arrows.item(i).addEventListener('click', panDoc, false);
}

function panDoc(evt) {
    var viewBox  = SVGRoot.getAttribute('viewBox');
    var viewVals    = viewBox.split(' ');
        viewVals[0] = parseFloat(viewVals[0]);
        viewVals[1] = parseFloat(viewVals[1]);

    switch (evt.target.id) {
        case 'upArrow':
            viewVals[1] += 20;
            break;
        case 'rightArrow':
            viewVals[0] -= 20;
            break;
        case 'downArrow':
            viewVals[1] -= 20;
            break;
```

LISTING 5.23   Continued

```
        case 'leftArrow':
            viewVals[0] += 20;
            break;
    }

    SVGRoot.setAttribute('viewBox', viewVals.join(' '));
}
  ]]>
  </script>
  <defs>
    <symbol id="panArrow" width="100" height="100">
      <path d="M 20 100 L 20 30 L 0 30 L 50 0 L 100 30 L 80 30 L 80 100"
stroke="red" fill="blue" />
    </symbol>
  </defs>
  <rect x="0" y="0" width="800px" height="600px"
   style="fill:none; stroke:red; stroke-width:4" />
  <rect x="370" y="270" width="60" height="60" fill="blue" />
  <use id="upArrow" xlink:href="#panArrow" x="350" y="170" />
  <use id="rightArrow" xlink:href="#panArrow" x="350" y="170"
transform="rotate(90, 400, 300)" />
  <use id="downArrow" xlink:href="#panArrow" x="350" y="170"
transform="rotate(180, 400, 300)" />
  <use id="leftArrow" xlink:href="#panArrow" x="350" y="170"
transform="rotate(270, 400, 300)" />
</svg>
```

Figure 5.21 shows the onscreen appearance when the screen loads. Clicking on any part of an arrow causes the SVG canvas to be panned in the corresponding direction by a distance of 20 pixels. The background rectangle is outlined in red and corresponds to the original boundaries of the initial viewport so that, as the image is panned, you can see how far it has moved.

An array, viewVals, contains the values that make up the value of the viewBox attribute.

When an arrow is clicked, the panDoc() function is called. The current value of the viewBox attribute is retrieved and parsed into the viewVals array. A switch statement manipulates the appropriate element of the array, depending on which arrow has been clicked. After each click, the elements of the array are assembled, and the value is written back to the viewBox attribute.

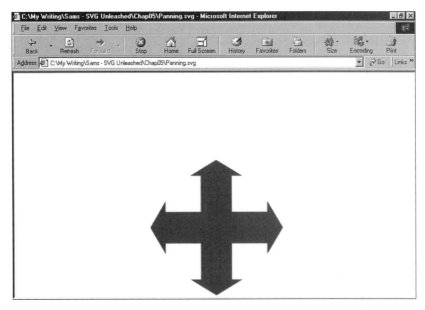

FIGURE 5.21   An arrow to allow panning of the SVG canvas by scripting the DOM.

Notice that if you right-click on the image after panning (in ASV3), the Original View menu option is grayed out. As far as ASV is concerned, what you see after the scripted panning *is* the original view, as defined by the viewBox attribute on the svg document element.

Scaling an Image

You can employ several techniques to script changes in scale. One technique is to manipulate the values contained in the value of the viewBox attribute on the svg document element.

Listing 5.24 shows an XHTML document that allows the scale of an embedded SVG image to be adjusted according to the user action.

LISTING 5.24   ScaleEvent.html—A Container XHTML Document for the SVG to Be Scaled

```
<?xml version="1.0"?>
<!DOCTYPE html PUBLIC "-//W3C//DTD XHTML 1.0 Transitional//EN"
    "http://www.w3.org/TR/xhtml1/DTD/xhtml1-transitional.dtd">
<html xmlns="http://www.w3.org/1999/xhtml">
  <head>
    <title>Scaling by changing viewBox attribute</title>
    <script type="text/javascript">
```

LISTING 5.24   Continued

```
var XHMTLObj, SVGDoc, SVGRoot;

function Initialize() {
    window.XHTMLObj   = document.getElementById('XHTMLObj');
    window.SVGDoc     = XHTMLObj.getSVGDocument();
    window.SVGRoot = SVGDoc.documentElement;
}

function zoomSVG(evt) {
    var viewBox     = SVGRoot.getAttribute('viewBox');
    var viewVals    = viewBox.split(' ');
    for (var i=0; i<viewVals.length; i++)
        viewVals[i] = parseFloat(viewVals[i]);

    if (evt.button == 0) {
        viewVals[2] *= 1.5;
        viewVals[3] *= 1.5;
    }
    else {
        viewVals[2] /= 1.5;
        viewVals[3] /= 1.5;
    }

    SVGRoot.setAttribute('viewBox', viewVals.join(' '));
    evt.preventDefault();
}

    </script>
  </head>
  <body onload="Initialize()">
    <p>Click in the SVG document below. This will change the values
       in the viewBox attribute. </p>
    <p>Left clicking makes the circles smaller.
➥Right clicking makes them bigger.</p>
    <embed id="XHTMLObj" src="ScaleEvent.svg" type="image/svg+xml"
➥style="width:
600px; height: 400px; border: solid #000 1px" />
  </body>
</html>
```

Listing 5.25 shows the SVG image that is scaled.

LISTING 5.25 ScaleEvent.svg—The viewBox Attribute Is Changed Under Script Control from the XHTML Document

```
<?xml version="1.0" standalone="no"?>
<!DOCTYPE svg PUBLIC "-//W3C//DTD SVG 20010904//EN"
"http://www.w3.org/TR/2001/REC-SVG-20010904/DTD/svg10.dtd">
<svg width="600px" height="400px" xmlns="http://www.w3.org/2000/svg"
xmlns:xlink="http://www.w3.org/1999/xlink" viewBox="0 0 600 400"
onmousedown="zoomSVG(evt)">
  <rect x="0" y="0" width="100%" height="100%" fill="white" />
<g transform="translate(300,200)">
  <circle cx="0" cy="0" r="200" fill="none" stroke="red" stroke-width="10"
/>
  <circle cx="0" cy="0" r="150" fill="none" stroke="red" stroke-width="10"
/>
  <circle cx="0" cy="0" r="100" fill="none" stroke="red" stroke-width="10"
/>
  <circle cx="0" cy="0" r="50"  fill="none" stroke="red" stroke-width="10"
/>
</g>
</svg>
```

Figure 5.22 shows the result of running Listing 5.24. The XHTML document contains the script that controls what happens in the SVG document. Left-clicking causes a change in the viewBox attribute, making the image smaller. Right-clicking (or middle-clicking) causes the circles to be rendered larger due to a change in the viewBox attribute. There is no if statement in the script, and the mousedown event is captured on the SVG document (not the circles), so if you carry on clicking, in principle, you can continue scaling the image infinitely.

When the XHTML document loads, an Initialize() function is called, ensuring that the SVG document is scriptable from the XHTML document. When a mousedown event is detected in the SVG document, the zoomSVG() function is called. The value of the viewBox attribute is parsed into its component parts. The third and fourth values in an array (array elements [2] and [3] because arrays are numbered from zero) are scaled, according to whether the right or left mouse button was pressed. The value of the viewBox attribute is reassembled, and the SVG image is rendered in accordance with the new values in the viewBox attribute.

Perhaps you are wondering why the Adobe SVG Viewer menu doesn't appear when you right-click. The script in the XHTML document captures the mousedown event in the SVG document. When the mousedown event is captured, the image is scaled. When the mouse button is released, a mouseup event happens, but this doesn't cause the Adobe SVG Viewer menu to appear. The ASV3 menu appears on click, and a click consists of both mousedown and mouseup. The mousedown event is handled by the zoomSVG() function, so only the mouseup event is left. It is only part of a click; therefore, the ASV3 menu does not appear.

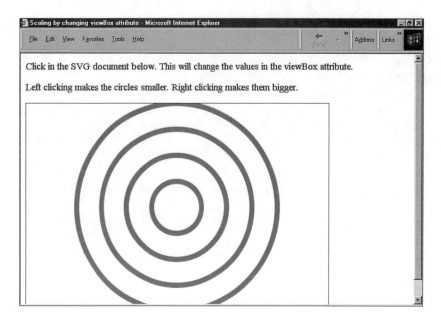

FIGURE 5.22   Controlling scaling by altering the viewBox attribute on a mousedown event.

Marker Example

The SVG DOM SVGMarkerElement object mentioned earlier in this chapter is not yet implemented in the Adobe SVG Viewer version 3.0. However, we can use generic DOM methods to access and manipulate attributes of a marker element until such time as ASV implements the SVGMarkerElement object.

Listing 5.26 shows an example of manipulating the attributes of a marker element using DOM core methods.

LISTING 5.26   MarkerExample.svg—Altering the Angle of a Marker

```
<?xml version="1.0" standalone="no"?>
<!DOCTYPE svg PUBLIC "-//W3C//DTD SVG 20010904//EN"
"http://www.w3.org/TR/2001/REC-SVG-20010904/DTD/svg10.dtd">
<svg width="200px" height="200px" xmlns="http://www.w3.org/2000/svg"
onload="Initialize()">
  <script type="text/javascript">
  <![CDATA[

var marker1;
var marker1Angle = 10;

function Initialize() {
```

LISTING 5.26   Continued

```
    marker1 = document.getElementById('marker1');
    moveMarker();
}

function moveMarker() {
    marker1Angle *= -1;
    marker1.setAttribute('orient', marker1Angle);
    setTimeout('moveMarker()', 1000);
}

/*

SVGMarkerElement should have the following properties and methods:
  refX
  refY
  markerUnits
  markerWidth
  markerHeight
  orientType
  orientAngle
  setOrientToAuto()
  setOrientToAngle(angle)

The SVGMarkerElement object corresponds to the marker element. Although the
marker element is recognized and its attributes correctly applied by ASV, its
properties and methods are not yet implemented in the DOM as of ASV3. However,
it is still possible to manipulate the attributes of a marker element by using
the Core methods getAttribute() and setAttribute() as demonstrated in this
example.

*/

  ]]>
  </script>
  <defs>
    <marker id="marker1" viewBox="0 0 10 10" refX="5" refY="9"
markerUnits="strokeWidth" markerWidth="4" markerHeight="3" orient="0">
      <path d="M 0 10 L 5 0 L 10 10 z" />
    </marker>
  </defs>
  <line x1="100" y1="170" x2="100" y2="50" fill="none" stroke="black"
stroke-width="10" marker-end="url(#marker1)" />
</svg>
```

The `moveMarker()` function is called from the `Initialize()` function, which is called when the document loads.

We create the movement of part of the marker by reversing the applied angle, within the `moveMarker()` function.

CAUTION

Be careful if you embed SVG images in HTML or XHTML. If you have onload attributes on the body element of the HTML/XHTML and on the svg document element, you may get unexpected effects if you use the convention of naming the function called from the onload attribute Initialize().

Summary

This chapter explored what the SVG viewport is and how the initial viewport is created. The viewport is the area of the SVG canvas that you can see onscreen. We looked at how the `viewBox` attribute can be used to scale or pan objects within its scope. We also looked at the `preserveAspectRatio` attribute and examined many of the values it can take.

Finally, we described the SVG DOM objects relevant to coordinates and showed some examples of using the DOM.

CHAPTER **6**

Paths in SVG

The basic SVG graphic shapes to which you were introduced in Chapter 3, "Basic SVG Elements and Shapes," are limited in the range of shapes that they can create. You can use the SVG path element, by contrast, to create almost any arbitrary two-dimensional shape, including those that can be created using the basic graphic shapes. The exceptions are circles and ellipses.

A path in SVG is an arbitrary graphic shape that can be filled, stroked, or used as a clipping path. A path can consist of a straight line or a curved line or any combination of straight and curved lines. It can be an open shape or a closed object of any arbitrary shape. Inevitably, because the path element supports the creation of such a potentially large number of shapes, the syntax of the path element can be somewhat complex.

In addition to examining how to use the path element in the early sections of the chapter, the final section of the chapter will describe the SVG DOM interfaces that are particularly relevant for manipulating paths.

Using the path Element

The path element is the SVG element used to define shapes of almost any arbitrary two-dimensional form.

Any of the basic graphic shapes that you saw in Chapter 3 can also be represented by a path element. The rect, line, and other basic graphic shapes simply provide an easier way to define and manipulate commonly used graphic shapes. The path element can also be used to create shapes approximating to a circle or ellipse element. For example, we could represent a square using either a rect element or a path element.

Listing 6.1 creates a square with a dashed outline using a rect element.

LISTING 6.1   Rect01.svg—Creating a Square Using a rect Element

```
<?xml version="1.0" standalone="no"?>
<!DOCTYPE svg PUBLIC "-//W3C//DTD SVG 20010904//EN"
"http://www.w3.org/TR/2001/REC-SVG-20010904/DTD/svg10.dtd">
<svg width="500px" height="300px">
<rect x="50px" y="50px" width="150px" height="150px"
 style="fill:none; stroke:red; stroke-dasharray:3,3; stroke-width:5"/>
</svg>
```

Listing 6.2 produces an identical square using the path element.

LISTING 6.2   Rect02.svg—Creating a Square Using a path Element

```
<?xml version="1.0" standalone="no"?>
<!DOCTYPE svg PUBLIC "-//W3C//DTD SVG 20010904//EN"
"http://www.w3.org/TR/2001/REC-SVG-20010904/DTD/svg10.dtd">
<svg width="500px" height="300px">
<path d="M50 50, L200 50, 200 200, 50 200, z"
style="fill:none; stroke:red; stroke-dasharray:3,3; stroke-width:5"
/>
</svg>
```

The syntax of the d attribute of the path element is explained in detail in the following section.

If you run either Listing 6.1 or Listing 6.2, the onscreen appearance will be similar to that shown in Figure 6.1.

The d Attribute

An examination of the path element in Listing 6.2 shows that, apart from the styling information contained in the style attribute, the shape of the path is controlled by the content of the d attribute. The d attribute is the **path data** attribute.

The value of the d attribute can be extremely lengthy and complex, for any shape other than simple ones. Therefore, it was decided during development of the SVG 1.0 specification to make the syntax used within the d attribute as succinct as possible, to minimize code length.

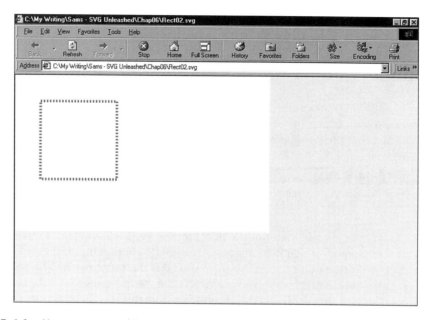

FIGURE 6.1   You can create this square using either a rect or path element.

The creation of a path in SVG can be viewed as similar to instructions to a plotter. The value of the path data contained in the d attribute consists of a series of instructions of the following types:

- moveto—Moves the pen to a particular point, while it is raised above the rendering surface

- lineto—Draws a straight line to a defined point

- curveto—Draws a Bezier curve to a defined point

- arc—Draws an elliptical or circular arc to a defined point

- closepath—Closes a path

We will examine each of these commands in turn during the next several sections of this chapter.

The d attribute of the path element provides two forms of syntax for its content—using absolute path coordinates and using relative path coordinates. First, we will look at the use of absolute path coordinates.

Absolute Path Coordinates

For the sake of simplicity, we will consider the default (untransformed) user coordinates in this section.

As mentioned in the previous section, the path data consists of several possible parts. In Listing 6.2, we see examples of the moveto, lineto, and closepath commands:

```
<path d="M50 50, L200 50, 200 200, 50 200, z"
style="fill:none; stroke:red; stroke-dasharray:3,3; stroke-width:5"
/>
```

The uppercase M with which the value of the d attribute begins is the abbreviation for moveto. The fact that the M is uppercase indicates that absolute coordinates are being used.

> **NOTE**
>
> The first instruction in a d attribute must be a moveto instruction.

The 50 50 indicates the coordinates of the point moved to. The comma is a separator from the next command, which is a lineto with absolute coordinates, indicated by the uppercase L. The starting point for a lineto command is the point reached by the previous (for example, moveto or lineto) command. So L200 50 indicates that a line is drawn from the point moved to, (50,50), to the absolute coordinates specified by the L, that is (200,50).

When two commands of the same type follow each other, such as

```
L200 50, L200 200,
```

the second L can be omitted. Thus, in our extract from Listing 6.2, the 200 200 is short for L200 200. Similarly, 50 200 is short for L50 200.

Finally, the closepath command is indicated by the lowercase character z.

Translating the content of the d attribute to English gives us a series of commands, like this: "Move the pen to (50,50), draw a straight line to (200,50), then draw a straight line to (200,200), and then draw a straight line to (50,200), and finally close the path (implicitly by drawing a straight line to (50,50)).

Syntax Options
SVG provides several options for writing absolute path instructions in compact form. The "full" version of the path data contained in the d attribute of the path element in Listing 6.2 can be written like this:

```
M 50 50, L 200 50, L 200 200, L 50 200, z
```

Notice the spaces between the instructions and each coordinate. We don't need to repeat an instruction if two successive instructions are the same, so we can omit two L instructions, as shown in the following:

```
M 50 50, L200 50, 200 200, 50 200, z
```

In addition, we can omit the commas, as long as whitespace separates numerical values:

```
M 50 50 L200 50 200 200 50 200 z
```

And we can omit whitespace between an instruction and the numerical value that follows, as in M50 in the following code, or between a numerical value and the instruction that follows it, as in 50L in the following code:

```
M50 50L200 50 200 200 50 200 z
```

When one d attribute contains multiple lineto and curveto commands and so on, omission of the comma separator and whitespace can reduce file size significantly, but it does so at the expense of code readability. Where the optimum balance lies is for you to decide.

If you want, you can even omit the L instruction. If an M instruction is followed by several pairs of coordinates, all but the first are treated as implicit lineto instructions. Thus, the following means the same as the previous lines of code:

```
M50 50 200 50 200 200 50 200 z
```

Horizontal and Vertical lineto Instructions

Drawing horizontal and vertical lines is common in technical drawing, mapping, and so on. Therefore, SVG provides an abbreviated syntax for drawing such lines. To draw a horizontal line to an absolute coordinate pair, we use the H instruction. To draw a vertical line to an absolute coordinate pair, we use a V instruction.

When using the H instruction, we can omit the y coordinate. Thus, if the current point is (50,50) and we want to draw to (200,50), we can use L 200 50 or H 200. Because the line is known to be horizontal, the y coordinate does not change and need not be expressed.

Similarly, to draw a vertical line from (200,50) to (200,200), we can write L 200 200 or V 200. Because the line is known to be vertical, we need not express the x coordinate. It will not change from the x coordinate of the start of the line.

Thus, we could rewrite the code

```
M 50 50, L 200 50, L 200 200, L 50 200, z
```

as

```
M 50 50, H 200 V 200 H 50   z
```

Listing 6.3 draws the same visual appearance as Listing 6.2, but instead of using L instructions, it uses H and V instructions.

LISTING 6.3   HorizVertLines.svg—Using H and V lineto Instructions

```
<?xml version="1.0" standalone="no"?>
<!DOCTYPE svg PUBLIC "-//W3C//DTD SVG 20010904//EN"
"http://www.w3.org/TR/2001/REC-SVG-20010904/DTD/svg10.dtd">
<svg width="500px" height="300px">
<path d="M50 50, H 200, V 200, H 50, z"
style="fill:none; stroke:red; stroke-dasharray:3,3; stroke-width:5"
/>
</svg>
```

Now we can remove the whitespace and comma separators from Listing 6.3, as shown earlier. The revised code is shown in Listing 6.4.

LISTING 6.4   HorizVertLines02.svg—Listing 6.3 After Removal of Whitespace and Separators

```
<?xml version="1.0" standalone="no"?>
<!DOCTYPE svg PUBLIC "-//W3C//DTD SVG 20010904//EN"
"http://www.w3.org/TR/2001/REC-SVG-20010904/DTD/svg10.dtd">
<svg width="500px" height="300px">
<path d="M50 50H200V200H50z"
style="fill:none; stroke:red; stroke-dasharray:3,3; stroke-width:5"
/>
</svg>
```

In Listing 6.4, the length of the d attribute's value is shorter. Readability, however, is significantly less good.

Subpaths

An SVG path need not be drawable using a single continuous line. We can, for example, use two separate **subpaths** to draw doughnut-like shapes. A simple example is shown in Listing 6.5.

LISTING 6.5   Subpaths.svg—A Square Doughnut Drawn Using Subpaths

```
<?xml version="1.0" standalone="no"?>
<!DOCTYPE svg PUBLIC "-//W3C//DTD SVG 20010904//EN"
"http://www.w3.org/TR/2001/REC-SVG-20010904/DTD/svg10.dtd">
<svg width="" height="">
<defs>
<path id="myDoughnut" d="M50 50, L300 50, 300 300, 50 300, z,
 M150 150, L200 150, 200 200, 150 200, z"
style="fill:none; stroke:green; stroke-width:4"/>
</defs>
```

LISTING 6.5   Continued

```
<use xlink:href="#myDoughnut" />
</svg>
```

The first subpath creates the outer square. The z closepath instruction when immediately followed by a moveto instruction means that a new subpath is to be started. Then the "pen" is lifted and moved to (150,150) and a further, smaller square is drawn. Figure 6.2 shows the appearance onscreen.

> **NOTE**
>
> If you use a closepath instruction, using the z character, to complete a path, the lines are joined using the current value of stroke-linejoin. If the value of stroke-linejoin is miter, the ends of the lines are joined at an angle; if the value is round, the place where the lines join is rounded; and if it is bevel, the corner is beveled (the sharp point is cut off). If, instead of using closepath, you draw a line to the initial coordinates of the subpath, the current value of stroke-linecap is applied to the end of each line.

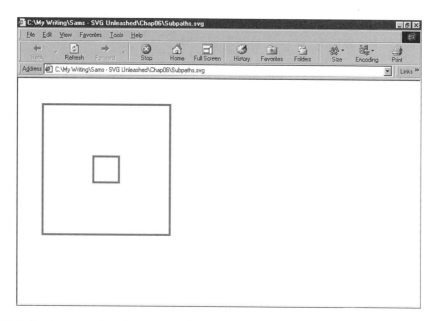

FIGURE 6.2   A square doughnut created using subpaths.

Filling Paths

If we want to fill a shape like the one we created in Listing 6.5, we can use the fill-rule attribute to specify which rule is to be used.

Listing 6.6 shows the use of the `fill-rule` attribute on Listing 6.5.

LISTING 6.6   SubpathsFilled.svg—Using the fill-rule Attribute

```
<?xml version="1.0" standalone="no"?>
<!DOCTYPE svg PUBLIC "-//W3C//DTD SVG 20010904//EN"
"http://www.w3.org/TR/2001/REC-SVG-20010904/DTD/svg10.dtd">
<svg width="" height="">
<defs>
<path id="myDoughnut" d="M50 50, L300 50, 300 300, 50 300, z,
 M150 150, L200 150, 200 200, 150 200, z"
style="fill:#CCCCCC; stroke:green"
fill-rule="evenodd"/>
</defs>
<use xlink:href="#myDoughnut" />
</svg>
```

Figure 6.3 shows the onscreen result of running Listing 6.6.

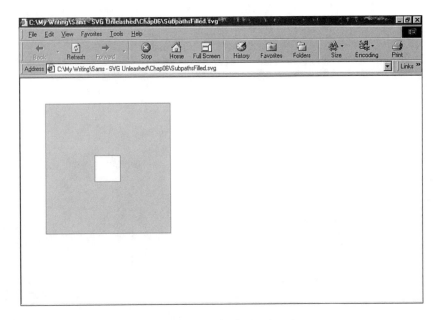

FIGURE 6.3   A filled square doughnut created using subpaths.

The permitted values of `fill-rule` are `nonzero` (the default), `evenodd`, or `inherit`. The rules determine whether and where an object is filled. To take a simple example, when we enter a rectangle, we cross one line so that is not zero, and it is an odd number of lines crossed. So, under both rules a rectangle is filled in the obvious place. For very complex shapes, setting the value of the fill-rule attribute to nonzero may give a different fill pattern compared to setting it to evenodd. If an object is part of a group, when the value of fill-rule is set to inherit, the value of the parent (or ancestor) definition of fill-rule will be applied.

Relative Path Coordinates

We can also use an alternate syntax for path data that uses relative coordinates. Suppose we are again drawing the simple square used in earlier examples. After the initial moveto command, we might, in English, express the next instruction as "Draw a line 150 units horizontally to the right." That is an instruction expressed as a relative change in coordinates. To use relative path coordinates, we simply use a lowercase l rather than an uppercase L for drawing lines. Similarly, we use m rather than M for moveto.

Listing 6.7 shows the doughnut drawn using relative path coordinates.

LISTING 6.7   Subpaths02.svg—Using Relative Coordinates in Two Subpaths

```
<?xml version="1.0" standalone="no"?>
<!DOCTYPE svg PUBLIC "-//W3C//DTD SVG 20010904//EN"
"http://www.w3.org/TR/2001/REC-SVG-20010904/DTD/svg10.dtd">
<svg width="" height="">
<defs>
<path id="myDoughnut" d="M50 50, l 250 0, 0 250, -250 0, z,
 m 100 100, 150 0, 0 50, -50 0, z"
style="fill:none; stroke:green"/>
</defs>
<use xlink:href="#myDoughnut" />
</svg>
```

In the value of the d attribute, a lowercase *L*, written as l, is used for drawing a line relative to a starting position. A lowercase *M*, written as m, is used for a relative moveto. You can see the use of both these relative path commands in the seventh line of Listing 6.7.

This code produces the same appearance onscreen as Listing 6.6. The value of the d attribute, expressed in English, is as follows "Move to (50,50), then draw a line to a position 250 units to the right, then draw a line 250 units vertically downward, then draw a line 250 units horizontally to the left and, finally, close the path by drawing a line back to coordinates (50,50). Then move the 'pen' 100 units to the right and 100 units down (to 150,150), draw a line 50 units horizontally to the right, then 50 units vertically down, then 50 units to the left, and finally close the path by drawing a line back to (150,150)."

CAUTION

The SVG 1.0 syntax for relative line drawing—a lowercase *L*, written as l, is very similar in appearance to the number 1. When you're creating code, you can easily introduce a number 1 for the character l.

In SVG 1.1 or 1.2, it is likely that an alternative syntax for relative line drawing, perhaps a lowercase r, will be introduced to avoid this problem.

The onscreen appearance is the same as Figure 6.1.

That is pretty much all there is to drawing paths that consist solely of straight lines. As long as you know the coordinates you want to draw to and understand how to express the moveto, lineto, and closepath instructions inside a d attribute, using either absolute or relative coordinates, the procedure is straightforward.

Creating curves can be significantly less easy to grasp.

Creating Curves Using the path Element

Creating graphic shapes that consist only of straight lines would be very limiting in many situations. Therefore, the path element provides support for rendering of curved path segments.

Three types of curves can be expressed as subpaths within the d attribute of a path element:

- **Cubic Bezier curve**—Expressed as C (absolute) or c (relative) instructions. There is also a shorthand syntax using S (absolute) and s (relative) instructions.

- **Quadratic Bezier curves**—Expressed as Q (absolute) or q (relative). There is also a shorthand syntax using T (absolute) and t (relative) instructions.

- **Elliptical arc curves**—Expressed as A (absolute) or a (relative).

Let's briefly look at each in turn.

Cubic Bezier Curves

A cubic Bezier curve is drawn using the coordinates of four points: a start point (also called the current point), an endpoint, and two **control points**.

The general form is

```
d="M x0 y0
  C x1 y1 x2 y2 x y "
```

where x0 and y0 are the coordinates of the start point of the curve, x1 and y1 are the coordinates of the control point for the start point of the curve, x2 and y2 are the coordinates of the control point for the endpoint of the curve, and x and y are the coordinates of the endpoint itself.

The notion of control points will be familiar if you have used vector graphics packages. Listing 6.8 shows an example of a simple curve created using a cubic Bezier curve.

> **TIP**
>
> Jasc WebDraw allows you to create curved shapes with one or more cubic Bezier curves. You can alter the control points on the Canvas tab or on the Source tab. This helps you get a feel for how to use the control points quantitatively.

LISTING 6.8   Cubic01.svg—A Bezier Curve

```
<?xml version="1.0"?>
<!DOCTYPE svg PUBLIC "-//W3C//DTD SVG 1.0//EN"
 "http://www.w3.org/TR/2001/REC-SVG-20010904/DTD/svg10.dtd">
<svg width="500" height="500">
<path
 d="M90.7895 235.526
 C7.91503 121.776 30.9618 38.2115 226.316 207.895"
 style="fill:none;stroke:rgb(0,0,0);stroke-width:4"/>
</svg>
```

Figure 6.4 shows the onscreen appearance when you run Listing 6.8.

Listing 6.9 shows a cubic Bezier curve with multiple segments.

LISTING 6.9   Cubic02.svg—A More Complex Bezier Curve

```
<?xml version="1.0"?>
<!DOCTYPE svg PUBLIC "-//W3C//DTD SVG 1.0//EN"
"http://www.w3.org/TR/2001/REC-SVG-20010904/DTD/svg10.dtd">
<svg width="500" height="500">
<path d="M96.0526 151.316
 C102.973 102.874 229.734 24.9198 214.474 122.368
 C207.901 164.344 191.176 238.14 227.632 226.316
 C284.063 208.012 375.766 35.3111 367.105 203.947"
 style="fill:none;stroke:rgb(0,0,0);stroke-width:4"/>
</svg>
```

6

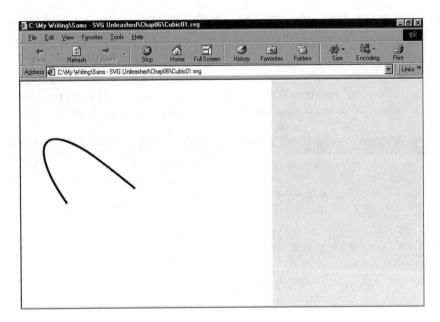

FIGURE 6.4   A cubic Bezier curve.

Listing 6.9 was produced using a drawing tool, as you might guess by the multiple figures after the decimal point for many coordinates.

> **TIP**
>
> When you are creating curves with multiple cubic Bezier curves, it can be useful to start the code for each segment on a separate line.

Figure 6.5 shows the onscreen result when you run Listing 6.9.

The Shorthand Cubic Bezier Syntax

The shorthand cubic Bezier syntax allows the creation of smooth cubic Bezier curves.

The general form is

```
d="M x0 y0
 S x2 y2 x y "
```

where x0 and y0 are the coordinates of the start point of the curve, x2 and y2 are the coordinates of the control point for the endpoint of the curve, and x and y are the coordinates of the endpoint itself. The control point for the start point of the curve is either the reflection of the second control point on the previous segment or, if there is no preceding command, the control point is the same point as the start point.

FIGURE 6.5   A cubic Bezier curve with multiple segments.

A corresponding s instruction can be used with relative coordinates.

Quadratic Bezier Curves

A Quadratic Bezier curve has only a single control point, rather than the two control points that a cubic Bezier curve has.

The general form for a Quadratic Bezier curve is

```
d="M x0 y0
 Q x1 y1 x y "
```

where x0 and y0 are the coordinates of the start point of the curve, x1 and y1 are the coordinates of the control point for the curve, and x and y are the coordinates of the endpoint itself.

The Shorthand Quadratic Bezier Syntax

The Quadratic Bezier curve has a shorthand form comparable to the s instruction for the cubic Bezier curves.

The general form for a Quadratic Bezier curve is

```
d="M x0 y0
  T x y "
```

where x0 and y0 are the coordinates of the start point of the curve and x and y are the coordinates of the endpoint itself. The control point is assumed to be the same as the start point (if there is no previous segment) or the reflection of the control point on the previous segment.

A corresponding t instruction can be used with relative coordinates.

Arc Curves

An elliptical arc curve is visually simple, but to draw an elliptical arc, you need several pieces of information.

Suppose we want to draw an elliptical arc from (300,300) to (500,200). Listing 6.10 shows two possible ellipses along which the elliptical arc can be drawn.

LISTING 6.10   Arc01.svg—Elliptical Arc Between Two Points

```
<?xml version="1.0" standalone="no"?>
<!DOCTYPE svg PUBLIC "-//W3C//DTD SVG 20010904//EN"
"http://www.w3.org/TR/2001/REC-SVG-20010904/DTD/svg10.dtd">
<svg width="" height="">
<ellipse cx="500px" cy="300px" rx="200px" ry="100px"
 style="stroke:red; fill:none; stroke-width:4"/>
<ellipse cx="300px" cy="200px" rx="200px" ry="100px"
 style="stroke:red; fill:none; stroke-width:4"/>
</svg>
```

Figure 6.6 shows the onscreen appearance when Listing 6.10 is run.

But we have two unanswered questions. Along which ellipse is the arc to be drawn? Is the arc to be the "long way around" or a "shortcut"?

The general form for an A instruction, which is used within a d attribute to create an arc, is as follows:

```
A rx ry x-axis-rotation large-arc-flag sweep-flag x y
```

To draw an elliptical arc from (300,300) to (500,200), we first specify the start point (300,300) by means of a moveto instruction. Next, we specify the A instruction. The next two parameters specify the x and y radii of the ellipse. Then we add a value of any rotation of the ellipse around the current user coordinate system—in this case, 0. If we want to go the "long way around," we set large-arc-flag to 1, and we set it to 0 if we want to take the "shortcut." Next, we set the sweep-flag to 1 if we want to go clockwise, and to 0 if we want to go counterclockwise. Finally, we specify the end of the arc—in this case, using the coordinates (500,200):

```
d="M300 300, A 200 100 0 1 1 500 200"
```

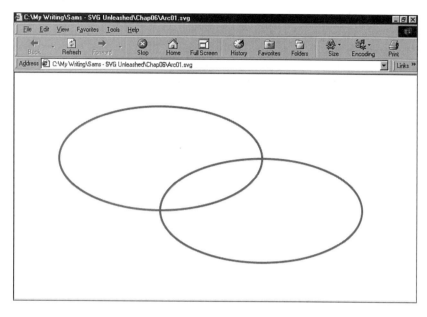

FIGURE 6.6   Two ellipses between (300,300) and (500,200).

Listing 6.11 shows four elliptical arcs specified to traverse between (300,300) and (500,200).

LISTING 6.11   Arc02.svg—Four Elliptical Arcs

```
<?xml version="1.0" standalone="no"?>
<!DOCTYPE svg PUBLIC "-//W3C//DTD SVG 20010904//EN"
"http://www.w3.org/TR/2001/REC-SVG-20010904/DTD/svg10.dtd">
<svg width="" height="">
<ellipse cx="500px" cy="300px" rx="200px" ry="100px"
 style="stroke:red; fill:none"/>
<ellipse cx="300px" cy="200px" rx="200px" ry="100px"
 style="stroke:red; fill:none"/>
<path d="M300 300, A 200 100 0 1 1 500 200"
 style="stroke:green; stroke-width:4; fill:none"/>
<path d="M300 300, A 200 100 0 1 0 500 200"
 style="stroke:green; stroke-width:4; stroke-dasharray: 2,2; fill:none"/>
<path d="M300 300, A 200 100 0 0 1 500 200"
 style="stroke:green; stroke-width:4; fill:none"/>
<path d="M300 300, A 200 100 0 0 0 500 200"
 style="stroke:green; stroke-width:4; stroke-dasharray: 6,6; fill:none"/>
</svg>
```

The first path element has the `large-arc-flag` set to 1 and the `sweep-flag` also set to 1. It is displayed in solid green and goes the long way around, clockwise. The second path element has the `large-arc-flag` set to 1 and the `sweep-flag` set to 0. It is displayed in very short dashes in green and goes the long way around, counterclockwise. The third path element has the `large-arc-flag` set to 0 and the `sweep-flag` set to 1. It is displayed in solid green and goes the short way around, clockwise. The fourth path element has the `large-arc-flag` set to 0 and the `sweep-flag` also set to 0. It is displayed in dashed green and goes the short way around, counterclockwise.

Figure 6.7 shows the onscreen appearance when you run Listing 6.11.

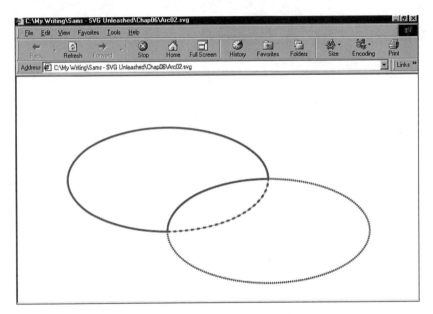

FIGURE 6.7   Four elliptical arcs between (300,300) and (500,200).

Applying Text to a Path

It is not uncommon for designers to want to place text along any arbitrary path, rather than simply along a straight line. SVG supports the placement of text on any path shape you might want to choose. If readability of the text is important, however, there are practical constraints on which paths it might be appropriate to place text on.

> **NOTE**
>
> You can find general information about laying out text in Chapter 8, "Laying Out Text in SVG."

The textPath Element

The textPath element is nested within a text element. The path onto which the text is to be placed is defined in a path element that possesses an id attribute and that is nested within the defs element. The textPath element references the path element by means of an xlink:href attribute whose value matches the value of the id attribute of the path element.

If we wanted to display text on an elliptical arc, such as the first arc in Listing 6.11, we would use code like that in Listing 6.12.

LISTING 6.12   TextPath.svg—Text on a Path

```
<?xml version="1.0" standalone="no"?>
<!DOCTYPE svg PUBLIC "-//W3C//DTD SVG 20010904//EN"
"http://www.w3.org/TR/2001/REC-SVG-20010904/DTD/svg10.dtd">
<svg width="" height="">
<defs>
<path id="LongWayRound"
 d="M300 300, A 200 100 0 1 1 500 200"
 style="stroke:green; stroke-width:4; fill:none"/>
</defs>
<text>
<textPath xlink:href="#LongWayRound">
The long way round an elliptical arc defined on a path element
</textPath>
</text>
</svg>
```

Figure 6.8 shows the zoomed onscreen appearance when Listing 6.12 is run.

You can find further information on text layout and on the use of the textPath element in Chapter 8.

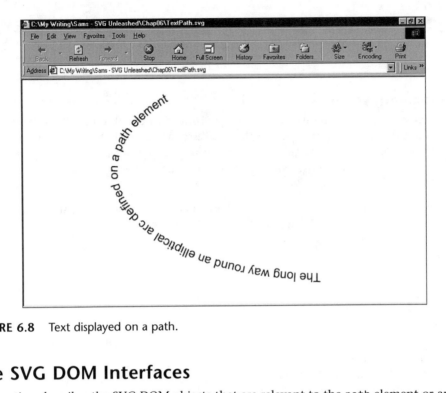

FIGURE 6.8   Text displayed on a path.

The SVG DOM Interfaces

This section describes the SVG DOM objects that are relevant to the path element or are otherwise relevant to the use of paths in SVG.

The SVGPathElement object will be described first. Other SVG DOM objects are listed in alphabetical order.

The SVGPathElement Object

The SVGPathElement object corresponds to a path element in an SVG document.

The SVGPathElement object has the properties and methods of the SVGElement object, the SVGTests object, the SVGLangSpace object, the SVGExternalResourcesRequired object, the SVGStylable object, the SVGTransformable object, the DOM Level 2 Events EventTarget object (events::EventTarget), and the SVGAnimatedPathData object.

The SVGPathElement object has the following property specific to it:

- pathLength—of type SVGAnimatedNumber

The SVGPathElement object has the following methods:

- `getTotalLength()`—The method returns a value of type `float`. The method takes no argument.

- `getPointAtLength(`*`distance`*`)`—The method returns a value of type `SVGPoint`. The distance argument is of type `float`.

- `getPathSegAtLength(`*`distance`*`)`—The method returns a value of type `unsigned long`. The distance argument is of type `float`.

- `createSVGPathSegClosePath()`—The method returns a value of type `SVGPathSegClosePath`. The method takes no argument.

- `createSVGPathSegMovetoAbs(`*`x`*`,`*`y`*`)`—The method returns a value of type `SVGPathSegMovetoAbs`. The x and y arguments are of type `float`.

- `createSVGPathSegMovetoRel(`*`x`*`,`*`y`*`)`—The method returns a value of type `SVGPathSegMovetoRel`. The x and y arguments are of type `float`.

- `createSVGPathSegLinetoAbs(`*`x`*`,`*`y`*`)`—The method returns a value of type `SVGPathSegLinetoAbs`. The x and y arguments are of type `float`.

- `createSVGPathSegLinetoRel(`*`x`*`,`*`y`*`)`—The method returns a value of type `SVGPathSegLinetoRel`. The x and y arguments are of type `float`.

- `createSVGPathSegCurvetoCubicAbs(`*`x`*`,`*`y`*`,`*`x1`*`,`*`y1`*`,`*`x2`*`,`*`y2`*`)`—The method returns a value of type `SVGPathSegCurvetoCubicAbs`. The x, y, x1, y1, x2, and y2 arguments are of type `float`.

- `createSVGPathSegCurvetoCubicRel(`*`x`*`,`*`y`*`,`*`x1`*`,`*`y1`*`,`*`x2`*`,`*`y2`*`)`—The method returns a value of type `SVGPathSegCurvetoCubicRel`. The x, y, x1, y1, x2, and y2 arguments are of type `float`.

- `createSVGPathSegCurvetoQuadraticAbs(`*`x`*`,`*`y`*`,`*`x1`*`,`*`y1`*`)`—The method returns a value of type `SVGPathSegCurvetoQuadraticAbs`. The x, y, x1, and y1 arguments are of type `float`.

- `createSVGPathSegCurvetoQuadraticRel(`*`x`*`,`*`y`*`,`*`x1`*`,`*`y1`*`)`—The method returns a value of type `SVGPathSegCurvetoQuadraticRel`. The x, y, x1, and y1 arguments are of type `float`.

- `createSVGPathSegArcAbs(`*`x`*`,`*`y`*`,`*`r1`*`,`*`r2`*`,`*`angle`*`,`*`largeArc`*`Flag,`*`sweepFlag`*`)`—The method returns a value of type `SVGPathSegArcAbs`. The x, y, r1, r2, and angle arguments are of type `float`. The `largeArcFlag` and `sweepFlag` arguments are of type `boolean`.

- `createSVGPathSegArcRel(`*`x`*`,`*`y`*`,`*`r1`*`,`*`r2`*`,`*`angle`*`,`*`largeArcFlag`*`,`*`sweepFlag`*`)`—The method returns a value of type `SVGPathSegArcRel`. The x, y, r1, r2, and angle arguments are of type `float`. The `largeArcFlag` and `sweepFlag` arguments are of type `boolean`.

- `createSVGPathSegLinetoHorizontalAbs(`*`x`*`)`—The method returns a value of type `SVGPathSegLinetoHorizontalAbs`. The x argument is of type `float`.

- `createSVGPathSegLinetoHorizontalRel(x)`—The method returns a value of type SVGPathSegLinetoHorizontalRel. The x argument is of type `float`.

- `createSVGPathSegLinetoVerticalAbs(y)`—The method returns a value of type SVGPathSegLinetoVerticalAbs. The y argument is of type `float`.

- `createSVGPathSegLinetoVerticalRel(y)`—The method returns a value of type SVGPathSegLinetoVerticalRel. The y argument is of type `float`.

- `createSVGPathSegCurvetoCubicSmoothAbs(x,y,x2,y2)`—The method returns a value of type SVGPathSegCurvetoCubicSmoothAbs. The x, y, x2, and y2 arguments are of type `float`.

- `createSVGPathSegCurvetoCubicSmoothRel(x,y,x2,y2)`—The method returns a value of type SVGPathSegCurvetoCubicSmoothRel. The x, y, x2, and y2 arguments are of type `float`.

- `createSVGPathSegCurvetoQuadraticSmoothAbs(x,y)`—The method returns a value of type SVGPathSegCurvetoQuadraticSmoothAbs. The x and y arguments are of type `float`.

- `createSVGPathSegCurvetoQuadraticSmoothRel(x,y)`—The method returns a value of type SVGPathSegCurvetoQuadraticSmoothRel. The x and y arguments are of type `float`.

The SVGMPath Object

The `SVGMPath` object corresponds to an `mpath` element in an SVG document.

The `SVGMPath` object has the properties and methods of the `SVGElement` object, the `SVGURIReference` object, and the `SVGExternalResourcesRequired` object.

The SVGPathSeg Object

The `SVGPathSeg` object has the following constants associated with it:

- `SVGPathSeg.PATHSEG_UNKNOWN`—The constant is of type `short` and has a value of `0`.

- `SVGPathSeg.PATHSEG_CLOSEPATH`—The constant is of type `short` and has a value of `1`.

- `SVGPathSeg.PATHSEG_MOVETO_ABS`—The constant is of type `short` and has a value of `2`.

- `SVGPathSeg.PATHSEG_MOVETO_REL`—The constant is of type `short` and has a value of `3`.

- `SVGPathSeg.PATHSEG_LINETO_ABS`—The constant is of type `short` and has a value of `4`.

- `SVGPathSeg.PATHSEG_LINETO_REL`—The constant is of type `short` and has a value of 5.

- `SVGPathSeg.PATHSEG_CURVETO_CUBIC_ABS`—The constant is of type `short` and has a value of 6.

- `SVGPathSeg.PATHSEG_CURVETO_CUBIC_REL`—The constant is of type `short` and has a value of 7.

- `SVGPathSeg.PATHSEG_CURVETO_QUADRATIC_ABS`—The constant is of type `short` and has a value of 8.

- `SVGPathSeg.PATHSEG_CURVETO_QUADRATIC_REL`—The constant is of type `short` and has a value of 9.

- `SVGPathSeg.PATHSEG_ARC_ABS`—The constant is of type `short` and has a value of 10.

- `SVGPathSeg.PATHSEG_ARC_REL`—The constant is of type `short` and has a value of 11.

- `SVGPathSeg.PATHSEG_LINETO_HORIZONTAL_ABS`—The constant is of type `short` and has a value of 12.

- `SVGPathSeg.PATHSEG_LINETO_HORIZONTAL_REL`—The constant is of type `short` and has a value of 13.

- `SVGPathSeg.PATHSEG_LINETO_VERTICAL_ABS`—The constant is of type `short` and has a value of 14.

- `SVGPathSeg.PATHSEG_LINETO_VERTICAL_REL`—The constant is of type `short` and has a value of 15.

- `SVGPathSeg.PATHSEG_CURVETO_CUBIC_SMOOTH_ABS`—The constant is of type `short` and has a value of 16.

- `SVGPathSeg.PATHSEG_CURVETO_CUBIC_SMOOTH_REL`—The constant is of type `short` and has a value of 17.

- `SVGPathSeg.PATHSEG_CURVETO_QUADRATIC_SMOOTH_ABS`—The constant is of type `short` and has a value of 18.

- `SVGPathSeg.PATHSEG_CURVETO_QUADRATIC_SMOOTH_REL`—The constant is of type `short` and has a value of 19.

The `SVGPathSeg` object has the following properties specific to it:

- `pathSegType`—of type `unsigned short`
- `pathSegTypeAsLetter`—of type `DOMString`

The `SVGPathSeg` object has no methods specific to it.

The SVGPathSegArcAbs Object

The SVGPathSegArcAbs object has all the properties and methods of the SVGPathSeg object.

The SVGPathSegArcAbs object has the following properties:

- x—of type float
- y—of type float
- r1—of type float
- r2—of type float
- angle—of type float
- largeArcFlag—of type boolean
- sweepFlag—of type boolean

The SVGPathSegArcAbs object has no methods specific to it.

The SVGPathSegArcRel Object

The SVGPathSegArcRel object has all the properties and methods of the SVGPathSeg object.

The SVGPathSegArcRel object has the following properties:

- x—of type float
- y—of type float
- r1—of type float
- r2—of type float
- angle—of type float
- largeArcFlag—of type boolean
- sweepFlag—of type boolean

The SVGPathSegArcRel object has no methods specific to it.

The SVGPathSegClosePath Object

The SVGPathSegClosePath object has all the properties and methods of the SVGPathSeg object.

The SVGPathSegCurvetoCubicAbs Object

The SVGPathSegCurvetoCubicAbs object has all the properties and methods of the SVGPathSeg object.

The `SVGPathSegCurvetoCubicAbs` object has the following properties:

- x—of type `float`
- y—of type `float`
- x1—of type `float`
- x2—of type `float`
- y1—of type `float`
- y2—of type `float`

The `SVGPathSegCurvetoCubicAbs` object has no methods specific to it.

The SVGPathSegCurvetoCubicRel Object

The `SVGPathSegCurvetoCubicRel` object has all the properties and methods of the `SVGPathSeg` object.

The `SVGPathSegCurvetoCubicRel` object has the following properties:

- x—of type `float`
- y—of type `float`
- x1—of type `float`
- x2—of type `float`
- y1—of type `float`
- y2—of type `float`

The `SVGPathSegCurvetoCubicRel` object has no methods specific to it.

The SVGPathSegCurvetoCubicSmoothAbs Object

The `SVGPathSegCurvetoCubicSmoothAbs` object has all the properties and methods of the `SVGPathSeg` object.

The `SVGPathSegCurvetoCubicSmoothAbs` object has the following properties:

- x—of type `float`
- y—of type `float`
- x2—of type `float`
- y2—of type `float`

The `SVGPathSegCurvetoCubicSmoothAbs` object has no methods specific to it.

The SVGPathSegCurvetoCubicSmoothRel Object

The SVGPathSegCurvetoCubicSmoothRel object has all the properties and methods of the SVGPathSeg object.

The SVGPathSegCurvetoCubicSmoothRel object has the following properties:

- x—of type float
- y—of type float
- x2—of type float
- y2—of type float

The SVGPathSegCurvetoCubicSmoothRel object has no methods specific to it.

The SVGPathSegCurvetoQuadraticAbs Object

The SVGPathSegCurvetoQuadraticAbs object has all the properties and methods of the SVGPathSeg object.

The SVGPathSegCurvetoQuadraticAbs object has the following properties:

- x—of type float
- y—of type float
- x1—of type float
- y1—of type float

The SVGPathSegCurvetoQuadraticAbs object has no methods specific to it.

The SVGPathSegCurvetoQuadraticRel Object

The SVGPathSegCurvetoQuadraticRel object has all the properties and methods of the SVGPathSeg object.

The SVGPathSegCurvetoQuadraticRel object has the following properties:

- x—of type float
- y—of type float
- x1—of type float
- y1—of type float

The SVGPathSegCurvetoQuadraticRel object has no methods specific to it.

The SVGPathSegCurvetoQuadraticSmoothAbs Object

The SVGPathSegCurvetoQuadraticSmoothAbs object has all the properties and methods of the SVGPathSeg object.

The SVGPathSegCurvetoQuadraticSmoothAbs object has the following properties:

- x—of type float
- y—of type float

The SVGPathSegCurvetoQuadraticSmoothAbs object has no methods specific to it.

The SVGPathSegCurvetoQuadraticSmoothRel Object

The SVGPathSegCurvetoQuadraticSmoothRel object has all the properties and methods of the SVGPathSeg object.

The SVGPathSegCurvetoQuadraticSmoothRel object has the following properties:

- x—of type float
- y—of type float

The SVGPathSegCurvetoQuadraticSmoothRel object has no methods specific to it.

The SVGPathSegLinetoAbs Object

The SVGPathSegLinetoAbs object has the properties and methods of the SVGPathSeg object.

The SVGPathSegLinetoAbs object has the following properties:

- x—of type float
- y—of type float

The SVGPathSegLinetoAbs object has no methods specific to it.

The SVGPathSegLinetoRel Object

The SVGPathSegLinetoRel object has the properties and methods of the SVGPathSeg object.

The SVGPathSegLinetoRel object has the following properties:

- x—of type float
- y—of type float

The SVGPathSegLinetoRel object has no methods specific to it.

The SVGPathSegLinetoHorizontalAbs Object

The SVGPathSegLinetoHorizontalAbs object has all the properties and methods of the SVGPathSeg object.

The SVGPathSegLinetoHorizontalAbs object has the following property:

- x—of type float

The SVGPathSegLinetoHorizontalAbs object has no methods specific to it.

The SVGPathSegLinetoHorizontalRel Object

The SVGPathSegLinetoHorizontalRel object has all the properties and methods of the SVGPathSeg object.

The SVGPathSegLinetoHorizontalRel object has the following property:

- x—of type float

The SVGPathSegLinetoHorizontalRel object has no methods specific to it.

The SVGPathSegLinetoVerticalAbs Object

The SVGPathSegLinetoVerticalAbs object has all the properties and methods of the SVGPathSeg object.

The SVGPathSegLinetoVerticalAbs object has the following property:

- y—of type float

The SVGPathSegLinetoVerticalAbs object has no methods specific to it.

The SVGPathSegLinetoVerticalRel Object

The SVGPathSegLinetoVerticalRel object has all the properties and methods of the SVGPathSeg object.

The SVGPathSegLinetoVerticalRel object has the following property:

- y—of type float

The SVGPathSegLinetoVerticalRel object has no methods specific to it.

The SVGPathSegList Object

The SVGPathSegList object has the following property:

- numberOfItems—of type unsigned long

The `SVGPathSegList` object has the following methods:

- `clear()`—The method returns a value of type `void`. The method takes no arguments.
- `initialize(newItem)`—The method returns a value of type `SVGPathSeg`. The `newItem` argument is of type `SVGPathSeg`.
- `getItem(index)`—The method returns a value of type `SVGPathSeg`. The `index` argument is of type `unsigned long`.
- `insertItemBefore(newItem, index)`—The method returns a value of type `SVGPathSeg`. The `newItem` argument is of type `SVGPathSeg`. The `index` argument is of type `unsigned long`.
- `replaceItem(newItem, index)`—The method returns a value of type `SVGPathSeg`. The `newItem` argument is of type `SVGPathSeg`. The `index` argument is of type `unsigned long`.
- `removeItem(index)`—The method returns a value of type `SVGPathSeg`. The `index` argument is of type `unsigned long`.
- `appendItem(newItem)`—The method returns a value of type `SVGPathSeg`. The `newItem` argument is of type `SVGPathSeg`.

The SVGPathSegMovetoAbs Object

The `SVGPathSegMovetoAbs` object has the properties and methods of the `SVGPathSeg` object.

The `SVGPathSegMovetoAbs` object has the following properties:

- x—of type `float`
- y—of type `float`

The `SVGPathSegMovetoAbs` object has no methods specific to it.

The SVGPathSegMovetoRel Object

The `SVGPathSegMovetoRel` object has the properties and methods of the `SVGPathSeg` object.

The `SVGPathSegMovetoRel` object has the following properties:

- x—of type `float`
- y—of type `float`

The `SVGPathSegMovetoRel` object has no methods specific to it.

The SVGTextPathElement Object

The SVGTextPathElement object corresponds to a textPath element in an SVG document.

The SVGTextPathElement object has the properties and methods of the SVGTextContentElement object and the SVGURIReference object.

The SVGTextPathElement object has the following constants associated with it:

- SVGTextPathElement.TEXTPATH_METHODTYPE_UNKNOWN—The constant is of type short and has a value of 0.

- SVGTextPathElement.TEXTPATH_METHODTYPE_ALIGN—The constant is of type short and has a value of 1.

- SVGTextPathElement.TEXTPATH_METHODTYPE_STRETCH—The constant is of type short and has a value of 2.

- SVGTextPathElement.TEXTPATH_SPACINGTYPE_UNKNOWN—The constant is of type short and has a value of 0.

- SVGTextPathElement.TEXTPATH_SPACINGTYPE_AUTO—The constant is of type short and has a value of 1.

- SVGTextPathElement.TEXTPATH_SPACINGTYPE_EXACT—The constant is of type short and has a value of 2.

The SVGTextPathElement object has the following properties:

- startOffset—of type SVGAnimatedLength

- method—of type SVGAnimatedEnumeration

- spacing—of type SVGAnimatedEnumeration

The SVGTextPathElement object has no methods specific to it.

Manipulating Paths Using the DOM

In this section, we will create some examples in which we manipulate the DOM to alter the onscreen appearance produced by paths.

Altering the Shape of a Path

In this example, we will alter the shape of a path element that has four corners. When the SVG document loads, it looks like a square with a circle at each corner. If you press the mouse button on one of the circles, you can drag the corner to any point onscreen. Listing 6.13 shows the code.

LISTING 6.13   ElasticPath.svg—A Shape Whose Corners Can Be Moved to New Positions

```
<?xml version="1.0" standalone="no"?>
<!DOCTYPE svg PUBLIC "-//W3C//DTD SVG 20010904//EN"
"http://www.w3.org/TR/2001/REC-SVG-20010904/DTD/svg10.dtd">
<svg width="500px" height="300px" xmlns="http://www.w3.org/2000/svg"
onload="Initialize(evt)">
  <script type="text/javascript">
  <![CDATA[

var SVGRoot = document.documentElement;
    SVGRoot.addEventListener('mousemove', dragPoint, false);
var rectPath, rectPoints;

var dragedPoint = null;

function Initialize() {
    rectPath = document.getElementById('rectPath');
    var d = rectPath.getAttribute('d').split(', ');
    rectPoints = [];
    for (var i=0; i<4; i++) {
        rectPoints[i] = document.createElement('circle');
        rectPoints[i].setAttribute('fill', 'blue');
        d[i] = /(\d+) (\d+)/.exec(d[i]);
        rectPoints[i].setAttribute('id', 'pt' + i);
        rectPoints[i].setAttribute('r', '7');
        rectPoints[i].setAttribute('cx', d[i][1]);
        rectPoints[i].setAttribute('cy', d[i][2]);
        rectPoints[i].addEventListener('mousedown', startDrag, false);
        rectPoints[i].addEventListener('mouseup', endDrag, false);
        SVGRoot.appendChild(rectPoints[i]);
    }
}

function startDrag(evt) {
    dragedPoint = evt.target;
}

function endDrag() {
    dragedPoint = null;
}

function dragPoint(evt) {
```

LISTING 6.13   Continued

```
    if (dragedPoint == null)
        return;

    var newX = evt.clientX;
    var newY = evt.clientY;
    var point = /\d+/.exec(dragedPoint.id)[0];
    rectPoints[point].setAttribute('cx', newX);
    rectPoints[point].setAttribute('cy', newY);
    var d = rectPath.getAttribute('d').split(', ');
        d[point]  = (point == 0)? 'M': 'L';
        d[point] += newX + ' ' + newY;
        d = d.join(', ');
    rectPath.setAttribute('d', d);
}


/*

As of ASV3 the only methods of SVGPathElement that are supported are
'getTotalLength' and 'getPointAtLength'. Therefore to manipulate the object we
need to use string manipulation to work with it's 'd' attribute.

*/

    ]]>
    </script>
    <rect x="0" y="0" width="100%" height="100%" fill="white" />
    <path id="rectPath" d="M50 50, L200 50, 200 200, 50 200, z" style="fill:none;
stroke:red; stroke-width:5" />
</svg>
```

First, let's look at Figures 6.9 and 6.10, which show how the shape looks when it is loaded and after one permutation of reshaping, respectively.

When the document loads, the `Initialize()` function is called. The `Initialize()` function, among other things, locates the `path` element by means of its `id` attribute and applies a small circle to each corner.

The mouse position is continuously monitored. When a mouse button is pressed, if the mouse pointer is over one of the circles, that corner of the `path` element is repositioned to correspond to the position of the mouse pointer. This is done by retrieving the value of the d attribute, parsing it, adjusting values to correspond to the new mouse pointer position, combining those coordinates into a new d attribute, and rendering the new position of the circle on the screen. At the same time, the lines joining two positions on the path are redrawn.

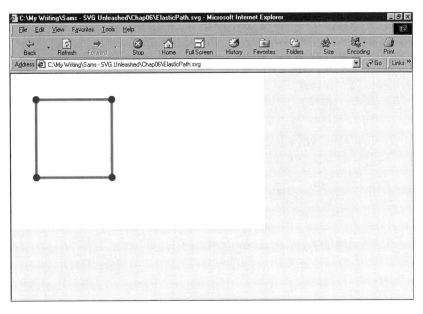

FIGURE 6.9   The shape, defined by a path element, on loading.

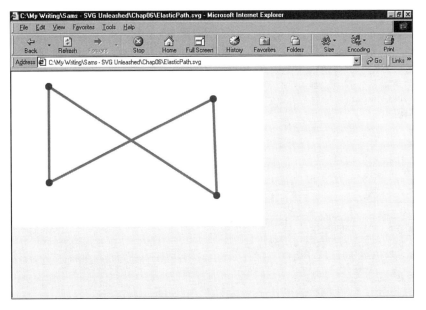

FIGURE 6.10   The shape, defined by a path element, after corners have been moved.

Manipulating the Start Offset of Text on a Path

As you saw earlier in this chapter, you can lay text out on a path. The `textPath` element has a `startOffset` attribute, which can be used to control, or animate, the position of a piece of text on a path. In the following example, we will use DOM methods to manipulate the value of the `startOffset` attribute, causing text to animate along a path. This example is a timed animation, but you can readily adapt it to respond to user-initiated events.

Listing 6.14 contains the code for the animated text. The example works correctly only for text strings that are no longer than the length of the path.

LISTING 6.14   SVGWave.svg—Using DOM to Animate Text Along a Path

```
<?xml version="1.0" standalone="no"?>
<!DOCTYPE svg PUBLIC "-//W3C//DTD SVG 20010904//EN"
"http://www.w3.org/TR/2001/REC-SVG-20010904/DTD/svg10.dtd">
<svg width="500px" height="300px" xmlns="http://www.w3.org/2000/svg"
onload="Initialize(evt)">
  <script type="text/javascript">
  <![CDATA[

var wavePath, waveLength, waveText;

function Initialize() {
    wavePath    = document.getElementById('wavePath');
    waveLength = wavePath.getTotalLength();
    waveText    = document.getElementById('waveText');
    waveText.setAttribute('startOffset', waveLength);
    moveText();
}

function moveText() {
    var currentOffset = parseInt(waveText.getAttribute('startOffset'));
    var newOffset = (currentOffset < -waveLength)? waveLength:
➥currentOffset - 5;
    waveText.setAttribute('startOffset', newOffset);
    setTimeout('moveText()', 100);
}

  ]]>
  </script>
  <defs>
    <path id="wavePath" d="M 50 150 C 125 75 175 75 250 150 C 325 225 375 225
450 150" />
```

LISTING 6.14   Continued

```
  </defs>
  <use xlink:href="#wavePath" fill="none" stroke="black" />
  <text font-family="Verdana" font-size="30" fill="blue" >
    <textPath id="waveText" xlink:href="#wavePath" startOffset="40">
    Text on an SVG wave.</textPath>
  </text>
</svg>
```

Figure 6.11 shows the onscreen appearance when the animation is partway complete.

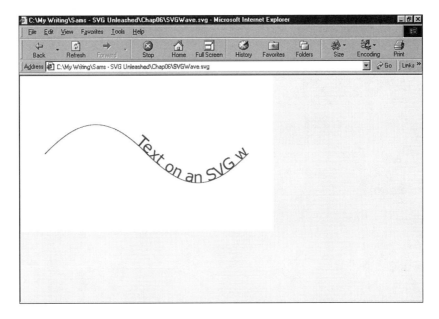

FIGURE 6.11   Text being animated along a path using DOM methods to manipulate the startOffset attribute.

When the document loads, the Initialize() function is called. Initialize() references the path element contained in the defs element, using the value of the path element's id attribute. The getTotalLength() method determines the length of the path. The value of the startOffset attribute is set to place the text just at the end of the path. The moveText() function is then called.

The moveText() function retrieves the current value of startOffset, parses out its numerical value, reduces the value by 5, and so moves the text 5 units along the path. Then, using the setTimeout() method, the moveText() function calls itself recursively every 100 milliseconds, each time moving the text 5 units along the path. As the animation proceeds, the value of `startOffset` becomes progressively less positive, then `0`, then progressively more negative. When the value of `startOffset` is less than `-waveLength`, the value of `startOffset` is reset to the length of the path. The text is then repositioned at the right end of the path, and the animation begins again.

Summary

This chapter introduced the SVG `path` element and the ways the information contained in its d attribute allows you to create any arbitrary two-dimensional graphic shape. The techniques to create straight lines and various types of curves were discussed, and some were demonstrated.

In the final sections of the chapter, we described the SVG DOM interfaces relevant to the creation of paths and provided a couple of examples of using the DOM to manipulate paths.

CHAPTER 7

Transformations in SVG

Transformations are an important part of SVG's functionality and can take many forms. The ability to place objects in a precise position relative to a fixed point, rotation of an object, scaling of an object, skew of an object—all these are supported in SVG. In addition, as you will see in Chapter 11, "SVG Animation Elements," you can animate transformations in SVG.

A full understanding of SVG transformations depends, in part, on an understanding of SVG coordinate systems. You may find it useful as you read this chapter to refer to some of the topics covered in Chapter 5, "Coordinate Systems in SVG."

The final section of the chapter will introduce SVG DOM interfaces that are relevant to SVG transformations.

Introduction to Transformations

First, let's demonstrate some of the transformations that are possible in SVG. Listing 7.1 shows several simple transformations available in SVG. SVG also allows us to combine such transformations.

LISTING 7.1   SimpleTransformations.svg—Some Examples of Simple SVG Transformations

```
<?xml version="1.0" standalone="no"?>
<!DOCTYPE svg PUBLIC "-//W3C//DTD SVG 20010904//EN"
"http://www.w3.org/TR/2001/REC-SVG-20010904/DTD/svg10.dtd">
<svg width="100%" height="100%">
<text x="30px" y="50px">I am normal text</text>
<text x="30px" y="50px" transform="translate(0,300px)">
I am translated vertically
</text>
<text x="30px" y="50px" transform="translate(200px,0)">
I am translated horizontally
</text>
<text x="30px" y="50px" transform="scale(5)">
I am scaled text
</text>
<text x="30px" y="50px" transform="rotate(315, 100px, 100px)">
I am rotated
</text>
<text x="330px" y="150px" transform="skewX(45)">
I am skewed X
</text>
<text x="330px" y="250px" transform="skewY(25)">
I am skewed Y
</text>
</svg>
```

The untransformed text and several simple transformations are shown in Figure 7.1 (which is slightly panned). Each piece of text states the type of transformation that has been applied to it.

> **NOTE**
>
> Many of the examples in this chapter use the text element. If you find any of the code difficult to follow, layout of text is covered in more detail in Chapter 8, "Laying Out Text in SVG."

Each piece of text is layed out in a text element, whose x and y attributes define its position onscreen. The x and y attributes of a text element define its bottom-left corner, differing from a rect element, for example, where the x and y attributes define the top-left corner.

Each transformation is specified within a transform attribute. So let's look a little closer at it and its syntax.

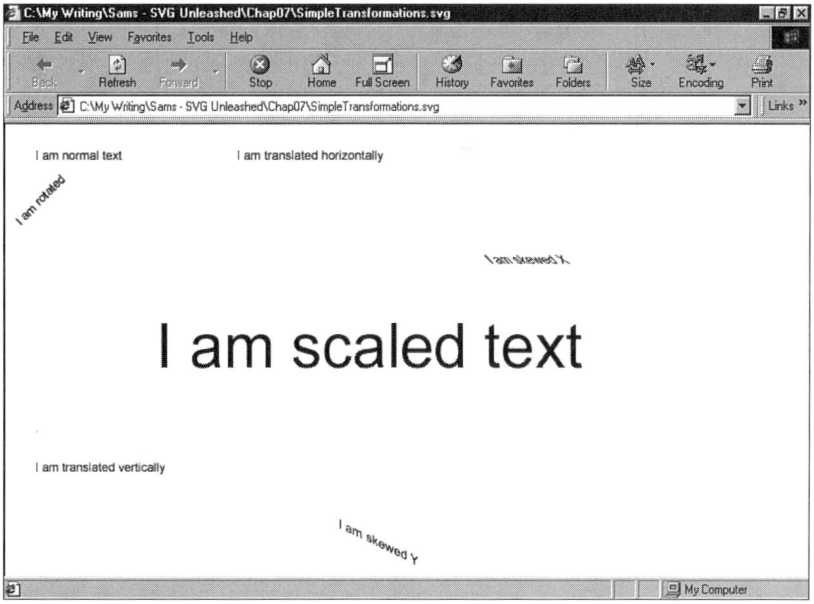

FIGURE 7.1   Simple transformations of text.

The transform Attribute

You can add the `transform` attribute to many of the SVG elements that were discussed in earlier chapters. The value of the `transform` attribute consists of one or more **transform definitions** separated by whitespace.

So, the general form of the `transform` attribute is as follows:

```
transform="transformtype1(argument(s))
 transformtype2(argument(s)) ..."
```

The types of transform definition supported by the `transform` attribute are as follows:

- `translate()`—Moves an object to a new position without scaling or rotating the object

- `scale()`—Scales an object to a smaller or larger size

- `rotate()`—Rotates an object around the origin of the coordinate system or around a defined point

- `skewX()`—Skews an object horizontally

- `skewY()`—Skews an object vertically

- `matrix()`—Is used to express a combination of one or more of the previously mentioned simple transformations

---

NOTE

The transform attribute cannot be placed on an svg element. If you want to group elements and also transform them, you need to use the g element.

In the following sections, we will look at several aspects of how SVG transformations are used.

The g Element

Transformations can be applied to single SVG graphic elements or to the g grouping element (discussed in Chapter 2, "Document Structure in SVG"). In the latter case, the transformation or transformations specified are applied to all elements nested within the g element.

Listings 7.2 and 7.3 show a brief example of applying a transformation to a pair of rectangles by grouping them using a g element and transforming the g element.

LISTING 7.2   TransformRects00.svg—A Pair of Rectangles

```
<?xml version="1.0" standalone="no"?>
<!DOCTYPE svg PUBLIC "-//W3C//DTD SVG 20010904//EN"
"http://www.w3.org/TR/2001/REC-SVG-20010904/DTD/svg10.dtd">
<svg width="800px" height="600px">
<rect x="0px" y="0px" width="100px" height="100px" style="fill:red"/>
<rect x="120px" y="0px" width="100px" height="100px" style="fill:red"/>
</svg>
```

If you run the code in Listing 7.2 and view the result onscreen, you will see that both squares have their top edge against the top edge of the browser window.

LISTING 7.3   TransformRects01.svg—Applying a Transformation to a Pair of Rectangles

```
<?xml version="1.0" standalone="no"?>
<!DOCTYPE svg PUBLIC "-//W3C//DTD SVG 20010904//EN"
"http://www.w3.org/TR/2001/REC-SVG-20010904/DTD/svg10.dtd">
<svg width="800px" height="600px">
<g transform="translate(200px, 200px)">
<rect x="0px" y="0px" width="100px" height="100px" style="fill:red"/>
<rect x="120px" y="0px" width="100px" height="100px" style="fill:red"/>
</g>
</svg>
```

If we nest the two rect elements within the g element, any transformation that we apply to the g element is applied to each element nested within it. In Listing 7.3, the transformation is a translate(200px, 200px) transformation.

The use Element

The use element provides an alternative way to apply a transformation to a group of elements when either a g element or a symbol element is defined within the defs element in an SVG document fragment.

Listing 7.4 shows how the use element can be employed to apply a transformation to a group of elements.

LISTING 7.4   GroupAndUse.svg—Using the use and g Elements

```
<?xml version="1.0" standalone="no"?>
<!DOCTYPE svg PUBLIC "-//W3C//DTD SVG 20010904//EN"
"http://www.w3.org/TR/2001/REC-SVG-20010904/DTD/svg10.dtd">
<svg width="1000px" height="600px">
<defs>
<g id="someGroup">
<rect x="100px" y="100px" width="250px" height="125px"
 style="fill:#cccccc; stroke:red;"/>
<text x="110px" y="140px"
 style="font-size:20; fill:red; stroke:none;">
Hello Grouped World!
</text>
</g>
</defs>
<use xlink:href="#someGroup" />
<use xlink:href="#someGroup" transform="translate(600, 200)" />
<use xlink:href="#someGroup" transform="scale(1.75)" />
</svg>
```

The first use element displays the group at the top-left shape in Figure 7.2 (slightly panned), the second use displays the large shape and text in the middle of the screen, and the third use element displays the shape and text to the right of the screen.

> **NOTE**
>
> A use element may also be translated by using x and y attributes. The value of the x attribute corresponds to the x-axis translation and the value of the y attribute corresponds to the y-axis translation.

Now let's examine in a little more detail each type of transformation available in SVG.

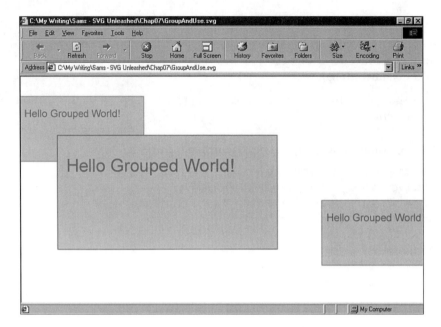

FIGURE 7.2   Grouped transformations using the use element.

Translation Transformations

To translate an object is to move it—horizontally, vertically, or diagonally—from some position, without rotating it or changing its size.

If you have an object on a flat surface such as a desk and move the object, then, in SVG terminology, that is a translation. When you translate an object in SVG, it appears as if you are moving the object to a new place on the existing user coordinate system. What is actually happening is that a new user coordinate system is created, and an object is put in its right place on that new system. If you think again of the object on the desk, then, in SVG, you move the desk to a new position to move the object. You may want to refresh your understanding of this concept by reviewing the discussion of transformations and user coordinate systems in Chapter 5.

A `translate()` transformation uses the following general syntax:

```
transform="translate(x-distance, y-distance)"
```

If you want to make a horizontal translation, you can use only one argument to `translate()`:

```
transform="translate(x-distance)"
```

Listing 7.5 shows a simple translation transformation.

LISTING 7.5   Translation01.svg—A Translation Example

```
<?xml version="1.0" standalone="no"?>
<!DOCTYPE svg PUBLIC "-//W3C//DTD SVG 20010904//EN"
"http://www.w3.org/TR/2001/REC-SVG-20010904/DTD/svg10.dtd">
<svg width="800px" height="600px">
<defs>
<g id="myGroup">
<line x1="0" y1="0" x2="800px" y2="0px"
 style="stroke:black; stroke-width:8"/>
<line x1="0" y1="0" x2="0px" y2="600px"
 style="stroke:black; stroke-width:8"/>
<rect x="0" y="0" width="100px" height="100px"
 style="fill:#CCCCCC; stroke:#FF6600; stroke-width:4;"/>
<text x="300" y="40" style="fill:#FF6600; stroke:none; font-size:24">
The horizontal axis, y=0
</text>
<text x="20" y="140" transform="rotate(90, 20, 140)"
 style="fill:#FF6600; stroke:none; font-size:24">
The vertical axis, x=0
</text>
</g>
</defs>
<use xlink:href="#myGroup" />
<g transform="translate(150,150)">
<use xlink:href="#myGroup" />
</g>
</svg>
```

The `transform` attribute we are interested in for this example is the one on the g element. As you can see in Figure 7.3, the x- and y-axes of the coordinate system are moved by the `translate()` transformation, which is specified on the g element within which the second use element is nested. The horizontal and vertical movement of the axes is defined in the `transform` attribute of the g element. The positions of the `rect` element and the `text` elements stay the same, relative to the moved axes.

Translation transformations can be animated by using SVG animation techniques (see Chapter 11).

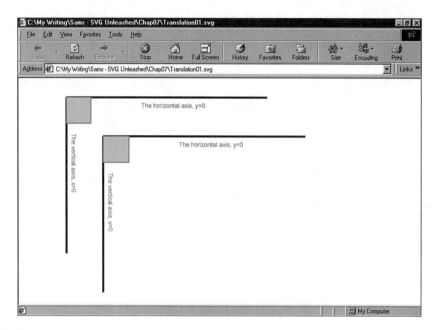

FIGURE 7.3   A translate() transformation moves the coordinate axes.

Rotation Transformations

A rotate() transformation causes an SVG object to be rotated around a specific point. If the coordinates of a point are not specified, as a default, the object is rotated around the origin of the current coordinate system.

Thus, to rotate around the origin, you use the following general syntax:

```
transform="rotate(rotate-angle)"
```

To rotate around a point other than the origin, you can use the following form:

```
transform="rotate(rotate-angle, x-coordinate, y-coordinate)"
```

Listing 7.6 shows rotate() transformations around both the origin and several defined pairs of coordinates.

LISTING 7.6   Rotate01.svg—Rotation Around the Origin and Other Points

```
<?xml version="1.0" standalone="no"?>
<!DOCTYPE svg PUBLIC "-//W3C//DTD SVG 20010904//EN"
"http://www.w3.org/TR/2001/REC-SVG-20010904/DTD/svg10.dtd">
<svg width="1000px" height="700px">
```

LISTING 7.6 Continued

```
<text x="100px" y="20px"
 style="fill:red; stroke:none; font-size:20">
 Text at rest
</text>
<text x="100px" y="20px" transform="rotate(30)"
 style="fill:red; stroke:none; font-size:20">
 Text rotated 30 degrees around origin
</text>
<text x="100px" y="20px" transform="rotate(45)"
 style="fill:red; stroke:none; font-size:20">
 Text rotated 45 degrees around origin
</text>
<text x="100px" y="20px" transform="rotate(60)"
 style="fill:red; stroke:none; font-size:20">
 Text rotated 60 degrees around origin
</text>
<text x="100px" y="20px" transform="rotate(30, 200, 0)"
 style="fill:blue; stroke:none; font-size:20">
 Text rotated 30 degrees around (200,0)
</text>
<text x="100px" y="20px" transform="rotate(30, 400, 0)"
 style="fill:blue; stroke:none; font-size:20">
 Text rotated 30 degrees around (400,0)
</text>
<text x="100px" y="20px" transform="rotate(30, 0, 300)"
 style="fill:blue; stroke:none; font-size:20">
 Text rotated 30 degrees around (0,300)
</text>
<text x="100px" y="20px" transform="rotate(30, 0, 500)"
 style="fill:blue; stroke:none; font-size:20">
 Text rotated 30 degrees around (0,500)
</text>
</svg>
```

Each transform attribute in Listing 7.6 defines a rotate() transformation. The text contained within each text element describes whether the text is rotated, how much it is rotated, and what point it is rotated around.

The x and y attributes for each text element have the same values. Remember that it is the coordinate system that is transformed—in this case, rotated.

Figure 7.4 shows the onscreen appearance (unzoomed) when Listing 7.6 is run.

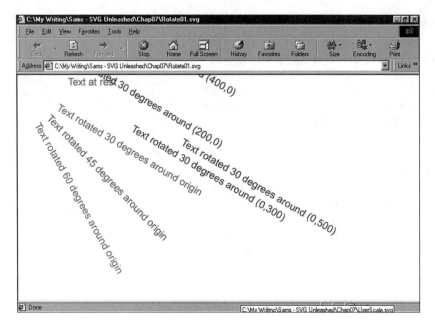

FIGURE 7.4 Several rotate() transformations.

You may find that the onscreen position of text that is rotated around points other than the origin is not where you expected it to be. Listing 7.7 shows `rotate()` transformations with their corresponding axes. Remember, from the earlier discussion, that the whole coordinate system is rotated.

LISTING 7.7 Rotate02.svg—Rotation of Axes and Text

```
<?xml version="1.0" standalone="no"?>
<!DOCTYPE svg PUBLIC "-//W3C//DTD SVG 20010904//EN"
"http://www.w3.org/TR/2001/REC-SVG-20010904/DTD/svg10.dtd">
<svg width="1000px" height="700px">
<defs>
<g id="myAxes">
<line x1="0" y1="0" x2="1000" y2="0"
 style="stroke:black; stroke-width:5"/>
<line x1="0" y1="0" x2="0" y2="700"
 style="stroke:black; stroke-width:5"/>
</g>
</defs>
<use xlink:href="#myAxes" transform="rotate(0)"/>
<use xlink:href="#myAxes" transform="rotate(30)" stroke-dasharray="5,5"/>
<text x="100px" y="20px" transform="rotate(30)"
 style="fill:red; stroke:none; font-size:20">
 Text rotated 30 degrees around origin
```

LISTING 7.7 Continued

```
</text>
<use xlink:href="#myAxes" transform="rotate(30, 200,0)"/>
<text x="100px" y="20px" transform="rotate(30, 200, 0)"
 style="fill:blue; stroke:none; font-size:20">
 Text rotated 30 degrees around (200,0)
</text>
<use xlink:href="#myAxes" transform="rotate(30, 400,0)"/>
<text x="100px" y="20px" transform="rotate(30, 400, 0)"
 style="fill:blue; stroke:none; font-size:20">
 Text rotated 30 degrees around (400,0)
</text>
<use xlink:href="#myAxes" transform="rotate(30, 600, 0)"/>
<text x="100px" y="20px" transform="rotate(30, 600, 0)"
 style="fill:blue; stroke:none; font-size:20">
 Text rotated 30 degrees around (600,0)
</text>
</svg>
```

Figure 7.5 shows the onscreen appearance (zoomed out and panned to show the various axes) when Listing 7.7 is run. The origin, (0,0), of the unrotated axes are horizontal and vertical. The image has been panned so you can see the origins of the rotated axes too.

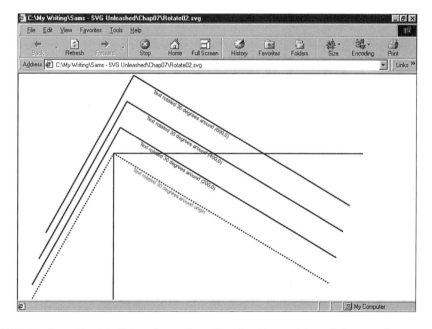

FIGURE 7.5 Several rotate() transformations showing the position of the coordinate axes.

The first `rotate()` transformation rotates the text and its associated axes 30 degrees around the origin. The next `rotate()` transformation rotates the text and axes around the coordinates (200,0). In Figure 7.5, you can see that the rotated axes intersect with the original x-axis at the point (200,0). The later rotation transformations are around (400,0) and (600,0). You can see that the rotated text maintains its position relative to its own rotated axes.

It isn't simple to grasp how rotations around various points will appear onscreen. I suggest you adapt Listing 7.7 and explore the onscreen appearance produced by varying the angle and center of rotation.

Listing 7.8 shows a full 360-degree rotation transformation in 45-degree steps.

LISTING 7.8   Rotate03.svg—Rotation Transformations in 45-Degree Steps

```
<?xml version="1.0" standalone="no"?>
<!DOCTYPE svg PUBLIC "-//W3C//DTD SVG 20010904//EN"
"http://www.w3.org/TR/2001/REC-SVG-20010904/DTD/svg10.dtd">
<svg width="1000px" height="700px">
<text x="500px" y="350px" transform="rotate(0, 500px, 350px)"
 style="fill:red; stroke:none; font-size:20">
 Text not rotated
</text>
<text x="500px" y="350px" transform="rotate(45 500px, 350px)"
 style="fill:red; stroke:none; font-size:20">
 Text rotated 45 degrees around (500, 350)
</text>
<text x="500px" y="350px" transform="rotate(90 500px, 350px)"
 style="fill:red; stroke:none; font-size:20">
 Text rotated 90 degrees around (500, 350)
</text>
<text x="500px" y="350px" transform="rotate(135 500px, 350px)"
 style="fill:red; stroke:none; font-size:20">
 Text rotated 135 degrees around (500, 350)
</text>
<text x="500px" y="350px" transform="rotate(180 500px, 350px)"
 style="fill:red; stroke:none; font-size:20">
 Text rotated 180 degrees around (500, 350)
</text>
<text x="500px" y="350px" transform="rotate(225 500px, 350px)"
 style="fill:red; stroke:none; font-size:20">
 Text rotated 225 degrees around (500, 350)
</text>
<text x="500px" y="350px" transform="rotate(270 500px, 350px)"
 style="fill:red; stroke:none; font-size:20">
 Text rotated 270 degrees around (500, 350)
```

LISTING 7.8   Continued

```
</text>
<text x="500px" y="350px" transform="rotate(315 500px, 350px)"
 style="fill:red; stroke:none; font-size:20">
 Text rotated 315 degrees around (500, 350)
</text>
</svg>
```

Each text element is positioned at (500,350), and the text is rotated around that point.

Figure 7.6 shows the onscreen appearance (slightly zoomed out but not panned) when Listing 7.8 is run.

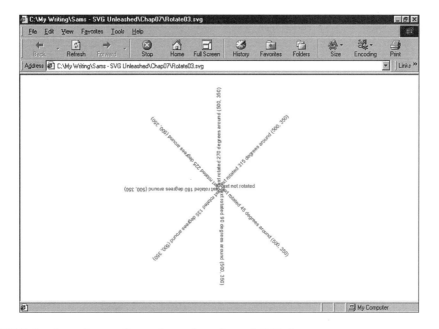

FIGURE 7.6   Several rotate() transformations through 360 degrees.

Listing 7.5, which was used to demonstrate a translate() transformation, also showed a rotate() transformation applied to the text that labels the y-axis with and without the translate() transformation.

A rotate() transformation can be animated using the techniques similar to those described in Chapter 11. By animating a rotate() transformation, we can animate visual appearances such as a moving second hand of a watch or clock or the pointer of a pressure gauge or similar instrument.

Scale Transformations

The scale() transformation alters all parts of the coordinates of an SVG graphic object. The scale() transformation uses two general forms. To scale the x and y directions by the same scale factor, you write

```
transform="scale(scale-factor)"
```

If you want to scale the x and y directions by different scale factors, you can write

```
transform="scale(x-scale-factor, y-scale-factor)"
```

Listing 7.9 shows an example. Several pieces of text are scaled by different factors. Each piece of text describes the scaling factor that has been applied to it.

LISTING 7.9   scaleText.svg—Applying the Scale Transformation to SVG Text

```
<?xml version="1.0" standalone="no"?>
<!DOCTYPE svg PUBLIC "-//W3C//DTD SVG 20010904//EN"
"http://www.w3.org/TR/2001/REC-SVG-20010904/DTD/svg10.dtd">
<svg width="100%" height="100%">
<text x="50px" y="100px" transform="scale(1.0)" style="font-family:Arial,
sans-serif; font-size:24;">
Text at natural size
</text>
<text x="50px" y="100px" transform="scale(1.5)" style="font-family:Arial,
sans-serif; font-size:24;">
Text scaled by 1.5
</text>
<text x="50px" y="100px" transform="scale(2.0)" style="font-family:Arial,
sans-serif; font-size:24;">
Text scaled by 2.0
</text>
<text x="50px" y="100px" transform="scale(2.5)" style="font-family:Arial,
sans-serif; font-size:24;">
Text scaled by 2.5
</text>
<text x="50px" y="100px" transform="scale(3.0)" style="font-family:Arial,
sans-serif; font-size:24;">
Text scaled by 3.0
</text>
</svg>
```

Figure 7.7 shows the onscreen appearance after a scale transformation is applied to each piece of text.

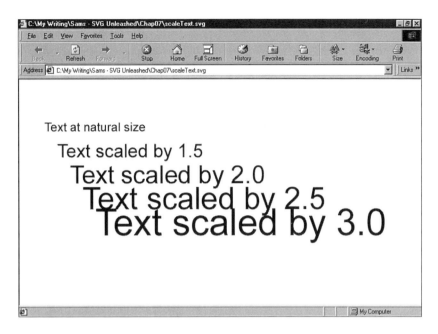

FIGURE 7.7   Applying a scale transformation to text.

You can, of course, apply a scaling factor less than 1 and greater than 0 to make text smaller.

When you apply a negative scale transformation, all parts of the coordinate system are scaled in that way. The text is therefore above and to the left of the top-left corner of the viewport. Listing 7.10 includes some negative scale transformations. Figure 7.8 shows the result zoomed out and panned to place the origin of the coordinate system near the middle of the screen. The line elements were added to show the axes of the coordinate system. The place where the axes cross is the original position of the top-left corner of the initial viewport.

LISTING 7.10   scaleText02.svg—Negative Scaling of Text

```
<?xml version="1.0" standalone="no"?>
<!DOCTYPE svg PUBLIC "-//W3C//DTD SVG 20010904//EN"
"http://www.w3.org/TR/2001/REC-SVG-20010904/DTD/svg10.dtd">
<svg width="100%" height="100%">
<line x1="-1000px" y1="0px" x2="1000px" y2="0px"
 style="stroke-width:15; stroke:red"/>
<line x1="0px" y1="-1000px" x2="0px" y2="1000px"
 style="stroke-width:15; stroke:red"/>
<text x="50px" y="300px" transform="scale(1.0)"
```

LISTING 7.10   Continued

```
  style="font-family:Arial,
sans-serif; font-size:24;">
Text at natural size
</text>
<text x="50px" y="300px" transform="scale(-1.25)"
 style="font-family:Arial,
sans-serif; font-size:24;">
Text scaled by -1.25
</text>
<text x="50px" y="300px" transform="scale(1.5)"
 style="font-family:Arial,
sans-serif; font-size:24;">
Text scaled by 1.5
</text>
<text x="50px" y="300px" transform="scale(-1.5)"
 style="font-family:Arial,
sans-serif; font-size:24;">
Text scaled by -1.5
</text>
<text x="50px" y="300px" transform="scale(2.0)"
 style="font-family:Arial,
sans-serif; font-size:24;">
Text scaled by 2.0
</text>
</svg>
```

Figure 7.8 shows the onscreen appearance after a negative scale transformation is applied to text. The screenshot is of a panned and zoomed-out version of the onscreen result. Notice that the text to which a negative scaling factor has been applied is inverted and reversed.

Unfortunately, SVG 1.0 does not provide a `scale()` transformation about a point other than the origin of the current coordinate system. If you want to create a group of elements scaled around a particular point, you need to combine a translation transformation with the desired scale transformation.

Listing 7.11 combines a translation transformation and a scale transformation to produce a number of progressively scaling circles centered around a common point.

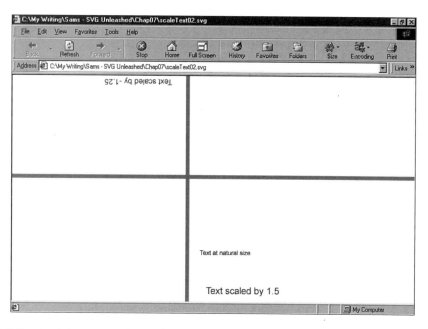

FIGURE 7.8   Applying a negative scale transformation to text.

LISTING 7.11   CenteredScale.svg—Concentric Circles

```
<?xml version="1.0" standalone="no"?>
<!DOCTYPE svg PUBLIC "-//W3C//DTD SVG 20010904//EN"
"http://www.w3.org/TR/2001/REC-SVG-20010904/DTD/svg10.dtd">
<svg width="800px" height="600px">
<defs>
<circle id="myCircle" cx="200px" cy="200px" r="10"
 style="stroke:red; fill:none;"/>
</defs>
<use xlink:href="#myCircle"/>
<use xlink:href="#myCircle"
 transform=" translate(-100, -100) scale(1.5)"/>
<use xlink:href="#myCircle"
 transform=" translate(-200, -200) scale(2.0)"/>
<use xlink:href="#myCircle"
 transform=" translate(-300, -300) scale(2.5)"/>
<use xlink:href="#myCircle"
 transform=" translate(-400, -400) scale(3.0)"/>
</svg>
```

Figure 7.9 shows the onscreen appearance after zooming when Listing 7.11 is run.

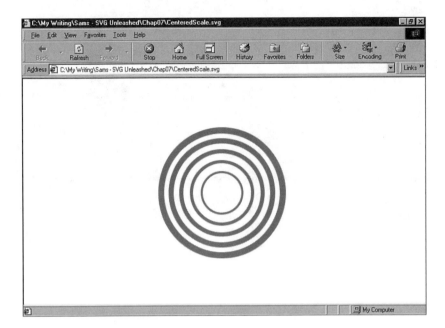

FIGURE 7.9   Concentric circles created using translation and scale transformations.

Notice in Figure 7.9 that the stroke width increases as the circle is scaled. The value of the `stroke-width` property is constant for all the circles, but the visual appearance it produces is scaled progressively. If you want to maintain the stroke width at a constant value onscreen, you need to scale the value of the `stroke-width` property downward by the inverse of the scale factor applied to that particular circle. Listing 7.12 shows how this is done.

LISTING 7.12   CenteredScale02.svg—Concentric Circles with Constant Onscreen Stroke Width

```
<?xml version="1.0" standalone="no"?>
<!DOCTYPE svg PUBLIC "-//W3C//DTD SVG 20010904//EN"
"http://www.w3.org/TR/2001/REC-SVG-20010904/DTD/svg10.dtd">
<svg width="800px" height="600px">
<defs>
<circle id="myCircle" cx="200px" cy="200px" r="10"
 style="stroke:red; fill:none;"/>
</defs>
<use xlink:href="#myCircle" stroke-width="1"/>
<use xlink:href="#myCircle" stroke-width="0.67"
 transform=" translate(-100, -100) scale(1.5)"/>
<use xlink:href="#myCircle" stroke-width="0.5"
 transform=" translate(-200, -200) scale(2.0)"/>
<use xlink:href="#myCircle" stroke-width="0.4"
```

LISTING 7.12 Continued

```
 transform=" translate(-300, -300) scale(2.5)"/>
<use xlink:href="#myCircle" stroke-width="0.33"
 transform=" translate(-400, -400) scale(3.0)"/>
</svg>
```

Figure 7.10 shows the zoomed onscreen appearance after running Listing 7.12. As you can see, the stroke width onscreen is constant. Perhaps paradoxically, we had to alter the value of the stroke-width property on each use element to achieve a constant visual appearance onscreen.

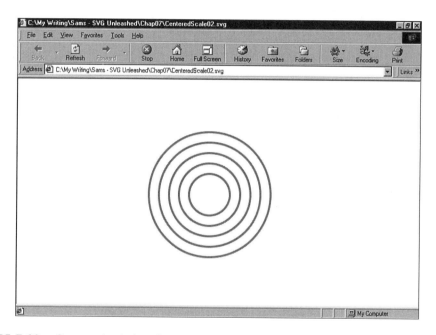

FIGURE 7.10 Concentric circles of constant stroke width created using translation and scale transformations.

Skew Transformations

SVG provides two skew transformations: skewX() and skewY().

The skewX() Transformation

The skewX() transformation skews SVG text or graphic shapes along a horizontal axis. You may want to review Figure 5.16 to see the effect on the axes of a skewX() transformation.

Listing 7.13 shows the effect of several degrees of skewX() applied to text.

LISTING 7.13   skewXText.svg—Applying the skewX() Transformation to Text

```
<?xml version="1.0" standalone="no"?>
<!DOCTYPE svg PUBLIC "-//W3C//DTD SVG 20010904//EN"
"http://www.w3.org/TR/2001/REC-SVG-20010904/DTD/svg10.dtd">
<svg width="100%" height="100%">
<text x="50px" y="50px" transform="skewX(0)"
 style="font-family:Arial, sans-serif; font-size:24;">
Unskewed text
</text>
<text x="50px" y="100px" transform="skewX(10)"
 style="font-family:Arial, sans-serif; font-size:24;">
Skewed by 10 degrees text
</text>
<text x="50px" y="150px" transform="skewX(30)"
 style="font-family:Arial, sans-serif; font-size:24;">
Skewed by 30 degrees text
</text>
<text x="50px" y="200px" transform="skewX(45)"
 style="font-family:Arial, sans-serif; font-size:24;">
Skewed by 45 degrees text
</text>
<text x="50px" y="250px" transform="skewX(60)"
 style="font-family:Arial, sans-serif; font-size:24;">
Skewed by 60 degrees text
</text>
</svg>
```

The first text element has a skewX(0) transformation applied; in other words, a zero skew is applied so the text appears normal. Each of the four succeeding text elements has a larger skewX() transformation applied, from 10 degrees to 60 degrees. Each piece of text content describes the transformation that has been applied to it.

Figure 7.11 shows the appearance onscreen when Listing 7.13 is run. Notice that there is both a distortion of the characters in the text and a movement in the horizontal direction from that specified in the x attribute of the text element.

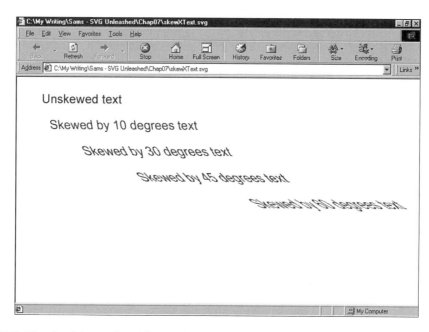

FIGURE 7.11   Applying a skewX() transformation with positive values for the argument.

Listing 7.14 applies the skewX() transformation with negative values for the argument.

LISTING 7.14   skewXText02.svg—Using the skewX() Transformation with Negative Values for the Argument

```
<?xml version="1.0" standalone="no"?>
<!DOCTYPE svg PUBLIC "-//W3C//DTD SVG 20010904//EN"
"http://www.w3.org/TR/2001/REC-SVG-20010904/DTD/svg10.dtd">
<svg width="100%" height="100%">
<text x="650px" y="50px" transform="skewX(0)"
 style="font-family:Arial, sans-serif; font-size:24;">
Unskewed text
</text>
<text x="650px" y="100px" transform="skewX(-10)"
 style="font-family:Arial, sans-serif; font-size:24;">
Skewed by -10 degrees text
</text>
<text x="650px" y="150px" transform="skewX(-30)"
 style="font-family:Arial, sans-serif; font-size:24;">
Skewed by -30 degrees text
</text>
<text x="650px" y="200px" transform="skewX(-45)"
 style="font-family:Arial, sans-serif; font-size:24;">
```

LISTING 7.14   Continued

```
Skewed by -45 degrees text
</text>
<text x="650px" y="250px" transform="skewX(-60)"
 style="font-family:Arial, sans-serif; font-size:24;">
Skewed by -60 degrees text
</text>
</svg>
```

Listing 7.14 begins with a text element that has a zero skew applied. Then each of the following four text elements has an increasing skewX() transformation applied. The text content of each text element describes the skew that has been applied.

Figure 7.12, which is slightly panned, shows the movement of the text to the left and the distortion of the text as the values of the argument become more negative.

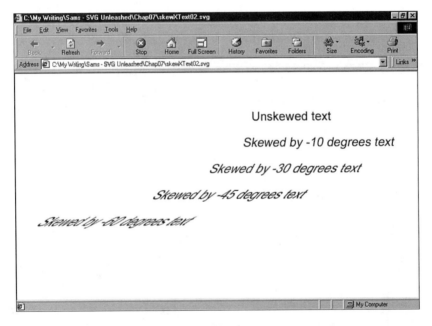

FIGURE 7.12   Using negative values for the argument of the skewX() transformation.

The skewY() Transformation

The skewY() transformation skews SVG text or graphic shapes along a vertical axis. You may want to review Figure 5.17 to see the effect on the axes of a skewY() transformation.

Listing 7.15 shows the skewY() transformation with positive values for the argument, which skews the text downward.

LISTING 7.15   skewYText.svg—Applying the skewY() Transformation to Text with Positive Values for the Argument

```
<?xml version="1.0" standalone="no"?>
<!DOCTYPE svg PUBLIC "-//W3C//DTD SVG 20010904//EN"
"http://www.w3.org/TR/2001/REC-SVG-20010904/DTD/svg10.dtd">
<svg width="100%" height="100%">
<text x="50px" y="50px" transform="skewY(0)" style="font-family:Arial,
sans-serif; font-size:24;">
Unskewed text
</text>
<text x="50px" y="100px" transform="skewY(10)" style="font-family:Arial,
sans-serif; font-size:24;">
Skewed by 10 degrees text
</text>
<text x="50px" y="150px" transform="skewY(30)" style="font-family:Arial,
sans-serif; font-size:24;">
Skewed by 30 degrees text
</text>
<text x="50px" y="200px" transform="skewY(45)" style="font-family:Arial,
sans-serif; font-size:24;">
Skewed by 45 degrees text
</text>
<text x="50px" y="250px" transform="skewY(60)" style="font-family:Arial,
sans-serif; font-size:24;">
Skewed by 60 degrees text
</text>
</svg>
```

Figure 7.13 shows the result onscreen of applying the skewY() transformation with positive values for the argument. Notice the downward displacement of the text as well as its distortion as the argument values become more positive.

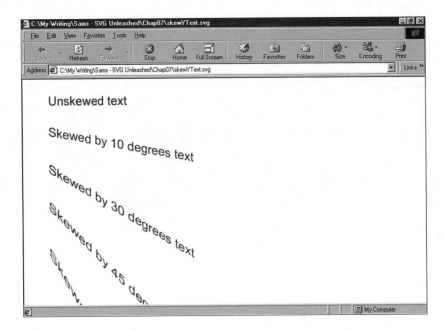

FIGURE 7.13   The skewY() transformation with positive argument values.

Listing 7.16 shows the skewY() transformation applied with negative values for the argument.

LISTING 7.16   skewYText02.svg—The skewY Transformation with Negative Argument Values

```
<?xml version="1.0" standalone="no"?>
<!DOCTYPE svg PUBLIC "-//W3C//DTD SVG 20010904//EN"
"http://www.w3.org/TR/2001/REC-SVG-20010904/DTD/svg10.dtd">
<svg width="100%" height="100%">
<text x="650px" y="450px" transform="skewY(0)"
 style="font-family:Arial, sans-serif; font-size:24;">
Unskewed text
</text>
<text x="650px" y="450px" transform="skewY(-10)"
 style="font-family:Arial, sans-serif; font-size:24;">
Skewed by -10 degrees text
</text>
<text x="650px" y="450px" transform="skewY(-20)"
 style="font-family:Arial, sans-serif; font-size:24;">
Skewed by -20 degrees text
</text>
```

LISTING 7.16 Continued

```
<text x="650px" y="450px" transform="skewY(-30)"
 style="font-family:Arial, sans-serif; font-size:24;">
Skewed by -30 degrees text
</text>
<text x="650px" y="450px" transform="skewY(-45)"
 style="font-family:Arial, sans-serif; font-size:24;">
Skewed by -45 degrees text
</text>
<text x="650px" y="450px" transform="skewY(-60)"
 style="font-family:Arial, sans-serif; font-size:24;">
Skewed by -60 degrees text
</text>
<text x="650px" y="450px" transform="skewY(-80)"
 style="font-family:Arial, sans-serif; font-size:24;">
Skewed by -80 degrees text
</text>
<text x="650px" y="450px" transform="skewY(-160)"
 style="font-family:Arial, sans-serif; font-size:24;">
Skewed by -160 degrees text
</text>
</svg>
```

Figure 7.14 shows the results onscreen, slightly zoomed out and panned. To fully appreciate the changes produced by skewY() transformations of this type, you should run the code and view the changes onscreen. Without zooming out, some text is off the screen. Notice the vertical displacement and distortion of the text. For values close to –90 degrees, you may not easily find the text. The text displayed for skewY(-80), for example, is a *long* way above the top of the initial viewport. To find it, use the Zoom Out option several times in the Adobe SVG Viewer. The result from skewY(-160) is below the initial viewport.

Having looked at the individual types of transformation available in SVG, we are now ready to take a closer look at the transformation matrix that SVG provides.

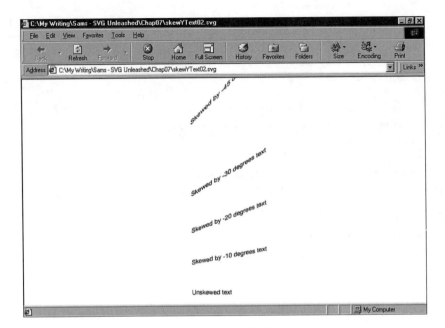

FIGURE 7.14   Using negative values for the argument of the skewY() transformation.

The Transformation Matrix

The SVG transformations that have been described so far in this chapter have been described in terms of single types of transformations. They can also be viewed as component parts of a 3×3 **matrix** transformation. In practice only six of the nine possible parts of the matrix are used; therefore, an SVG matrix transformation can be expressed as a six-value **vector**. You generally can write the six-value vector representation as follows:

```
transform="matrix(a b c d e f)"
```

Or, using commas with whitespace as separators, you can write this representation as follows:

```
transform="matrix(a, b, c, d, e, f)"
```

A `translate()` transformation can be written as

```
transform="matrix(1 0 0 1 x-displacement y-displacement)"
```

A `rotate()` transformation around the origin can be written as

```
transform="matrix(cos(a) sin(a) -sin(a) cos(a) 0 0)"
```

where *a* is the angle of rotation.

A skewX() transformation can be written as

```
transform="matrix(1 0 tan(a) 1 0 0)"
```

where the skew is of angle *a*.

A skewY() transformation can be written as

```
transform="matrix(1 tan(a) 0 1 0 0)"
```

where the skew is of angle *a*.

> **NOTE**
>
> Chapter 7 of the SVG 1.0 Recommendation, at http://www.w3.org/TR/SVG/coords.html,
> provides a brief introduction to matrix algebra applied to SVG transformations.

Combining Transformations

You can combine transformations to produce any arbitrary transformation you want.
There are two basic techniques to do that: to supply several values within a single
transform attribute or to nest several grouping, g, elements, each with a single transformation.

The following two pieces of code are equivalent.

```
<g transform="translate (150,150) scale(2.5)
 rotate(33) translate(25,0)">
<!-- Code goes here. -->
</g>
```

is equivalent to

```
<g transform="translate(150,150)">
 <g transform="scale(2.5)">
  <g transform="rotate(33)">
   <g translate(25,0)>
    <!-- Code goes here. -->
   </g>
  </g>
 </g>
</g>
```

The order in which you apply transformations is important in defining the final onscreen position. Listing 7.17 illustrates this principle.

LISTING 7.17   OrderedTransforms.svg—The Order of Transformations Can Affect the Result

```
<?xml version="1.0" standalone="no"?>
<!DOCTYPE svg PUBLIC "-//W3C//DTD SVG 20010904//EN"
"http://www.w3.org/TR/2001/REC-SVG-20010904/DTD/svg10.dtd">
<svg width="1000px" height="750px">
<defs>
<text id="myText" x="20" y="20"
style="fill:red; stroke:none; font-size:20">
Some test text
</text>
</defs>
<use xlink:href="#myText"
 transform="scale(2.0) translate(150,80) rotate(45) translate(200,-100)"/>
<use xlink:href="#myText"
 transform="translate(150,80) scale(2.0) rotate(45) translate(200,-100)"/>
<use xlink:href="#myText"
 transform="translate(150,80) rotate(45) translate(200,-100) scale(2.0)"/>
<use xlink:href="#myText"
 transform="rotate(45) translate(150,80) scale(2.0)  translate(200,-100)"/>
</svg>
```

Each of the use elements in Listing 7.17 has the same four transformations specified—scale(2.0), translate(150,80), rotate(45), and translate (200,-100). The only difference among the use elements is that the order of the transformations is different on each use element. Figure 7.15 shows the slightly panned onscreen result of running Listing 7.17. As you can see, the four pieces of text are rendered in different places onscreen. It isn't important that you understand exactly where the final position for any combination is, but it is important to grasp the idea that the order of transformations affects the final position of any SVG object onscreen.

In the final part of the chapter, the SVG DOM interfaces for SVG transformations are described.

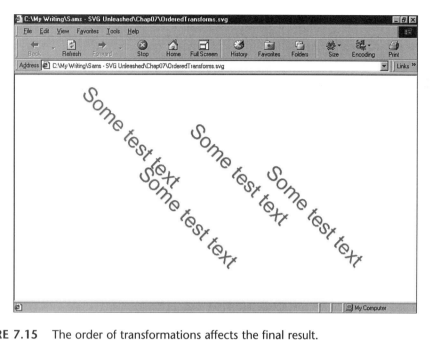

FIGURE 7.15   The order of transformations affects the final result.

Transformation SVG DOM Interfaces

In this section, we will describe the SVG DOM interfaces that are relevant to SVG transformations.

The SVGMatrix Object

As mentioned earlier in this chapter, transformations can be viewed as representing matrix transformations. The SVGMatrix object is used to express the six parts of the matrix in its properties listed below. Its methods include methods to produce transformations similar to those we can produce using the declarative syntax described earlier in this chapter.

The SVGMatrix object has the following properties:

- a—of type float

- b—of type float

- c—of type float

- d—of type float

- e—of type float

- f—of type float

The SVGMatrix object has the following methods:

- multiply(*secondMatrix*)—The method returns a value of type SVGMatrix. The *secondMatrix* argument is of type SVGMatrix.

- inverse()—The method returns a value of type SVGMatrix.

- translate(*x*,*y*)—The method returns a value of type SVGMatrix. The *x* and *y* arguments are of type float.

- scale(*scaleFactor*)—The method returns a value of type SVGMatrix. The *scaleFactor* argument is of type float.

- scaleNonUniform(*scaleFactorX*, *scaleFactorY*)—The method returns a value of type SVGMatrix. The *scaleFactorX* and *scaleFactorY* arguments are of type float.

- rotate(*angle*)—The method returns a value of type SVGMatrix. The *angle* argument is of type float.

- rotateFromVector(*x*,*y*)—The method returns a value of type SVGMatrix. The *x* and *y* arguments are of type float.

- flipX()—The method returns a value of type SVGMatrix. The method takes no argument.

- flipY()—The method returns a value of type SVGMatrix. The method takes no argument.

- skewX(*angle*)—The method returns a value of type SVGMatrix. The *angle* argument is of type float.

- skewY(*angle*)—The method returns a value of type SVGMatrix. The *angle* argument is of type float.

The SVGPoint Object

The SVGPoint object has the following properties specific to it:

- x—of type float
- y—of type float

The SVGPoint object has the following method:

- matrixTransform(*matrix*)—The method returns a value of type SVGPoint. The *matrix* argument is of type SVGMatrix.

The SVGPointList Object

The SVGPointList object has the following property:

- numberOfItems—of type unsigned long

The SVGPointList object has the following methods:

- clear()—The method returns a value of type void. The method takes no arguments.

- initialize(*newItem*)—The method returns a value of type SVGPoint. The *newItem* argument is of type SVGPoint.

- getItem(*index*)—The method returns a value of type SVGPoint. The *index* argument is of type unsigned long.

- insertItemBefore(*newItem*, *index*)—The method returns a value of type SVGPoint. The *newItem* argument is of type SVGPoint. The *index* argument is of type unsigned long.

- replaceItem(*newItem*, *index*)—The method returns a value of type SVGPoint. The *newItem* argument is of type SVGPoint. The *index* argument is of type unsigned long.

- removeItem(*index*)—The method returns a value of type SVGPoint. The *index* argument is of type unsigned long.

- appendItem(*newItem*)—The method returns a value of type SVGPoint. The *newItem* argument is of type SVGPoint.

The SVGTransform Object

The SVGTransform object provides properties and methods that express the type of a transformation. The SVGTransform object has as one of its properties the SVGMatrix object described earlier.

The SVGTransform object has the following constants associated with it:

- SVGTransform.SVG_TRANSFORM_UNKNOWN—The constant is type short and has a value of 0.

- SVGTransform.SVG_TRANSFORM_MATRIX—The constant is type short and has a value of 1.

- SVGTransform.SVG_TRANSFORM_TRANSLATE—The constant is type short and has a value of 2.

- SVGTransform.SVG_TRANSFORM_SCALE—The constant is type short and has a value of 3.

- SVGTransform.SVG_TRANSFORM_ROTATE—The constant is type short and has a value of 4.

- `SVGTransform.SVG_TRANSFORM_SKEWX`—The constant is type short and has a value of 5.

- `SVGTransform.SVG_TRANSFORM_SKEWY`—The constant is type short and has a value of 6.

The `SVGTransform` object has the following properties specific to it:

- `type`—of type unsigned short

- `matrix`—of type SVGMatrix

- `angle`—of type float

The `SVGTransform` object has the following methods:

- `setMatrix(matrix)`—The method returns a value of type void. The *matrix* argument is of type SVGMatrix.

- `setTranslate(tx,ty)`—The method returns a value of type void. The *tx* and *ty* arguments are of type float.

- `setScale(sx, sy)`—The method returns a value of type void. The *sx* and *sy* arguments are of type float.

- `setRotate(angle, cx, cy)`—The method returns a value of type void. The *angle*, *cx,* and *cy* arguments are of type float.

- `setSkewX(angle)`—The method returns a value of type void. The *angle* argument is of type float.

- `setSkewY(angle)`—The method returns a value of type void. The *angle* argument is of type float.

The SVGTransformable Object

The `SVGTransformable` object has the properties of the `SVGLocatable` object. The `SVGLocatable` object is described in Chapter 2.

The `SVGTransformable` object has the following property specific to it:

- `transform`—of type SVGAnimatedTransformList

The `SVGTransformable` object has no methods specific to it.

The SVGTransformList Object

The `SVGTransformList` object has the following property specific to it:

- `numberOfItems`—of type unsigned long

The `SVGTransformList` object has the following methods specific to it:

- `clear()`—The method returns a value of type `void`. The method takes no arguments.

- `initialize(newItem)`—The method returns a value of type `SVGTransform`. The *newItem* argument is of type `SVGTransform`.

- `getItem(index)`—The method returns a value of type `SVGTransform`. The *index* argument is of type `unsigned long`.

- `insertItemBefore(newItem, index)`—The method returns a value of type `SVGTransform`. The *newItem* argument is of type `SVGTransform`. The *index* argument is of type `unsigned long`.

- `replaceItem(newItem, index)`—The method returns a value of type `SVGTransform`. The *newItem* argument is of type `SVGTransform`. The *index* argument is of type `unsigned long`.

- `removeItem(index)`—The method returns a value of type `SVGTransform`. The *index* argument is of type `unsigned long`.

- `appendItem(newItem)`—The method returns a value of type `SVGTransform`. The *newItem* argument is of type `SVGTransform`.

- `createSVGTransformFromMatrix(matrix)`—The method returns a value of type `SVGTransform`. The *matrix* argument is of type `SVGMatrix`.

- `consolidate()`—The method returns a value of type `SVGTransform`. The method takes no argument.

Scripting Transformation Examples

In this section, we will look at a couple of examples of scripting transformations.

A skewX() Transformation Example

Listing 7.18 shows a simple vehicle being skewed in shape as it stops.

LISTING 7.18 Braking.svg—A skewX()Transformation

```
<?xml version="1.0" standalone="no"?>
<!DOCTYPE svg PUBLIC "-//W3C//DTD SVG 20010904//EN"
"http://www.w3.org/TR/2001/REC-SVG-20010904/DTD/svg10.dtd">
<svg width="600px" height="300px" xmlns="http://www.w3.org/2000/svg"
onload="Initialize()">
  <script type="text/javascript">
  <![CDATA[
```

LISTING 7.18   Continued

```
var time = 0;
var van;

function Initialize() {
    van = document.getElementById('van');
    parkVan();
}

function parkVan() {
    time += 0.01;
    if (time > 1) {
        bounceBack();
    }
    else {
        var x = displacement();
        var angle = -0.015 * acceleration();
        var transform = 'translate(' + x + ',0) skewX(' + angle + ')';
        van.setAttribute('transform', transform);
        setTimeout('parkVan()', 10);
    }
}

function acceleration() {
    return -1200*time;
}

function displacement() {
    return -200*Math.pow(time,3) + 600*time - 100;
}

function bounceBack() {
    var transform = van.getAttribute('transform');
    var reSkewX = /skewX\(([\d\.]+)/;
    var skewX = parseInt( reSkewX.exec(transform)[1] ) - 1;
    if (skewX == 0)
        return;
    if (skewX < 0)
        skewX = 0;
    transform = transform.replace(reSkewX, 'skewX(' + skewX);
    van.setAttribute('transform', transform);
```

LISTING 7.18 Continued

```
      setTimeout('bounceBack()', 10);
}

  ]]>
  </script>
  <defs>
    <symbol id="vanSymbol">
     <g transform="scale(2.0)">
      <path d="M0,10 L100,10 100,25 C100,35 95,38 85,38 L70,38 60,58 0,58 z"
fill="red" />
      <path d="M66,38 57,55 40,55 40,38 z" fill="black" />
      <circle cx="20" cy="10" r="10" fill="black" />
      <circle cx="75" cy="10" r="10" fill="black" />
      </g>
    </symbol>
  </defs>
  <!-- the following matrix creates a coordinate system
       at 0,200 with the Y-axes pointing towards the
       top of the screen -->
  <g transform="matrix(1 0 0 -1 0 200)">
    <use id="van" x="0" y="0" xlink:href="#vanSymbol" />
  </g>
</svg>
```

When the document loads, the Initialize() function is called. That function identifies a use element by the value of its id attribute. The parkVan() function is then called.

The parkVan() function manipulates the value of the transform attribute of the use element by using the setAttribute() method. A translate() transformation and a skewX() transformation are applied. The parkVan() function calls itself recursively, each time increasing the value of the time variable. When the time variable is 1, the parkVan() function calls the bounceBack() function.

Visually, the van appears to move across the screen and then decelerate as if its brakes had been applied. The van leans forward as if the braking were extreme (the effect is produced using the skewX() transformation). After the van stops, the skewX() transformation effect is removed, as if the vehicle were rebounding from its severe braking.

Figure 7.16 shows the van leaning forward when "braking." Figure 7.17 shows the final position of the van, after the skewX() transformation returns to 0.

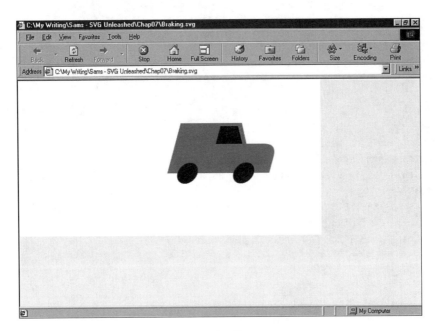

FIGURE 7.16   The van leaning forward when braking.

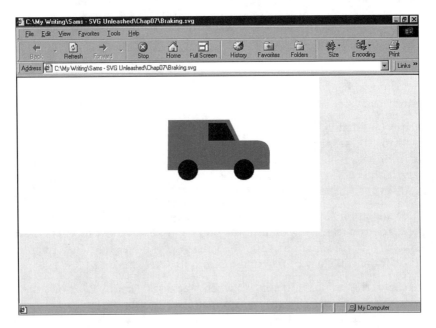

FIGURE 7.17   The van in its final position after braking.

Scaling Under User Control

Listing 7.19 shows an example of setting the scale() transform on a circle under user control, by clicking on the text Up or Down.

LISTING 7.19   A scale() Transformation

```
<?xml version="1.0" standalone="no"?>
<!DOCTYPE svg PUBLIC "-//W3C//DTD SVG 20010904//EN"
"http://www.w3.org/TR/2001/REC-SVG-20010904/DTD/svg10.dtd">
<svg width="" height="" onload="Initialize(evt)">
<script type="text/javascript">
<![CDATA[
var up = false;
var scaleFactor = 1;
var newTransform;

function Initialize(){
SVGRoot = document.documentElement;
myCircle = SVGRoot.getElementById("theCircle");
}

function adjustScale(){
if (up==true){
scaleFactor = scaleFactor * 1.25;
newTransform = "translate(100,150), scale(" + scaleFactor + ")";
myCircle.setAttribute("transform", newTransform);

} // end if
else {
scaleFactor = scaleFactor / 1.25;
newTransform = "translate(100,150), scale(" + scaleFactor + ")";
myCircle.setAttribute("transform", newTransform);
} // end else

}

]]>
</script>
<g transform="translate(200,200)">
<text x="75" y="75" onclick="up=true;adjustScale(evt)">Up</text>
<text x="115" y="75" onclick="up=false;adjustScale(evt)">Down</text>
```

LISTING 7.19   Continued

```
<circle id="theCircle" cx="0" cy="0" transform="translate(100,150),
➥scale(1.0)" r="50"
 style="stroke:#FF00FF; stroke-width:4; fill:none; pointer-events:none" />
</g>
</svg>
```

When the page loads, the `Initialize()` function is called. Within the `Initialize()` function, the `myCircle` variable is set using the `getElementById()` method.

When the text is clicked, the `onclick` attribute sets the value of the global up variable to an appropriate value. The `adjustScale()` function is then called. Within that function, an `if else` statement controls whether the circle, represented by the `myCircle` variable, is increased or decreased in size. The `newTransform` variable is used to create the new value of the `transform` attribute. The `setAttribute()` method is used to apply the value of the `newTransform` variable to the `transform` attribute. Onscreen the circle increases or decreases in size, as shown in Figure 7.18.

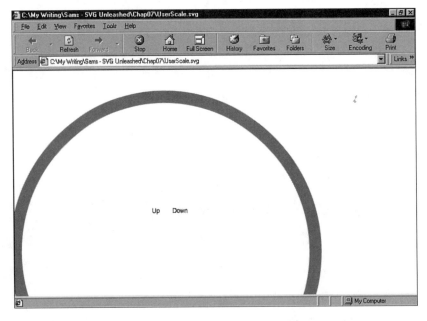

FIGURE 7.18 The circle enlarged by clicking on up a few times.

Summary

This chapter described each type of transformation that SVG provides, building on your understanding of coordinate systems from Chapter 5. Transformations can consist of moving an object to a new position onscreen (`translate()` transformations), rotating an object onscreen (`rotate()` transformations), changing the size of an object (`scale()` transformations), or distorting the shape of an object (`skewX()` and `skewY()` transformations). All simple transformation types were demonstrated.

The SVG DOM Interfaces for transformation were also described. Some examples of scripting the DOM to produce timed or interactive changes in transformation were shown.

7

Laying Out Text in SVG

It is essential that you be able to lay out text in SVG. For example, a map may need text to name towns or other features, a technical diagram may need text to label parts of a piece of machinery, and so on. In other settings, a logo may contain text whose positioning may in turn be animated. SVG can even be used to create SVG Web pages, where predictable text layout is vital to communication. If SVG is to be used effectively in such ways, the ability to lay out text precisely and predictably is essential.

This chapter will first look at some general text and text layout concepts and then introduce the SVG elements that are used in the layout of text on straight lines, both horizontal and vertical. Then we will introduce you to a variety of practical techniques, using the SVG elements for text, which are used for aligning text, creating subscript text, and so on. Next, we will examine the layout of text on any arbitrary path, using the `textPath` element. In the final section of the chapter, we will describe the SVG DOM interfaces relevant to text layout.

Overview of Text in SVG

If you are comfortable with general text terminology and can, without struggling, easily distinguish between a **character**, a **glyph**, and a **font** and know the meanings of terms such as **baseline**, **descender**, and **ascender**, feel free to skip this section.

Some Text Terms

In this section, we will briefly look at some foundational text terms.

What Is a Character?

A **character** in XML is essentially a numerical value represented as one or more bytes in the Unicode standard.

Listing 8.1 allows us to place three XML or Unicode characters—S, V, and G—onscreen by referencing their values using character references, S, V, and G.

LISTING 8.1   Character.svg—SVG Using Character References

```
<?xml version="1.0" standalone="no"?>
<!DOCTYPE svg PUBLIC "-//W3C//DTD SVG 20010904//EN"
"http://www.w3.org/TR/2001/REC-SVG-20010904/DTD/svg10.dtd">
<svg width="" height="">
<text x="250" y="250"
 style="font-size:40; font-family:Arial, sans-serif; fill:red; stroke:none" >
&#83;&#86;&#71;</text>
</svg>
```

The character references are nested between the start tag and the end tag of an SVG `text` element. Use of the `text` element will be discussed in more detail later in this chapter.

If you run Listing 8.1, you will see the string SVG displayed onscreen. The three character references are displayed as glyphs that you should recognize.

All SVG text consists of XML (and therefore Unicode) characters. Typically, you simply type them as normal keyboard characters without using character references.

SVG text remains as text in the SVG document. That means that XML-capable search engines can search for text strings. In addition, a user can select text from an SVG Web page or image and copy and paste that text. The text always remains accessible as text, not simply as a pattern of pixels. SVG text promotes accessibility, as discussed in Chapter 13, "Accessibility, Internationalization, and Metadata."

What Is a Glyph?

A **glyph** is a visual representation of a character. Any character may have an arbitrarily large number of glyphs that can visually represent it. Listing 8.2 displays onscreen three glyphs for each of the characters S, V, and G.

LISTING 8.2   Character02.svg—Displaying Three Glyphs for Each Character

```
<?xml version="1.0" standalone="no"?>
<!DOCTYPE svg PUBLIC "-//W3C//DTD SVG 20010904//EN"
"http://www.w3.org/TR/2001/REC-SVG-20010904/DTD/svg10.dtd">
<svg width="" height="">
<text x="250" y="150"
 style="font-size:40; font-family:Arial, sans-serif;
 fill:red; stroke:none" >
&#83;&#86;&#71;</text>
<text x="250" y="250"
 style="font-size:40; font-family:'Times New Roman', serif;
 fill:red; stroke:none" >
&#83;&#86;&#71;</text>
```

LISTING 8.2 Continued

```
<text x="250" y="350"
 style="font-size:40; font-family:'Courier New'; fill:red; stroke:none" >
&#83;&#86;&#71;</text>
</svg>
```

In Listing 8.2, you can see that within each text element the character references are unchanged. Onscreen the visual appearance is different for each line, because on each line we are using different glyphs to represent each of the three characters. The glyph displayed for, say, the S of SVG depends on the font of which it forms part. In SVG, we specify the font using the style attribute (or one of the alternative styling techniques discussed in Chapter 4, "Using CSS with SVG"). The glyph for S in Arial font, Times New Roman font, and Courier New font are visually different but represent the same character.

Figure 8.1 shows the onscreen appearance when Listing 8.2 is run.

> **CAUTION**
>
> Be careful when placing named fonts, whose name contains more than one word, in a style attribute. If you used paired quotation marks to delimit the value of the style attribute, you must use paired apostrophes to delimit the font name. If you used paired apostrophes to delimit the value of the style attribute, you must use paired quotation marks to delimit the font name.

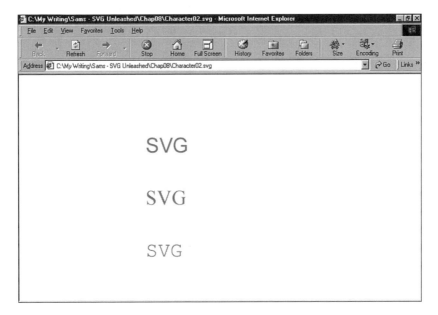

FIGURE 8.1   Each character may have many glyphs.

We will touch on the topic of glyph orientation later in the chapter.

What Is a Font?

A **font** is collection of **glyphs**. A font typically includes a **font table**, which is a mapping from characters to glyphs. The font table also typically includes additional information that allows correct positioning and sizing of a glyph. A collection of glyphs plus the corresponding **font table** is often termed the **font data**. Detailed consideration of onscreen geometry for glyphs is beyond the scope of this chapter but is described in the SVG 1.0 and CSS2 recommendations.

For many fonts intended to display English text, the glyphs include those to display the lowercase characters a to z and the uppercase characters A to Z, likely with numerical characters and some other punctuation and similar characters.

The glyphs in a font typically have visual appearances in common. For example, the glyphs on the top line in Figure 8.1 have no **serifs**—small decorative extensions at the ends of the strokes of glyphs—whereas in the second line, we can see serifs on the ends of strokes on each glyph. A font whose glyphs lack serifs is called **sans serif**. A font whose glyphs typically possess serifs is called a **serif** font.

A font may have a name, such as Times New Roman, Arial, or Courier New. Fonts with generally similar appearances can be grouped together into font families. Typically, a font family has a generic font of a particular type such as **serif** or **sans serif**. Times New Roman is a serif font. However, not all users have that particular serif font available, so we can specify an alternative, often the default, font in the same family such as **serif**.

Let's move on to discuss some terms that are used in describing glyphs. We will need to understand these terms because they are used in SVG when the display appearance or positioning is adjusted.

NOTE

A character can be represented by more than one glyph. For example, some accented characters may have two glyphs—one for the main part of the character and another for the accent. On the other hand, some character combinations, including **ligatures** such as ffi, may be represented by a single glyph. A ligature is a visual representation of a combination of characters. The mapping from characters to glyphs is often system dependent.

Some Glyph Terminology

One of the important terms when describing a glyph in detail is the notion of a **baseline**. Crudely, it is sometimes described as the line on which glyphs sit, but as you can see from Figure 8.2, not all glyphs sit on the baseline in exactly the same way.

Listing 8.3 displays a diagram that serves to illustrate some significant glyph terms.

LISTING 8.3   SVG.svg—A Diagram of Glyph Terms

```
<?xml version="1.0" standalone="no"?>
<!DOCTYPE svg PUBLIC "-//W3C//DTD SVG 20010904//EN"
"http://www.w3.org/TR/2001/REC-SVG-20010904/DTD/svg10.dtd">
<svg width="" height="">
<defs>
<line id="myDottedLine" x1="0" y1="0" x2="100%" y2="0"
 style="stroke:black; stroke-width:0.5; stroke-dasharray:2,2;"/>
 <line id="mySolidLine" x1="0" y1="0" x2="100%" y2="0"
 style="stroke:black; stroke-width:0.5;"/>
</defs>
<use xlink:href="#myDottedLine" transform="translate(0,202)"/>
<use xlink:href="#myDottedLine" transform="translate(0,235)"/>
<use xlink:href="#mySolidLine" transform="translate(0,302)"/>
<use xlink:href="#myDottedLine" transform="translate(0,330)"/>
<text x="100" y="300"
 style="font-family:'Times New Roman', serif; font-size:144;
 fill:red; stroke:none;">
Svg
</text>
<text x="330" y="300"
 style="font-family:'Arial', sans-serif; font-size:14;
 fill:black; stroke:none;">
baseline
</text>
</svg>
```

Figure 8.2 shows the zoomed onscreen appearance when Listing 8.3 is run.

The **baseline** is labeled in Figure 8.2. The distance from the baseline (solid line in the figure) to the dotted line above it is termed the **x-height**. The part of the letter that extends from that dotted line to the top dotted line is termed the **ascender**. The part of the letter, such as g, that extends below the baseline is termed the **descender**.

Having looked at these foundational terms, let's now move on and take a general look at the three SVG elements used for normal text layout—that is, text laid out in straight lines, either horizontal or vertical. The textPath element (that allows you to lay out text on a path) will be considered later in this chapter.

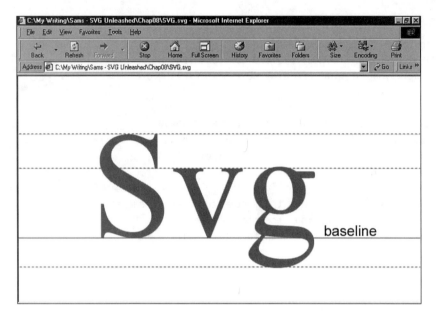

FIGURE 8.2   Baseline for glyphs.

The SVG Text Layout Elements

SVG provides four elements for layout of text: `text`, `tspan`, `tref`, and `textPath`.

The first three of these elements will be introduced in the following sections. Later in the chapter, we will explore how to use these elements on their own or in various combinations to achieve a range of desired text layout options onscreen.

The text Element

The `text` element is the essential element for any text layout in an SVG document. All text layout in SVG uses the `text` element, either alone or in combination with other text-related elements. Text may be laid out in straight lines using the `text` element alone or using the `text` element in combination with the `tspan` element and/or the `tref` element (discussed later in this chapter). If you want to display text along an arbitrary path, you must use the `text` element combined with the `textPath` element.

The display of text onscreen requires that you define the placement of the text, which you do by using the x and y attributes of the `text` element. The default behavior is that the value of the x attribute defines the left edge of the text, and the value of the y attribute defines the **baseline** for the glyphs. This contrasts with the y attribute of a `rect` element, where it indicates the top of the rectangle.

In addition to placing text, the `text` element is typically styled using one or more of the **styling properties** discussed in Chapter 4.

> **CAUTION**
>
> Using text elements alone to lay out text has an adverse effect on accessibility. Using tspan elements, described later in this chapter, promotes accessibility by allowing you to select related text chunks together.

Listing 8.4 shows the usage of `text` elements to lay out a paragraph of text.

LISTING 8.4   TextElements.svg—Using text Elements to Lay Out Text

```
<?xml version="1.0" standalone="no"?>
<!DOCTYPE svg PUBLIC "-//W3C//DTD SVG 20010904//EN"
"http://www.w3.org/TR/2001/REC-SVG-20010904/DTD/svg10.dtd">
<svg width="" height="">
<defs>
<style type="text/css">
<![CDATA[
text{
font-family:Arial, sans-serif;
font-size:16;
fill:#000099;
}
]]>
</style>
</defs>
<text x="25" y="35">
Laying out text in SVG can be done using &lt;text&gt; elements alone.
 A separate &lt;text&gt;
</text>
<text x="25" y="55">
element is needed for each line of text. The absolute coordinate in
 the y direction must be
</text>
<text x="25" y="75">
specified and must be determined manually. Text cannot be selected
 from more than one &lt;text&gt;
</text>
<text x="25" y="95">
element, which can be inconvenient for a user who wants to copy and
 paste. It also has a negative
</text>
<text x="25" y="115">
impact on accessibility for the disabled.
</text>
</svg>
```

Figure 8.3 shows the onscreen appearance when Listing 8.4 is run. An attempt to select the sentence beginning "The absolute coordinate…" cannot proceed beyond the end of the line; that is, it is confined within a single text element.

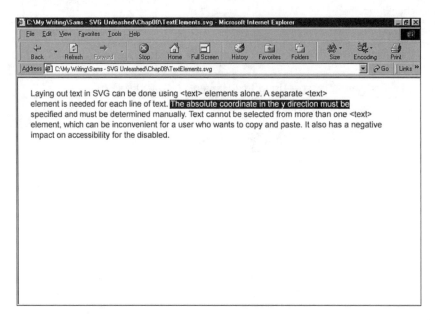

FIGURE 8.3   The situation when using text elements alone.

The text in Listing 8.4 describes some of the realities of using text elements alone. It isn't convenient for copying and pasting, nor for accessibility. You will find that you cannot select a sentence that spreads over two lines; you can select text within a single text element only. In addition, if you later want to convert text from static to animated text, the use of multiple text elements is inconvenient.

The tspan Element

The tspan element provides an alternative, and more accessible, way to contain text. The tspan element is always nested within a text element. It cannot be used alone. The position of a tspan element is specified using x and y attributes (to define an absolute position on page) or dx and dy attributes (to define a position relative to its parent text element or the preceding tspan element). Style on a tspan element is specified using the same techniques used on a text element. If no style is specified for tspan elements, they inherit styling from their parent text element.

Any arbitrary number of tspan elements can be nested in a text element. A user can select all the text within a single text element; therefore, if tspan elements are used within a single text element to lay out related lines of text, the user can select a whole paragraph, or equivalent text chunk.

Listing 8.5 shows a paragraph of text that is created using tspan elements nested within a text element.

LISTING 8.5   TSpan.svg—Using tspan Elements to Lay Out a Paragraph

```
<?xml version="1.0" standalone="no"?>
<!DOCTYPE svg PUBLIC "-//W3C//DTD SVG 20010904//EN"
"http://www.w3.org/TR/2001/REC-SVG-20010904/DTD/svg10.dtd">
<svg width="" height="">
<defs>
<style type="text/css">
<![CDATA[
text, tspan{
font-family:Arial, sans-serif;
font-size:16;
fill:#000099;
}
]]>
</style>
</defs>
<text x="25" y="35">
<tspan>
Laying out text in SVG can be done using &lt;text&gt; together
 with &lt;tspan&gt; elements. A single &lt;text&gt;
</tspan>
<tspan x="25" dy="1.5em">
element can be used for each paragraph (or other related chunk) of text,
 so that related text can be selected,
</tspan>
<tspan x="25" dy="1.5em">
cut and pasted. The y coordinate of each line can be specified using
 a dy attribute on each &lt;tspan&gt; element,
</tspan>
<tspan x="25" dy="1.5em">
so adjusting line spacing automatically when font size is changed.
 Additionally using the dy attribute makes it
</tspan>
<tspan x="25" dy="1.5em">
easy to vertically animate blocks of text to display an animated news
 feed, for example.
</tspan>
</text>
</svg>
```

8

Figure 8.4 shows the onscreen appearance when Listing 8.5 is run. Selecting all the text in the sentence beginning "The y coordinate..." is straightforward.

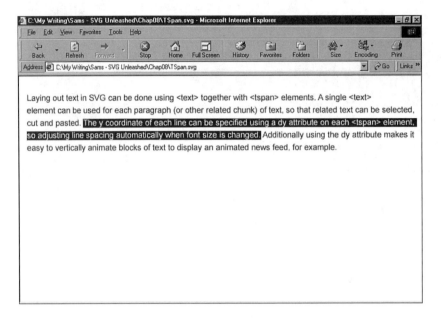

FIGURE 8.4   Improved accessibility when tspan elements are used.

Run both Listing 8.4 and Listing 8.5 and compare how much easier it is to select text when you're using tspan elements.

The tref Element

In XML 1.0, an ENTITY can be used to contain text that is used repeatedly in a document. The ENTITY is declared and can then be referenced multiple times from elsewhere in the document. The tref element works in a similar way to that and to the use element.

The tref element is most useful where a particular piece of text is used multiple times in a long document. For reasons of space, it is more practical to demonstrate the technique using a short document. Listing 8.6 provides an example of using the tref element.

LISTING 8.6   TRef.svg—A tref Element Example

```
<?xml version="1.0" standalone="no"?>
<!DOCTYPE svg PUBLIC "-//W3C//DTD SVG 20010904//EN"
"http://www.w3.org/TR/2001/REC-SVG-20010904/DTD/svg10.dtd">
```

LISTING 8.6 Continued

```
<svg width="" height="">
<defs>
<style type="text/css">
<![CDATA[
text, tspan{
font-family:Arial, sans-serif;
font-size:16;
fill:#000099;
}
]]>
</style>
<text id="Copyright">
Copyright &#0169; Sams Publishing 2002
</text>
</defs>
<text x="25" y="35">
<tspan>
SVG Unleashed <tref xlink:href="#Copyright"/>
</tspan>
<tspan x="25" dy="2em">
<tref xlink:href="#Copyright" fill="red"/>
</tspan>
</text>
</svg>
```

A text element with an id attribute of value Copyright is defined within the defs element early in Listing 8.6. The tref elements reference that text element by using an xlink:href attribute whose value, #Copyright, is a bare names XPointer. The content of the referenced text element, in effect, replaces the tref element.

Figure 8.5 shows the zoomed onscreen appearance when Listing 8.6 is run.

As the second use of the tref element shows in Listing 8.6, you can apply style locally to override any unwanted style properties present in the text definition. In the example, the fill property has been redefined locally.

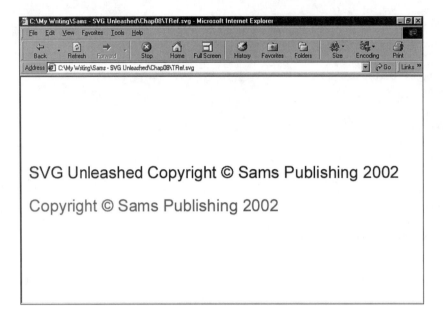

FIGURE 8.5   The defined text is used where the tref element appears.

Text Layout Tasks in SVG

In the various parts of this section, we will look at several text layout issues and how they are solved using an appropriate combination of the text, tspan, and tref elements and their attributes and properties.

Indenting and Outdenting Text

As well as the x attribute, there is also a dx attribute, which allows relative positioning in a horizontal direction. You can use the dx attribute to indent or outdent text. Listing 8.7 shows an example.

LISTING 8.7   dx.svg—Using the dx Attribute to Adjust Horizontal Positioning

```
<?xml version="1.0" standalone="no"?>
<!DOCTYPE svg PUBLIC "-//W3C//DTD SVG 20010904//EN"
"http://www.w3.org/TR/2001/REC-SVG-20010904/DTD/svg10.dtd">
<svg width="" height="">
<defs>
<style type="text/css">
<![CDATA[
text, tspan {
font-family:Arial, sans-serif;
font-size:16;
```

LISTING 8.7   Continued

```
fill:#000099;
}
]]>
</style>
</defs>
<text x="50" dx="1.5em" y="50">
You can use the dx attribute to adjust the precise horizontal positioning of text.
<tspan x="50" dy="1.5em">
For example by using the dx attribute on the first line of a paragraph, it is
</tspan>
<tspan x="50" dy="1.5em">
straightforward to indent the first line, as you can see above.
</tspan>
<tspan x="50" dy="2.5em">
Similarly if you want to outdent text for some reason you can use a negative value
</tspan>
<tspan x="50" dx="-1em" dy="1.5em">
on the dx attribute to achieve the effect, as on this line. Other lines in the text
</tspan>
<tspan x="50" dy="1.5em">
are displayed in the position defined by the x attribute.
</tspan>
</text>
</svg>
```

The text in Listing 8.7 explains how you can use dx. Figure 8.6 shows the onscreen appearance when Listing 8.7 is run. The use of the dy attribute, used in Listing 8.7, will be explained in a following section.

The text-rendering Property

When rendering an SVG graphic, particularly if it includes animated text, you might want to indicate the priorities to be given to the ways text is rendered. For example, priority might be given to legibility, rendering speed, or geometric precision. The text-rendering property allows the developer to specify the priority for rendering of a particular block of text.

Aligning Text Using the text-anchor Property

The ability to align text accurately is an important aspect of the layout of text. In SVG, we can left-align, center, or right-align text by means of the text-anchor property. Listing 8.8 demonstrates the use of the text-anchor property.

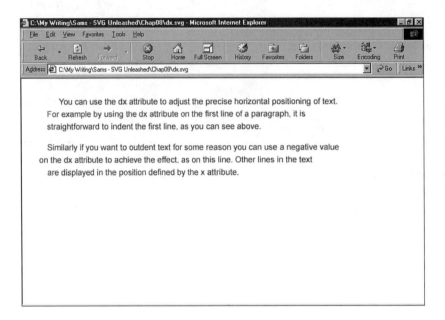

FIGURE 8.6   Using the dx attribute to indent and outdent text.

LISTING 8.8   TextAnchor.svg—Demonstrating the text-anchor Property

```
<?xml version="1.0" standalone="no"?>
<!DOCTYPE svg PUBLIC "-//W3C//DTD SVG 20010904//EN"
"http://www.w3.org/TR/2001/REC-SVG-20010904/DTD/svg10.dtd">
<svg width="1000px" height="750px">
<defs>
<style type="text/css">
<![CDATA[
text {
  fill:red;
  stroke:none;
  font-family:Arial, sans-serif;
  font-size:18;
  }
]]>
</style>
</defs>
<rect x="0" y="0" width="100%" height="100%"
 style="fill:none; stroke:red;"/>
<line x1="300px" y1="0px" x2="300px" y2="750px"
 style="stroke:black; stroke-width:1.5;"/>
<text x="300px" y="50px" text-anchor="start">
```

LISTING 8.8 Continued

```
SVG gets its ducks in a row
</text>
<text x="300px" y="100px" text-anchor="middle">
SVG gets its ducks in a row
</text>
<text x="300px" y="150px" text-anchor="end">
SVG gets its ducks in a row
</text>
</svg>
```

Figure 8.7 shows the zoomed onscreen appearance. The black vertical line corresponds to the x attribute of each `text` element. In examples earlier in this chapter, you saw that text has its left edge at the position indicated by the x attribute, which matches what you see in the first line of text. In other words, the default value of `text-anchor` is `start`. When the value of the `text-anchor` attribute is `middle`, the midpoint of the text string is aligned with the value of the x attribute. When the value of `text-anchor` is end, the right edge of the text aligns with the position indicated by the x attribute.

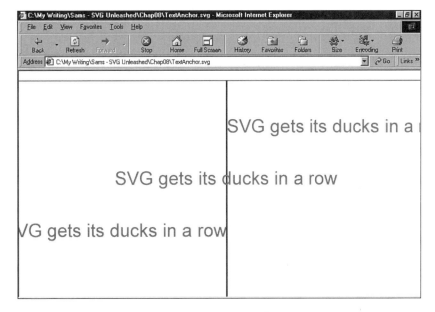

FIGURE 8.7 Text-alignment in SVG using the text-anchor property.

> **CAUTION**
>
> If you are accustomed to aligning text in HTML, it is easy to carry over HTML values and attempt to apply them to the text-anchor attribute in SVG. They won't work. The allowed values are start, middle, and end.

Vertical Text

You may want to use vertical text when working with one of the Asian languages, or you may want to use vertical text in English—for example, when labeling the vertical axis of a graph. SVG provides several techniques for displaying text vertically.

In Chapter 7, "Transformations in SVG" (refer to Figure 7.3), you saw that we could present text vertically by applying a rotate() transformation to text. SVG also provides a writing-mode property. When the value of the writing-mode property is tb, meaning top to bottom, text is presented vertically. When writing-mode is tb, we can adjust whether the text is displayed as if it were horizontal text rotated by 90 degrees (with each character turned on its side) or whether each character is right way up. To achieve the latter, we set glyph-vertical-direction to 0.

Listing 8.9 shows an example using each of the three techniques.

LISTING 8.9   VerticalText.svg—Vertical Text

```
<?xml version="1.0" standalone="no"?>
<!DOCTYPE svg PUBLIC "-//W3C//DTD SVG 20010904//EN"
"http://www.w3.org/TR/2001/REC-SVG-20010904/DTD/svg10.dtd">
<svg width="1000px" height="750px">
<defs>
<style type="text/css">
<![CDATA[
text {
  fill:red;
  stroke:none;
  font-family:Arial, sans-serif;
  font-size:18;
  }
]]>
</style>
</defs>
<rect x="0" y="0" width="100%" height="100%"
 style="fill:none; stroke:red;"/>
<text x="200px" y="50px" transform="rotate(90, 100, 100)">
Rotated horizontal text
</text>
```

LISTING 8.9   Continued

```
<text x="300px" y="100px" writing-mode="tb">
writing-mode is tb
</text>
<text x="400px" y="10px" writing-mode="tb"
 glyph-orientation-vertical="0">
Using glyph-orientation-vertical = 0
</text>
</svg>
```

Figure 8.8 shows the onscreen appearance using each of the three techniques to produce vertical text.

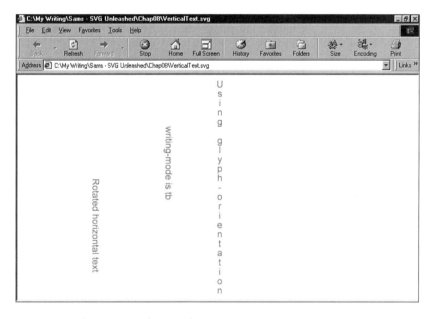

FIGURE 8.8   Vertical text using three techniques in SVG.

Bidirectional Text

SVG supports rendering of text that has a left-to-right inline direction (such as English) or a right-to-left inline direction (such as Arabic). The `direction` attribute on a `text` element can explicitly specify the direction in which text is to be rendered. For example, a `direction` attribute with value `rtl` would define text to be rendered right to left. To achieve a reversal of the natural direction, you may also have to specify a `unicode-bidi` attribute. Listing 8.10 shows a short example of reversing the direction for English text.

LISTING 8.10   Reverse.svg—Reversing the Direction of Text

```
<?xml version="1.0" standalone="no"?>
<!DOCTYPE svg PUBLIC "-//W3C//DTD SVG 20010904//EN"
"http://www.w3.org/TR/2001/REC-SVG-20010904/DTD/svg10.dtd">
<svg width="" height="">
<defs>
<style type="text/css">
<![CDATA[
text, tspan {
font-family:Arial, sans-serif;
font-size:16;
fill:#000099;
}
]]>
</style>
</defs>
<text x="50" y="50">
You can display text left to right.
<tspan x="50" y="70" direction="rtl" unicode-bidi="bidi-override">
Or right to left.
</tspan>
</text>
</svg>
```

Figure 8.9 shows the onscreen appearance after running Listing 8.10. The characters in the second line are written the right way round but from the right of the screen. To reverse the direction of the text, we must set both the `direction` and `unicode-bidi` attributes as shown in the code.

Rotating Text

In labeling diagrams, maps, or other SVG images, you may find it useful to rotate some text to align with axes or components. The `rotate()` transformation introduced in Chapter 7 allows us to rotate text to any desired angle. Rotating text was also shown in Listing 8.10.

Kerning

If you want to produce a visually attractive presentation of glyphs, it is customary to use kerning to adjust the spacing between certain character pairs. The distances between certain glyph pairs are stored in **kerning tables**.

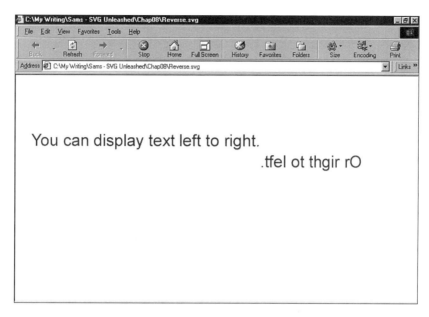

FIGURE 8.9   Altering the direction and unicode-bidi properties to reverse text direction.

If you do not specify any kerning for a piece of text, automatic kerning will be applied. If you want to override that automatic kerning, you specify a `kerning` property and give it a length value.

Listing 8.11 shows a short kerning example.

LISTING 8.11   Kerning.svg—Automatic and Manual Kerning

```
<?xml version="1.0" standalone="no"?>
<!DOCTYPE svg PUBLIC "-//W3C//DTD SVG 20010904//EN"
"http://www.w3.org/TR/2001/REC-SVG-20010904/DTD/svg10.dtd">
<svg width="" height="">
<defs>
<style type="text/css">
<![CDATA[
text, tspan {
font-family:Arial, sans-serif;
font-size:16;
fill:#000099;
}
]]>
</style>
</defs>
<text x="50" y="50">
```

LISTING 8.11 Continued

```
This uses automatic kerning
<tspan x="50" y="70" kerning="0">
This has kerning turned off, kerning="0"
</tspan>
<tspan x="50" y="90" kerning="2">
This has manual kerning, kerning="2"
</tspan>
<tspan x="50" y="110" kerning="4">
This has manual kerning, kerning="4"
</tspan>
</text>
</svg>
```

Figure 8.10 shows the zoomed onscreen appearance after running Listing 8.11. The text message onscreen describes the kerning value that is applied to the tspan element.

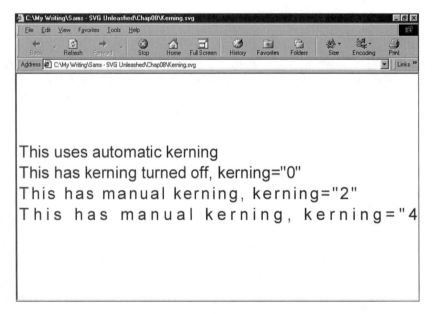

FIGURE 8.10 The effect of automatic kerning and manual kerning.

Letter Spacing

The kerning attribute specifies the spacing between glyphs based on kerning tables. In addition to the spacing between glyphs determined by a kerning attribute, a letter-spacing attribute allows you to specify additional spacing, independent of any values in kerning tables for a particular font.

Whichever setting of kerning is applied to a particular piece of text, SVG allows you to adjust the spacing between letters using the letter-spacing property. Listing 8.12 shows an example.

LISTING 8.12   LetterSpacing.svg—Adjusting the letter-spacing Property

```
<?xml version="1.0" standalone="no"?>
<!DOCTYPE svg PUBLIC "-//W3C//DTD SVG 20010904//EN"
"http://www.w3.org/TR/2001/REC-SVG-20010904/DTD/svg10.dtd">
<svg width="" height="">
<defs>
<style type="text/css">
<![CDATA[
text, tspan {
font-family:Arial, sans-serif;
font-size:16;
fill:#000099;
}
]]>
</style>
</defs>
<text x="50" y="50" kerning="0">
This uses zero kerning and default letter spacing
<tspan x="50" y="70" letter-spacing="0">
Zero kerning, letter-spacing="0"
</tspan>
<tspan x="50" y="90" letter-spacing="0.5">
Zero kerning, letter-spacing="0.5"
</tspan>
<tspan x="50" y="110" letter-spacing="1.0">
Zero kerning, letter-spacing="1.0"
</tspan>
</text>
</svg>
```

Figure 8.11 shows the onscreen appearance after running Listing 8.12. The text message onscreen describes the letter-spacing property value that is applied to the tspan element. The kerning property is 0 for all the text.

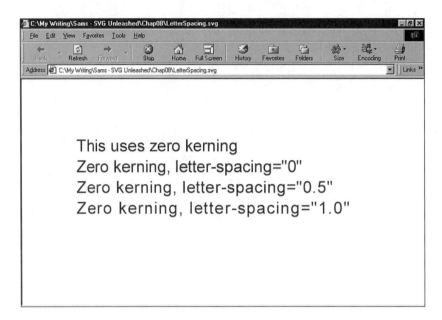

FIGURE 8.11   Adjusting the letter-spacing property.

Word Spacing

SVG also provides a way to adjust spacing between words—the word-spacing property.
Listing 8.13 shows a short example.

LISTING 8.13   WordSpacing.svg—Adjusting the word-spacing Property

```
<?xml version="1.0" standalone="no"?>
<!DOCTYPE svg PUBLIC "-//W3C//DTD SVG 20010904//EN"
"http://www.w3.org/TR/2001/REC-SVG-20010904/DTD/svg10.dtd">
<svg width="" height="">
<defs>
<style type="text/css">
<![CDATA[
text, tspan {
font-family:Arial, sans-serif;
font-size:16;
fill:#000099;
}
]]>
</style>
</defs>
<text x="50" y="50" kerning="0" letter-spacing="0">
This uses zero kerning and zero letter spacing with default word spacing
```

LISTING 8.13   Continued

```
<tspan x="50" y="70" word-spacing="0">
Zero kerning and letter spacing, word-spacing="0"
</tspan>
<tspan x="50" y="90" word-spacing="1.0">
Zero kerning and letter spacing, word-spacing="1.0"
</tspan>
<tspan x="50" y="110" word-spacing="2.0">
Zero kerning and letter spacing, word-spacing="2.0"
</tspan>
<tspan x="50" y="130" word-spacing="4.0">
Zero kerning and letter spacing, word-spacing="4.0"
</tspan>
</text>
</svg>
```

Figure 8.12 shows the onscreen appearance after running Listing 8.13. The text message onscreen describes the word-spacing property value that is applied to the tspan element. The kerning and letter-spacing properties are 0 for all the text.

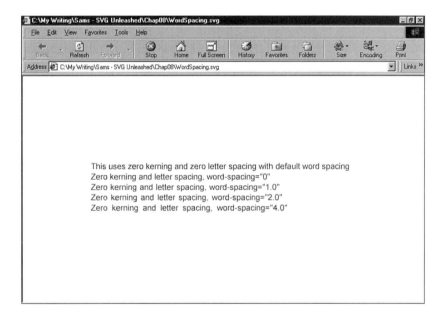

FIGURE 8.12   Adjusting the word-spacing property.

Subscript and Superscript

Many scientific or bibliographic uses of text require the use of subscript and/or superscript text. SVG supports both, using the `baseline-shift` property. Listing 8.14 shows an example of using the `baseline-shift` property to create superscript and subscript text.

LISTING 8.14   SuperSub.svg—Creating Superscript and Subscript Text

```
<?xml version="1.0" standalone="no"?>
<!DOCTYPE svg PUBLIC "-//W3C//DTD SVG 20010904//EN"
"http://www.w3.org/TR/2001/REC-SVG-20010904/DTD/svg10.dtd">
<svg width="1000px" height="750px">
<text x="100" y="100"
 style="fill:red; stroke:none; font-family:Arial, sans-serif; font-size:28">
This is text with a
<tspan baseline-shift="super">superscript</tspan> part and a
<tspan baseline-shift="sub">subscript</tspan> part to follow.
</text>
<text x="100" y="200"
 style="fill:red; stroke:none; font-family:Arial, sans-serif; font-size:28">
X times X = X
<tspan baseline-shift="super">2</tspan>
</text>
<text x="100" y="300"
 style="fill:red; stroke:none; font-family:Arial, sans-serif; font-size:28">
Water is made of H
<tspan baseline-shift="sub">2</tspan>O.
</text>
</svg>
```

Figure 8.13 shows the onscreen appearance when Listing 8.14 is run.

If you want to adjust the superscript or subscript text to a smaller size, you can do so by modifying the `font-size` on the `tspan` element that has the `baseline-shift` attribute.

An alternative way to create superscript and subscript is to use the dy attribute. Using the `baseline-shift` property, however, is more convenient than adjusting dy for multiple font sizes.

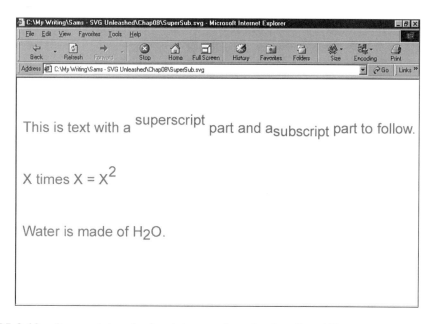

FIGURE 8.13 Superscript and subscript examples using baseline-shift.

The textPath Element

As well as laying out text on a straight line, SVG allows us to apply text to any arbitrary path. The creation of paths in SVG, using the `path` element, was described in Chapter 6, "Paths in SVG." The `SVGTextPathElement` object was described in "The SVG DOM Interfaces" section of Chapter 6.

The `textPath` element is nested within a `text` element and has an `xlink:href` attribute that references a `path` element, elsewhere in the document, which possesses an `id` attribute. Listing 8.15 shows a basic example using the `textPath` element. The text is displayed twice—first without showing the underlying path, and second with the underlying path displayed beneath the text.

LISTING 8.15 TextPath01.svg—A textPath Element Example

```
<?xml version="1.0"?>
<!DOCTYPE svg PUBLIC "-//W3C//DTD SVG 1.0//EN"
    "http://www.w3.org/TR/2001/REC-SVG-20010904/DTD/svg10.dtd">
<svg width="500px" height="500px">
<defs>
<path id="myCurve"
style="stroke-dasharray:4,4; stroke-width:2; stroke:red; fill:none;"
d="M57.8947 178.947
C74.7025 160.272 85.0084 151.316 110.526 151.316
```

LISTING 8.15   Continued

```
C178.042 151.316 154.753 213.768 201.316 238.158
C270.765 274.536 311.267 143.3 359.211 263.158"
/>
</defs>
<text style="font-family:Arial, sans serif">
<textPath xlink:href="#myCurve">
This is my very own curve and hopefully you can see it all
</textPath>
</text>
<g transform="translate(0,200)">
<use xlink:href="#myCurve" />
<text>
<textPath xlink:href="#myCurve">
This is my very own curve and hopefully you can see it all
</textPath>
</text>
</g>
</svg>
```

The path to which the text is to be applied is defined within a path element nested within the defs element. The path element has an id attribute with a value of myCurve.

The first textPath element references the path element by means of the xlink:href attribute. The text is then laid out along the curve defined by the referenced path element.

The second textPath element also references the path element. The use element which precedes it causes the outline of the path to be displayed onscreen so that you can see that the text follows the outline of the path.

Notice too that the alignment of each character is adjusted automatically to allow for alteration in the direction of a segment of the path.

Figure 8.14 shows the onscreen appearance after running Listing 8.15.

The startOffset Attribute

The startOffset attribute allows you to specify how far from the start of a path the text is to be displayed. The value of the startOffset attribute may be either a percentage value or a length that is interpreted as being in the current user coordinate system. Listing 8.16 gives an example of how you can use the startOffset attribute.

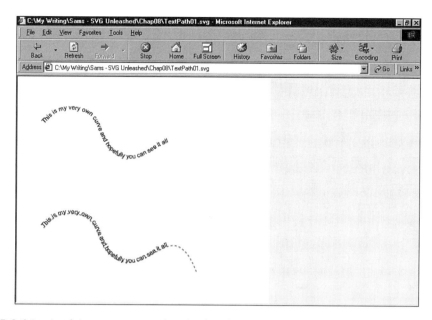

FIGURE 8.14   Applying text to a path, whether the path is visible or not.

LISTING 8.16   StartOffset.svg—Using the startOffset Attribute

```
<?xml version="1.0"?>
<!DOCTYPE svg PUBLIC "-//W3C//DTD SVG 1.0//EN"
    "http://www.w3.org/TR/2001/REC-SVG-20010904/DTD/svg10.dtd">
<svg width="1000px" height="600px">
<defs>
<path id="myCurve" style="stroke-dasharray:4,4; stroke-width:2;
 stroke:red; fill:none;"
d="M57.8947 178.947
C74.7025 160.272 85.0084 151.316 110.526 151.316
C178.042 151.316 154.753 213.768 201.316 238.158
C270.765 274.536 311.267 143.3 359.211 263.158"
/>
</defs>
<g transform="translate(0,0)">
<use xlink:href="#myCurve" />
<text>
<textPath xlink:href="#myCurve" startOffset="0%">
This is my very own curve and hopefully you can see it all
```

LISTING 8.16   Continued

```
</textPath>
</text>
</g>
<g transform="translate(0,100)">
<use xlink:href="#myCurve" />
<text>
<textPath xlink:href="#myCurve" startOffset="15%">
This is my very own curve and hopefully you can see it all
</textPath>
</text>
</g>
<g transform="translate(0,200)">
<use xlink:href="#myCurve" />
<text>
<textPath xlink:href="#myCurve" startOffset="25%">
This is my very own curve and hopefully you can see it all
</textPath>
</text>
</g>
<g transform="translate(0,300)">
<use xlink:href="#myCurve" />
<text>
<textPath xlink:href="#myCurve" startOffset="15">
This is my very own curve and hopefully you can see it all
</textPath>
</text>
</g>
</svg>
```

Figure 8.15 shows the panned appearance onscreen after running Listing 8.16.

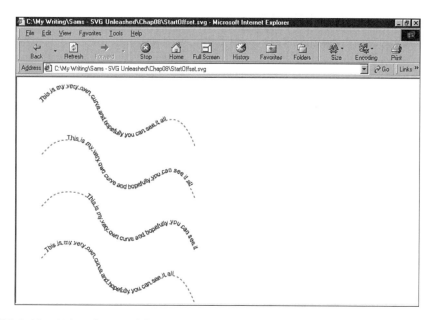

FIGURE 8.15   Using the startOffset attribute expressed as a percentage or length.

The switch Element

In a document, you may want to render content depending on particular conditions that apply. For example, if the user's language settings were for German content, you might want to render a greeting or description in German rather than English. Adjusting what is rendered according to the conditions that apply is termed **conditional processing**.

SVG allows conditional processing of content by means of a switch element. One use of the switch element is to allow localization of SVG content. Typically, such conditional processing controls which of several optional pieces of text are rendered onscreen.

The Test Attributes

Three attributes that are allowed on SVG elements, which may be child elements of a switch element, are sometimes termed **test attributes**. The test attributes are requiredFeatures, requiredExtensions, and systemLanguage. The value of a systemLanguage attribute is particularly relevant to conditional rendering of text.

When an SVG rendering engine meets a child element of a switch element for which the value of a test attribute evaluates to true, that element is rendered and all other child elements of the switch element are bypassed.

For example, suppose we had a background and text, each of which we wanted to depend on the system language settings of the user. In this case, we could use code like that shown in Listing 8.17 to control which background (in this example, a `rect` element) and which text would display.

LISTING 8.17 International02.svg—Controlling Display of a Graphics Background and of Text Depending on System Language Settings

```
<?xml version="1.0" standalone="no"?>
<!DOCTYPE svg PUBLIC "-//W3C//DTD SVG 20010904//EN"
"http://www.w3.org/TR/2001/REC-SVG-20010904/DTD/svg10.dtd">
<svg width="400" height="150">
<switch>
<rect x="40" y="40" rx="8" ry="8" width="200" height="40"
 style="fill:#FF0000;stroke:none" systemLanguage="en"/>
<rect x="40" y="40" rx="8" ry="8" width="200" height="40"
 style="fill:#00FF00;stroke:none" systemLanguage="fr"/>
<rect x="40" y="40" rx="8" ry="8" width="200" height="40"
 style="fill:#0000FF;stroke:none" systemLanguage="de"/>
<rect x="40" y="40" rx="8" ry="8" width="200" height="40"
 style="fill:#000000;stroke:none" />
</switch>
<switch>
<text x="65" y="65" style="stroke:none; fill:#FFFFFF; font-family:Arial,
sans-serif; font-size:18" systemLanguage="en"
>
Good Evening!
</text>
<text x="65" y="65" style="stroke:none; fill:#FFFFFF; font-family:Arial,
sans-serif; font-size:18"
 systemLanguage="fr">
Bonsoir!
</text>
<text x="65" y="65" style="stroke:none; fill:#FFFFFF; font-family:Arial,
sans-serif; font-size:18"
 systemLanguage="de">
Guten Abend!
</text>
<text x="65" y="65" style="stroke:none; fill:#FFFFFF; font-family:Arial,
sans-serif; font-size:18">
Good Evening!
</text>
</switch>
</svg>
```

Listing 8.17, when the system language is set to English, causes the greeting "Good Evening!" to be displayed against a red rectangle. When the system language is French, the greeting "Bonsoir!" is displayed on a green rectangle. When it is German, "Guten Abend!" is displayed on a blue background. When the system language is none of the three specified languages, the greeting is in English but the background rectangle is black.

The Batik SVG Viewer makes testing language settings easy using the Edit, Preferences menu choice. Figure 8.16 shows the appearance produced in Batik 1.1, after zooming, by Listing 8.17 when the system language is set to German.

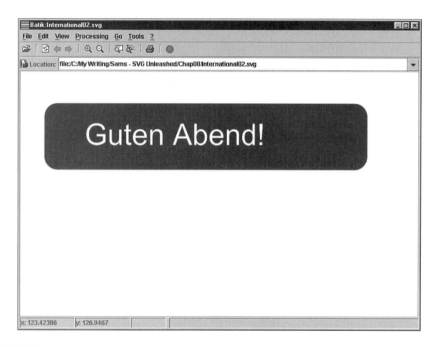

FIGURE 8.16
The greeting displayed when the system language is German.

You don't need to use multiple switch elements as was done in Listing 8.17. The switch element also allows you to group SVG elements that are to be displayed under certain circumstances. Listing 8.18 uses the g element with appropriate systemLanguage attribute settings to group elements to be displayed.

LISTING 8.18   International03.svg—Using a g Element to Group Elements to Be Displayed Within a switch Element

```
<?xml version="1.0" standalone="no"?>
<!DOCTYPE svg PUBLIC "-//W3C//DTD SVG 20010904//EN"
"http://www.w3.org/TR/2001/REC-SVG-20010904/DTD/svg10.dtd">
```

LISTING 8.18   Continued

```
<svg width="400" height="150">

<switch>
<g systemLanguage="en">
<rect x="40" y="40" rx="8" ry="8" width="200" height="40"
 style="fill:#FF0000;stroke:none" />
<text x="65" y="65" style="stroke:none; fill:#FFFFFF; font-family:Arial,
sans-serif; font-size:18" >
Good Evening!
</text>
</g>
<g systemLanguage="fr">
<rect x="40" y="40" rx="8" ry="8" width="200" height="40"
 style="fill:#00FF00;stroke:none" />
<text x="65" y="65" style="stroke:none; fill:#FFFFFF; font-family:Arial,
sans-serif; font-size:18">
Bonsoir!
</text>
</g>
<g systemLanguage="de">
<rect x="40" y="40" rx="8" ry="8" width="200" height="40"
 style="fill:#0000FF;stroke:none" />
<text x="65" y="65" style="stroke:none; fill:#FFFFFF; font-family:Arial,
sans-serif; font-size:18">
Guten Abend!
</text>
</g>
<g>
<rect x="40" y="40" rx="8" ry="8" width="200" height="40"
 style="fill:#000000;stroke:none" />
<text x="65" y="65" style="stroke:none; fill:#FFFFFF; font-family:Arial,
sans-serif; font-size:18">
Good Evening!
</text>
</g>
</switch>
</svg>
```

The ability to group allows a single `switch` element to control major changes to the rendered appearance of an SVG document.

The requiredFeatures Attribute

The SVG Recommendation allows an SVG rendering engine to optionally implement some features. Thus, for example, an SVG rendering engine on a mobile browser might choose optionally not to implement some computationally intensive filter primitives. To allow for such situations, you might want to use a `switch` element with its `requiredFeatures` attribute listing some necessary functionality. In the absence of the required functionality, you might have a default option that is visually simpler (but still coherent) and that does not rely on the functionality not implemented in the mobile browser.

The requiredExtensions Attribute

The `requiredExtensions` attribute defines a list of language extensions that go beyond the functionality described in the SVG 1.0 Recommendation.

Comparison of Text Layout in SVG and HTML

To developers who have used HTML, the absence of automatic text flow among the techniques of text layout available in SVG 1.0 may come as something of a shock. This does mean that laying out significant amounts of text requires much more thought and effort than simply using an XHTML p element.

> **NOTE**
>
> Word wrapping has been named in the Requirements for SVG 1.2. See http://www.w3.org/TR/SVG2Reqs/. Working drafts for SVG 1.2 are likely to be located at http://www.w3.org/tr/svg12.

Layout Options in SVG

The lack of automatic text flowing in SVG 1.0 means that we must use other options. The options available in SVG 1.0 are as follows:

- Create multiple `text` elements, one for each line of text. This process involves calculating appropriate lengths of text to be placed in each `text` element.

- Nest an appropriate number of `tspan` elements within a `text` element, one `tspan` element for each line of text.

- Use the SVG 1.0 `foreignObject` element (discussed in Chapter 5, "Coordinate Systems in SVG") to allow XHTML to be used for automatically wrapping text layout.

The use of multiple `tspan` elements for text layout in SVG Web pages will be discussed in Chapter 12, "SVG for Web Authoring."

Text-Related SVG DOM Interfaces

In this section, the SVG DOM objects that correspond to the SVG text-control elements are defined, together with definitions for other SVG DOM objects from which those objects inherit properties and methods.

The SVGTextElement, SVGTSpanElement, and SVGTRefElement objects will be described in this section. Other SVG DOM objects will be listed in alphabetical order. The SVGTextPathElement object was described in Chapter 6.

The SVGTextElement Object

The SVGTextElement object corresponds to the text element and has the properties and methods of the SVGTextPositioningElement object (described later in this section) and the SVGTransformable object.

The SVGTSpanElement Object

The SVGTSpanElement object corresponds to the tspan element and has the properties and methods of the SVGTextPositioningElement object.

The SVGTRefElement Object

The SVGTRefElement object corresponds to the tref element and has the properties and methods of the SVGTextPositioningElement object and the SVGURIReference object.

Other SVG DOM Text and Font Objects

In addition to the SVG DOM objects that correspond to the text, tspan, and tref elements, several additional DOM objects are relevant to text.

The SVGAltGlyphDefElement Object

The SVGAltGlyphDefElement object has the properties and methods of the SVGElement object.

The SVGAltGlyphDefElement object has no properties or methods specific to it.

The SVGAltGlyphElement Object

The SVGAltGlyphElement object has the properties and methods of the SVGTextPositioningElement object and the SVGURIReference object.

In addition, the SVGAltGlyphElement object has the following properties:

- glyphRef—of type DOMString
- format—of type DOMString

The SVGAltGlyphElement object has no methods specific to it.

The SVGAltGlyphItemElement Object

The `SVGAltGlyphItemElement` object has the properties and methods of the `SVGElement` object.

The `SVGAltGlyphItemElement` object has no properties or methods specific to it.

The SVGAltGlyphRefElement Object

The `SVGAltGlyphRefElement` object has the properties and methods of the `SVGElement` object, the `SVGURIReference` object, and the `SVGStylable` object.

The `SVGAltGlyphRefElement` object has the following properties specific to it:

- `glyphRef`—of type `DOMString`
- `format`—of type `DOMString`
- `x`—of type `float`
- `y`—of type `float`
- `dx`—of type `float`
- `dy`—of type `float`

The `SVGAltGlyphRefElement` object has no methods specific to it.

The SVGDefinitionsSrcElement Object

The `SVGDefinitionsSrcElement` object has the properties and methods of the `SVGElement` object.

The SVGFontElement Object

The `SVGFontElement` object has the properties and methods of the `SVGElement` object, the `SVGStylable` object, and the `SVGExternalResourcesRequired` object.

The SVGFontFaceElement Object

The `SVGFontFaceElement` object has the properties and methods of the `SVGElement` object.

The SVGFontFaceFormatElement Object

The `SVGFontFaceFormatElement` object has the properties and methods of the `SVGElement` object.

The SVGFontFaceNameElement Object

The `SVGFontFaceNameElement` object has the properties and methods of the `SVGElement` object.

The SVGFontFaceSrcElement Object

The SVGFontFaceSrcElement object has the properties and methods of the SVGElement object.

The SVGFontFaceUriElement Object

The SVGFontFaceUriElement object has the properties and methods of the SVGElement object.

The SVGGlyphElement Object

The SVGGlyphElement object has the properties and methods of the SVGElement object and the SVGStylable object.

The SVGHKernElement Object

The SVGHKernElement object has the properties and methods of the SVGElement object.

The SVGMissingGlyphElement Object

The SVGMissingGlyphElement object has the properties and methods of the SVGElement object and the SVGStylable object.

The SVGTextContentElement Object

The SVGTextContentElement object has the properties and methods of the SVGElement, SVGTests, SVGLangSpace, SVGExternalResourcesRequired, SVGStylable, and events::EventTarget objects.

The SVGTextContentElement object has the following constants associated with it:

- SVGTextContentElement.LENGTHADJUST_UNKNOWN—The constant is of type short and has a value of 0.

- SVGTextContentElement.LENGTHADJUST_SPACING—The constant is of type short and has a value of 1.

- SVGTextContentElement.LENGTHADJUST_SPACINGANDGLYPHS—The constant is of type short and has a value of 2.

The SVGTextContentElement object has the following properties:

- textLength—of type SVGAnimatedLength

- lengthAdjust—of type SVGAnimatedEnumeration

The `SVGTextContentElement` object has the following methods specific to it:

- `getNumberOfChars()`—The method returns a value of type `long`. The method takes no arguments.

- `getComputedTextLength()`—The method returns a value of type `float`. The method takes no arguments.

- `getSubstringLength(`*charnum, nchars*`)`—The method returns a value of type `float`. The *charnum* and *nchars* arguments are of type unsigned `long`.

- `getStartPositionOfChar(`*charnum*`)`—The method returns a value of type `SVGPoint`. The *charnum* argument is of type unsigned `long`.

- `getEndPositionOfChar(`*charnum*`)`—The method returns a value of type `SVGPoint`. The *charnum* argument is of type unsigned `long`.

- `getExtentOfChar(`*charnum*`)`—The method returns a value of type `SVGRect`. The *charnum* argument is of type unsigned `long`.

- `getRotationOfChar(`*charnum*`)`—The method returns a value of type `float`. The *charnum* argument is of type unsigned `long`.

- `getCharNumAtPosition(`*point*`)`—The method returns a value of type `long`. The *charnum* argument is of type `SVGPoint`.

- `selectSubString(`*charnum, nchars*`)`—The method returns a value of type `void`. The *charnum* and *nchars* arguments are of type unsigned `long`.

The SVGTextPositioningElement Object

The `SVGTextPositioningElement` object has the properties and methods of the `SVGTextContentElement` object.

The `SVGTextPositioningElement` object has the following properties:

- x—of type `SVGAnimatedLengthList`
- y—of type `SVGAnimatedLengthList`
- dx—of type `SVGAnimatedLengthList`
- dy—of type `SVGAnimatedLengthList`
- rotate—of type `SVGAnimatedNumberList`

The `SVGTextPositioningElement` object has no methods specific to it.

The SVGVKernElement Object

The SVGVKernElement object has the properties and methods of the SVGElement object.

Examples of Accessing and Manipulating the DOM

In this section, we will create examples that show how to access and manipulate the DOM.

Accessing Text Content

Listing 8.19 shows how to access the length of the content of a text element by using the getNumberofChars() method.

LISTING 8.19   AccessingText.svg—Using the getNumberofChars() Method

```
<?xml version="1.0" standalone="no"?>
<!DOCTYPE svg PUBLIC "-//W3C//DTD SVG 20010904//EN"
"http://www.w3.org/TR/2001/REC-SVG-20010904/DTD/svg10.dtd">
<svg width="" height="">
<script type="text/javascript">
<![CDATA[
var SVGDoc = document;
var SVGRoot = document.documentElement;
var MyContent;

function displayContent() {
var MyText = SVGRoot.getElementById("myText");
MyContent = MyText.getNumberOfChars();
alert (MyContent);
}
]]>
</script>
<text id="myText" x="75" y="75" onclick="displayContent(evt)">
This is some sample text. Click it to be told the length of the content of
➥ the &lt;text&gt; element.</text>
</svg>
```

Listing 8.19 accesses the number of characters contained within the text element and displays the result in an alert box. Figure 8.17 shows the result of running Listing 8.19.

If you take a moment to count the number of characters contained in the text element in Listing 8.19, you may think that the number is too low. However, the entities < and > are converted to the literal characters they stand for before the number of characters is counted.

FIGURE 8.17   An alert box displays the number of characters in the text content.

Leaning Text

The following example allows individual letters of the content of a text element to be manipulated—in this case, rotated—thus creating interesting animations not possible with declarative SVG animation.

It is significantly more complicated than the preceding example but is visually much more interesting too. Listing 8.20 shows the code.

LISTING 8.20   Pisa.svg—Manipulating Individual Characters Within a Piece of Text

```
<?xml version="1.0" standalone="no"?>
<!DOCTYPE svg PUBLIC "-//W3C//DTD SVG 20010904//EN"
"http://www.w3.org/TR/2001/REC-SVG-20010904/DTD/svg10.dtd">
<svg width="600px" height="400px" viewBox="0 0 300 200"
xmlns="http://www.w3.org/2000/svg" onload="Initialize(evt)">
  <script type="text/javascript">
  <![CDATA[

var txt1, numChars, txtInterval;
var moveRotateRight = false;

function Initialize() {
    txt1 = document.getElementById('txt1');
```

LISTING 8.20   Continued

```
    numChars = txt1.getNumberOfChars();
    var rotate = '-10 ';
    for (var i=1; i<numChars; i++) {
        rotate += ' 0';
    }
    txt1.setAttribute('rotate', rotate);
    txtInterval = setInterval('knockText()', 100);
}

function knockText() {
    var rotate = txt1.getAttribute('rotate');
    var rParts = /^([-\d]+) (.*) ([-\d]+)/.exec(rotate);
    if (rParts[1] != 0 || rParts[3] != 0) {
        moveRotateRight = !moveRotateRight;
        rParts[1] *= -1;
        rParts[3] *= -1;
    }
    if (moveRotateRight) {
        rotate = rParts[3] + ' ' + rParts[1] + ' ' + rParts[2];
    }
    else {
        rotate = rParts[2] + ' ' + rParts[3] + ' ' + rParts[1];
    }
    txt1.setAttribute('rotate', rotate);
}

    ]]>
    </script>
    <rect x="0" y="0" width="100%" height="100%" fill="white" />
    <text id="txt1" x="20" y="100"
    style="font-size:28">Leaning text of Pisa</text>
</svg>
```

It isn't very important that you understand the details of the scripting (see Part II for more information on scripting), but the example in Listing 8.20 is intended to give you a flavor of what can be done in manipulating text.

When the document loads, the `Initialize()` function is called. `Initialize()` starts the process by creating a string with each character in the text content separated by a space character from its neighbor. It sets up the characters as if the rotate had just reached the left coming in from the right. The rotate is `-10` on the first character, and the variable `moveRotateRight` had already been set to `false` at the top of the page, indicating that the rotate was moving left.

The `knockText()` function is called every tenth of a second by an interval assigned to `txtInterval`. Each time `knockText()` is called, it checks the value of `txt1`'s `rotate` attribute with a regular expression. The regular expression is set to match a group of digits (and a minus sign), followed by a space, a group of characters, another space, and finally another group of digits (and a minus sign). In this way, it separates the first and last digits in the `rotate` attribute from those between.

Next, the values of the first and last digits are checked in the `if` statement to determine whether they are nonzero. The first time that `knockText()` is called, the first digit is not. It is `-10`, so the statements inside the `if` statement are evaluated. They change the direction of travel of `rotate` by reversing the Boolean value stored in `moveRotateRight` so that its value is now `true`. They also reverse the sign of the first digits (to `+10`) by multiplying `rParts[1]` by `-1` so that the rotate will now be clockwise. The multiplication of `rParts[3]` has no effect, as its value is `0`. It is simply there for when the `+10` reaches the far right.

In the next `if else` statement, the last digits are moved to the start of the rotate string—the first time `knockText()` is called, this is the `0` at the end. This effectively moves the `+10` to the right so that when the rotate string is reassigned to the `rotate` attribute on `txt1`, it will move the rotate to the next character.

Figure 8.18 shows the uppercase *P* of Pisa, leaning forward. You need to run the code and view it onscreen to get a realistic impression of the scripted animation.

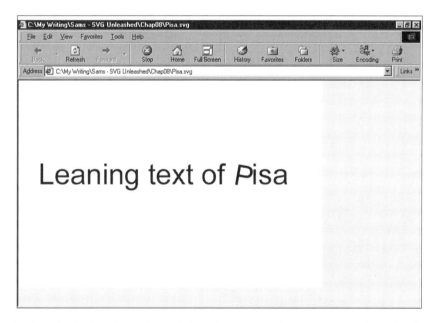

FIGURE 8.18   The text partway through its animation, with the uppercase *P* leaning forward.

Summary

This chapter introduced many general issues that apply to the layout of character data in SVG document. You were introduced to the text, tspan, and tref elements and shown how to use them to lay out text in straight lines. You were also shown the textPath element and how to use it. The switch element was described, and you were shown how to use it to achieve conditional rendering based on the user's language settings.

The SVG DOM interfaces for manipulation of text were described and examples of how to manipulate text were demonstrated.

CHAPTER 9

Clipping, Masking, Compositing

In earlier chapters, we looked at the use of various types of SVG "paint"—solid colors, gradients, patterns, and so on. In this chapter, we will look at the use of clipping and masking in SVG. If you don't have a background in graphics, you may not be familiar with exactly what clipping and masking are.

Clipping and masking can be viewed as techniques to modify where SVG paint is to be applied and some of the characteristics of SVG paint. An alternative, and less formal, way to view clipping and masking is to view clipping as cutting (clipping) out an arbitrary shape from an image and masking as applying potentially semi-transparent clipping paths to an image to modify its appearance.

First, we will review terminology that is relevant to clipping, masking, and compositing. We will also look at the SVG elements and properties that are necessary to achieve the desired clipping and masking effects and apply those elements and properties in several clipping and masking examples.

In the final section of the chapter, we will describe the SVG DOM interfaces that are relevant to clipping and masking.

A Terminology Review

SVG Unleashed is intended primarily for those readers who want to program SVG. Quite possibly, many readers won't be familiar with the jargon of clipping, masking, and compositing. For such readers, this section provides a review of terminology with which you may be unfamiliar. If you use the same or similar terms in other graphics contexts, you may find that the usage of terms in SVG differs from the usage with which you are familiar and that it is helpful to study what the terms mean in SVG.

> **NOTE**
>
> The use of terminology in various graphics disciplines can vary substantially. The descriptions given here are of the terms as they are used in SVG. The use of the same or similar terms in other disciplines may differ.

What Is Clipping?

Imagine you see something in a newspaper that is of sufficient interest that you want to cut it out and keep it. What do you likely do? You cut around the outline of the material that interests you and discard the material that isn't of ongoing interest. You have just **clipped** a newspaper article or photograph. That newspaper clipping has a shape and content.

Depending on how the newspaper article was laid out on the page, you may have a rectangle, an L-shaped piece of paper, or even several distinct pieces of paper that contain the item or items you clipped.

It's just the same with clipping in SVG. What you clip can be any arbitrary shape or combination of shapes, because clipping paths can use the path and text elements and any of the basic graphic shapes that were described in Chapter 3, "Basic SVG Elements and Shapes." Several graphics objects together can be used to create a complex clipping path.

Similarly, the content of the chosen shape you cut from the newspaper has, perhaps, only text or may have text plus one or more images. An SVG clipping path may also consist of or incorporate text and/or images within the clipping path.

> **NOTE**
>
> What is termed a **clipping path** in SVG might well come under the term **mask** in other contexts.

When you cut out a shape with scissors, a point is either within the shape you want, or it is outside that shape. An SVG clipping path is similar. When there is no antialiasing on a clipping path, a pixel is either within the clipping path and is displayed normally, or it is outside the clipping path and is not displayed at all.

> **NOTE**
>
> Antialiasing is a technique that is used to smooth the edges of objects such as individual glyphs in a piece of text. It works by creating intermediate color values in pixels close to the edge between the object and its surroundings.

What Is a Mask?

In SVG terminology, applying a **mask** is a little like overlaying a shape you cut out of an existing picture with a semi-transparent acetate sheet. The more opaque the acetate sheet is, the less definition of the underlying image you see. The more transparent the acetate sheet is, the more fully you see the underlying picture.

What Is Compositing?

Compositing is the process of combining colors in the generation of a final onscreen color.

Clipping in SVG

Clipping in SVG is done using a **clipping path**. A clipping path is the shape or shapes that you, effectively, cut out. A clipping path is created using a `clipPath` element. A `clipPath` element has an `id` attribute that allows it to be referenced and used.

The shape of clipping paths in SVG may be defined using any of the following SVG elements nested within a `clipPath` element: `path`, `text`, `line`, `rect`, `circle`, `ellipse`, `polyline`, `polygon`, and `use`. Given the enormous range of shapes available onscreen using an element from the available choices, it should be clear that the available shapes of a clipping path in SVG are enormously flexible.

> **NOTE**
>
> An SVG clipping path can, if antialiasing is turned off, be viewed as being a 1-bit mask. In other words, parts of the underlying image within the clipping path are seen normally, and parts of the underlying image outside the clipping path are totally concealed.

The clipPath Element

The `clipPath` element has similarities to the `symbol` element in how it is used. The `clipPath` element is never rendered onscreen directly and is typically defined in a `defs` element. It is defined within a `defs` element and then referenced using the `clip-path` property of another element.

The shapes defined by the SVG elements nested within the `clipPath` element define the shape of the clipping path. All of the image or other object to which the clipping path is applied and which is within the shape defined by the nested elements is shown. Everything outside that shape is not rendered. In other words, a point is within the clipping path if it is within any of the elements nested within the `clipPath` element.

The `clipPathUnits` property determines which coordinate system is to be applied to a clipping path. The permitted values are `userSpaceOnUse` and `objectBoundingBox`. The default is `userSpaceOnUse`. When the value is `userSpaceOnUse`, the clipping is relative to the initial SVG viewport. When the value is `objectBoundingBox`, the clipping is relative to the object that is being clipped.

> **CAUTION**
>
> Don't attempt to display a clipping path directly by setting a display property on a clipPath element. It won't work.

The `clip-rule` property defines the way in which a point is determined to be inside or outside the clipping path. The `clip-rule` property may take the values `nonzero`, `evenodd`, or `inherit`. The default value is `nonzero`.

The way this works is that you count the edges you cross in a shape. First, take the example of a simple rectangle. If we enter the rectangle, coming from the edge of the viewport, we cross an edge; so the number of edges crossed is one. That value is both nonzero and odd. When the value of the `clip-rule` property is nonzero, the interior of the rectangle is within the clip because the number of edges crossed is nonzero. Similarly, the value of one is odd, so the interior of the rectangle is within the clip.

When a shape is very irregular or has several edges—clipping to a piece of text, for example—whether a particular point is inside or outside the clipping path is more complex.

The clip-path Property

The `clip-path` property is used on an SVG element or group of elements within the main part of an SVG document fragment to reference a clipping path defined within a `clipPath` element. If the value of the `clip-path` property matches the value of the id attribute of a `clipPath` element in the same document, that clipping path is applied to the referencing element.

> **NOTE**
>
> A clipPath element may itself possess a clip-path property. In that case, the final clipping path is the intersection of the referenced clipping path and the clipping path defined within the clipPath element.

The clip and overflow Properties

When an `svg` element is used, the `overflow` and `clip` properties can be used to define an **initial clipping path**.

The `overflow` property applies to elements that establish new viewports—svg, image, symbol, foreignObject, pattern, and marker elements.

The `overflow` property may take the following values: `visible`, `hidden`, `auto`, `scroll`, and `inherit`. The default value in SVG is `hidden`. In other words, content that lies outside the current viewport is not displayed.

CAUTION

In CSS2, the default value of the overflow property is visible. SVG's overflow property behaves similarly to CSS2's overflow; however, the default value of overflow in SVG is hidden.

The clip property may take the following values: shape, auto, or inherit. In SVG, the default value is auto, which means that the object is clipped along the edges of the current viewport.

The following sections demonstrate some examples of the ways in which you can use a clipping path.

NOTE

Several of the following examples use SVG animation elements. Those elements are described more fully in Chapter 11, "SVG Animation Elements."

Using Text in Clipping

SVG text can be used as the shape into which clipping takes place. Listing 9.1 uses a text element to define a clipping path on an external SVG image.

LISTING 9.1   TextClip.svg—A Text Element–Based Clipping Path

```
<?xml version='1.0'?>
<!DOCTYPE svg PUBLIC "-//W3C//DTD SVG 20010904//EN"
"http://www.w3.org/TR/2001/REC-SVG-20010904/DTD/svg10.dtd">

<svg width="800" height="600">
<defs>
 <clipPath id="Clip1">
  <text x="60" y="80" class="Clipstyle">
   SVG Unleashed
  </text>
 </clipPath>
<style type="text/css">
<![CDATA[
  .Clipstyle
  {stroke:#FF0000;
   stroke-width:1;
   font-family: Arial, sans-serif;
   font-size:32;
   font-weight:bold;}
     ]]>
```

LISTING 9.1   Continued

```
</style>
</defs>
<image x="0" y="20" width="600" height="500"
 xlink:href="FillGradients.svg"
 style="clip-path:url(#Clip1)" />
</svg>
```

Figure 9.1 shows the onscreen appearance when Listing 9.1 is run. The shape of the clipping path is defined by the `text` element that is nested within the `clipPath` element. It is as if we cut the text "SVG Unleashed" out of an image created by the SVG file FillGradients.svg. If you run FillGradients.svg (refer to Listing 3.18) onscreen and then run Listing 9.1 in another browser window, you will be able to see that the fill of the text contains a green-to-red gradient, which comes from the top rectangle of FillGradients.svg.

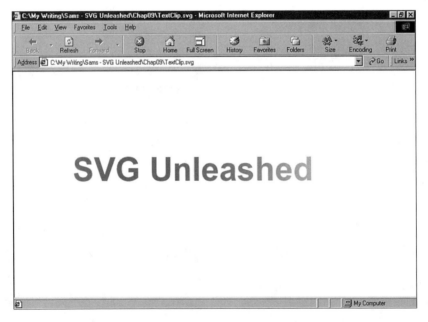

FIGURE 9.1   A text-shaped clipping path.

If you want to adjust the clipped part of the image, you can adjust the x or y attribute values of the `image` element. Listing 9.2 clips 300 pixels further down in FillGradients.svg, producing text that is filled with yellow on the left with a gradient toward blue on the right.

LISTING 9.2   TextClip02.svg—Clipping Lower Down the Referenced Image

```
<?xml version='1.0'?>
<!DOCTYPE svg PUBLIC "-//W3C//DTD SVG 20010904//EN"
"http://www.w3.org/TR/2001/REC-SVG-20010904/DTD/svg10.dtd">

<svg width="800" height="600">
<defs>
 <clipPath id="Clip1">
  <text x="60" y="80" class="Clipstyle">SVG Unleashed

  </text>
 </clipPath>
<style type="text/css">
 <![CDATA[
  .Clipstyle
   {stroke:#FF0000;
    stroke-width:1;
    font-family: Arial, sans-serif;
    font-size:32;
    font-weight:bold;}
      ]]>
</style>
</defs>
<image x="0" y="-320" width="600" height="500" xlink:href="FillGradients.svg"
 style="clip-path:url(#Clip1)" />
</svg>
```

To clip further down the image, make the value of the y attribute of the image element
(introduced in Chapter 5, "Coordinate Systems in SVG") less positive or more negative. To
clip further to the right, make the value of the x attribute less positive or more negative.

Creating a Binocular-Shaped Clip Path

One of the advantages of SVG clipping paths is that they allow us to use any arbitrary
shape as our clipping path. The example shown in Listing 9.3 creates a shape like a pair of
binoculars viewed end-on to give us a fixed viewpoint onto an underlying image, which
in this example happens to be an SVG image. You can apply a similar technique to select
part of a static bitmap image for display.

LISTING 9.3   MyBinocs.svg—Creating a Binocular-Shaped Clipping Path

```
<?xml version="1.0" standalone="no"?>
<!DOCTYPE svg PUBLIC "-//W3C//DTD SVG 20010904//EN"
"http://www.w3.org/TR/2001/REC-SVG-20010904/DTD/svg10.dtd">
```

LISTING 9.3   Continued

```
<svg width="" height="">
<defs>

<g id="myBinocs">
 <clipPath id="myClip">
 <circle cx="40px" cy="40px" r="50px" class="clipstyle"/>
 <circle cx="110px" cy="40px" r="50px" class="clipstyle"/>
 </clipPath>
</g>
<style type="text/css">
<![CDATA[
.clipstyle{

}
]]>
</style>
</defs>
<svg x="80px" y="80px" width="400px" height="500px">
<image x="0px" y="0px" width="400px" height="500px"
xlink:href="FillGradients.svg" clip-path="url(#myClip)" />

</svg> <!-- Ends nested <svg> element -->
</svg> <!-- Ends document <svg> element -->
```

Figure 9.2 shows the onscreen appearance when Listing 9.3 is run.

The appearance may initially be surprising, so let's examine what we are looking at. What you see onscreen is a shape that represents the intersection of the binocular shape and the upper rectangle in FillGradients.svg. Part of the binocular shape lies above and to the left of the rectangular shape that is being clipped. The shape displayed onscreen is that part of the rectangle which is also covered by the binocular shape.

A static view of an image may be useful, but an animated view could help direct a user's attention to specific areas of interest—for example, in a map or technical diagram. Listing 9.4 adds a predefined animation to Listing 9.3. The animation causes the binoculars to pan horizontally to the right across the underlying image and then vertically downward. As the animation proceeds, you can see more (or less) of the binocular shape, depending on whether or not it is overlapping much or little of one of the underlying rectangles. The animation uses the animateTransform element, which is described in Chapter 11.

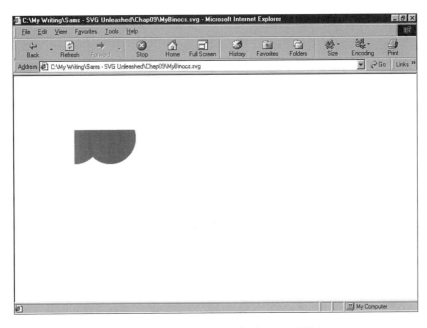

FIGURE 9.2   A binocular-shaped clipping path applied to an SVG image.

LISTING 9.4   AnimMyBinocs.svg—Animating a Binocular Clipping Path

```
<?xml version="1.0" standalone="no"?>
<!DOCTYPE svg PUBLIC "-//W3C//DTD SVG 20010904//EN"
"http://www.w3.org/TR/2001/REC-SVG-20010904/DTD/svg10.dtd">
<svg width="" height="">
<defs>

<g id="myBinocs">
 <clipPath id="myClip" transform="translate(0,0)">
 <animateTransform id="horiz" attributeName="transform"
  type="translate" begin="3s" from="0,0" to="200,0" dur="5s" />
 <animateTransform id="vert" attributeName="transform"
  type="translate" begin="horiz.end" from="200,0" to="200,350" dur="8s"
fill="freeze"/>
 <circle cx="40px" cy="40px" r="50px" class="clipstyle"/>
 <circle cx="110px" cy="40px" r="50px" class="clipstyle"/>
 </clipPath>
</g>
<style type="text/css">
<![CDATA[
.clipstyle{
```

LISTING 9.4   Continued

```
}
]]>
</style>
</defs>
<svg x="80px" y="80px" width="400px" height="500px">
<image x="0px" y="0px" width="400px" height="500px"
xlink:href="FillGradients.svg" clip-path="url(#myClip)" />

</svg> <!-- Ends nested <svg> element -->
</svg> <!-- Ends document <svg> element -->
```

Figure 9.3 shows the onscreen appearance after the first (horizontal) animation has completed when Listing 9.4 is run. Figure 9.4 shows the onscreen appearance after the vertical part of the animation has completed. To appreciate fully what is happening, you need to run the code and watch the clipped shape changing its position onscreen.

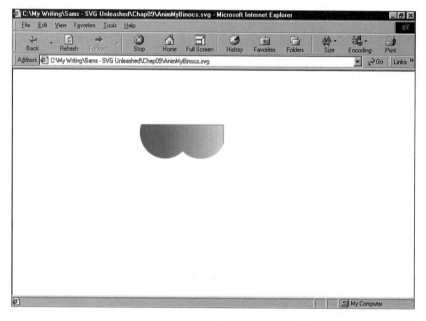

FIGURE 9.3   Appearance after the end of the first (horizontal) part of the animation.

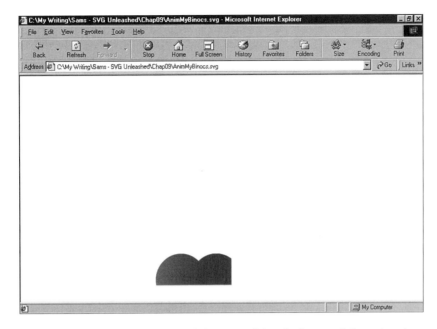

FIGURE 9.4   Appearance after the end of the second (vertical) part of the animation.

The animation in Listing 9.4 moves the binocular around the screen. An alternative approach to placing similar parts of the underlying image within the clipping path is to move the underlying image rather than the clipping path. This means that the binocular-shaped viewport stays stationary onscreen and the image being viewed moves within it. Listing 9.5 shows code to produce that type of effect.

LISTING 9.5   Anim2MyBinocs.svg—Animating an Image Within a Clipping Path

```
<?xml version="1.0" standalone="no"?>
<!DOCTYPE svg PUBLIC "-//W3C//DTD SVG 20010904//EN"
"http://www.w3.org/TR/2001/REC-SVG-20010904/DTD/svg10.dtd">
<svg width="" height="">
<defs>

<g id="myBinocs">
 <clipPath id="myClip" >
 <circle cx="40px" cy="40px" r="50px" class="clipstyle"/>
 <circle cx="110px" cy="40px" r="50px" class="clipstyle"/>
 </clipPath>
</g>
```

LISTING 9.5   Continued

```
<style type="text/css">
<![CDATA[
.clipstyle{
/* Use this to style any text in clipping path */
}
]]>
</style>
</defs>
<svg x="80px" y="80px" width="400px" height="500px">

<image x="0px" y="0px" width="400px" height="500px"
xlink:href="FillGradients.svg" clip-path="url(#myClip)" >
<animate id="horiz" attributeName="x" begin="3s" from="0px"
 to="-200px" dur="5s" fill="freeze"/>
<!-- Must set fill="freeze" or the clipping path will flip back horizontally -->
<animate attributeName="y" begin="horiz.end" from="0px" to="-350px"
 dur="8s" fill="freeze" />
</image>

</svg> <!-- Ends nested <svg> element -->
</svg> <!-- Ends document <svg> element -->
```

Figure 9.5 shows the onscreen appearance after the first (horizontal) animation has completed when Listing 9.5 is run. When you run the animation onscreen, you will notice that the binocular shape stays static onscreen but the background image scrolls horizontally within it. In the second part of the animation, the background image scrolls vertically within the binocular-shaped viewport. Figure 9.6 shows the onscreen appearance after the second (vertical) part of the animation has completed. To fully appreciate what is happening, you need to run the code and watch the animation onscreen.

You can go on to create any shape you want as a clipping path, using the basic shapes, text, and so on. Listings 9.4 and 9.5 have given you some examples of how to animate clipping paths. Studying the huge range of SVG animations described in Chapter 11 will likely give you ideas for other animation options.

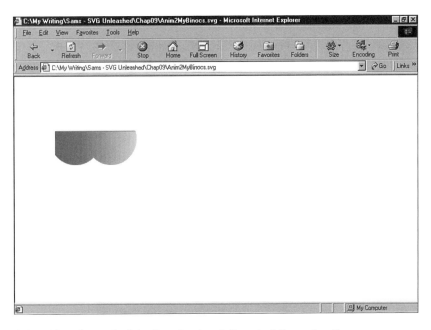

FIGURE 9.5   After the end of the first (horizontal) part of the animation.

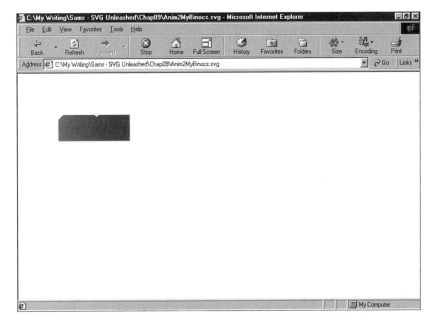

FIGURE 9.6   After the end of the second (vertical) part of the animation.

Masking

Understanding masking in SVG depends on an understanding of transparency or opacity in SVG. The key difference between a clipping path and an SVG mask is that the shape selected by a mask can be fully opaque (just like a clipping path) or can have its appearance modulated by the mask, which may be semi-transparent, including linear or radial gradients that can vary the opacity among various locations within the mask.

The mask Element

A mask element is used to define an SVG mask. A mask element is a **container element** that contains one or more SVG graphics elements. The content of the mask element defines the shape of the mask and provides a semi-transparent mask for compositing foreground graphics objects into the background of the image.

The definition of the shape and fill of a mask is situated within the defs element of an SVG document fragment. A mask element has similarities to a rect element in that it possesses x, y, width, and height attributes. However, a mask need not be rectangular in shape.

The general form for the definition of a mask is as follows:

```
<?xml version="1.0" standalone="no"?>
<!DOCTYPE svg PUBLIC "-//W3C//DTD SVG 20010904//EN"
"http://www.w3.org/TR/2001/REC-SVG-20010904/DTD/svg10.dtd">
<svg width="" height="">
<defs>
<mask id="myMaskName"
 x="some-x-position" y="some-y-position"
 width="some-width" height="some-height"
 style="someStyle">
<!-- Other elements can go here. -->
</mask>
</defs>
<!-- One or more references to the mask element can go here
placed on a graphics element or group. -->
</svg>
```

A mask element may also possess a maskUnits attribute, which may take the values userSpaceOnUse or objectBoundingBox. If no maskUnits attribute is specified, a default value of objectBoundingBox is assumed. When the value is userSpaceOnUse, the mask is relative to the initial SVG viewport. When the value is objectBoundingBox, the mask is relative to the object that is being masked.

TIP

Remember to include an id attribute on each mask element. Without the id attribute, you cannot reference the mask you have defined.

A `mask` element may also possess a `maskContentUnits` attribute. The permitted values of the `maskContentUnits` attribute are `userSpaceOnUse` or `objectBoundingBox`, with `objectBoundingBox` being the default if no `maskContentUnits` attribute is specified. The value of `maskContentUnits` specifies the coordinate system to be used. When `maskContentUnits` is `userSpaceOnUse`, the coordinate system of the current viewport is applied. When `maskContentUnits` is `objectBoundingBox`, the bounding box of the SVG object to which the mask is applied is used.

NOTE

Properties of a mask element may be inherited from its ancestor elements. Properties of a mask element are never inherited from an element that only references the mask element.

The mask Property

To apply a mask, you must place the `mask` property on the appropriate element and provide a valid value for the `mask` property.

The `mask` property may be present on any of the SVG graphics elements or on text-related elements.

Some Masking Examples

In this section, we will apply some of the theory that has just been described. Listing 9.6 shows an SVG animation that applies three different masks, one after the other, to a graphic shape. The purpose of the example is not to illustrate SVG animation elements, but if you run the code, the onscreen appearance will allow you to compare the effect of different masks on the same object.

LISTING 9.6   AnimatedMask01.svg—Applying Masks to an Ellipse

```
<?xml version="1.0" standalone="no"?>
<!DOCTYPE svg PUBLIC "-//W3C//DTD SVG 20010904//EN"
"http://www.w3.org/TR/2001/REC-SVG-20010904/DTD/svg10.dtd">
<svg width="" height="">
<defs>
<style type="text/css">
<![CDATA[
ellipse{
```

LISTING 9.6   Continued

```
stroke:red;
stroke-width:5;
fill:#CCFFCC;
}
]]>
</style>
<mask id="myMask1" maskUnits="userSpaceOnUse">
 <rect x="200px" y="300px" width="600px" height="30px"
  fill="#CCCCCC"/>
</mask>
<mask id="myMask2" maskUnits="userSpaceOnUse">
 <rect x="200px" y="300px" width="600px" height="30px"
  fill="black"/>
</mask>
<mask id="myMask3" maskUnits="userSpaceOnUse">
 <rect x="200px" y="300px" width="600px" height="30px"
  fill="#333333"/>
</mask>
<mask id="myMask4" maskUnits="userSpaceOnUse">
 <rect x="200px" y="300px" width="600px" height="30px"
  fill="#FFFFFF"/>
</mask>
</defs>
<g mask="">
<set id="set1" begin="4s" attributeName="mask"
 from="" to="url(#myMask1)" />
<set id="set1" begin="8s" attributeName="mask"
 from="url(#myMask1)" to="url(#myMask2)" />
<set id="set1" begin="12s" attributeName="mask"
 from="url(#myMask1)" to="url(#myMask2)" />
<set id="set2" begin="16s" attributeName="mask"
 from="url(#myMask2)" to="url(#myMask3)" />
<set id="set3" begin="20s" attributeName="mask"
 from="url(#myMask3)" to="url(#myMask4)" />
 <ellipse cx="500px" cy="300px" rx="250px" ry="100px" />
</g>
</svg>
```

Figure 9.7 shows the onscreen appearance when Listing 9.6 is first run and before the mask is applied. Figure 9.8 shows the onscreen appearance after Listing 9.8 has been run and after the final of the four masks has been applied.

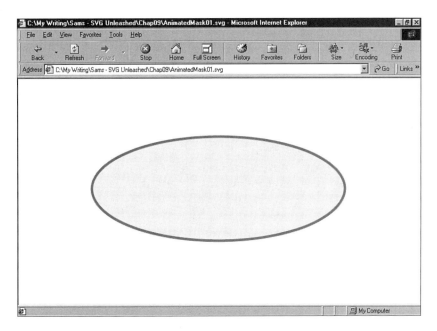

FIGURE 9.7   The appearance immediately after the document has loaded.

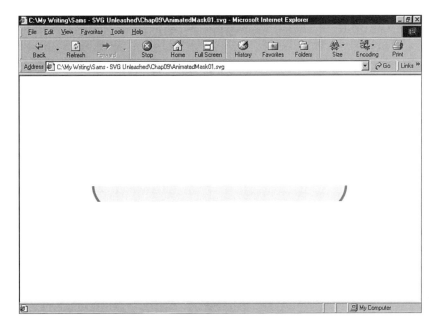

FIGURE 9.8   The appearance after the final mask has been applied.

Where a mask has the color black (whether expressed as a named color or using the hexadecimal or rgb() syntax), the part of the masked image is not shown onscreen.

Listing 9.7 shows a mask applied to some text. A horizontal linear gradient is applied to the text that affects the text differently depending on whether the stop-color property of the linear gradient is black or white.

LISTING 9.7   MaskedText01.svg—A Mask Applied to Text

```
<?xml version="1.0" standalone="no"?>
<!DOCTYPE svg PUBLIC "-//W3C//DTD SVG 20010904//EN"
"http://www.w3.org/TR/2001/REC-SVG-20010904/DTD/svg10.dtd">
<svg width="" height="">
<defs>
<linearGradient id="myMaskGradient" units="userSpaceOnUse">
 <stop offset="0%" stop-color="black"/>
 <stop offset="20%" stop-color="white"/>
 <stop offset="40%" stop-color="black"/>
 <stop offset="60%" stop-color="white"/>
 <stop offset="80%" stop-color="black"/>
 <stop offset="100%" stop-color="white"/>
</linearGradient>
<mask id="myMask" maskUnits="objectBoundingBox">
 <rect x="20px" y="30px" width="980px" height="200px"
  fill="url(#myMaskGradient)"/>
</mask>
</defs>
<g mask="url(#myMask)">
<text x="20px" y="100px"
 style="fill:red; stroke:none; font-family:Arial, sans-serif; font-size:80">
Some text which is masked
</text>
</g>
<text x="20px" y="120px"
 style="fill:black; stroke:none; font-size:20">
B
<tspan dx="185px" dy="0">
W
</tspan>
<tspan dx="175px" dy="0">
B
</tspan>
<tspan dx="175px" dy="0">
W
```

LISTING 9.7   Continued

```
</tspan>
<tspan dx="175px" dy="0">
B
</tspan>
<tspan dx="175px" dy="0">
W
</tspan>
</text>
</svg>
```

Figure 9.9 shows the onscreen appearance when Listing 9.9 is run. The letters "B" and "W" onscreen indicate the stop-color property at different points in the linear gradient that makes up the mask.

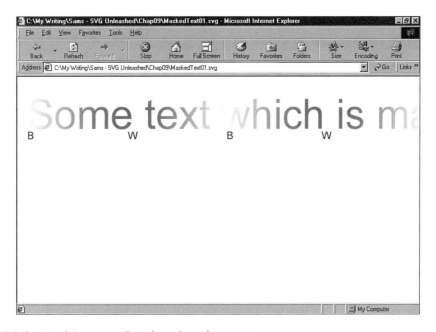

FIGURE 9.9   Applying a gradient-based mask to text.

An Animated Spotlight Example

In the example in this section, we will create a "spotlight" that travels across a piece of text. Listing 9.8 shows the code.

LISTING 9.8   MovingSpotlight.svg—Using a Mask to Simulate a Spotlight

```
<?xml version="1.0" standalone="no"?>
<!DOCTYPE svg PUBLIC "-//W3C//DTD SVG 20010904//EN"
"http://www.w3.org/TR/2001/REC-SVG-20010904/DTD/svg10.dtd">
<svg width="" height="">
<defs>
<style type="text/css">
<![CDATA[
circle{
stroke:none;
fill:white;
}
ellipse{
fill:green;
}
rect{
fill:black;
}
text{
fill:#CCCCCC;
stroke:none;
font-size:40;
}
text.masked{
mask:url(#myMask1);
fill:red;
font-size:40;
}
]]>
</style>
<mask id="myMask1" maskUnits="userSpaceOnUse">
 <circle cx="55px" cy="135px" r="25px">
 <animate attributeName="cx" from="55px" to="460px" begin="3s" dur="8s"
 repeatCount="indefinite"/>
 </circle>
</mask>
</defs>
<rect x="50px" y="60px" width="400px" height="150px" />
<text x="80px" y="150px" >
Some test text
</text>
<text x="80px" y="150px" class="masked">
```

LISTING 9.8   Continued

```
Some test text
</text>
</svg>
```

Let's look more closely at the definition of the `mask` element. The shape of the mask is a circle, defined by the `circle` element, which is nested within the `mask` element. The fill of that mask is red—because the text is in the class `masked` and the CSS rule for `text.masked` in the `style` element specifies a fill of `red`. The initial position of the circle is to the left of the text because the value of the `cx` attribute is `55px`. The `animate` element (described in Chapter 11) moves the center of the circle, specified by the value of the `cx` attribute, from `55px` to `460px`. Onscreen a red circle moves across the screen but, because the mask is applied only to the text and not the background, the red color is visible only on the text.

Figure 9.10 shows the initial onscreen appearance when Listing 9.8 is run. Figure 9.11 shows the appearance partway through the animation of the "spotlight."

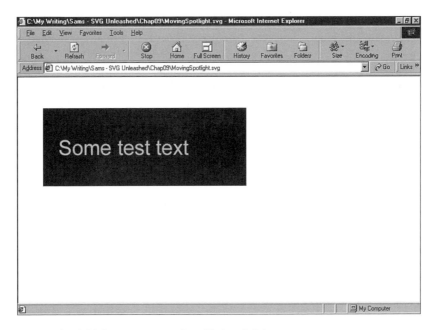

FIGURE 9.10   The initial appearance when Listing 9.8 is run.

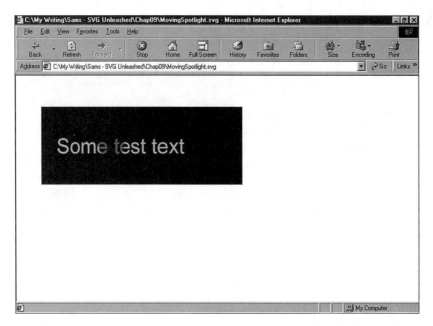

FIGURE 9.11   The appearance when the "spotlight" is partway through its animation.

You can use a similar approach to make text partly visible. Listing 9.9 modifies the code in Listing 9.8. In Listing 9.8, we had pale text against a black background. In Listing 9.9, we have white text against a white background. So it appears to the user as if there is no text there. When we animate the red circle across the screen, we make part of the text visible because the masked area of the text is red and so can be seen by the user, while most of the text remains white against a white background and so appears not to be there.

LISTING 9.9   MovingSpotlight02.svg—Using a Mask to Make Part of Text Visible

```
<?xml version="1.0" standalone="no"?>
<!DOCTYPE svg PUBLIC "-//W3C//DTD SVG 20010904//EN"
"http://www.w3.org/TR/2001/REC-SVG-20010904/DTD/svg10.dtd">
<svg width="" height="">
<defs>
<style type="text/css">
<![CDATA[
circle{
stroke:none;
fill:white;
}
ellipse{
fill:green;
}
rect{
```

LISTING 9.9   Continued

```
fill:white;
}
text{
fill:white;
stroke:none;
font-size:40;
}
text.masked{
mask:url(#myMask1);
fill:red;
font-size:40;
}
]]>
</style>
<mask id="myMask1" maskUnits="userSpaceOnUse">
 <circle cx="50px" cy="135px" r="30px">
 <animate attributeName="cx" from="50px" to="460px" begin="3s" dur="8s"
  repeatCount="indefinite"/>
 </circle>
</mask>
</defs>
<rect x="50px" y="60px" width="400px" height="150px" />
<text x="80px" y="150px" >
Some test text
</text>
<text x="80px" y="150px" class="masked">
Some test text
</text>
</svg>
```

Figure 9.12 shows the onscreen appearance when Listing 9.9 is run. In this animation, all the text is invisible except for the part defined by the mask.

Expanding Window on Text

Animated masks can be used to create many attractive effects. Listing 9.10 shows the size of a mask being animated so that progressively more of a text message is revealed as the mask is animated. Again, we used white text against a white background. The circular mask initially has a radius of zero pixels, and so isn't visible. An animation increases the radius of the mask and so seems to fill the text progressively with a red fill.

9

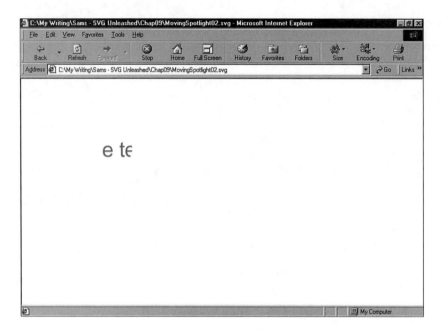

FIGURE 9.12   Part of the text is visible as the mask animates across it.

LISTING 9.10   PulsingText.svg—Using an Animated Mask to Show Text

```
<?xml version="1.0" standalone="no"?>
<!DOCTYPE svg PUBLIC "-//W3C//DTD SVG 20010904//EN"
"http://www.w3.org/TR/2001/REC-SVG-20010904/DTD/svg10.dtd">
<svg width="" height="">
<defs>
<style type="text/css">
<![CDATA[
circle{
stroke:none;
fill:#666666;
}
ellipse{
fill:green;
}
rect{
fill:white;
}
text{
fill:white;
```

LISTING 9.10   Continued

```
stroke:none;
font-size:40;
}
text.masked{
mask:url(#myMask1);
fill:red;
font-size:40;
}
]]>
</style>
<mask id="myMask1" maskUnits="userSpaceOnUse">
 <circle cx="210px" cy="135px" r="0px">
 <animate attributeName="r" from="0px" to="200px"
 begin="3s" dur="8s" repeatCount="indefinite"/>
 </circle>
</mask>
</defs>
<rect x="50px" y="60px" width="400px" height="150px" />
<text x="80px" y="120px" class="masked">
Some test text
<tspan x="80px" dy="1.5em">
A second line
</tspan>
<tspan x="80px" dy="1.5em">
And a third line
</tspan>
</text>
</svg>
```

Notice that the fill rule for the `circle` element specifies a fill of #666666. This applies partial transparency to the mask, making the red text paler than it would be if the fill for a `circle` element were `white`, in which case the red fill would be fully opaque. A fill of white on the circle is equivalent to producing a similar effect using a clipping path.

Figure 9.13 shows the onscreen appearance when Listing 9.10 is run.

9

FIGURE 9.13   The mask expands to progressively show more of the text.

Animated Gradients on Masked Text

The masked text you saw produced by Listing 9.7 uses a linear gradient in the mask. That gradient can, of course, be animated. Listing 9.11 shows one way to animate the gradient.

LISTING 9.11   AnimatedMaskedText01.svg—Animating the Gradient of a Mask

```
<?xml version="1.0" standalone="no"?>
<!DOCTYPE svg PUBLIC "-//W3C//DTD SVG 20010904//EN"
"http://www.w3.org/TR/2001/REC-SVG-20010904/DTD/svg10.dtd">
<svg width="" height="">
<defs>
<linearGradient id="myMaskGradient" units="userSpaceOnUse">
 <stop offset="0%" stop-color="black">
 <animate attributeName="stop-color" begin="2s"
 calcMode="Linear" values="black; white; black"
 dur="8s" repeatCount="indefinite"/>
 </stop>
 <stop offset="20%" stop-color="white">
  <animate attributeName="stop-color" begin="2s"
 calcMode="Linear" values="white; black; white"
 dur="8s" repeatCount="indefinite"/>
 </stop>
```

LISTING 9.11   Continued

```
<stop offset="40%" stop-color="black">
 <animate attributeName="stop-color" begin="2s"
calcMode="Linear" values="black; white; black"
dur="8s" repeatCount="indefinite"/>
 </stop>
 <stop offset="60%" stop-color="white">
 <animate attributeName="stop-color" begin="2s"
calcMode="Linear" values="white; black; white"
dur="8s" repeatCount="indefinite"/>
 </stop>
 <stop offset="80%" stop-color="black">
 <animate attributeName="stop-color" begin="2s"
calcMode="Linear" values="black; white; black"
dur="8s" repeatCount="indefinite"/>
 </stop>
 <stop offset="100%" stop-color="white">
  <animate attributeName="stop-color" begin="2s"
calcMode="Linear" values="white; black; white"
dur="8s" repeatCount="indefinite"/>
 </stop>
</linearGradient>
<mask id="myMask" maskUnits="objectBoundingBox">
 <rect x="20px" y="30px" width="980px" height="200px"
  fill="url(#myMaskGradient)"/>
</mask>
</defs>
<g mask="url(#myMask)">
<text x="20px" y="100px"
 style="fill:red; stroke:none; font-family:Arial, sans-serif; font-size:80">
Some text which is masked
</text>
</g>
<text x="20px" y="120px"
 style="fill:black; stroke:none; font-size:20">
B
<tspan dx="185px" dy="0">
W
</tspan>
<tspan dx="175px" dy="0">
B
</tspan>
<tspan dx="175px" dy="0">
```

LISTING 9.11   Continued

```
W
</tspan>
<tspan dx="175px" dy="0">
B
</tspan>
<tspan dx="175px" dy="0">
W
</tspan>
</text>
</svg>
```

Figure 9.14 shows the onscreen appearance when Listing 9.11 is run. The letters "B" and "W" indicate the starting value of the mask—black and white, respectively. Each animation simply animates the stop-color of one part of the linear gradient over 4 seconds to the opposite color and during a further 4 seconds back to the original color. If you run the code onscreen, you will see some quite subtle blinking of text. This blinking could be used to attract a user's attention in a way that is significantly more subtle than that produced by alternative techniques.

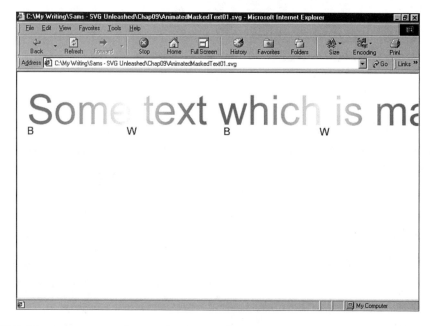

FIGURE 9.14   Appearance of text as it changes during application of the animated mask.

The animation of the individual `stop-color` properties of the linear gradient is carried out over the same time period, and the start times are synchronized.

Compositing

I indicated earlier in this chapter that compositing is the process of combining colors to produce a final color onscreen. Compositing makes use of the values of the alpha, red, green, and blue parts of an element's color value.

The alpha channel indicates full opacity if it has a value of 1 and indicates full transparency when it has a value of 0.

Suppose the following abbreviations apply:

- `Er`, `Eg`, and `Eb` stand for an element's red, green, and blue color values.

- `Ea` stands for an element's alpha value.

- `Or`, `Og`, and `Ob` stand for the original red, green, and blue color values of the SVG canvas.

- `Oa` stands for the original alpha value of the SVG canvas.

- `Fr`, `Fg`, and `Fb` stand for the final red, green, and blue color values of the SVG canvas.

- `Fa` stands for the final alpha value of the SVG canvas.

The formulae for compositing are as follows:

- `Fa = 1-(1 - Ea) * (1 - Oa)`

- `Fr = (1 - Ea) * Or + Er`

- `Fg = (1 - Ea) * Og + Eg`

- `Fb = (1 - Ea) * Ob + Eb`

Let's take the formula for the final value of red as an example (see the second bullet point in the preceding list).

First, if the element's paint is fully opaque, the value `(1 - Ea)` is zero. Therefore, `(1 - Ea) * Or` is also zero. Thus, the final value is `0 + Er`, which is equal simply to `Er`. In other words, the value for red on the element, `Er`, is the final color value of the canvas, `Fr`.

However, if the element's paint is fully transparent, `(1 - Ea)` equals one. Therefore, `(1 - Ea) * Or` is the same as `Or`. Thus, the final value of red, `Fr`, is the sum of `Or` plus `Er`.

The more opaque the element is, the closer the `Fr` value becomes to the `Er`. That makes sense intuitively. The more opaque the element's paint, the more impact it has on the onscreen color.

The color-interpolation Property

The color-interpolation property provides information about the color space in which compositing takes place. As well as providing information for alpha compositing, the color-interpolation property is used in determining intermediate colors in gradients and in animations of colors.

The color-interpolation property has four permitted values: auto, sRGB, linearRGB, and inherit. A value of auto indicates that interpolation may take place in either the sRGB or linearized RGB color spaces. When the value is sRGB or linearRGB, interpolation should take place in the color specified. A value of inherit indicates that interpolation is determined by the value of the color-interpolation property on the nearest ancestor element where it is specified.

The color-rendering Property

The color-rendering property provides information about prioritization during compositing. The permitted values of the color-rendering property are auto, optimizeSpeed, optimizeQuality, and inherit. A value of auto indicates that competing priorities are balanced optimizing speed or quality, but giving some priority to quality. When the value is optimizeSpeed or optimizeQuality, rendering takes place with speed or quality, respectively, being given priority. A value of inherit indicates that rendering is determined by the value of the color-rendering property on the nearest ancestor element where it is specified.

Let's move on to examine the SVG DOM interfaces that are particularly relevant to clipping and masking.

The SVG DOM Interfaces

Two SVG DOM interfaces are particularly relevant to clipping and masking: the SVGClipPathElement and SVGMaskElement objects.

The SVGClipPathElement Object

The SVGClipPathElement object is the SVG DOM representation of the clipPath element.

> **CAUTION**
>
> Remember that the "c" of the element type name of the clipPath element is lowercase, and the "c" of the SVGClipPathElement object is uppercase.

The SVGClipPathElement object has the properties and methods of the SVGElement object, the SVGTests object, the SVGLangSpace object, the SVGExternalResourcesRequired object, the SVGStylable object, the SVGTransformable object, and the SVGUnitTypes object.

In addition, the `SVGClipPathElement` object has the following property:

- `clipPathUnits`—of type `SVGAnimatedEnumeration`

The `SVGClipPathElement` object has no methods specific to it.

The SVGMaskElement Object

The `SVGMaskElement` object is the SVG DOM representation of the SVG mask element.

The `SVGMaskElement` object has the properties and methods of the `SVGElement` object, the `SVGTests` object, the `SVGLangSpace` object, the `SVGExternalResourcesRequired` object, the `SVGStylable` object, and the `SVGUnitTypes` object.

In addition, the `SVGMaskElement` object has the following properties:

- `maskUnits`—of type `SVGAnimatedEnumeration`
- `maskContentUnits`—of type `SVGAnimatedEnumeration`
- `x`—of type `SVGAnimatedLength`
- `y`—of type `SVGAnimatedLength`
- `width`—of type `SVGAnimatedLength`
- `height`—of type `SVGAnimatedLength`

The `SVGMaskElement` object has no methods specific to it.

Example Using a Clipping Path

A clipping path or mask, as you saw in Listings 9.8 and 9.9, can be used to create a timed animation similar to a searchlight. The example to be developed in this section allows the "searchlight" to be under user control. The code is shown in Listing 9.12.

LISTING 9.12   Searchlight.svg—Creating a Searchlight That Follows the User's Mouse

```
<?xml version="1.0" standalone="no"?>
<!DOCTYPE svg PUBLIC "-//W3C//DTD SVG 20010904//EN"
"http://www.w3.org/TR/2001/REC-SVG-20010904/DTD/svg10.dtd">
<svg width="500px" height="300px" xmlns="http://www.w3.org/2000/svg"
onload="Initialize(evt)">
  <script type="text/javascript">
  <![CDATA[

var SVGRoot = document.documentElement;
    SVGRoot.addEventListener('mousemove', moveLight, false);
var searchLight, slCircle;
```

LISTING 9.12   Continued

```
function Initialize() {
    searchLight = document.getElementById('searchLight');
    slCircle = searchLight.getElementsByTagName('circle').item(0);
}

function moveLight(evt) {
    slCircle.setAttribute('cx', evt.clientX);
    slCircle.setAttribute('cy', evt.clientY);
}

    ]]>
    </script>
    <defs>
      <clipPath id="searchLight">
        <circle cx="40" cy="40" r="40" />
      </clipPath>
    </defs>
    <rect x="0" y="0" width="100%" height="100%" fill="black" />
    <g clip-path="url(#searchLight)">
      <rect x="0" y="0" width="100%" height="100%" fill="white" />
      <text x="50%" y="50%" fill="red" text-anchor="middle" style="font-size:
40px; pointer-events:none">Interactive Searchlight!</text>
    </g>
</svg>
```

When the file loads, a white circle is displayed against a plain black background. If you place your mouse pointer anywhere in the black rectangle, the white circle follows the mouse. If you move the mouse pointer over the area where the text Interactive Searchlight is placed, that part of the text displays in red.

The code adds an event listener to detect movement of the mouse within the black rectangle. When the file loads, the Initialize() function is called. The clipping path is retrieved by means of its id attribute using the getElementById() method.

The variable slCircle is assigned the circle element. The event listener is triggered each time the mouse is moved. The moveLight() function is called and uses the setAttribute() method to change the value of the cx and cy attributes of the circle to correspond with the new onscreen position of the circle.

The effect is that the circle follows the mouse position onscreen, thus allowing the user to point the searchlight at any desired point of the black rectangle. In this case, the text Interactive Searchlight can be illuminated as the user moves the mouse to an appropriate position.

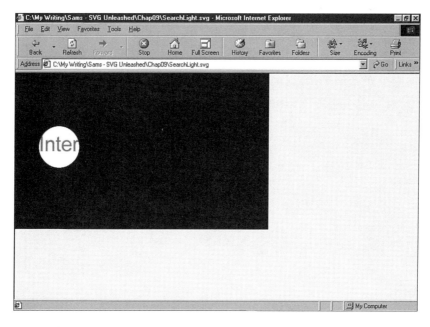

FIGURE 9.15   The "searchlight" displays part of the text.

Summary

This chapter introduced the topics of clipping, masking, and compositing in SVG. Clipping "cuts out" a defined shape for rendering. Masking additionally allows the transparency (or opacity, if you prefer) of the shape to be adjusted, in potentially complex and subtle ways. You also saw some of the ways you can apply these techniques of clipping and masking in SVG images.

The final section of the chapter described the SVG DOM interfaces related to clipping and masking.

CHAPTER 10

SVG Filters

In this chapter, we will look at some of the techniques available in SVG to apply **filters** to SVG graphics objects. Filters in SVG apply visual effects that are typically associated with bitmap graphics and allow such effects as drop shadows to be created declaratively using SVG.

In the final section of the chapter, we will describe the SVG DOM interfaces.

First, let's look at some general issues that relate to SVG filters.

SVG Filters

SVG filters provide many visual effects that correspond to effects found in bitmap graphics packages. An SVG filter is defined within the defs element and is referenced from an element within the main part of an SVG document.

SVG filters are defined using a filter element within which are nested one or more elements that describe **filter primitives**. A filter primitive can be seen as a component of a filter effect. For example, when a drop shadow is created, it is typically also offset. In SVG, that class of filter effect is created using an feGaussianBlur filter primitive, an feOffset filter primitive, and an feMerge filter primitive.

A filter primitive may take as its input some aspect of the graphic on which the filter is to be applied or may use the output of another filter primitive that is part of the same filter or, in some circumstances, may reference an external image.

A source graphic can be used multiple times within a filter—for example, to create a drop shadow that is then displaced and combined with the original image.

SVG filters can be animated, using the techniques described in Chapter 11, "SVG Animation Elements." There is a temptation to animate filters just because it can be done. Computation of filters can be very demanding of CPU resources, and images that animate filters can run slowly or jerkily on slower CPUs.

The filter Element

The `filter` element is typically found nested within a `defs` element. A `filter` element always has an `id` attribute, whose value allows the filter to be referenced from other elements within the SVG document fragment.

The `filter` element may take `x`, `y`, `width`, and `height` attributes, which define the position and dimensions of the part of the viewport on which the filter will be applied.

It is important that you adjust the values of these attributes to allow the filter to be applied to the appropriate area. For example, if you are creating a blur on text, that blur will often extend outside the rectangle that would contain the text. To avoid inadvertently creating a hard, straight edge to the blur, allow a larger area—for example, by setting the `x` attribute to `-10%`, the `width` attribute to `120%`, the `y` attribute to `-10%`, and the `height` attribute to `130%`. To check whether the filter has the desired quality of edge, zoom in on the image.

> **CAUTION**
>
> Be careful not to omit the x, y, width, and height attributes on a filter element. Some filters will not render unless these attributes are specified.

When the shapes to which the filter is applied do not form a regular shape, the tightest possible rectangular bounding box is applied.

The filter Property

If you want to apply a filter to a graphics element, the value of the `filter` property on that graphics element must correspond to the value of the `id` attribute of a `filter` element in the same SVG document.

The `filter` property is treated as a styling property. It can be expressed as a presentation attribute:

```
<someSVGElement filter="url(#myFilterName)" ... />
```

Or it can be expressed as a part of the value of a `style` attribute:

```
<someSVGElement style="filter:url(#myFilterName); ..."   ... />
```

For example, suppose we had a filter definition like the following:

```
<defs>
<filter id="myFilter" x="-10%" y="-10%" width="120%" height="130%" ... >
<!-- Filter primitives go here -->
</filter>
</defs>
```

In this case, we could reference it from some text using code like the following:

```
<text style="filter:url(#myFilter) ..." >
The filter is applied to this text
</text>
```

The SVG Filter Primitives

In this section, we will provide brief descriptions of all the SVG filter primitives and examples to indicate the types of appearance that several of the filter primitives can produce. Within a single chapter, it is possible to convey only a few of the huge number of possible visual effects. If they interest you, I encourage you to experiment with some of the examples to better understand how altering attribute values alters the onscreen appearance.

Common Attributes for the SVG Filter Primitives

SVG filter primitives share several attributes. They will be described in this preliminary section. However, you may find the description of the attributes easier to follow after you have studied the effects and usage of the individual filter primitives.

The x, y, width, and height Attributes

The x and y attributes define the top-left corner of the **clipping region** within which a filter primitive is to be applied. The width and height attributes define the horizontal and vertical extent of the clipping region within which the filter primitive is applied. All these attributes can be animated.

The in Attribute

A filter primitive is typically applied to a graphic image of some type. You use the in attribute on a filter primitive to specify the graphic input to be used by the filter primitive.

It is not compulsory for all filter primitives to possess an in attribute. If an in attribute is absent from the first filter primitive contained within a filter element, the default value is SourceGraphic. For all later filter primitives, if no in attribute is specified, the result of the immediately preceding filter primitive is used as the input.

10

The permitted values of the in attribute are as follows:

- SourceGraphic—The SVG element or group of elements that references the filter. In other words, the element or group of elements that possess a filter property which matches the id attribute of the filter element.

- SourceAlpha—The value of the alpha for the source graphic. If the source graphic is fully opaque, the alpha will have a value of 1.0, and less if the source graphic is at least partly transparent.

- BackgroundImage—The SVG canvas within the *filter region* at the time the filter was applied.

- BackgroundAlpha—The alpha value for the BackgroundImage.

- FillPaint—The value of the fill property on the element that references the filter.

- StrokePaint—The value of the stroke property on the element that references the filter.

- *filter-primitive-reference*—A reference to the value of a result attribute on another filter primitive.

CAUTION

Many values or attribute names in SVG use "camel case," that is, *likeThis* with a lowercase initial character on the first word and uppercase initial character on all succeeding words. The values of the in attribute do not follow that convention and use an uppercase initial letter for the first word of the value—for example, SourceGraphic. Failing to use the correct case can cause potentially puzzling failures of filters to render as anticipated.

The enable-background Attribute

The enable-background attribute provides an alternative to applying a filter to a single SVG element. Using the enable-background attribute allows you to apply a filter to a defined area of the SVG canvas, which may have been defined by more than one SVG element.

Applying the enable-background attribute to a g element enables you to apply a filter to the background in the context of that g element:

```
<defs>
<filter id="backgroundBlur" x="-10%" y="-20%" width="130%" height="140%">
<feGaussianBlur in="BackgroundImage" stdDeviation="2" />
</filter>
</defs>
<g enable-background="new" >
<text x="20" y="20" >Hello World!</text>
```

```
<circle cx="70" cy="50" r="20" fill="red" />
<rect x="20" y="20" width="200" height="100" fill="none"
 filter="url(#backgroundBlur)" />
</g>
```

The filter in the preceding snippet is applied to the background image—notice that the `in` attribute of the `feGaussianBlur` element has the value of `BackgroundImage`—so the filter is applied to both the text and circle.

The `enable-background` attribute can take values of `accumulate`, `new` (with optional `x`, `y`, `width`, and `height` parameters), or `inherit`. The default value is `accumulate`.

The result Attribute

The value of the `result` attribute is the name for the output from a filter primitive.

The `result` attribute is available to allow another SVG filter primitive nested within the same `filter` element to reference that `result` by means of its in attribute. The general format is as follows:

```
<filter id="myFilter" ...>
<somePrimitive ..... result="myResult"/>
<someOtherPrimitive .. in="myResult" ... />
</filter>
```

CAUTION

If you are using several filter primitives in a cascade, with the result of one being used as the value of the in attribute on another, make sure that the filter primitive whose result you are using comes earlier in the code. A forward reference to the value of a result attribute is an error.

If a `result` attribute is omitted from a filter primitive, its output is still available, but only to the next filter primitive in sequence, and only if the latter filter primitive has no other value specified for its `in` attribute.

CAUTION

Don't attempt to access the value of a result attribute from outside the filter element within which the filter primitive is nested. The name that is the value of a result attribute is in scope only within its own filter element.

The value of a `result` attribute may occur on more than one filter primitive within a filter element. A filter primitive that has one of the repeat values of a `result` attribute as the value for its `in` attribute will use the `result` attribute on the nearest preceding matching filter primitive.

Now let's move on to explore the SVG filter primitives.

10

The feBlend Filter Primitive

The feBlend filter primitive composites two objects together to produce a single image. As well as an in attribute, the feBlend element has an in2 attribute, which references the second image to be blended.

The feBlend element may take a mode attribute, whose permitted values are normal, multiply, screen, darken, and lighten. The default mode is normal.

Listing 10.1 shows a simple feBlend example.

LISTING 10.1   Blend.svg—The Various Modes Using feBlend

```
<?xml version="1.0"?>
<!DOCTYPE svg PUBLIC "-//W3C//DTD SVG 20010904//EN"
"http://www.w3.org/TR/2001/REC-SVG-20010904/DTD/svg10.dtd">
<svg width="500px" height="500px" viewBox="0 0 500 500"
xmlns="http://www.w3.org/2000/svg">
<defs>
<linearGradient id="myGradient" gradientUnits="userSpaceOnUse"
x1="0" y1="0" x2="600" y2="0">
<stop offset="0" stop-color="#FFFF00" />
<stop offset="0.25" stop-color="#FF0000" />
<stop offset="0.50" stop-color="#FFFF00" />
<stop offset="0.75" stop-color="#FF0000" />
<stop offset="1" stop-color="#999999" />
</linearGradient>
<filter id="Normal">
<feBlend mode="normal" in2="BackgroundImage" in="SourceGraphic"/>
</filter>
<filter id="Multiply">
<feBlend mode="multiply" in2="BackgroundImage" in="SourceGraphic"/>
</filter>
<filter id="Screen">
<feBlend mode="screen" in2="BackgroundImage" in="SourceGraphic"/>
</filter>
<filter id="Darken">
<feBlend mode="darken" in2="BackgroundImage" in="SourceGraphic"/>
</filter>
<filter id="Lighten">
<feBlend mode="lighten" in2="BackgroundImage" in="SourceGraphic"/>
</filter>
</defs>
<g enable-background="new">
<rect x="30" y="20" width="320" height="460" fill="url(#myGradient)" />
```

LISTING 10.1 Continued

```
<g font-family="Arial, sans-serif" font-size="75"
 fill="#666666" fill-opacity="0.8" >
<text x="50" y="90" filter="url(#Normal)" >Normal</text>
<text x="50" y="180" filter="url(#Multiply)" >Multiply</text>
<text x="50" y="270" filter="url(#Screen)" >Screen</text>
<text x="50" y="360" filter="url(#Darken)" >Darken</text>
<text x="50" y="450" filter="url(#Lighten)" >Lighten</text>
</g>
</g>
</svg>
```

Figure 10.1 shows the onscreen appearance when Listing 10.1 is run.

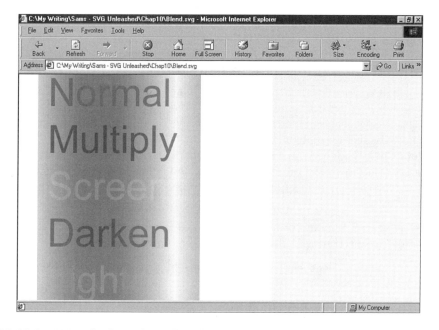

FIGURE 10.1 Using the five values of mode in feBlend.

The details of how the color values are calculated for each mode are described in the SVG 1.0 Recommendation.

The feColorMatrix Filter Primitive

The feColorMatrix element applies a matrix transformation to the red, green, blue, and alpha values of each pixel of an input image. Matrix transformations allow you to change color values in an SVG object in many possible ways.

The `type` attribute of `feColorMatrix` may take any of the following values:

- `matrix`
- `saturate`
- `hueRotate`
- `luminanceToAlpha`

When the value of the `type` attribute is `matrix`, a full 5 by 4 matrix operation is applied. The other permitted values are convenient labels for commonly used matrix operations. Details of the calculations are provided in the SVG 1.0 Recommendation.

The `values` attribute of `feColorMatrix` contains a list of numbers. When the `type` attribute has a value of `matrix`, the `values` attribute contains a list of 20 matrix values. When `type` is `saturate`, the `values` attribute contains a single number in the range `0` to `1.0`. When `type` is `hueRotate`, `values` has a single number (in degrees). When `type` has the value `luminanceToAlpha`, the `values` attribute is inapplicable.

The feComponentTransfer Filter Primitive

Sometimes when you're adjusting the appearance of an image, or part of an image, you may want to adjust values from one or more of the red, green, blue, or alpha components of the image. The `feComponentTransfer` filter primitive can provide such selective changes by remapping the red, green, blue, and alpha values for every pixel to which the filter of which it forms part is applied. An `feComponentTransfer` element has nested within it elements that, respectively, act on red, green, blue, and alpha: `feFuncR`, `feFuncG`, `feFuncB`, and `feFuncA`. The combined effect of the latter four filter primitives controls the overall remapping of values.

The `feComponentTransfer` filter primitive can be used to provide functionality such as brightness adjustment, contrast adjustment, and color balance.

The `type` attribute of `feComponentTransfer` specifies the type of component transfer function to be applied:

- `identity`—$C' = C$.
- `table`—A function is defined by applying linear interpolation to the values contained in the `tableValues` attribute.
- `discrete`—A function is defined by applying a step function based on the values in the `tableValues` attribute.
- `linear`—A function defined by $C' = slope * C + intercept$.
- `gamma`—A function defined by $C' = amplitude * pow(C, exponent) + offset$.

Full details of the functions are provided in the SVG 1.0 Recommendation.

The `tableValues` attribute contains values to be used by the component transfer functions. When the `type` attribute has a value of `linear`, the `slope` attribute contains the value of *slope*, and the `intercept` attribute contains the value of *intercept*. When the `type` attribute has a value of `gamma`, the `amplitude`, `exponent`, and `offset` attributes, respectively, contain the values of *amplitude*, *exponent,* and *offset*.

The feComposite Filter Primitive

When a filter is being constructed using multiple filter primitives, the result can be rendered with one result in front of the other using the SVG painter's model (using the `feMerge` element), or the result of individual filter primitives can be mathematically manipulated to alter the final result of the filter (using the `feComposite` filter primitive).

The `feComposite` filter primitive takes two inputs. The input images are specified using the `in` and `in2` attributes. The `operator` attribute of `feComposite` defines the mathematical operation to be applied and may take any of the following values:

- `over`—The input defined by the `in` attribute is rendered in front of the input defined by the `in2` attribute.

- `in`—The input defined by the `in` attribute is rendered only where it is included within the area of the image defined by the `in2` attribute.

- `atop`—The input defined by the `in` attribute is rendered within the area of the image defined by the `in2` attribute. The rest of the area is covered by the image that is the input to `in2`.

- `out`—Only the part of the input specified in the `in` attribute that is outside the image specified by the `in2` attribute is rendered.

- `xor`—Both the part of the `in` input that lies outside the `in2` image and the part of the `in2` image that lies outside the `in` input are rendered.

In addition, a component-wise arithmetic operation can be applied (with the result clamped to the range `0` to `1.0`). Being able to apply this operation can be useful for combining the output from `feDiffuseLighting` and `feSpecularLighting` with texture data.

When the `operator` attribute has a value of `arithmetic`, you can use the `k1`, `k2`, `k3`, and `k4` attributes.

The feConvolveMatrix Filter Primitive

You can use the `feConvolveMatrix` filter primitive to apply a convolution matrix transformation to an image. It combines pixels within the image with neighboring pixels. The `feConvolveMatrix` element can be used to achieve blurring, sharpening, embossing, and beveling.

Details of `feConvolveMatrix` are beyond the scope of this chapter.

10

The feDistantLight Filter Primitive

The feDistantLight filter primitive is one of three light source filter primitives, the others being fePointLight and feSpotLight. The feDistantLight element is intended to resemble a distant light source.

The value of the azimuth attribute of the feDistantLight element is an angle expressed in the plane of the SVG canvas. The value of the elevation attribute is an angle in the YZ plane, that is, at right angles to the SVG canvas. The default for both attributes is 0, if the attribute is not specified.

Listing 10.2 shows an example using the feDistantLight filter primitive.

LISTING 10.2   DistantLight.svg—Using feDistantLight

```
<?xml version="1.0" standalone="no"?>
<!DOCTYPE svg PUBLIC "-//W3C//DTD SVG 20010904//EN"
"http://www.w3.org/TR/2001/REC-SVG-20010904/DTD/svg10.dtd">
<svg width="" height="" xmlns:xlink="http://www.w3.org/1999/xlink">
<defs>

<filter id="distLight1" filterUnits="objectBoundingBox"
 x="-10%" y="-10%" width="120%" height="120%">
<feGaussianBlur in="SourceGraphic" stdDeviation="3" result="blur" />
<feSpecularLighting in="blur" surfaceScale="30" specularConstant="0.75"
 specularComponent="20" lighting-color="#00FF00" result="specOut">
<feDistantLight azimuth="45" elevation="45"/>
</feSpecularLighting>
<feComposite in="specOut" in2="SourceAlpha" operator="in" result="specOut2"/>
<feComposite in="SourceGraphic" in2="specOut2" operator="arithmetic" k1="0"
 k2="1" k3="1" k4="0" />
</filter>

<filter id="distLight2" filterUnits="objectBoundingBox"
 x="-10%" y="-10%" width="120%" height="120%">
<feGaussianBlur in="SourceGraphic" stdDeviation="3" result="blur" />
<feSpecularLighting in="blur" surfaceScale="30" specularConstant="0.75"
 specularComponent="20" lighting-color="#00FF00" result="specOut">
<feDistantLight azimuth="45" elevation="270"/>
</feSpecularLighting>
<feComposite in="specOut" in2="SourceAlpha" operator="in" result="specOut2"/>
<feComposite in="SourceGraphic" in2="specOut2" operator="arithmetic" k1="0"
 k2="1" k3="1" k4="0" />
</filter>
```

LISTING 10.2   Continued

```
</defs>
<g id="myGraphic" filter="url(#distLight1)" transform="scale(0.8)">
<ellipse cx="220px" cy="100px" rx="200px" ry="90px" fill="none" stroke="red"
stroke-width="5"/>
<ellipse cx="220px" cy="100px" rx="140px" ry="70px" fill="red" stroke="none"/>
</g>
<g id="myGraphic" filter="url(#distLight2)" transform="scale(0.8)">
<ellipse cx="640px" cy="100px" rx="200px" ry="90px" fill="none" stroke="red"
stroke-width="5"/>
<ellipse cx="640px" cy="100px" rx="140px" ry="70px" fill="red" stroke="none"/>
</g>

</svg>
```

Figure 10.2 shows the onscreen appearance when Listing 10.2 is run. When the elevation attribute of the feDistantLight attribute has a value of 45 (degrees), the front of the graphic is lit and is mostly yellow. When the elevation attribute has a value of 270, the flat front surface of the graphic is unlit, so the native color of the graphic, red, dominates.

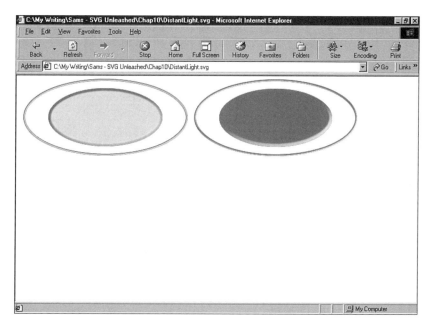

FIGURE 10.2   Effect of feDistantLight with two values for the elevation attribute.

The feDiffuseLighting Filter Primitive

The feDiffuseLighting filter primitive can be used to suggest a three-dimensional shape. The onscreen rendering depends on the type of incident light. You can use the feDiffuseLighting filter primitive with nested feDistantLight, fePointLight, and feSpotLight elements.

The feDisplacementMap Filter Primitive

The feDisplacementMap filter is used to create artistic effects where an image is moved (displaced) relative to its original position.

The feDisplacementMap filter primitive makes use of two images, defined by the values of its in and in2 attributes. The pixel values of the image defined by in2 are used to displace pixels from the image defined by the in attribute.

The value of the scale attribute is used to define the displacement scale factor. The values of the xChannelSelector and yChannelSelector attributes, which each may take the values of R, G, B, and A, indicate which channel from the in2 image to use in displacement in X-direction and Y-direction, respectively.

The feFlood Filter Primitive

The color of light falling on an object determines its appearance. Photographers use colored gels (acetate sheets) to manipulate the color of light falling on an object. The feFlood filter primitive produces a corresponding effect onscreen.

The feFlood filter primitive provides a rectangle filled with a color defined by the element's flood-color and flood-opacity attributes. The feFlood element takes x, y, width, and height attributes, which define the position and dimensions of the colored rectangle.

The feGaussianBlur Filter Primitive

The feGaussianBlur filter primitive can be used to create that perennial favorite, the drop shadow.

Listing 10.3 demonstrates the variation in result produced by the feGaussianBlur filter primitive with variation in opacity of the input graphic. When a source graphic is fully opaque, the alpha value (the opacity) is equal to 1.0. The closer to transparent that the input graphic is, the fainter the result of applying the feGaussianBlur filter primitive.

LISTING 10.3   OpacityTest.svg—The feGaussianBlur Filter Primitive and Opacity of the Source Graphic

```
<?xml version="1.0" standalone="no"?>
<!DOCTYPE svg PUBLIC "-//W3C//DTD SVG 20010904//EN"
"http://www.w3.org/TR/2001/REC-SVG-20010904/DTD/svg10.dtd">
<svg width="" height="">
```

LISTING 10.3   Continued

```
<defs>
<filter id="OpacityTest">
<feGaussianBlur in="SourceAlpha" stdDeviation="5" />
</filter>
</defs>
<rect x="20" y="20" width="300" height="100" rx="20" ry="20"
 style="filter:url(#OpacityTest); fill:red; opacity:1;"/>
<rect x="20" y="130" width="300" height="100" rx="20" ry="20"
 style="filter:url(#OpacityTest); fill:red; opacity:0.7;"/>
<rect x="20" y="240" width="300" height="100" rx="20" ry="20"
 style="filter:url(#OpacityTest); fill:red; opacity:0.4;"/>
<rect x="20" y="350" width="300" height="100" rx="20" ry="20"
 style="filter:url(#OpacityTest); fill:red; opacity:0.1;"/>
</svg>
```

Figure 10.3 shows the onscreen appearance when Listing 10.3 is run.

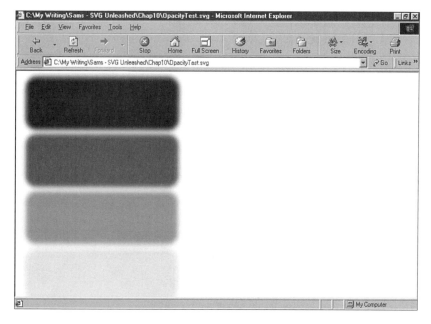

FIGURE 10.3   Effect of feGaussianBlur with source graphics of different opacity.

A drop shadow is created later in this chapter in Listing 10.4.

The feImage Filter Primitive

The feImage filter primitive allows an external image to be referenced to provide input to a filter. By allowing access to an external image, you can use a bitmap image as the input to an SVG filter.

The feImage filter primitive references an image that is external to the filter element. The referenced image may be external to the document that contains the filter element or may be a part of its SVG content.

You can use the xlink:href attribute to reference an external image file, such as SVG, PNG, or JPEG. The referenced external file is rendered as if it were referenced using the image element. If the image is not external, it is rendered as if it were a use element. For both scenarios, the primitiveUnits attribute of the feImage element determines the user coordinate system to be applied.

The feMerge Filter Primitive

In all but the simplest filters, you will want to merge the output from more than one filter primitive. For example, to create an effect of text with an offset drop shadow, you would want to merge the text with the offset drop shadow. The feMerge filter primitive allows intermediate results of an SVG filter to be merged.

The feMerge filter primitive allows the result from other filter primitives to be merged into one image. The images to be merged are referenced by feMergeNode elements, which are nested within the feMerge element.

An feMerge element may have two or more feMergeNode elements nested within it. Each feMergeNode element may possess an in attribute, the value of which will often match the value of a result attribute on another filter primitive.

Listing 10.4 shows an example of using feMerge to create a drop shadow.

LISTING 10.4   Merge.svg—An feMerge Example

```
<?xml version="1.0" standalone="no"?>
<!DOCTYPE svg PUBLIC "-//W3C//DTD SVG 20010904//EN"
"http://www.w3.org/TR/2001/REC-SVG-20010904/DTD/svg10.dtd">
<svg width="" height="">
<defs>
<filter id="dropShadow" x="0%" y="0%" height="100%">
<feGaussianBlur in="SourceAlpha" stdDeviation="3" />
<feOffset dx="4px" dy="4px" result="offsetBlur" />
<feMerge>
 <feMergeNode in="offsetBlur"/>
 <feMergeNode in="SourceGraphic"/>
</feMerge>
```

LISTING 10.4   Continued

```
</filter>
</defs>
<text x="40px" y="80px"
 style="font-size:48; fill:red; stroke:none; font-family:Arial, sans-serif;
  filter:url(#dropShadow);">
SVG Unleashed!
</text>

</svg>
```

Figure 10.4 shows the zoomed onscreen appearance when Listing 10.4 is run. Notice that the bottom of the drop shadow is very tightly clipped to the text size. We get this result because we have not increased the size of the filter region beyond the default, which is to limit the filter to 100% of the height and width of the SVG object to which the filter is applied.

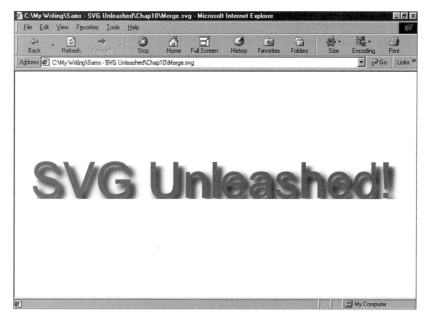

FIGURE 10.4   Applying feMerge without enlarging the filter region.

To avoid undesirable straight edges on some filters, you need to adjust the values of the x, y, width, and/or height attributes of the filter element. Listing 10.5 shows an enlarged filter region, achieved by modifying the height attribute of the filter element.

LISTING 10.5   Merge02.svg—Adjusting the Filter Region Size

```
<?xml version="1.0" standalone="no"?>
<!DOCTYPE svg PUBLIC "-//W3C//DTD SVG 20010904//EN"
"http://www.w3.org/TR/2001/REC-SVG-20010904/DTD/svg10.dtd">
<svg width="" height="">
<defs>
<filter id="dropShadow" x="0%" y="-10%" height="140%">
<feGaussianBlur in="SourceAlpha" stdDeviation="3" />
<feOffset dx="4px" dy="4px" result="offsetBlur" />
<feMerge>
 <feMergeNode in="offsetBlur"/>
 <feMergeNode in="SourceGraphic"/>
</feMerge>
</filter>
</defs>
<text x="40px" y="80px"
 style="font-size:48; fill:red; stroke:none;
 font-family:Arial, sans-serif;
  filter:url(#dropShadow);">
SVG Unleashed!
</text>

</svg>
```

Figure 10.5 shows the zoomed onscreen appearance when Listing 10.5 is run. Notice that the bottom of the drop shadow now extends well below the text size. This improvement occurs because we have increased the height of the filter region to 140%. The increase in size that is needed will vary according to, for example, the displacement applied using feOffset and the stdDeviation attribute value of the feGaussianBlur filter primitive.

The feMorphology Filter Primitive

The feMorphology filter primitive allows you to fatten or thin artwork. The operator attribute of feMorphology may take values of dilate (which fattens) or erode (which thins).

The radius attribute of feMorphology may take one or two values. If it takes one value, the same value is applied in the X and Y directions. If two values are supplied in the radius attribute, the first is applied to the X direction and the second to the Y direction.

Listing 10.6 shows an example using both erode and dilate.

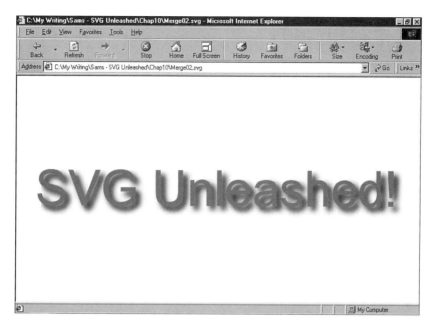

FIGURE 10.5   Applying feMerge with appropriate enlargement of the filter region.

LISTING 10.6   Morphology.svg—An feMorphology Example

```
<?xml version="1.0" standalone="no"?>
<!DOCTYPE svg PUBLIC "-//W3C//DTD SVG 20010904//EN"
"http://www.w3.org/TR/2001/REC-SVG-20010904/DTD/svg10.dtd">
<svg width="" height="">
<defs>
<filter id="morph1" x="0" y="0" width="100%" height="100%">
<feMorphology in="SourceGraphic" operator="erode" radius="1" />
</filter>
<filter id="morph2" x="0" y="0" width="100%" height="100%">
<feMorphology in="SourceGraphic" operator="dilate" radius="1" />
</filter>
</defs>
<g style="font-size:48; fill:red; stroke:none;
 font-family:Arial, sans-serif;">
<text x="40px" y="40px" fill="red">
SVG Unleashed!
</text>
<text x="40px" y="90px" filter="url(#morph1)">
SVG Unleashed!
</text>
```

10

LISTING 10.6   Continued

```
<text x="40px" y="140px" filter="url(#morph2)">
SVG Unleashed!
</text>
</g>
</svg>
```

Figure 10.6 shows the onscreen appearance when Listing 10.6 is run. The top piece of text is normal. The middle piece of text has the morph1 filter applied to it, which includes an feMorphology filter primitive with the operator attribute having a value of erode. The bottom piece of text has the morph2 filter applied, which includes an feMorphology filter primitive with the operator attribute having a value of dilate. On the bottom text, notice that there are straight line cutoffs because the x, y, width, and height attributes of the morph2 filter element weren't adjusted, so the dilated text overflowed the filter area.

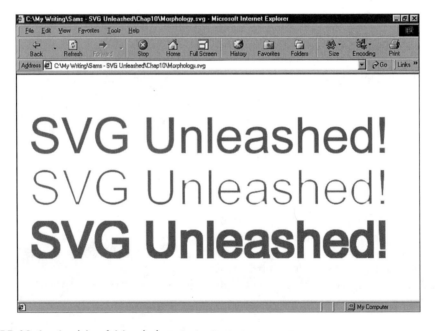

FIGURE 10.6   Applying feMorphology to text.

> **CAUTION**
>
> Be careful when you use the operator attribute with a value of erode. If you set the value for the radius attribute too high, the object to which the feMorphology is applied won't render onscreen because it has been totally eroded.

The feOffset Filter Primitive

When creating effects such as a drop shadow, you will typically want to offset the drop shadow from the original text or shape by a defined amount. The feOffset filter primitive is used to define the offset image.

The feOffset filter primitive displaces an input image. The input image is defined by the in attribute. The displacement is defined by the dx and dy attributes of feOffset.

The feOffset filter primitive was used in Listing 10.5.

The fePointLight Filter Primitive

The fePointLight filter primitive is one of three light source filter primitives, the others being feDistantLight and feSpotLight. The fePointLight filter primitive is intended to represent a point light source.

The position of the point light is expressed using x, y, and z attributes. The x attribute holds the value in the horizontal direction in the SVG canvas. If the value of the x attribute is greater than the X coordinate of the right side of an object, the light shines from the right. If the value of x is less than the X coordinate of the left side of the object, the light shines from the left. The y attribute holds the value of the coordinate of the light in the vertical direction. If the value of y is greater than the bottom of the object, the light shines from below. If y is less (less positive or more negative) than the top of the object, the light shines from above. The z attribute holds the value of the Z coordinate of the light, that is, in the plane at right angles to the SVG canvas. If z is positive, the light shines from in front of the SVG canvas.

Listing 10.7 shows a beveled graphic created using four slightly different filters. Each of the four graphics is lit from four different directions. The lighting direction is modified by adjusting the values of the x and y attributes of the fePointLight element contained within each of the filters.

LISTING 10.7   PointLight.svg—Modifying Lighting Direction

```
<?xml version="1.0" standalone="no"?>
<!DOCTYPE svg PUBLIC "-//W3C//DTD SVG 20010904//EN"
"http://www.w3.org/TR/2001/REC-SVG-20010904/DTD/svg10.dtd">
<svg width="" height="" xmlns:xlink="http://www.w3.org/1999/xlink">
<defs>

<filter id="fromLeftAbove" filterUnits="objectBoundingBox"
 x="-10%" y="-10%" width="120%" height="120%">
<feGaussianBlur in="SourceGraphic" stdDeviation="1" result="blur" />
<feSpecularLighting in="blur" surfaceScale="10" specularConstant="0.75"
 specularComponent="20" lighting-color="#00FF00" result="specOut">
<fePointLight x="-5000" y="-5000" z="200"/>
</feSpecularLighting>
```

LISTING 10.7   Continued

```
<feComposite in="specOut" in2="SourceAlpha" operator="in" result="specOut2"/>
<feComposite in="SourceGraphic" in2="specOut2" operator="arithmetic" k1="0"
 k2="1" k3="1" k4="0" result="litPaint"/>
</filter>
<filter id="fromLeftBelow" filterUnits="objectBoundingBox"
 x="-10%" y="-10%" width="120%" height="120%">
<feGaussianBlur in="SourceGraphic" stdDeviation="1" result="blur" />
<feSpecularLighting in="blur" surfaceScale="10" specularConstant="0.75"
 specularComponent="20" lighting-color="#00FF00" result="specOut">
<fePointLight x="-5000" y="5000" z="200"/>
</feSpecularLighting>
<feComposite in="specOut" in2="SourceAlpha" operator="in" result="specOut2"/>
<feComposite in="SourceGraphic" in2="specOut2" operator="arithmetic" k1="0"
 k2="1" k3="1" k4="0" result="litPaint"/>
</filter>
<filter id="fromRightAbove" filterUnits="objectBoundingBox"
 x="-10%" y="-10%" width="120%" height="120%">
<feGaussianBlur in="SourceGraphic" stdDeviation="1" result="blur" />
<feSpecularLighting in="blur" surfaceScale="10" specularConstant="0.75"
 specularComponent="20" lighting-color="#00FF00" result="specOut">
<fePointLight x="5000" y="-5000" z="200"/>
</feSpecularLighting>
<feComposite in="specOut" in2="SourceAlpha" operator="in" result="specOut2"/>
<feComposite in="SourceGraphic" in2="specOut2" operator="arithmetic" k1="0"
 k2="1" k3="1" k4="0" result="litPaint"/>
</filter>
<filter id="fromRightBelow" filterUnits="objectBoundingBox"
 x="-10%" y="-10%" width="120%" height="120%">
<feGaussianBlur in="SourceGraphic" stdDeviation="1" result="blur" />
<feSpecularLighting in="blur" surfaceScale="10" specularConstant="0.75"
 specularComponent="20" lighting-color="#00FF00" result="specOut">
<fePointLight x="5000" y="5000" z="200"/>
</feSpecularLighting>
<feComposite in="specOut" in2="SourceAlpha" operator="in" result="specOut2"/>
<feComposite in="SourceGraphic" in2="specOut2" operator="arithmetic" k1="0"
 k2="1" k3="1" k4="0" result="litPaint"/>
</filter>
<g id="myGraphic" >
<ellipse cx="300px" cy="300px" rx="200px" ry="90px" fill="none" stroke="red"
stroke-width="5"/>
<ellipse cx="300px" cy="300px" rx="140px" ry="70px" fill="red" stroke="none"/>
</g>
```

LISTING 10.7 Continued

```
</defs>
<g transform="scale(0.8)">
<use xlink:href="#myGraphic" transform="translate(-80px, -200px)"
 filter="url(#fromLeftAbove)"/>
<use xlink:href="#myGraphic" transform="translate(-80px, 30px)"
filter="url(#fromLeftBelow)"/>
<use xlink:href="#myGraphic" transform="translate(400px, -200px)"
filter="url(#fromRightAbove)"/>
<use xlink:href="#myGraphic" transform="translate(400px, 30px)"
filter="url(#fromRightBelow)"/>
</g>
</svg>
```

Figure 10.7 shows the onscreen appearance when Listing 10.7 is run. The color transitions are best seen onscreen. The top-left graphic is lit from the top left; the bottom left graphic, from the bottom left; and so on. Perhaps the easiest place on the graphic to spot the direction of the light source is on the rim of the inner graphic. In the top-left graphic, for example, you will be able to see onscreen that it is yellow around the top left because the point light is coming from that direction. The basic color of the graphic is red, but where the green point light impacts on it, the visual appearance is close to yellow, #FFFF00, because the red and green interact. On the parts of the graphic shaded from the point light, the red color dominates.

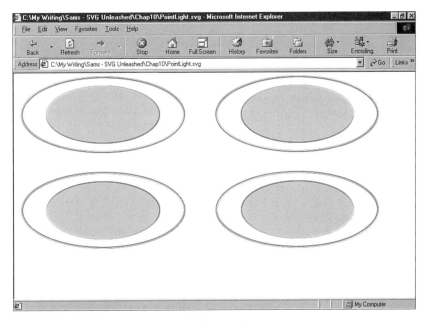

FIGURE 10.7 Effect of fePointLight from different directions.

10

The feSpecularLighting Filter Primitive

Specular lighting is the light that is reflected from a highlight on a shape. Light reflected from nonhighlight regions of a shape is diffuse lighting.

Listing 10.8 shows how you can create a couple of types of bevels on a graphic shape.

LISTING 10.8   SpecularLighting.svg—Using feSpecularLighting to Create a Bevel

```
<?xml version="1.0" standalone="no"?>
<!DOCTYPE svg PUBLIC "-//W3C//DTD SVG 20010904//EN"
"http://www.w3.org/TR/2001/REC-SVG-20010904/DTD/svg10.dtd">
<svg width="" height="">
<defs>
<filter id="myBevel" filterUnits="objectBoundingBox"
 x="-10%" y="-10%" width="120%" height="120%">
<feGaussianBlur in="SourceGraphic" stdDeviation="5" result="blur" />
<feSpecularLighting in="blur" surfaceScale="5" specularConstant="0.75"
 specularComponent="20" lighting-color="#00FF00" >
<fePointLight x="-5000" y="-10000" z="200"/>
</feSpecularLighting>
</filter>
<filter id="myBigBevel" filterUnits="objectBoundingBox"
 x="-10%" y="-10%" width="120%" height="120%">
<feGaussianBlur in="SourceGraphic" stdDeviation="3" result="blur" />
<feSpecularLighting in="blur" surfaceScale="15" specularConstant="0.75"
 specularComponent="20" lighting-color="#00FF00" >
<fePointLight x="-5000" y="-10000" z="200"/>
</feSpecularLighting>
</filter>
<g id="myGraphic" filter="url(#myBevel)">
<ellipse cx="300px" cy="300px" rx="200px" ry="90px"
 fill="none" stroke="red" stroke-width="5"/>
<ellipse cx="300px" cy="300px" rx="140px"
 ry="70px" fill="red" stroke="none"/>
</g>
</defs>
<use xlink:href="#myGraphic" transform="translate(-80px, -200px)"/>
<use xlink:href="#myGraphic"
 transform="translate(-80px, 30px)" filter="url(#myBigBevel)"/>
</svg>
```

Figure 10.8 shows the onscreen appearance when Listing 10.8 is run. The upper graphic has a surfaceScale attribute value of 5. The lower graphic has a surfaceScale attribute value of 15. Increasing the value of surfaceScale gives a more defined bevel. Decreasing the value of the stdDeviation attribute on the input feGaussianBlur gives a sharper edge.

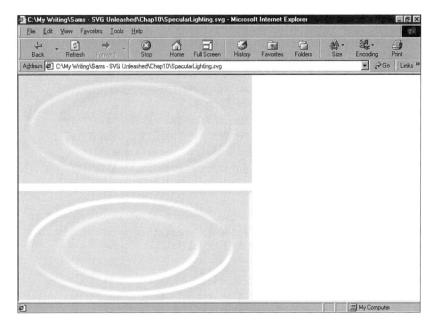

FIGURE 10.8   Graphics created using the feSpecularLighting filter primitive.

The feSpotLight Filter Primitive

A spotlight, in real life, produces a fairly linear beam of light. The SVG feSpotlight filter primitive is intended to provide an onscreen approximation of a spotlight. The feSpotLight filter primitive is one of three light source filter primitives, the others being feDistantLight and fePointLight.

The x, y, and z attributes of feSpotLight indicate the position of the spotlight in the x-, y-, and z-axes. The pointsAtX, pointsAtY, and pointsAtZ attributes indicate the X, Y, and Z coordinates of the point at which the spotlight is pointing towards. You use the specularExponent attribute to control the focus of the spotlight, and you can use the limitingConeAngle attribute to limit the area onto which the spotlight shines.

Listing 10.9 shows the effect of changing the value of the z attribute on the area covered by the feSpotLight primitive, with a defined value for limitingConeAngle. The more positive the value of z—that is, the further from the SVG canvas—the more the light spreads.

LISTING 10.9   SpotLight01.svg—Effect of Altering z on the Area Covered by the Spotlight

```
<?xml version="1.0" standalone="no"?>
<!DOCTYPE svg PUBLIC "-//W3C//DTD SVG 20010904//EN"
"http://www.w3.org/TR/2001/REC-SVG-20010904/DTD/svg10.dtd">
<svg width="" height="" xmlns:xlink="http://www.w3.org/1999/xlink">
<defs>

<filter id="spotLight1" filterUnits="objectBoundingBox"
 x="-10%" y="-10%" width="120%" height="120%">
<feGaussianBlur in="SourceGraphic" stdDeviation="3" result="blur" />
<feSpecularLighting in="blur" surfaceScale="30" specularConstant="0.75"
 specularComponent="20" lighting-color="#0000FF" result="specOut">
<feSpotLight x="220" y="100" z="100" pointsAtX="220" pointsAtY="100" pointsAtZ="0"
 limitingConeAngle="10"/>
</feSpecularLighting>
<feComposite in="specOut" in2="SourceAlpha" operator="in" result="specOut2"/>
<feComposite in="SourceGraphic" in2="specOut2" operator="arithmetic" k1="0"
 k2="1" k3="1" k4="0" />
</filter>

<filter id="spotLight2" filterUnits="objectBoundingBox"
 x="-10%" y="-10%" width="120%" height="120%">
<feGaussianBlur in="SourceGraphic" stdDeviation="3" result="blur" />
<feSpecularLighting in="blur" surfaceScale="30" specularConstant="0.75"
 specularComponent="20" lighting-color="#0000FF" result="specOut">
<feSpotLight x="640" y="100" z="250" pointsAtX="640" pointsAtY="100"
 pointsAtZ="0"
 limitingConeAngle="10"/>
</feSpecularLighting>
<feComposite in="specOut" in2="SourceAlpha" operator="in" result="specOut2"/>
<feComposite in="SourceGraphic" in2="specOut2" operator="arithmetic" k1="0"
 k2="1" k3="1" k4="0" />
</filter>

<filter id="spotLight3" filterUnits="objectBoundingBox"
 x="-10%" y="-10%" width="120%" height="120%">
<feGaussianBlur in="SourceGraphic" stdDeviation="3" result="blur" />
<feSpecularLighting in="blur" surfaceScale="30" specularConstant="0.75"
 specularComponent="20" lighting-color="#0000FF" result="specOut">
<feSpotLight x="220" y="400" z="500" pointsAtX="220" pointsAtY="400"
 pointsAtZ="0" limitingConeAngle="10"/>
```

LISTING 10.9   Continued

```
</feSpecularLighting>
<feComposite in="specOut" in2="SourceAlpha" operator="in" result="specOut2"/>
<feComposite in="SourceGraphic" in2="specOut2" operator="arithmetic" k1="0"
 k2="1" k3="1" k4="0" />
</filter>
</defs>
<g transform="scale(0.8)">
<g id="myGraphic1" filter="url(#spotLight1)">
<ellipse cx="220px" cy="100px" rx="200px" ry="90px" fill="none"
 stroke="#CCCCCC" stroke-width="5"/>
<ellipse cx="220px" cy="100px" rx="140px" ry="70px" fill="#CCCCCC"
 stroke="none"/>
</g>
<g id="myGraphic2" filter="url(#spotLight2)">
<ellipse cx="640px" cy="100px" rx="200px" ry="90px" fill="none"
 stroke="#CCCCCC"
stroke-width="5"/>
<ellipse cx="640px" cy="100px" rx="140px" ry="70px" fill="#CCCCCC"
 stroke="none"/>
</g>
<g id="myGraphic3" filter="url(#spotLight3)">
<ellipse cx="220px" cy="400px" rx="200px" ry="90px" fill="none"
 stroke="#CCCCCC" stroke-width="5"/>
<ellipse cx="220px" cy="400px" rx="140px" ry="70px" fill="#CCCCCC"
 stroke="none"/>
</g>
</g>
</svg>
```

Figure 10.9 shows the onscreen appearance when Listing 10.9 is run. In the center of the top-left graphic, the blue circle is very small, when z is 100. In the center of the top-right graphic, the blue circle is larger because z is 250. In the center of the bottom-left graphic, the circle is again larger, with z now being 500. The pools of light are circular because each spotlight is positioned exactly above the center of the ellipses. If the light is moved but still has the same values for pointsAtX, pointsAtY, and pointsAtZ, the pool of light becomes more elliptical the further the light's position is from the point to which it is pointing.

10

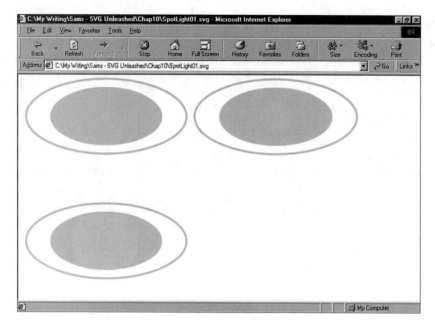

FIGURE 10.9   Using a defined limitingConeAngle from different lighting distances.

The feTile Filter Primitive

The feTile filter primitive fills a target rectangle with a repeated, tiled pattern of an input image. The x, y, width, and height attributes of the feTile element define the position and size of the target rectangle. The input image is defined using the in attribute.

Listing 10.10 shows a short example using the feTile filter primitive.

LISTING 10.10   Tile.svg—Creating a Pattern of Circles Using feTile

```
<?xml version="1.0" standalone="no"?>
<!DOCTYPE svg PUBLIC "-//W3C//DTD SVG 20010904//EN"
"http://www.w3.org/TR/2001/REC-SVG-20010904/DTD/svg10.dtd">
<svg width="" height="">
<defs>
<circle id="myCircle" cx="10" cy="10" r="7"
 style="fill:green; stroke:red;"/>
<filter id="myTile" x="0" y="0" width="100%" height="100%">
<feImage xlink:href="#myCircle" result="tileIn" width="20" height="20" />
<feTile in="tileIn" result="tileOut"  x="0" y="0" width="200" height="150"/>
<feBlend in="tileOut" in2="SourceGraphic" mode="screen" />
</filter>
</defs>
```

LISTING 10.10   Continued

```
<rect x="0px" y="0px" width="200px" height="150px"
 filter="url(#myTile)" fill="#333333">
SVG Unleashed!
</rect>
</svg>
```

Figure 10.10 shows the zoomed and panned appearance when Listing 10.10 is run.

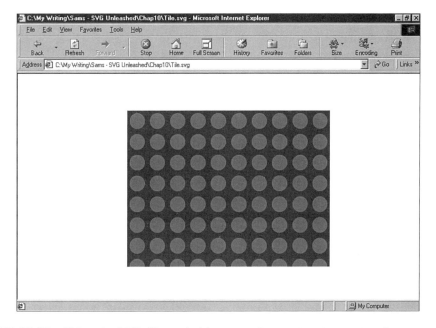

FIGURE 10.10   Using the feTile filter primitive to apply a pattern to a rectangle.

The feTurbulence Filter Primitive

You can use the feTurbulence filter to create effects that look like clouds or like marble.

The type attribute of feTurbulence takes two values: fractalNoise or turbulence. The stitchTiles attribute may take values of stitch and noStitch, the former indicating that some smoothing is applied to the edges of tiles that contain turbulence. The seed attribute contains a starting number for the pseudo-random number generator. The numOctaves attribute contains the parameter for the noise function, with a default value of 1. The value of the baseFrequency attribute may contain one or two values. If there is one value, it is the base frequency parameter to the noise function in both the X and Y directions. If two values are in the baseFrequency attribute, the first value defines the base frequency in the X direction, and the second value defines the base frequency in the Y direction.

10

Listing 10.11 demonstrates a few appearances produced by the `feTurbulence` filter primitive.

LISTING 10.11 TurbulenceExamples.svg—Some feTurbulence Examples

```
<?xml version="1.0" standalone="no"?>
<!DOCTYPE svg PUBLIC "-//W3C//DTD SVG 20010904//EN"
"http://www.w3.org/TR/2001/REC-SVG-20010904/DTD/svg10.dtd">
<svg width="" height="">
<defs>
<filter id="myTurb1" x="0" y="0" width="100%" height="100%">
<feTurbulence seed="3" type="turbulence" baseFrequency="0.01" numOctaves="2" />
</filter>
<filter id="myTurb2" x="0" y="0" width="100%" height="100%">
<feTurbulence seed="1" type="turbulence" baseFrequency="0.1" numOctaves="2" />
</filter>
<filter id="myTurb3" x="0" y="0" width="100%" height="100%">
<feTurbulence seed="4" type="turbulence" baseFrequency="0.002" numOctaves="3" />
</filter>
<filter id="myTurb4" x="0" y="0" width="100%" height="100%">
<feTurbulence seed="9" type="fractalNoise" baseFrequency="0.1" numOctaves="3" />
</filter>
<filter id="myTurb5" x="0" y="0" width="100%" height="100%">
<feTurbulence seed="1" type="fractalNoise" baseFrequency="0.01" numOctaves="4" />
</filter>
<filter id="myTurb6" x="0" y="0" width="100%" height="100%">
<feTurbulence seed="2" type="fractalNoise" baseFrequency="0.005" numOctaves="2" />
</filter>
</defs>
<g transform="scale(0.8)">
<rect x="0px" y="0px" width="200px" height="150px"
 filter="url(#myTurb1)" fill="#333333"/>
<rect x="300px" y="0px" width="200px" height="150px"
 filter="url(#myTurb2)" fill="#333333"/>
<rect x="600px" y="0px" width="200px" height="150px"
 filter="url(#myTurb3)" fill="#333333"/>
<rect x="0px" y="200px" width="200px" height="150px"
 filter="url(#myTurb4)" fill="#333333"/>
<rect x="300px" y="200px" width="200px" height="150px"
 filter="url(#myTurb5)" fill="#333333"/>
 <rect x="600px" y="200px" width="200px" height="150px"
 filter="url(#myTurb6)" fill="#333333"/>
</g>
</svg>
```

Figure 10.11 shows the onscreen appearance when Listing 10.11 is run. You can see six different appearances produced by manipulating the values of the attributes of the feTurbulence filter primitive. The three images in the top row of Figure 10.11 are produced by setting the type attribute on the feTurbulence filter primitive to a value of turbulence. The images in the bottom row have the type attribute with value of fractalNoise. Notice that within a row, the values of the baseFrequency, seed, and numOctaves attributes vary.

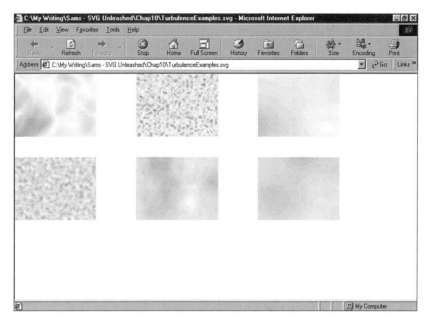

FIGURE 10.11   Six sample appearances using the feTurbulence filter primitive.

The SVG DOM Filter Interfaces

In this section, we will describe the interfaces of the SVG DOM that relate to filters. Many of the DOM interfaces correspond one to one with either the filter element or filter primitive elements.

The SVGFilterElement Object

The SVGFilterElement object can be viewed as the SVG DOM representation of the SVG filter element.

The SVGFilterElement object has the properties and methods of the SVGElement object, the SVGURIReference object, the SVGLangSpace object, the SVGExternalResourcesRequired object, the SVGStylable object, and the SVGUnitTypes object.

In addition, the SVGFilterElement object has the following properties:

- filterUnits—of type SVGAnimatedEnumeration

- primitiveUnits—of type SVGAnimatedEnumeration

- x—of type SVGAnimatedLength

- y—of type SVGAnimatedLength

- width—of type SVGAnimatedLength

- height—of type SVGAnimatedLength

- filterResX—of type SVGAnimatedInteger

- filterResY—of type SVGAnimatedInteger

The SVGFilterElement object has the following method:

- setFilterRes(*filterResX*, *filterResY*)—The method returns a value of type void. The *filterResX* and *filterResY* arguments are both of type unsigned long.

As well as the SVGFilterElement object, we will need to understand the various SVG DOM objects that relate to the SVG filter primitive elements. First, let's look at the SVGFilterPrimitiveStandardAttributes object.

The SVGFilterPrimitiveStandardAttributes Object

The SVGFilterPrimitiveStandardAttributes object is the SVG DOM representation of the attributes that are common to the SVG filter primitive elements: feBlend, feColorMatrix, feComponentTransfer, feComposite, feConvolveMatrix, feDiffuseLighting, feDisplacementMap, feDistantLight, feFlood, feGaussianBlur, feImage, feMerge, feMorphology, feOffset, fePointLight, feSpecularLighting, feSpotLight, feTile, and feTurbulence. Typically, the SVG DOM objects representing filter primitive elements inherit the properties and methods of the SVGFilterPrimitiveStandardAttributes object.

The SVGFilterPrimitiveStandardAttributes object has the following properties:

- x—of type SVGAnimatedLength

- y—of type SVGAnimatedLength

- width—of type SVGAnimatedLength

- height—of type SVGAnimatedLength

- result—of type SVGAnimatedString

The SVGFilterPrimitiveStandardAttributes object has no methods specific to it.

The SVG DOM Objects for Filter Primitives

In this section, we will describe the SVG DOM object for each of the SVG filter primitive elements.

The SVGFEBlendElement Object

The SVGFEBlendElement object is the SVG DOM representation of the feBlend filter primitive.

The SVGFEBlendElement object has the properties and methods of the SVGElement object and the SVGFilterPrimitiveStandardAttributes object.

In addition, the SVGFEBlendElement object has the following constants:

- SVGFEBlendElement.SVG_FEBLEND_MODE_UNKNOWN—The constant is of type short and has a value of 0.

- SVGFEBlendElement.SVG_FEBLEND_MODE_NORMAL—The constant is of type short and has a value of 1.

- SVGFEBlendElement.SVG_FEBLEND_MODE_MULTIPLY—The constant is of type short and has a value of 2.

- SVGFEBlendElement.SVG_FEBLEND_MODE_SCREEN—The constant is of type short and has a value of 3.

- SVGFEBlendElement.SVG_FEBLEND_MODE_DARKEN—The constant is of type short and has a value of 4.

- SVGFEBlendElement.SVG_FEBLEND_MODE_LIGHTEN—The constant is of type short and has a value of 5.

The SVGFEBlendElement object has the following properties:

- in1—of type SVGAnimatedString

- in2—of type SVGAnimatedString

- mode—of type SVGAnimatedEnumeration

The SVGFEBlendElement object has no methods specific to it.

The SVGFEColorMatrixElement Object

The SVGFEColorMatrixElement object is the SVG DOM representation of the feColorMatrix filter primitive.

The SVGFEColorMatrixElement object has the properties and methods of the SVGElement object and the SVGFilterPrimitiveStandardAttributes object.

10

The SVGFEColorMatrixElement object has the following associated constants:

- SVGFEColorMatrixElement.SVG_FECOLORMATRIX_TYPE_UNKNOWN—The constant is of type short and has a value of 0.

- SVGFEColorMatrixElement.SVG_FECOLORMATRIX_TYPE_MATRIX—The constant is of type short and has a value of 1.

- SVGFEColorMatrixElement.SVG_FECOLORMATRIX_TYPE_SATURATE—The constant is of type short and has a value of 2.

- SVGFEColorMatrixElement.SVG_FECOLORMATRIX_TYPE_HUEROTATE—The constant is of type short and has a value of 3.

- SVGFEColorMatrixElement.SVG_FECOLORMATRIX_TYPE_LUMINANCETOALPHA—The constant is of type short and has a value of 4.

In addition, the SVGFEColorMatrixElement object has the following properties:

- in1—of type SVGAnimatedString

- type—of type SVGAnimatedEnumeration

- values—of type SVGAnimatedNumberList

The SVGFEColorMatrixElement object has no methods specific to it.

The SVGFEComponentTransferElement Object

The SVGFEComponentTransferElement object is the SVG DOM representation of the feComponentTransfer filter primitive.

The SVGFEComponentTransferElement object has the properties and methods of the SVGElement object and the SVGFilterPrimitiveStandardAttributes object.

In addition, the SVGFEComponentTransferElement object has the following property:

- in1—of type SVGAnimatedString

The SVGFEComponentTransferElement object has no methods specific to it.

Several other objects in the SVG DOM are relevant to the feComponentTransfer element. They are listed in the following sections.

The SVGFEComponentTransferFunctionElement Object

The SVGFEComponentTransferFunctionElement object has the following constants associated with it:

- SVGFEComponentTransferFunctionElement.SVG_FECOMPONENTTRANSFER_TYPE_ UNKNOWN—The constant is of type short and has a value of 0.

- SVGFEComponentTransferFunctionElement.SVG_FECOMPONENTTRANSFER_TYPE_ IDENTITY—The constant is of type short and has a value of 1.

- SVGFEComponentTransferFunctionElement.SVG_FECOMPONENTTRANSFER_TYPE_TABLE— The constant is of type short and has a value of 2.

- SVGFEComponentTransferFunctionElement.SVG_FECOMPONENTTRANSFER_TYPE_ DISCRETE—The constant is of type short and has a value of 3.

- SVGFEComponentTransferFunctionElement.SVG_FECOMPONENTTRANSFER_TYPE_LINEAR— The constant is of type short and has a value of 4.

- SVGFEComponentTransferFunctionElement.SVG_FECOMPONENTTRANSFER_TYPE_GAMMA— The constant is of type short and has a value of 5.

In addition, the SVGFEComponentTransferFunctionElement object has the following properties:

- type—of type SVGAnimatedEnumeration

- tableValues—of type SVGAnimatedNumberList

- slope—of type SVGAnimatedNumber

- intercept—of type SVGAnimatedNumber

- amplitude—of type SVGAnimatedNumber

- exponent—of type SVGAnimatedNumber

- offset—of type SVGAnimatedNumber

The SVGFEComponentTransferFunctionElement object has no methods specific to it.

The SVGFEFuncAElement Object
The SVGFEFuncAElement object has all the properties and methods of the SVGFEComponentTransferFunctionElement object.

The SVGFEFuncBElement Object
The SVGFEFuncBElement object has all the properties and methods of the SVGFEComponentTransferFunctionElement object.

The SVGFEFuncGElement Object
The SVGFEFuncGElement object has all the properties and methods of the SVGFEComponentTransferFunctionElement object.

The SVGFEFuncRElement Object

The SVGFEFuncRElement object has all the properties and methods of the SVGFEComponentTransferFunctionElement object.

The SVGFECompositeElement Object

The SVGFECompositeElement object is the SVG DOM representation of the feComposite filter primitive.

The SVGFECompositeElement object has the properties and methods of the SVGElement object and the SVGFilterPrimitiveStandardAttributes object.

The SVGFECompositeElement object has the following constants associated with it:

- SVGFECompositeElement.SVG_FECOMPOSITE_OPERATOR_UNKNOWN—The constant is of type short and has a value of 0.

- SVGFECompositeElement.SVG_FECOMPOSITE_OPERATOR_OVER—The constant is of type short and has a value of 1.

- SVGFECompositeElement.SVG_FECOMPOSITE_OPERATOR_IN—The constant is of type short and has a value of 2.

- SVGFECompositeElement.SVG_FECOMPOSITE_OPERATOR_OUT—The constant is of type short and has a value of 3.

- SVGFECompositeElement.SVG_FECOMPOSITE_OPERATOR_ATOP—The constant is of type short and has a value of 4.

- SVGFECompositeElement.SVG_FECOMPOSITE_OPERATOR_XOR—The constant is of type short and has a value of 5.

- SVGFECompositeElement.SVG_FECOMPOSITE_OPERATOR_ARITHMETIC—The constant is of type short and has a value of 6.

The SVGFECompositeElement object has the following properties:

- in1—of type SVGAnimatedString

- in2—of type SVGAnimatedString

- operator—of type SVGAnimatedEnumeration

- k1—of type SVGAnimatedNumber

- k2—of type SVGAnimatedNumber

- k3—of type SVGAnimatedNumber

- k4—of type SVGAnimatedNumber

The SVGFECompositeElement object has no methods specific to it.

The SVGFEConvolveMatrixElement Object

The SVGFEConvolveMatrixElement object is the SVG DOM representation of the feConvolveMatrix filter primitive.

The SVGFEConvolveMatrixElement object has the properties and methods of the SVGElement object and the SVGFilterPrimitiveStandardAttributes object.

The SVGFEConvolveMatrixElement object has the following constants associated with it:

- SVGFEConvolveMatrixElement.SVG_EDGEMODE_UNKNOWN—The constant is of type short and has a value of 0.

- SVGFEConvolveMatrixElement.SVG_EDGEMODE_DUPLICATE—The constant is of type short and has a value of 1.

- SVGFEConvolveMatrixElement.SVG_EDGEMODE_WRAP—The constant is of type short and has a value of 2.

- SVGFEConvolveMatrixElement.SVG_EDGEMODE_NONE—The constant is of type short and has a value of 3.

The SVGFEConvolveMatrixElement object has the following properties:

- orderX—of type SVGAnimatedInteger

- orderY—of type SVGAnimatedInteger

- kernelMatrix—of type SVGAnimatedNumberList

- divisor—of type SVGAnimatedNumber

- bias—of type SVGAnimatedNumber

- targetX—of type SVGAnimatedInteger

- targetY—of type SVGAnimatedInteger

- edgeMode—of type SVGAnimatedEnumeration

- kernelUnitLengthX—of type SVGAnimatedLength

- kernelUnitLengthY—of type SVGAnimatedLength

- preserveAlpha—of type SVGAnimatedBoolean

The SVGFEConvolveMatrixElement object has no methods specific to it.

The SVGFEDiffuseLightingElement Object

The SVGFEDiffuseLightingElement object is the SVG DOM representation of the feDiffuseLighting filter primitive.

10

The SVGFEDiffuseLightingElement object has the properties and methods of the SVGElement object and the SVGFilterPrimitiveStandardAttributes object.

The SVGFEDiffuseLightingElement object has the following properties:

- in1—of type SVGAnimatedString

- surfaceScale—of type SVGAnimatedNumber

- diffuseConstant—of type SVGAnimatedNumber

The SVGFEDiffuseLightingElement object has no methods specific to it.

The SVGFEDisplacementMapElement Object

The SVGFEDisplacementMapElement object is the SVG DOM representation of the feDisplacementMap filter primitive.

The SVGFEDisplacementMapElement object has the properties and methods of the SVGElement object and the SVGFilterPrimitiveStandardAttributes object.

The SVGFEDisplacementMapElement object has the following constants associated with it:

- SVGFEDisplacementMapElement.SVG_CHANNEL_UNKNOWN—The constant is of type short and has a value of 0.

- SVGFEDisplacementMapElement.SVG_CHANNEL_R—The constant is of type short and has a value of 1.

- SVGFEDisplacementMapElement.SVG_CHANNEL_G—The constant is of type short and has a value of 2.

- SVGFEDisplacementMapElement.SVG_CHANNEL_B—The constant is of type short and has a value of 3.

- SVGFEDisplacementMapElement.SVG_CHANNEL_A—The constant is of type short and has a value of 4.

The SVGFEDisplacementMapElement object has the following properties:

- in1—of type SVGAnimatedString

- in2—of type SVGAnimatedString

- scale—of type SVGAnimatedNumber

- xChannelSelector—of type SVGAnimatedEnumeration

- yChannelSelector—of type SVGAnimatedEnumeration

The SVGFEDisplacementMapElement object has no objects specific to it.

The SVGFEDistantLightElement Object

The `SVGFEDistantLightElement` object is the SVG DOM representation of the `feDistantLight` filter primitive.

The `SVGFEDistantLightElement` object has the properties and methods of the `SVGElement` object.

The `SVGFEDistantLightElement` object has the following properties:

- azimuth—of type `SVGAnimatedNumber`
- elevation—of type `SVGAnimatedNumber`

The `SVGFEDistantLightElement` object has no methods specific to it.

The SVGFEFloodElement Object

The `SVGFEFloodElement` object is the SVG DOM representation of the `feFlood` filter primitive.

The `SVGFEFloodElement` object has the properties and methods of the `SVGElement` object and the `SVGFilterPrimitiveStandardAttributes` object.

The `SVGFEFloodElement` object has the following specific property:

- in1—of type `SVGAnimatedString`

The `SVGFEFloodElement` object has no methods specific to it.

The SVGFEGaussianBlurElement Object

The `SVGFEGaussianBlurElement` object is the SVG DOM representation of the `feGaussianBlur` filter primitive.

The `SVGFEGaussianBlurElement` object has the properties and methods of the `SVGElement` object and the `SVGFilterPrimitiveStandardAttributes` object.

The `SVGFEGaussianBlurElement` object has the following properties:

- in1—of type `SVGAnimatedString`
- stdDeviationX—of type `SVGAnimatedNumber`
- stdDeviationY—of type `SVGAnimatedNumber`

The `SVGFEGaussianBlurElement` object has the following method specific to it:

- setStdDeviation(*stdDeviationX*, *stdDeviationY*)—The method returns a value of type void. The arguments *stdDeviationX* and *stdDeviationY* are of type `float`.

10

The SVGFEImageElement Object

The SVGFEImageElement object is the SVG DOM representation of the feImage filter primitive.

The SVGFEImageElement object has the properties and methods of the SVGElement object, the SVGURIReference object, the SVGLangSpace object, the SVGExternalResourcesRequired object, and the SVGFilterPrimitiveStandardAttributes object.

The SVGFEImageElement object has no properties or methods specific to it.

The SVGFEMergeElement Object

The SVGFEMergeElement object is the SVG DOM representation of the feMerge filter primitive.

The SVGFEMergeElement object has the properties and methods of the SVGElement object and the SVGFilterPrimitiveStandardAttributes object.

The SVGFEMergeElement object has no properties or methods specific to it.

Associated with the SVGFEMergeElement object is the SVGFEMergeNodeElement object.

The SVGFEMergeNodeElement Object

The SVGFEMergeNodeElement object is the SVG DOM representation of the feMergeNode filter primitive.

The SVGFEMergeNodeElement object has the properties and methods of the SVGElement object.

The SVGFEMergeNodeElement object has the following property specific to it:

- in1—of type SVGAnimatedString

The SVGFEMergeNodeElement object has no methods specific to it.

The SVGFEMorphologyElement Object

The SVGFEMorphologyElement object is the SVG DOM representation of the feMorphology filter primitive.

The SVGFEMorphologyElement object has the properties and methods of the SVGElement object and the SVGFilterPrimitiveStandardAttributes object.

The SVGFEMorphologyElement object has the following constants associated with it:

- SVGFEMorphologyElement.SVG_MORPHOLOGY_OPERATOR_UNKNOWN—The constant is of type short and has a value of 0.

- SVGFEMorphologyElement.SVG_MORPHOLOGY_OPERATOR_ERODE—The constant is of type short and has a value of 1.

- SVGFEMorphologyElement.SVG_MORPHOLOGY_OPERATOR_DILATE—The constant is of type short and has a value of 2.

The `SVGFEMorphologyElement` object has the following properties associated with it:

- `in1`—of type `SVGAnimatedString`

- `operator`—of type `SVGAnimatedEnumeration`

- `radiusX`—of type `SVGAnimatedLength`

- `radiusY`—of type `SVGAnimatedLength`

The `SVGFEMorphologyElement` object has no methods specific to it.

The SVGFEOffsetElement Object

The `SVGFEOffsetElement` object is the SVG DOM representation of the `feOffset` filter primitive.

The `SVGFEOffsetElement` object has the properties and methods of the `SVGElement` object and the `SVGFilterPrimitiveStandardAttributes` object.

The `SVGFEOffsetElement` object has the following properties:

- `in1`—of type `SVGAnimatedString`

- `dx`—of type `SVGAnimatedNumber`

- `dy`—of type `SVGAnimatedNumber`

The `SVGFEOffsetElement` object has no methods specific to it.

The SVGFEPointLightElement Object

The `SVGFEPointLightElement` object is the SVG DOM representation of the `fePointLight` filter primitive.

The `SVGFEPointLightElement` object has the properties and methods of the `SVGElement` object.

The `SVGFEPointLightElement` object has the following properties:

- `x`—of type `SVGAnimatedNumber`

- `y`—of type `SVGAnimatedNumber`

- `z`—of type `SVGAnimatedNumber`

The `SVGFEPointLightElement` object has no methods specific to it.

The SVGFESpecularLightingElement Object

The `SVGFESpecularLightingElement` object is the SVG DOM representation of the `feSpecularLighting` filter primitive.

10

The SVGFESpecularLightingElement object has the properties and methods of the SVGElement object and the SVGFilterPrimitiveStandardAttributes object.

The SVGFESpecularLightingElement object has the following properties:

- in1—of type SVGAnimatedString
- surfaceScale—of type SVGAnimatedNumber
- specularConstant—of type SVGAnimatedNumber
- specularExponent—of type SVGAnimatedNumber

The SVGFESpecularLightingElement object has no methods specific to it.

The SVGFESpotLightElement Object

The SVGFESpotLightElement object is the SVG DOM representation of the feSpotLight filter primitive.

The SVGFESpotLightElement object has the properties and methods of the SVGElement object.

The SVGFESpotLightElement object has the following properties:

- x—of type SVGAnimatedNumber
- y—of type SVGAnimatedNumber
- z—of type SVGAnimatedNumber
- pointsAtX—of type SVGAnimatedNumber
- pointsAtY—of type SVGAnimatedNumber
- pointsAtZ—of type SVGAnimatedNumber
- specularExponent—of type SVGAnimatedNumber
- limitingConeAngle—of type SVGAnimatedNumber

The SVGFESpotLightElement object has no methods specific to it.

The SVGFETileElement Object

The SVGFETileElement object is the SVG DOM representation of the feTile filter primitive.

The SVGFETileElement object has the properties and methods of the SVGElement object and the SVGFilterPrimitiveStandardAttributes object.

The SVGFETileElement object has the following property:

- in1—of type SVGAnimatedString

The SVGFETileElement object has no methods specific to it.

The SVGFETurbulenceElement Object

The SVGFETurbulenceElement object is the SVG DOM representation of the feTurbulence filter primitive.

The SVGFETurbulenceElement object has the properties and methods of the SVGElement object and the SVGFilterPrimitiveStandardAttributes object.

The SVGFETurbulenceElement object has the following constants associated with it:

- SVGFETurbulenceElement.SVG_TURBULENCE_TYPE_UNKNOWN—The constant is of type short and has a value of 0.

- SVGFETurbulenceElement.SVG_TURBULENCE_TYPE_FRACTALNOISE—The constant is of type short and has a value of 1.

- SVGFETurbulenceElement.SVG_TURBULENCE_TYPE_TURBULENCE—The constant is of type short and has a value of 2.

- SVGFETurbulenceElement.SVG_STITCHTYPE_UNKNOWN—The constant is of type short and has a value of 0.

- SVGFETurbulenceElement.SVG_STITCHTYPE_STITCH—The constant is of type short and has a value of 1.

- SVGFETurbulenceElement.SVG_STITCHTYPE_NOSTITCH—The constant is of type short and has a value of 2.

The SVGFETurbulenceElement object has the following properties associated with it:

- baseFrequencyX—of type SVGAnimatedNumber
- baseFrequencyY—of type SVGAnimatedNumber
- numOctaves—of type SVGAnimatedInteger
- seed—of type SVGAnimatedNumber
- stitchTiles—of type SVGAnimatedEnumeration
- type—of type SVGAnimatedEnumeration

The SVGFETurbulenceElement object has no methods specific to it.

Interactive Turbulence Example

The example in this section allows you to examine the effects of different attribute settings for the feTurbulence filter primitive. Listing 10.12 shows the code. Clicking on the viewport toggles the type attribute from turbulence to fractalNoise or vice versa. Moving the mouse alters the values of the baseFrequency and numOctaves attributes.

10

LISTING 10.12   InteractiveTurbulence.svg—Altering feTurbulence Attribute Values in Response to Mouse Movements

```
<?xml version="1.0"?>
<!DOCTYPE svg PUBLIC "-//W3C//DTD SVG 20010904//EN"
"http://www.w3.org/TR/2001/REC-SVG-20010904/DTD/svg10.dtd">
<svg width="500px" height="300px" xmlns="http://www.w3.org/2000/svg"
onload="Initialize(evt)">
  <script type="text/javascript">
  <![CDATA[

var SVGRoot = document.documentElement;
    SVGRoot.addEventListener('mousemove', mouseMoved, false);
var ftTPrim, feDisplay, type, baseFrequency, numOctaves;

function Initialize() {
    ftTPrim = document.getElementById('feTPrim');
    feDisplay = document.getElementById('feDisplay');
    feDisplay.addEventListener('click', mouseClicked, false);
    type = document.getElementById('type');
    baseFrequency = document.getElementById('baseFrequency');
    numOctaves = document.getElementById('numOctaves');
}

function mouseMoved(evt) {
    var x = evt.clientX;
    var y = evt.clientY;
    var newBF = x / 500;
    var newNO = y / 30;
    ftTPrim.setAttribute('baseFrequency', newBF);
    ftTPrim.setAttribute('numOctaves', newNO);
    newBF = document.createTextNode(newBF);
    newNO = document.createTextNode(newNO);
    baseFrequency.replaceChild(newBF, baseFrequency.firstChild);
    numOctaves.replaceChild(newNO, numOctaves.firstChild);
}

function mouseClicked() {
    var oldType = ftTPrim.getAttribute('type');
    var newType = (oldType=='turbulence')? 'fractalNoise': 'turbulence';
    ftTPrim.setAttribute('type', newType);
    newType = document.createTextNode(newType);
    type.replaceChild(newType, type.firstChild);
}
```

LISTING 10.12 Continued

```
   ]]>
   </script>
   <defs>
     <filter id="feT" x="0%" y="0%" width="100%" height="100%">
       <feTurbulence id="feTPrim" type="fractalNoise" baseFrequency="0.05"
numOctaves="1"/>
     </filter>
   </defs>
   <rect width="100%" height="100%" fill="white"/>
   <rect id="feDisplay" x="20" y="20" width="460" height="200"
filter="url(#feT)" />
   <text x="250" y="260" text-anchor="middle">&lt;feTurbulence
     type="<tspan id="type">turbulence</tspan>"
     baseFrequency="<tspan id="baseFrequency">0.05</tspan>"
     numOctaves="<tspan id="numOctaves">1</tspan>"
     /&gt;
   </text>
</svg>
```

Event listeners monitor whether the mouse is clicked or moved. Moving the mouse is best done very slowly because there are potentially very many mouse movements if you move the mouse rapidly. I find the appearance most attractive when the mouse is in the upper-left part of the viewport. Very subtle mouse movements in that region of the viewport can make a significant difference to the onscreen appearance.

Summary

This chapter introduced the principles that lie behind SVG filters and the associated filter primitives. SVG filters permit you to apply mathematically determined adjustments to the appearance of an SVG object or a bitmap image.

We described and demonstrated the use of the SVG filter element and how to reference a filter. Each SVG filter primitive was described, and several were demonstrated.

In the final section of the chapter, we described the SVG DOM interfaces that are relevant to filters.

10

SVG Animation Elements

The visual communication of information is greatly helped by animations. When a change in visual appearance of a graphic occurs, it often communicates a change in the underlying information much more succinctly and effectively than expressing the same change in words or numbers.

SVG supports powerful and flexible animation facilities that can be exploited using simply the declarative animation elements supported by SVG rendering engines. SVG declarative animation can be carried out in association with particular points in time or in response to events occurring in an SVG document fragment. Animations can take the form of instantaneous changes in color, visibility, or other parameters or can be more gradual changes in color, position, size, orientation onscreen, and so on. SVG animations can be chained so that the end of one animation triggers the beginning of another, or animations can run in parallel.

As well as powerful declarative animation, the functionality of those animation elements can be augmented by scripting techniques using JavaScript and other scripting languages. The use of JavaScript with SVG is introduced in Part II, "Programming SVG Client-Side."

In this chapter, we will first look at the context in which SVG animations function and examine a number of attributes and techniques that are common to several of the SVG animation elements. Then we will discuss each of the SVG animation elements in turn and demonstrate some uses of each animation element. The final section of the chapter will describe the SVG DOM interfaces that relate to the SVG animation elements.

SVG Animation in Context

Effective and rapid communication of information is becoming a crucial aspect of online information exchange. Visual communication, assuming that the consumer of information is familiar with the visual metaphor being used, can be an immensely powerful communication tool.

The need for and benefits of such visual communication can arise in many settings. In the financial sector, a user might want to know through a live SVG data feed when a share price goes above or below some limits set on business criteria. An engineer monitoring the function of a piece of equipment using an SVG control panel might want to know when various parameters of operation went outside defined safety limits. A teacher explaining how a piece of machinery works might want to be able to show geared wheels rotating in synchrony. Animations may help to convey a range of scientific or engineering concepts.

> **NOTE**
>
> Several animation examples, including animation of SVG clipping paths and masks, are included in Chapter 9, "Clipping, Masking, Compositing."

To be able to make use of the power of communication of SVG animations, we need to understand a little about its context and then move on to examine how to code SVG animations.

SVG Animation and SMIL 2.0

Four of the five animation elements in SVG 1.0 are derived from elements defined in SMIL 2.0. SMIL is the Synchronized Multimedia Integration Language. The SMIL 2.0 Recommendation was finalized by the W3C in August 2001 and is located at `http://www.w3.org/TR/2001/REC-smil20-20010807/`. A subset of SMIL 2.0, SMIL Animation, is located at `http://www.w3.org/TR/2001/REC-smil-animation-20010904/`.

In the terminology used in SMIL Animation, SVG is a **host language**. This allows SVG to amend or extend SMIL Animation in appropriate circumstances. For example, SVG has added the `animateTransform` element to the elements made available by SMIL Animation— `set`, `animate`, `animateColor`, and `animateMotion`.

The following summarizes the functionality available with the SVG animation elements:

- `animate`—A general-purpose animation element that allows time-based or event-based changes in scalar values of SVG attributes

- `animateColor`—Allows you to modify the values of color-related attributes and properties

- `animateMotion`—Allows animations that move an object along a motion path

- animateTransform—Allows you to create animated transforms, for example, by adjusting the value of a transform attribute

- set—Allows stepwise changes of attribute or property values

Timing is crucially important to some types of SVG animations. For example, you may want an animation to start either when an SVG image loads or a defined period after that. So it is important that SVG is able to time intervals, based from the common starting point of the time when the document completes loading. **Document begin** is defined as being the time when the onload event of the document element svg element is triggered.

In SVG, the **presentation time** is the time on the timeline relative to the **document begin** of the SVG document. We will look a little later at how the begin attribute allows us to specify a desired presentation time.

> **CAUTION**
>
> SVG is stricter in how it handles errors than SMIL. Any error in an SVG document fragment will stop the rendering of SVG animations within that SVG document fragment.

SMIL, like SVG, is a declarative XML application language. In SVG, we provide syntax that specifies what is to happen, such as "Five seconds after the document loads, the fill of this rectangle should change to green." In SVG, the syntax is declarative, corresponding broadly to the English sentence you have just read. Understanding how the SVG rendering engine achieves an animation isn't generally necessary. We simply specify the desired result. SVG rendering engines then animate SVG elements on the basis of such declarative syntax. That can be supplemented by scripting, which can provide the logic to control animations depending on, for example, time, the current onscreen position of an object, and so on.

> **TIP**
>
> To avoid jerkiness or delays in animations, keep the animation to a size adequate to communicate the relevant information. Large SVG animations that, for example, include filters and gradients can be very CPU intensive. The larger the SVG graphic, the more demand on the CPU.

Let's move on to see how the theory is put into practice.

Specifying the Target Element for Animation

SMIL Animation and therefore SVG provide several techniques to specify which element or elements are to be animated in a particular situation.

One technique is simply to nest the animation element within the element to be animated. Thus, we might have the following:

```
<text ...>SVG Unleashed
<animate ..... />
</text>
```

An alternative approach is to use the `xlink:href` attribute on the animation element to specify that an element that possesses a matching `id` attribute is to be animated. Thus, in two separate parts of an SVG document fragment, we might have code like this:

```
<text id="myIDText" ....>
SVG Unleashed
</text>
....
<animate xlink:href="#myIDText" .... />
```

The URI value specified by the `xlink:href` attribute must reference an element in the same SVG document fragment.

CAUTION

In SVG 1.0, you can use xlink:href to animate a single target element only. An attempt to animate more than one target element will cause an error. You can, however, animate a group of SVG elements in the same way by animating a grouping g element.

When an SVG animation element lacks an `xlink:href` attribute, the target for animation is the parent element of the animation element.

Identifying the Target Attribute for Animation

In the preceding section, we examined how to specify which element is to be animated. However, we also need to know which attribute or property of that element is to be animated.

The `attributeName` attribute is used to specify the attribute or property to be animated. For example, if we wanted to alter the fill color of an element, we would use syntax like this:

```
<text ...>
<animate attributeName="fill" .... />
Some text
</text>
```

SVG 1.0 also provides an `attributeType` attribute, which relates to whether an attribute or property is an XML attribute or a CSS property. The permitted values of the `attributeType` attribute are `CSS`, `XML`, and `auto`. The default value is `auto`.

If you specify `attributeType` as `CSS`, you are indicating that the property to be animated is a CSS property. If you specify a value of `XML`, the attribute is an XML attribute. If you specify that `attributeType` is `auto`, first any CSS property is matched, if it exists, and then an XML attribute is matched. Because `auto` is the default value, typically you needn't specify the `attributeType` attribute if you are dealing with SVG images in HTML/XHTML or as stand-alone SVG Web pages.

Timing-Related Attributes

Timing of animations is important; therefore, it is not surprising that SVG provides several attributes on its animation elements that specify or modify the timing of an animation.

The begin Attribute

A basic question is when an animation begins. The `begin` attribute is used to specify that information.

To specify that an animation begins a specified number of seconds after a document loads—for example, 5 seconds—we simply write

```
<animate begin="5s" ... />
```

We can also use the `begin` attribute to specify the timing of one animation in relation to another. If we had two animations related to each other, with the first animation having an `id` attribute of value `myFirst`, we can specify that the second animation starts when the first finishes as follows:

```
<animate begin="myFirst.end" .... />
```

If we want to specify that the second animation starts 2 seconds after the first finishes, we can write

```
<animate begin="myFirst.end+2s" .... />
```

If we want an animation to begin on more than one occasion, we can use a semicolon-separated list of values to specify that fact within the `begin` attribute. The following specifies an animation that begins at 2 seconds, 17 seconds, and 33 seconds after the document loads:

```
<animate begin="2s; 17s; 33s" ... />
```

Time may be expressed as hours, minutes, seconds, or milliseconds. For many animations, using seconds as a measure of time is appropriate.

CAUTION

Be careful not to include a trailing semicolon at the end of the list of values. If you do, some very strange and difficult-to-diagnose behavior can occur. In a long SVG document, working out where the problem is can waste a lot of time. You have been warned! A trailing semicolon is something to avoid (except within the style attribute or CSS rules where it does not cause a problem).

We can also use the begin attribute to respond to events. For example, to begin an animation when an element is moused, we would write something like this:

```
<animate begin="mouseover" .... />
```

Or if an element is clicked, we might write the following:

```
<animate begin="click" .... />
```

The event may be specified to occur on another object, rather than the object on which the event occurs. If that object had an id attribute of value anOther, we could write

```
<animate begin="anOther.mouseover" .... />
```

or

```
<animate begin="anOther.click" .... />
```

If you want to use the beginElement() method to start an animation, you set the begin attribute to a value of indefinite, until such time as the method is called.

The dur Attribute

The dur attribute specifies how long a simple animation will last. For example, if we wanted to create a color transition that takes place over 5 seconds, we would write

```
<animateColor ... dur="5s" ... />
```

An alternative way to specify the duration is to use both the begin and end attributes. So, to specify a color transition beginning at 3 seconds after the document loads and ending at 8 seconds, we have two options:

```
<animateColor begin="3s" dur="5s" ... />
```

or

```
<animateColor begin="3s" end="8s" ... />
```

The restart Attribute

After an animation is started, you may want to specify that it cannot restart before the animation has completed. The `restart` attribute allows you to do so.

When the `restart` attribute has a value of `whenNotActive`, an animation will not restart when it is partway through. If it is permissible that an animation can be restarted when it is partway completed, you can set the value of the `restart` attribute to `always`.

If you want to specify that an animation runs only once, you can set the `restart` attribute to a value of `never`.

The repeatCount Attribute

If you want an animation to run a specified number of times, you can specify that the `repeatCount` attribute has the appropriate numerical value. For example, to specify that an animation runs exactly 5 times, you would write the following:

```
<animate .... repeatCount="5" ... />
```

If you want an animation to repeat indefinitely, you would set the value of the `repeatCount` attribute to `indefinite`:

```
<animate ... repeatCount="indefinite" ... />
```

The fill Attribute

The `fill` attribute of an SVG animation element specifies what happens when an animation completes. Suppose you animate a rectangle from the left of the screen to the right side. Do you want it to stay in its new position or return to its original position? The `fill` attribute provides the control to choose from those two options.

If you want the rectangle to return to its original position when the animation is complete, you can simply omit the `fill` attribute on the animation element. Doing so is equivalent to using the `fill` attribute with a value of `remove`, which indicates that the animated value is removed.

If you want the rectangle to stay on the right of the screen, you can specify the `fill` attribute with a value of `freeze`. Setting `fill` to `freeze` causes the animated position, size, color, and so on to be held at the completion of the animation.

> **CAUTION**
>
> Be sure not to confuse the CSS fill property (which modifies the SVG paint inside the outline of an SVG object) with the fill attribute on SVG animation elements. The CSS fill property is allowed only on nonanimation elements whose shape is painted. The fill attribute is found only on SVG animation elements.

Animation Attributes

SVG animation elements also have several attributes that specify the animated value at the beginning and end of an animation and during the animation.

The from Attribute

The from attribute specifies the value of an attribute or property at the beginning of the animation. For example, if we wanted to specify that an animation of color began with the color blue, we could write

```
<animateColor ... from="blue" ... />
```

> **TIP**
>
> To avoid flicker at the beginning of your animations, make sure that the from attribute has the same value as the corresponding attribute or property on the element being animated. Alternatively, omit the from attribute from the animation element.

The to Attribute

To specify the final value of an animation, we can use the to attribute. So, if we wanted to carry out a color animation to red, we could write

```
<animateColor ... to="red" ... />
```

The by Attribute

You may want to specify by how much the animated attribute or property changes rather than specifying a to attribute. The by attribute allows us to specify a change from a starting value. For example, to increase the value of the width attribute of a rect element by 50 pixels, we could write

```
<rect .... >
<animate attributeName="width" ... by="50px" ... />
</rect>
```

The calcMode Attribute

The calcMode attribute allows us to define several ways in which an animation may be calculated. The permitted values of the calcMode attribute are as follows:

- discrete—The animation function will jump from one value to another without any interpolated values.

- linear—Simple linear interpolated values will be applied between the start and end values.

- `paced`—Interpolation will be carried out to produce an even pace of change throughout the animation.

- `spline`—Interpolation will take place using a cubic Bezier spline function.

The values Attribute

You may want to create an animation that varies in speed or direction over the duration of the animation. For example, you might want to create an animation that increases font size from 12 to 16 and then back to 14. To do that, you could use the `values` attribute, as follows:

```
<animate ... attributeName="font-size" values="12; 16; 14" />
```

You specify the timing of when the specified values apply using the `keyTimes` attribute.

The keyTimes Attribute

The `keyTimes` attribute is used to control the speed of parts of an animation. The `keyTimes` attribute contains a semicolon-separated list of time values between 0 and 1. The value 0 corresponds to the beginning of the animation, and the value 1 corresponds to the end of the animation.

The value that corresponds to an individual time within a `keyTimes` attribute is to be found in a corresponding value in the list that makes up a `values` attribute. The number of values in the list in a `keyTimes` attribute must match the number of values in the `values` attribute. An example using the `values` and `keyTimes` attributes is shown in Listing 11.12.

Attributes Controlling Additive Animation

The `additive` attribute specifies animations that add to the existing value of an animated attribute, rather than specifying absolute values for the beginning and end of the animation. An example using the `additive` attribute is shown in Listing 11.6 later in the chapter.

In addition, you can use the `accumulate` attribute to allow a value to progressively accumulate each time an animation is run. Listing 11.6 also shows how you can use the `accumulate` attribute.

Having taken a general look at attributes that can be used on several SVG animation elements, let's now look at the syntax of each SVG animation element in turn, with examples of using each element.

The set Element

The `set` element provides a means to create stepwise virtually instantaneous transitions between two states. It can be used, for example, to create mouseover effects where a CSS style property is altered stepwise. Clicking an SVG object may alter the appearance of the same or another object or may hide or make visible another object.

You don't need to set the `fill` attribute to a value of `freeze` on the `set` element. Using a `set` element to animate a value causes the animated value to be held, unless the `set` element has an `end` attribute and the event specified in the value of the `end` attribute is satisfied. Listing 11.1 shows an example of this usage.

LISTING 11.1   Set.svg—Using set With and Without an end Attribute

```
<?xml version="1.0" standalone="no"?>
<!DOCTYPE svg PUBLIC "-//W3C//DTD SVG 20010904//EN"
"http://www.w3.org/TR/2001/REC-SVG-20010904/DTD/svg10.dtd">
<svg width="" height="">
<rect x="50px" y="50px" width="200px" height="100px"
 style="fill:red; stroke:black; stroke-width:4">
<set attributeName="fill" begin="click" from="red" to="#00FF00"/>
</rect>
<rect x="50px" y="250px" width="200px" height="100px"
 style="fill:red; stroke:black; stroke-width:4">
<set attributeName="fill" begin="mouseover" dur="2s" from="red" to="#00FF00"/>
</rect>
</svg>
```

If you run Listing 11.1, you will see two rectangles onscreen. If you click the top rectangle (animated using `set` with no `end` attribute), the fill of the `rect` changes when the rectangle is clicked and then maintains that color without a need for a `fill="freeze"`. The bottom rectangle responds to being moused and has a value specified for the `dur` attribute, so the change in `fill` color lasts only 2 seconds.

A single `set` element is not capable of producing progressive animations with multiple intermediate steps. However, multiple `set` elements can be used to produce such effects.

> **TIP**
>
> If you want numerous set elements to respond to one event, you can specify an id attribute for the element or object where the event takes place—say an id attribute of keyAnim. Then each set element can have a begin attribute with a value such as keyAnim.click.

A Simple Rollover Effect

To create rollover effects in HTML/XHTML, we need to add a scripting language. In SVG, the rollover effect can be achieved using declarative syntax. Listing 11.2 shows a simple rollover using the `set` element to change the fill of text and addition of an SVG filter in response to mousing some text.

LISTING 11.2   Rollover01.svg—A Rollover Effect Using the set Element

```
<?xml version="1.0" standalone="no"?>
<!DOCTYPE svg PUBLIC "-//W3C//DTD SVG 20010904//EN"
"http://www.w3.org/TR/2001/REC-SVG-20010904/DTD/svg10.dtd">
<svg width="" height="">
<defs>
<filter id="myBlur" x="-10%" y="-10%" width="120%" height="140%">
<feGaussianBlur in="SourceAlpha" stdDeviation="3"
 x="-10%" y="-10%" width="120%" height="140%"/>
<feOffset dx="4px" dy="5px" result="outOffset"/>
<feMerge>
<feMergeNode in="outOffset" />
<feMergeNode in="SourceGraphic" />
</feMerge>
</filter>
</defs>
<text x="50px" y="50px"
 style="fill:red; stroke:none; font-size:48;
 font-family:Arial, sans-serif;" >
<set attributeName="fill" begin="mouseover"
 end="mouseout" from="red" to="green"/>
<set attributeName="filter" begin="mouseover"
 end="mouseout" from="" to="url(#myBlur)"/>
SVG Unleashed!
</text>
</svg>
```

The begin attribute on each of the two set elements has a value of mouseover. So, when the text is moused, the two animations begin. The fill of the text changes to green, and the filter myBlur is applied too.

The value of the end attribute, mouseout, of the set elements defines when the animation ends, that is, when the mouse is moved away from the text.

Figure 11.1 shows the zoomed initial appearance when Listing 11.2 is run. When the text is moused, the fill changes from red to green, and the drop shadow filter named myBlur is applied. The moused appearance is shown in Figure 11.2. When the mouse is removed, the text returns to its starting appearance.

Time-Controlled Animation of Visibility

The set element is well suited for controlling the visibility of an element or group of elements.

Listing 11.3 shows a time-based animation using the set element, which causes a change in the visibility of text at a defined time after the document loads.

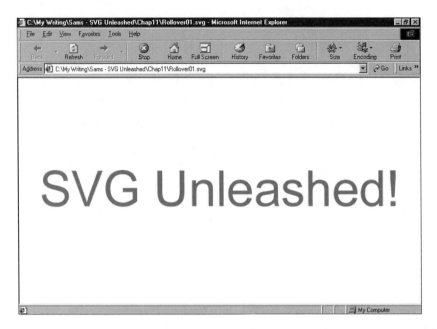

FIGURE 11.1   The appearance when Listing 11.1 is first run.

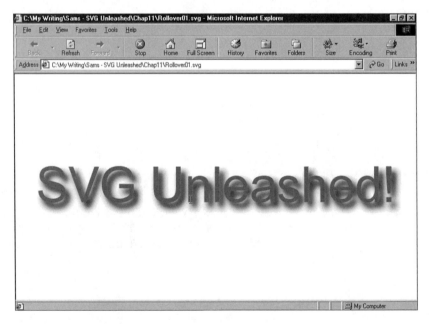

FIGURE 11.2   The appearance when the text is moused.

LISTING 11.3   SetVisibility.svg—A Time-Based set Animation

```
<?xml version="1.0" standalone="no"?>
<!DOCTYPE svg PUBLIC "-//W3C//DTD SVG 20010904//EN"
"http://www.w3.org/TR/2001/REC-SVG-20010904/DTD/svg10.dtd">
<svg width="" height="">
<text visibility="visible" x="40px" y="40px"
 style="fill:blue; stroke:none; font-size:48; font-family:Arial, sans-serif;">
<set attributeName="visibility" from="visible" to="hidden" begin="4s" />
Now you see me!
</text>
<text visibility="hidden" x="40px" y="40px"
 style="fill:red; stroke:none; font-size:48; font-family:Arial, sans-serif;">
<set attributeName="visibility" from="hidden" to="visible" begin="4s" />
Now you don't!
</text>
</svg>
```

Figure 11.3 shows the onscreen appearance when Listing 11.3 is first run. After 4 seconds, the visibility attribute of the first text element is set to hidden. Simultaneously, the visibility attribute of the second text element is set to visible. Onscreen the text content and its color appear to change. Figure 11.4 shows the appearance after the animation has taken place.

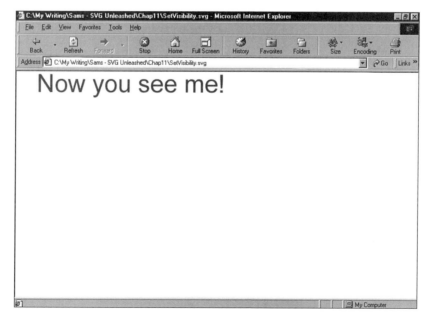

FIGURE 11.3   The appearance when Listing 11.3 is first run.

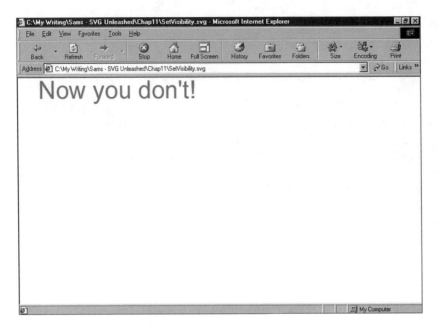

FIGURE 11.4   After the animation in Listing 11.3 has taken place.

Event-Related Animation of Another Element

The set element allows us to process events occurring on one element to cause an animation on another SVG element or elements. Listing 11.4 shows an example.

LISTING 11.4   AnimAnother.svg—Animating Another Element in Response to an Event

```
<?xml version="1.0" standalone="no"?>
<!DOCTYPE svg PUBLIC "-//W3C//DTD SVG 20010904//EN"
"http://www.w3.org/TR/2001/REC-SVG-20010904/DTD/svg10.dtd">
<svg width="" height="">
<text x="40px" y="40px"
 style="fill:red; stroke:none; font-size:20;
 font-family:Arial,sans-serif;">
Click the rectangle below
</text>
<rect id="myRect" x="40px" y="50px" width="200px" height="100px"
 style="fill:#CCCCCC; stroke:red;" />
<text   x="40px" y="180px" visibility="hidden"
 style="fill:red; stroke:none; font-size:20;
```

LISTING 11.4   Continued

```
font-family:Arial,sans-serif;">
<set id="myAnim" attributeName="visibility"
 begin="myRect.click" from="hidden" to="visible" />
You clicked the rectangle!
</text>
</svg>
```

Notice the id attribute on the rect element with a value of myRect. The begin attribute of the set element has the value of myRect.click, indicating that the animation begins when the myRect rectangle is clicked. The animation simply causes the visibility property of the second text element to change from hidden to visible, and so the text appears onscreen when the rectangle is clicked.

Figure 11.5 shows the onscreen appearance after Listing 11.4 has been run. After the rectangle has been clicked, the content of the second text element becomes visible. Figure 11.6 shows the onscreen appearance after the rectangle has been clicked.

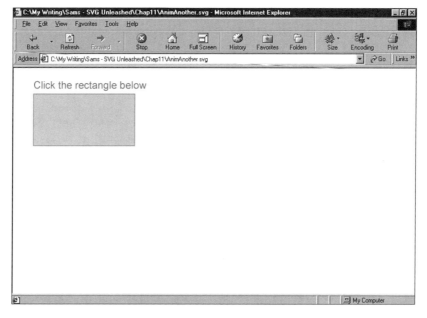

FIGURE 11.5   The appearance when Listing 11.4 is first run.

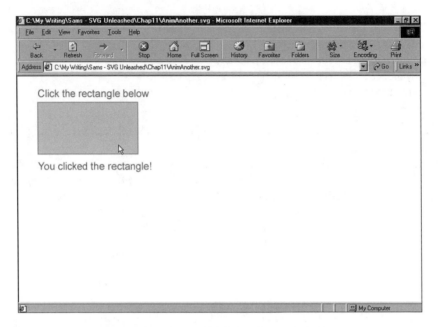

FIGURE 11.6   The appearance after the rectangle has been clicked.

Let's move on and look at the animate element.

The animate Element

The animate element is the most general purpose of the SVG, or SMIL, animation elements. The set element can be more succinct in some circumstances, and the animateTransform element can describe animations beyond the scope of the animate element. However, many commonly used animations can be expressed using the animate element, without using the more specialized animateColor and animateMotion elements.

The animate element is also useful for animations that are time based or event based.

A Color Fade Example

The animate element is ideal for creating gradual transitions of various types, including transitions of color, opacity, or position. Listing 11.5 demonstrates four simple animations using the animate element, a couple of color changes, and a couple of changes of opacity.

LISTING 11.5   ColorFade.svg—Brief animate Element Examples

```
<?xml version="1.0" standalone="no"?>
<!DOCTYPE svg PUBLIC "-//W3C//DTD SVG 20010904//EN"
"http://www.w3.org/TR/2001/REC-SVG-20010904/DTD/svg10.dtd">
<svg width="" height="">
```

LISTING 11.5   Continued

```
<defs>
<style type="text/css">
<![CDATA[
ellipse {
fill:#FF0000;
stroke:#000000;
stroke-width:5;
}
]]>
</style>
</defs>

<ellipse cx="150px" cy="100px" rx="100px" ry="50px" >
<animate attributeName="fill" begin="3s"
 from="#FF0000" to="#00FF00" dur="8s" repeatCount="5" />
</ellipse>
<ellipse cx="450px" cy="100px" rx="100px" ry="50px" >
<animate attributeName="fill" begin="3s"
 values="#FF0000; #FFFF00; #00FF00" dur="8s" repeatCount="5" />
</ellipse>
<ellipse cx="150px" cy="300px" rx="100px" ry="50px" >
<animate attributeName="opacity" begin="3s"
 from="1.0" to="0.2" dur="8s" repeatCount="5" />
</ellipse>
<ellipse cx="450px" cy="300px" rx="100px" ry="50px" >
<animate attributeName="fill" begin="3s"
 values="#FF0000; #FFFF00; #00FF00" dur="8s" repeatCount="5" />
<animate attributeName="opacity" begin="8s"
 from="1.0" to="0.2" dur="3s" repeatCount="5" />
</ellipse>
</svg>
```

The first two animate elements, which relate to the ellipses on the top row, define a change in the fill property. The first animation simply specifies a from value of red and a to value of green. If you run the animation, you will see that there are muddy intermediate colors during the transition from red to green. The second animation provides an alternative approach, using the values attribute, specifying an intermediate color of #FFFF00 (yellow), thus avoiding the muddy intermediate colors during the transition.

The third animate element provides a fade effect from full opacity to an opacity value of 0.2. The fourth animation uses two animate elements, one of which uses the values attribute to change the fill color and the other to produce a late fade.

To appreciate the color and opacity changes, you need to run these animations and view the transitions as they happen.

Example Using additive and accumulate Attributes

Listing 11.6 shows how the additive and accumulate attributes can be used with the animate element.

LISTING 11.6   Additive.svg—Using the additive and accumulate Attributes

```
<?xml version="1.0" standalone="no"?>
<!DOCTYPE svg PUBLIC "-//W3C//DTD SVG 20010904//EN"
"http://www.w3.org/TR/2001/REC-SVG-20010904/DTD/svg10.dtd">
<svg width="" height="">
<defs>
<style type="text/css">
<![CDATA[
rect{
fill:#FFFF33;
stroke:#000099;
stroke-width:4;
}
text{
fill:red;
stroke:none;
font-size:14;
font-family:Arial, sans-serif;
}
]]>
</style>
</defs>
<text x="40px" y="40px">
This rectangle returns to its original size
 and doesn't use additive attribute
</text>
<rect x="40px" y="50px" width="100px" height="50px">
<animate attributeName="width" from="100px" to="200px"
 begin="click" dur="7s" restart="whenNotActive"
 repeatCount="5" fill="freeze" />
</rect>
<text x="40px" y="140px">
```

LISTING 11.6   Continued

```
This rectangle uses additive attribute but returns
 to its original size for each repeat
</text>
<rect x="40px" y="150px" width="100px" height="50px">
<animate attributeName="width" from="0px" to="100px"
 begin="click" dur="7s" restart="whenNotActive"
 additive="sum" accumulate="none"
 repeatCount="5" fill="freeze"/>
</rect>
<text x="40px" y="240px">
This animation grows further when it repeats
</text>
<rect x="40px" y="250px" width="100px" height="50px">
<animate attributeName="width" from="0px" to="100px"
 begin="click" dur="7s" restart="whenNotActive"
 fill="freeze" additive="sum" accumulate="sum"
 repeatCount="5"/>
</rect>
</svg>
```

Listing 11.6 defines three animations, each of which is started when a rectangle is clicked. The first animation uses the from and to attributes to express the value of the rectangle's width at the beginning and end of the animation. The second animation uses the additive attribute to express an addition to the rectangle's width attribute. The third animation uses the additive attribute together with the accumulate attribute with the value of sum. So, on each repeat, the third animation adds a further 100 pixels to the value achieved at the end of the preceding animation. At the end of the first two animations, the rectangle width is 200 pixels. At the end of the third animation, the rectangle width is 600 pixels, due to accumulate="sum".

Figure 11.7 shows the initial onscreen appearance after Listing 11.6 has been run. Onscreen the top two rectangles behave the same after they have been clicked. They cycle five times through an animation where the width grows from 100px to 200px. The bottom rectangle has the accumulate attribute set to sum, so each time the animation repeats, the growth of 100px in width is added to the growth during the previous cycle. The final width is 500 pixels for the bottom rectangle and 200 pixels for the other two rectangles. Figure 11.8 shows the onscreen appearance after all the animations have completed.

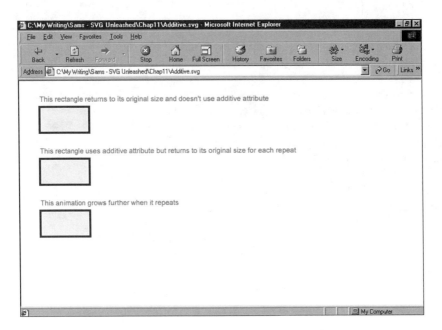

FIGURE 11.7   The initial appearance when Listing 11.6 is run.

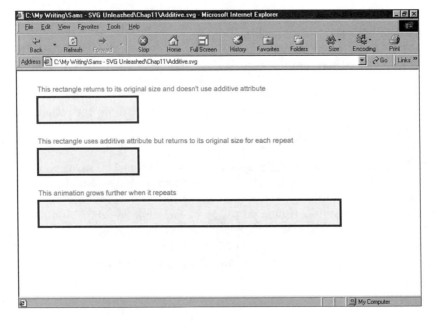

FIGURE 11.8   The appearance after the animations have repeated.

Chaining Animations

The capability to chain SVG animations can be very useful. The techniques are not specific to the animate element, but because of the broad animation capabilities of the animate element, chaining animations is described here.

Syntax to Chain Animations

The begin attribute is used to determine when an animation starts. If, as part of the permitted syntax for the value of a begin attribute, we can express information about the state—for example, the end—of other animations, we can create animations that are synchronized to each other. If we synchronize an animation with the end of another, we are chaining the animations.

Listing 11.7 shows an example of chaining animations.

LISTING 11.7   ChainAnim.svg—An Example of Chaining Animations

```
<?xml version="1.0" standalone="no"?>
<!DOCTYPE svg PUBLIC "-//W3C//DTD SVG 20010904//EN"
"http://www.w3.org/TR/2001/REC-SVG-20010904/DTD/svg10.dtd">
<svg width="" height="">
<defs>
<style type="text/css">
<![CDATA[
text {
font-size:48;
font-family:Arial, sans-serif;
fill:red;
stroke:none;
}
]]>
</style>
</defs>
<svg x="200px" y="200px" width="0px" height="200px" >
<animate id="Width1" attributeName="width" begin="1s"
 from="0px" to="400px" dur="5s" fill="freeze" />
<animate id="Visibility1" attributeName="visibility" begin="Width1.end+1s"
 from="visible" to="hidden" dur="5s" fill="freeze" />
<text x="10px" y="50px" >
SVG Unleashed!
</text>
</svg> <!-- Close the nested <svg> element -->

<svg x="100px" y="200px" width="0px" height="200px" >
<animate id="Width2" attributeName="width" begin="Visibility1.end+1s"
 from="0px" to="700px" dur="6s" fill="freeze" />
```

LISTING 11.7 Continued

```
<animate id="Visibility2" attributeName="visibility" begin="Width2.end+1s"
 from="visible" to="hidden" dur="5s" fill="freeze" />
<text x="10px" y="50px" >
Introducing SVG to Developers
</text>
</svg> <!-- Close the nested <svg> element -->
</svg>
```

Onscreen the animation wipes a line of text across the screen and then causes it to disappear. A second line of text is then wiped onto the screen and, in turn, is hidden.

Listing 11.7 has four `animate` elements. The first `animate` element, with `id` attribute of `Width1`, begins its animation 1 second after the document loads (`begin="1s"`). It animates the `width` attribute of a nested `svg` element from `0px` to `400px`. The `Visibility1` animation begins 1 second after `Width1` ends (`begin="Width1.end+1s"`) and causes the initial text to be hidden.

The animation `Width2` is similar to `Width1`, except that its `begin` attribute has the value `Visibility1.end+1s`. In other words, the animation of the second `text` element begins 1 second after the first piece of text disappears. The `Width2` animation is followed by the `Visibility2` animation.

Figure 11.9 shows the first piece of text partly revealed as the value of the `width` attribute of the first nested `svg` element is increased.

> **CAUTION**
>
> Be careful how you use whitespace within the begin attribute when chaining animations. Errors can occur if you include whitespace except around the + sign.

As written in Listing 11.7, the code runs only once. However, we might want to create an endless loop of such information using a suitable size font for use in a banner ad or similar size message. To do that, we can add a second value to the `begin` attribute of the `animate` element with `id` of `Width1`:

```
<animate id="Width1" attributeName="width" begin="1s; Visibility2.end+1s"
 from="0px" to="400px" dur="5s" fill="freeze" />
```

The value added to the `begin` attribute links the beginning of `Width1` to the end of `Visibility2`. To make the endless loop work correctly, we need to "reset" the values for the `width` and `visibility` properties of each text element after its pair of animations completes. The chained animation then becomes an endlessly repeating loop. Listing 11.8 shows code to create an endless loop by chaining animations to keep the visible animations working and also to reset the values of animated properties behind the scenes.

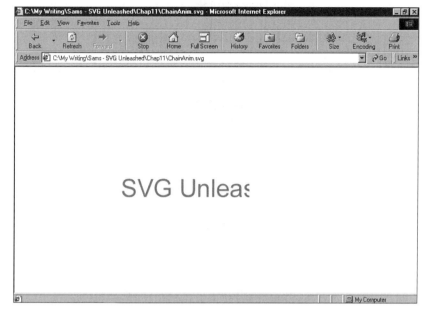

FIGURE 11.9   The text partly revealed by the first animation.

LISTING 11.8   ChainAnim02.svg—Creating an Endless Loop Using Chained Animations

```
<?xml version="1.0" standalone="no"?>
<!DOCTYPE svg PUBLIC "-//W3C//DTD SVG 20010904//EN"
"http://www.w3.org/TR/2001/REC-SVG-20010904/DTD/svg10.dtd">
<svg width="" height="">
<defs>
<style type="text/css">
<![CDATA[
text {
font-size:48;
font-family:Arial, sans-serif;
fill:red;
stroke:none;
}
]]>
</style>
</defs>
<svg x="200px" y="200px" width="0px" height="200px" >
<animate id="Width1" attributeName="width" begin="1s; Visibility2.end+1s"
 from="0px" to="400px" dur="5s" fill="freeze" />
```

LISTING 11.8 Continued

```
<animate id="Visibility1" attributeName="visibility" begin="Width1.end+1s"
 from="visible" to="hidden" dur="5s" fill="freeze" />
<set attributeName="width" from="400px" to="0px" begin="Visibility1.end+1s" />
<set attributeName="visibility" from="hidden" to="visible"
 begin="Visibility2.end" />
<text x="10px" y="50px" >
SVG Unleashed!
</text>
</svg> <!-- Close the nested <svg> element -->

<svg x="100px" y="200px" width="0px" height="200px" >
<animate id="Width2" attributeName="width" begin="Visibility1.end+1s"
 from="0px" to="700px" dur="6s" fill="freeze" />
<animate id="Visibility2" attributeName="visibility" begin="Width2.end+1s"
 from="visible" to="hidden" dur="5s" fill="freeze" />
<set attributeName="width" from="400px" to="0px" begin="Visibility2.end+1s" />
<set attributeName="visibility" from="hidden" to="visible"
 begin="Visibility1.end" />
<text x="10px" y="50px" >
Introducing SVG to Developers
</text>
</svg> <!-- Close the nested <svg> element -->
</svg>
```

In Listing 11.8, notice that four set elements are used to reset the values of the width and visibility properties of the nested svg elements. Using these elements ensures that each property is correctly reset before the corresponding animate element animations are begun again.

Scrolling Text Output

Scrolling text is frequently used in Web pages, sometimes within Java applets. SVG animation elements provide straightforward ways to animate text both horizontally and vertically. Examples of both types of animation are shown in the following sections.

Horizontal Scrolling Text

Horizontal text animations can be used for ticker-tape information announcements or advertising purposes. Listing 11.9 shows an animation using the animate element to horizontally animate text.

LISTING 11.9   HorizText.svg—Horizontally Scrolling SVG Text

```
<?xml version="1.0" standalone="no"?>
<!DOCTYPE svg PUBLIC "-//W3C//DTD SVG 20010904//EN"
"http://www.w3.org/TR/2001/REC-SVG-20010904/DTD/svg10.dtd">
<svg width="" height="">
<defs>
<style type="text/css">
<![CDATA[
text{
font-size:16;
font-family:Arial, sans-serif;
fill:url(#myLinGrad);
stroke:none;
}
]]>
</style>
<linearGradient id="myLinGrad" units="userSpaceOnUse">
 <stop offset="0%" style="stop-color:#FF00FF"/>
 <stop offset="10%" style="stop-color:#0000FF"/>
 <stop offset="20%" style="stop-color:#FF0000"/>
 <stop offset="40%" style="stop-color:#0000FF"/>
 <stop offset="70%" style="stop-color:#FF00FF"/>
 <stop offset="100%" style="stop-color:#FF0000"/>
</linearGradient>
</defs>

<svg x="200px" y="20px" width="468px" height="60px">
<rect x="0" y="0" width="100%" height="100%"
 style="fill:#CCFFCC; stroke:red; stroke-width:2;"/>
<text x="440px" y="35px" >
<animate attributeName="x" begin="0s" from="440px" to="-500px" dur="10s"
 repeatCount="indefinite" />
XMML.com - Consultancy services in XML &amp; SVG
</text>
</svg>
</svg>
```

The animation is created using an animate element to alter the value of the x attribute of a text element. Figure 11.10 shows the animated text zoomed onscreen.

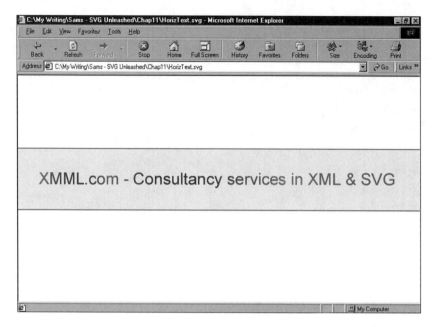

FIGURE 11.10   The animated text partway through its animation.

Vertical Scrolling Text

Vertically scrolling text is useful for displaying news feeds or other series of text-based messages. Creating these scrolling displays is straightforward using SVG `text` and `tspan` elements combined with SVG animation elements.

Let's create an example that might be a Web page advertisement for *SVG Unleashed* and that will display the book title, together with the titles for Chapters 1 to 12. Listing 11.10 shows the code.

LISTING 11.10   VertText.svg—An SVG Advertisement for *SVG Unleashed*

```
<?xml version="1.0" standalone="no"?>
<!DOCTYPE svg PUBLIC "-//W3C//DTD SVG 20010904//EN"
"http://www.w3.org/TR/2001/REC-SVG-20010904/DTD/svg10.dtd">
<svg width="" height="">
<defs>
<style type="text/css">
<![CDATA[
text{
font-size:16;
```

LISTING 11.10   Continued

```
font-family:Arial, sans-serif;
fill:#990066;
stroke:none;
}
tspan{
font-size:14;
font-family:Arial, sans-serif;
fill:black;
stroke:none;
}
]]>
</style>
</defs>

<svg x="200px" y="20px" width="300px" height="250px">
<rect x="0" y="0" width="100%" height="100%"
 style="fill:white; stroke:#990066; stroke-width:2;"/>
<text x="40px" y="" >
<animate attributeName="y" begin="0s" from="210px"
 to="-300px" dur="10s" repeatCount="indefinite" />
SVG Unleashed
<tspan x="40px" dy="2em">
1 - SVG Overview
</tspan>
<tspan x="40px" dy="1.5em">
2 - Document Structure in SVG
</tspan>
<tspan x="40px" dy="1.5em">
3 - Basic SVG Elements &amp; Shapes
</tspan>
<tspan x="40px" dy="1.5em">
4 - Using CSS with SVG
</tspan>
<tspan x="40px" dy="1.5em">
5 - Coordinate Systems in SVG
</tspan>
<tspan x="40px" dy="1.5em">
6 - Paths in SVG
</tspan>
<tspan x="40px" dy="1.5em">
```

LISTING 11.10   Continued

```
7 - Transformations in SVG
</tspan>
<tspan x="40px" dy="1.5em">
8 - Laying Out Text in SVG
</tspan>
<tspan x="40px" dy="1.5em">
9 - Clipping, Masking and Compositing
</tspan>
<tspan x="40px" dy="1.5em">
10 - SVG Filters
</tspan>
<tspan x="40px" dy="1.5em">
11 - SVG Animation Elements
</tspan>
<tspan x="40px" dy="1.5em">
12 - SVG for Web Authoring
</tspan>
</text>
</svg>
</svg>
```

We have multiple lines of text in the animation, but we need have only one `animate` element. The `animate` element causes the value of the y attribute of the `text` element to be changed over time. The vertical position of each of the `tspan` elements is specified relative to the `text` element or a preceding `tspan` element, using the dy attribute. Each time the position of the `text` element is animated upward, the position of each of the `tspan` elements is adjusted to maintain the same position relative to the `text` element. In other words, they are animated upward too.

The `from` attribute on the `animate` element could be adjusted to alter the starting position onscreen. If you find that the text is scrolling a little faster or slower than you prefer, simply adjust the value of the `dur` attribute on the `animate` element.

Figure 11.11 shows the zoomed and panned onscreen view when Listing 11.10 is run.

Controlling Animation Restarting

You can use the `restart` attribute to control whether or when an animation will restart. Listing 11.11 includes three animations using the `animate` element to demonstrate the use of different values for the `restart` attribute.

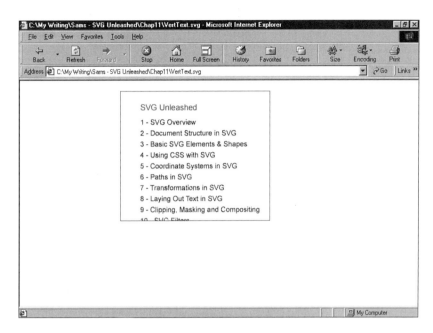

FIGURE 11.11   The vertically scrolling animated text partway through its animation.

LISTING 11.11   Restart.svg—Testing Values of the restart Attribute

```
<?xml version="1.0" standalone="no"?>
<!DOCTYPE svg PUBLIC "-//W3C//DTD SVG 20010904//EN"
"http://www.w3.org/TR/2001/REC-SVG-20010904/DTD/svg10.dtd">
<svg width="" height="">
<defs>
<style type="text/css">
<![CDATA[
rect{
fill:#FFFF33;
stroke:#000099;
stroke-width:4;
}
text{
fill:red;
stroke:none;
font-size:14;
font-family:Arial, sans-serif;
}
]]>
</style>
```

11

LISTING 11.11   Continued

```
</defs>
<text x="40px" y="40px">
This animation will run once only
</text>
<rect x="40px" y="50px" width="100px" height="50px">
<animate attributeName="width" from="100px" to="800px"
 begin="click" dur="7s" restart="never" />
</rect>
<text x="40px" y="140px">
This animation will restart any time
</text>
<rect x="40px" y="150px" width="100px" height="50px">
<animate attributeName="width" from="100px" to="800px"
 begin="click" dur="7s" restart="always" />
</rect>
<text x="40px" y="240px">
This animation will not restart when active
</text>
<rect x="40px" y="250px" width="100px" height="50px">
<animate attributeName="width" from="100px" to="800px"
 begin="click" dur="7s" restart="whenNotActive" />
</rect>
</svg>
```

Figure 11.12 shows the onscreen appearance after Listing 11.11 has been run and before the rectangles have been clicked. Three rectangles appear onscreen, each with descriptive text about when it will or will not restart. Each rectangle will increase in width in response to being clicked. The top rectangle has the restart attribute set to never. You can click it once, and it will animate, but reclicking will have no effect. The middle rectangle has the restart attribute set to always and will animate any number of times, and the animation will restart if you click the rectangle while the animation is in progress. The bottom rectangle has the restart attribute with a value of whenNotActive. That means that the animation will not restart while the rectangle is being animated. However, if you wait until the rectangle has finished its animation, you can restart a similar animation.

Using the values Attribute

The values attribute allows you to create animations that are not necessarily linear.

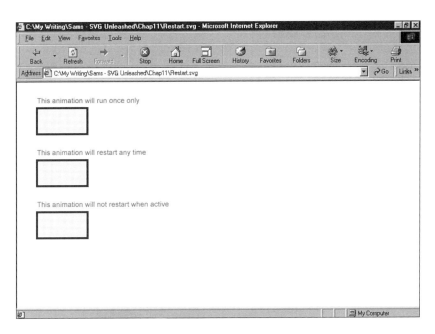

FIGURE 11.12   The appearance after Listing 11.12 has been run.

> **CAUTION**
>
> Remember, when using the style attribute (described in Chapter 4, "Using CSS with SVG"), you can leave a trailing semicolon at the end of a list of properties without causing an error. When you use the values attribute with an animation, leaving a trailing semicolon at the end of a list of values will likely cause unpredictable animation behavior. Spotting where the problem is located can be very difficult.

Listing 11.12 contains an example of using the values and keyTimes attributes with the animate element.

LISTING 11.12   Values.svg—A values and keyTimes Attributes Example

```
<?xml version="1.0" standalone="no"?>
<!DOCTYPE svg PUBLIC "-//W3C//DTD SVG 20010904//EN"
"http://www.w3.org/TR/2001/REC-SVG-20010904/DTD/svg10.dtd">
<svg width="" height="">
<defs>
<style type="text/css">
<![CDATA[
```

LISTING 11.12   Continued

```
rect{
fill:#FFFF33;
stroke:#000099;
stroke-width:4;
}
text{
fill:red;
stroke:none;
font-size:14;
font-family:Arial, sans-serif;
}
]]>
</style>
</defs>
<text x="40px" y="40px">
This rectangle uses values and keyTimes attributes
</text>
<rect x="40px" y="50px" width="100px" height="50px">
<animate attributeName="width" values="100px; 150px; 750px; 800px"
 keyTimes="0; 0.33; 0.667; 1.0"
 begin="click" dur="6s" restart="whenNotActive"
 repeatCount="5" fill="freeze" />
</rect>
</svg>
```

The rectangle, when clicked, grows slowly for the first 2 seconds, faster for the next 2 seconds, and slowly for the final 2 seconds (of each cycle, up to a repeat count of 5).

Notice the value of the values attribute:

```
values="100px; 150px; 750px; 800px"
```

Also, notice the keyTimes attribute:

```
keyTimes="0; 0.33; 0.667; 1.0"
```

The total duration of the animation is 6 seconds, as defined by the value of the dur attribute. In the first third of the animation (from key times 0 to 0.33), the width of the rectangle grows by only 50 pixels (from 100px to 150px). In the second third of the animation (from key times 0.33 to 0.667), the rectangle grows by 600 pixels (from 150px to 750px). In the final third of the animation (from key times 0.667 to 1.0), the width again grows by only 50 pixels (from 750px to 800px).

No figure is provided because you can really appreciate the changes in speed of the animation only by running the code and viewing it onscreen.

The animateColor Element

The animateColor element is, as its name suggests, a specialized animation element that changes a color value over time. Listing 11.13 shows an animateColor example.

LISTING 11.13   AnimColor.svg—Altering the fill Property Using animateColor

```
<?xml version="1.0" standalone="no"?>
<!DOCTYPE svg PUBLIC "-//W3C//DTD SVG 20010904//EN"
"http://www.w3.org/TR/2001/REC-SVG-20010904/DTD/svg10.dtd">
<svg width="" height="">
<defs>
<style type="text/css">
<![CDATA[
text{
font-size:28;
font-family:Arial, sans-serif;
fill:green;
stroke:none;
}
]]>
</style>
</defs>
<text x="50px" y="80px" >
SVG is RED hot when moused!
<animateColor attributeName="fill" from="green" to="red"
 begin="mouseover" dur="0.01s" fill="freeze" />
<animateColor attributeName="fill" from="red" to="green"
 begin="mouseout" dur="0.01s" fill="freeze" />
</text>
</svg>
```

The animation is a straightforward rollover effect. When the text is moused, the animation, which uses the animateColor element, changes the text from green to red. When the user moves the mouse away, begin="mouseout" causes the text to change from red to green.

If you recall the rollover effect using the set element earlier in the chapter, you will see why the set element is preferable for such effects. With the set element, you need only a single animation with begin="mouseover" and end="mouseout".

There is no accompanying figure. It is best to view the visual color change onscreen when you run the code.

The animateMotion Element

The `animateMotion` element, as its name suggests, is intended to specify motion along a path. The path along which the animation is to take place is indicated by a `path` attribute on the `animateMotion` element whose values take the same form as the values of the `d` attribute of the `path` element.

In a path element, the syntax

```
<path d="M 0 0, L 200 200" ... />
```

would cause a line to be drawn from coordinates (0,0) to coordinates (200,200). When you use the `animateMotion` element, the syntax

```
<animateMotion path="M 0 0, L 200 200" ... />
```

causes a translate transformation corresponding to an initial `translate(0,0)` to a final `translate(200,200)`.

The `rotate` attribute of `animateMotion` can be used to make an object remain in alignment with the current direction of a path. The `keyTimes` and `keyPoints` attributes contain semicolon-separated lists of values, which can be used to control progress along a path in relation to elapsed time.

The SVG `animateMotion` element extends the functionality of the SMIL `animateMotion` element so that all the content of SVG `path` elements can be animated. The SVG `animateMotion` element may also have a nested `mpath` element, which references an SVG `path` element, which defines the motion path. The `keyPoints` and `rotate` attributes of the SVG `animateMotion` element are also extensions of the functionality that SMIL Animation provides.

To follow SMIL 2.0 syntax, the SVG `animateMotion` element has an `origin` attribute. In SVG, the `origin` attribute has no effect.

Listing 11.14 uses a pair of `animateMotion` animations. The first animation causes a green rectangle to move to the right when the gray rectangle is clicked. When the green rectangle is clicked, a second `animateMotion` animation returns the green rectangle to its starting point (out of sight).

LISTING 11.14   AnimMotion01.svg—A Pair of animateMotion Animations

```
<?xml version="1.0" standalone="no"?>
<!DOCTYPE svg PUBLIC "-//W3C//DTD SVG 20010904//EN"
"http://www.w3.org/TR/2001/REC-SVG-20010904/DTD/svg10.dtd">
<svg width="" height="">
<defs>
<style type="text/css">
```

LISTING 11.14   Continued

```
<![CDATA[
text{
font-size:14;
font-family:Arial, sans-serif;
fill:blue;
stroke:none;
}
text.whiteText{
fill:white;
}
rect{
stroke:#006600;
fill:#CCCCCC
}
rect.greenClass{
fill:green;
stroke:#006600;
}
]]>
</style>

</defs>
<text x="50px" y="50px" >
Click the gray rectangle and a green rectangle will appear.
<tspan x="50px" dy="2em">
Click the green rectangle and it will move back out of sight
</tspan>
</text>
<svg x="50px" y="90px" width="410px" height="100px" >
<rect id="backRect" x="0px" y="0px" width="200px"
 height="100px" rx="10px" ry="10px" class="greenClass">
<animateMotion id="wasClicked" path="M 0 0 L 200 0"
 begin="frontRect.click" dur="2s" fill="freeze" restart="whenNotActive"/>
<animateMotion id="" path="M 200 0 L 0 0"
 begin="click" dur="2s" fill="freeze" restart="whenNotActive"/>
</rect>
<text x="220px" y="50px" class="whiteText" visibility="hidden"
 pointer-events="none">
<animate attributeName="visibility" begin="wasClicked.end"
 dur="0.01s" fill="freeze" from="hidden" to="visible"
 restart="whenNotActive"/>
```

LISTING 11.14   Continued

```
<animate attributeName="visibility" begin="backRect.click"
 dur="0.01s" fill="freeze" from="visible" to="hidden"
 restart="whenNotActive"/>
You clicked the rectangle!
</text>
<rect id="frontRect" x="0px" y="0px" width="200px"
 height="100px" rx="10px" ry="10px"/>
</svg> <!-- End tag of the nested <svg> element. -->
</svg>
```

When the document first loads, a single gray-filled rectangle is visible onscreen with some descriptive text indicating that, when it is clicked, another rectangle will appear. Figure 11.13 shows the initial onscreen appearance. The gray rectangle has an id attribute with the value frontRect, and the begin attribute of the first animateMotion element (begin="frontRect.click") uses that id value. The path attribute of the animateMotion element has a value of M 0 0 L 200 0, which causes the rectangle to be moved 200 pixels to the right. The animateMotion element has an id attribute of value wasClicked. That allows us to chain an animate animation to it, displaying a simple text message on the green rectangle. Figure 11.14 shows the onscreen appearance at that point.

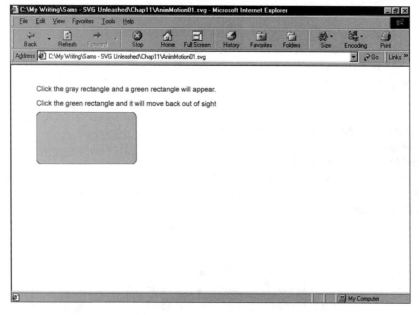

FIGURE 11.13   The single rectangle visible when the document first loads.

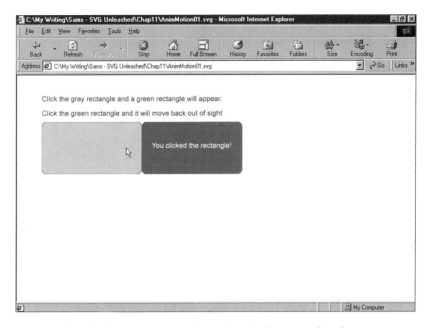

FIGURE 11.14   After the first animateMotion animation has completed.

The keyPoints Attribute

When used together with the keyTimes attribute, the keyPoints attribute allows the portion of an animation along a path to be specified at particular points in time. The values of both keyTimes and keyPoints are semicolon-separated lists. If the two attributes have different numbers of values, an error occurs. Listing 11.15 shows Listing 11.14 adapted so that the appearance of the green rectangle starts slowly, speeds up during the middle third of the animation, and ends slowly. This process is controlled by the values of the keyTimes and keyPoints attributes on the first animateMotion element in the code.

LISTING 11.15   AnimMotion02.svg—Altering Speed of an Animation Using keyTimes and keyPoints Attributes

```
<?xml version="1.0" standalone="no"?>
<!DOCTYPE svg PUBLIC "-//W3C//DTD SVG 20010904//EN"
"http://www.w3.org/TR/2001/REC-SVG-20010904/DTD/svg10.dtd">
<svg width="" height="">
<defs>
<style type="text/css">
<![CDATA[
text{
font-size:14;
```

LISTING 11.15   Continued

```
font-family:Arial, sans-serif;
fill:blue;
stroke:none;
}
text.whiteText{
fill:white;
}
rect{
stroke:#006600;
fill:#CCCCCC
}
rect.greenClass{
fill:green;
stroke:#006600;
}
]]>
</style>

</defs>
<text x="50px" y="50px" >
Click the gray rectangle and a green rectangle will appear.
<tspan x="50px" dy="2em">
Click the green rectangle and it will move back out of sight
</tspan>
</text>
<svg x="50px" y="90px" width="410px" height="100px" >
<rect id="backRect" x="0px" y="0px" width="200px" height="100px" rx="10px"
 ry="10px" class="greenClass">
<animateMotion id="wasClicked" path="M 0 0 L 200 0" begin="frontRect.click"
 dur="2s" fill="freeze" restart="whenNotActive"
 keyTimes="0; 0.33; 0.67; 1.0" keyPoints="0; 0.1; 0.9; 1.0"/>
<animateMotion id="" path="M 200 0 L 0 0" begin="click" dur="2s"
 fill="freeze" restart="whenNotActive"
 />
</rect>
<text x="220px" y="50px" class="whiteText" visibility="hidden"
 pointer-events="none">
<animate attributeName="visibility" begin="wasClicked.end" dur="0.01s"
 fill="freeze" from="hidden" to="visible" restart="whenNotActive"/>
<animate attributeName="visibility" begin="backRect.click" dur="0.01s"
 fill="freeze" from="visible" to="hidden" restart="whenNotActive"/>
You clicked the rectangle!
</text>
```

LISTING 11.15   Continued

```
<rect id="frontRect" x="0px" y="0px" width="200px" height="100px" rx="10px"
 ry="10px"/>
</svg> <!-- End tag of the nested <svg> element. -->
</svg>
```

No figure is shown; at present, the Adobe SVG Viewer 3.0 appears not to implement this feature.

The rotate Attribute

The rotate attribute is designed to allow you to define the rotation of an object that is traveling along a motion path. The default value of rotate is 0, which means that the orientation of an object being animated along a path remains the same with respect to the user coordinate system. If rotate is auto, an object being animated changes its orientation as the orientation of the path changes. The onscreen behavior is similar to the progressive change in direction of a car as it goes around a bend. The value of the rotate attribute may take any arbitrary angle as its value or a value of auto-reverse.

Listing 11.16 shows an example of an animateMotion animation with and without rotate="auto".

LISTING 11.16   Rotate.svg—The Effect of the rotate Attribute

```
<?xml version="1.0" standalone="no"?>
<!DOCTYPE svg PUBLIC "-//W3C//DTD SVG 20010904//EN"
"http://www.w3.org/TR/2001/REC-SVG-20010904/DTD/svg10.dtd">
<svg width="" height="">

<path d="M200 200 l200 0 0 200 -200 0 z"
 style="fill:none; stroke:black; stroke-width:4" />
<g style="fill:none; stroke:red; stroke-width:7;"
 transform="translate(200,200)">
<animateMotion path="M 0 0, l 200 0, 0 200, -200 0, 0 -200"
 begin="2s" dur="8s" repeatCount="indefinite" rotate="auto"/>
<line x1="0" y1="0" x2="50" y2="0" />
<line x1="50" y1="1" x2="35" y2="-15" />
<line x1="50" y1="-1" x2="35" y2="15" />
</g>

<g transform="translate(400,0)">
<path d="M200 200 l200 0 0 200 -200 0 z"
 style="fill:none; stroke:black; stroke-width:4" />
<g style="fill:none; stroke:red; stroke-width:7;"
 transform="translate(200,200)">
```

LISTING 11.16   Continued

```
<animateMotion path="M 0 0, l 200 0, 0 200, -200 0, 0 -200"
 begin="2s" dur="8s" repeatCount="indefinite" />
<line x1="0" y1="0" x2="50" y2="0" />
<line x1="50" y1="1" x2="35" y2="-15" />
<line x1="50" y1="-1" x2="35" y2="15" />
</g>
</g>
</svg>
```

When the document first loads, the panned onscreen appearance is as shown in Figure 11.15. You can see two square paths with a red arrow placed at the top left of each.

On each square is an `animateMotion` element, which animates the arrow around the square. On the `animateMotion` element that applies to the left square, the value of `rotate` is `auto`. On the corresponding `animateMotion` element for the right square, the `rotate` attribute is not specified and therefore takes the default value of `0`.

When the arrows are animated, the left arrow changes its orientation at each corner. The right arrow doesn't rotate in response to a change in the direction of the path and always points to the right. Figure 11.16 shows the animation partway through. In this figure, you can see the difference in the orientation of the arrows produced by the different values of the `rotate` attribute.

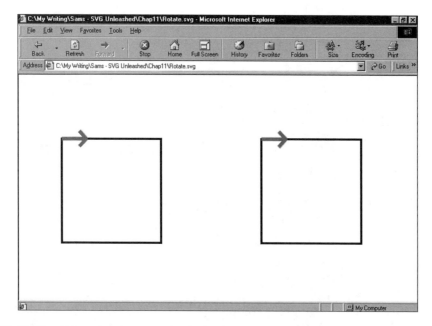

FIGURE 11.15   When the document loads, both arrows point the same way.

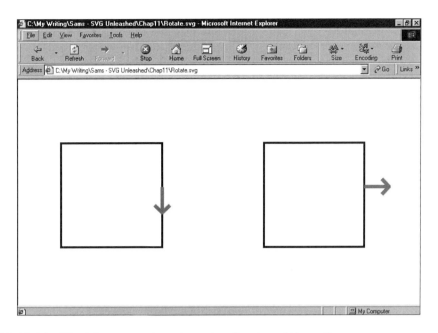

FIGURE 11.16   The left arrow points along the direction of the path.

The mpath Element

You nest the mpath element within an animateMotion element. The mpath element references, through an xlink:href attribute, a path that may be defined within a path element nested in the defs element. Listing 11.17 shows an example of a path being reused, by using an mpath element, in several animateMotion elements.

LISTING 11.17   MPath.svg—Using the mpath Element with animateMotion

```
<?xml version="1.0" standalone="no"?>
<!DOCTYPE svg PUBLIC "-//W3C//DTD SVG 20010904//EN"
"http://www.w3.org/TR/2001/REC-SVG-20010904/DTD/svg10.dtd">
<svg width="" height="">
<defs>
<path id="roundTheSquare" d="M0 0 l200 0 0 200 -200 0 0 -200"
style="fill:none; stroke:black; stroke-width:4"/>
</defs>
<path d="M200 200 l200 0 0 200 -200 0 z"
 style="fill:none; stroke:black; stroke-width:4" />
<g style="fill:none; stroke:red; stroke-width:7;"
 transform="translate(200,200)">
<animateMotion  begin="2s" dur="8s" repeatCount="indefinite" rotate="auto">
```

LISTING 11.17   Continued

```
<mpath xlink:href="#roundTheSquare" />
</animateMotion>
<line x1="0" y1="0" x2="50" y2="0" />
<line x1="50" y1="1" x2="35" y2="-15" />
<line x1="50" y1="-1" x2="35" y2="15" />
</g>
<g style="fill:none; stroke:red; stroke-width:7;"
 transform="translate(200,200)">
<animateMotion  begin="6s" dur="8s" repeatCount="indefinite" rotate="auto">
<mpath xlink:href="#roundTheSquare" />
</animateMotion>
<line x1="0" y1="0" x2="50" y2="0" />
<line x1="50" y1="1" x2="35" y2="-15" />
<line x1="50" y1="-1" x2="35" y2="15" />
</g>

<g transform="translate(400,0)">
<path d="M200 200 l200 0 0 200 -200 0 z"
 style="fill:none; stroke:black; stroke-width:4" />
<g style="fill:none; stroke:red; stroke-width:7;"
 transform="translate(200,200)">
<animateMotion  begin="4s" dur="8s" repeatCount="indefinite" rotate="auto">
<mpath xlink:href="#roundTheSquare" />
</animateMotion>
<line x1="0" y1="0" x2="50" y2="0" />
<line x1="50" y1="1" x2="35" y2="-15" />
<line x1="50" y1="-1" x2="35" y2="15" />
</g>
<g style="fill:none; stroke:red; stroke-width:7;"
 transform="translate(200,200)">
<animateMotion  begin="8s" dur="8s" repeatCount="indefinite" rotate="auto">
<mpath xlink:href="#roundTheSquare" />
</animateMotion>
<line x1="0" y1="0" x2="50" y2="0" />
<line x1="50" y1="1" x2="35" y2="-15" />
<line x1="50" y1="-1" x2="35" y2="15" />
</g>
</g>

</svg>
```

The path to be traversed by each of the animated arrows is defined on a path element with the id attribute having a value of roundTheSquare. Each animateMotion element has nested within it an mpath element whose xlink:href attribute references the defined path along which the arrow is to be animated.

Each animateMotion element has a different value for its begin attribute, so although each animation follows the same path (subject to a further translation when on the right rectangle), each arrow's animation is separated by 2 seconds from any other. Figure 11.17 shows the animation underway.

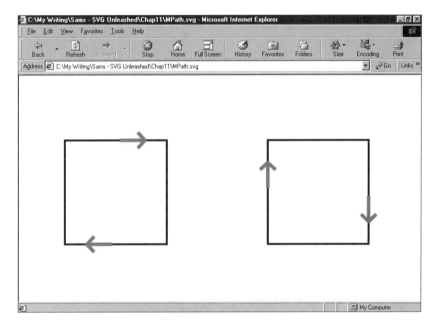

FIGURE 11.17   Four arrows being animated using the same path referenced in the mpath element.

The animateTransform Element

The animateTransform element is the only SVG 1.0 animation element that is not defined in the SMIL specifications. The animateTransform element allows animations that support translate, scale, rotate, and skewing (skewX and skewY) transformations.

Each animateTransform element must have a type attribute, which may take any of the following as permitted values: translate, scale, rotate, skewX, and skewY. The default value of the type attribute is translate.

The permitted structure of the content of the from, by, and to attributes depends on the value of the type attribute. Similarly, if a values attribute is present, its content must be a semicolon-separated list with individual values that are separated by commas having a structure determined by the value of the `type` attribute.

Animations of the translate Transformation

One of the animation options with the `animateTransform` element is the `translate` animation.

Listing 11.18 shows a short `translate` animation created using the `animateTransform` element. The code also includes an `animateMotion` animation that produces the same translation onscreen, for comparison of the visual effect and the code.

LISTING 11.18   Translate.svg—A translate Animation

```
<?xml version="1.0" standalone="no"?>
<!DOCTYPE svg PUBLIC "-//W3C//DTD SVG 20010904//EN"
"http://www.w3.org/TR/2001/REC-SVG-20010904/DTD/svg10.dtd">
<svg width="" height="">
<text x="50px" y="55px" font-size="16">
animateTransform :
</text>
<g style="fill:none; stroke:red; stroke-width:7;"
 transform="translate(200,50)">
<animateTransform attributeName="transform" type="translate"
 attributeType="XML" begin="2s" dur="8s"
 repeatCount="3" from="200,50" to="600,50" fill="freeze">
</animateTransform>
<line x1="0" y1="0" x2="50" y2="0" />
<line x1="50" y1="1" x2="35" y2="-15" />
<line x1="50" y1="-1" x2="35" y2="15" />
</g>

<text x="50px" y="205px" font-size="16">
animateMotion :
</text>
<g style="fill:none; stroke:red; stroke-width:7;"
 transform="translate(200,200)">

<animateMotion  begin="2s" dur="8s" repeatCount="3"
 path="M 0 0 L 400 0" fill="freeze"/>
<line x1="0" y1="0" x2="50" y2="0" />
<line x1="50" y1="1" x2="35" y2="-15" />
<line x1="50" y1="-1" x2="35" y2="15" />
</g>

</svg>
```

Figure 11.18 shows the onscreen appearance when Listing 11.18 is loaded. Two seconds after document loading, each arrow begins an animation to the right. The top arrow is animated using `animateTransform`. The bottom is animated using `animateMotion`.

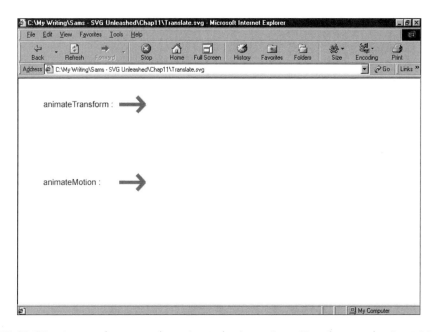

FIGURE 11.18   Arrows that are to be animated using animateTransform and animateMotion.

> **TIP**
>
> Remember to specify attributeName="transform" in all your animateTransform elements. The only value that attributeName can take is transform, but the animation won't run at all if it is absent.

Animations of the scale Transformation

To create a scale animation, we use the `animateTransform` element with the `type` attribute having a value of `scale`. Listing 11.19 shows a brief example.

LISTING 11.19   Scale.svg—A Scale Animation

```
<?xml version="1.0" standalone="no"?>
<!DOCTYPE svg PUBLIC "-//W3C//DTD SVG 20010904//EN"
"http://www.w3.org/TR/2001/REC-SVG-20010904/DTD/svg10.dtd">
<svg width="" height="">
```

LISTING 11.19   Continued

```
<text x="100px" y="100px"
 style="font-size:14; fill:red;">
 SVG grows on you!
</text>

<text x="100px" y="100px"
 style="font-size:14; fill:red;">
 <animateTransform attributeName="transform" type="scale" begin="2s"
  from="1" to="3" dur="5s" repeatCount="1" fill="freeze"/>
 SVG grows on you!
</text>

</svg>
```

When Listing 11.19 loads, you can see the text toward the top left of the screen. The first text element is not animated and is included in the code to allow you to compare the initial and animated positions and size of the text, as shown in Figure 11.19. The `from` and `to` attributes on the `animateTransform` element define the scale at the start and end of the animation.

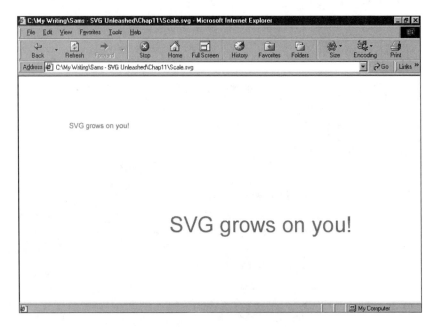

FIGURE 11.19   Initial and scaled text shown together for comparison.

You may want to scale a graphic object around its center point. SVG offers two ways to do that. Listing 11.20 shows one way. It shows a scale example that appears to pulse at a specific location because the change in coordinates due to the scale is balanced by a translate animation. Paradoxically, this way to achieve an onscreen appearance of no translation while scaling is to apply a translate animation in parallel with the scaling animation.

LISTING 11.20   Scale02.svg—Scaling Without Visible Translation

```
<?xml version="1.0" standalone="no"?>
<!DOCTYPE svg PUBLIC "-//W3C//DTD SVG 20010904//EN"
"http://www.w3.org/TR/2001/REC-SVG-20010904/DTD/svg10.dtd">
<svg width="" height="">

<text x="100px" y="100px" transform="translate(0,0) scale(1)"
 style="font-size:14; fill:red;">
 <animateTransform attributeName="transform" attributeType="XML"
 type="translate" begin="2s"
  from="0,0" to="-200,-200" dur="5s" repeatCount="1" fill="freeze"/>
 <animateTransform attributeName="transform" attributeType="XML"
 type="scale" begin="2s"
  from="1" to="3" dur="5s" repeatCount="1" fill="freeze" additive="sum" />
 SVG grows on you!
</text>

</svg>
```

The text increases to three times its original size, as indicated by the values of the to and from attributes.

The alternative approach is to nest the animated object within a g element that has a transform attribute. When a scale animation is applied to the object within the g element, whose coordinates are centered approximately on (0,0), the object grows in size while staying approximately stationary onscreen. Listing 11.21 shows the technique used with text. If you use this approach with regular shapes such as rectangles and circles, ensure that the center of the object is placed at (0,0) by adjusting the values of the x and y attributes (or their equivalent) appropriately.

LISTING 11.21   Scale03.svg—Scaling Around the Origin and Then Translating

```
<?xml version="1.0" standalone="no"?>
<!DOCTYPE svg PUBLIC "-//W3C//DTD SVG 20010904//EN"
"http://www.w3.org/TR/2001/REC-SVG-20010904/DTD/svg10.dtd">
<svg width="" height="">
```

LISTING 11.21   Continued

```
<g transform="translate(100,100)">
<text x="-30px" y="0px" transform="translate(0,0) scale(1)"
 style="font-size:14; fill:red;">
 <animateTransform attributeName="transform" attributeType="XML" type="scale"
 begin="2s" from="1" to="3" dur="5s" repeatCount="1" fill="freeze"
 additive="sum" />
 SVG grows on you!
</text>
</g>
</svg>
```

No figure is shown because the text simply grows in size, according to the from and to attributes on the animateTransform element.

You can use the values attribute on the animateTransform element to create a multiple-step scaling, as shown in Listing 11.22.

LISTING 11.22   Scale04.svg—A Multiple-Step Scaling

```
<?xml version="1.0" standalone="no"?>
<!DOCTYPE svg PUBLIC "-//W3C//DTD SVG 20010904//EN"
"http://www.w3.org/TR/2001/REC-SVG-20010904/DTD/svg10.dtd">
<svg width="" height="">

<rect x="100px" y="100px" width="150px" height="80px"
 transform="translate(0,0) scale(1)"
 style="font-size:14; fill:red;">
 <animateTransform attributeName="transform" attributeType="XML"
 type="translate" begin="2s"
  values="0,0; -133,-133; 0,0; -300,-300; -133,-133"
 keyTimes="0; 0.25; 0.5; 0.75; 1.0" dur="10s" repeatCount="1" fill="freeze"/>
 <animateTransform attributeName="transform" attributeType="XML"
 type="scale" begin="2s"
  values="1; 2; 1; 3; 2" keyTimes="0; 0.25; 0.5; 0.75; 1.0"
 dur="10s" repeatCount="1" fill="freeze" additive="sum" />
 SVG grows on you!
</rect>

</svg>
```

Onscreen the rectangle appears to pulse. Its size is first doubled, then returned to its original size, then tripled, and then reduced by one-third as indicated by the value of the values attribute, 1; 2; 1; 3; 2.

No figure is provided because the growth and shrinking of the shape are best appreciated onscreen.

Animations of the rotate Transformation

The rotate type of animated transformation allows the display of time—for example, in the creation of an onscreen clock—or values in a pressure gauge or similar measuring apparatus. Listing 11.23 shows a simple rotate transformation that animates a line through 360 degrees in 60 seconds.

LISTING 11.23   RotateAnim.svg—A rotate animateTransform Animation

```
<?xml version="1.0" standalone="no"?>
<!DOCTYPE svg PUBLIC "-//W3C//DTD SVG 20010904//EN"
"http://www.w3.org/TR/2001/REC-SVG-20010904/DTD/svg10.dtd">
<svg width="" height="">
<circle cx="200px" cy="200px" r="100px"
 style="fill:none; stroke:red; stroke-width:3;"/>
<g transform="translate(200,200)">
<line x1="0" y1="0" x2="0" y2="-100"
 style="stroke:#999999">
<animateTransform attributeName="transform" type="rotate" from="0" to="360"
 begin="0s" dur="60s" repeatCount="indefinite"/>
</line>
</g>
</svg>
```

Onscreen the line element is animated through 360 degrees in 60 seconds; that is, it makes one full sweep around the circle in a minute. It could function as the second hand of a clock. Notice that one end of the line is fixed on (0,0), then subject to the transform on the g element within which it is nested.

Animations of the skewX and skewY Transformations

The following two examples illustrate the use of the skewX and skewY animated transformations.

Listing 11.24 shows an example of a skewX animation.

LISTING 11.24   SkewX.svg—A skewX animateTransform Animation

```
<?xml version="1.0" standalone="no"?>
<!DOCTYPE svg PUBLIC "-//W3C//DTD SVG 20010904//EN"
"http://www.w3.org/TR/2001/REC-SVG-20010904/DTD/svg10.dtd">
<svg width="" height="">
<rect x="100px" y="100px" width="200px" height="100px"
 style="fill:none; stroke:red; stroke-width:3;">
<animateTransform attributeName="transform" attributeType="XML" type="skewX"
 from="0" to="60" begin="3s" dur="10s" repeatCount="1" fill="freeze"/>
</rect>
<text x="40px" y="40px" font-size="28">
SVG Unleashed
<animateTransform attributeName="transform" attributeType="XML" type="skewX"
 from="0" to="45" begin="3s" dur="10s" repeatCount="1" fill="freeze"/>
</text>
<g transform="translate(0,200)">
<rect x="100px" y="100px" width="200px" height="100px"
 style="fill:none; stroke:red; stroke-width:3;" />
<text x="40px" y="40px" font-size="28">
SVG Unleashed
</text>
</g>
</svg>
```

In Figure 11.20, the top text and rectangle are both animated using an animateTransform element whose type attribute has the value of skewX. The bottom text and rectangle are shown to allow comparison of the distortion and change in position on the horizontal axis.

Listing 11.25 shows a skewY animated transformation.

LISTING 11.25   SkewY.svg—A skewY animateTransform Animation

```
<?xml version="1.0" standalone="no"?>
<!DOCTYPE svg PUBLIC "-//W3C//DTD SVG 20010904//EN"
"http://www.w3.org/TR/2001/REC-SVG-20010904/DTD/svg10.dtd">
<svg width="" height="">
<rect x="100px" y="100px" width="200px" height="100px"
 style="fill:none; stroke:red; stroke-width:3;">
<animateTransform attributeName="transform" attributeType="XML" type="skewY"
 from="0" to="45" begin="3s" dur="10s" repeatCount="1" fill="freeze"/>
</rect>
<text x="40px" y="40px" font-size="28">
```

LISTING 11.25   Continued

```
SVG Unleashed
<animateTransform attributeName="transform" attributeType="XML" type="skewY"
 from="0" to="45" begin="3s" dur="10s" repeatCount="1" fill="freeze"/>
</text>
<g transform="translate(300,0)">
<rect x="100px" y="100px" width="200px" height="100px"
 style="fill:none; stroke:red; stroke-width:3;" />
<text x="40px" y="40px" font-size="28">
SVG Unleashed
</text>
</g>
</svg>
```

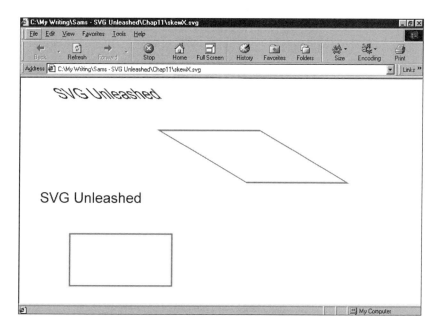

FIGURE 11.20   The top text and rectangle have had a *skewX* animation applied.

The text and rectangle on the left of Figure 11.21 have been subject to a skewY animated transformation. The text and rectangle are shown for comparison of the shapes and position on the vertical axis produced by the skewY transformation.

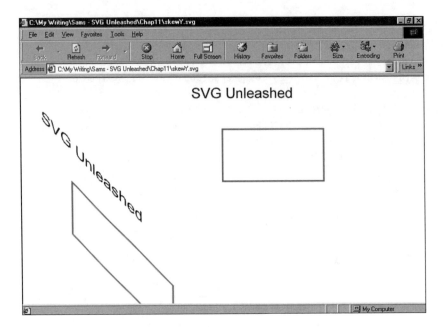

FIGURE 11.21   The text and rectangle on the left have had a skewY animation applied.

Animation Element-Related SVG DOM Interfaces

In the sections related to the SVG DOM in many earlier chapters, we mentioned objects that relate to animation. In this section, we will, now that you have looked at the SVG animation elements, take a closer look at how some of these animation-related objects and their properties and methods can be used.

First, let's look at the SVGAnimationElement object from which several of the element-specific objects inherit.

The SVGAnimationElement Object

The SVGAnimationElement object has properties and methods that are inherited by the other SVG DOM objects that represent animation elements.

The SVGAnimationElement object has the properties and methods of the SVGElement object, the SVGTests object, the SVGExternalResourcesRequired object, the ElementTimeControl object from the SMIL 2 Recommendation, and the EventTarget object from the DOM Level 2 Events specification.

In addition, the SVGAnimationElement object has the following property:

- targetElement—of type SVGElement

The `SVGAnimationElement` object has the following methods specific to it:

- `getStartTime()`—The method returns a value of type `float`. It takes no argument.
- `getCurrentTime()`—The method returns a value of type `float`. It takes no argument.
- `getSimpleDuration()`—The method returns a value of type `float`. It takes no argument.

The SVGSetElement Object

The `SVGSetElement` object is the SVG DOM representation of the set element.

The `SVGSetElement` object has the properties and methods of the `SVGAnimationElement` object.

The SVGAnimateElement Object

The `SVGAnimateElement` object is the SVG DOM representation of the animate element.

The `SVGAnimateElement` object has the properties and methods of the `SVGAnimationElement` object.

The SVGAnimateColorElement Object

The `SVGAnimateColorElement` object is the SVG DOM representation of the `animateColor` element.

The `SVGAnimateColorElement` object has the properties and methods of the `SVGAnimationElement` object.

The SVGAnimateMotionElement Object

The `SVGAnimateMotionElement` object is the SVG DOM representation of the `animateMotion` element.

The `SVGAnimateMotionElement` object has the properties and methods of the `SVGAnimationElement` object.

The SVGAnimateTransformElement Object

The `SVGAnimateTransformElement` object is the SVG DOM representation of the `animateTransform` element.

The `SVGAnimateTransformElement` object has the properties and methods of the `SVGAnimationElement` object.

Miscellaneous Animation-Related Objects

In this section, we will describe a number of miscellaneous animation-related SVG DOM objects. Many of these objects relate to the definitions of objects described elsewhere.

The SVGAnimatedAngle Object

The SVGAnimatedAngle object has the following properties:

- baseVal—of type SVGAngle
- animVal—of type SVGAngle

The SVGAnimatedAngle object has no methods specific to it.

The SVGAnimatedBoolean Object

The SVGAnimatedBoolean object has the following properties:

- baseVal—of type boolean
- animVal—of type boolean

The SVGAnimatedBoolean object has no methods specific to it.

The SVGAnimatedEnumeration Object

The SVGAnimatedEnumeration object has the following properties:

- baseVal—of type unsigned short
- animVal—of type unsigned short

The SVGAnimatedEnumeration object has no methods specific to it.

The SVGAnimatedInteger Object

The SVGAnimatedInteger object has the following properties:

- baseVal—of type long
- animVal—of type long

The SVGAnimatedInteger object has no methods specific to it.

The SVGAnimatedLength Object

The SVGAnimatedLength object has two properties:

- baseVal—of type SVGLength
- animVal—of type SVGLength

> **NOTE**
>
> Adobe SVG Viewer 3.0 does not support the scripting of the baseVal or animVal properties of an animated length.

The SVGAnimatedLength object has no methods specific to it.

The SVGAnimatedLengthList Object

The SVGAnimatedLengthList object has the following properties:

- baseVal—of type SVGLengthList

- animVal—of type SVGLengthList

The SVGAnimatedLengthList object has no methods specific to it.

The SVGAnimatedNumber Object

The SVGAnimatedNumber object has the following properties:

- baseVal—of type float

- animVal—of type float

The SVGAnimatedNumber object has no methods specific to it.

The SVGAnimatedNumberList Object

The SVGAnimatedNumberList object has the following properties:

- baseVal—of type SVGNumberList

- animVal—of type SVGNumberList

The SVGAnimatedNumberList object has no methods specific to it.

The SVGAnimatedPathData Object

The SVGAnimatedPathData object has the following properties:

- pathSegList—of type SVGPathSegList

- normalizedPathSegList—of type SVGPathSegList

- animatedPathSegList—of type SVGPathSegList

- animatedNormalizedPathSegList—of type SVGPathSegList

The SVGAnimatedPathData object has no methods specific to it.

The SVGAnimatedPoints Object

The `SVGAnimatedPoints` object has the following properties specific to it:

- `points`—of type `SVGPointsList`
- `animatedPoints`—of type `SVGPointsList`

The `SVGAnimatedPoints` object has no methods specific to it.

The SVGAnimatedPreserveAspectRatio Object

The `SVGAnimatedPreserveAspectRatio` object has the following properties:

- `baseVal`—of type `SVGPreserveAspectRatio`
- `animVal`—of type `SVGPreserveAspectRatio`

The `SVGAnimatedPreserveAspectRatio` object has no methods specific to it.

The SVGAnimatedRect Object

The `SVGAnimatedRect` object has the following properties:

- `baseVal`—of type `SVGRect`
- `animVal`—of type `SVGRect`

The `SVGAnimatedRect` object has no methods specific to it.

The SVGAnimatedString Object

The `SVGAnimatedString` object has the following properties:

- `baseVal`—of type `DOMString`
- `animVal`—of type `DOMString`

The `SVGAnimatedString` object has no methods specific to it.

The SVGAnimatedTransformList Object

The `SVGAnimatedTransformList` object has the following properties:

- `baseVal`—of type `SVGTransformList`
- `animVal`—of type `SVGTransformList`

The `SVGAnimatedTransformList` object has no methods specific to it.

Summary

This chapter introduced the principles of SVG animation and the methods to use the SVG animation elements. You saw several ways to create SVG animations. The set element is used to achieve stepwise transitions in the properties of an element. The animate element is a general-purpose animation element that can animate color, position, visibility, and so on. The animateColor and animateMotion elements are specialized animation elements for animating color properties and position, respectively. The animateTransform element is used to animate the range of transformations available in SVG.

In the final section of the chapter, we described the SVG DOM interfaces that are relevant to animation.

CHAPTER 12

SVG for Web Authoring

The Web is one of the most important places where SVG images and documents can be displayed. The interactivity and animation capabilities of SVG can be used to maximize the communication capabilities of SVG both in conventional HTML/XHTML Web pages by adding interactive and/or animated SVG graphics or in SVG Web pages.

SVG can be used in Web authoring in several ways. SVG images can be used as substitutes for, or improvements on, other bitmap or vector graphics formats in conventional HTML or XHTML Web pages. Equally, SVG can be used in places where you might otherwise consider using proprietary vector formats such as SWF and VML. Alternatively, Web pages can be created entirely from SVG. In this chapter, we will look at both approaches.

Using SVG with HTML/XHTML

One basic task that you will need to perform is to embed SVG images within a conventional HTML/XHTML Web page.

In the following sections, we will explore the use of the `object` and `embed` elements and will use Listing 12.1 as one of the test SVG images to be embedded.

LISTING 12.1   TestSVG.svg—A Test SVG Image

```
<?xml version="1.0" standalone="no"?>
<!DOCTYPE svg PUBLIC "-//W3C//DTD SVG 20010904//EN"
"http://www.w3.org/TR/2001/REC-SVG-20010904/DTD/svg10.dtd">
<svg width="400px" height="300px">
<rect x="0" y="0" width="398" height="298"
 style="fill:white; stroke:blue; stroke-width:5;" />
<text x="80px" y="20px">
This is the top of the SVG image
</text>
<text x="80px" y="295px">
This is the bottom of the SVG image
</text>
<g transform="translate(10,30) rotate(90)">
<text x="0" y="0">
This is the left side of the SVG image
</text>
</g>
<g transform="translate(390,230) rotate(270)">
<text x="0" y="0">
This is the right side of the SVG image
</text>
</g>
</svg>
```

Figure 12.1 shows the unzoomed onscreen appearance when the SVG image is displayed on its own. Notice that the outline of the `rect` element outlines the SVG image and that each edge of the image is labeled. The image size is 400 pixels by 300 pixels.

In the next two sections, we will look at how we can embed this SVG image in an XHTML Web page using the `object` or `embed` elements.

The object Element

The W3C-approved method of embedding an SVG image in an HTML or XHTML Web page is the `object` element. The `object` element is a general-purpose element that can be used to embed various objects within an HTML or XHTML Web page. Despite its being the officially recommended element, it is not problem free, due to variable support in Web browsers.

Listing 12.2 shows the code to embed the test SVG image using the `object` element.

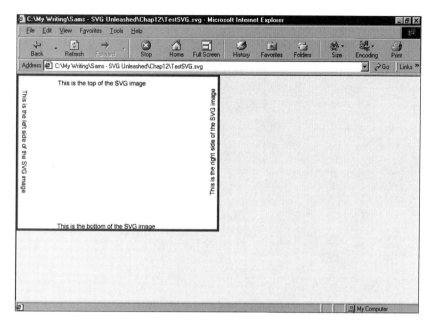

FIGURE 12.1   A test SVG image.

LISTING 12.2   ObjectTest.html—An Example Using the object Element

```
<!DOCTYPE html
PUBLIC "-//W3C//DTD XHTML 1.0 Transitional//EN"
"DTD/xhtml1-transitional.dtd">
<html>
<head>
<title>Embedding SVG in XHTML</title>
</head>
<body marginwidth="0" marginheight="0" >
<object data="TestSVG.svg" width="400px" height="300px" type="image/svg+xml" />

</body>
</html>
```

Figure 12.2 shows the onscreen appearance when Listing 12.2 is run in the Mozilla 0.9.9 browser. As you can see, you can place the SVG image right against the browser window edges, if you want. If you want to allow some space around the SVG image, you can adjust the dimensions of the margins.

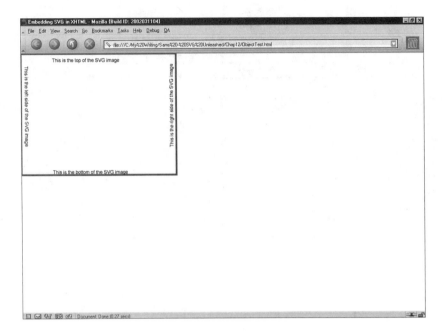

FIGURE 12.2   Using the object element to embed an SVG image.

Internet Explorer may add, on some machines, a three-dimensional border to an SVG image embedded using the object element and/or may add scrollbars around the image to allow the user to scroll to all the image. To allow for the space taken up by the 3D border and to avoid the scrollbars, you can add, say, 10 or 20 pixels all around so that all the SVG image will be displayed.

> **CAUTION**
>
> On occasional Windows machines using Internet Explorer, the object element seems not to work at all for SVG images. The reasons are unclear.

The bottom line, at the time of writing, is that using the object element is problematic, yielding different visual results when using different browsers. There are known issues with using the object element in Internet Explorer for other types of objects too, so it is not surprising that problems can occur when using the object element with SVG images.

So, if the official object element isn't reliable at the time of writing, how should SVG images be embedded in HTML or XHTML Web pages? The answer is to use the unofficial embed element, which is well supported by browsers despite its unofficial status.

The embed Element

The embed element does not exist in XHTML 1.0. In fact, the embed element has never been an official W3C HTML element at all but was a Netscape proprietary element that has been implemented widely in Web browsers, despite being frowned on by the tag police at the W3C.

Listing 12.3 shows the basic technique for using the embed element to embed an SVG image in an XHTML Web page.

LISTING 12.3 EmbedTest.html—Using the embed Element

```
<!DOCTYPE html
PUBLIC "-//W3C//DTD XHTML 1.0 Transitional//EN"
"DTD/xhtml1-transitional.dtd">
<html>
<head>
<title>Embedding SVG in XHTML</title>
</head>
<body leftmargin="0" marginwidth="0" topmargin="0" marginheight="0"
bottommargin="0">
<embed src="TestSVG.svg" width="400px" height="300px" type="image/svg+xml" />

</body>
</html>
```

Figure 12.3 shows the onscreen appearance when Listing 12.3 is run in the Internet Explorer 5.5 browser. The assortment of attributes on the body element may look distinctly odd. That combination does work. It achieves zero margins essentially all around the image, allowing you to place it precisely where you want in the HTML or XHTML Web page.

Using the embed element works correctly in Internet Explorer 5.5 and higher, Netscape 4.5 and higher, Netscape 6.0 and higher, and in Opera 5.1 and higher.

So, the embed element is the element of choice if you are planning to embed SVG in HTML or XHTML Web pages.

Zooming and Panning in Embedded SVG

One issue that you will want to consider about an SVG image embedded within an HTML or XHTML Web page is whether zooming and panning should be allowed on the image. Listing 12.4 lets us examine some of the issues that arise when we allow zooming and panning.

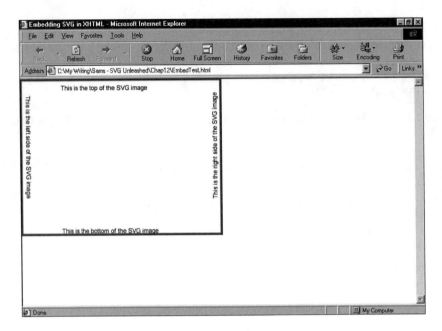

FIGURE 12.3   Using the embed element to embed an SVG image.

LISTING 12.4   TestSVG02.svg—An SVG Image Allowing Zooming and Panning

```
<?xml version="1.0" standalone="no"?>
<!DOCTYPE svg PUBLIC "-//W3C//DTD SVG 20010904//EN"
"http://www.w3.org/TR/2001/REC-SVG-20010904/DTD/svg10.dtd">
<svg width="600px" height="450px">
<g transform="scale(1.3)">
<rect x="0" y="0" width="398px" height="298px"
 style="fill:white; stroke:blue; stroke-width:5;" />
<text x="80px" y="20px">
This is the top of the SVG image
</text>
<text x="80px" y="295px">
This is the bottom of the SVG image
</text>
<g transform="translate(10,30) rotate(90)">
<text x="0" y="0">
This is the left side of the SVG image
</text>
</g>
```

LISTING 12.4   Continued

```
<g transform="translate(390,230) rotate(270)">
<text x="0" y="0">
This is the right side of the SVG image
</text>
</g>
</g>
</svg>
```

Listing 12.5 is a modified XHTML file to contain Listing 12.4.

LISTING 12.5   EmbedTest02.html—An XHTML File to Hold an SVG Image That Can Be Zoomed

```
<!DOCTYPE html
PUBLIC "-//W3C//DTD XHTML 1.0 Transitional//EN"
"DTD/xhtml1-transitional.dtd">
<html>
<head>
<title>Embedding SVG in XHTML</title>
</head>
<body leftmargin="0" marginwidth="0" topmargin="0" marginheight="0"
bottommargin="0">
<embed src="TestSVG02.svg" width="600px" height="450px" type="image/svg+xml" />

</body>
</html>
```

Figure 12.4 shows the onscreen appearance when Listing 12.5 is run.

Zooming and panning is enabled for this image because the default value for the `zoomAndPan` attribute is `magnify`. If we, in the Adobe SVG Viewer 3.0, right-click on the center of the image and zoom, we are presented with a blank screen. For many users, seeing a blank screen will be disorientating. Of course, the users can pan the image to regain a comprehensible image. But parts of the image will be invisible because the screen real estate set aside for the image is 800 pixels by 600 pixels. Figure 12.5 shows the zoomed and panned image. You can see that text extends beyond the viewbox and is therefore not visible beyond its boundaries.

Listing 12.6 is modified to disable zooming and panning on the SVG image. To do that, we add a `zoomAndPan` attribute to the document element `svg` element and set its value to `disable`.

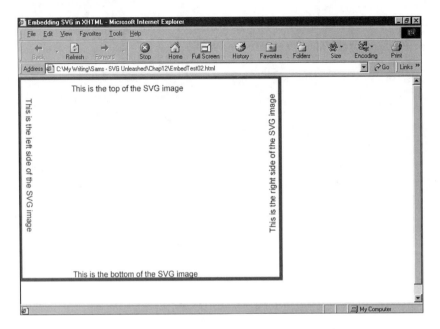

FIGURE 12.4   Unzoomed onscreen appearance when running Listing 12.5.

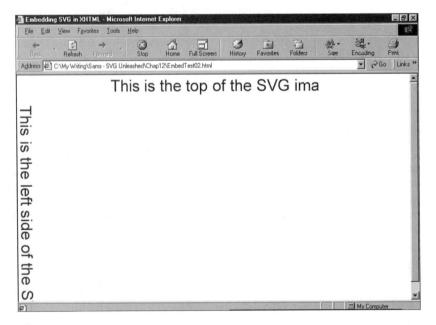

FIGURE 12.5   Zoomed and panned onscreen appearance when running Listing 12.5.

LISTING 12.6   TestSVG03.svg—An SVG Image with Zooming and Panning Disabled

```
<?xml version="1.0" standalone="no"?>
<!DOCTYPE svg PUBLIC "-//W3C//DTD SVG 20010904//EN"
"http://www.w3.org/TR/2001/REC-SVG-20010904/DTD/svg10.dtd">
<svg width="600px" height="450px" zoomAndPan="disable">
<g transform="scale(1.3)">
<rect x="0" y="0" width="398px" height="298px"
 style="fill:white; stroke:blue; stroke-width:5;" />
<text x="80px" y="20px">
This is the top of the SVG image
</text>
<text x="80px" y="295px">
This is the bottom of the SVG image
</text>
<g transform="translate(10,30) rotate(90)">
<text x="0" y="0">
This is the left side of the SVG image
</text>
</g>
<g transform="translate(390,230) rotate(270)">
<text x="0" y="0">
This is the right side of the SVG image
</text>
</g>
</g>
</svg>
```

We need to amend the XTHML file to reference the desired SVG image, as in Listing 12.7.

LISTING 12.7   EmbedTest03.html—An XHTML File to Reference a Zoom-Disabled SVG Image

```
<!DOCTYPE html
PUBLIC "-//W3C//DTD XHTML 1.0 Transitional//EN"
"DTD/xhtml1-transitional.dtd">
<html>
<head>
<title>Embedding SVG in XHTML</title>
</head>
<body leftmargin="0" marginwidth="0" topmargin="0" marginheight="0"
bottommargin="0">
<embed src="TestSVG03.svg" width="600px" height="450px" type="image/svg+xml" />
```

LISTING 12.7   Continued

```
</body>
</html>
```

When you run Listing 12.7 and attempt to zoom or pan the image, you will find that you can't. When you right-click on the image, you will find that the zooming options on the Adobe SVG Viewer menu are grayed out, as shown in Figure 12.6.

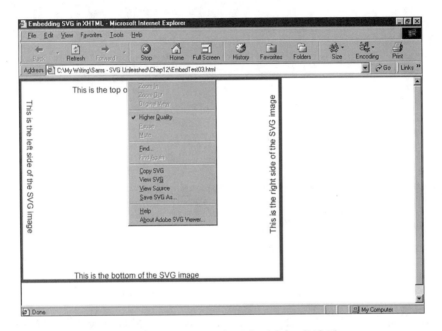

FIGURE 12.6   The zooming options are grayed out in Adobe SVG Viewer.

If you decide that the zooming and panning facility is desirable, you will likely want to make the screen real estate devoted to the SVG image pretty large. You also should consider whether to provide some instructions within the HTML/XHTML part of the page to guide inexperienced users about the ways to use the zooming and panning facility effectively.

Server Settings

The correct Internet Media type (sometimes called MIME type) for an SVG document or image is `image/svg+xml`. You should ask the system administrator for your company's Web server or at your ISP to apply the appropriate settings to ensure that SVG can be served correctly.

CAUTION

Early drafts of SVG had an Internet Media type of image/svg-xml. The Adobe SVG Viewer will correctly render both image/svg-xml and image/svg+xml. However, it is wise to correct any reference to image/svg-xml to avoid problems with other current or future SVG viewers.

DOCTYPE Declarations

You may find SVG code on the Internet or produced by graphics software such as CorelDRAW 9 or Adobe Illustrator 9 that contains a DOCTYPE declaration different from that which is defined in the SVG 1.0 Recommendation. The Adobe SVG Viewer will, typically, recognize and render most such code without problems. However, several syntax changes were made during the development of the final SVG 1.0 Recommendation. So, if you have code produced by one of these older versions of drawing tools that uses one of the old DOCTYPE declarations and won't render as you expect, be sure to check its syntax carefully.

Laying Out Web Pages in SVG

In this section, we will look at some issues relating to how you can create Web pages using only SVG. Chapter 8, "Laying Out Text in SVG," introduced the text and tspan elements, which are fundamental to laying out significant pieces of text to create an SVG Web page.

Laying Out Text in SVG Web Pages

In Chapter 8, we described the available options for laying out significant bodies of text in SVG. In this section, we will look at the option that, at the time of writing, provides the best combination of practicality and accessibility—using multiple tspan elements for text layout.

NOTE

It is likely that SVG version 1.2, whose Requirements document is currently at Working Draft status at the W3C, will add at least some automatic text flow functionality to SVG. The Requirements document for SVG 1.2 (as well as 1.1 and 2.0) is located at http://www.w3.org/TR/SVG2Reqs/. The SVG 1.2 specification itself is likely to be located at http://www.w3.org/TR/svg12.

Until automatic text flow is provided in SVG, the best option for text layout is to use text elements with tspan elements nested within them. It is important to have text content finalized before you add the content to an SVG 1.0 Web page because adjusting screen layout is a clumsy and time-consuming process. Much better to get it right the first time. In addition, it makes sense to agree to a desired font size up front rather than changing font sizes later on and finding that text overflows its view box and the end of a line can't be seen without panning (assuming that the page author hasn't turned off that feature).

What follows is a description for hand coding. If you generate such code automatically, you will need to locate an algorithm for doing something similar.

The `text` element can be used either as a container only for `tspan` elements or may contain some text before the first `tspan` element. I assume you have a chosen font size for paragraph text to be nested within the `text` and/or `tspan` elements. The number of glyphs that will fit on a line will depend on both the font and the font size.

A `text` element is created with appropriate values for the x and y attributes. Style is defined by one of the several techniques available. Within the `text` element, a `tspan` element is nested with an x attribute matching the x attribute on the `text` element and a dy attribute having a value of `1.5em` or `2em`. The length of a line of text needs to be decided on the basis of the allowed screen real estate for text and is influenced, of course, by the font size used. When you're hand coding, you make these choices by eye. If you plan to automatically generate text, you will need to explore what is an appropriate line length for the font and font size you choose to use, also taking into consideration the length of a line as constrained by the dimensions of the viewbox that the text is to be displayed in.

> **NOTE**
>
> Using the dy attribute in the manner described corresponds to *leading* in other approaches to text layout. Setting the dy attribute to 1.5em corresponds to 150% leading.

A section of text would look like this:

```
<text x="30px" y="40px">
<tspan x="30px" dy="1.5em">
This is a first line of text.
</tspan>
<tspan x="30px" dy="1.5em">
A second line of similar length.
</tspan>
<tspan x="30px" dy="2em">
dy = 2em for a new paragraph
</tspan>
<tspan x="30px" dy="1.5em">
But only 1.5em for normal lines
</tspan>
</text>
```

As you can imagine, this code snippet does not produce the nice, automatically adjusted lines of text you are used to in a word processor or Web browser. But it handles the job of getting text onto an SVG Web page. You can view examples at http://www.svgspider.com/, http://www.XMML.com/, and http://www.editITwrite.com/.

I find it convenient to copy and paste three lines at a time:

```
<tspan x="30px" dy="1.5em">
This is a first line of text.
</tspan>
```

Then I adjust the value of the dy attribute, for example. I find it is visually acceptable to use dy="2em" between paragraphs and dy="1.5em" between lines in the same paragraph. However, you may need to adjust that amount depending on the line height you choose. Then I simply paste an appropriate length of the desired text between the start tag and the end tag of the tspan element. I frequently preview the text to ensure that most lines are as close to the same length as I can make them. If you allow a line to overflow its viewbox and go on to write several more tspan elements, you will have unnecessary cutting and pasting to do to get the visual appearance correct.

This process is much more tedious than simply adding paragraphs of text using p elements in an HTML or XHTML Web page.

Using CSS to Separate Content and Presentation

Many examples in this book use style attributes or individual presentation properties or an internal CSS style sheet for convenience of presentation. In practice, for a production site, the choice for applying styling will lie between using an external CSS style sheet or an internal CSS style sheet, nested within a style element. Styling was discussed at greater length in Chapter 4, "Using CSS with SVG."

Internal Versus External CSS Style Sheets

The choice between internal and external CSS style sheets is one between smoothness of presentation versus efficiency of maintenance.

You can write an external CSS style sheet to control style throughout an SVG Web site. Such a style sheet is very convenient and efficient to write and to maintain. However, an external CSS style sheet can cause a transient, undesirable appearance when a page first loads.

The SVG Web pages at http://www.XMML.com/default.svg and http://www.editITwrite.com/default.svg both use external CSS style sheets. If you view these SVG Web pages using a dial-up connection on a 56K modem, you will notice a perceptible delay between the initial rendering of the page (using black and shades of gray) and the definitive rendering of the page when the external CSS style sheet has been retrieved and that styling information applied.

Internal style sheets avoid the initial rendering problem just described. However, they are less convenient and efficient to update than a single external CSS style sheet.

Controlling Cursor Appearance

You may want to control onscreen cursor appearance for several reasons.

If you want to give a hint to users that a certain part of the SVG image or document can usefully be clicked, you may want the cursor to display as a hand. You can do so by nesting the object of interest within an a element whose xlink:href value is the empty string. Listing 12.8 shows an example. The top text has the standard effect on the cursor appearance; that is, the cursor changes to an I-bar (or I-beam). The middle text has no effect on the cursor, a situation created by setting the pointer-events property to none. The a element on the bottom text causes the cursor to change to a pointing hand.

LISTING 12.8   Cursor01.svg—Controlling Cursor Appearance

```
<?xml version="1.0" standalone="no"?>
<!DOCTYPE svg PUBLIC "-//W3C//DTD SVG 20010904//EN"
"http://www.w3.org/TR/2001/REC-SVG-20010904/DTD/svg10.dtd">
<svg width="" height="">
<style type="text/css">
<![CDATA[
text{
font-size:20;
font-family:Arial, sans-serif;
fill:#000099;
stroke:none;
font-weight:normal;
}
]]>
</style>
<text x="50px" y="50px" >
This text is normal. An I-bar shows when it is moused
</text>
<text x="50px" y="150px" pointer-events="none" >
This text doesn't change the cursor because pointer-events is set to none.
</text>
<a xlink:href="">
<text x="50px" y="250px" >
This text produces a pointing hand cursor. It is wrapped in an &lt;a&gt;
 element
</text>
</a>
</svg>
```

Figure 12.7 shows a zoomed and panned onscreen appearance with the bottom text producing a pointing hand cursor.

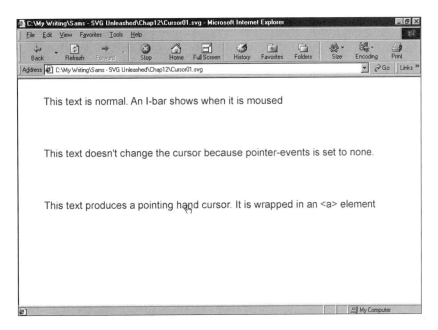

FIGURE 12.7   The pointing hand cursor created by an a element.

By using the a element and the pointing hand cursor, you can hint to users that the object is to be clicked. You can see examples of using the a element in this way online at http://www.XMML.com/default.svg and SVGPage.svg, where the technique is used within the SVG mini-pages.

Creating SVG Mini-Pages

SVG can be used to create conventionally laid out all-SVG Web pages such as those at http://www.svgspider.com/. However, SVG can also be used to create SVG "mini-pages" within a conventional page layout.

Figure 12.8 shows a sample mini-page on the http://www.XMML.com/ all-SVG Web site.

Figure 12.9 shows a zoomed view of the lower part of the mini-page with the navigation Next producing a pointing hand cursor. This is achieved using an a element with xlink:href="". The click event is captured and used to provide the transition between mini-pages.

SVG can provide many different, visually pleasing transition effects between mini-pages. You can view a few examples on the www.XMML.com and www.editITwrite.com, plus all other SVG Web sites.

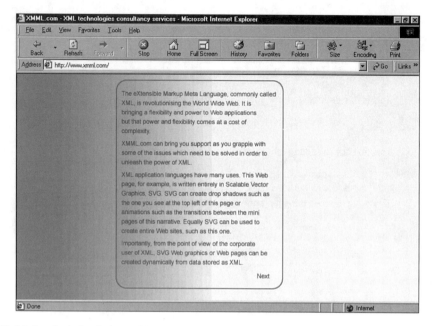

FIGURE 12.8   A general view of a page containing an SVG mini-page.

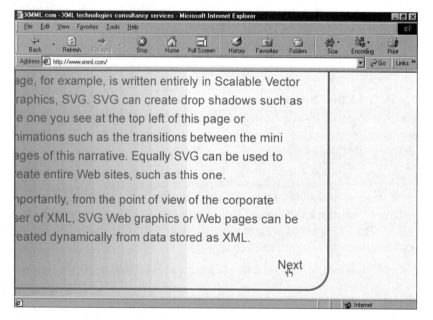

FIGURE 12.9   The pointing hand cursor created by an a element to turn mini-pages.

Reusing Visual Components

The image element of SVG 1.0 is intended to allow SVG document fragments to be imported into another SVG document fragment. In designing the SVG Web page at http://www.XMML.com/default.svg, it would have been ideal to have the code for the SVG banner ad at the top of the page as a separate SVG file to be referenced using the image element. However, ASV3 does not support referencing of SVG files that include animations. Therefore, the code for the animated SVG banner ad had to be included within the SVG Web page itself.

Similarly, the basic Web page design could have been created as a template from which various parts were referenced using the image element. Possible candidates are the mini-pages that make up the focus of the page and a navigation bar at the left. Having the mini-pages as separate components would be convenient. The navigation bar could simply be referenced from each appropriate page in the site, rather than written for each page (or copied and pasted into each page).

Creating SVG Web Pages with Scrollbars

One of the disappointing omissions in the Adobe implementation of SVG is that the Adobe SVG Viewer does not communicate with its containing browser to indicate to the browser that scrollbars are needed. So, if you create an SVG image that is larger than its containing browser window, you will find that, contrary to your experience with HTML/XHTML Web pages, no scrollbars will appear automatically.

This lack of scrollbars is a significant impediment to navigation when you want to navigate horizontally or vertically. You are able to pan, but not predictably in horizontal or vertical directions. In addition, the absence of automatically created scrollbars poses hurdles for disabled users compared to using scrollbars. If you have only one arm and try to (in Windows) hold down the Alt key, hold down the left mouse button, and at the same time move the mouse, it is almost impossible to do all that with one hand.

So, if you want to create large SVG Web pages, you may want to add scrollbars to improve the experience of visitors to your Web site. You can employ two techniques: embedding the SVG Web page within a blank HTML/XHTML Web page or using JavaScript to create scrollbars that are part of the SVG image.

Adding Scrollbars by Embedding

It is straightforward to add scrollbars to large SVG Web pages by embedding them in an empty HTML/XHTML Web page. Remember, if you choose to use the embed element, you may run into problems at some future date, depending on how and whether Web browsers tightly implement the XHTML 1.0 specification. At the time of writing, you can use embed within XHTML Web pages and are likely to do so for the foreseeable future.

Listing 12.9 is a simple but large, 1300 pixel by 800 pixel, SVG image that is a short substitute for a lengthy Web page. We will use it to test the creation of scrollbars. If your screen size is greater than 1300 by 800, adjust the numbers accordingly in the `width` and `height` attributes of the document element `svg` element to ensure that scrollbars are produced on your system.

LISTING 12.9   BigTest.svg—A Simple, Large SVG Image

```
<?xml version="1.0" standalone="no"?>
<!DOCTYPE svg PUBLIC "-//W3C//DTD SVG 20010904//EN"
"http://www.w3.org/TR/2001/REC-SVG-20010904/DTD/svg10.dtd">
<svg width="1300px" height="800px">
<rect x="0px" y="0px" width="100%" height="100%"
 style="stroke:red; stroke-width:4; fill:blue"/>
</svg>
```

Listing 12.10 shows a basic HTML shell that we can use to embed Listing 12.9 to provide scrollbars, using the `embed` element.

LISTING 12.10   ScrollBars01.html—Using the embed Element to Add Scrollbars

```
<!DOCTYPE html
PUBLIC "-//W3C//DTD XHTML 1.0 Transitional//EN"
"DTD/xhtml1-transitional.dtd">
<html>
<head>
<title>Embedding SVG in XHTML</title>
</head>
<body leftmargin="0" marginwidth="0" topmargin="0" marginheight="0"
 bottommargin="0">
<embed src="BigTest.svg" width="1300px" height="800px" type="image/svg+xml" />

</body>
</html>
```

If you test and run the code in Listing 12.10, you will have scrollbars available to you; whereas if you load BigTest.svg in a browser without an HTML or XHTML shell, no scrollbars will be automatically created. Depending on how you want the users to interact with the SVG content, you could, for example, provide scrollbars to enable the users to see the whole SVG image/Web page, but at the same time you could prevent them from zooming and panning by setting the `zoomAndPan` attribute to `disable`.

Many of the attributes used in the code for the body element are not officially recognized. They will place the top, left, and right of the SVG image right at the edge of the browser window in Internet Explorer, Netscape 6, and Mozilla 0.9.9, as well as Opera.

In theory, you ought to be able to use the W3C-approved object element and achieve the same result. In practice, it isn't so easy. Listing 12.11 creates scrollbars for Listing 12.9 using the object element, but the SVG file itself isn't displayed in Internet Explorer 5.5, Netscape 4.7, or Opera 5. However, it is displayed correctly in Netscape 6 and Mozilla 0.9.9.

LISTING 12.11   ScrollBars02.html—Embedding Using the object Element

```
<!DOCTYPE html
PUBLIC "-//W3C//DTD XHTML 1.0 Transitional//EN"
"DTD/xhtml1-transitional.dtd">
<html>
<head>
<title>Embedding SVG in XHTML</title>
</head>
<body marginwidth="0" marginheight="0" >
<object data="BigTest.svg" width="1300px" height="800px"
 type="image/svg+xml" />

</body>
</html>
```

In practice, then, it is safer—although not W3C-approved—to use the embed element rather than the object element to create scrollbars for large SVG Web pages.

Creating Scrollbars Using JavaScript

If you want to display all-SVG Web pages with scrollbars, you will, at least at the time of writing, need to use JavaScript and SVG to simulate the scrollbars that the browser automatically provides for HTML/XHTML.

Peter Sorotokin created a vertical scrollbar in SVG using JavaScript. Members of the SVG-Developers mailing list can access this code at `http://groups.yahoo.com/group/svg-developers/files/Scrollbar/map.svgz`. To subscribe to the list, send an e-mail to `svg-developers-subscribe@yahoogroups.com`. The files are mirrored at `http://www.svgfaq.com/scrollbars/scrollbars.zip`. The use of JavaScript with SVG is introduced in more detail in Part II of this book.

Adding mailto Links

A commonly used link on a Web page is a mailto link. To add a mailto link to an SVG Web page, simply add an a element and set the value of its xlink:href attribute to a value such as `mailto:consultancy@XMML.com`.

A sample mailto link in SVG is shown on the third SVG mini-page at `http://www.XMML.com/default.svg`.

Using the image Element

The existence of the `image` element in SVG ought to allow developers to create SVG visual components and include them when and where required by using the `image` element.

At the time of writing, there are practical impediments to taking full advantage of the flexibility that SVG 1.0 should provide. The Adobe SVG Viewer version 3.0 does not fully support the inclusion of SVG documents that include animations. The Batik SVG Viewer 1.1 (the latest full release version at the time of writing) does not support animations at all, although version 1.5 (in beta at the time of writing) promises to significantly improve functionality.

Therefore, any SVG code that might otherwise be suitable for inclusion by using an `image` element will have to be included in the primary SVG document, likely within a nested `svg` element. When support in SVG rendering engines improves, the nested `svg` element and its content can simply be excised and replaced by an `image` element with appropriate attributes.

To check on the current capabilities of the Batik browser, visit `http://xml.apache.org/batik/`.

The `image` element was introduced in Chapter 5, "Coordinate Systems in SVG."

Using the foreignObject Element

The absence of automatic text flow in SVG 1.0 is a distinct disadvantage to the developer, compared to the convenience of automatic text flow of HTML text content provided by the major Web browsers. In principle, the existence of the SVG 1.0 `foreignObject` element would allow SVG authors to simply place significant amounts of text in an XHTML foreign object and embed it in an SVG Web page. However, at the time of writing, the `foreignObject` element is not supported in Adobe SVG Viewer 3.0, the SVG viewer that has the most complete all-around SVG capabilities.

The X-Smiles browser, currently under development, allows SVG and XHTML to be mixed. Further information is available at `http://www.x-smiles.org/`. The latest information about the Adobe SVG Viewer should be accessible at `http://www.adobe.com/svg/`.

Using SVG with Bitmap Images

If you want to use bitmap images within SVG Web pages, you can do so by using the `image` element. A conforming SVG viewer is required to support PNG and JPEG formats (as well as supporting SVG images) and may optionally support other formats such as GIFs.

To make use of a PNG image, you simply use the `image` element with its `x`, `y`, `width`, and `height` attributes set to values appropriate to the size of the image that you want to display and use the `xlink:href` attribute, as follows, to specify the location of the bitmap image:

```
<image ... xlink:href="myPNGImage.png" />
```

Optionally, you may want to add a `type` attribute whose value indicates the MIME type of the bitmap image.

Summary

This chapter introduced a number of techniques to allow the use of SVG in Web pages, either conventional HTML/XHTML Web pages or all-SVG Web pages. The `embed` element is the element of choice to embed SVG images in HTML/XHTML Web pages. In addition, you can create all-SVG Web pages, so we discussed a number of issues relating to that topic.

CHAPTER 13

Accessibility, Internationalization, and Metadata

The purpose of a Web site is communication, and this chapter will look at three ways in which SVG can help you communicate your message to as large a proportion of your target audience as possible. Accessibility, internationalization, and metadata are important topics at a time when it is getting harder to stand out from the crowd, and each area has seen major advances in recent years, largely thanks to the development of XML. Being an application of XML, SVG inherently offers considerable support for these three techniques, and designers of the language have built on this support in a big way. In brief, the concerns of accessibility, internationalization, and metadata are as follows:

- **Accessibility**—Web accessibility may be defined as making content available for the target audience regardless of any disability it may have. This means Web design free from unnecessary barriers to the information, such as limited options in navigation (for example, mouse-only menus) that can block people with physical disabilities who rely on the keyboard. Accessibility should be considered a necessary part of Web design, and it is relatively easy to follow guidelines such as those of the W3C's Web Accessibility Initiative (http://www.w3.org/WAI/). SVG recognizes the importance of accessibility, and it is part of the specification. By following what essentially boils down to good coding practice, use of SVG means that to a great extent accessibility comes without extra effort. More information about accessibility with SVG can be found in the note at http://www.w3.org/TR/SVG-access.

- **Internationalization**—Internationalization (i18n) is primarily concerned with making content available in different languages. With markets becoming ever more global, the commercial potential is obvious. It may be a while before the results of information in general being globally available become apparent, but significant benefits to humanity as a whole are probable. SVG is a technology that, through its graphical nature (as well as its XML foundations), is supremely placed for communicating to any corner of the world.

> **NOTE**
>
> To save on typing, the term **internationalization** is commonly abbreviated to **i18n**, to represent "i + 18 letters + n."

- **Metadata**—This book is all about handling data that describes visual information. But what about data that describes that visual information's data? This is, of course, where metadata comes into the picture. An analogy has been made between the Web in its present form and a library without an index—or card catalog—the information might be there, but it's very hard to find. Metadata not only offers potential for improved indexing, cataloging, and searching, but also for applications that can reason further with the information, adding a layer of meaning to the Web.

Improving Code

For an example here, we'll use a rather simplistic architectural diagram of a house, as shown in Figure 13.1.

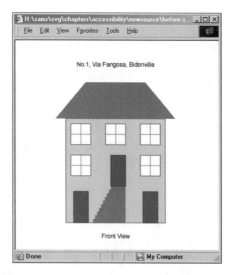

FIGURE 13.1 A simple architectural diagram.

The figure illustrates a fairly typical northern Italian house, with two ground floor "cantina" wine and food stores with doors leading onto the yard. Stone steps lead up to the front door. The code for this house, shown in Listing 13.1, is based on basic shapes as you learned in the first chapters of this book, and is reasonably self-explanatory (although it would be a lot less clear without the comments).

LISTING 13.1   before.svg—First Version of Architectural SVG

```
<svg xmlns="http://www.w3.org/2000/svg">

   <!-- house body -->
   <rect x="100" y="150" width="200" height="200" style="fill:lightgrey;
      stroke:black; stroke-width:1"/>

   <!-- roof -->
   <polygon fill="red" points="80,150 140,80 260,80 320,150"/>

   <!-- top floor windows -->
   <rect x="110" y="160" width="40" height="40" style="fill:white;
      stroke:black; stroke-width:1"/>
   <line x1="110" y1="180" x2="150" y2="180"
      style="stroke:grey; stroke-width:1"/>
   <line x1="130" y1="160" x2="130" y2="200"
      style="stroke:grey; stroke-width:1"/>

   <rect x="180" y="160" width="40" height="40" style="fill:white;
      stroke:black; stroke-width:1"/>
   <line x1="180" y1="180" x2="220" y2="180"
      style="stroke:grey; stroke-width:1"/>
   <line x1="200" y1="160" x2="200" y2="200"
      style="stroke:grey; stroke-width:1"/>

   <rect x="250" y="160" width="40" height="40"
      style="fill:white; stroke:black; stroke-width:1"/>
   <line x1="250" y1="180" x2="290" y2="180"
      style="stroke:grey; stroke-width:1"/>
   <line x1="270" y1="160" x2="270" y2="200"
      style="stroke:grey; stroke-width:1"/>

   <!-- middle floor windows -->
   <rect x="110" y="220" width="40" height="40" style="fill:white;
      stroke:black; stroke-width:1"/>
   <line x1="110" y1="240" x2="150" y2="240"
```

13

LISTING 13.1   Continued

```
          style="stroke:grey; stroke-width:1"/>
      <line x1="130" y1="220" x2="130" y2="260"
          style="stroke:grey; stroke-width:1"/>

      <rect x="250" y="220" width="40" height="40" style="fill:white;
          stroke:black; stroke-width:1"/>
      <line x1="250" y1="240" x2="290" y2="240"
          style="stroke:grey; stroke-width:1"/>
      <line x1="270" y1="220" x2="270" y2="260"
          style="stroke:grey; stroke-width:1"/>

      <!-- front door -->
      <rect x="190" y="220" width="30" height="60" style="fill:brown;
          stroke:black; stroke-width:1"/>

      <!-- cantina doors -->
      <rect x="115" y="290" width="30" height="60" style="fill:brown;
          stroke:black; stroke-width:1"/>
      <rect x="255" y="290" width="30" height="60" style="fill:brown;
          stroke:black; stroke-width:1"/>

      <!-- steps -->
      <polygon transform="translate(155, 280) scale(0.4,0.7)"
          style="fill:grey; stroke:black; stroke-width:1"
             points="0,100 0,90 10,90 10,80 20,80
                  20,70 30,70 30,60 40,60 40,50
                  50,50 50,40 60,40 60,30 70,30
                  70,20 80,20 80,10 90,10 90,0
                  100,0 160,0 160,100"/>

      <text x="200" y="50" text-anchor="middle">No.1, Via Fangosa, Bidonville
          </text>
      <text x="200" y="380" text-anchor="middle">Front View</text>
</svg>
```

The most obvious fault of Listing 13.1 is the amount of repetition; for instance, five windows look identical, apart from their position. From a programmer's point of view, the main reason this is undesirable is that repetition of code means extra work. From an accessibility perspective, the same applies, in that a nonvisual representation of this code (which we will be looking at shortly) would involve repetition of the description of each basic element. The underlying flaw from both points of view is that structural information is being neglected.

A good first step in maximizing the accessibility of SVG material is to make the structure of the document as clear as possible.

The easiest way of doing this is to use defs (these elements are introduced in Chapter 2, "Document Structure in SVG") to define the more complex symbols such as house windows. Listing 13.2 incorporates the defs element.

LISTING 13.2   Windows Using Symbol Definitions

```
...
<defs>
    <symbol id="window">
        <rect width="40" height="40" style="fill:white; stroke:black;
          stroke-width:1"/>
        <line x1="0" y1="20" x2="40" y2="20" style="stroke:grey;
          stroke-width:1"/>
        <line x1="20" y1="0" x2="20" y2="40" style="stroke:grey;
          stroke-width:1"/>
    </symbol>
...
</defs>
...
    <!-- top floor windows -->
    <use xlink:href="#window" transform="translate(110, 160)"/>
    <use xlink:href="#window" transform="translate(180, 160)"/>
    <use xlink:href="#window" transform="translate(250, 160)"/>
...
```

For the moment, we have kept the styling attributes of the shapes that make up a window, but we will be moving them out later as they are solely related to presentation.

> **NOTE**
>
> To use the xlink attributes, we need to declare the prefix. This declaration can be to the SVG element:
>
> ```
> <svg xmlns="http://www.w3.org/2000/svg"
>     xmlns:xlink="http://www.w3.org/1999/xlink">
> ```
>
> For more information on using xlink, see Chapter 2.

According to the specification, the symbol definitions can be placed in a separate file and referenced. You would use a URI with a fragment identifier (starting with #) to specify which element to point to. So, if we wanted to reference the symbol definition with an `id` attribute of `window` in a file named housebits.svg, we would use

```
<use xlink:href="housebits.svg#window" transform="translate(180, 160)"/>
```

An alternative is to embed an image:

```
<image x="110" y="160" width="40" height="40" xlink:href="window.svg"/>
```

Note that the height and width of the image have to be given.

NOTE

At present, the support for the specifications in the implementations breaks down here. In particular, Adobe's SVG Viewer 3 (ASV3) doesn't support cross-file element linking on the use element, and CSS styling from an embedded image is lost.

Now that we have made the structure of the SVG document clear, we can look at how SVG and accessibility can work together.

General Accessibility Features of SVG

There is a very useful accessibility feature inherent in SVG—it's scalable. Being able to zoom in and out of an image means that someone with limited vision can blow up a part of an image to get a better view. This feature is, however, only the tip of the iceberg. The more ways in which data can be represented, the more ways in which information can be communicated. SVG can be used to present static graphics, text, sound, and animation—and this is only the front end of the technology. Underneath we have XML, the DOM, and programming language support. For communication, the limiting factor with SVG is now the developer's imagination. In this book, the limiting factor is page count, so in this chapter, we will look only at the relatively low-level features of SVG that enhance accessibility.

No Viewer, No Comment?

One fundamental problem with discussing SVG as an aid to accessibility is that this technology is only beginning to receive widespread adoption. If a user doesn't have a suitable viewer, graphic SVG information is essentially inaccessible. Additionally, some browsers and browsing tools (such as screen readers) by design don't support graphics. This is really the worst-case scenario. After all, text is one of the three basic graphic objects (along with shape and image), so at least this information can be presented more or less directly on a screen reader. Additionally, XML is intended to be reasonably human-readable, and it may be appropriate sometimes to present SVG as plain text. However, lack of a dedicated SVG viewer is often an issue, so we need to repeat the accessibility mantra: "Provide a text alternative."

The simple act of adding alternate text makes any graphical material significantly more accessible and therefore makes the information more widely available. HTML provides this facility primarily in the form of the alt attribute for <img> elements, and pop-up tooltips using the title attribute are now quite familiar. SVG provides the alternate text facility in the form of desc and title elements, though the benefit might not be as obvious as a pop-up. The title element, as we saw in Chapter 2, can be used to assign a title to any container or graphical element. The desc element has a similar role and is used in the same fashion to provide a description of the associated element or group of elements.

> **NOTE**
>
> The way in which the title and desc elements are handled is largely browser- or agent-specific. For instance, the Adobe plug-in for Internet Explorer uses the outermost title element for the title of the browser window, other title elements and descriptions remaining invisible. But these elements can also be utilized by the developer within scripts for much more interesting purposes, to create voiceovers, for example, to speak the contained text.

According to the specifications, authors should always provide a title for an SVG document, and it is good practice to supply a description at this level too. So a reasonable minimum use of alternate text would be something like this:

```
<svg xmlns="http://www.w3.org/2000/svg">
    <title>No.1, Via Fangosa, Bidonville</title>
    <desc>Front View of a House</desc>
    ...
</svg>
```

It is no coincidence that the text here is the same as the text on the diagram shown in Figure 13.1; it is convenient to leverage alternate text a little by using the same content within the visual representation. You can do so by assigning the <title> and <desc> elements unique IDs and referring to them through <tref> elements (discussed in Chapter 8, "Laying Out Text in SVG"):

```
...
<title id="mainTitle">No.1, Via Fangosa, Bidonville</title>
<desc id="subTitle">Front View of a House</desc>
...
<text x="200" y="50"><tref xlink:href="#mainTitle"/></text>
<text x="200" y="380"><tref xlink:href="#subTitle"/></text>
...
```

We can provide a description of the contents of an SVG document with whatever level of granularity we deem appropriate, grouping the elements together as necessary. It is worth remembering that the description should actually add some information. "Front View" wouldn't convey much information to someone using a screen reader, whereas "Front View of a House" is more useful. For instance, we might have the following:

```
<g>
    <title>Front Bedroom Window</title>
    <desc>Modern aluminum frame</desc>
    <use xlink:href="#window" transform="translate(110, 160)"/>
</g>
```

Styling for Accessibility

With most browsers, we can apply a default CSS style sheet with features that can be made to take precedence over those specified by the author. For instance, a partially sighted user may be able to see an image more clearly with a particular high-contrast color scheme. The following CSS declaration will produce a bold yellow outline on a black background:

```
.background {
    fill:black !important
}

svg {
    stroke:yellow ! important;
    stroke-width:1 ! important;
    text-anchor:middle ! important;
    fill:black ! important
}
```

The ! important operator gives these user styles precedence, overriding whatever else is associated with the document. As usual, we can make the styling more fine-grained, which is desirable for this example because the stroke-width of 1 applied to shapes appears very light, and it also is applied to the text, which comes out fuzzy:

```
svg {
    stroke:yellow ! important;
    stroke-width:2 ! important;
    text-anchor:middle ! important;
    fill:black ! important
}

text {
    fill:yellow ! important;
    font-size:14 ! important;
    stroke:none ! important
}
```

> **NOTE**
>
> An ! important declaration within a presentation attribute definition is an error. For more information on the use of presentation attributes, see section 6.4 of the specification.

The result is rather more balanced, as shown in Figure 13.2.

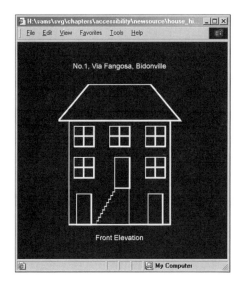

FIGURE 13.2   High-contrast style.

Styling the Document

A paradigm that crops up regularly in Web programming is the separation of content from appearance. With an SVG document, we can pull out the local styling information and place it in a separate CSS file. In Listing 13.3, we have a restructured version of the house diagram with added element titles and descriptions, with the attributes that define appearance now linked in from a style sheet. The styling information will be in a file named after.css, which we will look at shortly. We want to use links to symbols in this document, so we need to declare the XLink namespace.

LISTING 13.3   house_after.svg

```
<?xml version="1.0"?>
<?xml-stylesheet href="css/after.css" type="text/css"?>
<svg    xmlns="http://www.w3.org/2000/svg"
    xmlns:xlink="http://www.w3.org/1999/xlink">
```

Next, we have the definitions of the symbols we will be using in the diagram. Each symbol has an `id` attribute so that we can refer to it later and also a `class` attribute through which we can supply styling information:

```
<defs>
    <symbol id="houseBody">
        <rect width="200" height="200" class="houseBody"/>
    </symbol>

    <symbol id="houseRoof">
        <polygon points="0,70 60,0 180,0 240,70" class="roof"/>
    </symbol>

    <symbol id="window">
        <rect width="40" height="40" class="window"/>
        <line x1="0" y1="20" x2="40" y2="20" class="window"/>
        <line x1="20" y1="0" x2="20" y2="40" class="window"/>
    </symbol>

    <symbol id="door">
        <rect width="30" height="60" class="door"/>
    </symbol>

    <symbol id="steps">
        <polygon transform="scale(0.4,0.7)" class="steps"
                points="0,100 0,90 10,90 10,80 20,80
                        20,70 30,70 30,60 40,60 40,50
                        50,50 50,40 60,40 60,30 70,30
                        70,20 80,20 80,10 90,10 90,0
                        100,0 160,0 160,100"/>
    </symbol>
</defs>
```

As mentioned earlier, recycling the document title and description can be convenient. We've given each one an `id` here so that we can display this text later:

```
<title id="mainTitle">No.1, Via Fangosa, Bidonville</title>
<desc id="subTitle">Front View of a House </desc>
```

Now we start the diagram proper, with each part of the house being given by means of a use element to access the symbols described previously. First, we have the roof and body of the house, and nested within the use element, we now have additional textual information giving the title and description of this part of the house:

```
<use x="80" y="80" xlink:href="#houseRoof">
    <title>Roof</title>
    <desc>terracotta tiles</desc>
</use>

<use x="100" y="150" xlink:href="#houseBody">
    <title>House Body</title>
    <desc>grey stucco</desc>
</use>
```

We could supply titles and descriptions for every single part of the diagram, but here instead we group together the upper floor windows in a g element so that they can share the same title> and desc:

```
<g>
    <title>Top floor windows</title>
    <desc>three in a row, modern aluminum</desc>

    <use x="110" y="160" xlink:href="#window"/>
    <use x="180" y="160" xlink:href="#window"/>
    <use x="250" y="160" xlink:href="#window"/>
</g>
```

We continue in the same fashion for the rest of the diagram, with extra textual information included as deemed appropriate:

```
<g>
    <title>Middle floor windows</title>
    <desc>one either side of front door, modern aluminum</desc>

    <use x="110" y="220" xlink:href="#window"/>
    <use x="250" y="220" xlink:href="#window"/>
</g>

<use x="190" y="220" xlink:href="#door">
    <title>Front door</title>
    <desc>modern aluminum</desc>
</use>

<g>
    <title>Cantina doors</title>
    <desc>one either side of steps, painted wood</desc>
    <use x="115" y="290" xlink:href="#door"/>
```

```
    <use x="255" y="290" xlink:href="#door"/>
</g>

<use x="155" y="280" xlink:href="#steps">
    <title>Steps</title>
    <desc>stucco-faced stone</desc>
</use>
```

Finally, we have the diagram labels, the text obtained from the document title and description:

```
    <text x="200" y="50" class="mainTitle"><tref xlink:href="#mainTitle"/></text>
    <text x="200" y="380" class="subTitle"><tref xlink:href="#subTitle"/></text>
</svg>
```

The style sheet the preceding document uses—after.css—begins by styling the outermost element to give a white background:

```
svg {
    fill:white
}
```

Next, we deal with the way in which text will be displayed. For a little variety, we can make a minor change to the original diagram so that all the text on the page will inherit some common characteristics, but the font size will be different for the main title and subtitle:

```
text {
    fill:black;
    stroke:none;
    text-anchor:middle;
}

text.mainTitle {
    font-size:14
}

text.subTitle {
    font-size:12
}
```

Next is the styling for each symbol used in the diagram, with the declaration properties and values taken from the attributes in the original house document:

```
rect.houseBody {
    fill:lightgrey;
    stroke:black;
    stroke-width:1
}

polygon.roof {
    fill:red;
    stroke:none;
}

rect.window {
    fill:white;
    stroke:black;
    stroke-width:1
}

line.window {
    stroke:grey;
    stroke-width:1
}

rect.door {
    fill:brown;
    stroke:black;
    stroke-width:1
}

polygon.steps {
    fill:grey;
    stroke:black;
    stroke-width:1
}
```

Finally, we have a couple of declarations whose purpose isn't immediately obvious (the title> and desc aren't normally visible in an SVG viewer):

```
title {
    display: block;
    font-weight: bolder
}

desc {
    display: block
}
```

Earlier, we stated that if someone doesn't have a suitable viewer, graphic SVG information is inaccessible. This is perfectly true, but given the fact that many browsers make an effort to render XML, it is still possible to convey some of the information in an SVG document. If we open the SVG file named house_after.svg in Internet Explorer 6 without having a viewer installed, we get the window shown in Figure 13.3.

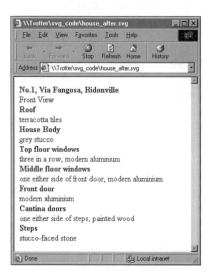

FIGURE 13.3   A message displayed in IE6 without the SVG plug-in.

As you can see in the figure, the contents of the title and desc elements have been interpreted as text nodes, and what's more, the rendering has been governed by the style declarations for these elements in the CSS file.

The CSS support offeredby SVG means that it is possible to use aural style sheets to provide audio equivalents for text content, but this is a standard practice that goes beyond the scope of this book. You can find further information at http://www.w3.org/TR/REC-CSS2/aural.html.

Device Independence

Earlier, we briefly mentioned the need to provide keyboard support for navigation, and this extends to anything that calls for user interaction. Basically, the requirement is to be able to tab through items on a page until the one of interest has focus, and then to activate that item (corresponding to a mouse click). SVG 1.0 does not cover keyboard events because of complications with the DOM Level 2 specification, but the Adobe viewer incorporates support for these events as described in the draft spec (see http://www.adobe.com/svg/indepth/pdfs/CurrentSupport.pdf). It is probable that by the time SVG 1.1 becomes a recommendation this issue will be resolved in the specification through reference to DOM Level 3 events. This issue is discussed (with an ECMAScript partial workaround) on the SVG Wiki (http://www.protocol7.com/svg-wiki/).

As well as providing information that can be accessed using different input devices, we must also consider different output devices such as audio channels. In a few year's time, it is likely that the facilities provided by user agents (such as SVG browsers) will cover audio output well enough that it won't be an issue for developers, but at present, work in this area is largely experimental. An example of an approach to this is "Self-Voicing SVG" (http://www.dpawson.co.uk/svg/), a system in which annotations can be added to an SVG document that can later be rendered back using speech software.

Accessible Navigation

We will now look at one way of augmenting the mouse/visual interface to a page with keyboard access and audio. The page initially displays four arrows, corresponding to different directions in which the user can navigate (see Figure 13.4). In this example, clicking on an arrow will open one of four linked HTML pages.

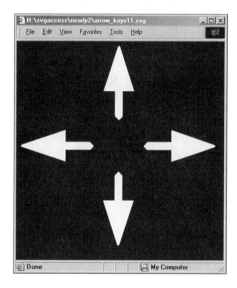

FIGURE 13.4   Initial view of the navigator.

With the aid of ECMAScript, we are going to make it possible to select a direction using the keyboard, and give audio cues to indicate which direction is currently selected.

> **NOTE**
>
> You'll learn more about SVG with ECMAScript/JavaScript in Part II of this book.

An additional feature in this example will be the use of "tooltip" type pop-ups. As an arrow receives attention either from the mouse pointer being over it or being selected by the keyboard, a label will be displayed (see Figure 13.5). The text used in the pop-ups will be derived from the `title` element associated with the area of interest. Due to the limitations of current implementations, a couple of hacks will be used, so this code should very much be considered experimental.

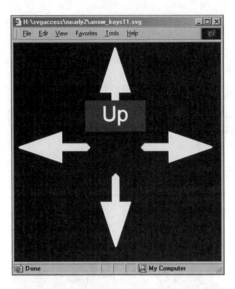

FIGURE 13.5　View of navigator when the "up" direction is selected.

The user can also move between the four points by pressing the spacebar. The pop-up for each arrow will then be displayed in turn, and pressing the Return or Enter key will cause the appropriate linked page to load. This approximates the way a user can normally navigate around links on a Web page using the Tab key.

The code for this is all contained in `navigator.svg`, shown in Listing 13.4, and is available from the Sams Web site. To operate, the code uses five MP3 format sound files also available from the site. Four of these files contain recordings of the words *up*, *down*, *left*, and *right*, and the fifth contains silence. To demonstrate that the navigation to other pages actually works, we will also use four HTML pages that just display the word *Up*, *Left*, and so on.

Having four arrows suggests some logical grouping in the code. In fact, what we'll have in the SVG is four `g` groups, each corresponding to one of the directions. We want some of the same results whether the page elements are accessed through a mouse or keyboard: a pop-up and a sound played. This means much of the code can be common for both kinds of access. Every time the mouse pointer moves over a particular arrow (group) or that arrow (group) is selected using the keyboard, we need to display a pop-up containing the corresponding `<title>` text, play the corresponding sound, and enable the appropriate link.

If we had to deal only with mouse events, we *could* easily get all these values directly from the DOM. To be able to select each arrow in turn from the keyboard means we will have to remember which arrow we are looking at, and one straightforward way of doing this is to have an index. So, in the code, we have a variable called direction that can have one of four values: 0 for up, 1 for left, 2 for right, and 3 for down. If we are going to have such an index, we can also avoid having to query the DOM every time for the values we need and instead keep them in a lookup table. The approach taken here falls between the two extremes; we will keep a lookup table containing the <title> text along with each DOM element that represents each g group. Links can be set up to respond to mouse events using a elements in the usual fashion, so half the work is already done for them, and we won't store them in the lookup table but will extract them from the DOM as demanded by keyboard actions.

The lookup table will, in fact, be a hashtable of g elements and their associated <title> text. This table will also be indexed, so we can step through the alternatives with the keyboard. The table will be loaded right at the start; then if an arrow is selected by the user using the keyboard, the table will be used to get the appropriate element and pop-up text. If the user presses Return or Enter, the code will examine the selected element (through DOM methods) to get the appropriate page address.

If the user points the mouse at an arrow, we will find the required g element based on the mouse event and use the lookup table to find the corresponding pop-up text.

Most of the code, in fact, consists of functions that wrap up a series of DOM operations. For example, the addText(text, x, y) method will create a new text element and rect element (to act as the pop-up background), with the supplied values for x and y attributes, and insert them in the DOM tree, thus displaying a pop-up.

The code begins by declaring the namespaces that will be used; they are standard SVG, XLink, and a namespace that includes Adobe's extension for audio. The svg element also contains some event-handling code to grab the focus and call an initialization function on loading, call a keypress-handling function and again the grab the focus when a key is pressed, and grab the focus when the mouse pointer moves over this element. The init() and getKey() functions are shown in Listing 13.4. The focus is needed to be able to respond to keyboard events.

LISTING 13.4   navigator.svg

```
<?xml version="1.0" encoding="ISO-8859-1" standalone="yes"?>

<svg xmlns="http://www.w3.org/2000/svg"
    xmlns:xlink="http://www.w3.org/1999/xlink"
    xmlns:a="http://www.adobe.com/svg10-extensions"
        onload="focus();init(evt)"
        onkeypress="getKey(evt);focus()"
        onmouseover="window.focus()">
```

> **NOTE**
>
> This example uses a proprietary extension declared through the http://www.adobe.com/svg10-extensions namespace. Some unreliability has been noted using this namespace with ASV3 (though not with this sample code). You can substitute the ASV3 extension namespace http://ns.adobe.com/AdobeSVGViewerExtensions/3.0/ if you encounter problems.

Within the `<defs>` block, we have the definition of the arrow symbol that will be displayed:

```
<defs>
    <symbol id="Arrow" viewBox="0 0 100 100">
        <line x1="0" y1="0" x2="80" y2="80" stroke="yellow" stroke-width="15"/>
        <path d="M 100 100 L 60 20 L 20 60 z" fill="yellow"
         stroke="yellow" stroke-width="3" />
    </symbol>
</defs>
```

The next line is a hack needed for the SVG document to gain the focus, simply one huge rectangle. Discussion of this hack and the issues relating to focus can be found on the SVG Wiki (http://www.protocol7.com/svg-wiki/).

```
<rect x="-10000" y="-10000" width="30000" height="30000" fill="black"/>
```

In the future, the best way of getting audio into SVG is likely to be using SMIL (Synchronized Multimedia Integration Language, http://www.w3.org/AudioVideo/), but until implementations catch up with specifications, one alternative is to use the Adobe extensions. The following line will cause a sound to play and repeat whenever the page has focus:

```
<a:audio xlink:href="nothing.mp3" dur="1s" repeatCount="indefinite" />
```

This is part of the second hack; documentation describing how the Adobe extensions work isn't currently available, but experimentation suggests that it isn't yet possible to trigger the playing of a new sound from an ECMAScript event. Instead, what we do here is to continually loop the sound (here, nothing.mp3 is empty; it is just silence) and substitute into the DOM a different link reference when we want a different sound to play. This second sound will also be looped indefinitely, which, although far from ideal, is reasonably acceptable in use.

Next, in the SVG we have four blocks, each of which describes one of the four possible navigation directions (up, left, right, down). The arrow is produced by using the symbol defined previously, with a rotation used to get it to point in the right direction. The arrow is linked to an external file (up.html, and so on) by its parent a element. The location of the arrow onscreen is determined by a transform on the g element, and we are going to be using this information later. The g elements form a grouping to enclose the use and other elements associated with each arrow. Each group also includes a title element, which under normal circumstances wouldn't be displayed. Two events are picked up by attributes on the g elements, calling the following ECMAScript methods when the mouse pointer passes over the arrow:

```
<g transform="translate(200,150)"  onmouseover="showTitle(evt)"
                        onmouseout="hideTitle()">
    <title>Up</title>
    <a xlink:href="up.html">
        <use xlink:href="#Arrow" width="100" height="100"
                        transform="rotate(-135)"/>
    </a>
</g>

<g transform="translate(150,200)"  onmouseover="showTitle(evt)"
                        onmouseout="hideTitle()">
    <title>Left</title>
    <a xlink:href="left.html">
        <use xlink:href="#Arrow" width="100" height="100"
                        transform="rotate(135)" />
    </a>
</g>

<g transform="translate(250,200)"  onmouseover="showTitle(evt)"
                        onmouseout="hideTitle()">
    <title>Right</title>
    <a xlink:href="right.html">
        <use xlink:href="#Arrow" width="100" height="100"
                        transform="rotate(-45)" />
    </a>
</g>

<g transform="translate(200,250)" onmouseover="showTitle(evt)"
                        onmouseout="hideTitle()">
    <title>Down</title>
    <a xlink:href="down.html">
        <use xlink:href="#Arrow" width="100" height="100"
                        transform="rotate(45)" />
    </a>
</g>
```

The ECMAScript begins by declaring a handful of variables that will be shared across different functions in the script. The groups contained in the SVG shown earlier will be represented as items in a custom data structure called groups. As the user sequences through the four alternatives by pressing the spacebar, currentGroup will contain data related to the currently selected direction. Similarly, direction (an index) and element (a DOM text element) will relate to one of the four arrows. The rectElement variable will contain the rectangle that will act as the background for each pop-up. The init() function initializes the direction variable to the first option (up) and loads data from the document into the groups data structure. The audio element described in SVG earlier is then found in the document and pointed to by the variable soundElement:

```
<script type="text/ecmascript"><![CDATA[

var groups;
var currentGroup;
var direction;
var element;
var rectElement;
var soundElement;

function init(){
    direction = 0;
    loadGroups();
    var allSoundElements = svgDocument.getElementsByTagName("a:audio");
    soundElement = allSoundElements.item(0);
}
```

Next in the code, we make use of ECMAScript's object-awareness and create a custom data structure called Hashtable to contain a list of data pairs. As well as the usual hashtable put(key, value) and get(key) methods (to store the pair {key, value} and retrieve a value given the key), the data structure also has an item(index) method, which will allow access to the keys in the order in which they were put into the data structure.

The data pairs we will be storing in a Hashtable object will consist of a g element and the string of text extracted from the group's associated title element, which is reflected in the naming of local variables within the object's definition:

```
function Hashtable(){
    this.elements = new Array();
    this.titles = new Array();
    this.size = 0;
    this.put = put;
    this.get = get;
    this.item = item;
}
```

```
function put(element, title){
    this.elements[this.size] = element;
    this.titles[this.size] = title;
    this.size++;
}

function get(element){
    for(i=0;i<this.size;i++){
        if(element == this.elements[i])
            return this.titles[i];
        }
    return null;
}

function item(index){
    return this.elements[index];
}
```

The Hashtable instance groups is filled by the following method, which is called when the page is first loaded. First, the title elements are gathered into a node set from the document. For each of these elements, the text they contain is extracted using a helper method. Similarly, the g element that contains each title element is found using a helper method, and each g element and its associated title is put into the hashtable:

```
function loadGroups(){
    groups = new Hashtable();
    var titleElements = svgDocument.getElementsByTagName("title");

    var title, container;

    for(var i=0;i<titleElements.getLength();i++){
        title = extractText(titleElements.item(i));
        container = getContainerElement(titleElements.item(i));
        groups.put(container, title);
    }
}
```

The helper methods that loadGroups() calls are as follows. The method to extract text is fairly generic, in that it will pull out all the text from below any element it is sent. The getContainerElement() method is more specific, looking for an ancestor g element.

```
// gets the text from an element
function extractText(element) {
try {
```

```
        var children = element ? element.getChildNodes() : null;
        var text = "";

        for (var i=0; children && i<children.getLength(); i++) {

            if (children.item(i).getNodeType() == 3) { // text node
                text += children.item(i).getNodeValue();
            }
        }
    } catch(exception){
        alert("Error in extractText :"+exception);
     }
        return text;
}


// steps up to find a parent <g>
function getContainerElement(element){
    while(element.nodeName != "g"){
        element = element.parentNode;
    }
    return element;
}
```

The next two methods also carry out simple operations on the DOM. The first will pull out the URL given as an attribute in an <a> child of the element it has been supplied. It does so by using the second method that obtains and then checks child nodes for an element with a particular name:

```
// gets the link text from a contained <a> element
function getLink(element){
    var aElement = extractElement(element, "a");
    return aElement.getAttributeNS("http://www.w3.org/1999/xlink","href");
}


// pull out a single named element child
function extractElement(parent, name) {
try{
    var children = parent.getChildNodes();
    var child;

    for (var i=0; i<children.getLength(); i++) {
        child = children.item(i);
    if (child.getNodeType() == 1 && child.getNodeName() == name)
```

```
        return child;
    }
    } catch(exception){
        alert("Error in extractElement :"+exception);
    }
    return null;
}
```

We will be placing the pop-up text at a position determined by the transform made on the g elements, and the next two methods are crude but adequate parsers to extract the coordinates from an attribute of the form transform="translate(x, y)":

```
function getTransformX(element){
    var transform = element.getAttribute("transform");
    var leftBrace = transform.indexOf("(");
    var comma = transform.indexOf(",");
    return transform.substring(leftBrace+1, comma);
}


function getTransformY(element){
    var transform = element.getAttribute("transform");
    var comma = transform.indexOf(",");
    var rightBrace = transform.indexOf(")");
    return transform.substring(comma+1, rightBrace);
}
```

When the user moves his or her mouse pointer over an arrow, the following showTitle() method will be called. It uses the getContainerElement() method listed earlier to get the g element that contains the element that the mouse pointer is over. This element is used as a key in the groups hashtable to find the text to display, as well as in the previous methods to find the x and y coordinates to locate the pop-up. The text and coordinates are then passed to the addText() method, which will add new elements to the document to display the pop-up.

```
function showTitle(evt){
    var container = getContainerElement(evt.target);
    addText(groups.get(container), getTransformX(container),
    getTransformY(container));
}
```

The first thing addText() does is to remove any existing pop-up by calling the hideTitle() method. Next, the sound element (<a:audio...> listed in the SVG part of the code) is updated with the name of the new sound file. The text element and its background rectangle are then created programmatically using DOM methods, and then they are appended to the document. The painting order ensures that these elements will appear on top of the arrows. The `element` and `rectElement` variables are global to this script, so we will have no trouble referring back to them later should we need to remove them.

```
function addText(text, x, y) {

    hideTitle(); // make sure previous is cleared

    soundElement.setAttributeNS("http://www.w3.org/1999/xlink","xlink:href",
      text+".mp3");

   try{
    var textNode = svgDocument.createTextNode(text);
    element = svgDocument.createElement("text");

    element.setAttributeNS(null, "fill", "white");
    element.setAttributeNS(null, "stroke", "white");
    element.setAttributeNS(null, "font-size", "40");
    element.setAttributeNS(null, "text-anchor","middle");

    element.setAttributeNS(null, "x", x);
    element.setAttributeNS(null, "y", y);

// background for 'tooltip'
    rectElement = svgDocument.createElement("rect");
    rectElement.setAttributeNS(null, "fill", "blue");
    rectElement.setAttributeNS(null, "width", "120");
    rectElement.setAttributeNS(null, "height", "60");

    rectElement.setAttributeNS(null, "x", ""+(parseInt(x)-60));
    rectElement.setAttributeNS(null, "y", ""+(parseInt(y)-40));

    svgDocument.documentElement.appendChild(rectElement);  // added to root

    element.appendChild(textNode);
    svgDocument.documentElement.appendChild(element); // added to root
    } catch(exception){
        alert("Error in addText :"+exception);
    }
}
```

The `hideTitle()` method resets the audio file being looped back to the sound of silence, before removing the pop-up elements. Because this method may be called before any pop-up is displayed (from the first call to addText()), we will catch and ignore the exception generated in such circumstances:

```
function hideTitle() {
    soundElement.setAttributeNS("http://www.w3.org/1999/xlink",
            "xlink:href", "nothing.mp3");
    try{
        svgDocument.documentElement.removeChild(element);
        svgDocument.documentElement.removeChild(rectElement);
    } catch(exception){
    // ignore 'not found' exception
     }
}
```

The last part of navigator.svg is a function that is called when the user hits the keyboard. We are on the lookout for two particular keys: the spacebar and the Return key. The first we check for by translating the keypress event into a corresponding string and comparing it with " "; we check for the Return key i for more directly by comparing it with the character code (13). This approach could be rationalized to use one method or the other, but both are left here as a reminder of how it can be done. If the key pressed is the spacebar, the direction index (0...3) is used to find the appropriate g element in the groups data structure. The addText() method, shown previously, is then called to display the pop-up and change the sound using parameters derived from this element. The direction index is then moved to the next value in its cycle. If the Return key is pressed, the URL given in the current group is extracted and given as a new target page for the browser, producing the same effect as clicking on a regular hyperlink.

```
function getKey(e) {

    key = e.getCharCode();

    var pressed = String.fromCharCode(key);

    if(pressed == " "){
        currentGroup = groups.item(direction);
        hideTitle();
        addText(groups.get(currentGroup), getTransformX(currentGroup),
            getTransformY(currentGroup));
      if(++direction == 4){
          direction = 0;
      }
        return;
    }
    if(key == 13){ // return key
```

```
        if(currentGroup == undefined){
            currentGroup = groups.item(direction);
        }
        var link = getLink(currentGroup);
        window.open(link, "_self",null);
    }
}
]]>
</script>
```

Performance Issues

The example in the preceding section works well running locally, but over the Internet, the sounds are heard after a relatively long delay. Unfortunately, ASV3 cannot cache audio, so every time a different sound is required, it must be downloaded again. One workaround is to include the audio data inside the SVG document using base64 encoding, an output option on many audio tools. Each of the sounds can then be referenced by ID, which will look something like this:

```
<a:audio id="up" xlink:href="data:audio/mp3;base64,//qQQMPUAAAAAABLBQAAAAAACWC
➥gAAALzT9VuTUAAWWnarcmoAAAAEDAIBAECAUCgUDADwN9wPt
```

...

We can switch the sounds on and off by means of their duration, modifying the addText() method to read

```
function addText(text, x, y) {
    hideTitle(); // make sure previous is cleared
//    soundElement.setAttribute("xlink:href", text+".mp3");
svgDocument.getElementById('up').setAttribute('dur','0s')
svgDocument.getElementById('left').setAttribute('dur','0s')
svgDocument.getElementById('right').setAttribute('dur','0s')
svgDocument.getElementById('down').setAttribute('dur','0s')
svgDocument.getElementById(text.toLowerCase()).setAttribute('dur','2s')
```

...

Bear in mind that the need for hacks and workarounds will only be temporary. Implementations of SVG are improving at a rapid pace, and the work on the specifications themselves continues. The fact that so much can already be done with such a young technology is a very promising sign.

Internationalization

SVG again has a head start regarding internationalization, thanks to its XML base. The availability of Unicode encoding allows us to present material in any of the major world languages. Features of SVG make it possible to define character sets and also to determine the way text is laid out, so in effect this means that text can be rendered in potentially any written language. In addition, there is a simple mechanism by which different language material can be presented according to locale.

> **NOTE**
>
> Internationalization is often discussed alongside localization. This is where material is adapted to suit the customs and preferences of a particular culture (usually a geographic locale). SVG's versatility in graphic and textual presentation makes localization an area open for exploitation using this technology.

Alternate Languages

Different elements can be rendered according to the language a client system is configured for, according to a test made on the elements' attributes.

In the following example, an SVG renderer will display the word English if the system language corresponds to the identification tag en (you can find these tags in ISO 639, and you can find a list at http://www.oasis-open.org/cover/iso639a.html). If the systemLanguage corresponds to fr, the word French will be displayed:

```
<text x="10" y="10" systemLanguage="en">English</text>
<text x="10" y="10" systemLanguage="fr">French</text>
```

Using a <switch>

Slightly more sophisticated operation is possible using the switch element:

```
<switch>
    <text x="10" y="10" systemLanguage="en">English</text>
    <text x="10" y="10" systemLanguage="fr">French</text>
</switch>
```

The switch operates by checking each descendant element within the <switch> block until it reaches an attribute that returns a true value. The attributes that it checks (if they exist) are requiredFeatures, requiredExtensions, and the one of interest here, systemLanguage. In the preceding example, if the system isn't English or French, nothing will be displayed. Any true statements after the first statement will be ignored, which gives greater control than not using the <switch>.

When we want more than a single element for each language, we can simply place the systemLanguage attribute within a container element. Listing 13.5 will display a predefined symbol and some text according to the system language.

LISTING 13.5   europe.svg

```
<svg       xmlns="http://www.w3.org/2000/svg"
     xmlns:xlink="http://www.w3.org/1999/xlink">

<defs>
    <symbol id="flag_it">
          <rect x="0" y="0" width="10" height="20" fill="green"/>
          <rect x="10" y="0" width="10" height="20" fill="white"/>
          <rect x="20" y="0" width="10" height="20" fill="red"/>
    </symbol>
    <symbol id="flag_fr">
          <rect x="0" y="0" width="10" height="20" fill="blue"/>
          <rect x="10" y="0" width="10" height="20" fill="white"/>
          <rect x="20" y="0" width="10" height="20" fill="red"/>
    </symbol>
</defs>

<switch>
    <g systemLanguage="it">
          <use xlink:href="#flag_it" x="10" y="10"/>
          <text x="10" y="20">Italian</text>
    </g>
    <g systemLanguage="fr">
          <use xlink:href="#flag_fr" x="10" y="10"/>
          <text x="10" y="20">French</text>
    </g>
    <g>
          <text x="10" y="10">I don't understand...</text>
    </g>
</switch>
</svg>
```

If the `systemLanguage` attribute equals `fr`, the result shown in Figure 13.6 will be displayed.

FIGURE 13.6   Display seen on French systems (blue, white, red flag).

On an Italian system, the result shown in Figure 13.7 will be rendered.

FIGURE 13.7   Display seen on Italian systems (green, white, red flag).

NOTE

The images displayed directly from the code were too small for publication, but fortunately SVG is scalable, and these screenshots were taken after zooming in.

It is unlikely that the developer will want to provide an alternative for every possible language, so a default is included in Listing 13.4. If an element doesn't contain any of the three testable attributes, it is considered `true`, and as long as it is the first `true` element in the block, its contents are rendered. So the last of the three `<g>` blocks within the `switch` is coded without any extra attributes. If the system detected by the renderer seeing the SVG isn't French or Italian, the result shown in Figure 13.8 will be displayed.

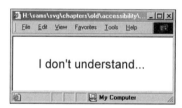

FIGURE 13.8   View seen on systems that aren't French or Italian.

Switching on Features

Another issue that relates to accessibility in general is that particular features described in the specification might not be implemented in a particular viewer. As well as `systemLanguage`, we can also have different material displayed depending on two other tests: `requiredFeatures` and `requiredExtensions`. The latter of these tests has yet to find that much application; very few extensions to SVG 1.0 are presently available, although support for them is provided in several places, such as the Batik toolkit. This could well become a significant feature within support for different kinds of browsers/viewers such as screen readers or, for that matter, mass-marketed mobile devices. The `requiredFeatures` test already has direct applications; for instance, the following snippet will display differently according to whether the viewer supports SVG animation:

```
<?xml version="1.0"?>
<svg     xmlns="http://www.w3.org/2000/svg"
     xmlns:xlink="http://www.w3.org/1999/xlink">

    <text x="100" y="200" font-size="30" fill="green">Double</text>

    <switch>
        <g requiredFeatures="org.w3c.svg.animation">
            <text id="moving" x="100" y="200" font-size="30"
                                    fill="red">Double</text>
            <animate attributeName="dy" attributeType="XML"
                begin="0s" dur="4s"
                from="-100" to="0"
                xlink:href="#moving" fill="freeze" />
            <animate attributeName="font-size" attributeType="XML"
                begin="0s" dur="3s"
                from="0" to="30"
                xlink:href="#moving" fill="freeze" />
        </g>

            <text x="100" y="210" font-size="30"
                            fill="blue">Double</text>

    </switch>
</svg>
```

The first piece of text, the word Double in green, will be displayed whatever happens. A switch controls what happens next: If the viewer supports animation, the attribute requiredFeatures="org.w3c.svg.animation" will be seen as a true statement, and the contents of this <g> block will be rendered. The rendering flow will then continue after the closing </switch> tag. The result will be the text Double, only this time in red, apparently coming closer until it drops down over the green text (as shown in Figure 13.9).

FIGURE 13.9   Snapshot of animation-capable view.

If animation isn't supported, the <g> block will be ignored, and the next element in the switch will be tested. Here, we have a text element without any conditional attributes that will thus be considered true and rendered. The result, shown in Figure 13.10, is intended to provide the same information as the animated version in a static form. Whether this is the case is a matter of opinion.

FIGURE 13.10   Display seen on viewers without animation support.

Unicode Support

SVG inherits from XML the ability to use Unicode character encoding. In practice, for most languages, this means that as long as the Web server is correctly configured to send the charset parameter in the HTTP headers, and the client's browser supports that character set, they will receive the information correctly.

Having Unicode support is a major plus for i18n. If, for example, we want to use the Greek letter *pi*, we can check the relevant Unicode charts (Greek and Coptic at http://www.unicode.org), where we find the following:

03C0 π GREEK SMALL LETTER PI

Inserting this character into our text is straightforward; we can just use the Numeric Character Reference (NCR) as follows:

```
...
<text x="100" y="100" font-size="36">Easy as &#x3C0;!</text>
...
```

Here, the &#x3C0 sequence will be rendered as the *pi* character. The NCR is specified in hexadecimal, which is easier to find in the Unicode charts.

> **NOTE**
>
> Each character in a Unicode character set can be represented by a numeric character reference (NCR), which may be either decimal or hexadecimal. A hexadecimal reference takes the form &#x*hhh*; where *hhh* is the appropriate hexadecimal number. For example, the decimal reference for the copyright symbol is &169; and the hexadecimal version is ©.

In a viewer, the result looks like Figure 13.11.

FIGURE 13.11   The pi symbol displayed in a standard font.

Using Glyphs

Sometimes the character we want isn't available using Unicode, or for aesthetic or other reasons, we want to use something out of the ordinary. In these circumstances, SVG provides a simple mechanism by which we can define our own character representation. To allow arbitrary character representations, the SVG specification contains the glyph element. A **glyph** is a set of instructions describing how to draw a character, part of a character, or even a series of characters. Often there is a one-to-one mapping between a single glyph and a Unicode character, although the complexities of various written languages have led the specification developers to include a lot of flexibility in representation within SVG.

Looking at a simple case, let's say we want to draw our own version of the Greek letter *pi* (look at Figure 13.11 for a reason). We already know its Unicode identifier; now all we need is the instructions to draw the representation we want. As you might expect, these instructions will be expressed in familiar SVG terms. We can write an expression in two different ways: We can either use a single d expression to draw the symbol or use any SVG content we like. There are (slightly involved) differences in the way each is rendered, notably that the first approach will be treated like a system font and can be cached. Using the first approach, we define a glyph like this:

```
...
<glyph unicode="&#x3C0;" glyph-name="GREEK SMALL LETTER PI"
    d="M200 7 C304 55 282 219 326 317
        L358 433 C378 467 452 443 492 447 L448 201 C458 49 462 29 474 11
        C496 1 522 11 536 29 C504 161 476 313 522 449 L654 449
```

```
C682 445 712 461 706 493 C516 503 178 599 90 355
C146 379 226 491 330 447
C324 295 166 133 200 7 z"/>
```

...

The Unicode number and name of the glyph are given as attributes, followed by the d attribute, which follows the same pattern as in path elements.

Using the second approach, we have essentially the whole range of SVG elements available. For example, we can define a crude exclamation mark (!) using a tall, slim ellipse and an accompanying circle:

```
...
<glyph unicode="&#x021;" glyph-name="EXCLAMATION MARK">
    <ellipse transform="translate(100, 700)" rx="40" ry="350"/>
    <circle transform="translate(100, 0)" r="50"/>
</glyph>
...
```

A common feature of these two approaches is that the coordinate system for glyphs begins from the bottom left, that is, is the other way up to regular SVG. This might cause problems because at present not all SVG drawing applications allow transformations, and drawing upside down isn't easy. There is a way around this problem: We can use a raster-based drawing application such as MS Paint or Photoshop to draw the image the right way up, flip it, and save the result. Going into the SVG application (here using the free Amaya browser/editor at http://www.w3.org/Amaya/), we can load in this image (which will be an image element in the source) and trace over it using SVG path tools. We end up with something like Figure 13.12 (simplicity wins over accuracy here).

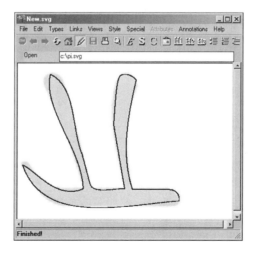

FIGURE 13.12   Tracing an image in Amaya.

NOTE

The credit for generating SVG paths by tracing lies with the RDFWeb codepiction experiments into creating photo metadata. See http://rdfweb.org/2002/01/photo/.

We can then manually edit the source to pull out the image reference and, if necessary, combine multiple path elements into one. The resulting d attribute can now be used inside a glyph.

It is possible to build font packages (you can find some nice examples at http://nagoya.apache.org/svgfonts/samples.svg), where full or partial character sets can be enclosed in an SVG file and referenced using XLink, but here we'll include the definitions of the *pi* and exclamation mark in the same document as the text we want to display:

```
<svg    xmlns="http://www.w3.org/2000/svg">
    <title>Demonstration of Glyphs</title>
    <desc>Shows how to make custom characters</desc>
        <defs>
            <font id="SAMS">
                <font-face font-family="SAMS"/>
```

The id attribute of the font element serves to give the element a reference point if these glyphs are to be linked into from another file. The font-face element comes straight from CSS2 and contains the description of the font—the font-family attribute we will be calling on when we want to use the glyph. Here we are going to define a small part of a font called SAMS. Next, we have the glyph definitions themselves:

```
<glyph unicode="&#x3C0;" glyph-name="GREEK SMALL LETTER PI"
    d="M200 7 C304 55 282 219 326 317
        L358 433 C378 467 452 443 492 447 L448 201 C458 49 462 29 474 11
        C496 1 522 11 536 29 C504 161 476 313 522 449 L654 449
        C682 445 712 461 706 493 C516 503 178 599 90 355
        C146 379 226 491 330 447
        C324 295 166 133 200 7 z"/>

<glyph unicode="&#x021;" glyph-name="EXCLAMATION MARK">
    <ellipse transform="translate(100, 700)" rx="40" ry="350"/>
    <circle transform="translate(100, 0)" r="50"/>
</glyph>

</font>
</defs>
```

Now we have the bit of code that uses the glyphs. First, we have some text in a standard serif font and then the two characters from the SAMS font:

```
<text x="100" y="100" font-size="36">
<tspan font-family="serif">Easy as </tspan>
<tspan font-family="SAMS">&#x3C0;!</tspan>
</text>
</svg>
```

The result looks like Figure 13.13.

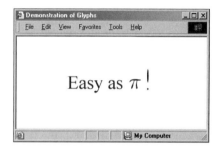

FIGURE 13.13   The pi character rendered using a custom glyph.

Text Direction and Orientation

The layout of text varies between languages. Whereas Latin scripts normally read left-to-right, others run vertically (such as various Asian languages) or bidirectionally (such as Arabic). Text can also be made to run along an arbitrary path using the `textPath` element as you saw in Chapter 8. An SVG renderer can determine the orientation of text based on several factors, the first of which is the reference orientation. In the initial coordinate system, the orientation is straight up. The next factor is the value of the `writing-mode` attribute of the `text` element, which is used in combination with the reference orientation to decide the text progression directions. The decision is based on a series of rules, and to complicate matters further, the `text` element can have `direction` and `unicode-bidi` (bidirectional) properties as well. There is also the orientation of individual glyphs to take into account. All in all, text layout can get somewhat convoluted, and the best bet is to refer to the specification on a case-by-case basis. Rather than regurgitate the specification's description of how the various factors can combine, Figure 13.14 provides a simple example.

In the figure, we use various combinations of writing mode and glyph orientation. The small circles show the position from which each piece of text flows:

```
<svg     xmlns="http://www.w3.org/2000/svg">
<g font-size="24">
```

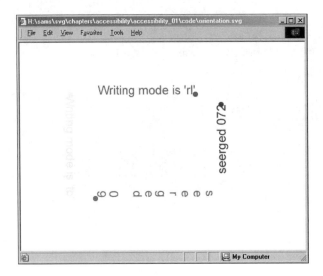

FIGURE 13.14   Examples of text orientation.

In yellow, we have top-to-bottom text (on the left in Figure 13.14), with the default layout being modified by the `writing-mode` property:

```
<g fill="yellow">
    <text writing-mode="tb" x="100" y="100">Writing mode is 'tb'</text>
    <circle cx="100" cy="100" r="5"/>
</g>
```

In green, we have right-to-left text (at the top of Figure 13.12); layout again is affected by the `writing-mode` property. Note that although the text runs from right to left, the glyph orientation is unchanged:

```
<g fill="green">
    <text x="350" y="100" writing-mode="rl">Writing mode is 'rl'</text>
    <circle cx="350" cy="100" r="5"/>
</g>
```

For red (at the bottom of the figure), we have kept the default left-to-right layout, but using the `glyph-alignment-horizontal` property rotated the glyphs by 90 degrees. Here, `glyph-orientation-horizontal` controls glyph orientation because the `inline-progression-direction` is horizontal:

```
<g fill="red">
    <text x="150" y="300" glyph-orientation-horizontal="90">90 degrees</text>
    <circle cx="150" cy="300" r="5"/>
</g>
```

Last, the blue text (at the right of the figure) is rendered based on a combination of a top-to-bottom writing mode and a glyph orientation of 270 degrees. Here, `glyph-orientation-vertical` controls glyph orientation because the `inline-progression-direction` is vertical:

```
<g fill="blue">
    <text x="400" y="120" writing-mode="tb"
        glyph-orientation-vertical="270">270 degrees</text>
    <circle cx="400" cy="120" r="5"/>
</g>
</g>
</svg>
```

Metadata

Metadata is familiar on the Web in the shape of HTML `<meta>` tags, as used to provide a description and keywords for a page. Metadata isn't new in the computer graphics world either; for instance, within JPEG (JFIF) files, marker segments describe the data that in turn describes the visual representation. Work has been done on embedding metadata in the PNG format at a higher level—for example, describing the subject of the image. SVG, however, can take the notion of a self-describing image a few stages further. Not only does an SVG file automatically describe itself in a common text-based format (XML), but it also allows information in other languages to be included. Description and title elements within an SVG document are really metadata, and a bonus here is that they can contain marked-up information from other namespaces. For example, using a hypothetical architectural markup language, we could use the following:

```
<g>
    <title>Front Bedroom Window</title>
    <desc xmlns:arch="http://example.org/windows">
        <arch:material>aluminum</arch:material>
        <arch:dimensions height="1" width="1"/>
    </desc>
    <use xlink:href="#window" transform="translate(110, 160)"/>
</g>
```

To be able to make use of this information, an agent must be able to extract and interpret it. To allow interoperability between systems, it is advantageous to use standards, and languages have been developed specifically for providing metadata. Although several other metadata languages that can use XML syntax are in circulation (notably XTM; see `http://www.topicmaps.org`), the predominant metadata language at present comes from the Resource Description Framework (RDF; see `http://www.w3.org/RDF/`).

Resource Description Framework

RDF is based around the concepts of resources and their description. Essentially, every-thing that can be given a unique identifier (a URI) can be considered a resource, whether it be a Web page, an image, a person, or a planet. We can easily give a document on the Web such an identifier; normally, we would use its URL. To say things about a resource, metadata is expressed in the form of three-part statements known as **triples**, which consist of a subject, predicate, and object. The subject is the resource in question; the predicate, some property of that resource; and the object, the value of that property. For example, let's say that the plan of the Italian house had been designed by an architect named Brunello. We could express this information visually as shown in Figure 13.15.

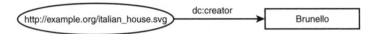

FIGURE 13.15   A typical RDF statement.

In this figure, the house plan is identified by the document's location and has a property called dc:creator with the value Brunello. This diagram actually expresses the information in RDF (albeit in a shorthand form). The ellipse represents the resource and is labeled with the resource's URI, and the rectangle contains a literal value, the architect's name. The dc: prefix on the property is a namespace prefix and here refers to the Dublin Core (DC) namespace.

> **NOTE**
>
> The Dublin Core Metadata Initiative (http://dublincore.org/) is responsible for a vocabulary that defines a set of terms that frequently occur in relation to electronic documents. An RDF Schema for this vocabulary can be found at http://dublincore.org/2001/08/14/dces#.

Namespaces are critical to the operation of RDF because they allow unambiguous defini-tion of terms. Though there are other syntaxes for RDF, the most appropriate for use within SVG is, as you would expect, XML. The information from Figure 13.13 expressed in this format looks like this:

```
<rdf:RDF xmlns:rdf='http://www.w3.org/1999/02/22-rdf-syntax-ns#'
     xmlns:dc='http://purl.org/dc/elements/1.1/'>

    <rdf:Description rdf:about='http://example.org/italian_house.svg'>
        <dc:creator>Brunello</dc:creator>
    </rdf:Description>
</rdf:RDF>
```

The rdf:RDF element identifies the nature of this information, and gives prefixes for two namespaces. The first is the namespace of one of the RDF specifications, and the second is Dublin Core. Within the RDF namespace is the Description element, which is used to contain a statement about a resource. The resource that the statement is about is given as an XML attribute here. The creator element is defined as a property in the DC namespace, and the value it takes is here given as the contained text, Brunello. To add metadata of this kind to an SVG document, we simply place the block of RDF inside a metadata element. Any number of metadata elements can be added to a document at any point in the document, and the specification states the following: "Authors should provide a 'metadata' child element to the outermost 'svg' element within a standalone SVG document."

Model, Syntax, and Schemas

RDF is specified in a suite of documents from the W3C, which cover the underlying theoretical model, the RDF/XML syntax, an introductory text (the "RDF Primer"), and a series of test cases for the benefit of developers. Part of the suite, the "RDF Schema Specification," describes how vocabularies can be constructed using the model and syntax. These vocabularies define properties relevant to the field of interest that resources may have; for instance, another property from Dublin Core is publisher, "An entity responsible for making the resource available." Definitions for the terms within the vocabularies are usually to be found both in human language and expressed as RDF Schemas. RDF Schemas resemble schemas in other contexts, such as database or XML schemas, though their main purpose is to enable inference (once terms are agreed upon, they can be argued upon). They can help with validation and ensuring data integrity, but this has to be achieved through inference using languages or processors built on top, rather than using any constraints within RDFS.

There is a lot of ongoing development in the metadata world, particularly surrounding RDF and the idea of a "Semantic Web," (see http://www.w3.org/2001/sw/) which is the existing Web with added intelligence. As a result of this activity, the specifications are subject to change, so it's worth checking out the current status at http://www.w3.org before embarking on any major project.

Summary

In this chapter, we saw several ways SVG can increase the potential audience for documents. Using straightforward techniques, we can include users with particular requirements such as enhanced visibility, users with different preferred languages, and even end users that aren't human—the applications and agents that can understand metadata.

PART II

Programming SVG Client-Side

IN THIS PART

The SVG DOM

SVG by itself is cool, but it's really interactive when you use a programming language such as JavaScript, VBScript, or Java. Therefore, it needs a system that gives the programming language access to the SVG elements and attributes. The World Wide Web Consortium (or W3C, creator of SVG) solved this problem by using the Document Object Model (DOM) as the basis for its own SVG DOM. The SVG DOM is a language-neutral Application Programming Interface (API), which gives any programming language access to the parts of the SVG document. As soon as the programming language has access to the SVG document, it can do virtually everything—create, delete, change, or otherwise manipulate the elements.

In this book, the topic of scripting the SVG DOM is divided among three chapters. The "real programming" will be done in the next two chapters, which will be filled with examples. However, we first need to lay a solid foundation about the theoretical concepts of DOM and SVG DOM. Therefore, this chapter provides an inside view into the SVG Document Object Model.

DOM Background

In August 1997, the W3C first started developing a Document Object Model specification. The goal was to create a language-independent interface to access and modify structured documents. DOM itself is divided into several different modules. In DOM Level 1, there were only two modules: HTML and XML 1.0. In Level 2, support for style sheets and events were added. With this functionality, DOM 2 (DOM Level 2) became interesting for developing SVG because it provided everything you need: access to the document structure, Cascading Style Sheet (CSS) elements, and event-handling mechanisms. SVG DOM uses DOM 2 as a basis and extends it in some areas. For example, SVG DOM extends support for more events than are defined in DOM 2. Some SVG-specific events could not be included in DOM 2 because then DOM would not be an independent interface anymore. The Adobe SVG Viewer extended the SVG DOM even more by adding keyboard events. This functionality once was part of the DOM Level 2 draft but did not make it to the final version (and is now a candidate for DOM Level 3, the to-be-successor standard).

The most important modules of the DOM for SVG are as follows:

- **Core**—Contains the tree view of the document (you can find more information in the section "DOM2 Core"). This module allows access to all elements of a document via a hierarchical system.

- **CSS**—Includes different ways to access and change styles.

- **Events**—Provides access to different events such as mouse actions.

- **SVG**—Delivers SVG-specific interfaces for direct access to SVG elements.

DOM Level 2

This section describes the most important parts of DOM2, as defined by the W3C. You must understand the opportunities DOM2 offers you as an SVG developer before we go on to the description of the SVG DOM later in this chapter.

DOM2 Core

In the DOM view, the elements of a document are divided into objects. These objects are arranged in a tree-like structure. The tree consists of nodes, and every node represents one element, attribute, event, or object.

The node at the top of the tree is the svg element. It is also called a **root element** because, in a visual representation of the tree, the uppermost element is the root.

Listing 14.1 is a simple SVG document that illustrates the node principle.

LISTING 14.1   14code01.svg—A Simple SVG Document

```
<?xml version="1.0" encoding="iso-8859-1"?>
<svg width="300" height="150">
   <defs>
      <radialGradient id="gradient"
                      cx="70%" cy="30%" r="50%" fx="50%" fy="50%">
         <stop offset="0%" style="stop-color:green"/>
         <stop offset="100%" style="stop-color:black"/>
      </radialGradient>
   </defs>
```

LISTING 14.1   Continued

```
    <text x="15" y="40" id="text">Hello SVG World!</text>
    <circle id="circle" cx="60" cy="80" r="20" style="fill:url(#gradient)"/>
</svg>
```

The top node is the svg element. It must not be confused with the SVGDocument object. This object contains all the elements of the SVG document.

On the second level of the tree are three elements, as shown in Figure 14.1. The hierarchical relationship is often described as a **parent-child** relationship. Using this analogy, the svg element is the **parent** (element) of the text element. All elements on Level 2 are **siblings** (and obviously children of the parent). Some node elements such as text or attributes have no children.

In Figure 14.1, you can see how Listing 14.1 looks in the Batik SVG Viewer (with whitespace removed). You can clearly see the different elements in the SVG document and their level in the tree.

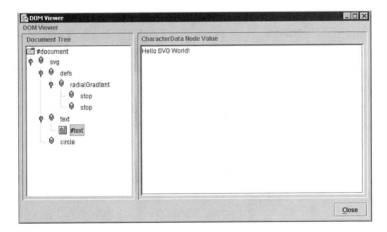

FIGURE 14.1   The example from Listing 14.1 in the Batik SVG Viewer.

In the DOM core, every node has properties. With the properties, you can navigate the document hierarchy. Table 14.1 lists the possible node properties.

TABLE 14.1   Node Properties

Property	Description
childNodes	Contains a list with all child nodes of the actual node. The list is an array. The index starts at 0.
firstChild	Contains the first child node of the actual node. If a node has no child, the value is 0.

TABLE 14.1   Continued

Property	Description
lastChild	Contains the last child node of the actual node. If a node has no child, the value is 0.
nextSibling	Contains the node next to the actual one, on the same level (if available).
nodeList	Contains a list of all nodes of an SVG document.
nodeName	Contains the name of the node (name attribute).
nodeType	Contains the type of the node by number: 1 = element, 2 = attribute, 3 = text, and so on. You can find more information about node types in the section "Different Node Types."
nodeValue	Contains the value of the node (value attribute).
parentNode	Delivers the node above the actual node, that is, the parent node (if available).
previousSibling	Contains the node before the actual one, on the same level (if available).

Figure 14.2 shows the relationships between the different elements for the preceding example.

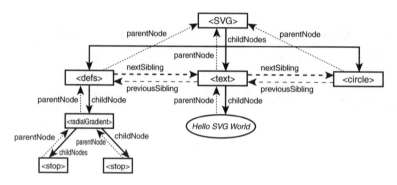

FIGURE 14.2   The relationship between the elements of our example.

The different properties give you a hint to the methods that allow you to access the nodes.

Of course, you can also directly access the properties of the given element. However, SVG offers a method to access these properties: Just put get in front of the attribute name and capitalize the first letter of the next word. So firstChild turns into getFirstChild(), and you have your method. The same trick works for setting a property. Just put set in front of it: firstChild becomes setfirstChild(). We will cover this method in detail in Chapter 15, "Scripting SVG."

Next, we will use JavaScript to get the text of our example. Let's assume that the variable s is a reference to the svg node. We will now loop through the array childNodes (the number of elements can be determined with the property length) and look at the name of each node:

```
var output = "";
for (var i=0; i<s.childNodes.length; i++)
  output += s.childNodes[i].nodeName + "\n";
alert(output);
```

The `nodeName` property contains the name of a node; thus, the name of the node is appended to the string variable named `output`.

Methods

Table 14.2 lists the most important methods that can be used to modify nodes.

TABLE 14.2   Node Methods

Method	Description
appendChild	Adds a child node under the actual node.
cloneNode	Copies the actual node and pastes a perfect clone.
insertBefore	Inserts a child node under the actual node before a sibling, which can be named.
removeNode	Deletes the actual node.
replaceNode	Replaces the actual node with another.
setAttribute	Adds a new attribute with name and value. If another attribute has the same name, its value will be replaced.

These methods will be covered in more detail in the next chapter, when we manipulate the SVG DOM tree.

Different Node Types

In the SVG DOM, there are different kinds of nodes. In the official specification, you can find 12 different types. In the preceding section, we worked with the general type Node, which is a kind of metatype.

The other most important types are the following:

- **Element**—This type represents all SVG elements such as geometric forms, gradients, and so on.

- **Attribute**—This type covers all attributes. Attributes are, in most cases, children of elements. An attribute cannot have children itself.

- **Text**—This type contains pure text. It also cannot have children.

- **Document**—The document type stands for the complete document. It is the root of the document tree. On the other hand, the root element is a child of the document node. In the document node, you can create other nodes or document objects. Some methods are `createElement()`, `createTextNode()`, and `createAttribute()`.

You can check the node type by using the `getNodeType()` function. This function returns a number that identifies the node type.

Table 14.3 provides a complete overview of all types.

TABLE 14.3   Node Types

Node Type—No.	Name	Value	Children
Attribute—2	name	value	Text, Entity Reference
CDATA Section—4	#cdata-section	content	none
Comment—8	#comment	content	none
Document—9	#document	0	Element (max. 1), Processing Instruction, Comment, Document Type
Document Fragment—11	#document-fragment	0	Element, Processing Instruction, Comment, Text, CDATA Section, Entity Reference
Document Type—10	name	0	none
Element—1	name	0	Element, Text, Comment, Entity Reference, CDATA Section, Processing Instruction
Entity—6	name	0	Element, Comment, Processing Instruction, Text, CDATA Section, Entity Reference
Entity Reference—5	name	0	Element, Comment, Processing Instruction, Text, CDATA Section, Entity Reference
Notation—12	name	0	none
Processing Instruction—7	name (target of Processing Instruction)	content	none
Text—3	#text	content	none

Depending on the node type, you have different options. For instance, it makes no sense at all to read the value of a document node because it has none.

Accessing Nodes

In the real world, the most interesting function is to get the name or the value of a node. Two methods—`getNodeName()` and `getNodeValue()`—serve this purpose.

The next question is how you can get access to the nodes. There are different possible ways:

- **Using methods and properties**—For instance, by using the `nextSibling` property, you get access to the adjacent node, if any. The property returns an object of type Node, and you can work with it. However, to achieve this, you must somehow get access to the original node. Thus, you need some way to access a node "from scratch."

- **Using `getElementById()`, `getElementsByTagName()`, and others**—These methods of the `Document` object (or `SVGDocument`) return node objects or lists of nodes.

  `getElementById()` takes the id attribute of an element as a parameter and returns a reference to the element. On the other hand, `getElementsByTagName()` also takes a tag name as parameter (for example, `svg` for the `<svg>` element) and returns a list of all elements in the current document that bear this tag name.

In the real world, the `getElementById()` approach is most widely used because directly accessing an element in the document by using its id attribute is very practical. Walking through the DOM—that is, using the methods of the `Node` interface—is less often seen. This approach takes longer to implement (you must always have the DOM tree in mind) and does not offer many advantages.

In the next chapter, we will provide several examples; however, most often we will use `getElementById()`.

DOM2 CSS

The DOM2 CSS delivers a module for all style elements of an SVG document. The module consists of different interfaces, and most of the interfaces in the SVG DOM start with `CSS`. The DOM2 style sheet module is not focused on CSS; it provides support for all types of style sheets and all style sheets in a document. For SVG, CSS is the most important choice; therefore, we'll use it throughout this chapter. In reality, there is also only one style sheet per site.

The interface named `CSSStyleSheet` represents a single style sheet in a document. It contains a collection of all the rules in the style sheet. The base interface for all style rules is `CSSRule`. It contains all CSS statements for a document. The interface named `CSSRuleList` provides a full list of all rules in the document. By using the attribute length, you can determine how many elements are in the list.

Table 14.4 details the most important interfaces. In the Adobe SVG Viewer, most of these interfaces have been implemented since version 3.0 beta. (See the introductory chapters of this book for more detailed information about which interface is supported by which version of the Adobe SVG Viewer.)

TABLE 14.4   CSS Interfaces

Interface	Description
Counter	Contains the value of a counter or a counter function, which is realized with style sheets. If you use a counter to number paragraphs of a site, you can read the style properties of the counter by using this interface.
CSSCharsetRule	Inherited by CSSRule. It contains the properties of a charset rule.
CSSFontFaceRule	Inherited by CSSRule. It provides the properties of a font face rule, which consists of font face descriptions.
CSSImportRule	Inherited by CSSRule. It contains all imported styles from other style sheets.
CSSMediaRule	Inherited by CSSRule. It contains all rules relating to the media type. In CSS, you can make different style definitions for different media types, such as print or screen.
CSSPageRule	Inherited by CSSRule. This interface provides page rules, which consist of information about the page, such as page size and margin width.
CSSRule	Provides the basic interface for all rules.
CSSRuleList	Delivers an array with all rules listed.
CSSStyleDeclaration	Contains the elements of a style sheet block (*Syntax {Block}*). Delivers methods to change the properties of the style declaration.
CSSStyleRule	Inherited by CSSRule. Contains a single rule set.
CSSStyleSheet	Provides the properties of a complete CSS style sheet. It inherits from the interface StyleSheet of the DOM2 Style Sheet module.
CSSUnknownRule	Inherited by CSSRule. Catches every rule that is unknown to the user agent.
CSSValue	Represents a value of a style sheet property. The additional interfaces CSSValueList and CSSValueType are not supported by the Adobe SVG Viewer 3.
ElementCSSInlineStyle	Provides the content of the style attribute in SVG tags.

You can find the methods and properties for the interfaces in the official specification (for Level 2, the URL is `http://www.w3.org/TR/2000/REC-DOM-Level-2-Style-20001113/css.html`).

DOM 2 Events

So far, you have seen what DOM 2 is all about, how the DOM tree is structured, and even how you can access nodes in the tree—theoretically, of course, because we will introduce the "real stuff," that is, scripting the SVG DOM, in the next chapter.

Knowing *how* to access the tree is one thing, but knowing *when* to access the tree is another. The SVG viewer does not just define a random moment to execute your scripts, but it waits until some special event has occurred. There are many different events; here are just some examples:

- Clicking the mouse

- Moving the mouse pointer over an object

- Fully loading a document

Events are also standardized in DOM2. So, in this section, we will take a closer look at the DOM 2 event model and present the supported events. We will also show which SVG-specific events exist. Additionally, we will show which events are supported by the most widely used SVG viewer to date, the Adobe SVG Viewer—although they are not defined in the W3C's SVG specification. You'll see how you can connect script code to events and how you can find out which event has been triggered within this script code.

The DOM 2 Event Model

On November 13, 2000, version 1.0 of the Document Object Model (DOM) Level 2 Events Specification became a W3C Recommendation; that's the highest level any specification can get in W3C terms. In this specification, the different approaches of event handling were defined per the W3C. The main goal of this standardization was to enable the organization of event handling within the DOM tree structure defined by the DOM Level 2 Core.

Types of Events

As we explained previously, the W3C defines many different events. These events are divided into the following categories:

- **User interface events, or short UI events**—These events can be triggered by the user. Examples of such events are keyboard input and mouse interactions (moving, clicking). Generally, anything the user can do with an external device may generate a UI event.

- **User interface logical events, or short UI logical events**—These events are essentially the same as UI events; however, no external device is included. One example of such an event occurs when the focus is taken from or assigned to an element. Any events that are triggered by the user but are device independent are UI logical events.

- **Mouse events**—These events are basically UI events; however, because they can be achieved only by using a mouse or any other pointing device (trackball, mouse pen), they are represented in this special group of events.

- **Mutation events**—As you will see later, the logical structure of the document, or the DOM tree, may be manipulated by different means. Whenever this happens, a mutation event occurs. Mutation events are always triggered by script execution, for example, when nodes in the DOM tree are deleted or modified in some way.

Where Do Events Go?

As you may have guessed, events are always associated with elements in the DOM tree. When the user clicks on a special element of an SVG page (or an HTML page), a UI event is triggered in this element. If the page is fully loaded, an event is triggered—in the main element of the page, in the uppermost level of the DOM structure. In technical terms, every event has a target, an object it is sent to. This is also called an **event target**; the appropriate SVG interface is called `EventTarget`. The event target receives this event and must decide what to do next. For this, the concept of event listeners (using—as defined per DOM Level 2 Events specification—the interface `EventListener`) was introduced. An event listener is a mechanism that does nothing but wait for an event to be triggered. It is like someone who watches the street, waiting for the bus to arrive. An event listener can be used with any event target; however, you must decide which event target to associate with which event listener. Going back to the bus analogy, the person who watches for the bus can be anywhere in the city, but you must tell this person which bus to look out for.

An event target may have an arbitrary number of event listeners associated with it. So you can react not only if the user clicks on an object of your page, but also if the mouse pointer moves over this object. The question then becomes which event listener will become active first, if more than one of them is registered with an event target. The W3C specification does not answer this question, so it's up to the implementation to decide what to do first and which event listeners have to wait.

Bubbling Events

Depending on the implementation and the desired effect, the programmer can choose how events behave. The first step is always the same: As soon as an event is triggered, the associated event target element is sought and all associated event listeners there are executed. However, if an event is designed as a bubbling event, the event does not stop at the associated event target but bubbles up the DOM tree. Thus, at first, the parent element of the object is visited, and the DOM implementation checks (and executes) any associated event listeners with this object. After that, the event tries to bubble up further, moving to the parent object's parent object, looking for event listeners there. If it is not stopped (see next paragraph for details), the event will move up to the top level of the DOM structure, where it finally comes to a full stop.

You can, however, stop the bubbling mechanism. As you will see later, the DOM implementation grants programmatic access to the different aspects of the DOM specification via so-called **interfaces**. Using the `Event` interface, you gain access to a DOM event. If you use the `stopPropagation()` method, the event will not bubble further up. However, all event listeners on the current event target will still be executed. Because the order in which event listeners will be called is not defined in the specification, all remaining event listeners on the current object must be executed; otherwise, it would be pure chance which event listeners are used and which are not.

Let's look at a practical example. Here, you see the sample code we used earlier in this chapter:

```
<?xml version="1.0" encoding="iso-8859-1"?>
<svg width="300" height="150">
<defs>
  <radialGradient id="gradient" cx="70%" cy="30%" r="50%" fx="50%" fy="50%">
    <stop offset="0%" style="stop-color:green" />
    <stop offset="100%" style="stop-color:black" />
  </radialGradient>
</defs>
<text x="15" y="40" id="text">Hello SVG-World!</text>
<circle id="circle" cx="60" cy="80" r="20" style="fill:url(#gradient)" />
</svg>
```

The DOM tree looks like Figure 14.3.

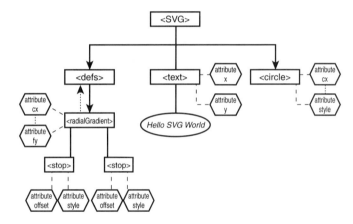

FIGURE 14.3   The DOM tree.

Now assume that you want to attach an event listener to this element:

```
<stop offset="0%" style="stop-color:green" />
```

If this event listener calls `stopPropagation()` after its execution, the event does not bubble up further. If, however, this method is not called (and the event is set to bubbling, obviously), the next element you see is `<radialGradient>`. If an event listener is attached, it is executed. Again, if `stopPropagation()` is not called, the event then moves further up the DOM tree. The next element on the way is the `<defs>` element and finally the `<svg>` element. This movement is illustrated in Figure 14.4.

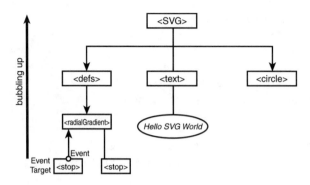

FIGURE 14.4   The DOM tree with an event listener.

Capturing Events

Sometimes you do not want an event to reach its event target. One example from the HTML world is that programmers do not want the users to use the right mouse button to access the context menu of a given page. To prevent this, the right-click event of the mouse must not reach the target element; thus, it must be captured somewhere on the way there.

Remember the bubbling mechanism described in the preceding section? There, events made their way up to the top, starting at the event target of the given event. Event capturing works the other way around. Event capturing takes place before the "usual" execution of event listeners is completed. Remember that the execution of events starts at the event target, and then events can bubble up. Event capturing can take place while the event is on its way to the event target. The event starts at the uppermost element of the DOM tree (or root element) and then makes its way down the tree until the event target is reached. On any element along the way, an event listener for event capturing may be defined. When such an event listener is found, it is executed.

If several capturing event listeners are found along the way, all of them are executed. Finally, the event reaches its event target and may execute the associated event listener or listeners. If the event is a bubbling event, it then climbs up the DOM tree.

However, as you saw with bubbling events in the preceding section, the propagation of the event may be stopped by calling a special method called stopPropagation(). This method is valid while capturing events as well. One call to stopPropagation(), and the event will not climb down the DOM tree any further. However, for the same reasons as with stopping bubbling events, all event listeners of the current element still will be executed. The next level, however, will not be reached, which may mean that the original event target will not even receive the event. However, this might be just the effect you want to achieve.

We want to present a practical example here as well. We again will use the SVG code we presented in the preceding section. Again, we assume that an event is triggered, and the first <stop> element in the page is the associated event target.

This event starts at the top of the DOM tree and then makes its way down. The following elements are passed by:

- `<svg>`
- `<defs>`
- `<radialGradient>`

At any of these elements, an event listener can intercept the way of the event and get to execution. If none of these event listeners call `stopPropagation()`, the event, however, does finally reach the event target. You can see the path of the event in Figure 14.5.

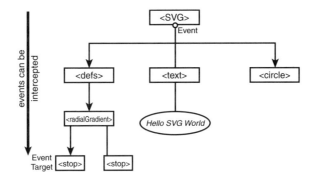

FIGURE 14.5   The path of the event.

Canceling Events

Here's another HTML analogy for you: If you click on a link on a Web page, another page is loaded immediately. What if an event listener is associated with this link? You might expect that this event listener will never execute because the default action of this element (in this case, the loading of another page) overrides any other actions that should be taken.

By canceling events, you can prevent the loading of the next page or prevent the default action of the element from being taken—if you cancel the default action. Not every event is cancelable (this neologism is the term used in the specification), but if so, you can call the `preventDefault()` method from any event listener associated with the event target and thus intercept the default action of the given element.

This ends our overview over the DOM Level 2 event specification. For more detailed information, visit the associated W3C Web page at `http://www.w3.org/DOM/`. Currently, you can find the latest version of the specification at `http://www.w3.org/TR/2000/REC-DOM-Level-2-Events-20001113/`. But now let's look at which of these concepts is still available in SVG, what is new, and what has changed.

Supported Events

Now that you know which kinds of events exist (see the section "Types of Events," earlier in this chapter), the next logical step is to look at which of these events specifically exist in SVG. We separate this discussion into the different types of events so that you can quickly find what you specifically are looking for.

UI Events

UI events are events that a user can trigger with an external device such as a mouse or a keyboard (called a UI event) or are device independently called (called a UI logical event). Table 14.5 shows the name and a description of each event and an attribute name. As you may know from HTML, you can not only attach event listeners to elements, but also use attributes for that task.

TABLE 14.5   UI Events

Event	Description	Attribute Name
activate	Occurs when an element is "activated" using an external device. A user can click on the element or press a key. From a programmatic point of view, you can decide what kind of activation happened. The value 1 means a "standard" activation, a mouse click, or a key press; whereas 2 means a "strong" activation, such as a double-click.	Onactivate
focusin	Occurs when an element receives the focus. This may happen when, for instance, the content of a <text> element is selected.	onfocusin
focusout	Occurs when an element loses the focus— it must have received the focus before (thus, a focusin event previously occurred). For example, the content of a <text> element, once selected, becomes deselected.	onfocusout

Here's a simple example. The SVG file in Listing 14.2 contains only a square. As soon as it is activated (that is, as soon as you click on it), a modal text box is created using JavaScript's `alert()` method (see Figure 14.6).

LISTING 14.2   14code02.svg—A Text Box

```
<?xml version="1.0" encoding="iso-8859-1" ?>
<svg>
  <g id="test" onactivate="alert('Good morning, I am awake now')">
    <rect x="0" y="0" width="100" height="100"/>
  </g>
</svg>
```

FIGURE 14.6   A text box opens when Listing 14.2 is run.

Mouse Events

Mouse events—by definition—cannot be triggered by a nonpointing device such as a keyboard. By moving and/or clicking a mouse button, you can trigger one of the events listed in Table 14.6.

> **NOTE**
>
> The developer of the DOM-compliant software can decide whether to allow keyboard input to trigger mouse events. Special keyboards for disabled people who cannot use a pointing device may offer this possibility, thus enabling the users to trigger mouse events even though no mouse is available.

TABLE 14.6   Mouse Events

Event	Description	Attribute Name
click	Occurs when the mouse (or the device used, such as a mouse pen) clicks over an element. Related events are mousedown and mouseup.	onclick
mousedown	Occurs when the mouse button (or the pointing device used) is pressed and held down over an element. Mouse clicking events occur in the following order: mousedown, mouseup, click.	onmousedown
mousemove	Occurs when the mouse (or pointing device used) is moved while over an element.	onmousemove
mouseout	Occurs when the mouse pointer (or the pointer of the pointing device used) leaves an element. The pointer must have been over this element previously; thus, the onmouseover event occurred previously.	onmouseout

TABLE 14.6   Continued

Event	Description	Attribute Name
mouseover	Occurs when the mouse pointer (or the pointer of the pointing device used) is moved over an element.	onmouseover
mouseup	Occurs when the (held-down) mouse button (or the pointing device used) is released over an element. Mouse clicking events occur in the following order: mousedown, mouseup, click.	onmouseup

Now let's look at an example similar to the one we used with the UI events. In the SVG document shown in Listing 14.3, a message box pops up as soon as the mouse pointer is moved on the square (shown in Figure 14.7).

LISTING 14.3   14code03.svg—onmouseover

```
<?xml version="1.0" encoding="iso-8859-1" ?>
<svg>
   <g id="test" onmouseover="alert('That tickles!')">
      <rect x="0" y="0" width="100" height="100"/>
   </g>
</svg>
```

FIGURE 14.7   A message box pops up when the mouse pointer is moved over the square.

Mutation Events

Modifications in the DOM tree are also called **mutations**; thus, mutation events are triggered whenever something is changed in the tree structure. Remember that event listeners are attached to elements, so you must decide which node or nodes you want to monitor. Mutation events can be attached to nodes only via event listeners, not attributes; thus, the Attribute Name column remains empty in Table 14.7, which lists the mutation events.

TABLE 14.7   Mutation Events

Event	Description	Attribute Name
DOMAttrModified	Occurs when an attribute of the node has been modified.	N/A
DOMCharacterDataModified	Occurs when the CDATA portion of a node has been modified; the node itself, however, remains unchanged (that is, it is not deleted from or inserted into the tree).	N/A
DOMNodeInserted	Occurs when a node is directly inserted into the tree, as the child node of another, existing node.	N/A
DOMNodeInsertedIntoDocument	Occurs when a node is directly or indirectly inserted into the tree, either as a child node of another, existing node, or as part of a subtree that is inserted into the DOM tree.	N/A
DOMNodeRemoved	Occurs when a node is directly removed into the tree, as the child node of another, existing node.	N/A
DOMNodeRemovedIntoDocument	Occurs when a node is directly or indirectly removed from the tree, either as a child node of another, existing node, or as part of a subtree that is removed from the DOM tree.	N/A
DOMSubtreeModified	Occurs when the DOM subtree of the given node is modified in any way. This event is more general than the events presented previously.	N/A

Mutation events are not yet supported by Adobe SVG Viewer and thus should not be used unless you can be absolutely sure that your user base uses an SVG viewer that can handle mutation events (such as Batik).

SVG-Specific Events

The SVG specification introduces some new events that were not part of the DOM Level 2 Specification by the World Wide Web Consortium. You might wonder why the W3C added something new, thus trying to extend an existing, approved standard? The answer to that question is quite simple: The W3C specification works very well; however, SVG has some special capabilities that are not covered by the predefined DOM2 events. To be able to deal with these special capabilities with the event-handling mechanism of SVG, some new events had to be introduced.

14

> **NOTE**
>
> Some new events were also introduced in HTML. For example, the dragdrop event occurs when the user drags and drops an element, and the abort event is triggered when the loading of a file (such as a graphic) is aborted before it finishes.

The first set of special events is very SVG specific and deals with the loading and rendering of SVG graphics. You can find a complete list in Table 14.8.

TABLE 14.8   SVG-Specific Events

Event	Description	Attribute Name
SVGAbort	Occurs when loading of an SVG page is aborted before all data has been completely transmitted.	onabort
SVGError	Occurs when an error is found, either while loading an element or during script execution. Thus, this event either means there are problems with the connection or problems in the coding (which are two quite different things).	onerror
SVGLoad	Occurs when the element has been fully loaded (including referenced, external resources) and has been completely parsed. Optional external resources do not have to be completely loaded. This event occurs right before the element (and its subelements) is rendered.	onload
SVGResize	Occurs when the page is resized. This event works only with the root element, <svg>.	onresize
SVGScroll	Occurs when the page is scrolled, horizontally or vertically or both. This event works only with the root element, <svg>.	onscroll
SVGUnload	Occurs when the document is unloaded (that is, another document is loaded in the same window or frame).	onunload
SVGZoom	Occurs when the user zooms in or out of the document. This event is not fired if the zooming is the result of script code; only user interaction counts here.	onzoom

The following minimalistic example shows one of these events. As soon as the SVG document is loaded, a message box is displayed:

```
<?xml version="1.0" encoding="iso-8859-1" ?>
<svg onload="alert('I am ready now!')">
</svg>
```

Apart from these SVG-specific events, three animation events are defined in the SMIL Animation specification available at `http://www.w3.org/AudioVideo/` or `http://www.w3.org/TR/2001/REC-smil-animation-20010904/` (see Table 14.9).

TABLE 14.9 Animation Events

Event	Description	Attribute Name
beginEvent	Occurs when the animation element begins.	onbegin
endEvent	Occurs when the animation element ends. If there are iterations, it is fired after the last iteration.	onend
repeatEvent	Occurs each time the animation element is repeated. That means if the animation has several iterations, each iteration after the first one fires the event.	onrepeat

Key Events

Keyboard interaction was part of the DOM Level 2 Event specification but was later removed and is now no longer part of it. However, it is expected that keyboard events will return to the DOM specification with Level 3, which is currently in progress.

The Adobe SVG Viewer, at the time of writing the most widely used SVG viewer, does support keyboard events. You should keep in mind the fact that if you use keyboard events, they will work only with the Adobe SVG Viewer, not with all other viewers (and maybe no other viewer at all). Keyboard events are listed in Table 14.10.

TABLE 14.10 Keyboard Events

Event	Description	Attribute Name
keydown	Occurs when a key on the keyboard is pressed and held down.	onkeydown
keypress	Occurs when a key on the keyboard is pressed and released.	onkeypress
keyup	Occurs when a (held-down) key on the keyboard is released.	onkeyup

> **NOTE**
>
> Key events occur in the following order: keydown, keyup, keypress.

Now we'll look at how to add event listeners to elements of an SVG document.

Event Listeners

Earlier in this chapter, you saw a quick overview of event listeners and looked at the
`EventTarget` interface. You now will see how to use the `EventTarget` interface to add
event listeners to your nodes.

> **NOTE**
>
> Programming the DOM using JavaScript/ECMAScript will be covered no earlier than in the next
> chapter, so we cannot present many examples here. The intention of this chapter is to introduce
> you to the concepts so that you can dive right into programming your SVG documents in the
> next chapter.

Adding an Event Listener

To add an event listener to an event target, you can call the `addEventListener()` method
by using the `EventTarget` interface. This method expects the following three parameters
to be passed to it:

- *type*—The event type of the event listener (for example, `activate` or `SVGLoad`).

- *listener*—The code to be executed when the event is fired and the event listener
  becomes active. The parameter must be passed as a reference to a function.

- *useCapture*—A Boolean value defining whether this event listener should capture
  events before it reaches the designated event target (`true`) or not (`false`). If this parameter is set to `true`, events bubbling up the DOM tree will not activate this event
  handler.

Listing 14.4 uses JavaScript/ECMAScript syntax, but the basic concepts are also valid for
other languages. Now assume that variable et is of type `EventTarget`. The following code
adds some event listeners to this element.

LISTING 14.4   14code04.svg—Adding Event Listeners

```
// First, when the activate event occurs, call function doSomething()
et.addEventListener("activate",
                    doSomething,
                    false);
// Now, call function doSomethingElse() if mouse pointer moves over element
et.addEventListener("mouseover",
                    doSomethingElse,
                    false);
// doSomethingDifferent() shall be called on mouseover, too
// this declaration does not overwrite doSomethingElse() !
et.addEventListener("mouseover",
```

LISTING 14.4   Continued

```
                    doSomethingDifferent,
                    false);

// click events for elements below et should be captured,
// capture() shall be called in this case
et.addEventListener("click",
                    capture,
                    true);
```

> **NOTE**
>
> No parentheses follow the function names because you must supply references to the functions. Therefore, you must remove the parentheses.

If you do not want to use addEventListener(), you might follow the old HTML way and use the attribute names provided in Tables 14.5 through 14.10. The code would now look similar to this:

```
...
<elementname
   onactivate="doSomething()"
   onmouseover="doSomethingElse(); doSomethingDifferent()"
   onclick="capture()";
/>
...
```

However, note the following:

- This time, you need to provide real code; thus, you have to end function references with parentheses.

- Capturing events is not possible; if you are using attributes, *useCapture* has a default value of false.

- As you will see later in this chapter, from within the called function, you can determine which element and which event called this function. If you are using attributes, this is not possible anymore, according to the DOM Level 2 specification. However, the Adobe SVG Viewer does offer this capability, but according to the specs, it needn't do so.

To summarize: Using addEventListener() (and the other functions) is recommended if you want flexibility and functionality. For easier tasks, if you do not need to capture and/or bubble events, and if you do not need to determine why the function was called, you can use attribute names.

Removing an Event Listener

After an event listener is added to an event target, you can easily remove it. Just call the removeEventListener() method and be careful to use the same parameters you used for addEventListener(). If you fail to do so, removeEventListener() will find nothing to remove, so nothing will happen.

Like addEventListener(), removeEventListener() expects the following three parameters:

- *type*—The event type

- *listener*—The code to be executed

- *useCapture*—A Boolean value indicating whether this event listener will capture events before they reach the designated EventTarget (true) or not (false)

Now we will expand Listing 14.4 and try to remove some of the event listeners in Listing 14.5.

LISTING 14.5   14code05.svg—Removing the Event Listeners

```
// First, when the activate event occurs, call function doSomething()
et.addEventListener("activate",
                    doSomething,
                    false);
// Now, call function doSomethingElse() if mouse pointer moves over element
et.addEventListener("mouseover",
                    doSomethingElse,
                    false);
// doSomethingDifferent() shall be called on mouseover, too
// this declaration does not overwrite doSomethingElse() !
et.addEventListener("mouseover",
                    doSomethingDifferent,
                    false);

// click events for elements below et should be captured,
// capture() shall be called in this case
et.addEventListener("click",
                    capture,
                    true);
// NEW CODE:
//
// First of all, the event listener that calls doSomethingDifferent()
```

LISTING 14.5   Continued

```
// is removed
et.removeEventListener("mouseover",
                       doSomethingDifferent,
                       false);
// The following code will NOT work - the third parameter is not
// the same as was used when adding the event listener
// (now false, back then true)
et.removeEventListener("click",
                       capture,
                       false);
// The following code is correct and does remove the click event listener
et.removeEventListener("click",
                       capture,
                       true);
```

Dispatching Events

The last method for handling events sounds at first quite banal: `dispatchEvent()` dispatches an event, that is, calls the event-handling function for a given event. You might say that this capability is not really extraordinary because you could call the functions directly and not have to use `dispatchEvent()`.

If you use SVG quite a lot, and especially do a lot of DOM work (including adding or removing nodes and so on, as will be explained in the next chapter), someday you might need `dispatchEvent()`. Say you have a reference to an `EventTarget` object but do not know what exactly the event listener associated to it does. Here, `dispatchEvent()` comes into play. This function pretends that a given event has been fired so that the appropriate event listener or listeners can be activated.

The event target is the `EventTarget` object that calls `dispatchEvent()`. The parameter for this function is the event that will be fired.

Note that this function is seldom used. A lot of event handling can be done with attribute names, and almost all the rest can be done with `addEventListener()`and `removeEventListener()`.

Getting Information About Events

As we mentioned several times before, when an event listener becomes active and an event is handled by one or more functions, you can always find out which event and which element triggered the function and what the event target was.

Whenever an event-handling function is called, this function automatically receives one parameter: a reference to the event that triggered the execution of the function. Thus, the following code reads out this event and opens an alert box with its textual representation:

```
function handler(evt) {
  alert(evt);
}
```

The event parameter from the preceding code snippet, given the name evt, contains quite a lot of useful information. To access this information, you must use the interfaces Event and EventTarget.

The latter of these interfaces, EventTarget, was introduced previously. It has only three methods: addEventListener(), removeEventListener(),and dispatchEvent().

Event Interface

Now let's look at the interface you can use to get further information about a variable of type Event. The Event interface is part of DOM Level 2 and has the properties listed in Table 14.11.

TABLE 14.11 Event Properties

Property	Description	Read-only?
type	Type of event (for example, click, activate).	yes
target	The target of the event (the object it is sent to).	yes
currentTarget	The element that is currently executing event listeners (and thus calling the current function).	yes
eventPhase	The current so-called phase in event flow. It is basically a numeric value that is incremented by 1 at every turn.	yes
bubbles	A Boolean value indicating whether the event is a bubbling event (true) or not (false).	yet
cancelable	A Boolean value indicating whether the default action of the event may be canceled with preventDefault() (true) or not (false).	yes
timeStamp	Epoch time value (that is, milliseconds since January 1, 1970) at which the event was created.	yes
currentNode	Reference to the node that is currently being processed; specific to Adobe SVG Viewer.	yes

As you can see, all the properties in Table 14.11 are read-only, which means you cannot change them after an event has been created.

The Event interface offers three methods, which are listed in Table 14.12.

TABLE 14.12   Event Methods

Method	Description
initEvent(eventtype, bubble, cancelable)	Initializes an event. Parameters are the event type (String), whether the event can bubble or not (Boolean), and whether the event's default action can be canceled or not (Boolean).
preventDefault()	Cancels the event (if it is cancelable; that is, the cancelable property is true).
stopPropagation()	Prevents any further propagation of the event, both during the "capturing phase" and during the "bubbling phase."

Other Interfaces

If you want specific information about a given event—for example, if the Alt key was held down while a mouse click occurred (yes, that's an event, too!)—the Event interface doesn't allow you to access this information; you must use these more specific interfaces for the different types of events:

- KeyEvent—Gives information for a key event (not part of DOM Level 2 but implemented in Adobe SVG Viewer nonetheless)

- MouseEvent—Gives information for a mouse event

- MutationEvent—Gives information for a mutation event (but currently not supported in Adobe SVG Viewer)

These interfaces—or to be more specific, the interesting properties—will be covered in Chapter 15.

A Working Example

Although we have not talked about JavaScript and ECMAScript or incorporating script code within SVG code yet, we do not want to end this section without an example. This example will do nothing more than tell the user which kind of event has occurred. To accomplish that, we have to put some pieces together.

First, we will use attribute names to generate the event handler:

```
<?xml version="1.0" encoding="iso-8859-1" ?>
<svg>
   <g id="test" onclick="...">
      <rect x="0" y="0" width="100" height="100"/>
   </g>
</svg>
```

14

Now let's look at the value of these attributes. Calling a function is not a good idea because you have not seen yet where to put these functions within the SVG file. So, we have to use pure JavaScript code. The special variable evt contains a reference to the current event; you have seen something like it before, when we mentioned that a reference to the triggered event is automatically passed to each function.

The alert() method creates a modal window that displays any given text. Thus, alert(evt) creates a pop-up window that contains the string representation of the event:

```
<?xml version="1.0" encoding="iso-8859-1" ?>
<svg>
    <g id="test" onclick="alert(evt)">
        <rect x="0" y="0" width="100" height="100"/>
    </g>
</svg>
```

You will see something like [object MouseEvent] when you click on the black square. However, we are interested in what kind of mouse event was triggered. Thus, we need a property of the Event interface, type. Using the dot syntax almost every object-oriented language uses, evt.type returns the type property of evt—in this case, the type of event:

```
<?xml version="1.0" encoding="iso-8859-1" ?>
<svg>
    <g id="test" onclick="alert(evt.type)">
        <rect x="0" y="0" width="100" height="100"/>
    </g>
</svg>
```

In the final step, shown in Listing 14.6, we use more event attributes so that there is something to distinguish.

LISTING 14.6   14code06.svg—Event Attributes

```
<?xml version="1.0" encoding="iso-8859-1" ?>
<svg>
    <g id="test" onclick="alert(evt.type)"
                 onmouseout="alert(evt.type)">
        <rect x="0" y="0" width="100" height="100"/>
    </g>
</svg>
```

When you load this SVG file now, you see an alert box when you click on the square and when you move your mouse pointer away from it. Depending on which of these two events occurred, the text in the modal window is different—either click or mouseout. The latter is shown in Figure 14.8.

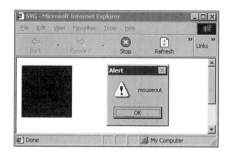

FIGURE 14.8   An alert box after moving the mouse pointer away from the square.

SVG DOM-Specific Interfaces

In some cases, getting an element with the core functionality of the DOM is not very useful. The alternative way is to access an element with interfaces of the SVG module. The interfaces in the SVG module are called **specific interfaces**. With specific interfaces, you can access elements like definitions with <desc> more quickly. However, you must not check where and how often an element occurs.

Using specific interfaces is sometimes the faster way to access elements. But are there interfaces for all-important SVG elements? Yes, more or less for all SVG elements. The base interface for most of the others is SVGElement. It contains all elements of an SVG graphic. Other interfaces inherit from SVGElement.

In the following list, we have collected the most important SVG-specific interfaces. In most chapters of Part I, you will find all relevant interfaces for the SVG elements that are the topic of this chapter.

- SVGElement—This interface is the basic element of the SVG module. It contains all elements of an SVG graphic. All other SVG interfaces with Element in their names are derivatives of SVGElement. One example is SVGLineElement, which represents all lines in an SVG graphic.

- SVGSVGElement—This element represents the svg element. For example, it contains methods to get the current time or to create a matrix. Many other elements have their own SVG interfaces. For the defs element, the interface is SVGDefsElement.

The SVGRect interface is one example of a specialized interface. It contains the rectangle forms of the SVG graphic. It has four methods to get attributes of the rectangle: x and y for the position, height and width for the size.

Listing 14.7 shows the relationship between events, DOM core methods, and SVG DOM methods. In this example, we want to get the first style definition of a style sheet in an SVG document. To do so, we use the target property and the getOwnerDocument()

method in connection with the evt variable to get the actual document. Using getElementById() and the sty ID, we change into the style sheet part of the site. The resulting object is of type SVGStyleElement. Finally, the firstChild property contains the first—and here only—style definition text.

LISTING 14.7   14code07.svg—Get the Actual Document

```
<?xml version="1.0" encoding="iso-8859-1"?>
<svg width="300" height="200" id="svgdoc"
    onload =
      "alert(evt.target.getOwnerDocument().getElementById('sty').firstChild);">
  <defs>
    <style type="text/css" id="sty"><![CDATA[
        text {font-size:12pt;}
    ]]>
    </style>
  </defs>
  <text x="25" y="20" id="text1">Hello SVG-World</text>
</svg>
```

You can see the output of Listing 14.7 in Figure 14.9.

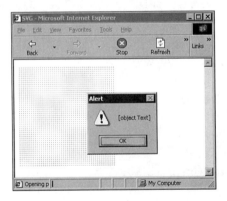

FIGURE 14.9   The output of our code.

Summary

This chapter did not contain very much code. The reason is obvious: We provided you with the theoretical side of the SVG DOM, thus laying the foundation for the next chapter, where you will find less text but much more code. Then we will script the SVG DOM.

So far, we have looked at the following topics:

- We looked at the W3C's DOM 2 specification and explained the motivation behind it and the basic concepts.

- We had a closer look at the tree structure of DOM and the DOM 2 event mechanisms.

- Finally, we switched over to SVG and looked at what is left of DOM 2 there, what has been changed, and what is new.

- At the end of the chapter, we introduced some of the SVG DOM-specific interfaces to give you an idea of what interfaces are good for.

Now we're ready to get down to the nitty-gritty of scripting SVG. The next two chapters feature—after some more theoretical basis—code, code, and more code.

14

Scripting SVG

Chapter 14, "The SVG DOM," provided a lot of information about standards—the W3C DOM Level 2 specification, the DOM Level 2 Event specification, and so on. Now that this foundation has been laid, it's time to put these standards into practice. This chapter will introduce you to the various possibilities to make SVG even more dynamic using script languages such as ECMAScript/JavaScript. Fasten your seatbelts, and load your favorite text editor; here we go!

Introduction to Scripting SVG

The W3C SVG specification does not say much about scripting SVG. In fact, the data provided there adheres to the DOM Level 2 specification, and as we explained in the preceding chapter, it covers what's new, what's different, and what has been left out. So, basically, you are moving into the great wide open in this chapter.

In real-world examples, however, you will find only a few different approaches for scripting SVG. In this section, we will explain which approaches are used and why they are so popular.

Which Language?

Although SVG is language independent in terms of scripting, you will find that ECMAScript is used most often for scripting SVG. There are several reasons for that:

- If possible, people want to avoid learning a new programming language if they can use another language they have already mastered. This is especially true in companies where tight schedules and cut budgets force programmers to improvise a lot.

- When starting to learn a programming language or ways to use a programming language to extend the possibilities of a markup language (as we do now), people always try to learn from others, so they can look on the Web for examples. It is logical that they also tend to use the programming language that they find in these examples.

> **NOTE**
>
> The last point is one of the main reasons that most ASP programming is done using VBScript, although programming in JScript is possible as well, and JScript does have some advantages over VBScript.

The first of these reasons presumably has led the developers of the SVG specification to use ECMAScript as the default scripting language for SVG documents. ECMAScript is a standardized language, developed from Netscape's JavaScript (the default scripting language for Web browsers). You will find only very few, primarily cosmetic differences between JavaScript and ECMAScript. JavaScript version 1.5, which is available within the Netscape 6 browser series and Mozilla, is fully ECMAScript-compliant.

The creators of Adobe's SVG Viewer seem to like ECMAScript as well. Prior to version 3.0, the viewer used the browser's scripting engine. However, the scripting engine did not work with some browsers that didn't allow such connections; Internet Explorer for Macintosh is one example. So, beginning with version 3.0, the Adobe SVG Viewer has a built-in ECMAScript scripting engine that is used whenever the browser's scripting engine is not accessible from within an SVG document.

For this reason, we stick to JavaScript/ECMAScript in this chapter. If you insist on using another language for accessing the DOM, you should still read this chapter. The basic principles of interaction with SVG we provide here are true for other languages as well, so you still receive a lot of information you can use for your programming experiments. And, of course, a first step into scripting SVG could be to port the examples here into your language of choice!

> **NOTE**
>
> In this chapter, we do not have the space to give you a full introduction to the JavaScript/ECMAScript language, but we will thoroughly explain every code example.

Specifying the Scripting Language

The standard scripting language is, as we have already told you, ECMAScript. So, if you are using only ECMAScript (and we recommend that you do so), you do not need to change anything in your code to use the ECMAScript interpreter. Chances are close to zero that the default scripting language will change within the next few releases of the SVG specification.

If you want to use another scripting language, however, or are uncertain whether all scripting-capable SVG viewers use ECMAScript as their default (according to the SVG spec, they should), you can tell the SVG viewer precisely which language you are planning to use. For that, the `contentScriptType` attribute of the `svg` element comes into play. There, you can set the default scripting language for the whole SVG document. You do not have to provide the name of the language as a value, but its MIME type as defined in RFC2045 (see `http://www.faqs.org/rfcs/rfc2045.html` for details). For ECMAScript, the type is `text/ecmascript`; for JavaScript, it is `text/javascript`. If you want to use Microsoft's JScript (the JavaScript clone) that is available only on the Windows platform, your code would look like this:

```
<?xml version="1.0" encoding="iso-8859-1"?>
<svg contentScriptType="text/jscript">
<!-- ... -->
</svg>
```

The content types for the scripting language supported by Adobe SVG Viewer are shown in Table 15.1.

TABLE 15.1   Content Types

Content Type	Description
text/ecmascript	ECMAScript
text/javascript	JavaScript
text/jscript	JScript (Windows only)

As mentioned previously, the Adobe SVG Viewer comes with a built-in script interpreter, beginning with version 3. By default, this built-in engine is used only in environments that do not offer access to the browser's scripting engine—for example, Microsoft Internet Explorer on the Macintosh platform. In other environments that do grant access to the browser's scripting capabilities (such as Microsoft Internet Explorer on Windows platforms), the browser's engine is used. If, however, you want to avoid that and make the Adobe SVG Viewer's scripting engine the default engine, you can use the `scriptImplementation` attribute of the `<svg>` tag and set it to `"Adobe"`:

```
<?xml version="1.0" encoding="iso-8859-1"?>
<svg scriptImplementation="Adobe">
<!-- ... -->
</svg>
```

All scripting within this SVG document will be done by Adobe's internal ECMAScript engine. But be aware that this currently works only with Adobe SVG Viewer, and only with version 3 and higher.

The `scriptImplementation` attribute accepts several values; they are described in Table 15.2.

TABLE 15.2   Values of the scriptImplementation Attribute

Value	Description
Adobe	Use Adobe's built-in engine.
browser	Use the browser's engine.
Microsoft	Use Microsoft's engine (thus, this value works only within Internet Explorer).
Netscape	Use Netscape's engine (thus, this value works only within Netscape browsers).
"" (empty string, or alternatively, attribute not set)	Use the default. In this case, use the browser's engine, if available, and if you don't succeed, use Adobe's engine.

In this chapter, we will not set the `contentScriptType` and `scriptImplementation` attributes because we always use ECMAScript. If you plan to use another language, you can find the necessary information to accomplish that in this section.

The script Element

While reading the preceding chapter, you may have noticed the examples there always had event-handler attributes for SVG tags and very long, one-lined code after that, as in this example:

```
<?xml version="1.0" encoding="iso-8859-1"?>
<svg width="300" height="200" id="svgdoc"
    onload="alert(evt.target.getOwnerDocument().
➥getElementById('sty').firstChild);">
  <defs>
    <style type="text/css" id="sty"><![CDATA[
      text {font-size:12pt;}
    ]]>
    </style>
  </defs>
  <text x="25" y="20" id="text1">Hello SVG-World</text>
</svg>
```

The reason for coding this way is obvious: We would really have liked to just call an ECMAScript function there, but where would we have put these functions? In HTML, you can use a `script` element for that job, but how about SVG?

The answer: SVG can use a `script` element as well. However, there is a specialty that does not exist in HTML. Because SVG is XML-compliant, the contents of a `script` element—functions, variable declarations, and other code—are of type #CDATA and thus must be surrounded by `<![CDATA[` and `]]>`. So, this simple example incorporates a `script` element into your SVG code:

```
<?xml version="1.0" encoding="iso-8859-1"?>
<svg>
   <defs>
      <script type="text/ecmascript"><![CDATA[
         // nothing happens here ...
      ]]></script>
   </defs>
   <!-- ... -->
</svg>
```

You should note the following points about this example:

- The script element is contained within the defs element (which sounds logical because style sheets are also located between <defs> and </defs>).

- The type attribute of the script element is set to "text/ecmascript"; this is also the default. As with the contentScriptType attribute of the svg element, other values are possible; the following values are supported by Adobe SVG Viewer:

  "text/ecmascript" (ECMAScript)

  "text/javascript" (JavaScript)

  "text/jscript" (JScript, Windows platforms only)

The Adobe SVG Viewer, version 3.0 and higher, again offers the scriptImplementation attribute where you can specify which scripting engine should be used. You have the following choices:

- "Adobe"—Use Adobe's built-in ECMAScript/JavaScript engine.

- "browser"—Use the browser's engine.

- "Microsoft"—Use the Microsoft engine (available only in Internet Explorer).

- "Netscape"—Use the Netscape engine (available only in Netscape browsers).

- "" or attribute not set at all—Use the default; that is, try the browser's engine first, and if that fails, use Adobe's built-in engine.

With this setting, you can override the settings for the whole document provided in the svg element. In the following example, the default scripting language is ECMAScript and the Adobe scripting engine is used; however, the <script> block is executed only on Internet Explorer and uses JScript:

```
<?xml version="1.0" encoding="iso-8859-1"?>
<svg contentScriptType="text/ecmascript" scriptImplementation="Adobe">
   <defs>
      <script type="text/jscript" scriptImplementation="Microsoft"><![CDATA[
         // this is only seen by Microsoft browsers...
```

```
      ]]></script>
   </defs>
   <!-- ... -->
</svg>
```

All functions you define within a `<script>` block and all variables you declare within `<script>` (but not within a function) are globally available. So one function from one `<script>` block may call another function from another `<script>` block; however, you should really put all script code into one `<script>` block like this:

```
<?xml version="1.0" encoding="iso-8859-1"?>
<svg>
   <defs>
      <script type="text/ecmascript"><![CDATA[
         function ecma1() {
            return ecma2();
         }
      ]]></script>
      <script type="text/ecmascript"><![CDATA[
         function ecma2() {
            return "Scripting SVG is fun!";
         }
      ]]></script>
   </defs>
   <!-- ... -->
</svg>
```

Now you know where to put your script code, and thanks to Chapter 14, you also know (or at least have a basic idea) how to call this script code. We're ready to get down to the nitty-gritty and do some stuff with SVG documents!

Manipulating the DOM

For changing the DOM, you have to know quite well which functions are offered as per the W3C DOM Level 2 specification, a specification SVG quite exactly implements. In this section, we will present the different methods, and this time, you will see several examples. So, fasten your seatbelts.

Getting to the Top

In this section, we will provide some ways to access the different elements of an SVG document and some ways to change these elements. However, a basic problem is knowing where to start. First, we must have some way to access the basic SVG document because this element also offers (via interface) several methods we need throughout the rest of this chapter. So, the first question is, How do we get to this top-level document?

In the preceding chapter, we told you that, by using the special variable `evt`, you gain access to the current event that triggered script execution. If you are calling a function from an event handler (remember, this is an attribute of any SVG element that calls a function upon receiving an event), a reference to this object should be submitted to the called function as a parameter.

Now you must complete two steps to get a reference to the SVG document:

1. Call the `getTarget()` method or use the property target. As you know from Chapter 14, you can use this method to get to the SVG element that is the event target for the current event. However, you don't need to use exactly the event target element; any element will do for this example. Because accessing any other elements is quite hard, `getTarget()` or target should be your first choice.

2. Access the owner document of the event target. This document, in fact, is the SVG document we want you to access for this example. To accomplish that, you can use the `getOwnerDocument()` method or the `ownerDocument` property of the event target.

> **NOTE**
>
> You might have noticed that you always seem to have the choice between a property *xxx* and an associated method get*Xxx*(). In fact, that's correct; for every property, there exists a get*Xxx*() method to read the property (and also a set*Xxx*() method for setting the property, but we'll discuss such methods more later). Note the "camel case" notation: The first letter of the property name is capitalized in the method name. Throughout this chapter, we will stick to the method access because we do not want to mix different notations. Furthermore, the Netscape browser cannot directly write properties of plug-ins; changes can be made only via methods.

To summarize, the following line of code sets the `svgdoc` variable to the current SVG document:

```
var svgdoc = event.getTarget().getOwnerDocument();
```

You should use this code in all your functions, or maybe even define the `svgdoc` variable as global so that you can access the SVG document from anywhere within your `script` element.

The following code illustrates this approach: As soon as the SVG document is loaded (using the event handler `onload`), a reference to the document is saved in the `svgdoc` variable, which is globally available. To demonstrate that this approach works, the variable's content is presented to the user via an alert box:

```
<?xml version="1.0" encoding="iso-8859-1"?>
<svg onload="init(evt)">
   <defs>
      <script type="text/ecmascript"><![CDATA[
         var svgdoc;   //global variable

         function init(evt) {
            svgdoc = evt.getTarget().getOwnerDocument();
            alert(svgdoc);
         }
      ]]></script>
   </defs>
   <!-- ... -->
</svg>
```

As you can see, the svgdoc variable is of type SVGDocument, so we have successfully accessed the actual SVG document.

Finding Elements

Let's take a quick look at the DOM implementations of current Web browsers. As you probably know, elements can be accessed using their id attribute, in combination with the getElementById() method. This method returns the object with the desired ID. In HTML/JavaScript, this method can be called from the document object, the object that represents the HTML document. Thus, you need to call document.getElementById(). In SVG, however, implementing this functionality is not so easy because the document object just doesn't exist there. However, as you saw in the preceding section, you can access the SVG document object by using the following code line:

```
var svgdoc = evt.getTarget().getOwnerDocument();
```

Thus, if you want to access an element by its ID, you can now use svgdoc.getElementById().

To try out this method, run Listing 15.1, an SVG document that creates a digital clock.

LISTING 15.1   15code01.svg—A Digital Clock with SVG

```
<?xml version="1.0" encoding="iso-8859-1"?>
<svg width="300" height="300">
   <defs>
      <script type="text/ecmascript"><![CDATA[
         // ...
      ]]></script>
```

LISTING 15.1   Continued

```
            <linearGradient id="linear_bw" x1="0%" y1="0%" x2="100%" y2="0%"
               spreadMethod="pad" gradientUnits="userSpaceOnUse">
               <stop offset="0%" stop-color="rgb(255,255,255)" stop-opacity="1"/>
               <stop offset="100%" stop-color="rgb(0,0,0)" stop-opacity="1"/>
            </linearGradient>
            <linearGradient id="linear_bw_tr" x1="0%" y1="0%" x2="100%" y2="0%"
               spreadMethod="pad" gradientUnits="userSpaceOnUse"
               gradientTransform="matrix(0.819152 0.573576 -0.573576 0.819152 0 0)">
               <stop offset="0%" stop-color="rgb(255,255,255)" stop-opacity="1"/>
               <stop offset="100%" stop-color="rgb(0,0,0)" stop-opacity="1"/>
            </linearGradient>
         </defs>
         <path
            d="M158 139 L34 139 L56 106 L180 106 L180 172 L158 205 L158 139 L180 106"
            fill="url(#linear_bw_tr)" stroke="rgb(0,0,128)" stroke-width="0"/>
         <rect x="31" y="136" width="130" height="71" rx="9" ry="9"
            fill="url(#linear_bw)" stroke-width="0"/>
         <rect x="36" y="141" width="120" height="61" rx="8" ry="8" fill="rgb(0,0,0)"
            stroke-width="0"/>
         <text id="hours" x="34px" y="186px" fill="rgb(255,255,255)" font-size="30"
            font-family="Arial">12</text>
         <text x="68px" y="183px" fill="rgb(255,255,255)" font-size="30"
            font-family="Arial">:</text>
         <text id="minutes" x="76px" y="186px" fill="rgb(255,255,255)" font-size="30"
            font-family="Arial">34</text>
         <text x="111px" y="184px" fill="rgb(255,255,255)" font-size="30"
            font-family="Arial">:</text>
         <text id="seconds" x="121px" y="186px" fill="rgb(255,255,255)"
            font-size="30" font-family="Arial">56</text>
      </svg>
```

The digital clock is initialized with 12:34:56, as shown in Figure 15.1.

Now we want to manipulate the appearance of the clock. First, look again at the SVG code. You will see five `text` elements, three for hours, minutes, and seconds, respectively, and two for the colons separating the different values. The naming scheme is also quite straightforward:

- The `text` element for hours has the ID `hours`.
- The `text` element for minutes has the ID `minutes`.
- The `text` element for seconds has the ID `seconds`.

FIGURE 15.1   A digital clock.

We now want to access the elements using ECMAScript. To achieve that, we need to assemble our listing step by step.

We again need the code that puts a reference to the SVG document in a global variable:

```
var svgdoc;  //global variable

function init(evt) {
    svgdoc = evt.getTarget().getOwnerDocument();
}
```

Here, the init() function is called via the onload attribute of the <svg> tag.

In the next step, the text elements for hours, minutes, and seconds should be accessed when the user clicks on them. Additionally, only the element that the user clicks on should be accessed. Thus, one idea is to use the onclick event handler for each of the three elements:

```
<text onclick="sayHello('hours')"> ......
```

As you can see, a sayHello() function is called. The only parameter is the name (that is, id attribute) of the text element. So, the function sayHello() could look like this:

```
function sayHello(id) {
    var el = svgdoc.getElementById(id);
    if (el)
        alert(el);
}
```

The function sayHello() calls getElementById() as a method of the SVG document saved in the variable svgdoc. If an element with the desired id is found, the element is shown to the user. Of course, the user still sees only that the element is of type TextElement, but nothing more. We will approach this problem in the following section.

But first, look at the complete example in Listing 15.2.

LISTING 15.2   15code02.svg—The Complete Listing for Our Digital Clock Example

```
<?xml version="1.0" encoding="iso-8859-1"?>
<svg width="300" height="300" onload="init(evt)">
   <defs>
      <script type="text/ecmascript"><![CDATA[
         var svgdoc;   //global variable

         function init(evt) {
            svgdoc = evt.getTarget().getOwnerDocument();
         }

         function sayHello(id) {
            var el = svgdoc.getElementById(id);
            if (el)
               alert(el);
         }
      ]]></script>
      <linearGradient id="linear_bw" x1="0%" y1="0%" x2="100%" y2="0%"
         spreadMethod="pad" gradientUnits="userSpaceOnUse">
         <stop offset="0%" stop-color="rgb(255,255,255)" stop-opacity="1"/>
         <stop offset="100%" stop-color="rgb(0,0,0)" stop-opacity="1"/>
      </linearGradient>
      <linearGradient id="linear_bw_tr" x1="0%" y1="0%" x2="100%" y2="0%"
         spreadMethod="pad" gradientUnits="userSpaceOnUse"
         gradientTransform="matrix(0.819152 0.573576 -0.573576 0.819152 0 0)">
         <stop offset="0%" stop-color="rgb(255,255,255)" stop-opacity="1"/>
         <stop offset="100%" stop-color="rgb(0,0,0)" stop-opacity="1"/>
      </linearGradient>
   </defs>
   <path
      d="M158 139 L34 139 L56 106 L180 106 L180 172 L158 205 L158 139 L180 106"
      fill="url(#linear_bw_tr)" stroke="rgb(0,0,128)" stroke-width="0"/>
   <rect x="31" y="136" width="130" height="71" rx="9" ry="9"
      fill="url(#linear_bw)" stroke-width="0"/>
   <rect x="36" y="141" width="120" height="61" rx="8" ry="8" fill="rgb(0,0,0)"
      stroke-width="0"/>
```

LISTING 15.2   Continued

```
  <text id="hours" x="34px" y="186px" fill="rgb(255,255,255)" font-size="30"
    onclick="sayHello('hours')"
    font-family="Arial">12</text>
  <text x="68px" y="183px" fill="rgb(255,255,255)" font-size="30"
    font-family="Arial">:</text>
  <text id="minutes" x="76px" y="186px" fill="rgb(255,255,255)" font-size="30"
    onclick="sayHello('minutes')"
    font-family="Arial">34</text>
  <text x="111px" y="184px" fill="rgb(255,255,255)" font-size="30"
    font-family="Arial">:</text>
  <text id="seconds" x="121px" y="186px" fill="rgb(255,255,255)"
    onclick="sayHello('seconds')"
    font-size="30" font-family="Arial">56</text>
</svg>
```

Figure 15.2 shows the results of running Listing 15.2.

FIGURE 15.2   A message appears after running Listing 15.2.

Apart from getElementById(), where you can search for elements using their identifiers, you can also search by the tag names used. For this task, you need the getElementsByTagName() method. Note the *s* in the method name; this function does not return one, but all elements with the tag name provided as a parameter. The return value of this method is of type NodeList. In the following code, getElementById() is called and all text elements are returned:

```
...
function showMeText(evt) {
```

```
    var elements = svgdoc.getElementsByTagName("text");
    if (elements)  //if there are any "text" elements
        alert(el);
}
```

Accessing Attributes

Now comes the fun stuff. Accessing elements is one thing, and now you should know quite well how you can do that. However, this procedure makes sense only if you know how you can access attributes of these elements.

We want to demonstrate how to access attributes and extend the digital clock example. First, let's examine some theory. To access (and manipulate) attributes, you need two methods:

- getAttribute()—This method returns the value of the attribute provided as a parameter to the method.

- setAttribute()—This method sets an attribute (the first parameter) to a given value (the second parameter).

These two methods exist for each SVG element, and it is logical that they are always called for the element you want to modify.

Reading Attributes

For the next step in expanding the digital clock example, we are interested in the vertical position of the text elements. They can be read from the y attributes of the elements. So, we again need a function that accepts the id attribute as a parameter. Then the y attribute is accessed and presented to the user:

```
function sayHello(id) {
    var el = svgdoc.getElementById(id);
    if (el) {
        var y = el.getAttribute("y");
        alert(y);
    }
}
```

Now you can reload your document in your browser to see the current vertical position of the element.

Now may be the right time to reconsider the code so far. Every time you call sayHello(), you must provide the id attribute as a parameter. This is not good style: If you later change the element's id attribute, the code will not run any longer.

From Chapter 14, you know that you can find out which element triggered the event, the event target. One easy way to get access to the event target and its attributes is to call getTarget(); this way, you have your reference to the object, without getElementById():

```
function sayHello(evt) {
   var el = evt.getTarget();
   if (el) {
      var y = el.getAttribute("y");
      alert(y);
   }
}
```

Now you just need to change the event handler for the three text elements in your code. You have to submit evt as a parameter, not the id attribute:

```
<text onclick="sayHello(evt)"> ......
```

This piece of code is *reusable*. You can—using copy and paste—use this code over and over again, for all elements, and you do not have to change the onclick attribute.

Writing Attributes

In the next step, we will write these attributes. For this step, we will rewrite the sayHello() function. In this case, the vertical position of the text element will be changed. When the user clicks on the element the first time, the element will be moved up by five pixels. The next time, the element will be moved back to its original position.

To achieve this functionality, we will use a small trick: We will assume that the original vertical values of the elements are even. If the position is altered by five pixels, the position is odd. We know that an odd vertical position means that the element has been moved from its original position; otherwise, the element is at its original position.

The vertical position is read using getAttribute(), and then written back, changed plus or minus five pixels, using setAttribute():

```
function sayHello(evt) {
   var el = evt.getTarget();
   if (el) {
      var y = parseInt(el.getAttribute("y"));
      if (y % 2 == 0) //if even
         el.setAttribute("y", y+5);
      else
         el.setAttribute("y", y-5);
   }
}
```

> **NOTE**
>
> The parseInt() method converts a string into an integer value. We use this method here just to avoid error messages if the return value of getAttribute() contains letters, for any reason whatsoever.

Now you can rerun your script. When you click on a number, its position changes (see Figure 15.3); when you click again, the original position is restored.

FIGURE 15.3   The position changes.

Using Interfaces

Throughout the chapters in Part I of this book and on the Adobe and the W3C Web sites, you can find an exhaustive list of interfaces that are supported from SVG. Using this list, you can easily access a number of attributes and call a series of methods that this element supports. Let's look at this: We want to see what we can change in the text element. As you know from the alert boxes created earlier in the chapter, these elements are of type SVGTextElement. In Chapter 8, "Laying Out Text in SVG," you saw that this element inherits from SVGTextPositioningElement and SVGTextTransformable. SVGTextPositioningElement, however, inherits from SVGTextContentElement. This interface has the selectSubString method that selects a given substring in the text element. We now want to try that: As soon as the user clicks on a text element, the text will be selected.

The selectSubString method takes two parameters. The first parameter is the index of the first character to be selected (counting starts at 0), whereas the second parameter is the index of the first character that is *not* selected. Thus, selectSubString(0, 2) selects the first two characters.

We can now rewrite the `sayHello()` function. When the user clicks on a `text` element, not only is the position changed, but the text is also selected (see Figure 15.4):

```
function sayHello(evt) {
    var el = evt.getTarget();
    if (el) {
        var y = parseInt(el.getAttribute("y"));
        if (y % 2 == 0) //if not odd
            el.setAttribute("y", y+5);
        else
            el.setAttribute("y", y-5);
        el.selectSubString(0, 2);
    }
}
```

FIGURE 15.4   The text is selected.

Of course, you can walk further up the interface hierarchy: `SVGTextContentElement` inherits from several other elements, including `SVGStylable`. This interface has the read-only attribute `style` (thus, the `getStyle()` method) that contains style information about the given element. Let's look at this `style` element:

```
function sayHello(evt) {
    var el = evt.getTarget();
    if (el) {
        var y = parseInt(el.getAttribute("y"));
        if (y % 2 == 0) //if not odd
            el.setAttribute("y", y+5);
```

```
        else
            el.setAttribute("y", y-5);
        alert(el.getStyle());
    }
}
```

The result of this code is shown in Figure 15.5.

FIGURE 15.5   The style element.

The returned object is of type `CSSStyleDeclaration`. For more information on this object type, refer to the spec. Among others, this interface has the `cssText` attribute (and, as mentioned previously, the `getCssText()` method). Now let's look at its contents:

```
function sayHello(evt) {
    var el = evt.getTarget();
    if (el) {
        var y = parseInt(el.getAttribute("y"));
        if (y % 2 == 0) //if not odd
            el.setAttribute("y", y+5);
        else
            el.setAttribute("y", y-5);
        alert(el.getStyle().getCssText());
    }
}
```

When you click on one of the text elements, nothing happens. Why? Because there is no style attribute set. Just for fun, set the style attribute of one of the SVG elements to "font-family: Courier":

```
<text id="seconds" x="121px" y="186px" fill="rgb(255,255,255)"
   font-size="30" onclick="sayHello(evt)"
   style="font-family: Courier">56</text>
```

Run the example again. Now the script interpreter shows the contents of the style attribute and even automatically adds a semicolon at the end of the style, as required by the CSS specification (see Figure 15.6).

FIGURE 15.6   Style information.

> **NOTE**
>
> If you want to avoid the effect that nothing happens if an empty string is sent to an alert box (which occurs only with Adobe SVG Viewer), you could concatenate the string for the alert box with the space character. This way, the alert box always appears.

Changing style Attributes

If you want to change the style attributes of your document, you have several possible ways to do so. The techniques also depend on how you integrate style elements into your SVG document.

Styles in Attributes

Not all the text elements in our digital clock example have a style attribute, but several styles have been applied using the appropriate attributes. Let's look at the font size, for example. It has been set using the font-size attribute. Thus, if you want to change the font size, you can use getAttribute and setAttribute(), as you have seen before.

The following rewrite of the sayHello() function changes the font size from 30 to 24 and vice versa (see Figure 15.7), when the user clicks on one of the three "digits" text elements:

```
function sayHello(evt) {
   var el = evt.getTarget();
   if (el) {
      var fontsize = parseInt(el.getAttribute("font-size"));
      if (fontsize == 30)
        el.setAttribute("font-size", 24);
      else
        el.setAttribute("font-size", 30);
   }
}
```

FIGURE 15.7 The style is changed.

Using this technique, you can also change other styles that have been applied as attributes.

The style Attribute

What if styles have been applied using the style attribute for an element? To experiment with those styles, we first have to rewrite the SVG code so that the style attribute is used for formatting elements (at least to some degree):

```
<text id="hours" x="34px" y="186px" fill="rgb(255,255,255)"
   onclick="sayHello(evt)"
   style="font-family: Arial; font-size: 30;">12</text>
<text x="68px" y="183px" fill="rgb(255,255,255)" font-size="30"
   font-family="Arial">:</text>
<text id="minutes" x="76px" y="186px" fill="rgb(255,255,255)"
   onclick="sayHello(evt)"
   style="font-family: Arial; font-size: 30;">34</text>
<text x="111px" y="184px" fill="rgb(255,255,255)" font-size="30"
   font-family="Arial">:</text>
<text id="seconds" x="121px" y="186px" fill="rgb(255,255,255)"
   onclick="sayHello(evt)"
   style="font-family: Arial; font-size: 30;">56</text>
```

As you can see, the font size and font face are assigned via a style attribute. Now you can use the style interfaces of SVG to access this information.

Previously, you saw that by using the style attribute (or, to remain consistent in our coding conventions, the getStyle() method), you gain access to the CSSStyleDeclaration interface for an element; there, cssText contains (or getCssText() returns) the complete style information as a string. The CSSStyleDeclaration interface, however, offers some more methods that are interesting for programmers:

- getPropertyValue() reads the given property.

- setProperty() writes the given property (note that there is no Value in the method name).

The interface offers several other methods and attributes; however, these two are the most commonly used. Now we can rewrite our sayHello() function, this time using the CSSStyleDeclaration interface for style access:

```
function sayHello(evt) {
   var el = evt.getTarget();
   if (el) {
      var css = el.getStyle();
      var fontsize = css.getPropertyValue("font-size");
      if (fontsize == 30)
         css.setProperty("font-size", 24);
      else
         css.setProperty("font-size", 30);
```

```
    }
}
```

The effect of this script is the same as the previous script, except that this time we used the `style` attribute.

At this point, you might wonder why we use these two different approaches. Why not stick to `getAttribute()` and `setAttribute()`, which offer the same capabilities?

The answer is ease of programming. When you use the `style` attribute, you can certainly access this attribute and read the data from the string. However, reading this way is quite painful. First, you have to read the contents of the `style` attribute:

```
var css = el.getAttribute("style");
```

Then you have to look for the desired `style` command. Let's say it's `font-size`. In that case, you first have to search for that command:

```
var searchfor = "font-size";
var begin = css.indexOf(searchfor);
```

Then you have to look for the end of the assignment, either a semicolon or the end of the string:

```
var end = css.indexOf(";", begin);
if (end == -1)
    end = css.length;
```

Now you can finally extract the important data:

```
var data = css.substring(begin + searchfor.length, end);
```

But wait—the variable data now contains something like `": 30"`. That means that you have to remove all colons and spaces from the beginning of the string:

```
while (data.charAt(0) == " " || data.charAt(0) == ":")
    data = data.substring(1, data.length);
```

This example makes it clear why using the `CSSStyleDeclaration` interface is the better way here and why interfaces generally are a good thing. This approach can make programming quite a lot easier. Instead of writing 10 lines of code, you just access one attribute or call one method.

Inline Styles

There is, however, one more way to apply styles to SVG elements: using inline styles with the `style` element.

To do so, we will once again change our SVG document with the digital clock (see Listing 15.3). This time, we will remove the `style` attribute from the `text` elements and define a style class instead.

LISTING 15.3   15code03.svg—The Digital Clock (Body)

```
<?xml version="1.0" encoding="iso-8859-1"?>
<svg width="300" height="300" onload="init(evt)">
   <defs>
      <style type="text/css"><![CDATA[
         text.normal {font-family: Arial; font-size: 30;}
         text.small {font-family: Arial; font-size: 24;}
      ]]></style>
      <script type="text/ecmascript"><![CDATA[
         var svgdoc;  //global variable

         function init(evt) {
            svgdoc = evt.getTarget().getOwnerDocument();
         }
         function sayHello(evt) {
            //...
         }
      ]]></script>
      <linearGradient id="linear_bw" x1="0%" y1="0%" x2="100%" y2="0%"
         spreadMethod="pad" gradientUnits="userSpaceOnUse">
         <stop offset="0%" stop-color="rgb(255,255,255)" stop-opacity="1"/>
         <stop offset="100%" stop-color="rgb(0,0,0)" stop-opacity="1"/>
      </linearGradient>
      <linearGradient id="linear_bw_tr" x1="0%" y1="0%" x2="100%" y2="0%"
         spreadMethod="pad" gradientUnits="userSpaceOnUse"
         gradientTransform="matrix(0.819152 0.573576 -0.573576 0.819152 0 0)">
         <stop offset="0%" stop-color="rgb(255,255,255)" stop-opacity="1"/>
         <stop offset="100%" stop-color="rgb(0,0,0)" stop-opacity="1"/>
      </linearGradient>
   </defs>
   <path d="M158 139 L34 139 L56 106 L180 106 L180 172 L158 205 L158 139 L180 106"
      fill="url(#linear_bw_tr)" stroke="rgb(0,0,128)" stroke-width="0"/>
   <rect x="31" y="136" width="130" height="71" rx="9" ry="9"
      fill="url(#linear_bw)" stroke-width="0"/>
   <rect x="36" y="141" width="120" height="61" rx="8" ry="8" fill="rgb(0,0,0)"
      stroke-width="0"/>
   <text id="hours" x="34px" y="186px" fill="rgb(255,255,255)"
      onclick="sayHello(evt)"
      class="normal">12</text>
   <text x="68px" y="183px" fill="rgb(255,255,255)" font-size="30"
```

LISTING 15.3 Continued

```
        font-family="Arial">:</text>
    <text id="minutes" x="76px" y="186px" fill="rgb(255,255,255)"
        onclick="sayHello(evt)"
        class="normal">34</text>
    <text x="111px" y="184px" fill="rgb(255,255,255)" font-size="30"
        font-family="Arial">:</text>
    <text id="seconds" x="121px" y="186px" fill="rgb(255,255,255)"
        onclick="sayHello(evt)"
        class="normal">56</text>
</svg>
```

Now if we change the definition of the `normal` class, all three `text` elements change. However, to do so, we must directly access the element and change the text within the element, a clumsy thing to do. But achieving this effect is quite simple because a second style class called `small` is defined. If we assign this class name to an element, it changes immediately.

Accomplishing this task is very easy. Because `class` is an attribute of the `text` element, a simple call to `getAttribute()` and `setAttribute()` will do the trick:

```
function sayHello(evt) {
    var el = evt.getTarget();
    if (el) {
        var c = el.getAttribute("class");
        if (c == "normal")
            el.setAttribute("class", "small");
        else
            el.setAttribute("class", "normal");
    }
}
```

In fact, this approach is nothing new; we're simply using an old trick to accomplish a new effect. If you are using inline styles, you can define all the classes that you need and then just swap classes using `setAttribute()`. This way, you keep your code short and easily expandable. Are new effects required? Just add a few more classes and a few more lines of code.

Of course, we could show numerous other examples, but they would all follow the same concept:

- You can use `getElementById()` or `getTarget()` to access an element of the SVG document.

- You can use `getAttribute()` and `setAttribute()` or the different interfaces to access and/or change the elements.

15

Now take a look back at the SVG interfaces and explore the possibilities of scripting SVG. But note that there is more to come!

Changing the Tree

Have you ever wondered why we exhaustively covered the DOM structure of SVG? It's obvious: Because SVG mostly complies with the DOM Level 2 specification, the required methods and properties are implemented (or ought to be implemented—the Adobe SVG Viewer does an excellent job with that; other viewers are catching up).

Overview of DOM Methods

Table 15.3 recaps the most important node-manipulating methods that DOM2 and SVG support.

TABLE 15.3   Node-Manipulating Methods

Method or Property	Description
appendChild(*node*)	Adds a child node under the current node.
childNodes	Returns a list with all child nodes of the current node.
cloneNode(*node, deep*)	Returns a copy of the current node. If *deep* is true, all subnodes are copied as well.
firstChild	Returns the first child of the current node.
insertBefore(*newnode, nextnode*)	Inserts the current node before a node.
lastChild	Returns the last child of the current node.
nextSibling	Returns the next node to the current node on the same hierarchy level.
nodeList	Returns a list of all nodes in SVGdocument.
nodeName	Returns the name of the current node.
nodeType	Returns the (numeric) type of the current node.
nodeValue	Returns the value of a node.
parentNode	Returns the parent node.
previousSibling	Returns the node previous to the current node on the same hierarchy level.
removeChild(*childnode*)	Removes a child from the current node.
removeNode()	Removes the current node.
replaceNode(*node*)	Replaces the current node with another node.

As you can see, you can do virtually everything with nodes—adding, cloning, and removing them. To change a single node, though, you need to use the methods presented in the previous section.

We want to demonstrate the use of these functions using a new example. We'll start off with a document that defines a logo (see Listing 15.4).

LISTING 15.4   15code04.svg—A Logo in SVG (Body)

```
<?xml version="1.0" standalone="no"?>
<svg width="500" height="500" onload="init(evt)" onclick="modifyTree()">
    <defs>
        <script type="text/ecmascript"><![CDATA[
            var svgdoc;  //global variable
            var logo; //another variable
            var counter = 0 //helper variable for different stages

            function init(evt) {
                svgdoc = evt.getTarget().getOwnerDocument();
                logo = svgdoc.getElementById("logo");
            }
            function modifyTree() {
                //...
            }
        ]]></script>
    </defs>
    <g id="logo">
        <text id="abbr" x="32px" y="60px"
            style="fill:rgb(0,0,0);font-size:36;font-family:Courier New">
            SVG
        </text>
        <text id="long" x="33px" y="88px"
            style="fill-opacity:0.5;fill:rgb(0,0,128);
            font-size:24;font-family:Arial">
            Scalable Vector Graphics
        </text>
        <text id="text" x="33px" y="111px"
            style="fill-opacity:1;fill:rgb(0,0,128);
            font-size:14;font-family:Arial">
            Teach Yourself SVG in 24 Hours by SAMS
        </text>
        <line x1="25" y1="30" x2="25" y2="150"
            style="fill:none;stroke:rgb(0,0,0);stroke-width:2;stroke-opacity:0.5"/>
    </g>
</svg>
```

Figure 15.8 is the result of running Listing 15.4.

As you can see, after the document is loaded, a reference to the SVG document is saved in the variable svgdoc, whereas logo holds a reference to the group of text elements. Also, whenever the user clicks on the document, the function `modifyTree()` is executed. The global variable counter counts these clicks. Our goal is that with every click, the next phase of DOM modification will be done.

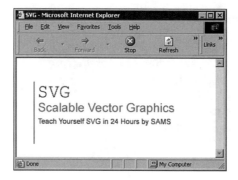

FIGURE 15.8   A simple logo.

Cloning and Inserting

First, we want to give the `"SVG"` text a shadow. We can do this in three steps:

1. First, we clone the text node.

2. Then we change the `style` attributes and the position so that the shadow can be seen.

3. Finally, we insert the new text node after the original node.

We need to change the `modifyTree()` function as follows. Let's start with the cloning:

```
function modifyTree() {
   counter ++;
   switch (counter) {
     case 1:
         //step 1: cloning the text node
         var svgtext = svgdoc.getElementById("abbr");
         var svgtext2 = svgtext.cloneNode(true, true);
         //step 2: changing style attributes
         //...
         //step 3: inserting the node
         //...
         break;
   }
}
```

Changing `style` attributes is no problem, as soon as you have access to the right element. Using `getElementById()` is quite easy, but the new element currently exists only in memory or in the `svgtext2` variable. But before we continue coding, let's pause and think about what a node element is all about.

In the section "Different Node Types" in Chapter 14, we showed you that the `nodeType` property of a node returns a numeric value that tells you what kind of node you have. In this case, `svgtext2.nodeType` returns 1, which means `element`. It also means that you can change `style` attributes with this variable.

So, without any further ado, we will change the new node, saved in the `svgtext2` variable:

```
function modifyTree() {
    counter ++;
    switch (counter) {
      case 1:
          //step 1: cloning the text node
          var svgtext = svgdoc.getElementById("abbr");
          var svgtext2 = svgtext.cloneNode(true);
          //step 2: changing style attributes
          var css = svgtext2.getStyle();
          css.setProperty("fill", "rgb(0,128,0)");
          svgtext2.setAttribute("x",
              parseInt(svgtext.getAttribute("x")) + 5);
          svgtext2.setAttribute("y",
              parseInt(svgtext.getAttribute("y")) + 4);
          //step 3: inserting the node
          //...
          break;
    }
}
```

Only one final step remains: We must insert the new node into the g element. We also said that we wanted to insert this node next to the original node. The `insertBefore()` method expects as a parameter the node in the position to the right of the new node. This node, however, is in the position to the right of the original node, which can be read using `nextSibling` or `getNextSibling()`. Thus, we can use the following:

```
function modifyTree() {
    counter ++;
    switch (counter) {
      case 1:
          //step 1: cloning the text node
          var svgtext = svgdoc.getElementById("abbr");
          var svgtext2 = svgtext.cloneNode(true);
          //step 2: changing style attributes
          var css = svgtext2.getStyle();
          css.setProperty("fill", "rgb(0,128,0)");
```

```
        svgtext2.setAttribute("x",
           parseInt(svgtext.getAttribute("x")) + 5);
        svgtext2.setAttribute("y",
           parseInt(svgtext.getAttribute("y")) + 4);
        //step 3: inserting the node
        svgtext2 = logo.insertBefore(svgtext2, svgtext.getNextSibling());
        break;
    }
}
```

Load this example in your browser or SVG viewer, and click on the SVG document. The shadow then appears, as shown in Figure 15.9.

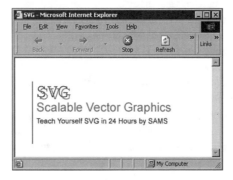

FIGURE 15.9　A logo with a shadow.

Changing Text

In the next step, we want to change the text in one of the `text` elements: *Teach Yourself SVG in 24 Hours by Sams* is not the correct title of this book (but the title of another SVG book by the same publisher). The correct title is *SVG Unleashed*. So the question is how to access the text within the `text` element. Remember the node types? The `text` element is of type 1; it is an element. However, this element contains several children, including attributes and the #CDATA text portion of the element. Thus, to access the text portion of the `text` element, we have to cycle through all children of the `text` element until we find the text. A quick look in Chapter 14 shows that text nodes are of type 3.

We need to find out how to cycle through all nodes. You already know that the `childNodes` property—and the associated method `getChildNodes()`—returns a list of all child nodes of the current element. Now you need only two more details:

- You can find the number of elements in a list of nodes in the property `length` or via the `getLength()` method.

- You gain access to a node in a list by using the item collection; the index of the element is provided in parentheses: `nodelist.item(1)` returns the second element because counting starts at `0`.

Now you can easily extend the `modifyTree()` function and set the value of the text node:

```
function modifyTree() {
    counter ++;
    switch (counter) {
        case 1:
            //step 1: cloning the text node
            var svgtext = svgdoc.getElementById("abbr");
            var svgtext2 = svgtext.cloneNode(true);
            //step 2: changing style attributes
            var css = svgtext2.getStyle();
            css.setProperty("fill", "rgb(0,128,0)");
            svgtext2.setAttribute("x",
                parseInt(svgtext.getAttribute("x")) + 5);
            svgtext2.setAttribute("y",
                parseInt(svgtext.getAttribute("y")) + 4);
            //step 3: inserting the node
            svgtext2 = logo.insertBefore(svgtext2, svgtext.getNextSibling());
            break;
        case 2:
            var tagline = svgdoc.getElementById("text");
            var children = tagline.getChildNodes();
            for (var i=0; i<children.length; i++)
                if (children.item(i).getNodeType() == 3) //text node
                    children.item(i)
                            .setNodeValue("SVG Unleashed");
            break;
    }
}
```

As you can see in your SVG viewer, this code actually works—the text has changed.

In some sources, you may find code similar to this; instead of cycling through all child nodes, looking for a node with type 3, you can just use `getFirstChild()` to access the text. But there is one drawback to this approach. If there are any other attributes, they are child nodes as well, and DOM Level 2 does not force implementations to stick to a certain order in which these attributes will be turned into nodes. Thus, cycling always is the most secure way to go.

Creating New Elements

In the next step, we want to create a new text node. This time we do not want to clone one of the available nodes, but we want to create a new one.

We start by using the `createElement()` method. This method of the `SVGDocument` interface creates a new SVG document. The tag name of this document (without the angle brackets) must be provided as a parameter:

```
var newText = svgdoc.createElement("text");
```

In the next step, we set some attributes:

```
newText.setAttribute("x", 32);
newText.setAttribute("y", 140);
```

Then we set some style properties:

```
var css = newText.getStyle();
css.setProperty("fill", "rgb(128,0,0)");
css.setProperty("font-size", 12);
css.setProperty("font-family", "Verdana,Arial");
```

Then we need to create the text. For this step, the `SVGDocument` interface provides the `createTextNode()` method, which creates a text node with the given text:

```
var samsText = svgdoc.createTextNode("by SAMS");
```

This text node now has to be appended as a child to the new `text` element:

```
newText.appendChild(samsText);
```

Finally, this new node must be appended to the g element in the SVG document:

```
logo.appendChild(newText);
```

And that's it. The SVG viewer displays the new text node. Listing 15.5 shows the current state of the code.

LISTING 15.5   15code05.svg—Adding a New Text Node

```
function modifyTree() {
    counter ++;
    switch (counter) {
        case 1:
            //step 1: cloning the text node
            var svgtext = svgdoc.getElementById("abbr");
            var svgtext2 = svgtext.cloneNode(true);
            //step 2: changing style attributes
            var css = svgtext2.getStyle();
            css.setProperty("fill", "rgb(0,128,0)");
            svgtext2.setAttribute("x",
                parseInt(svgtext.getAttribute("x")) + 5);
```

LISTING 15.5   Continued

```
            svgtext2.setAttribute("y",
               parseInt(svgtext.getAttribute("y")) + 4);
            //step 3: inserting the node
            svgtext2 = logo.insertBefore(svgtext2, svgtext.getNextSibling());
            break;
        case 2:
            var tagline = svgdoc.getElementById("text");
            var children = tagline.getChildNodes();
            for (var i=0; i<children.length; i++)
               if (children.item(i).getNodeType() == 3) //text node
                   children.item(i).setNodeValue("SVG Unleashed");
            break;
        // new code; a new "text" element is created and added
        case 3:
            var newText = svgdoc.createElement("text");
            newText.setAttribute("x", 32);
            newText.setAttribute("y", 140);
            var css = newText.getStyle();
            css.setProperty("fill", "rgb(128,0,0)");
            css.setProperty("font-size", 12);
            css.setProperty("font-family", "Verdana,Arial");
            var samsText = svgdoc.createTextNode("by SAMS");
            newText.appendChild(samsText);
            logo.appendChild(newText);
            break;
    }
}
```

Removing Nodes

Looking back at the original version of the code (see Listing 15.4) and comparing it to the current state, we find that we corrected the error in the book title and put the publisher's name in a new text element. But the shadow does not look good here. So we decided to remove it on the fourth click. To do so, we must call the removeNode() or removeChild() method. In this case, we decided to use removeChild(). The node to be removed is the shadow node, which we created dynamically. Because we didn't provide this node with an id attribute, we must think of another way to access this node. Remember where we put this node—next to the node with the id attribute "abbr"—so we can access this node by using getElementById("abbr").getNextSibling(). The rest is easy. This node is a child of the g element; thus, we can use the following:

```
var shadow = svgdoc.getElementById("abbr").getNextSibling();
logo.removeChild(shadow);
```

Incorporating these lines into the code, here is the final version of our modifyTree()function:

```
function modifyTree() {
    counter ++;
    switch (counter) {
        case 1:
            //step 1: cloning the text node
            var svgtext = svgdoc.getElementById("abbr");
            var svgtext2 = svgtext.cloneNode(true);
            //step 2: changing style attributes
            var css = svgtext2.getStyle();
            css.setProperty("fill", "rgb(0,128,0)");
            svgtext2.setAttribute("x",
                parseInt(svgtext.getAttribute("x")) + 5);
            svgtext2.setAttribute("y",
                parseInt(svgtext.getAttribute("y")) + 4);
            //step 3: inserting the node
            svgtext2 = logo.insertBefore(svgtext2, svgtext.getNextSibling());
            break;
        case 2:
            var tagline = svgdoc.getElementById("text");
            var children = tagline.getChildNodes();
            for (var i=0; i<children.length; i++)
                if (children.item(i).getNodeType() == 3) //text node
                    children.item(i).setNodeValue("SVG Unleashed");
            break;
        case 3:
            var newText = svgdoc.createElement("text");
            newText.setAttribute("x", 32);
            newText.setAttribute("y", 140);
            var css = newText.getStyle();
            css.setProperty("fill", "rgb(128,0,0)");
            css.setProperty("font-size", 12);
            css.setProperty("font-family", "Verdana,Arial");
            var samsText = svgdoc.createTextNode("by SAMS");
            newText.appendChild(samsText);
            logo.appendChild(newText);
            break;
        case 4:
            var shadow = svgdoc.getElementById("abbr").getNextSibling();
```

```
        logo.removeChild(shadow);
        break;
    }
}
```

After four clicks, the shadow disappears, as shown in Figure 15.10.

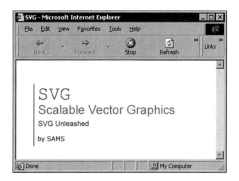

FIGURE 15.10   No shadow again.

Of course, you can use the DOM manipulating methods of SVG in many more ways, but you have seen several of them now. For the rest of this chapter, you can stick to the various details of the DOM covered in Part I and explore this subject further. You now have all the basic knowledge you need.

SVG Events

In Chapter 14, we showed you the basic principles of event capturing with the SVG implementation of DOM Level 2. We also provided a list of available events and how to deal with them.

In the previous examples in this chapter, we used the load and click events. This section is dedicated to the other events. Of course, we will cover only a few to give you some pointers because you already know the theoretical background from the preceding chapter. We will also cover some really cool features, such as capturing keyboard events, which is currently supported only by Adobe SVG Viewer version 3 and higher.

Event Listeners

Event listeners provide a flexible alternative to the event handlers we used in the previous examples.

Adding an Event Listener

Let's recap the most important points about event listeners. To attach an event listener to an SVG element, you have to call the addEventListener()function, which expects three parameters:

- The name of the event that will be captured as a string (for example, "click").

- The function that will be executed when the event listener is activated; you must provide a reference here (such as functionname, not functionname() or "functionname").

- Whether the event handler can capture events (true) or not (false).

Remember the clock example? Whenever the virtual digits of the clock are clicked, its size changes. Previously, you had to stick an event handler attribute at every text element you wanted to change. This time, though, you can try a clever new way. This approach requires a little bit more code, but it makes the code more flexible.

The idea is the following: We cycle through all SVG elements in the document. If we find a text element and its text is not ":" (meaning it's a separator between hours, minutes, and seconds), we add an event listener that calls the sayHello() function whenever the user clicks on the text element.

Adding the event listener is the easy part:

```
element.addEventListener("click", sayHello, false);
```

Cycling through all elements is a little bit trickier, but you can do so by using the knowledge you acquired from the previous sections.

The getElementsByTagName("text") method call returns a list of all text nodes in the SVG document:

```
var list = svgdoc.getElementsByTagName("text");
```

As you have seen before, you can cycle through all elements of a node list by using a for loop, with the following parameters:

- Counting starts at 0.

- Counting ends at list.length.

- The current node can be accessed using list.item(current_list_index).

So here is the piece of code that loops over all list items:

```
for (var i=0; i<list.length; i++) {
   var el = list.item(i);
```

```
        var children = el.getChildNodes();
            for (var j=0; j<children.length; j++)
                if (children.item(j).getNodeType() == 3) //text node
                    if (children.item(j).getNodeValue() != ":")
                        el.addEventListener("click", showMe, false);
}
```

This code must be put in the `init()` function of the SVG document. Then you can get rid of those pesky `onclick` event handlers because they are automatically added to the three `text` elements in question. As you will find out in your SVG viewer, the script runs exactly as before.

Listing 15.6 is the complete listing, with the changes commented.

LISTING 15.6   15code06.svg—The Clock with Event Listeners

```
<?xml version="1.0" encoding="iso-8859-1"?>
<svg width="300" height="300" onload="init(evt)">
   <defs>
      <style type="text/css"><![CDATA[
         text.normal {font-family: Arial; font-size: 30;}
         text.small {font-family: Arial; font-size: 24;}
      ]]></style>
      <script type="text/ecmascript"><![CDATA[
         var svgdoc;  //global variable

         function init(evt) {
            svgdoc = evt.getTarget().getOwnerDocument();
            var list = svgdoc.getElementsByTagName("text");
            // looping through all elements, adding event listeners
            for (var i=0; i<list.length; i++) {
               var el = list.item(i);
               var children = el.getChildNodes();
               for (var j=0; j<children.length; j++)
                  if (children.item(j).getNodeType() == 3) //text node
                     if (children.item(j).getNodeValue() != ":")
                        el.addEventListener("click", sayHello, false);
            }
         }
         function sayHello(evt) {
            var el = evt.getTarget();
            if (el) {
               var c = el.getAttribute("class");
               if (c == "normal")
```

LISTING 15.6   Continued

```
                     el.setAttribute("class", "small");
               else
                     el.setAttribute("class", "normal");
          }
       }
    ]]></script>
    <linearGradient id="linear_bw" x1="0%" y1="0%" x2="100%" y2="0%"
       spreadMethod="pad" gradientUnits="userSpaceOnUse">
       <stop offset="0%" stop-color="rgb(255,255,255)" stop-opacity="1"/>
       <stop offset="100%" stop-color="rgb(0,0,0)" stop-opacity="1"/>
    </linearGradient>
    <linearGradient id="linear_bw_tr" x1="0%" y1="0%" x2="100%" y2="0%"
       spreadMethod="pad" gradientUnits="userSpaceOnUse"
       gradientTransform="matrix(0.819152 0.573576 -0.573576 0.819152 0 0)">
       <stop offset="0%" stop-color="rgb(255,255,255)" stop-opacity="1"/>
       <stop offset="100%" stop-color="rgb(0,0,0)" stop-opacity="1"/>
    </linearGradient>
  </defs>
  <path d="M158 139 L34 139 L56 106 L180 106 L180 172 L158 205 L158 139 L180 106"
    fill="url(#linear_bw_tr)" stroke="rgb(0,0,128)" stroke-width="0"/>
  <rect x="31" y="136" width="130" height="71" rx="9" ry="9"
    fill="url(#linear_bw)" stroke-width="0"/>
  <rect x="36" y="141" width="120" height="61" rx="8" ry="8" fill="rgb(0,0,0)"
    stroke-width="0"/>
  <text id="hours" x="34px" y="186px" fill="rgb(255,255,255)"
    class="normal">12</text>
  <text x="68px" y="183px" fill="rgb(255,255,255)" font-size="30"
    font-family="Arial">:</text>
  <text id="minutes" x="76px" y="186px" fill="rgb(255,255,255)"
    class="normal">34</text>
  <text x="111px" y="184px" fill="rgb(255,255,255)" font-size="30"
    font-family="Arial">:</text>
  <text id="seconds" x="121px" y="186px" fill="rgb(255,255,255)"
    class="normal">56</text>
</svg>
```

If you think about it, you might wonder why the code in Listing 15.6 runs at all. Look at the sayHello() function. It expects an evt variable as a parameter. You might think that if the parameter is not provided, the ECMAScript interpreter will assume that this variable is undefined or null; thus, the script interpretation will continue.

In the first line of code within the function body, evt is used (and needed). So where does this variable come from?

Whenever you add an event listener to an SVG element, the triggered event is always automatically submitted to the function as a parameter. So evt contains the current event, and that's why the script still runs. A very nice design.

Removing an Event Listener

If—for any reason whatsoever—you feel that you do not need a specific event listener any longer, you can remove it by using the removeEventListener() method. This method takes the same parameters as addEventListener(), so you have to take care that all three parameters are the same as in addEventListener(); otherwise, the event listener is not removed.

Let's get back to our digital clock example. If the user clicks on one of the two colons, the event listener for the digits will be removed. No problem! First, we locate the two colons and add event listeners to them. To do so, we just add two lines to the previous code:

```
list = svgdoc.getElementsByTagName("text");
for (var i=0; i<list.length; i++) {
   var el = list.item(i);
   var children = el.getChildNodes();
      for (var j=0; j<children.length; j++)
         if (children.item(j).getNodeType() == 3) //text node
            if (children.item(j).getNodeValue != ":")
               el.addEventListener("click", showMe, false);
            else  // 1st new line
               el.addEventListener("click", removeEv, false);  // 2nd new line
}
```

The removeEv() function now must remove the event listeners from the three text elements for the digits. We can achieve this by using a slight modification of the preceding code:

```
function removeEv(evt) {
   list = svgdoc.getElementsByTagName("text");
   for (var i=0; i<list.length; i++) {
      var el = list.item(i);
      var children = el.getChildNodes();
         for (var j=0; j<children.length; j++)
            if (children.item(j).getNodeType() == 3) //text node
               if (children.item(j).getNodeValue != ":")
                  el.removeEventListener("click", showMe, false);
   }
}
```

Note that the code is almost identical, but removeEventListener() is now called.

Bubbling Up

As you know, events bubble up from their target to the top of the SVG document. We can see this functionality in the example with the different `text` elements (refer to Listing 15.4). Listing 15.7 is a slightly changed version.

LISTING 15.7   15code07.svg—Events Bubble Up

```
<?xml version="1.0" standalone="no"?>
<svg width="500" height="500" onload="init(evt)">
    <defs>
        <script type="text/ecmascript"><![CDATA[
            var svgdoc;  //global variable
            var logo; //another variable

            function init(evt) {
                svgdoc = evt.getTarget().getOwnerDocument();
                logo = svgdoc.getElementById("logo");
                svgdoc.getElementById("abbr")
                        .addEventListener("click", identifyYourself, false);
                svgdoc.getElementById("long")
                        .addEventListener("click", identifyYourself, false);
                svgdoc.getElementById("text")
                        .addEventListener("click", identifyYourself, false);
                svgdoc.getElementById("logo")
                        .addEventListener("click", identifyYourself, false);
            }
            function identifyYourself(evt) {
                //...
            }
        ]]></script>
    </defs>
    <g id="logo">
        <text id="abbr" x="32px" y="60px"
            style="fill:rgb(0,0,0);font-size:36;font-family:Courier New">
            SVG
        </text>
        <text id="long" x="33px" y="88px"
            style="fill-opacity:0.5;fill:rgb(0,0,128);
            font-size:24;font-family:Arial">
            Scalable Vector Graphics
        </text>
        <text id="text" x="33px" y="111px"
            style="fill-opacity:1;fill:rgb(0,0,128);
            font-size:14;font-family:Arial">
            SVG Unleashed by SAMS
```

LISTING 15.7   Continued

```
        </text>
        <line x1="25" y1="30" x2="25" y2="150"
            style="fill:none;stroke:rgb(0,0,0);stroke-width:2;stroke-opacity:0.5"/>
    </g>
</svg>
```

As you can see, the identifyYourself() function is called whenever you click on one of the three text elements. An event handler for the click event is also attached to the g element.

The identifyYourself() function gets only one task: It provides information about the current node where the event is located (it can be accessed through currentNode or getCurrentNode() in the Adobe SVG Viewer only). Looking at the interface section in Chapter 2, "Document Structure in SVG," we see that the SVGElement interface offers the id attribute and logically the getId() method, which returns the ID of the element that receives the event. The identifyYourself() function must create an alert box with this value:

```
function identifyYourself(evt) {
    var el = evt.getCurrentNode();
    alert(el.getId() + " says: 'Ouch!'");
}
```

Run this code and click on "Scalable Vector Graphics", for instance. You will see two alert boxes: one for "long" (the text "Scalable Vector Graphics") and one for "logo" (the g element that contains the text elements). The reason: The event is bubbling up.

Now let's change identifyYourself() a bit, to stop the event from bubbling up. For that, we use stopPropagation():

```
function identifyYourself(evt) {
    var el = evt.getCurrentNode();
    alert(el.getId() + " says: 'Ouch!'");
    evt.stopPropagation();
}
```

As you might expect, when you click on a text element, you get only one alert box; after that, event propagation is stopped and the event never reaches the next higher level.

Capturing Events

Before an event hits its event target, it travels down the DOM tree, starting at the top element and then making its way to its destination. Along the way, the event may be intercepted. For that to happen, however, you first have to create event handlers that are able to capture events.

15

In our previous example, the need to capture events does not apply for the click event handler for the g element; it makes no sense because not all elements on a higher level have an active event listener. It does make sense, however, to enable capturing for the text elements, so we have to change one line in the init() function:

```
function init(evt) {
   svgdoc = evt.getTarget().getOwnerDocument();
   logo = svgdoc.getElementById("logo");
   svgdoc.getElementById("abbr")
      .addEventListener("click", identifyYourself, true);
   svgdoc.getElementById("long")
      .addEventListener("click", identifyYourself, false);
   svgdoc.getElementById("text")
      .addEventListener("click", identifyYourself, false);
   svgdoc.getElementById("logo")
      .addEventListener("click", identifyYourself, false);
}
```

The last parameter of addEventListener() for the first text element is set to true, enabling capturing.

Now we can go to the identifyYourself() function and remove this line:

```
evt.stopPropagation();
```

Before you try the code in your SVG viewer, think about what you see. When you click on "Scalable Vector Graphics", you see two alert boxes (remember that you have just removed the call to stopPropagation()). But what will happen when you click on "SVG" (see Figure 15.11)?

FIGURE 15.11   An alert.

The answer: The g element (id="logo") captures the event and creates an alert box.

Now you have seen how to attach and remove event listeners, and how to capture them and stop them from bubbling up.

Keyboard Events

If you scan the W3C DOM Level 2 specification, you will notice that keyboard events are not covered at all there. They are supposed to reappear in the next level, DOM3. For more information on keyboard events in W3C DOM, see Chapter 27, "SVG 1.1, 1.2, and SVG 2.0."

> **NOTE**
>
> In early versions of DOM2, keyboard events were part of the spec but were later removed.

The Adobe SVG Viewer, however, does support keyboard events, which is reason enough for us to cover these events in this book. Note that you should not overuse these effects or let your application rely on them. Users who do not have Adobe SVG Viewer will not be able to see the effects or might even receive error messages from their viewers.

These three events are relevant for keyboard interaction:

- keydown

- keypress

- keyup

In general, it does not really matter which of these three events you use. In most cases, you use keypress. When the event is fired, you can use the evt variable to find out which key was pressed. Table 15.4 lists the most important attributes for this task, all supported by the Adobe SVG Viewer starting at version 1.0.

TABLE 15.4   keypress Event Attributes

Attribute	Description
altKey	Returns whether the Alt key was pressed.
charCode	Returns the ASCII char code of the pressed key.
clientX	Returns the relative horizontal position of the place where the event occurred.
clientY	Returns the relative vertical position of the place where the event occurred.
ctrlKey	Returns whether the Ctrl key was pressed.
keyCode	Returns the ASCII code for the capitalized key.
metaKey	Returns whether the meta key (such as the Windows key on Windows keyboards) was pressed.
screenX	Returns the absolute horizontal position of the place where the event occurred.
screenY	Returns the absolute vertical position of the place where the event occurred.
shiftKey	Returns whether the Shift key was pressed.

15

To stay consistent in our coding and to support Netscape browsers, we will use the associated methods instead of these attributes; for example, we'll use `getAltKey()` instead of `altKey`.

The difference between `charCode` and `keyCode` is quite tricky: If the `keydown` or `keyup` event is triggered, and `charCode` contains 0, `keyCode` will contain the ASCII code of the capitalized character. So, if you press A, `keyCode` will contain 65, the ASCII code for the letter *A*. If, however, you press A, you get 65, as well. So you should not use `keydown` and `keyup`. The `keypress` event, however, works quite nicely, as `charCode` contains the correct ASCII code for the pressed key—`keyCode` is 0, however.

Now let's have some fun with these events. First, let's create a simple SVG document. To visualize the effect, we'll add a circle that tries to catch keyboard input. The code for this event is shown in Listing 15.8.

LISTING 15.8   15code08.svg—Capturing Keyboard Events (Body)

```
<?xml version="1.0" standalone="no"?>
<svg width="500" height="500" onload="init(evt)">
    <defs>
        <script type="text/ecmascript"><![CDATA[
            var svgdoc;  //global variable

            function init(evt) {
                svgdoc = evt.getTarget().getOwnerDocument();
                svgdoc.getElementById("c").addEventListener("keypress",
                                                            showKeys,
                                                            false);
            }
        ]]></script>
    </defs>
    <circle id="c" cx="50" cy="50" r="40" fill="rgb(128,0,0)"/>
</svg>
```

Now we're ready for the `showKeys()` function. In this function, all attributes from Table 15.4 are shown to the user in an alert box:

```
function showKeys(evt) {
    var info = "";
    info += "altKey: " + evt.getAltKey() + "\n";
    info += "charCode: " + evt.getCharCode() + "\n";
    info += "clientX: " + evt.getClientX() + "\n";
    info += "clientY: " + evt.getClientY() + "\n";
    info += "ctrlKey: " + evt.getCtrlKey() + "\n";
    info += "keyCode: " + evt.getKeyCode() + "\n";
```

```
    info += "metaKey: " + evt.getMetaKey() + "\n";
    info += "screenX: " + evt.getScreenX() + "\n";
    info += "screenY: " + evt.getScreenY() + "\n";
    info += "shiftKey: " + evt.getShiftKey() + "\n";
    info += "Key: " + String.fromCharCode(evt.getCharCode());
    alert(info);
}
```

Now look at the last string that is appended to the variable info:

```
info += "Key: " + String.fromCharCode(evt.getCharCode());
```

The fromCharCode() method of the String object—that is, the JavaScript String object—converts an ASCII value into the appropriate character. Thus, this call tries to find out which key was pressed.

Try this example in the Adobe SVG Viewer. As you can see in Figure 15.12, the key you pressed (in this example, *S*) is also shown in the alert box.

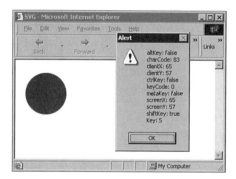

FIGURE 15.12   The key you pressed also appears in the alert box.

We will now use this functionality in a more complex example. We want to enable the user to enter his or her own text into a text field. To accomplish this task, we first must create a basic SVG document like the one in Listing 15.9.

LISTING 15.9   15code09.svg—Displaying Captured Keys (Body)

```
<?xml version="1.0" standalone="no"?>
<svg width="500" height="500" onload="init(evt)">
    <defs>
        <script type="text/ecmascript"><![CDATA[
            var svgdoc;   //global variable
            var t;
```

LISTING 15.9   Continued

```
        function init(evt) {
            svgdoc = evt.getTarget().getOwnerDocument();
            t = svgdoc.getElementById("t")
            t.addEventListener("keypress", showText, false);
        }
    ]]></script>
  </defs>
  <text id="t" x="10" y="50" fill="rgb(0, 0, 0)"
      font-size="30">Look here: </text>
</svg>
```

As you can see in Listing 15.9, whenever a keypress event occurs in the text element, the showText() function is called. Note that you might have to click into the text element to send the events to the element.

Now we can move on to showText(). This function first checks which key was pressed:

```
var character = String.fromCharCode(evt.getCharCode());
```

This character is now appended to the text that already resides in the text element. As you know from previous examples, accessing this text is no trivial task. You have to cycle through all child nodes:

```
var children = evt.getTarget().getChildNodes();
for (var i=0; i<children.length; i++)
   if (children.item(i).getNodeType() == 3) //text node
      children.item(i).setNodeValue(
         children.item(i).getNodeValue() + character);
```

If, however, the Enter key is pressed, the text input will stop. For that, the character code must be checked. The ASCII code for the Enter key is 13, so you use the following code:

```
if (evt.getCharCode() == 13)
   evt.getTarget().removeEventListener("keypress", showText, false);
```

If we put all these pieces together, we get the final SVG code for this example, shown in Listing 15.10.

LISTING 15.10   15code10.svg—The Entered Text Is Displayed

```
<?xml version="1.0" standalone="no"?>
<svg width="500" height="500" onload="init(evt)">
   <defs>
      <script type="text/ecmascript"><![CDATA[
```

LISTING 15.10   Continued

```
        var svgdoc;  //global variable
        var t;

        function init(evt) {
           svgdoc = evt.getTarget().getOwnerDocument();
           t = svgdoc.getElementById("t")
           t.addEventListener("keypress", showText, false);
        }

        function showText(evt) {
           if (evt.getCharCode() == 13)
              evt.getTarget().removeEventListener("keypress",
                                                  showText,
                                                  false);
           else {
              var character = String.fromCharCode(evt.getCharCode());
              var children = evt.getTarget().getChildNodes();
              for (var i=0; i<children.length; i++)
                 if (children.item(i).getNodeType() == 3) //text node
                    children.item(i).setNodeValue(
                       children.item(i).getNodeValue() + character);
           }
        }
     ]]></script>
  </defs>
  <text id="t" x="10" y="50" fill="rgb(0, 0, 0)"
     font-size="30">Look here: </text>
</svg>
```

Now your (Adobe) SVG Viewer enables you to change SVG documents at your fingertips—literally. However, the text element must receive the focus for this example to work (you have to click into it).

Figure 15.13 shows this script after some keys have been pressed.

Mouse Events

We've covered mouse events several times throughout this chapter. To find out how many times, just count how often you find onclick. In contrast to key events, mouse events are part of the DOM Level 2 Event specification and thus are supported by more browsers than only the Adobe SVG Viewer. The event variable uses the attributes detailed in Table 15.5.

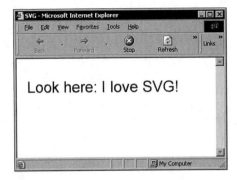

FIGURE 15.13   Changing the text.

TABLE 15.5   event Variable Attributes

Attribute	Description
altKey	Returns whether the Alt key was pressed.
button	Returns the number of the mouse button that changed state (was pressed or released). The left mouse button is 0, the middle mouse button is 1, and the right mouse button is 2. For left-handed mouse devices, this order is reversed (if the mouse driver correctly identifies the pointing device as "left-handed").
clientX	Returns the relative horizontal position of the place where the event occurred.
clientY	Returns the relative vertical position of the place where the event occurred.
ctrlKey	Returns whether the Ctrl key was pressed.
metaKey	Returns whether the meta key (such as the Windows key on Windows keyboards) was pressed.
relatedTarget	Returns the element the mouse came from (for mouseover events) or the element the mouse entered (for mouseout events).
screenX	Returns the absolute horizontal position of the place where the event occurred.
screenY	Returns the absolute vertical position of the place where the event occurred.
shiftKey	Returns whether the Shift key was pressed.

To try out these attributes, we will again create a fairly simple example using a circle, as shown in Listing 15.11, that returns all attributes of the mouse event.

LISTING 15.11   15code11.svg—Mouse Events

```
<?xml version="1.0" standalone="no"?>
<svg width="500" height="500" onload="init(evt)">
   <defs>
      <script type="text/ecmascript"><![CDATA[
         var svgdoc;  //global variable

         function init(evt) {
```

LISTING 15.11   Continued

```
            svgdoc = evt.getTarget().getOwnerDocument();
            svgdoc.getElementById("c").addEventListener("click", showMouse, false);
        }

    function showMouse(evt) {
        var info = "";
        info += "altKey: " + evt.getAltKey() + "\n";
        info += "button: " + evt.getButton() + "\n";
        info += "clientX: " + evt.getClientX() + "\n";
        info += "clientY: " + evt.getClientY() + "\n";
        info += "ctrlKey: " + evt.getCtrlKey() + "\n";
        info += "metaKey: " + evt.getMetaKey() + "\n";
        info += "relatedTarget: " + evt.getRelatedTarget() + "\n";
        info += "screenX: " + evt.getScreenX() + "\n";
        info += "screenY: " + evt.getScreenY() + "\n";
        info += "shiftKey: " + evt.getShiftKey() + "\n";
        alert(info);
        }
    ]]></script>
    </defs>
    <circle id="c" cx="50" cy="50" r="40" fill="rgb(128,0,0)"/>
</svg>
```

Now try clicking on the circle with your mouse, and watch the results (see Figure 15.14).

FIGURE 15.14   The coordinates of the mouse click are displayed in the alert box.

Using the coordinates of the mouse click, you can find out which section of an element was clicked. Thus, you can create a kind of imagemap. However, given the possibilities of

SVG, you do not need these kinds of tricks. Remember: Not every viewer supports ECMAScript, so the less often you use it, the better (if you want to reach the broadest audience possible).

Summary

This chapter showed how to include client-side script code in SVG documents. We also showed you how to react to events and how to use keyboard events, which did not make it into the final version of DOM Level 2 but are supported by the Adobe SVG Viewer. Now we've laid the necessary foundation for the next chapter, where we will use this knowledge (and some other nifty JavaScript tricks) to create SVG animations that could not have been created without client-side script support.

CHAPTER **16**

Animating SVG with Scripting

IN THIS CHAPTER

- HTML and SVG Interaction
- Animating with ECMAScript

In Chapter 15, "Scripting SVG," you saw how to modify SVG—from within SVG (or embedded script code). This chapter features techniques to access HTML data from within SVG and vice versa. We will also look at ways to animate SVG using client-side ECMAScript/JavaScript.

HTML and SVG Interaction

If you know JavaScript, you probably know how to change HTML content—from within HTML (or embedded script code). In this chapter, we go over the border and access HTML data from within SVG and vice versa.

From SVG to HTML

In JavaScript terms, the most important objects for accessing HTML data are the following two:

- The document object represents the HTML document, including all elements within the document (yes, newer browsers such as Internet Explorer 5 and higher and Netscape 6 support DOM2).

- The window object represents the top window, including access to window functions such as setTimeout() and setInterval() to enable SVG animations from JavaScript, as you will see in the next section.

From within SVG, you can access any of these objects directly from within an SVG file.

Setting Timeouts

For our trip from SVG to HTML, let's start with the window object. This object has many useful methods, including the four methods described in Table 16.1.

TABLE 16.1   window Object Methods

Method	Description
setTimeout(*code, interval*)	Runs *code* (a string variable) after *interval* (in milliseconds). Returns a numeric identifier for the timeout.
clearTimeout(*id*)	Clears the timeout with the given *id*; that is, the code is not executed.
setInterval(*code, interval*)	Runs *code* (a string variable) every *interval* milliseconds. Returns a numeric identifier for the timeout.
clearInterval(*id*)	Clears the interval with the given *id*; that is, the code is not executed again.

SVG brings its own Window interface (yes, within SVG, it is capitalized), but you can work with the ECMAScript/JavaScript window object as well. Both offer the same capabilities.

Setting the Status Bar

SVG also offers several other nice methods and properties. With window.status, you can write data into the browser's status bar. We will return to our example from the preceding chapter that utilized mouse events—upon clicking on a circle, information about this mouse click is shown (coordinates, clicked mouse button, and so on). This time, though, we will write the gathered information in the window's status bar, as shown in Listing 16.1. Obviously, this example will work only within a Web browser, so no standalone viewer will execute this code.

LISTING 16.1   16code01.svg—Writing Information in the Status Bar

```
<?xml version="1.0" standalone="no"?>
<svg width="500" height="500" onload="init(evt)">
   <defs>
      <script type="text/ecmascript"><![CDATA[
         var svgdoc;  //global variable

         function init(evt) {
            svgdoc = evt.getTarget().getOwnerDocument();
            svgdoc.getElementById("c").addEventListener("click",
                                                 showMouse,
                                                 false);

         }

         function showMouse(evt) {
            var info = "";
            info += "altKey: " + evt.getAltKey() + "; ";
            info += "button: " + evt.getButton() + "; ";
            info += "clientX: " + evt.getClientX() + "; ";
            info += "clientY: " + evt.getClientY() + "; ";
```

LISTING 16.1 Continued

```
            info += "ctrlKey: " + evt.getCtrlKey() + "; ";
            info += "metaKey: " + evt.getMetaKey() + "; ";
            info += "relatedTarget: " +
                    evt.getRelatedTarget() + "; ";
            info += "screenX: " + evt.getScreenX() + "; ";
            info += "screenY: " + evt.getScreenY() + "; ";
            info += "shiftKey: " + evt.getShiftKey() + ".";
            window.status = info;
        }
    ]]></script>
  </defs>
  <circle id="c" cx="50" cy="50" r="40" fill="rgb(128,0,0)"/>
</svg>
```

Load Listing 16.1 in the browser and click the circle to see how the code works (see Figure 16.1).

FIGURE 16.1 Clicking on the circle writes information to the status bar.

> **NOTE**
>
> To be exact, we used this technique many times in Chapter 14, "The SVG DOM." The alert() function is a method of the window object, and the reference to window has been omitted (because the window object is the default). If you want to use the long syntax, you always have to use window.alert().

The document object can be used to access all elements in the HTML document. So this gives us the opportunity to output data in any HTML element.

In the next example, we'll use DHTML. With DHTML, you can access most elements on your Web page.

> **NOTE**
>
> Netscape 4 gives you access to very few elements, but Internet Explorer and more recent Netscape versions grant access to many more elements.

In this next example, we want to again reveal information about the mouse click to the user. However, we want to use HTML means to do so. Thus, we define a special area in our HTML code where we want to put the output:

```
<div id="output" style="position:absolute;"></div>
```

Now we can use the following JavaScript code to write something into this element:

```
if (document.layers)  //code for Netscape Navigator 4.x
   with (document.layers["output"].document) {
      open();
      write(info);
      close();
   }
else if (document.all)  //code for Internet Explorer 4+
   document.all("output").innerHTML = info;
else if (document.getElementById)  //code for Netscape 6, Opera
   document.getElementById("output").innerHTML = info;
```

In the preceding code, you can see how to access the div HTML element and write text into it, for the different flavors of browsers:

- For Netscape 4.x, you have to access the element using
  document.layers["*id_of_element*"] and then use document.open(),
  document.write("..."), and document.close().

- Internet Explorer versions 4 and higher grant access via
  document.all("*id_of_element*"). Then you just have to set the innerHTML attribute.

- Netscape 6 and, by the way, Opera 5 and Internet Explorer 5, too (but they are already covered by the previous code) are DOM2-compliant and thus implement getElementById("*id_of_element*"). If you use this method, you also have to set the innerHTML attribute.

To make this code run within your Web browser, you need to change it a little bit because document or window.document returns a reference to the SVGDocument interface, that is, the current SVG document. To access the HTML's document object, you have to use a special syntax:

```
var d = self.document;
```

The keyword `self` is a JavaScript/ECMAScript specialty: It contains a reference to the current window. The `document` object is a subobject of the `window` object. Thus, you get access to the HTML document object.

The complete code for this circle example is shown in Listing 16.2.

LISTING 16.2   16code02.svg—The Complete Code for Our Circle Example

```
<?xml version="1.0" standalone="no"?>
<svg width="500" height="500" onload="init(evt)">
   <defs>
      <script type="text/ecmascript"><![CDATA[
         var svgdoc;  //global variable

         function init(evt) {
            svgdoc = evt.getTarget().getOwnerDocument();
            svgdoc.getElementById("c").addEventListener("click",
                                                       showMouse,
                                                       false);
         }


         function showMouse(evt) {
            var info = "";
            info += "altKey: " + evt.getAltKey() + "<br>";
            info += "button: " + evt.getButton() + "<br>";
            info += "clientX: " + evt.getClientX() + "<br>";
            info += "clientY: " + evt.getClientY() + "<br>";
            info += "ctrlKey: " + evt.getCtrlKey() + "<br>";
            info += "metaKey: " + evt.getMetaKey() + "<br>";
            info += "relatedTarget: " + evt.getRelatedTarget() + "<br>";
            info += "screenX: " + evt.getScreenX() + "<br>";
            info += "screenY: " + evt.getScreenY() + "<br>";
            info += "shiftKey: " + evt.getShiftKey();
            var d = self.document;
            if (d.layers && d.layers["output"])  //NN 4.x
               with (d.layers["output"].document) {
                  open();
                  write(info);
                  close();
               }
            else if (d.all && d.all("output"))  //IE 4+, Opera
               d.all("output").innerHTML = info;
            else if (d.getElementById && d.getElementById("output")) //N6
               d.getElementById("output").innerHTML = info;
```

16

LISTING 16.2   Continued

```
        }
    ]]></script>
  </defs>
  <circle id="c" cx="50" cy="50" r="40" fill="rgb(128,0,0)"/>
</svg>
```

NOTE

Netscape 4 sometimes tends to be quite unreliable when it comes to plug-in scripting; you will get no results at all or will not even see the red circle (especially after clicking the Reload button several times).

As you can see in Listing 16.2, we have added some extra code to check whether the target div element exists, in order to avoid silly error messages.

Now the only thing you have to do is to run an HTML file that contains both a reference to this svg document and the div element, and you're ready to go!

After you click on the circle, further information about this event appears in the div element, as shown in Figure 16.2.

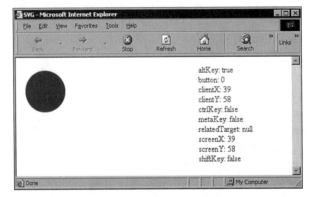

FIGURE 16.2   Further information appears when you click on the circle.

From HTML to SVG

You can embed SVG elements into HTML code in two different ways:

- Using the <object> tag
- Using the <embed> tag

The `object` element is the official W3C recommendation; however, it is supported only by Internet Explorer and Netscape 6. On Netscape 4.x, some systems/configurations seem to support `object`s, whereas some others don't (so you cannot rely on it).

You should always use the `<embed>` tag, or you can combine both tags: the `<embed>` tag for Netscape 4.x and `<object>` tags for more recent browsers. In this case, you have to nest these two tags:

```
<object>
   <embed>
   <!-- ... -->
   </embed>
</object>
```

To access the embedded element, you have different choices:

- You can use the `id` attribute of the element and then use `document.getElementById()`. But note that this approach works only on browsers that support `document.getElementById()`: Internet Explorer 5 and higher, Opera 4 and higher, and Netscape 6.

- You can use the `name` attribute of the element and use `document.name_attribute` to access the embedded element. Note that you can use this approach only if the SVG document has been embedded using `<embed>`.

Usually, Netscape would allow you to access the embedded data using `document.embeds[name_attribute]`; however, due to a bug, this technique does not always work. Thus, using `document.name_attribute` is the preferred method.

As soon as you access the embedded element, you can access all elements there. Using the `getDocument()` method, you gain access to the `SVGDocument` element. From there, you can do virtually everything.

To demonstrate how to use these elements, we will recycle one of the old examples. This time, we want to reuse the digital clock from Chapter 15 so that we can set the time correctly.

First, look at Listing 16.3, which creates the digital clock.

LISTING 16.3   16code03.svg—The Digital Clock

```
<?xml version="1.0" encoding="iso-8859-1"?>
<svg width="300" height="300">
   <defs>
      <linearGradient id="linear_bw" x1="0%" y1="0%" x2="100%" y2="0%"
         spreadMethod="pad" gradientUnits="userSpaceOnUse">
         <stop offset="0%" stop-color="rgb(255,255,255)" stop-opacity="1"/>
```

16

LISTING 16.3   Continued

```
        <stop offset="100%" stop-color="rgb(0,0,0)" stop-opacity="1"/>
    </linearGradient>
    <linearGradient id="linear_bw_tr" x1="0%" y1="0%" x2="100%" y2="0%"
        spreadMethod="pad" gradientUnits="userSpaceOnUse"
        gradientTransform="matrix(0.819152 0.573576 -0.573576 0.819152 0 0)">
        <stop offset="0%" stop-color="rgb(255,255,255)" stop-opacity="1"/>
        <stop offset="100%" stop-color="rgb(0,0,0)" stop-opacity="1"/>
    </linearGradient>
</defs>
<path d="M158 139 L34 139 L56 106 L180 106 L180 172 L158 205 L158 139 L180 106"
    fill="url(#linear_bw_tr)" stroke="rgb(0,0,128)" stroke-width="0"/>
<rect x="31" y="136" width="130" height="71" rx="9" ry="9"
    fill="url(#linear_bw)" stroke-width="0"/>
<rect x="36" y="141" width="120" height="61" rx="8" ry="8" fill="rgb(0,0,0)"
    stroke-width="0"/>
<text id="hours" x="34px" y="186px" fill="rgb(255,255,255)" font-size="30"
    font-family="Arial">12</text>
<text x="68px" y="183px" fill="rgb(255,255,255)" font-size="30"
    font-family="Arial">:</text>
<text id="minutes" x="76px" y="186px" fill="rgb(255,255,255)" font-size="30"
    font-family="Arial">34</text>
<text x="111px" y="184px" fill="rgb(255,255,255)" font-size="30"
    font-family="Arial">:</text>
<text id="seconds" x="121px" y="186px" fill="rgb(255,255,255)" font-size="30"
    font-family="Arial">56</text>
</svg>
```

Then we need to find the correct values for hours, minutes, and seconds. We can do so by using JavaScript's Date object:

```
var d = new Date();
var h = d.getHours() + "";
if (h.length < 2)
    h = "0" + h;
var m = d.getMinutes() + "";
if (m.length < 2)
    m = "0" + m;
var s = d.getSeconds() + "";
if (s.length < 2)
    s = "0" + s;
```

In the next step, we need to access the SVG text nodes in the digital clock and write the current time there. As before, this procedure entails several steps; you need to do the following:

1. Find the text element.

2. Find the appropriate text element (nodeType = 3).

3. Set the text element to the calculated value.

The following code implements that functionality; here, we use the techniques we introduced in the preceding two chapters:

```
var svgdoc = document.SVGEmbed.getSVGDocument();

hours = svgdoc.getElementById("hours");
var children = hours.getChildNodes();
for (var i=0; i<children.length; i++)
   if (children.item(i).getNodeType() == 3)
      children.item(i).setNodeValue(h);

minutes = svgdoc.getElementById("minutes");
children = minutes.getChildNodes();
for (var i=0; i<children.length; i++)
   if (children.item(i).getNodeType() == 3)
      children.item(i).setNodeValue(m);

seconds = svgdoc.getElementById("seconds");
var children = secconds.getChildNodes();
for (var i=0; i<children.length; i++)
   if (children.item(i).getNodeType() == 3)
      children.item(i).setNodeValue(s);
```

To get the code to work, we now have to set the name attribute of the <embed> tag to "SVGEmbed". Now, to make the example work, we put all this code into a function and add an HTML button. When you click on this button, the function is called and the clock is updated. Here is an excerpt of this HTML code:

```
<html>
<head>
<title>SVG</title>
<script language="JavaScript"><!--
function updateClock() {
```

16

```
    var d = new Date();
    var h = d.getHours() + "";
    if (h.length < 2)
        h = "0" + h;
    var m = d.getMinutes() + "";
    if (m.length < 2)
        m = "0" + m;
    var s = d.getSeconds() + "";
    if (s.length < 2)
        s = "0" + s;

    var svgdoc = document.SVGEmbed.getSVGDocument();

    hours = svgdoc.getElementById("hours");
    var children = hours.getChildNodes();
    for (var i=0; i<children.length; i++)
        if (children.item(i).getNodeType() == 3)
            children.item(i).setNodeValue(h);

    minutes = svgdoc.getElementById("minutes");
    children = minutes.getChildNodes();
    for (var i=0; i<children.length; i++)
        if (children.item(i).getNodeType() == 3)
            children.item(i).setNodeValue(m);

    seconds = svgdoc.getElementById("seconds");
    var children = seconds.getChildNodes();
    for (var i=0; i<children.length; i++)
        if (children.item(i).getNodeType() == 3)
            children.item(i).setNodeValue(s);
}

//--></script>
<body>
<embed name="SVGEmbed" type="image/svg-xml" src="..."></embed>
<form>
   <input type="button" value="update clock" onClick="updateClock()">
</form>
</body>
</html>
```

Now, whenever you click the HTML button, the clock is updated with the current time.

Animating with ECMAScript

Because you now know what is possible when you want to script SVG, it's time to show you some more examples, with a focus on animation. The intention of this section is not only to show you how to create animation even without the built-in animation techniques (as you learned in Chapter 11, "SVG Animation Elements"), but also to elaborate on the advantages and disadvantages of each approach.

Animated Clock

One animation that certainly cannot be created using SVG means alone is our digital clock. We cannot calculate the current time in SVG; we can use only ECMAScript or another scripting language. In the previous versions of this clock example, either the time was constantly 12:34:56, or the time was updated only upon user interaction (in our case, clicking an o button). If we use the `setTimeout()` and `setInterval()` methods of the `window` object, however, the clock can be updated automatically as well.

Digital Clock

To update the clock automatically, you can use the `updateClock()` function from the previous section and modify the `SVGDocument` reference so that it can be called within the SVG document. (We do not want to call it from HTML; this is SVG only.) The rest is quite easy: Use `setInterval()` to call the function that updates the clock every second. That means the second parameter to `setInterval()` must be `1000` (1000 milliseconds equal one second). Listing 16.4 shows the complete code for the automatically updated clock.

LISTING 16.4   16code04.svg—The Animated Digital Clock

```
<?xml version="1.0" encoding="iso-8859-1"?>
<svg width="400" height="400" onload="init(evt)">
   <defs>
      <script type="text/ecmascript"><![CDATA[
         var svgdoc;  //global variable
         var id; //interval id

         function init(evt) {
            svgdoc = evt.getTarget().getOwnerDocument();
            startClock();
         }

         function startClock(evt) {
            id = window.setInterval("updateClock()", 1000); //every second
         }

         function updateClock() {
```

LISTING 16.4   Continued

```
        var d = new Date();
        var h = d.getHours() + "";
        if (h.length < 2)
            h = "0" + h;
        var m = d.getMinutes() + "";
        if (m.length < 2)
            m = "0" + m;
        var s = d.getSeconds() + "";
        if (s.length < 2)
            s = "0" + s;

        hours = svgdoc.getElementById("hours");
        var children = hours.getChildNodes();
        for (var i=0; i<children.length; i++)
            if (children.item(i).getNodeType() == 3)
                children.item(i).setNodeValue(h);

        minutes = svgdoc.getElementById("minutes");
        children = minutes.getChildNodes();
        for (var i=0; i<children.length; i++)
            if (children.item(i).getNodeType() == 3)
                children.item(i).setNodeValue(m);

        seconds = svgdoc.getElementById("seconds");
        var children = seconds.getChildNodes();
        for (var i=0; i<children.length; i++)
            if (children.item(i).getNodeType() == 3)
                children.item(i).setNodeValue(s);
    }

]]></script>
<linearGradient id="linear_bw" x1="0%" y1="0%" x2="100%" y2="0%"
    spreadMethod="pad" gradientUnits="userSpaceOnUse">
    <stop offset="0%" stop-color="rgb(255,255,255)" stop-opacity="1"/>
    <stop offset="100%" stop-color="rgb(0,0,0)" stop-opacity="1"/>
</linearGradient>
<linearGradient id="linear_bw_tr" x1="0%" y1="0%" x2="100%" y2="0%"
    spreadMethod="pad" gradientUnits="userSpaceOnUse"
    gradientTransform="matrix(0.819152 0.573576 -0.573576 0.819152 0 0)">
    <stop offset="0%" stop-color="rgb(255,255,255)" stop-opacity="1"/>
    <stop offset="100%" stop-color="rgb(0,0,0)" stop-opacity="1"/>
</linearGradient>
```

LISTING 16.4 Continued

```
    </defs>
    <path
       d="M158 139 L34 139 L56 106 L180 106 L180 172 L158 205 L158 139 L180 106"
       fill="url(#linear_bw_tr)" stroke="rgb(0,0,128)" stroke-width="0"/>
    <rect x="31" y="136" width="130" height="71" rx="9" ry="9"
       fill="url(#linear_bw)" stroke-width="0"/>
    <rect x="36" y="141" width="120" height="61" rx="8" ry="8" fill="rgb(0,0,0)"
       stroke-width="0"/>
    <text id="hours" x="34px" y="186px" fill="rgb(255,255,255)" font-size="30"
       font-family="Arial">12</text>
    <text x="68px" y="183px" fill="rgb(255,255,255)" font-size="30"
       font-family="Arial">:</text>
    <text id="minutes" x="76px" y="186px" fill="rgb(255,255,255)" font-size="30"
        font-family="Arial">34</text>
    <text x="111px" y="184px" fill="rgb(255,255,255)" font-size="30"
       font-family="Arial">:</text>
    <text id="seconds" x="121px" y="186px" fill="rgb(255,255,255)"
       font-size="30" font-family="Arial">56</text>
</svg>
```

The clock that gets updated each second is shown in Figure 16.3.

FIGURE 16.3 Updating the clock.

We want to add some more functionality to the clock example. For those users who get nervous when there is too much animation on a Web site (or in a graphic), we add the possibility to start and stop the animation in Listing 16.4.

We already have a function for starting the clock, startClock(); here, we add one for stopping it. The id variable that holds the timeout ID is global and thus also accessible within other functions.

So, we write stopClock() like this:

```
function stopClock(evt) {
    window.clearInterval(id);
}
```

Furthermore, we need some kind of user interface. So we add two more text fields to the SVG document:

```
<text id="start" x="50px" y="230px" fill="rgb(128,0,0)" font-size="12"
    font-family="Arial">start</text>
<text id="stop" x="100px" y="230px" fill="rgb(128,0,0)" font-size="12"
    font-family="Arial">stop</text>
```

Now we can put the pieces together. The init() function must be extended to add event handlers to the two new text fields:

```
function init(evt) {
    svgdoc = evt.getTarget().getOwnerDocument();
    svgdoc.getElementById("start")
          .addEventListener("click", startClock, false);
    svgdoc.getElementById("stop")
          .addEventListener("click", stopClock, false);
    startClock()
}
```

The clock can now be stopped or restarted with one click (see Figure 16.4).

Analog Clock

SVG is a graphics format, so why not use an analog clock, which is more sophisticated in terms of graphics than a digital clock that uses a computer font for its digits? Sounds like a good idea, and it's fun, too! Let's start with the clock itself, as shown in Listing 16.5.

FIGURE 16.4   Starting and stopping the clock.

LISTING 16.5   16code05.svg—The Analog Clock

```
<?xml version="1.0" standalone="no"?>
<svg width="500" height="500" onload="init(evt)">
   <defs>
      <script type="text/ecmascript"><![CDATA[
         var svgdoc;   //global variable

         function init(evt) {
            svgdoc = evt.getTarget().getOwnerDocument();
            startClock();
         }

         function startClock(evt) {
            id = window.setInterval("updateClock()", 1000); //every second
         }

         function updateClock() {
            //...
         }
      ]]></script>
```

16

LISTING 16.5   Continued

```
    <filter id="Drop_Shadow" filterUnits="objectBoundingBox"
        x="-15%" y="-15%" width="150%" height="150%">
        <feGaussianBlur in="SourceAlpha" stdDeviation="1.5"
            result="blurredAlpha"/>
        <feOffset in="blurredAlpha" dx="3" dy="3"
            result="offsetBlurredAlpha"/>
        <feFlood result="flooded"
            style="flood-color:rgb(0,0,0);flood-opacity:0.55"/>
        <feComposite in="flooded" operator="in" in2="offsetBlurredAlpha"
            result="coloredShadow"/>
        <feComposite in="SourceGraphic" in2="coloredShadow" operator="over"/>
    </filter>
    <radialGradient id="gradient" cx="50%" cy="50%" r="50%" fx="50%" fy="50%"
        spreadMethod="pad" gradientUnits="objectBoundingBox">
        <stop offset="78%"
            style="stop-color:rgb(255,255,255);stop-opacity:1"/>
        <stop offset="80%" style="stop-color:rgb(0,0,153);stop-opacity:1"/>
        <stop offset="89%" style="stop-color:rgb(0,0,128);stop-opacity:1"/>
        <stop offset="98%" style="stop-color:rgb(0,0,153);stop-opacity:1"/>
        <stop offset="100%"
            style="stop-color:rgb(255,255,255);stop-opacity:0"/>
    </radialGradient>
</defs>
<ellipse cx="250" cy="250" rx="75" ry="75"
    style="filter:url(#Drop_Shadow);fill:url(#gradient)"/>
<line id="seconds" x1="250" y1="250" x2="250" y2="303"
    style="fill:none;stroke:rgb(128,0,128);stroke-width:1"/>
<line id="minutes" x1="250" y1="250" x2="250" y2="197"
    style="fill:none;stroke:rgb(0,0,0);stroke-width:3"/>
<line id="hours" x1="250" y1="250" x2="283" y2="250"
    style="fill:none;stroke:rgb(0,0,128);stroke-width:2"/>
<line x1="250" y1="185" x2="250" y2="195"
    style="fill:none;stroke:rgb(0,0,128);stroke-width:2"/>
<line x1="250" y1="305" x2="250" y2="315"
    style="fill:none;stroke:rgb(0,0,128);stroke-width:2"/>
<line x1="306" y1="250" x2="316" y2="250"
    style="fill:none;stroke:rgb(0,0,128);stroke-width:2"/>
<line x1="185" y1="250" x2="195" y2="250"
    style="fill:none;stroke:rgb(0,0,128);stroke-width:2"/>
<text x="243px" y="187px"
    style="fill:rgb(255,255,255);font-size:11;font-family:Arial">12</text>
```

LISTING 16.5   Continued

```
    <text x="248px" y="321px"
       style="fill:rgb(255,255,255);font-size:11;font-family:Arial">6</text>
    <text x="314px" y="254px"
       style="fill:rgb(255,255,255);font-size:11;font-family:Arial">3</text>
    <text x="180px" y="254px"
       style="fill:rgb(255,255,255);font-size:11;font-family:Arial">9</text>
</svg>
```

As you can see, the SVG document in Listing 16.5 contains

- An ellipse that represents the clock

- Three lines that represent the hands of the clock

- The numbers 3, 6, 9, and 12 and four short lines that provide some visual orientation

Your SVG viewer will render this clock, and it should look like Figure 16.5.

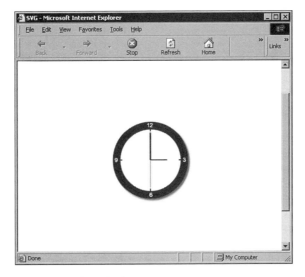

FIGURE 16.5   Rendering an analog clock.

Also, you will find a call to a `startClock()` function. This function creates an interval that calls the `updateClock()` function as we did in the digital clock example. The only thing left to do is update this function.

The first step, the calculation of the time of day, stays mostly the same as before. However, because the clock goes only from 0 to 11, any hour value between 12 and 24 is decremented by 12:

```
var d = new Date();
var h = d.getHours();
if (h >= 12)
    h -= 12;
var m = d.getMinutes();
var s = d.getSeconds();
```

Now comes the math (we will keep this discussion as short as possible).

To calculate the appropriate positions of the clock hands, we must find the second coordinates. For this, we must calculate the angle of the hand. To do so, we need to use a little bit of trigonometry.

Let's start with the hour hand: In the first step, the angle to the y-axis is calculated. Twelve hours equal 360 degrees, or 2π (the radial measurement). Thus, each hour stands for $\pi/6$. If you multiply this angle by the number of hours, you get the appropriate angle—almost. You also have to take the minutes into account; 30 minutes move the hour hand halfway to the next hour. So this value (minutes divided by 60) must be added to the hour value before it is multiplied by $\pi/6$.

> **NOTE**
>
> To be exact, we must also take the number of seconds into account. One hour equals 3600 seconds, so the number of seconds divided by 3600 must be added to the hour value, as well:
>
> ```
> var hoursYAngle = (h + m/60 + s/3600) * Math.PI / 6;
> ```

When you understand this principle, calculating the angles to the y-axis of the minute and the second hands is quite easy. For minutes, you have to take into account the minutes and the seconds, and bear in mind that 60 seconds make up one minute, so one minute stands for $360/60 = 6$ degrees, or $\pi/30$:

```
var minutesYAngle = (m + s/60) * Math.PI / 30;
```

Finally, the second hand must be adjusted. Sixty seconds equal one minute, so one second moves the hand's angle to the y-axis by $\pi/30$, as previously one minute moved the minute hand by $\pi/30$:

```
var secondsYAngle = s * Math.PI / 30;
```

Now we somehow have to calculate the angles to the x-axis; we can use the sine and cosine functions to get the coordinates of the hands. An angle of 0 degrees to the y-axis means an angle of 270 degrees—or –90 degrees—to the x-axis. An angle of 90 degrees to the y-axis leads to an angle of 0 degrees to the x-axis. So it's obvious that we can calculate the angle to the x-axis by subtracting 90 degrees—or $\pi/2$—from the angle to the y-axis:

```
hoursXAngle = hoursYAngle - Math.PI/2;
minutesXAngle = minutesYAngle - Math.PI/2;
secondsXAngle = secondsYAngle - Math.PI/2;
```

Now calculating the coordinates has become easier. First, we save the coordinates of the center of the clock in variables:

```
var centerX = 250;   //position of the circle's center
var centerY = 250;
```

Then we need the length of the hands:

```
var hoursLength = 33;
var minutesLength = 53;
var secondsLength = 53;
```

The next step is crucial: We use the trigonometric functions of ECMAScript to calculate the coordinates of the second end of each hand. For this, we multiply the cosine (for the x coordinate) or the sine (for the y coordinate) of the angle to the x-axis by the length of the hand, and we have the desired coordinates:

```
var hoursX = centerX + hoursLength * Math.cos(hoursXAngle);
var hoursY = centerY + hoursLength * Math.sin(hoursXAngle);
var minutesX = centerX + minutesLength * Math.cos(minutesXAngle);
var minutesY = centerY + minutesLength * Math.sin(minutesXAngle);
var secondsX = centerX + secondsLength * Math.cos(secondsXAngle);
var secondsY = centerY + secondsLength * Math.sin(secondsXAngle);
```

We are almost done now. All we have left to do is to apply the new coordinates, by setting the x2 and y2 attributes of the three hands:

```
svgdoc.getElementById("hours").setAttribute("x2", hoursX);
svgdoc.getElementById("hours").setAttribute("y2", hoursY);
svgdoc.getElementById("minutes").setAttribute("x2", minutesX);
svgdoc.getElementById("minutes").setAttribute("y2", minutesY);
svgdoc.getElementById("seconds").setAttribute("x2", secondsX);
svgdoc.getElementById("seconds").setAttribute("y2", secondsY);
```

And now we're done! Let's put all this code in the updateClock() function, and thanks to the call to setInterval() in startClock(), the updateClock() function is executed every second, keeping the clock at the current time, all the time.

16

Here is the complete code for this function:

```
function updateClock() {
    var d = new Date();
    var h = d.getHours();
    if (h >= 12)
        h -= 12;
    var m = d.getMinutes();
    var s = d.getSeconds();

    var hoursYAngle = (h + m/60 + s/3600) * Math.PI / 6;
    var minutesYAngle = (m + s/60) * Math.PI / 30;
    var secondsYAngle = s * Math.PI / 30;
    hoursXAngle = hoursYAngle - Math.PI/2;
    minutesXAngle = minutesYAngle - Math.PI/2;
    secondsXAngle = secondsYAngle - Math.PI/2;

    var centerX = 250;   //position of the circle's center
    var centerY = 250;
    var hoursLength = 33;
    var minutesLength = 53;
    var secondsLength = 53;

    var hoursX = centerX + hoursLength * Math.cos(hoursXAngle);
    var hoursY = centerY + hoursLength * Math.sin(hoursXAngle);
    var minutesX = centerX + minutesLength * Math.cos(minutesXAngle);
    var minutesY = centerY + minutesLength * Math.sin(minutesXAngle);
    var secondsX = centerX + secondsLength * Math.cos(secondsXAngle);
    var secondsY = centerY + secondsLength * Math.sin(secondsXAngle);

    svgdoc.getElementById("hours").setAttribute("x2", hoursX);
    svgdoc.getElementById("hours").setAttribute("y2", hoursY);
    svgdoc.getElementById("minutes").setAttribute("x2", minutesX);
    svgdoc.getElementById("minutes").setAttribute("y2", minutesY);
    svgdoc.getElementById("seconds").setAttribute("x2", secondsX);
    svgdoc.getElementById("seconds").setAttribute("y2", secondsY);
}
```

NOTE

If you place the three hands in a group whose center is at the center of the clock, you can also use the rotate() transformation to rotate the hands. Just rotate each hand each second.

Pull-Down Menus

Many Web sites have menus that expand when you move your mouse pointer over them and collapse as soon as you move your mouse away. In HTML, you create this functionality by using DHTML, which can be difficult when you want to support different browsers.

With SVG, creating fancy pull-down menus is easy. You just have to do the following:

1. Create the headings for the menu.

2. Create the collapsed version of each menu, but make it invisible with the value of the style attribute set to "visibility:hidden".

3. Write two functions, one for the mouseover event (over()) and one for the mouseout event (out()). The first function makes the menu visible; the second function makes it invisible again. You can use these functions over and over again, if you supply the id attribute of the to-be-shown or to-be-concealed menu as a function parameter.

And that's about it!

Programming an effect like this is a really easy task, as you can see in Listing 16.6.

LISTING 16.6   16code06.svg—A Pull-Down Menu

```
<?xml version="1.0" standalone="no"?>
<svg width="400" height="400" onload="init(evt)">
  <desc>
    <script language="text/ecmascript"><![CDATA[
      var svgdoc;

      function init(evt) {
        svgdoc = evt.getTarget().getOwnerDocument();
      }

      function over(name) {
        var group=svgdoc.getElementById(name);
        var sty=group.getStyle();
        sty.setProperty("visibility", "visible");
        }
      function out(name) {
        var group=svgdoc.getElementById(name);
        var sty=group.getStyle();
        sty.setProperty("visibility", "hidden");
      }
    ]]></script>
  </desc>
   <g id="books" onmouseover="over('books_menu')"
                 onmouseout="out('books_menu')">
```

16

LISTING 16.6   Continued

```
        <rect fill="rgb(204,0,51)" stroke="rgb(204,0,51)" stroke-width="1" x="75"
          y="35" width="70" height="30"/>
        <text fill="rgb(255,255,255)" font-size="18" font-family="Arial" x="85px"
          y="56px">Books</text>
    </g>
    <g id="sources" onmouseover="over('sources_menu')"
                    onmouseout="out('sources_menu')">
        <rect fill="rgb(204,0,51)" stroke="rgb(204,0,51)" stroke-width="1"
          x="145.5" y="35" width="90" height="30"/>
        <text fill="rgb(255,255,255)" font-size="18" font-family="Arial"
          x="155px" y="56px">Sources</text>
    </g>
    <g id="books_menu" style="visibility:hidden"
      onmouseover="over('books_menu')" onmouseout="out('books_menu')">
        <rect fill="rgb(255,255,255)" stroke="rgb(0,0,0)" stroke-width="1" x="75"
          y="66" width="70" height="50"/>
            <a xlink:href="http://www.amazon.com/exec/obidos/ASIN/0672322900">
        <text fill="rgb(0,0,0)" font-size="10" font-family="Arial"
          x="75px" y="80px">TY SVG 24 Hrs</text>
            </a>
            <a xlink:href="http://www.amazon.com/exec/obidos/ASIN/0672324296">
        <text fill="rgb(0,0,0)" font-size="10" font-family="Arial"
          x="75px" y="100px">SVG Unleashed</text>
            </a>
    </g>
    <g id="sources_menu" style="visibility:hidden"
      onmouseover="over('sources_menu')" onmouseout="out('sources_menu')">
        <rect fill="rgb(255,255,255)" stroke="rgb(0,0,0)"
          stroke-width="1" x="146" y="66" width="90" height="60"/>
            <a xlink:href="http://www.w3.org/Graphics/SVG">
        <text fill="rgb(0,0,0)" font-size="10" font-family="Arial"
          x="150px" y="80px">W3C Specification</text>
            </a>
            <a xlink:href="http://xml.apache.org/batik">
        <text fill="rgb(0,0,0)" font-size="10" font-family="Arial"
          x="150px" y="100px">Batik</text>
            </a>
            <a xlink:href="http://www.adobe.com/svg">
        <text fill="rgb(0,0,0)" font-size="10" font-family="Arial"
          x="150px" y="120px">Adobe SVG</text>
            </a>
    </g>
</svg>
```

The result of running Listing 16.6 is shown in Figure 16.6. The right menu (Sources) is expanded; the left one (Books) is collapsed.

FIGURE 16.6   Navigation with SVG.

Animating the Sky

In this section, we show you how to create SVG animations using JavaScript/ECMAScript. We want to create an *X-Files*-like scenario. A UFO appears and flies around, most probably seeking out human test subjects for some medical experiments.

Take a look at Figure 16.7.

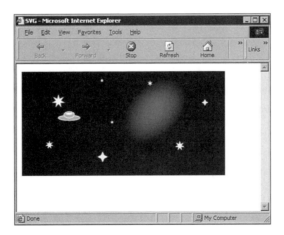

FIGURE 16.7   A UFO sighting.

Figure 16.7 was created by the (truly extra-terrestrial) piece of SVG code shown in Listing 16.7.

LISTING 16.7   16code07.svg—Animated Sky

```
<?xml version="1.0" standalone="no"?>
<svg width="400" height="200" style="fill:rgb(0,0,0)">
    <defs>
        <radialGradient id="milkyway" cx="50%" cy="50%" r="50%" fx="50%" fy="50%"
            spreadMethod="pad" gradientUnits="objectBoundingBox">
            <stop offset="0%"
                style="stop-color:rgb(255,255,255);stop-opacity:0.5"/>
            <stop offset="100%" style="stop-color:rgb(0,0,0);stop-opacity:1"/>
        </radialGradient>
        <animateMotion xlink:href="#ufo" dur="10s"
            path="M399 96.5 Q331 48.5 290 45.5 Q191 67.5 215 115.5 Q301 163.5
                336 134.5 Q398 50.5 340 29.5 Q181 -1.5 130 19.5 Q88 98.5 67
                103.5 Q0 113.5 0 113.5"
            repeatCount="indefinite" />
    </defs>
    <rect x="0" y="0" width="400" height="200"
        style="fill:rgb(0,0,0);stroke-width:0"/>
    <rect x="175" y="30" width="150" height="100"
        style="fill:url(#milkyway);stroke-width:0"
        transform="rotate(-45,250,65)"/>
    <polygon
        points="72,44.3009 74.1362,52.1736 81.6233,48.9352 76.8,55.5139 84,
                59.3484 75.8493,59.6792 77.3405,67.6991 72,61.5329 66.6595,67.6991
                68.1507,59.6792 60,59.3484 67.2,55.5139
                62.3767,48.9352 69.8638,52.1736"
        style="fill:rgb(255,255,204);stroke-width:0"/>
    <polygon
        points="310.719,134.301 312.271,140.021 317.71,137.668 314.206,
                142.448 319.437,145.234 313.515,145.474 314.599,151.301
                310.719,146.821 306.838,151.301 307.922,145.474 302,145.234
                307.231,142.448 303.727,137.668 309.167,140.021"
        style="fill:rgb(255,255,192);stroke-width:0"/>
    <polygon
        points="54.2189,133.301 55.5039,138.012 60.0071,136.074 57.106,
                140.01 61.437,142.305 56.5339,142.502 57.4314,147.301
                54.2189,143.612 51.0056,147.301 51.9031,142.502 47,142.305
                51.331,140.01 48.4299,136.074 52.9339,138.012"
        style="fill:rgb(255,255,180);stroke-width:0"/>
    <polygon
        points="252,18 252.75,21.701 256.33,20.5 253.5,23 256.33,25.5 252.75,
                24.299 252,28 251.25,24.299 247.67,25.5 250.5,
                23 247.67,20.5 251.25,21.701"
```

LISTING 16.7   Continued

```
          style="fill:rgb(255,255,164);stroke-width:0"/>
    <polygon
       points="177,94.1468 177.649,96.408 180,96.3265 178.05,97.6424
               178.854,99.8532 177,98.4053 175.146,99.8532 175.95,97.6424
               174,96.3265 176.351,96.408"
       style="fill:rgb(255,255,153);stroke-width:0"/>
    <polygon
       points="157,14.1468 157.649,16.408 160,16.3265 158.05,17.6424
               158.854,19.8532 157,18.4053 155.146,19.8532 155.95,17.6424
               154,16.3265 156.351,16.408"
       style="fill:rgb(255,255,128);stroke-width:0"/>
    <polygon
       points="361,54 362.909,58.0908 367,60 362.909,61.9092 361,66 359.091,61.9092
               355,60 359.091,58.0908"
       style="fill:rgb(255,255,102);stroke-width:0"/>
    <polygon
       points="158,154 161.182,160.818 168,164 161.182,167.182 158,174
               154.818,167.182 148,164 154.818,160.818"
       style="fill:rgb(255,255,78);stroke-width:0"/>
    <g id="ufo">
       <ellipse cx="0" cy="8" rx="21" ry="5"
          style="fill:rgb(192,192,192);stroke:rgb(255,255,255);stroke-width:1"/>
       <ellipse cx="0" cy="2" rx="10" ry="6"
          style="fill:rgb(192,192,192);stroke:rgb(255,255,255);stroke-width:1"/>
       <ellipse cx="0" cy="0" rx="6" ry="1.5"
          style="fill:rgb(255,255,255);stroke:rgb(255,255,255);stroke-width:0.5"/>
    </g>
</svg>
```

Some polygon elements in Listing 16.7 represent the different stars in the sky, whereas the flying saucer is generated by combining three ellipses and a radial gradient.

Animation Using ECMAScript

This chapter is about animation, right? So now we want to transform the SVG sky created in Listing 16.7 into an ECMAScript-empowered animation. Let's first look at the path that is used for the SVG-only animation:

```
<animateMotion xlink:href="#ufo" dur="10s"
   path="M399 96.5 Q331 48.5 290 45.5 Q191 67.5 215 115.5 Q301 163.5 336
         134.5 Q398 50.5 340 29.5 Q181 -1.5 130 19.5 Q88 98.5
         67 103.5 Q0 113.5 0 113.5"
   repeatCount="indefinite" />
```

As you can see, thanks to the Q command (see Chapter 6, "Paths in SVG"), cubic Bezier curves are used. Because ECMAScript does not have direct support for such curves, we need to create the animation using a special technique:

- A list of points that the object has to be moved to must be saved in variables.

- Using timeouts and/or intervals, we must repeatedly move the object to the next point in the list.

It would be quite tricky to extract all the points the UFO visits during its journey from the path printed at the beginning of this section. So we want to make this code a little bit easier and just provide a list of arbitrary points. But don't worry; the basic principle of ECMAScript animation is the same: Provide a list of points, and then iterate through this list.

So, here is the list, in an easy array. The order of points is always x coordinate, y coordinate, x coordinate, y coordinate, and so on:

```
var points = new Array(
    400, 100, 397,  98, 394,  96, 392,  94,  390,  96,  385,  98,
    380, 100, 375, 105, 370, 110, 365, 115,  360, 120,  355, 125,
    350, 130, 345, 135, 340, 140, 335, 145,  330, 150,  325, 155,
    305, 154, 290, 153, 275, 152, 260, 151,  245, 150,  230, 149,
    215, 148, 200, 147, 185, 146, 170, 145,  160, 140,  150, 135,
    140, 130, 130, 125, 120, 120, 110, 115,  100, 110,   90, 109,
     80, 108,  70, 107,  60, 106,  50, 105,   40, 104,   30, 103,
     20, 102,  10, 101,   0, 100);
```

Now we need to move the object along these points. For that task, we introduce a global variable that holds the current position of the UFO's coordinates in the list of points:

```
var position = 0;
```

A moveUFO() function now moves the UFO, that means the <g> object containing the three ellipses, to the coordinates that can be found at the given position in the points array. Because each coordinate consists of two parts, we need to extract two values from the array:

```
var x = points[position];
var y = points[position + 1];
```

Moving the object to the specific coordinates is no longer a big problem. Just remember that we put the UFO within a g element. So, to move the flying saucer to coordinates (50, 50), we must execute the transformation command translate(50, 50):

```
var ufo = svgdoc.getElementById("ufo");
ufo.setAttribute("transform", "translate("+x+","+y+")");
```

Finally, the position counter must be incremented. If the counter exceeds the number of elements in the array, it is reset to 0, and the animation restarts:

```
position += 2;
if (position >= points.length)
   position = 0;
```

And that's it! The remaining tasks on the to-do list are putting up the functions, using setInterval() to repeat execution of the animation, and making other minor improvements (such as moving the declaration of the ufo variable into the init() function because this must be done only once).

Listing 16.8 shows the complete SVG code for our UFO example, with the script elements identified.

LISTING 16.8   16code08.svg—Animated UFO

```
<?xml version="1.0" standalone="no"?>
<svg width="400" height="200" style="fill:rgb(0,0,0)" onload="init(evt)">
   <defs>
      <script type="text/ecmascript"><![CDATA[
         var svgdoc;  //global variable
         var ufo;  //flying saucer
         // points the UFO must be moved to
         var points = new Array(
            400, 100, 397,  98, 394,  96, 392,  94, 390,  96, 385,  98,
            380, 100, 375, 105, 370, 110, 365, 115, 360, 120, 355, 125,
            350, 130, 345, 135, 340, 140, 335, 145, 330, 150, 325, 155,
            305, 154, 290, 153, 275, 152, 260, 151, 245, 150, 230, 149,
            215, 148, 200, 147, 185, 146, 170, 145, 160, 140, 150, 135,
            140, 130, 130, 125, 120, 120, 110, 115, 100, 110,  90, 109,
             80, 108,  70, 107,  60, 106,  50, 105,  40, 104,  30, 103,
             20, 102,  10, 101,   0, 100);
         var position = 0; //position in array

         function init(evt) {
            svgdoc = evt.getTarget().getOwnerDocument();
            ufo = svgdoc.getElementById("ufo");
            startUFO();
         }

         function startUFO() { // calles updateUFO() periodically
            window.setInterval("updateUFO()", 100);
         }

         function updateUFO() {
```

16

LISTING 16.8   Continued

```
            // retrieve coordinates of next point
            var x = points[position];
            var y = points[position + 1];
            // updates position of UFO
            ufo.setAttribute("transform", "translate("+x+","+y+")");
            // moves to next position in array "points"
            position += 2;
            if (position >= points.length)
                position = 0;
        }
    ]]></script>
    <radialGradient id="milkyway" cx="50%" cy="50%" r="50%" fx="50%" fy="50%"
        spreadMethod="pad" gradientUnits="objectBoundingBox">
        <stop offset="0%"
            style="stop-color:rgb(255,255,255);stop-opacity:0.5"/>
        <stop offset="100%" style="stop-color:rgb(0,0,0);stop-opacity:1"/>
    </radialGradient>
</defs>
<rect x="0" y="0" width="400" height="200"
    style="fill:rgb(0,0,0);stroke-width:0"/>
<rect x="175" y="30" width="150" height="100"
    style="fill:url(#milkyway);stroke-width:0"
    transform="rotate(-45,250,65)"/>
<polygon
    points="72,44.3009 74.1362,52.1736 81.6233,48.9352 76.8,
            55.5139 84,59.3484 75.8493,59.6792 77.3405,67.6991
            72,61.5329 66.6595,67.6991 68.1507,59.6792 60,59.3484
            67.2,55.5139 62.3767,48.9352 69.8638,52.1736"
    style="fill:rgb(255,255,204);stroke-width:0"/>
<polygon
    points="310.719,134.301 312.271,140.021 317.71,137.668
            314.206,142.448 319.437,145.234 313.515,145.474 314.599,
            151.301 310.719,146.821 306.838,151.301 307.922,145.474 302,
            145.234 307.231,142.448 303.727,137.668 309.167,140.021"
    style="fill:rgb(255,255,192);stroke-width:0"/>
<polygon
    points="54.2189,133.301 55.5039,138.012 60.0071,136.074 57.106,140.01
            61.437,142.305 56.5339,142.502 57.4314,147.301 54.2189,
            143.612 51.0056,147.301 51.9031,142.502 47,142.305 51.331,
            140.01 48.4299,136.074 52.9339,138.012"
    style="fill:rgb(255,255,180);stroke-width:0"/>
```

LISTING 16.8   Continued

```
<polygon
  points="252,18 252.75,21.701 256.33,20.5 253.5,23 256.33,25.5
          252.75,24.299 252,28 251.25,24.299 247.67,25.5 250.5,23
          247.67,20.5 251.25,21.701"
  style="fill:rgb(255,255,164);stroke-width:0"/>
<polygon
  points="177,94.1468 177.649,96.408 180,96.3265 178.05,97.6424 178.854,
          99.8532 177,98.4053 175.146,99.8532 175.95,97.6424 174,96.3265
          176.351,96.408"
  style="fill:rgb(255,255,153);stroke-width:0"/>
<polygon
  points="157,14.1468 157.649,16.408 160,16.3265 158.05,17.6424 158.854,
          19.8532 157,18.4053 155.146,19.8532 155.95,17.6424 154,16.3265
          156.351,16.408"
  style="fill:rgb(255,255,128);stroke-width:0"/>
<polygon
  points="361,54 362.909,58.0908 367,60 362.909,61.9092 361,66
          359.091,61.9092 355,60 359.091,58.0908"
  style="fill:rgb(255,255,102);stroke-width:0"/>
<polygon
  points="158,154 161.182,160.818 168,164 161.182,167.182 158,174
          154.818,167.182 148,164 154.818,160.818"
  style="fill:rgb(255,255,78);stroke-width:0"/>
<g id="ufo">
  <ellipse id="ufo1" cx="0" cy="8" rx="21" ry="5"
    style="fill:rgb(192,192,192);stroke:rgb(255,255,255);stroke-width:1"/>
  <ellipse id="ufo2" cx="0" cy="2" rx="10" ry="6"
    style="fill:rgb(192,192,192);stroke:rgb(255,255,255);stroke-width:1"/>
  <ellipse id="ufo3" cx="0" cy="0" rx="6" ry="1.5"
    style="fill:rgb(255,255,255);stroke:rgb(255,255,255);stroke-width:0.5"/>
</g>
</svg>
```

Note that the final coordinate on the path of the UFO is very close to the starting coordinate. By locating these coordinates close together, you ensure a smooth transition when the animation starts all over again at the end.

Random Animations

Another great feature of ECMAScript is the possibility to generate random values. A call to `Math.random()` returns a decimal between 0 and 1; thus, you can generate an arbitrary

number of random numbers. For example, the following code generates a number
between 0 and 9:

```
var between_0_and_9 = Math.floor(10 * Math.random());
```

Now let's move on to our sample application. Maybe you noticed the eight stars in the sky
in Figure 16.7. Each star consists of one polygon. Well, supernovas tend to happen, so we
want the stars to disappear at a random point in time. To do so, we first have to assign an
id attribute to all eight stars. Note our naming scheme—"star" plus the number of the
star:

```
<polygon
    id="star1"
    points="72,44.3009 74.1362,52.1736 81.6233,48.9352 76.8,55.5139
            84,59.3484 75.8493,59.6792 77.3405,67.6991 72,61.5329 66.6595,67.6991
            68.1507,59.6792 60,59.3484 67.2,55.5139 62.3767,
            48.9352 69.8638,52.1736"
    style="fill:rgb(255,255,204);stroke-width:0"/>
<polygon
    id="star2"
    points="310.719,134.301 312.271,140.021 317.71,137.668 314.206,142.448
            319.437,145.234 313.515,145.474 314.599,151.301 310.719,146.821
            306.838,151.301 307.922,145.474 302,145.234 307.231,142.448 303.727,
            137.668 309.167,140.021"
    style="fill:rgb(255,255,192);stroke-width:0"/>
<polygon
    id="star3"
    points="54.2189,133.301 55.5039,138.012 60.0071,136.074 57.106,140.01
            61.437,142.305 56.5339,142.502 57.4314,147.301 54.2189,143.612
            51.0056,147.301 51.9031,142.502 47,142.305 51.331,140.01 48.4299,136.074
            52.9339,138.012"
    style="fill:rgb(255,255,180);stroke-width:0"/>
<polygon
    id="star4"
    points="252,18 252.75,21.701 256.33,20.5 253.5,23 256.33,25.5 252.75,24.299
            252,28 251.25,24.299 247.67,25.5 250.5,23 247.67,20.5 251.25,21.701"
    style="fill:rgb(255,255,164);stroke-width:0"/>
<polygon
    id="star5"
    points="177,94.1468 177.649,96.408 180,96.3265 178.05,97.6424 178.854
            ,99.8532 177,98.4053 175.146,99.8532 175.95,97.6424 174,96.3265
            176.351,96.408"
    style="fill:rgb(255,255,153);stroke-width:0"/>
<polygon
```

```
      id="star6"
   points="157,14.1468 157.649,16.408 160,16.3265 158.05,17.6424
          158.854,19.8532 157,18.4053 155.146,19.8532 155.95,17.6424 154,
          16.3265 156.351,16.408"
   style="fill:rgb(255,255,128);stroke-width:0"/>
<polygon
   id="star7"
   points="361,54 362.909,58.0908 367,60 362.909,61.9092 361,66 359.091,61.9092
          355,60 359.091,58.0908"
   style="fill:rgb(255,255,102);stroke-width:0"/>
<polygon
   id="star8"
   points="158,154 161.182,160.818 168,164 161.182,167.182 158,174
          154.818,167.182 148,164 154.818,160.818"
   style="fill:rgb(255,255,78);stroke-width:0"/>
```

Now we want to make these stars disappear at random moments in time. First, we have to create a `startSuperNova()` function that starts this process and creates an interval:

```
function startSuperNova() {
   window.setInterval("createSuperNova()", 6000);
}
```

This function must be called from within the `init()` function. The referenced `createSuperNova()` function performs several tasks:

- It finds a random star (that is, a random number between 1 and 8).

- It finds a random starting point in milliseconds (a random number between 1 and 3000).

- It finds a random duration indicating how long that star should not be visible (a random number between 1 and 3000). In a world with UFOs, supernovas can be undone.

- It creates a timeout that lets the star disappear in the randomly calculated amount of time.

- It creates a timeout to make the star visible again.

First, let's generate the random numbers:

```
var nr = Math.floor(8*Math.random()) + 1;
var start = Math.floor(3000*Math.random()) + 1;
var duration = Math.floor(3000*Math.random()) + 1;
```

To make the example more sophisticated, we do not use the visibility attributes of the different stars, but we assign colors. So we set the fill color of the star to black to make it disappear in black space. However, to be able to undo this, we first must save the original color:

```
var star = svgdoc.getElementById("star" + nr);
var originalColor = star.getStyle().getPropertyValue("fill");
```

Now we can create the timeout. The first timeout calls a function to make the star disappear, using the number of the star as a parameter:

```
window.setTimeout("hideStar(" + nr + ")", start);
```

The second timeout makes the star reappear. For this, we need two parameters, the number of the star and the original fill color (as a string):

```
window.setTimeout("showStar(" + nr + ", \""
    + originalColor + "\")", start + duration);
```

The hideStar() function now assigns a black fill color to the star whose number was provided as a parameter to this function:

```
function hideStar(nr) {
    var star = svgdoc.getElementById("star" + nr);
    star.getStyle().setProperty("fill", "rbg(0,0,0)");
}
```

The showStar() function makes the star visible again, using the original color:

```
function showStar(nr, color) {
    var star = svgdoc.getElementById("star" + nr);
    star.getStyle().setProperty("fill", color);
}
```

If you run this script, you will notice that every few seconds a star disappears and mysteriously appears again a few seconds later.

> **NOTE**
>
> If you want the stars to fade very slowly, you should consider using <colorTransformation>; however, you have no trivial random access to that.

Here is the complete code for this example (script portions only):

```
var svgdoc;

function init(evt) {
```

```
      svgdoc = evt.getTarget().getOwnerDocument();
      startSuperNova();
   }

   function startSuperNova() {
      window.setInterval("createSuperNova()", 6000);
   }
   function createSuperNova() {
      var nr = Math.floor(8*Math.random()) + 1;
      var start = Math.floor(3000*Math.random()) + 1;
      var duration = Math.floor(3000*Math.random()) + 1;

      var star = svgdoc.getElementById("star" + nr);
      var originalColor = star.getStyle().getPropertyValue("fill");

      window.setTimeout("hideStar(" + nr + ")", start);
      window.setTimeout("showStar(" + nr + ", \""
          + originalColor + "\")", start + duration);
   }

   function hideStar(nr) {
      var star = svgdoc.getElementById("star" + nr);
      star.getStyle().setProperty("fill", "rbg(0,0,0)");
   }

   function showStar(nr, color) {
      var star = svgdoc.getElementById("star" + nr);
      star.getStyle().setProperty("fill", color);
   }
```

Scripted Versus Declarative Animation

Now that you've seen all these kinds of animations, it's time to look back and reconsider whether animation using SVG's built-in mechanism is better. When should you prefer an ECMAScript approach to support your SVG? In the following sections, we'll give you a few pointers.

Scripting Advantages

- Adobe SVG Viewer has problems with animating two transformations for one object. With scripts, you can solve this problem by scripting the animation.

- You can use randomized functions.

- You can combine animations with events.

- Scripting generally is more flexible, as you can extend SVG's possibilities. Virtually everything is possible.

Scripting Disadvantages

- The user must have enabled ECMAScript/JavaScript in the browser, or the viewer must bring its own script interpreter.

- For animations along paths, the calculations are too complex. For example, you saw that the UFO animation was not as smooth as the SVG-only animation. We could have achieved that level of smoothness but would also have had to provide nearly 500 different coordinates where the UFO must move to. You can do the same thing much faster with paths.

- Scripted animations are normally slower than declarative animations because the script interpreter has to jump in. Plus, the optimized, built-in animation functions of the viewers are not used.

Animation Advantages

- The SVG animations are easy to use.

- Very complex animations can be realized.

- Durations and repeats can be defined with only one value for a specific attribute.

Basically, you should always try the SVG-only way first. But if you come upon a barrier you cannot surpass, try using ECMAScript to solve your problems. With combined efforts, you often can achieve amazing results (not that SVG itself isn't amazing enough.

Summary

This chapter provided several examples showing how you can dynamically extend the capabilities of SVG, making this file format even more dynamic and flexible than it already is. However, you should note that not every viewer supports scripting, so currently you have to assume that your users have the Adobe SVG Viewer installed.

To summarize, this chapter covered the following:

- We built a bridge between SVG and HTML, accessing one part of a page from the other.

- We animated SVG using script languages, most of the time getting results that were not possible using SVG-only approaches.

- Finally, we looked back at what we had created, elaborating advantages and disad-vantages of scripting versus pure SVG.

This chapter concludes coverage of ECMAScript/JavaScript. In the next chapter, you will learn how you can use SVG in Java applications.

16

Using SVG in Java Applications

The focus of this chapter is the Batik SVG Toolkit. After an overview of the contents of the Toolkit, we will look at how desktop applications constructed using standard Java programming techniques can be given SVG viewing and export capabilities using two modules from the Toolkit.

Applications in Java

SVG is a specification of the World Wide Web Consortium (W3C), and clearly the Web and SVG are intimately linked. The Web has moved on from being just the HTML language and the HTTP protocol, and the application has moved on from its old-fashioned disconnected desktop roots. But desktop applications still play a big role in this new environment, particularly when it comes to creating content.

There are many reasons why Java is great for SVG work; in particular, its relative platform-independence at least approaches the claim of "Write Once, Run Anywhere." Another good reason for using Java is that it is an object-oriented language. This issue is open to debate, but whereas ECMAScript is certainly capable of using objects, Java is truly object-oriented. Object-oriented code is generally more likely to be reusable than procedural scripts, and systems built from objects are more likely to be scalable. Though nowadays it's true for many languages, it's worth mentioning that Java offers sophisticated support for XML technologies.

One more *very* good reason for using Java for SVG work is the Batik Toolkit.

Apache Batik

Even if you're not a Java developer, the Batik Toolkit has quite a lot to offer. It is tightly coupled to the SVG specifications and comes from the Apache Software Foundation, which means that it is quality, nonproprietary material under continual development and supported by a proven open-source infrastructure.

It wouldn't be easy to do Batik justice in a whole book, so in this chapter, we give an overview of the tools and demonstrate two modules that are particularly suitable for use in desktop applications.

The Batik Toolkit, consisting of applications, code, and documentation, is available free from http://xml.apache.org/batik, and support in the form of FAQs and mailing lists can be found at the site as well.

The Toolkit is layered into three sets of modules:

- Application modules
- Core modules
- Low-level modules

Applications

The Batik team built the Applications set of SVG tools primarily to give some idea of the capabilities of the programming tools, though each tool is useful in its own right.

SVG Browser

You saw the Batik browser in earlier chapters of this book. The appearance and user interface of the SVG browser is very much like that of a conventional Web browser. In terms of specification implementation, it is some way behind the Adobe plug-in but is improving all the time. As well as your being able to view SVG in its rendered form, you can view the source SVG, and the browser also provides a DOM tree view, in which you can examine the structure and element contents of the SVG. Other notable items on the feature list include the ability to export the image as a PNG, JPEG, or TIFF file and the printing capability.

SVG Rasterizer

The rasterizer is a straightforward command-line tool to convert SVG images into PNG, JPEG, or TIFF files. When you use this tool with the Apache Ant build tool, together with the FOP (Formatting Objects Processor) print formatter, you can convert the SVG into PDF.

SVG Pretty-Printer

The Pretty-Printer is a command-line tool for reformatting the XML in an SVG file. As well as setting layout properties such as indentation, you also can set the XML declaration and DOCTYPE. This capability might be useful when various files have come from different sources and they need standardizing for a specific viewer. Being able to automatically tidy hand-hacked source is nice, too.

SVG Font Converter

The Font Converter is a command-line tool for converting TrueType fonts into SVG fonts so that they can be embedded in or linked to from SVG files. This means that their appearance will be more standard across platforms, and that there is no need for the end users to have the particular TrueType font installed on their system.

These applications are built from standard Java and programming modules of Batik, and you can easily build the kind of functionality they offer into your own applications. Of course, you also could use their source code as a starting point for custom applications.

Core Modules

The key tools for the SVG-Java developer are as follows:

- SVG DOM
- SVG Generator
- SVG Canvas Component
- Transcoder API
- Bridge

The key module here is the SVG DOM, an implementation of the API defined in the SVG specification. Most applications built from Batik use this DOM, though in many cases they do so indirectly through the other core modules. We will look at how this module can be used directly in the server-side Java chapter (Chapter 19, "JSP, Servlets, and SVG"), but it is worth pointing out here that virtually everything in this book in any language that refers to the SVG DOM could equally apply to the Batik Java implementation, used either in a desktop or server-side application.

The SVG Generator (`SVGGraphics2D`) is a "Wow!" tool, in that any visuals that can be created using Java2D can be very simply converted to SVG. The SVG Canvas Component (`JSVGCanvas`) is a `Swing` component for displaying SVG content. The Transcoder API aims to provide a generic way of converting from input to output, where the input could, for instance, be an SVG DOM tree and the output could be a `FileOutputStream` containing JPEG image data. The Bridge module is used to convert SVG documents into Batik's internal representation.

Low-Level Modules

The low-level modules are the modules from which the core modules are built. For most practical purposes, developers don't need to directly use these modules:

- SVG Parsers—These parsers are used for extracting information from SVG attributes, which can get quite complex.

- Graphics Vector Toolkit (GVT)—The GVT are classes that provide the view of the SVG DOM tree used internally by Batik.

- Renderer—The Renderer takes the GVT representation and renders it into an image object.

Scripting Support

The Scripting Support feature of Batik falls outside the modules but demonstrates the versatility of building systems in Java. Following the SVG specification, Batik supports ECMAScript (through the Mozilla Rhino interpreter), but also it is possible to add support to SVG for other scripted languages such as Tcl and Python through Java implementations. As it happens, interpreter interfaces for these two languages (using Jacl and JPython) are already included in Batik.

Displaying SVG in a Java Application

The features listed in the preceding section give you an idea of the power and versatility of the Toolkit. The capability to display SVG is certainly something that will have a place in many applications. Batik provides a component specifically for rendering SVG files in Swing applications: JSVGCanvas. This component is an extension of the standard Java JComponent class, which is the base for most visual components found in Swing. In use, the JSVGCanvas will be placed in a container in the same fashion as other Swing components, and then by using its loadSVGDocument() method, an SVG file can be loaded from a given URL or file. To demonstrate this usage, in Figure 17.1 we have created an SVG viewer application. We will look at the code shortly, but first here is a preview.

The application has three main components: at the top, a button that will launch a dialog box for selection of the required file; in the middle, the canvas on which the SVG file is painted (here a bar chart sample); and at the bottom, a text area that reports the time of events in the display process. For the SVG displayed here, the total time taken was 501 milliseconds.

Display Process

The display process is made up of three steps:

1. **Loading**—This is the process of parsing an SVG file and constructing a DOM tree from the elements encountered.

2. **Building**—The next step takes the DOM tree and builds a GVT (Graphics Vector Toolkit) tree from it. The GVT is really a view of the DOM used within Batik from which an image can be constructed.

3. **Rendering**—In this step, the image itself is constructed from the GVT.

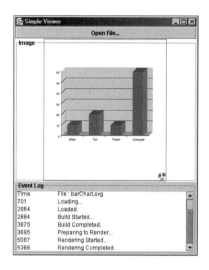

FIGURE 17.1   Our viewer in action.

Viewer Source Code

Thanks to Batik, we can build our viewer in a single Java file (see Listing 17.1). The imports needed for this application are a selection of standard Java classes, the JSVGCanvas class itself, and the event and listener classes used to track the display process.

LISTING 17.1   SimpleViewer.java—SVG Viewer Source

```
import java.awt.*;
import java.awt.event.*;
import java.util.*;
import java.io.*;
import javax.swing.*;

import org.apache.batik.swing.JSVGCanvas;

import org.apache.batik.swing.svg.SVGDocumentLoaderListener;
import org.apache.batik.swing.svg.SVGDocumentLoaderEvent;
import org.apache.batik.swing.svg.GVTTreeBuilderListener;
import org.apache.batik.swing.svg.GVTTreeBuilderEvent;
import org.apache.batik.swing.gvt.GVTTreeRendererListener;
import org.apache.batik.swing.gvt.GVTTreeRendererEvent;
```

The class implements the ActionListener interface because we are going to use it to respond to button clicks. The other listener interfaces correspond to the three stages of the display process. In the member variables, we have a JFrame, which is used to create the application window; a JPanel, which will house our components; and the JSVGCanvas object, which we'll use to display SVG. The time at which the display process started will be recorded in the startTime long integer. The main() method acts as an entry point into the application, simply creating a new instance of the SimpleViewer class:

```
public class SimpleViewer
    implements ActionListener, SVGDocumentLoaderListener,
        GVTTreeBuilderListener, GVTTreeRendererListener {

    private JFrame frame;
    private JPanel panel;
    private JTextArea textArea;
    private JSVGCanvas svgCanvas;
    private long startTime;

    public static void main(String[] args) {
        new SimpleViewer();
    }
```

The code in the class constructor is mostly composed of typical GUI construction operations, although the SVGCanvas object has extra listeners added, all the methods of which will be implemented by this class:

```
public SimpleViewer() {

    // construct the application window
    frame = new JFrame("Simple Viewer");

    // create the button and give it a listener
    JButton button = new JButton("Open File...");
    button.addActionListener(this);

    // create the log text area, make it scrollable and give it a pretty border
    textArea = new JTextArea();
    JScrollPane scrollPane = new JScrollPane(textArea);
    scrollPane.setPreferredSize(new Dimension(250, 150));
    scrollPane.setBorder(BorderFactory.createTitledBorder("Event Log"));

    // create the SVG area, and give that a pretty border
    svgCanvas = new JSVGCanvas();
    svgCanvas.setBorder(BorderFactory.createTitledBorder("Image"));

    // add the display process listeners
```

```
    svgCanvas.addSVGDocumentLoaderListener(this);
    svgCanvas.addGVTTreeBuilderListener(this);
    svgCanvas.addGVTTreeRendererListener(this);

    // create the panel and place the components on it
    panel = new JPanel(new BorderLayout());
    panel.add("North", button);
    panel.add("Center", svgCanvas);
    panel.add("South", scrollPane);

    // put the panel in the app frame, and set up the frame
    frame.getContentPane().add(panel);
    frame.addWindowListener(new WindowAdapter() {
        public void windowClosing(WindowEvent exception) {
            System.exit(0);
        }
    });
    frame.setSize(400, 500);
    frame.setVisible(true);
}
```

When the user clicks on the Open File button, the `actionPerformed` method will be called. This action invokes a standard `Swing` dialog component (`JFileChooser`), which will allow the user to select the file he or she wants to view. After a file is selected, its path and name will be converted to a URI, which is passed the `setURI()` method. This will cause `JSVGCanvas` to start the display process, so prior to this, a note is taken of the time, and a string is sent to the `logEvent()` method, which will show the filename in the event log text area:

```
// ActionListener method - responds to mouse clicks
public void actionPerformed(ActionEvent ae) {
    JFileChooser filechooser = new JFileChooser();
    int choice = filechooser.showOpenDialog(panel);
    if (choice == JFileChooser.APPROVE_OPTION) {
        File file = filechooser.getSelectedFile();
        try {
            startTime = System.currentTimeMillis();
            logEvent("\nTime\tFile : " + file.getName());
            svgCanvas.setURI(file.toURL().toString());
        } catch (IOException exception) {
            logEvent(exception.toString());
            exception.printStackTrace();
        }
```

```
        }
}
```

The `logEvent()` method simply appends the time since the `startTime` was set and whatever string it has been sent to the text area:

```
private void logEvent(String string) {
    textArea.append("\n"
        + (System.currentTimeMillis() - startTime) + "\t" + string);
}
```

Finally, we have the methods that will be called as `JSVGCanvas` goes through its display process. Whenever one of these methods is called, it will pass an appropriate text message to the event log:

```
// SVGDocumentLoaderListener methods
public void documentLoadingStarted(SVGDocumentLoaderEvent exception) {
    logEvent("Loading...");
}
public void documentLoadingCompleted(SVGDocumentLoaderEvent exception) {
    logEvent("Loaded.");
}

public void documentLoadingCancelled(SVGDocumentLoaderEvent exception) {
    logEvent("Loading Cancelled.");
}

public void documentLoadingFailed(SVGDocumentLoaderEvent exception) {
    logEvent("Loading Failed.");
}

// GVTTreeBuilderListener methods
public void gvtBuildStarted(GVTTreeBuilderEvent exception) {
    logEvent("Build Started...");
}
public void gvtBuildCompleted(GVTTreeBuilderEvent exception) {
    logEvent("Build Completed.");
}

public void gvtBuildCancelled(GVTTreeBuilderEvent exception) {
    logEvent("Build Cancelled");
}

public void gvtBuildFailed(GVTTreeBuilderEvent exception) {
    logEvent("Build Failed");
```

```
    }

    // GVTTreeRendererListener methods
    public void gvtRenderingPrepare(GVTTreeRendererEvent exception) {
        logEvent("Preparing to Render...");
    }

    public void gvtRenderingStarted(GVTTreeRendererEvent exception) {
        logEvent("Rendering Started...");
    }

    public void gvtRenderingCompleted(GVTTreeRendererEvent exception) {
        logEvent("Rendering Completed.");
    }

    public void gvtRenderingCancelled(GVTTreeRendererEvent exception) {
        logEvent("Rendering Cancelled.");
    }

    public void gvtRenderingFailed(GVTTreeRendererEvent exception) {
        logEvent("Rendering Failed.");
    }
```

Compiling and Running the Example

To compile and run the example we've been creating, and any code in this chapter (available from the Sams Web site), you need to have Java 2 Standard Edition installed (see http://java.sun.com for details). Batik comes as a zipped set of compiled libraries (along with source and documentation), so installation is simply a matter of unzipping to a convenient directory. It is advisable to obtain recent versions of Java and Batik; at the time of writing, the latest full releases are J2SE 1.4 and Batik 1.5.

The Java compiler (javac) and bytecode runner (java or javaw) need to see the Batik library files, of which there are many (although individual applications are unlikely to need all of them). One convenient way to compile and run applications is through batch files or scripts. On Windows machines, we can use a utility batch file like the one in Listing 17.2 to prepare a couple of system variables to make life easier.

LISTING 17.2   set_variables.bat—Batch File to Set classpath

```
ECHO OFF
SET JBIN=C:\java\jdk\bin
SET BL=C:\batik\batik-1.5\lib

SET BC=%BL%\batik-awt-util.jar;%BL%\batik-bridge.jar;%BL%\batik-css.jar;
```

LISTING 17.2   Continued

```
➥%BL%\batik-dom.jar;%BL%\batik-ext.jar;%BL%\batik-extension.jar;
➥%BL%\batik-gui-util.jar;%BL%\batik-gvt.jar;%BL%\batik-parser.jar;
➥%BL%\batik-script.jar;%BL%\batik-svg-dom.jar;%BL%\batik-svggen.jar;
➥%BL%\batik-transcoder.jar;%BL%\batik-util.jar;%BL%\batik-xml.jar;
➥%BL%\crimson-parser.jar;%BL%\js.jar;%BL%\batik-swing.jar
ECHO ON
```

To use Listing 17.2 on your machine, change the directory description passed to `JBIN` to reflect the location of the `\bin` directory of J2SE, and `BL` to that of the Batik `\lib` directory. You can then compile the preceding code by running Listing 17.3 (this and `set_variables.bat` should be in the same directory as the source file).

LISTING 17.3   compile_sv.bat

```
CALL set_variables
%JBIN%\javac -classpath .;%BC% SimpleViewer.java
```

You can run the application by using a similar batch file (see Listing 17.4).

LISTING 17.4   run_simpleviewer.bat

```
CALL set_variables
%JBIN%\java -classpath .;%BC% SimpleViewer
```

All being well, Listing 17.4 will launch the application, and clicking the Open File button will allow you to choose a file to view. Batik comes with a handful of SVG examples (in the `\samples` directory), and it is interesting to compare the time taken for each stage of processing with the complexity of the SVG.

Generating SVG with a Java Application

The ability to display SVG in Java has its uses, but probably your first requirement as a Java developer is to get your application to generate SVG. Using Batik, you can do so in two main ways: using the SVG Generator (`SVGGraphics2D`) and using the SVG DOM.

When you use the first method—which, for want of a better word, is "shallow"—the generator is normally sent a completely drawn `Swing` object, and it pumps out a complete SVG representation of this object. This approach is eminently suitable for tagging onto existing applications. The code needed to use the generator is minimal, and the only other step required is to add the necessary user interface (such as an Export to SVG menu item) and use it to pick up the object to draw and pass it to the generator.

Using the SVG DOM is a more versatile approach to generation. We can build up a DOM tree element by element in whatever programmatic manner we want. This allows us to construct SVG closer to the core operations of an application, and so could be called a "deep" approach. We will cover the Java SVG DOM in Chapter 19.

Using the SVG Generator

Within Java, the key to graphics is, predictably, the Graphics class. This class allows drawing of basic shapes, but an extension of this class, Graphics2D, goes much further, allowing sophisticated control over the creation of two-dimensional forms. Both of these classes are abstract and represent a context in which drawing can take place. Instances of objects that implement Graphics or Graphics2D are normally created by a Swing component or obtained from image objects. Within Java2D, various different graphical classes approximately correspond to the primitives of SVG—line (Line2D), rect (Rectangle2D), path (GeneralPath), and so on. These classes have member variables that correspond, again approximately, to the attributes found in SVG elements. The following sample Java code could be used to draw a filled-in red circle:

```
Shape ellipse = new Ellipse2D.Float(50, 50, 100, 100);
graphics2D.setPaint(Color.red);
graphic2D.fill(ellipse);
```

A Shape object is created—here, an instance of Ellipse2D.Float—based on the given parameters. The graphics context has its paint color set, and then calling the fill method causes the shape to be drawn in the Graphics2D context, which would normally mean on the surface of a component such as Canvas or JPanel.

> **NOTE**
>
> Most of the Java2D shapes come in two flavors, one specified using normal floating-point numerical precision, and another double-precision, such as Line2D.Float and Line2D.Double. Under most circumstances, it doesn't make much difference which you use, although it is a good idea to pick a level of precision and stick to it.

You may be wondering what this all has to do with the SVG Generator. The answer is...everything. The SVG Generator, SVGGraphics2D, is an implementation of the Graphics2D abstract class, which we can substitute wherever we might have used a Graphics2D context referring to a component. This internally builds an SVG DOM representation, which we can serialize out via the SVGGraphics2D object when required. This process is all done as if by magic; we only have to think about getting the Java2D right. In Listing 17.5, we use an SVG Generator to create a simple SVG file.

LISTING 17.5   SimpleSVGGen.java

```
import java.awt.*;
import java.awt.geom.*;
```

LISTING 17.5 Continued

```java
import java.io.*;

import org.w3c.dom.Document;
import org.w3c.dom.DOMImplementation;

import org.apache.batik.svggen.SVGGraphics2D;
import org.apache.batik.dom.GenericDOMImplementation;


public class SimpleSVGGen {

    public static void main(String[] args) {

        // Get a DOMImplementation
        DOMImplementation domImpl =
            GenericDOMImplementation.getDOMImplementation();

        // Create a SVG DOM Document
        Document document = domImpl.createDocument(null, "svg", null);

        // Create an instance of the SVG Generator
        SVGGraphics2D svgGenerator = new SVGGraphics2D(document);

        // Create a Java2D shape
        Shape ellipse = new Ellipse2D.Float(50, 50, 100, 100);

        // Render into the SVG Graphics2D implementation
        svgGenerator.setPaint(Color.red);
        svgGenerator.fill(ellipse);

        // Stream out SVG to the named file
        try {
            svgGenerator.stream("generated.svg");
        } catch (IOException exception) {
            exception.printStackTrace();
        }
    }
}
```

Listing 17.5 begins as usual with the package imports, including imports of standard Java 2 packages for the Java2D classes, and file input/output. Next, we have the interfaces defined in the Java binding part of the SVG specification: the DOM Document and

DOMImplementation, which is a factory for DOM documents. The last two imports refer to the Batik Toolkit: the SVGGraphics2D class in question and GenericDOMImplementation, which is an implementation of the (questionably named) DOMImplementation interface.

The code proper starts with the creation of domImpl, an object factory that is subsequently used to create an instance of a DOM document. The two null parameters correspond to namespace and DOCTYPE, neither of which is needed here, as supplying "svg" for the qualified name is enough to get us an instance of an SVG DOM document. This document is used to create an SVGGraphics2D object. This construction sums up the elegant conceptual core of the SVG Generator: Rather than having a Swing component to draw on, we have a DOM document.

The ellipse is created and then rendered to the SVGGraphics2D object—drawn on the SVG DOM. The developers of Batik have added convenience to elegance by providing the SVG Generator with a simple method (stream) that will stream the SVG out to the named file. The stream may cause an I/O exception, so it needs to be contained in a try-catch block. The whole of this program is within the main() method, so the program has an entry point.

If you compile and run the code (you can use batch files like those you saw earlier), you will find a new file, generated.svg, in the same directory.

Opened in a viewer, this file looks like Figure 17.2.

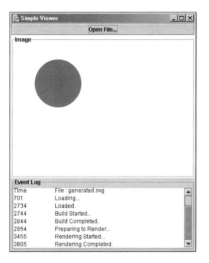

FIGURE 17.2   Generated SVG in viewer.

The generated SVG looks like Listing 17.6.

LISTING 17.6   generated.svg

```
<?xml version="1.0" encoding="ISO-8859-1"?>
<!DOCTYPE svg PUBLIC '-//W3C//DTD SVG 1.0//EN'
```

LISTING 17.6   Continued

```
   'http://www.w3.org/TR/2001/REC-SVG-20010904/DTD/svg10.dtd'>
<svg fill-opacity="1" xmlns:xlink="http://www.w3.org/1999/xlink"
    color-rendering="auto" color-interpolation="auto" text-rendering="auto"
    stroke="black" stroke-linecap="square" stroke-miterlimit="10"
    shape-rendering="auto" stroke-opacity="1" fill="black"
    stroke-dasharray="none" font-weight="normal" stroke-width="1"
    xmlns="http://www.w3.org/2000/svg" font-family="&apos;dialog&apos;"
    font-style="normal" stroke-linejoin="miter" font-size="12"
    stroke-dashoffset="0" image-rendering="auto">
  <!--Generated by the Batik Graphics2D SVG Generator-->
  <defs id="genericDefs" />
  <g>
    <g fill="red" stroke="red">
      <circle r="50" cx="100" cy="100" stroke="none" />
    </g>
  </g>
</svg>
```

As you can see, the SVG Generator has left no property unstyled, but following this, the drawing code itself is clear.

For comparison, here are the relevant Java2D statements again:

```
Shape ellipse = new Ellipse2D.Float(50, 50, 100, 100);
svgGenerator.setPaint(Color.red);
svgGenerator.fill(ellipse);
```

Notice that the Java2D ellipse was specified using four parameters: x-position, y-position, width, and height. The x and y coordinates refer to the top-left corner of a rectangle that would enclose the ellipse, and the width and height values give its dimensions. Ellipse2D belongs to a set of Java2D shapes that extend the RectangularShape class; these shapes are defined in terms of an enclosing rectangle. SVG, on the other hand, views ellipses in terms of the position of the center and radii in the x and y directions. In the case of the preceding code, Batik recognizes that the width and height (corresponding to the rx and ry attributes of the enclosing ellipse) are equal and produce an SVG circle element. The radius is, of course, half the value of the dimensions of the enclosing rectangle (actually a square in this case). Though this mapping between the Java2D representation of shapes and their SVG equivalents can seem a little awkward at times, this is as bad as it gets. If you are drawing with Java2D and use the SVG Generator (with one reservation we will come to later), you can forget about the details of the SVG and let Batik do its magic.

Do-It-Yourself Objects

The example from the preceding section shows how the SVG generator can be used to generate SVG from Java2D objects. However, the real benefits of an object-oriented language like Java start to kick in only when more complex systems are required, and a starting point for desktop applications is interactivity.

Interactive Graphic Java

We have already seen a little interaction, with the button click for loading images in the viewer application. The following example will demonstrate how interactions can be extended to graphical elements. The application will allow us to find the coordinates of points on an image and export an SVG representation of these points. Potential uses for such interactivity might include taking measurements from charts or perhaps easing the pain of babysitting by providing dot-to-dot pictures for children to connect.

The application has a drawing area in the center and a button at the top that allows an image to be loaded as the background to the drawing area. Clicking in the drawing area results in a cross being marked at the mouse pointer's location, along with a reference number and the coordinates of the point (see Figure 17.3). Right-clicking on the drawing area will remove all the points. A button below the drawing area will allow the contents of the drawing area (without the background) to be exported as SVG.

FIGURE 17.3   Point Marker application.

Application Classes

This application is built from five Java source files, which contain the following classes:

- `PointMarkerApp`—This class builds the application window and the components it contains, and also looks after user interaction with the buttons.

- `LocatorMouseListener`—This is actually an inner class of `PointMarkerApp`, which handles interaction with the drawing area.

- `ImagePanel`—An instance of this component will hold the background image.

- `LocatorScreen`—This class contains the points marked over the image.

- `PointLocator`—Each point marked on the screen is an instance of this class, which holds the coordinates of the point and also renders the Java2D representation (a labeled cross).

- `SVGWriter`—This class renders the SVG to a file.

Starting with the simplest class, in Listing 17.7 we have the source for the `ImagePanel` class.

LISTING 17.7   ImagePanel.java

```java
package com.sams.swingsvg;

import java.awt.*;
import javax.swing.*;

public class ImagePanel extends JPanel {

    private Image image;

    public void setImage(Image image) {
        this.image = image;
    }

    public void paintComponent(Graphics graphics) {
        super.paintComponent(graphics);
        if (image != null) {
            graphics.drawImage(image, 0, 0, this);
        }
    }
}
```

So that we can keep things organized, all the classes in this application go in the com\sams\swingsvg directory, which corresponds to com.sams.swingsvg package, as in the first line of Listing 17.7. The ImagePanel is an extension of the standard JPanel container component onto which an Image object can be drawn. The setImage() method gives an instance of this class its image. The paintComponent() method first calls the same method of its superclass (JPanel) to render any visual characteristics given there and then proceeds to render the image.

> **NOTE**
>
> The paintComponent() method is called as part of a JComponent's rendering process, and by overriding this method, we can add any custom drawing we like. If we want visual aspects of the parent component to be drawn (for instance, to paint a background), we use the super.paintComponent() call.

The image (if one exists—it is possible to mark points on a blank screen) will be drawn at point (0,0) on this panel, with the last parameter given to drawImage() being an ImageObserver (here, this is the container JPanel component) to notify of drawing progress.

Containing the Objects

The LocatorScreen class, shown in Listing 17.8, is another extension of a standard Swing class—in this case, JComponent. It acts as a store for the graphical points onscreen (here called locators), which it keeps as objects in an ArrayList, and will draw them when it is asked to paint itself.

LISTING 17.8   LocatorScreen.java

```java
package com.sams.swingsvg;

import java.awt.*;
import java.awt.geom.*;
import javax.swing.*;

import java.util.*;

public class LocatorScreen extends JComponent {

    java.util.List locators = new ArrayList();

    public void addLocator(PointLocator locator) {
        locators.add(locator);
        repaint();
    }

    public int getCount(){
        return locators.size();
    }

    public void clear() {
        locators.clear();
```

LISTING 17.8   Continued

```
        repaint();
    }

    public void paintComponent(Graphics graphics) {
        super.paintComponent(graphics);
        Graphics2D graphics2D = (Graphics2D) graphics;
        graphics2D.setRenderingHint(RenderingHints.KEY_ANTIALIASING,
            RenderingHints.VALUE_ANTIALIAS_ON);
        PointLocator locator;
        for (int i = 0; i < locators.size(); i++) {
            locator = (PointLocator) locators.get(i);
            locator.draw(graphics2D);
        }
    }
}
```

The LocatorScreen class in Listing 17.8 has a method for adding the locator objects, which pass them to the ArrayList locators and then call its superclass's repaint() method to make sure the new point gets drawn. We will discuss the representation of the points in a moment; all we (and this class) need to know right now is that the locator objects have a draw() method. When this component is called upon to draw itself, the paintComponent() method is called, and it runs through the contents of the locators List, calling the draw() method of each PointLocator object in turn. Before drawing, the graphics object is cast into a Graphics2D object, and a rendering hint is suggested to improve the appearance of the painted cross. The getCount() method returns the number of locators contained in the List, and the clear() method removes them all. Each of these methods calls the repaint() method of the JComponent superclass, which will in turn call paintComponent(), and this will update the view to reflect the change in the list's contents.

Now we come to the representation of points onscreen, our locator objects. We want a cross at each point and some text nearby. Such an item could be represented in various different ways—there is the abstract idea of a point in 2D space, the associated text, and the way in which they should be rendered. For more complex items, it would make sense to keep the visual representation separate from the abstract model, and for something like this, possibly even the point separate from associated text. Here, things are simple enough that we can lump everything about the locator together, so it knows its x and y coordinates, its text, and also how to draw itself.

Listing 17.9 begins with three constants for the "view" representation: the size of the cross to be drawn (its radius), the stroke to be used, and the color. The path variable will contain the cross object to draw. The other three member variables—x, y, and text—make up the "model" of the point locator. The values of the x, y, and text variables are set using a couple of trivial methods. The draw() method receives a Graphics2D object, onto which the cross and text will be rendered. The path itself is a `GeneralPath` object and consists of two lines, specified using two `moveTo()` and `lineTo()` calls. The color and stroke of subsequent drawing operations are then specified, and the cross drawn. Note that the draw method on each object may be called many times, and to avoid accumulating move/line elements, the `GeneralPath` object is created afresh within this method on every call.

When text is drawn with Java2D using the `drawString(text, x, y)` method, the x and y refer to the baseline of the first character, so a little adjustment is needed to get the label in a good position relative to the cross. The graphics context includes a `FontMetrics` object from which it is possible to obtain dimensional information about the current font (in this case, the default). The adjustment is calculated, and finally the text is drawn.

LISTING 17.9   PointLocator.java

```java
package com.sams.swingsvg;

import java.awt.*;
import java.awt.geom.*;

public class PointLocator {

    public final static int crossSize = 3;
    public final Stroke stroke = new BasicStroke(2);
    public final Color color = Color.red;

    private GeneralPath path;

    private int x;
    private int y;
    private String text;

    public void setLocation(int x, int y) {
        this.x = x;
        this.y = y;
    }

    public void setText(String text) {
        this.text = text;
    }


    public void draw(Graphics2D graphics2D) {
```

LISTING 17.9   Continued

```
        path = new GeneralPath();

        // trace the path of the cross
        path.moveTo(x - crossSize, y - crossSize); // north-west
        path.lineTo(x + crossSize, y + crossSize); // south-east
        path.moveTo(x - crossSize, y + crossSize); // south-west
        path.lineTo(x + crossSize, y - crossSize); // north-east

        // draw the cross
        graphics2D.setPaint(color);
        graphics2D.setStroke(stroke);
        graphics2D.draw(path);

        // tweak text position
        FontMetrics metrics = graphics2D.getFontMetrics();
        int widthOffset = -metrics.stringWidth(text) / 2;
        int heightOffset =
    4 * crossSize + metrics.getHeight() / 2 - metrics.getMaxDescent();

        // draw the text
        graphics2D.drawString(text, x + widthOffset, y + heightOffset);
    }
}
```

The main application class (PointMarkerApp) that ties everything together is quite long, so we'll look at it in chunks (Listing 17.10 is the first part of this code; the rest of it is broken up with discussion so that it's easy to follow). After the imports, the class definition shows that the class will implement the ActionListener interface, which will allow us to capture button clicks with this class. The member variables include the application window (frame); a JPanel to contain the drawing area and two buttons (panel); the background image (image); and the panel (imagePanel) that will contain it. We also have a Swing file chooser object (fileChooser), which will look after the Load and Save File dialogs. Lastly, there is the text (title) to go in the title bar of the application window. Once again, we use the main() method to create a new instance of the application class to get things started.

LISTING 17.10   PointMarkerApp.java

```
package com.sams.swingsvg;

import java.awt.*;
import java.awt.event.*;
import javax.swing.*;
```

LISTING 17.10   Continued

```java
import javax.swing.event.*;
import java.util.*;
import java.io.*;

public class PointMarkerApp implements ActionListener {

    private JFrame frame;
    private JPanel panel;
    private Image image;
    private final JFileChooser fileChooser;
    private LocatorScreen locatorScreen;
    private ImagePanel imagePanel;
    private final String title = "Point Marker";

    public static void main(String args[]) {
        new PointMarkerApp();
    }
}
```

The class constructor creates all the visual components and glues them together. This is very much standard Swing code. The method calls on instances of our custom LocatorScreen and ImagePanel objects will be handled by their Swing superclasses (JComponent and JPanel, respectively):

```java
public PointMarkerApp() {

    // prepare a file selector dialog
    fileChooser = new JFileChooser();

    // set up the component panel
    panel = new JPanel();
    panel.setLayout(new BorderLayout());
    panel.setPreferredSize(new Dimension(300, 250));

    // create and add the load button
    JButton loadButton = new JButton("Load Image");
    loadButton.addActionListener(this);
    panel.add(loadButton, BorderLayout.NORTH);

    // create and add the save button
    JButton saveButton = new JButton("Save SVG");
    saveButton.addActionListener(this);
    panel.add(saveButton, BorderLayout.SOUTH);
```

17

```
    // create and add the image component
    imagePanel = new ImagePanel();
    imagePanel.setBackground(Color.white);
    panel.add(imagePanel, BorderLayout.CENTER);

    // create the drawing component
    locatorScreen = new LocatorScreen();
    locatorScreen.setPreferredSize(new Dimension(300, 300));
    locatorScreen.setBackground(Color.white);

    // listen for clicks
    locatorScreen.addMouseListener(new LocatorMouseListener());

    // put the drawing component on top of the image component
    imagePanel.add(locatorScreen, BorderLayout.CENTER);

    // build and show the app window
    frame = new JFrame(title);
    frame.getContentPane().add(panel);
    frame.addWindowListener(new WindowAdapter() {
        public void windowClosing(WindowEvent event) {
            System.exit(0);
        }
    });
    frame.pack();
    frame.setVisible(true);
}
```

This class implements `ActionListener`, which demands an `actionPerformed()` method. As a listener, the instance of this class has been passed to the two buttons on our application window, and clicking either of them will cause the following method to be called. The `ActionEvent` object passed to the method is aware of the source of the action, and by default, the action command of a button is its label, so here we use this information to decide which of two other methods to call:

```
public void actionPerformed(ActionEvent event) {

    if (event.getActionCommand().equals("Save SVG")) {
        exportFile();
    }
    if (event.getActionCommand().equals("Load Image")) {
        loadImage();
    }
}
```

The next method first uses the file chooser created in the constructor to make an Open File dialog box to get a file path and name from the user. The Toolkit referred to is actually the superclass of the Abstract Windows Toolkit (AWT), which is very rarely used directly, but here one of its utility methods is called to load an image from the file. The image object is then passed to the imagePanel, which is repainted to make the image visible:

```
private void loadImage() {

    int returnVal = fileChooser.showOpenDialog(frame);

    if (returnVal == JFileChooser.APPROVE_OPTION) {
        Toolkit toolkit = Toolkit.getDefaultToolkit();
        File imageFile = fileChooser.getSelectedFile();
        try {
            image = toolkit.getImage(imageFile.toURL());
        } catch (Exception exception) {
            exception.printStackTrace();
        }
        imagePanel.setImage(image);
        imagePanel.repaint();
    }
}
```

The exportFile() method, which will save the SVG representation, also uses the file chooser, this time for a Save File type dialog box. The core code behind the file-saving process is essentially the same as that we saw in the simple SVG Generator example earlier, but generalized out into a separate class (SVGWriter). As we will see in a moment, this class requires a Writer object to know where to stream the data, and here we create a buffered writer for this purpose. This approach is somewhat more complicated than simply calling SVGGraphics2D.stream(*filename*), but allows a lot more control over the operation. In this case, for example, we specify the encoding to use as UTF-8. As well as a target Writer, the SVGWriter also needs to know what to render into SVG, and here we pass it the locatorScreen component, which will contain the locator points:

```
private void exportFile() {
    int returnVal = fileChooser.showSaveDialog(frame);

    if (returnVal == JFileChooser.APPROVE_OPTION) {
        Writer writer = null;
        try {
            OutputStream fileOutputStream
                = new FileOutputStream(fileChooser.getSelectedFile());
            writer =
 new BufferedWriter(new OutputStreamWriter(fileOutputStream, "UTF-8"));
```

```
    } catch (Exception event) {
        event.printStackTrace();
    }
    SVGWriter svgWriter = new SVGWriter();
    svgWriter.setComment(title);

    svgWriter.write(locatorScreen, writer);
    }
}
```

The code that deals with mouse clicks on the drawing screen is straightforward. We have only two kinds of events to consider: right-clicks to clear the screen and left-clicks to add a point. The listener is set up as an inner class, so we can take advantage of the MouseInputAdapter class, which includes dummy methods to implement all the listener interfaces corresponding to mouse actions: mouseDragged(), mouseReleased(), and so on. A utility method is used to catch the right-clicks, and the locatorScreen is asked to clear itself. For any other click, a new PointLocator is constructed and given the coordinates that came along with the mouse event. Text is then put together from the count of objects onscreen and the coordinates, and this too is passed to the PointLocator. This object is then added to the locatorScreen, and a call to the underlying panel is made so that the whole screen gets refreshed:

```
class LocatorMouseListener extends MouseInputAdapter {
    public void mouseClicked(MouseEvent event) {
        if (SwingUtilities.isRightMouseButton(event)) {
            locatorScreen.clear();
            return;
        }
        PointLocator locator = new PointLocator();
        locator.setLocation(event.getX(), event.getY());
        String label
        = (locatorScreen.getCount() + 1)
            + "  (" + event.getX() + "," + event.getY() + ")";
        locator.setText(label);
        locatorScreen.addLocator(locator);
        panel.repaint();
    }
}
}
```

Render Unto SVG...

The remaining class is used to create the SVG serialization of any Swing container component. In this application, the code in the preceding section will pass the locatorScreen component, along with a file writer to act as a destination for the stream of data. Once again, things look a lot more complicated than the Java2D-to-SVG code we saw earlier in `SimpleSVGGen`, shown in Listing 17.5. One reason is that it is good practice to encapsulate behavior like this to make a reusable class. Another (which accounts for the extra code) is that we are using `Swing` in this application, and `Swing` isn't thread-safe. In the earlier GUI-less example, it was reasonable to do the file writing in the main application thread. In this application, however, we want the file save to occur as the result of a mouse-click. Though file saving shouldn't take long, it certainly isn't instantaneous, and delays here would cause problems with the redrawing of the application window. A half-pressed button isn't a very inspiring sight. The answer to this problem is simple: We spark up another thread, the sole purpose of which is to write the data to a stream. When the appropriate method is called to stream a file, a new thread is created, and the method returns almost immediately. This way, the `Swing` GUI can flow along smoothly, with the streaming happening in the background.

Listing 17.11 begins with the imports, including those we saw earlier from Batik. A `Container` and `Writer` are declared as member variables because we need them to be available to different methods. A string `comment` will hold the text that will end up in the generated stream, to show the providence of the SVG. In the class constructor, we create an SVG DOM document as we did before so that the Java2D rendering will take place. Here, we use a two-parameter constructor, which can be used to specify whether text from the Java2D should be rendered as SVG `text` elements or drawn as SVG paths. In Listing 17.11, the boolean value is declared as a constant `TEXT_AS_SHAPES`, though for more flexibility `get`/`set` methods could easily be added.

LISTING 17.11   SVGWriter.java

```
package com.sams.swingsvg;

import java.awt.*;
import java.io.*;

import org.apache.batik.svggen.*;
import org.apache.batik.dom.GenericDOMImplementation;
import org.w3c.dom.Document;
import org.w3c.dom.DOMImplementation;

public class SVGWriter implements Runnable {

    private Container container;
    private Writer writer;
    private String comment;
    private SVGGraphics2D svgGenerator;
    private SVGGeneratorContext context;
```

LISTING 17.11   Continued

```
    private final boolean TEXT_AS_SHAPES = false;

    public SVGWriter() {
        DOMImplementation domImpl =
            GenericDOMImplementation.getDOMImplementation();
        Document document = domImpl.createDocument(null, "svg", null);
        context = SVGGeneratorContext.createDefault(document);
        svgGenerator = new SVGGraphics2D(context, TEXT_AS_SHAPES);
    }

    public void setComment(String comment) {
        context.setComment(comment);
    }
```

The setComment() method in Listing 17.11 replaces the default <!--Generated by the Batik Graphics2D SVG Generator--> comment. The SVGWriter class implements Runnable, and so must have a run() method like the following. It paints the Container object into the graphics context and then serializes the resulting data:

```
public void run() {
    container.paint(svgGenerator);
    try {
        svgGenerator.stream(writer);
        writer.close();
    } catch (Exception exception) {
        exception.printStackTrace();
    }
}
```

After an instance of this class is constructed, when we want to stream out some visuals, we call the write() method, which follows. It sets the container and writer variables and then creates a new Thread from this class definition. The thread's start() method is called, which causes the preceding run() method to be called on the new thread, that is, asynchronously.

```
    public void write(Container container, Writer writer) {
        this.container = container;
        this.writer = writer;
        Thread writeThread = new Thread(this);
        writeThread.start();
    }
}
```

Running the Application

We can compile and run the application using batch/script files like we saw earlier. However, note that the code is all in the package com.sams.swingsvg, so the java and javac commands must reflect this fact:

```
CALL set_variables
%JBIN%\javac -classpath .;%BC% com\sams\swingsvg\PointMarkerApp.java
```

and

```
CALL set_variables
%JBIN%\java -classpath .;%BC% com.sams.swingsvg.PointMarkerApp
```

Generated SVG

If we run the application now and click a few times on the screen (with or without loading a background image), and then click the Save SVG button, the file saved will have contents like those in Listing 17.12.

LISTING 17.12   points.svg—Sample Output from Point Marker

```
<?xml version="1.0"?>
<!DOCTYPE svg PUBLIC '-//W3C//DTD SVG 1.0//EN'
'http://www.w3.org/TR/2001/REC-SVG-20010904/DTD/svg10.dtd'>
<svg fill-opacity="1" xmlns:xlink="http://www.w3.org/1999/xlink"
    color-rendering="auto" color-interpolation="auto" text-rendering="auto"
    stroke="black" stroke-linecap="square" stroke-miterlimit="10"
    shape-rendering="auto" stroke-opacity="1" fill="black"
    stroke-dasharray="none" font-weight="normal" stroke-width="1"
    xmlns="http://www.w3.org/2000/svg" font-family="&apos;sansserif&apos;"
    font-style="normal" stroke-linejoin="miter" font-size="12"
    stroke-dashoffset="0" image-rendering="auto">
  <!--Point Marker-->
  <defs id="genericDefs" />
  <g>
    <defs id="defs1">
      <clipPath clipPathUnits="userSpaceOnUse" id="clipPath1">
        <path d="M0 0 L300 0 L300 300 L0 300 L0 0 Z" />
      </clipPath>
    </defs>
    <g fill="red" text-rendering="optimizeLegibility" font-family="sans-serif"
        shape-rendering="geometricPrecision" stroke="red" stroke-width="2">
      <path fill="none" d="M104 123 L110 129 M104 129 L110 123"
            clip-path="url(#clipPath1)" />
      <text xml:space="preserve" x="74" y="143" clip-path="url(#clipPath1)"
```

17

LISTING 17.12   Continued

```
          stroke="none">1   (107,126)</text>
      <path fill="none" d="M221 129 L227 135 M221 135 L227 129"
          clip-path="url(#clipPath1)" />
      <text xml:space="preserve" x="191" y="149" clip-path="url(#clipPath1)"
          stroke="none">2   (224,132)</text>
    </g>
  </g>
</svg>
```

The crosses and their associated text can be seen in the alternating `path` and `text` elements. Opening this file in a viewer will show something like Figure 17.4.

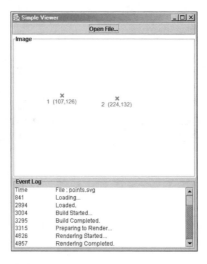

FIGURE 17.4   Viewing data saved from Point Marker.

Summary

Batik contains a set of powerful tools that allow SVG developers to concentrate more on what they want to create than the details of the creation process. This chapter provided an overview of the three sets of modules included in the Toolkit and examples of how two of these modules (`JSVGCanvas` and `SVGGraphics2D`) could be used to give a Java application basic SVG capabilities. These capabilities (viewing and exporting) are limited in being peripheral to the application itself. In Chapter 19, we'll look at SVG with server-side Java and examine the powerful SVG DOM. If you want SVG right in the core of your application (desktop or server), stay tuned.

PART III

Producing SVG
Server-Side

IN THIS PART

Server-Side Basics

In Part II of this book, we learned how to manipulate SVG with client-side scripts. Even more possibilities are offered with server-side scripting, as we'll learn throughout Part III.

However, before you start serving SVG files from your site, you need to understand MIME types and how browsers use them. You also have to configure your Web server for sending SVG files with the correct MIME type. Finally, we show you how to set the MIME type within server-side scripts with selected scripting languages.

MIME Types

Web servers send files, including SVG files, to requesting clients, which then try to display those files. For the clients, there must be a mechanism to identify which type of content arrives. The solution for this problem is to use the document's MIME type.

MIME stands for multipurpose Internet mail extensions. Originally, MIME was a definition to distinguish the media type of mail attachments in different formats.

You can find the MIME standard in RFC-2045 to RFC-2049 of the Internet Engineering Task Force (IETF) at http://www.ietf.org/. This organization maintains Internet standards. Another famous IETF standard (among many others) is the Hypertext Transfer Protocol (HTTP). MIME types are part of this protocol. That means a MIME type is sent in the HTTP stream, as illustrated in Figure 18.1.

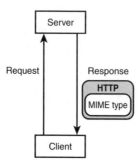

FIGURE 18.1   The client/server principle.

> **NOTE**
>
> HTTP 1.1 sends MIME information with the Accept statement of the requested object from the client to the server. This information describes which MIME types the client supports or accepts. The problem is that SVG is not one of the MIME types for which the actual browsers send this information. Therefore, you cannot use this method to check for SVG.

The SVG MIME type is `image/svg+xml`. It identifies SVG files for the browser.

> **NOTE**
>
> The W3C changed the SVG MIME type in the standardization phase. So, on many Web sites, you may find the older MIME type image/svg-xml, which was the actual MIME type before November 2, 2000.

The next section describes how current browsers handle the SVG MIME type.

Browsers and MIME Types

In some ways, using Internet Explorer and SVG is very simple: IE recognizes SVG in most cases. But the news is not all good: Older versions of IE do not use the MIME type as the first indicator. Instead, they use the file extension. This means that your SVG document can have the correct MIME type, but if it has the wrong extension, Internet Explorer 5.x and earlier will not display it correctly. Let's say a server-side Perl script generates SVG code. This script is executed by calling `http://servername/scriptname.pl`. Some IE versions now look at the extension .pl and think it's a Perl file, not an SVG file.

> **NOTE**
>
> Since version 4, Internet Explorer has used a technology called Moniker. This technology identifies the file type by examining the document data. You can find more information about it at the following site: http://msdn.microsoft.com/library/default.asp?url=/workshop/networking/moniker/overview/appendix_a.asp.

The best way to avoid this problem is to add the correct file extension .svg and the correct MIME type on your server.

An alternative is to add the extension .svg to the URL. This can be part of a link, such as `?IE=.svg`. (Note that this parameter is only a dummy.) We will use this technique in many examples in this part of the book. You'll recognize it when you see an URL that looks like this:

```
http://servername/scriptname.pl?IE=.svg.
```

`?IE=.svg` does not change the output of the script. However, Internet Explorer sees that the URL ends with .svg, thus taking .svg as a file extension and treating the results as they should be treated—as SVG files.

Netscape 4.x does check the MIME type, so there are no special "hacks" for this browser.

Netscape 6 supports SVG (with the Adobe SVG plug-in), but only when the MIME type is set correctly. Be careful; local files can be opened without the MIME type set, but files that are transferred via HTTP from the Web server must have the MIME type. In the next section, we will show you how to add the SVG MIME type to your Web server.

The SVG MIME type also must be set on the client. In Netscape, you can find it by opening Netscape, Preferences, Navigator, Applications. In the resulting dialog box, you should have an entry like this: SVG Document, MIME Type: `image/svg+xml`, Extension: `svg`, `svgz`, Handled by: Plugin SVG Plug In. Usually, the Adobe SVG plug-in makes this entry itself, but if that goes wrong, you can update these settings accordingly.

Mozilla (`www.mozilla.org`) has built-in SVG support. Note that not all builds that come from mozilla.org contain the SVG module; on the Windows platform, for instance, the latest Mozilla release build with SVG support is available for version 0.9.7.

Mozilla does not accept the normal SVG MIME type. Instead, it uses `text/xml` or `application/xml+xhtml`.

MIME Types on the Server

The browser needs the MIME type and gets that information from a server response. Therefore, you must activate the SVG MIME type on the server. In this section, we'll show you the procedure for the most popular Web servers, Apache and Microsoft Internet Information Server (IIS).

On Apache, activating the MIME type is easy; you can also activate it if your page or Web space is located on a host's server. You simply put an .htaccess file in the folder with your SVG files. To do so, you must add the following lines in the file:

```
AddType image/svg+xml svg
AddType image/svg+xml svgz
```

That's all there is to it; the SVG MIME type is now active.

If you want to include the SVG MIME type not only for one project, but for all webs on the server, simply edit the file named mime.types. You need to add the following line:

```
image/svg+xml    svg svgz
```

This line tells Apache to send the MIME type `image/svg+xml` with both file extensions .svg and .svgz.

With the Internet Information Server, part of Windows NT/2000/XP Professional, you cannot set MIME types in text files. Instead, you use the Internet Service Manager or Microsoft Management Console. You can find it by choosing Start, Settings, Control Panel. Depending on your version of Windows, you might first have to access the Administration section in the Control Panel (starting with Windows 2000).

If you want to add the MIME type only for one special Web application, follow these steps:

1. Start the Internet Service Manager or, on other operating systems, the Microsoft Management Console.

2. Right-click the Web site you want to configure for SVG (on a fresh install, there is only one entry, Default Web Site), and select Properties.

3. When the Default Web Site Properties dialog box opens, change to the HTTP Headers tab.

4. Click on File Types.

5. Click on New Type to create a new entry.

6. In the File Type dialog box, enter **.svg** as the extension and **image/svg+xml** as the MIME type.

7. Repeat step 6 to add the extension **.svgz** and MIME type **image/svg+xml**.

If, however, you want to register the MIME type for SVG for all Web sites that are running under your IIS, complete the following steps:

1. Start the Internet Service Manager.

2. Right-click the computer name and choose Properties.

3. Choose Edit.

4. Click on New Type to create two new mappings. In the File Type dialog box, enter the extension **.svg** and the MIME type **image/svg+xml** for one, and create another with the extension **.svgz** and MIME type **image/svg+xml**.

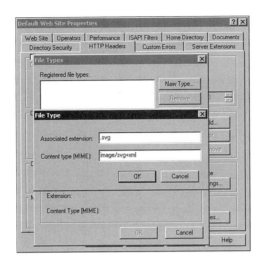

FIGURE 18.2   Configuring the IIS.

Finally, if you are using a non-server version of Microsoft Windows, especially Windows 95, 98, or Me, you might be using Microsoft's Personal Web Server (PWS). It is the little brother of IIS and does not have much functionality (basically, it provides ASP support). In particular, you cannot add MIME types within the server administration console. Instead, you must register the MIME types system-wide.

To register them, launch Windows Explorer and select Tools, Folder Options, File Types (on older versions of Windows Explorer, you access this dialog box by choosing View, Options, File Types). Click on New (or New Type on older versions) and create new mappings for extensions .svg and .svgz, both with the content type (MIME) image/svg+xml.

SVG with the Most Important Scripting Languages

After you complete the necessary steps to prepare your Web site for SVG files, all data served from your server that bears the extension .svg will have the correct MIME type, satisfying the client browser (if the plug-in is installed, obviously). However, when you're generating SVG files on the server side, as we will do in the next few chapters, you need to set the MIME type by hand. In this section, we will show you how to achieve this with some of the most popular scripting languages.

To test these scripts in your browser, call the scripts and append ?IE=.svg to the URL to trick older Internet Explorer versions into handling the results as actual SVG files (for example, http://servername/scriptname.ext?IE=.svg). However, note that some browsers do not like to show SVG files as the top document in the browser but require an

18

HTML file that contains an `<embed>` element (`<object>` is not supported by Netscape 4.x and earlier) that references the script:

```
<html>
<head>
<title>SVG serverside</title>
</head>
<body>
<embed width="100" height="100" type="image/svg+xml"
       src="/path/to/script/name.ext?IE=.svg"></embed>
</body>
</html>
```

The respective server-side scripting language must already be correctly set up on your system; just pick the language of your choice.

PHP

When you're using PHP, the most important step is to set the correct MIME type. You can do so by using the `header()` function, which must be called before the first text output is sent to the client:

```
header("Content-type: image/svg+xml");
```

But there is another issue. Look at the first line of an XML document—and therefore the first line of an SVG file, too:

```
<?xml version="1.0" ?>
```

In PHP—depending on the settings in the global configuration file php.ini—`<?` starts PHP code; PHP tends to think that `<?` starts some PHP code, which in this case would lead to a syntax error. So you either have to deactivate the short open tags (`<?`) for PHP commands in php.ini or write the first line of the SVG file using PHP's `echo()` function:

```
echo('<?xml version="1.0"?>');
```

Here is a complete script:

```
<?php
  header("Content-type: image/svg+xml");
  echo('<?xml version="1.0"?>');
?>
<svg width="100px" height="20px">
  <text x="10" y="20">SVG serverside</text>
</svg>
```

> **NOTE**
>
> Currently, some extensions for creating SVG from PHP are in development; however, only one of them has made it into PEAR (the PHP Extension and Application Repository, http://pear.php.net/) so far (converting graphics into SVG code).

ASP/ASP.NET

No matter whether you use ASP or ASP.NET, you can always set the MIME type of the response by setting the `ContentType` property of the `Response` object:

```
Response.ContentType = "image/svg+xml"
```

> **NOTE**
>
> If you are using ASP.NET and C#, you need to put a semicolon at the end of the preceding line.

This complete script works both under ASP (file extension .asp) and under ASP.NET (file extension .aspx):

```
<%
  Response.ContentType = "image/svg+xml"
%>
<?xml version="1.0"?>
<svg width="100px" height="20px">
  <text x="10" y="20" >SVG serverside</text>
</svg>
```

Perl

Perl is still very widespread on the Web, mainly because it is part of Linux systems and thus is ready to use, especially for Web applications. As you will see in the Perl case study (Chapter 21, "SVG and Perl"), you can create SVG from Perl with the help of mighty modules (for example, SVG.pm). In this section, however, we will show you the basics, how to set the MIME type of the HTTP response and to create SVG output from Perl.

With Perl, you need to output the complete HTTP header when creating server-side scripts. Thus, you can set the MIME type by hand. Here is a working listing:

```
#!/usr/bin/perl
print "Content-type: image/svg+xml\n\n";
print <<'EOF';
<?xml version="1.0"?>
<svg width="100px" height="20px">
```

18

```
   <text x="10" y="20" >SVG serverside</text>
</svg>
EOF
```

JSP and Java Servlets

You can set the response's MIME type from within JSP by using the following line:

```
<%@ page contentType="image/svg+xml" %>
```

Unlike in other languages and/or technologies, you can put this directive virtually anywhere on your page, also after the first HTML/SVG output. However, it is good style to use this directive as early as possible. Here is a complete example:

```
<%@ page contentType="image/svg+xml" %>
<?xml version="1.0"?>
<svg width="100px" height="20px">
   <text x="10" y="20" >SVG serverside</text>
</svg>
```

When using Java servlets, you must use `response.setContentType()`; for the parameter, you must provide the required MIME type—in this case, of course, `image/svg+xml`:

```
package SVGUnleashed;

import java.io.*;
import javax.servlet.*;
import javax.servlet.http.*;

public class SVGServerSide extends HttpServlet {
  public void doGet(HttpServletRequest request,
                    HttpServletResponse response)
     throws ServletException, IOException {
    response.setContentType("image/svg+xml");
    PrintWriter out = response.getWriter();
    out.println("<?xml version=\"1.0\"?>\n" +
                "<svg width=\"100px\" height=\"20px\">\n" +
                "  <text x=\"10\" y=\"20\" >SVG serverside</text>\n" +
                "</svg>");
  }
}
```

Summary

This chapter explained what a MIME type is and why it is important to set this MIME type. We have also shown how to set up your Web server correctly for the SVG MIME type, `image/svg+xml`, and how to set this MIME type manually from within your server-side scripts for various programming languages. The remaining chapters in Part III show several rather practical examples. You will see case studies of various kinds that combine the power of server-side scripting with the power of SVG.

18

JSP, Servlets, and SVG

In earlier chapters, we saw how to use client-side techniques to generate and manipulate SVG and briefly discussed how SVG can be generated on the server. The combination of client- and server-side techniques can be extremely powerful, perhaps more so with SVG than any other system or format, thanks to the language's built-in scripting capabilities. Allowing processing at either end produces an explosion in the number of solutions to any given problem. In this chapter, we will look at producing SVG with server-side Java, but to keep things simple, we won't do any real processing on the client.

We will first look at a quick and easy way of using Java Server Pages (JSP) to create SVG using scripts. We will then see how JSP can be used for more sophisticated SVG applications by building and using a simple JavaBean. After an overview of the SVG DOM and a simple example, the rest of the chapter will be devoted to a complete, practical servlet-based SVG application. The earlier parts of the chapter require only a knowledge of the basics of Java (or any other object-oriented language), though the code to the servlet-based example is likely to make more sense if you have already encountered servlets and are reasonably familiar with the XML DOM.

We won't look at applets in this chapter, despite their relevance to the Web. Generally speaking, they can be considered as client-side applications, even though they are designed to run in a browser. The information in Chapter 17, "Using SVG in Java Applications," together with any applets tutorial will cover that angle.

JSP for Scripting

As we saw in Chapter 18, "Server-Side Basics," serving up SVG using Java Server Pages (JSP) is only a matter of specifying the appropriate MIME type and then listing the SVG content. There isn't much point in doing so unless some use is made of the Java programming language, and the simplest way of using JSP to dynamically generate SVG is to treat it as a scripting language.

SVG Fractals

Unfortunately, many of the appealing images that are loosely categorized as "fractals" are pixel-based, which means that they aren't a very good fit for a vector-based system like SVG. However, many are produced by repeatedly applying an affine transformation to a simple shape. Such transformations are combinations of linear operations such as translation, rotation, and reflection, and SVG is good at shapes and can do these operations. One such fractal image is the Sierpinsky Triangle. It is formed by initially drawing a triangle and then applying a scaling and translation transformation three times to produce three new triangles, located at the corner positions of the original shape. The scaling and triplication is then repeated for as many times as required (see Figure 19.1).

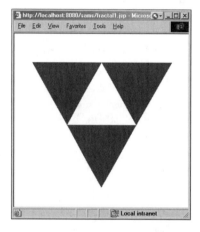

FIGURE 19.1   Sierpinsky Triangle (one iteration).

The MecXpert site (`http://www.mecxpert.de/`, SVG for mechanical engineering) describes how to draw a Sierpinsky Triangle with SVG, and Listing 19.1 uses this technique to draw the shape after two iterations of the transformation. Within the `defs` section, the initial triangle is defined using a path and given the ID `level_0`. The group of elements that follows it represents three shapes that are scaled and translated versions of the shape defined as `level_0`. This group has the ID `level_1`. The next group defines three shapes as transformed versions of the `level_1` shape. Notice that the applied transforms are identical to those in the previous group. After the `defs` section, a single `level_2` shape is drawn, with a little translation and scaling to give it a good position and size in the window.

LISTING 19.1   fractal.svg—Hand-Coded SVG Fractal

```
<svg width="600" height="400">
   <defs>
     <path id="level_0" fill="#003399" d="M0 0,2 0,1 1.732,z" />
     <g id="level_1">
         <use xlink:href="#level_0"
            transform="matrix(0.5 0 0 0.5   0  0)" />
         <use xlink:href="#level_0"
            transform="matrix(0.5 0 0 0.5   1  0)" />
         <use xlink:href="#level_0"
            transform="matrix(0.5 0 0 0.5  0.5 0.866)" />
     </g>
     <g id="level_2">
         <use xlink:href="#level_1"
            transform="matrix(0.5 0 0 0.5   0  0)" />
         <use xlink:href="#level_1"
            transform="matrix(0.5 0 0 0.5   1  0)" />
         <use xlink:href="#level_1"
            transform="matrix(0.5 0 0 0.5  0.5 0.866)" />
     </g>
     </defs>
   <use xlink:href="#level_2"
            transform="translate(200,200) scale(100)" />
</svg>
```

Loading Listing 19.1 into a browser produces Figure 19.2.

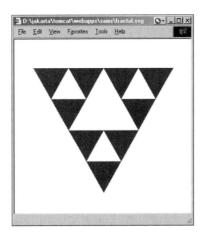

FIGURE 19.2   Two-step fractal.

The iterative nature of the code is clear, and is a good candidate for automation. Step forward JSP. The iteration through the levels can obviously be put into a loop. If the contents of the transform attributes are held in an array of strings, we can produce each of the three use elements in each group using another loop. The result is Listing 19.2.

LISTING 19.2 fractal1.jsp—JSP-Automated SVG Fractal

```
<%@ page contentType="image/svg+xml" %>
<%
    String transforms[] = new String[3];
    transforms[0] =  "matrix(0.5 0 0 0.5   0   0)";
    transforms[1] =  "matrix(0.5 0 0 0.5   1   0)";
    transforms[2] =  "matrix(0.5 0 0 0.5  0.5 0.866)";
%>

<svg width="400" height="400">
   <defs>
     <path id="level_0" fill="#0000FF" d="M0 0,2 0,1 1.732,z" />
     <%
     int level;
     for(level=0;level<8;level++){
     %>
         <g id="level_<%=level+1%>">
         <%
         for(int i=0;i<3;i++){ %>
                 <use xlink:href="#level_<%=level%>"
                     transform="<%=transforms[i]%>" />
         <% } %>
             </g>
     <% } %>
   </defs>
   <use xlink:href="#level_<%=level%>"
       transform="translate(40,60) scale(150)" />
</svg>
```

The code contained within the <% ... %> blocks is interpreted as standard Java, and variables such as level can be placed in the generated code using the syntax <%=level%>. Putting this code onto a JSP-capable server and opening the page in a browser produces the image in Figure 19.3.

JSP and JavaBeans
The real benefits of JSP only really begin beyond the script with sophisticated JSP-specific techniques such as custom tags and more generic techniques such as JavaBeans. The field

is wide open for SVG developers, so for a taste, we will now look at a simple example using a JavaBean.

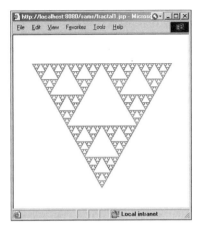

FIGURE 19.3   Eight-step machine-generated fractal.

What Is a JavaBean?

JavaBeans are components built from Java classes that can be as simple or complex as required. Certain patterns such as providing get/set methods for accessing and modifying properties of the bean objects allow them to be used in systems like JSP. Any Java class can be treated as a JavaBean as long as it obeys two rules: It implements the Serializable interface, and it provides a no-argument constructor. The Serializable interface doesn't specify any methods, so just saying that the class implements it is usually enough. Providing a no-argument constructor is rarely a problem.

A Moderately Useful Bean

Figure 19.4 shows a line running from an arbitrary point outside a rectangle to the center of the rectangle.

We are going to use a JavaBean to locate the point at which the line intersects one of the sides of the rectangle. This might seem like a pointless exercise in geometry, but imagine that the rectangle is part of a diagram, and you want an arrow to point to it. The solution to this problem will tell you where to put the arrowhead. We will approach this problem from the point of view of the line, as we can get some of the basic functionality we need by extending the Line2D.Double class. This class is part of the standard Java2D library we looked at in Chapter 17. The code for the bean begins as in Listing 19.3.

19

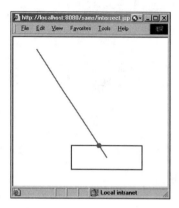

FIGURE 19.4   Finding the intersection.

LISTING 19.3   SmartLine.java

```java
package com.sams.beans;

import java.io.*;
import java.awt.*;
import java.awt.geom.*;

public class SmartLine extends Line2D.Double implements Serializable {

    private Rectangle2D rectangle;
    private double x;
    private double y;

    public SmartLine() {
        super();
    }
```

Note that we have now fulfilled the contract that allows this class to be a JavaBean: It implements `Serializable`, and it has a no-argument constructor. That didn't hurt at all. The next method receives the characteristics of the rectangle, specified in the Java2D fashion using the coordinates of its center. A new Java2D rectangle object is created, and the method that will carry out the calculations is called:

```java
public void setRect(int cx, int cy, int width, int height) {
    rectangle = new Rectangle2D.Double(cx, cy, width, height);
    calculateRectangleIntersection();
}
```

```
public int getX(){
    return (int)x;
}

public int getY(){
    return (int)y;
}
```

In the preceding code, we have the methods that will be used to obtain the coordinates of the point of intersection. The following code shows the four methods that will be used within the calculation. The getP1() and getP2() methods used here belong to this class's parent class; they return the start and end points of the line as Point2D objects:

```
public double getXDistance() {
    return getP1().getX() - getP2().getX();
}

public double getYDistance() {
    return getP1().getY() - getP2().getY();
}

private double getYValue() {
    return (rectangle.getHeight() / 2)
        * ((rectangle.getWidth() / 2) / getXDistance());
}

private double getXValue() {
    return (rectangle.getWidth() / 2)
        * ((rectangle.getHeight() / 2) / getYDistance());
}

private void calculateRectangleIntersection() {

    double yValue = (getYDistance())
        * ((rectangle.getWidth() / 2) / getXDistance());
    double xValue = (getXDistance())
        * ((rectangle.getHeight() / 2) / getYDistance());

    boolean eastside = (Math.abs(yValue) < rectangle.getHeight() / 2)
        && (getXDistance() >= 0);
    boolean westside = (Math.abs(yValue) < rectangle.getHeight() / 2)
        && (getXDistance() < 0);
    boolean northside = (Math.abs(xValue) < rectangle.getWidth() / 2)
```

```
            && (getYDistance() < 0);
    boolean southside = (Math.abs(xValue) < rectangle.getWidth() / 2)
            && (getYDistance() >= 0);

    if (westside){
        x = rectangle.getMinX();
        y = rectangle.getCenterY() - yValue;
    }

    if (eastside) { // right
        x = rectangle.getMaxX();
        y = rectangle.getCenterY() + yValue;
    }

    if (northside) { // top
        x = rectangle.getCenterX() - xValue;
        y = rectangle.getMinY();
    }

    if (southside) { // bottom
        x = rectangle.getCenterX() + xValue;
        y = rectangle.getMaxY();
    }
    }
}
```

The preceding calculation first finds the distance from the center along each axis of the intersection point. Next, we determine which side of the rectangle the line is running through. The conditionals that follow combine these pieces of information to locate the point. This method is by no means foolproof; division by zero could mess things up, not to mention the behavior if the line doesn't actually intersect the rectangle. But this example works well enough for demonstration purposes. Now that we have a JavaBean, how do we use it?

Beans in JSP

The following code uses the bean created in the preceding section. To use a bean, we need to declare it and give it a name. By doing so, we are, in effect, creating an instance of the bean's class. The jsp:useBean element does this, calling this instance of the bean sLine and giving it the scope of this page only (it is possible to persist the bean further, for instance, by giving it session scope). The next code block sets the location of the line and rectangle, with the rectangle being centered on one end of the line. We can then pass these values to the bean, using standard method calls. This isn't the only way of accessing beans, however; in a moment, we'll see another way.

```
<%@ page contentType="image/svg+xml" %>
<jsp:useBean id='sLine' scope='page' class='com.sams.beans.SmartLine' />
<%
// define the line ends
    int x1 = 50;
    int y1 = 25;
    int x2 = 200;
    int y2 = 250;

// define the rect
    int rectWidth = 150;
    int rectHeight = 50;

    int rectX = x2 - rectWidth/2;
    int rectY = y2 - rectHeight/2;

// set the values in the bean
    sLine.setLine(x1, y1, x2, y2);
    sLine.setRect(x2, y2, rectWidth, rectHeight);
%>
```

Next, we have the SVG itself. The line and rectangle are positioned using variables defined in the preceding Java code. The circle that marks their intersection is, however, positioned using properties of the bean; the JSP elements here are equivalent to calling the getX() and getY() methods of the object's class:

```
<svg width="400" height="400">
    <line x1="<%=x1%>" y1="<%=y1%>" x2="<%=x2%>" y2="<%=y2%>"
            stroke="green"     stroke-width="2"  />

    <rect x="<%=rectX%>" y="<%=rectY%>" width="<%=rectWidth%>"
          height="<%=rectHeight%>"
           fill="none" stroke="blue" stroke-width="2"/>

    <circle    cx="<jsp:getProperty name="sLine" property="x"/>"
          cy="<jsp:getProperty name="sLine" property="y"/>"
          r="5" fill="red" />
</svg>
```

If the preceding Java code compiled, and the resulting class and the JSP file were placed on a suitable server, pointing a browser at the JSP file will result in the browser view shown in Figure 19.4.

19

Java SVG DOM

Appendix D of the SVG 1.0 specification, "Java Language Binding," points to a Zip file containing 160 small Java files, each of which contains an interface corresponding to an SVG component. What Java binds to is the SVG Document Object Model (DOM), which stands independent of any specific language. This is apparent if you compare it with Appendix E of the specification, which is the ECMAScript binding that is provided as an HTML document. Because it is tied to the same underlying model as the Java binding, it could almost be mistaken for documentation of the Java interfaces. As you learned earlier in the book, the SVG DOM is built on DOM Level 2, so pretty much anything you can do with regular DOM, you can do with SVG DOM as long as the implementation you're using supports it. If you've used the SVG DOM in ECMAScript, the Java version will seem very familiar.

There is at least one other implementation of the Java SVG DOM, but here we will use Batik's implementation, which offers wide support of the specification and is open source.

> **NOTE**
>
> The CSIRO SVG Toolkit (available from http://sis.cmis.csiro.au/svg/) is another open-source imple-mentation of SVG 1.0, but parts of the specification aren't supported and no further develop-ment is planned.

A Simple Example

Listing 19.4 is a sample command-line application that will load an SVG document file into a DOM object, add a circle element at random coordinates, and then save the result back to file. If the file doesn't exist when the program is run, a new DOM object will be created. The application will also save a JPEG image of the SVG representation. The imports come from Java I/O (to allow loading and saving of the data), the W3C DOM namespace (which contains the interfaces for Document and Element objects), and various parts of the Batik Toolkit. The class has a DOM Document object as a member variable, along with a couple of values to give the height and width of the image we want to gener-ate. The main() method simply creates a new instance of this class to start the process.

LISTING 19.4   SimpleDOM.java

```
import java.io.*;

import org.w3c.dom.*;

import org.apache.batik.dom.svg.*;
import org.apache.batik.util.*;
```

LISTING 19.4   Continued

```
import org.apache.batik.transcoder.*;
import org.apache.batik.transcoder.svg2svg.*;
import org.apache.batik.transcoder.image.*;

import org.apache.batik.dom.svg.*;

public class SimpleDOM {

    Document document;
    int WIDTH = 100;
    int HEIGHT = 100;

    public static void main(String[] args) {
        new SimpleDOM();
    }
```

The class constructor SimpleDOM() calls various methods in sequence. First, it tries to load SVG data into the Document object from the c:/circles.svg file using the load() method. If this attempt fails, a new Document will be created. A circle element will be added to the Document, and then it will be stored back to disk as an SVG XML file and also a JPEG image file.

```
public SimpleDOM() {
        if (!load("c:/circles.svg")) {
            createDocument();
        }
        addCircle();

        try {
            store("c:/circles.svg", "svg");
            store("c:/circles.jpg", "jpg");
        } catch (Exception exception) {
            exception.printStackTrace();
        }
    }
```

The first method called from the preceding code begins by getting an instance of a DOM implementation (as defined in the DOM interface), using a static factory method call on one of the Batik classes. The default namespace to be used for SVG documents is obtained from a property of the implementation (in this case, it is http://www.w3.org/2000/svg). An SVG DOM document is then created using the implementation, with the specified

namespace, the qualified name to use in the root element, and the DOCTYPE (if the
DOCTYPE is null, the owner document is set to the document being created).

```
public void createDocument() {
    DOMImplementation impl = SVGDOMImplementation.getDOMImplementation();
    String svgNS = SVGDOMImplementation.SVG_NAMESPACE_URI;
    document = impl.createDocument(svgNS, "svg", null);
}
```

To add a circle element to the SVG document, we begin by getting the document's root
svg element. We then give this element a couple of attributes (the width and height we
want our image to be) by calling the Element.setAttribute() method. Note that the
WIDTH and HEIGHT variables are of type int, whereas setAttribute() expects a String
object, so a conversion is needed. A couple of random numbers are then generated, within
the range of our image's dimensions. The circle element is created using a conventional
call to the DOM, and similarly the attributes are set using methods from DOM. Before
returning, the method attaches the newly created element to the root of the tree. For such
an example, the fact that we are using an SVG DOM object is irrelevant.

```
public void addCircle() {

    // get the root element (the svg element)
    Element svgRoot = document.getDocumentElement();

    // set the width and height attribute on the root svg element
    svgRoot.setAttribute("width", Integer.toString(WIDTH));
    svgRoot.setAttribute("height", Integer.toString(HEIGHT));

    // a couple of random coordinates
    int x = (int) (Math.random() * WIDTH);
    int y = (int) (Math.random() * HEIGHT);

    // create the circle
    Element circle = document.createElement("circle");
    circle.setAttribute("cx", Integer.toString(x));
    circle.setAttribute("cy", Integer.toString(y));
    circle.setAttribute("r", "5");
    circle.setAttribute("style", "fill:green");

    // attach the circle to the root element
    svgRoot.appendChild(circle);
}
```

```java
public boolean load(String filename) {
    System.out.println("Loading " + filename);
    File file = new File(filename);
    try {
        String parser = XMLResourceDescriptor.getXMLParserClassName();
        SAXSVGDocumentFactory factory = new SAXSVGDocumentFactory(parser);

        document = factory.createDocument(file.toURL().toString());
    } catch (Exception exception) {
        System.out.println(filename + " not found");
        return false;
    }
    return true;
}

public void store(String filename, String format) throws Exception {
    OutputStream outputStream = new FileOutputStream(filename);

    TranscoderInput input = new TranscoderInput(document);

    System.out.println("Saving " + filename);
    Transcoder transcoder;
    TranscoderOutput output;
    OutputStreamWriter outWriter = null;

    if (format == "svg") {
        transcoder = new SVGTranscoder();
        outWriter = new OutputStreamWriter(outputStream);
        output = new TranscoderOutput(outWriter);
    } else {
        transcoder = new JPEGTranscoder();
        output = new TranscoderOutput(outputStream);
    }
    transcoder.transcode(input, output);
    outputStream.flush();
    outputStream.close();
    if (outWriter != null) {
        outWriter.flush();
        outWriter.close();
    }
}
}
```

19

NOTE

To be able to serve up SVG with Java, we will need a servlet-capable Web server. The Apache Tomcat server is the reference implementation of the Servlet and JSP specification, and what's more, it is free and will run on virtually any machine. It can be downloaded from http://jakarta.apache.org/tomcat/index.html. Documentation is supplied, but additional information specific to the application described in this chapter can be found with the software download from the Sams Web site and at http://www.isacat.net/squirrel.

SVG DOM Specifics

The SVG specification defines various characteristics of the SVG DOM and its elements that extend the DOM2 model. They add a great deal of functionality, but unfortunately much of this functionality has yet to find its way into the implementations. However, the power of DOM being what it is means that this isn't a problem in practice, and the application we are now going to look at barely uses the extensions at all.

Squirrel: A DOM-Based Server Application

We will now look at a practical server-side Java application that uses DOM to generate SVG. The application is essentially an XML tree browser, but rather than showing the usual tree-centric explorer type of view, it provides an element-centric view. Elements are displayed as labeled shapes onscreen using dynamically generated SVG. In each display, an element is considered the focus, and only the other elements that are directly linked to it are displayed, that is, its parent and immediate children. Clicking on one of the peripheral elements brings up another view, with the element clicked as the new focus. This could be likened to what a short-sighted squirrel sees as it clambers around a tree, hence, the name. The application shows DOM elements as shapes labeled with the element name and any text contained in the elements. The focus also has a listing of the corresponding element's attributes. This parent + focus + offshoots representation can be considered an abstract data structure, which we'll be referring to as a "sprig" ("twig" is already overloaded by XML-ers).

The application is relatively simple and could probably be implemented using fewer lines of code in a scripting language or using XSLT transformations. The advantages of using Java here include the fact that many of the resultant classes may be reused in other applications, but much more importantly, the system can be modified and extended with great ease.

Figure 19.5 shows the view after loading data from the URL in the form's text box. This example shows contact details for an organization.

The data in test.xml is in an arbitrary XML language; the code is shown in Listing 19.5.

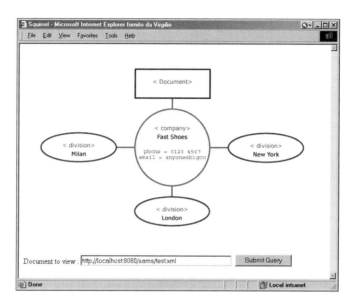

FIGURE 19.5   A top-level view of the application.

LISTING 19.5   test.xml—Example XML File to View

```xml
<?xml version="1.0" encoding="ISO-8859-1"?>
<company phone="0123 4567" email="anyone@bigco">
    Fast Shoes
    <division phone="0123 4567" email="anyone@bigco">
    New York
        <dept contact="Ashok" email="ashok@bigco">Marketing</dept>
        <dept contact="Stephanie" email="steph@bigco">Sales</dept>
        <dept contact="Joe" email="joe@bigco">HR</dept>
        <dept contact="John" email="john@bigco">R&amp;D</dept>
    </division>
    <division phone="0234 4567">
    London
        <dept contact="John" email="steph@bigco">Sales</dept>
    </division>
    <division phone="0456 4567">
    Milan
        <dept contact="Antonio" email="toni@bigco">Sales</dept>
    </division>
</company>
```

19

As you can see in Figure 19.5, the focus is the root element company, and the attributes of this element are displayed. The data in the next level down the tree is contained in <division> tags. This level is displayed as the ellipses in the figure, and although the text locally contained by the element is displayed, the attributes are hidden. The rectangle at the top corresponds to the parent of the focus element, and in this case, it is labeled <Document> because the focus currently represents the root of the tree. If we click on the New York item, the browser will load a new page, as shown in Figure 19.6.

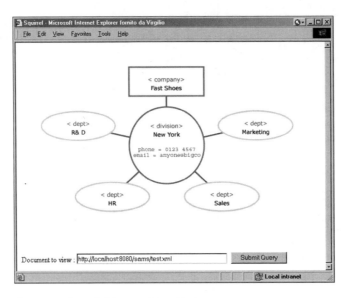

FIGURE 19.6   The page after clicking on New York.

Now that the previous focus (<company>) has moved to the parent position, the item clicked to the focus and the children of this division element are laid out around the focus.

The shapes displayed are color-coded according to the position of the element in the source tree and where in the sprig view they appear: The document rectangle is black, the root of the source tree is red, leaf nodes (those without children) are green, and so on. The three levels of text (element name, text, and attributes) are also styled differently. The styling, as you might have guessed, is specified in a standard external CSS file, as shown in Listing 19.6.

LISTING 19.6   squirrel.css—CSS Style Sheet Used by the Application

```
svg {fill:white; stroke-width:3}

line {stroke:green}
```

LISTING 19.6 Continued

```
circle.normal {stroke:gray}
circle.root {stroke:red}
circle.leaf {stroke:lightgreen}

ellipse.normal {stroke:blue}
ellipse.leaf {stroke:lightgreen}

rect.normal {stroke:blue}
rect.document {stroke:black}
rect.root {stroke:red}

text {text-anchor:middle; stroke:none;}
text.title {fill:gray; font-family:Verdana}
text.content {fill:black; font-family:Verdana}
text.detail {fill:gray; font-family:Courier}
```

Clicking on the Sales item brings up the view in Figure 19.7. Here, the division is the new parent; and Sales, the focus. Referring to Listing 19.5, test.xml, we can see that this dept element doesn't have any child elements, so no offshoots appear below the focus. The focus shape is also now colored green because it is a leaf element.

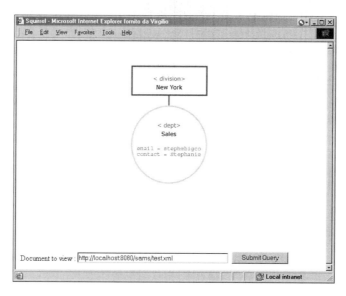

FIGURE 19.7 The page after clicking on Sales.

Clicking on the parent item, New York, will return us to the previous view, from where we can either explore other departments of the company's New York base, or click on the parent item again to return to the root view.

The key difference between the Squirrel view and that of regular tree browsers is that the former offers a much simpler view. Such a view would be appropriate where the information is hierarchical and the user doesn't want to be bombarded with too much information at once. Potential applications might be site navigation or product catalogs. Or imagine a tourist information console with a touch screen.

Application Package

The source code, classes, and documentation for this application are available from the Sams Web site. Decompressing the package will reveal a `sams` directory containing the following subdirectories:

- `backup`—This directory contains backup copies of the source code.

- `css`—This directory contains the stylesheet used by the application.

- `javadoc`—This directory contains the automatically generated documentation of the application.

- `WEB-INF`—This directory contains the following subdirectories:

    - `src`—The application source files

    - `classes`—The compiled application classes

    - `lib`—The library jars the application depends on (Batik and the Crimson parser)

Rebuilding the Application

You can rebuild the application by using an IDE or by typing in the appropriate commands at the command line. For a simple alternative, a Windows batch file and an Ant build file (build.xml) are included in the package. You need to install the Apache Ant application to use this file, and you need to edit the batch file to give appropriate values for the Ant and Java home directories. When you're prepared, running `build` at the command line (in the same directory as build.bat) will make a backup of the source code, compile all the classes, and make a jar file out of the classes. Running `build javadoc` will reconstruct the documentation.

The award-winning Ant (`http://jakarta.apache.org/ant/`) is another open-source Apache project. It resembles the Unix `make` tool but is easier to use. In use, a series of operations such as compilation and packaging are specified in an XML file. Running Ant carries out the operations as specified. This automation can make the building of software distributions a one-command task. Ant is written in Java and so is ideal for cross-platform use. Documentation and installation instructions (you just unzip and set a couple of environment variables) are included with the download.

Running the Application

From a default installation of Tomcat, you can install the application by copying the `sams` directory (that is, the whole extracted package) into Tomcat's `webapps` directory. You also will need to edit the Tomcat conf\server.xml file to include the following lines:

```
<Context path="/sams" docBase="sams" debug="0" reloadable="true"
         crossContext="true">
</Context>
```

You can now start Tomcat, either by running one of the scripts/batch files in the `bin` directory (or simply entering `catalina run` at the command line in this directory).

Pointing a browser at

```
http://localhost:8080/sams/servlet/com.sams.squirrel.control.SquirrelServlet
```

should then run the servlet, which will display a text box containing the test file's address. Clicking the submit button should then produce the view shown in Figure 19.5.

> **NOTE**
>
> SVG's built-in scripting capabilities provide a lot of power, but in practice they will often be unsuitable for building larger-scale applications. The primary role of SVG is as a presentation language, and thanks to its (XML) standards base, it can be plugged into virtually any language. In the code we'll be looking at, we have an SVG face on a Java back end. For us to describe a complete application here means that sections of this code won't be directly related to the SVG presentation, but it is important to see how all parts of a system can work together. We have chosen an XML-based modeling task, so all the techniques used for manipulating this arbitrary XML can be applied just the same to SVG.

Application Architecture

Like the desktop application we saw in Chapter 17, this application follows the Model-View-Controller paradigm. In this case, it doesn't depend on Swing architecture, so the different parts are somewhat more clearly differentiated. The user interface in this case is an SVG-capable browser, which communicates with the application over HTTP through Java servlets.

The application classes are located in four different package groups, all under the umbrella of `com.sams.squirrel`. Three of these packages are named for their primary role in the M-V-C architecture. The fourth package contains classes concerned with generating sprig objects from a source XML file. The package groups are as follows:

- `model`—Interfaces and base implementations that define the sprig data structure
- `view`—Classes that implement the model interfaces to generate an SVG-based visualization of the sprig

19

- control—Servlet classes that control program flow and interact with the browser front end

- xml—Classes that implement the model interfaces to create sprig objects from an arbitrary DOM tree

We will look at the code for the packages later, but the manner in which communication to the server is made definitely falls under the heading of application architecture. What will be received by the browser is an HTML Web page containing an embedded SVG object. What will be served up by the application is a dynamically generated stream of HTML and SVG that is created only when the browser tries to retrieve the embedded object. We will, in fact, have two servlets: one to serve up the HTML and one to serve up the SVG. When an XML file is loaded into the application for viewing, chances are that the user will want to go beyond the initial sprig view of the root. It is, therefore, desirable to retain the loaded tree and just present different views until the user selects a different source file. This caching is reasonably straightforward to achieve using servlet sessions.

The SVG representations will be created at the end of a chain. This chain begins with the XML being loaded into a DOM tree in a class that can create objects that conform to a model we will look at in a moment. These objects are then passed on to another set of classes that implement an extension of the model to produce the required SVG. This approach means that the source data and visualization result are effectively decoupled by the model. If we wanted to view a different tree structure—for example, a file system—from the squirrel's point of view, we would only have to deal with adapters between the file system tree and the interfaces found in the model part of the application, with the SVG generation part (which is a significant proportion of the code) being reused without modification.

Model Classes

The SVG we're going to be generating will present a visual representation of an abstract model. This model is based around four interfaces. First, the Sprig interface outlines a container in which to place the items found in a Sprig object. Implementation of the Sprig will wrap up the parent element + focus element + offshoot elements data structure we mentioned earlier. The TreeItem interface defines a series of get/set methods that relate to characteristics of an item found in a tree structure. SprigItem, which is an extension of TreeItem, defines methods to look after characteristics of an individual part of a Sprig. Finally, the SprigSource interface defines methods that a class designed to generate Sprig objects must have. Also in the com.sams.squirrel.model package are base implementations of the Sprig (SprigImpl) and SprigItem (AbstractSprigItem) interfaces. We will now look at the source for each of these interfaces and classes, beginning with the Sprig interface in Listing 19.7.

> **NOTE**
>
> Most of the comments in the original source code have been removed from the listings in this chapter in the interest of space, so for more detail on the operation of the code, you can consult the source download, as well as its javadoc.

LISTING 19.7   Sprig.java

```java
package com.sams.squirrel.model;

import java.util.*;

public interface Sprig {

    public void add(SprigItem item);

    public SprigItem getFocus();

    public SprigItem getParent();

    public int size();

    public List getItems();

    public SprigItem item(int item);
}
```

The methods in Listing 19.7 are (we hope) reasonably self-explanatory. A sprig is essentially a collection of items, so this listing contains methods to add items, to get all the items (as a Java 2 List collection), or to get a single item by an index number. We will look at the interfaces and classes describing the items themselves shortly. The size() method here will return the total number of items in the sprig, including the focus and parent, and these two particular items can be retrieved using the corresponding get methods. Listing 19.8 is the code for the SprigImpl class, which provides a basic implementation of each method in Listing 19.7.

LISTING 19.8   SprigImpl.java—Base Implementation of Sprig Interface

```java
package com.sams.squirrel.model;

import java.util.*;

import com.sams.squirrel.model.*;
```

19

LISTING 19.8   Continued

```
public class SprigImpl implements Sprig {

    private SprigItem focus;
    private SprigItem parent;
    private List items;

        // constructs an empty Sprig
    public SprigImpl() {
        items = new ArrayList();
    }

        // constructs a Sprig with the given focus item
    public SprigImpl(SprigItem focus) {
        this();
        focus.setType(SprigItem.FOCUS);
        this.focus = focus;
        items.add(focus);
    }

        // adds an item to this Sprig
    public void add(SprigItem item) {
        if (item.getType() == SprigItem.FOCUS) {
            this.focus = focus;
        }
        if (item.getType() == SprigItem.PARENT) {
            this.parent = parent;
        }
        items.add(item);
    }

        // gets the focus item
    public SprigItem getFocus() {
        return focus;
    }

        // gets the parent item
    public SprigItem getParent() {
        return parent;
    }

        // gets the number of items in this Sprig
    public int size() {
```

LISTING 19.8 Continued

```
        return items.size();
    }

        // gets all the items in this Sprig
    public List getItems() {
        return items;
    }

        // gets the item at the specified index
    public SprigItem item(int item) {
        return (SprigItem) items.get(item);
    }

        // gets the String representation of this Sprig
    public String toString() {
        String string = "FOCUS : " + focus;
        string += "\nPARENT : " + parent;
        string += "\nall items : \n" + items;
        return string;
    }
}
```

The base implementation is straightforward, wrapping the Sprig interface definitions around a List collection, which will contain all the items. For convenience, the focus and parent are also contained as objects in their own right. When an item is added, it is tested for type, and if it is the focus or parent, the corresponding member variable will be set to refer to it.

The TreeItem interface in Listing 19.9 contains methods relating to the tree that is used as the source for sprigs. The methods simply get or set whether or not the item corresponds to the root of the tree, a leaf of the tree, or the (conceptual) document item that is the parent of the root.

LISTING 19.9 TreeItem.java

```
package com.sams.squirrel.model;

public interface TreeItem {

    public void setDocument(boolean isDocument);

    public boolean isDocument();
```

19

LISTING 19.9   Continued

```
    public void setRoot(boolean isRoot);

    public boolean isRoot();

    public void setLeaf(boolean isLeaf);

    public boolean isLeaf();

    public void setDataSource(Object object);

    public Object getDataSource();
}
```

Note that the interface makes no attempt to relate an instance of `TreeItem` to its parent or children. From a sprig's point of view, this isn't really important because it represents only a restricted picture of the tree. In fact, whether or not an item in a sprig is the root, document item, or a leaf is significant only in implementation terms; for example, in this application we will use this information to decide the displayed color of items.

The final two method skeletons in this interface are also auxiliary; they are intended to enable a back linking to whatever source object was used to provide the characteristics of this item. These methods aren't actually used in the Squirrel application, but their potential utility meant they were considered worth including. An example of their use would be in an extension of the Squirrel application that allowed editing of the source XML data.

As you can see from Listing 19.10, the items in a sprig will have various properties associated with them, and these properties will be contained within an implementation of the `SprigItem` interface. The constants defined at the start of this interface relate to an item's position in a sprig, which will be determined using the `setType()` and `getType()` methods, the parameter of which will either be `SprigItem.FOCUS`, `SprigItem.PARENT`, or `SprigItem.OFFSHOOT`. The item will also be aware of the sprig that contains it, through the `setSprig()`/`getSprig()` methods. Each of the offshoot items will be given an identifying number that is accessed through another `get`/`set` pair. The last three methods allow operations on a collection of properties associated with this item that will be implementation-specific. In this application, these attributes will be the XML attributes of an element in the source XML.

LISTING 19.10   SprigItem.java—Interface for the Individual Parts of a Sprig

```
package com.sams.squirrel.model;

import java.util.*;
```

LISTING 19.10   Continued

```java
public interface SprigItem extends TreeItem {

    public static final char FOCUS = 0;

    public static final char PARENT = 1;

    public static final char OFFSHOOT = 2;

    public void setType(char type);

    public char getType();

    public void setSprig(Sprig sprig);

    public Sprig getSprig();

    public void setOffshootID(String id);

    public String getOffshootID();

    public void setAttribute(Object key, Object value);

    public void setAttributes(Map attributes);

    public Map getAttributes();
}
```

The base class for `SprigItem` implementations (actually an `abstract` class because it doesn't implement all the methods of the interface) is another straightforward series of get/set methods backed by standard Java member variables (see Listing 19.11).

LISTING 19.11   AbstractSprigItem.java—Abstract Class Containing SprigItem's Accessor Methods

```java
package com.sams.squirrel.model;

import java.util.*;

public abstract class AbstractSprigItem implements SprigItem {

    private Sprig sprig;
    private char type;
```

LISTING 19.11   Continued

```
    private String id;
    private boolean isDocument;
    private boolean isRoot;
    private boolean isLeaf;
    private Object dataSource;
    private Map attributes;

    public AbstractSprigItem() {
        attributes = new HashMap();
    }

    public void setOffshootID(String id) {
        this.id = id;
    }

    public String getOffshootID() {
        return id;
    }

    public void setSprig(Sprig sprig) {
        this.sprig = sprig;
    }

    public Sprig getSprig() {
        return sprig;
    }

    public List getItems() {
        return sprig.getItems();
    }

    public void setType(char type) {
        this.type = type;
    }

    public char getType() {
        return type;
    }

    public void setDocument(boolean isDocument) {
        this.isDocument = isDocument;
```

LISTING 19.11 Continued

```java
    }

    public boolean isDocument() {
        return isDocument;
    }

    public void setRoot(boolean isRoot) {
        this.isRoot = isRoot;
    }

    public boolean isRoot() {
        return isRoot;
    }

    public void setLeaf(boolean isLeaf) {
        this.isLeaf = isLeaf;
    }

    public boolean isLeaf() {
        return isLeaf;
    }

    public void setDataSource(Object object) {
        this.dataSource = object;
    }

    public Object getDataSource() {
        return dataSource;
    }

    public void setAttribute(Object key, Object value) {
        attributes.put(key, value);
    }

    public void setAttributes(Map attributes) {
        this.attributes = attributes;
    }

    public Map getAttributes() {
        return attributes;
    }
```

LISTING 19.11   Continued

```java
    public String typeAsString(){
            switch (type) {
            case SprigItem.FOCUS :
                return "focus";
            case SprigItem.PARENT :
                return "parent";
            default:
                return "offshoot";
        }
    }

    public String toString() {
        String string = "id" + getOffshootID();
        string += typeAsString();
        string += isDocument ? "(document)" : "";
        string += isRoot ? "(root)" : "";
        string += isLeaf ? "(leaf)" : "";
        string += attributes.toString();
        return string;
    }
}
```

A major aid in the development and debugging of Java classes is the `toString()` method. When in doubt, call `System.out.println(object)`, and if a reasonable `toString()` method has been provided, the internal state of the object is described. In the `AbstractSprigItem` class in Listing 19.11, two methods build up a textual representation of the item from its various characteristics. The `type` variable is a `char`, so to produce a textual representation of it, we use a switch in the `typeAsString()` method. The document, root, and leaf properties are Boolean variables, so in the `toString()` method, we use the tertiary operator to add either a descriptive word or an empty string, depending on the property value.

The `SprigSource` interface in Listing 19.12 is very simple; it has a method to get the sprig at the root of the source tree and a method to get the sprig with the specified focus. These two methods are sufficient to let a squirrel go where it likes around a tree, from one sprig to another, starting through the offshoots of the first sprig.

LISTING 19.12   SprigSource.java

```java
package com.sams.squirrel.model;

public interface SprigSource {
```

LISTING 19.12 Continued

```
    public Sprig getRootSprig();

    public Sprig getSprig(SprigItem focus);
}
```

View

In the `com.sams.squirrel.view` package, we find SVG-oriented implementations of the `Sprig` and `SprigItem` interfaces, appropriately named `SVGSprig` and `SVGSprigItem`. These two implementation classes form the heart of the view package, but in building up an SVG representation, they have a lot to do. To prevent these classes from becoming unwieldy, we pass much of the detailed work over to two other classes, one of which, `SVGHelpers`, is composed of helper methods. For the most part, these methods combine a series of SVG DOM operations to create an element and set its attributes. This class also contains methods for creating the SVG document and storing it to a file. Another class in this package, `SVGLabelGroup`, encapsulates the elements that will form the text labels in a single group element. This package also has an interface that uses a convenient Java idiom (values defined in an interface are available to any class that implements the interface) to provide constant values that will be used in the SVG classes. This interface can be seen in Listing 19.13.

LISTING 19.13 SVGConstants.java—Package Constants

```
package com.sams.squirrel.view;
public interface SVGConstants {

    // namespaces
    public static final String XLINK_NS ="http://www.w3.org/1999/xlink";
    public static final String SVG_NS="http://www.w3.org/2000/svg";

    // view
    public static final int VIEW_WIDTH = 600;
    public static final int VIEW_HEIGHT = 400;

    // rectangle (parent) & ellipse (normal offshoots)
    public static int ITEM_WIDTH = 160;
    public static int ITEM_HEIGHT = 60;

    // circle (focus)
    public static int RADIUS = 80;

    // text labels
```

19

LISTING 19.13   Continued

```
        public static final int TEXT_SPACING = 12;
}
```

In Listing 19.13, the namespaces are used in the creation of the SVG document and its elements. The view height and width are values that will be passed on to the root element of the document to set its dimensions. Values that will be used to give the size of the SVG shapes are then defined, and finally the value to use for vertically separating lines of text used as labels for the shapes.

Listing 19.14 is the implementation of the Sprig interface that will be used to generate the SVG. The constructor takes two objects: a String, which will be used when generating links from the SVG file, and another Sprig object, from which this Sprig object will obtain its properties. With this constructor, we can create SVG-oriented Sprig objects based on objects from any other domain, as long as they implement the Sprig interface. The String and Sprig are retained as member variables, among which there are also an SVGDocument object, which will contain the SVG representation, and the root element of the SVGDocument. The document is created using the appropriate helper method in SVGHelpers. When the member variables are all in place, the createSVGItems() method is called to build the individual item in this sprig. The constructor is followed by methods to allow access to the member variables.

LISTING 19.14   SVGSprig.java

```java
package com.sams.squirrel.view;

import org.w3c.dom.*;
import org.w3c.dom.svg.*;

import com.sams.squirrel.model.*;

public class SVGSprig extends SprigImpl implements SVGConstants {

    private SVGDocument svgDocument;
    private Element svgRoot;
    private String linkBaseURL;
    private Sprig sourceSprig;

    public SVGSprig(String linkBaseURL, Sprig sourceSprig) {
        super();
        this.linkBaseURL = linkBaseURL;
        svgDocument = SVGHelpers.createSVGDocument();
```

LISTING 19.14 Continued

```
            svgRoot = svgDocument.getDocumentElement();
            this.sourceSprig = sourceSprig;
            createSVGItems();
        }
        public String getLinkBaseURL() {
            return linkBaseURL;
        }

        public SVGDocument getDocument() {
            return svgDocument;
        }

        public Element getRoot() {
            return svgRoot;
        }

        public Element createSVGElement(String type) {
            return svgDocument.createElementNS(SVG_NS, type);
        }

        public void appendChildElement(Element element) {
            svgRoot.appendChild(element);
        }
```

The following method builds up SVGItem objects from the SprigItem objects contained in the sprig supplied to the constructor. A key part of the SVG representation is the onscreen location of the items, and part of the calculation of these coordinates is carried out here. The number of nonfocus items is obtained (that is, those that will be laid out in a circle around the focus) and the required angle between them calculated. Then, for each item required (based on the contents of the source sprig object), an SVGSprigItem is created, and the properties of the corresponding source items are copied across to the new item. A count is kept of the nonparent items to place each at the appropriate position around the circle. As we will see shortly, the SVGItem class contains an SVG g element that is used to hold the shape and text elements. These elements are prepared by calling the buildSVGElements() method, and the populated SVG g element is then obtained and added to the SVG tree of this SVGSprig.

The SVG elements that are created include the lines linking the focus and peripheral items. These lines will be drawn between the centers of these items, and the order in which the elements occur in the SVG file very much matter (because of the "painter's model"). We want the last element drawn to be the focus, to obscure the continuation of these lines to the center of the circle. Within this application, the focus will be generated first, so the following iterator counts down:

```
public void createSVGItems() {
    int size = sourceSprig.size();
    double anglePerItem = 2 * Math.PI / (size - 1); // ignore focus

    SVGSprigItem svgItem = null;
    int offshootCount = 0;
    double x, y;
    boolean isOffshoot;
    for (int i = size - 1; i > -1; i--) {
        svgItem = new SVGSprigItem();
        svgItem.setSprig(this);
        svgItem.copyProperties(sourceSprig.item(i));
        if (svgItem.getType() == SprigItem.OFFSHOOT) {
            offshootCount++;
        }
        svgItem.locate(offshootCount * anglePerItem);
        svgItem.buildSVGElements();
        appendChildElement(svgItem.getSVGElement());
        add(svgItem);
    } // end for
[ch1][ch2]}
```

The last method in the SVGSprig class, shown here, isn't used in the "live" Squirrel application. It allows the SVG representation to be saved to file, which is useful during development.

```
    public void store(String filename) {
        SVGHelpers.store((SVGDocument) svgDocument, filename);
    }
}
```

The SVGSprigItem, shown in Listing 19.15, adds the notion of two-dimensional location to its parent abstract class by having x and y coordinates as member variables, along with values obtained from the SVGConstants interface to help locate the item. It also contains a DOM element as a member variable, which will be used to build and contain this individual item's SVG representation. One key part of this representation will be the text displayed on this item, and it is contained within an instance of SVGLabelGroup.

LISTING 19.15   SVGSprigItem.java

```
package com.sams.squirrel.view;

import java.util.*;
```

LISTING 19.15   Continued

```java
import org.w3c.dom.*;

import com.sams.squirrel.model.*;

public class SVGSprigItem extends AbstractSprigItem implements SVGConstants {

    int centerX = VIEW_WIDTH / 2;
    int centerY = VIEW_HEIGHT / 2;
    double scaleX = 2 * centerX / 3;
    double scaleY = 2 * centerY / 3;

    private Element svgElement;

    private int x;
    private int y;

    private SVGLabelGroup label;

    public Element getSVGElement() {
        return svgElement;
    }

    public void setX(int x) {
        this.x = x;
    }

    public void setY(int y) {
        this.y = y;
    }

    public int getX() {
        return x;
    }

    public int getY() {
        return y;
    }

    public void copyProperties(SprigItem sourceItem) {
        setOffshootID(sourceItem.getOffshootID());
        setType(sourceItem.getType());
```

LISTING 19.15   Continued

```
        setDocument(sourceItem.isDocument());
        setRoot(sourceItem.isRoot());
        setLeaf(sourceItem.isLeaf());
        setAttributes(sourceItem.getAttributes());
    }
```

Most of the methods in Listing 19.15 are trivial getters/setters, apart from the barely more complex copyProperties() method, which obtains the values of the supplied item's properties and copies them directly into the properties of this instance. The following method is a little more interesting; it receives the angle of rotation around the center to apply to this item's coordinates to position it correctly in the squirrel's field of vision. If the item is the focus, the angle value is ignored and the item is placed right in the center. Similarly, we want the parent item to appear directly above the focus, so we just subtract an offset from the center to the parent object's y coordinate. In the default case, that is, when the type is SprigItem.OFFSHOOT, the position onscreen is calculated using a bit of fundamental trigonometry.

```
public void locate(double angle) {

    switch (getType()) {
        case SprigItem.FOCUS :
            x = centerX;
            y = centerY;
            break;
        case SprigItem.PARENT :
            x = centerX;
            y = (int) (centerY - scaleY);
            break;
        default :
            x =  (int) (centerX -scaleX * Math.sin(angle));
            y =  (int) (centerY - scaleY * Math.cos(angle));
    }
}
```

As mentioned earlier, most of the detailed SVG element constructing work is handled by the SVGLabelGroup and SVGHelpers classes. The method that knits together the elements created using the helper methods is buildSVGElements(), which follows. This method starts by casting the Sprig object into an SVGSprig, so more specific operations can be carried out with it. The operations that follow create elements in the SVG DOM. The SVGLabelGroup constructor is given an SVGItem (this) as a parameter, and also a boolean value that will be used to determine how much information to put into the label. If this item is the focus, a value of true will be given, which will result in a label containing more detail.

```
public void buildSVGElements() {
    SVGSprig svgSprig = (SVGSprig)getSprig();

    Element lineElement =
        SVGHelpers.createLineElement(svgSprig, centerX, centerY, x, y);
    svgSprig.getRoot().appendChild(lineElement);

    Element groupElement = svgSprig.createSVGElement("g");
    Element linkElement = SVGHelpers.createLinkElement(svgSprig, this);
    Element shapeElement = SVGHelpers.createShapeElement(svgSprig, this);

    SVGLabelGroup labelGroup =
        new SVGLabelGroup(this, (getType() == SprigItem.FOCUS));

    linkElement.appendChild(shapeElement);
    linkElement.appendChild(labelGroup.getLabelElement());
    groupElement.appendChild(linkElement);
    String transform = "translate(" + x + "," + y + ")";
    groupElement.setAttribute("transform", transform);
    svgElement = groupElement;
    }
}
```

If we look at an excerpt from the SVG generated from this application (see Listing 19.16), we can see that the correspondence between the elements in the end product and the preceding construction is fairly clear. You may also want to refer to Figure 19.5 and note the appearance of the item labeled Milan.

LISTING 19.16   output.svg

```
...
    <line y2="200" x1="300" x2="100" y1="200"/>
    <g transform="translate(100,200)">
        <a xlink:type="simple" xlink:actuate="onRequest" xlink:show="replace"
xmlns:xlink="http://www.w3.org/1999/xlink"xlink:href="/sams/servlet/com.sams.
➥squirrel.
➥control.SquirrelServlet?sprigID=7">
            <ellipse rx="80" ry="30" class="normal"/>
            <g>
                <text class="title" dy="0">&lt;
                    division&gt;
```

LISTING 19.16   Continued

```
            </text>
            <text class="content" dy="18">
                Milan
            </text>
        </g>
    </a>
</g>
...
```

The SVG is all based on simple group, shape, and text elements, although the a element deserves a little explanation. It uses an attribute from the XLink namespace (href) to define the behavior when the contained elements are clicked. The way the links are used in this application, this behavior is exactly the same as familiar HTML <a href="... elements. In this case, clicking the item will redirect the browser to a servlet-generated HTML page.

Note that each of the SVG elements is given a class, which allows the application of CSS styles. Listing 19.17 will also make more sense when viewed alongside the preceding SVG extract. This listing shows the SVGHelpers class, which is composed of static methods because no state information needs to be maintained. To ensure that instances cannot be created, we give the default constructor private scope. The createDocument() method is essentially the same as that in the simple example we saw earlier, with a document being created from an SVGDOMImplementation. The XLink namespace is added to the root, along with values for height and width. The store() method, included for testing purposes, is also the same as that of the simple example, except that here we don't need to consider a JPEG representation. The rest of the methods follow the same basic pattern—creating an element and then adding its attributes. The createShape() method calls one of three different helper methods, depending on whether the item is the parent (an SVG rect required), the focus (circle), or an offshoot (ellipse).

LISTING 19.17   SVGHelpers.java

```java
package com.sams.squirrel.view;

import java.util.*;
import java.io.*;

import org.w3c.dom.*;
import org.w3c.dom.svg.*;

import org.apache.batik.dom.svg.SVGDOMImplementation;
import org.apache.batik.transcoder.*;
```

LISTING 19.17   Continued

```java
import org.apache.batik.transcoder.svg2svg.*;

import com.sams.squirrel.model.*;
import com.sams.squirrel.view.*;

public class SVGHelpers implements SVGConstants {

    private SVGHelpers() {
    }

    public static SVGDocument createSVGDocument() {

        DOMImplementation impl = SVGDOMImplementation.getDOMImplementation();
        String SVG_NS = SVGDOMImplementation.SVG_NAMESPACE_URI;
        SVGDocument svgDocument =
            (SVGDocument) impl.createDocument(SVG_NS, "svg", null);
        Element svgRoot = svgDocument.getDocumentElement();

        svgRoot.setAttribute("xmlns:xlink", SVGConstants.XLINK_NS);

        svgRoot.setAttribute("width", Integer.toString(VIEW_WIDTH));
        svgRoot.setAttribute("height", Integer.toString(VIEW_HEIGHT));
        return svgDocument;
    }

    public static void store(SVGDocument svgDocument, String filename) {
        Transcoder transcoder = new SVGTranscoder();

        TranscoderInput input = new TranscoderInput(svgDocument);
        try {
            OutputStream ostream = new FileOutputStream(filename);
            OutputStreamWriter out = new OutputStreamWriter(ostream);
            TranscoderOutput output = new TranscoderOutput(out); //ostream

            transcoder.transcode(input, output);
            ostream.flush();
            ostream.close();
        } catch (Exception exception) {
            exception.printStackTrace();
        }
    }
```

19

LISTING 19.17   Continued

```
public static Element
      createShapeElement(SVGSprig svgSprig, SprigItem sprigItem) {

    Element shapeElement = null;
    switch (sprigItem.getType()) {
        case SprigItem.PARENT :
            shapeElement = createParentShape(svgSprig);
            break;
        case SprigItem.FOCUS :
            shapeElement = createFocusShape(svgSprig);
            break;
        case SprigItem.OFFSHOOT :
            shapeElement = createOffshootShape(svgSprig);
            break;
    }
    setCSSClass(sprigItem, shapeElement);
    return shapeElement;
}

public static Element createParentShape(SVGSprig svgSprig) {
    Element shapeElement = svgSprig.createSVGElement("rect");
    shapeElement.setAttribute("width", Integer.toString(ITEM_WIDTH));
    shapeElement.setAttribute("height", Integer.toString(ITEM_HEIGHT));
    shapeElement.setAttribute("x", Integer.toString(-ITEM_WIDTH / 2));
    shapeElement.setAttribute("y", Integer.toString(-ITEM_HEIGHT / 2));
    return shapeElement;
}

public static void setCSSClass(SprigItem sprigItem, Element shapeElement) {

    if (sprigItem.isDocument()) {
        shapeElement.setAttribute("class", "document");
        return;
    }
    if (sprigItem.isRoot()) {
        shapeElement.setAttribute("class", "root");
        return;
    }
    if (sprigItem.isLeaf()) {
        shapeElement.setAttribute("class", "leaf");
        return;
```

LISTING 19.17   Continued

```
        }
        shapeElement.setAttribute("class", "normal");
    }

    public static Element createFocusShape(SVGSprig svgSprig) {
        Element shapeElement = svgSprig.createSVGElement("circle");
        shapeElement.setAttribute("r", Integer.toString(RADIUS));
        return shapeElement;
    }

    public static Element createOffshootShape(SVGSprig svgSprig) {
        Element shapeElement = svgSprig.createSVGElement("ellipse");
        shapeElement.setAttribute("rx", Integer.toString(ITEM_WIDTH / 2));
        shapeElement.setAttribute("ry", Integer.toString(ITEM_HEIGHT / 2));
        return shapeElement;
    }

    public static Element
        createLineElement(SVGSprig svgSprig, int x1, int y1, int x2, int y2) {

        Element line = svgSprig.createSVGElement("line");
        line.setAttribute("x1", Integer.toString(x1));
        line.setAttribute("y1", Integer.toString(y1));
        line.setAttribute("x2", Integer.toString(x2));
        line.setAttribute("y2", Integer.toString(y2));
        return line;
    }

    public static Element
        createLinkElement(SVGSprig svgSprig, SVGSprigItem svgSprigItem) {

        String link =
            svgSprig.getLinkBaseURL()
                + "/servlet/com.sams.squirrel.control.SquirrelServlet"
                + "?sprigID="
                + svgSprigItem.getOffshootID();
        Element linkElement = svgSprig.createSVGElement("a");
        linkElement.setAttributeNS(SVGConstants.XLINK_NS, "xlink:href", link);
        return linkElement;
    }
}
```

The last method creates the link associated with the item using the XLink namespace on the attribute. The linked URL will be of the form

```
"/sams/servlet/com.sams.squirrel.control.SquirrelServlet?sprigID=7"
```

which, when the item is clicked, will carry out a GET call on the Squirrel servlet, passing along the ID of this item.

Listing 19.18 encapsulates the text that an item will be labeled with. In this application, the label has three parts: the name of the element, the text the element contains, and the attributes of the element. The latter will be generated only if the item is the focus. This code looks a lot more complicated than it really is because of the need to calculate the spacing between the lines of text (which is based on the TEXT_SPACING constant). The constructor obtains the container objects it will be manipulating, that is, the sprig that is currently being generated, the DOM document that will contain the SVG data, and the SVG group element that will contain all the text elements created by this class. In generating the label, we are looking only at the information made available by the SprigItem interface, and the text is held in the Map attributes available from implementations of this class. Specifically, in this application, the attribute with the key "sprigName" will be presented as the first line of text, the attribute with the key "sprigText" will be presented as the second line, and the remaining attributes will form the subsequent lines when a detailed label is required. There is an exception—the "sprigID" attribute is used by the SVG link-to-servlet-to-SVG generation communication and is introduced by the application rather than being part of the information to be viewed. This attribute is not displayed. The buildGroup() method calls on the buildTitle() method to create the first line of the label, and for creation of subsequent lines, the addDetail() method is used instead. The different SVG text elements are given different "dy" attributes to look after the vertical spacing.

LISTING 19.18   SVGLabelGroup.java—Wrapper for Elements That Form a Label

```java
package com.sams.squirrel.view;

import java.util.*;

import org.w3c.dom.*;

public class SVGLabelGroup {

    private Element groupElement;
    private Document document;
    private SVGSprig svgSprig;

    private boolean detailed;
```

LISTING 19.18   Continued

```java
public SVGLabelGroup(SVGSprigItem svgSprigItem, boolean detailed) {
    this.detailed = detailed;
    svgSprig = (SVGSprig) svgSprigItem.getSprig();
    document = svgSprig.getDocument();
    buildGroup(svgSprigItem);
}

public Element getLabelElement() {
    return groupElement;
}

private void buildGroup(SVGSprigItem svgSprigItem) {

    groupElement = svgSprig.createSVGElement("g");
    Map attributes = svgSprigItem.getAttributes();
    Iterator iterator = attributes.keySet().iterator();
    String key;
    String value;
    int vOffset = 0;
    if (detailed) {
        vOffset = -SVGConstants.TEXT_SPACING * ((2+attributes.size()) / 2);
    }
    value = (String) attributes.get("sprigName");
    if (value != null) {
        groupElement.appendChild(buildTitle(value, vOffset));
    }
    groupElement.appendChild(
        addDetail("sprigText",
        (String)attributes.get("sprigText"),
        (int)(vOffset+1.5*SVGConstants.TEXT_SPACING)));

    if (!detailed) {
        return;
    }
    int lineNumber = 4;
    while (iterator.hasNext()) {
        key = (String) iterator.next();
        value = (String) attributes.get(key);
        if (!key.equals("sprigName")
            && !key.equals("sprigID")
            && !key.equals("sprigText")) {
```

19

LISTING 19.18   Continued

```java
                groupElement.appendChild(
                    addDetail(key,
                        value,
                        vOffset+(lineNumber++) * SVGConstants.TEXT_SPACING) );
            }
        }
    }

    private Element buildTitle(String text, int vOffset) {

        Element titleElement = svgSprig.createSVGElement("text");
        titleElement.setAttribute("class", "title");
        Node textNode = document.createTextNode("<" + text.trim() + ">");
        titleElement.appendChild(textNode);
        titleElement.setAttribute("dy", Integer.toString(vOffset));
        return titleElement;
    }

    private Element addDetail(String name, String value, int vOffset) {
        Element detailElement = svgSprig.createSVGElement("text");

        Node textNode;

        if (name.equals("sprigText")) {
            detailElement.setAttribute("class", "content");
            textNode = document.createTextNode(value);
        } else {
            detailElement.setAttribute("class", "detail");
            textNode = document.createTextNode(name + " = " + value);
        }

        detailElement.appendChild(textNode);
        detailElement.setAttribute("dy", Integer.toString(vOffset));
        return detailElement;
    }

}
```

Data Source

We have looked at the model and viewed parts of the M-V-C architecture, but before moving on to the controller, we will now look at the classes that are responsible for loading the source XML file and creating the `Sprig` objects that the application displays. The contents of the `com.sams.squirrel.xml` package are essentially implementations of the model interfaces wrapped around a conventional DOM document. This document is contained in the `DOMSprigSource` class, which is also responsible for delivering `Sprig` objects based on the contents of the DOM tree (see Listing 19.19). For convenience, this class uses the Crimson parser, parts of which are also used in Batik, although it should be noted that the full `crimson.jar` package (from apache.org) is required here. The `load()` method loads the source XML into the DOM document and then calls the local `addIdentifiers()` method. We use this approach to add a `sprigID="x"` attribute to all the elements in the tree that will be used for identification purposes. The `getSprig()` methods use the `DOMSprig` and `DOMSprigItem` classes to construct a `Sprig` object based on elements in the DOM tree.

LISTING 19.19   DOMSprigSource.java—Sprig Objects Built from the DOM Tree

```
package com.sams.squirrel.xml;

import java.io.*;

import org.xml.sax.*;
import javax.xml.parsers.*;
import org.xml.sax.helpers.*;

import org.w3c.dom.*;

import org.apache.batik.dom.svg.SAXSVGDocumentFactory;
import org.apache.batik.util.XMLResourceDescriptor;

import com.sams.squirrel.model.*;

// An adapter, DOM+SprigSource

public class DOMSprigSource implements SprigSource {

    private static final String PARSER_NAME = "dom.wrappers.DOMParser";

    private Document document;


    public void load(String uri) {

        DocumentBuilderFactory factory = DocumentBuilderFactory.newInstance();

        // default value from JAXP 1.0 was defined to be false.
```

LISTING 19.19   Continued

```java
        factory.setNamespaceAware(true);
        factory.setValidating(false);
        factory.setIgnoringComments(true);
        DocumentBuilder builder = null;
        try {
            builder = factory.newDocumentBuilder();
            document = builder.parse(uri);
        } catch (Exception exception) {
            exception.printStackTrace();
        }
        addIdentifiers();
    }

    public Sprig getRootSprig() {
        Element root = document.getDocumentElement();
        SprigItem sprigItem = new DOMSprigItem(root);
        return getSprig(sprigItem);
    }

    public Sprig getSprig(String focusID) {
        if (focusID.equals("-1")) {
            return getRootSprig();
        }
        NodeList elements = document.getElementsByTagName("*");
        Element element;
        for (int i = 0; i < elements.getLength(); i++) {
            element = (Element) elements.item(i);
            if (element.getAttribute("sprigID").equals(focusID)) {
                SprigItem sprigItem = new DOMSprigItem(element);
                return getSprig(sprigItem);
            }
        }
        return null;
    }

    public Sprig getSprig(SprigItem focus) {
        Sprig sprig = new DOMSprig(focus);
        return sprig;
    }

    private void addIdentifiers() {
```

LISTING 19.19   Continued

```
        NodeList elements =
    document.getDocumentElement().getElementsByTagNameNS("*", "*");
        Element element;
        for (int i = 0; i < elements.getLength(); i++) {
            element = (Element) elements.item(i);
            element.setAttribute("sprigID", Integer.toString(i));
        }
    }
}
```

The `DOMSprig` class, shown in Listing 19.20, uses the `DOMSprigItem` class to build the parent and offshoot items surrounding a given focus item. The characteristics of these items are determined by the position of their corresponding DOM element in the source tree.

LISTING 19.20   DOMSprig.java—HeadSprig Implementation for XML DOM Domain

```
package com.sams.squirrel.xml;

import java.util.*;

import org.w3c.dom.*;

import com.sams.squirrel.model.*;

public class DOMSprig extends SprigImpl {

    private Element focusElement;

    public DOMSprig(SprigItem focus) {
        super(focus);
        focus.setSprig(this);
        focusElement = ((DOMSprigItem) focus).getDOMElement();
        createParent();
        createOffshoots();
    }

    private void createParent() {
        Element parent = Utils.getParentElement(focusElement);
        SprigItem sprigItem = new DOMSprigItem(parent);
        sprigItem.setType(SprigItem.PARENT);
```

LISTING 19.19   Continued

```
            super.add(sprigItem);
    }

    private void createOffshoots() {
        List childElements = Utils.getChildElements(focusElement);
        SprigItem sprigItem;
        for (int i = 0; i < childElements.size(); i++) {
            sprigItem = new DOMSprigItem((Element) childElements.get(i));
            sprigItem.setType(SprigItem.OFFSHOOT);
            super.add(sprigItem);
        }
    }
}
```

The DOMSprig class in Listing 19.20 makes calls to a class called Utils, shown in Listing 19.21. This is another class of static utility methods that encapsulate various sequences of operations. The first is a convenience method for creating a Map object that contains just a single pair of items. The next, attributesAsMap(), obtains the attributes of a DOM element as a standard Java collection; likewise, getChildElements() returns a collection of the child elements of a given node. The getParentElement() method is just a wrapper to narrow the behavior of Node.getParentNode() to only returning elements.

LISTING 19.21   Utils.java

```
package com.sams.squirrel.xml;

import java.util.*;

import org.w3c.dom.*;

public class Utils {

    public static Map mapFromPair(Object key, Object value) {
        Map map = new HashMap();
        map.put(key, value);
        return map;
    }

    public static Map attributesAsMap(Element element) {
        Map attributes = new HashMap();
        NamedNodeMap nnMap = element.getAttributes();
```

LISTING 19.21   Continued

```
        Node node;
        for (int i = 0; i < nnMap.getLength(); i++) {
            node = nnMap.item(i);
            attributes.put(node.getNodeName(), node.getNodeValue());
        }
        return attributes;
    }

    public static List getChildElements(Node parent) {
        List children = new ArrayList();
        NodeList nodes = parent.getChildNodes();
        Node node;
        for (int i = 0; i < nodes.getLength(); i++) {
            node = nodes.item(i);
            if (node.getNodeType() == Node.ELEMENT_NODE) {
                children.add(node);
            }
        }
        return children;
    }

    public static Element getParentElement(Node node) {
        Node parent = node.getParentNode();
        if ((parent == null) ||
                !(parent.getNodeType() == Element.ELEMENT_NODE)) {
            return null;
        }
        return (Element)parent;
    }
}
```

The role of the DOMSprigItem class in Listing 19.22 is to examine the DOM element from which it is created and to set its own properties based on the properties of that item. The loadAttributes() method pulls out all the DOM attributes of the element that an instance of this class will wrap and puts them in the attribute map of this SprigItem. It also adds an attribute to this SprigItem's map corresponding to the text content of the element (sprigText) and the name of the element's tag (sprigName). These two attributes are given special status by the class that generates the SVG representation from a SprigItem, so customization for viewing a specific XML language would probably start here.

LISTING 19.22   DOMSprigItem.java—Adapter Between XML DOM Elements and SprigItems

```java
package com.sams.squirrel.xml;

import java.util.*;

import org.w3c.dom.*;

import com.sams.squirrel.model.*;


public class DOMSprigItem extends AbstractSprigItem {

    private Element element;

    public DOMSprigItem(Element element) {
        this.element = element;
        super.setDataSource(element);
        setRoot(false);
        setDocument(false);
        setLeaf(false);
        if (element == null) { // document
            setDocument(true);
            setOffshootID("-1");

        } else { // doc root
            setOffshootID(element.getAttribute("sprigID"));
            if (element.getParentNode().equals(element.getOwnerDocument())) {
                setRoot(true);
                setOffshootID("-1");
            } else {
                setLeaf(Utils.getChildElements(element).size() == 0);
            }
        }
        loadAttributes();
    }

    public Element getDOMElement() {
        return element;
    }

    public List getItems() {
        return super.getSprig().getItems();
    }
```

LISTING 19.22   Continued

```java
    private void loadAttributes() {
        // code for customizing labels could go here
        if (element != null) {
            setAttributes(Utils.attributesAsMap((Element) element));
            setAttribute("sprigName", element.getTagName());
            String text = "";
            NodeList childNodes = element.getChildNodes();
            for(int i=0;i<childNodes.getLength();i++){
                if(childNodes.item(i).getNodeType() == Node.TEXT_NODE){
                    text += childNodes.item(i).getNodeValue();
                }
            }
            setAttribute("sprigText", text.trim());
        } else {
            setAttribute("sprigName", "Document");
            setDocument(true);
        }
    }
}
```

Controller

The behavior of the application is coordinated by classes located in the com.sams.squirrel.control package. This behavior is somewhat convoluted due to the need for separate servlets to generate the HTML and the SVG. You can see the general idea behind the creation of the SVG more clearly in Listing 19.23, which is a command-line application that will use the previously described classes to read an XML file; it also will generate the SVG for the sprig view of the root element of the XML, which is saved to file. The place to save the file (svgLocation), the source document (sourceDocument), and the base URL (baseURL) to use in the links within the SVG are all hard-coded here.

This mini-application begins by creating a new DOMSprigSource object. This object's load() method is then called to populate the DOM tree contained in the object from the source XML. The root sprig is then obtained from the source using the getRootSprig() method. This can be seen as a generic Sprig object, with the characteristics defined in the Sprig interface. The constructor of the SVGSprig class takes this object, along with the URL to use in links, producing a sprig with SVG properties. The store() method is then called to save this new object to a file.

LISTING 19.23   CommandLineTest.java—Simplified Application for Testing

```java
package com.sams.squirrel.control;

import java.io.*;
```

19

LISTING 19.23   Continued

```java
import com.sams.squirrel.model.*;
import com.sams.squirrel.view.*;
import com.sams.squirrel.xml.*;

public class CommandLineTest {

    static final String svgLocation =
    "C:/output.svg";
    static final String sourceDocument
            = "http://localhost:8080/sams/test.xml";
    static final String baseURL =
    "http://localhost:8080/sams/servlet/com.sams.squirrel.control.Squirrel";

    public static void main(String[] args) {
        new CommandLineTest(sourceDocument, svgLocation);
    }

    public CommandLineTest(String sourceDocument, String targetFilename) {
        DOMSprigSource domSprigSource = new DOMSprigSource();

        try {
            domSprigSource.load(sourceDocument);
        } catch (Exception exception) {
            exception.printStackTrace();
        }

        Sprig domRootSprig = domSprigSource.getRootSprig();

        SVGSprig start = new SVGSprig(baseURL, domRootSprig);
        start.store(targetFilename);
    }
}
```

Note that you may have to modify the addresses in Listing 19.23 and recompile to suit your system. The use of hard-coded addresses in this listing is just about acceptable, as the code is disposable, merely intended as a quick test.

> **NOTE**
>
> We have used hard-coded addresses several times in this chapter to reduce listing complexity and save space on paper. Under normal circumstances, coding this way is bad practice. For more

robust applications, environment-dependent constants such as addresses should be specified outside the code, in custom property files or in purpose-built files such as Tomcat's web.xml file.

The control side of Squirrel is handled by four classes. The first, shown in Listing 19.24, merely defines a couple of constants that are used by the servlets.

LISTING 19.24   SystemConstants.java—System-Specific Constants

```
package com.sams.squirrel.control;

public interface SystemConstants {
    public static final String DEFAULT_SOURCE =
                    "http://localhost:8080/sams/test.xml";
    public static final String STYLESHEET = "/sams/css/squirrel.css";
}
```

SquirrelServlet looks after the generation of HTML, and SVGServlet looks after the generation of SVG. The latter servlet will build SVGSprig objects based on supplied parameters from a cached copy of the DOM tree of the source XML. To simplify its job, we use the SprigBridge class, which ties the HTTP operations of SVGServlet to the classes that look after loading and building sprigs in the other packages. The caching of the DOM tree is achieved by storing instances of SprigBridge in the session object of an SVGServlet.

SquirrelServlet, shown in Listing 19.25, is really the application front end and isn't far from a minimal "print HTML" servlet. It will normally be accessed through HTTP GET calls generated by an HTML form in the browser. In fact, the first time this servlet is accessed, it will respond by presenting a simple HTML form with a single-line text entry box (for the URL of the source XML to explore) and a submit button. The URL of the XML of interest is persisted in the session attribute with the key "source". This value will be used as part of the request for the SVG. Clicking on the button will make the following request of the Web server:

```
http://localhost:8080/sams/servlet/com.sams.squirrel.control.SquirrelServlet?
➥sourceDocument=http://localhost:8080sams/test.xml&sprigID=root
```

As in Figures 19.5 through 19.7, the first image displayed will be the root sprig of the source tree. Each item in the tree has a link, and within the link string is a parameter corresponding to the ID of that item within the sprig. When one of the items is clicked, a SquirrelServlet will be called again, and this time the HTTP request will contain a parameter called "sprigID". The request will look something like this:

```
http://localhost:8080/sams/servlet/com.sams.squirrel.control.SquirrelServlet?
➥sprigID=5
```

The values of these GET parameters are picked up in the servlet and used to determine whether this is the first time the servlet has been run, and also to provide a parameter within the embedded (SVG) object.

LISTING 19.25   SquirrelServlet.java—HTML-Generation Servlet

```java
package com.sams.squirrel.control;

import java.io.*;
import javax.servlet.*;
import javax.servlet.http.*;

import com.sams.squirrel.view.*;

public class SquirrelServlet extends HttpServlet implements SystemConstants {

    private HttpSession session;
    private String requestURI;
    private String sourceDocument;
    private String previousDocument;
    private String sprigID;

    private boolean firstRun;

    public void doGet(HttpServletRequest request,
                          HttpServletResponse response)
        throws IOException, ServletException {

        session = request.getSession(true);

        previousDocument = (String) session.getAttribute("source");
        sourceDocument = request.getParameter("sourceDocument");
        sprigID = request.getParameter("sprigID");

        // this finds out if it's the first time it's been run
        if ((sourceDocument == null) && (sprigID == null)) {
            firstRun = true;
        } else {
            session.setAttribute("source", sourceDocument);
            firstRun = false;
        }
        generateResponse(request, response);
    }

    public void doPost(HttpServletRequest request,
```

LISTING 19.25   Continued

```
                         HttpServletResponse response)
    throws IOException, ServletException {
    doGet(request, response);
}

private void generateResponse(HttpServletRequest request,
                              HttpServletResponse response)
    throws IOException {

    response.setContentType("text/html");

    PrintWriter out = response.getWriter();
    out.print("<?xml version=\"1.0\"?>");

    out.print("<?xml-stylesheet href=\""
            + STYLESHEET + "\" type=\"text/css\"?>");
    out.print("<html>");
    out.println("<head>");
    out.println("<title>Squirrel</title>");
    out.println("</head>");
    out.println("<body>");
    out.println("<!-- generated by SquirrelServlet -->");

    if (!firstRun) {
        out.print("<object type=\"image/svg+xml\"
        ➥name=\"SVGObject\" width=\"600\" height=\"400\">");
        out.print("<param name=\"src\" value = \"");
        out.print(
            request.getContextPath()
+ "/servlet/com.sams.squirrel.control.SVGServlet?sourceDocument="
                + sourceDocument
                + "&sprigID="
                + sprigID
                + "&extension=is.svg");
        out.print("\" /></object>");
    }

    out.println("<form action=
    ➥\"com.sams.squirrel.control.SquirrelServlet\" method=\"GET\">");
    out.println("Document to view :");
    out.println(
```

LISTING 19.25   Continued

```
                "<input type=\"text\" size=\"50\" name=\"sourceDocument\" value=\""
            ➥+ DEFAULT_SOURCE + "\"/>");
        out.println("<input type=\"hidden\"
        ➥name=\"sprigID\" value=\"root\"/>");
        out.println("<input type=\"submit\"/>");
        out.println("</form>");
        out.println("</body>");
        out.println("</html>");
    }

}
```

The XHTML generated by this servlet will look something like Listing 19.26.

LISTING 19.26   Dynamically Generated HTML

```
<?xml version="1.0"?>
<?xml-stylesheet href="/sams/css/squirrel.css" type="text/css"?>
<html><head>
<title>Squirrel</title>
</head>
<body>
<!-- generated by SquirrelServlet -->
<object type="image/svg+xml" name="SVGObject" width="600" height="400">
<param name="src" value =
"/sams/servlet/com.sams.squirrel.control.SVGServlet?
sourceDocument=null&sprigID=-1&extension=is.svg" />
</object>
<form action="com.sams.squirrel.control.SquirrelServlet" method="GET">
Document to view :
<input type="text" size="50" name="sourceDocument"
value="http://localhost:8080/sams/test.xml"/>
<input type="hidden" name="sprigID" value="root"/>
<input type="submit"/>
</form></body></html>
```

In Listing 19.26, note the use of the dummy parameter `extension=is.svg` to give the browser a hint that this object should be served up as SVG. The servlet called by the browser when it encounters the embedded `<object>` in the XHTML is also relatively simple; it is shown in Listing 19.27.

LISTING 19.27   SVGServlet.java

```java
package com.sams.squirrel.control;

import java.io.*;
import javax.servlet.*;
import javax.servlet.http.*;

import com.sams.squirrel.view.*;

public class SVGServlet extends HttpServlet implements SystemConstants {

    private HttpSession session;
    private String requestURI;
    private String sourceDocument;
    private String previousDocument;
    private String sprigID;

    private boolean newDocument;

    public void doGet(HttpServletRequest request,
                      HttpServletResponse response)
        throws IOException, ServletException {

        session = request.getSession(true);

        sourceDocument = request.getParameter("sourceDocument");
        sprigID = (String) request.getParameter("sprigID");

        sourceDocument = request.getParameter("sourceDocument");

        if (sprigID.equals("root")) {
            newDocument = true;
            session.setAttribute("source", sourceDocument);
        } else {
            newDocument = false;
            sourceDocument = (String) session.getAttribute("source");
        }
        generateResponse(request, response);
    }

    public void doPost(HttpServletRequest request,
                       HttpServletResponse response)
        throws IOException, ServletException {
```

LISTING 19.27 Continued

```
        doGet(request, response);
    }


    private void generateResponse(HttpServletRequest request,
                                  HttpServletResponse response)
        throws IOException {

        response.setContentType("text/html");

        PrintWriter out = response.getWriter();
        SprigBridge bridge;

        if (newDocument) {
            bridge = new SprigBridge();
            session.setAttribute("bridge", bridge);
            bridge.setBaseURL(request.getContextPath());
            bridge.prepareRootSprig(sourceDocument);
        } else {
            bridge = (SprigBridge) session.getAttribute("bridge");
            bridge.prepareSprig(sprigID);
        }

        out.print("<?xml version=\"1.0\"?>");

        out.print("<?xml-stylesheet href=\"" + STYLESHEET +
        ➥ "\" type=\"text/css\"?>");
        out.println("<!-- generated by SVGServlet -->");
        bridge.outputSVG(out);
    }
```

The name of the document requested is stored in a session variable; this way, a check can be made whether the URL refers to a new document. If so, a new SprigBridge object is created (to wrap the back-end classes) and is stored in a session variable. The source code for the SprigBridge class appears in Listing 19.28. The first time around, a method is called in this object to create the root sprig view. If the document URL isn't new, the previously created SprigBridge object is retrieved from the session and its prepareSprig() method called, with the ID of the SprigItem to use as the focus. Either way, the HTTP response generated will begin with a couple of XML processing instructions and a comment, followed by a serialization of the SVG obtained from the SprigBridge.

LISTING 19.28   SprigBridge.java—Bridge Between Sprig Classes and Servlets

```java
package com.sams.squirrel.control;

import java.io.*;

import org.w3c.dom.*;
import org.w3c.dom.svg.*;

import org.apache.batik.transcoder.*;
import org.apache.batik.transcoder.svg2svg.*;

import com.sams.squirrel.model.*;
import com.sams.squirrel.xml.*;
import com.sams.squirrel.view.*;

public class SprigBridge {

    private DOMSprigSource domSprigSource;
    private String baseURL;
    private SVGSprig svgSprig;

    public void prepareRootSprig(String sourceDocument) {
        domSprigSource = new DOMSprigSource();
        try {
            domSprigSource.load(sourceDocument);
        } catch (Exception exception) {
            exception.printStackTrace();
        }

        Sprig domSprig = domSprigSource.getRootSprig();
        convertToSVG(domSprig);
    }

    public void setBaseURL(String baseURL) {
        this.baseURL = baseURL;
    }

    public void prepareSprig(String focusID) {
        Sprig domSprig = domSprigSource.getSprig(focusID);
        convertToSVG(domSprig);
    }

    private void convertToSVG(Sprig sprig) { //requestURI
```

LISTING 19.28   Continued

```
            svgSprig = new SVGSprig(baseURL, sprig);
    }


    public void outputSVG(PrintWriter writer) {
        SVGDocument svgDocument = svgSprig.getDocument();
        Transcoder transcoder = new SVGTranscoder();
        TranscoderInput input = new TranscoderInput(svgDocument);
        try {
            TranscoderOutput output = new TranscoderOutput(writer);
            transcoder.transcode(input, output);
        } catch (Exception exception) {
            exception.printStackTrace();
        }
    }
}
```

When asked to prepare the root sprig in Listing 19.28, the `SprigBridge` class follows a similar procedure to that of the `CommandLineTest` code. The `prepareSprig()` method is also similar, except in this case the ID of the item to use as the focus is provided. The `outputSVG()` method is like the `store()` method in `SVGHelpers`, except this time the data is sent to a `PrintWriter` object, which in this case will pass it back to the calling browser.

Summary

This chapter showed several ways in which server-side Java can be used to generate SVG. First, we used JSP as a scripting language to generate simple fractal images. This approach is perfectly good, but the real benefits of server-side Java really start only when we start building Java classes behind the scenes. One range of possibilities is offered by JavaBeans, like this chapter's example which finds where a line intersects a rectangle. We can build all manner of JavaBean components, which we can call directly with JSP to provide information that can be represented in SVG.

By using the SVG DOM, as we did in the simple example in which we drew a circle and then in the Squirrel application, we get a degree of control over the SVG that goes beyond text-based manipulation. SVG DOM is, of course, available on the client-side too, but its sophistication is soon appreciated in the server-side environment.

The Squirrel application demonstrated one way that servlets can generate SVG. A nontrivial structure was loaded (from the source XML file) so that the user could explore interactively. The SVG was visually trivial, but in other chapters we saw how straightforward it is to make sophisticated imagery with SVG. What we demonstrated here is that linking SVG presentation to nontrivial back-end abstract models is also straightforward. These models required quite a lot of code, but the individual classes weren't particularly complex. The Model-View-Controller architecture allows relatively loose coupling between different aspects of the code, making extension and reuse straightforward.

In this chapter, we saw in isolation only two key parts of the most prominent approaches to server-side Java and SVG. Many more options are available. Servlets and JSP are commonly used together, and this combination is well suited for SVG use. There is a major amount of potential for the use of other Java techniques with SVG, such as custom tags, which extend the capabilities of JSP, and JDBC, which provides database connectivity. Countless readily available Java-based systems such as the Tomcat server and the Jena RDF Toolkit mean that sophisticated systems can be easily developed, and tools such as Batik mean that sophisticated SVG user interfaces are possible. Java is a great tool for building applications with machine-to-machine interconnectivity, and SVG is excellent for human-to-machine connectivity. The combination of these technologies is likely to play a significant role in the evolution of the Web.

CHAPTER **20**

SVG and XSLT

In this chapter, we will see how XSLT (Extensible Stylesheet Language Transformations) can be used to generate SVG from XML. This chapter is not intended as a complete XSLT tutorial, but we will begin with a brief overview and work through examples with aspects of the language brought in just a few at a time.

After the overview and a look at the XSLT processors available, we will work step by step toward generating SVG from some source data—in this case, a piece of XHTML. We will then show how this generation can be carried out on the server. Afterward, we will look at how source data can be obtained from an HTML form and how XSLT transformations can be chained, leading to a simple but nontrivial client/server application.

Little of the code presented here will contain much in the way of surprises for the experienced XSLT programmer. There is, however, one simple underlying idea, the implications of which can come as a major revelation: SVG is XML, so all those clever XSLT tricks can be used *directly* to generate SVG.

Whatever your background, we hope that this chapter will demonstrate that XSLT can form a versatile and powerful part of your toolkit as an SVG developer.

XSLT Overview

So far in this book, we have looked at creating SVG using procedural and object-oriented techniques. A great many operations, however, can be carried out in a far more straightforward fashion by moving away from the more familiar programming paradigms. XSLT is a declarative language, based on rules rather than objects or functions. Though powerful, it is essentially a very simple language, but after you learn other languages, it can be difficult to grasp at first because of the paradigm shift. The initial steep climb is very much worthwhile, though, because XSLT offers very neat solutions to a vast number of common problems.

Declarative Languages

Nowadays the database language SQL is probably the best-known example of a declarative language, though functional languages such as Lisp and logic languages such as Prolog also fall into this category. Within such languages, we don't write dozens of lines of procedure that describe how to get a result; we just state the result we want and let the processor do the work. In SQL we might make a statement to, say, add a bonus $100 to the salaries of all employees who have a birthday in January. Once given the statement, the database system will just go away and carry out the operation, hiding the internal details of how it does its work.

XSLT works this way in principle, but instead of records, it deals with an XML tree, and operations are specified using templates to select parts of the tree and describe what to do with them, with the output being a transformed version of the input XML. The input is XML, but the output can be any (text-based) format we like, and we determine how the two are related. Despite the different basis, XSLT also has many facilities found in other languages, and it is possible, for example, to carry out tasks such as numeric calculations based on source data.

The transformation approach is extremely good for presentation purposes, because for a given input structure, we can specify the target format and layout, and the XSLT will take care of putting the content in the right places. SVG is primarily a presentation language, and XSLT is perfect for preparing information for presentation. As we will see in this chapter, XSLT fits SVG like a glove.

The XSLT specification can be found at `http://www.w3.org/TR/xslt`, and a large part of it depends on XPath.

XPath

Template matching and entity selection in XSLT are carried out using the XPath language. Comparable to SQL SELECT statements, XPath expressions are used to select sets of nodes from an XML tree. XPath is used to describe a path through to the nodes of interest, and this is specified as a series of steps separated by forward slashes. The location steps can be given in either of two forms, abbreviated or unabbreviated. Most of the time the abbreviated form will be used, and paths in this form appear very similar to those of file system directories: / is the root, /foo/bar specifies the bar element contained in the foo element contained in the root, . is the current location, .. is the parent, and so on. The general form of each step is as follows:

```
axis::node-test[predicate]*
```

The `axis` part describes which way to look from the current node; it can have values such as `self` (.), `attribute` (@), or `descendants` (//). The `node-test` part is a basic test of the nodes found at the current path. The `predicate` is a logical test in which we can use a range of functions to further filter down the node set.

The easiest way to understand how XSLT works is to see it in practice, so we'll move on to some practical code shortly. First, though, we'll look at what software we need to use XSLT.

XSLT Processors

An XSLT processor is an engine that converts XML to another format, based on rules provided in an XSLT style sheet. These processors appear in various forms, either as stand-alone command-line applications, as built-in development tools, as a functional unit in a programming language, or as a single aspect of a larger application.

For developing style sheets in isolation, the tools available include XML Spy (lots of features; `http://www.xmlspy.com/`) and XML Cooktop (Windows platform only, but simple and *free*; `http://www.xmlcooktop.com/`).

The following is a list of language-specific implementations that is by no means exhaustive. Many of these implementations (such as Xalan) include command-line tools based on the libraries. Most can be used client- or server-side.

- **C**—libxml2/libxslt (`http://xmlsoft.org/`)

- **C++**—Apache Xalan (`http://xml.apache.org/xalan-c`)

- **Java**—XT (`http://www.blnz.com/xt/`)

  Apache Xalan (`http://xml.apache.org/xalan-j`)

- **Microsoft Only**—Application and ASP support is provided in MSXML and the .NET Framework (`http://msdn.microsoft.com/xml`)

- **Perl**—XML::XSLT (`http://xmlxslt.sourceforge.net/`)

- **PHP**—Sabletron XSLT processor (`http://www.php.net/manual/en/ref.xslt.php`)

- **Python**—4XSLT (`http://www.4suite.org`)

When we begin demonstrating XSLT-based applications on the server, we will use ASP JScript code, which might not be appropriate for your target system. However, exactly the same techniques can be used in virtually any language, the differences in the code for various systems being more a matter of syntax than anything else.

In this chapter, we are looking at XSLT techniques in isolation, but you should bear in mind that XSLT is entirely compatible with other XML programming techniques and can be used in conjunction with them.

Three Steps to SVG

To explain how we can arrive at an SVG representation of XML data using XSLT, we will break down the process into three steps. We are aiming for a single style sheet to make the complete transformation, but we'll get there by progressively moving the output of a style sheet closer to SVG.

In the first step, we will concentrate on getting at the pieces of data of interest, which will be demonstrated using a simple style sheet that delivers text output. We will then use a couple more language features to help us get an XML output and finally add the extra bits needed for a stylish SVG output.

For a practical application, we'll see how XSLT and SVG can be used together to make a simple piece of (X)HTML appear somewhat more stylish than usual. We're talking about presentation, so without wasting any imagination we'll use for our source data a slide from a presentation. The code for this slide is shown in Listing 20.1.

LISTING 20.1   source.htm—HTML Slide Presentation

```
<html>
<head><title>Slide One</title></head>
<body>
<h1>XSLT and SVG</h1>
        <ul>
          <li>Versatility</li>
          <li>Interoperability</li>
          <li>Presentation Consistency</li>
          <li>Eye Candy</li>
        </ul>
</body>
</html>
```

XSLT processors expect well-formed XML, so all the elements here have closing tags. In a browser, running Listing 20.1 returns the result shown in Figure 20.1.

We have only two kinds of information displayed in the slide itself, the heading and bullet points, but we also have the title ("Slide One"), which is used to label the browser window.

Outputting Text

Getting at this information is straightforward in XSLT. Listing 20.2 will extract the parts we are interested in and format them in an arbitrary layout. When the XSLT processor is run, it will attempt to match templates in the style sheet. The code begins with the opening tag of the xsl:stylesheet element, which declares this as a style sheet and specifies the version and namespace. The kind of output data required—here, "text"—is then specified. The transformation features three templates, the first two of which use the XPath wildcard reference `//` to move the context to each of any `h1` or `li` elements, respectively, no matter how nested they are within the document tree. The third template uses the expression `/html/head/title` to specifically target the `title` element of an HTML document. This matching moves the frame of reference, so the context within the template is the element in question, and the statement `<xsl:value-of select="."/>` will address its content. Within each template is a piece of text, `Title =` and so on, that will be quoted literally in the output.

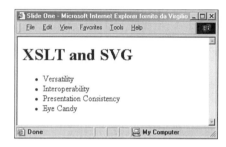

FIGURE 20.1   Presentation slide.

LISTING 20.2   stylesheet01.xsl—Arbitrary Text from XML

```
<xsl:stylesheet version = '1.0'
    xmlns:xsl='http://www.w3.org/1999/XSL/Transform'>

<xsl:output method = "text" />

<xsl:template match="//h1">
    Heading =
        <xsl:value-of select="."/>
</xsl:template>

<xsl:template match="//li">
    Bullet =
        <xsl:value-of select="."/>
</xsl:template>

<xsl:template match="/html/head/title">
    Title =
        <xsl:value-of select="."/>
</xsl:template>

</xsl:stylesheet>
```

20

The result of applying the transformation in Listing 20.2 (with some whitespace removed) looks like the output shown in Listing 20.3.

LISTING 20.3 stylesheet01.txt—Result of Transformation

```
        Title =
            Slide One
    Heading =
            XSLT and SVG
    Bullet =
            Versatility
    Bullet =
            Interoperability
    Bullet =
            Presentation Consistency
    Bullet =
            Eye Candy
```

Note that the templates in the style sheet appear in the order h1, li, title, and yet the output shown in Listing 20.3 follows the order of the source HTML document. This is evidence of the declarative nature of XSLT, in that the code states the rules, but the order in which they are applied is up to the processor. If two different rules can apply to the same item or items in the tree, the more specific rule takes precedence. We can demonstrate this principle by adding the following template anywhere within Listing 20.2:

```
<xsl:template match="/html/body/h1">
    Top thing =
            <xsl:value-of select="."/>
</xsl:template>
```

The path here is very specific, which gives this template precedence over the one with a wildcard-rooted (//h1) match, so the output would include Top thing =... instead of Heading =....

Outputting XML

We will now look at a style sheet designed to output XML (see Listing 20.4), in a language invented for demonstration purposes, based on the source HTML. The first change we need to make is to tell the processor that we want XML output, which we do by changing the method attribute of the xsl:output element. The indent attribute simply makes the output XML easier on the eye.

XML is tree-structured, whereas the output we saw in the preceding section is flat—what's lacking is a root. We can insert this root by starting at the context of the root in the source data tree. The XPath expression corresponding to the root is /, so we have a template match on this. Within the template in Listing 20.4, we have a `<slide>` element (from the invented language), which will serve as the root of our tree. Between this element's tags, we have the XSLT `<xsl:apply-templates select="*">` instruction. The asterisk is a wildcard that represents all child elements of the current context node, and the instruction is to find any templates in the style sheet that match the elements. The `select` attribute is actually redundant in this case because the default behavior without a `select` is to apply templates that match all child nodes (elements, text nodes, comments, and so on) of the current node, and the root element of our source document has only elements as children.

LISTING 20.4   stylesheet02.xsl—SimpleXML Output

```
<xsl:stylesheet version = '1.0'
    xmlns:xsl='http://www.w3.org/1999/XSL/Transform'>


<xsl:output method = "xml" indent="yes"/>


<xsl:template match="/">
    <slide>
        <xsl:apply-templates select="*"/>
    </slide>
</xsl:template>
```

The next two templates are essentially the same as in the text-output example, except that now the literal text is in the form of tags (again from the invented language), which will wrap the content of the elements from the source document. The use of literal text to form XML elements in the output may seem a little inelegant. In fact, the elements could be constructed using the `xsl:element` element, but unless the characteristics of the element are to be determined by the contents of the source document, the literal text approach keeps things simple:

```
<xsl:template match="//h1">
    <heading>
            <xsl:value-of select="."/>
        </heading>
</xsl:template>


<xsl:template match="//li">
    <bullet>
            <xsl:value-of select="."/>
        </bullet>
</xsl:template>
```

The template that will match the title of the source document has been changed a little here. We are going to keep this as a `title` element in our output, so we use the `copy-of` instruction to pass the element on, together with its descendant nodes (that is, the text it contains):

```
<xsl:template match="/html/head/title">
         <xsl:copy-of select="."/>
</xsl:template>

</xsl:stylesheet>
```

Running the source.htm file from Listing 20.1 through an XSLT processor using this style sheet produces Listing 20.5.

LISTING 20.5   stylesheet02.xml—Result of Transformation

```
<?xml version="1.0" encoding="UTF-16"?>
<slide>
<title>Slide One</title>
<heading>XSLT and SVG</heading>
<bullet>Versatility</bullet>
<bullet>Interoperability</bullet>
<bullet>Presentation Consistency</bullet>
<bullet>Eye Candy</bullet>
</slide>
```

Now that we can generate arbitrary XML based on the source document, we are most of the way to producing SVG.

Outputting SVG

The next version of our style sheet is structurally identical to the last, except this time we replace the pieces of the invented language with SVG elements and attributes, as shown in Listing 20.6.

LISTING 20.6   stylesheet03.xsl—Transforming to SVG

```
<xsl:stylesheet version = '1.0'
    xmlns:xsl='http://www.w3.org/1999/XSL/Transform'>

<xsl:output method = "xml" indent="yes"/>

<xsl:template match="/">
    <svg width="600" height="400">
    <xsl:apply-templates/>
    </svg>
```

LISTING 20.6   Continued

```
</xsl:template>

<xsl:template match="//h1">
    <g>
    <text class ="heading">
        <xsl:value-of select="."/>
    </text>
    </g>
</xsl:template>

<xsl:template match="//li">
    <g>
    <circle class="bullet" r="10" />
    <text class="bullet">
        <xsl:value-of select="."/>
    </text>
    </g>
</xsl:template>

<xsl:template match="/html/head/title">
        <xsl:copy-of select="."/>
        <desc>Generated using XSLT</desc>
</xsl:template>

</xsl:stylesheet>
```

Running source.htm (refer to Listing 20.1) through this style sheet produces something that is recognizably SVG but still not quite presentable. We are going to use an additional CSS style sheet alongside the SVG for final presentation, so we've included an appropriately named `class` attribute in all the visible elements in Listing 20.7. The heading we will represent as a single line of text, and the bullet points will be displayed as a circle (with a radius of 10 pixels) alongside the text.

LISTING 20.7   stylesheet03.xml—Generated SVG

```
<?xml version="1.0" encoding="UTF-16"?>
<svg width="600" height="400">
    <title>Slide One</title>
    <desc> Generated using XSLT </desc>
    <g>
        <text class="heading">XSLT and SVG</text>
    </g>
```

LISTING 20.7   Continued

```
        <g>
                <circle class="bullet" r="10" />
                <text class="bullet">Versatility</text>
        </g>
        <g>

                <circle class="bullet" r="10" />
                <text class="bullet">Interoperability</text>
        </g>
        <g>

                <circle class="bullet" r="10" />
                <text class="bullet">Presentation Consistency</text>
        </g>
        <g>

                <circle class="bullet" r="10" />
                <text class="bullet">Eye Candy</text>
        </g>
</svg>
```

NOTE

It has been reported that some installations of the Adobe viewer crash with UTF-16 encoding. A simple workaround is to specify UTF-8 instead.

The main thing that is missing from Listing 20.7 is the information relating to the onscreen positioning of the elements. We want each item of bullet text to stay in position relative to its associated circle, so we will place the pair using a translate transform applied to the enclosing g> element. Shortly, we will be adding an effects filter to the heading that we want to apply only to an area local to the element. For this reason, we will give the text> element fixed x and y coordinates and also use a transform on the enclosing group to do the positioning. Listing 20.8 shows the (almost) complete HTML slide-to-SVG style sheet.

LISTING 20.8   stylesheet04.xsl—HTML-to-SVG Transformation

```
<xsl:stylesheet version = '1.0'
    xmlns:xsl='http://www.w3.org/1999/XSL/Transform'><xsl:output method = "xml"
indent="yes" encoding="iso-8859-1"
    media-type="image/svg+xml"/>
```

To give the result a better chance of being visible in SVG viewers, we have added encoding and MIME-type information to the output element in Listing 20.8. Next, we are going to create a variable to hold the number of bullet points on the slide. We do so, hardly surprisingly, by using the XSLT `variable` element. The variable will take whatever string value appears between the element's tags. Here, we are using a built-in XSLT function to count the number of nodes in the tree that the expression matches. The `value-of` element makes this value explicit, so it can be placed in the variable:

```
<xsl:variable name="totalBullets">
    <xsl:value-of select="count(//li)"/>
</xsl:variable>
```

Next, we have the root template, which is as shown previously, but with the addition of a `processing-instruction` element. We are going to be using an external CSS style sheet with the result of this transformation, which is specified in a processing instruction (PI). The `xsl:text` element is another way of entering literal text into the output, which preserves the whitespace and doesn't escape any characters. We will be inserting a block of SVG `<defs>` later on, and the comment here is just a marker for future (human) reference:

```
<xsl:template match="/">

<xsl:processing-instruction name="xml-stylesheet">
    <xsl:text>href="css/presentation.css" type="text/css"</xsl:text>
</xsl:processing-instruction>

<svg width="600" height="400">

<!-- defs here -->

    <xsl:apply-templates/>
    </svg>
</xsl:template>

<xsl:template match="//h1">
    <g transform="translate(100,40)">
    <text class="heading" x="0" y="30" >
        <xsl:value-of select="."/>
    </text>
    </g>
</xsl:template>
```

The preceding template, which is applied to h1 elements, is essentially the same as before, except this time we've added a `transform` attribute and coordinates for the `text` element. For this example, the use of coordinates for the text and transformation for the group is relatively unnecessary, but by separating the two, we have better control if, for example, we want to use a logo as a background to the title.

In the template that will address the bullet point items, we use another variable to temporarily hold the number of the item as it appears in the list of nodes that //li matches. This number is used in combination with the totalBullets value we obtained earlier to calculate the y coordinate at which the bullet item will be displayed. Variables and literals such as 60 are generally treated as strings, so the number() function must be used on each part of the calculation. The / character has special status in XSLT, so the div keyword is used for division instead. The result of the calculation shown here is stored in the variable y:

```
<xsl:template match="//li">

<xsl:variable name="bulletNumber"><xsl:number/></xsl:variable>

<xsl:variable name="y">
  <xsl:value-of select=
"number(60) + number(250) * number($bulletNumber) div number($totalBullets)"/>
</xsl:variable>
```

Next, we need to output the <g> element for the bullet item, and we do so by using an xsl:element element. The attribute value depends on the value of the y variable, so here we explicitly construct the transform attribute using an xsl:attribute element within the xsl:element block:

```
<xsl:element name="g">
    <xsl:attribute
name="transform">translate(150, <xsl:value-of select="$y"/>)</xsl:attribute>

    <circle class="bullet" r="10" />
    <text class="bullet">
        <xsl:value-of select="."/>
    </text>
</xsl:element>
```

The final template copies across the <title> element of the source document to the output document, and here we have added an SVG desc element containing a little information about the output document:

```
</xsl:template>

<xsl:template match="/html/head/title">
        <xsl:copy-of select="."/>
        <desc> Generated using XSLT </desc>
</xsl:template>

</xsl:stylesheet>
```

As a reminder, here is the source document again:

```
<html>
<head><title>Slide One</title></head>
<body>
<h1>XSLT and SVG</h1>
<ul>
    <li>Versatility</li>
    <li>Interoperability</li>
    <li>Presentation Consistency</li>
    <li>Eye Candy</li>
</ul>
</body>
</html>
```

The output produced by applying the preceding style sheet on this document looks like this (indented for clarity):

```
<?xml version="1.0" encoding="iso-8859-1"?>
<?xml-stylesheet href="css/presentation.css" type="text/css"?>

<svg width="600" height="400">

    <title>Slide One</title>
    <desc> Generated using XSLT </desc>

    <g transform="translate(100,40)">
        <text class="heading" x="0" y="30">XSLT and SVG</text>
    </g>
    <g transform="translate(150, 122.51)">
        <circle class="bullet" r="10" />
        <text class="bullet">Versatility</text>
    </g>
    <g transform="translate(150, 1852)">
        <circle class="bullet" r="10" />
        <text class="bullet">Interoperability</text>
    </g>
    <g transform="translate(150, 247.53)">
        <circle class="bullet" r="10" />
        <text class="bullet">Presentation Consistency</text>
    </g>
    <g transform="translate(150, 3104)">
        <circle class="bullet" r="10" />
        <text class="bullet">Eye Candy</text>
```

```
          </g>
</svg>
```

We're nearly there! As it stands, rendering this code as SVG wouldn't really offer much advantage over the HTML view, no matter what flourish we put in the CSS. In the XSLT Listing 20.8, we mentioned some `<defs>`. These elements are two filters. The first produces the familiar drop-shadow effect by blurring and displacing the source's alpha channel, and the second gives a pseudo-3D appearance to text using specular lighting and again adding a shadow.

```
<defs>
        <filter id="dropShadow">
        <feGaussianBlur in="SourceAlpha" stdDeviation=".8" result="blur"/>
        <feOffset in="blur" dx="1" dy="1" result="offsetBlurredAlpha"/>
            <feMerge>
              <feMergeNode in="offsetBlurredAlpha"/>
              <feMergeNode in="SourceGraphic"/>
            </feMerge>
        </filter>

        <filter id="3D" filterUnits="userSpaceOnUse" x="0" y="0"
                width="400" height="150">
          <feGaussianBlur in="SourceAlpha" stdDeviation="1" result="blur"/>
           <feSpecularLighting in="blur" surfaceScale="3"
                       specularConstant=".5"
                       specularExponent="3" lighting-color="#ffffff"
                       result="specOut">
               <fePointLight x="-5000" y="-5000" z="500"/>
           </feSpecularLighting>
          <feOffset in="blur" dx="1" dy="1" result="offsetBlur"/>
           <feComposite in="specOut" in2="SourceAlpha" operator="in"
                   result="specOut"/>
           <feComposite in="SourceGraphic" in2="specOut" operator="arithmetic"
              k1="0" k2="1" k3="1" k4="0" result="litPaint"/>
           <feMerge>
                <feMergeNode in="offsetBlur"/>
                <feMergeNode in="litPaint"/>
           </feMerge>
        </filter>
</defs>
```

Ideally, it would have been nice to keep the filters in another file, but unfortunately the ASV3 viewer at least doesn't support this kind of linking. What we can and do have in a separate file, however, is the CSS style sheet (see Listing 20.9).

LISTING 20.9   presentation.css—CSS Used by the SVG

```
text.heading{filter:url(#3D); font-size:36; font-weight:bold; fill:brown}

.bullet {filter:url(#dropShadow)}
circle.bullet {fill:lightblue }
text.bullet {font-size:18; font-weight:bold; text-anchor:left; fill:orange}
```

As you can see, there's not a great deal to Listing 20.9. The # references get the filters applied. Putting all this code together, we see a result that looks like Figure 20.2.

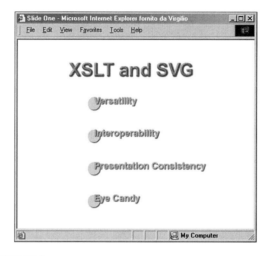

FIGURE 20.2   Final SVG Slide.

Server-Side Transformations

Very little code is needed on the server to run a transformation. The JScript in Listing 20.10 uses MSXML 4.0 to apply the style sheet we've just been looking at to a local copy of source.htm (refer to Listing 20.1). We simply create a DOM document to contain the source data and a DOM document to contain the style sheet and then use one of the source document's methods to carry out the transformation. The source and style sheet files are in the same directory as this ASP file, and we address them with the help of a `Server` method to obtain the correct path. The transformation method we are using here is `transformNode()`. It returns a string, which we write to the `Response` object after setting the MIME type. If we point a browser at slide01.asp (Listing 20.10), we will be presented with the SVG as shown in Figure 20.2.

> **NOTE**
>
> MSXML 4.0 is a DLL that provides core XML functionality on Microsoft platforms, including parsing and XSLT. For more information, see http://msdn.microsoft.com/downloads.

LISTING 20.10   slide01.asp—Simple Server-Side XSLT

```
<%@ LANGUAGE=JScript %>
<%
    var source = Server.CreateObject("Msxml2.DOMDocument.4.0");
    source.async = false;
    source.load(Server.MapPath("source.htm"));

    var stylesheet = Server.CreateObject("Msxml2.DOMDocument.4.0");
    stylesheet.async = false;
    stylesheet.load(Server.MapPath("stylesheet05.xsl"));

    var result = source.transformNode(stylesheet);

    Response.contenttype="image/svg+xml";
    Response.write(result);
    Response.end();
%>
```

Although this code works fine with MSXML4, the result given by MSXML3 cannot be viewed with ASV3 because the transformNode() method in this version always forces the encoding of the output XML to UTF-16. We can avoid this problem by using the transformNodeToObject() method instead, which pushes the transformed document into a specified object. The target can be the Response object, which not only fixes the MSXML3 problem, but also gives us simpler and more efficient code. The code lines starting at var result... in Listing 20.10 should be replaced with those in Listing 20.11.

LISTING 20.11   slide02.asp—Using transformNodetoObject

```
    ...
Response.contenttype="image/svg+xml";
    source.transformNodeToObject(stylesheet, Response);
    Response.end();
%>
```

Preprocessing

XSLT processors need their source data to be in XML. This is ubiquitous nowadays, but there are still many situations in which data needs processing to produce an XML representation. The representation can be in-memory as a DOM object or in the form of a file or stream. Usually, there are a variety of alternative methods of preparing data for the processor.

Remember that XSLT isn't necessarily the best choice for generating SVG. In many cases where non-XML data is being dealt with, creating the SVG directly is preferable to having an intermediate XML representation that then has to be transformed. The advantage of using an intermediate XML format is that it can contain the data in a fashion independent of the way it will be displayed; in other words, this is a way of separating content from presentation.

Form Data

When using HTML forms, we have two basic options for producing something the XSLT processor will recognize. The first is to create a smart form that will pass ready-built XML to the server. We can achieve this result by building a DOM object using script (assuming it is supported), or a simpler alternative is to wrap the strings obtained from form elements in preset strings to act as tags.

The second option is to carry out the form data-to-XML processing on the server. We will be looking at a way of doing this shortly.

Although we are talking about handling data from HTML forms here, very much the same principles apply if the data comes from a different source, such as a hyperlink containing query parameters or a server-side agent that constructs an HTTP GET or POST request.

Arbitrary Data Sources

Of course, the category of data sources is extremely wide, but the primary choice is likely to be between manipulating the source data into a string representation of XML or building a DOM tree programmatically.

HTML

If the source data is likely to be legacy or just plain messy HTML, we can avoid manual editing by using HTML Tidy (http://tidy.sourceforge.net/), which has an option to output XML. The engine behind this project has been ported to various languages and in most environments can be run server-side to carry out its tidying on the fly.

Slide Maker

We will now look at how a standard HTML form can be used to provide source data for the HTML-to-SVG transformation we saw earlier. The form appears in a browser, as in Figure 20.3, where text has already been entered into most of the fields.

20

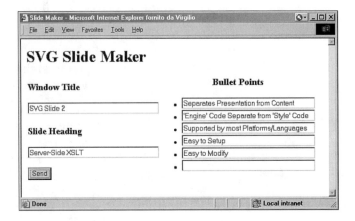

FIGURE 20.3   Entering slide data.

The straightforward HTML code for this form is shown in Listing 20.12.

LISTING 20.12   slidemaker.htm—Data Entry Form

```
<!DOCTYPE HTML PUBLIC "-//W3C//DTD HTML 4.01 Transitional//EN"
          "http://www.w3.org/TR/html4/loose.dtd">
<html>
<head>
<title>Slide Maker</title>
<meta http-equiv="Content-Type" content="text/html; charset=utf-8">
</head><body>

<form name="slideForm" method="get" action="slidemaker.asp">

<h1>SVG Slide Maker</h1>
<table>
<tr><td>

<h3>Window Title</h3>
<input type="text" name="title"  size="40" tabindex="1"/>

</td><td rowspan="3">
<center><h3>Bullet Points</h3></center>
<ul>
    <li><input type="text" name="bullet1" size="40" tabindex="3"/></li>
    <li><input type="text" name="bullet2" size="40" tabindex="4"/></li>
    <li><input type="text" name="bullet3" size="40" tabindex="5"/></li>
    <li><input type="text" name="bullet4" size="40" tabindex="6"/></li>
```

LISTING 20.12   Continued

```
    <li><input type="text" name="bullet5" size="40" tabindex="7"/></li>
    <li><input type="text" name="bullet6" size="40" tabindex="8"/></li>
</ul>
</td></tr><tr><td>

<h3>Slide Heading</h3>
<input type="text" name="heading" size="40" tabindex="2"/>

</td></tr><tr><td>
<input type="hidden" name="IE" value=".svg"/>
<input type="submit" value="Send" tabindex="9"/>

</td></tr>
</table>
</form>
</body></html>
```

> **NOTE**
>
> Listing 20.12 uses old-fashioned HTML formatting elements, following the "transitional" DTD to avoid confusion. True XHTML with CSS styling would be more correct for machine-readability.

The form in Listing 20.12 uses the GET method to make a request of slidemaker.asp (shown later in Listing 20.15) when the Send button is clicked. This action will deliver a string containing the name and content of each of the text boxes on the form. The only unconventional part of this code is the use of the hidden field to make the query string with the characters '.svg'. This workaround is necessary for all but the most recent versions of Internet Explorer with ASV3 because the MIME type is not recognized correctly.

The query string contains a series of name/value pairs based on the contents of the fields in the form. What goes into the address box of the browser will look something like this:

```
http://localhost/sams/slidemaker.asp?
    ➥title=TITLE
    ➥&bullet1=bullet1&bullet2=&bullet3=
    ➥&bullet4=&bullet5=&bullet6=bullet6
    ➥&heading=HEADING&IE=.svg
```

Note that this would appear as one long string, without spaces.

Here, the title and heading fields have been filled in (using uppercase letters), along with the first and last bullet points. Normally, we would get at these values with server code using convenience methods or properties of the `Request` object; for instance, `Request.Form("bullet3")` would give us the value of the third bullet-point string (we should also use an HTTP `POST` method on the form rather than a `GET` with this method). What we want to produce using these values is valid XML that we can use as input to an XSLT processor. Whatever we do, the XML is going to be relatively arbitrary, but if we base it on the name/value pairs, we can at least reuse the code in other applications. By implementing our own mini-parser, we can take away the need to know the names of the fields in advance and produce elements of the form:

```
<fieldName>fieldValue</fieldName>
```

The code, which will be contained in its own file, is shown in Listing 20.13. In this code, two operations are actually carried out: the supplied query string is broken into an array of individual token strings (that is, {*name*, *value*, *name*, *value*...}), and then this array is used to build up a string in XML format.

> **NOTE**
>
> An alternative to building up a string containing the XML is to create an XML DOM document and populate it by creating and appending elements based on the text found in the query string. This would also avoid the need for the MS-specific loadXML method (but because we are using MSXML anyway, this isn't an issue). Generally, working directly with DOM is preferable to manipulating strings because XML validity will always be maintained. Here, however, we have divided up the operations to make it easier to see what is going on.

A regular expression (`/[^&=]+\b|=&/gi`) is used in the parsing of the query string, which will recognize any sequence of characters that doesn't contain & or = (`[^&=]`) but is terminated by a word break (`\b`) or any sequence =& (`|=&`). If no value is given to an item in the query string, the string will contain the block =& (for example, one=1&two=&three=3). The latter test avoids the array getting out of sequence (such as *name*, *value*, *name*, *name*, and so on).

> **NOTE**
>
> Regular expressions have been a feature of most server-side languages for many years, with the exception of Java, which until recently needed a GNU library. Java 2 version 1.4 makes up for this deficit.

LISTING 20.13   querytoxml.asp—Converter from GET Query to Arbitrary XML

```
<%

function queryToXML(queryString){
```

LISTING 20.13   Continued

```
    var headString = "<?xml version='1.0' ?>";
    var root = "root";

    var reg = /[^&=]+\b|=&/gi;
    var strings = new Array();
    var i = 0;
    var token;

    while ((token = reg.exec(queryString)) != null){
        strings[i++] = token;
}
```

At this point, the tokens have been loaded into the array, so we can start building the XML string. This step is essentially a matter of taking alternate items in the array and wrapping them up to look like elements. A few minor tweaks are needed. The query string will contain + characters where there were spaces in the original text field, which we swap using another regular expression. Punctuation is replaced with escape characters, which need unescaping, and if the last named field in the query string is empty, it gets the value undefined, so we skip any pairs with this value:

```
    var xmlString = headString +"\n"+"<"+root+">";

    var tag, text;

    var plusreg = /\+/g;

    for(var j=0;j<i;j+=2){

        tag = strings[j];
        text = new String(strings[j+1]);
        text = unescape(text);
        text = text.replace(plusreg," ");

        if((text != "=&") && (text != "undefined")){
            xmlString += "\n\t<"+tag+">"+text+"</"+tag+">";
        }
    }

    xmlString += "\n"+"</"+root+">";

    return xmlString;
```

20

```
}
%>
```

When we pass this function the query string

```
title=TITLE&bullet1=BULLET1&bullet2=&bullet3=&bullet4➡
    =&bullet5=&bullet6=BULLET6&heading=HEADING&IE=.svg
```

it will return the following:

```
<?xml version='1.0' ?>
<root>
    <title>TITLE</title>
    <bullet1>BULLET1</bullet1>
    <bullet6>BULLET6</bullet6>
    <heading>HEADING</heading>
    <IE>.svg</IE>
</root>
```

Now that we have our data in XML, we can transform it into SVG. As it happens, we already have a style sheet (refer to Listing 20.8) to transform the HTML representation of a slide into SVG, so rather than building a style sheet to go all the way from the preceding arbitrary XML into SVG, we can just transform the preceding code into HTML. Apart from the fact that this step will demonstrate how XSLT style sheets can be chained, it also has a potential use in practice: We could make the HTML representation available for users who don't have SVG-capable viewers.

The HTML we are after here, based on the query string just given, will look something like this:

```
<html><head>
<title>TITLE</title>
</head>
<body>
        <h1>HEADING</h1>
        <ul>
                <li>BULLET1</li>
                <li>BULLET6</li>
        </ul>
</body></html>
```

The style sheet to transform arbitrary XML into XHTML is shown in Listing 20.14.

LISTING 20.14   tohtml.xsl—Simple XML-to-XHTML Transformation

```
<xsl:stylesheet version = '1.0'
    xmlns:xsl='http://www.w3.org/1999/XSL/Transform'>


<xsl:output method = "xml" indent = "yes" encoding="iso-8859-1" />


<xsl:template match="/">
    <html><head>
    <xsl:copy-of select="/root/title"/>
    </head>
    <body>
    <h1>
    <xsl:value-of select="/root/heading"/>
    </h1>
    <ul>
    <xsl:apply-templates/>
    </ul>
    </body></html>
</xsl:template>
```

The template in Listing 20.14 matches the root of the source document and uses simple `xsl:copy-of` and `xsl:value-of` elements to place the title and heading in the right positions in the output tree. The root context will also be picked up by the `xsl:apply-templates` instruction. The following template will check all the nodes it receives to see, first, whether they are elements (*), and then whether the predicate [`starts-with(name(), 'bullet')`] is true—in other words, whether the name of the element begins with `bullet`. If this is the case, the template will pass to the output the contents of the element wrapped in `<li>` tags.

```
<xsl:template match="//*[starts-with(name(), 'bullet')]">
    <li>
      <xsl:value-of select="."/>
     </li>
</xsl:template>
```

One aspect of XSLT we haven't touched on so far is the default behavior of style sheets. In effect, several templates are already defined for matching elements, attributes, and text nodes, and of significance here is the rule that text nodes, by default, will be delivered to the output. This would result in the contents of all the elements in the source document winding up in the output. To prevent this situation, we now have a template to eat text nodes without producing any output:

20

```
<xsl:template match="text()">
</xsl:template>

</xsl:stylesheet>
```

We will now look at the code that first calls the JScript function we saw in Listing 20.13 to convert the form data into arbitrary XML and then applies the style sheet in Listing 20.14 to convert this into HTML, and finally applies the style sheet to turn HTML into SVG before passing the result back to the browser. There's quite a lot going on, but XSLT lends itself to a modular approach with the result that any individual piece of code is relatively simple.

Listing 20.15 is the JScript that ties everything together. The code begins by using the queryToXML function to convert the query string from the client into a string of XML. Three DOM documents are then created: source, which will be loaded with the string of XML; intermediate, which will be used to hold the (X)HTML representation; and style sheet, which will be used to hold first the XML-to-XHTML and then the XHTML-to-SVG transforms.

LISTING 20.15 slidemaker.asp—JScript Tying Everything Together

```
<%@ LANGUAGE=JScript %>
<!-- #INCLUDE FILE="querytoxml.asp" -->
<%
    var xmlString = queryToXML(Request.QueryString);

    var source = Server.CreateObject("Msxml2.DOMDocument.4.0");
    source.async = false;

    var intermediate = Server.CreateObject("Msxml2.DOMDocument.4.0");
    intermediate.async = false;

    var stylesheet = Server.CreateObject("Msxml2.DOMDocument.4.0");
  stylesheet.async = false;

    source.loadXML(xmlString);

    stylesheet.load(Server.MapPath("tohtml.xsl"));
```

The source and the first style sheet have now been loaded into documents and have run the transformation on source, putting the result into intermediate:

```
source.transformNodeToObject(stylesheet, intermediate);
```

Now we load the second style sheet, set the MIME type of the Response object, and apply the transformation. The result is passed directly back to the client:

```
    stylesheet.load(Server.MapPath("tosvg.xsl"));

    Response.contenttype="image/svg+xml";

    intermediate.transformNodeToObject(stylesheet, Response);

    Response.end();
%>
```

In practice, a user of this application might want to take away individual SVG slides, and a minor modification to the HTML-to-SVG code (stylesheet04.xsl, in Listing 20.8) makes them self-contained. We simply remove the link to the external CSS stylesheet (the xsl:processing-instruction block) and add the styling inline to the <defs> section like this:

```
...
<defs>
    <style type="text/css"><![CDATA[
    text.heading{filter:url(#3D); font-size:36; font-weight:bold; fill:brown}

.bullet {filter:url(#dropShadow)}
circle.bullet {fill:lightblue }
text.bullet {font-size:18; font-weight:bold; text-anchor:left; fill:orange}
        ]]></style>
...
</defs>
...
```

We have named the modified version tosvg.xsl. If we now place all these files on the server, point a browser at slidemaker.htm (Listing 20.12), and enter the details as shown in Figure 20.3, clicking on the Send button will produce the result shown in Figure 20.4.

Going Further

In the examples throughout this chapter, we have only scraped the surface of the potential of XSLT in the creation of SVG. For a simple extension of the presentation slide, if we wanted to include company sales performance, we could take the raw figures and use XSLT to transform them into SVG bar charts.

Any aspect of source XML data can be mapped to any individual characteristics of the target SVG, or to whole blocks of SVG. Additionally, there is the interactive capability of SVG. It can be used to apply different style sheets to the source data according to the user's behavior—for example, choosing between bar and pie charts of the company figures.

20

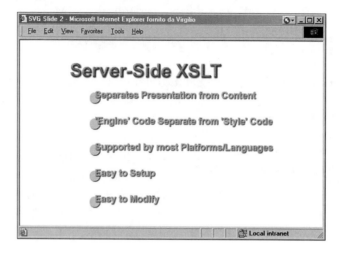

FIGURE 20.4   Slide generated with server-side XSLT.

SVG is of course suitable for input to transformations as well, and there is a lot of potential in the use of XSLT as an SVG-to-SVG filtering mechanism to perhaps highlight particular elements of a diagram or to add or remove detail.

For a more complex possibility, imagine creating a set of animated characters using SVG. Whole cartoons could be scripted by describing the activities of these characters in XML, and letting XSLT translate high-level descriptions into appropriate code. Add interaction, and you have the basis for games.

Summary

In this chapter, we looked at the ideas behind XSLT and the ways XML in general can be transformed. We saw the purpose of a good number of processing elements and the ways they can be used to create SVG. We also demonstrated that data in a non-XML source (an HTML form) can be made suitable for transformation and the ways intermediate representations can be used in style sheet chains.

We also saw the way a simple XSLT application can be constructed in the Web environment, using a conventional client/server architecture.

We have, however, only seen the tip of the XSLT and SVG iceberg here, but we hope this chapter is enough to demonstrate that these technologies combine very well indeed and that the XSLT approach can simplify a whole range of SVG tasks.

CHAPTER 21

SVG and Perl

In this chapter, we will explore the generation of SVG using Perl. We will start by converting a sample SVG file to a "templatized" version to allow the creation of a more dynamic version of the original. Then we will explore three methods of SVG document generation and provide a brief analysis of the pros and cons of each approach.

Generating SVG with Perl

Perl has been a standard tool in the Web developer's toolbox for many years. Perl's string-manipulating functionality serves as an excellent means for creating documents for the World Wide Web. And in its latest incarnation, Perl offers the full features (and more) of any mainstream programming language.

As the Web matured and XML began to show itself, Perl once again showed its technical prowess. Many talented Perl developers have created numerous Perl modules for the generation and manipulation of XML documents. We can use these modules to ease the generation of SVG because SVG is an application of XML.

One of the mottos of Perl is TIMTOWTDI (pronounced *tim toadie*), which stands for "There is more than one way to do it." As you will see in this chapter, this philosophy continues into Perl's XML capabilities. We cannot cover all the myriad ways of generating SVG with Perl within a single chapter. As a result, this chapter will discuss three popular methods for generating SVG.

Viewing the Quote of the Day

Our project is to create an SVG document that displays a quote of the day. We've supplied an SVG file (see Figure 21.1) to be used as a reference for building our template.

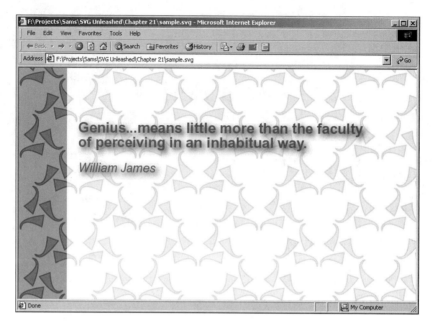

FIGURE 21.1   The Quote of the Day template.

We will step through the lines of code in the SVG file to discover the document's structure. This process will reveal hard-coded values that, when replaced by a variable value, will allow our sample to serve as a template for our "Quote of the Day" system.

SVG Header

In Listing 21.1, we see that our sample begins with an XML declaration, followed by a Document Type Declaration. Next, the topmost `svg` element is defined, along with its default namespace declaration and `xlink` namespace declaration.

LISTING 21.1   sample.svg—Sample File: Headers

```
<?xml version="1.0" encoding="ISO-8859-1" standalone="no"?>
<!DOCTYPE svg PUBLIC "-//W3C//DTD SVG 20010904//EN"
    "http://www.w3.org/TR/2001/REC-SVG-200100904/DTD/svg10.dtd">
<svg xmlns="http://www.w3.org/2000/svg"
    xmlns:xlink="http://www.w3.org/1999/xlink">
    .
    .
    .
```

Style Sheet

As we proceed to Listing 21.2, we see that a style sheet has been defined. Two classes are created: one for the text in the quote and one for the text of the author's name.

LISTING 21.2   sample.svg continued—Sample File: Styles

```
.
.
.
<style type="text/css"><![CDATA[
    .quote {
        font-size:   28;
        font-weight: bold
    }
    .author {
        font-size:   24;
        font-weight: normal;
        font-style:  italic
    }
]]></style>
.
.
.
```

Before continuing on to Listing 21.3, we need to discuss how patterns are created in SVG, specifically, how to create a hexagonal tiling.

Patterns and Tilings

SVG defines a facility for generating patterns by defining a graphic within a rectangular region. This invisible rectangle and its contents are tiled horizontally and vertically across an SVG element to fill it with a pattern.

> **NOTE**
>
> Patterns may be used to fill and stroke SVG elements.

In our sample, we see that we have a hexagonal tiling. This type of tiling tends to be more pleasing to the eye because it avoids the strong horizontal and vertical lines that are associated with simple rectangular patterns. However, SVG allows us to use only a rectangular region for our unit pattern. Fortunately, a hexagonal tiling can be converted to a rectangular tiling.

Figure 21.2 shows a rectangle with lines indicating the edges of four hexagons. The rectangle is the unit rectangle that we need for our pattern. This unit rectangle will also be referred to as a **unit tile** in this chapter. The circle in the upper-left corner corresponds to the origin of the unit tile and is displayed here for reference only. The additional circles on the hexagon vertices are the exact locations on which we need to place our repeating shape. Placing our shapes at those points will create our hexagonal tiling.

FIGURE 21.2 A unit tile for a hexagonal tiling.

If you look closely at each of the repeating shapes in Figure 21.1, two properties will be revealed: Our basic shape (the green, hooked triangle) is grouped into clusters of three, and some of these clusters are rotated and reflected from the other clusters. Figure 21.3 reveals this underlying organization by placing a triangle at each hexagon vertex. The triangle points in the direction in which the cluster must point, and the letter *L* reveals whether a cluster has been reflected.

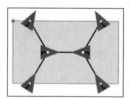

FIGURE 21.3 The underlying organization of the unit tile.

We now have a general overview of the way clusters of our basic shape are laid out within the unit tile; however, we need to discuss how these clusters are built.

First, we start with an element that will be used to create our cluster (see Figure 21.4). The circle indicates the origin of the not-yet-complete cluster.

FIGURE 21.4 The tiling element.

The cluster is constructed by making two duplicates of the original element. The first duplicate is rotated 120° about the cluster's origin (the dot mentioned earlier), and the second duplicate is rotated 240° about the cluster's origin. Figure 21.5 shows the resulting cluster, along with a mirror image.

FIGURE 21.5   A cluster and its mirror image.

Now we are ready to construct our unit tile. Referring to Figure 21.3 as a guide, we place a single cluster at each hexagon vertex honoring the rotation and reflection as indicated by the green triangle. Figure 21.6 shows the results after completing one half of the tile. The dots to the right correspond to a cluster's origin and its associated hexagon vertex. The dot on the left is a reference point used when constructing this half of the unit tile and will be discussed later in this section. As before, the dots are for reference only and are not included in the final unit tile.

FIGURE 21.6   Half of a unit tile.

We apply a reflection of the same process to the other half of the unit tile, as in Figure 21.7, to create our finished product, as shown in Figure 21.8.

FIGURE 21.7   The complete unit tile (with reference points).

FIGURE 21.8   The complete unit tile (without reference points).

Now we are ready to enter the defs section of the document. In Listing 21.3, the path element defines the basic shape for the tile pattern.

LISTING 21.3   sample.svg continued—Sample File: Basic Shape

```
.
.
.
<defs>
    <path id="elem" d="M-6,29.5 Q33.5,10 35.5,34.5 Q44,14.5 -10,7.5 z"
          stroke="rgb(0,100,0)" stroke-width="2"
          fill="rgb(0,128,0)" fill-opacity="0.5"/>
.
.
.
```

In Listing 21.4, the first g element creates a single cluster by building three rotated copies of our basic shape.

LISTING 21.4   sample.svg continued—Sample File: Cluster

```
.
.
.
<g id="cluster">
    <use xlink:href="#elem" transform="rotate(0)"/>
    <use xlink:href="#elem" transform="rotate(120)"/>
    <use xlink:href="#elem" transform="rotate(240)"/>
</g>
.
.
.
```

21

In Listing 21.5, the second g element builds a supercluster (a cluster of clusters) through a series of transformations. Let's look at the first use element to get an idea of what's going on in the `transform` attribute.

NOTE

From an element's perspective, transformations are applied in the reverse order that they are listed within a transform attribute.

A cluster's origin is initially aligned with the supercluster's origin—the dot on the left side in Figure 21.6. The first cluster is reflected horizontally using scale(–1,1), rotated 60° about its origin, moved 79.674 units in the positive x direction, and rotated 60° about the supercluster's origin. The combination of all these transformations places the first cluster at the lower-left vertex in the unit tile. In case you're wondering, 79.674 is the distance from the center of the hexagon to one of its vertices; that is, this is equivalent to the radius of the hexagon.

LISTING 21.5   sample.svg continued—Sample File: Supercluster

```
        .
        .
        .
<g id="supercluster">
    <use xlink:href="#cluster"
        transform="rotate(60) translate(79.674,0) rotate(60) scale(-1,1)"/>
    <use xlink:href="#cluster"
        transform="rotate(0) translate(79.674,0)"/>
    <use xlink:href="#cluster"
        transform="rotate(-60) translate(79.674,0) scale(1,-1)"/>
</g>
        .
        .
        .
```

The last g element creates one half of our unit tile. The `pattern` element in Listing 21.6 transforms two superclusters to create the complete unit tile for our background pattern.

A supercluster's origin is initially aligned with the unit tile's origin. The transformations in the `pattern` element move these origins to correspond to the leftmost and rightmost dots in Figure 21.7.

LISTING 21.6   sample.svg continued—Sample File: The Pattern

```
        .
        .
        .
```

LISTING 21.6   Continued

```
<pattern id="tile" height="138" width="239.023"
        patternUnits="userSpaceOnUse" overflow="visible">
    <use xlink:href="#supercluster" transform="translate(0,69)"/>
    <use xlink:href="#supercluster" transform="translate(239.023,69)
        scale(-1,1)"/>
</pattern>
    .

    .

    .
```

Next, we move on to the drop shadow that gives our text dimension. A shadow can be viewed as a larger, blurrier, grayish version of the object from which it is cast. The feGaussianBlur element in Listing 21.7 generates this effect.

LISTING 21.7   sample.svg continued—Sample File: Drop Shadow Blur

```
    .

    .

    .
<filter id="dropShadow" height="130%" width="130%">
    <feGaussianBlur in="SourceAlpha" stdDeviation="4" result="shadow"/>
    .

    .

    .
```

Figure 21.9 shows the result of running Listing 21.7.

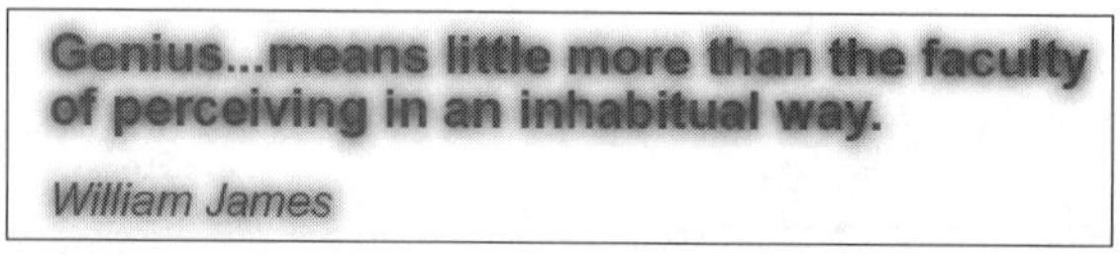

FIGURE 21.9   A drop shadow filter.

The text has a larger, blurrier, grayish border, but we end up with blurry text as opposed to shadowed text. We create the illusion of the text coming off the page (see Figure 21.10) by offsetting the shadow from the type. The feOffset element in Listing 21.8 creates the offset.

LISTING 21.8   sample.svg continued—Sample File: Drop Shadow Offset

```
    .

    .

    .
```

LISTING 21.8   Continued

```
<feOffset in="shadow" dx="5" dy="5" result="offsetShadow"/>
    .
    .
    .
```

Figure 21.10 shows the result of running Listing 21.8.

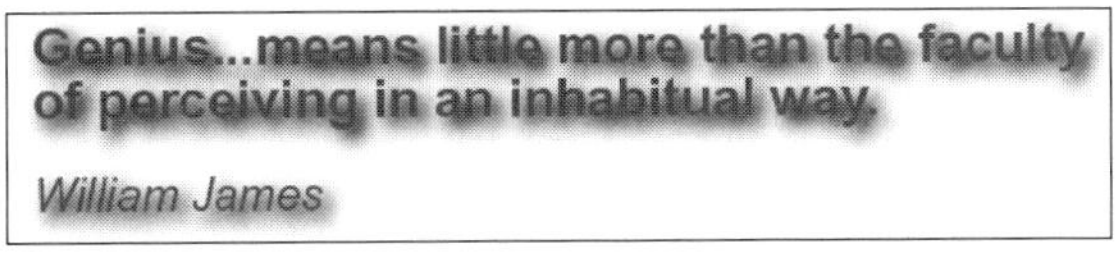

FIGURE 21.10   Offset text.

The result in Figure 21.10 is a definite improvement; however, the shadow is too dark, making it difficult to read the text. The feComponentTransfer in Listing 21.9 remaps each of the color channels of the drop shadow, resulting in a lighter shadow and more legible text.

LISTING 21.9   sample.svg continued—Sample File: Lighter Drop Shadow

```
    .
    .
    .
<feComponentTransfer in="offsetShadow" result="lighterOffsetShadow">
    <feFuncR type="linear" intercept="0.1"/>
    <feFuncG type="linear" intercept="0.1"/>
    <feFuncB type="linear" intercept="0.1"/>
</feComponentTransfer>
    .
    .
    .
```

The text and all these effects are merged together in Listing 21.10 to form the final drop shadow effect. This listing completes the defs section of the SVG document.

LISTING 21.10   sample.svg continued—Sample File: The Composite Drop Shadow

```
    .
    .
    .
        <feMerge>
            <feMergeNode in="lighterOffsetShadow"/>
```

LISTING 21.10   Continued

```
            <feMergeNode in="SourceGraphic"/>
        </feMerge>
    </filter>
</defs>
.

.

.
```

Figure 21.11 shows the final drop shadow effect produced by the filter effect defined in the defs section of the SVG document.

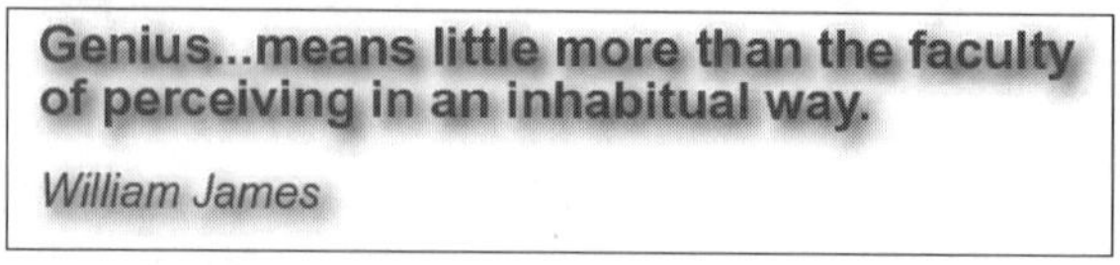

> **Genius...means little more than the faculty of perceiving in an inhabitual way.**
>
> *William James*

FIGURE 21.11   The final quote section of the document.

All the work in the defs section is now used to build our final "Quote of the Day" SVG layout. Listing 21.11 draws a solid color rectangle behind what will become the sidebar of our image. Next, the sidebar is drawn on top of the solid rectangle using the tiling pattern that we defined earlier. A lighter version of the tiling pattern is used to finish the rest of the background of the image (see Figure 21.12).

LISTING 21.11   sample.svg continued—Sample File: Quote and Author

```
.

.

.

<g>
    <desc>A quote with a tiled background</desc>
    <g>
        <desc>The tiled background</desc>
        <rect width="1in" height="100%" fill="rgb(128,192,128)"/>
        <rect width="1in" height="100%" fill="url(#tile)"/>
        <rect x="1in" width="100%" height="100%" opacity="0.15"
              fill="url(#tile)"/>
    </g>
.

.

.
```

Figure 21.12 shows the result of running Listing 21.11.

FIGURE 21.12   The background and sidebar tilings.

In Listing 21.12, the lines of our quotation are positioned on the background, use the drop shadow effect, and use the "quote" class to style the text. The author's name goes through a similar process to complete our sample image, as shown in Figure 21.1.

LISTING 21.12   sample.svg continued—Sample File: Quote and Author

```
.
.
.
        <text class="quote" y="1in" fill="rgb(96,96,144)"
            filter="url(#dropShadow)">
          <desc>The quote</desc>
          <tspan x="1.25in" dy="1em">
              Genius…means little more than the faculty
          </tspan>
          <tspan x="1.25in" dy="1em">
              of perceiving in an inhabitual way.
          </tspan>
          <tspan class="author" x="1.25in" dy="2em">William James</tspan>
        </text>
    </g>
</svg>
```

Generalizing Our Sample File

Now that we have completed our analysis of our sample image, we have more information to use in deciding how to make this document more dynamic. We can randomize many aspects to give each quotation a unique appearance while retaining the overall layout and look of the original design.

The size of the pattern rectangle determines how tightly or how loosely our background pattern repeats. As we saw earlier in the chapter, the tile is based on a hexagon. The hexagon has many characteristics, one being that the proportion of a hexagon's width to its height remains constant. This tells us that if we want to change the size of our tile, we must change both dimensions in proportion to the hexagon. Actually, this quality turns out to be nice because we can define our tile's size using only a single value. In this case, we will use the hexagon's height and then, through a little geometry and trigonometry, we will calculate the tile's width.

Other areas of potential dynamism are as follows:

- We can vary the shape of the element used in our pattern.
- We can vary the shape's color.
- We can vary the drop shadow's size and offset.
- We can vary the sidebar's size and color.
- We can vary the background's opacity.

All these properties allow us to build a large amount of flexibility into our template. Each visitor will be presented with his or her own unique quotation.

Common Code

Now we can begin to write Perl to generate SVG. The common code in each of our SVG generation techniques will be contained within a single Perl module.

The code in Listing 21.13 configures the visual characteristics of the basic shape used in our unit tile. This shape corresponds to the image in Figure 21.4.

LISTING 21.13   QOTDCommon.pm—Basic Shape Characteristics

```
.
.
.
my $path_data          = "M-6,29.5 Q33.5,10 35.5,34.5 Q44,14.5 -10,7.5 z";
my $path_stroke_color  = "rgb(0,100,0)";
my $path_stroke_width  = 2;
my $path_fill_color    = "rgb(0,128,0)";
```

LISTING 21.13   QOTDCommon.pm—Basic Shape Characteristics

```
my $path_fill_opacity   = 0.5;
.
.
.
```

The code in Listing 21.14 determines the dimensions of the pattern tile and the unit hexagon used within the tile. These values are used in the SVG code to create the tile pattern.

LISTING 21.14   QOTDCommon.pm continued—Pattern Characteristics

```
.
.
.
my $pattern_height      = generate_integer(50,200);
my $pattern_half_height = $pattern_height / 2;
my $hexagon_side_length = $pattern_half_height / cos(PI/6);
my $hexagon_offset      = $pattern_half_height * sin(PI/6)/cos(PI/6);
my $hexagon_radius      = $hexagon_side_length/2 + $hexagon_offset;
my $pattern_width       = 2*$hexagon_radius + $hexagon_side_length;
.
.
.
```

The code in Listing 21.15 configures the size, offset, and lightness of the drop shadow.

LISTING 21.15   QOTDCommon.pm continued—Drop Shadow Characteristics

```
.
.
.
my $blur_amount         = 4;
my $blur_offset_x       = 5;
my $blur_offset_y       = 5;
my $blur_lighten_amount = 0.1;
.
.
.
```

The code in Listing 21.16 configures the size and color of the sidebar. background_opacity sets the overall lightness of the background pattern.

LISTING 21.16   QOTDCommon.pm continued—Sidebar and Background Characteristics

```
 .
 .
 .
my $sidebar_width          = "1in";
my $sidebar_background_color = "rgb(128,192,128)";
my $background_opacity     = "0.15";
 .
 .
 .
```

The code in Listing 21.17 configures the position and color of the quoted text.

LISTING 21.17   QOTDCommon.pm continued—Text Characteristics

```
 .
 .
 .
my $quote_top_margin  = "1in";
my $quote_left_margin = "1.25in";
my $quote_color       = "rgb(96,96,144)";
 .
 .
 .
```

> **NOTE**
>
> The configuration values just described have been hard-coded for brevity. A more realistic appli-
> cation would store these values in a configuration file or acquire the values from a data store.

The generate_integer() function in Listing 21.18 generates random integers in a specified range. This function randomly selects the unit tile dimensions and randomly selects
the quote that will appear in the final SVG image.

LISTING 21.18   QOTDCommon.pm continued—generate_integer()

```
 .
 .
 .
sub generate_integer {
    my $low  = shift;
    my $high = shift;
```

LISTING 21.18   Continued

```
    my $diff = $high - $low;

    return int( rand($diff) + $low + 0.5 );
}
    .
    .
    .
```

The quotes are hard-coded into the common Perl module. Listing 21.19 shows an excerpt
of the data structure that is used to store the quotes.

LISTING 21.19   QOTDCommon.pm continued—Loading Quotes

```
    .
    .
    .
$quotes = [
    {
        author => "Anton Checkov",
        lines  => [
            "Man is what he believes."
        ]
    },
    {
        author => "Buddha",
        lines  => [
            "All that we are is the result",
            "of what we have thought."
        ]
    },
        .
        .
        .
];
    .
    .
    .
```

> **NOTE**
>
> Similarly to our configuration information, the quote data would be more realistically stored in a
> quote file or data store. The data has been included in the example for simplicity.

That completes the common configuration information that will be used in the following sections. We have captured all the dynamic properties of our Quote of the Day in one place for easy editing. With these properties, we can adjust the tiling's size, the drop shadow's size and offset, the sidebar's size, and the background opacity. We can also define as many quotes as we like.

Generating SVG Using print Statements

Perhaps the most straightforward way to generate SVG in Perl is to use the venerable print statement. For small files, this option may be your best choice. This approach uses very little memory and is undoubtedly the fastest way to generate any text file in Perl.

Regardless of which approach you take to generating SVG with Perl, you will need to let the client's browsers know that you are serving up an SVG document. Listing 21.20 accomplishes this by sending the Content-type header with a value of image/svg+xml.

Another header that we need to use is Pragma. By sending that header with a value of no-cache, we prevent most browsers from caching our SVG file. Normally, you'll want a page to be cached, but in our case, we need the client to poll the server each time so that the server can generate a new quote for each request.

All headers must be sent before any content, and they must be followed by a blank line.

LISTING 21.20   svg_via_print.pl—Emitting Custom HTTP Headers

```
print "Pragma: no-cache\n";
print "Content-type: image/svg+xml\n\n";
```

Listing 21.21 shows the majority of the code used to generate our "Quote of the Day" using the print statement. If you compare this listing to the code in the original sample, you will see that not much has changed. We have replaced all attributes with Perl scalars (our configuration). We are free to make adjustments to our configuration without worrying about the actual SVG code itself.

LISTING 21.21   svg_via_print.pl continued—Generating SVG

```
print <<EOF;
<?xml version="1.0" standalone="no"?>
<!DOCTYPE svg PUBLIC "-//W3C//DTD SVG 20010904//EN"
    "http://www.w3.org/TR/2001/REC-SVG-20010904/DTD/svg10.dtd">
<svg xmlns="http://www.w3.org/2000/svg"
    xmlns:xlink="http://www.w3.org/1999/xlink">
    <style type="text/css"><![CDATA[
        .quote {
            font-size: 28;
```

LISTING 21.21   Continued

```
            font-weight: bold
        }
        .author {
            font-size: 24;
            font-weight: normal;
            font-style: italic
        }
    ]]></style>
    <defs>
        <path id="elem" d="$path_data"
            stroke="$path_stroke_color" stroke-width="$path_stroke_width"
            fill="$path_fill_color" fill-opacity="$path_fill_opacity"/>
        <g id="cluster">
            <use xlink:href="#elem" transform="rotate(0)"/>
            <use xlink:href="#elem" transform="rotate(120)"/>
            <use xlink:href="#elem" transform="rotate(240)"/>
        </g>
        <g id="supercluster">
            <use xlink:href="#cluster"
                transform="rotate(60)  translate($hexagon_radius,0)
                        rotate(60) scale(-1,1)"/>
            <use xlink:href="#cluster"
                transform="rotate(0)    translate($hexagon_radius,0)"/>
            <use xlink:href="#cluster"
                transform="rotate(-60) translate($hexagon_radius,0)
                rotate(-60) scale(-1,1)"/>
        </g>
        <pattern id="tile" height="$pattern_height" width="$pattern_width"
                patternUnits="userSpaceOnUse" overflow="visible">
            <use xlink:href="#supercluster"
                transform="translate(0,$pattern_half_height)"/>
            <use xlink:href="#supercluster"
                transform="translate($pattern_width,$pattern_half_height)
                    scale(-1,1)"/>
        </pattern>
        <filter id="dropShadow" height="130%" width="130%">
            <feGaussianBlur in="SourceAlpha" stdDeviation="$blur_amount"
                    result="shadow"/>
            <feOffset in="shadow" dx="$blur_offset_x" dy="$blur_offset_y"
                    result="offsetShadow"/>
            <feComponentTransfer in="offsetShadow"
```

LISTING 21.21   Continued

```
                                    result="lighterOffsetShadow">
                <feFuncR type="linear" intercept="$blur_lighten_amount"/>
                <feFuncG type="linear" intercept="$blur_lighten_amount"/>
                <feFuncB type="linear" intercept="$blur_lighten_amount"/>
            </feComponentTransfer>
            <feMerge>
                <feMergeNode in="lighterOffsetShadow"/>
                <feMergeNode in="SourceGraphic"/>
            </feMerge>
        </filter>
    </defs>
    <g>
        <desc>A quote with a tiled background</desc>
        <g>
            <desc>The tiled background</desc>
            <rect width="$sidebar_width" height="100%"
                  fill="$sidebar_background_color"/>
            <rect width="$sidebar_width" height="100%" fill="url(#tile)"/>
            <rect x="$sidebar_width" width="100%" height="100%"
                  opacity="$background_opacity" fill="url(#tile)"/>
        </g>
        <text class="quote" y="$quote_top_margin" fill="$quote_color"
              filter="url(#dropShadow)">
            <desc>The quote</desc>
EOF
    .
    .
    .
```

We need to randomly pick a quote and the associated author to impart our user with some new wisdom of the world. In Listing 21.22, we generate a number between 0 and the size of the array holding all our quotes. We grab the quote record at that position in the quotes array. We pull out the lines and the author and generate tspan elements to create the text in our SVG image.

LISTING 21.22   svg_via_print.pl continued—Generating SVG Text

```
    .
    .
    .
my $index  = generate_integer( 0, @$quotes - 1 );
my $quote  = $quotes->[$index];
```

21

LISTING 21.22   Continued

```perl
my $author = $quote->{author};
my $lines  = $quote->{lines};

foreach ( @$lines ) {
    print "              <tspan x=\"$quote_left_margin\" dy=\"1em\">$_</tspan>\n";
}

print <<EOF;
          <tspan class="author" x="$quote_left_margin" dy="2em">$author</tspan>
        </text>
     </g>
</svg>
EOF
```

Listing 21.22 completes the coding for this example.

Pros and Cons of Using the print Statement

Code generation via the `print` statement has the advantage of being very fast, lean on memory, and straightforward to write. Often, for short documents, you can quickly "templatize" the original document and then use Perl to fill in the holes.

The simplicity of this method does not come without its drawbacks, however. This style of SVG generation makes it difficult to modularize your code.

Other problems include the fact that after you output text, you cannot change it. You can use various techniques to get around this problem, but they tend to be cumbersome and end up slowing down your SVG generation. At that point, you need to consider using another method, perhaps one mentioned in one of the following sections.

Generating SVG Using the W3C DOM API

You've seen a lot about the DOM in earlier chapters of this book. Not surprisingly, a Perl module, `XML::DOM`, has been written to implement the DOM Level 1 API. Although SVG is built on the DOM Level 2 API, we can still generate any type of SVG document we need using this module.

> **NOTE**
>
> The DOM APIs are available at http://www.w3.org/DOM/DOMTR.

Listing 21.23 shows the high-level approach used to generate our "Quote of the Day" document with this module. For the sake of space, we will not show all the code from this example. The code has been modularized and, as a result, is highly repetitive in the way it generates the SVG document fragments. With these points in mind, you should find the creation pattern clear enough that you can determine how the complete document is generated. The complete code is available online at `http://www.samspublishing.com`.

At the highest level, we need to create a document node to contain the DOM tree that we will build. When we have that object, we can create the style sheet section, the `defs` section, and the text for the quote and author name.

LISTING 21.23   svg_via_dom.pl—Generating SVG with the W3C DOM API

```
.
.
.

create_SVG_Document();
$svgRoot->appendChild( create_style() );
$svgRoot->appendChild( create_defs()  );
$svgRoot->appendChild( create_quote() );

.
.
.
```

Let's take a closer look at the `create_SVG_Document()` function in Listing 21.24. All XML documents have a document node at the top of the node hierarchy. First, we create the document node. Next, we create the XML declaration and the document type, and then append them to the document node. Finally, the topmost svg element is generated and appended to the document node. The svg element is attached to the document node, as all nodes are attached to their parent, using the `appendChild` method. You will see the `createElement`, `setAttribute`, and `appendChild` patterns used repeatedly in this example.

LISTING 21.24   svg_via_dom.pl continued—Creating the SVG Document Node

```
.
.
.

sub create_SVG_Document {
    $svgDocument = new XML::DOM::Document();

    my $xmlDecl = new XML::DOM::XMLDecl($svgDocument, "1.0", "ISO-8859-1", 0);
    my $doctype = new XML::DOM::DocumentType($svgDocument);

    $svgDocument->setXMLDecl($xmlDecl);
```

LISTING 21.24   Continued

```
$doctype->setParams(
    "svg",
    "http://www.w3.org/TR/2001/REC-SVG-200100904/DTD/svg10.dtd",
    "-//W3C//DTD SVG 20010904//EN"
);
$svgDocument->setDoctype($doctype);

$svgRoot = $svgDocument->createElement("svg");
$svgRoot->setAttribute("xmlns", "http://www.w3.org/2000/svg");
$svgRoot->setAttribute("xmlns:xlink", "http://www.w3.org/1999/xlink");
$svgDocument->appendChild($svgRoot);
}
.
.
.
```

Listing 21.25 builds the style sheet by creating a new style element. This function introduces a new method on the document node: `createCDATASection`.

A `CDATASection` is a special node type used to contain text in the DOM tree. A `CDATASection` prevents the text it contains from being processed by the XML processor. Using this node type is particularly important if you know that you are including text that has any special XML identifiers. For example, an opening angle bracket, <, indicates the beginning of a start tag or an end tag. If your text has some code that contains if (x < 10), for example, the XML parser would treat the less than sign as the beginning of a tag. If you place your text in a `CDATASection`, the parser will incorporate the `CDATASection`'s text without processing it. This use is similar in nature to the use of the single quotation mark in Perl.

> **NOTE**
>
> A CDATASection section is typically used to embed ECMAScript within an SVG document for script-based interactivity.

> **NOTE**
>
> You can avoid using a CDATASection if you replace the less than sign with an entity reference, specifically <. In this case, however, placing style sheet information and code within a CDATASection prevents the obfuscation of these uses of text.

LISTING 21.25   svg_via_dom.pl continued—Creating a Style Sheet

```
.
.
.
sub create_style {
    my $style = $svgDocument->createElement("style");
    my $cdata = $svgDocument->createCDATASection(<<EOL);
    .quote { font-size: 28; font-weight: bold }
    .author { font-size: 24; font-weight: normal; font-style: italic }
EOL

    $style->setAttribute("type", "text/css");
    $style->appendChild($cdata);

    return $style;
}
.
.
.
```

In Listing 21.26, the text for the quotation and the author's name is created. We use the same technique we used in the previous example to randomly pick a quotation. Again, we use the standard `createElement`, `setAttribute`, and `appendChild` patterns to build this document fragment.

This section of code introduces another document node method: `createTextNode`. The text node is functionally equivalent to a `CDATASection`, but you will need to take special care if your text contains any characters that have special meaning for the XML parser. These special characters must be replaced by entity references. Typically, a regular expression is used to replace special characters with entity references, but for the sake of simplicity, we will assume that our quotes already have entity references in place where needed.

LISTING 21.26   svg_via_dom.pl continued—Creating Text

```
.
.
.
sub create_text {
    my $text  = $svgDocument->createElement("text");
    my $desc  = $svgDocument->createElement("desc");
    my $tnode = $svgDocument->createTextNode("The quote");
    my $index = generate_integer( 0, @$quotes - 1 );
    my $quote = $quotes->[$index];
```

LISTING 21.26   Continued

```perl
    my $author = $quote->{author};
    my $lines  = $quote->{lines};

    $desc->appendChild($tnode);
    $text->appendChild($desc);

    $text->setAttribute("class", "quote");
    $text->setAttribute("y", $quote_top_margin);
    $text->setAttribute("fill", $quote_color);
    $text->setAttribute("filter", "url(#dropShadow)");

    foreach ( @$lines ) {
        my $tspan = $svgDocument->createElement("tspan");
        my $tnode = $svgDocument->createTextNode($_);

        $tspan->setAttribute("x", $quote_left_margin);
        $tspan->setAttribute("dy", "1em");
        $tspan->appendChild($tnode);

        $text->appendChild($tspan);
    }

    my $tspan = $svgDocument->createElement("tspan");

    $tnode = $svgDocument->createTextNode($author);

    $tspan->setAttribute("class", "author");
    $tspan->setAttribute("x", $quote_left_margin);
    $tspan->setAttribute("dy", "2em");
    $tspan->appendChild($tnode);

    $text->appendChild($tspan);

    return $text;
}
```

Listing 21.26 completes our example using the DOM API.

Now that we've constructed the document in its entirety, we can use the toString method on the document node to convert the tree to text. Listing 21.27 outputs the necessary HTTP headers and the string version of the SVG DOM tree.

LISTING 21.27   svg_via_dom.pl continued—Outputting the SVG File

```
.

.

.

print "Pragma: no-cache\n";
print "Content-type: image/svg+xml\n\n";
print $svgDocument->toString();

.

.

.
```

Listing 21.27 completes this example.

The XML::DOM Perl module is a great way to start creating SVG content if you are already familiar with the DOM API. We have seen how this module can be used to create most, if not all, of the node types needed to generate an SVG document.

Pros and Cons of Using the DOM API

The DOM API is a standard interface that has been implemented in many languages. Among the beauties of this API is that you have a distinct advantage in that, once you learn the API, you will be able to move from place to place without having to relearn a new API.

This style of SVG generation produces much larger Perl files. This example is more than four times larger than the example that used only print statements. Having more lines of code means more potential places for failures and bugs in your code.

The DOM API is a flexible and general model for manipulating document trees; however, this flexibility and generality are memory intensive. The entire SVG document tree must be created in memory before it is output. It is not uncommon to see estimates of memory usage being six times larger than the resulting document size. This can become a problem when you're generating very large SVG files.

Generating SVG Using the SVG.pm Module

In our last example, we will look at a Perl module, SVG.pm, written by Ronan Oger for the specific purpose of generating SVG with Perl.

> **NOTE**
>
> Additional SVG.pm documentation and tutorials are available at http://www.roasp.com.

SVG.pm differs from the DOM in that, by default, the equivalent of the document node and the svg root node are created simultaneously. When you use the default functionality during the creation of the SVG object, you will need to specify a mixture of attributes that are typically associated with separate nodes within the DOM. Listing 21.28 creates the XML declaration, the topmost `svg` element, and customizes the indentation used when outputting the final SVG tree.

The last few lines go behind the scenes to find the topmost `svg` element. The commented line shows a case in which this may be necessary. That line shows an example of how you can add a `viewBox` attribute to the `svg` element. The remaining lines show how to access an element's attributes.

> **NOTE**
>
> The default value for the height and width attributes is 100%. Removing these attributes will have no effect on our final SVG image.

LISTING 21.28   svg_via_svgpm.pl—Creating an SVG Document

```
.
.
.
sub create_SVG_Document {
    $svgDocument = new SVG(
        "xmlns"       => "http://www.w3.org/2000/svg",
        "xmlns:xlink" => "http://www.w3.org/1999/xlink",
        -standalone   => "no",
        -encoding     => "ISO-8859-1",
        -indent       => "    "
    );

    $svgRoot = $svgDocument->{-childs}[0];
    #$svgRoot->{'viewBox'} = "0 0 100 100";
    delete $svgRoot->{width};
    delete $svgRoot->{height};
}
.
.
.
```

> **NOTE**
>
> You can generate the document container using "-nostub=1" in the SVG constructor. Consequently, you have to create the SVG node using the svg method on the document container.

You can easily create a child element and append it to its parent with SVG.pm. In most cases, on the parent node to which you want to append, you invoke a method with a name that matches the element name you want to create. Then you pass in a list of attribute name/value pairs to set the new element's attributes.

In some cases, SVG.pm defines a method name that matches an element name. You cannot create the element using the steps mentioned in the preceding paragraph. The `tag` method is used in these situations. The first parameter is the name of the element that you want to create followed by the attribute name/value pairs.

Listing 21.29 creates the document style sheet. In this listing, we encounter a case in which we need to generate a style element. The `style` method is used to set the `style` attribute of an element, so we need to use the `tag` method to create the style element.

SVG.pm recognizes that certain text must be wrapped within a `CDATASection`. The `CDATA` method is used to populate our style object with the actual text of the style sheet.

LISTING 21.29   svg_via_svgpm.pl continued—Creating a Style Sheet

```
.
.
.
sub create_style {
    my $parent = shift;
    my $style  = $parent->tag("style", type => "text/css");
    my $cdata  = $style->CDATA(<<EOL);
    .quote { font-size: 28; font-weight: bold }
    .author { font-size: 24; font-weight: normal; font-style: italic }
EOL
}
.
.
.
```

Listing 21.30 creates the text of the quotation and the author's name. This code introduces a few new methods.

Whenever you need to add text to an element, you will need to use the `cdata` method. This listing creates a `desc` element, attaches a text node whose value is `"The quote"`, and then appends the `desc` element to a text element.

> **NOTE**
>
> SVG.pm includes two methods with similar names: CDATA and cdata. CDATA is used to create CDATASections, whereas cdata is used to create character data in text elements. These names

could be a source for confusion, so it is important to understand when it is appropriate to use these methods.

Once again, we randomly pick a quote to display. You may recall that our text is contained within individual tspan elements, one for each line of text. The text method allows us to pass a parameter, -type, to indicate that we want to create a tspan. The last statement in the listing creates a tspan element, sets the tspan's attributes, appends a text node containing the author's name, and appends the tspan element to the text element.

LISTING 21.30   svg_via_svgpm.pl continued—Creating Text

```
.
.
.
sub create_text {
    my $parent = shift;
    my $text   = $parent->text(
        class  => "quote",
        y      => $quote_top_margin,
        fill   => $quote_color,
        filter => "url(#dropShadow)"
    );

    $text->desc()->cdata("The quote");

    my $index  = generate_integer( 0, @$quotes - 1 );
    my $quote  = $quotes->[$index];
    my $author = $quote->{author};
    my $lines  = $quote->{lines};

    foreach ( @$lines ) {
        $text->text(
            -type => "span",
            x     => $quote_left_margin,
            dy    => "1em"
        )->cdata($_);
    }

    $text->text(
        -type => "span",
        x     => $quote_left_margin,
        dy    => "2em",
        class => "author"
```

LISTING 21.30   Continued

```
    )->cdata($author);
}
```

Listing 21.31 concludes our example using SVG.pm to generate our "Quote of the Day" SVG image.

Now that we've constructed our SVG document, we can use the `xmlify` method on the topmost SVG document container to convert the tree to text. Listing 21.31 outputs the necessary HTTP headers and the string version of the SVG tree.

LISTING 21.31   svg_via_svgpm.pl continued—Outputting the SVG File

```
print "Pragma: no-cache\n";
print "Content-type: image/svg+xml\n\n";
print $svgDocument->xmlify();
```

This concludes our SVG.pm example.

Pros and Cons of SVG.pm

SVG.pm is quite easy to use. You gain the same flexibilities gained using the DOM API, but with substantially fewer lines of code.

SVG.pm is similar to the DOM approach in that you must construct the entire document tree in memory before outputting it. However, the data structure that represents the tree is much leaner than the DOM approach. SVG.pm should not be as susceptible to the memory problems usually associated with the DOM.

This module is relatively new, and as such, it still has a few areas that need smoothing out. A standard API for accessing previously created elements would be useful. Also, the attributes are output in a seemingly random order as opposed to the order in which they were created. These are only minor problems that do not affect the overall utility of this module. SVG.pm shows the best compromise between the pros and cons of all three methods.

Summary

In this chapter, we analyzed a sample SVG file and subsequently converted it to a templatized version, allowing for more dynamism in our final SVG document.

We discussed a method for creating hexagonal tiles using SVG's `pattern` element and created a flexible drop shadow on text within our "Quote of the Day" document.

We also covered three methods for generating SVG using Perl: using the `print` statement, using the DOM API, and using the SVG.pm module. Each method brings its own set of pros and cons:

- The clear winner for speed and conciseness goes to the `print` statement method; however, this approach suffers from manageability problems as documents grow in size and complexity.

- The DOM API presents a natural approach to individuals who already use it in other development environments. The DOM API produces longer Perl programs and uses more memory per document than the other two methods.

- SVG.pm finds a happy compromise between these two methods. The API is easy to learn, code is shorter than the code written using the DOM API, and the data structure is lean on memory usage.

You should look at each method as a basic tool to keep in your toolbox. There are arguments for using each method. It is a matter of recognizing the right tool for the right job.

CHAPTER 22

SVG and PHP: Building an Online Survey

PHP is one of the most widely used server-side scripting languages today. Among many other reasons, the easy syntax, the rich set of features, and the availability on a huge number of systems (due to the public availability of the source code) have led to its rise from a private programming project to one of the hottest technologies around.

PHP has its origins in Linux/Unix, and typically when you think of PHP, you also think of MySQL as the underlying database. Like PHP, MySQL also is available as open source and will run on Linux/Unix as well as under the Windows platform. In fact, several books out there bear the words **PHP** and **MySQL** in their names.

Using databases with PHP does not necessarily mean that you have to use MySQL. PHP supports various different RDBMSs (Relational Database Management Systems), and on some platforms (such as Windows), there are better choices than MySQL. Nevertheless, we will use the PHP-MySQL combination throughout this case study because both products are available for most major platforms at no cost. You can download PHP from `http://www.php.net/` and MySQL from `http://www.mysql.com/`.

In this chapter, we will assume that you already have PHP and MySQL installed and configured on your system and that you are ready to go. If you have configuration problems, look at the support sections of either the PHP or the MySQL home page; both offer a great deal of information that will assist you in getting the PHP and MySQL installations to run. For the code in this chapter, you need a recent version of both PHP 4 and MySQL 3 or 4. Furthermore, the PHP code in this chapter expects the variable `error_reporting` in the php.ini file to be set to `E_ALL & ~E_NOTICE` (all errors and warnings are displayed; the use of uninitialized variables, however, will result in no warning, which saves us some time and coding effort). However, some people do not have access to their Web server's php.ini file (for example, when the Web host does not allow access to that file); therefore, we use the following code in all our PHP scripts:

```php
<?php
error_reporting(E_ALL ^ E_NOTICE);
?>
```

The goal of this case study is to create an online survey tool. Using some simple HTML forms, we will create new surveys and alter old surveys (or even delete them). Users can take these surveys and answer the prepared questions. As soon as the users finish the surveys, we can look at the survey results—to determine which percentage of people gave which answer to which question. This is where SVG comes in—to create charts showing the results. Creating graphics with SVG is quite easy and elegant (as you saw especially in Part I of this book); this time, though, we will retrieve the data for our charts from a data source.

In the next chapter, you will see a similar case study with ASP.NET. However, the applications are totally different.

Database Structure

To get started, we need to create a database and some tables for our survey application. There are several different approaches; we tried to choose a simple one so that we could create a complex but yet conceivable application.

The GUIs that ship with the MySQL distribution are very weak (one reason is that on the Windows platform, for instance, people tend to use primarily Microsoft Access or Microsoft SQL server). However, from `http://www.phpmyadmin.net/`, you can freely download a Web-based MySQL management tool (see Figure 22.1). When you use phpMyAdmin, you can easily create and edit MySQL databases and tables.

Our first step is to create the database for the survey application. We recommend that it be named svg. Of course, you are free to choose some other identifier for the database and all tables; however, you also will need to change the table and database names in the code listings.

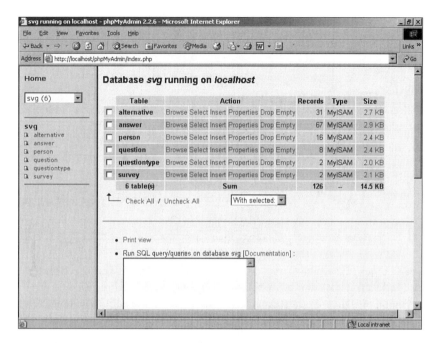

FIGURE 22.1   Running phpMyAdmin.

Survey

The first table we will create, named survey, will hold the general information about the survey. The table consists of the following fields:

Field Name	Data Type	Description
id	int(11) auto_increment	Identifier; primary key
name	varchar(50)	Name/title of the survey
status	enum('active','inactive')	Whether the survey currently is active (can be taken) or not
persons	int(11)	Number of persons who have already taken the survey

The appropriate SQL statement for creating this table looks like this:

```
CREATE TABLE `survey` (
  `id` int(11) NOT NULL auto_increment,
  `name` varchar(50) default NULL,
  `status` enum('active','inactive') NOT NULL default 'inactive',
  `persons` int(11) NOT NULL default '0',
  PRIMARY KEY  (`id`)
) TYPE=MyISAM;
```

While you are creating a new survey, you certainly do not want users to take (or test) this survey; thus, we introduced the status field that has as its value either active or inactive, providing the status of the survey.

Survey Questions

Each survey consists of several questions. These questions are saved in a table named question that has the following fields:

Field Name	Data Type	Description
id	int(11) auto_increment	Identifier; primary key
text	varchar(255)	Text of the question
type	tinyint(4)	Type of question (for example, multiple answers may be selected or only one)
survey_id	int(11)	Identifier of the survey the questions belong to

The survey and question tables are quite independent. The only connection between them is that question contains a field named survey_id that corresponds to the id field in the survey table. Thus, all questions for all surveys are stored in the question table. With the value in the survey_id field, we can find out which survey the current question belongs to.

Here is the SQL code for creating the question table:

```
CREATE TABLE `question` (
  `id` int(11) NOT NULL auto_increment,
  `text` varchar(255) NOT NULL default '',
  `type` tinyint(4) NOT NULL default '0',
  `survey_id` int(11) NOT NULL default '0',
  PRIMARY KEY  (`id`)
) TYPE=MyISAM;
```

You may have noticed the type field that contains the type of question. Here are some possibilities for question types:

- **Radio button questions**—Only one of the answers or alternatives may be selected.

- **Check box questions**—Any number of answers or alternatives may be selected.

- **Free text questions**—The user may answer with any arbitrary text.

In this case study, we will concentrate on the first two question types—radio buttons and check boxes. However, to make the system flexible and expandable, we will not hard-code the question types in the question table but create a new table, named questiontype, that holds the question type information. The following two fields are required for this table:

Field Name	Data Type	Description
id	tinyint(4) auto_increment	Identifier; primary key
name	varchar(50)	Textual description of the question type

Here is the SQL statement that creates the `questiontype` table:

```
CREATE TABLE `questiontype` (
  `id` tinyint(4) NOT NULL auto_increment,
  `name` varchar(50) NOT NULL default '',
  PRIMARY KEY  (`id`)
) TYPE=MyISAM;
```

We will also fill this table with two values for radio button questions and check box questions:

```
INSERT INTO `questiontype` (`id`, `name`) VALUES (1, 'radio'), (2, 'checkbox');
```

Survey Answers

For each question, some number of alternatives (or answers) exists. Because this number may change from question to question, we cannot store the information in the `question` table but need to create a new table named `alternative`. In this table, we will store the different alternatives and also the identifier of the associated question (the id field in the question table). The fields in this table are as follows:

Field Name	Data Type	Description
id	int(11) auto_increment	Identifier; primary key
text	varchar(50)	Text of the alternative
question_id	int(11)	Identifier of the question this alternative belongs to

Here is the associated SQL command to create the alternative table:

```
CREATE TABLE `alternative` (
  `id` int(11) NOT NULL auto_increment,
  `text` varchar(255) default NULL,
  `question_id` int(11) NOT NULL default '0',
  PRIMARY KEY  (`id`)
) TYPE=MyISAM;
```

Via the `question_id` field, we can find out which question the current alternative belongs to, so it is possible to store all alternatives for all questions for all surveys in one database.

When a person takes the test, his or her answers are stored in the `answers` table, which contains the following fields:

Field Name	Data Type	Description
id	int(11) auto_increment	Identifier; primary key
question_id	int(11)	Identifier of the question
alternative_id	int(11)	Identifier of the alternative

Here is the associated SQL command to create the table:

```
CREATE TABLE `answer` (
  `id` int(11) NOT NULL auto_increment,
  `question_id` int(11) NOT NULL default '0',
  `alternative_id` int(11) NOT NULL default '0',
  PRIMARY KEY  (`id`)
) TYPE=MyISAM;
```

Persons

Finally, we want to make sure that no one can fill out a survey more than once; otherwise, it would be too easy to manipulate the survey's results. Thus, we will store the e-mail address of each person who takes a survey. Of course, one person may take several surveys; however, the surveys must be different. So we can store the following information in a table named person:

Field Name	Data Type	Description
id	int(11) auto_increment	Identifier; primary key
email	varchar(50)	E-mail address of the test taker
survey_id	int(11)	Identifier of the survey this person has taken

Here is the associated SQL command to create this table:

```
CREATE TABLE `person` (
  `id` int(11) NOT NULL auto_increment,
  `email` varchar(50) default NULL,
  `survey_id` int(11) NOT NULL default '0',
  PRIMARY KEY  (`id`)
) TYPE=MyISAM;
```

> **NOTE**
>
> You could, of course, use the id field to create a profile of your users; however, it is a nice gesture to use only anonymous surveys. We are interested only in the percentages that come out after many persons have taken the survey, not in each person's individual answers.

We've now completed the database structure for this application. In Figure 22.2, you can see all the tables and fields and how they are connected.

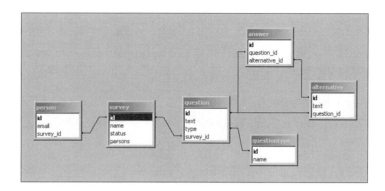

FIGURE 22.2 Tables, fields, and their connections.

> **NOTE**
>
> If you want to make the creation of this database as easy as possible, use the SQL file you can download with this chapter's listings from http://www.samspublishing.com/. Create a database named svg within phpMyAdmin and then load this SQL file into MySQL; the databases will be created automatically for you.

Survey Administration Tool

In this section, we will create the PHP pages that allow us to create, change, and delete surveys, questions, and alternatives. We will show the code bit by bit; the complete files can be downloaded (as all source code from this book) from http:// www.samspublishing.com/. However, before we start with PHP, let's look at some prerequisites.

To get started, we need to put the files in the virtual directory /svgsurvey/admin on the Web server so that we can access the files via http://servername/svgsurvey/admin/ filename.php.

Next, let's ensure that MySQL runs. We can connect to the database by using the following statement:

```
$conn = mysql_connect("localhost");
```

As you can see, we provide no password because this database is stored in our local system. If your configuration is different, add a username and password to the connect statements as follows:

```
$conn = mysql_connect("localhost", "user", "pwd");
```

And finally, to add at least a minimum of style to the application, we created the style sheet named survey.css in Listing 22.1.

LISTING 22.1   survey.css—The Style Sheet

```
.heading {font-family:Arial, Geneva, Helvetica, sans-serif;
          font-weight: bold;
          font-size: 12pt}
.bold {font-family:Arial, Geneva, Helvetica, sans-serif;
       font-weight: bold;
       font-size: 10pt}
body,td {font-family:Arial, Geneva, Helvetica, sans-serif;
          font-size: 10pt}
```

On all our PHP pages, we include this style sheet by using the following directive in the <head> segment of the page:

```
<head>
<!-- ... -->
<link href="survey.css" type="text/css" rel="stylesheet" />
</head>
```

Listing Surveys

On the front page of our administration tool, logically called index.php, we will first show a list of all surveys in the system. To do so, we send a SELECT * FROM survey statement to the MySQL database:

```
<p class="heading">Available Surveys:</p>
<ul>
<?php
$conn = mysql_connect("localhost");
mysql_select_db("svg", $conn) or die("error connecting to db!");
$rows = mysql_query("SELECT * FROM survey", $conn);
while ($row = mysql_fetch_array($rows)) {
```

```
    $id = $row["id"];
    echo("<li><span class=\"bold\">" . htmlspecialchars($row["name"]) .
    "</span>" .
        " (" . $row["status"] . ")" .
        " [<a href=\"index.php?survey=$id&toggle=" . $row["status"] .
    "\">toggle status</a>]" .
        " [<a href=\"edit.php?survey=$id\">edit</a>]" .
        " [<a href=\"eval.php?survey=$id\">statistics</a>]" .
        " [<a href=\"index.php?survey=$id&delete=ok\">delete</a>]</li>");
}
mysql_close($conn);
?>
</ul>
```

Next, we create a connection to the database and then loop through all surveys. Apart from the name and the status of the survey, we also provide the following links:

- A link to toggle the status of the survey, from `active` to `inactive` and vice versa; the link goes to index.php (the current page) and submits the survey's `id` value and the current status via URL.

- A link to edit the survey, linking to edit.php and providing the survey's `id` value in the URL.

- A link to look at the statistics of the survey, linking to eval.php and providing the survey's `id` field in the URL.

- Finally, a link to delete the survey, linking to index.php and providing via URL the `id` of the survey and `delete=ok`.

If you look at the `while` loop in the example, you will see that it links to several PHP scripts. The first is index.php, which we will look at first to see how the `toggle` parameter is processed by this script.

We will analyze how the survey's status is toggled. To accomplish that, we can look at the current status, which is provided as a parameter in the URL. If it is `active`, we will change it to `inactive` and vice versa:

```
if (isset($HTTP_GET_VARS["toggle"])) {
  $status = ($HTTP_GET_VARS["toggle"] == "active") ? "in" : "";
  $status .= "active";
```

After that, we will connect to the database, read the survey ID from the URL, and update the status by sending an UPDATE statement to the database:

```
$conn = mysql_connect("localhost");
  $survey = $HTTP_GET_VARS["survey"];
  mysql_select_db("svg", $conn) or die("error connecting to db!");
  mysql_query("UPDATE survey SET status='$status' WHERE id='$survey'", $conn);
  mysql_close($conn);
  $message = "Status toggled!";
}
```

> **NOTE**
>
> Starting with PHP 4.1.0, you can access GET data by using the $_GET array and can retrieve POST data via $_POST. However, because older PHP versions do not support this capability, we have used the old-fashioned approach in this chapter.

Deleting a question is a similar task. Again, we read the survey ID from the URL and generate an SQL statement from it, this time a DELETE statement. To be exact, we create two statements:

- One statement to delete all questions that belong to the to-be-deleted survey

- One statement to delete the survey itself

> **NOTE**
>
> To be exact, we need three more statements to delete all data relevant to the deleted survey from the alternative, answer, and person tables. The way the application is written, we can delete only the entry in the survey table so that the survey no longer appears in the survey list.

Here is the code to create these statements:

```
if ($HTTP_GET_VARS["delete"] == "ok") {
  $conn = mysql_connect("localhost");
  $survey = $HTTP_GET_VARS["survey"];
  mysql_select_db("svg", $conn) or die("error connecting to db!");
  mysql_query("DELETE FROM question WHERE survey_id='$survey'", $conn);
  mysql_query("DELETE FROM survey WHERE id='$survey'", $conn);
  mysql_close($conn);
  $message = "Question deleted!";
}
```

Both code fragments, for toggling the status and deleting a survey, must be put in a PHP segment above the first html element.

Creating Surveys

Apart from listing existing surveys, the user also can create new surveys. The following HTML form serves this purpose:

```
<p class="heading">Create new survey</p>
<form method="post" action="index.php">
Survey name:
  <input type="text" name="name" />
  <input type="submit" name="Submit" value="Create!" />
</form>
```

When the user clicks the submit button, the form data is posted to the index.php file, where—at the top of the page—the following code reads out the form data and writes the survey data into the database. However, there is one caveat: If a survey with the given name already exists, an error message is created.

```
if (isset($HTTP_POST_VARS["Submit"])) {
  $conn = mysql_connect("localhost");
  $name = $HTTP_POST_VARS["name"];
  mysql_select_db("svg", $conn) or die("error connecting to db!");
  $rows = mysql_query("SELECT * FROM survey WHERE name='$name'", $conn);
  if (mysql_num_rows($rows) == 0) {
    mysql_query("INSERT INTO survey (name) VALUES ('$name')", $conn);
    $id = mysql_insert_id($conn);
    $message = "Survey created! <a href=\"edit.php?survey=$id\">edit survey</a>";
    mysql_close($conn);
  } else {
    $message = "Survey with name '$name' already exists!";
  }
}
```

As you may have noticed in the previous code fragments, sometimes we have set a variable named $message to show information to the user. The value of this variable is printed in the body of the HTML page:

```
<p class="bold"><?=$message?></p>
```

However, for this to work, short_open_tag has to be set to on in the php.ini file; otherwise, you would have to use

```
<p class="bold"><?php echo($message); ?></p>
```

We have now completed the code for index.php (apart from some cosmetic additions). In Figure 22.3, you can see what the final page looks like.

The complete code for index.php is shown in Listing 22.2.

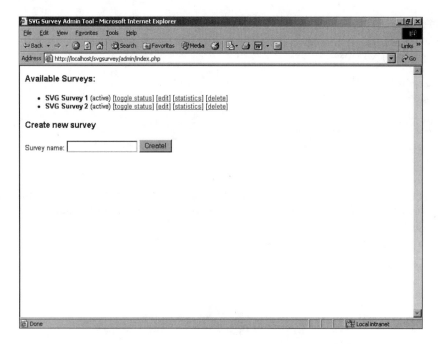

FIGURE 22.3   The final page of the form to create new surveys.

LISTING 22.2   index.php—Creating New Surveys

```php
<?php
error_reporting(E_ALL ^ E_NOTICE);

if (isset($HTTP_POST_VARS["Submit"])) {
  $conn = mysql_connect("localhost");
  $name = $HTTP_POST_VARS["name"];
  mysql_select_db("svg", $conn) or die("error connecting to db!");
  $rows = mysql_query("SELECT * FROM survey WHERE name='$name'", $conn);
  if (mysql_num_rows($rows) == 0) {
    mysql_query("INSERT INTO survey (name) VALUES ('$name')", $conn);
    $id = mysql_insert_id($conn);
    $message = "Survey created! <a href=\"edit.php?survey=$id\">edit
     survey</a>";
    mysql_close($conn);
  } else {
    $message = "Survey with name '$name' already exists!";
  }
}
```

LISTING 22.2 Continued

```php
if ($HTTP_GET_VARS["delete"] == "ok") {
  $conn = mysql_connect("localhost");
  $survey = $HTTP_GET_VARS["survey"];
  mysql_select_db("svg", $conn) or die("error connecting to db!");
  mysql_query("DELETE FROM question WHERE survey_id='$survey'", $conn);
  mysql_query("DELETE FROM survey WHERE id='$survey'", $conn);
  mysql_close($conn);
  $message = "Question deleted!";
}
if (isset($HTTP_GET_VARS["toggle"])) {
  $status = ($HTTP_GET_VARS["toggle"] == "active") ? "in" : "";
  $status .= "active";
  $conn = mysql_connect("localhost");
  $survey = $HTTP_GET_VARS["survey"];
  mysql_select_db("svg", $conn) or die("error connecting to db!");
  mysql_query("UPDATE survey SET status='$status' WHERE id='$survey'", $conn);
  mysql_close($conn);
  $message = "Status toggled!";
}
?>
<html>
<head>
<title>SVG Survey Admin Tool</title>
<link href="survey.css" type="text/css" rel="stylesheet" />
</head>
<body>
<p class="heading">Available Surveys:</p>
<ul>
<?php
$conn = mysql_connect("localhost");
mysql_select_db("svg", $conn) or die("error connecting to db!");
$rows = mysql_query("SELECT * FROM survey", $conn);
while ($row = mysql_fetch_array($rows)) {
  $id = $row["id"];
  echo("<li><span class=\"bold\">" . htmlspecialchars($row["name"]) .
      "</span>" .
      " (" . $row["status"] . ")" .
      " [<a href=\"index.php?survey=$id&toggle=" . $row["status"] .
      "\">toggle status</a>]" .
      " [<a href=\"edit.php?survey=$id\">edit</a>]" .
      " [<a href=\"eval.php?survey=$id\">statistics</a>]" .
```

LISTING 22.2   Continued

```
            " [<a href=\"index.php?survey=$id&delete=ok\">delete</a>]</li>");
}
mysql_close($conn);
?>
</ul>
<p class="heading">Create new survey</p>
<p class="bold"><?=$message?></p>
<form method="post" action="index.php">
Survey name:
  <input type="text" name="name" />
  <input type="submit" name="Submit" value="Create!" />
</form>
</body>
</html>
```

Listing Questions

As you have seen, after creating a survey, the user gets a link to edit.php, where he or she can change the survey information, including creating questions. All this work will be done on the edit.php page. As a URL parameter, the id field of the current survey will be provided to the script.

In edit.php, the user first gets a list of all questions in the survey; the code is analogous to the one for listing all existing surveys in index.php.

First, a SELECT statement is sent to the database:

```
<p class="heading">Edit survey</p>
<?php
$conn = mysql_connect("localhost");
$survey = $HTTP_GET_VARS["survey"];
mysql_select_db("svg", $conn) or die("error connecting to db!");
$rows = mysql_query("SELECT * FROM survey WHERE id='$survey'", $conn);
```

Then we check whether the survey exists. If it does not, an error message is created:

```
if (mysql_num_rows($rows) == 0) {
?>
  <p class="bold">Error: survey does not exist! <a href="index.php">Back</a></p>
```

Otherwise, all questions from the survey are shown to the user; the questions' titles are retrieved from the question table:

```
<?php
} else {
```

```
    $row = mysql_fetch_array($rows);
    echo("<p class=\"bold\">Survey name: " . htmlspecialchars($row["name"]) .
        "</p>");
    echo("<ul>");
    $rows1 = mysql_query("SELECT question.id, question.text, questiontype.name
      FROM question, questiontype WHERE question.survey_id='$survey' AND
      question.type = questiontype.id ORDER BY question.id", $conn);
    while ($row1 = mysql_fetch_array($rows1)) {
      $id = $row1["id"];
      echo("<li><span class=\"bold\">" . htmlspecialchars($row1["text"]) .
          "</span>" .
          " (" . $row1["name"] . ")" .
          " [<a href=\"editq.php?survey=$survey&question=$id\">edit</a>]" .
          " [<a href=\"edit.php?survey=$survey&question=$id&delete=ok\">delete
            </a>]</li><ul>");
      $rows2 = mysql_query("SELECT * FROM alternative WHERE question_id='$id'",
                          $conn);
      while ($row2 = mysql_fetch_array($rows2)) {
        echo("<li>" . $row2["text"] . "</li>");
      }
      echo("</ul>");
    }
    echo("</ul>");
}
?>
```

For each question, two links are offered:

- A link to edit the question, linking to editq.php and providing the survey's ID (not necessary, but this link saves one database access in editq.php) and the question's ID.

- A link to delete the question, calling edit.php and providing the survey's and the question's IDs and delete=ok in the URL.

Now let's look at the code to delete a question. An appropriate SQL DELETE statement is created and sent to the database. This code must reside at the top of the PHP script, before the HTML output:

```
if ($HTTP_GET_VARS["delete"] == "ok") {
  $conn = mysql_connect("localhost");
  $question = $HTTP_GET_VARS["question"];
  $survey = $HTTP_GET_VARS["survey"];
  mysql_select_db("svg", $conn) or die("error connecting to db!");
  mysql_query("DELETE FROM question WHERE survey_id='$survey' AND id=
    '$question'", $conn);
```

```
  mysql_query("DELETE FROM alternative WHERE question_id='$question'", $conn);
  mysql_close($conn);
  $message = "Question deleted!";
}
```

As you can see, two DELETE statements are executed. Not only the question itself but also all alternatives are removed from the database.

Creating Questions

Apart from viewing and editing single questions, the user also can create new questions by using an HTML form:

```
<form method="post">
New question:
  <input type="text" name="text" /><br />
```

The question type is retrieved from table "questiontype"; this makes the application flexible for additional question types:

```
Type:
  <select name="type">
<?php

$rows = mysql_query("SELECT * FROM questiontype", $conn);
while ($row = mysql_fetch_array($rows)) {
  echo("<option value=\"" . $row["id"] . "\">" . $row["name"] . "</option>");
}
mysql_close($conn);
?>
</select>
<input type="hidden" name="survey" value="<?=$survey?>" />
<input type="submit" name="Submit" value="Add!" />
</form>
```

The data from this form is interpreted on edit.php, as well (because no action attribute for the <form> tag was provided, data is posted to the current page). The question and its type are written into the database:

```
if (isset($HTTP_POST_VARS["Submit"])) {
  $conn = mysql_connect("localhost");
  $text = $HTTP_POST_VARS["text"];
  $type = $HTTP_POST_VARS["type"];
  $survey = $HTTP_POST_VARS["survey"];
  mysql_select_db("svg", $conn) or die("error connecting to db!");
  mysql_query("INSERT INTO question (text, type, survey_id) VALUES
```

```
                ('$text', '$type', '$survey')",
                  $conn);
```

After that, the user is automatically (or rather automagically) redirected to the editq.php script where the question can be edited (see Figure 22.4). So it is possible to add alternatives to the question and save one mouse click. As a parameter for editq.php, the ID of the new question is required; it can be retrieved by calling the PHP function `mysql_insert_id()` that returns the ID created by the last INSERT statement:

```
header("Location: editq.php?question=" . mysql_insert_id($conn) .
       "&survey=$survey");
  mysql_close($conn);
}
```

And now we've completed the vital parts of the edit.php code. In Listing 22.3, you can find it all.

LISTING 22.3 edit.php—Editing Surveys

```
<?php
error_reporting(E_ALL ^ E_NOTICE);

if (isset($HTTP_POST_VARS["Submit"])) {
  $conn = mysql_connect("localhost");
  $text = $HTTP_POST_VARS["text"];
  $type = $HTTP_POST_VARS["type"];
  $survey = $HTTP_POST_VARS["survey"];
  mysql_select_db("svg", $conn) or die("error connecting to db!");
  mysql_query("INSERT INTO question (text, type, survey_id) VALUES
            ('$text', '$type', '$survey')", $conn);
  header("Location: editq.php?question=" . mysql_insert_id($conn) .
         "&survey=$survey");
  mysql_close($conn);
}
if ($HTTP_GET_VARS["delete"] == "ok") {
  $conn = mysql_connect("localhost");
  $question = $HTTP_GET_VARS["question"];
  $survey = $HTTP_GET_VARS["survey"];
  mysql_select_db("svg", $conn) or die("error connecting to db!");
  mysql_query("DELETE FROM question WHERE survey_id='$survey' AND
    id='$question'", $conn);
  mysql_query("DELETE FROM alternative WHERE question_id='$question'", $conn);
  mysql_close($conn);
  $message = "Question deleted!";
```

LISTING 22.3   Continued

```php
}
?>
<html>
<head>
<title>SVG Survey Admin Tool</title>
<link href="survey.css" type="text/css" rel="stylesheet" />
</head>
<body>
<p class="heading">Edit survey</p>
<p class="bold"><?=$message?></p>
<?php
$conn = mysql_connect("localhost");
$survey = $HTTP_GET_VARS["survey"];
mysql_select_db("svg", $conn) or die("error connecting to db!");
$rows = mysql_query("SELECT * FROM survey WHERE id='$survey'", $conn);
if (mysql_num_rows($rows) == 0) {
?>
  <p class="bold">Error: survey does not exist!
    <a href="index.php">Back</a></p>
<?php
} else {
  $row = mysql_fetch_array($rows);
  echo("<p class=\"bold\">Survey name: " . htmlspecialchars($row["name"]) .
      "</p>");
  echo("<ul>");
  $rows1 = mysql_query("SELECT question.id, question.text, questiontype.name
    FROM question, questiontype WHERE question.survey_id='$survey' AND
    question.type = questiontype.id ORDER BY question.id", $conn);
  while ($row1 = mysql_fetch_array($rows1)) {
    $id = $row1["id"];
    echo("<li><span class=\"bold\">" . htmlspecialchars($row1["text"]) .
        "</span>" .
        " (" . $row1["name"] . ")" .
        " [<a href=\"editq.php?survey=$survey&question=$id\">edit</a>]" .
        " [<a href=\"edit.php?survey=$survey&question=$id&delete=ok\">delete
          </a>]</li><ul>");
    $rows2 = mysql_query("SELECT * FROM alternative WHERE question_id='$id'",
                          $conn);
    while ($row2 = mysql_fetch_array($rows2)) {
      echo("<li>" . $row2["text"] . "</li>");
    }
    echo("</ul>");
```

LISTING 22.3 Continued

```
  }
  echo("</ul>");
}
?>
<form method="post">
New question:
  <input type="text" name="text" /><br />
Type:
  <select name="type">
<?php
$rows = mysql_query("SELECT * FROM questiontype", $conn);
while ($row = mysql_fetch_array($rows)) {
  echo("<option value=\"" . $row["id"] . "\">" . $row["name"] . "</option>");
}
mysql_close($conn);
?>
</select>
<input type="hidden" name="survey" value="<?=$survey?>" />
<input type="submit" name="Submit" value="Add!" />
</form>
<a href="index.php">back to overview</a>
</body>
</html>
```

Listing Alternatives

On the editq.php page, the alternatives for a question may be listed and deleted; editing is not possible (because of space constraints of this chapter). The code again is a while loop that reads and prints the results from an SQL SELECT statement. Apart from the single alternatives, the name of the question and—more important—its type are also shown:

```
<p class="heading">Edit survey</p>
<?php
$question = $HTTP_GET_VARS["question"];
$conn = mysql_connect("localhost");
$survey = $HTTP_GET_VARS["survey"];
mysql_select_db("svg", $conn) or die("error connecting to db!");
$rows = mysql_query("SELECT * FROM question, questiontype WHERE question.id=
  '$question' AND question.survey_id='$survey' AND
  question.type=questiontype.id", $conn);
if (mysql_num_rows($rows) == 0) {
?>
```

```
      <p class="bold">Error: question does not exist!
                     <a href="edit.php?survey=<?=$survey?>">Back</a></p>
<?php
} else {
  $row = mysql_fetch_array($rows);
  echo("<p><span class=\"bold\">" . htmlspecialchars($row["text"]) .
       "</span> (type: " . $row["name"] . ")</p>");
  echo("<ul>");
  $rows1 = mysql_query("SELECT * FROM alternative WHERE question_id='$question'",
                       $conn);
  while ($row1 = mysql_fetch_array($rows1)) {
    $id = $row1["id"];
    echo("<li>" . htmlspecialchars($row1["text"]) .
         " [<a href=\"editq.php?survey=$survey&question=$question&alternative=
           $id&delete=ok\">delete</a>]</li>");
  }
  echo("</ul>");
}
mysql_close($conn);
?>
```

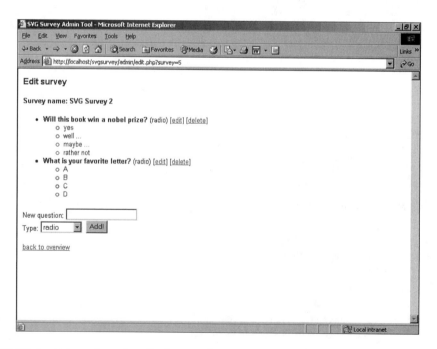

FIGURE 22.4   Using a form to edit the questions.

Again, we offer a delete link that deletes—if clicked—the current alternative. This action is taken by the following piece of code that resides at the top of the PHP page:

```
if ($HTTP_GET_VARS["delete"] == "ok") {
  $conn = mysql_connect("localhost");
  $alternative = $HTTP_GET_VARS["alternative"];
  mysql_select_db("svg", $conn) or die("error connecting to db!");
  mysql_query("DELETE FROM alternative WHERE id='$alternative'", $conn);
  mysql_close($conn);
  $message = "Question deleted!";
}
```

Creating Alternatives

To create a new alternative, the user must fill out the following form that requests the name of the alternative (that is, the possible answer to the question). Other information is transmitted via hidden form fields. Hidden fields are used because browser bugs sometimes cut the query string from URLs when posting a form.

```
<form method="post">
  <input type="text" name="text" />
  <input type="hidden" name="question" value="<?=$question?>" />
  <input type="hidden" name="survey" value="<?=$survey?>" />
  <input type="submit" name="Submit" value="Add!" />
</form>
```

The data entered in the form is written into the database as follows:

```
if (isset($HTTP_POST_VARS["Submit"])) {
  $conn = mysql_connect("localhost");
  $text = $HTTP_POST_VARS["text"];
  $question = $HTTP_POST_VARS["question"];
  $survey = $HTTP_POST_VARS["survey"];
  mysql_select_db("svg", $conn) or die("error connecting to db!");
  mysql_query("INSERT INTO alternative (text, question_id) VALUES
          ('$text', '$question')", $conn);
  mysql_close($conn);
  $message = "Alternative added!";
```

For practical reasons, the $question and $survey variables that are used throughout the code are set at this position as well. Remember that we used hidden form fields to transmit the question ID and the survey ID. However, if the page is called via a link from edit.php, this data must be retrieved from the query string as follows:

```
} else {
  $question = $HTTP_GET_VARS["question"];
```

```
    $survey = $HTTP_GET_VARS["survey"];
}
```

The output of this script run in the browser is shown in Figure 22.5.

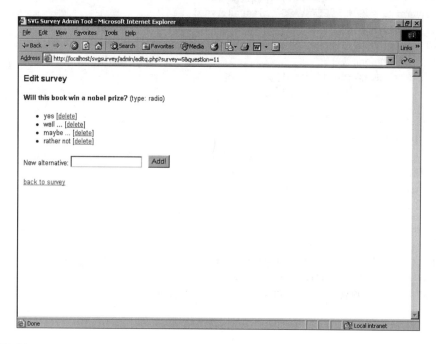

FIGURE 22.5   Creating new alternatives.

Now let's add the style sheet to the page, and we'll be done; the complete code is shown in Listing 22.4.

LISTING 22.4   editq.php—Creating and Editing Questions

```php
<?php
error_reporting(E_ALL ^ E_NOTICE);
if (isset($HTTP_POST_VARS["Submit"])) {
  $conn = mysql_connect("localhost");
  $text = $HTTP_POST_VARS["text"];
  $question = $HTTP_POST_VARS["question"];
  $survey = $HTTP_POST_VARS["survey"];
  mysql_select_db("svg", $conn) or die("error connecting to db!");
  mysql_query("INSERT INTO alternative (text, question_id) VALUES
            ('$text', '$question')", $conn);
  mysql_close($conn);
```

LISTING 22.4 Continued

```php
  $message = "Alternative added!";
} else {
  $question = $HTTP_GET_VARS["question"];
  $survey = $HTTP_GET_VARS["survey"];
}
if ($HTTP_GET_VARS["delete"] == "ok") {
  $conn = mysql_connect("localhost");
  $alternative = $HTTP_GET_VARS["alternative"];
  mysql_select_db("svg", $conn) or die("error connecting to db!");
  mysql_query("DELETE FROM alternative WHERE id='$alternative'", $conn);
  mysql_close($conn);
  $message = "Question deleted!";
}
?>
<html>
<head>
<title>SVG Survey Admin Tool</title>
<link href="survey.css" type="text/css" rel="stylesheet" />
</head>
<body>
<p class="heading">Edit survey</p>
<p class="bold"><?=$message?></p>
<?php
$conn = mysql_connect("localhost");
$survey = $HTTP_GET_VARS["survey"];
mysql_select_db("svg", $conn) or die("error connecting to db!");
$rows = mysql_query("SELECT * FROM question, questiontype WHERE question.id=
  '$question' AND question.survey_id='$survey' AND question.type=
  questiontype.id", $conn);
if (mysql_num_rows($rows) == 0) {
?>
  <p class="bold">Error: question does not exist!
    <a href="edit.php?survey=<?=$survey?>">Back</a></p>
<?php
} else {
  $row = mysql_fetch_array($rows);
  echo("<p><span class=\"bold\">" . htmlspecialchars($row["text"]) .
      "</span> (type: " . $row["name"] . ")</p>");
  echo("<ul>");
  $rows1 = mysql_query("SELECT * FROM alternative WHERE question_id=
    '$question'", $conn);
```

LISTING 22.4   Continued

```php
  while ($row1 = mysql_fetch_array($rows1)) {
    $id = $row1["id"];
    echo("<li>" . htmlspecialchars($row1["text"]) .
        " [<a href=\"editq.php?survey=$survey&question=$question&alternative=
          $id&delete=ok\">delete</a>]</li>");
  }
  echo("</ul>");
}
mysql_close($conn);
?>
<form method="post">
New alternative:
  <input type="text" name="text">
<input type="hidden" name="question" value="<?=$question?>">
<input type="hidden" name="survey" value="<?=$survey?>">
<input type="submit" name="Submit" value="Add!">
</form>
<a href="edit.php?survey=<?=$survey?>">back to survey</a>
</body>
</html>
```

So far, we have created a PHP online survey administration tool. To avoid attacks on your system, you should now secure the admin directory, using HTTP authentication, so that no one but you (or other authorized persons) can access this tool.

Online Survey Tool

Now that we have created the administrative tools for the survey application, we also want users to complete our surveys.

Registering Users and Listing Surveys

To register users, we will write two pages that reside in the /svgsurvey directory. We will start with index.php, where all available surveys are shown. Before that, however, each user must provide his or her e-mail address. As mentioned previously, we ask for this information so that we can prevent users from completing the same survey twice (or at least make it a little bit harder to do so).

> **NOTE**
>
> The following approach is quite simple. You could, of course, think of a more complex mechanism, such as verifying the entered e-mail address by sending e-mail to the user, asking for a reply.

To store the e-mail address (and later the answers to the various questions as well), we will use sessions that are part of the PHP core distribution, starting with PHP version 4. Before using that script, check the session settings in your php.ini file. Take a special look at the value of session.save_path; the given directory must exist, and the PHP interpreter must have write access to this directory.

Now we're ready for the script itself (remember: we start with index.php). On top of the page, the following PHP code checks whether there is a session variable for the user's e-mail address or whether the e-mail address has been submitted to the script via POST. If so, a new session variable is created.

```
session_start();
if (isset($HTTP_POST_VARS["Submit"]) && $HTTP_POST_VARS["email"] != "") {
  $email = $HTTP_POST_VARS["email"];
  session_register("email");
} else {
  $email = $HTTP_SESSION_VARS["email"];
}
```

After that, the user's e-mail address—if provided—is stored in the $email variable. If the e-mail address is valid (to keep it simple, we check only if there is any value in $email)), all available surveys are listed. This is achieved by sending a SELECT statement to the database and printing the results.

NOTE

However, be aware that you must use WHERE status='active' in your SQL statement, as follows; otherwise, inactive surveys would also be shown.

```
<?php
if ($email != "") {
?>
<p class="heading">Available Surveys:</p>
<ul>
<?php
$conn = mysql_connect("localhost");
mysql_select_db("svg", $conn) or die("error connecting to db!");
$rows = mysql_query("SELECT * FROM survey WHERE status='active'", $conn);
while ($row = mysql_fetch_array($rows)) {
  $id = $row["id"];
  $rows1 = mysql_query("SELECT * FROM person WHERE survey_id='$id' AND
                        email LIKE '$email'", $conn);
  if (mysql_num_rows($rows1) == 0) {
    echo("<li><span class=\"bold\">" . htmlspecialchars($row["name"]) .
```

```
             "</span>" ." [<a href=\"survey.php?survey=$id\">go to survey</a>]</li>");
  }
}
mysql_close($conn);
?>
</ul>
```

A link to survey.php sends the user to the page where he or she can answer the questions stored in the database; we will take a closer look at that file in the next section.

If, however, no e-mail address is provided, an HTML form is created using the following code, and the user is prompted to enter his or her address:

```
<?php
} else {
?>
<p class="heading">Please provide your email address!</p>
<form method="post" action="index.php">
  <input type="text" name="email" />
  <input type="submit" name="Submit" value="Start!" />
</form>
<?php
}
?>
```

This form will submit the data to the same page, and the e-mail address will be saved into the session variable as we have coded at the top of this page.

Listing 22.5 shows the complete source code for index.php.

LISTING 22.5   index.php—The Start Page for the Survey

```
<?php
error_reporting(E_ALL ^ E_NOTICE);

session_start();
if (isset($HTTP_POST_VARS["Submit"]) && $HTTP_POST_VARS["email"] != "") {
  $email = $HTTP_POST_VARS["email"];
  session_register("email");
} else {
  $email = $HTTP_SESSION_VARS["email"];
}
?>
<html>
<head>
```

LISTING 22.5 Continued

```
<title>SVG Survey</title>
<link href="survey.css" type="text/css" rel="stylesheet" />
</head>
<body>
<?php
if ($email != "") {
?>
<p class="heading">Available Surveys:</p>
<ul>
<?php
$conn = mysql_connect("localhost");
mysql_select_db("svg", $conn) or die("error connecting to db!");
$rows = mysql_query("SELECT * FROM survey WHERE status='active'", $conn);
while ($row = mysql_fetch_array($rows)) {
  $id = $row["id"];
  $rows1 = mysql_query("SELECT * FROM person WHERE survey_id='$id' AND
                        email LIKE '$email'", $conn);
  if (mysql_num_rows($rows1) == 0) {
    echo("<li><span class=\"bold\">" . htmlspecialchars($row["name"]) .
         "</span>" .
         " [<a href=\"survey.php?survey=$id\">go to survey</a>]</li>");
  }
}
mysql_close($conn);
?>
</ul>
<?php
} else {
?>
<p class="heading">Please provide your email address!</p>
<form method="post" action="index.php">
  <input type="text" name="email">
  <input type="submit" name="Submit" value="Start!">
</form>
<?php
}
?>
</body>
</html>
```

Figure 22.6 shows the available surveys after the e-mail address has been entered.

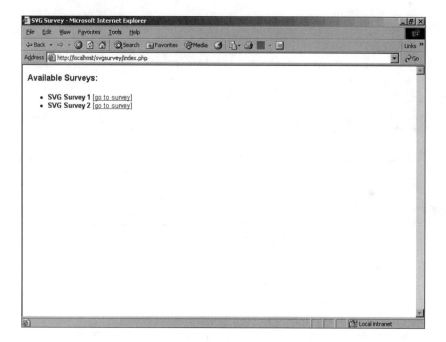

FIGURE 22.6   After the user enters his or her e-mail address, the available surveys are shown.

Taking the Survey

The survey.php file handles the survey itself; it asks the questions and saves the answers. For practical reasons, the answers are stored in session variables and saved in the database only after the last question is answered. The reason for that is simple: Only complete surveys are stored in the database; if a user decides to cancel a survey in the middle, the answers given do not count.

The page starts by checking whether an e-mail address is saved in the session variable. If not, the user is redirected to index.php as follows:

```
session_start();
$email = $HTTP_SESSION_VARS["email"];
if ($email == "") {
  header("Location: index.php");
}
```

Now let's look at some background information about the approach we are taking. PHP sessions can not only accept string or numeric values, but can also save objects (such as arrays) in a session variable; PHP performs the serialization (transformation in a string representation) and deserialization (the same, backward) automatically. The underlying concept of serialization is to transform an object into a byte stream; deserialization decodes serialized data, transforming the byte stream back into an object.

In an array named $question, we save all questions of the current survey that the user has not yet answered. This variable is initialized, as shown here, if the page is loaded for the first time:

```
if (count($HTTP_SESSION_VARS["questions"]) == 0) {
  $questions = array();
  $answers = array();
  $conn = mysql_connect("localhost");
  $survey = $HTTP_GET_VARS["survey"];
  mysql_select_db("svg", $conn) or die("error connecting to db!");
  $rows = mysql_query("SELECT * FROM question WHERE survey_id='$survey' ORDER
                      by id", $conn);
  while ($row = mysql_fetch_array($rows)) {
    array_push($questions, $row["id"]);
  }
  mysql_close($conn);
  session_register("questions");
} else {
  $questions = $HTTP_SESSION_VARS["questions"];
}
```

Now comes the fun part. Another session variable, named $lastquestion, is introduced. In this variable, the ID of the last question is saved. The standard value for $lastquestion is the first element in $question:

```
$lastquestion = $questions[0];
session_register("lastquestion");
```

Now, a connection to the database is established, and the new question is read (using a SELECT statement). Furthermore, the question type is determined. If it's a radio button question, the resulting HTML code looks something like this:

```
<input type="radio" name="q42[]" value="5" />alternative 1<br />
<input type="radio" name="q42[]" value="6" />alternative 2<br />
<input type="radio" name="q42[]" value="7" />alternative 3<br />
```

If, however, it's a check box question, the following HTML code is generated:

```
<input type="checkbox" name="q42[]" value="5" />alternative 1<br />
<input type="checkbox" name="q42[]" value="6" />alternative 2<br />
<input type="checkbox" name="q42[]" value="7" />alternative 3<br />
```

Here, 42 is the question ID, and 5, 6, and 7 are the IDs of the three alternatives.

22

The following code reads the question type and creates the HTML form:

```
$conn = mysql_connect("localhost");
mysql_select_db("svg", $conn) or die("error connecting to db!");
$rows = mysql_query("SELECT question.id, question.text, questiontype.name FROM
                    question, questiontype WHERE question.id='$lastquestion'
                    AND question.type = questiontype.id", $conn);
$rows1 = mysql_query("SELECT * FROM alternative WHERE question_id=
                    '$lastquestion'", $conn);
$row = mysql_fetch_array($rows);
echo("<p class=\"bold\">" . htmlspecialchars($row["text"]) . "</p>");
echo("<form method=\"post\">");
  while ($row1 = mysql_fetch_array($rows1)) {
    $questiontype = $row["name"];
    $alternative = $row1["text"];
    $id = $row1["id"];
    echo("<input type=\"$questiontype\" name=\"q" . $lastquestion .
        "[]\" value=\"$id\" />");
    echo(htmlspecialchars($alternative) . "<br />");
  }
mysql_close($conn);
echo("<input type=\"submit\" name=\"Submit\" value=\"Continue\" />");
echo("</form>");
```

At the top of the PHP page, the user's answer or answers are stored in the $answer array that will be stored in a session variable. Each element of the $answer array is an array itself, containing a question ID and alternative ID. Due to the structure of the database, the alternative ID alone would be enough information, but we later need less database traffic when we write the data to the answer table.

```
if (isset($HTTP_POST_VARS["Submit"])) {
  $answers = $HTTP_SESSION_VARS["answers"];
  $lastquestion = $HTTP_SESSION_VARS["lastquestion"];
  for ($i=0; $i<count($HTTP_POST_VARS["q$lastquestion"]); $i++) {
    $id = $HTTP_POST_VARS["q$lastquestion"][$i];
    if ($id != "") {
      $answers[] = array($lastquestion, $id);
    }
  }
  session_register("answers");
}
```

Figure 22.7 shows a sample survey in the browser.

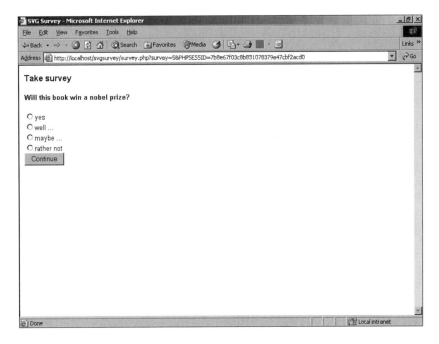

FIGURE 22.7   A user takes the survey.

Ending the Survey

If the survey.php page is reloaded (and a value is found in $lastquestion), the question ID must be removed from the $questions array like this:

```php
<?php
if ($HTTP_SESSION_VARS["lastquestion"] > 0) {
  array_shift($questions);
  session_register("questions");
}
```

If, after removal, the $questions array is empty, there is only one explanation: The user has answered all questions. Then the data in $array must be saved into the database, as follows, to end the survey:

```php
if (count($questions) == 0) {
  // write to DB
  $conn = mysql_connect("localhost");
  mysql_select_db("svg", $conn) or die("error connecting to db!");
  while (count($answers) > 0) {
    $q = $answers[0][0]; // question id
    $a = $answers[0][1]; // alternative id
```

```
    array_shift($answers);
    mysql_query("INSERT INTO answer (question_id, alternative_id) VALUES
              ('$q', '$a')", $conn);
  }
  $survey = $HTTP_GET_VARS["survey"];
  mysql_query("INSERT INTO person (email, survey_id) VALUES ('$email',
            '$survey')", $conn);
  mysql_query("UPDATE survey SET persons = persons + 1", $conn);
  mysql_close($conn);
  $lastquestion = 0;
  session_register("lastquestion");
  $questions = array();
  session_register("questions");
  $answers = array();
  session_register("answers");
?>
<p class="bold">Thanks for participating in this survey!
Click <a href="index.php">here</a> to check if other surveys are available.</p>
<?php
} else {
// ... code from previous section to output question and alternatives
}
?>
```

At this point, the session variables are reset, and the user may return to the main page and complete another survey, if one is available.

We've now concluded the survey.php file; in Listing 22.6, you will find the complete source code (you can also download it from `http://www.samspublishing.com/`).

LISTING 22.6   survey.php—Taking the Survey

```
<?php
error_reporting(E_ALL ^ E_NOTICE);
session_start();
$email = $HTTP_SESSION_VARS["email"];
if ($email == "") {
  header("Location: index.php");
}
if (count($HTTP_SESSION_VARS["questions"]) == 0) {
  $questions = array();
  $answers = array();
  $conn = mysql_connect("localhost");
  $survey = $HTTP_GET_VARS["survey"];
```

LISTING 22.6 Continued

```php
  mysql_select_db("svg", $conn) or die("error connecting to db!");
  $rows = mysql_query(
    "SELECT * FROM question WHERE survey_id='$survey' ORDER by id", $conn);
  while ($row = mysql_fetch_array($rows)) {
    array_push($questions, $row["id"]);
  }
  mysql_close($conn);
  session_register("questions");
} else {
  $questions = $HTTP_SESSION_VARS["questions"];
}
if (isset($HTTP_POST_VARS["Submit"])) {
  $answers = $HTTP_SESSION_VARS["answers"];
  $lastquestion = $HTTP_SESSION_VARS["lastquestion"];
  for ($i=0; $i<count($HTTP_POST_VARS["q$lastquestion"]); $i++) {
    $id = $HTTP_POST_VARS["q$lastquestion"][$i];
    if ($id != "") {
      $answers[] = array($lastquestion, $id);
    }
  }
  session_register("answers");
}
?>
<html>
<head>
<title>SVG Survey</title>
<link href="survey.css" type="text/css" rel="stylesheet" />
</head>
<body>
<p class="heading">Take survey</p>
<?php
if ($HTTP_SESSION_VARS["lastquestion"] > 0) {
  array_shift($questions);
  session_register("questions");
}
if (count($questions) == 0) {
  // write to DB
  $conn = mysql_connect("localhost");
  mysql_select_db("svg", $conn) or die("error connecting to db!");
  while (count($answers) > 0) {
    $q = $answers[0][0]; // question id
```

LISTING 22.6   Continued

```
    $a = $answers[0][1]; // alternative id
    array_shift($answers);
    mysql_query(
      "INSERT INTO answer (question_id, alternative_id) VALUES ('$q', '$a')",
      $conn);
  }
  $survey = $HTTP_GET_VARS["survey"];
  mysql_query(
    "INSERT INTO person (email, survey_id) VALUES ('$email', '$survey')",
      $conn);
  mysql_query("UPDATE survey SET persons = persons + 1", $conn);
  mysql_close($conn);
  $lastquestion = 0;
  session_register("lastquestion");
  $questions = array();
  session_register("questions");
  $answers = array();
  session_register("answers");
?>
<p class="bold">Thanks for participating in this survey!
Click <a href="index.php">here</a> to check if other surveys are available.</p>
<?php
} else {
  $lastquestion = $questions[0];
  session_register("lastquestion");
  $conn = mysql_connect("localhost");
  mysql_select_db("svg", $conn) or die("error connecting to db!");
  $rows = mysql_query("SELECT question.id, question.text, questiontype.name
    FROM question, questiontype WHERE question.id='$lastquestion' AND
    question.type = questiontype.id", $conn);
  $rows1 = mysql_query(
    "SELECT * FROM alternative WHERE question_id='$lastquestion'", $conn);
  $row = mysql_fetch_array($rows);
  echo("<p class=\"bold\">" . htmlspecialchars($row["text"]) . "</p>");
  echo("<form method=\"post\">");
    while ($row1 = mysql_fetch_array($rows1)) {
      $questiontype = $row["name"];
      $alternative = $row1["text"];
      $id = $row1["id"];
      echo("<input type=\"$questiontype\" name=\"q" . $lastquestion .
```

LISTING 22.6   Continued

```
            "[]\" value=\"$id\" />");
        echo(htmlspecialchars($alternative) . "<br />");
    }
  mysql_close($conn);
  echo("<input type=\"submit\" name=\"Submit\" value=\"Continue\" />");
  echo("</form>");
}
?>
</body>
</html>
```

Survey Statistics

And now, finally, we will look at SVG. In the previous sections, we developed quite complex code that created the data structure for a survey, established a framework for administering Web-based surveys, and wrote a script that allowed users to complete the surveys. Now we are interested in looking at graphic results of the surveys. SVG is a great technology for creating nice-looking graphics. And you can create your program with XML elements; that is, you "program" the chart, you do not paint it. It is a logical step to compute these graphics dynamically, given an existing data source.

The previous listings in this chapter laid the foundation for a great amount of data. This is the place where we will interpret this data, but instead of tons of boring numbers and statistics, we will add some eye candy and create pie charts.

> **NOTE**
>
> Due to the very nature of pie charts, all segments add up to 360° or 100%. So, if you use check box questions, for example, the pie chart depicts the percentage each alternative received when compared to the total number of votes.

Creating Pie Charts

Let's first look at a static pie chart to examine the basic idea behind our approach. We have this basic header:

```
<?xml version="1.0" ?>
<!DOCTYPE svg PUBLIC "-//W3C//DTD SVG 20001102//EN"
  "http://www.w3.org/TR/2000/CR-SVG-20001102/DTD/svg-20001102.dtd">
<svg width="300px" height="270px"
  style="shape-rendering:optimizeSpeed;text-rendering:optimizeLegibility">
```

We start with a text element that will hold the name of the question:

```
<text x="60" y="40" id="title"
     style="font-family:Arial, Geneva, Helvetica, sans-serif;
     font-size:10pt;font-weight:bold;color:white;alignment-baseline:baseline">
     What is your favorite letter?
</text>
```

Then comes the pie. We start with the shadow of the pie; when it is first generated, it does not overlap with the pie chart itself:

```
<g id="shadow" transform="skewX(-25) translate(75,0)">
   <circle cx="105" cy="155" r="50" style="fill:rgb(100,100,100)" />
</g>
```

Next comes the pie chart itself. Each section of the circle has another color. To create the arc, we must use a path element. Here are four of them:

```
<g id="pie" transform="skewX(-25) translate(75,0)">
  <path d="M 150,150 A50,50 0 0,1 85,198 L100,150 L150,150"
    style="fill:aqua;stroke:black;stroke-width:1" id="part1" />
  <path d="M 85,198 A50,50 0 0,1 85,102 L100,150 L85,198"
    style="fill:blue;stroke:black;stroke-width:1" id="part2" />
  <path d="M 85,102 A50,50 0 0,1 140,121 L100,150 L85,102"
    style="fill:fuchsia;stroke:black;stroke-width:1" id="part3" />
  <path d="M 140,121 A50,50 0 0,1 150,150 L100,150 L140,121"
    style="fill:gray;stroke:black;stroke-width:1" id="part4" />
</g>
```

In a box in the lower-right corner of our graphic, we will explain which color stands for which answer to the question and will also provide the percentage each answer received:

```
<g id="description">
  <rect id="bgdescription" x="180" y="200" width="115" height="45"
     style="fill:none;stroke:black;stroke-width:1" />
  <rect id="d1" x="185" y="205" width="5" height="5" style="fill:aqua;
   stroke:black;stroke-width:1" /><text id="d1t" x="195" y="211" style=
   "font-family:Arial, Geneva, Helvetica, sans-serif;font-size:6pt;
   font-weight:bold;color:white;alignment-baseline:baseline">A (30%)</text>
  <rect id="d2" x="185" y="215" width="5" height="5" style="fill:blue;
   stroke:black;stroke-width:1" /><text id="d2t" x="195" y="221" style=
   "font-family:Arial, Geneva, Helvetica, sans-serif;font-size:6pt;
   font-weight:bold;color:white;alignment-baseline:baseline">B (40%)</text>
  <rect id="d3" x="185" y="225" width="5" height="5" style="fill:fuchsia;
   stroke:black;stroke-width:1" /><text id="d3t" x="195" y="231" style=
   "font-family:Arial, Geneva, Helvetica, sans-serif;font-size:6pt;
```

```
      font-weight:bold;color:white;alignment-baseline:baseline">C (20%)</text>
    <rect id="d4" x="185" y="235" width="5" height="5" style="fill:gray;
      stroke:black;stroke-width:1" /><text id="d4t" x="195" y="241" style=
      "font-family:Arial, Geneva, Helvetica, sans-serif;font-size:6pt;
      font-weight:bold;color:white;alignment-baseline:baseline">D (10%)</text>
  </g>
  </svg>
```

In Figure 22.8, you can see the output of this SVG file in your viewer.

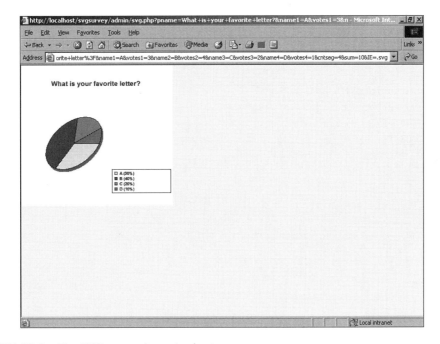

FIGURE 22.8   The SVG output in a pie chart.

Dynamically Creating a Graphic

To dynamically create the graphic, we use a **torso** (skeleton), a simplified version of the
SVG code with placeholders for the dynamic values such as circle segments and height of
the description box and of the graphic itself. The file, shown in Listing 22.7, will be called
torso.svg and must reside in the admin directory of the SVG Survey application.

LISTING 22.7   torso.svg—The Skeleton for the SVG Chart

```
<?xml version="1.0" ?>
<!DOCTYPE svg PUBLIC "-//W3C//DTD SVG 20001102//EN"
  "http://www.w3.org/TR/2000/CR-SVG-20001102/DTD/svg-20001102.dtd">
```

LISTING 22.7   Continued

```
<svg width="300px" height="%SVGHEIGHT%px" style="shape-rendering:optimizeSpeed;
  text-rendering:optimizeLegibility">
  <text x="60" y="40" id="title"
      style="font-family:Arial, Geneva, Helvetica, sans-serif;
      font-size:10pt;font-weight:bold;color:white;alignment-baseline:baseline">
      %SURVEYNAME%
  </text>
  <g id="shadow" transform="skewX(-25) translate(75,0)">
      <circle cx="105" cy="155" r="50" style="fill:rgb(100,100,100)" />
  </g>
  <g id="pie" transform="skewX(-25) translate(75,0)">
      %SEGMENTS%
  </g>
  <g id="description">
      <rect id="bgdescription" x="180" y="200" width="115" height="%DESCHEIGHT%"
       style="fill:none;stroke:black;stroke-width:1" />
      %DESCRIPTIONS%
  </g>
</svg>
```

As you can see, placeholders start and end with %. There are five of them:

- %SVGHEIGHT% stands for the height of the whole SVG graphic.

- %SURVEYNAME% is the title of the question.

- %SEGMENTS% will later be replaced by the circle segments, one for each alternative (that received at least one vote).

- %DESCHEIGHT% is the height of the description box.

- %DESCRIPTIONS% are the text elements for the description text.

We will now create a PHP page named svg.php that will return an SVG document. All important parameters will be provided via a URL. A typical call to this page would look like the following; we added some line breaks to make the different parameters more obvious:

```
http://servername/svgsurvey/admin/svg.php
  ?pname=What+is+your+favorite+letter%3F
  &name1=A&votes1=3
  &name2=B&votes2=4
  &name3=C&votes3=2
  &name4=D&votes4=1
  &cntseg=4&sum=10&IE=.svg
```

As you can see, this call contains several parameters:

- pname contains the name of the question.

- cntseg provides the number of alternatives.

- name1, name2, ... are the names of the different alternatives, and votes1, votes2, ... are the number of votes each alternative received in the survey.

- sum contains the number of votes that were given. (Using this parameter saves some calculations.)

- IE=.svg is a hack for Internet Explorer (see Chapter 18, "Server-Side Basics") to let this browser assume that the file returned from the server has the extension .svg and therefore must be an SVG graphic.

The code for generating the SVG file itself is quite straightforward. It starts by setting the correct MIME type for the SVG graphic:

```
header("Content-type: image/svg+xml");
```

After that, we define a list of colors to be used to fill the circle sections. We use 14 of the 16 standard HTML colors, omitting white and black:

```
$colors = array("aqua",
                "blue",
                "fuchsia",
                "gray",
                "green",
                "lime",
                "maroon",
                "navy",
                "olive",
                "purple",
                "red",
                "silver",
                "teal",
                "yellow");
```

Next, we define some variables and retrieve data from the URL:

```
$segments = "";
$descriptions = "";
$sname = $HTTP_GET_VARS["pname"];
$sum = $HTTP_GET_VARS["sum"];
$cntseg = $HTTP_GET_VARS["cntseg"];
```

Then we loop through all $cntseg alternatives. We start with an angle to the x-axis of 0 degrees. After each segment, we add the angle used for the segment so that we know where the next segment will start.

Within the loop, we pick the next color to use. Instead of accessing `$colors[$loopvariable]`, we use `$colors[$loopvariable % count($colors)]` so that we do not run out of colors when we have more segments than predefined colors.

The parameters for the `path` elements are retrieved using simple trigonometry. Using the cosine of the angle, we can calculate the x coordinate; using the sine, the y coordinate:

```
for ($i=1; $i<=$cntseg; $i++) {
  $color = $colors[($i-1) % count($colors)];
  $vote = $HTTP_GET_VARS["votes" . $i];
  $arc = ($vote/$sum >= .5) ? "1,1" : "0,1";   //parameter for <path>
  $x1 = round(100 + 50*cos($angle), 0);
  $y1 = round(150 + 50*sin($angle), 0);
  $angle += 2*Pi() * $vote / $sum;
  $x2 = round(100 + 50*cos($angle), 0);
  $y2 = round(150 + 50*sin($angle), 0);
  if ($vote > 0) {
    $segments .= "<path d=\"M $x1,$y1 A50,50 0 $arc $x2,$y2 L100,150 L$x1,$y1\"
      style=\"fill:$color;stroke:black;stroke-width:1\" id=\"part$i\" />\n";
  }
```

Next, we add the box for the descriptions. Each description has a height of 10 pixels:

```
$descriptions .= "<rect id=\"d$i\" x=\"185\" y=\"" . (195 + 10*$i) . "\"
 width=\"5\" height=\"5\" style=\"fill:$color;stroke:black;
 stroke-width:1\" />";
$descriptions .= "<text id=\"d" . $i . "t\" x=\"195\" y=\"" . (201 + 10*$i) .
 "\" style=\"font-family:Arial,
```

Geneva, Helvetica, sans-serif;font-size:6pt;font-weight:bold;color:white;
alignment-baseline:baseline\">";

```
  $descriptions .= htmlspecialchars($HTTP_GET_VARS["name" . $i]) ;
  $descriptions .= " (" . round(100*$vote/$sum, 0) . "%)</text>\n";
}
```

Now it is time to read in the torso (torso.svg) we previously prepared:

```
$svg = "";
if ($fh = fopen("torso.svg", "r")) {
  while (!feof($fh)) {
```

```
    $svg .= fgets($fh, 1024) . "\n";
  }
}
fclose($fh);
```

In this torso, we replace the five placeholders with the appropriate values:

```
$svg = str_replace("%SEGMENTS%", $segments, $svg);
$svg = str_replace("%SURVEYNAME%", $sname, $svg);

$svg = str_replace("%SVGHEIGHT%", 230 + 10*$cntseg, $svg);
$svg = str_replace("%DESCHEIGHT%", 5 + 10*$cntseg, $svg);
$svg = str_replace("%DESCRIPTIONS%", $descriptions, $svg);
Finally, we send the SVG code directly to the browser - and we are done!
echo($svg);
```

To wrap it all up, look at the complete code for svg.php in Listing 22.8. Remember to put this file in the admin directory of the application.

LISTING 22.8   svg.php—The Script That Generates the SVG Charts

```
<?php
  error_reporting(E_ALL ^ E_NOTICE);

  header("Content-type: image/svg+xml");
  $colors = array("aqua",
                  "blue",
                  "fuchsia",
                  "gray",
                  "green",
                  "lime",
                  "maroon",
                  "navy",
                  "olive",
                  "purple",
                  "red",
                  "silver",
                  "teal",
                  "yellow");
  $segments = "";
  $descriptions = "";
  $sname = $HTTP_GET_VARS["pname"];
  $sum = $HTTP_GET_VARS["sum"];
```

LISTING 22.8   Continued

```php
$cntseg = $HTTP_GET_VARS["cntseg"];
$angle = 0;   // middle 100 150; radius = 50!
for ($i=1; $i<=$cntseg; $i++) {
  $color = $colors[($i-1) % count($colors)];
  $vote = $HTTP_GET_VARS["votes" . $i];
  $arc = ($vote/$sum >= .5) ? "1,1" : "0,1";
  $x1 = round(100 + 50*cos($angle), 0);
  $y1 = round(150 + 50*sin($angle), 0);
  $angle += 2*Pi() * $vote / $sum;
  $x2 = round(100 + 50*cos($angle), 0);
  $y2 = round(150 + 50*sin($angle), 0);
  if ($vote > 0) {
    $segments .= "<path d=\"M $x1,$y1 A50,50 0 $arc $x2,$y2 L100,150 L$x1,
      $y1\" style=\"fill:$color;stroke:black;stroke-width:1\" id=\"part$i\"
      />\n";
  }
  $descriptions .= "<rect id=\"d$i\" x=\"185\" y=\"" . (195 + 10*$i) . "\"
   width=\"5\" height=\"5\" style=\"fill:$color;stroke:black;
   stroke-width:1\" />";
  $descriptions .= "<text id=\"d" . $i . "t\" x=\"195\" y=\"" . (201 + 10*$i)
   . "\" style=\"font-family:Arial, Geneva, Helvetica, sans-serif;font-size:
   6pt;font-weight:bold;color:white;alignment-baseline:baseline\">";
  $descriptions .= htmlspecialchars($HTTP_GET_VARS["name" . $i]) ;
  $descriptions .= " (" . round(100*$vote/$sum, 0) . "%)</text>\n";
}
$svg = "";
if ($fh = fopen("torso.svg", "r")) {
  while (!feof($fh)) {
    $svg .= fgets($fh, 1024) . "\n";
  }
}
fclose($fh);

$svg = str_replace("%SEGMENTS%", $segments, $svg);
$svg = str_replace("%SURVEYNAME%", $sname, $svg);

$svg = str_replace("%SVGHEIGHT%", 230 + 10*$cntseg, $svg);
$svg = str_replace("%DESCHEIGHT%", 5 + 10*$cntseg, $svg);
$svg = str_replace("%DESCRIPTIONS%", $descriptions, $svg);
echo($svg);
?>
```

Serving the Survey Statistics

All we have left to do now is to create a page (we call it eval.php) that calls the svg.php
script several times—once for each question in the current survey. First, we try to fetch the
survey data from the database. If we cannot fetch it, as follows, an error message is sent to
the client browser:

```php
<?php
$conn = mysql_connect("localhost");
$survey = $HTTP_GET_VARS["survey"];
mysql_select_db("svg", $conn) or die("error connecting to db!");
$rows = mysql_query("SELECT * FROM survey WHERE id='$survey'", $conn);
if (mysql_num_rows($rows) == 0) {
?>
  <p class="bold">Error: survey does not exist! <a href="index.php">Back</a></p>
```

Otherwise, data is retrieved from the MySQL data source. From the answer table, all
answers to questions within the given survey are read and stored in an array named $a:

```php
<?php
} else {
  $row = mysql_fetch_array($rows);
  $persons = $row["persons"]; // number of persons that took the survey
  echo("<p class=\"bold\">Survey name: " . htmlspecialchars($row["name"]) .
      " (" . $persons . " testees)</p>");
  $rows1 = mysql_query("SELECT answer.alternative_id FROM answer, question
   WHERE question.survey_id='$survey' AND answer.question_id = question.id",
   $conn);
  $a = array();
  while ($row1 = mysql_fetch_array($rows1)) {
    $id = $row1["alternative_id"]; // alternative id
    if ($a[$id] == "") {
      $a[$id] = 1;
    } else {
      $a[$id]++;
    }
  }
}
```

If you recall the data required for the query string we need to provide for calling svg.php,
we also need the names of the alternatives. They can be read from the alternative table.
While they are being read, the number of alternatives and the sum of votes are counted
and the query string is assembled as follows:

```php
  $rows2 = mysql_query("SELECT id, text FROM question WHERE
question.survey_id='$survey'", $conn);
```

```
  while ($row2 = mysql_fetch_array($rows2)) {
    $question = $row2["id"];
    $querystring = "?pname=" . urlencode($row2["text"]);
    $rows3 = mysql_query("SELECT id, text FROM alternative WHERE question_id
     = '$question'", $conn);
    $cntseg = 0;
    $sum = 0;
    while ($row3 = mysql_fetch_array($rows3)) {
      $cntseg++;
      $querystring .= "&name$cntseg=" . urlencode($row3["text"]);
      $querystring .= "&votes$cntseg=" . $a[$row3["id"]];
      $sum += $a[$row3["id"]];
    }
    $querystring .= "&cntseg=$cntseg&sum=$sum&IE=.svg";
```

Finally, the <embed> HTML tag with the appropriate src attribute (where you provide the URL of the SVG file—in our case, the URL of the script that generates the SVG file) is sent to the client:

```
    echo("<embed type=\"image/svg+xml\" width=\"300\" height=\"");
    echo((230 + 10*$cntseg) . "\" ");
    echo("src=\"svg.php$querystring\"></embed><hr noshade=\"noshade\" />");
  }
}
mysql_close($conn);
?>
```

Et voilà—that's it! You now have a fully functional survey tool, as shown in Listing 22.9, and really nice-looking pie charts depicting the result of your questionnaires, as shown in Figure 22.9.

LISTING 22.9   eval.php—The Survey Statistics Are Displayed

```
<?php
error_reporting(E_ALL ^ E_NOTICE);
?>
<html>
<head>
<title>SVG Survey Admin Tool</title>
<link href="survey.css" type="text/css" rel="stylesheet" />
</head>
<body>
<p class="heading">Survey statistics</p>
<?php
$conn = mysql_connect("localhost");
$survey = $HTTP_GET_VARS["survey"];
```

LISTING 22.9   Continued

```php
mysql_select_db("svg", $conn) or die("error connecting to db!");
$rows = mysql_query("SELECT * FROM survey WHERE id='$survey'", $conn);
if (mysql_num_rows($rows) == 0) {
?>
  <p class="bold">Error: survey does not exist!
    <a href="index.php">Back</a></p>
<?php
} else {
  $row = mysql_fetch_array($rows);
  $persons = $row["persons"]; // number of persons that took the survey
  echo("<p class=\"bold\">Survey name: " . htmlspecialchars($row["name"]) .
        " (" . $persons . " testees)</p>");
  $rows1 = mysql_query("SELECT answer.alternative_id FROM answer, question
   WHERE question.survey_id='$survey' AND answer.question_id = question.id",
   $conn);
  $a = array();
  while ($row1 = mysql_fetch_array($rows1)) {
    $id = $row1["alternative_id"]; // alternative id
    if ($a[$id] == "") {
      $a[$id] = 1;
    } else {
      $a[$id]++;
    }
  }
  $rows2 = mysql_query(
    "SELECT id, text FROM question WHERE question.survey_id='$survey'", $conn);
  while ($row2 = mysql_fetch_array($rows2)) {
    $question = $row2["id"];
    $querystring = "?pname=" . urlencode($row2["text"]);
    $rows3 = mysql_query(
      "SELECT id, text FROM alternative WHERE question_id = '$question'",
      $conn);
    $cntseg = 0;
    $sum = 0;
    while ($row3 = mysql_fetch_array($rows3)) {
      $cntseg++;
      $querystring .= "&name$cntseg=" . urlencode($row3["text"]);
      $querystring .= "&votes$cntseg=" . $a[$row3["id"]];
      $sum += $a[$row3["id"]];
    }
    $querystring .= "&cntseg=$cntseg&sum=$sum&IE=.svg";

    echo("<embed type=\"image/svg+xml\" width=\"300\" height=\"");
```

LISTING 22.9   Continued

```
    echo((230 + 10*$cntseg) . "\" ");
    echo("src=\"svg.php$querystring\"></embed><hr noshade=\"noshade\" />");
  }
}
mysql_close($conn);
?>
<a href="index.php">back to overview</a>
</body>
</html>
```

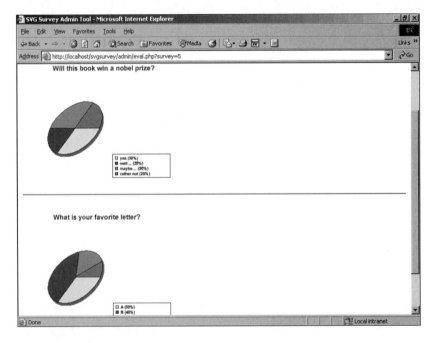

FIGURE 22.9   The survey statistics.

Summary

This chapter provided a quite complex but still manageable demonstration of the ways to combine the powers of MySQL, PHP, and SVG. There are many possibilities for improving and expanding the features of the survey tool. You will also need to take some additional security precautions—for instance, checking each user input, especially data in the query string.

We just wanted to give you some pointers here; feel free to use this case study as a starting point for your own data-mining adventures.

CHAPTER **23**

SVG .NET: Creating an Online Poll

In the Web world, very few announcements lead to unrivaled interest in both the open source and the closed source communities. In 1999 when Bill Gates first told the press about Microsoft's new .NET strategy, people were interested, but the strategy itself consisted of some theory and concepts without getting down to the nitty-gritty. This changed, however, when the first beta of the .NET Framework came out and, accompanying it, ASP.NET, the next generation of ASP.

ASP, short for Active Server Pages (not to be confused with Application Service Provider/Providing), is Microsoft's technology for serving dynamic Web content. ASP itself is only a technology, not a language. ASP supported a few scripting languages, mainly VBScript and JScript (the Microsoft variation of JavaScript). Most developers choose VBScript as their main scripting language.

ASP was very easy to install (unlike many other languages, including PHP, JSP, and Perl), quite easy to learn (unlike other languages), and lacked some very important features (unlike many other languages). Additionally, ASP was only (freely) available on the Windows platform (unlike ... you get the picture). With Chili!ASP (`http://www.chiliasp.com/`), there exists an ASP port to other systems; however, this option is not free. As you might guess, ASP was quite successful on Windows and nonexistent on other platforms. When PHP came up, however—it was quite easy to learn and had an impressive feature set—ASP began to fall, and many people say it earned this outcome.

With ASP.NET, however, this situation might change. At the time of writing, ASP.NET is available only on Windows server platforms (that is, even fewer platforms than "classic" ASP), but ports of the .NET Framework to other platforms are currently being developed. The feature set of the .NET Framework (a class library, basically) rivals that of PHP and other technologies. Unlike Java, which comes with many libraries and can be used from Java servlets and JSP pages, ASP.NET aims directly at Web development and includes a collection of really useful classes, methods, and functions. Form handling is worth noting as it is very smooth with ASP.NET and can be quite painful with other technologies, especially when it comes to prefilling form elements.

For this chapter, we assume that you already have a thorough knowledge of ASP.NET and C#, the scripting language we will use throughout this chapter. We will use a simple Microsoft Access file for the data source. If you do not have Access, don't worry; you can download a sample database file for this example from `http://www.samspublishing.com/`. Just search for this book's ISBN.

Finally, we'll look at some information about the example presented on the following pages (the complete source code is also available from the Sams Publishing Web site). Many Web pages contain simple polls: A question is asked, and several alternatives are offered. Often, the question is about current trends and news in the computer industry—for example, "What do you think the new Xbox should cost?" or "Will Mozilla 1.0 be successful?" After the user selects an appropriate alternative, the current poll results are shown.

In this case study, we want to rely heavily on SVG to create a Web-based poll. We will create both the poll itself (the question and alternative responses) and the poll results (as percentage, or progress, bars) using SVG. We will also program a Web-based administration tool to create and update new and existing polls. And now—let the games, er... poll begin!

In the preceding chapter, you saw a similar application, but it was created using PHP and had other features.

Database Structure

For our example, we will use an Access .mdb file named svg.mdb. You can find such a file on the Web site, as mentioned previously; however, we will show you how this file was generated and—even more important—what the meanings of the various database fields are.

Poll

The name of the main table is `poll`, obviously. In this table, the name of the poll and some other basic information are stored. Here is a list of the used fields, their SQL field types (Access type names vary), and their descriptions:

Field Name	Data Type	Description
id	identity	Identifier; primary key
name	varchar(50)	Name/title of the poll (the question)
status	varchar(8)	Whether the poll is active or not; the default value is inactive

Note the `status` field; it will later contain either the value `active` or `inactive`. Only one poll can be displayed on the (virtual) home page, but old polls can still reside in the database and new ones might be added.

Alternatives

The different answer possibilities for each poll are individually stored in the `alternative` table. Because the number of alternatives may vary from poll to poll, we cannot store this information in the `poll` table itself but must create another table. The fields in `alternative` are as follows:

Field Name	Data Type	Description
id	identity	Identifier; primary key
name	varchar(50)	Name of the answer
poll_id	integer	Identifier of the poll this answer belongs to
count	integer	Number of votes this answer has already received (the default value is 0)

Persons

Usually, we could stop now and start coding. However, one common problem with Web polls is that many of them are quite easy to manipulate. Just click the Reload button a few times, and the percentage of your favorite answer grows. To avoid this situation (or at least to make it quite hard to achieve), we will save each user's Internet Protocol address. Furthermore, we will generate for each user a globally unique ID (GUID) and send him or her this GUID via a cookie. In the `person` table, we will store which IP and which GUID have voted at which poll. Later, we will be able to check in this table whether a given IP address or a GUID has already taken the poll.

The `person` table consists of the following four fields:

Field Name	Data Type	Description
id	identity	Identifier; primary key
ip	varchar(50)	IP address
guid	varchar(50)	GUID
poll_id	integer	Identifier (field ID) of the poll

In Figure 23.1, you can see the three tables and their relationships.

FIGURE 23.1   The tables and their relationships.

> **NOTE**
>
> In this chapter's code, we assume that the svg.mdb file resides in the c:\inetpub\db directory. If you want to use another directory, change the code appropriately.

Survey Administration Tool

Our first step is to create an administration tool that allows us to create and edit polls. The tools consist of one index.aspx file and one poll.css style sheet that is used to add some (well, quite a bit of) eye candy. We will start with the style sheet; Listing 23.1 defines two classes and sets the standard font for the page to Arial.

LISTING 23.1   poll.css—The Style Sheet

```
.heading {font-family:Arial, Geneva, Helvetica, sans-serif;
        font-weight: bold;
        font-size: 12pt}
.bold {font-family:Arial, Geneva, Helvetica, sans-serif;
      font-weight: bold;
      font-size: 10pt}
body,td {font-family:Arial, Geneva, Helvetica, sans-serif;
        font-size: 10pt}
```

This style sheet is incorporated in all .aspx files, within the <head> section, as follows:

```
<link href="poll.css" type="text/css" rel="stylesheet" />
```

Now let's get started with the tool named index.aspx. Put the file in a virtual directory so that you can access it via http://servername/svgpoll/admin/index.aspx. Additionally, take some security precautions; for example, secure this directory so that only you have access to it.

Listing Polls

Now we can use two <asp:Panel> elements: one for the polls and one for the individual alternatives to one poll. We will start with the panel for the polls:

```
<asp:Panel id="PollPanel" runat="server">
...
</asp:Panel>
```

Within this panel, we have an <asp:DataGrid> element. Datagrids allow programmers to easily display information from a data source and even edit them.

```
<asp:DataGrid id="polls"
  AutoGenerateColumns="False"
  DataKeyField="id"
  OnItemCommand="PollCommand"
  OnEditCommand="PollEdit"
  OnUpdateCommand="PollUpdate"
  OnCancelCommand="PollCancel"
  runat="server">
```

Later, we will bind the data from the database to this datagrid. But first, we must take care of the columns of the datagrid. When we give an overview of the polls, we are primarily interested in the IDs, the names, and the status of each poll. So we will define a special column for each of them. We start with the column for the ID:

```
<Columns>
  <asp:BoundColumn DataField="id" HeaderText="<b>id</b>" ReadOnly="True" />
```

Next comes the column for the poll question:

```
<asp:BoundColumn DataField="name" HeaderText="<b>name</b>" />
```

Next up is the status. However, we do not want to allow the user to freely change the status of the survey—for example, to bogus. Thus, we have to think of something else. With the <ItemTemplate> and <EditItemTemplate> elements of ASP.NET, we can make sure that the status is shown, but when the user switches to edit mode, a special link will be provided to allow him or her to toggle the status of the poll. This is how it's done:

```
  <asp:TemplateColumn HeaderText="<b>status</b>">
    <ItemTemplate>
      <asp:Label Text='<%# DataBinder.Eval(Container.DataItem, "status")
      %>' runat="server" />
    </ItemTemplate>
    <EditItemTemplate>
      <asp:LinkButton Text='<%# "toggle status to " + ((DataBinder.Eval
          (Container.DataItem, "status").ToString() == "active") ? "inactive" :
          "active") %>'
        CommandName="Toggle"
        CommandArgument='<%# DataBinder.Eval(Container.DataItem, "status") %>'
        runat="server" />
    </EditItemTemplate>
  </asp:TemplateColumn>
```

If the status of the poll is active, the link has the text "toggle status to inactive"; otherwise, it is "toggle status to active".

In the next column, we want to present links to switch to edit mode. We can do so easily by using an `<asp:EditCommandColumn>` element:

```
<asp:EditCommandColumn
  EditText="Edit"
  UpdateText="Update"
  CancelText="Cancel" />
```

In the next—and next-to-last column—we want to offer a link to add and edit possible answers to the poll. We again use an `<ItemTemplate>` for that task:

```
<asp:TemplateColumn HeaderText="<b>alternatives</b>">
  <ItemTemplate>
    <asp:LinkButton
      Text="Add/Remove alternatives"
      CommandName="Alternatives"
      CommandArgument='<%# DataBinder.Eval(Container.DataItem, "id") %>'
      runat="server" />
  </ItemTemplate>
</asp:TemplateColumn>
```

The final column contains a link to remove the whole poll:

```
  <asp:TemplateColumn HeaderText="<b>remove</b>">
    <ItemTemplate>
      <asp:LinkButton
        CommandName="Delete"
        CommandArgument='<%# DataBinder.Eval(Container.DataItem, "id") %>'
        Text="Delete"
        runat="server"/>
    </ItemTemplate>
  </asp:TemplateColumn>
</Columns>
</asp:DataGrid>
```

Binding Data to the Datagrid

To get the poll data into the datagrid, we write a function named `FillPollGrid()` that queries the database and binds the data to the dataset:

```
void FillPollGrid() {
  PollPanel.Visible = true;
  AltPanel.Visible = false;
  OleDbConnection conn = new OleDbConnection(
```

```
    "Provider=Microsoft.Jet.OleDb.4.0; Data Source=c:\\inetpub\\db\\svg.mdb");
  conn.Open();
  OleDbDataAdapter adapter = new OleDbDataAdapter("SELECT * FROM poll", conn);
  DataSet data = new DataSet();
  adapter.Fill(data, "poll");
  polls.DataSource = data.Tables["poll"].DefaultView;
  polls.DataBind();
  conn.Close();
}
```

Coding Datagrid Functionality for the Polls

Before we can really edit the polls, we still need to write handler functions for the various commands that can occur in the datagrid:

- PollEdit()—When the user wants to switch to editing mode

- PollUpdate()—When the user is done with editing and wants to write his or her changes to the database

- PollCancel()—When the user wants to leave the editing mode, discarding changes

- PollCommand()—When the user wants to handle special commands—for example, toggling the status, deleting a poll, or switching to the poll alternatives

Let's start with PollEdit(); the ASP.NET interpreter is advised to switch to editing mode and the FillPollGrid() function is again called to update the datagrid:

```
void PollEdit(Object o, DataGridCommandEventArgs e) {
  polls.EditItemIndex = e.Item.ItemIndex;
  FillPollGrid();
}
```

Updating the poll (using PollEdit()) is not easy because we must create an SQL statement and send it to the database. Also, we must set polls.EditItemIndex to -1, forcing ASP.NET back in normal mode, leaving editing mode:

```
void PollUpdate(Object o, DataGridCommandEventArgs e) {
  string sql = "UPDATE poll ";
  sql += "SET name='" + ((TextBox)e.Item.Cells[1].Controls[0]).Text + "' ";
  sql += "WHERE id=" + polls.DataKeys[e.Item.ItemIndex];
  RunSQL(sql);
  polls.EditItemIndex = -1;
  FillPollGrid();
}
```

The RunSQL() function is not part of ASP.NET; it is a simple function we wrote to simplify programming. It does nothing more than open a connection to the database, execute the query, and close the connection again, as shown here:

```
int RunSQL(string sql) {
  OleDbConnection conn = new OleDbConnection(
    "Provider=Microsoft.Jet.OleDb.4.0; Data Source=c:\\inetpub\\db\\svg.mdb");
  conn.Open();
  OleDbCommand comm = new OleDbCommand(sql, conn);
  int ret = comm.ExecuteNonQuery();
  conn.Close();
  return ret;
}
```

The next function on our to-do list is PollCancel(). Here, we leave editing mode and repaint the datagrid, but don't send any SQL statements to the database:

```
void PollCancel(Object o, DataGridCommandEventArgs e) {
  polls.EditItemIndex = -1;
  FillPollGrid();
}
```

Finally, we come to the PollCommand() function, which handles all special functionality. The CommandName property determines what to do. The following values must be taken care of:

- "Toggle"—The status of the poll must be toggled. It is obvious that only one poll can be active at a time. So, first, all polls are deactivated; then the status is toggled.

- "Alternatives"—The answers to the poll must be sent to the client. For that, the FillAltGrid() function (a variation of FillPollGrid(), which we will write later) must be called; also, we save the ID of the poll that will be edited in a session variable.

- "Delete"—The poll and all alternatives for the given poll are deleted via specially constructed SQL DELETE statements.

The complete PollCommand() function is shown here:

```
void PollCommand(Object o, DataGridCommandEventArgs e) {
  if (e.CommandName == "Toggle") {
    string sql = "UPDATE poll SET status='inactive'";
    RunSQL(sql);
    sql = "UPDATE poll ";
```

```
      sql += "SET status='" + ((e.CommandArgument.ToString() == "active") ?
                              "inactive" : "active") + "' ";
      sql += "WHERE id=" + polls.DataKeys[e.Item.ItemIndex];
      RunSQL(sql);
      polls.EditItemIndex = -1;
      FillPollGrid();
    } else if (e.CommandName == "Alternatives") {
      Session["pid"] = Convert.ToInt32(e.CommandArgument.ToString());
      FillAltGrid();
    } else if (e.CommandName == "Delete") {
      string sql = "DELETE FROM poll ";
      sql += "WHERE id=" + polls.DataKeys[e.Item.ItemIndex];
      RunSQL(sql);
      sql = "DELETE FROM alternative ";
      sql += "WHERE poll_id=" + polls.DataKeys[e.Item.ItemIndex];
      RunSQL(sql);
      FillPollGrid();
    }
}
```

In Figures 23.2 and 23.3, you can see both modes, normal and editing.

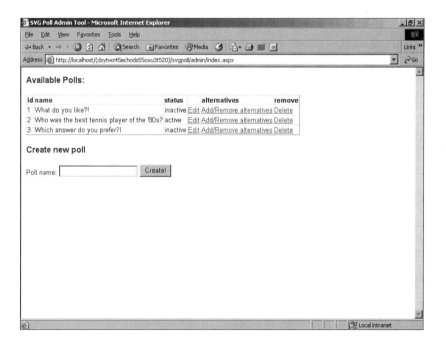

FIGURE 23.2   Viewing the poll in normal mode.

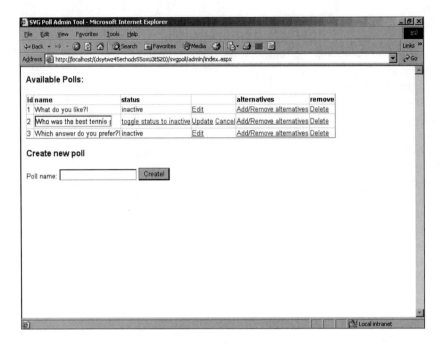

FIGURE 23.3   Viewing the poll in editing mode.

Creating New Polls

To create a new poll, we provide a form field for the name of the poll—within the poll panel, obviously:

```
<p class="heading">Create new poll</p>
```

We also provide the poll name as follows:

```
<asp:TextBox id="pollname" EnableViewState="False" runat="server" />
<asp:Button Text="Create!"
  OnClick="CreatePoll" runat="server" />
```

The CreatePoll() function creates the poll, writes it to the database, and, of course, updates the datagrid so that the new poll is visible. But this step is completed only if no other poll with the same name already exists:

```
void CreatePoll(Object o, EventArgs e) {
  OleDbConnection conn = new OleDbConnection(
    "Provider=Microsoft.Jet.OleDb.4.0; Data Source=c:\\inetpub\\db\\svg.mdb");
  conn.Open();
  OleDbCommand comm = new OleDbCommand("SELECT * FROM poll WHERE name='" +
  pollname.Text + "'", conn);
```

```
OleDbDataReader reader = comm.ExecuteReader();
if (reader.Read()) {
  message.Text = "Poll with name '" + pollname.Text + "' already exists!";
  reader.Close();
} else {
  message.Text = "";
  reader.Close();
  OleDbCommand comm1 = new OleDbCommand(
    "INSERT INTO poll (name) VALUES ('" + pollname.Text + "')", conn);
  comm1.ExecuteNonQuery();
  OleDbCommand comm2 = new OleDbCommand("SELECT id FROM poll WHERE name='" +
    pollname.Text + "'", conn);
  OleDbDataReader reader2 = comm2.ExecuteReader();
  reader2.Read();
  int id = (int)reader2["id"];
  reader2.Close();
  FillPollGrid();
  Session["pid"] = id;
  FillAltGrid();
}
reader.Close();
conn.Close();
}
```

Listing Alternatives

Now that we are done with the polls, we need to take care of the alternative responses for each poll. They are also presented via an <asp:DataGrid> element:

```
<asp:Panel id="AltPanel" runat="server">
  <p><b><asp:Label CssClass="bold" id="pname" runat="server" /></b></p>
  <p class="heading">Alternatives:</p>
  <asp:DataGrid id="alternatives"
    AutoGenerateColumns="False"
    DataKeyField="id"
    OnEditCommand="AltEdit"
    OnUpdateCommand="AltUpdate"
    OnCancelCommand="AltCancel"
    OnDeleteCommand="AltDelete"
    runat="server">
```

Again, some columns are defined. In our case, we will just define the ID and name of the alternative and columns for editing and deleting the alternative:

```
    <Columns>
      <asp:BoundColumn DataField="id" HeaderText="id" ReadOnly="True" />
      <asp:BoundColumn DataField="name" HeaderText="name" />
      <asp:EditCommandColumn
        EditText="Edit"
        UpdateText="Update"
        CancelText="Cancel" />
      <asp:TemplateColumn HeaderText="remove">
        <ItemTemplate>
          <asp:LinkButton
            CommandName="Delete"
            CommandArgument='<%# DataBinder.Eval(Container.DataItem, "id") %>'
            Text="Delete"
            runat="server"/>
        </ItemTemplate>
      </asp:TemplateColumn>
    </Columns>
    </asp:DataGrid>
</asp:Panel>
```

This datagrid is filled by the FillAltGrid() function, which is quite similar to
FillPollGrid(). The ID of the current poll is retrieved from the session variable pid:

```
void FillAltGrid() {
  PollPanel.Visible = false;
  AltPanel.Visible = true;
  OleDbConnection conn = new OleDbConnection(
    "Provider=Microsoft.Jet.OleDb.4.0; Data Source=c:\\inetpub\\db\\svg.mdb");
  conn.Open();
  OleDbCommand comm = new OleDbCommand("SELECT name FROM poll WHERE id=" +
    Session["pid"], conn);
  OleDbDataReader reader = comm.ExecuteReader();
  if (reader.Read()) {
    pname.Text = reader["name"].ToString();
  }
  reader.Close();
  OleDbDataAdapter adapter = new OleDbDataAdapter(
    "SELECT id, name FROM alternative WHERE poll_id=" + Session["pid"], conn);
  DataSet data = new DataSet();
  adapter.Fill(data, "alternative");
  alternatives.DataSource = data.Tables["alternative"].DefaultView;
  alternatives.DataBind();
  conn.Close();
}
```

Coding Datagrid Functionality for the Alternatives

As with the datagrid for the polls, we need some special handling functions for the alternatives datagrid as well. We will start with `AltEdit()`, which switches to editing mode:

```
void AltEdit(Object o, DataGridCommandEventArgs e) {
  alternatives.EditItemIndex = e.Item.ItemIndex;
  FillAltGrid();
}
```

Next up is `AltUpdate()`, in which the `alternative` table is updated. An SQL statement is created and sent to the database via `RunSQL()`:

```
void AltUpdate(Object o, DataGridCommandEventArgs e) {
  string sql = "UPDATE alternative ";
  sql += "SET name='" + ((TextBox)e.Item.Cells[1].Controls[0]).Text + "' ";
  sql += "WHERE id=" + alternatives.DataKeys[e.Item.ItemIndex];
  RunSQL(sql);
  alternatives.EditItemIndex = -1;
  FillAltGrid();
}
```

When the user wants to leave the editing mode by clicking on Cancel, the `AltCancel()` function is called:

```
void AltCancel(Object o, DataGridCommandEventArgs e) {
  alternatives.EditItemIndex = -1;
  FillAltGrid();
}
```

Finally, `AltDelete()` removes a given alternative from the database:

```
void AltDelete(Object o, DataGridCommandEventArgs e) {
  string sql = "DELETE FROM alternative ";
  sql += "WHERE id=" + e.CommandArgument;
  RunSQL(sql);
  FillAltGrid();
}
```

You can see both the editing and the normal view mode of the datagrid in Figures 23.4 and 23.5.

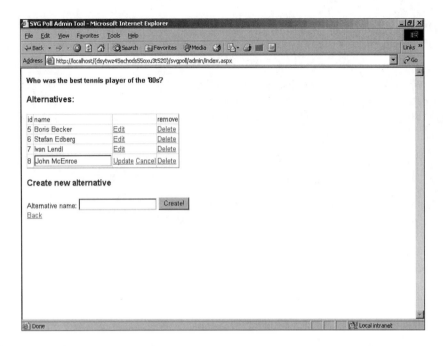

FIGURE 23.4   The datagrid in editing view.

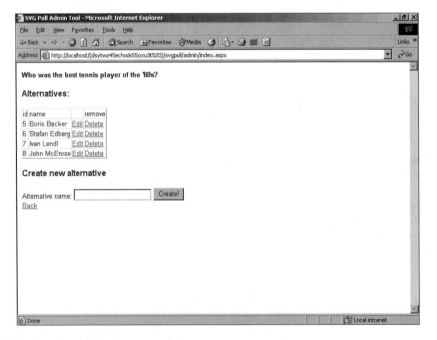

FIGURE 23.5   The datagrid in normal view.

Creating New Alternatives

We can insert new alternatives in the system by using an HTML form at the bottom of the page:

```
<p class="heading">Create new alternative</p>
```

We add the alternative name as follows:

```
<asp:TextBox id="altname" EnableViewState="False" runat="server" />
<asp:Button Text="Create!"
  OnClick="CreateAlternative" runat="server" />
```

CreateAlternative() is similar to CreatePoll(), but this time a new entry into the alternative table is created:

```
void CreateAlternative(Object o, EventArgs e) {
  OleDbConnection conn = new OleDbConnection(
    "Provider=Microsoft.Jet.OleDb.4.0; Data Source=c:\\inetpub\\db\\svg.mdb");
  conn.Open();
  OleDbCommand comm = new OleDbCommand(
    "SELECT * FROM alternative WHERE name='" + altname.Text + "'", conn);
  OleDbDataReader reader = comm.ExecuteReader();
  if (reader.Read()) {
    message.Text = "Alternative with name '" + altname.Text +
      "' already exists!";
    reader.Close();
  } else {
    message.Text = "";
    reader.Close();
    OleDbCommand comm1 = new OleDbCommand(
      "INSERT INTO alternative (name, poll_id) VALUES ('" + altname.Text +
      "', " + Session["pid"] + ")", conn);
    comm1.ExecuteNonQuery();
  }
  reader.Close();
  conn.Close();
  FillAltGrid();
}
```

Making Small Additions

To allow the user to get back from the alternatives overview to the polls overview, we will create a special back link that calls the ShowPollGrid() function:

```
<asp:LinkButton Text="Back" OnClick="ShowPollGrid" runat="server" />
```

This function just makes the poll data visible, hiding the (currently visible) alternatives grid:

```
void ShowPollGrid(Object o, EventArgs e) {
  PollPanel.Visible = true;
  AltPanel.Visible = false;
}
```

Finally, in Page_Load(), the session variable is initialized, and the two fill functions for the two datagrids are called. Each fill function—as you can see from the previous code fragments—makes the associated datagrid visible; thus, FillAltGrid() is called *before* FillPollGrid() so that the poll grid is initially visible:

```
void Page_Load() {
  if (Session["pid"] == null) {
    Session["pid"] = 0;
  };
  if (!Page.IsPostBack) {
    FillAltGrid();
    FillPollGrid();
  }
}
```

And that's it! The administration tool is now ready. You need to put together all the pieces of code shown in this chapter into one single index.aspx file that will lie in the admin directory of the SVG Poll application directory. Listing 23.2 shows the complete code, including the required Import statements and an asp:Label element used for writing a message to the user. Of course, you can find the code on the Sams Publishing Web site (http://www.samspublishing.com/) as well.

LISTING 23.2   index.aspx—The Poll Administration Tool

```
<%@ Page Language="c#" %>
<%@ Import Namespace="System.Data" %>
<%@ Import Namespace="System.Data.OleDb" %>
<script runat="server">
int RunSQL(string sql) {
  OleDbConnection conn = new OleDbConnection(
    "Provider=Microsoft.Jet.OleDb.4.0; Data Source=c:\\inetpub\\db\\svg.mdb");
  conn.Open();
  OleDbCommand comm = new OleDbCommand(sql, conn);
  int ret = comm.ExecuteNonQuery();
  conn.Close();
  return ret;
}
```

LISTING 23.2   Continued

```
void CreatePoll(Object o, EventArgs e) {
  OleDbConnection conn = new OleDbConnection(
    "Provider=Microsoft.Jet.OleDb.4.0; Data Source=c:\\inetpub\\db\\svg.mdb");
  conn.Open();
  OleDbCommand comm = new OleDbCommand("SELECT * FROM poll WHERE name='" +
    pollname.Text + "'", conn);
  OleDbDataReader reader = comm.ExecuteReader();
  if (reader.Read()) {
    message.Text = "Poll with name '" + pollname.Text + "' already exists!";
    reader.Close();
  } else {
    message.Text = "";
    reader.Close();
    OleDbCommand comm1 = new OleDbCommand("INSERT INTO poll (name) VALUES ('" +
      pollname.Text + "')", conn);
    comm1.ExecuteNonQuery();
    OleDbCommand comm2 = new OleDbCommand("SELECT id FROM poll WHERE name='" +
      pollname.Text + "'", conn);
    OleDbDataReader reader2 = comm2.ExecuteReader();
    reader2.Read();
    int id = (int)reader2["id"];
    reader2.Close();
    FillPollGrid();
    Session["pid"] = id;
    FillAltGrid();
  }
  reader.Close();
  conn.Close();
}

void FillPollGrid() {
  PollPanel.Visible = true;
  AltPanel.Visible = false;
  OleDbConnection conn = new OleDbConnection(
    "Provider=Microsoft.Jet.OleDb.4.0; Data Source=c:\\inetpub\\db\\svg.mdb");
  conn.Open();
  OleDbDataAdapter adapter = new OleDbDataAdapter("SELECT * FROM poll", conn);
  DataSet data = new DataSet();
  adapter.Fill(data, "poll");
  polls.DataSource = data.Tables["poll"].DefaultView;
  polls.DataBind();
  conn.Close();
}
```

23

LISTING 23.2   Continued

```
void PollEdit(Object o, DataGridCommandEventArgs e) {
  polls.EditItemIndex = e.Item.ItemIndex;
  FillPollGrid();
}

void PollUpdate(Object o, DataGridCommandEventArgs e) {
  string sql = "UPDATE poll ";
  sql += "SET name='" + ((TextBox)e.Item.Cells[1].Controls[0]).Text + "' ";
  sql += "WHERE id=" + polls.DataKeys[e.Item.ItemIndex];
  RunSQL(sql);
  polls.EditItemIndex = -1;
  FillPollGrid();
}

void PollCancel(Object o, DataGridCommandEventArgs e) {
  polls.EditItemIndex = -1;
  FillPollGrid();
}

void PollCommand(Object o, DataGridCommandEventArgs e) {
  if (e.CommandName == "Toggle") {
    string sql = "UPDATE poll SET status='inactive'";
    RunSQL(sql);
    sql = "UPDATE poll ";
    sql += "SET status='" + ((e.CommandArgument.ToString() == "active") ?
      "inactive" : "active") + "' ";
    sql += "WHERE id=" + polls.DataKeys[e.Item.ItemIndex];
    RunSQL(sql);
    polls.EditItemIndex = -1;
    FillPollGrid();
  } else if (e.CommandName == "Alternatives") {
    Session["pid"] = Convert.ToInt32(e.CommandArgument.ToString());
    FillAltGrid();
  } else if (e.CommandName == "Delete") {
    string sql = "DELETE FROM poll ";
    sql += "WHERE id=" + polls.DataKeys[e.Item.ItemIndex];
    RunSQL(sql);
    sql = "DELETE FROM alternative ";
    sql += "WHERE poll_id=" + polls.DataKeys[e.Item.ItemIndex];
    RunSQL(sql);
    FillPollGrid();
  }
}
```

LISTING 23.2   Continued

```
/* ------------------------------------------------------------------ */

void CreateAlternative(Object o, EventArgs e) {
  OleDbConnection conn = new OleDbConnection(
    "Provider=Microsoft.Jet.OleDb.4.0; Data Source=c:\\inetpub\\db\\svg.mdb");
  conn.Open();
  OleDbCommand comm = new OleDbCommand("SELECT * FROM alternative WHERE name='"
    + altname.Text + "'", conn);
  OleDbDataReader reader = comm.ExecuteReader();
  if (reader.Read()) {
    message.Text = "Alternative with name '" + altname.Text +
      "' already exists!";
    reader.Close();
  } else {
    message.Text = "";
    reader.Close();
    OleDbCommand comm1 = new OleDbCommand("INSERT INTO alternative
      (name, poll_id) VALUES ('" + altname.Text + "', " + Session["pid"] +
        ")", conn);
    comm1.ExecuteNonQuery();
  }
  reader.Close();
  conn.Close();
  FillAltGrid();
}

void FillAltGrid() {
  PollPanel.Visible = false;
  AltPanel.Visible = true;
  OleDbConnection conn = new OleDbConnection(
    "Provider=Microsoft.Jet.OleDb.4.0; Data Source=c:\\inetpub\\db\\svg.mdb");
  conn.Open();
  OleDbCommand comm = new OleDbCommand("SELECT name FROM poll WHERE id=" +
    Session["pid"], conn);
  OleDbDataReader reader = comm.ExecuteReader();
  if (reader.Read()) {
    pname.Text = reader["name"].ToString();
  }
  reader.Close();
  OleDbDataAdapter adapter = new OleDbDataAdapter("SELECT id, name FROM
    alternative WHERE poll_id=" + Session["pid"], conn);
  DataSet data = new DataSet();
  adapter.Fill(data, "alternative");
  alternatives.DataSource = data.Tables["alternative"].DefaultView;
```

LISTING 23.2   Continued

```
    alternatives.DataBind();
    conn.Close();
}

void AltEdit(Object o, DataGridCommandEventArgs e) {
    alternatives.EditItemIndex = e.Item.ItemIndex;
    FillAltGrid();
}

void AltUpdate(Object o, DataGridCommandEventArgs e) {
    string sql = "UPDATE alternative ";
    sql += "SET name='" + ((TextBox)e.Item.Cells[1].Controls[0]).Text + "' ";
    sql += "WHERE id=" + alternatives.DataKeys[e.Item.ItemIndex];
    RunSQL(sql);
    alternatives.EditItemIndex = -1;
    FillAltGrid();
}

void AltCancel(Object o, DataGridCommandEventArgs e) {
    alternatives.EditItemIndex = -1;
    FillAltGrid();
}

void AltDelete(Object o, DataGridCommandEventArgs e) {
    string sql = "DELETE FROM alternative ";
    sql += "WHERE id=" + e.CommandArgument;
    RunSQL(sql);
    FillAltGrid();
}

void ShowPollGrid(Object o, EventArgs e) {
    PollPanel.Visible = true;
    AltPanel.Visible = false;
}

void Page_Load() {
    if (Session["pid"] == null) {
        Session["pid"] = 0;
    };
    if (!Page.IsPostBack) {
        FillAltGrid();
        FillPollGrid();
```

LISTING 23.2 Continued

```
  }
}
</script>
<html>
<head>
<title>SVG Poll Admin Tool</title>
<link href="poll.css" type="text/css" rel="stylesheet" />
</head>
<body>
<form runat="server">
<asp:Panel id="PollPanel" runat="server">
  <p class="heading">Available Polls:</p>
  <asp:DataGrid id="polls"
    AutoGenerateColumns="False"
    DataKeyField="id"
    OnItemCommand="PollCommand"
    OnEditCommand="PollEdit"
    OnUpdateCommand="PollUpdate"
    OnCancelCommand="PollCancel"
    runat="server">
  <Columns>
    <asp:BoundColumn DataField="id" HeaderText="<b>id</b>" ReadOnly="True" />
    <asp:BoundColumn DataField="name" HeaderText="<b>name</b>" />
    <asp:TemplateColumn HeaderText="<b>status</b>">
      <ItemTemplate>
        <asp:Label Text='<%# DataBinder.Eval(Container.DataItem, "status")
          %>' runat="server" />
      </ItemTemplate>
      <EditItemTemplate>
        <asp:LinkButton Text='<%# "toggle status to " + ((DataBinder.Eval
          (Container.DataItem, "status").ToString() == "active") ? "inactive"
          : "active") %>'
          CommandName="Toggle"
          CommandArgument='<%# DataBinder.Eval(Container.DataItem, "status") %>'
          runat="server" />
      </EditItemTemplate>
    </asp:TemplateColumn>
    <asp:EditCommandColumn
      EditText="Edit"
      UpdateText="Update"
      CancelText="Cancel" />
    <asp:TemplateColumn HeaderText="<b>alternatives</b>">
      <ItemTemplate>
```

23

LISTING 23.2   Continued

```
        <asp:LinkButton
          Text="Add/Remove alternatives"
          CommandName="Alternatives"
          CommandArgument='<%# DataBinder.Eval(Container.DataItem, "id") %>'
          runat="server" />
      </ItemTemplate>
    </asp:TemplateColumn>
    <asp:TemplateColumn HeaderText="<b>remove</b>">
      <ItemTemplate>
        <asp:LinkButton
          CommandName="Delete"
          CommandArgument='<%# DataBinder.Eval(Container.DataItem, "id") %>'
          Text="Delete"
          runat="server"/>
      </ItemTemplate>
    </asp:TemplateColumn>
  </Columns>
  </asp:DataGrid>
  <p class="heading">Create new poll</p>
  Poll name:
    <asp:TextBox id="pollname" EnableViewState="False" runat="server" />
    <asp:Button Text="Create!"
      OnClick="CreatePoll" runat="server" />
</asp:Panel>

<asp:Panel id="AltPanel" runat="server">
  <p><b><asp:Label CssClass="bold" id="pname" runat="server" /></b></p>
  <p class="heading">Alternatives:</p>
  <asp:DataGrid id="alternatives"
    AutoGenerateColumns="False"
    DataKeyField="id"
    OnEditCommand="AltEdit"
    OnUpdateCommand="AltUpdate"
    OnCancelCommand="AltCancel"
    OnDeleteCommand="AltDelete"
    runat="server">
    <Columns>
      <asp:BoundColumn DataField="id" HeaderText="id" ReadOnly="True" />
      <asp:BoundColumn DataField="name" HeaderText="name" />
```

LISTING 23.2   Continued

```
        <asp:EditCommandColumn
          EditText="Edit"
          UpdateText="Update"
          CancelText="Cancel" />
        <asp:TemplateColumn HeaderText="remove">
          <ItemTemplate>
            <asp:LinkButton
              CommandName="Delete"
              CommandArgument='<%# DataBinder.Eval(Container.DataItem, "id") %>'
              Text="Delete"
              runat="server"/>
          </ItemTemplate>
        </asp:TemplateColumn>
      </Columns>
    </asp:DataGrid>
    <p class="heading">Create new alternative</p>
    Alternative name:
      <asp:TextBox id="altname" EnableViewState="False" runat="server" />
      <asp:Button Text="Create!"
        OnClick="CreateAlternative" runat="server" />
      <br /><asp:LinkButton Text="Back" OnClick="ShowPollGrid" runat="server" />
</asp:Panel>
    <p><asp:Label id="message" CssClass="bold" runat="server" /></p>
</form>
</body>
</html>
```

Load it in your browser and create at least one survey and a few alternatives so that creating the poll input and output pages makes sense.

The Poll

Next, we will display the poll. We will first show how the SVG for the poll is constructed; then we will present ways to prevent people from getting more than one vote per survey.

SVG Representation of the Poll

For the SVG representation of the poll, we will create a `rect` element that contains the text of each possible alternative. The voting button consists of a circle that represents the button and another circle that creates a shadow for the button. Additionally, we will create a hook or check mark that resembles a cross you can make on your voting sheet (even in Florida ;-)). Using a little bit of ECMAScript, the hook appears when the user moves the mouse pointer over the button. The sample in Listing 23.3 shows two alternatives.

LISTING 23.3   alternatives.svg—Two Alternatives in SVG

```
<?xml version="1.0" ?>
<!DOCTYPE svg PUBLIC "-//W3C//DTD SVG 20001102//EN"
 "http://www.w3.org/TR/2000/CR-SVG-20001102/DTD/svg-20001102.dtd">
<svg width="300px" height="250px" style="shape-rendering:optimizeSpeed;
 text-rendering:optimizeQuality" onload="init(evt);">
    <defs>
     <script type="text/ecmascript"><![CDATA[
        var svgdoc;  //global variable

        function init(evt) {
            svgdoc = evt.getTarget().getOwnerDocument();
            for (var i=1; i<=2; i++) {
               var el = svgdoc.getElementById("button" + i);
               el.addEventListener("mouseover", toggle, false);
               el.addEventListener("mouseout", toggle, false);
            }
        }
        function toggle(evt) {
            var el = evt.getTarget();
            if (el) {
               var id = el.getAttribute("id");
               id = id.substring(6, id.length);
               var hook = svgdoc.getElementById("hook" + id);
               if (hook) {
                 var s = hook.getStyle();
                 var v = s.getPropertyValue("visibility");
                 s.setProperty("visibility", (v == "visible") ? "hidden" :
"visible");
               }
            }
        }
     ]]></script>
        <radialGradient id="radGrad" cx="50%" cy="50%" r="60%">
            <stop offset="0%" style="stop-color:white;stop-opacity:1" />
            <stop offset="80%" style="stop-color:blue;stop-opacity:1" />
        </radialGradient>
        <filter id="shadow">
            <feGaussianBlur in="SourceAlpha" stdDeviation="1" />
        </filter>
```

LISTING 23.3 Continued

```
    </defs>
    <text id="title" x="60" y="30" style="font-face:Arial, Geneva, Helvetica,
              sans-serif;font-size:14pt;font-weight:bold;
              alignment-baseline:baseline">
             Place your vote
    </text>
    <g><text id="vote1" x="50" y="80" style="font-face:Arial, Geneva,
      Helvetica, sans-serif;font-size:12pt;alignment-baseline:baseline">
      Boris Becker</text>
<rect x="35" y="55" width="200" height="40" style="fill:none;stroke-width:1;
  stroke:rgb(204,204,204)" />
<circle cx="202" cy="77" r="10" style="fill:black;filter:url(#shadow)" />
<a xlink:href="...">
<circle id="button1" cx="200" cy="75" r="10" style="fill:url(#radGrad)">
<set attributeName="cx" begin="mouseover" end="mouseout" to="202" />
<set attributeName="cy" begin="mouseover" end="mouseout" to="77" />
</circle></a>
<g id="hook1" style="visibility:hidden">
<path transform="translate(0,2)" d="M200 75 C200 75 212 82 216 91 C216 91 220
  65 233 61" style="fill:none;filter:url(#shadow);stroke-width:4;
  stroke:rgb(100,100,100)" />
<path d="M200 75 C200 75 212 82 216 91 C216 91 220 64 233 61" style="fill:none;
  stroke-width:4;stroke:rgb(100,100,100)" />
</g>
<text id="vote2" x="50" y="130" style="font-face:Arial, Geneva, Helvetica,
  sans-serif;font-size:12pt;alignment-baseline:baseline">Stefan Edberg</text>
<rect x="35" y="105" width="200" height="40" style="fill:none;stroke-width:1;
  stroke:rgb(204,204,204)" />
<circle cx="202" cy="127" r="10" style="fill:black;filter:url(#shadow)" />
<a xlink:href="...">
<circle id="button2" cx="200" cy="125" r="10" style="fill:url(#radGrad)">
<set attributeName="cx" begin="mouseover" end="mouseout" to="202" />
<set attributeName="cy" begin="mouseover" end="mouseout" to="127" />
</circle></a>
<g id="hook2" style="visibility:hidden">
<path transform="translate(0,2)" d="M200 125 C200 125 212 132 216 141 C216 141
  220 115 233 111" style="fill:none;filter:url(#shadow);stroke-width:4;
  stroke:rgb(100,100,100)" />
<path d="M200 125 C200 125 212 132 216 141 C216 141 220 114 233 111" style=
 "fill:none;stroke-width:4;stroke:rgb(100,100,100)" />
</g>
</g>
</svg>
```

Figure 23.6 shows the result in an SVG viewer; note that when you run the code that a hook appears when the mouse pointer is over one of the buttons.

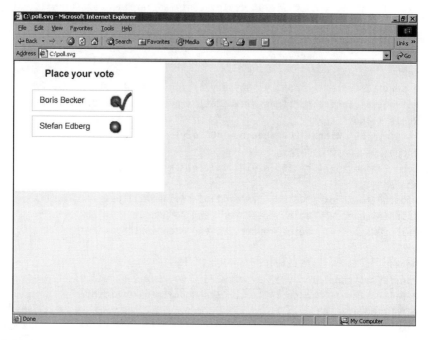

FIGURE 23.6　Viewing the result on the SVG site.

To achieve this result, we must create a skeleton or torso, a simplified version of the previous SVG code. Via ASP.NET, this skeleton will be filled with the actual values from the database. Listing 23.4, named torso1.svg, shows what the skeleton looks like.

LISTING 23.4　torso1.svg—The Skeleton for the Alternatives

```
<?xml version="1.0" ?>
<!DOCTYPE svg PUBLIC "-//W3C//DTD SVG 20001102//EN"
 "http://www.w3.org/TR/2000/CR-SVG-20001102/DTD/svg-20001102.dtd">
<svg width="300px" height="%SVGHEIGHT%px" style="shape-rendering:optimizeSpeed;
  text-rendering:optimizeQuality" onload="init(evt);">
    <defs>
     <script type="text/ecmascript"><![CDATA[
        var svgdoc;  //global variable

        function init(evt) {
           svgdoc = evt.getTarget().getOwnerDocument();
           for (var i=1; i<=%CNTALT%; i++) {
              var el = svgdoc.getElementById("button"+i);
```

LISTING 23.4   Continued

```
            el.addEventListener("mouseover", toggle, false);
            el.addEventListener("mouseout", toggle, false);
          }
        }

        function toggle(evt) {
          var el = evt.getTarget();
          if (el) {
            var id = el.getAttribute("id");
            id = id.substring(6, id.length);
            var hook = svgdoc.getElementById("hook" + id);
            if (hook) {
              var s = hook.getStyle();
              var v = s.getPropertyValue("visibility");
              s.setProperty("visibility",
                            (v == "visible") ? "hidden" : "visible");
            }
          }
        }
    ]]></script>
      <radialGradient id="radGrad" cx="50%" cy="50%" r="60%">
        <stop offset="0%" style="stop-color:white;stop-opacity:1" />
        <stop offset="80%" style="stop-color:blue;stop-opacity:1" />
      </radialGradient>
      <filter id="shadow">
        <feGaussianBlur in="SourceAlpha" stdDeviation="1" />
      </filter>
    </defs>
    <text id="title" x="60" y="30"
        style="font-face:Arial, Geneva, Helvetica, sans-serif;
               font-size:14pt;font-weight:bold;alignment-baseline:baseline">
                Place your vote
    </text>
    <g>%ALTERNATIVES%</g>
</svg>
```

Note the three placeholders:

- %SVGHEIGHT%—The height of the SVG document measured in pixels

- %CNTALT%—The number of alternatives

- %ALTERNATIVES%—SVG code for the alternatives

We will now develop a script named svg1.aspx that will create SVG output based on torso1.svg. The script will be called as follows:

```
svg1.aspx?pid=1&cntalt=4&text1=Boris+Becker&id1=5&text2=Stefan+Edberg&IE=.svg
```

The IDs of the alternatives (here, 4 and 5) are submitted in the GET variables id1, id2, and so on; whereas the text for the alternatives comes in variables text1, text2, and so on and the poll ID comes in variable pid. Finally, IE=.svg is a nonused variable that tricks some versions of Internet Explorer into treating the output as an SVG file (see Chapter 18, "Server-Side Basics," for more information).

The following script generates the SVG file based on the GET variables. Everything takes place in the Page_Load() function:

```
<%@ Page Language="c#" %>
<%@ Import Namespace="System.IO" %>
<script runat="server">
void Page_Load() {
```

First, the MIME type that is sent to the client is set to the SVG MIME type:

```
Response.ContentType = "image/svg+xml";
```

Now the GET variable cntalt, which contains the number of alternatives, is retrieved. String variable a, which follows, will contain the SVG representation of the alternatives:

```
string a = "";
int cntalt = Convert.ToInt32(Request.QueryString["cntalt"]);
string poll_id = Request.QueryString["pid"];
```

In the next step, we loop through all alternatives and start with the text for the alternatives. The coordinates of the first alternative are (50, 80), and the next alternative will be (50, 130). Thus, the y variable of the current alternative can be retrieved rather easily:

```
for (int i=1; i<=cntalt; i++) {
  a += "<text id=\"vote" + i + "\" x=\"50\" y=\"" + (30 + 50*i) +
      "\" style=\"font-face:Arial, Geneva, Helvetica, sans-serif;
      font-size:12pt;alignment-baseline:baseline\">";
  a += Server.HtmlEncode(Request.QueryString["text"+i]);
  a += "</text>\n";
```

We then continue with the bounding box and the shadow circle:

```
  a += "<rect x=\"35\" y=\"" + (5 + 50*i) +
      "\" width=\"200\" height=\"40\" style=\"fill:none;stroke-width:1;
      stroke:rgb(204,204,204)\" />\n";
  a += "<circle cx=\"202\" cy=\"" + (27 + 50*i) +
      "\" r=\"10\" style=\"fill:black;filter:url(#shadow)\" />\n";
```

Then the blue button is painted. Furthermore, a link will be added to the link that sends—when clicked—the browser to `index.aspx?alt=42&amp;id=1`, where 42 is the ID of the selected alternative and 1 is the ID of the poll. Additionally, we use the `<set>` element to create the 3D effect achieved by moving the blue button when the mouse pointer is over it:

```
a += "<a xlink:href=\"index.aspx?alt=" + Request.QueryString["id"+i] +
     "&amp;id=" + poll_id + "\">\n";
a += "<circle id=\"button" + i + "\" cx=\"200\" cy=\"" + (25 + 50*i) +
     "\" r=\"10\" style=\"fill:url(#radGrad)\">\n";
a += "<set attributeName=\"cx\" begin=\"mouseover\" end=\"mouseout\"
     to=\"202\" />\n";
a += "<set attributeName=\"cy\" begin=\"mouseover\" end=\"mouseout\" to=\"" +
     (27 + 50*i) + "\" />  \n";
a += "</circle></a>\n";
```

Finally, we create the hook. Again, we calculate the y coordinates of each element, knowing that each alternative has a height of 50 pixels:

```
    a += "<g id=\"hook" + i + "\" style=\"visibility:hidden\">\n";
    a += "<path transform=\"translate(0,2)\" d=\"M200 " + (25 + 50*i) +
         " C200 " + (25 + 50*i) + " 212 " + (32 + 50*i) + " 216 " +
         (41 + 50*i) + " C216 " + (41 + 50*i) + " 220 " + (15 + 50*i) +
         " 233 " + (11 + 50*i) + "\"";
    a += " style=\"fill:none;filter:url(#shadow);stroke-width:4;
         stroke:rgb(100,100,100)\" />\n";
    a += "<path d=\"M200 " + (25 + 50*i) + " C200 " + (25 + 50*i) + " 212 " +
         (32 + 50*i) + " 216 " + (41 + 50*i) + " C216 " + (41 + 50*i) +
         " 220 " + (14 + 50*i) + " 233 " + (11 + 50*i) + "\"";
    a += " style=\"fill:none;stroke-width:4;stroke:rgb(100,100,100)\" />\n";
    a += "</g>\n";
}
```

In the next step, the data from torso1.svg is read in and the three placeholders are replaced by the actual values:

```
StreamReader sr = new StreamReader(Server.MapPath("torso1.svg"));
string svg = sr.ReadToEnd();
sr.Close();

svg = svg.Replace("%SVGHEIGHT%", (50*(cntalt+1)).ToString());
svg = svg.Replace("%CNTALT%", cntalt.ToString());
svg = svg.Replace("%ALTERNATIVES%", a);
```

In the final step, the result (residing in the svg variable) is sent to the client, ending the script:

```
  Response.Write(svg);
}
</script>
```

SVG Representation of the Results

The vote results will be presented using a progress bar. As a special bonus, the bars will be animated; they start at 0% and grow to their final length. Thus, a little bit of tension will be generated—a great eye-catcher.

We will start with the coordinate system, including the text of the poll question:

```
<?xml version="1.0" ?>
<!DOCTYPE svg PUBLIC "-//W3C//DTD SVG 20001102//EN"
 "http://www.w3.org/TR/2000/CR-SVG-20001102/DTD/svg-20001102.dtd">
<svg width="300px" height="250px" style="shape-rendering:optimizeSpeed;
  text-rendering:optimizeQuality">
        <g id="coordinates">
          <path d="M 20,245 L 20,20" style="fill:black;stroke:black;
            stroke-width: 2" id="xaxis" />
          <line x1="15" y1="25" x2="20" y2="20" style="fill:black;stroke:black;
            stroke-width: 2" />
          <line x1="20" y1="20" x2="25" y2="25" style="fill:black;stroke:black;
            stroke-width: 2" />
          <path d="M 20,245 L 210,245" style="fill:black;stroke:black;
            stroke-width: 2" id="yaxis"/>
        <text x="40" y="265" id="y"
                style="font-face:Arial, Geneva, Helvetica, sans-serif;
                font-size:10pt;color:black;alignment-baseline:baseline">
                Who was the best tennis player of the '80s?</text>
          <line x1="205" y1="240" x2="210" y2="245" style="fill:black;
            stroke:black; stroke-width: 2" />
          <line x1="210" y1="245" x2="205" y2="250" style="fill:black;
            stroke:black; stroke-width: 2" />
        </g>
```

Next come the percentage bars. Obviously, they all consist of a rect element:

```
<g id="rows"><rect width="0" height="30" x="20" y="50" style="fill:aqua;
stroke:black" id="row1">
```

Using two animations, the rect element will grow to its final length. This animation will be completed in two steps. The first step is the same for all progress bars; this ensures that the first two seconds the animations will grow simultaneously up to a certain point. Unfortunately, SVG does not offer any means to synchronize different animations; thus, we take this step:

```
<animate attributeName="width" from="0" to="33" begin="1s" dur="2s"
 repeatCount="1" fill="freeze" />
<animate attributeName="width" from="33" to="157" begin="3s" dur="4s"
 repeatCount="1" fill="freeze" /></rect>
```

Finally, the text of the alternative is shown, after 6 seconds. Most of the time, the display of text coincides with the end of the animation.

```
<text x="40" y="70" id="text1" style="font-face:Arial, Geneva,
 Helvetica, sans-serif; font-size:9pt;color:black;visibility:hidden"
 >Boris Becker (37%)<set attributeType="CSS" attributeName="visibility"
 to="visible" begin="6s" dur="1s" repeatCount="1" fill="freeze" />
</text></g>
<text x="75" y="20" id="title"
        style="font-face:Arial, Geneva, Helvetica, sans-serif;
        font-size:10pt;font-weight:bold;color:white;
        alignment-baseline:baseline">
        Online Poll
</text>
</svg>
```

In Figure 23.7, you can see the final stage of the animation (for multiple progress bars), with the description text already visible.

To generate such SVG output, we will again create a skeleton (this time called torso2.svg) that contains some placeholders we will replace with ASP.NET. Listing 23.5 contains this code.

LISTING 23.5   torso2.svg—The Skeleton for the Poll Results

```
<?xml version="1.0" ?>
<!DOCTYPE svg PUBLIC "-//W3C//DTD SVG 20001102//EN"
 "http://www.w3.org/TR/2000/CR-SVG-20001102/DTD/svg-20001102.dtd">
<svg width="300px" height="%SVGHEIGHT%px" style="shape-rendering:optimizeSpeed;
 text-rendering:optimizeQuality">
        <g id="coordinates">
            <path d="M 20,%AXISY% L 20,20" style="fill:black;stroke:black;
             stroke-width: 2" id="xaxis" />
            <line x1="15" y1="25" x2="20" y2="20" style="fill:black;stroke:black;
             stroke-width: 2" />
            <line x1="20" y1="20" x2="25" y2="25" style="fill:black;stroke:black;
             stroke-width: 2" />
```

LISTING 23.5   Continued

```
            <path d="M 20,%AXISY% L 210,%AXISY%" style="fill:black;stroke:black;
              stroke-width: 2" id="yaxis"/>
          <text x="40" y="%AXISTEXTY%" id="y"
                  style="font-face:Arial, Geneva, Helvetica, sans-serif;
                  font-size:10pt;color:black;alignment-baseline:baseline"
                  >%POLLNAME%</text>
            <line x1="205" y1="%AXISY-%" x2="210" y2="%AXISY%" style="fill:black;
              stroke:black; stroke-width: 2" />
            <line x1="210" y1="%AXISY%" x2="205" y2="%AXISY+%" style="fill:black;
              stroke:black; stroke-width: 2" />
        </g>
        <g id="rows">%BARS%</g>
        <text x="75" y="20" id="title"
                  style="font-face:Arial, Geneva, Helvetica, sans-serif;
                  font-size:10pt;font-weight:bold;color:white;
                  alignment-baseline:baseline">
                  Online Poll
        </text>
    </svg>
```

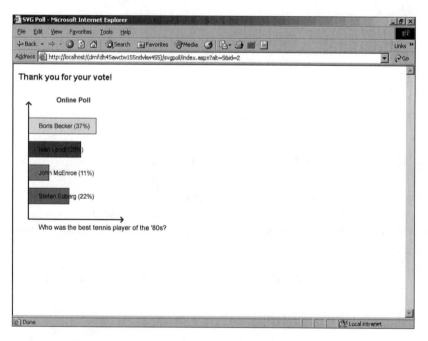

FIGURE 23.7   The final stage of the progress bar animation.

The following placeholders are used:

- `%SVGHEIGHT%`—The (computed) height of the SVG document

- `%AXISY%`—The y coordinate of the x-axis

- `%AXISY+%`—The y coordinate of the x-axis plus 5 pixels (used for the arrow at the end of the axis)

- `%AXISY-%`—The y coordinate of the x-axis minus 5 pixels (used for the arrow at the end of the axis)

- `%AXISTEXTY%`—The y coordinate of the text at the axis (the name of the poll)

- `%POLLNAME%`—The name of the poll

- `%BARS%`—To be replaced by the SVG code for the percentage bars (including the animation)

To create the SVG file, we will use a script called svg2.aspx (essentially, the brother or sister of svg1.aspx). This script will return SVG code (and the associated MIME type). A sample call to this script looks like this:

```
svg2.aspx?pname=Who+is+the+best+tennis+player+of+the+%2780s%3f&name1=
Boris+Becker&votes1=1&name2=Stefan+Edberg&votes2=2&cntbars=2&sum=
3&minvote=1&maxvote=23&IE=.svg
```

Following is a list of all GET variables that are appended to the URL (apart from IE=.svg, the well-known hack for Internet Explorer as you saw in Chapter 18:

- `pname`—Name of the poll

- `name1, name2, ...`—The names of the alternatives

- `votes1, votes2, ...`—The number of votes of the alternatives

- `cntbars`—The number of alternatives

- `sum`—The sum of all votes for this poll

- `min`—The smallest number of votes for this poll

- `max`—The largest number of votes for this poll

> **NOTE**
>
> The last three values in the preceding list can also be computed within svg2.aspx, but they are easier to retrieve in the script that calls svg2.aspx.

Using torso2.svg, we are now ready to create the svg2.aspx script. As usual, we start by setting the MIME type:

```
<%@ Page Language="c#" %>
<%@ Import Namespace="System.IO" %>
<script runat="server">
void Page_Load() {
  Response.ContentType = "image/svg+xml";
```

Then we define an array of colors. We use 14 of the 16 standard colors, omitting only white and black (the latter because the black alternative text could not be seen):

```
string[] colors = {"aqua",
                   "blue",
                   "fuchsia",
                   "gray",
                   "green",
                   "lime",
                   "maroon",
                   "navy",
                   "olive",
                   "purple",
                   "red",
                   "silver",
                   "teal",
                   "yellow"};
```

Next, we read some variables from the URL:

```
string bars = ""; //will contain the SVG code for the progress bars
string pname = Request.QueryString["pname"];
int cntbars = Convert.ToInt32(Request.QueryString["cntbars"]);
int sum = Convert.ToInt32(Request.QueryString["sum"]);
```

Now comes the fun part. The maximum length of the bar is around 170 pixels. But we do not want to use all that space; we also do not want the maximum length to equal 100% (because the bars would be very short if there were, say, four alternatives with 25% each). So we will choose the maximum vote and let this bar become 85% of the available width. We can now compute a factor with which we multiply each percentage:

```
double factor = 170*85/(Convert.ToInt32(Request.QueryString["maxvote"]));
```

Now we can loop through all alternatives. The first SVG element is the <text> element for the bar itself. The color is retrieved from the colors array. Instead of colors[loopvariable], though, we will use colors[loopvariable % colors.Length] because the 15th bar (if available) will also get a color instead of generating an index out of bounds error:

```
for (int i=1; i<=cntbars; i++) {
  bars += "<rect width=\"0\" height=\"30\" x=\"20\" y=\"" + (5 + 45*i) +
          "\" style=\"fill:";
  bars += colors[(i-1) % colors.Length];
  bars += ";stroke:black\" id=\"row" + i + "\">\n";
```

Then come the animations. The first animation goes from 0 to 33 pixels (which corresponds to somewhat less than a fifth of the 170 pixels); the second animation goes from 33 pixels to the computed length of the bar:

```
bars += "<animate attributeName=\"width\" from=\"0\" to=\"33\" begin=\"1s\"
➥dur=\"2s\" repeatCount=\"1\"fill=\"freeze\" />\n";
bars += "<animate attributeName=\"width\" from=\"33\" to=\"";
bars += Convert.ToInt32(factor*Convert.ToInt32(
                        Request.QueryString["votes" + i])/sum);
bars += "\" begin=\"3s\" dur=\"4s\" repeatCount=\"1\" fill=\"freeze\"
                        /></rect>\n";
```

> **NOTE**
>
> With this approach, the first phase of the animation always gives the bar a width of 33 pixels, even if the bar will later be shorter (it will shrink). If you want to avoid that, you need to use the value of the GET variable minvote and let the first phase of the animation go only up to this mark. However, if one alternative has only a very small number of votes, this would influence the animations of all the other alternatives as well. Thus, we chose to give the first animation a fixed width.

In the next step, the name of the alternative is written and the animation set up so that the text appears after 6 seconds have elapsed:

```
  bars += "<text x=\"40\" y=\"" + (25 + 45*i) + "\" id=\"text" + i + "\"
  style=\"font-face:Arial, Geneva, Helvetica, sans-serif; font-size:9pt;
  color:black;visibility:hidden\" >";
  bars += Server.HtmlEncode(Request.QueryString["name" + i]);
  bars += " (" + Convert.ToInt32(100*Convert.ToInt32(
                          Request.QueryString["votes" + i])/sum) + "%)";
  bars += "<set attributeType=\"CSS\" attributeName=\"visibility\" to=
  \"visible\" begin=\"6s\" dur=\"1s\" repeatCount=\"1\" fill=\"freeze\"
  /></text>";
}
```

Note that the position of the text (and in the previous fragment, of the bars) is computed using the loop variable and the fixed height of the element. Each alternative gets a height of 45 pixels.

We are almost done now. In the next step, the torso, torso2.svg, is read in:

```
StreamReader sr = new StreamReader(Server.MapPath("torso2.svg"));
string svg = sr.ReadToEnd();
sr.Close();
```

Now, the placeholders in the SVG torso can be replaced by the actual, computed values:

```
svg = svg.Replace("%BARS%", bars);
svg = svg.Replace("%SVGHEIGHT%", (115 + 45*cntbars).ToString());
svg = svg.Replace("%POLLNAME%", pname);
svg = svg.Replace("%AXISY%", (65 + 45*cntbars).ToString());
svg = svg.Replace("%AXISY-%", (60 + 45*cntbars).ToString());
svg = svg.Replace("%AXISY+%", (70 + 45*cntbars).ToString());
svg = svg.Replace("%AXISTEXTY%", (85 + 45*cntbars).ToString());
```

Finally, the SVG output, currently residing in the svg variable, is sent to the client, usually the Web browser:

```
  Response.Write(svg);
}
</script>
```

And that's it! This script dynamically generates some progress bars and the associated animations. The only piece that is still missing is the code that calls the svg1.aspx and svg2.aspx scripts and checks whether the user is allowed to vote or has already voted.

Voting

We will now create an index.aspx page that will reside in the same directory as the two torso files and svg1.aspx and svg2.aspx. This page will have to fulfill the following tasks:

- Decide whether to show the poll or the results
- Call the script to generate the SVG representation of the poll
- Save votes in the database
- Call the script to generate the SVG representation of the poll results

We will start with the HTML portion of the script. In this code, we use two ASP.NET controls: one to display a message to the user (<asp:Label>) and one HTML control to put the <embed> element for the SVG graphic into:

```
<html>
<head>
<title>SVG Poll</title>
<link href="poll.css" type="text/css" rel="stylesheet" />
```

```
</head>
<body>
<form runat="server">
<p><asp:Label id="message" CssClass="heading" runat="server" /></p>
<div id="PollGrid" runat="server" />
</form>
</body>
</html>
```

> **NOTE**
>
> Using <embed runat="server"> does *not* work. When you try to set the src attribute of that element using ASP.NET, all ampersands (&) are converted into &, so the call to svg1.aspx might look like
>
> svg1.aspx?cntalt=1&name1=X&id1=1
>
> This itself is no problem, but Internet Explorer does not convert the & occurrences back to & when calling svg1.aspx; thus, svg1.aspx does not return the desired SVG file.

As you saw in the "Database Structure" section, we have a guid field in the person table that will contain a globally unique ID (GUID). ASP.NET can create such a GUID with the NewGuid() method in the System.Guid class. The following function generates a new GUID and tries to write this GUID into a cookie (that will last 30 days in the user's browser). If the cookie already exists, the GUID is taken from this cookie. The return value of the function is the GUID.

```
string getGUID() {
  string guid;
  if (Request.Cookies["svgGUID"] != null) {
    guid = Request.Cookies["svgGUID"].Value;
  } else {
    guid = Guid.NewGuid().ToString();
    Response.Cookies["svgGUID"].Value = guid;
    Response.Cookies["svgGUID"].Expires = DateTime.Now.AddDays(30);
  }
  return guid;
}
```

For testing purposes, we will define two variables that trigger whether the IP and the GUID checking should be done. In particular, the IP checking might irritate your users. People within a corporate network often access the Web via a proxy server; they therefore all have the same IP address, the IP of the proxy server. If you receive complaints, you should disable the IP checking option.

```
bool ipcheck = true; // whether to check IP
bool idcheck = true; // whether to check GUID from cookie
```

In Page_Load(), the main work is done. The user's IP and the GUID are retrieved. For the GUID, we use the getGUID() function, so either an existing GUID is used or a new one is generated by ASP.NET:

```
void Page_Load() {
  if (!Page.IsPostBack && Request.QueryString["alt"] == null) {
    string ip = Request.ServerVariables["REMOTE_ADDR"];
    string guid = getGUID();
```

Now the script retrieves the available poll (if any) from the database. Depending on the values of ipcheck and idcheck, an appropriate query is sent to the database, checking in the person table whether the same IP address or GUID already has voted:

```
OleDbConnection conn = new OleDbConnection(
  "Provider=Microsoft.Jet.OleDb.4.0; Data Source=c:\\inetpub\\db\\svg.mdb");
conn.Open();
OleDbCommand comm;
if (ipcheck && idcheck) {
  comm = new OleDbCommand("SELECT poll.id FROM poll WHERE poll.status='active'
    AND id NOT IN (SELECT poll_id FROM person, poll WHERE person.ip='" + ip + "'
    OR person.guid='" + guid + "')", conn);
} else if (ipcheck) {
  comm = new OleDbCommand("SELECT poll.id FROM poll WHERE poll.status='active'
    AND id NOT IN (SELECT poll_id FROM person, poll WHERE person.ip='" + ip +
    "')", conn);
} else if (idcheck) {
  comm = new OleDbCommand("SELECT poll.id FROM poll WHERE poll.status='active'
    AND id NOT IN (SELECT poll_id FROM person, poll WHERE person.guid='" + guid
    + "')", conn);
} else {
  comm = new OleDbCommand("SELECT poll.id FROM poll WHERE poll.status=
    'active'", conn);
}
OleDbDataReader reader = comm.ExecuteReader();
```

If a suitable poll exists, Show_Poll() is called (we will take care of that function later, but its effect is obvious); if not, Show_Results() is executed. The ID of the current poll is submitted to Show_Poll() as follows:

```
if (reader.Read()) {
  Show_Poll(Convert.ToInt32(reader["id"]));
} else {
```

```
    Show_Results();
}
reader.Close();
conn.Close();
```

> **NOTE**
>
> In the standard configuration, ASP.NET sessions require cookies. If you do not want to use them, configure your web.config file for cookieless session management.

Remember the start of the Page_Load() function? We checked whether the page was posted back and a URL alt parameter was submitted:

```
if (!Page.IsPostBack && Request.QueryString["alt"] == null) {
```

If there is a parameter called alt, that means a vote has been submitted; we then must call a (still-to-be-written) function named Vote():

```
} else {
  Vote();
}
}
```

What now remains is to write these three missing functions:

- Show_Poll()
- Show_Results()
- Vote()

We will start with Show_Poll(), which displays a poll. (To be honest, the main work is to create the correct call to svg1.aspx.) First, the function retrieves the given poll's data from the database and also all data from the alternative table:

```
void Show_Poll(int poll_id) {
  OleDbConnection conn = new OleDbConnection(
    "Provider=Microsoft.Jet.OleDb.4.0; Data Source=c:\\inetpub\\db\\svg.mdb");
  conn.Open();
  OleDbCommand comm1 = new OleDbCommand("SELECT * FROM poll WHERE id=" +
                                        poll_id + " ORDER BY id", conn);
  OleDbDataReader reader1 = comm1.ExecuteReader();
  reader1.Read();
  string pname = reader1["name"].ToString();
  reader1.Close();
  OleDbCommand comm2 = new OleDbCommand(
```

```
  "SELECT * FROM alternative WHERE poll_id=" + poll_id +
    " ORDER BY id", conn);
  OleDbDataReader reader2 = comm2.ExecuteReader();
```

Then the query string is assembled. The text of all the alternatives and their IDs must occur, as well as the number of alternatives, the ID of the poll, and the hack for Internet Explorer:

```
string querystring = "";
int cntalt = 0;
while (reader2.Read()) {
  cntalt++;
  querystring += "&text" + cntalt + "=" +
                 Server.UrlEncode(reader2["name"].ToString());
  querystring += "&id" + cntalt + "=" + reader2["id"];
}
reader2.Close();
conn.Close();
querystring = "?cntalt=" + cntalt + querystring;
querystring += "&pid=" + poll_id;
querystring += "&IE=.svg";
```

Finally, the HTML embed element is written into the <div> element and the name of the poll to the <asp:Label> element:

```
  PollGrid.InnerHtml = "<embed type=\"image/svg+xml\" width=\"300\" ";
  PollGrid.InnerHtml += "src=\"svg1.aspx" + querystring + "\" ";
  PollGrid.InnerHtml += "height=\"" + (50*(cntalt+1)) + "\"></embed>";

  message.Text = pname;
}
```

Showing the results, the main task of the Show_Results() function, works basically the same way. First, the function looks up the active poll in the database:

```
void Show_Results() {
  int pid, sum;
  string pname = "";
  OleDbConnection conn = new OleDbConnection(
    "Provider=Microsoft.Jet.OleDb.4.0; Data Source=c:\\inetpub\\db\\svg.mdb");
  conn.Open();
  OleDbCommand comm1 = new OleDbCommand(
    "SELECT id, name FROM poll WHERE status='active'", conn);
  OleDbDataReader reader1 = comm1.ExecuteReader();
```

If such a poll exists, the voting information is retrieved from the `alternative` table; also, the sum of all votes is fetched from the table:

```
if (reader1.Read()) {
  pid = Convert.ToInt32(reader1["id"]);
  pname = (string)reader1["name"];
  reader1.Close();
  OleDbCommand comm2 = new OleDbCommand(
    "SELECT SUM(votes) FROM alternative WHERE poll_id=" + pid, conn);
  OleDbDataReader reader2 = comm2.ExecuteReader();
  reader2.Read();
  sum = Convert.ToInt32(reader2[0]);
  reader2.Close();
  OleDbCommand comm3 = new OleDbCommand(
    "SELECT DISTINCT name, votes FROM alternative WHERE poll_id=" + pid +
    " GROUP BY name, votes", conn);
  OleDbDataReader reader3 = comm3.ExecuteReader();
```

Now it is time to assemble the query string for svg2.aspx. The sum of all votes must be written to the query string, along with the minimum and maximum number of votes and some other information:

```
string querystring = "?pname=" + Server.UrlEncode(pname);
int cntbars = 0;
int maxvote = 0, minvote = 0, currentvote;
while (reader3.Read()) {
  currentvote = Convert.ToInt32(reader3["votes"].ToString());
  if (maxvote == 0) { maxvote = currentvote; minvote = currentvote; }
  if (maxvote < currentvote) { maxvote = currentvote; }
  if (minvote > currentvote) { minvote = currentvote; }
  cntbars++;
  querystring += "&name" + cntbars + "=" +
                 Server.UrlEncode(reader3["name"].ToString());
  querystring += "&votes" + cntbars + "=" +
                 Convert.ToInt32(reader3["votes"].ToString());
}
reader3.Close();
querystring += "&cntbars=" + cntbars;
querystring += "&sum=" + sum;
querystring += "&minvote=" + minvote;
querystring += "&maxvote=" + maxvote;
querystring += "&IE=.svg";
```

Finally, the <embed> element is written to the page:

```
PollGrid.InnerHtml = "<embed type=\"image/svg+xml\" width=\"300\" ";
PollGrid.InnerHtml += "src=\"svg2.aspx" + querystring + "\" ";
PollGrid.InnerHtml += "height=\"" + (115 + 45*cntbars) + "\"></embed>";
```

If, however, no active poll is found, an error message is written to the <asp:Label> element:

```
  } else {
    reader1.Close();
    message.Text = "no poll available!";
  }
  conn.Close();
}
```

The last function on our to-do list is Vote(), in which the vote is counted. The URL parameters alt and id must exist; otherwise, the vote cannot count.

```
void Vote() {
  if (Request.QueryString["alt"] != null && Request.QueryString["id"] != null) {
```

The URL parameters are then saved in local variables as follows:

```
string poll_id = Request.QueryString["id"];
string id = Request.QueryString["alt"];
```

Then the IP and the GUID are checked. Otherwise, a clever person could try to call index.aspx directly using the parameters id and alt.

```
string ip = Request.ServerVariables["REMOTE_ADDR"];
string guid = getGUID();
OleDbConnection conn = new OleDbConnection(
  "Provider=Microsoft.Jet.OleDb.4.0; Data Source=c:\\inetpub\\db\\svg.mdb");
conn.Open();
OleDbCommand comm;
if (ipcheck && idcheck) {
  comm = new OleDbCommand("SELECT * FROM poll, person WHERE (person.ip='" +
                          ip + "' OR person.guid='" + guid +
                          "') AND person.poll_id = poll.id AND poll.id=" +
                          poll_id, conn);
} else if (ipcheck) {
  comm = new OleDbCommand("SELECT * FROM poll, person WHERE (person.ip='" +
                          ip + "') AND person.poll_id = poll.id AND poll.id=" +
                          poll_id, conn);
} else if (idcheck) {
```

```
comm = new OleDbCommand("SELECT * FROM poll, person WHERE (person.guid='" +
                        guid + "') AND person.poll_id = poll.id AND poll.id="
                        + poll_id, conn);
} else {
  // bogus SELECT
  comm = new OleDbCommand("SELECT * FROM poll WHERE status='bogus'", conn);
}
OleDbDataReader reader = comm.ExecuteReader();
```

The last SQL statement, `SELECT * FROM poll WHERE status='bogus'`, will never return a result. It will be executed only when the IP address and the GUID should not be checked; in that case, we can be certain that no entry will be found. If no entry is found, that means the person probably has not voted before on this poll, so his or her vote can count:

```
if (!reader.Read()) {
  reader.Close();
  OleDbCommand comm1 = new OleDbCommand("UPDATE alternative SET votes=votes+1
   WHERE poll_id IN (SELECT id FROM poll WHERE status='active') AND
   id=" + id, conn);
  comm1.ExecuteNonQuery();
  OleDbCommand comm2 = new OleDbCommand("INSERT INTO person
   (ip, [guid], poll_id) VALUES ('" + ip + "', '" + guid + "',
    " + poll_id + ")", conn);
  comm2.ExecuteNonQuery();
} else {
  reader.Close();
}
```

Finally, the connection to the database is closed and the results of the vote are displayed:

```
    conn.Close();
    message.Text = "Thank you for your vote!";
    Show_Results();
  }
}
```

The complete code is shown in Listing 23.6.

LISTING 23.6   index.aspx—The SVG Poll

```
<%@ Page Language="c#" %>
<%@ Import Namespace="System.Data" %>
<%@ Import Namespace="System.Data.OleDb" %>
<%@ Import Namespace="System.IO" %>
<script runat="server">
```

LISTING 23.6   Continued

```
bool ipcheck = false; // whether to check IP
bool idcheck = false; // whether to check GUID from cookie

void Show_Poll(int poll_id) {
  OleDbConnection conn = new OleDbConnection(
    "Provider=Microsoft.Jet.OleDb.4.0; Data Source=c:\\inetpub\\db\\svg.mdb");
  conn.Open();
  OleDbCommand comm1 = new OleDbCommand("SELECT * FROM poll WHERE id=" + poll_id
    + " ORDER BY id", conn);
  OleDbDataReader reader1 = comm1.ExecuteReader();
  reader1.Read();
  string pname = reader1["name"].ToString();
  reader1.Close();
  OleDbCommand comm2 = new OleDbCommand("SELECT * FROM alternative WHERE
    poll_id=" + poll_id + " ORDER BY id", conn);
  OleDbDataReader reader2 = comm2.ExecuteReader();
  string querystring = "";
  int cntalt = 0;
  while (reader2.Read()) {
    cntalt++;
    querystring += "&text" + cntalt + "=" + Server.UrlEncode
      (reader2["name"].ToString());
    querystring += "&id" + cntalt + "=" + reader2["id"];
  }
  reader2.Close();
  conn.Close();
  querystring = "?cntalt=" + cntalt + querystring;
  querystring += "&pid=" + poll_id;
  querystring += "&IE=.svg";

  PollGrid.InnerHtml = "<embed type=\"image/svg+xml\" width=\"300\" ";
  PollGrid.InnerHtml += "src=\"svg1.aspx" + querystring + "\" ";
  PollGrid.InnerHtml += "height=\"" + (50*(cntalt+1)) + "\"></embed>";

  message.Text = pname;
}

void Show_Results() {
  int pid, sum;
  string pname = "";
  OleDbConnection conn = new OleDbConnection(
    "Provider=Microsoft.Jet.OleDb.4.0; Data Source=c:\\inetpub\\db\\svg.mdb");
```

LISTING 23.6 Continued

```
conn.Open();
OleDbCommand comm1 = new OleDbCommand("SELECT id, name FROM poll WHERE
  status='active'", conn);
OleDbDataReader reader1 = comm1.ExecuteReader();
if (reader1.Read()) {
  pid = Convert.ToInt32(reader1["id"]);
  pname = (string)reader1["name"];
  reader1.Close();
  OleDbCommand comm2 = new OleDbCommand("SELECT SUM(votes) FROM alternative
    WHERE poll_id=" + pid, conn);
  OleDbDataReader reader2 = comm2.ExecuteReader();
  reader2.Read();
  sum = Convert.ToInt32(reader2[0]);
  reader2.Close();
  OleDbCommand comm3 = new OleDbCommand("SELECT DISTINCT name, votes FROM
    alternative WHERE poll_id=" + pid + " GROUP BY name, votes", conn);
  OleDbDataReader reader3 = comm3.ExecuteReader();
  string querystring = "?pname=" + Server.UrlEncode(pname);
  int cntbars = 0;
  int maxvote = 0, minvote = 0, currentvote;
  while (reader3.Read()) {
    currentvote = Convert.ToInt32(reader3["votes"].ToString());
    if (maxvote == 0) { maxvote = currentvote; minvote = currentvote; }
    if (maxvote < currentvote) { maxvote = currentvote; }
    if (minvote > currentvote) { minvote = currentvote; }
    cntbars++;
    querystring += "&name" + cntbars + "=" + Server.UrlEncode
      (reader3["name"].ToString());
    querystring += "&votes" + cntbars + "=" + Convert.ToInt32
      (reader3["votes"].ToString());
  }
  reader3.Close();
  querystring += "&cntbars=" + cntbars;
  querystring += "&sum=" + sum;
  querystring += "&minvote=" + minvote;
  querystring += "&maxvote=" + maxvote;
  querystring += "&IE=.svg";
  PollGrid.InnerHtml = "<embed type=\"image/svg+xml\" width=\"300\" ";
  PollGrid.InnerHtml += "src=\"svg2.aspx" + querystring + "\" ";
  PollGrid.InnerHtml += "height=\"" + (115 + 45*cntbars) + "\"></embed>";
} else {
  reader1.Close();
```

LISTING 23.6   Continued

```
    message.Text = "no poll available!";
  }
  conn.Close();
}

void Vote() {
  if (Request.QueryString["alt"]  != null) {
    string poll_id = Request.QueryString["id"];
    string id = Request.QueryString["alt"];
    string ip = Request.ServerVariables["REMOTE_ADDR"];
    string guid = getGUID();
    OleDbConnection conn = new OleDbConnection(
      "Provider=Microsoft.Jet.OleDb.4.0; Data Source=c:\\inetpub\\db\\svg.mdb");
    conn.Open();
    OleDbCommand comm;
    if (ipcheck && idcheck) {
      comm = new OleDbCommand("SELECT * FROM poll, person WHERE
        (person.ip='" + ip + "' OR person.guid='" + guid + "') AND
         person.poll_id = poll.id AND poll.id=" + poll_id, conn);
    } else if (ipcheck) {
      comm = new OleDbCommand("SELECT * FROM poll, person WHERE
        (person.ip='" + ip + "') AND person.poll_id = poll.id AND
         poll.id=" + poll_id, conn);
    } else if (idcheck) {
      comm = new OleDbCommand("SELECT * FROM poll, person WHERE
        (person.guid='" + guid + "') AND person.poll_id = poll.id
         AND poll.id=" + poll_id, conn);
    } else {
      // bogus SELECT
      comm = new OleDbCommand("SELECT * FROM poll WHERE status='bogus'", conn);
    }
    OleDbDataReader reader = comm.ExecuteReader();
    if (!reader.Read()) {
      reader.Close();
      OleDbCommand comm1 = new OleDbCommand("UPDATE alternative SET
        votes=votes+1 WHERE poll_id IN (SELECT id FROM poll WHERE
        status='active') AND
        id=" + id, conn);
      comm1.ExecuteNonQuery();
      OleDbCommand comm2 = new OleDbCommand("INSERT INTO person (ip, [guid],
       poll_id) VALUES ('" + ip + "', '" + guid + "', " + poll_id + ")", conn);
      comm2.ExecuteNonQuery();
```

LISTING 23.6   Continued

```
    } else {
      reader.Close();
    }
    conn.Close();
    message.Text = "Thank you for your vote!";
    Show_Results();
  }
}

string getGUID() {
  string guid;
  if (Request.Cookies["svgGUID"] != null) {
    guid = Request.Cookies["svgGUID"].Value;
  } else {
    guid = Guid.NewGuid().ToString();
    Response.Cookies["svgGUID"].Value = guid;
    Response.Cookies["svgGUID"].Expires = DateTime.Now.AddDays(30);
  }
  return guid;
}

void Page_Load() {
  if (!Page.IsPostBack && Request.QueryString["alt"] == null) {
    string ip = Request.ServerVariables["REMOTE_ADDR"];
    string guid = getGUID();
    OleDbConnection conn = new OleDbConnection(
      "Provider=Microsoft.Jet.OleDb.4.0; Data Source=c:\\inetpub\\db\\svg.mdb");
    conn.Open();
    OleDbCommand comm;
    if (ipcheck && idcheck) {
      comm = new OleDbCommand("SELECT poll.id FROM poll WHERE poll.status=
        'active' AND id NOT IN (SELECT poll_id FROM person, poll WHERE
        person.ip='" + ip + "' OR person.guid='" + guid + "')", conn);
    } else if (ipcheck) {
      comm = new OleDbCommand("SELECT poll.id FROM poll WHERE poll.status=
        'active' AND id NOT IN (SELECT poll_id FROM person, poll WHERE
        person.ip='" + ip + "')", conn);
    } else if (idcheck) {
      comm = new OleDbCommand("SELECT poll.id FROM poll WHERE poll.status=
        'active' AND id NOT IN (SELECT poll_id FROM person, poll WHERE
        person.guid='" + guid + "')", conn);
    } else {
```

LISTING 23.6   Continued

```
      comm = new OleDbCommand("SELECT poll.id FROM poll WHERE poll.status=
        'active'", conn);
    }
    OleDbDataReader reader = comm.ExecuteReader();
    if (reader.Read()) {
      Show_Poll(Convert.ToInt32(reader["id"]));
    } else {
      Show_Results();
    }
    reader.Close();
    conn.Close();
  } else {
    Vote();
  }
}
}
</script>
<html>
<head>
<title>SVG Poll</title>
<link href="poll.css" type="text/css" rel="stylesheet" />
</head>
<body>
<form runat="server">
<p><asp:Label id="message" CssClass="heading" runat="server" /></p>
<div id="PollGrid" runat="server" />
</form>
</body>
</html>
```

Summary

This chapter provided a real-life example showing how you can combine the amazing power of ASP.NET with the amazing possibilities of SVG. Using this example, you can create an online poll that can be administered and generated dynamically, so you do not have to paint the poll statistics individually but can display them live. As with the other case studies, you might want to add some more security features into the application—for example, to check each and every form input for invalid characters.

PART IV

Case Studies

IN THIS PART

Case Study: SVG for Blueprints

The Architectural Engineering Construction industry, or AEC, depends heavily on vector design files. The classic blueprint set, rolled and fastened with a rubber band, is still the primary communication tool at any construction site. Whether up on the high steel or down in the superintendent's trailer, blueprints still rule. Back in the office, CAD software has long since replaced drafting tables, but most of the design files produced with CAD never pass further than the plotter. The Internet has really not affected distribution of engineering designs. This is all about to change with the introduction of XML and especially SVG.

Although there have been a few attempts at defining a vector standard for the Internet prior to SVG, they have generally been proprietary binary formats. SVG, as a self-describing open standard, sanctioned and protected by the W3C, finally brings vectors to the Internet in a format accessible to anyone. No special tools, no reverse engineering, no extensive training required.

SVG is more than a simple static presentation view of vector drawings. As XML, it represents a human-readable grammar with a tree hierarchy rich in relationship information well suited to describing real-world systems. JavaScript/ECMAScript access to the DOM adds a dimension of dynamic interactivity (as you saw in Part II), while server-side linkage opens the wide world of Internet collaboration.

The purpose of this case study is to examine a typical AEC design and explore ways to structure our design in SVG. We will need to look at ways to move our design files from a CAD world into SVG. Then we will explore client-side ECMAScript enhancements that glue our individual SVG files into a cohesive design system. Finally, we will look at a simple server-side enhancement to connect our SVG design to the larger world of databases.

A variety of technologies will be used in this example, including

- CAD-to-SVG translation tools
- ECMAScript customization
- MySQL database
- Java servlets and a JDBC database connection

Some Blueprint Basics

Finding your way around a blueprint may be difficult unless you are familiar with its structure. Blueprints follow an early pattern of linkage, perhaps a primitive paper precursor to the hyperlink. Starting with a plan view, you will find elevation symbols and section cuts. They identify a page number to find the actual elevation or more detailed drawing. Drilling deeper into the design are further links to even more detailed sections. These links are often identified with a bubble showing a page number and the detail number. This pattern of primitive icon linkage maps very well to an Internet scheme. The simple addition of href links to the existing bubble icons reproduces a hyperlinked version of our traditional blueprint pattern.

In addition, designs follow a composition rule with more complex features built up from basic features. For example, a detail may be composed of a variety of fasteners, structural items, extrusions, and caulking. This design also maps very well to XML element hierarchies. As an XML grammar, SVG has a natural expression for grouping graphically represented items into a tree structure. In this way, SVG can be both the presentation grammar and, at a deeper level, a model of object relationships. We will not have a chance to dig into this aspect of SVG, but you should look for hierarchical composition of SVG to play an important role in process and manufacturing automation as XML systems become more sophisticated.

From CAD to SVG

Computer Aided Design (CAD) software started trickling into architectural engineering offices in the early 1980s. By the mid '80s, the trickle had turned into a flood, and by the end of the decade, CAD had overwhelmed every engineering discipline. Out of that disruptive technology wave, one software company emerged to dominate the field, Autodesk. Autodesk's flagship product AutoCAD® has become a *de facto* standard in the industry. One reason AutoCAD became so popular was its early adoption of an open system that encouraged a community of third-party developers. From its very beginning, Autodesk published an open ASCII interchange format called DXF©. This allowed third-party developers, as well as end users, access to the graphic entities of their designs. DXF has been leveraged to provide many innovative design tools over the years, but because it is proprietary and limited, it never evolved much beyond a simple exchange format.

Because nearly all CAD software supports DXF, it is a good place to start in our move from CAD to SVG. Listing 24.1 shows a small section of a DXF ENTITIES section. AutoCAD DXF ENTITIES are roughly equivalent to XML elements and provide details for a variety of graphic objects.

LISTING 24.1   DXF ENTITIES

```
  0
SECTION
  2
ENTITIES
  0
LWPOLYLINE
  5
41
330
2
100
AcDbEntity
  8
3-6a
  6
Continuous
100
AcDbPolyline
 90
        6
 70
      1
 43
0.0
 10
2193.825674600704
 20
1955.287984956111
 10
2182.799701168565
 20
1974.385531143482
 10
  .
  .
```

DXF to SVG Using Java

DXF is an ASCII format that describes a number of AutoCAD-specific entities. It has some complexities that can make a full translator a bigger project than this chapter can cover. However, we can develop a small translator for just a couple of entity types, CIRCLE and LWPOLYLINE. This is a useful subset that will help us activate existing entities when we start connecting SVG to ECMAScript events. Listing 24.2 shows the main class for our sample translator.

LISTING 24.2   DXFtoSVG.java—Main Class for DXFtoSVG Translator

```java
import java.io.*;

public class DXFToSVG {
  static boolean events = true;

  public static void main(String[] args) {
    if (args.length <2) {
      displayUsage();
      System.exit(-1);
    }
    else if (!((new File(args[0])).isFile())) {
      displayUsage();
      System.exit(-1);
    } else {
      if (args[1].toLowerCase().equals("true")) events = true;
      else events = false;
      DxfToSVG(args[0]);
    }
  }

  private static void displayUsage() {
    System.err.println("Usage: DXFtoSVG <DXF file> <add event true/false>");
  }

  private static void DxfToSVG(String Infile) {
    String name = new String(Infile.substring(0,Infile.lastIndexOf('.')));
    String line = "";
    try {
      BufferedReader in = new BufferedReader(new FileReader(Infile));
      PrintWriter out = new PrintWriter(new BufferedWriter
                                   (new FileWriter(name + ".svg")));

      // Output svg head
```

LISTING 24.2   Continued

```
    out.println("<?xml version=\"1.0\" encoding=\"iso-8859-1\"?>");
    out.println("<!DOCTYPE svg PUBLIC \"-//W3C//DTD SVG 1.0//EN\"");
    out.println("\"http://www.w3.org/TR/SVG/DTD/svg10.dtd\">");
    out.println("<svg width='100%' height='100%' ");
    out.print("preserveAspectRatio='xMidYMax'");
    out.println("\txmlns='http://www.w3.org/2000/svg'");
    out.println("\txmlns:xlink='http://www.w3.org/1999/xlink'");
    out.println("\txmlns:aec='http://www.sams.com/2002/aec'>");
    out.println("<title>"+ name +"</title>");
    out.println("<g id='ACTIVE' style='fill:none;stroke:black'>");
    // skip DXF header
    while (((line = in.readLine()) != null) &&
            (!line.equalsIgnoreCase("ENTITIES"))) {
    }
    // read entities section
    while (((line = in.readLine()) != null) &&
            (!line.equalsIgnoreCase("ENDSEC"))) {
      // translate circle entities
      if (line.equalsIgnoreCase("CIRCLE")) {
        Circle c = new Circle();
        c.readDXFCircle(in);
        c.writeSVGCircle(out);
      }
      // translate light weight polyline entities
      else if (line.equalsIgnoreCase("LWPOLYLINE")) {
        LWPolyline lwp = new LWPolyline();
        lwp.readDXFLWPolyline(in);
        lwp.writeSVGLWPolyline(out);
      }
    }

    // Output svg tail
    out.println("</g>");
    out.println("</svg>");

    in.close();
    out.close();
  } catch (IOException e) {
    System.out.println("IO Exception:" + Infile);
  }
  }
}
```

24

The events `true`/`false` toggle allows us to optionally add mouse events to the features we are translating. We have also customized a generic svg element to include a specialized namespace prefix declaration, aec. This will allow us to add our own custom attributes for information we might need to reference in our ECMAScript. Remember that this name-space URL must be unique but does not actually point to any content. You will want to substitute your own URL to guarantee uniqueness. (See Chapter 2, "Document Structure in SVG," for more information on namespaces.) After outputting our specialized svg element, the program skips through the DXF file until it reaches the ENTITIES section. There are numerous possible entities, but we are checking for only two types: circles (CIRCLE) and lightweight polylines (LWPOLYLINES). The real action takes place in the entity classes. Listing 24.3 shows the entity class for translating circles.

LISTING 24.3   Circle.java—CIRCLE Entity Class for DXFtoSVG Translator

```java
import java.io.*;

public class Circle {
  private double x;
  private double y;
  private double r;
  private String layer = "";

  static int id = 0;

  public void readDXFCircle(BufferedReader in) throws IOException  {
    String line;
    // read DF file until next entity
    while ((((line = in.readLine()) != null)&&(!line.equals("  0"))) {
      // pick up layer name
      if (line.equals("  8"))
        this.layer = in.readLine();
      // get center point x value
      else if (line.equals(" 10"))
        this.x= Double.parseDouble(in.readLine());
      // get center point y value
      else if (line.equals(" 20"))
        this.y= Double.parseDouble(in.readLine());
      // get circle radius
      else if (line.equals(" 40")) {
        this.r = Double.parseDouble(in.readLine());
        return;
      }
    }
  }
}
```

LISTING 24.3   Continued

```java
    public void writeSVGCircle(PrintWriter svg) throws IOException {
      svg.print("<circle cx='" + x + "' cy='" + (-y) + "' r='" + r + "'");
      // if the events flag is set add mouse events
      if (DXFToSVG.events) {
        svg.print(" id='CIR" + id++ + "' onmouseover='over(evt)' ");
        svg.print("onmouseout='out(evt)' onclick='click(evt)' ");
        svg.print("style='fill:yellow;fill-opacity:0.25'");        }
      if (!layer.equals("")) svg.print(" aec:page='"+layer+"'");
      svg.println("/>");
    }
}
```

DXF format uses numeric flags to indicate the data type that follows. The DXF 8 flag indicates the next line is a layer name. There are several ways to attach additional information to AutoCAD entities, but the layer name is one of the simplest approaches for DXF. Collecting the layer name following the DXF 8 flag will allow us to add some additional information to our specialized aec namespace attribute. We can use this custom attribute to provide target page information when we start linking a project together. To read the CIRCLE entity, we simply check for the x-value flag, which is 10; the y-value flag, which is 20; and the 40 flag, which indicates that the radius value follows. After we capture the CIRCLE entity values, we can plug them into the SVG output. Note that the y value is inverted. CAD software uses a normal Cartesian plane, while svg uses an inverted Cartesian system with y down. Our DXFtoSVG translator inverts the y coordinate, ensuring that the SVG version of our drawing is not shown upside down.

The only other issue is the events flag, which indicates whether to add some mouse events to our new svg element or leave our circle a static SVG feature. We can use this capability to add ECMAScript functionality to a project.

Listing 24.4 is somewhat more involved showing the LWPolyline class, which is made up of a list of vertices.

LISTING 24.4   LWPolyline.java—LWPolyline Class for DXFtoSVG Translator

```java
import java.io.*;
import java.util.*;

public class LWPolyline {
  private ArrayList pts = new ArrayList();
  private boolean closed = false;
  private String layer = "";

  static int id = 0;
```

LISTING 24.4   Continued

```java
public void readDXFLWPolyline(BufferedReader in) throws IOException  {
  String line;
  Point pt = new Point();
  // read DXF file until next entity
  while (((line = in.readLine()) != null) && (!line.equals("  0"))) {
    // pick up layer name
    if (line.equals("  8"))
      this.layer = in.readLine();
    // check for polyline closure flag
    else if (line.equals(" 70")) {
      line = in.readLine();
      if (line.equals("      1")) closed = true;
      else closed = false;
    }
    // get vertex x value
    else if (line.equals(" 10")) {
      pt = new Point();
      pt.x= Double.parseDouble(in.readLine());
    }
    // get vertex y value
    else if (line.equals(" 20")) {
      pt.y= Double.parseDouble(in.readLine());
      pts.add(pt);
    }
  }
  return;
}

public void writeSVGLWPolyline(PrintWriter svg) {
  Point pt;

  svg.print("<polyline ");
  // if events flag is set add mouse events
  if (DXFToSVG.events) {
    svg.print("id='LWP" + id++ +"' onmouseover='over(evt)' ");
    svg.print("onmouseout='out(evt)' onclick='click(evt)' ");
    svg.print("style='fill:yellow;fill-opacity:0.25'");
  }
  svg.print(" points='");
  // add all the vertices to the points attribute
  Iterator it = pts.iterator();
  while (it.hasNext()) {
```

LISTING 24.4   Continued

```
      pt = (Point)it.next();
      svg.print(pt.x + "," + (-pt.y));
      if (it.hasNext()) svg.print(" ");
    }
    if this DXF polyline is closed add a closing point to the svg polyline
    if (closed) {
      it = pts.iterator();
      pt = (Point)it.next();
      svg.print(" " + pt.x + "," + (-pt.y));
    }
    // add the layer name to our svg element
    if (!layer.equals("")) svg.print("' aec:page='"+layer);
    svg.println("'/>");
  }

  public class Point {
    double x;
    double y;

    Point () {
      x = 0.0;
      y = 0.0;
    }

    public Point(double x, double y) {
      this.x = x;
      this.y = y;
    }
  }
}
```

In addition to collecting the x and y values for each vertex, we check the 70 flag for a value indicating whether this LWPOLYLINE is closed or open. If our LWPOLYLINE is closed, we will need to add one more vertex to our svg polyline, repeating our first point at the end of the point list. Again, we are picking up the DXF layer as a method of adding some specialized information to our features in the aec namespace. We are ignoring any DXF flag 42 bulge factors in this simplified translator, which means any arcs or curved segments in our LWPOLYLINE entities will be flattened.

Our simplified DXFtoSVG translator can read AutoCAD r2000 DXF files and extract circles as well as simple lightweight polylines to a generic SVG file. We also have a custom namespace that we can use for specialized information. We have a command-line option to add mouse events if we want. Chapter 26, "Case Study: FMS—Monitor and Control," will revisit our skeleton DXFtoSVG translator and put it to use. However, for a general-purpose translator, we would need to add classes for all the DXF entity types and account for DXF header information, layer tables, line styles, font styles, images, and recursive blocks. DXF can also get tangled with hatching patterns, hidden dimension blocks, block attributes, and extended entities. Because enhancing our translator to account for all the complexities of DXF is a huge task, it makes sense to use tools available from commercial sources.

Commercial Translation Tools

DXF has been around for almost 20 years, but SVG is still relatively new. This means there are still only a few tools available to choose from. Autodesk, Inc., unfortunately, does not yet support SVG export in any of its products.

Adobe Illustrator 10 allows DXF and DWG import/export as well as SVG export (DWG is the proprietary binary drawing format used by AutoCAD). Adobe has had a lot of experience using AutoCAD files, and its translator is very complete. As the creator of the popular, free SVG Viewer plug-in, Adobe obviously has a lot of expertise in SVG as well. The Adobe Web site (`http://www.adobe.com/products/illustrator/`) provides information on the Illustrator product. However, Adobe Illustrator is a powerful package and might be overkill for simply moving CAD files to SVG. The Adobe orientation is toward graphic design rather than engineering design. As a graphic design tool, Illustrator pays a lot of attention to font and style sheet details but does not always reflect the original AutoCAD structure. The result is a somewhat flattened SVG tree without SVG `<defs>` for AutoCAD block structures. Also, DXF-specific nomenclature is missing, which may make Adobe SVGs seem less familiar to the CAD world.

Some less well-known CAD tools currently support SVG export as well as DXF. One of these tools is CAD 5 by the German company Malz++Kassner (`www.malz-kassner.com`). CAD 5 is a complete 2D CAD tool that recently added SVG export to its features. Because CAD 5 can already import DWG and DXF, it can also become a tool for moving from DXF to SVG. Unfortunately, it flattens the SVG tree, losing some of the structures that are important to AEC. At this early stage, there will likely be rapid evolution of these types of tools.

Another tool for DXF-to-SVG translation is CAD2SVG by Savage Software (`www.savagesoftware.com`). CAD2SVG is a standalone batch-oriented conversion package for translating DWG/DXF to SVG. Savage Software has a good deal of expertise in the DWG format, and this expertise shows in the quality of its SVG output. All the block and layer structures are preserved in the resulting SVG. Savage Software also markets a Web server–oriented package that can serve DWG design files directly to SVG.

In addition to serving DWG as SVG, DataSlinger can be used to dynamically serve SVG with additional customized "manipulator" code. This can extend static SVG by decorating the SVG output stream with custom ECMAScript. DataSlinger provides an early glimpse of the power inherent in SVG for Web services.

NOTE

There is a demo version of DataSlinger available for experimenting with DWG translation.

For this sample project, we will use the output SVG from both CAD2SVG and Adobe Illustrator 10. The concepts covered may be adapted to SVG output from a variety of translation packages.

Translating an AEC Design to SVG

It's now time to get into the main part of our AEC case study. The set of drawings we will use is a subset of a curtain wall design for an Oracle office building. Curtain wall systems are the exterior wall systems found on nearly all high-rise construction since William Le Baron Jenney designed the first steel frame office structure with non–load-bearing walls. Curtain walls are hung from the building's structure and typically consist of extruded aluminum frames filled in with glass, vision or opaque, as well as a variety of panel materials. The particular system we are using in this illustration was designed and manufactured by Elward, Inc., and incorporates an aluminum-clad plastic core panel system called Alucobond™. We will use just a subset of seven AutoCAD drawings from the complete design set: two plan views, pages 1.3a and 3.5a; one elevation view, page 3.6a; and four detail sections, pages 5.1a, 5.2a, 5.4a, and 5.7a. Figure 24.1 shows an AutoCAD view of elevation page 3.6a.dwg.

FIGURE 24.1 The elevation page 3.6a.

We will be working in a project subdirectory called `.\aec` with at least three subdirectories, `.\aec\svg-savage`, `.\aec\js`, and `.\aec\svg-adobe`.

Here is an overview of the steps for turning our individual CAD files into a basic SVG design:

1. Translate the DWG files into SVG using Savage Software CAD2SVG and/or Adobe Illustrator.

2. Create the ECMAScript for navigation.

3. Modify the SVG files with the Apache Xerces DOM parser:

   3a. Add namespace declarations and a `script` element.

   3b. Add ECMAScript events to active elements.

   3c. Add an HTML table for layer control.

4. Add a Java servlet for database queries and updates.

Translating DWG to SVG

Starting with Adobe Illustrator, we can choose Open from the File menu to open the DWG files one at a time. In the DWG/DXF Options dialog box, deselect the Merge Layers options because we will need to preserve the layer structure. Because the DWG position coordinates are not needed, we can leave the Fit option selected. The only other option, Unite Separate Paths, does not affect our project. After the DWG is loaded, we can choose Save As from the File menu, selecting SVG from the Save Type list. At this point, an SVG Options dialog box appears. Select Advanced and leave the CSS Properties set to Presentation Attributes, and the Encoding set to Unicode (UTF-8). All the other selection boxes should be deselected for this project, especially Preserve Illustrator Editing Capabilities. After we click OK to accept changes and close the dialog boxes, our file will be saved in SVG format. Repeating this process for all the DWG files will complete the initial conversion.

If our project were made up of dozens or hundreds of individual DWG files, Savage Software's CAD2SVG translator would make life easier.

This single-minded tool simply translates all the DWG files from a selected subdirectory to SVG. A command line such as the following will convert all the DWG files in the `d:\aec\dwg` subdirectory:

```
D:\CAD2SVGprog.exe -i -d d:\cad2svgconv\lib\ d:\aec\dwg\*.dwg
```

The –i option indicates that background color will be inverted, and the –d option is a path to a set of font libraries.

Figure 24.2 shows design page 3.6a as SVG in a browser window.

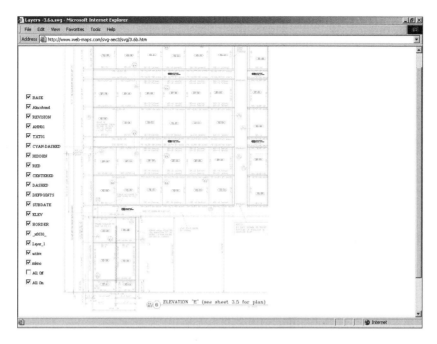

FIGURE 24.2   Elevation 3.6a as SVG.

Although we can now view our design files in an SVG-enabled browser, we will explore some possible enhancements. Our design is more than a series of pages; it encompasses a set of relationships, which we want to reflect in our SVG structure. At the very minimum, we want to navigate through the system with visual links.

Adding ECMAScript Functions

To connect our individual SVG files into a project, we need to add some ECMAScript events. We want to move from one drawing to the next by adding an `onclick` event to the bubble callouts and the elevation icons. We also would like to have some rollover effects to indicate live features. This can all be done with a few functions in an ECMAScript file named aec.js. Because all the pages in our design will be able to use this same code, we will later modify our SVG files to add a `script` element with a reference to this file. Note that we are not using the Adobe SVG Viewer's internal scripting engine in this example (see Chapter 15, "Scripting SVG," for more information on scripting engines). This may cause some difficulty in supporting all possible browsers due to browser compatibility issues. However, it does allow us to reference an enclosing HTML. Cross browser issues will be less of a problem for the AEC community because AutoCAD is available only on the Windows platform.

The ECMAScript file named aec.js is shown in Listing 24.5.

LISTING 24.5   ECMAScript Functions aec.js

```
var detailWin;
var oldstyle;

 // mouse over
function over(evt) {
  var svgstyle = evt.currentTarget.style;
  oldstyle = svgstyle.getPropertyValue('fill');
  svgstyle.setProperty ('fill','red');
}

//mouse out
function out(evt) {
  var svgstyle = evt.currentTarget.style;
  svgstyle.setProperty ('fill',oldstyle);
}


//mouse click
function click(evt) {
  if (evt.button==0) {
    var page = evt.currentTarget.getAttributeNS
              ('http://www.sams.com/2002/SVGUnleashed/ch24/aec','page');
    if ((page=="3.5a")||(page=="3.6a")) {
      window.location.href= page+".svg";
    } else if ((page=="5.1a")||(page=="5.2a")||
              (page=="5.4a")||(page=="5.7a")) {
      if (detailWin!=null) detailWin.close();
      detailWin=window.open(page+".svg","detailWin","width=600,height=600,
➥left=400,top=0,scrollbars=yes,toolbar=yes, location=yes, menubar=yes,
➥ resizable=yes,status=yes");
      detailWin.focus();
    } else {
      alert("Only pages 3.5a, 3.6a, 5.1a, 5.2a, 5.4a, 5.7a are activated");
    }
  }
}
```

Our ECMAScript contains only three functions. The over(evt) function changes the style attribute fill color when our mouse rolls over an active svg element. Here, we first obtain the style attribute of whatever element triggered the event: var svgstyle = evt.currentTarget.style. The next line, oldstyle =

svgstyle.getPropertyValue('fill');, stores our current fill property in a global variable to be used later in the out(evt) function. The last line, svgstyle.setProperty ('fill','red');, changes the current fill property to a more visible red color.

The out(evt) function simply resets our fill property back to its original color.

The click(evt) function is the glue for this project, connecting the various pages for navigation through the design. After verifying the left mouse button has been clicked, this function gets the aec namespace page attribute from the currentTarget. The page value becomes a link deeper into the design. When we actually add active elements to our SVG files, we will be able to navigate through the design. For some of the pages, we just want to change the window.location.href, but for design details, we would like to open a new window. This allows us to see the details in one window while also viewing the plans or elevations. if (detailWin!=null) detailWin.close(); ensures only one detail window at a time will be opened, while detailWin.focus(); forces the detail window to the foreground. Figure 24.3 shows design page 3.6a open in a browser window with a detail page opened in a separate window.

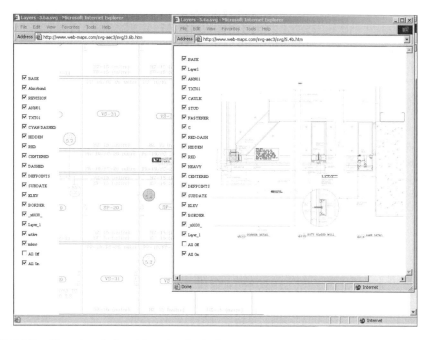

FIGURE 24.3   Elevation 3.6a with a detail window.

Modifying the SVG Files

When we have a set of SVG versions of our DWG files, we can begin adding features. We could make simple modifications to our SVG files in a text editor, but because our files are now XML, we have some powerful tools available for processing them. Xerces is an Apache open-source project providing parser APIs and utilities for working with XML. Xerces-J 2.0 was used for this project and can be obtained from `http://xml.apache.org/xerces2-j/index.html`.

Because Apache Xerces provides parsing and serializing capability, let's start with Listing 24.6 instead of the text editor approach.

LISTING 24.6   ModifyDOM.java—Using Xerces's XMLSerializer

```java
import java.io.*;
import java.util.*;
import org.w3c.dom.*;
import javax.xml.parsers.*;
import org.xml.sax.SAXException;
import org.apache.xml.serialize.XMLSerializer;
import org.apache.xml.serialize.OutputFormat;

public class ModifyDOM {

  public static void main(String[] args) {
    if (args.length == 0) {
      displayUsage();
      System.exit(-1);
    }
    else if (!((new File(args[0])).isFile())) {
      displayUsage();
      System.exit(-1);
    } else {
      SVGOutput(args[0]);
    }
  }

  private static void displayUsage() {
    System.err.println("Usage: ModifyDOM <svg file>");
  }

  private static void SVGOutput(String infile) {
    Document svgdoc;
    Element svgroot;
    Element activeLyr;
    NodeList nl;
    ArrayList layers = new ArrayList();
    String name;
```

LISTING 24.6 Continued

```
    try {
      System.out.println("Translating:" + infile);
      name = infile.substring(0,infile.lastIndexOf(".")-1);
      PrintWriter out = new PrintWriter(new BufferedWriter
        (new FileWriter(name + "b.svg")));

      // setup a parser factory
      DocumentBuilderFactory factory = DocumentBuilderFactory.newInstance();
      factory.setValidating(false);
      factory.setNamespaceAware(true);

      DocumentBuilder builder = factory.newDocumentBuilder();

      // read in our file and parse into a DOM tree
      svgdoc = builder.parse(infile);

      // now output our new DOM using the XMLSerializer
      OutputFormat format = new OutputFormat(svgdoc,"UTF-8",true);
      format.setIndent(1);
      format.setLineWidth(0);
      format.setOmitComments(true);

      XMLSerializer serializer = new XMLSerializer((Writer)out,format);
      serializer.serialize(svgdoc);

      out.close();
      System.out.print(" ... Finished");
    } catch (IOException e) {
      System.out.println("IO Error: " + e.getMessage());
    } catch (SAXException e) {
      System.out.println("SAX Excepion: " + e.getMessage());
    } catch (ParserConfigurationException e) {
      System.out.println("Parser Configuration Exception: " + e.getMessage());
    }
  }
}
```

Here, in our ModifyDOM program, we are simply parsing our SVG into a DOM and then using XMLSerializer to output the DOM to a new file. First, we set up DocumentBuilderFactory and set a few parameters. In this case, we do not need to validate the SVG from our translator. In fact, if we did set validating to true, we would need to modify each of the SVG DOCTYPE declarations with additional internal subset DTD ATTLST declarations for any non-svg namespaces such as xlink. For example, Listing 24.7 shows a modified DOCTYPE declaration that would allow us to turn on validation for SVG files generated by Adobe Illustrator.

LISTING 24.7   DOCTYPE with ATTLST Declarations

```
<!DOCTYPE svg PUBLIC "-//W3C//DTD SVG 1.0//EN"
"http://www.w3.org/TR/SVG/DTD/svg10.dtd"[
<!ATTLIST svg
    a:scriptImplementation CDATA #IMPLIED
    xmlns:a CDATA #IMPLIED
    xmlns:xlink CDATA #IMPLIED
    xmlns:aec CDATA #IMPLIED>
<!ATTLIST script
    a:scriptImplementation CDATA #IMPLIED>
<!ATTLIST circle
    aec:page CDATA #IMPLIED
    xmlns:aec CDATA #IMPLIED>
<!ATTLIST polyline
    aec:page CDATA #IMPLIED
    aec:panel CDATA #IMPLIED
    xmlns:aec CDATA #IMPLIED>
<!ENTITY ns_flows 'http://ns.adobe.com/Flows/1.0/'>
<!ENTITY ns_svg 'http://www.w3.org/2000/svg'>
<!ENTITY ns_xlink 'http://www.w3.org/1999/xlink'>
]>
```

We do want our DOM to be namespace-aware so that later we can add custom namespace attributes, so we set our factory accordingly. When we have a factory, we use it to create a document builder and then parse the SVG file into a DOM:

```
svgdoc = builder.parse(infile);
```

Now that we have a DOM, we can make modifications, but for now we just write a new SVG file with XMLSerializer. We provide an OutputFormat class customizing the indent to 1 and turning off the line width by setting LineWidth to 0. We also omit any comments to simplify our new output. We now have the skeleton of a DOM processor and can begin customizing our SVG files by adding new features.

Adding a script Element and Namespace Declarations

Navigating through the design is handled in our ECMAScript click function shown in Listing 24.5, but we still need to add event listeners to the bubble callouts and the elevation icons. Because the same ECMAScript can be used for several drawings, we will reference an external ECMAScript text file by adding a `script` element to our SVG file right after the `svg` element. We want the `script` element to look like this:

```
<script xlink:href="../js/aec.js" type="text/ecmascript"/>
```

To create this element, we must add the code in Listing 24.8 to our `ModifyDOM` program.

LISTING 24.8   Adding a script Element

```
    .

    .
// read in our file and parse into a DOM tree
svgdoc = builder.parse(fname);
svgroot = svgdoc.getDocumentElement();

// create a new script element
Element element = svgdoc.createElementNS(
                    "http://www.w3.org/2000/svg","script");
element.setAttribute("type","text/ecmascript");
element.setAttributeNS("http://www.w3.org/1999/xlink","href",
                                        "../js/aec.js");
svgroot.insertBefore(element,svgroot.getFirstChild());

    .

    .
```

Our `script` element uses an `xlink:href` namespace, so we must use `createElementNS` to create our `script` element with the correct reference to the `svg` namespace. We add one ordinary attribute indicating the type. Then we add a namespace attribute to our `script` element to reference the external ECMAScript source file, aec.js. The `setAttributeNS` method uses the full namespace URL, `"http://www.w3.org/1999/xlink"`, rather than just the `"xlink"` prefix. We are referencing the aec.js relative to the location of our SVG file. This means we will need to create our subdirectory on the server similar to this:

```
aec-project
  svg
    1.3b.htm
    1.3b.svg
      .

      .

  js
    aec.js
```

Namespaces complicate life a bit, so we must also declare our `xlink` namespace prefix in the enclosing `svg` element. We also add a custom namespace called aec, which will be used later for adding custom attributes to some of our elements. Listing 24.9 shows these additions to our `ModifyDOM` main class.

LISTING 24.9   Namespace Declarations

```
    .
    .
// declare the xlink namespace
svgroot.setAttribute("xmlns:xlink","http://www.w3.org/1999/xlink");
// declare the aec namespace
svgroot.setAttribute("xmlns:aec",
                "http://www.sams.com/2002/SVGUnleashed/ch24/aec");
    .
    .
```

Just as in the previous code for the DXFtoSVG translator, you should specify your own URL for the custom namespace to guarantee unique fully qualified names.

The changes we have made will allow us to view our SVG file in a browser, and although this is "well-formed" SVG, it is not a strictly "valid" SVG file. This is not a problem for our particular project, but in some instances a valid version may be necessary. By adding a `DOCTYPE` declaration with an internal subset DTD, we can turn our well-formed SVG files into valid SVG files, as shown in Listing 24.7. Unfortunately, changing the `DOCTYPE` using Xerces 2.0 requires creating a whole new document with a new `DOCTYPE` and transferring all the elements of our existing DOM to this new document. There is not yet a way to edit existing `DOCTYPE` declarations. Because we do not need validation in this project, we will leave `DOCTYPE` editing as an exercise for you.

Extracting Active Entities

Now we can go back to our SVG file and add some active elements. Creating active elements involves adding ECMAScript events to the elements we want to activate. For example, adding our three functions to an `svg circle` element would look like this:

```
<circle cx='346.69' cy='-426.27' r='39.01' id='CIR1' onmouseover='over(evt)'
onmouseout='out(evt)' onclick='click(evt)'/>
```

We could search through our SVG files looking for elements we want to activate and adding our mouse events manually, but doing so would quickly become tedious. Because our DWG files are from the real world, we do not have the benefit of decreeing a standard process for the designers as they engineer the project. For this project, SVG is a retrofit, and we are forced to add some information after the fact. There are many possible ways to identify features for activation, but the simplest approach is to use the layer structure of our original DWG files. We will look at three different approaches, but they all involve editing the layers of our original design.

Our first approach will activate elements using LAYER identifiers. We go all the way back to our original 1.3a.dwg AutoCAD DWG file. Using the AutoCAD LAYER command, we first create a couple of new layers, named "activate-3.5a" and "activate-3.6a". These layer names have been chosen to identify the target pages for links. Next, we select all the features that need to link to page 3.5a and change them to the layer named "activate-3.5a". We do the same for all the features that link to page 3.6a. We have now added some new information to our design, identifying a target page in the layer name. After we translate this new DWG to SVG, we can utilize our information back in the ModifyDOM program. Listing 24.10 shows the additional code for our main ModifyDOM class.

LISTING 24.10 Activating Elements Using Layer Identifiers

```
    .
    .
    .
ActivateLayer al = new ActivateLayer();
activeLyr = al.activate(svgdoc.getElementById("activate-3.5a"));
// move activated layer to the end of the svg
if (activeLyr!=null) svgroot.appendChild(
    activeLyr.getParentNode().removeChild(activeLyr));

activeLyr = al.activate(svgdoc.getElementById("activate-3.6a"));
// move activated layer to the end of the svg
if (activeLyr!=null) svgroot.appendChild(
    activeLyr.getParentNode().removeChild(activeLyr));
    .
    .
```

Here, we create a new ActivateLayer object called al and then use its activate method to modify the element we give it. We are taking advantage of the new layer information by using getElementById() to quickly find all the elements to modify. This technique can work only because our translators happen to preserve DWG layer structures as group id attributes. As you recall, using Adobe Illustrator, we were careful to turn off the Merge Layer option when opening a DWG file just so that we could use these layer group id attributes. Because CAD2SVG more carefully follows DWG structures in its SVG translation, layers are always provided. After al.activate is done with changes to activeLyr, we move it to the end of our SVG file to make sure that any new event listeners will be on top of the rendering stack. Listing 24.11 shows the details of our ActivateLayer class, which does most of the work.

LISTING 24.11 ActivateLayer.java—ActivateLayer Class (Adobe)

```
import org.w3c.dom.*;

public class ActivateLayer {
```

24

LISTING 24.11   Continued

```
public ActivateLayer() {
}

public Element activate(Element activeLyr) {
  if (activeLyr != null) {
    String id = activeLyr.getAttribute("id");
    String page = id.substring(id.indexOf("-")+1,id.length()-1);
    NodeList nl = activeLyr.getChildNodes();
    for (int i=0;i<nl.getLength();i++) {
      if ((nl.item(i).getNodeType()!=Element.TEXT_NODE) &&
          (nl.item(i).getNodeName().equals("path"))) {
        Element e = (Element)nl.item(i);
        e.setAttribute("onmouseover","over(evt)");
        e.setAttribute("onmouseout","out(evt)");
        e.setAttribute("onclick","click(evt)");
        e.setAttribute("style","fill:yellow;fill-opacity:0.25");
        e.setAttributeNS(
        "http://www.sams.com/2002/SVGUnleashed/ch24/aec","aec:page",page+"b");
      }
    }
  }
  return activeLyr;
}
}
```

If the `activeLyr` element exists, its `id` will be the layer name we assigned in our DWG file. We can clip the page name out of the `id`, which will be added to each activated element as a custom aec namespace page attribute. We loop through the children nodes of our layer looking for `path` elements and then adding all the event listener attributes as well as our `aec:page` attribute. We also make sure the `fill` style property is yellow and has a `fill-opacity:0.25`, which allows elements underneath to show through. We need to be concerned only with `path` elements in this case because Adobe Illustrator happens to change all the DWG `CIRCLE` entities into SVG `path` elements. On the other hand, CAD2SVG more accurately reflects DWG entities and translates DWG `CIRCLE` entities into SVG `ellipse` elements. Neither translator uses the SVG `circle` element. Because we are using both CAD2SVG and Adobe, Listing 24.12 shows the corresponding `ActivateLayer` class for SVG files generated by CAD2SVG.

LISTING 24.12   ActivateLayer.java—ActivateLayer Class (CAD2SVG)

```
import org.w3c.dom.*;

public class ActivateLayer {
```

LISTING 24.12   Continued

```
public ActivateLayer() {
}

public Element activate(Element activeLyr) {
  if (activeLyr != null) {
    String id = activeLyr.getAttribute("id");
    String page = id.substring(id.indexOf("-")+1,id.length()-1);
    NodeList nl = activeLyr.getChildNodes();
    for (int i=0;i<nl.getLength();i++) {
      if ((nl.item(i).getNodeType()!=Element.TEXT_NODE) &&
         (nl.item(i).getNodeName().equals("ellipse"))) {
        Element e = (Element)nl.item(i);
        e.setAttribute("onmouseover","over(evt)");
        e.setAttribute("onmouseout","out(evt)");
        e.setAttribute("onclick","click(evt)");
        e.setAttribute("style","fill:yellow;fill-opacity:0.25");
        e.setAttributeNS("http://www.sams.com/2002/SVGUnleashed/ch24/aec",
➥ "aec:page",page+"b");
      }
      else if ((nl.item(i).getNodeType()!=Element.TEXT_NODE) &&
         (nl.item(i).getNodeName().equals("g"))) {
        Element e = (Element)nl.item(i).getFirstChild().getNextSibling();
        e.setAttribute("onmouseover","over(evt)");
        e.setAttribute("onmouseout","out(evt)");
        e.setAttribute("onclick","click(evt)");
        e.setAttribute("style","fill:yellow;fill-opacity:0.25");
        e.setAttributeNS("http://www.sams.com/2002/SVGUnleashed/ch24/aec",
➥ "aec:page",page+"b");
      }
    }
  }
  return activeLyr;
}
}
```

Using layer names to connect resulting SVG elements to event listeners is one approach. But, what if our design included links to hundreds of parts diagrams and manufacturing drawings? We would then end up with a myriad of layer names, one for each link target.

The next approach will make life simpler for more complex projects. In this method, we will use a relationship between the graphic CIRCLE entity and the page number text found in the DWG bubble icons. Again, we must go back to our original DWG file. This time we open the 3.6a.dwg page in AutoCAD. We create a new layer called `"active"`. Then we change all the bubble icon `CIRCLE` entities and the page reference `TEXT` entities to this new layer. We do not need the bubble divider `LINE` entities or the detail number `TEXT` entities. In fact, changing additional entities will only clutter our `"active"` layer and make sorting out relationships in `ModifyDOM` more complex. After we make our changes, we save the 3.6a.dwg and translate it to SVG. Back to our `ModifyDOM` main class, we add Listing 24.13.

LISTING 24.13   ModifyDOM.java—Adding ActivateLayerByText Class

```
    .
    .
ActivateLayerByText altext = new ActivateLayerByText();
activeLyr = altext.activate(svgdoc.getElementById("active"));
if (activeLyr!=null) svgroot.appendChild(
     activeLyr.getParentNode().removeChild(activeLyr));
    .
    .
```

Here, we use `getElementById()` again to find our new `"active"` layer in the SVG DOM. The actual work is accomplished in our new `ActivateLayerByText` class shown in Listing 24.14.

LISTING 24.14   ActivateLayerByText.java—ActivateLayerByText Class (Adobe)

```
public class ActivateLayerByText {

  public ActivateLayerByText() {
  }

  public Element activate(Element activeLyr) {
    if (activeLyr != null) {
      NodeList nl = activeLyr.getChildNodes();
      for (int i=0;i<nl.getLength();i++) {
        if ((nl.item(i).getNodeType()!=Element.TEXT_NODE) &&
           (nl.item(i).getNodeName().equals("path"))) {
          Element e = (Element)nl.item(i);
          String page = e.getNextSibling().getNextSibling().getFirstChild().
    getFirstChild().getNodeValue();
          e.setAttribute("onmouseover","over(evt)");
          e.setAttribute("onmouseout","out(evt)");
          e.setAttribute("onclick","click(evt)");
          e.setAttribute("style","fill:yellow;fill-opacity:0.25");
          e.setAttributeNS(
          "http://www.sams.com/2002/SVGUnleashed/ch24/aec","aec:page",page+"b");
```

LISTING 24.14 Continued

```
        }
      }
    }
    return activeLyr;
  }
}
```

`ActivateLayerByText` is similar to the previous `ActivateLayer` class. In this class, we are not clipping page information from the layer `id` but looking forward in the DOM to get the `text` element value that follows. If you are wondering about the complex series of `getNextSibling` and `getFirstChild` functions, remember that we did not ignore white-space in our original factory. Consequently, there are additional whitespace `#TEXT` nodes in between the elements we want. We could have filtered out this whitespace by setting up our factory to ignore it, but this setting is checked only if validation is also set to `true`. However, setting validation to `true` requires special editing of the `DOCTYPE` declaration. Even if we make all these changes, the resulting SVG files are not formatted very well. So, for this project, we just live with the extra `getNextSibling` and `getFirstChild` functions required to skip over extra `#TEXT` whitespace. Making two minor changes to this class will allow it to be used for CAD2SVG files. First, we'll change `"path"` to `"ellipse"` and next substitute the following code for capturing the page:

```
String page = e.getNextSibling().getNextSibling().getFirstChild().
➥getNextSibling().getFirstChild().getNodeValue();
```

This method of activating entities is an improvement over the layer approach. However, it depends on the `text` element following the correct `path` or `ellipse` element. This happens to be the case for this DWG file and these translators, but there is no guarantee. It would be nice to force this relationship in the AutoCAD DWG file.

Our third approach uses DWG blocks to guarantee a proximity relationship in the resulting SVG element hierarchy. Again, we open page 3.6a.dwg in the AutoCAD editor and make some changes. First, we create a new layer called `"mkno"`. We also create a new block called `"MkNos"`. This new block consists of an `LWPolyline` entity with a single `Block Attribute` for the mark number text. The elevation page 3.6a has a number of these mark number symbols identifying individual panels and glass units. They have been inserted on layer `"mkno"`. After this edited DWG is saved and translated to SVG, we have a layer group with `id` value `"mkno"`, which contains a series of `path` elements and `text` elements. Because the relationship is bound by the DWG `BLOCK` entity, the resulting SVG is guaranteed to preserve this relationship.

Now that we have these `mknos`, we would like to make use of them in our SVG design. Instead of navigating deeper into the design project, by perhaps linking to the manufacturing drawings for each panel type, we will use our `mknos` to link to a database table. First,

Listing 24.15 shows the `ModifyDOM` additions, and Listing 24.16 shows the `ActivateByMkno` class for activating the `mkno` symbols.

LISTING 24.15   ModifyDOM.java—Using ActivateByMkno

```
   .

   .

ActivateLayerByMkno almkno = new ActivateLayerByMkno();
activeLyr = almkno.activate(svgdoc.getElementById("mkno"));
if (activeLyr!=null) svgroot.appendChild(
     activeLyr.getParentNode().removeChild(activeLyr));

   .

   .
```

LISTING 24.16   ActivateLayerByMkno.java—ActivateByMkno Class (Adobe)

```
import org.w3c.dom.*;

public class ActivateLayerByMkno {

  public ActivateLayerByMkno() {
  }

  public Element activate(Element activeLyr) {
    if (activeLyr != null) {
      NodeList nl = activeLyr.getChildNodes();
      for (int i=0;i<nl.getLength();i++) {
        if ((nl.item(i).getNodeType()!=Element.TEXT_NODE) &&
            (nl.item(i).getNodeName().equals("g"))) {
          Element e = (Element)nl.item(i).getFirstChild().getNextSibling();
          String panel = e.getParentNode().getNextSibling().getNextSibling().
➥getFirstChild().getFirstChild().getNodeValue();
          e.setAttribute("onmouseover","over(evt)");
          e.setAttribute("onmouseout","out(evt)");
          e.setAttribute("onclick","click(evt)");
          e.setAttribute("style","fill:yellow;fill-opacity:0.25");
          e.setAttributeNS(
          "http://www.sams.com/2002/SVGUnleashed/ch24/aec","aec:panel",panel);
        }
      }
    }
    return activeLyr;
  }
}
```

We have changed our namespace attribute to reflect the different purpose of this new activation. The namespace attribute, aec:panel, stores the panel mkno for use in our ECMAScript. Next we go back to our ECMAScript click function in aec.js. We need to edit this function to read the aec:panel attribute value and use it to connect to a server-side database. Listing 24.17 shows these changes.

LISTING 24.17   aec.js—New click Function

```
//mouse click
function click(evt) {
  if (evt.button==0) {
    var page = evt.currentTarget.getAttributeNS
            ('http://www.sams.com/2002/SVGUnleashed/ch24/aec','page');
    if (page!= "") {
        if ((page=="3.5b")||(page=="3.6b")) {
        window.location.href = page + ".htm";
        } else if ((page=="5.1b")||(page=="5.2b")||
                (page=="5.4b")||(page=="5.7b")) {
          if (detailWin!=null) detailWin.close();
          detailWin=window.open(page+".htm","detailWin",
    "width=600,height=600,left=400,top=0,scrollbars=yes,toolbar=yes,
➥location=yes,menubar=yes,resizable=yes,status=yes");
          detailWin.focus();
        }
    }
      else {
        var panel = evt.currentTarget.getAttributeNS
            ('http://www.sams.com/2002/SVGUnleashed/ch24/aec','panel');
      if (dataWin!=null) dataWin.close();
      dataWin=window.open(servlet_path +
"PanelQuery?cmd=query&mkno=" + panel,
"dataWin","width=400,height=500,left=500,top=0,scrollbars=yes,toolbar=yes,
➥location=yes, menubar=yes,resizable=yes,status=yes");
      dataWin.focus();
      }
    }
  }
```

If we click on an mkno symbol, there will be no aec:page attribute, so our function will skip to the panel section. Here, we use getAttributeNS() to pick up a panel value. After we obtain a panel value, our function opens a third window type called dataWin. Instead of opening a new SVG file, however, this window is opened with a URL reference to a server-side Java servlet. This servlet handles the details of connecting to a database table and returning an HTML table showing the query result. In this project, we have used a server with the free MySQL database available. Listing 24.18 shows a SQL dump of a simple MySQL table, which was created just to illustrate linking to a database. A database for an actual project would include much more information on all the parts making up a panel and could, in fact, be created from SVG shop drawings. However, for simplicity, we leave out all those details.

> **NOTE**
>
> You can also see MySQL examples in Chapter 22, "SVG and PHP: Building an Online Survey," and Chapter 25, "Case Study: SVG Web Map for Population Demographics."

LISTING 24.18   panel.sql—MySQL Dump for Sample aec_panel Table

```
CREATE TABLE aec_panels (
  width double NOT NULL default '0',
  height double NOT NULL default '0',
  perimeter double NOT NULL default '0',
  area double NOT NULL default '0',
  R_Ext varchar(10) NOT NULL default '',
  L_Ext varchar(10) NOT NULL default '',
  T_Ext varchar(10) NOT NULL default '',
  B_Ext varchar(10) NOT NULL default '',
  MkNo varchar(10) NOT NULL default '',
  PRIMARY KEY  (MkNo)
) TYPE=MyISAM;


INSERT INTO aec_panels VALUES ('','','','','','','','','SP-18');
INSERT INTO aec_panels VALUES ('','','','','','','','','SP-19');
INSERT INTO aec_panels VALUES ('','','','','','','','','SP-20');
INSERT INTO aec_panels VALUES ('','','','','','','','','SP-21');
INSERT INTO aec_panels VALUES ('','','','','','','','','VS-29');
INSERT INTO aec_panels VALUES ('','','','','','','','','VS-30');
INSERT INTO aec_panels VALUES ('','','','','','','','','VS-31');
INSERT INTO aec_panels VALUES ('','','','','','','','','VS-32');
INSERT INTO aec_panels VALUES ('','','','','','','','','VS-27');
INSERT INTO aec_panels VALUES ('','','','','','','','','VS-28');
INSERT INTO aec_panels VALUES ('','','','','','','','','VS-38');
INSERT INTO aec_panels VALUES ('','','','','','','','','VT-8');
INSERT INTO aec_panels VALUES ('','','','','','','','','VT-14');
```

As you can see, we left most of the fields empty. As we get into our Java servlet, we will see how to update these fields from our activated mkno symbols. The doGet() method of the

Java servlet, shown in Listing 24.19, provides a sample JDBC query with its results returned to the client as an HTML table. Remember, as discussed in Chapter 19, "JSP, Servlets, and SVG," the action in a servlet happens back at the server.

LISTING 24.19   PanelQuery.java—PanelQuery Servlet doGet() Method

```java
/**Process the HTTP Get request*/
public void doGet(HttpServletRequest request, HttpServletResponse response)
                            throws ServletException, IOException {
 //initialize variables
  response.setContentType(CONTENT_TYPE);
  PrintWriter out = response.getWriter();

  String line = "";
  String mkno = "";
  String cmd = "";
  StringBuffer sql;
  String [] values = new String[35];
  HashMap columns = new HashMap();
  ResultSet rs;
  ResultSetMetaData rsmd;

  Enumeration enum  = request.getParameterNames();
  while (enum.hasMoreElements()) {
    String name = (String)enum.nextElement();
    if (name.toLowerCase().equals("mkno")) {
      values = request.getParameterValues(name);
      mkno = values[0];
      columns.put(name,values[0]);
    }
    else if (name.equals("cmd")) {
      values = request.getParameterValues(name);
      cmd = values[0];
    }
    else {
      values = request.getParameterValues(name);
      columns.put(name,values[0]);
    }
  }
  out.println("<HTML>");
  out.println("<HEAD>");
  out.println("    <TITLE>AEC Panel Query</TITLE>");
  out.println("</HEAD>");
  out.println(" <BODY>");
```

24

LISTING 24.19   Continued

```java
    if (mkno.charAt(0)=='V') out.println("<H3>Vision lite</H3>");
    else out.println("<H3>Alucobond Panel</H3>");

    try {
     Statement stmt = con.createStatement();
     if (cmd.equals("query")) {
       sql = new StringBuffer(
           "SELECT * FROM aec_panels WHERE MkNo=\"" + mkno + "\"" );
       if (stmt.execute(sql.toString())) {
         rs = stmt.getResultSet();
         rsmd = rs.getMetaData();
         out.println(
           "<FORM ACTION=\""+SERVLET_PATH+"PanelQuery?
 METHOD=\"POST\" ENCTYPE=\"application/x-www-form-urlencoded\">");
         out.println("<TABLE>");
         while (rs.next()) {
           for (int i = 1; i <= rsmd.getColumnCount(); i++) {
             out.println("<tr><TD WIDTH=\"26%\">" +
                       rsmd.getColumnName(i).toUpperCase() + "</td>");
           out.print("<TD WIDTH=\"74%\"> <INPUT TYPE=\"TEXT\" NAME=\"" +
                       rsmd.getColumnName(i) +"\" SIZE=\"35\" VALUE=\"");
             if (rsmd.getColumnType(i)== Types.INTEGER)
                                       out.print(rs.getInt(i));
             else if (rsmd.getColumnType(i)== Types.VARCHAR)
                                       out.print(rs.getString(i));
             else if (rsmd.getColumnType(i)== Types.CHAR)
                                       out.print(rs.getString(i));
             else if (rsmd.getColumnType(i)== Types.DATE)
                                       out.print(rs.getDate(i));
             else if (rsmd.getColumnType(i)== Types.FLOAT)
                                       out.print(rs.getFloat(i));
             out.println("\"></td></tr>");
           }
         }
         out.println("</TABLE>");
         out.println("<INPUT TYPE='SUBMIT' VALUE='update' NAME='cmd'>");
         out.println(" </FORM>");
       }

     }
     else if (cmd.equals("update")) {
       sql =  new StringBuffer("UPDATE aec_panels SET " );
```

LISTING 24.19   Continued

```java
      //out.println("sql: " + sql.toString());
      int f = 0;
      Object[] fields = columns.keySet().toArray();
      for (int i = 0; i<fields.length;i++) {
        if ((!columns.get(fields[i]).equals("")) &&
                      (!fields[i].equals("MkNo"))) {
          if (f > 0) sql.append(",");
          f++;
          sql.append(fields[i]+"='"+columns.get(fields[i])+"'");
        }
      }
      sql.append(" WHERE MkNo='"+mkno+"';");
      out.println("sql: " + sql.toString());
      stmt.executeUpdate(sql.toString());
      out.println("<H3>Update successful</H3>");
    }
    out.println(" </BODY>");
    out.println("</HTML>");
    stmt.close();
  } catch (SQLException e) {
    out.println("<pre>ERROR:Mysql: " + e.getMessage());
    out.println(e.getSQLState());
    if (e.getSQLState().equals("08S01")) {
      out.println("Connection lost");
    }
    out.println("</pre>");
  } catch (Exception e) {
    throw new UnavailableException("General Access error");
  }
}
```

The complete servlet code is available in the download for this chapter. Just remember to substitute your own server-specific URL, username, and password.

When our click function calls the servlet, our servlet collects the URL-encoded parameters cmd and mkno. The cmd value tells our servlet whether this is a query or an update. The mkno value is the key field in our aec_panel table. Because the cmd is coming from our click function, its value will be "query". The doGet() method builds a SQL statement, executes the statement, and then uses the returned result for building an HTML table. We have modified an ordinary HTML table to be part of a FORM with a SUBMIT button. The form ACTION declaration

```
ACTION=\""+SERVLET_PATH+"PanelQuery?
```

refers back again to our servlet. As a result, the `dataWin` opened in the client browser can be edited with new information and resubmitted to our servlet with the Update button. This button has a value of `"update"` and the name `"cmd"`, which are returned to the servlet in the URL-encoded string. Because our servlet is checking for a parameter named `"cmd"`, it will be assigned a value of `"update"`. The `update` command will then skip our previous query and create a SQL `UPDATE` statement. If the `UPDATE` statement executes successfully, we send an `Update Successful` message back to the HTML window. In this way, `PanelQuery` is connected to our design `mknos` through the ECMAScript `click` function. We can now view the database record for each panel and then edit the fields for updating the panel record.

This is a quick overview of a JDBC query servlet. We will discuss this type of servlet again in more detail in Chapter 25. Figure 24.4 shows our design with a third `PanelQuery` HTML window.

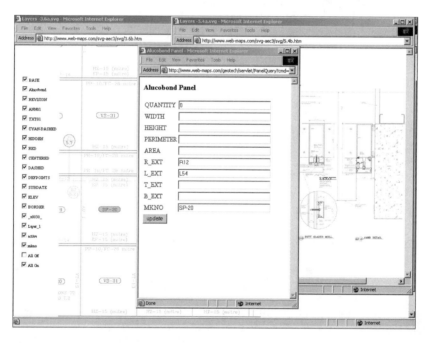

FIGURE 24.4   PanelQuery HTML response.

Adding Layer Control with an HTML Sidebar

We can now navigate through our design, we can look up panels in our database, and we can even update our panel records. We left our `ModifyDOM` program after activating the panel mark number symbols, but we can do more than simply activate elements. One feature that is useful to CAD designers is layer control. It would be nice to add a layer control capability to our Internet SVG design. This can be accomplished for page 1.3a with the HTML file shown in Listing 24.20.

LISTING 24.20   HTML for a Layer Control

```
<?xml version="1.0" encoding="UTF-8"?>
<HTML>
 <head>
  <title>Layers -3.6a.svg</title>
 </head>
 <body onload="init()">
  <script>
   <!--
var layers = new Array(
"BASE",
"Alucobond",
"REVISION",
"ANN01",

    .
    .
    .

"active",
"mkno",
"All Off",
"All On");

function init() {
  for (var i=0;i<layers.length;i++)
    // initialize with all boxes checked except 'All Off'
    window.document.layer_form[i].checked = true;
    window.document.layer_form[layers.length-2].checked = false;
}

function Layerclick(button) {
// function called when a box is clicked
var svgobj;
var svgstyle;
// get the associated svg document
var svgdoc = window.SVGPage.getSVGDocument();
// all on button clicked
if (button=="on") {
    var i;
    // loop through all layers and boxes
```

LISTING 24.20   Continued

```
  for (i=0;i<layers.length;i++) {
    // check the boxes
    window.document.layer_form[i].checked = true;
    // set svg visibility attribute to visible
    svgobj = svgdoc.getElementById(layers[i]);
    if (svgobj!=null){
      svgstyle = svgobj.getStyle();
        svgstyle.setProperty('visibility', 'visible');
    }
  }
  // uncheck the all off box to
  window.document.layer_form[layers.length-2].checked = false;
}
// all off box checked
else if (button=="off") { // all off
  // loop through all layers and boxes
  for (i=0;i<layers.length;i++) {
    // uncheck the boxes
    window.document.layer_form[i].checked = false;
    // set svg visibility attribute to hidden
    svgobj = svgdoc.getElementById(layers[i]);
    if (svgobj!=null){
      svgstyle = svgobj.getStyle();
      svgstyle.setProperty("visibility", "hidden");
    }
  }
  // check the all off box
  window.document.layer_form[layers.length-2].checked = true;
}
// change just the clicked box
else { // change
    // get the associated svg layer group
    svgobj = svgdoc.getElementById(button);
    if (svgobj!=null){
      svgstyle = svgobj.getStyle();
      // toggle visibility depending on current setting
      if (window.document.layer_form[button].checked) {
        svgstyle.setProperty("visibility", "visible");
      } else {
        svgstyle.setProperty("visibility", "hidden");
      }
    }
```

LISTING 24.20   Continued

```
        }
    }
}
\\-->
  </script>

  <table>
   <td>
     <form name="layer_form">
     <table name="layers" style="font-size:10">
      <tr><td>
<input name="BASE" onclick="Layerclick('BASE')" type="checkbox">BASE</input>
        </td></tr>
        <tr><td>
<input name="Alucobond" onclick="Layerclick('Alucobond')" type="checkbox">
  Alucobond
</input>
        </td></tr>
        <tr><td>
<input name="REVISION" onclick="Layerclick('REVISION')" type="checkbox">
REVISION
</input>
        </td></tr>
        <tr><td>
<input name="ANN01" onclick="Layerclick('ANN01')" type="checkbox">
ANN01
</input>
        </td></tr>
     .
     .
     .
      <tr><td>
<input name="active" onclick="Layerclick('active')" type="checkbox">
active
</input>
        </td></tr>
        <tr><td>
<input name="mkno" onclick="Layerclick('mkno')" type="checkbox">
mkno
</input>
        </td></tr>
```

LISTING 24.20   Continued

```
      <tr><td>
<input name="All Off" onclick="Layerclick('off')" type="checkbox">
All Off
</input>
        </td></tr>
        <tr><td>
<input name="All On" onclick="Layerclick('on')" type="checkbox">
All On
</input>
        </td></tr>
      </table>
    </form>
  </td>

  <td>

<object height="776.057" name="SVGPage" type="image/svg+xml" width="516.935">
    <param name="src" value="3.6b.svg"/>
</object>
  </td>

 </table>
 </body>
</HTML>
```

The HTML is made up of some inline ECMAScript and an OBJECT element whose source value is our page 3.6 SVG file. Note that we change our SVG page name from 3.6a to 3.6b whenever we run it through our ModifyDOM program. The ECMAScript will be different for each page because the layers will change. This means it is not very beneficial to reference our script from an external file. Our script starts by setting up an Array variable containing all the layer names. Our first function, init(), is called from the BODY element when our HTML is first loaded. This function loops through all the layer check boxes in the layer_form and sets them to checked before returning to the All Off check box and setting it to checked=false.

The onclick event for each input check box calls the main function in our code, Layerclick(button). This function first obtains the enclosed svgdoc from our OBJECT element:

```
var svgdoc = window.SVGPage.getSVGDocument();
```

If the All On check box triggered our `Layerclick`, the script loops through all the layers setting the HTML check boxes to `checked` and setting the `svgdoc` layer groups to the style property `visibility:visible`. After this loop, it resets the All Off check box to unchecked. Clicking on the All Off check box also loops through the layers but changes the `svgdoc` layer group style property to `visibility:hidden`. Any of the other check boxes toggle the individual layers between `visibility:visible` and `visibility:hidden`. The effect of this script is to allow us to turn layers on and off in our SVG file using ordinary HTML check box input.

This feature is nice, but imagine trying to build each of these HTML files for every SVG page in even a small project. To make this feature feasible, we need to go back to our `ModifyDOM` program and add some new code to create these HTML files for us. Listing 24.21 shows the necessary additions to our main class.

LISTING 24.21   ModifyDOM.java—Revised ModifyDOM with HTML Layer Control (Adobe)

```
     .
     .
     .
PrintWriter htm = new PrintWriter(new BufferedWriter
  (new FileWriter(name + "b.htm")));

//layers for html sidebar
nl = svgroot.getChildNodes();
for (int i=0;i<nl.getLength();i++) {
  if ((nl.item(i).getNodeType()!=Element.TEXT_NODE) &&
      (nl.item(i).getNodeName().equals("g"))) {
    Element e = (Element)nl.item(i);
    layers.add(e.getAttribute("id"));
  }
}
layers.add("All Off");
layers.add("All On");

DOMImplementation dm = builder.getDOMImplementation();
Document newdoc = dm.createDocument(null,"HTML",null);
Element newroot = newdoc.getDocumentElement();

LayerSidebar ls = new LayerSidebar(newdoc,newroot,
    svgroot.getAttribute("width"),svgroot.getAttribute("height"));
newdoc = ls.createLayerSidebar(layers.toArray(), name);

format = new OutputFormat(newdoc,"UTF-8",true);
format.setIndent(1);
format.setLineWidth(0);
```

LISTING 24.21   Continued

```
XMLSerializer htmserializer = new XMLSerializer((Writer)htm,format);
htmserializer.serialize(newdoc);

htm.close();
      .
      .
```

First, we scan through the layer level of our original svgdoc document adding all the g element id attributes to our ArrayList layers. At the end of the ArrayList, we add two more items: "All Off" and "All On". Now that we have a list of all the layers, we need to create a new HTML document. We can use our original builder to get a new DOMImplementation. We then use this DOMImplementation to create a new document, newdoc. We leave the namespace URL null, make the document root element "HTML", and ignore the DOCTYPE with a second null. Now we have a new document and can start filling in the HTML element hierarchy. We actually do this in a separate class named LayerSidebar. After we fill in our root element, we make a new XMLSerializer and write out newdoc to the htm PrintWriter. Listing 24.22 provides the details of filling in our newdoc root.

LISTING 24.22   LayerSidebar.java—LayerSidebar Class (Adobe)

```
import org.w3c.dom.*;

public class LayerSidebar {
  private Document newdoc;
  private Element newroot;
  private String width;
  private String height;

  public LayerSidebar(Document newdoc, Element newroot,
                              String width, String height) {
    this.newdoc = newdoc;
    this.newroot = newroot;
    this.width = width;
    this.height = height;
  }

  public Document createLayerSidebar(Object[] lyrTable, String name) {
    Node head = newdoc.createElement("head");
    Node title = newdoc.createElement("title");
    Text text = newdoc.createTextNode("Layers -" + name + "a.svg");
```

LISTING 24.22 Continued

```
    title.appendChild(text);
    head.appendChild(title);
    newroot.appendChild(head);

    //create an inline javascript
    StringBuffer js = new StringBuffer();
    js.append("\nvar layers = new Array(\n");

      boolean first=true;
      for (int i = 0; i < lyrTable.length; i++) {
        String l = (String)lyrTable[i];
        if (!first) { js.append(",\n"); }
        first = false;
        js.append("\"" + l + "\"");
      }
    js.append(");\n");

    js.append("function init() {\n");
    js.append("  for (var i=0;i<layers.length;i++)\n");
    js.append("    window.document.layer_form[i].checked = true;\n");
    js.append("    window.document.layer_form[layers.length-2].checked
= false;\n");
    js.append("}\n");

    js.append("function Layerclick(button) {\n");
    js.append("var svgobj;\n");
    js.append("var svgstyle;\n");
            .
            .
            .
    js.append("            svgstyle.setProperty(\"visibility\", \"hidden\");\n");
    js.append("        }\n");
    js.append("        }\n");
    js.append("  }\n");
    js.append("}\n\\\\");

    Element script =  newdoc.createElement("script");
    Comment comment = newdoc.createComment(js.toString());
    script.appendChild(comment);
    Element body = newdoc.createElement("body");
    body.setAttribute("onload","init()");
```

LISTING 24.22   Continued

```
body.appendChild(script);

Element table = newdoc.createElement("table");
table.setAttribute("name","layers");
table.setAttribute("style","font-size:10");
for (int i = 0; i < lyrTable.length; i++) {
  String l = (String)lyrTable[i];
  Element tr = newdoc.createElement("tr");
  Element td = newdoc.createElement("td");
  Element input = newdoc.createElement("input");
  input.setAttribute("type","checkbox");
  input.setAttribute("name",l);
  if (l.equals("All On"))
            input.setAttribute("onclick","Layerclick(\"on\")");
  else if (l.equals("All Off"))
            input.setAttribute("onclick","Layerclick(\"off\")");
  else input.setAttribute("onclick","Layerclick(\"" + l +"\")");
  text = newdoc.createTextNode(l);
  input.appendChild(text);
  td.appendChild(input);
  tr.appendChild(td);
  table.appendChild(tr);
}
Element form = newdoc.createElement("form");
form.setAttribute("name","layer_form");
form.appendChild(table);
Element td = newdoc.createElement("td");
td.appendChild(form);
table = newdoc.createElement("table");
table.appendChild(td);

Element param = newdoc.createElement("param");
param.setAttribute("name","src");
param.setAttribute("value",name+"b.svg");
Element object = newdoc.createElement("object");
object.setAttribute("type","image/svg+xml");
object.setAttribute("name","SVGPage");
object.setAttribute("width",width);
object.setAttribute("height",height);
object.appendChild(param);
td = newdoc.createElement("td");
```

LISTING 24.22   Continued

```
    td.appendChild(object);

    table.appendChild(td);
    body.appendChild(table);
    newroot.appendChild(body);

    return newdoc;
  }
}
```

After creating the head and title elements, the createSidebar method builds the
ECMAScript as a comment inside a script element. The script is the same code shown in
Listing 24.19, built with a series of StringBuffer append statements. We can build much
of the table structure with a for loop, but there is still a lot of tedious DOM building.
Fortunately, we need to build it only once, and all our SVG files can benefit.

One last helpful addition to ModifyDOM makes processing a set of files easier. Listing 24.23
adds some code to allow us to process all of the SVG files in a subdirectory.

LISTING 24.23   ModifyDOM.java—Revised for File Sets (Adobe)

```
          .
          .
public static void main(String[] args) {
   if (args.length == 0) {
    displayUsage();
    System.exit(-1);
  }
  else if (!(new File(args[0])).isDirectory()) {
    displayUsage();
    System.exit(-1);
  }
  else {
    String path = args[0];
    File dirPath = new File(path);
    String [] fileLst;
    fileLst = dirPath.list(new DirFilter("a.svg"));
    Arrays.sort(fileLst);
    for (int i=0;i<fileLst.length;i++) {
      SVGOutput(dirPath.getAbsolutePath(),fileLst[i]);
    }
  }
```

LISTING 24.23   Continued

```
}
        .
        .
```

We can now point our ModifyDOM program at a subdirectory and process everything at once like this:

```
java -jar ModifyDOM.jar <path to folders>
```

Uploading to the Server

After we process all our design files using ModifyDOM, we can upload the resulting *b.htm and *b.svg files to the aec-project/svg subdirectory. If the aec.js file has also been copied to the aec-project/js subdirectory, we can point our browser to the first design page, substituting our server URL for localhost:8080, http://localhost:8080/svg/1.3b.htm. Moving through the design simply involves clicking on the detail bubbles or activated polygons.

To view the attributes of our panels, we will also need to upload the PanelQuery servlet to the Web server's servlet subdirectory. This location will vary depending on your server's configuration. Remember that we need to edit server-specific path references in both the aec.js and the PanelQuery.java files, which are noted with comments. The panel.sql file provides a sample MySQL table for populating the aec_panels table with some data. Again, you will need to modify the PanelQuery database connection to work with your particular database.

Using our new tools, we can transfer our CAD design in just a few steps:

1. Edit our CAD files to identify active entities.

   We have outlined three approaches, but many more could be adapted, such as the use of data objects or extended entities.

2. Translate our DWGs to SVGs using CAD2SVG, Adobe, or some other commercial translator.

   CAD2SVG can automate this step with a simple script to translate thousands of DWGs at a time.

3. Run each of the files through our ModifyDOM.

4. Save all the .svg, .htm, and ECMAScript aec.js files to a Web server.

   Apache/Tomcat is a very popular free Web server that can be set up on a local LAN, with an ISP, or on a dedicated Web server. The .svg files can also be gzip-compressed to .svgz format to minimize download times and disk space, but this will require changes to the references in each of the .htm files.

5. Load the .sql table into your Web server's favorite SQL RDBMS.

   MySQL and PostgreSQL are a couple of popular open-source database programs, but any database with a JDBC driver can be used.

6. Open a browser and start using XML/SVG anywhere in the world.

   This project has been developed with the Internet Explorer browser in mind, largely because Windows is the only operating system that will run AutoCAD.

We have now gone through all the steps necessary to turn a CAD design into a Web-enabled SVG design with some simple ECMAScript functionality and database connectivity.

Summary

Much more can be done to transfer CAD designs to SVG. We have opened the door only a small crack to show some ways the power of SVG can be used in the AEC design world. It is easy to see that XML/SVG will affect the AEC design world in a couple of major ways.

First, SVG makes design collaboration and distribution mainstream. The office, field, and shop can all share and use SVG designs from any location worldwide. Version control and updates are instantly available to all project participants. Because the W3C is rapidly proceeding with a new SVG Mobile specification, the client range will soon extend to PDAs, tablets, and even cell phones.

Second, SVG/XML will be adapted to process automation. We have not really touched on this issue for our example, but a whole additional layer of shop fabrication is involved in this type of project. Much of the fabrication is done from shop drawings showing all the specialized manufacturing processes. XML hierarchies, along with the geometry implicit in SVG, can be leveraged into design rules to automate many of these processes. When they are treated as a whole system, changes at any level can easily be connected, reminiscent of database triggers, allowing revisions to propagate back and forth from manufacturing to architectural review and back again. Parametric design systems like this have been around for a while, but never before with an open exchange language, accessible in a simple browser, from anywhere on the planet.

Finally, as a human-readable XML language, SVG is an enabling technology. It pushes technology down the pyramid into the hands of those closer to the problem domains of AEC. Add a bit of SVG to the existing domain expertise of engineers, and the possibilities really are endless.

CHAPTER 25

Case Study: SVG Web Map for Population Demographics

Svg provides a foundation for publishing vector maps over the Internet. SVG Web maps can have very flexible database linkage and a full range of customization, while still remaining accessible to generic browsers over the Internet. The purpose of this case study is to look at the details of a typical Web-mapping application using SVG as the presentation of both map data and database query results. Along the way, we will have a chance to look at several approaches to manipulating SVG templates on the server.

A number of technologies will be used in this example, including

- SVG vector maps
- JavaScript/ECMAScript customization
- MySQL database
- Java servlets
    - JDBC database connection
    - SAX parser template processing
    - DOM parser template processing
    - JDOM API template processing

Some Map Basics

Computer mapping has evolved around the convergence of three technologies: vector drawing, raster images, and databases. SVG directly addresses vector and raster capabilities, but until future standards like XML Query are widely implemented, additional non-XML tools are needed to provide database access. There are several approaches to database access, all requiring some type of server technology for database linkage. CGI, ASP, and PHP can all be used in this capacity. However, this case study will focus on Java solutions, which are portable to a wide spectrum of servers, as well as being highly extensible with an apparently unending stream of APIs.

There are some issues to keep in mind when dealing with maps. First, the amount of map data can be overwhelming. Even though vectors describe lines much more efficiently than raster images, terrestrial features will easily outpace existing bandwidth. Cartographers have developed several approaches to this problem, generally implementing some form of "divide and conquer" to split a map project into many smaller files. A regular tile grid and a hierarchical approach are two common methods of reducing the world to manageable chunks. This case study uses the hierarchical approach to present map data in successive levels of detail, as illustrated in Figure 25.1.

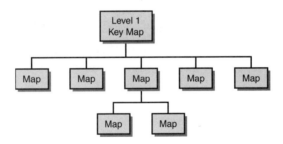

FIGURE 25.1   Map hierarchy.

A second issue that will necessarily come up in almost any Web map application is the coordinate system. Cartographers have developed innumerable ways of projecting the surface of the earth's oblate spheroid onto a 2D plane. Choosing a coordinate system that best represents the required extent of a map application can be complex. With map hierarchies that are potentially worldwide in extent, the easiest coordinate system is simply longitude and latitude, which is used in this example. By convention, western hemisphere longitudes are negative, as are southern hemisphere latitudes. Figure 25.2 shows a simple null-projected, Longitude, Latitude world map. The mathematics of projections is a fascinating field with a long history. Additional information about coordinate system projections can be found at this link: http://mathworld.wolfram.com/topics/MapProjections.html.

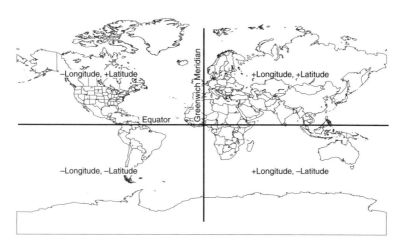

FIGURE 25.2   Longitude, Latitude projection.

Obtaining Map Data

Map data is available by the terabyte. Much of the existing map data is copyrighted material, which requires some form of release or compensation for use. Fortunately, the U.S. government has taken a liberal perspective on data compiled with tax dollars, releasing huge collections of map data to the public without copyright restriction, and at minimal cost. We will take advantage of this for our simple case study utilizing map data as well as demographic data from the U.S. Census Bureau. We will be looking at a county map of Massachusetts and then drilling down to a more detailed census tract map of a single county, Plymouth, MA. Census tracts are just one of several sets of boundary polygons for which the U.S. Census aggregates demographic data. This data, as well as data for any state in the U.S., is freely available from the Census Bureau Web site (`http://www.census.gov`).

Although this data is freely available, it will still need to be converted into the SVG format. At present, map data can be found in dozens of formats with generally widely published specifications. The standard Census Bureau format is TIGER, which stands for Topologically Integrated Geographic Encoded Reference. However, there are sources on the Census Web site for other well-known data formats. The data for this example has been converted to SVG format and made available for download from `http://www.samspublishing.com`.

This project uses .shp format data files from the Census Web site and a SHPtoSVG translator. See the official W3C SVG site (`http://www.w3.org/Graphics/SVG/Overview.htm8`) or the Adobe site (`http://www.adobe.com/svg/tools/3party.html`) for links to numerous conversion tools for legacy data formats. The .SHP or shape format is a popular map format containing graphic elements for points, polylines, and polygons along with attached database attributes. Chapter 24, "Case Study: SVG for Blueprints," discussed some common issues and techniques for SVG translation.

> **NOTE**
>
> At this early stage, translation can be an important issue. Because there are literally thousands of existing graphic formats, you may be faced with finding a translator for the particular data set you want to use. Eventually, SVG, as a nonproprietary open standard with very complete graphics capability will provide a common intermediary or replacement for many of these current formats. In the meantime tools are available for the most common formats such as DXF, PDF, and SHP. Because these formats have a longer history, they can often be used as an intermediary. For our example, the original TIGER census data can be converted to .DXF or .SHP with existing translators and then moved to SVG. Multistep translations are not the ideal, and SVG/XML holds the promise of becoming a universal graphics interchange format, at least for 2D.

Web Map Project Overview

For many Web-mapping applications that use SVG, there is a three-step progression. In the first phase, the required map data is converted to SVG. This process will require an examination of the map structure, the way features will be grouped, and the way events will be tied to particular features. Recall from Chapter 1, "SVG Overview," that SVG specifies a "painter's model" of rendering, with features rendered in the order they occur. This first phase of a Web map project may require consideration of feature order in the final SVG file.

As the project progresses, the natural second phase is the development of custom ECMAScript/JavaScript functions, which are connected to event listeners in the SVG file. ECMAScript/JavaScript affords a great deal of flexibility when developing the user interaction with the map. Some common functions we will include in our Web map are rollover effects, color-change and cursor-following labels, as well as database linkage.

The next distinct phase of development is on the server side. In this phase of our project, Java servlets are developed to access a behind-the-scenes database and produce different views of the Census population data associated with the Web map. The JDBC query results will be displayed with a variety of technologies, starting with the simplest HTML table output and then moving to an SVG bar chart output. The bar chart will utilize a simple SVG template processed with several alternative XML technologies, including

- Java text strings
- SAX `ContentHandler`
- DOM editing
- JDOM

Our sample project will deal with a single smaller state and a single county. This is a representative subset of a larger project, which illustrates some common SVG mapping approaches without becoming overwhelmed by the data. A complete project would likely have a three-level hierarchy starting at the U.S., then linking to individual states, and finally to individual counties within a state. The resulting project would have a single U.S. key map, with 50 state SVG files on level two, and several thousand county SVG files on level three. Also, keep in mind that saving our files as compressed .svgz will save space on the server and, more importantly, bandwidth for slower Internet connections.

Massachusetts Key Map: Level One

For our simplified project, the first map to consider is the root map (or key map) for the project, shown in Figure 25.3. This will be the top level in our simple two-step hierarchy. In this project, we have converted the Census TIGER county map for Massachusetts into a set of SVG closed paths, as shown in Figure 25.3.

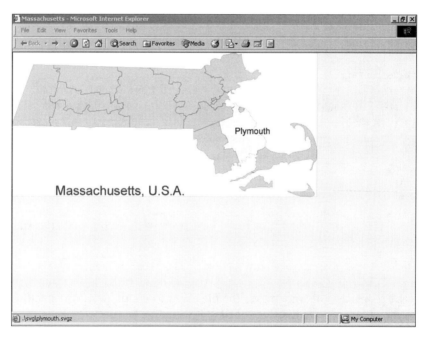

FIGURE 25.3   Massachusetts county key map.

The corresponding SVG for the Massachusetts key map is shown in Listing 25.1.

LISTING 25.1   ma.svg—Massachusetts SVG

```
<?xml version="1.0" encoding="UTF-8"?>
<!DOCTYPE svg PUBLIC "-//W3C//DTD SVG 1.0//EN"
```

LISTING 25.1   Continued

```
                "http://www.w3.org/TR/SVG/DTD/svg10.dtd" [
<!ENTITY MA  "stroke:blue;stroke-width:0.0001;fill:blue;fill-opacity:0.15">
<!ENTITY Hilite  "stroke:red;stroke-width:0.0001;fill:red;fill-opacity:0.15">
<!ENTITY BOUNDARY   "stroke:magenta;stroke-width:0.0001;fill:none;">
<!ENTITY TEXT   "stroke:black;stroke-width:0.0001;fill:blue;font-size:0.15;">
]>
<svg width="600" height="276.3"  preserveAspectRatio="xMinYMin"
  viewBox="-73.508142 -42.886589 3.579881 1.648625" onload="on_load(evt)"
  xmlns="http://www.w3.org/2000/svg"
  xmlns:xlink="http://www.w3.org/1999/xlink">
<title>Massachusetts</title>
<text x="-73.0" y="-41.25" style="&TEXT;">Massachusetts, U.S.A.</text>

<g id="canvas" onmousemove="DoOnMouseMove(evt)">
<polyline style="&BOUNDARY;"
  points="-73.508142,-42.886589 -69.928261,-42.886589 -69.928261,-41.237964
          -73.508142,-41.237964 -73.508142,-42.886589 "/>

  <g id="Massachusetts">
<path id="Essex" style="&MA;" onmouseover="over(evt)" onmouseout="out(evt)"
 d="M-70.914899,-42.886589 L-70.914886,-42.886564 L-70.902768,-42.88653
L-70.886136,-42.88261  L-70.8837340828846,-42.88122235515428 L-70.848625,
-42.8609370.82420578217194,-42.87108033804639 L-70.821769,-42.87188
L-70.817296,-42.87229 L-70.81729906081927,-42.87213747269107
.
.
```

Here, we have included the style properties in the DOCTYPE as an internal DTD subset
rather than referencing an external CSS file:

```
<!ENTITY MA  "stroke:blue;stroke-width:0.0001;fill:blue;fill-opacity:0.15">
```

Including the properties this way makes the file easier to maintain in this small project. In
a large project with repetitive map sets or tiles, it would be beneficial to keep the style
sheet separate and reference it with each similar SVG map. Refer to Chapter 4, "Using CSS
with SVG," for more details on internal and external style sheets.

The svg element attributes include a width and height, which are scaled to match the
ratio of map extents. This information will allow us to later calculate screen position for
ECMAScript/JavaScript labels. Our Massachusetts key map has been left in the native
TIGER coordinate system using decimal longitude for x values and decimal latitude for y
values. The horizontal extent of 3.579881 degrees longitude corresponds to the pixel

width of 600, while the vertical dimension 1.648625 degrees latitude determines the ratio for the height of 276.3 pixels. The `preserveAspectRatio` is explicitly set to the upper-left corner, `xMinYMin`, again to allow coordinate calculations for ECMAScript/JavaScript labels:

```
<svg width="600" height="276.3"  preserveAspectRatio="xMinYMin"
  viewBox=" -73.508142 -42.886589 3.579881 1.648625" onload="on_load(evt)"
  xmlns=http://www.w3.org/2000/svg
  xmlns:xlink="http://www.w3.org/1999/xlink">
```

One important detail that affects map conversion is the origin of SVG coordinates. The SVG specification follows programmer conventions, using the upper-left corner as the origin. This means that positive x values will act as expected, increasing to the right. However, positive y values will increase toward the bottom of the screen. The effect is to invert map coordinates around the x-axis. At first, it might seem appropriate to handle correction of this map inversion inside the `svg` element by applying a simple `transform=` `"scale(1,-1)"`. This type of transform will correct the map orientation, but unfortunately it will also invert any text in the map. If you want to avoid lengthy transform corrections on every text feature, it is easiest to take the external approach and invert all the y values on translation. In our Massachusetts example, the longitude values are negative because Massachusetts is in the western hemisphere, but the latitude values are negative because we want to correct the map orientation in SVG coordinates.

The purpose of the `viewBox` attribute is to map our world coordinates onto screen coordinates:

```
viewBox="-73.508142 -42.886589 3.579881 1.648625"
```

Finally, we add an event listener to the `svg` element, `onload="on_load(evt)"`. This is standard practice for calling an ECMAScript/JavaScript setup function at the initial `svg` load. We will look at this in more detail when examining the ECMAScript/JavaScript code.

The `title` and `text` elements are standard `svg` format. They are followed by a `g` grouping with an associated event listener for mouse movements:

```
<g id="canvas" onmousemove="DoOnMouseMove(evt)">
```

Here, we are adding a `g` element to hold the entire set of map features and collect mouse movement events that will be used in the ECMAScript/JavaScript. In our Massachusetts map, we are not interested in collecting mouse move events anywhere outside the defined county paths. However, in some cases it is necessary to collect these events even outside map features; an example might be a floating toolbar. We would then need to use the boundary `polyline` as the event boundary. However, by default, events will be triggered only on filled surfaces, which means the `polyline` style would need to be changed from `fill:none` to some color such as `fill:white`. If the boundary is offensive, its visibility can be controlled by setting its `style` attribute property to `opacity:0` or `visibility:hidden`.

Within the canvas, we add another g element for all of Massachusetts and then start adding county path elements. Each county has its own unique id as well as mouse event listeners. The absolute Moveto, M, and absolute Lineto, L, prefixes to the path element's d attribute have been explicitly included by the translation. The TIGER translator also furnished a closing coordinate on each path, so the Z closure prefix is not needed. Note that events will be associated only with the stroke or bounding line of our closed paths unless we have set a fill to something other than none. In this case, we set the style fill with a color and a fill-opacity that would allow any underlying features to remain visible. If a color is distracting, we can set the fill-opacity to 0, but we still need some fill to grab events as our cursor moves across the inside of our path.

There is one added twist with Suffolk, Norfolk, and Duke counties. Each of these counties is disjoint, that is, made up of more than one polygon. They could have been handled within a single path element's d attribute using Moveto (M) prefixes for jumping to additional external boundaries, but in this case the translator has grouped the separate polygonal features into a <g> feature and attached the id attribute value and event listeners to this enclosing group:

```
<g id="Norfolk" style="&MA;" onmouseover="over(evt)" onmouseout="out(evt)">
  <path d="M-71.2611,-42.326796 L-71.259348,-42 . . . L-71.123087,-42.35155"/>
  <path d="M-70.824660,-42.265934 . . . L-70.82466085670549,-42.265934676602"/>
</g>
```

We can now use this group for events associated with both of the distinct polygons making up Norfolk.

Referring to Figure 25.3, you can see that Plymouth has the additional distinction of being the only active link in our key map:

```
<a xlink:href="plymouth.svgz" target="blank">
  <path id="Plymouth" style="&Hilite;" onmouseover="over(evt)"
   onmouseout="out(evt)" d="M-70.90630201246992,-42.27163620517878
       .
       .
  L-70.90630201246992,-42.27163620517878"/>
</a>
```

Here, we have made a direct hyperlink to the next level of the map hierarchy. Because we use a target="blank", a new window creation is forced. Refer to Chapter 2, "Document Structure in SVG," for more information on linking.

At the next level of the map hierarchy, we will see another approach to linking, but first let's look at the ECMAScript/JavaScript used to make this key map interact with the user. Our script will add two rollover effects, cursor labels, and fill color changes.

Following the example of the style sheet, we will include the ECMAScript/JavaScript in our Massachusetts SVG to make it more compact. Again, in more complex map projects, it would be better to reference the ECMAScript/JavaScript externally from each of the presumably numerous map tiles. We will see this second approach in our next map of Plymouth County. However, for Massachusetts, the ECMAScript/JavaScript is included as CDATA shown in Listing 25.2.

LISTING 25.2   ma.svg—Massachusetts ECMAScript/JavaScript

```
<script language="JavaScript"><![CDATA[
  var label = "";
  var style;
  var offset = 0.05;

  // must be calculated from viewbox to w x h
  var x0 = 0;
  var y0 = 0;
  var vboxW = 0;
  var vboxH = 0;
  var svgW = 0;
  var svgH = 0;

  function on_load(e){
    svgdoc = evt.target.getOwnerDocument();
    svgroot = svgdoc.getDocumentElement();

    //initialize cursor parameters
    var vbox = (svgroot.getAttribute("viewBox")).split(' ');
    x0 = parseFloat(vbox[0]);
    y0 = parseFloat(vbox[1]);
    vboxW = parseFloat(vbox[2]);
    vboxH = parseFloat(vbox[3]);
    svgW = parseFloat(svgroot.getAttribute("width"));
    svgH = parseFloat(svgroot.getAttribute("height"));

    // initialize label text
    var data = svgdoc.createTextNode("");
    var text = svgdoc.createElement("text");
    text.setAttribute("transform","translate("+ x0 + "," + y0 + ")");
    text.setAttribute("style",
"stroke:black;stroke-width:0.001;fill:black;font-size:0.1;font-family:arial;");
    text.setAttribute("id", "label");
    text.appendChild(data);
```

25

LISTING 25.2   Continued

```
    svgroot.appendChild(text);
  }

  function DoOnMouseMove(e) {
    var X = x0 + (e.clientX - svgroot.currentTranslate.x)*
                                (vboxW/(svgW*svgroot.currentScale));
    var Y = y0 - offset + (e.clientY - svgroot.currentTranslate.y)*
                                (vboxH/(svgH*svgroot.currentScale));
    label = svgdoc.getElementById("label");
    label.setAttribute("transform","translate("+ X + "," + Y + ")");
  }

  // mouse_over
  function over(e) {
    target = e.currentTarget;
    var id = target.id;
    if (id!="") {
      //rollover label on
      label = svgdoc.getElementById("label");
      label.firstChild.setData(id);
      var svgstyle = e.currentTarget.style;
      style = svgstyle.getPropertyValue('fill');
      svgstyle.setProperty ('fill','yellow');
    }
  }

  //mouse_out
  function out(e) {
    //rollover label off
    var label = svgdoc.getElementById("label");
    label.firstChild.setData(" ");
    var svgstyle = e.currentTarget.style;
    svgstyle.setProperty('fill',style);
  }
]]></script>
```

The on_load function is called when the document is loaded. It is used to initialize cursor parameters and create an additional label text element:

```
function on_load(e){
  svgdoc = evt.target.getOwnerDocument();
  svgroot = svgdoc.getDocumentElement();
```

After getting the document and the root, we can start initializing the origin and other parameters, which are used to track the cursor. These parameters are obtained by splitting the viewBox attribute. Note that we are assuming a space separator, which may not always be the case:

```
//initialize cursor parameters
var vbox = (svgroot.getAttribute("viewBox")).split(' ');
x0 = parseFloat(vbox[0]);
y0 = parseFloat(vbox[1]);
vboxW = parseFloat(vbox[2]);
vboxH = parseFloat(vbox[3]);
svgW = parseFloat(svgroot.getAttribute("width"));
svgH = parseFloat(svgroot.getAttribute("height"));
```

A blank text node is initialized at the origin. We will position the text with a transform attribute instead of x and y, making position changes a bit easier later:

```
    // initialize label text
    var data = svgdoc.createTextNode("");
    var text = svgdoc.createElement("text");
    text.setAttribute("transform","translate("+ x0 + "," + y0 + ")");
    text.setAttribute("style",
"stroke:black;stroke-width:0.001;fill:black;font-size:0.1;font-family:arial;");
    text.setAttribute("id", "label");
    text.appendChild(data);
    svgroot.appendChild(text);
```

The mouse movement event was associated with the canvas group in our SVG map, which includes all the features in the map. Because SVG allows zooming and panning, we need to keep track of the currentScale and currentTranslate transforms to properly calculate positions in the map. This calculation will work only as long as the svg element is explicitly positioned at the origin. Future SVG viewing tools may provide better methods for obtaining X,Y positions even when there is no prior knowledge of svg width and height, as in the case of percentage dimensions, width="100%" and height="100%". The offset value will position the text slightly away from the cursor. If this offset is not provided, whenever the cursor is over the text feature, it will be blocked from the mouseover event, resulting in a continuously blinking text label. Alternatively, we could handle this situation by adding a style property pointer-events:none to the label text element:

```
function DoOnMouseMove(e) {
  var X = x0 + (e.clientX - svgroot.currentTranslate.x)*
                              (vboxW/(svgW*svgroot.currentScale));
  var Y = y0 - offset + (e.clientY - svgroot.currentTranslate.y)*
                              (vboxH/(svgH*svgroot.currentScale));
```

25

Finally, we can look up our label by its id and change its position by setting a new translation transform. This moves our label text to follow the cursor position:

```
label =  svgdoc.getElementById("label");
label.setAttribute("transform","translate("+ X + "," + Y + ")");
```

The mouseover event is triggered the first time our cursor enters an associated path feature. We use this event to add text to our label:

```
// mouse_over
function over(e) {
```

First, we find the id attribute of the feature triggering the event:

```
// mouse_over
function over(e) {
  target = e.currentTarget;
  var id = target.id;
```

If there is an id, we use it as the new label text:

```
if (id!="") {
  //rollover label on
  label =  svgdoc.getElementById("label");
  label.firstChild.setData(id);
```

In addition to setting the label text, we also change the fill color as a rollover hint. We first save the current fill color in a variable to use later when we restore the original color:

```
var svgstyle = e.currentTarget.style;
style = svgstyle.getPropertyValue('fill');
svgstyle.setProperty ('fill','yellow');
```

The mouseout event occurs whenever our cursor leaves the associated path feature:

```
//mouse_out
function out(e) {
  //rollover label off
```

First, we turn off the label by setting the text to blank:

```
var label =  svgdoc.getElementById("label");
label.firstChild.setData("");
```

Next, we change the fill color back to its original color:

```
var svgstyle = e.currentTarget.style;
svgstyle.setProperty('fill',style);
```

We've now completed the top level of our Web map. We have set up a county map of Massachusetts with cursor-following county labels and a single `href` link to the more detailed second level, Plymouth County.

Plymouth County Map: Level Two

The next level of the hierarchy moves to Plymouth County and the Census tract polygons shown in Figure 25.4.

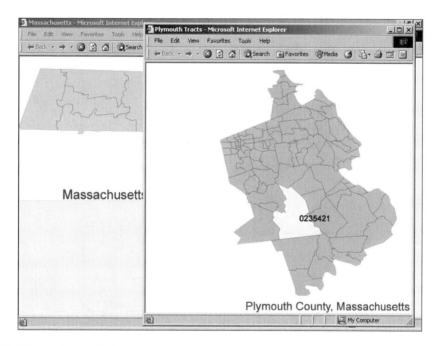

FIGURE 25.4   Plymouth County Census tracts.

The associated SVG for Plymouth County Census tracts is shown in Listing 25.3.

LISTING 25.3   plymouth.svg—Plymouth Census Tracts SVG

```
<?xml version="1.0" encoding="UTF-8"?>
<!DOCTYPE svg PUBLIC "-//W3C//DTD SVG 1.0//EN"
            "http://www.w3.org/TR/SVG/DTD/svg10.dtd" [
<!ENTITY Plymouth
            "stroke:purple;stroke-width:0.0001;fill:purple;fill-opacity:0.25">
<!ENTITY BOUNDARY  "stroke:magenta;stroke-width:0.0001;fill:none;">
<!ENTITY TEXT   "stroke:black;stroke-width:0.0001;fill:blue;font-size:0.035;">
]>
```

LISTING 25.3   Continued

```
<svg width="700" height="700"  preserveAspectRatio="xMinYMin"
  viewBox="-71.25 -42.35 1 1" onload="on_load(evt)"
  xmlns="http://www.w3.org/2000/svg"
  xmlns:xlink="http://www.w3.org/1999/xlink">
<script type="text/javascript" xlink:href="../js/map.js"/>
<title>Plymouth Tracts</title>
<text transform="translate(-71.0,-41.58)" style="&TEXT;">
  Plymouth County, Massachusetts
</text>
<g id="canvas" onmousemove="DoOnMouseMove(evt)">
<g id="Plymouth">
<path id="0235001.01" style="&Plymouth;"
onmouseover="over(evt)" onmouseout="out(evt)" onclick="click(evt)"
d="M-70.89612186423385,-42.28728004812354
L-70.89603267844453,-42.28861783885205 L-70.89577810704088,-42.29243642100662
L-70.89621068473353,-42.29353753284876 L-70.89712319627394,-42.29586030001939
L-70.91558769004943,. . . .

L-70.89612186423385,-42.28728004812354"/>
<path id="0235001.02" style="&Plymouth;"
onmouseover="over(evt)" onmouseout="out(evt)" onclick="click(evt)"
d="M-70.876004,-42.29277 . . .
   .

   .
<path id="0235601" style="&Plymouth;"
onmouseover="over(evt)" onmouseout="out(evt)" onclick="click(evt)"
d="M-70.803848,-41.705399 L-70.808424,-41.69148 . . . L-70.803848,-41.705399"/>
</g><!-- Plymouth -->
</g><!-- canvas -->
</svg>
```

The structure of plymouth.svg is virtually identical to the top-level Massachusetts map. Adjustments have been made to the svg width, height, and viewBox attributes to accommodate the difference in size and location. An additional event listener is also attached to each polygon, onclick="click(evt)". The only other difference is moving the ECMAScript/JavaScript to an external file with this line:

```
<script type="text/ecmascript" xlink:href="../js/map.js"/>
```

The map.js ECMAScript/JavaScript is also very similar to the internal Massachusetts ECMAScript/JavaScript, with the addition of one more function that checks for events from the left mouse button. This additional click function is shown in Listing 25.4.

LISTING 25.4   map.js—The click Function

```
//mouse click
function click(e) {
  if (e.getButton()==0) {
    if (dataWin!=null) dataWin.close();
    if (e.getShiftKey()==1) {
    dataWin=window.open(servlet_path+"dataQuery1?table="+
      e.currentTarget.parentNode.id + "&id=" + e.currentTarget.id +
      "&chart=false", "dataWindow",
       "width=400, height=300, left=500, top=0, scrollbars=yes, toolbar=yes,
➥location=yes, menubar=yes, resizable=yes, status=yes");
    }
    else {
    dataWin=window.open(servlet_path+"dataQuery1?table="+
      e.currentTarget.parentNode.id + "&id=" + e.currentTarget.id +
      "&chart=true", "dataWindow",
       "width=400, height=300, left=500, top=0,scrollbars=yes, toolbar=yes,
➥ location=yes, menubar=yes, resizable=yes, status=yes");
    }
    dataWin.focus();
  }
}
```

This new `click` function will check mouse click events for the left mouse button, `e.getButton()==0`. If the query window is already opened, it is first closed in preparation for a new window and then a call is made to a servlet. The servlet in this case has three URL-encoded parameters, that is, parameters added to the URL address of the servlet:

- The `table` parameter provides the enclosing `<g>` parent `id` to identify the table for a database access. In this case, the table is `Plymouth`.

- The `id` parameter provides the current feature `id` as the database record `id`.

- The `chart` parameter is a toggle for returning a population bar chart.

`e.getShiftKey()==1` indicates that a Shift key is being pressed. Holding the Shift key while clicking the left mouse button triggers a `window.open` to a servlet with a `chart` parameter set to `false`. A single left-click will call the same servlet with `chart` set to `true`.

> **NOTE**
>
> Due to internationalization issues, the key events currently implemented in the Adobe SVG Viewer will be changed in DOM Level 3 and SVG 1.1 to text events. Consequently, the use of key events in our ECMAScript/JavaScript will need to be revised at some point.

We've now completed the SVG and ECMAScript/JavaScript portion of the Web map application. It's time to switch over to the server side. We will first look at a servlet that returns a simple HTML query result and then move to four different approaches to producing a bar chart from our database.

Server-Side Processing

Many options are available for server-side processing, but we will explore several approaches using basic Java servlets. We will first illustrate a simple HTML query result using JDBC in our servlet to connect to a MySQL database. Recall from Chapter 22, "SVG and PHP: Building an Online Survey," that MySQL was used with PHP and Perl, but here we connect using the Java JDBC API. We will then enhance our query result with an alternative SVG bar chart display. Because we can choose from several methods of handling XML, we will illustrate four common ways of customizing the SVG chart template with the results of our database query.

Servlet 1: Database Access—Query Database and Return HTML Table

First, we need to set up a database on the server. Any SQL database will do, but our project uses MySQL as a freely available example (http://www.mysql.org/). Again, this population data was taken from the U.S. Census Bureau Web site. Census population figures are available for several levels of detail: city, county, tract, block group, and block in progressively finer grain. For this case study, we've chosen to use the tract-level polygons. Numerous additional population figures are available, including age, income, race, and gender. In this example, we pulled a limited subset of age and gender. There are more than 100 population categories to choose from, but we will arbitrarily limit the example to just 12 categories. First, we create a simple flat table in our MySQL database on the server with two Integer fields per record plus a primary key id field. Listing 25.5 shows the SQL CREATE TABLE command to set up this table.

LISTING 25.5   Plymouth-tracts.sql—SQL CREATE TABLE Statement

```
CREATE TABLE Plymouth (
total int(8),
totalMale int(8),
totalFemale int(8),
under18 int(8),
under18Male int(8),
under18Female int(8),
adult int(8),
adultMale int(8),
adultFemale int(8),
over65 int(8),
over65Male int(8),
```

LISTING 25.5 Continued

```
over65Female int(8),
ID varchar(12) DEFAULT '' NOT NULL,
PRIMARY KEY (ID) );
```

We then populate the records one per tract polygon and use a combination of county FIPS code, 023, and census tract number as our unique record id. FIPS stands for Federal Index Processing System and identifies unique numeric codes for common U.S. governmental entities. If this application were expanded to the entire U.S., we would have to add the State FIPS code, 25 for Massachusetts, to guarantee a unique id—for example, 250235001.01.

```
INSERT INTO Plymouth VALUES
('4259','2080','2179','1022','537','485','2762','1324','1438','475','219',
'256','0235001.01');
    .
    .
    .
INSERT INTO Plymouth VALUES
('5123','2461','2662','1285','667','618','2931','1402','1529','907','392',
'515','0235611');
```

After a database table is set up, we are ready to start looking at Java servlet options. The first servlet connects to the new database table and, using the SVG path id, looks up the corresponding table record. The dataQuery1 servlet, shown in Listing 25.6, is normal servlet code setting up the JDBC connection and using the doGet method for catching parameters and responding to the client. Here, we return ordinary HTML to the client browser, so we need to set the CONTENT TYPE=text/html.

LISTING 25.6 dataQuery1.java—Java Servlet for Data Query

```
import javax.servlet.*;
import javax.servlet.http.*;
import java.io.*;
import java.util.*;
import java.sql.*;

public class dataQuery1 extends HttpServlet  {
  private static final String CONTENT_TYPE = "text/html";
  private Connection con = null;
  //Note: set this to the file path for your server
  public static final String FILE_PATH = "/home/httpd/html/svgtest/svg/";
```

25

LISTING 25.6   Continued

```
/**Initialize global variables*/
public void init(ServletConfig config) throws ServletException {
  super.init(config);
  try {
    // Load the MYSQL MM driver
    Class.forName("org.gjt.mm.mysql.Driver").newInstance();

    //establish connection to database
// Note: this will need to be edited to your system database name, user,
// and password
    con = DriverManager.getConnection("jdbc:mysql://localhost/sams","user",
        "password");
  }
  catch (ClassNotFoundException e) {
    throw new UnavailableException("Couldn't load database driver");
  }
  catch (SQLException e) {
    throw new UnavailableException("Couldn't get db connection");
  }
  catch (IllegalAccessException e) {
    throw new UnavailableException("Illegal access");
  }
  catch (Exception e) {
    throw new UnavailableException("General Access error");
  }
}

/**Process the HTTP Get request*/
public void doGet(HttpServletRequest request, HttpServletResponse response)
                                    throws ServletException, IOException {
  response.setContentType(CONTENT_TYPE);
  PrintWriter out = response.getWriter();


  //initialize variables
  String table = "";
  String id = "";
  String sql = "";
  boolean chart = false;
```

LISTING 25.6   Continued

```java
    String [] values = new String[10];

    //collect parameters
    Enumeration enum  = request.getParameterNames();
    while (enum.hasMoreElements()) {
      String name = (String) enum.nextElement();
      if (name.equals("table")) {
        values = request.getParameterValues(name);
        table = values[0];
      }
      else if (name.equals("id")){
        values = request.getParameterValues(name);
        id =  values[0];
      }
      else if (name.equals("chart")){
        values = request.getParameterValues(name);
        chart =  values[0].equals("true");
      }
    }
    // setup the HtmlTable
    HtmlTable1 outTable = new HtmlTable1(con,table,id);
    //return HtmlTable to the client
    outTable.write(response.getWriter());
  }

  /**Process the HTTP Post request*/
  public void doPost(HttpServletRequest request, HttpServletResponse response)
                                      throws ServletException, IOException {
    doGet(request,response);
  }

  /**Clean up resources*/
  public void destroy() {
    // Clean up.
    try {
      if (con != null) con.close();
    }
    catch (SQLException ignored) { };
  }
```

The more interesting work goes on in the `HtmlTable` class. Here, the JDBC connection, created in the servlet initialization, is used with the table name and `id` string to query our Plymouth table. Remember that the table name and `id` are passed from our SVG map as parameters in the ECMAScript/JavaScript `click` function:

```
import java.io.*;
import java.util.*;
import java.sql.*;


public class HtmlTable {
  private Connection con = null;
  private String table;
  private String id;


  public HtmlTable(Connection con, String table, String id) {
    this.con = con;
    this.table = table;
    this.id = id;
  }
```

The `HtmlTable.write` method uses the servlet response `PrintWriter` to send our response back to the client as `text/html`:

```
public void write(PrintWriter out) {
  String sql = "";
```

First, we send the HTML header information, which will allow us to write any errors that might occur as legible HTML code:

```
out.println("<html>");
out.println("<head>");
out.println("<title>Data Query</title>");
out.println("</head>");
out.println(" <body>");
if ((table!=null) && (id!=null)) {
  out.println("<h3>Query - " + table + "</h3>");
  try {
```

Next, we attempt to set up and execute the query using the table name and `id`:

```
Statement stmt = con.createStatement();
sql = "SELECT * FROM " + table + " WHERE id=\"" + id + "\";";
if (stmt.execute(sql)) {
```

If the `sql` statement executes and a result set is returned, we can use the first, and only, record to populate our HTML table:

```
// There is a ResultSet
ResultSet rs = stmt.getResultSet();
ResultSetMetaData rsmd = rs.getMetaData();
```

The Java JDBC `ResultSetMetaData` is handy for looping through all the fields and then providing a field label and field type. In our database, we have used only `VarChar` and `Int` fields, as you can see here, but the JDBC API has a full complement of type accessors:

```
      out.println("<table>");
      while (rs.next()) {
        for (int i = 1; i <= rsmd.getColumnCount(); i++) {
out.println("<tr><td width=\"26%\">" + rsmd.getColumnName(i) + "</td>");
out.print("<td width=\"74%\"> <input type=\"text\" size=\"25\" value=\"");
          switch (rsmd.getColumnType(i)) {
            case Types.INTEGER: out.print(rs.getInt(i)); break;
            case Types.VARCHAR: out.print(rs.getString(i)); break;
            case Types.TIMESTAMP: out.print(rs.getTimestamp(i)); break;
            case Types.CHAR: out.print(rs.getString(i)); break;
            case Types.DATE: out.print(rs.getDate(i)); break;
            case Types.FLOAT: out.print(rs.getFloat(i)); break;
          }
          out.println("\"></td></tr>");
        }
      }
      rs.close();
      out.println("</table>");
    } else {
```

If errors occur, we can still print a meaningful message in HTML:

```
        out.println("<p>" + table + " has no record for Id =" + id + "</p>");
        }
        stmt.close();
      } catch (SQLException e) {
        out.println("<h1>ERROR:MySQL</h1>" + e.getMessage());
      }
    } else {
      out.println("<p>Error: the Table or Id Parameter is null</p>");
    }
    out.println(" </body>");
    out.println(" </html>");
  }
}
```

25

However, if everything works correctly, the result of a query will appear in its own HTML window, as shown in Figure 25.5.

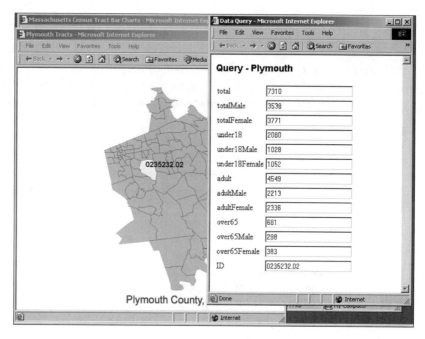

FIGURE 25.5   HTML table result of query.

Servlet 2: Database query2—Return SVG Bar Chart or HTML Table

Now we want to extend our database query servlet to return either an HTML table or a bar chart. First, we modify the dataQuery servlet slightly to branch on the results of the chart parameter sent from the ECMAScript/JavaScript click function. Here, we set the ContentType according to the type of response. An image/svg+xml MIME type is required for SVG output, whereas a text/html type is required for the HtmlTable.

.

.

```
if (chart) {
  response.setContentType("image/svg+xml");
  SvgChart2 outChart = new SvgChart2(con,table,id);
  outChart.write(response.getWriter());
} else {
  response.setContentType("text/html");
  HtmlTable2 outTable = new HtmlTable2(con,table,id);
  outTable.write(response.getWriter());
```

```
    }
.
.
```

> **CAUTION**
>
> Important: It is also necessary to add this image/svg+xml MIME type to your Web server configuration. If your server is the Apache Jakarta Tomcat, you accomplish this by creating an additional MIME type record in the \tomcat\conf\web.xml configuration file. There should also be a record for the .svgz extension, which is the gzipped version of svg used to compress file sizes and reduce bandwidth load. When you add the necessary information, remember that you need to restart Tomcat before the new settings take effect.

Listing 25.7 shows a sample <mime-mapping> record.

LISTING 25.7   Sample <mime-mapping> Record

```
<mime-mapping>
  <extension>
    svg
  </extension>
  <mime-type>
    image/svg+xml
  </mime-type>
</mime-mapping>
<mime-mapping>
  <extension>
    svgz
  </extension>
  <mime-type>
    image/svg+xml
  </mime-type>
</mime-mapping>
```

If the `chart` parameter is `true`, which will be the case when we simply click a census tract polygon, we will create a bar chart. If we hold down the Shift key while clicking with our mouse, our `chart` parameter will be `false` and the previous HTML table will be returned.

Let's look at the `SvgChart2` class in this iteration. This class will be similar to the `HtmlTable` class except for the `SvgChart.write` method. In this version, the bar chart SVG is created by reading a previously created chart.svg file, stored on the server. `Text` content and `rect` attributes are modified to reflect the database fields from our query. This "template" approach allows us to create the chart visually with any SVG editing tool and verify its appearance manually before feeding it through the servlet. Listing 25.8 is the chart template.

LISTING 25.8   chart.svg—The Chart Template

```
<?xml version="1.0" standalone="no"?>
<!DOCTYPE svg PUBLIC "-//W3C//DTD SVG 1.0//EN"
                    "http://www.w3.org/TR/SVG/DTD/svg10.dtd" [
<!ENTITY AXIS  "stroke:black;stroke-width:1;stroke-linejoin:round;fill:none;">
<!ENTITY LABEL "stroke:black;stroke-width:0.01;fill:black;font-size:5;">
<!ENTITY TITLE "stroke:black;stroke-width:0.01;fill:blue;font-size:6;">
<!ENTITY BAR
"stroke:black;stroke-width:0.001;fill:black;fill-opacity:0.5;font-size:3.5;">
<!ENTITY TIC "stroke:black;stroke-width:0.1;fill:black;font-size:3.0;">
]>
<svg width="100%" height="100%"  preserveAspectRatio="xMidYMid"
     viewBox=" 0 0 120 130">
<text id="title" style="&TITLE;" x="25" y="10">Plymouth</text>
<g id="axis" style="&AXIS;">
<path d="M14.5,10 14.5,110.5 125,110.5"/>
<g id="test" style="&TIC;">
<line x1="12" y1="10" x2="15" y2="10"/>
<text x="3" y="10">100%</text>
<line x1="12" y1="35" x2="15" y2="35"/>
<text x="3" y="35">75%</text>
<line x1="12" y1="60" x2="15" y2="60"/>
<text x="3" y="60">50%</text>
<line x1="12" y1="85" x2="15" y2="85"/>
<text x="3" y="85">25%</text>
</g>
<text style="&LABEL;" x="-5" y="90" transform="rotate(-90,-5,90)">
  Population %
</text>
<text style="&LABEL;" x="25" y="117">Total</text>
<text style="&LABEL;" x="65" y="117">Male</text>
<text style="&LABEL;" x="100" y="117">Female</text>
</g>

<g id="totals">
<text id="totalTxt" style="&LABEL;" x="25" y="125">total</text>
<text id="totalMaleTxt" style="&LABEL;" x="65" y="125">totalMale</text>
<text id="totalFemaleTxt" style="&LABEL;" x="100" y="125">totalFemale</text>
</g>
<g id="total" style="&BAR;">
<rect id="under18" x="25" y="110" width="10" height="30" style="fill:green"
 transform="rotate(180,25,110)"/>
<text x="20" y="108" transform="rotate(-90,20,108)">under 18</text>
```

LISTING 25.8   Continued

```
<rect id="adult" x="35" y="110" width="10" height="50" style="fill:red"
 transform="rotate(180,35,110)"/>
<text x="30" y="108" transform="rotate(-90,30,108)">18 to 65</text>
<rect id="over65" x="45" y="110" width="10" height="20" style="fill:blue"
 transform="rotate(180,45,110)"/>
<text x="40" y="108" transform="rotate(-90,40,108)">over 65</text>
</g>

<g id="male" style="&BAR;">
<rect id="under18Male" x="65" y="110" width="10" height="30"
  style="fill:green" transform= "rotate(180,65,110)"/>
<text x="60" y="108" transform="rotate(-90,60,108)">under 18</text>
<rect id="adultMale" x="75" y="110" width="10" height="50"
  style="fill:red" transform="rotate(180,75,110)"/>
<text x="70" y="108" transform="rotate(-90,70,108)">18 to 65</text>
<rect id="over65Male" x="85" y="110" width="10" height="20"
  style="fill:blue" transform="rotate(180,85,110)"/>
<text x="80" y="108" transform="rotate(-90,80,108)">over 65</text>
</g>

<g id="female" style="&BAR;">
<rect id="under18Female" x="105" y="110" width="10" height="30"
  style="fill:green" transform="rotate(180,105,110)"/>
<text x="100" y="108" transform="rotate(-90,100,108)">under 18</text>
<rect id="adultFemale" x="115" y="110" width="10" height="50"
  style="fill:red" transform="rotate(180,115,110)"/>
<text x="110" y="108" transform="rotate(-90,110,108)">18 to 65</text>
<rect id="over65Female" x="125" y="110" width="10" height="20"
  style="fill:blue" transform="rotate(180,125,110)"/>
<text x="120" y="108" transform="rotate(-90,120,108)">over 65</text>
</g>

</svg>
```

The only thing to note on this chart template is the liberal use of id attributes, which will make editing our template easier. The <rect> shapes have been positioned with a transform to minimize the number of edits required in the servlet processing. By rotating the rectangle 180 degrees, we can position all the rectangles on the bottom axis of our chart. Only a modification of the height attribute will be required with this approach. Again, we are taking into account the inverted Cartesian plane of the SVG specification. Listing 25.9 shows the SvgChart2 class.

LISTING 25.9   SvgChart2.java—Processing XML as Strings

```
import java.io.*;
import java.util.*;
import java.sql.*;

public class SvgChart2 {
  private Connection con = null;
  private String table;
  private String id;


  public SvgChart2(Connection con, String table, String id) {
    this.con = con;
    this.table = table;
    this.id = id;
  }

  public void write(PrintWriter out) {
    String sql = "";
    int total;
    String line;
    StringBuffer buf;

    if ((table!=null) && (id!=null)) {
      try {
        Statement stmt = con.createStatement();
        sql = "SELECT * FROM " + table + " WHERE id=\"" + id + "\";";

        if (stmt.execute(sql)) {
          // There is a ResultSet
          ResultSet rs = stmt.getResultSet();
          // There is only one record
          if (rs.next()) {
            total = rs.getInt("total");
            BufferedReader infile = new BufferedReader(
                      new FileReader(dataQuery2.FILE_PATH+"chart.svg"));

            while (((line = infile.readLine()) != null)) {
              if (line.startsWith("<text id=\"title\"")) {
                buf = new StringBuffer(line.substring(0,line.indexOf(">")+1));
                buf = buf.append(table + " tract: " + id);
                line = buf.append(
```

LISTING 25.9 Continued

```
                          line.substring(line.indexOf("</"))).toString();
      }
      else if (line.startsWith("<text id=\"totalTxt\"")) {
        buf = new StringBuffer(line.substring(0,line.indexOf(">")+1));
        buf = buf.append("Total: " + total);
        line = buf.append(
                          line.substring(line.indexOf("</"))).toString();
      }
      else if (line.startsWith("<text id=\"totalMaleTxt\"")) {
        buf = new StringBuffer(line.substring(0,line.indexOf(">")+1));
        buf = buf.append(Integer.toString(rs.getInt("totalMale")));
        line = buf.append(
                          line.substring(line.indexOf("</"))).toString();
      }
      else if (line.startsWith("<text id=\"totalFemaleTxt\"")) {
        buf = new StringBuffer(line.substring(0,line.indexOf(">")+1));
        buf = buf.append(Integer.toString(rs.getInt("totalFemale")));
      line = buf.append(
                          line.substring(line.indexOf("</"))).toString();
      }

      if (line.startsWith("<rect id=\"under18\"")) {
        buf = new StringBuffer(
                          line.substring(0,line.indexOf("height=")+8));
        buf = buf.append(
                   Double.toString(rs.getInt("under18")*100.0/total));
        line = buf.append(
                line.substring(line.indexOf("\" style="))).toString();
      }
      else if (line.startsWith("<rect id=\"adult\"")) {
        buf = new StringBuffer(
                          line.substring(0,line.indexOf("height=")+8));
        buf = buf.append(
                     Double.toString(rs.getInt("adult")*100.0/total));
        line = buf.append(
                line.substring(line.indexOf("\" style="))).toString();
       }
      else if (line.startsWith("<rect id=\"over65\"")) {
        buf = new StringBuffer(
                          line.substring(0,line.indexOf("height=")+8));
        buf = buf.append(
```

LISTING 25.9   Continued

```java
                                Double.toString(rs.getInt("over65")*100.0/total));
        line = buf.append(
                    line.substring(line.indexOf("\" style="))).toString();
    }
    if (line.startsWith("<rect id=\"under18Male\"")) {
        buf = new StringBuffer(
                        line.substring(0,line.indexOf("height=")+8));
        buf = buf.append(
                    Double.toString(rs.getInt("under18Male")*100.0/total));
        line = buf.append(
                    line.substring(line.indexOf("\" style="))).toString();
    }
    else if (line.startsWith("<rect id=\"adultMale\"")) {
        buf = new StringBuffer(
                        line.substring(0,line.indexOf("height=")+8));
        buf = buf.append(
                        Double.toString(rs.getInt("adultMale")*100.0/total));
        line = buf.append(
                    line.substring(line.indexOf("\" style="))).toString();
    }
    else if (line.startsWith("<rect id=\"over65Male\"")) {
        buf = new StringBuffer(
                        line.substring(0,line.indexOf("height=")+8));
        buf = buf.append(
                    Double.toString(rs.getInt("over65Male")*100.0/total));
        line = buf.append(
                    line.substring(line.indexOf("\" style="))).toString();
    }

    if (line.startsWith("<rect id=\"under18Female\"")) {
        buf = new StringBuffer(
                        line.substring(0,line.indexOf("height=")+8));
        buf = buf.append(
                Double.toString(rs.getInt("under18Female")*100.0/total));
        line = buf.append(
                    line.substring(line.indexOf("\" style="))).toString();
    }
    else if (line.startsWith("<rect id=\"adultFemale\"")) {
        buf = new StringBuffer(
                        line.substring(0,line.indexOf("height=")+8));
        buf = buf.append(
                Double.toString(rs.getInt("adultFemale")*100.0/total));
```

LISTING 25.9   Continued

```
                  line = buf.append(
                          line.substring(line.indexOf("\" style="))).toString();
              }
              else if (line.startsWith("<rect id=\"over65Female\"")) {
                buf = new StringBuffer(
                                line.substring(0,line.indexOf("height=")+8));
                buf = buf.append(
                        Double.toString(rs.getInt("over65Female")*100.0/total));
                line = buf.append(
                          line.substring(line.indexOf("\" style="))).toString();
              }
                out.println(line);

              } //while
              infile.close();
            }
            rs.close();
          } else {
            out.println("<text style=\"&LABEL;\" x=\"25\" y=\"125\">" + table
                              + " has no record for Id =" + id+"</text></svg>");
          }
          stmt.close();
        } catch (SQLException e) {
          out.println("<text style=\"&LABEL;\" x=\"25\" y=\"125\">ERROR:Mysql  "
                                      + e.getMessage()+"</text></svg>");
        } catch (IOException e) {
         out.println(
                 "<text style=\"&LABEL;\" x=\"25\" y=\"125\">IO ERROR:Infile  "
                                      + e.getMessage()+"</text></svg>");
        }
      } else {
        out.println("<text style=\"&LABEL;\" x=\"25\" y=\"125\">
➥Error: table or id parameter is null</text></svg>");
      }
    }
```

Again, we are using our JDBC connection and obtaining a result set from the same SQL statement, `"SELECT * FROM " + table + " WHERE id=" + id;"`. However, instead of populating a table of HTML tags, we are creating SVG output. Creating all the features from scratch could be quite tedious, especially if our template SVG is quite large. In this example, we read a premade template, chart.svg, and just modify the parts that change from one record to the next. Even with this very small chart.svg template, this approach leads to a significant number of repetitious `else if` clauses.

Figure 25.6 shows the output of the SvgChart.

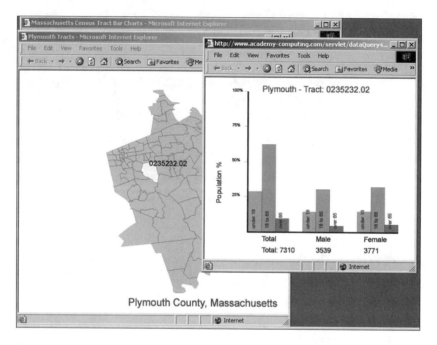

FIGURE 25.6   SVG bar chart of query result.

Servlet 3: Database query3—Return SVG Bar Chart Using a SAX Parser ContentHandler

As we saw in servlet 2, modifying a template with text filters can be tedious even with a simple template. Let's explore some other possibilities. First, we want to look at using a SAX parser to read our template and modify the output with a `ContentHandler`.

> **NOTE**
>
> SAX stands for Simple API for XML and is an event-based approach to XML processing, which reads the XML serially without building a DOM in memory.

Several popular parsers are available, but we have chosen to use the Xerces parser available from Apache (`http://xml.apache.org/`). Listing 25.10 shows the main class, `DataQuery3`, which sets up the SAX parsing if `chart` is `true`.

LISTING 25.10 dataQuery3.java—Java Servlet Using SAX Parser

.

.

```java
    if (chart) {
      response.setContentType("image/svg+xml");
      PrintWriter out = response.getWriter();

        // setup SAX Parser with result set
        SVGContentHandler svgHandler =
                            new SVGContentHandler(out, con, table, id);

        try {
          String template =  FILE_PATH+"/chart.svg";

          XMLReader reader =
    XMLReaderFactory.createXMLReader("org.apache.xerces.parsers.SAXParser");
          ContentHandler svg = new SVGContentHandler(out, con, table, id);
          ErrorHandler svgError = new SVGErrorHandler(out);
          //Register the SVG contentHandler
          reader.setContentHandler(svg);

          //Register the SVG ErrorHandler
          reader.setErrorHandler(svgError);

          //Set validation only if interested
          //reader.setFeature("http://xml.org/sax/features/validation",true);

          //Parse SVG to client browser
          InputSource inputSource = new InputSource(template);
          reader.parse(inputSource);

          out.flush();
        } catch (IOException e) {
          out.println("IO Error: " + e.getMessage());
        } catch (SAXException e) {
          out.println("SAX Exception: " + e.getMessage());
        }
    } else {
      response.setContentType("text/html");
      HtmlTable3 outTable = new HtmlTable3(con,table,id);
      outTable.write(response.getWriter());
    }
```

.

.

25

Here, we are using the `XMLReaderFactory` to set up our SAX parser from the `Xerces.jar` for this project. After we have a parser and begin to parse our template, the action moves to the `SVGContentHandler`, shown in Listing 25.11.

LISTING 25.11   SVGContentHandler.java —SAX ContentHandler for DataQuery3

```java
import java.io.*;
import org.xml.sax.*;
import org.xml.sax.helpers.DefaultHandler;
import java.sql.*;

public class SVGContentHandler extends DefaultHandler {
  private PrintWriter out;
  private Connection con = null;
  private String table;
  private String id;

  private ResultSet rs;
  private boolean results;
  private boolean skipTxt = false;
  private int total;

  public SVGContentHandler(PrintWriter out, Connection con,
                                        String table, String id) {
    this.out = out;
    this.con = con;
    this.table = table;
    this.id = id;

    String sql = "";

      // Collect query results
      try {
        Statement stmt = con.createStatement();
        sql = "SELECT * FROM " + table + " WHERE id=\"" + id + "\";";
        //out.println(sql);
        if (stmt.execute(sql)) {
          // There is a ResultSet
          rs = stmt.getResultSet();

          if (rs.next()) {
            results = true;
            total = rs.getInt("total");
```

LISTING 25.11 Continued

```
        }
        stmt.close();
      }
    } catch (SQLException e) {
      out.println("MySQL Error: " + e.getMessage());
    }
}

public void processingInstruction(String target, String data)
                                          throws SAXException {
  out.println(target+data);
}

public void startElement(String namespaceURI, String localName,
                   String rawName, Attributes atts) throws SAXException {
    try {
      out.print("<"+localName);
      for (int i=0; i<atts.getLength(); i++) {
        if (results && (localName.equals("rect") &&
            atts.getLocalName(i).equals("height"))) {
          out.print(" "+atts.getLocalName(i)+"=\""+
                  (rs.getInt(atts.getValue("id"))*100.0/total)+"\"");
        }
        else out.print(" "+atts.getLocalName(i)+"=\""+atts.getValue(i)+"\"");
      }
      out.print(">");
      if (results) {
        if (localName.equals("text") &&
              atts.getValue("id")!=null &&
               atts.getValue("id").equals("title")){
          out.print(table + " - Tract: " + id);
          skipTxt = true;
        }
        else if (localName.equals("text") &&
              atts.getValue("id")!=null &&
               atts.getValue("id").equals("totalTxt")){
          out.print("Total: " + rs.getInt("total"));
          skipTxt = true;
        }
        else if (localName.equals("text") &&
              atts.getValue("id")!=null &&
```

LISTING 25.11   Continued

```
                           atts.getValue("id").equals("totalMaleTxt")){
                out.print(rs.getInt("totalMale"));
                skipTxt = true;
            }
            else if (localName.equals("text") &&
                    atts.getValue("id")!=null &&
                       atts.getValue("id").equals("totalFemaleTxt")){
                out.print(rs.getInt("totalFemale"));
                skipTxt = true;
            }
        }
    } catch (SQLException e) {
        out.print("Sql error");
    }
}


public void endElement(String namespaceURI, String localName, String rawName)
                                               throws SAXException {
    out.print("</"+localName+">");
    skipTxt = false;
}


public void characters(char[] characters, int start, int end)
                                               throws SAXException {
    if (!skipTxt) {
        String line = new String(characters,start,end);
        out.print(line);
    }
}


public void ignorableWhitespace(char[] characters, int start, int end)
                                               throws SAXException {
    String line = new String(characters,start,end);
    out.print(line);
}


public void endDocument() throws SAXException {
    try {
        rs.close();
    } catch (SQLException e) {
        out.println("MySQL Error: " + e.getMessage());
```

LISTING 25.11   Continued

```
    }
  }
}
```

The `SVGContentHandler` extends the `DefaultHandler` and furnishes callback methods for the important events as they occur in the parsing. As soon as we receive a notice of the document start, we collect the usual result set from our database query. It is saved in a class variable for use when needed. We also set a results flag to let us know that a result is available.

The main parsing event of interest is the `startElement`. Here, we check elements and `id` attributes looking for the elements that need to be changed. As we loop through the attributes, we check for `rect` elements and replace the `height` attribute with a new calculated height. Otherwise, we simply print the elements and their attributes to the servlet response. The new height calculation takes advantage of information in the chart `id` attributes:

```
(rs.getInt(atts.getValue("id"))*100.0/total
```

We have used the table field names as `id` values in our premade chart.svg file. This helps us grab the correct field value from our result set because `atts.getValue("id")` will return the Plymouth table field name needed for the calculation.

A few of the `text` elements of our chart.svg template need to have their character data modified. We must check for the appropriate `text` elements and print out the new text content:

```
if (localName.equals("text") &&
    atts.getValue("id")!=null &&
    atts.getValue("id").equals("title")){
  out.print(table + " - Tract: " + id);
  skipTxt = true;
}
```

However, we do not want the old text content to print, so we must also set a `skipTxt` flag and check this flag in the character callback:

```
public void characters(char[] characters, int start, int end)
                                            throws SAXException {
  if (!skipTxt) {
    String line = new String(characters,start,end);
    out.print(line);
  }
}
```

If the `skipTxt` flag has been set to `true`, we know that the character content should not be printed.

At the end of our document, we simply close our result set.

The SAX parser approach to template processing adds some advantages. First, we are able to do some checking, if desired. We can set the validation to `true` and verify that our SVG template is "valid" in addition to "well-formed." However, the SAX parser approach is somewhat cumbersome to implement. We break up our processing code across several of the callback methods, which can get complicated. There are additional flags to set and check whenever a replacement is needed. However, the SAX parser has one big advantage. It does not create and store the entire SVG template in memory as a DOM tree. This means very large templates could be processed through a SAX parser without running into memory constraints. Our sample uses a very small template, but if the template size is large, a SAX parser might be the better choice. Because bandwidth constraints are still a real issue, it is unlikely that SVG projects will use very large templates. As we will see in our next servlet iteration, the DOM parser is much cleaner to code, but the SAX parser will always be faster. In fact, the DOM parser actually uses the SAX parser to create its in-memory DOM tree.

Servlet 4: Database query4—Return SVG Bar Chart Using DOM Parser

Changing our template process from a SAX parser to a DOM parser is not very complex. Instead of using a `ContentHandler` that triggers responses to individual elements of our template file, a DOM parser reads the entire file into memory. When we have a DOM tree in memory, we can use DOM methods to make the necessary changes to reflect our database record. This process will be familiar because it is similar to DOM processing used in ECMAScript/JavaScript. Listing 25.12 shows the necessary changes to our main class, `DataQuery4`.

LISTING 25.12   dataQuery4.java—Java Servlet Using DOM Parser

```
import javax.servlet.*;
import javax.servlet.http.*;
import java.io.*;
import java.util.*;
import java.sql.*;


public class dataQuery4 extends HttpServlet  {
    private Connection con = null;
    //Note: set this to the file path for your server
    public static final String FILE_PATH = "/home/httpd/html/svgtest/svg/";

    /**Initialize global variables*/
```

LISTING 25.12   Continued

```java
public void init(ServletConfig config) throws ServletException {
  super.init(config);
  try {
    // Load (and therefore register) the MYSQL MM driver
    Class.forName("org.gjt.mm.mysql.Driver").newInstance();
    //establish connection to database
    // Note: this will need to be edited to your system database name, user,
    // and password
    con = DriverManager.getConnection("jdbc:mysql://localhost/sams", "user",
                                      "password");
  }
  catch (ClassNotFoundException e) {
    throw new UnavailableException("Couldn't load database driver");
  }
  catch (SQLException e) {
    throw new UnavailableException("Couldn't get db connection");
  }
  catch (IllegalAccessException e) {
    throw new UnavailableException("Illegal access");
  }
  catch (Exception e) {
    throw new UnavailableException("General Access error");
  }
}

/**Process the HTTP Get request*/
public void doGet(HttpServletRequest request, HttpServletResponse response)
                                throws ServletException, IOException {

  //initialize variables
  String table = "";
  String id = "";
  boolean chart = false;
  String sql = "";
  String [] values = new String[10];
  int total;

  //collect parameters
  Enumeration enum  = request.getParameterNames();
  while (enum.hasMoreElements()) {
    String name = (String) enum.nextElement();
    if (name.equals("table")) {
```

25

LISTING 25.12   Continued

```java
      values = request.getParameterValues(name);
      table = values[0];
    }
    else if (name.equals("id")){
      values = request.getParameterValues(name);
      id =  values[0];
    }
    else if (name.equals("chart")){
      values = request.getParameterValues(name);
      chart =  values[0].equals("true");
    }
  }

  if ((table!="") && (id!="")) {
    if (chart) {
      response.setContentType("image/svg+xml");
      SvgChart4 outChart = new SvgChart4(con,table,id);
      outChart.write(response.getWriter());
    } else {
      response.setContentType("text/html");
      HtmlTable4 outTable = new HtmlTable4(con,table,id);
      outTable.write(response.getWriter());
    }
  }
}


/**Process the HTTP Post request*/
public void doPost(HttpServletRequest request, HttpServletResponse response)
                                    throws ServletException, IOException {
  doGet(request,response);
}

/**Clean up resources*/
public void destroy() {
  // Clean up.
  try {
    if (con != null) con.close();
  }
  catch (SQLException ignored) { };
  }
}
```

This class is identical to the `dataQuery2` class in servlet 2, allowing the `chart` parameter from the SVG ECMAScript/JavaScript to choose between the HTML output and the SVG bar chart output. Again, the real work goes on in the `SvgChart4` class, shown in Listing 25.13.

LISTING 25.13   SvgChart4.java—SvgChart4 Class

```java
import java.io.*;
import java.util.*;
import java.sql.*;
import javax.xml.parsers.DocumentBuilder;
import javax.xml.parsers.DocumentBuilderFactory;
import javax.xml.parsers.ParserConfigurationException;
import org.xml.sax.SAXException;
import org.apache.xml.serialize.XMLSerializer;
import org.apache.xml.serialize.OutputFormat;
import org.w3c.dom.*;

public class SvgChart4 {
  private Connection con = null;
  private String table;
  private String id;


  public SvgChart4(Connection con, String table, String id) {
    this.con = con;
    this.table = table;
    this.id = id;
  }

  public void write(PrintWriter out) {
    String sql = "";
    int total;

    if ((table!=null) && (id!=null)) {
      String template = dataQuery4.FILE_PATH+"/chart.svg";
      // setup DOM Parser with result set
      try {
        DocumentBuilderFactory factory = DocumentBuilderFactory.newInstance();
        DocumentBuilder svgParser = factory.newDocumentBuilder();
        // read in our template and parse into a DOM tree
        Document doc = svgParser.parse( new File(template));
        try {
          //collect a result set from our sql query
```

LISTING 25.13   Continued

```
        Statement stmt = con.createStatement();
        sql = "SELECT * FROM " + table + " WHERE id=\"" + id + "\"";
        if (stmt.execute(sql)) {
          // There is a ResultSet
          ResultSet rs = stmt.getResultSet();
          // There is only one record
          while (rs.next()) {
            total = rs.getInt("total");
// use org.w3c.dom methods to change dom tree according to the result record
            Element obj;
            obj = doc.getElementById("title");
            obj.getFirstChild().setNodeValue(table + " - tract: " + id);

            obj = doc.getElementById("totalTxt");
            obj.getFirstChild().setNodeValue("Total: " + total);
            obj = doc.getElementById("totalMaleTxt");
            obj.getFirstChild().setNodeValue(
                                    "Total: " + rs.getInt("totalMale"));
            obj = doc.getElementById("totalFemaleTxt");
            obj.getFirstChild().setNodeValue(
                                    "Total: " + rs.getInt("totalFemale"));

            obj = doc.getElementById("under18");
            obj.setAttribute("height",
                        Double.toString(rs.getInt("under18")*100.0/total));
            obj = doc.getElementById("adult");
            obj.setAttribute("height",
                          Double.toString(rs.getInt("adult")*100.0/total));
            obj = doc.getElementById("over65");
            obj.setAttribute("height",
                          Double.toString(rs.getInt("over65")*100.0/total));

            obj = doc.getElementById("under18Male");
            obj.setAttribute("height",
                      Double.toString(rs.getInt("under18Male")*100.0/total));
            obj = doc.getElementById("adultMale");
            obj.setAttribute("height",
                        Double.toString(rs.getInt("adultMale")*100.0/total));
            obj = doc.getElementById("over65Male");
            obj.setAttribute("height",
                        Double.toString(rs.getInt("over65Male")*100.0/total));
```

LISTING 25.13   Continued

```
            obj = doc.getElementById("under18Female");
            obj.setAttribute("height",
                    Double.toString(rs.getInt("under18Female")*100.0/total));
            obj = doc.getElementById("adultFemale");
            obj.setAttribute("height",
                    Double.toString(rs.getInt("adultFemale")*100.0/total));
            obj = doc.getElementById("over65Female");
            obj.setAttribute("height",
                    Double.toString(rs.getInt("over65Female")*100.0/total));
          }
          rs.close();
        } else {
          out.println("<text style=\"&LABEL;\" x=\"25\" y=\"125\">"+table
 + " has no record for Id =" + id+"</text>");
        }
        stmt.close();
      } catch (SQLException e) {
        out.println("<text style=\"&LABEL;\" x=\"25\" y=\"125\">
ERROR:Mysql   " + e.getMessage()+"</text>");
      }


      // now that the changes are done output the doc to our servlet response
      XMLSerializer serializer =
          new XMLSerializer((Writer)out, new OutputFormat(doc,"UTF-8",true));
      serializer.serialize(doc);
    } catch (IOException e) {
      out.println("IO Error: " + e.getMessage());
      e.printStackTrace(out);
    } catch (ParserConfigurationException e) {
      out.println("Parser Configuration Error: " + e.getMessage());
    } catch (SAXException e) {
      out.println("SAX Exception: " + e.getMessage());
    }
  }
 }
}
```

First, a parser is obtained using the JAXP DocumentBuilderFactory:

```
DocumentBuilderFactory factory = DocumentBuilderFactory.newInstance();
DocumentBuilder svgParser = factory.newDocumentBuilder();
```

In our case, we used the Xerces 2.0 .jar file for the actual DOM parser. When we have a parser, we use it to read and parse the chart.svg template:

```
Document doc = svgParser.parse( new File(template));
```

We can now use DOM methods on the SVG document in memory. Because we have carefully provided id attributes for all our elements, the DOM Level 2 getElementById() method is very useful for minimizing DOM manipulation:

```
obj = doc.getElementById("under18");
obj.setAttribute("height", Double.toString(rs.getInt("under18")*100.0/total));
```

The actual modification of our template is much cleaner and straightforward using the DOM methods. We are not tangling with convoluted String calculations as in servlet 2, nor do we have code spread all over a contentHandler as in servlet 3. This demonstrates some of the advantages of choosing a DOM parser for our template processing. The only difficulty occurs when the template file is large. If our chart.svg template were moderately large, the SAX parser would provide an advantage in processing time even though it is more complex to set up. Let's take this example through one more iteration and look at template processing using JDOM.

Servlet 5: Database query5—Return SVG Bar Chart Using JDOM

Our final iteration (see Listing 25.14) will look at the JDOM approach to our template processing. JDOM is a Java-centric open-source DOM API. It is currently in the Java Community Process as a Java Specification Request, JSR-102. Eventually, it will work its way into a consolidated Java XML offering, along with several other rapidly evolving Java/XML APIs: JAXP, JAXB, JAX-RPC, JAXM, and JAXR. JDOM beta 0.7 was used for this iteration, and more information is available at http://www.jdom.org/. JDOM offers a couple of advantages for the Java programmer. It provides a lightweight API for XML processing that takes advantage of Java collections. Consequently, JDOM provides access to a Java-optimized DOM that consumes less memory and is more familiar to the Java community than some of the other parsers.

LISTING 25.14   SvgChart5.java—SVGChart Class Using JDOM

```
import java.io.*;
import java.util.*;
import java.sql.*;
import java.net.*;

import org.jdom.*;
import org.jdom.JDOMException;
import org.jdom.input.SAXBuilder;
import org.jdom.output.XMLOutputter;
```

LISTING 25.14   Continued

```java
public class SvgChart5 {
  private Connection con = null;
  private String table;
  private String id;

  public SvgChart5(Connection con, String table, String id) {
    this.con = con;
    this.table = table;
    this.id = id;
  }

  public void write(PrintWriter out) {
    String sql = "";
    int total;

    if ((table!=null) && (id!=null)) {
      String template = dataQuery5.FILE_PATH+"chart.svg";
      // setup DOM Parser with result set
      try {
      // create a SAX document builder using default Xerces without validation
        SAXBuilder builder = new SAXBuilder();
        // create the svg JDOM document from our chart.svg template
        Document svg = builder.build( new File(template));

        try {
          //collect a result set from our sql query
          Statement stmt = con.createStatement();
          sql = "SELECT * FROM " + table + " WHERE id=\"" + id + "\"";
          if (stmt.execute(sql)) {
            // There is a ResultSet
            ResultSet rs = stmt.getResultSet();
            // There is only one record
            while (rs.next()) {
              total = rs.getInt("total");
              Element root = svg.getRootElement();

          // change all the text elements
          Iterator it = root.getChildren("text").iterator();
          while (it.hasNext()) {
            Element obj = (Element)it.next();
            if (obj.getAttribute("id").getValue().equals("title")) {
```

25

LISTING 25.14   Continued

```
        obj.setText(table + " - tract: " + id);
      }
      else if (obj.getAttribute("id").getValue().equals("totalTxt")) {
        obj.setText("Total: " + total);
      }
      else if (obj.getAttribute("id").getValue().equals("totalMaleTxt")) {
        obj.setText("Total: " + rs.getInt("totalMale"));
      }
      else if (obj.getAttribute("id").getValue().equals("totalFemaleTxt")) {
          obj.setText("Total: " + rs.getInt("totalFemale"));
      }
    }
    // change all the rect elements
    it = root.getChildren("rect").iterator();
    while (it.hasNext()) {
      Element obj = (Element)it.next();
      if (obj.getAttribute("id").getValue().equals("under18")) {
        obj.setAttribute("height",
                    Double.toString(rs.getInt("under18")*100.0/total));
      }
      else if (obj.getAttribute("id").getValue().equals("adult")) {
        obj.setAttribute("height",
                      Double.toString(rs.getInt("adult")*100.0/total));
      }
      else if (obj.getAttribute("id").getValue().equals("over65")) {
        obj.setAttribute("height",
                      Double.toString(rs.getInt("over65")*100.0/total));
      }
      if (obj.getAttribute("id").getValue().equals("under18Male")) {
        obj.setAttribute("height",
                  Double.toString(rs.getInt("under18Male")*100.0/total));
      }
      else if (obj.getAttribute("id").getValue().equals("adultMale")) {
        obj.setAttribute("height",
                    Double.toString(rs.getInt("adultMale")*100.0/total));
      }
      else if (obj.getAttribute("id").getValue().equals("over65Male")) {
        obj.setAttribute("height",
                  Double.toString(rs.getInt("over65Male")*100.0/total));
      }
      if (obj.getAttribute("id").getValue().equals("under18Female")) {
```

LISTING 25.14   Continued

```
            obj.setAttribute("height",
                        Double.toString(rs.getInt("under18Female")*100.0/total));
        }
        else if (obj.getAttribute("id").getValue().equals("adultFemale")) {
          obj.setAttribute("height",
                        Double.toString(rs.getInt("adultFemale")*100.0/total));
        }
        else if (obj.getAttribute("id").getValue().equals("over65Female")) {
          obj.setAttribute("height",
                        Double.toString(rs.getInt("over65Female")*100.0/total));
        }
      } //while

          }
          rs.close();
        } else {
          out.println("<text style=\"&LABEL;\" x=\"25\" y=\"125\">"+table +
                              " has no record for Id =" + id+"</text>");
        }
        stmt.close();
      } catch (SQLException e) {
        out.println("<text style=\"&LABEL;\" x=\"25\" y=\"125\">ERROR:Mysql   "
                              + e.getMessage()+"</text>");
      }

      // now that the changes are done output the doc to our servlet response
      XMLOutputter outputter = new XMLOutputter();
      outputter.output(svg, out);
    } catch (JDOMException e) {
      e.getMessage();
    } catch (Exception e) {
      e.getMessage();
    }
  }
 }
}
```

JDOM is still not in a final release, but at this stage we have fewer DOM methods to choose from, when moving around the DOM tree. Instead of directly accessing an element with the convenient getElementById("name") as in the DOM parser, we need to iterate through different levels and check for a desired id. We could have altered the chart.svg template to better suit JDOM parsing tools by eliminating nesting. However, that is an unlikely possibility in a real-world template. Perhaps a better approach would be creating a custom namespace with custom elements specifically for the JDOM parsing. In that case, `Element.GetChild(tagName, tagNameSpace)` could conveniently locate individual elements that require modification.

Summary

In this case study, we showed you how to develop a small but full-scale Web-mapping application with SVG. Server-side XML tools can be used for more than just template processing. For example, server-side layer selection, data merging, data attribute filtering, and geo-spatial queries are just a few areas of Geographic Information Systems (GIS) that would lend themselves to server-side solutions. Combining open source SVG with server-side Java APIs provides an extremely powerful and flexible approach to Internet GIS. The technologies illustrated have equal application across a wide spectrum of engineering design fields requiring the flexibility of vectors capable of linking to server-side functions and database interaction.

Here are the specific technologies we can now apply to new projects:

- Organizing a set of SVG Web maps into a map hierarchy

- Adding ECMAScript/JavaScript functions for labeling and linking

- Attaching a database for visual SQL query linkage

- Processing our SQL query results into an HTML table

- Adding a choice to output SQL queries as bar charts

    - Using Java string methods to produce bar charts from an SVG template

    - Using a SAX parser to produce bar charts from an SVG template

    - Using a DOM parser to produce bar charts from an SVG template

    - Using the JDOM API to produce bar charts from an SVG template

CHAPTER **26**

Case Study: FMS— Monitor and Control

In Chapter 24, we looked at SVG for the Architectural Engineering Construction industry (AEC), and in Chapter 25, for Geographic Information Systems (GIS) Web-mapping systems. In this chapter, we want to look at an application area that falls at the intersection of GIS and AEC—Facilities Management Systems (FMS). FMS covers a broad spectrum of issues, and its definition can be a bit hazy. However, one of the most common and easiest understood applications of FMS revolves around office building maintenance and management. Essentially, FMS is the use of building maps to connect facilities and assets to floor plan locations. Viewed from a geometric perspective, FMS is simply GIS restricted to a smaller world, where assets are building-referenced instead of geo-referenced. Viewed from a timeline perspective, FMS is concerned with the life of a building after birth. As AEC hands over a new building, the owner would ideally take possession with FMS in hand.

This case study will look at a building from the FMS perspective and explore possible uses of SVG. Because we covered SVG and database connections in the preceding two case studies, we will not go into that type of application here. Instead, we will look at SVG as a possible approach to monitor and control systems.

Project Overview

After working with SVG to build the office building in Chapter 24, we are now moved in and hard at work. The contract documents were passed on to the new owner, who would like to see how SVG might help with maintenance and management. We can take our previous AEC project floor plans and apply them to the ongoing life of our new building. As you recall, the second-floor plan is page 1.3a.svg of the complete design set, shown in Figure 26.1.

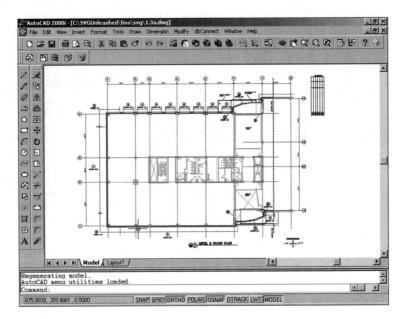

FIGURE 26.1   The office's second-floor plan.

However, we are no longer working with a construction community familiar with the common blueprint pattern. In this case, we want to create a model that is more familiar to building management staff. We will start with a photo view of our office building and use a hybrid raster/vector approach. Figure 26.2 shows the opening view of our FMS system.

From our opening photo view, the staff can select the floor of interest. Selecting floor two north will link to our page 1.3a floor plan. The second floor has three temperature zones, each controlled by its own thermostat control system. In this project, we want to monitor our zone temperatures and also provide a remote thermostat control. Our building management staff has recently been downsized, and in fact, all our offices are now managed from one location in Chicago. It would be nice to monitor our office temperature zones and control our thermostats from this central location so that cost-saving initiatives can be implemented uniformly across the United States. Fortunately, SVG can help us provide the visual interface to this system, which is then accessible via the Internet.

FIGURE 26.2   Hybrid raster vector SVG.

Elevation Photo

The first step of this project will be to create a front page with a photo of our building. The photo, office.jpg, is stored in the .\images subdirectory. We want to identify hotspots on our photo for linking to other parts of the FMS. Using AutoCAD, we insert our photo into a new drawing and then outline the various building segments using LWPOLYLINE entities. Remember, the DXFtoSVG translator developed in Chapter 24 can translate AutoCAD DXF files to SVG. We can use our DXFtoSVG translator to translate these hotspot link areas to SVG. As you recall, the easiest method of attaching information to DXF ENTITIES is by layer assignment. For this page, we will draw our LWPOLYLINEs on layers that identify the floor. For example, the polyline identifying floor 2 north will be placed on layer "Floor2-N." The AutoCAD drawing file, office.dwg, has been created with these additional polylines assigned to the correct layers. After exporting the office.dwg file to AutoCAD 2000 DXF format, we move to our DXFtoSVG translator.

Before translating our file, we first make some enhancements to our translator. It would be nice to have the translator add a viewbox to the top svg element. We can accomplish this by checking for DXF extent values, $EXTMIN and $EXTMAX, in the DXF header, as shown in Listing 26.1.

LISTING 26.1   Adding a viewbox to DXFtoSVG

```
       .
       .
       .
//  DXF header
while (((line = in.readLine()) != null) &&
        (!line.equalsIgnoreCase("ENTITIES"))) {
  // collect Extent Minimum and Maximum from DXF head
  if (line.equals("$EXTMIN")) {
    minpt.readDXFPoint(in);
  }
  else if (line.equals("$EXTMAX")) {
    maxpt.readDXFPoint(in);
    dx = maxpt.x-minpt.x;
    dy = maxpt.y-minpt.y;
        }
}
       .
       .
```

We can then plug these values into a viewbox that will make our SVG file load within the browser view window. We make some other changes to the svg element and add a script element, as shown in Listing 26.2.

LISTING 26.2   Modified SVG Heading in DXFtoSVG

```
       .
       .
out.println("<?xml version=\"1.0\" encoding=\"UTF-8\"?>");
out.println("<!DOCTYPE svg PUBLIC \"-//W3C//DTD SVG 1.0//EN\"");
out.println("\"http://www.w3.org/TR/SVG/DTD/svg10.dtd\">");
out.println("<svg width='800' height='"+(800*Math.abs(dy/dx))+"' ");
out.println("preserveAspectRatio='xMinYMin'");
out.println(" viewBox=\"" + minpt.x + " " + dy + " " + dx + " " + -dy + "\"");
out.println("\tonload=\"on_load(evt)\" onzoom=\"onZoom(evt)\"");
out.println("\txmlns='http://www.w3.org/2000/svg'");
out.println("\txmlns:xlink='http://www.w3.org/1999/xlink'");
out.println("\txmlns:fms='http://www.sams.com/2002/SVGUnleashed/ch26/fms'>");
out.println("<title>"+ name +"</title>");
out.println("<script xlink:href=\"../js/fms.js\"
                                      type=\"text/ecmascript\"/>");
out.println("<g id=\"canvas\" onmousemove=\"mousemove(evt)\">");
       .
       .
```

Refer to DXFtoSVG.java in the Chapter 26 file downloads to see all the minor changes. A new custom fms namespace for creating link attributes has also been added. Processing office.dxf through this revised DXFtoSVG translator creates office.svg. This SVG file now shows our outlines with some simple rollover effects and a cursor-following label defined by the ENTITY layer. Listing 26.3 shows the relevant ECMAScript in fms.js.

LISTING 26.3   ECMAScript, fms.js, Referenced by the Elevation SVG, office.svg

```
var svgdoc;
var svgroot;

var label = "";
var style;
var offset = 0.0;;

// must be calculated from viewbox to w x h
var x0 = 0;
var y0 = 0;
var vboxW = 0;
var vboxH = 0;
var svgW = 0;
var svgH = 0;
var sz = 0.25;
var zoom = 1.0;

function on_load(evt){
  svgdoc = evt.target.getOwnerDocument();
  svgroot = svgdoc.getDocumentElement();

  //initialize cursor parameters
  var vbox = (svgroot.getAttribute("viewBox")).split(' ');
  x0 = parseFloat(vbox[0]);
  y0 = parseFloat(vbox[1]);
  vboxW = parseFloat(vbox[2]);
  vboxH = parseFloat(vbox[3]);
  svgW = parseFloat(svgroot.getAttribute("width"));
  svgH = parseFloat(svgroot.getAttribute("height"));
  if (vboxW>vboxH) sz = (vboxW/70);
  else sz = vboxH/70.0;
  offset = sz ;

  // initialize label text
  var data = svgdoc.createTextNode(" ");
  var text = svgdoc.createElement("text");
```

LISTING 26.3   Continued

```
    text.setAttribute("transform","translate("+ x0 + "," + y0 + ")
                                        scale(" + 1.0/zoom + ")");
    text.setAttribute("style",
"stroke:white;stroke-width:0.001;fill:black;font-size:0.5;font-family:arial;");
    text.setAttribute("id", "label");
    text.appendChild(data);
    svgroot.appendChild(text);
    //alert(printNode(text));
}

function onZoom() {
        zoom = svgroot.currentScale;
}

function mousemove(evt) {
    var X = x0 + (evt.clientX - svgroot.currentTranslate.x)*
                                (vboxW/(svgW*svgroot.currentScale));
        var Y = y0 - offset + (evt.clientY - svgroot.currentTranslate.y)*
                                (vboxH/(svgH*svgroot.currentScale));
    label = svgdoc.getElementById("label");
    label.setAttribute("transform","translate("+ X + "," + Y + ") scale("
                                                + 1.0/zoom + ")");
}

// mouse over
function over(evt) {
    var link = evt.currentTarget.getAttributeNS
        ('http://www.sams.com/2002/SVGUnleashed/ch26/fms','link');
    if (link!="") {
        //rollover label on
        label = svgdoc.getElementById("label");
        label.firstChild.setData(link);
        var svgstyle = evt.currentTarget.style;
        svgstyle.setProperty('fill-opacity',0.25);
    }
}

//mouse out
function out(evt) {
    //rollover label off
    var label = svgdoc.getElementById("label");
    label.firstChild.setData(" ");
```

LISTING 26.3   Continued

```
  var svgstyle = evt.currentTarget.style;
  svgstyle.setProperty('fill-opacity',0.0);
}


//mouse click
function click(evt) {
  if (evt.getButton()==0) {
    var link = evt.currentTarget.getAttributeNS
        ('http://www.sams.com/2002/SVGUnleashed/ch26/fms','link');
  if (link=="Floor2-N") window.location.href = "1.3b.htm";
  else alert("Only Floor 2 North is active");
  }
}
```

Listing 26.3 is similar to the ECMAScript, map.js, discussed in Listing 25.2. Here, though, we are using our new fms namespace to add a link attribute, which becomes our label as well as the link identifier for the click function. This is a simple elevation skeleton, which is now filled in with an image reference to our photo. We manually add Listing 26.4 to office.svg before the ACTIVE group.

LISTING 26.4   Image Element for office.svg

```
    .
    .
<g id="ElevationPhoto">
<image x="0" y="-7.9" width="10.0" height="7.9"
      xlink:href="..\images\office.jpg"></image>
</g>
    .
    .
```

The width and height values for our image element come from the size of the .jpg image used in the AutoCAD office.dwg file. Because SVG uses a y down coordinate system, we have inverted all the y values in our translation and need to compensate by shifting the image's y insertion point by the height of the image, y="-7.9". The addition of a title text element, as shown in Listing 26.5, completes the FMS front page.

LISTING 26.5   Title Text Element

```
    .
    .
```

LISTING 26.5   Continued

```
<text transform="translate(3 -7)"
 style="Stroke:white;stroke-width:0.001;fill:white;font-size:0.5">
 <tspan x="0" dy="0">Office Elevation</tspan>
 <tspan x="0.5" dy="1em" style="font-size:0.35">(Select a Floor)</tspan>
</text>
        .
        .
        .
```

Plan View and Temperature Zones

Adding temperature zones to the second floor plan is similar. We add LWPOLYLINE entities to the 1.3a.dwg AutoCAD file on three layers called zone1, zone2, and zone3. These layers are then placed in a new file using the AutoCAD WBLOCK command. After translating this zone.dxf file to SVG, we copy our zone elements into 1.3a.svg. We can then make a few modifications to the header and to the zone g elements of 1.3a.svg, as shown in Listing 26.6.

LISTING 26.6   Adding Zone Polygons to 1.3a.svg

```
        .
        .
        .
<svg id="svgAll" width="900" height="600" style="shape-rendering:optimizeSpeed;
text-rendering:optimizeSpeed; image-rendering:optimizeSpeed"
viewBox="-48.608758 -2295.2036 3521.5775 2331.8821" xml:space="preserve"
  preserveAspectRatio="xMinYMin"
  onload="on_load(evt)" onzoom="onZoom(evt)"
  xmlns="http://www.w3.org/2000/svg"
  xmlns:xlink="http://www.w3.org/1999/xlink"
  xmlns:fms="http://www.sams.com/2002/SVGUnleashed/ch26/fms">
<script xlink:href="../js/fms.js" type="text/ecmascript"/>
        .
        .
        .
<g id="zones" onmousemove="mousemove(evt)" style="fill:magenta;fill-opacity:0">
    <polyline fms:link="zone1" onmouseover="over(evt)" onmouseout="out(evt)"
onclick="click(evt)" points="2115.973168482447,-1196.742022460513
2121.087990623123,-1706.149676578562 2081.473168482448,-1706.149676578562
2081.473168482448,-1722.83635067497 1049.473168482447,-1722.83635067497
1049.473168482447,-1706.024676578568 1025.473168482447,-1706.024676578568
1025.473168482447,-1196.524676578568 2115.973168482447,-1196.742022460513"/>
        .
        .
        .
</g><!--zones  -->
</svg>
```

At this point, we can move from our front elevation photo to a floor plan. The floor plan has been enhanced with zone areas that can be linked to additional SVG files.

Remote Monitoring

We would like to use our zones to monitor temperature data. We will have to assume these temperature readings have already been connected to a server using a messaging technology such as XML-RPC (XML-Remote Procedure Calls), JMS (Java Messaging Service), or even SOAP (Simple Object Access Protocol). Exploring these messaging options is outside the scope of this project. In this project, we look only into the SVG aspects of monitoring a live data stream, regardless of how the data is received at the server. The approach we will use takes advantage of a couple of extensions to the SVG specification, `getURL()` and `postURL()`. They are Adobe SVG Viewer–specific extensions that will not necessarily be available to other viewers.

Here is a brief overview of the monitoring process. First, the user selects a zone with a mouse click, which calls the ECMAScript click function to open a new window. This window is opened with an image/svg+xml stream from a servlet that creates a temperature cylinder graph and control panel. The graph is actuated with a start button in the control panel, which calls the `dataUpdate` function found in the associated ECMAScript file, graph.js. `dataUpdate` is a recursive function set up in a timer that uses `getURL(servlet_URL, call_back)` to get a temperature response from our servlet. The servlet collects the next available temperature data and sends back this information in the `status` object of the `call_back` function. When this temperature data is available to the ECMAScript, a new line segment, label, and point are inserted in the SVG graph.

Listing 26.7 shows the first step of connecting our zone polygons to a new window.

LISTING 26.7   New Click Function in fms.js

```
//mouse click
function click(evt) {
  if (evt.getButton()==0) {
    var link = evt.currentTarget.getAttributeNS
      ('http://www.sams.com/2002/SVGUnleashed/ch26/fms','link');
    if (link=="Floor2-N") window.location.href = "1.3a.svg";
    else if (link.indexOf("Floor")!=-1)
      alert("Only Floor 2 North is active");
    else if (link.indexOf("zone")!=-1) {
     if (dataWin!=null) dataWin.close();
       link = link.substring(link.indexOf("zone")+4,link.length);
       dataWin=window.open(servlet_path+"FMSGraph?cmd=initialize&zone="+link,
        dataWin", "width=600, height=300, left=200, top=0, scrollbars=yes,
        toolbar=yes, location=yes, menubar=yes, resizable=yes, status=yes");
       dataWin.focus();
```

LISTING 26.7   Continued

```
    }
  }
}
```

If the click event target has an `fms:link` attribute containing the string `"zone"`, a new dataWin is opened with `servlet_path` + `"FMSGraph?cmd=initialize&zone="+link`. This servlet writes an SVG template for a cylinder graph as well as a couple of control buttons. Figure 26.3 shows graph.svg template as it looks before starting the temperature data updates.

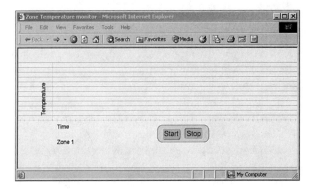

FIGURE 26.3   SVG cylinder graph.

The graph.svg template was created in a text editor, as shown in Listing 26.8.

LISTING 26.8   graph.svg

```
<?xml version="1.0" encoding="ISO-8859-1" standalone="no"?>
<!DOCTYPE svg PUBLIC "-//W3C//DTD SVG 20010904//EN"
    "http://www.w3.org/TR/SVG/DTD/svg10.dtd" [
    <!ENTITY SENSOR1   "stroke:black;stroke-width:0.01;fill:none;">
    <!ENTITY DATA     "stroke:green;stroke-width:1;fill:none;">
]>
<svg width="600" height="250"  preserveAspectRatio="xMinYMin"
        viewBox="-0.006 -200.0 600 250.0" onload="on_load(evt)">
<script xlink:href="http://www.yourserver.com/svg-fms/js/graph.js"
                                    type="text/ecmascript"/>
<title>Zone Temperature monitor</title>
<defs>
    <marker id="ticV"
      viewBox="0 0 10 10" refX="0" refY="2.5"
```

LISTING 26.8 Continued

```
      markerUnits="userSpaceOnUse"
      markerWidth="1000" markerHeight="10"
      orient="auto">
      <line x1="0" y1="0" x2="0" y2="5"/>
    </marker>
  </defs>

<g id="axis" fill="none" stroke="red" stroke-width="0.25" >
  <path d="M 0 -50 h5 h10 h10 h10 h10 h10 h10 h10 h10 h10 h10 h10 h10 h10
   h10 h10 h10 h10 h10 h10 h10 h10 h10 h10 h10 h10 h10 h10 h10 h10 h10 h10
   h10 h10 h10 h10 h10 h10 h10 h10 h10 h10 h10 h10 h10 h10 h10 h10 h10 h10
   h10 h10 h10 h10 h10 h10 h10 h5"
   marker-mid="url(#ticV)"/>
  <line x1="75" y1="-50" x2="75" y2="-170"/>
</g>


<g id="canvas">


<g id="SENSOR1"
    style="stroke:black;stroke-width:0.0001;fill:back;font-size:12.0;">
  <g transform="rotate(-90.0,60,-60)">
    <text transform="translate(60,-60)" >
      Temperature
    </text>
  </g>
  <text transform="translate(85,-32)">
    Time
  </text>
  <text transform="translate(85,0)">
    Zone <tspan id="zone">1</tspan>
  </text>
</g>

<g id="linerule" style="stroke:black;stroke-width:0.01">
  <line x1="0" y1="-60" x2="600;" y2="-60"/>
  <line x1="0" y1="-70" x2="600;" y2="-70"/>
  <line x1="0" y1="-80" x2="600;" y2="-80"/>
  <line x1="0" y1="-90" x2="600;" y2="-90"/>
  <line x1="0" y1="-100" x2="600;" y2="-100"/>
  <line x1="0" y1="-110" x2="600;" y2="-110"/>
  <line x1="0" y1="-120" x2="600;" y2="-120"/>
  <line x1="0" y1="-130" x2="600;" y2="-130"/>
```

LISTING 26.8   Continued

```
   <line x1="0" y1="-140" x2="600;" y2="-140"/>
   <line x1="0" y1="-150" x2="600;" y2="-150"/>
   <line x1="0" y1="-160" x2="600;" y2="-160"/>
   <line x1="0" y1="-170" x2="600;" y2="-170"/>
</g>

<g id="DATA" transform="translate(0,0)" style="&DATA;">
  <g id="DATA1">
    <path d="M75,-50L75,-51"/>
  </g>
</g>

<g id="control" transform="translate(300,-40) scale(0.75)">
  <rect x="1" y="1" rx="15" ry="15" width="148" height="48"
           style="stroke:black;strokewidth:10;fill:rgb(220,220,220)"/>

    <g id="start" onmousedown="Button_down(evt)">
      <g transform="translate(15 10)">
        <rect rx="5" ry="5" height="30" width="50" transform="translate(0,0)"
              style="fill:white"/>
        <rect rx="5" ry="5" height="30" width="50" transform="translate(2,2)"
              style="fill:black"/>
        <rect rx="5" ry="5" height="30" width="50" transform="translate(1,1)"
              style="fill:rgb(192,192,192)"/>
         <text transform="translate(5,22)" style="font-size:20;">
           Start
         </text>
    </g>
    </g>

    <g id="stop" onmousedown="Button_down(evt)">
      <g transform="translate(80 10)">
        <rect rx="5" ry="5" height="30" width="50" transform="translate(0,0)"
              style="fill:black"/>
        <rect rx="5" ry="5" height="30" width="50" transform="translate(2,2)"
              style="fill:white"/>
        <rect rx="5" ry="5" height="30" width="50" transform="translate(1,1)"
              style="fill:rgb(192,192,192)"/>
         <text transform="translate(5,22)" style="font-size:20;">
           Stop
         </text>
    </g>
    </g>
```

LISTING 26.8   Continued

```
  </g> <!-- control -->
</g><!-- canvas -->
</svg>
```

Note that you will need to edit `<script>` `href` to match the URL for your particular server. We are using a `marker` definition to create the vertical tics in the x-axis of our cylinder chart with a 10-unit interval. We also include a dummy `path` in `<g id="DATA1">`, which will be used later to create our live data graph. The servlet will also use `<tspan id="zone">` to store the zone number of the selected temperature zone. The button controls are created with overlapping `rect` elements, which we can manipulate in the `Button_down(evt)` function to provide a primitive pushbutton appearance. The interesting action takes place in the ECMAScript contained in graph.js, shown in Listing 26.9.

LISTING 26.9   graph.js

```
var svgdoc;
var svgroot;

var timer;
var sample = 0;
var sampleRate = 5000;//millisecond sampling rate
// note: set this to the servlet path for your server
var servlet_path = "/servlet/";
var dx = 75.0;
var shift = 0.0;
var style;
var graphLen = 575;

function on_load(evt){
  svgdoc = evt.target.getOwnerDocument();
  svgroot = svgdoc.getDocumentElement();
  zone = svgdoc.getElementById("zone").firstChild.data;
}

function dataUpdate() {
  getURL(servlet_path+"FMSGraph?cmd=data&zone="+zone,FmsBack);


  timer = setTimeout('dataUpdate()',sampleRate);
}
```

26

LISTING 26.9   Continued

```
function fmsback(status){
  //alert("Success = " + status.success + " type: " + status.contentType);
  //alert(status.content);
  if (status.success) {
    var temp = status.content;
    dx = dx + sampleRate*0.005;

    if (dx>(graphLen-50)) {
      // when dx is greater than graphLen-50 start scrolling graph paper
      shift = shift - sampleRate * 0.005;
      var data = svgdoc.getElementById("DATA");
      data.setAttribute("transform","translate(" + shift + ",0)");
    }

    var data1 = svgdoc.getElementById("DATA1");

    dy = -50 - temp;
    attr = data1.firstChild.nextSibling.getAttribute("d");
    if (dx>graphLen) {
      // when dx is greater than graphLen start dropping segments
      attr = newPath(attr);
      obj = data1.firstChild.nextSibling.nextSibling;
      obj.parentNode.removeChild(obj);
      obj = data1.firstChild.nextSibling.nextSibling.nextSibling;
      obj.parentNode.removeChild(obj);
    }
    data1.firstChild.nextSibling.setAttribute("d",attr+"L"+dx+","+dy);

    var pt1 = svgdoc.createElement("circle");
    pt1.setAttribute("id", "d1"+sample);
    pt1.setAttribute("style", "stroke:red;stroke-width:0.01;fill:red;");
    pt1.setAttribute("cx", dx);
    pt1.setAttribute("cy", dy);
    pt1.setAttribute("r", 1);
    pt1.setAttribute("onmouseover", "over(evt)");
    pt1.setAttribute("onmouseout", "out(evt)");
    data1.appendChild(pt1);

    var txtdata = svgdoc.createTextNode(temp.substring(0,6) + " degree F");
    var text = svgdoc.createElement("text");
    text.setAttribute("x", dx+2);
    text.setAttribute("y", dy);
    text.setAttribute("style",
```

LISTING 26.9 Continued

```
         "stroke:black;stroke-width:0.01;fill:black;font-size:10;opacity:0");
    text.appendChild(txtdata);
    data1.appendChild(text);
    //alert(printNode(data1));

    sample++;
  }
}

function newPath(attr) {
  var p = attr.split('L');
  attr = "M"+p[1];
  for (var i = 2;i<p.length;i++) {
  attr = attr +"L"+p[i];
  }
  return attr;
}

// --------------------------------------------------
//  rollover effects for our newly created data points
// --------------------------------------------------

// mouse_over_a
function over(evt) {
  var svgobj = evt.currentTarget;
  var svgstyle = svgobj.style;
  style = svgstyle.getPropertyValue('fill');
  svgstyle.setProperty ('fill','yellow');
  svgstyle = svgobj.nextSibling.style;
  svgstyle.setProperty ('opacity',1);
}

//mouse_out_b
function out(evt) {
  var svgobj = evt.currentTarget;
  var svgstyle = svgobj.style;
  svgstyle.setProperty ('fill',style);
  svgstyle = svgobj.nextSibling.style;
  svgstyle.setProperty ('opacity',0);
}

// --------------------------------------------------
//      graph control buttons
```

LISTING 26.9   Continued

```
// -------------------------------------------------

function Button_down(evt) {
  //toggle button down
  var button = evt.getCurrentTarget.id;
  var obj = evt.getCurrentTarget;
  obj = obj.firstChild.nextSibling.firstChild.nextSibling;
  obj.style.setProperty("fill","black");
  obj.nextSibling.nextSibling.style.setProperty("fill","white");
  if (button=="start") {
    Button_up("stop");
    dataUpdate();
  }
  else if (button=="stop") {
    Button_up("start");
    clearTimeout(timer);
  }
}

function Button_up(button) {
  //toggle button up
  var obj = svgdoc.getElementById(button);
  obj = obj.firstChild.nextSibling.firstChild.nextSibling;
  obj.style.setProperty("fill","white");
  obj.nextSibling.nextSibling.style.setProperty("fill","black");
}
```

Button_down(evt) controls the graph updates by calling the pivotal function of this project, updateData(). The recursive updateData() function first calls getURL(servlet,fmsback); and then creates a timer object that calls itself at the interval set by sampleRate. The initial sampleRate is set to 5000ms, but this rate may be changed depending on the update rate needed. Setting a rate below 500ms will not gain much because this is about the average response time of the getURL function. getURL calls a servlet called FMSGraph, which simply feeds the next data point to our SVG graph. After a data point is returned, the callback function fmsback(status) completes the tedious work of updating our graph line. The two commented alert lines at the beginning of the callback are useful for debugging the servlet's return status. The status object returned to our callback function, fmsback, has a couple of properties, but the really useful part of the status is the returned content:

```
alert("Success = " + status.success + " type: " + status.contentType);
alert(status.content);
```

status.content is a string returned from our servlet, which in this case is simply a temperature data value. When we have a new point, we create the next segment in our path element's d attribute. However, if the segment is near the right edge of our cylinder graph, we first scroll the paper by translating our Data1 group to the left:

```
data.setAttribute("transform","translate(" + shift + ",0)");
```

We could continue scrolling our graph indefinitely, except that eventually our path becomes so long that each transform takes an exorbitantly long time. To prevent this situation, we will also begin deleting path segments that fall off the paper at the left. In addition to the path segment, we create a data point circle element and a text label element. Initially, the text element is set with the style attribute opacity:0. However, we also add onmouseover and onmouseout events to our circle element. The over event function will reset the label text opacity to 1, which turns on the point label. An alternative approach for rollover labeling would be to manipulate a visibility style attribute property:

```
style="visibility:visible"
```

The last part of our temperature monitor is the FMSGraph servlet shown in Listing 26.10.

LISTING 26.10   FMSGraph Servlet

```
import javax.servlet.*;
import javax.servlet.http.*;
import java.util.*;
import java.io.*;

public class FMSGraph extends HttpServlet  {
  private static final String CONTENT_TYPE = "text/html";
  private static double[] thermostat = {70.0, 70.0, 70.0, 70.0};

  /**Initialize global variables*/
  public void init(ServletConfig config) throws ServletException {
    super.init(config);
  }

  /**Process the HTTP Get request*/
  public void doGet(HttpServletRequest request, HttpServletResponse response)
                                    throws ServletException, IOException {
    //initialize variables
    response.setContentType(CONTENT_TYPE);
    PrintWriter out = response.getWriter();
    BufferedReader in = request.getReader();
    String cmd = request.getParameter("cmd");
```

26

LISTING 26.10   Continued

```java
      int zone = Integer.parseInt(request.getParameter("zone"));

    if (cmd != null) {
      // write out the initial svg from the graph.svg template
      if (cmd.equals("initialize")) {
        String line;
        response.setContentType("image/svg+xml");
        try {
          BufferedReader infile = new BufferedReader(
                    new FileReader("/home/httpd/html/svg-fms/svg/graph.svg"));
          while (((line = infile.readLine()) != null)) {
            // edit the zone text to reflect the selected zone
            if (line.indexOf("id=\"zone\"")!=-1) {
              StringBuffer temp = new StringBuffer("Zone <tspan id=\"zone\">");
              temp.append(zone);
              temp.append("</tspan>");
              line = temp.toString();
            }
            out.println(line);
          }
          infile.close();
        } catch (IOException e) {
          out.println("IO ERROR:Infile  " + e.getMessage());
        }
      }
      else {      //this is a data command
        Random r1 = new Random();
        double d1 = (r1.nextGaussian()*5.0)+thermostat[zone] + 5.0;
        out.println(d1);
      }
    }
  }


  /**Process the HTTP Post request*/
  public void doPost(HttpServletRequest request, HttpServletResponse response)
            throws ServletException, IOException {
    doGet(request,response);
  }

  /**Clean up resources*/
  public void destroy() {
  }
}
```

The first iteration of our FMSGraph servlet can process two commands: `initialize` or `data`. If the `cmd` is `initialize`, FMSGraph will read the graph.svg template, replacing its zone `tspan` element with the selected zone number, and write this SVG to the output. For our example, the FMSGraph servlet merely generates a random data point to simulate a data stream from our building. Now we have all the parts in place to monitor our simulated temperature data. We have added a link from the floor plan, 1.3a.svg, using fms.js click events. We have a graph template, a servlet that will initially return the graph template, and a graph.js script for repeatedly calling our servlet with `getURL()`. This completes a temperature monitor presented as an SVG cylinder graph model. The monitor illustrates the use of `getURL()` to return data from the server at a set interval. But, what about going the other direction, from the monitor to the server? In the next section, we look at using the Adobe `postURL()` function to push thermostat input up to our servlet.

Remote Control

To control our thermostat, we will model an old-style thermostat slider. The input from our slider will then be sent, using Adobe's `postURL()`, back to FMSGraph on the server. `getURL()` could be used for this simple demonstration using a URL-encoded parameter such as

```
"/servlet/FMSGraph?data="+data;
```

However, `postURL()` allows us more options, including sending entire SVG nodes back to the server:

```
PostURL("/servlet/FMSGraph",printNode(obj),"text/plain",null);
```

We are changing graph.svg substantially, adding a slider, some text labels, and a temperature readout. Listing 26.11 shows the additional elements in our new graph.svg.

LISTING 26.11   graph.svg with a Slider Thermostat

```
<?xml version="1.0" encoding="ISO-8859-1" standalone="no"?>
<!DOCTYPE svg PUBLIC "-//W3C//DTD SVG 20010904//EN"
    "http://www.w3.org/TR/SVG/DTD/svg10.dtd" [
    <!ENTITY SENSOR1   "stroke:black;stroke-width:0.01;fill:none;">
    <!ENTITY DATA     "stroke:green;stroke-width:1;fill:none;">
]>
<svg width="600" height="250"  preserveAspectRatio="xMinYMin"
  viewBox="-0.006 -200.0 600 250.0" onload="on_load(evt)">
<script xlink:href="http://www.yourserver.com/svg-fms/js/graph.js"
                                        type="text/ecmascript"/>
<title>Zone Temperature monitor</title>
<defs>
    <marker id="ticV"
      viewBox="0 0 10 10" refX="0" refY="2.5"
```

26

LISTING 26.11   Continued

```
        markerUnits="userSpaceOnUse"
        markerWidth="1000" markerHeight="10"
        orient="auto">
        <line x1="0" y1="0" x2="0" y2="5"/>
      </marker>
      <linearGradient id="tempGradient">
        <stop offset="0%" stop-color="rgb(255,0,0)"/>
        <stop offset="30%" stop-color="rgb(255,255,0)"/>
        <stop offset="80%" stop-color="rgb(240,255,255)"/>
      </linearGradient>
    </defs>

      .

      .

<g id="thermostat" transform="translate(525,-175)">
  <rect x="1" y="1" rx="15" ry="15" width="58" height="150"
style="stroke:black;strokewidth:10;fill:rgb(220,220,220);fill-opacity:0.25"/>
  <text x="0" y="-5">Thermostat</text>
  <text style="font-size:10">
    <tspan x="5" dy="28">90</tspan>
    <tspan x="5" dy="10">80</tspan>
    <tspan x="5" dy="10">70</tspan>
    <tspan x="5" dy="10">60</tspan>
    <tspan x="5" dy="10">50</tspan>
    <tspan x="5" dy="10">40</tspan>
    <tspan x="5" dy="10">30</tspan>
    <tspan x="5" dy="10">20</tspan>
    <tspan x="5" dy="10">10</tspan>
    <tspan x="8" dy="10">0</tspan>
  </text>
  <text id="temp" x="25" y="145">70</text>
  <g id="slider" transform="translate(30 20) scale(1) rotate(90)"
                 onmousedown="SliderDown(evt)" onmouseup="SliderUp(evt)"
                 onmousemove="TempValue(evt)" onclick="TempValue(evt)">
    <g id="body" style="fill: none">
      <rect x="-9" y="-9" width="118" height="18"
                                       style="fill: rgb(128,128,128)"/>
      <rect x="-8" y="-8" width="116" height="16"
                                      style="fill: url(#tempGradient)"/>
      <polyline points="-7.5,7, -7.5,-7.5 108,-7.5"
                                      style="stroke: rgb(100,100,100)"/>
      <polyline points="-8,7.5 107.5,7.5 107.5,-8" style="stroke: white"/>
```

LISTING 26.11 Continued

```
      <g id="thumb" style="fill: none" transform="translate(25 0)">
        <rect x="-6" y="-6" width="12" height="12"
                                    style="fill: rgb(192,192,192)"/>
      <polyline points="-4,5.5 -0,12 4,5.5 -4,5.5"
                                    style="stroke:gray;fill:gray"/>
        <polyline points="-6,5.5 5.5,5.5 5.5,-6" style="stroke:black"/>
        <polyline points="-5,4.5 4.5,4.5 4.5,-5"
                                    style="stroke: rgb(128,128,128)"/>
        <polyline points="-5.5,5 -5.5,-5.5 5,-5.5" style="stroke: white"/>
      </g>
    </g>
  </g><!--slider-->
</g> <!-- thermostat-->

</g><!-- canvas -->
</svg>
```

In addition to the slider thermostat object, we have also added a linearGradient to the
<defs> section. We can use it as a color hint in the slider body showing a gradient from
arctic blue to yellow and then to red as temperatures increase. The slider itself was adapted
from a horizontal version, but the addition of a rotation(90) transform takes care of
setting it vertically. Now we need to look at the changes in graph.js, as shown in Listing
26.12.

LISTING 26.12 graph.js Updated for Slider Thermostat

```
var svgdoc;
var svgroot;
var zone;
// note: set this to the servlet path for your server
  var servlet_path = "/servlet/";

var timer;
var sample = 0;
var sampleRate = 5000;//millisecond sampling rate
var graphLen = 575;
var shift = 0.0;
var dx = 75.0;

var style;
var zoom = 1.0;
var active = false;
```

LISTING 26.12   Continued

```
var thermostat = 70;
var tempLabel;

// must be calculated from viewbox to w x h
var x0 = 0;
var y0 = 0;
var vboxW = 0;
var vboxH = 0;
var svgW = 0;
var svgH = 0;
var sz = 0.25;


function on_load(evt){
  svgdoc = evt.target.getOwnerDocument();
  svgroot = svgdoc.getDocumentElement();
  zone = svgdoc.getElementById("zone").firstChild.data;

  // slider initialization
  slider = svgdoc.getElementById("slider");
  thumb = svgdoc.getElementById("thumb");
  tempLabel = svgdoc.getElementById("temp");

  //initialize cursor parameters
  var vbox = (svgroot.getAttribute("viewBox")).split(' ');
  x0 = parseFloat(vbox[0]);
  y0 = parseFloat(vbox[1]);
  vboxW = parseFloat(vbox[2]);
  vboxH = parseFloat(vbox[3]);
  svgW = parseFloat(svgroot.getAttribute("width"));
  svgH = parseFloat(svgroot.getAttribute("height"));


  // get initial thermostat temperature
  getURL(servlet_path + "FMSGraph?cmd=get&zone="+zone,tempGet);
}

// call back for initial thermostat setting
function tempGet(status) {
  if (status.success) {
    thermostat = parseInt(status.content);
    svgdoc.getElementById("temp").firstChild.setData(thermostat);
```

LISTING 26.12   Continued

```
      thumb.setAttribute("transform", "translate(" + (95-thermostat)+ " 0)");
  }
}

function dataUpdate() {
  getURL(servlet_path + "FMSGraph?cmd=data&zone="+zone,FmsBack);
  timer = setTimeout('dataUpdate()',sampleRate);
}

        .
        .

// slider thermostat
function SliderDown(evt) {
  active = true;
}

function SliderUp(evt) {
  active = false;
  postURL(servlet_path + "FMSGraph?cmd=set&zone="+zone,
                              thermostat,TempSet,"text/plain",null);
}

function TempSet(status) {
//alert(status.content);
}

function TempValue(evt){
  if (active){
    value = 144-((evt.clientY - svgroot.currentTranslate.y)*
                          (vboxH/(svgH*svgroot.currentScale)));
    if (value>100) value = 100;
    if (value<0) value = 0;
    thumb.setAttribute("transform", "translate(" + (100-value)+ " 0)");
    thermostat = Math.round(value-5);
    tempLabel.firstChild.setData(thermostat);
  }
}
```

We have added some global variables to keep track of the slider, but also to provide the necessary view window support. They are initialized on loading the SVG file. The initialization code that is executed on loading also adds a getURL() function to our servlet. This time it is a single access to read the current thermostat setting. TempValue(evt) is called each time the user clicks in the thermostat control area or slides the thumb to a different temperature. The value is calculated in a manner that takes into account any scale changes made by zooming or panning. Although we are really interested only in the Y coordinate, we are reusing modified code from our cursor following labels discussed in Chapter 25.

The `value` is adjusted to the location of our thermostat in the `viewbox` and used to move the slider thumb. After updating the thumb position, we save the `value` adjusted to the temperature reading as `newTemp`. After the mouse is released, we call `postURL()` to send this `newTemp` value up to the server. There happens to be nothing exotic in this `postURL()` because we are merely sending the `newTemp` setting to our servlet. The callback function receives any response from the servlet, but in this case we are not using any response and include it just for debugging purposes.

Back at the servlet shown in Listing 26.13, we add some code to check for two additional commands: `set` and `get`. If the `cmd` is `set`, we can update the thermostat to the new value read from our `postURL()` message. We write back a string message just for debugging. If the `cmd` is `get`, we write the current thermostat setting back to the `getURL()`. Note that the thermostat setting is used for the random number offset so that the client will see feedback as the temperature settings change.

LISTING 26.13   Revised FMSGraph Servlet

```
       .
       .
       .
else if (cmd.equals("set")) {
  try {
    thermostat[zone] = Integer.parseInt(in.readLine());
    out.println("new temp: " + thermostat[zone]);
  } catch (NumberFormatException e) {
    out.println("error");
  }
}
else if (cmd.equals("get")) {
  out.println(thermostat[zone]);
}
       .
       .
```

Listing 26.3 is a simple loopback for our SVG control, but it shows the basic mechanism for updating our client from the server. However, what if several building managers are reviewing the thermostat setting, and they begin making adjustments? The thermostat settings at the servlet are a static array variable, which means changing the thermostat setting from any monitor will affect thermostat settings and temperature logs to anyone else monitoring the system. However, the only monitor that will be immediately updated with the new thermostat setting is the one that sent the change. What we need is an additional output with each of our temperature data points for the current thermostat setting. That way, any change across the system will update the other monitors within 5000ms, without having to refresh each browser. This requires only a single line revision on the server side in FMSGraph.java:

```
out.println(d1+";" + temperature);
```

The changes to graph.js are only a little more involved, as shown in Listing 26.14.

LISTING 26.14   graph.js with Thermostat Update

```
function FmsBack(status){
  //alert("Success = " + status.success + " type: " + status.contentType);
  //alert(status.content);
  if (status.success) {
    var temp = status.content.split(';');
    // thermostat has changed so update the slider thumb
    if (temp[zone]!= thermostat.toString()) {
      thermostat = temp[zone];
      thumb.setAttribute("transform", "translate(" + (95-thermostat)+ " 0)");
      tempLabel.firstChild.setData(thermostat);
    }
    dx = dx + sampleRate*0.005;
       .
       .
```

We are using the line var temp = status.content.split(';'); to split the two data values returned by our servlet. The first data value, temp[0], is the usual temperature reading, and the second value, temp[1], is the current thermostat setting. Any change to the servlet thermostat setting will be recognized and used to update the local thermostat setting as well as the slider thumb.

Our FMS system now has a basic remote Internet control that allows users to monitor simulated temperature on an SVG cylinder chart as well as control thermostat settings. Figure 26.4 shows the completed temperature monitor with thermostat control.

26

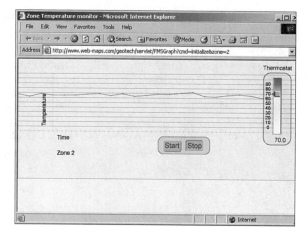

FIGURE 26.4   Graphing monitor with thermostat control.

Summary

This case study illustrates the use of SVG in a monitor control application for a simplified FMS. It demonstrates the power of SVG for visual models, but more importantly, it demonstrates a method of adding dynamic control to an online monitoring system. With SVG, FMS can easily be extended from a somewhat static report-and-query system to a dynamic loopback control. Admittedly, this example is simplified, and of course, you would not want to trust sensitive controls to the Internet world. However, even if SVG controls are not suitable for real-time heart monitors, innumerable, less critical, functions can fit into this model.

Mobile asset tracking is another area of FMS that can benefit from dynamic updating. For example, it is not difficult to envision an SVG map model capable of tracking shipping containers across a transportation system. The addition of a Java Messaging Service (JMS) to our server can loosely couple a publisher/subscriber pattern to an SVG visual display. The container's GPS unit is the JMS message publisher, and an SVG map servlet is the message subscriber. As units move across the real world, they also move across a map model accessible from any browser. Here, SVG slips across the threshold of dreams, eerily reminiscent of a Jorge Luis Borges novel, a semantic web of referential chains bridging mind and space, convoluting the virtual and real, until all the world is a text of singularly vast lineage.

PART V

Looking Ahead

IN THIS PART

CHAPTER **27**

SVG 1.1, 1.2, and 2.0

Version 1.0 of any specification cannot cover everything, and SVG is no exception. During development of SVG 1.0, the Working Group received a large amount of feedback from the user and developer community. Some was easily incorporated. Some, such as the lack of declarative animation syntax in early drafts, was important enough to warrant a delay to the specification. Other feedback, while deemed important, could not be integrated into SVG 1.0 and was deferred for a later version.

The preceding chapters were concerned with SVG 1.0, which is a stable Web standard. This chapter examines the SVG 1.1, 1.2, and 2.0 specifications, which, at the time of writing, are not finished; they are working drafts or requirements documents and, thus, subject to change. Be sure to check the latest status of these specifications on the W3C Web site (http://www.w3.org/Graphics/SVG).

The emerging developments in SVG will be considered in three parts: first, the mechanisms to adapt SVG for use on mobile browsers; second, the addition of requested features to versions of SVG beyond 1.0; and finally, the techniques for using SVG with other languages from the XML family of technologies.

Mobile SVG

The new generation of mobile devices such as palmtop and pocket computers or mobile phones have the sort of processing power, network speeds, and color displays that were commonplace on desktop machines less than a decade ago. They allow information to be delivered in situations in which a conventional laptop computer is too cumbersome. Use of graphics, rather than just text, allows complex information to be presented in a compact and easily understood manner. Thus, there is considerable interest in using SVG on this class of device.

The major use of SVG to date has been on desktop and laptop computers. Because it is scalable, SVG is also useful on the smaller screens of mobile devices; however, there are particular constraints that you should bear in mind when developing SVG for mobile usage.

Need for Mobile Profiles

During the year 2001, several partial implementations of SVG appeared on small, mobile devices. They were partial not only due to lack of development time, but also because they were approaching or meeting the capability limits of the devices on which they ran. There was often some commonality of features chosen for such subset implementations—for example, they could all render paths in solid colors—but there were also large differences between them. Clearly, there would be an interoperability problem unless there was an official subset or profile of SVG.

A wide variety of new mobile devices was also released onto the market, and the much-discussed third-generation (3G) phones started to become a reality. The "typical" capabilities of a device still vary in different countries. Cell phones in Japan have for several years had color displays and in some cases include small digital cameras and can run Java applets, for example. But these differences are starting to even out, and the gap between high-end cell phones and low-end palmtop devices has shrunk to zero; in some cases, these devices have merged. At the same time, new mobile processors, increased amounts of memory, large and clear color displays, and ubiquitous networking have raised the top end of the Pocket PC market.

It became clear that the spread of device capabilities meant that a single profile would not suffice. It would be too complex for the most limited hardware and insufficiently powerful to be attractive on the more capable machines. Equally, having a large number of profiles would lead to confusion among the public, cause difficulties in authoring, and limit interoperability.

After much discussion, two profiles called SVG Tiny and SVG Basic were seen as the optimal trade-off. SVG Tiny is aimed at the new generation of color cell phones, and SVG Basic is aimed at the handheld, palmtop, and Pocket PC market. To allow these profiles to be created while ensuring complete upward compatibility (SVG Tiny content will display on all SVG Basic and SVG Full players), the capabilities of the SVG 1.0 specification had to be broken down into small, functional building blocks or modules. These modules could then be combined in different ways to make profiles.

Implementers could then target the appropriate profile of SVG and implement all of it; content developers could select an appropriate profile and design content for it, rather than attempting to design content for each mobile device that they knew about or could obtain for testing.

The result of modularizing SVG 1.0 was called SVG 1.1. SVG Tiny and SVG Basic, collectively known as SVG Mobile, are thus profiles of SVG 1.1.

Figure 27.1 shows an SVG Basic implementation running on two handheld devices.

FIGURE 27.1   SVG Basic implementation by BitFlash, on a Palm Pilot and a Pocket PC. (Photographs by kind permission of Bitflash.)

SVG 1.1 and SVG Mobile both moved to Candidate Recommendation status on April 30, 2002. For the latest version of these specifications, see `http://www.w3.org/TR/SVGMobile` and `http://www.w3.org/TR/SVG11`.

Using only the features of the appropriate profile will help ensure that content displays well on the target device. Each of the two profiles is tuned for use on a particular class of hardware and includes a selection of elements and attributes suitable for that device. Care and thought still need to be exercised, however, to ensure that content is suitable. For example, a profile will stop you from creating filters in SVG Tiny content but will not prevent you from including a 2MB JPEG file in SVG Tiny content aimed at a cell phone.

In general, all SVG Tiny and SVG Basic examples will work on any conformant SVG 1.0 implementation, whether it is on a desktop or a mobile device.

Constraints of Mobile Devices

Compared to a desktop or laptop computer, mobile devices have much lower CPU power and memory capacity—or to put this into a more positive perspective, similar capabilities to a desktop machine of 10 years ago will now fit into your pocket. There is also a very wide spread of capabilities across the market—from highly constrained devices such as cell phones to very capable devices such as Pocket PCs. Even the most powerful devices, with 400MHz StrongARM CPUs, are less than one-fifth the speed of a desktop with a 2GHz Intel or AMD CPU.

The amount of memory available is also highly constrained—2 to 16MB on a palmtop, 32 to 64MB on a pocket PC, and a few hundred kilobytes on a phone.

27

Thus, care should be given to the facilities used. On very small devices, for example, filter effects should be avoided because they consume both CPU and memory (for offscreen compositing buffers); larger devices can use carefully selected filters with caution.

Desktop devices have large hard disks that can be used for storing content and as a network cache; long-term storage on mobile devices may be limited (megabytes, not giga-bytes) or indeed nonexistent. The lack of a cache can affect the way content is best struc-tured. For example, a raster image might be retransmitted for each SVG graphic that uses it, which increases total download time. A mobile content author might realize that there is no additional cost to having several slightly different versions, whereas an SVG devel-oper aiming at the desktop market would attempt to reuse the same raster graphic so that it is downloaded only once.

Typical display resolutions on desktop and laptop devices range from 800×600 at the lower end up to 1920×1280 for a workstation. Resolutions on the new generation of color cell phones are typically 120×90 up to 160×180; PDAs may go from 160×160 up to 360×480. The largest PDA screens therefore have one-third the number of pixels of the smallest laptops. Clearly, this means that SVG for mobile devices needs to be designed from the start for compact, information-dense representation. There is an unexpected benefit, however; because substantially fewer pixels are being updated, the limited CPU capabilities go much further in terms of achievable frame rates when updating animated content.

In terms of networking, too, mobile devices show differences from the desktop. The use of broadband networking, common in the office and becoming widespread in the home, has meant that desktop machines typically have ample bandwidth for displaying Web content. In the mobile space, bandwidth has a wide variation. In a business or industrial setting, wireless 802.11 networking provides a reliable 11 Mbps capacity within a small area such as a single building, comparable to bandwidth available on a desktop. Other mobile units that are used further afield may use GPRS, CDMA, and similar wireless network standards to provide 64Kbps bandwidth, similar to an analog modem or ISDN line but with much longer latency. Some cell phones and pagers will continue to use GSM, which is primarily aimed at voice traffic and gives only 9.6Kbps bandwidth. Lastly, connectivity on mobile phones may not always be available, and users may be paying by the packet or the megabyte.

High latency, rather than low bandwidth, has the greatest effect on structuring SVG for the mobile market. On the desktop, with latencies in the tens to low hundreds of millisec-onds, you can easily download an SVG file; parse it; discover that it needs two raster images, a font, and a symbol file; download each of these separately; and display the result. On mobile devices, latencies of several seconds mean that it is much faster to place all the resources inline in a single file that is fetched in a single transaction; this includes raster images, inlined using the data:protocol and base64 encoding.

When you're developing SVG for the mobile market, aim for a specific SVG profile and hardware capability. Ensure that your content will display on devices a little less capable, and rest assured that higher-powered devices will display it fine. Content aimed at cell phones may look plain, but will function correctly, on more capable devices; content aimed at fully featured PDAs may run poorly or not at all on cell phones.

Advantages of Mobile Devices

Mobile devices have advantages as well as drawbacks, of course; otherwise, no one would use them. They are much more convenient to carry and to use in situations in which people would not think to bring a laptop computer. Besides being lightweight, they can be operated with one hand. They can be used for long periods of time, longer than a laptop running without main power, and can be placed unobtrusively to one side. They are also significantly less expensive than laptop devices, opening up new and larger markets than traditional computing devices.

Rather than compare a mobile device unfavorably to a laptop, we can compare it favorably to a printout. With zooming and panning, and user-selectable layers, an SVG graphic on a mobile device can display similar levels of detail to a sheet of paper. Because a large (and increasing) number of mobile devices have some sort of wireless network connection—GSM, GPRS, up to 802.11—they can display an up-to-date view of the data at all times.

The mobile professional can be greatly aided by an up-to-date, wirelessly connected graphic display. A doctor making the rounds of a hospital ward can consult height/weight dosage charts, view graphs of laboratory test results over time, and read up-to-the-minute contraindications on prescribed drugs. A financial trader can produce comparative graphs of stock prices, currency exchange rates, and predictors of future performance. An aircraft electrical engineer, looking for a wiring fault in a confined space, can call up circuit diagrams, routing tables, and lists of modifications made to this particular aircraft and can log the repairs that have been made immediately rather than waiting until he or she is back in the office.

The general public, too, can benefit from SVG on a mobile device by sending multimedia messages rather than SMS. The third generation (3G) multimedia messaging service (MMS) is based on SMIL Basic, XHTML Basic, and SVG Tiny.

An important differentiating factor for mobile devices, as opposed to desktops, is that they move—their position changes over time. With a means of determining this position, such as the Global Positioning System (GPS) or by triangulation from towers of known position and signal strength, the current position can be incorporated into the graphical display. Clearly, this is aided by metadata that gives the geographical coverage of an SVG graphic that represents a map—something SVG 1.1 adds.

Beyond SVG 1.1

The preceding section described Mobile SVG profiles based on SVG 1.1, which has the SVG 1.0 feature set but with modularized DTDs. This section looks beyond the feature set of SVG 1.1. The examples in this section use a speculative syntax which, at the time of writing, might work only in specialized experimental software or not at all.

The intention of this discussion is to make you aware of current trends in the SVG community and to alert you to follow the ongoing work of the second SVG Working Group at W3C. You can find pointers to the latest information linked from the following: `http://www.w3.org/Graphics/SVG`.

SVG and Patents

The early growth of the Web, and of the Internet, was fueled by the ready availability of the specifications at no cost, and the ability to implement and use these specifications freely at no monetary cost. It is the stated intention of the W3C that this should continue to be the model for development of Web specifications. Unfortunately, this position was seen to be so self-evident that it was rarely put into writing.

On the other hand, software patents exist in the USA and in some other countries; ignoring their existence does not ensure that specifications are or continue to be freely implementable. In some cases, there are patent claims for existing specifications, but the claims are not enforced—either through goodwill, or because the patents are held in reserve to be used as a counterclaim defense.

The W3C has been taking steps to ensure that the existing, implicit culture is both preserved and made explicit. For example, participants in W3C Working Groups are required to disclose patents that might be necessary for implementation of a particular specification as soon as they become aware of them.

As a result, SVG 1.0 was one of the first specifications from the W3C that was published together with patent disclosures and associated licenses. See http://www.w3.org/2001/07/SVG10-IPR-statements.html.

The inclusion of this information caused some consternation in the community, whose members were unaccustomed to being presented with this sort of information. After the information was read and understood, however, the community saw that there was no problem. One patent claim, from Apple, had been disclosed to the Working Group early on and was avoided in the design of SVG 1.0. Another, from Kodak, was determined not essential for implementing SVG 1.0, according to the company. Furthermore, 8 of the 11 Working Group participants made Royalty Free (RF) licenses available on any as-yet-unknown patents that they might discover in the future and that might be necessary for implementing SVG 1.0.

Another change at the W3C requires newly chartered working groups to explicitly state whether they will produce an RF or fee-bearing (Reasonable and Non-Discriminatory, RAND) specification and to treat this as a technical constraint. The second SVG Working Group was the first group at the W3C to be created with such an explicit RF licensing mode. Thus, SVG 1.1, 1.2, and 2.0 will be freely implementable.

DOM Level 3 TextEvents

Early drafts of SVG used the keyboard events that were part of early drafts of DOM Level 2. This allowed an event listener to determine which key had been pressed. Early implementations of SVG also supported them in good faith.

These events were criticized from an internationalization standpoint; they were not equally applicable to all keyboard layouts, which vary by country as well as by operating system, and it was not clear what other input methods (as widely used in Japan and China) were supposed to do. The problems could not be corrected without holding up the specification for an unreasonable time, so this feature was removed. Keyboard events do not form part of the DOM Level 2 Recommendation published on November 13, 2000, which states:

> The DOM Level 2 Event specification does not provide a key event module. An event module designed for use with keyboard input devices will be included in a later version of the DOM specification.

In consequence, keyboard events were also removed from SVG long before publication of the SVG 1.0 Recommendation on September 4, 2001. SVG 1.1, the modularization of SVG 1.0, similarly has no keyboard events.

Any usage of keyboard events in current SVG content is thus outside the specification, and relies on legacy implementation. Newer SVG implementations do not have these legacy events; thus, the content *will not work* on conformant SVG implementations.

As noted in the DOM Level 2 specification, work was deferred rather than stopped. A working draft of DOM Level 3 Events was published on February 8, 2002; this draft includes something called TextEvents. Unlike the earlier keyboard events, TextEvents generate text strings—usually one character, but it could be more. Attributes on the event describe the string generated, the key pressed, and whether any visual output was generated. To check for a capital letter *S*, for example, it is enough to check the `outputString` attribute to look for *S* instead of checking for the S key, checking to see whether Shift was pressed at the same time, and checking the state of CapsLock.

It is still possible to do keyboard-like programming such as checking for a particular function key, Alt key, or Control key being pressed during a `textInput` event or starting animations on a `keyDown` or `keyUp` event. But it is also possible to input text, in any language, without having to worry whether the user had the CapsLock button pressed or used a kana-to-kanji input conversion for Japanese or a Bopomofo-to-Hanzi input conversion for Chinese (both of which would require several key presses for a single character) or indeed whether they used a radical-stroke index to select the Kanji character for Japanese (which would involve using the mouse to pick from a list, in addition to key presses). The power of the interface is increased, and the life of the programmer is made easier; it was worth waiting until DOM Level 3.

The intention is to add the DOM Level 3 TextEvents to SVG 1.2, assuming that both specifications are able to move through the maturity levels of Last Call, Candidate Recommendation, and Proposed Recommendation on similar timescales.

Thus, SVG 1.2 implementations will be able to reliably and interoperably interact with the keyboard or other text-generating device. The presence of DOM Level 3 TextEvents may be reliably detected in script as follows:

27

```
if (hasFeature("TextEvents", "3.0"))
  MyFunction();
else
  MyOtherFunction();
```

You can find the specification for DOM Level 3 TextEvents at the following address: http://www.w3.org/TR/DOM-Level-3-Events/events.html#Events-TextEvents-Interfaces.

Simple Text Wrapping

In HTML pages, text wrapping happens automatically. If the size of the text container is changed, the text will reflow. Exact control over the layout is not possible, even if the implementation supports CSS well.

In SVG 1.0, text wrapping is done at content creation time by the author or the authoring application. The basic text element in SVG is a single line; small variations in length caused by font metrics on different platforms can be accommodated by using the textLength attribute or eliminated entirely by using an SVG font.

As you saw in Chapter 12, "SVG for Web Authoring," you can achieve the effect of multiple lines in SVG 1.0 by inserting tspan elements with dx or dy attributes (depending on whether the text is horizontal, as it is in most Western languages, or vertical, as it sometimes is in Chinese and Japanese). It is also possible with x and y attributes, but this is bad practice if the text contains any bidirectional languages (Hebrew or Arabic) because these attributes cause the tspan element to create a new text chunk and break bidirectional reordering.

This sort of manual layout is fine for static text, but is of no use for text that is dynamically generated either at the server or as a result of scripting in the client. Such text will become ragged, overlap adjacent content, and will not reflow. Some users have tried to implement their own text reflowing in SVG 1.0 and ECMAScript, but it is hard.

It is the intention for SVG 1.2 to add elements that contain reflowing text. This will simplify applications that display dynamically changing information and SVG generators that take templates and fill them in on the server.

Listing 27.1 uses a speculative syntax that is certainly subject to change but serves to illustrate the concepts:

LISTING 27.1   textflow.svg—SVG 1.2 Text Flow

```
<?xml version="1.0" encoding="UTF-8"?>
<svg width="100%" height="100%" viewBox="0 0 650 550"
    xmlns="http://www.w3.org/2000/svg" version="1.2">
    <g fill="#FFD" stroke="#060" stroke-width="2">
        <rect x="40" y="40" width="270" height="480"/>
        <rect x="340" y="40" width="270" height="480"/>
    </g>
```

LISTING 27.1   Continued

```
<flowText font-size="26" xml:space="default">
    <flowRegion>
        <region x="50" y="50" width="250" height="460"/>
        <region x="350" y="50" width="250" height="460"/>
    </flowRegion>
    <flowDiv>
        <flowPara bottom-margin="10">
        This paragraph has lots of text that will wrap. It
        can contain <flowSpan fill="red">spans of text styled
        differently</flowSpan> as well as
        forced <flowLine/>line breaks.
        The text flows from one child of the 're&#xAD;gion'
        element to another, and is thrown away if
        there is too much.
    </flowPara>
        <flowPara bottom-margin="10">The simple algorithm
         wraps on spaces if it can
        find them, otherwise it will break in the middle
        of a word. This is needed for Japanese and
        Chinese text where there are no spaces between
        words like this:
        <flowSpan xml:lang="ja-JP" font-family="'MS Gothic',
            MS ゴシック,'MS Mincho',MS 明朝 , Code2000,'
            Arial Unicode MS',DFP-SMTWSong"
            > なぜ、みんな日本語を話してくれないのか ?</flowSpan>
        </flowPara>
        <flowPara bottom-margin="10">
        If you need to imp&#xAD;lement Japanese
      <flowSpan font-style="italic">kinsoku</flowSpan>
        rules for line breaking, use Unicode
        zero-width-joiner (zwj) characters to
        forbid certain line breaks.
    </flowPara>
    </flowDiv>
    </flowText>
</svg>
```

Within a `flowText` element, all the text is selectable. It forms a natural reading order, which enhances accessibility. A `flowText` element has a `region` child, which defines the geometry in which the text is laid out, and one (or possibly more) `flowDiv` children, which are block containers. Whether multiple `flowDiv` children are useful is a matter of debate.

The children of a `flowRegion` are likely to be restricted to rectangular shapes all aligned in the same direction. This is why a new `region` element is used; it's like a `rect` but has no `transform` attribute. Subsequent versions of SVG may allow more complex shapes, including arbitrary paths with holes.

The children of `flowDiv` are `flowPara` (unlike HTML, elements either contain blocks or they contain text, but never both; this simplifies implementation a great deal and is arguably cleaner and more structured). `flowPara` elements are also blocks; for the purposes of bidirectional text layout, they establish a new text chunk in SVG 1.0 terms.

The content model of the `flowPara` element is mixed (allows both elements and text), and is inline—text, `flowSpan`, and `flowLine` (the equivalent of the XHTML `br` element). For purposes of bidirectional reordering and ligature formation, each `flowPara` element is a text chunk. The `flowSpan` and `flowLine` elements never create new text chunks.

In HTML (and indeed in CSS and XSL), line breaking is application dependent. Implementations vary in the ways they approach line breaking. Some do a better job than others in terms of internationalization; perhaps they know all the JIS X-4051 rules for line breaking in Japanese text but cannot break Thai (which has no spaces between words and can be broken only by consulting a Thai dictionary).

This variability is fine for presentation of text, but not for graphically rich text and mixed text/graphics such as logos and artwork. Repeatability and consistency are highly important. For this reason, a simple line-breaking algorithm is specified, and all implementations must follow it. Line breaking can occur at a space character, an ideographic space character, or a soft hyphen. Line breaking cannot occur at a nonbreaking space or a zero-width joiner. If a line is too long (there are no spaces of soft hyphens, common in languages that do not separate words with spaces), the line is broken wherever it fits.

Figure 27.2 shows an experimental implementation of the text flow capabilities, rendered in a special build of Batik 1.5.

Background Colors

CSS1 defines a `background` property, which provides a colored background for text. It also allows an image to be positioned on this background and for the image to be tiled. CSS1 is aimed at flowing text layout, such as HTML pages. The widths and heights of individual elements such as paragraphs are not known in advance, but they are always rectangular and axis aligned; they are usually nested one inside the other and rarely overlap.

In the SVG example in the preceding section, colored rectangles were drawn behind the text to form a background. This technique works well if the size of the rectangles is known in advance, and the items whose background they form does not change. SVG can readily produce solid-colored or gradient backgrounds, can stretch an image to fit a given size (something proposed for CSS3), and can tile an image by referencing it as a pattern. It can do this for any arbitrary shape, not just rectangles, but only if the size and position are known.

This paragraph has lots of text that will wrap. It can contain spans of text styled differently as well as forced line breaks. The text flows from one child of the 'region' element to another, and is thrown away if there is too much.

The simple algorithm wraps on spaces if it can find them, otherwise it will break in the middle of a

word. This is needed for Japanese and Chinese text where there are no spaces between words like this:
なぜ、みんな日本語を話してくれないのか？

If you need to implement Japanese *kinsoku* rules for line breaking, use Unicode zero-width-joiner (zwj) characters to forbid certain line

FIGURE 27.2   SVG textflow in an extended build of the Batik Squiggle SVG browser.

The possibility of dynamically generated text in SVG 1.0, and the introduction of flowed text into SVG 1.2, highlights a need to produce colored backgrounds whose size is not known in advance but is calculated on the fly. It seems that rectangular areas will suffice—rectangular at least in their local coordinate system, but not necessarily axis aligned. Further transformations and clipping might make them into arbitrary polygons, but in the local coordinate system they are rectangles.

Thus, the CSS background property might be allowed in SVG 1.2 for those elements that generate a rectangular shape—elements that generate a viewport, and text elements.

Z-ordering

SVG 1.0 uses the painter's model to control rendering order, as described in Chapter 1, "SVG Overview." Thus, for a given SVG parse tree, the order of rendering is fixed: The object that is last in tree order will render on top of everything else.

In SVG 1.0, the usual way to manipulate the order of rendering is to physically move the element in the tree by scripting; the element is cloned to a new position and the original deleted. A variant of this strategy is to have multiple copies of an object and to animate the visibility property so that first one copy shows, and then a different copy that has a different place in the tree shows and thus is in front of, or behind, another object when rendered.

A commonly requested extension to SVG is control of the rendering order without recourse to scripting. This corresponds to the widely available functionality in many

27

graphics authoring tools whereby an object or group can be moved forward, backward, to the front, or to the back of the overall composition. It is also commonly observed that CSS2 has a z-index property that appears to provide this sort of functionality, but SVG 1.0 does not use it.

The problem with the CSS2 z-index property is that it was designed for a layout model of nested rectangular boxes. For each box, there is a limit to the amount of reordering that can be achieved. Siblings can be reordered, but no element can be placed above or below the stacking context of the parent. Thus, the CSS2 z-index property does not provide the commonly requested functionality for fully general control of z-order.

Is all that we need, then, a differently named property that provides the required functionality and allows any arbitrary z-ordering? Unfortunately, such a property would be very hard to specify while remaining compatible with the SVG 1.0 rendering model.

Two examples may demonstrate the problems. The group opacity property is defined to work by rendering the entire element, including its children, to an offscreen buffer, then adjusting the opacity of the result, and compositing it with the rest of the graphic. This approach works well with the painter's algorithm because all the children are adjacent in rendering order. Similarly, in filter effects, the enable-background property constructs an offscreen buffer consisting of everything that has been rendered so far, including preceding siblings of the element, and bringing this image into the network of filter nodes. Consider what would happen if some other element somewhere in the tree were given a z-index such that it should be rendered in among these siblings. Would its opacity be altered? Would it take part in the filtering operation?

Load and Save

Dynamic, data-driven applications need to access data on remote servers and update the display. Examples of such data-driven graphics range from stock quotes and sports scores through to industrial monitoring and process control.

It is most convenient if such data is in XML so that it can be parsed into a new tree, its DOM navigated to find the appropriate content, and new nodes created in the SVG graphic. This also allows for such applications as dynamically generated, time-changing graphics symbols—for example, on a weather chart that always displays the current weather in different parts of the country.

The DOM 3 Load and Save API is a prime candidate for such functionality and is under consideration as a required part of SVG 1.2. It is influenced by, but not identical to, the Java API for XML Processing (JAXP) and Simple API for XML (SAX). Similar functionality is also present in the Adobe SVG implementation, with the proprietary getURL, parseXML, and postURL methods. Addition of a standardized method would allow interoperable data-driven SVG graphics.

For further details, refer to the DOM 3 specifications at the following address:
http://www.w3.org/TR/DOM-Level-3-ASLS/load-save.html.

Vector Effects

Filter effects, introduced in SVG 1.0, perform image-processing operations on the rasterized rendering of a subtree of SVG before sending it for display. They are often used to add depth and texture to a vector graphic to make it look less "vectorial." Filter effects were described in Chapter 10, "SVG Filters."

In Listing 27.2, an `feDisplacement` filter whose input is random turbulence is applied to a simple geometric shape to give a rougher, more random look, while keeping the actual geometry small (see Figure 27.3). The path data to encode such a rough shape directly would be rather large.

LISTING 27.2   feDisplacement.svg—Rough Shapes Using Raster Filters

```
<?xml version="1.0" encoding="utf-8"?>
<!DOCTYPE svg PUBLIC "-//W3C//DTD SVG 1.0//EN"
"http://www.w3.org/TR/SVG/DTD/svg10.dtd">
<svg width="100%" height="100%" viewBox="0 0 295 105">
    <defs>
        <path id="star" d="M88.42,103.13L55.1,85.88L22,103.55l6.11-37.02
            L1.08, 40.51l37.1-5.63L54.56,
            1.13l16.82,33.54l37.16,5.16l-26.7,26.36l6.58,36.94z"/>
        <filter id="ragged" filterUnits="objectBoundingBox"
            x="-15%" y="-15%" width="130%" height="130%">
            <feTurbulence baseFrequency="0.1" numOctaves="2" result="turb"/>
            <feDisplacementMap in="SourceGraphic" in2="turb" scale="10"
                xChannelSelector="R" yChannelSelector="G" result="shifted"/>
            <feFlood flood-color="rgb(71,133,183)" result="color"/>
            <feComposite in2="shifted" in="color" operator="in"/>
        </filter>
    </defs>
    <g fill="#4785B7" stroke="black" stroke-miterlimit="4">
        <use xlink:href="#star" transform="translate(20,0)"/>
        <use xlink:href="#star" transform="translate(150,0)"
            filter="url(#ragged)"/>
    </g>
</svg>
```

The problem is that the elements to which the filter is applied must be rasterized before the filter is applied. Although the resolution of the filter can be controlled, using a high resolution (for example, suitable for printed output) consumes a great deal of memory.

An idea under consideration is to reuse the filter nodes concept, but to add a new set of vector filters that take vector data as input and generate new vector data as output. This technique would certainly improve printed output and might also allow some of the visual effects of raster filters to be implemented on mobile devices.

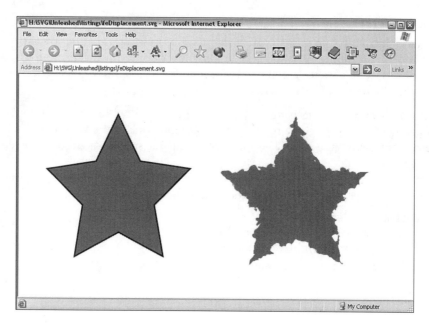

FIGURE 27.3   Raster effects to generate complex outlines.

In Figure 27.4, three different vector filter effects have been applied to a simple star shape. At the top right, a curve and swirl effect spins the star about its center. To the bottom right, a wave function makes each line in the original more complex, in a regular and symmetric way. To the bottom left, a random function gives an irregular, jagged appearance.

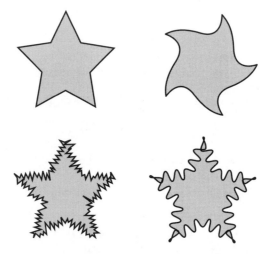

FIGURE 27.4   Four sample vector filter effects.

SVG and Multiple Namespaces

Some capabilities were not added to SVG 1.0 and are not planned for a subsequent version because another specification already provides the capability and a Web client can provide the functionality by implementing a combination of SVG and other XML namespaces. It may be, though, that the SVG Working Group has to define some "glue" to ensure that the two namespaces can be reliably used together and work the same way across multiple implementations.

This section gives some examples of what can be done, with a suitable client, by combining the SVG namespace and another XML namespace. In some cases, existing implementations can already implement this functionality; in other cases, the specifications are complete and await implementation; and in yet other cases, further design work needs to be done as specifically noted.

Linking and Synchronization for Audio

Addition of the SMIL `audio` element to SVG content is simple because it has no impact on the visual layout; the synchronization of the audio with the timeline and with events in the SVG tree is also straightforward because the underlying SMIL model is the same. This is an expected benefit of the joint work that the SVG and SYMM working groups undertook to produce the SMIL Animation subset of SMIL 2.0.

Adobe has already prototyped functionality in ASV3, as have CSIRO in its PocketSVG player. They both used the SMIL `audio` element as a basis but placed the element in its own namespace because it uses an XLink `href` rather than the `src` attribute used by SMIL. Although this design is arguably better, it is not what the specification says.

The X-Smiles browser (`http://www.x-smiles.org`) also implements a mixture of SVG and SMIL and can play streaming audio synchronized with SVG.

The one remaining issue is that of audio formats. To improve interoperability, it would be preferable to pick at least one format that all conformant players must support (as was done in SVG 1.0 with the image formats JPEG and PNG). Some commonly used audio formats are proprietary and not well documented. Others, such as MP3, are international standards but require implementers and content creators to pay license fees to the patent holders. A possible solution would be to use the open OGG Vorbis format, as implemented in X-Smiles.

> **NOTE**
>
> For further information about the Ogg Vorbis format, look at http://www.xiph.org/ogg/vorbis/index.html.

Full Text Layout with Flow

The limited text-wrapping capabilities of SVG are meant to deal with small amounts of text inside graphics. They are not a substitute for the full text-layout capabilities of CSS or

XSL, nor are they a substitute for the higher-level semantics of XHTML or MathML. When a combination of rich graphics and complex text is needed, a multinamespace solution is the best approach.

At the same time as the SVG 1.1 candidate recommendation, a first working draft of a multinamespace DTD combining XHTML 1.1, MathML 2.0, and SVG 1.1 was published. It allows DTD validation of mixed namespace documents that use these three namespaces (plus XLink, of course).

Listing 27.3 is a simple example.

LISTING 27.3   Mixed MathML, XHTML, and SVG Example

```
<?xml-stylesheet type="text/xsl"
    href="http://www.w3.org/Math/Group/XSL/pmathml.xsl"?>
<html xmlns="http://www.w3.org/1999/xhtml">
    <head>
        <meta http-equiv="Content-Type" content="text/html; charset=UTF-8"/>
        <title>Mixing MathML and SVG with XHTML</title>
        <meta content="amaya 6.1, see http://www.w3.org/Amaya/"
            name="generator" />
        <style type="text/css">
            p { text-indent: 15pt; line-height: 34pt}
        </style>
    </head>
    <body>
        <h1>Mixed Namespace Example</h1>
        <p>Inside this paragraph of
            XHTML text is an inline equation:
            x<math xmlns="http://www.w3.org/1998/Math/MathML">
                <mover>
                    <mo>&RightArrow;</mo>
                    <mtext>maps to</mtext>
                </mover>
            </math>y and then a small graphic.</p>
        <svg:svg xmlns:svg="http://www.w3.org/2000/svg">
            <svg:rect stroke="black" fill="none" y="15px" x="50px"
                width="89px" height="32px" style="stroke: #FF5F00;
                fill: #00B200"/>
            <svg:rect stroke="black" fill="none" y="3px" x="108px"
                width="18px" height="70px" style="stroke: #000000;
                fill: #E50073"/>
            <svg:ellipse stroke="black" fill="none" cy="26px" cx="67px"
                rx="7px" ry="6px" style="stroke: #0000E5; fill: #0000E5"/>
        </svg:svg>
```

LISTING 27.3 Continued

```
        <p>More SVG:</p>
        <svg:svg xmlns:svg="http://www.w3.org/2000/svg">
            <svg:rect stroke="black" fill="none" y="13px" x="24px"
                width="391px" height="145px" style="fill: #FFDA95"/>
            <svg:switch>
                <svg:foreignObject width="158px" height="85px"
                    y="20px" x="90px">
                    <div dir="ltr" xmlns="http://www.w3.org/1999/xhtml">
                        <math xmlns="http://www.w3.org/1998/Math/MathML">
                            <munderover>
                                <mo>&Sum;</mo>
                                <mrow>
                                    <mi>i</mi>
                                    <mo>=</mo>
                                    <mn>1</mn>
                                </mrow>
                                <mi>n</mi>
                            </munderover>
                        </math>
                    </div>
                </svg:foreignObject>
            </svg:switch>
            <svg:circle stroke="black" fill="none" cy="33px" cx="402px"
                r="7px" style="fill: #FFAA00"/>
            <svg:circle stroke="black" fill="none" cy="82px" cx="323px"
                r="42px" style="fill: #FFCB69"/>
            <svg:switch>
                <svg:foreignObject width="57px" height="35px"
                    y="50px" x="290px">
                    <div dir="ltr" xmlns="http://www.w3.org/1999/xhtml">
                        <p>Hi!</p>
                    </div>
                </svg:foreignObject>
            </svg:switch>
            <svg:circle stroke="black" fill="none" cy="44px" cx="55px"
                r="17px" style="fill: #FFAA00"/>
            <svg:circle stroke="black" fill="none" cy="89px" cx="43px"
                r="11px" style="fill: #FFAA00"/>
        </svg:svg>
    </body>
</html>
```

27

In this DTD, svg elements are permitted anywhere in the XHTML that a block-level element such as a paragraph could be placed. Within svg elements, the other namespaces are enclosed inside a foreignObject (to give a position, width, and height of the rendered result of the foreign namespace,) which is itself enclosed in a switch element as required by the SVG 1.0 and 1.1 DTDs (somewhat redundantly here because the switch has only a single child and no tests, to make the example shorter). Within the foreignObject elements are some simple (and nonsensical) MathML equations (see Figure 27.5).

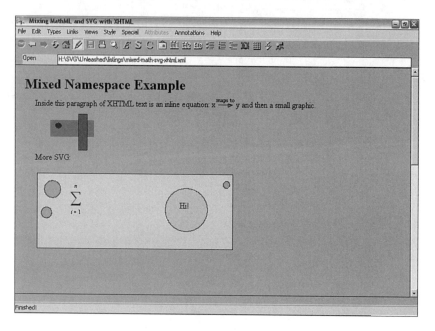

FIGURE 27.5   XHTML, SVG, and MathML created and rendered in W3C Amaya 6.1.

SVG and XForms

Currently, interactive SVG pages are often collected together in an HTML frameset that is used solely to allow HTML forms to be displayed along with the SVG. This has known problems—internationalization of the form results, lack of structure in the form (a list of name-value pairs is all that can be provided), difficulty of bookmarking framesets, and poor standards compliance of the legacy HTML browsers.

The combination of XForms and SVG allows the same or better functionality to be achieved in a single file. Dependence on legacy HTML rendering is avoided, and the result of submitting a form is itself an XML document with all the attendant advantages.

When you're developing an XForm, the first thing to design is the XML document that will be sent when the form is submitted. For this example, we will make a simple customer survey form for a coffee shop. This toy example will win no prizes for survey technique or artistic excellence, but it is short enough to explain the basic concepts.

Suppose the coffee shop is examining preferences among its regular espresso drinkers. Do they want a twist of lemon on the side, Italian style? Do they take sugar? To establish frequent espresso drinkers, we need to add two other questions: favorite drink and number of drinks per week.

The following XML captures this information:

```
<?xml version="1.0" encoding="UTF-8"?>
<survey>
    <drink>espresso</drink>
    <espressoPrefs>
        <numberPerWeek>6</numberPerWeek>
        <sugar>1</sugar>
        <lemon>Always</lemon>
    </espressoPrefs>
</survey>
```

The survey root element has two children. The first, drink, holds the favorite drink (espresso, latté, cappuccino, and so on), and the other, only relevant if drink is espresso, has the preferences—number of shots of espresso per week, whether the customers take sugar, whether they like lemon with it. None of these element names are standardized anywhere; they are made up just for this example.

The next thing to do is to create a W3C XML Schema that describes constraints on these values. We won't go into detail because XML Schemas are a complex topic, but this schema declares that drink can hold only one of the four values espresso, cappuccino, latté, or none; that numberPerWeek is a non-negative integer between 0 and 30; that sugar is (for the purposes of this example) a Boolean value, true or false, and so forth. The XForm processor will ensure that form entries comply with the constraints expressed in the schema, thus doing declaratively what current HTML forms have to do using scripting. The schema is available on the Web site (surveyschema.xsd).

NOTE

You can find out more about schemas here: http://www.w3.org/TR/xmlschema-0/.

The next task is to design the graphical layout of the SVG page. For the purposes of this example, we will keep things really simple—just text with small bullets, a little espresso cup for decoration. The spaces where the form elements go can be added to the design as rectangles, to aid placement. In this example, the actual cup is placed in a separate file referenced with an SVG image element, so it occupies a single line in the listing (survey-graphics.svg):

```
<?xml version="1.0" encoding="UTF-8" standalone="no"?>
<!DOCTYPE svg PUBLIC "-//W3C//DTD SVG 1.0//EN"
"http://www.w3.org/TR/SVG/DTD/svg10.dtd">
<svg xmlns="http://www.w3.org/2000/svg" width="700px" height="600px"
    viewBox="0 0 700 600" xmlns:xlink="http://www.w3.org/1999/xlink">
    <defs>
        <polygon id="bullet" points="-30,-30, -10,-10, -20,10" fill="#007138"/>
    </defs>
    <title>Espresso survey</title>
    <desc>Sample SVG  - espresso customer survey</desc>
    <g>
        <text x="50" y="70" font-size="40" font-family="Arial Black, sans-serif"
            font-weight="900">Customer Survey: Espresso</text>
        <g font-family="Arial, Helvetica, sans-serif" font-size="18">
            <g transform="translate(80, 140)">
                <use xlink:href="#bullet"/>
                <text>Your usual coffee drink is:</text>
            </g>
            <g transform="translate(80, 230)">
                <use xlink:href="#bullet"/>
                <text>Shots of espresso:</text>
            </g>
            <g transform="translate(80, 340)">
                <use xlink:href="#bullet"/>
                <text>Sugar?</text>
            </g>
            <g transform="translate(80, 410)">
                <use xlink:href="#bullet"/>
                <text>Lemon?</text>
            </g>
        </g>
        <use xlink:href="#bullet" x="101" y="64" transform="scale(7,3)"/>
        <!--- keep the graphics data out of this example listing -->
        <image xlink:href="espresso.svg"
            x="400" y="230" width="280" height="270"/>
    </g>
</svg>
```

Now, we combine the various namespaces into one XML file. Starting with the SVG file, we add namespace declarations for XForms, XML Events, and a namespace for our own survey vocabulary that we have just invented (it still needs a namespace, to distinguish it from the elements in other namespaces). It would be an error, for example, to add these elements to the SVG namespace.

```
<svg xmlns="http://www.w3.org/2000/svg"
    width="700px" height="600px"
    viewBox="0 0 700 600"
    xmlns:xlink="http://www.w3.org/1999/xlink"
    xmlns:xforms="http://www.w3.org/2002/01/xforms"
    xmlns:ev="http://www.w3.org/2001/xml-events"
    xmlns:s="http://example.com/survey">
```

The XForms model is added inside the SVG `defs` element because it is not something that is to be rendered; rather, it is defined for later use. The `model` element has an ID so that it can be pointed to and has three children. The first is an `instance` element that holds the `survey` xml that we defined earlier. This establishes the structure of the information that will be sent from the form and also provides default values for the form instance. If the form is reset, it will be reset to these values. The instance can either be placed inline, as here, or referenced with an external link.

The second child is a `schema` element that points to the W3C XML Schema. Again, it can be either inline, or external (as here).

The third child is a `submitInfo` element that describes what method (`GET` or `PUT` or `POST`) is used and the URL to which it is sent. There can be other information too, such as a P3P privacy profile, but not in this short example.

```
<xforms:model id="form1">
    <xforms:instance id="instance1" xmlns="http://example.com/survey">
        <survey xmlns="http://example.com/survey">
            <drink>none</drink>
            <espressoPrefs>
                <numberPerWeek>0</numberPerWeek>
                <sugar>0</sugar>
                <lemon>Always</lemon>
            </espressoPrefs>
        </survey>
    </xforms:instance>
    <xforms:schema xlink:href="surveyschema.xsd"/>
    <xforms:submitInfo id="submit1" method="post"
        action="http://www.example.org/surveyhandler"/>
</xforms:model>
```

We now have all the logical structure of the form in place, defining what information is to be collected and how it is structured; we also have the graphical shell of the survey but no actual form elements that the user could interact with. These elements are added into the body of the SVG graphic, using `foreignObject` elements because the rendering will be done by the XForms processor, not the SVG processor. So SVG needs to allocate a rectangle of space in which the XForms processor can draw. Here is one example, for a simple Boolean (yes/no) form control:

```
<foreignObject x="80" y="350" width="250" height="40">
    <xforms:selectBoolean model="form1"
        ref="/survey/espressoPrefs/sugar">
        <xforms:caption>Espresso needs sugar</xforms:caption>
    </xforms:selectBoolean>
</foreignObject>
```

Because one XML page can have several independent forms, there is a `model` attribute with the ID of the particular model that is being affected. Our example has only a single form, but the attribute is still needed. A child element `caption` holds the explanatory caption text that will be displayed beside the check box or whatever is used to collect an on/off Boolean value. There is also a `ref` attribute, which indicates the part of the model that this form control is affecting. The attribute contains an XPath expression; in this example, it identifies the `sugar` element, whose parent is `espressoPrefs`, whose parent is `survey` (the root of our survey instance).

> **NOTE**
>
> You can learn more about XPath 1.0 at http://www.w3.org/TR/xpath.

Listing 27.4 shows the complete worked example. For clarity, the graphics that make up the graphical trimmings (a coffee cup) and the XML Schema have been placed in separate files, linked with XLink hrefs. These extra files (surveyschema.xsd and espresso.svgz) together with this listing (survey.xml) are available on this book's Web site.

LISTING 27.4   survey.xml—XForms and SVG

```
<?xml version="1.0" encoding="UTF-8" standalone="no"?>
<!DOCTYPE svg PUBLIC "-//W3C//DTD SVG 1.0//EN"
"http://www.w3.org/TR/SVG/DTD/svg10.dtd">
<svg width="700px" height="600px" viewBox="0 0 700 600"
    xmlns="http://www.w3.org/2000/svg"
    xmlns:xlink="http://www.w3.org/1999/xlink"
    xmlns:xforms="http://www.w3.org/2002/01/xforms"
    xmlns:ev="http://www.w3.org/2001/xml-events"
    xmlns:s="http://example.com/survey">
    <defs>
        <polygon id="bullet" points="-30,-30, -10,-10, -20,10" fill="#007138"/>
        <xforms:model id="form1">
            <xforms:instance id="instance1" xmlns="http://example.com/survey">
                <survey xmlns="http://example.com/survey">
                    <drink>none</drink>
                    <espressoPrefs>
                        <numberPerWeek>0</numberPerWeek>
```

LISTING 27.4   Continued

```
                    <sugar>0</sugar>
                    <lemon>Always</lemon>
                </espressoPrefs>
            </survey>
        </xforms:instance>
        <xforms:schema xlink:href="surveyschema.xsd"/>
        <!--
        xforms:submitInfo id="submit1" method2="postxml"
        localfile="temp2.xml" target2="http://www.w3.org/"/-->
        <xforms:submitInfo id="submit1" method="post"
            action="http://www.example.org/surveyhandler"/>
    </xforms:model>
</defs>
<title>Espresso survey</title>
<desc>Sample SVG and XForms - espresso customer survey</desc>
<g>
    <text x="50" y="70" font-size="40" font-family="Arial Black, sans-serif"
        font-weight="900">Customer Survey: Espresso</text>
    <g font-family="Arial, Helvetica, sans-serif" font-size="18">
        <g transform="translate(80, 140)">
            <use xlink:href="#bullet"/>
            <text>Your usual coffee drink is:</text>
        </g>
        <foreignObject x="80" y="150" width="250" height="40">
            <xforms:selectOne selectUI="menu"
                model="form1" ref="/survey/drink">
                <xforms:item>
                    <xforms:caption>Rich, dark espresso</xforms:caption>
                    <xforms:value>espresso</xforms:value>
                </xforms:item>
                <xforms:item>
                    <xforms:caption>Creamy cappuccino</xforms:caption>
                    <xforms:value>cappuccino</xforms:value>
                </xforms:item>
                <xforms:item>
                    <xforms:caption>Long, milky latté</xforms:caption>
                    <xforms:value>latté</xforms:value>
                </xforms:item>
                <xforms:item>
                    <xforms:caption>Don't like coffee!</xforms:caption>
                    <xforms:value>none</xforms:value>
                </xforms:item>
            </xforms:selectOne>
```

27

LISTING 27.4   Continued

```
    </foreignObject>
    <g transform="translate(80, 230)">
        <use xlink:href="#bullet"/>
        <text>Shots of espresso:</text>
    </g>
    <foreignObject x="80" y="240" width="250" height="40">
        <xforms:range model="form1" start="0" end="30" stepsize="5"
            ref="/survey/espressoPrefs/numberPerWeek">
            <xforms:caption>On average, per week</xforms:caption>
        </xforms:range>
    </foreignObject>
    <g transform="translate(80, 340)">
        <use xlink:href="#bullet"/>
        <text>Sugar?</text>
    </g>
    <foreignObject x="80" y="350" width="250" height="40">
        <xforms:selectBoolean model="form1"
            ref="/survey/espressoPrefs/sugar">
            <xforms:caption>Espresso needs sugar</xforms:caption>
        </xforms:selectBoolean>
    </foreignObject>
    <g transform="translate(80, 410)">
        <use xlink:href="#bullet"/>
        <text>Lemon?</text>
    </g>
    <foreignObject x="80" y="420" width="250" height="90">
        <xforms:selectOne selectUi="radio" model="form1"
            ref="/survey/espressoPrefs/lemon">
            <xforms:item>
                <xforms:caption>Required for the full
                    experience</xforms:caption>
                <xforms:value>Always</xforms:value>
            </xforms:item>
            <xforms:item>
                <xforms:caption>Whatever</xforms:caption>
                <xforms:value>Indifferent</xforms:value>
            </xforms:item>
            <xforms:item>
                <xforms:caption>Keep that citrus to
                    yourself</xforms:caption>
                <xforms:value>Never</xforms:value>
```

LISTING 27.4   Continued

```
                    </xforms:item>
                </xforms:selectOne>
            </foreignObject>
        </g>
        <use xlink:href="#bullet" x="101" y="64" transform="scale(7,3)"/>
        <foreignObject y="150" x="500" height="60" width="100">
            <xforms:submit>
                <xforms:caption>Send survey</xforms:caption>
            </xforms:submit>
        </foreignObject>
        <!--- keep the graphics data out of this example listing -->
        <image xlink:href="espresso.svg" x="400" y="230"
            width="280" height="270"/>
    </g>
</svg>
```

Rendered in XSmiles, Listing 27.4 produces the output shown in Figure 27.6.

FIGURE 27.6   SVG and XForms in the XSmiles browser.

Summary

We have seen three directions in which SVG 1.0 is being developed. The first is by subsetting, to make the SVG implementations fit on a range of mobile devices that greatly outnumber personal computers. The second is by extension, to add capabilities to SVG that were not present in version 1.0. The third is by association with other XML namespaces, the combination being more powerful than the sum of the parts. It is the latter method that vindicates the entire design concept of SVG as an XML application and opens up the widest range of powerful solutions.

PART VI

Appendix

IN THIS PART

APPENDIX A

Glossary

The primary references for SVG are the specifications available from `http://www.w3.org/Graphics/SVG`. In the following glossary definitions, **SVG Spec**. refers to the SVG 1.0 Specification (`http://www.w3.org/TR/SVG/`) and **XML Spec**. refers to the Extensible Markup Language (XML) 1.0 (2nd Edition) Recommendation (`http://www.w3.org/TR/REC-xml`).

Absolute Positioning—Placing an element by means of x and y attributes relative to the point (0,0) in the current coordinate system, which, due to transformations, may not be the top-left corner. See also *Relative Positioning*.

Accessibility—In the sense of the W3C's Web Accessibility Initiative (WAI), providing a high degree of usability for people with disabilities. See `http://www.w3.org/WAI/`.

Alignment Point—A location within a glyph that is used to decide how to position the glyph in a given piece of text.

Alpha Channel—The portion of a pixel's data reserved for transparency, used in SVG alongside RGB channels.

Amaya—The free browser developed by the W3C to act as a testbed for Web technologies. Supports SVG.

Animated Value—The value of an attribute achieved during an animation.

Animation Target—The attribute that is the target of an SVG animation.

API—Application Programming Interface, a specification of how programming language elements should behave to allow code to work with different implementations of a system.

Arc—A line that follows the curve of a circle or ellipse, created in SVG using the A or a command as part of the value of a d attribute of a path element.

Aspect Ratio—The proportion of width to height; for example, 800×600 monitors have an aspect ratio of 4:3.

ASP—Active Server Pages, a system developed by Microsoft for dynamically generating Web pages.

ASV—Adobe SVG Viewer, a plug-in for Netscape/Internet Explorer available for Macintosh and Microsoft Windows systems. On version 3 at the time of writing (ASV3). See `http://www.adobe.com/svg/viewer/install/main.html`.

Attribute—A name-value pair associated with an element. See XML Spec. 3.3.

Aural Style Sheet—A style sheet used to specify the characteristics of an audio rendition of a document, using a screen reader, for example.

Baseline—The line along which text is drawn; it provides a series of reference points that determine where individual characters will be positioned.

Basic Shapes—Certain simple shapes (`rect`, `circle`, `ellipse`, `line`, `polyline`, and `polygon`) that are predefined as SVG elements.

Batik—A sophisticated open-source SVG toolkit from the Apache Foundation, built on Java technologies. It includes an SVG viewer and is in very active development. Strongly recommended for any SVG developer.

Bezier Curves—A way of drawing curved lines specified in terms of their start point, end point, and a number of control points. SVG supports quadratic (two control points) and cubic (three control points) Beziers. Bezier curves are used in the `path` element.

Bidirectionality (Bidi)—The ability of the characters in a piece of text to run from left to right or vice versa on the same line. This functionality is supported by SVG, based on an algorithm from the Unicode standard.

Binding—The way SVG DOM interfaces should be represented in a particular language. The specification includes bindings for ECMAScript and Java.

Bitmap—As opposed to vector graphics, the internal representation of an image using rows and columns of pixels. Also commonly known as **raster graphics**.

Block Progression Direction—The direction in which blocks of text progress. See SVG Spec. 10.7.1.

Bounding Box—The smallest rectangular area into which a given graphical element will fit.

Bump Map—A means of giving the impression of texture or relief to an image or part of an image. Used in SVG within filter effects such as `feDiffuseLighting`. See SVG Spec. 15.

Canvas—The infinite two-dimensional space into which SVG is potentially rendered. Rendering takes place only within a finite rectangular region of this space, which is called the **viewport**.

Cartesian Plane—A representation of a two-dimensional area, on which any point can be described using x and y (rectangular) coordinates.

CDATA Sections—The blocks used in XML to contain characters that should not be parsed by an XML parser. See XML Spec. 2.7.

Character Entity Reference—A way of referring to a character that cannot be expressed in a given encoding; for example, < represents the symbol <.

Clipping—Restricting the region in which painting can take place. See SVG Spec. 14.

Compositing—Blending objects according to their color and opacity at each individual pixel.

Container Element—An element that can have graphics elements and other elements as child elements, such as svg, g, and defs.

Convolution—A mathematical technique that can be used to add effects to a digital image, supported in the SVG filter primitive feConvolveMatrix. See SVG Spec. 15.13

CSS—Cascading Style Sheets, a means of specifying properties such as color or fonts for HTML/XML document elements. SVG uses many of the same property definitions as CSS2, and styling can be applied using external or inline style sheets. See SVG Spec. 6.9 and CSS2 Syntax and Data: http://www.w3.org/TR/REC-CSS2/syndata.html.

Current Transformation Matrix (CTM)—The mapping between the user coordinate system and the viewport coordinate system, specified as a 3×3 matrix.

Cursor—The pointer found in interactive display environments. SVG provides support for changing the cursor according to the document context. See SVG Spec. 16.8.

DOCTYPE Declaration—Within an XML document, the declaration that specifies the element type of the document element and may reference any DTD for the document, which allows validation of the document. See XML Spec. 2.8.

Document Fragment—Any number of SVG elements nested within an svg element.

DOM—Document Object Model, a tree-structured model behind interfaces for HTML, XML, and SVG that allows programs to dynamically access and modify the document content. SVG has a DOM based on DOM Level 2, with numerous additional interfaces. See http://www.w3.org/DOM/ and SVG Spec. Appendix B.

DTD—Document Type Definition, a grammar of legal structure for an XML application language. The SVG DTD can be found in the SVG Spec. Appendix A. See also XML Spec. 2.8.

Dublin Core—A widely used metadata standard suitable for use in SVG. An RDF vocabulary is available. See http://dublincore.org/.

ECMAScript—An open, internationally accepted scripting language specification. A popular implementation of ECMAScript is JavaScript.

Element—A component of XML that may contain attributes and other elements. SVG elements represent graphical components and containers for such elements, with attributes defining their properties.

Event—Communication between entities can be achieved using events and listeners. When a user carries out an action—for instance, clicking a button—this will create a message within the system that will be received by any parts of the system that have declared themselves as listeners. The message is described as an event. SVG supports a set of events that includes much of DOM2 events; these events can be used, for example, to make a script respond to clicking on an element. See SVG Spec. 16.

Feature Strings—A means by which an implementation can be queried using the `hasFeature` method to determine whether a specific part of the specification has been implemented. See SVG Spec. B.4.

Fill—The operation of painting the interior of a shape or character glyph.

Filter Effect—An operation or series of operations that dynamically change the appearance of an image or elements of an image. SVG includes a number of fundamental effects (the filter primitives) and provides the facility to combine them, allowing complex effects equivalent to those found in sophisticated commercial graphics applications. See SVG Spec. 15.

Filter Primitive—A filter effect that defines a single operation, such as `feGaussianBlur` or `feBlend`. See SVG Spec. 15.

FIPS Code—(U.S.) Federal Information Processing Standards code used to identify geographic entities such as states and counties.

Font—A collection of glyphs used to represent characters in a particular script or style.

FOP—Formatting Objects Processor, a print formatter from Apache that uses XSL.

Fragment Identifier—The # symbol followed by an identifier that URIs can use to refer to a location within a document. See SVG Spec. 17.2.2.

Gaussian Blur—A filter that follows the normal (bell-shaped) distribution curve found in nature and statistics.

Glyph—The representation of a character or part of a character in a font. In SVG, glyphs can be defined as a series of drawing instructions together with (Unicode) identifiers. See SVG Spec. 10.2.

Gradient—A smooth transition from one color to another. SVG supports linear and radial gradients. See SVG Spec. 13.2.

Group—In SVG, a set of graphics elements contained within a g element. Grouping allows the treatment of such a set of elements as a single unit.

HTML—Hypertext Markup Language, the primary language of the Web. See `http://www.w3.org`.

HTTP—Hypertext Transfer Protocol, the primary protocol of the Web. See `http://www.w3.org`.

i18n—i[18 letters]n. See also *Internationalization*.

IDL—Interface Definition Language, a programming-language-independent means of specifying interfaces of software objects. Used to specify the SVG DOM interfaces. See `http://www.omg.org/gettingstarted/omg_idl.htm`.

IETF—The Internet Engineering Task Force, an open organization concerned with Internet architecture that maintains an RFC (Request for Comments) document repository.

Inheritance—In SVG, the application of an element's painting and style properties to that element's children that will apply, unless explicitly overridden.

Initial User Coordinate System—The user coordinate system that applies when an SVG document loads. At this point, the user coordinate system is identical to the viewport coordinate system, with the root origin (0,0) in the top-left corner.

Inline Progression Direction—The direction in which text flows along a line. In English, the inline progression direction is left to right.

Internationalization (i18n)—The process of making software and standards work across differing writing systems, languages, and cultures. SVG has extensive support for i18n. See SVG Spec. Appendix I.

ISO—International Organization for Standardization, maintainers of various standards, several of which are important in SVG. See `http://www.iso.ch`.

JavaScript—An implementation of the ECMAScript language.

JAXP—Java API for XML Processing, a series of specifications from Sun Microsystems that incorporate SAX, DOM, and XSLT. Implementations of these specifications can be found in packages such as Xerces and Xalan. See `http://java.sun.com/xml/jaxp/index.html`.

JPEG—Joint Photographic Experts Group, the group that created an image format standard known by this acronym. A lossy, compressed bitmap format appropriate for use with images derived from photographs. Conforming SVG viewers must support JPEG images when using the `image` element.

JSP—Java Server Pages, a technology from Sun Microsystems that allows Java code to run server-side from Web pages.

Kerning—Adjusting the spacing between certain pairs of letters to improve appearance. See SVG Spec. 10.11.

Marker—A graphic found on a path or line, such as an arrowhead. See SVG Spec. 11.6.

Masking—Painting an object through a screen that can completely or partially mask parts of the object. In effect, painting blends objects into the background. See SVG Spec. 14.

A

Metadata—Machine-readable data about data. Supported in SVG through the `metadata` element. See SVG Spec. 21 and `http://www.w3.org/RDF`.

MIME Type—Multipurpose Internet Mail Extensions, used by a Web server to identify the type of content it is delivering. The MIME type for SVG is `image/svg+xml`.

Mozilla—An open-source browser on which Netscape browsers from version 6.0 onward are built. An SVG-capable version is under development; see `http://www.mozilla.org`.

MSXML—Microsoft XML Parser and related software.

Namespace—A way of removing ambiguity from XML names. In XML, namespaces are specified as URI references and apply to elements and attributes. The namespace of SVG is `http://www.w3.org/2000/svg`. See `http://www.w3.org/TR/REC-xml-names/`.

Node-Set—A collection of nodes (without duplicates) taken from a DOM tree. Produced by various operations in DOM and XSLT.

NURB—Non-Uniform Rational B-Spline, a mathematical representation of a shape commonly used in computer graphics. See also *Spline*.

Oblate Spheroid—A squashed-ball shape that is used as a mathematical approximation to the shape of the earth for mapping purposes, that is, a globe where the equatorial radius is greater than the polar radius.

Opacity—The opposite of transparency. SVG allows full control over the opacity of graphical elements and groups. See SVG Spec. 14.5.

Paint—A way of putting color onto the canvas. SVG has three types of paint built in: color, gradients, and patterns.

Painter's Model—The approach to rendering used by SVG which mimics an artist applying paint to a canvas, where each successive application partially or fully obscures whatever was on the canvas already. Elements in an SVG document are painted generally in the order in which they appear in the document.

Pan—The operation of moving the visible area of the SVG canvas horizontally, vertically, or diagonally. Implemented by most SVG viewers.

Path—A way to describe lines and curves and draw the outlines of shapes, which can subsequently be filled in as required. A path in SVG is analogous to drawing with a pen on paper. See SVG Spec. 8.

Pattern—In SVG, a set of graphical elements used to fill in areas by tiling.

PDF—Portable Document Format, an open standard developed by Adobe, typically used for print-like documents.

PI—See *Processing Instruction*.

PNG—Portable Network Graphics, a sophisticated bitmapped graphics format approved as a standard by the W3C. Similar to the GIF format but without patent restrictions.

Pointer—A user interface device such as a mouse or trackball.

Polyline—A set of connected straight line segments. See SVG Spec. 9.6.

Prefix—A short sequence of characters used indirectly to identify the namespace of a particular XML element or attribute, for example, `svg:rect`. Also known as a **namespace prefix**. See `http://www.w3.org/TR/REC-xml-names`.

Processing Instruction—An instruction declared in XML documents to specify the handling of the data by applications. See XML Spec. 2.6.

Property—A parameter that determines how an element or group of elements should be rendered. As well as SVG-specific properties, SVG also supports properties from other styling languages such as CSS. In general, properties are assigned using XML attributes. See SVG Spec. Appendix N.

QName—Qualified name, the name of an XML element or attribute expressed as `[namespace prefix]:[local name]`, for example, `svg:rect`. See `http://www.w3.org/TR/REC-xml-names`.

Range Clamping—Attaching out-of-range values to the nearest permitted value (such as 0 or 1 for opacity) because numeric values such as those determining colors or opacity have a restricted range of legal values. See SVG Spec. F.4.

RDF—Resource Description Framework, a metadata framework that allows anything that can be identified (a resource) to be described. A key element in the W3C's Semantic Web initiative. See `http://www.w3.org/RDF`.

Reference Orientation—This is the first consideration when determining the direction of flow of text. For standard horizontal or vertical text in the initial coordinate system, the reference orientation is up. See SVG Spec. 10.7.

Relative Positioning—Defining a coordinate pair relative to a point other than the origin, (0,0), of the current coordinate system. Relative positioning may be used, for example, within the value of the d attribute of a path element. See also *Absolute Positioning*.

Rendering Model—The ideal behavior of an SVG implementation, based on the "Painter's Model," with particular behavior defined for elements and groups. See SVG Spec. 3.

RGB—A way of describing a color (hue) in terms of the proportions of red, green, and blue.

SAX—Simple API for XML, a set of standard interfaces, implementations of which allow the parsing of XML data.

Scripting—In SVG, using interpreted languages such as ECMAScript and Python to control rendering behavior or interactivity. See SVG Spec. 18.

Semantic Web—A vision of the next generation of the Web, in which information is presented in such a way that machine interpretation is possible. See `http://www.w3.org/2001/sw/`.

Servlet—A Java class designed to respond to HTTP requests. See `http://www.java.sun.com`.

SGML—Standard Generalized Markup Language, the standard from which HTML and XML was derived.

SMIL—Synchronized Multimedia Integration Language, a "rich media" format from the W3C. SVG animation elements are based on SMIL version 2 elements. See `http://www.w3.org/AudioVideo/`.

Specular Lighting—An effect that mimics the reflective properties of a mirror. SVG has the filter primitive `feSpecularLighting` for this effect. See SVG Spec. 15.22.

Spline—A way of defining a curve by means of control points. SVG supports cubic and quadratic Bezier splines. See SVG Spec. 8.3.5.

Stroke—The operation of painting the outline of a shape or glyph.

Stylesheet—A way of defining how documents and their constituent elements should be rendered. The primary stylesheet languages are CSS and XSL(T), from which many of the properties within SVG are derived. The styling of an SVG document can be determined using these languages. See SVG Spec. 6.

SVG—Scalable Vector Graphics, an XML grammar for stylable graphics built from simple geometric objects such as lines and curves. See *SVG Unleashed*.

svgz—The usual extension of SVG files compressed using the gzip compression algorithm. See `http://www.ietf.org/rfc/rfc1952.txt`.

Swing—A set of classes in the Java language for building user interfaces.

TCL —Tool Command Language, a scripting language mainly used for user-interface inter-actions. See `http://www.neosoft.com/tcl/`.

TIGER—(U.S.) Topologically Integrated Geographic Encoding and Referencing system used by the Census Bureau, which includes a topographical database. See `http://www.census.gov/geo/www/tiger/index.html`.

Transformation—A way of modifying the rendering of a graphical element or group of elements. Transformations can either be specified using simple operations (scale, rotate, or translate) or by providing a matrix describing the required transformation. Transformations are applied on top of the Current Transformation Matrix (CTM), yielding a new CTM.

Transformation Matrix—The mathematical mapping from one coordinate system into another using a 3×3 matrix using the equation `[x' y' 1] = [x y 1] * matrix`.

Turbulence—(Perlin Turbulence) "Smooth" randomness that can be used to generate natural-looking effects. Supported in SVG through the `feTurbulence` filter primitive.

Unicode—A standard, "universal" character-encoding scheme supported by SVG. See `http://www.unicode.org/`.

URI—Uniform Resource Identifier, used in SVG to form references to files or elements within files.

User Agent—A generic term for applications that can retrieve, render, or process Web content. In the context of SVG, the term is usually used to refer to SVG-capable Web browsers or dedicated SVG viewers.

User Coordinate System/User Space—The coordinate system that is currently active, which is either the initial user coordinate system or that system with transformations applied.

Vector—A mathematical term for something with magnitude and direction. A vector can be represented geometrically as a movement from one point to another, and this representation forms the basis of vector graphics.

Viewport—The rectangular region into which content is rendered. See SVG Spec. 7.

VML—Vector Markup Language, a predecessor of SVG developed by Microsoft.

W3C—World Wide Web Consortium. See `http://www.w3.org`.

WAI—Web Accessibility Initiative.

XML Linking Language (XLink)—An XML-based linking language used in SVG.

XML Pointer Language (XPointer)—XPointer is a way of identifying a particular part of a document. It goes beyond XPath, in which a node can be addressed allowing any specific characters to be identified. See `http://www.w3.org/XML/Linking`, and for an example of its use, `http://www.w3.org/2001/Annotea/`.

XSL—Extensible Stylesheet Language, an XML-based language for expressing style sheets. See `http://www.w3.org/Style/XSL/`.

XSLT—XSL Transformations, a rule-based language that forms part of XSL that may be used to transform XML data into other representations (including other XML representations).

Z—In either upper- or lowercase—the `closepath` command.

A

Index

Symbols

A

How can we make this index more useful? Email us at indexes@samspublishing.com

F

G

I

How can we make this index more useful? Email us at indexes@samspublishing.com

How can we make this index more useful? Email us at indexes@samspublishing.com

How can we make this index more useful? Email us at indexes@sampspublishing.com

T

How can we make this index more useful? Email us at indexes@samspublishing.com

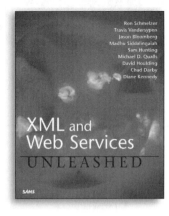

Related Titles from Sams Publishing

PHP and MySQL Web Development

Laura Thompson,
Luke Welling
0-672-31784-2
$49.99 US / $77.99 CAN

PHP Developer's Cookbook

Sterling Hughes,
Andrei Zmievski
0-672-32325-7
$39.99 US / $62.99 CAN

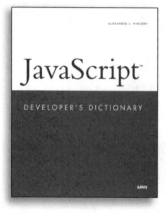

JavaScript Developer's Dictionary

Alexander Vincent
0-672-32201-3
$49.99 US / $77.99 CAN

Perl Developer's Dictionary

Clinton Pierce
0-672-32067-3
$39.99 US / $62.99 CAN

XML in Flash
Craig Swann and Gregg
Caines
0-672-32315-x
$49.99 US / $77.99 CAN

**PHP Developer's
Dictionary**
R. Allen Wyke
0-672-32029-0
$35.99 US / $55.99 CAN

Perl Web Site Workshop
Molly Holzschlag, Jason
Pellerin
0-672-32275-7
$39.99 US / $62.99 CAN

Pure JavaScript
Jason Gilliam; R.Allen Wyke;
Charlton Ting; Sean
Michaels
0-672-32141-6
$49.99 US / $77.99 CAN

**MySQL and JSP Web
Applications:
Programming Using
Tomcat and MySQL**
James Turner
0-672-32309-5
$39.99 US / $62.99 CAN

All prices are subject to change.

SAMS

www.samspublishing.com